West's Law School Advisory Board

INTERNATIONAL CIVIL DISPUTE RESOLUTION

A PROBLEM-ORIENTED COURSEBOOK

Second Edition

By

Charles S. Baldwin, IV
Rountree, Losee & Baldwin, LLP,
Wilmington, North Carolina

Ronald A. Brand
Professor of Law and Director, Center for International Legal Education
University of Pittsburgh

David Epstein
Former Director, Office of Foreign Litigation
U.S. Department of Justice

Michael Wallace Gordon
John H. & Mary Lou Dasburg Professor of Law
University of Florida

AMERICAN CASEBOOK SERIES®

Mat #40673428

American Casebook Series and West Group are trademarks
registered in the U.S. Patent and Trademark Office.

© West, a Thomson business, 2004
© 2008 Thomson/West
      610 Opperman Drive
      P.O. Box 64526
      St. Paul, MN 55123
      1–800–313–9378

Printed in the United States of America

ISBN 978–0–314–18792–5

 *TEXT IS PRINTED ON 10% POST CONSUMER RECYCLED PAPER*

We Dedicate This Book to:

Devon, Davis and Selden Baldwin
With gratefulness, love and appreciation

Mary

Arlene, Jennifer, Sarah, Susannah and Esther

Elsbeth, Elsbeth & Elsbeth

*

Preface

The vast increase over the past few decades in the movement of goods, services and people, accelerated by numerous trade agreements, has generated increased conflict and a need for lawyers to learn about the role and characteristics of judicial and arbitral resolution of international civil disputes. With this increased exchange comes an increase in disputes between parties on different sides of the borders. Increased disputes mean a greater need for lawyers to deal with the disputes. Americans sell goods abroad, such as induction molding devices, and they sell goods to foreign persons or entities that are in the United States, such as office furniture to a Chinese state-owned travel agency in Washington. Americans purchase goods from abroad, such as automobile tires from Canada, or cement from Indonesia. Sometimes transnational business results in personal injury, such as when foreign produced tire treads separate and automobiles crash, or when an explosion occurs in a Mexican subsidiary of a U.S. parent. Foreign governments are often involved, such as when they fail to fulfill a contract such as payment for the office furniture, or when the government expropriates U.S. property. The injured parties may all wish to sue, and quite possibly they may wish to bring the suit in a U.S. court. The defendants will also need lawyers—American lawyers if the suits are initiated in the United States. Whatever the source of the dispute, the existence of parties in more than one country requires special attention to issues of jurisdiction, service of process, taking of evidence, choice of law, special rules for sovereign parties, and ultimately of enforcement of any resulting judgment or arbitral award. While all of this may not change the nature of a lawyer's work, it dramatically changes the sources of both the procedural and substantive laws applicable to a dispute.

This book is designed to provide an introduction to the dispute resolution issues raised in the resolution of cross-border civil disputes. While the focus is on litigation, mediation and arbitration are also considered, and the choice of the dispute settlement mechanism should be a matter considered throughout the materials.

There is a Documents Supplement prepared especially for use with this book. References are made in problems to parts of the Documents Supplement that are important to an analysis of the problem.

Four and a half years have passed since the first edition was published. Revisions of first editions are unique in contrast to later editions. The first edition invariably includes some unintentional errors, some awkward phrasing that fails to convey the intended meaning, and may lack emphasis on areas that merit attention. Second editions offer the authors the opportunity to correct these, as well as to update the materials with new decisions and approaches to the issues. We hope that this second edition succeeds in these respects.

The format of this edition remains much the same. It is a problem oriented coursebook. We have added a new problem in chapter three, addressing preliminary relief, both the approach in the United States and the well established *Mareva* injunction in the United Kingdom. The final problem in chapter four that addressed both choice of law and the method of proof of foreign law has been divided into two problems. A new problem 10.3 was added in chapter ten to address important procedural issues in arbitration.

We especially hope that the revised Teacher's Manual proves as useful as faculty have told us.

CHARLES BALDWIN
RONALD BRAND
DAVID EPSTEIN
MICHAEL WALLACE GORDON

January 2008

Acknowledgments

We wish to acknowledge the aid that we have received from numerous colleagues. Special appreciation is due several persons who have thoughtfully commented on individual problems. They are, Volker Behr of the University of Augsburg Faculty of Law; Franklin Gill and Ted Occhialino of the University of New Mexico School of Law; Adolfo Jimenez of Holland & Knight in Miami; Jorge Ramirez, Carlos Loperera and Leonel Pereznieto Castro of Mexico City; George Rountree, III and Geoffrey A. Losee of Rountree, Losee & Baldwin of Wilmington; John A. Spanogle, Jr., of the George Washington University National Law Center; John Stevenson of Jackson Walker of Dallas.

Extraordinary patience, support and assistance has been given by legal assistants and staff at our respective locations, including Jamie Burchianti, Gina Clark, Dan Deane, LuAnn Driscoll, Giuseppi Fina, Marilyn Henderson, Scott Jablonski, Karen Knochel, Darleen Mocello, Valerie Pompe, Barbara Salopek, Lori Turner, Gail Warren, and the lawyers and staff of Rountree, Losee & Baldwin of Wilmington, and special thanks to Arlene.

We also appreciate the association with our editors at West, Ryan Pfeiffer, Roxanne Birkel, and Kathleen Vandergon, who had to deal with a generation of authors who have not yet worked out all the mysteries of the computer age.

*

Summary of Contents

*

Table of Contents

Table of Cases

The principal cases are in bold type. Cases cited or discussed in the text are roman type. References are to pages. Cases cited in principal cases and within other quoted materials are not included.

INTERNATIONAL CIVIL DISPUTE RESOLUTION

A PROBLEM-ORIENTED COURSEBOOK

Second Edition

*

Part One

INTERNATIONAL CIVIL
DISPUTE RESOLUTION

Chapter 1

THE FORMS OF CIVIL DISPUTE RESOLUTION

INTRODUCTION 1.0

With increasing frequency, lawyers are called on to identify and select the preferred means of resolving international legal controversies for their clients. Once an international dispute arises, it may be too late to select the jurisdiction for resolution of the dispute. If a lawsuit is filed against your client in X country concerning an international business transaction, you and your client may be forced to deal with the dispute under a totally unfamiliar legal system of different laws and procedures. Lawyers in the international arena are confronted with a bewildering array of dispute resolution mechanisms. Should the lawyer counseling the party to an international transaction advise the inclusion of an arbitration clause or forum selection clause in the contract in order to pre-determine the method or the choice of court for potential disputes? What factors contribute to deciding between litigation or an alternate form of dispute resolution? In order to provide effective legal representation, the international lawyer should be in a position to identify and plan the best strategy for the resolution of potential disputes involving international transactions.

The advance planning and strategy described above may not be possible in all situations. Not every international dispute arises out of an international transaction. With globalization of trade and commerce, there has been a corresponding increase in international issues in connection with otherwise domestic cases. In order to provide effective legal representation to his or her client, the lawyer needs to understand these issues and how they factor into achieving a favorable outcome in the case. In addition, the lawyer needs to be aware that the judge or presiding official in the proceeding may not have previously encountered the particular international litigation issue involved and may need a careful presentation of the background and the relevant law in order to achieve maximum effectiveness of the legal position asserted.

L. CHWIALKOWSKA, BE REALISTIC, LEADING
JUDGE TELLS LAWYERS

Toronto National Post.
April 12, 2002.

The Supreme Court is struggling to come to grips with a proliferation of international treaties and conventions signed by the Canadian government, and to cope with lawyers who rely on vaguely worded agreements and elusive international law principles to make their case, says a high court judge.

Justice Louis LeBel will today ask legal academics and lawyers to think through the proper relationship between international law and domestic laws passed by Parliament and the provinces, as well as decisions made by provincial and federal officials.

"In our opinion, as the use of international law continues to rise, the Court will need more guidance from counsel with respect to the scope and limitations of international law," states a draft of his paper to be delivered today at an annual constitutional law conference at Osgoode Hall Law School in Toronto, co-authored with law clerk Gloria Chao.

The number of cases making use of international law and conventions has increased dramatically since the adoption of the Charter of Rights and Freedoms in 1982, his draft text states.

The court has recently ruled on cases involving international agreements on the treatment of refugees, protection from torture, and the rights of children, for example. In one case currently before the court, lawyers relied on international agreements on social and economic rights to argue for the right to a guaranteed income.

Judge LeBel's draft speech seems to hint that the judges may be ready to call international experts or foreign officials to argue cases before the top court, rather than limiting their participation to written submissions as is presently the case.

"As the cases involving international matters become more complex, we foresee that there will be an increasing need for international law evidence," the speech states.

"The Court has generally relied on published documents provided by international interveners to fill this need. As issues grow in complexity, this method of evidence may not be sufficient to meet the demands of the issues examined by the Court," it states. The text chides Canadian lawyers for their simplistic attempts to base cases on international law.

"What has been unhelpful in the past are recitations of principles of public international law [as though] they are binding law without a discussion on their application in the domestic legal order," the speech states.

"The Court has greeted with skepticism such blanket statements on the relevance of international law principles to the case to be decided. As international law is generally non-binding or without effective control mechanisms, it does not suffice to simply states that international law requires a certain outcome," the paper says.

Judges themselves have sometimes been divided on the relevance of international agreements and principles of Canadian law.

For example, in the 1999 deportation case of Mavis Baker, the court ruled immigration officials must treat the best interests of her Canadian born children as a primary consideration in their deportation decision. The 5–2 majority, led by Justice Claire L'Heureux–Dubé, relied in part on the international Convention on the Rights of the Child to support the decision.

However two judges, led by Justice Frank Iacobucci, found that the Convention was not binding because it had been signed by the Executive but had not been ratified by Parliament.

The paper states that there are a number of challenges that arise with an increased use of international law.

Principles of public international law, for instance, are difficult to define, their application to constitutional law cases is "cumbersome as there are questions of their legitimacy" and the place they should occupy in or alongside domestic law, and there are many value-laden terms that do not translate automatically into legal principles.

In some cases, the court has fused international and domestic law, and kept them separate in other, the speech states.

In the 2001 case of Burns and Rafay, the court ruled that except in rare circumstances, suspected murderers could not be extradited to the United States without assurances they would not face the death penalty. Glen Sebastien Burns and Atif Ahmad Rafay were wanted for the July, 1994, murders of Rafay's father, mother and sister at their home in Bellevue, Wash.

As part of its reasons, the court relied on international initiatives to abolish the death penalty.

In that case, the court heard from two international bodies, the Italian Senate and a cross-border association of lawyers.

In contrast, extradition cases 10 years ago heard arguments from only one or two international interveners, according to Judge LeBel.

Earlier this year, the court also relied on a number of international conventions in ruling that a suspected terrorist fundraiser could not be deported to face a substantial risk of torture. That case involved eight interveners of which only two did not plead international law principles.

———

In international cases, the lawyer has added responsibilities. As the Toronto news article indicates, the court may need assistance from counsel in identifying and understanding international law materials and issues. Counsel will need to determine the most effective way of presenting and proving the international law relied on.

The lawyer handling a product liability case in the United States against a foreign party may not sense anything unique about the nature or character of the dispute. But what happens if the lawyer in the U.S. proceeding is called on to effect service of process and obtain evidence abroad or to prove foreign law as part of his/her case. Does this turn an otherwise domestic case into "international litigation" or an "international dispute"? How are those terms defined? Definitional problems exist in this area in large part because the term "international litigation" is somewhat of a hybrid and does not neatly fit within commercial litigation practice as we commonly think of that specialty of the law. For purposes of the discussion in this book, we should consider the term as a sub-category of litigation, commercial or otherwise, involving international transactions, parties, or foreign law. Similarly, if the dispute is subject to arbitration, we need to better understand the roles of those engaged in the practice of international arbitration and how it compares or contrasts with litigation.

Attorneys representing the parties to the international dispute need to know that its outcome may be materially affected by its international character. Chapter 1 seeks to identify special factors that are present in most definitions of "international litigation." Once the attorney is alerted to the presence of international issues in the case, it becomes easier to provide good advice to his/her client on the best means of resolving the dispute as well as the choice of the forum if the case is litigated.

SECTION 1.1   LITIGATION

PART A.   WHAT IS INTERNATIONAL LITIGATION?

Commentators have developed special lists containing the elements that delineate an international dispute. One such list follows:

ALAN H. KAUFMAN, MAJOR STRATEGIC ISSUES IN INTERNATIONAL LITIGATION

Course Handbook on International Business
Litigation and Arbitration 11.
Practicing Law Institute 2000.

1.   the existence of material foreign documents or witnesses;

2.   foreign parties;

3.   applicable foreign law, foreign events or other elements which could allow a foreign court to have jurisdiction over the matter or an American court to decline jurisdiction;

4.   material assets located abroad;

5.   the existence of multiple countries which could legitimately assert simultaneous jurisdiction over the dispute; and

6. the need to have the case adjudged in multiple jurisdictions either for purposes of obtaining discovery, for collection or for some other strategic purpose.

————

As Kaufman indicates, the international elements of the case should be identified and analyzed early. Failure to properly address these points at the beginning may have serious ramifications throughout the proceeding and into the post-enforcement/execution phase of the proceedings. Mr. Kaufman suggests that parties should develop their own checklists to pinpoint the international elements of the case.

For plaintiffs, Mr. Kaufman lists the following as the minimum threshold checklist:

1. The nature (or absence) of a dispute, forum, choice of law or enforcement clause in applicable documents;

2. possible venues for the litigation/arbitration (within the United States and in foreign countries);

3. location of documents and witnesses;

4. timing considerations which will impact the ultimate enforcement date;

5. speed of the docket (both domestic and foreign dockets need to be carefully evaluated for enforcement, estoppel and *res judicata* impacts);

6. location/s of assets: a critical issue in many cases which is linked to enforceability of judgments and the timing of collection, particularly for cases in initiated in U.S. courts;

7. need for attachment or other interlocutory remedies: is critical when collectability is at issue and also can significantly impact cases involving intellectual property; and

8. enforceability of judgments: the absence of treaties recognizing U.S. judgments has impacts on a country-by-country basis.

For defendants, Mr. Kaufman lists the following international dispute considerations as follows:

1. The nature (or absence) of a forum, choice of law or enforcement clause in any applicable documents;

2. existence of multiple venues;

3. damage award exposure in the initial venue chosen by the plaintiff (the U.S. is really the only jurisdiction that systematically allows major damage awards);

4. location of documents and witnesses;

5. whether key witnesses speak fluent English or will require interpreters;

6.   accessibility of and ability to communicate precisely with fact witnesses;

7.   availability of more favorable damage, discovery or other parameters in foreign venues;

8.   availability of *forum non conveniens*, "jurisdictional rule of reason", antisuit injunctions or other common law and statutory defenses or remedies; and

9.   cost factors should be seriously considered by both parties. International litigation is frequently more expensive than comparable domestic litigation.

Consider the following news article which describes a recent significant ruling of the Supreme Court of Australia on Internet jurisdiction in a defamation case. The case is replete with international litigation issues for both of the parties to the controversy.

JONATHAN KRIM, INTERNET LIBEL FENCE FALLS

Washington Post.
December 11, 2002.

An Australian businessman, in a court ruling that could change how publishers view their ability to distribute information around the world, won the right to sue a U.S. news organization in his home country over a story published on the Internet.

In the first decision of its kind in any country, Australia's highest court ruled yesterday that Dow Jones & Co., which publishes the Wall Street Journal and Baron's, must stand trial in Australia, not in the United States for allegedly defaming a mining executive from Melbourne. Like most countries, Australia offers fewer free-speech protections than are afforded by the First Amendment to the U.S. Constitution.

A group of U.S., European and Australian media organizations and Internet companies supported Dow Jones in the case, arguing that publishers could be subject to an array of different legal standards.

"The rule that the court adopted, if more broadly applied by other countries, could render the Internet unusable as a vehicle for mass communication," said David A. Schulz, a New York lawyer who helped the coalition prepare legal briefs supporting Dow Jones. The group includes the Washington Post Co., the New York Times Co., and Yahoo Inc. and Amazon.com Inc.

The case demonstrates the difficulty in applying laws to the Internet, which has no borders. Some legal experts said the ruling could crimp the increasingly free flow of information across borders that the Internet has unleashed.

"It's a significant case," said Ian C. Ballon, a lawyer and the executive director of Stanford Law School's Center for E–Commerce.

"What it says is that free accessibility of expression on the Internet carries risks."

Stuart D. Karle, a Dow Jones lawyer, said the ruling means that "you don't know what law will apply to what you're saying until someone sues you. At that point, it's a little late." He said the risk applies to news organizations, which have foreign correspondents based in many countries, and individuals whose personal Web sites contain political expression.

Others worry that the case could be a harbinger of a legal free-for-all that might undermine Internet commerce more broadly. If, for example, consumers or businesses in various countries could sue over a failed Internet transaction under myriad local laws and jurisdictions, doing business online would be jeopardized because it could be unclear which laws govern commercial liability.

It's going to have a snowball effect on other countries asserting jurisdictions over things going on in cyberspace," said Megan E. Gray, an Internet lawyer in Washington.

International treaty negotiations to deal with jurisdictional questions have been stymied thus far, and, Gray said, many countries may lose patience and begin to "put up fences in the ether."

More than 150 countries allow defamation or libel suits in some form, and none is bound by the decision of the High Court of Australia. But Australia's laws are grounded in the law of the British Commonwealth, and the decision could be viewed as a precedent by courts in other Commonwealth nations, such as Canada and New Zealand.

Dow Jones argued that the case should be heard in the United States, where Barron's, which carried the article at the heart of the case, is published. The company said in a prepared statement that it will vigorously defend the suit in Australian court, and is heartened by language in the ruling that allows the trial court to take into account the relevant libel laws where the story was produced.

The story, published in October 2000, questioned the propriety of business dealings by Joseph Gutnick, a mining entrepreneur and philanthropist in Melbourne.

In its ruling, the court said that publishers' concerns about legal uncertainty were overwrought. A news organization will know, the court said, which jurisdiction would be involved in a particular story, and it can adapt its story to those laws.

Gutnick told an Australian television station that the ruling puts the Internet on a par with a local newspaper.

Schulz said free expression could be jeopardized by the ruling. Foreign correspondents for U.S. news organizations report on other countries assuming U.S. libel standards. If they can be prosecuted under local laws, such stories might be less likely to be produced.

A British journalist recently was arrested in Zimbabwe under similar circumstances but was released on a technicality.

Karle said that in response to the ruling, news organizations probably will keep their financial assets out of countries that assert Internet jurisdiction, making it harder for anyone to collect damages if the new organization loses a case in local courts.

"Decisions like Gutnick are going to require some very careful thought," said Clifford M. Sloan, general counsel of the Washington Post Co.'s digital division, Washington Post Newsweek Interactive. "But an institution like ours has a commitment to doing the best job it can and spreading news widely."

––––––

Chapter 2 discusses various situations which illustrate the role of the lawyer when foreign and/or international law issues are presented. One of the examples, which is patterned after the case described in the Washington Post article, analyses the lawyer's responsibility to his/her client in a multiple jurisdictional context. The international lawyer needs to be prepared to transcend traditional domestic boundaries in providing legal advice to his/her client. This means that, in addition to servicing the client in the home forum, the international lawyer needs to advise of the potential impact and consequences of the legal action in other jurisdictions.

PART B.   WHAT HAPPENS WHEN THE METHOD OF RESOLVING THE DISPUTE IS PRE–DETERMINED?

Parties to an international dispute may have options in choosing the mechanism for the resolution of the dispute. Are there clauses in the international contract which bind the parties to the resolution of present or future disputes? These dispute clauses generally take the form of arbitration clauses or forum selection clauses providing adjudicatory authority in general or power to particular courts to resolve the matter. If there is no dispute clause, the parties may still choose a particular means of dealing with the dispute after it arises. Despite the absence of an arbitration clause, the parties may still select arbitration or an ADR alternative and the particular rules that will apply, even after the dispute arises. However, agreement after the dispute arises is frequently difficult to obtain.

Jurisdiction clauses, also known as prorogation agreements, serve as an alternative to arbitration. Forum selection clauses have become a standard component of international contracts where the parties seek to designate a particular place in which any disputes arising from the agreement should be resolved. For example, a contract between an American and foreign party could designate that the parties agree to submit to the exclusive jurisdiction of the courts of a particular country or specified tribunals within a given jurisdiction. U.S. courts have given effect to such clauses in recent years in order to provide predictability in international commerce. In *M/S Bremen v. Zapata Off–Shore Co.*, 407 U.S. 1, 92 S.Ct. 1907, 32 L.Ed.2d 513 (1972) (discussed in Problem 3.1) the Supreme Court held that "such clauses are prima facie valid and should be enforced unless enforcement is shown by the resisting party to be 'unreasonable' under the circumstances.

Enforcement of a forum selection clause serves as a guarantee that there will be a designated forum consented to by the parties to the transaction in which a dispute will be settled. Parties to an international transaction will usually try to designate their own courts in order to obtain the "home court" advantage. Certainly, American lawyers will try to designate U.S. courts in order to obtain the procedural and substantive benefits inherent in the U.S. legal system. Some commentators have noted, however, that designation of the U.S. forum can sometimes backfire since there is considerable judicial discretion to remove cases to other jurisdictions under the doctrine of *forum non conveniens* where other factors may favor resolving the case elsewhere.[1]

Is it preferable for international contracts to include either a forum selection or arbitration clause? Most commentators would agree that either one of these clauses gives more predictability and certainty to the international dispute to the international dispute resolution process. Why have these clauses become standard components of the international contract?

There is less consensus as to whether arbitration and/or litigation is the preferred dispute resolution mechanism for the international transaction. It is important for the international lawyer to be aware of the benefits and pitfalls of either process and the major factors that should be considered in determining which one to use.

CHARLES BROWER AND ABBY COHEN SMUTNY, ARBITRATION AGREEMENTS VERSUS FORUM SELECTION CLAUSES: LEGAL AND PRACTICAL CONSIDERATIONS

The Regulation of Forum Selection
Fourteenth Sokol Colloquium.
International Dispute Resolution 37.
Transnational Publishers 1997.

The first question faced by those considering whether to include an arbitration agreement or a forum selection clause in an international contract is whether either is necessary at all. The answer to that question certainly is "Yes." International contracts should always stipulate the means of resolving disputes between the parties, and, in addition, a governing law.

Parties failing to address these issues inevitably will face, should a dispute arise, significant and ultimately costly complications due to their

---

1. William Park, *the Relative Reliability of Arbitration Agreements and Court Selection Clauses, International Dispute Resolution 3, 8 (1997).*

uncertain ability to enforce their contractual rights. They then are faced with essentially two options, neither of which is appealing and both of which could prove impossible. The first option is to seek at this late stage to conclude a dispute resolution agreement with respect to the particular dispute that has arisen. The parties then must face the same choices they avoided earlier, this time, however, with the disadvantage that relations between them are likely to make teaching any agreement extremely difficult, if not downright impossible.

The second option is for the claiming party to locate a national jurisdiction with both personal jurisdiction over its adversary and subject matter jurisdiction over the dispute. Such a jurisdiction is very likely to be foreign to the claimant, and the law to be applied will be determined by that court in accordance with whatever conflict of laws rules are deemed to be applicable (with concomitantly unpredictable results). Moreover, in such a case the claimant's success ultimately depends on any resulting judgment being enforceable in a jurisdiction where the defendant has assets.

Hence, although at the outset of contract negotiations neither party may wish to contemplate the possibility of an eventual dispute, the unhappy consequences of any such dispute are almost certain to be far greater for those who fail to provide in advance for such an eventuality.

Parties negotiating commercial agreements naturally seek at the outset to mitigate risk in every respect possible. Thus, in considering how potential disputes might be resolved neither side generally is willing to submit itself in advance to the courts of the other's country, if not for fear of actual bias by national courts in favor of their own nations, then for fear of placing itself at a relative disadvantage having to defend its interest in an unfamiliar environment. The parties' ability to agree upon a neutral forum for resolving their disputes, therefore, is of paramount importance. Whereas a third-country court might be as neutral as an international arbitral forum, assuming it would accept jurisdiction, arbitration stands as the far more popular choice.

There are several practical reasons why this is so. One is that arbitration is perceived by some as being a friendlier means of resolving disputes than litigation. Relatedly, a growing number of standard form contracts used in international commerce provide for arbitration. Even where contracts are negotiated on an ad hoc basis, often one or both of the parties either will be a member of some trade association whose rules provide for arbitration, or will be familiar with the terms of some standard contract containing an arbitration clause, such as, for example, in the construction field, FIDIC contracts.

In addition, many businesspeople instinctively prefer arbitration because it is private and generally less formal, and because they believe it to be a less expensive and more efficient means of dispute resolution. Ultimately, these assumptions may not be accurate, however, and each is discussed further below in addition to several other considerations relevant for parties considering the choice between arbitration and litigation.

Two very significant factors for parties considering whether to choose arbitration or to elect litigation are ... (1) the relative enforceability both of agreements to arbitrate versus forum selection clauses and of arbitral awards versus national court judgments; and (2) the relative unavailability of "appellate" judicial review of arbitral awards as compared to national court judgments....

One other possibly critical factor to be considered in the choice between arbitration and litigation is the availability of provisional measures, sometimes referred to as conservatory or interim measures.... For many types of disputes, for example those dealing with intellectual property rights, which by their nature may be particularly vulnerable to infringing action, the availability of effective and enforceable provisional measures may be essential.

Clearly, such measures of protection are available in the majority of (if not all) national court systems for parties choosing to litigate their disputes, although naturally there is some variation as to the types of protection available and the conditions under which they might be granted.

Most sets of arbitral rules likewise provide that the tribunal has the authority to grant interim measures of protection, and also that the parties' agreement to arbitrate does not preclude petition by a party to national courts for interim relief, at least prior to constitution of the arbitral tribunal. In many cases provisional remedies, if they are to have practical effect, must be granted sooner than the time at which an arbitral tribunal normally is constituted, and there still is some disagreement among national courts as to the availability of provisional measures in aid of arbitration.

To address parties' needs in respect of provisional remedies prior to the constitution of the arbitral tribunal, and to give parties an alternative to going into court, the International Chamber of Commerce (ICC) in 1990 adopted a PreArbitral Referee Procedure, modeled on the French referee-judge procedure, for obtaining urgent interim relief before the constitution of the arbitral tribunal. One obvious disadvantage of such a mechanism, however, is that both parties must agree to submit to the procedure. In addition, an ICC Referee's decision is not an award, and hence not directly enforceable, although it binds the parties and a failure to comply may be sanctioned by the arbitral tribunal once constituted.

Considerations do not inevitably point to litigation, however, for those parties anticipating the need for some interim relief. Many national jurisdictions require a showing of irreparable harm and a likelihood of success on the merits in order to obtain any provisional relief. Arbitrators, however, might not be so limited. In addition, parties agreeing to arbitrate may get two bites at the apple. Should a party be refused interim relief from a court, it may still apply to the tribunal for relief. Courts, however, may be more likely than arbitral tribunals to grant interim relief on an ex parte basis, which might be necessary to prevent an opposing party from transferring its assets out of reach. Also, there is likely to be some question as to the enforceability in courts of tribunal-ordered provisional measures, depending in part on whether the tribunal styles its decision an "award" or an "order."

Is arbitration cheaper and faster? The short answer to that question is "Not necessarily." In fact, although many have the impression that a less expensive and less time-consuming procedure is one of the major advantages of arbitration over litigation, in the international context, this may well not be the case. As previously noted, when arbitration is preferred in the international context it most likely is because it offers a neutral, ostensibly amicable forum for dispute resolution, which considerations outweigh most others.

Arbitration, like nearly any adversarial process, may be costly and time-consuming so long as a respondent is willing to devote significant resources to defending its positions and dilatory tactics are possible. In some respects, the amicable and flexible nature of arbitration may give rise to even greater time delays and consequent costs than litigation. In that sense the disadvantage of arbitration can result from the every same attributes that give rise to its advantages.

The success of arbitration as a broadly acceptable means of dispute resolution generally depends upon instilling trust in the process among parties from a wide variety of cultural perspectives. In addition, the fact that individual arbitrators are engaged by the parties to resolve a dispute and hence wish to instill in each of them confidence that its case is being thoroughly considered militates against curtailing or appearing to curtail either party's opportunity to present its case. The result is a reluctance, on the one hand, to limit the opportunity of either party to present its case to the tribunal, and, on the other hand, to decide issues summarily. Hence, in arbitration one does not find the panoply of remedies often available in courts designed to limit the further development of a case, e.g., motions to dismiss, summary judgment motions, etc. For the claimant, having a full opportunity to present its case to the tribunal without fear of summary dismissal may be a distinct advantage. For a defendant faced with what it considers to be patently meritless claims, however, such limitation may create significant burdens as one may be forced to spend significant resources fighting a costly battle that might have been dismissed summarily by a court.

Other factors leading to the potentially high cost of arbitration include the disposition of arbitrators, like diplomats, to be accommodating and, hence, often willing to grant numerous extensions of time to the parties to submit their pleadings. In addition, arbitral tribunals most often consist of three members, who must be paid appropriately, whereas court fees often are negligible. Delays caused by the difficulty in fixing hearing dates are common as there are invariably difficulties in accommodating the schedules of all three members of the tribunal as well as the parties, their attorneys and witnesses, and long hearings at a single stretch will prove to be either impossible or extremely difficult to arrange.

If one party is intent on dragging its feet, there will be ample opportunity for doing so even at the outset of the proceeding. It may take months before the constitution of the arbitral tribunal is settled, and even afterwards there may be challenges and resignations and the necessity to reconstitute, all before the arbitration can commence in earnest.

For many, the private nature of arbitration is seen as a major advantage over litigation. Arbitral proceedings are closed to the public and awards normally are not matters of public record. (Unless there is a specific agreement to the contrary, however, the proceedings may not be confidential as a matter of law, in which case either party may choose to publish the award.)

Nevertheless, the privacy and potential confidentiality of arbitration may prove of significant advantage to a party concerned, for example, about the disclosure of trade secrets. Arbitration offers parties an opportunity to shield their business dealings from competitors and the public. It may also be valued as a means of protecting ongoing commercial relations from possible harm due to a publicized dispute.

For some, however, the advantages of privacy may turn out to be unimportant. In a small commercial community the fact of an arbitration is likely to become known, and in a large one litigation may well pass unnoticed.

The greater flexibility of arbitration procedures as compared to litigation in national courts can be a major advantage in the international context. Regardless of what neutral forum is chosen, parties to an international dispute often find themselves thrust into an altogether alien process. The ability to control that process to a certain degree therefore may be valuable.

Most international arbitrations are conducted before a tribunal of three arbitrators, each of whom is required to be independent and impartial, although two of them are appointed by the respective disputants, the chairman often being chosen by the two party-appointed arbitrators. Parties often seek to appoint as a party-appointed arbitrator someone from a similar economic, political and social milieu whom they hope may be receptive to their position. So long as the arbitrator is capable of applying his or her mind judicially and impartially to the evidence and arguments submitted by both parties, such presumed affinity toward the one party is desirable, as it may give comfort and confidence in the integrity of the process to the parties. Indeed, the fact that a party-appointed arbitrator often is in a position more readily to appreciate and to explain to the other arbitrators the legal and cultural assumptions of the party that appointed him or her does not denote bias toward one side or the other; rather it is a natural and useful result of the modes of appointment of the three-member panel.

Apart from participating directly in the selection of a three-member panel of arbitrators, arbitrating parties have the widest discretion to fashion the proceedings to suit their needs. True, they usually begin by choosing an established arbitral institution with an existing set of procedural rules, such as, for example, the International Court of Arbitration of the International Chamber of Commerce (ICC) or the London Court of International Arbitration (LCIA), or an existing set of noninstitutional procedural rules, such as the United Nations Commission on International Trade Law (UNCITRAL) Arbitration Rules, although, strictly speaking, they may agree to a wholly unique procedure that suits their particular needs. Parties to arbitration also may agree to supplement the basic set of rules on which they have agreed by acceptance of, for example, the International Bar Association's (IBA's) Supplementary Rules Governing the Presentation and Reception of Evidence in International Commercial Arbitration, which incorporates attributes of both the common law and civil law approaches as regards the reception of evidence.

All basic sets of arbitration rules tend to be very flexible, however, and since they ordinarily permit the parties to vary them to a considerable extent, may be adapted by the parties easily. Moreover, the established arbitration rules that exist are silent on many points giving the parties and the arbitrators wide latitude to determine the procedure to be followed. Thus, where the parties cannot agree on how to conduct themselves, the tribunal (or its chairman) has tremendous power to control the proceedings.

When both parties are cooperative, and when their dispute lends itself to an expedited proceeding, the inherent flexibility of arbitration may enable them to complete proceedings significantly faster than would be the case with litigation in a national court. Parties may even opt for a "fast track" arbitration, such as is offered by the ICC and the LCIA, and thus may obtain resolution of their entire dispute in very short order.

* * *

PART C. LITIGATION

If the parties designate a forum selection clause, they must consider where to litigate and the consequences of that selection under the particular forum chosen. The well-informed party will consider the substantial differences in procedure between the common law and civil law legal systems. Under U.S. procedure, for example, the proceedings are described as adversarial, i.e., a contest between the two sides. The attorneys play an active role in asserting, as well as protecting, the parties' interests. Each party is responsible for developing its case in the pre-trial development as well as the evidentiary trial of the proceeding. The court only becomes involved during the pre-trial phase when objections are raised by either side which require judicial consideration and rulings on how the discovery should be conducted. One of the essential elements of the common law system is a separate trial proceeding with examination and cross-examination of witnesses by the attorneys for the parties. The right to a trial by jury is preserved in the seventh amendment in suits at common law. State constitutions generally include express guarantees of the right to trial by jury.[2]

In civil law systems, the court plays an active role in the proceeding. The pre-trial portion does not exist in civil law countries, and the entire proceeding remains under court supervision and control. Unlike common law legal systems, there is no separate trial proceeding with examination and cross-examination of witnesses. In civil law countries, trials are generally conducted without a jury and there tends to be no separate trial proceeding. The court chooses who should be selected as witnesses and examines the witnesses as well. There is generally no right of cross-examination and it is within the court's discretion to decide whether the attorney can ask supplemental questions. There is no oath-taking requirement and no verbatim transcript. The court usually prepares a summary of the proceeding. There may be specific requirements for witness testimony. Parties may not be called as witnesses and the court, rather than the parties, selects the experts.

In certain civil law countries, there are restrictions on contacting or interviewing witnesses before and during the trial. For example, Article 271 of the Swiss Penal Code provides in pertinent part: "Whoever, on Swiss territory, without being authorized . . . takes on behalf of a foreign government any action which is solely within the province [of the Swiss authorities] . . . shall be punished or imprisoned." Foreign attorneys are barred under such provisions from interviewing witnesses or obtaining affidavits or other acts deemed to fall within notions of foreign judicial sovereignty.

The United States is viewed as a magnet forum for foreigners. The U.S. legal system is noted for pretrial discovery, technical rules of evidence, and the dilatory tactics of attorneys. Without question, foreign plaintiffs seeking to take advantage of the U.S. legal system are faced with a variety of distinctive features which are unknown elsewhere. These features are highlighted in Problem 3.

As pointed out in the Brower and Smutny article, one of critical factors in favor of choosing the litigation alternative may be the availability of preliminary or interim relief. Provisional remedies may be more readily available in litigation proceedings than in arbitration. A variety of interim relief measures are readily available in common law countries, *i.e.*, the United States and common law jurisdictions. A provisional measure may be defined as a temporary process available to a party in a civil action, which secures against loss, irreparable injury, dissipation of property or evidence, or other events, while the litigation is in progress. In assessing your case, consider whether it is necessary to maintain the status quo on your party's behalf. Is it necessary to attach

2. See David Epstein, Jeffrey L. Snyder and Charles S. Baldwin, IV, *International Litigation: A Guide to Jurisdiction, Practice & Strategy* 3–6—3–8 (Transnational Publishers 2003)(hereinafter Epstein).

assets, bank accounts, etc. prior to the hearing? It is established that most judicial systems provide for preliminary relief although the available measure of protection and the required showing necessary to obtain such relief may vary under different legal systems. For example, many national courts require a showing of irreparable harm and a likelihood of success on the merits in order to obtain interim relief. It may be possible to obtain the assistance of United States or other national courts in securing provisional measures, either prior to or during an international arbitration. Obtaining preliminary relief in arbitration proceedings involves the following considerations: (1) the applicability of international arbitration conventions; (2) the applicability of national law; (3) the parties' arbitration agreement; and (4) the rules of the arbitral tribunal.[3]

In addition, damage awards rendered by U.S. juries are likely to be higher across-the-board than those obtained in foreign jurisdictions. In addition, punitive damages, which are recognized under the U.S. legal system, are considered novel in other jurisdictions. The size of punitive damage awards rendered by U.S. courts has led other countries, such as Germany, to bar enforcement of that portion of U.S. judgments and to hinder efforts of the United States in attempting to negotiate a multilateral enforcement of judgments convention.[4]

Plaintiffs will engage in forum shopping in order to avail themselves of the procedural and substantive benefits available in U.S. courts. Even where the contacts or links are tenuous, plaintiffs will select the U.S. forum as their preferred choice. Significant obstacles are presented under the doctrine of *forum non conveniens*, however, when plaintiffs have only a minimal interest in litigating in the United States. The trial court is vested with considerable discretion in determining whether to exercise jurisdiction in a given case or to dismiss the case when the U.S. forum is inconvenient. *See Gulf Oil v. Gilbert,* 330 U.S. 501, 67 S.Ct. 839, 91 L.Ed. 1055 (1947); *Piper Aircraft v. Reyno,* 454 U.S. 235, 102 S.Ct. 252, 70 L.Ed.2d 419 (1981).

Arbitration may lack many of the procedural and other safeguards inherent in the U.S. litigation system. It may be advantageous for a party to rely on the full range of discovery offered by litigation, including the right to compel production of documents and to depose recalcitrant witnesses. The availability of discovery in litigation provides benefits to all parties to the dispute. Pretrial discovery is virtually unknown in civil law systems and is a feature of the U.S. legal system. This is a central factor in parties deciding whether or not to select U.S. courts as the forum of choice. In arbitration, discovery is more limited and depends on the discretion of the arbitrators. In the majority of cases, the discovery which is permitted is limited to the production of specified relevant documents. This is in contrast to discovery under the U.S. legal system, which generally permits the parties to obtain wide-ranging interrogato-

3. See Epstein, *supra* at 12.23 *et seq.*

4. Judgment of June 4, 1993, BGH 46 Westpapier–Mittehunger 1451, 1461 (1992).

Two German decisions dealing with judgment enforcement are reproduced and discussed in Problem 7.2.

ries, depositions, and production of documents from the other party. Rule 26, F.R.C.P. generally allows discovery to be had of any relevant information reasonably calculated to lead to discovery of admissible evidence.

28 U.S.C. 1782 provides that U.S. district courts may order discovery "for use in a proceeding in a foreign or international tribunal" upon the request of such a foreign or international tribunal, "or upon the application of any interested person . . .". It has generally been held that the provisions of Section 1782 do not extend to international arbitral tribunals. These courts have not considered a private commercial arbitration as a "proceeding in a foreign or international tribunal" or as adjudicatory in nature for purposes of Section 1782.[5] Commentators have noted that while discovery may be expensive and time-consuming, it serves to weed out meritless claims and defenses early in the process and may even deter parties from pursuing such claims altogether. Hence, the limitation on the availability of discovery in the context of arbitration may hinder fact development and lead to unjustified results.

There are key procedural differences between arbitration and litigation. While parties to arbitration must submit to the whole process, litigation may be disposed of by a motion to dismiss or summary judgment prior to trial. In addition, there is usually no appeals procedure in arbitration.

Additionally, on a comparative basis, the costs of arbitration may be higher since the expenses, including the fees of the arbitrators, are borne by the parties to the arbitration. These costs may vary depending on the rules of the appointing authorities selected by the parties. For example,

> [Assuming] a claim of $1,000,000, the AAA [American Arbitration Association] would charge $5,000 for its services as the appointing authority and administrator. The I.C.C. [International Chamber of Commerce] charges $16,800. The I.C.C generally has a more thorough review process, however, which probably improves the quality of the awards. The London Court of Arbitration charges $2250 plus time and expenses for administration plus approximately the amount the arbitrator would normally earn in his or her profession. The Japanese Commercial Arbitration Association would charge approximately $12,350, while the British Columbia Arbitration Centre would charge approximately $3,360 plus additional fees per quarter ($350 per party) as administrative fees.[6]

What is the preferred mechanism for international dispute resolution—arbitration or litigation? Does the answer depend on whether the party is considering resolution of the dispute from the perspective of an American businessman versus his or her foreign adversary?

---

5. *See National Broadcasting Company, Inc. v. Bear Stearns & Co., Inc.,* 165 F.3d 184 (2d Cir.1999); *Republic of Kazakhstan v. Biedermann Int'l,* 168 F.3d 880 (5th Cir. 1999).

6. ALI–ABA Continuing Legal Education Court of Study Nov. 2000. E. Charles Routh, Dispute Resolution–Representing the Foreign Client in Arbitration in Arbitration and Litigation.

PART D.   ARBITRATION

WILLIAM W. PARK, THE RELATIVE RELIABILITY OF ARBITRATION AGREEMENTS AND COURT SELECTION CLAUSES

The Regulation of Forum Selection.
Fourteenth Sokol Colloquium 3.
Transnational Publishers 1997.

In the broad field of international business transactions, for example, arbitration and court selection mechanisms level the playing field in resolving disputes between companies from different countries and cultures. In the garden of domestic transactions, however, a forum selection clause can become an instrument of oppression, inserted into the fine print of a standard form contract to designate a court or an arbitral tribunal predisposed in favor of the dominant party.

Context-related contrasts of a different nature present themselves when one compares the relative reliability of arbitration agreements and court-selection clauses, the two principal forum selection mechanisms. In a domestic transaction, American business managers normally expect, and often find, that submitting a claim to a court will provide a greater level of predictability than arbitration. When the adversary is foreign, however, commercial actors can often enhance the reliability of contract adjudication through abandoning recourse to judges, substituting instead arbitration under the rules of a neutral institution and subject to the New York Convention's treaty-based enforcement regime.

As a preliminary matter, one should be clear about what the relevant differences between court selection and arbitration are *not*. Despite the practitioners and scholars who wax eloquent about arbitration's high speed and low cost, arbitral proceedings in the real world are rarely either quicker or cheaper than court actions. Whether arbitration commends itself as speedy and cost efficient depends entirely on the factual configuration of each transaction.

Arbitration justifies itself in a cross-border business context principally as a tool to minimize the real or imagined dangers of litigation abroad: a mechanism to reduce the risk of ending up before a biased foreign judge who will apply unfamiliar procedures in a strange language. It is not so much that business managers "choose" to submit controversies to arbitrators, as that arbitration imposes itself on an international transaction for want of any better way to resolve a conflict between parties whose different cultures create a high degree of mutual suspicion toward each other's judicial system.

Few attorneys, however, seem to give much attention to the relative merits of arbitration in contrast to court selection. When lawyers in Boston learn that I teach a course on international business transactions, they often share with me the details of a cross-border venture in which they spent a considerable amount of their own time and the client's money negotiating a well-crafted contract with a foreign buyer, seller, or licensee. But when asked about the forum selection provision, not many of them can explain why they chose particular courts or arbitration rules. It is as if they assumed the contract would enforce itself automatically.

Such failure to consider adequately the selection of those individuals or institutions that will interpret a contract may not make much of a difference in a domestic context, where language and procedural alternatives in litigation are relatively minimal. In an international transaction, however, foreign litigation can be both dramatically different and dramatically disagreeable.

————

The pros and cons of arbitration versus litigation are frequently debated by practitioners in the field of international litigation and arbitration. There is no debate, however, that choosing the arbitral procedure together with the rules of a neutral institution lends certainty to the mechanisms of resolving the dispute. Of equal significance is the enforcement mechanism provided by the New York Convention's treaty-based enforcement regime.

WILLIAM W. PARK, AWARD ENFORCEMENT UNDER THE NEW YORK CONVENTION

Course Handbook on International Business.
Litigation and Arbitration 573.
Practicing Law Institute 2003.

Agreements to arbitrate are enforced in one hundred and thirty-three countries under the Convention on the Recognition and Enforcement of Foreign Arbitral Awards. Often referred to as the "New York Convention" (by virtue of its city of adoption), this treaty implements business managers' agreements to waive recourse to otherwise competent national courts in favor of binding private business dispute resolution. The Convention gives effect to both the arbitration clause and the resulting award even in countries that have resisted analogous treaties to enforce court selection agreements and foreign judgments.

* * *

The New York Convention operates both to enforce arbitration agreements and to promote recognition of awards at the place where the loser has assets. The Convention requires courts of contracting states to refer the parties to arbitration when a dispute is subject to a written arbitration agreement that is not "null and void, inoperative or incapable of being performed." Although this duty to refer the parties to arbitration will apply to judicial actions, the arbitration clause will not necessarily bar administrative proceedings.

In addition, courts must recognize foreign awards "in accordance with the rules of procedure of the territory where the award is relied upon" and subject to conditions no more onerous than those imposed on domestic awards. Thus the Convention's practical effectiveness can depend on national arbitration law.

* * *

There is no requirement that the litigants come from different states, or that the party seeking to enforce an award be from a country that has adhered to the Convention. Citizenship is relevant to Convention coverage only indirectly, when the parties' different nationalities add an element indicating an award is "not domestic," . . .

Geography is the principal trigger for application of the Convention, which covers primarily foreign awards. Under this test, an award rendered in New York would be covered by the Convention when presented for enforcement against assets in Zurich, Paris or London, but not when recognition is sought before courts in Atlanta or Los Angeles.

Inability to meet the geographical test, however, does not mean the award creditor is entirely out of luck. The Convention will also apply to "awards not considered as domestic," a subtle and multi-faceted notion. Thus in the above scenario, a New York award might be considered by a United States court as "not domestic" if the factual configuration of the case contained foreign parties or other significant cross-border elements.

The concept of a non-domestic award was given a wide scope in a decision holding that United States courts could apply the Convention to awards rendered in the United States in disputes entirely between United States corporations. Part of the contract was to be performed abroad, leading the court to consider the dispute within the scope of the Convention.

For better or worse, the Convention is less precise with respect to its coverage of arbitration agreements than awards. The Convention requires only that the agreement to arbitrate be in writing, and that it cover disputes "in respect to a defined legal relationship" (whether or not contractual) concerning a "subject matter capable of settlement by arbitration."

Whether through design or inadvertence, the Convention drafters did not indicate further limitations on the type of arbitration agreements covered. Commentators have suggested, however, that Convention coverage of arbitration agreements should be interpreted consistently with its scope as to awards. Applying by analogy the general provisions on Convention coverage of awards, the Convention would apply to agreements (i) providing for foreign arbitration (in a country other than the one in which the arbitration clause is invoked) or (ii) sufficiently international to be "not domestic."

* * *

A court of a Convention country may refuse recognition and enforcement to awards only on the basis of a limited list of procedural defenses. Divided into two groups, these defenses allow courts to avoid lending their power to support awards that result from unfair proceedings or which contravene the forum's fundamental notions of public policy.

The first group of defenses includes an invalid arbitration agreement, lack of opportunity to present one's case, arbitrator excess of jurisdiction and irregular composition of the arbitral tribunal. These defenses must be asserted and proven by the party resisting the award.

In addition, a court on its own motion, without any proof by the party resisting the award, may refuse to enforce an award whose subject matter is not arbitrable or which violates the forum's public policy (*ordre public*). While the first set of Convention defenses are intended to safeguard the parties against injustice, the second set serve as a explicit catch-all for the enforcement country's own vital interests and policies.

In the United States, New York Arbitration Convention defenses have traditionally been given a narrow scope, with the Conventions's public policy defense interpreted to include only violations of the "most basic notions of morality and justice." Many other nations have recognized that a broad interpretation of "public policy" would defeat one of the principal purposes of international arbitration, which is to permit business managers from different countries to secure some measure of neutral dispute resolution.

* * *

While some countries benefit from comprehensive treaties for enforcing court selection clauses and the resulting judgment, not all parts of the world are blessed with such a dependable framework for dealing with jurisdiction and judgments. Thus the New York Convention can be of special significance in business transactions in which enforcement of a court selection clause might be problematic.

For example, to date the United States has not concluded a single treaty on foreign judgments. Even its closest allies and trading partners have refused to enter into such treaties from fear of punitive damages, strict product liability, civil juries and other aspects of the United States' civil justice system unfamiliar in more civilized lands. While United States judgments might in some cases be enforced abroad as a matter of "comity" (a judicially created golden rule allowing courts to recognize foreign judgments) or common law actions on debt, this remains a matter of national discretion rather than international obligation.

However, the United States is a party to the New York Arbitration Convention, which permits American business managers and their foreign counter parties to maximize the certainty that commercial disputes will be resolved in a relatively neutral and predictable forum. The importance of such neutrality and predictability can hard by overestimated in contexts where there exists between the parties a high degree of mistrust of the other side's judicial system and a mutual interest in foreclosing multiple litigation options.

As stated in the Park article, there is no comparable treaty in force for the enforcement of United States judicial judgments. In fact, as will be discussed in Chapter Seven, enforcement of U.S. judgments by foreign courts is problematic and subject to the discretionary application of principles of international comity and variances in local law on a case-by-case basis. The wide-spread implementation by approximately 133 countries of the framework of the New York Convention enables parties to engage in the arbitration process in the selected forum with the likelihood that the courts will enforce the arbitral award obtained.

PART E.   MEDIATION

Parties to the international transaction may also consider the use of mediation in the dispute resolution process. Mediation operates differently from arbitration in that the parties and the mediator have no authority to bind the other to a decision unless there is agreement among the parties to the dispute. The international contract may include both mediation and arbitration clauses. The mediation clause may provide that the parties agree to submit the dispute, as a precondition to the filing or commencement of any litigation or arbitration proceeding, to mediation.... The mediation process is described in greater detail in Chapter 10.

NANCY A. ORETSKIN, A FASHIONABLE ALTERNATIVE TO RESOLVE INTERNATIONAL CONFLICTS

Course Handbook on International Business.
Litigation and Arbitration 513.
Practicing Law Institute (2003).

The interest and importance of using mediation domestically and internationally as a dispute resolution mechanism has been steadily increasing. This is clearly evidenced in the legal world by the promulgation and adopting of two model pieces of legislation. In the United States, the Uniform Mediation Act (UMA) was adopted in August 2001 by the National Conference of Commissioners on Uniform State Laws (NCCUSL) and by the American Bar Association (ABA) House of Delegates in February 2002; internationally, the United Nations adopted the Model Law on international Commercial Conciliation (Model Law) in 2002.

The UMA was drafted collaboratively between NCCUSL and the ABA over a four-year period that began in 1997. These two legal "powerhouses" had never before "joined" forces to create an Act. The drafting process included extensive public interaction from invited observers that represented the diverse mediation community. Written comments for those absent from the negotiating table were also considered. This open process created a space which allowed the drafting committee to approach their task fully, informed and ultimately allowed them to produce an acceptable Act to most of the mediation constituency.

The UMA was promulgated in an effort to enhance the use of mediation and its effectiveness yet preserve public confidence in the justice system. Some states have already adopted this Act. Both NCCUSSL and the ABA view this Act as priority and in 2003 will focus on the promotion of this Act in the legislative bodies of the fifty United States.

The United Nations Commission on International Trade Law (UNCITRAL) negotiated the Model Law over a two-year period rotating meetings between Vienna, Austria and New York. Over fifty United Nations member states participated in the drafting of this Model Law. Official observers from a variety of international organizations also participated in the process. Although drafted as an international document, it is believed this Model Law will be very useful in a number of countries for the promotion of domestic mediation. The Model Law is available in the six official U.N. languages. UNCITRAL has also designated this law as a top priority and is encouraging all of the 190 plus members of the United Nations to adopt this law.

In December 2002, NCCUSL reconvened its drafting group to explore possible ways to incorporate the content of the UNCITRAL Model Law into the UMA. As of this writing, the next drafting member is scheduled for March 2003.

Why has mediation moved so quickly to the forefront in the domestic and international world as a preferred legal method of dispute resolution?

1.   The mediation process allows disputing parties from a variety of business organizations (multi-national conglomerates to sole proprietorships), different cultures, different gender, different professions, a "level playing field" to use for the resolution of their dispute. Parties and the mediator are equally important in this dispute resolution (DR) process since no one has the authority to bind the other to a decision unless there is agreement among and between the disputing parties. The role of the mediator is not as a decision-maker, but rather as a facilitator assisting the parties to work together to reach a consensual settlement. The disputing parties retain a large control over this process rather than yielding this decision to a third party who is a stranger unfamiliar with either the business or the people involved in the dispute.

Legal procedure, (foreign or domestic) and evidentiary rules are not utilized in mediation since they are not germane and thus do not hinder the parties ability to address the conflict.

2.   Often, mediation is referred to as "facilitated negotiation". As this definition suggests, the "heart" of the mediation process is negotiation. Irrespective of the specific negotiation style one utilizes, (interest-based, narrative-based or identity-based negotiation), a "win-win" result rather than the adversarial "win-lose" result is an obtainable goal for the disputing parties.

Through the use of a mediator, parties are encouraged to minimize the coercive use of power, and utilize a cooperative approach of problem solving that permits the disputing parties to identify interests and share information and priorities related to these interests rather than focus on positions and bottom lines. Through the mutual process of brainstorming, the parties proffer idealized proposals and work through these suggestions until they identify a workable negotiated settlement. This process allows the parties through the assistance of the mediator to follow a flexible communication pattern where creativity is central and the view of a single-fixed pie [sic] is obsolete.

3. Mediation allows parties a venue to reach a quick and expedient resolution. Through the use of mediation, parties are not required to file legal documents with courts and comply with legal formalities. As soon as parties mutually agree to use mediation as a dispute resolution process, the process can begin. There is no delay or waiting period so long as the parties agree. Truly, mediation is the best business approach to resolve conflicts. The process can be quick, inexpensive and under the control of the disputing parties. Corporate CEO's and business managers have the ability without the interference of another bureaucracy to reach a negotiated settlement.

4. The mediation process is flexible and easily managed. Very often disputes can be minimized if parties have an opportunity to apologize to the other without sacrificing the perception that he/she is weak. This process allows one to save face. As a result of this characteristic of mediation, many business entities that have utilized mediation express very high customer satisfaction with the process thereby enhancing its value to the business community.

5. The mediation process allows trust to play an interesting as well as critical role in the DR process. Disputing parties work collaboratively from the onset of the dispute to identify and select an appropriate mediator. Opposing sides trust that the mediator will act in an impartial manner to assist in the resolution of the dispute. The mediator uses this element of trust as his or her power. Building on the shared belief of trust, a skillful mediator is able to "grow" the trust factor and eventually lead the disputing parties to begin to trust the other. Once this period of "enlightenment" has begun, the disputing parties are able to look with "new eyes" at the barriers creating the conflict. Slowly building on each other's trust, the parties are able to jointly identify and create a "space" for a solution.

Engendering trust between the parties and toward the entire process is one of the beautiful elements of mediation.

6. Reliable trading partners are considered a very valuable asset for all commercial entities; this is even more important from an international perspective. In the multinational marketplace, trading relationships are less fungible and more difficult to substitute or replace. Thus, it is very important, economically, emotionally and socially that this underlying business relationship be preserved and kept intact.

Mediation allows disputing parties an opportunity to work in an amicable style rather than an adversarial manner to resolve or settle the conflict. Through the use of mediation, disputing parties are able to "attack the problem" not the people behind the problem. Once the human element is emphasized and the underlying business relationship preserved, one can continue to transact business.

7.   Mediation offers disputing parties the ability to structure their own negotiated Confidential Settlement. Often, disputes are intertwined with confidential and proprietary information. Protecting this information from public exposure becomes the work of far too many lawyers during the litigation process. Through the use of mediation, this information is protected from public access since all aspects of the mediation process are confidential.

In summary, for the resolution of domestic and international commercial disputes, mediation is becoming a fashionable DR alternative since it focuses on the human aspect of dispute resolution while concurrently providing an expedient and acceptable business option.

.   .   .

Most commentators would agree that the inclusion of some type of dispute resolution mechanism, arbitration, mediation or forum selection, in the international contract is better than none at all. Otherwise, the claiming party is left to search for a suitable jurisdiction with perhaps an unfriendly forum applying unfamiliar procedures to the dispute. For these reasons, this option frequently leads to unhappy results and large uncertainties at the enforcement stage.

Comments

1.   The Chwialkowska article printed from the Toronto National Post points out the increasing need of courts for guidance concerning international law materials and evidence. While Chapter One focuses on identifying international law issues and cases, Chapter Two deals with the lawyer's responsibility in handling cross-border issues. The lawyer who fails to present international evidence in proper form may prejudice his/her client's case if the court has to grapple with their legal significance.

In a related context, any party intending to rely on foreign law as part of the proof of its case should be familiar with Rule 44.1 of the Federal Rules of Civil Procedure. That rule provides as follows:

> A party who intends to raise an issue concerning the law of a foreign country shall give notice in his pleadings or other reasonable written notice. The court, in determining foreign law, may consider any relevant material or source, including testimony, whether or not submitted by a party or admissible under the Federal Rules of Evidence. The court's determination shall be treated as a ruling on question of law.

In determining issues of foreign law, U.S. courts have considered a wide variety of sources, including affidavits and expert testimony. Under Rule 44.1, a court may conduct its own research or insist that the counsel engage in this task. It is incumbent on counsel to make a complete and convincing presentation of foreign law issues despite the court's authority under Rule 44.1 to conduct its own independent research. Under the adversarial legal system, if the party makes a weak showing on proof of foreign law, there is the risk that the opposing side will prevail. Similarly, counsel may lose control of the issue if the court has difficulty understanding the foreign law issue and decides to embark on its own research and review.

2. The case of *Bhatnagar v. Surrendra Overseas Ltd.*, 52 F.3d 1220 (3d Cir.1995) illustrates how submissions by experts on foreign law and procedure can become a "battle of the experts." In that case the Third Circuit analyzed the adequacy of an alternate forum under the doctrine of *forum non conveniens*. At issue was the factor of delay in establishing that an adequate alternative forum was available in the Indian courts for the subject litigation. Plaintiff relied on elaborate statistical data from its expert which showed that it would take in excess of 20 years to resolve the case in the Indian courts. Defendant submitted an affidavit of an Indian law expert noting that India had a well-developed legal system which would be able to handle the issues presented in the case and agreed to support expeditious hearing of the matter in India. In weighing the competing affidavits, the court was not convinced that defendant's willingness to cooperate in expediting the case in India would have any real effect in avoiding unreasonable delays there. Based on a comparison of the expert affidavits, it is not surprising that the Third Circuit found plaintiff's elaborate statistical analysis more persuasive than defendant's conclusory, self-serving submission.

3. Some courts view expert testimony as the basic mode of proving foreign law. Courts may question by testimony or other means the objectivity and reliability of experts engaged by the parties. Where close questions of foreign law are presented, courts retain the ability under FED.R.EVID. 706 to appoint their own experts to narrow the gap. Pursuant to FED.R.EVID. 706, the expert's duties may be clarified at a conference to be attended by the parties. In addition, the expert's findings must be provided to the parties, who may depose or cross-examine the expert. The witness may be called to testify before the court by any party and subject to cross-examination by each party, including the party calling the witness. See Chapter 4, problem 4.4 *infra*.

Chapter 2

THE ROLE OF THE INTERNATION-AL LAWYER IN INTERNATIONAL CIVIL DISPUTE RESOLUTION

SECTION 2.1 CROSS–BORDER PRACTICE

It has been observed that the lawyer who undertakes to handle an international case or one that involves the law or parties of more than one country may have broader responsibilities than his/her domestic counterpart. These responsibilities, which traditionally include issues involving the law of the forum, can extend well beyond those borders. Legal commentators have noted the expansive role of the U.S. lawyer engaged in the practice of international law.

> With greater emphasis on federal legislation in many areas of the law, and harmonization of state laws through 'uniform' laws promulgated by the National Conference of Commissioners on Uniform State Law, as well as case law that relies heavily on the Restatements of the American Law Institute, lawyers regularly must look beyond the law of their own state to provide competent legal counsel in both transactional and litigation matters. As private international law experiences the development of conventions and model laws designed to harmonize rules world-wide, this process is repeating itself on a global scale.[1]

This chapter describes situations in which the lawyer has to decide whether he or she is competent to undertake the international aspects of the matter. Is the professional responsibility owed to the client any different from that in a purely domestic case? How does a U.S. lawyer know when he or she should seek assistance from foreign counsel? What are the benchmarks that determine this evaluation in terms of the lawyer's professional and ethical responsibilities? Professor Ronald Brand has observed:

---

1. Ronald Brand, *Uni-State Lawyers and Multinational Practice: Dealing with* *International, Transnational, and Foreign Law*, 34 Vand. J. Transnat'l L. 1135 (2001).

Businesses in today's markets both want and fear transnational involvement. On the one hand, they want the extra profits and economies of scale that can come from global markets. At the same time they seek to avoid the increased uncertainty and risk resulting from the additional sets of rules that may apply to their conduct in those markets. Competent legal counsel is thus even more important in a cross-border transaction than in its domestic counterpart. This raises two fundamental questions regarding the lawyer's role in such a transaction: what is the benchmark by which we measure lawyer competence in such representation, and what is the threshold beyond which even the most competent lawyer should not pass in engaging in the practice of law outside his or her state of admission? The related question, by which we necessarily must judge our answers to the first two, is: what is the profession's obligation to a client involved in transnational transactions in terms of encouraging, allowing, and regulating competent provision of legal services?[2]

Some of the ethical and professional responsibility issues faced by the lawyer engaged in the practice of international law will be examined in Section 2.3.

Section 2.2 highlights special tools available in the conduct of legal research of foreign and international law. Such research can be difficult and frustrating for those unfamiliar with the special research tools available to acquire knowledge of foreign and international law. What sources are available to assist the U.S. lawyer in locating and employing the services of qualified foreign counsel to provide advice on foreign law and procedure? What are some of the basic rules in communicating and dealing with foreign counsel? Once issues involving international and/or foreign law have been identified, what resources may be employed to achieve success for your client? These are some of the areas to be covered in this chapter in dealing with the role of the international lawyer in resolving international civil disputes.

PART A.   HANDLING CROSS–BORDER ISSUES

A substantial number of attorneys in the United States have clients with needs in the international area. This increase has been attributed to growing global trade. Knowledge of international law will increasingly become an essential part of everyday practice. One recent study of international legal education in the United States points to the following factors as contributing to the growth in the practice in this area of the law:

> The need for the practitioner to know international law is not limited to the business attorney. The proliferation of international transactions will invariably result in a growth in international disputes. Litigators increasingly find themselves representing or suing foreigners. The modern day litigator, whether defending against a product's liability claim or bringing suit because a foreign

---

2. Id. at 1138.

purchaser failed to pay for delivery of a product, must know the peculiarities of transnational legal dispute settlement. Will a judgment from one jurisdiction be enforced in another? Might the case turn on how process was served? Which law will be applied to decide the case? How do these issues affect choice of venue? Litigators can no longer afford to be ignorant of international law.

Regardless of a lawyer's specialty, he or she must know something about international law to compete in tomorrow's market. The Internet further exacerbates this need. The World Wide Web allows inexpensive worldwide advertising for products in a way unprecedented in history—no doubt accelerating the brisk pace of international trade. Unfortunately, worldwide advertising via the Internet also allows the dishonest to infringe on an owner's copyright interest from the safety of a country that inadequately protects intellectual property. Furthermore, the ability to send solicitations instantaneously, and virtually without cost, by electronic mail creates the possibility of 'pyramid' schemes on a previously unheard-of-scale. Business attorneys and litigators certainly have significant international work to keep them busy for years to come.[3]

The following three examples serve to illustrate the role of the lawyer when pertinent international and/or foreign law issues emerge during the course of the dispute resolution process. These issues may appear at any stage of the process or even before the litigation or other dispute resolution process has commenced. The lawyer needs to consider the following factors in providing effective legal advice to his or her client: (1) awareness and identification of the international issues presented; (2) proper conduct of legal research as to foreign law and international law issues involved; (3) employment of foreign counsel or foreign legal consultants to assist, if needed; (4) consideration of strategy alternatives to effect the best results for the client.

Example 1

Your client sues a Japanese company in a court in the United States. Service of process of the summons and complaint needs to be effected on the defendant in Japan. You advise the client that Japan is a signatory to the Hague Service Convention and that service should be made in accordance with treaty procedures. Your client wishes to serve the documents in the least expensive manner and to avoid incurring costs for translating the documents into Japanese. The client expresses a preference to serve the documents by mail. This fact scenario implicates the following international law issues: 1) Is service of process by mail valid under the provisions of the Hague Service Convention, 2) How has the service by mail provision—Article 10—in the Hague Service Convention been interpreted under U.S. law?, 3) Is service by mail a valid means of

3. John A. Barrett, Jr., *International Legal Education in the United States: Being Educated for Domestic Practice While Living in a Global Society*, 12 Am. U.J. Int'l. L. & Pol'y 975 (1997).

service under the laws of Japan, and 4) Will a U.S. judgment be enforced in Japan if service is effected by mail?

A study of U.S. case law reveals that the validity of service by mail under the Hague Service Convention is unresolved and Article 10 has been the subject of conflicting interpretations. While there is no controlling point of law on the service by mail question, it is certainly more prudent to advise the client to transmit the documents by the formal method prescribed by the treaty. Your client would be provided with proof of service which could be used to support a subsequent enforcement of judgment action in Japan, if service of process became an issue in that proceeding. On the other hand, service by mail provides no record of proof of service and enforcement of the judgment in Japan may be challenged on grounds of insufficient notice. Should Japanese counsel be employed to provide an opinion on the validity of service by mail in Japan and its effect on enforceability of the judgment? While some of the general research issues under U.S. law might be conducted by the U.S. lawyer, a more definitive opinion on the law of Japan could be rendered by foreign counsel. Legal costs and attorneys fees factor into many of the decisions made in litigation. Frequently, shortcuts are taken which may not be in the client's best interests. It is the U.S. lawyer's responsibility, however, to present available options to the client under this example and the legal consequences of following a particular course of action.

Example Two

A commercial litigation dispute is filed in United States court. Both parties are domestic. As the case develops, plaintiff seeks to obtain crucial evidence from a third party located in Germany. Testimony is sought, including the production of documents for use at the trial. As counsel for the plaintiff, you need to determine the proper method of obtaining the evidence in Germany. This situation gives rise to issues under U.S. and German law. In order to place the evidence gathering issue in proper perspective, the lawyer should advise his or her client of the restrictive attitude in civil law countries, such as Germany, towards discovery as opposed to the liberal U.S. pretrial practice.[4] General guidance to the public in obtaining evidence abroad is available from the Bureau of Consular Affairs of the State Department.[5] The United States and Germany are signatories to the Hague Evidence Convention. A study of the Convention, including the declarations and reservations taken by Germany, reveal the applicable procedures for obtaining evidence in that country as well as the restrictive rules under Article 23 which preclude obtaining pretrial production of documents from Germany. The lawyer also will need to research the applicable law as to the exclusivity of the Hague Evidence Convention, i.e., whether the evidence-taking proceed-

---

4. Under Rule 26(b)(1) Fed.R.Civ.P., and similar state rules of civil procedure, a party may obtain all relevant information, not privileged, reasonably calculated to *lead to* the discovery of admissible evidence.

5. Judicial assistance information may be found at the following web-site (www.travel.state.gov/).

ing is governed by the treaty or state and federal rules of procedure when the evidence sought is to be obtained from a third-party.

All of the issues presented *supra,* can be researched under U.S. law. However, there is an important role for foreign counsel under this scenario. Under the civil law procedure in Germany, the evidence gathering is in the hands of the German judge who presides over the proceeding and asks all of the questions. There are, in addition, many procedural differences from a U.S. deposition proceeding, including no verbatim transcript, no oath taking and other differences. If the U.S. lawyer seeks to participate in the proceeding, the services of a German lawyer must be employed. In the evidence request, the U.S. party would request that counsel be permitted to attend the proceeding in order to ask supplemental questions. The German lawyer could also attempt to obtain selected documents despite the Article 23 restrictions noted above. Foreign counsel can also assist in drafting the evidence request to insure that it conforms to local law and procedure. There is no assurance that the U.S. party's request will be honored under German law and procedure. However, participation by the U.S. party in the proceeding may be the only way to insure that full and responsive evidence is obtained. While there are no guarantees that this strategy will work, the U.S. lawyer can demonstrate to the client that all efforts have been exhausted, thereby discharging the duties of zealous, competent representation.

The lawyer assigned to handle the international case may be called on to provide advice on cross-border issues at any stage of the dispute resolution process or even before the actual process has begun. For example, if your client intended to initiate a lawsuit against a multinational company, you may need to advise on the pros and cons of choosing a particular forum. In selecting the best place to bring suit, issues would have to be resolved, both practical and strategic, involving a number of key considerations, such as personal jurisdiction over the defendant, availability of interim relief such as injunction or seizure of assets, substantive law theories, damage concepts, location of assets, etc. Inherent in this type of analysis would be a description of the legal system in the potential forum.

If suit in a civil law country is contemplated, the attorney would need to compare the key differences between a civil versus a common law system. In a complex case, the attorney should exercise caution before embarking on a detailed examination of foreign or comparative law without special expertise or background as to those issues. The U.S. lawyer may find that employing the services of a foreign lawyer to resolve crucial issues of this nature is the most professional and responsible way to proceed. From an ethical standpoint, which will be examined in greater detail in Section 2.3, the duty of competent representation may be satisfied through increased understanding of foreign law, as well as through association with a foreign lawyer when advice on foreign law is necessary. As Professor Brand notes, the more difficult question is when a lawyer may rely on his or her own knowledge in providing competent representation.[6]

Example 3

Your client, a U.S. based company, is threatened with a libel suit by an individual in a foreign court for defamatory statements made over the Internet. The individual alleges there is personal jurisdiction in his home country since that is where the damage to his reputation occurred and where the defamatory statements were published. The libel laws in his home jurisdiction are much stricter than in the United States. Defendant publishing company states that jurisdiction should lie where the material is placed on the computer and not in the jurisdiction where the published material is read. The publishing company seeks legal advice from its U.S. lawyer on possible defenses as to lack of personal jurisdiction of the foreign court and liability on the merits under the foreign libel laws. The U.S. lawyer is faced with the following choices: 1) advise the client to be patient and wait until litigation is actually filed in order to better assess its defenses; 2) provide an opinion on the general law involved in both the home and foreign jurisdictions; 3) provide an opinion based solely on issues raised under U.S. law; 4) provide a comprehensive opinion researching questions involving U.S. law and employing overseas counsel for input on foreign law issues.

The U.S. lawyer identifies the following cross-border issues from a preliminary analysis of the facts:

(1) Does the foreign court have personal jurisdiction over the U.S. company? The body of law on this issue is still developing since the material was published on the Internet. This will likely be a controversial issue with little precedent under customary international law.

(2) What is the law on defamation in the foreign jurisdiction and what defenses are available to the U.S. defendant? The foreign defamation law will need to be examined in detail and compared with the U.S. libel law. The client should understand that its liability exposure may be greater under the foreign law versus liability in a U.S. proceeding.

(3) What are the categories of damages available under the foreign law, *i.e.,* punitive damages, damage to reputation, etc. and what is the usual range of damages awarded in this type of case in that jurisdiction?

(4) Should the defendant appear and defend the case in the foreign jurisdiction?

(5) If defendant decides not to appear in the foreign lawsuit, would a foreign default judgment in this type of case be recognized and enforced by a U.S. court? What defenses may be available to the defendant to the enforcement proceeding?

It may not be prudent under the above scenario to delay providing comprehensive advice pending the actual filing of the lawsuit. The client

---

6. *Id.* at 1139.

needs to be fully advised of the legal issues involved in his/her situation as soon as possible. Important decisions need to be made; namely, whether the foreign action will be defended or the matter settled. Advice on both U.S. and foreign law will greatly assist the client in making these decisions and deciding on an appropriate strategy once litigation commences. As stated, the need to employ legal services in multiple jurisdictions is often necessary and essential in complex international cases in order to provide effective legal advice to the client.

PART B.   HIRING A LAWYER ABROAD

As above discussed, it often becomes necessary during the course of international litigation to retain local counsel for legal advice in other countries. The U.S. attorney would neither be licensed nor qualified to appear in those proceedings without the presence of foreign counsel. The services of foreign counsel are also required when proof of foreign law or specific advice on foreign law is needed for the case. One good resource in selecting foreign counsel is the Bureau of Consular Affairs in the Department of State. On its web-site,[7] this office provides a country-by-country list of attorneys who practice in the particular foreign jurisdiction together with basic biographical information, specialities of practice, and language capabilities. The office also distributes a practical guide to retaining and utilizing a foreign attorney. There are suggested "Do's" and "Don't's" in dealing with foreign counsel as well as billing procedures and fee structures fixed by local law.

U.S. DEPARTMENT OF STATE INTERNATIONAL JUDICIAL ASSISTANCE CIRCULARS BUREAU OF CONSULAR AFFAIRS

RETAINING A FOREIGN ATTORNEY

RECOMMENDING A FOREIGN ATTORNEY: 22 CFR 92.82 provides that Foreign Service officers shall refrain from recommending a particular foreign attorney, but may furnish names of several attorneys, or refer inquiries to foreign law directories, bar associations or other organizations.

WHAT TYPE OF LAWYER WILL YOU NEED:

Barristers and Solicitors: In some foreign countries it may be necessary to retain the services of both a solicitor and a barrister. In such jurisdictions, barristers are allowed to appear in court, including trial courts and higher courts of appeal or other courts. Solicitors are allowed to advise clients and sometimes represent them in the lower courts. They may also prepare cases for barristers to try in the higher courts.

Notaries, "Notaires", "Notars", and "Huissiers": In some countries, notaries public, "notaires", "notars" and "huissiers" can perform many of the functions performed by attorneys in the United States. A notary in

7. www.travel.state.gov.

a civil law country is not comparable to a notary public in the United States. Their education and training differs from that of most notaries public in the United States. They frequently draft instruments such as wills and conveyances. In some countries a notary is a public official appointed by the Ministry of Justice, whose functions include not only preparing documents, but the administration and settlement of estates. Such notaries serve as repositories for wills and are empowered to serve legal documents. In some countries "huissiers" serve documents. They are not lawyers, but are very specialized members of the foreign legal profession. They may not plead cases in court. Your foreign attorney may delegate certain functions to a notary, "notaire", "notar" or "huissier".

GUIDELINES ON HOW TO DEAL WITH YOUR FOREIGN ATTORNEY:

Understanding Your Attorney: Ask your attorney to analyze your case, giving you the positive and negative aspects and probable outcome. Do not expect your attorney to give a simple answer to a complex legal question. Be sure that you understand the technical language in any contract or other legal document prepared by your attorney before you sign it.

Fees: Find out what fees the attorney charges and how the attorney expects to be paid. In some countries fees are fixed by local law. Establish a billing schedule that meets your requirements and is acceptable to the foreign attorney. Foreign lawyers may be unaccustomed to including a description of work performed in connection with billing. Some foreign attorneys may expect to be paid in advance; some may demand payment after each action they take on your behalf and refuse to take further action until they are paid; and some may take the case on a contingency or percentage basis, collecting a pre-arranged percentage of moneys awarded to you by the foreign court. Request an estimate of the total hours and costs of doing the work. Be clear who will be involved in the work and the fees charged by each participant. Determine costs if other attorneys or specialists need to be consulted, such as barristers. See "Payment of Attorneys and Litigation Expenses in Selected Foreign Nations", U.S. Library of Congress, Law Library, Doc. LL–95–2 (March 1995) (Includes information on Australia, Canada, China, France, Germany, Great Britain, Greece, India, Italy, Japan, Mexico, Netherlands, Poland, Sweden and Taiwan.)

Progress Reports: Ask that your attorney keep you informed of the progress of your case according to a pre-established schedule. Remember that most foreign courts work rather slowly. You may, therefore, wish the attorney to send you monthly reports, even though no real developments have ensured, simply to satisfy your doubts about the progress of the case. Ask what the fee will be for progress reports.

Language: Is the attorney fluent in English? This may or may not be important to you. If the foreign attorney does not speak or write in English, you can arrange for translation of correspondence. Attorneys on lists prepared by the U.S. embassies and consulates abroad do speak English.

Communication: Remember your responsibility to keep your attorney informed of any new developments in your case. Be honest and frank with your attorney. Tell the attorney every relevant fact in order to get the best representation of your interests. Establish how you be communicate with your foreign attorney (mail, phone, fax, Internet.)

FINDING A FOREIGN ATTORNEY:

U.S. Department of State, Bureau of Consular Affairs, Office of American Citizens Services and Crisis Management, (CA/OCS/ACS), Room 4811A, 2201 C Street N.W., Washington, D.C. 20520; tel: 202–647–5225 or 5226. Please send a stamped, self addressed envelope, 8 ½ x 11, to accommodate postage for 20 sheets of paper or more. These lists of attorneys are also being added to the Internet home pages of our U.S. embassies and consulates. Lists of attorneys are prepared by U.S. embassies and consulates triennially (every three years). The lists include names, addresses, telephone numbers, etc., and information concerning the foreign attorney's educational background, areas of specialization, and language capability. When compiling the lists, U.S. consular officers send letters and questionnaires to the attorneys in their consular district in the foreign country. American attorneys licensed to practice in the foreign country or working as foreign legal consultants are also included. Local foreign bar associations are used as a resource in determining whether an attorney is in good standing. See Volume 7, Department of State Foreign Affairs Manual 990 (8/30/94) and 22 CFR 92.82.

PART C.   FOREIGN LEGAL CONSULTANTS

An additional avenue to obtaining advice on foreign law is the employment of a foreign legal consultant in the United States. A number of states now allow foreign lawyers to practice as foreign legal consultants without taking the state bar examination. In the 1980's, a substantial number of foreign firms opened branch offices in the United States, pursuant to these new state bar rules. These local bar rules allow foreign attorneys who have been specially licensed by the local bar to work as foreign legal consultants and to render professional advice on the law of the foreign country in which they are admitted to practice. Advice on foreign law prior to entering into international transactions may help avoid problems in the future. In the pre-litigation stage of an international case, the consultant may be called upon to assess the viability of a claim under the applicable foreign law, and to interpret that law as it applies to the specific facts involved. During the litigation, the consultant may continue to advise on substantive aspects of the foreign law, as well as procedural considerations, such as the complex discovery or pretrial limitations found in many nations. At the trial, the consultant may be retained as an expert witness to advise the court of the law of the foreign jurisdiction. In many cases the court may have little understanding of the law of the foreign country and may rely on the consultant's testimony in order to become better informed of the foreign law. The consultant's services may also include the preparation of necessary affidavits to prove foreign law in support of summary judgment motions, etc.

CAROL A. NEEDHAM, THE LICENSING OF FOREIGN LEGAL CONSULTANTS IN THE UNITED STATES
21 Fordham Int'l L.J. 1126 (1998).*

1.   THE CURRENT OPERATION OF THE FOREIGN LEGAL CONSULTANT STATUS

Upon compliance with the requirements of a particular state's rule, foreign legal consultants are granted an official status in that state for the limited purpose of giving legal advice regarding the laws of jurisdictions other than the United States. In even the most narrowly worded regulations, the foreign legal consultants are permitted to give advice regarding the laws of the country in which they were originally licensed. The regulations address common topics, but there is a good deal of variation from state to state.

A.   Scope of Permitted Legal Work

All of the regulations in the United States predictably prohibit the foreign legal consultant from giving advice regarding the state's local law. This is not surprising, given the political realities surrounding any relaxation of the prohibition on the unauthorized practice of law. Locally licensed attorneys are likely to rule that their monopoly be protected. The narrowest regulations, such as those in effect in California, Connecticut, Florida, Georgia, Illinois, Missouri, Minnesota, and Texas restrict the foreign legal consultant to giving legal advice only on the laws of the country in which the attorney was originally licensed. Five jurisdictions permit foreign legal consultants licensed there to give legal advice regarding international law and third country law, as long as they do not give advice on U.S. law.

Eleven jurisdictions, including Alaska, Arizona, the District of Columbia, Hawaii, Indiana, New Jersey, New Mexico, New York, North Carolina, Ohio, and Oregon also permit the foreign legal consultant to pass along to a client advice regarding the law of the state granting the foreign legal consultant status as well as federal law, as long as the advice originates with a lawyer who holds a law license in that state.

The rule in the District of Columbia even permits the foreign legal consultant to advise a client on the law of any state, in addition to federal law or the law of the District of Columbia, as long as he is simply passing along to the client the opinion of a person qualified to render such legal advice in the District of Columbia. The person who is the source of the advice must have acted as counsel to the legal consultant, must have been consulted with regard to the particular matter at hand, and must have been identified by name to the client. The primary effect

* Reprinted with permission of the Fordham Law International Journal.

of this provision is to clarify that a foreign legal consultant who discusses all aspects of a transaction or other legal matter with a client will not be prosecuted for the unauthorized practice of law if he explains some legal issue which involves U.S. law.

A majority of the regulations, those in effect in fourteen jurisdictions, contains similar language specifying that the foreign legal consultant cannot prepare any papers to be filed with, or appear before, any court or administrative agency in the state granting the status, and cannot prepare any instrument affecting title to real estate located in the United States, prepare any wills or trust instruments, or prepare any instrument with respect to marital rights or custody of a child of a resident of the United States. The jurisdictions with this language are Alaska, California, the District of Columbia, Florida, Georgia, Hawaii, Illinois, Minnesota, New Jersey, North Carolina, Ohio, Oregon, Texas, and Washington. Four additional states' regulations omit the prohibition on preparing pleadings to be filed in court, but otherwise list the same restrictions: Arizona, Connecticut, Indiana, and New York. The regulation in effect in Illinois also provides that a foreign legal consultant cannot render legal advice regarding any personal injury occurring in the United States, immigration laws, custom laws, and U.S. trade laws. In five states, the wording of the regulation permits the foreign legal consultants to engage in additional activities. In addition to the same list of prohibitions, the regulations in Florida and Minnesota explicitly permit a foreign legal consultant to prepare documents relating to personal property in situations in which the instrument affecting title to the property is governed by the law of a jurisdiction in which the foreign legal consultant is admitted to practice. The rules in Missouri and New Mexico expressly prohibit foreign legal consultants only from appearing in court and preparing court pleadings, but omit any prohibition of preparation of documents related to real estate, wills, and marital rights or child custody. Connecticut is the only state that does not have any version of the list of prohibitions. Its regulation simply states that the foreign legal consultant can only give advice on the law of the jurisdiction where he or she is admitted to practice.

SECTION 2.2   RESEARCHING THE INTERNATIONAL CASE

Researching an international case presents U.S. lawyers with a particularly challenging obstacle—learning the laws of a foreign country, or of the international community as a whole. U.S. lawyers are often unfamiliar with the research tools and methods that are necessary to extract the international laws at issue. In recent years, however, the birth and expansion of the Internet and the World Wide Web has made the search for law much less burdensome. Proper use of the Internet can provide an easy and cost-effective method to find international law. This section attempts to summarize some of the tools which can be used to research the law of an international case.

The best way to begin is to start with fundamentals—acquaint or re-acquaint oneself with international legal research concepts and systems of documentation by reading books and articles on the subject.[8]

LINDA K. O'CONNOR, INTERNATIONAL AND FOREIGN LEGAL RESEARCH: TIPS, TRICKS AND SOURCES

28 Cornell Int'l L.J. 418–422 (1995).*

There is now greater interest in foreign and international legal issues. While once the exclusive concern of specialists, the general legal researcher and librarian can no longer avoid dealing with foreign and international documents. This essay contains practical tips, sources, and tricks for researching international and foreign legal topics. The discussions on locating documents online include sources available on the Internet as well as through Lexis and Westlaw.

Many law schools now publish international law reviews, introducing law students to non-American research early in their careers. As most law students are barely familiar with U.S. legal research at the end of their first year, it is not surprising when, given citations to both basic and esoteric documents cited by authors of articles on international topics, the students have no idea where to find documents for source collection and citation verification. Many authors of law review articles are experts in their fields and are present at the meetings where unpublished documents are distributed and discussed. Although these documents may not be distributed and published formally, authors often cite the unpublished draft documents in the interim. Students are also required to write publishable notes on topics appropriate for the journal; most librarians, but few students, know that the ability to write a note depends heavily on whether there are secondary sources on a topic, on whether there are relevant published documents, and on the law library's ability to obtain such sources.

Practicing lawyers often have difficulty locating current legal codes from municipalities and other jurisdictions, both in their own locales and in other states. Imagine the difficulties faced by U.S. lawyers representing domestic companies expanding their foreign markets. To conduct business in other countries, they must find relevant treaties and these countries' applicable national and local laws. This requires not only an understanding of international and foreign law, but also the ability to find and update the law. Unfortunately, most lawyers do not even know what questions to ask because they are working with a set of legal assumptions that they presume are universal.

---

8. Some good starting places include: Susan Van Syckel, *Strategies For Identifying Sources of Foreign Law: An Integrated Approach*, 13 Transnt'l Law. 289 (2000); Chad A. Freed, *Uncovering Global Resources: A Practitioner's Guide to Researching International Law on the Internet*, 6 Tul. J. Int'l & Comp. L. 487 (1998). *Guide to International Legal Research*, Geo. Wash. J. Int'l L. & Econ. (Vol. 20, nos. 1 & 2) (1986).

* Reprinted with the permission of the Cornell International Law Journal.

Fundamental differences in approach and philosophy exist between civil law and common law jurisdictions. For example, in many civil jurisdictions there is no principle of stare decisis. The law flows primarily from civil codes rather than from case law. Consequently, respected commentaries and doctrinal writings about the codes may be given more weight by practitioners and judges than are cases, even if on point. In these jurisdictions, less weight is given to the factual circumstances of the parties and more to the spirit and principles of applicable laws. More subtle distinctions exist in the traditions, social practices, and roles of attorneys or legal advisers in other countries. While it is common for a law firm whose client is doing business internationally to engage local counsel in foreign countries, it is still necessary to understand the issues and laws involved, and to review the documentation of laws upon which its client relies.

Most transnational legal transactions boil down to a choice of law and forum: which country's legal system and laws will be used to settle legal disputes. A lawyer familiar only with the U.S. legal system may blindly argue for the application of U.S. law. This is shortsighted. Another country's laws and forum might well be more advantageous to the client's interests and legal situation. It is always worth at least a cursory look a the laws of a country to see whether they protect a client's interests before arguing that those laws should not apply.

American legal researchers are often surprised to find that codes, published at the federal and state level, annotated and regularly updated, do not exist in many other countries. Another country may have a code, but it may have been published seventy years ago, with every statute passed since then appearing in an unindexed gazette. Once I had to find the service of process laws for a Caribbean country. Its laws were a sheaf of papers tied together. Only after I worked my way backwards through the sheaf, turning pages with a moistened finger, did I discover the warning on the first page: "This paper has been treated with insecticide." But this sheaf was indeed that country's published current laws.

One can find basic tools for international legal research in most large academic law libraries, in the larger county law libraries (most notably Los Angeles County Law Library), in law firms with transnational practices, and in a few court and bar association libraries. Legal researchers initially need introductions to the legal systems and legal bibliographies of the jurisdiction they are researching. This introductory information is found in encyclopedias, legal research guides, bibliographies, and occasional articles. Two sources have been invaluable in my search for legal documents of foreign and international entities.

Thomas H. Reynolds & Arthur A. Flores, Foreign Law: Current Sources of Codes and Legislation in Jurisdictions of the World (Littleton, CO: Rothman and Co., 1989).

Claire German, Germain's Transnational Law Research: A Guide for Attorneys (Ardsley-on-Hudson, NY: Transnational Juris Publications, 1991).

These two reference works provide practical information that leads to specific documents. Reynolds and Flores include a rich essay on each country's legal system and list titles of codes and case reporters. Germain's shorter treatise focuses on items of particular use to lawyers and provide both jurisdictional and substantive access points. If I could recommend only two titles for a small foreign and international reference collection, it would be these.

The Guide to International Legal Research is an extremely helpful book, worth reading thoroughly if your specialty is international legal research. There is a lot of practical information in this book and the bibliographic information is thorough. The introductory chapter, Research Tips in International Law by John W. Williams, presents a good overview of research techniques, tools and processes.

Other useful and extremely useful sources for gaining an understanding of a country's legal system are:

Modern Legal Systems Cyclopedia, Kenneth Robert Redden ed. (Buffalo, NY: William S. Hein & Co., 1988).

International Encyclopedia of Comparative Law (Tubingen: J.C. Mohr: New York: Oceana Publications, 1971).

While there is no substitute for consulting these excellent introductions to legal systems, Lexis, Westlaw, and the Internet increasingly provide many shortcuts and connections to actual documents. Most practitioners, scholars, and students reading this article are familiar with Lexis and Westlaw, but they may not have used the Internet to find legal sources. If you are interested in international and foreign law, or in online access to U.S. government and court decisions without paying for Lexis and Westlaw, I strongly recommend learning how to access Internet resources.

Foreign and international transactions also create a great need for bilingual dictionaries. Some experts prefer a good general, rather than legal, English/foreign language dictionary. An accurate translation of a legal term explains the word in the context of a legal system. Imagine a Spanish/English legal dictionary giving the contextual meaning of a term for all Spanish-speaking jurisdictions. False cognates abound, and the legal researcher must be cautiously aware.

Dictionaries of international terms are also useful. I recommend the following titles:

James R. Fox, Dictionary of International and Comparative Law (New York: Oceana Publications, 1992). This is the briefest and most concise of the international law dictionaries, and it often gives citations to treatise, cases, and other documents.

Clive Parry et al., Encyclopedia Dictionary of International Law (New York: Oceans Publications, 1986). This combines the features of a dictionary and an encyclopedia, with high-quality scholarly analysis and source references.

Robert L. Bledsoe & Boleslaw A. Boczek, The International Law Dictionary (Santa Barbara, CA: ABC–CLIO, 1987). The authors provide useful analysis, but the organization can be a barrier when one is in a rush.

Edward G. Hinkelman, Dictionary of International Trade (San Rafael, CA: World Trade Press, 1994). This is a good and inexpensive dictionary focused on trade. It includes extras like maps and addresses, phone numbers for organizations, and references to other useful materials.

Search tools and document collections exist in print, online, on CD–ROM, and in dreaded microfiche (though a handy collection in fiche will save you hours compared to finding individual documents). Lexis and Westlaw provide decisions from an increasing number of foreign jurisdictions. A full-text collection of treaties is also available on Lexis, although not through the academic law library subscription. The Internet has become a major resource of internationally significant documents, particularly U.N. documents. Some understanding of citation schemes will aid in finding particular documents and examples of citations are provided later in this essay.

Defining the updating process and verifying the authority of a particular foreign law, treaty, or case are especially difficult aspects of foreign and international law research. For good, basic, and quick identification and location of documents and updating processes, the base source is Germain's Transnational Law Research, which is arranged in a manner which reflects the structured approach of a European mind. For those of us with chaotic American minds and eyes, the journey from the index to the book page can be harrowing. But once you open to the relevant section, the practical advice and sources and there. Professor Germain is an enthusiastic Internet user and future supplements to her work will include Internet sources.

Foreign jurisdictions have no Shepard's citators or, in most cases, annotated codes, but U.S. lawyers expect to find them in translation. They will not. U.S. lawyers also expect to find all foreign cases online. Cases are increasingly available online, but they are in the vernacular, and coverage is far from comprehensive. The usefulness of Lexis and Westlaw customer service is limited regarding their foreign and international databases. They are unlikely to have foreign language skills, and they tend not to know an ECJ from and ICJ decision. Use what online sources are available for convenience, but do not confuse an online search with thorough research.

———

The best way to begin any research assignment in international law is to look for a general treatment of the subject under study. Sources of international law which must be considered include international conventions, international custom, general principles of law recognized by civilized nations, judicial decisions and scholarly writings. *The Digest of International Law*, which is issued by the Department of State, discusses international law topics, foreign policy and the law of diplomacy, and treaty matters. In this series, the Whiteman Digest covers the years 1963–1973 and the *Digest of United States Practice in International Law*, which has been published by the Department of State since 1973. The Restatement (Third) of the Law of Foreign Relations is a frequently used summary of United States practice in international law. The Restatement is intended to be a statement of the foreign relations law of the United States and not an official document. According to the Restatement, the foreign relations law consists of international law as applied in the United States under relevant domestic law. The rules of the Restatement are often relied on by the parties in framing the relevant international law issue in the case and cited in U.S. judicial decisions. For example, the balancing factors in Section 442 of the Restatement (Third) is frequently employed as a comity test when courts need to determine whether domestic or foreign law should be applied in resolving an international law issue.

Those using the Internet as a tool for finding international law have a tremendous advantage over the researcher who relies purely on traditional hard copy sources. The O'Connor article and others cited in that text contain lists of many useful web sites with foreign and international links. A competent researcher must also learn how to use the search tools available on the Internet. Each of these tools has its own advantages and disadvantages. Furthermore, these search tools and each particular version of a search tool (i.e., *Yahoo versus Google*) has its own set of instructions. A careful and efficient researcher should utilize multiple search tools and should read the instructions for each tool used.[9]

The U.S. State Department has posted general circulars in the area of international judicial assistance, *i.e.,* service of process and obtaining evidence abroad, on its web-site (*www.travel.state.gov*—click on Law and Policy) which should be reviewed in the international case. This web-site has country-specific information on applicable procedures to be followed when seeking international judicial assistance abroad. Included in this information are addresses of foreign government offices in each country (central authorities) where service and evidence requests are to be directed as well as procedures for the taking of a deposition before a diplomatic or consular official of the United States. As described in Chapter 3, Problem 3.5, these consular procedures are important when a U.S. styled deposition is to be taken in the case.

9. See Van Syckel, *supra* note 8.

This web-site provides general guidance in the following areas: enforcement of judgments, foreign attorney information including lists of attorneys; notarial and authentication services; obtaining evidence abroad; State Department treaty databases; service of process abroad; and State Department procedures concerning travel abroad for judicial assistance purposes. As shown in this information, U.S. attorneys are required to comply with foreign law and procedures when undertaking these functions abroad.

The treaty information section of this web-site includes circulars which describe U.S. practice and procedure under the Hague Service and Evidence Conventions. There is an invaluable link in the treaty section to the work of the Hague Conference on Private International Law. This data base includes the text of each Hague-sponsored treaty, a full status report of signatory countries showing the dates of signatures, ratifications and accessions and entry into force as well as the texts of declarations and reservations taken as to each treaty. This is a direct source which provides significant guidance in the field of international judicial assistance.

SECTION 2.3 ETHICAL CONSIDERATIONS

Those engaged in international litigation should be aware of the special ethical considerations that apply in that area of legal practice. Rule 1.1 of the ABA Model Rules of Professional Conduct requires the lawyer to provide competent representation to a client. The Rule further states that "[c]ompetent representation requires the legal knowledge, skill, thoroughness and preparation reasonably necessary for the representation."[10] In the transnational context, this does not mean that the lawyer has to be fully familiar with the foreign law at the time the representation is undertaken. Professor Ronald Brand has outlined the following options that are available to the transnational lawyer in satisfying the duty of competent representation:

> The duty of competent representation does not require that the lawyer know all the answers to a client's legal questions at the time representation is undertaken. A lawyer can provide adequate representation in a wholly novel field through necessary study. Competent representation can also be provided through the association of a lawyer of established competence in the field in question. Thus, it is wholly appropriate to develop new areas of competence through continued study and to associate with other lawyers to provide legal services on multiple issues. This process should allow satisfaction of the duty of competence through increased understanding of foreign law, as well as through association with a foreign lawyer when advice on foreign law is necessary. The more difficult question is when a lawyer may rely on his or her own knowledge of foreign law in providing competent representation.[11]

10. Model Rules of Prof'l Conduct R. 1.1. (1999) (hereinafter Model Rules).

11. See Brand, *supra* 1139.

If foreign counsel is employed, the U.S. lawyer may be held responsible for their selection and supervision.[12] Ignorance of the foreign law will not operate as an excuse for incompetent representation and through any of the means chosen by the lawyer to provide adequate representation, as outlined *supra,* the lawyer's responsibility to the client will extend to rendering advice on foreign law. [13]In this age of globalization, partnering between U.S. and foreign law firms may be an effective tool in providing comprehensive advice to clients in transnational cases. This type of arrangement may have ethical and professional responsibility implications for the transnational lawyer.

Mark Zimmett of the New York Bar has commented on the lawyer's responsibility under ABA model code provisions as well as local disciplinary rules for the supervision of co-counsel if he or she knew or reasonably should have known of the conduct in question.[14]

b. Model Rule 5.1(c):

A lawyer shall be responsible for another lawyer's violation of the Rules of Professional Conduct if:

(1) The lawyer orders or, with knowledge of the specific conduct, ratifies the conduct involved; or

(2) The lawyer is a partner in the law firm in which the other lawyer practices, or has direct supervisory authority over the other lawyer, and knows of the conduct at a time when its consequences can be avoided or mitigated but fails to take reasonable remedial action.

2. Division of Fees Among Lawyers.

a. Disciplinary Rule DR 2–107A.:

A lawyer shall not divide a fee for legal services with another lawyer who is not a partner in or associate of the lawyer's law firm, unless:

(1) The client consents to employment of the other lawyer after a full disclosure that a division of fees will be made.

(2) The division is in proportion to the services performed by each lawyer or, by a writing given the client, each lawyer assumes joint responsibility for the representation.

(3) The total fee of the lawyers does not exceed reasonable compensation for all legal services they rendered the client.

b. Model Rule 1.5(e):

---

12. *See e.g., Tormo v. Yormark,* 398 F.Supp. 1159 (D.N.J.1975); *Bluestein v. State Bar of California,*13 Cal.3d 162, 529 P.2d 599, 118 Cal.Rptr. 175 (1974).

13. *See Degan v. Steinbrink,* 202 App. Div. 477, 195 N.Y.S. 810 (App.Div.1922), *aff'd,* 236 N.Y. 669, 142 N.E. 328 (1923); *In re Roel,* 3 N.Y.2d 224, 144 N.E.2d 24, 165 N.Y.S.2d 31, 37 (1957), *appeal dismissed,* 355 U.S. 604 (1958).

14. M. Zimmett, *Ethics in International Commercial Litigation and Arbitration, Course Handbook on International Business Litigation & Arbitration* (PLI 2002) 475, 520–522.

A division of a fee between lawyers who are not in the same firm may be made only if:

(1) The division is in proportion to the services performed by each lawyer or, by written agreement with the client, each lawyer assumes joint responsibility for the representation;

(2) The client is advised of and does not object to the participation of all the lawyers involved; and

(3) The total fee is reasonable.

Mark Zimmett further comments on whether compensation for services performed by the U.S. lawyer in supervising the work of foreign co-counsel in international or transnational litigation or arbitration constitutes impermissible fee-splitting under local disciplinary rules and ABA model code provisions.[15] In order to consider this issue, an assessment must be made of the nature of the services performed by the U.S. lawyer through various arrangements with foreign counsel. Is the U.S. lawyer performing a special skill or using his or her expertise in dealing with foreign counsel?

Is charging a professional fee for supervising foreign co-counsel's work that you are not competent to do impermissible fee splitting? Or is the supervision of an international or transnational litigation or arbitration itself a professional skill, independent of the particular substantive domestic legal work involved? Consider the following:

1. [T]he American international lawyer has presumably acquired a degree of expertise in dealing with foreign transactions and certain foreign legal systems which he can present to the client as specialized competence. This expertise relates as much to the manner of conducting business abroad, and the legal and regulatory framework within which such business is conducted in different countries, as it does to the specific rules of law for a given transaction. The experienced international lawyer becomes, to some degree, a cultural intermediary, assisting clients to adapt their American (or other native) mode of business to one suitable for operations in radically different social or cultural contexts.

The trained American international lawyer will also normally have acquired competence in international conflicts of law, with special attention to choice of law and choice of forum. He will have developed a knowledge of international arbitration devices, the practical use of arbitration in various contexts, and the suitability or acceptability of different arbitration tribunals and procedures. He will also be aware of standard or customary patterns of international commercial contracts, such as CIF, FOB or other sales contracts, letters of credit, international financing devices, licensing, leasing, etc. Finally, he will have some awareness of areas of public international law as they may affect private commercial or investment transactions.

15. *Id. at 522.*

This then is the expert competence which the American international lawyer should develop and which he can then offer to clients, either directly or, where appropriate, in tandem with the customary domestic counsel, who can provide his specific knowledge of the client's particular requirements and business usages. Roger J. Goebel, *Professional Responsibility Issues in International Law Practice*, 29 Am.J.Comp. L. 1, 12 (1981).[16]

Questions and Comments

1. There are several important decisions for a lawyer who engages in a transaction where foreign law may be helpful or critical to know. One is at what point do you engage a foreign lawyer? Another is how do you find the best foreign lawyer for your needs? Failing to retain a foreign lawyer may be malpractice. One of the authors consulted on a case where a beach resort club incorporated in a Latin American country was sold in the United States from one U.S. national to another. The club owned valuable beach front property in the foreign country but the U.S. attorney for the buyer never thought it necessary to have an attorney in the foreign country help with transferring title to the property to comply with the foreign nation's property law. Not long after the "sale" the sellers returned to the foreign country and "sold" the property again. The negligent lawyer was sued for malpractice and settled.

Finding the proper foreign attorney is often difficult. Perhaps once a month an e-mail comes from some member of the ABA Section on International Law to all members asking for recommendations for a lawyer in a particular country. What they mean is "do you know someone who is good and reliable?" The readings offer numerous sources. But the best source may be a "friend of a friend."

2. The NAFTA in Article 1210 and Annex 120.5 Section B requires each party (Canada, Mexico, United States) to develop some means of licensing and certifying foreign legal consultants. About half of the states in the United States have not complied. Some Canadian provinces have complied but Mexico has not. See Mexican Lawyers Going North and U.S. Lawyers Going South: Interstate Legal Practice, NAFTA and U.S. State Bar Regulations, 9 U.S.—Mexico L.J. 189 (2001).

3. If a Foreign Legal Consultant (FLC) is allowed only to practice the law of his nation, for example a Mexican who is an FLC in New York, does that include international law?

4. If you were asked to help your state develop a foreign legal consultant rule, how would you control such issues as:

    a. Designation of status in letterheads.

    b. Should the foreign lawyer applicant be in good standing (still licensed) in the foreign nation, or only have been admitted previously?

    c. Amount of experience as a lawyer in the foreign country.

---

16. *Id.* at 522–524.

d.   If the annual fee for a full member of the bar of the state of practice is, for example, $300, should the FLC fee be similar?

e.   Once designated as a FLC, how can the bar be certain that the person is practicing only the law of his country?

5.   Some states seem to allow a FLC to give extensive advice on U.S. law, as long as the FLC does so by passing it to the client through a member of the bar. Can that be controlled?

6.   What about the role of the foreign lawyer who is, for example, a French resident and partner of a multinational law firm and who spends a year in the New York office engaging in mostly advice on French law with some work on domestic and international issues? That person is not likely to become a FLC. But are they not required to follow the FLC rules?

7.   If we allow a Canadian to become a FLC in Florida and give advice on Canadian law, is there an equal protection argument for the New York lawyer who wants to be a Florida FLC and give advice on New York law while vacationing in Florida? Would a foreign lawyer be more or less likely to take work from Florida bar members than would the N.Y. lawyer? Which lawyer would be more likely to abide by FLC restrictions on the practice of U.S. law?

8.   Courts may find it necessary to conduct independent legal research and apply foreign law in unique and difficult situations. For example, in *National Group for Communications & Computers, Ltd. v. Lucent Technologies Int'l, Inc.,* 331 F.Supp.2d 290 (D.N.J. 2004), the court enforced the parties' choice of law clause and applied the law of Saudi Arabia to relevant breach of contract issues in the action. In undertaking this research, the court stated as follows:

> The legal system in Saudi Arabia is fundamentally different from that of the United States. Western conceptions of the role that law plays in society, the legal process, and methods of legal interpretation, often mistakenly assumed to be universal in nature, are in many ways poles apart from those concepts in Islamic countries such as Saudi Arabia. The difficulties in understanding Islamic law are multiplied by the fact that there is a paucity of literature specifically targeted at those who, like this Court, are steeped in other legal mindsets and seek guidance as to Islamic laws' interpretation. Confronted with this formidable and difficult responsibility, this Court has examined various texts and treatises dealing with Saudi Arabian law and carefully considered the testimony of the experts presented and the submissions of the parties which included testimony and submissions from Saudi Arabian lawyers, Islamic scholars, and former Saudi Arabian judges.

In applying foreign law on the issue of permissible damages, the court rejected all damages for breach which were not actual and direct including all valuation means involving speculative and uncertain losses. The court held that under the choice of law clause the parties should be held to the full application of foreign law, including the law of damages, however uncompromising that application might be to their case.

Part Two

LITIGATION IN THE UNITED STATES

Chapter 3

U.S. PLAINTIFF/FOREIGN DEFENDANT

INTRODUCTION 3.0
U.S. PLAINTIFF SUING FOREIGN DEFENDANTS IN U.S. COURTS

As stated in Chapter 1, arbitration has become a frequently used alternative to litigation in resolving international legal disputes. Once the dispute arises, parties need to determine the most effective means of resolving the controversy. Despite the wide use of arbitration, there may be sound reasons for choosing to litigate the dispute in the U.S. forum. Arbitration may lack many of the procedural safeguards inherent in the U.S. legal system. A study of the U.S. legal system reveals distinctive features, such as liberal pretrial discovery and technical rules of evidence. Many of the litigation procedures in U.S. courts are unique and without parallel, even in other common law countries. Depending on the nature of the claim, it may be a decided advantage for the party to be able to develop its own case and strategy through recourse to a U.S. court.

In the issues for discussion in Problems 3.1–3.6, U.S. and foreign plaintiffs have initiated a product liability action arising from an automobile accident which occurred in the United States against foreign companies which either assembled or manufactured the allegedly defective product for distribution and sale in the United States. Plaintiffs have selected the U.S. forum as the preferred forum to litigate the controversy. Are there special reasons for selecting the U.S. forum in product liability claims? These problems discuss some of the advantages of choosing the U.S. forum to litigate certain types of disputes. Foreign litigants choose the U.S. forum because of our expansive theories of personal jurisdiction, jury trials, potentially large damage recoveries including the availability of punitive damages, and the full range of discovery tools/procedures. In addition, foreign plaintiffs are drawn to U.S. liability and choice-of-law rules. U.S. law, when compared with foreign law, is more likely to create liability and provide more generous compensation than will foreign law. There may be obstacles to keeping the international case in the United States such as where the court determines that the plaintiff has been forum shopping and under *forum non conveniens* there is a more convenient forum elsewhere. The doctrine of *forum non conveniens* is discussed in problem 4.3.

The question of alternative choices of the forum to litigate a particular dispute and the ultimate decision of where to sue depends on differences in substantive law, public policy, and procedures in effect in the potential countries involved. The cost of proceeding in a particular jurisdiction may also play an important part in forum selection. If there is jurisdiction over a dispute in the courts of two or more countries, an important consideration in selecting the right forum is the location in which sufficient assets exist to satisfy the judgment. This is a crucial factor since enforcement of the judgment in a foreign jurisdiction may be problematic and subject to varying conditions and exceptions. The issue of enforcement of U.S. judgments in foreign courts is discussed in Chapter 5.

Problem 3.1 addresses choice of forum issues when litigation is initiated in a U.S. court by a foreign plaintiff. Since there may be reasons for choosing the U.S. forum as the preferred forum in which to litigate an international legal dispute, the parties may be able to designate the choice of forum in a forum selection clause. Problem 3.1 focuses on some of the special features which make the United States a magnet forum. Parties to the international transaction need to know how U.S. courts have treated forum selection clauses and the extent to which they have been enforced. Problem 3.1 further examines the validity of arbitration clauses as a means of resolving international disputes. The subject of arbitration is discussed in greater detail in Chapter 10. Problem 3.1 addresses some of the pertinent issues the parties should consider in determining whether to arbitrate or litigate the international dispute.

Problem 3.2 focuses on an analysis of *in personam* jurisdiction in a typical product liability case where the foreign parties—the manufacturer and assembler of component parts—have been named as defendants to a U.S. action arising from their role in the chain of manufacture, sale and distribution of the product to plaintiffs in the United States. What are the contours of such an analysis in the context of international commercial litigation for due process purposes? The same jurisdictional principles and due process limits apply to foreign defendants as they do to domestic defendants in the United States. There have been a series of Supreme Court decisions, especially in *Asahi Metal Indus. Co. v. Superior Court of Cal.*, 480 U.S. 102, 107 S.Ct. 1026, 94 L.Ed.2d 92 (1987), discussed *infra*, Problem 3.2, which have left the law of activity-based jurisdiction unsettled. Problem 3.2 seeks to examine how the international features described in the hypothetical have factored into the courts' due process analysis.

Problem 3.3 discusses another method of obtaining jurisdiction, by piercing the veil of the U.S. subsidiary to reach the foreign parent. Since jurisdiction over the U.S. subsidiary is likely to be much easier to obtain than jurisdiction over the foreign parent, as discussed in Problem 3.2, veil piercing reaches the foreign parent without all the issues of long-arm effect of laws with extraterritorial reach. Veil piercing for purposes of jurisdiction differs from veil piercing that students have studied in the introductory corporations class. The latter is veil piercing for imposing liability, and may require greater proof.

Problem 3.4 discusses service of process as applied to the foreign defendants named in the product liability action. Effecting proper service of process in accordance with the law of the forum is an important issue which frequently arises in international cases. Proper service of process is another prerequisite for personal jurisdiction. Unwary plaintiffs may be faced with motions to dismiss for lack of personal jurisdiction based on invalid service. Certain service procedures may not be recognized to the foreign country involved. This could create problems for the plaintiff if subsequent recognition and enforcement of the U.S. judgment will eventually be sought in the foreign jurisdiction. Problem 3.4 examines how proper service of process can be effected in compliance with the law of the forum and applicable international treaties such as the Hague Service Convention which cover the subject.

The issues in Problem 3.5 explore options and procedures for obtaining foreign-based evidence for use in U.S. courts. Are there special rules which govern foreign evidence gathering? Obtaining foreign evidence provides an interesting contrast to the issues considered in problem 3.2 which deals with service of process. As with service of process, the procedural variations for obtaining evidence between the U.S. legal system and civil law systems are considerable. Problem 3.5 discusses foreign attitudes about U.S. discovery practice and how U.S. courts have considered the Hague Evidence Convention—the only multi-lateral treaty in the field—in order to accommodate both domestic and foreign interests.

Problem 3.6 discusses parallel proceedings and anti-suit injunctions. While the above problems have dealt with suits initiated in the United States, there may be similar suits initiated in foreign courts dealing with the same issues. These are parallel proceedings. Similar to and a form of parallel proceeding is the anti-suit injunction, where one of the foreign defendants in the U.S. litigation goes into a foreign court and asks that the court enjoin one or more of the plaintiffs in the U.S. litigation from proceeding in the U.S. courts. Courts have struggled in dealing with these issues.

PROBLEM 3.1   CHOICE OF FORUM

SECTION I.   THE SETTING

Plaintiffs are two U.S. citizens residing in the State of New Jersey and two UK citizens. While traveling in their 1999 SUV through New Jersey on a sightseeing trip to view "on location" scenes in a popular TV series, they experienced a sudden blowout causing the car to roll over, resulting in severe medical injuries and emotional trauma to the U.S. parties and to their U.K. friends, who were sitting in the rear of the vehicle. The SUV was originally purchased by the U.S. plaintiffs from VUSCO, a distributor which held a distribution franchise for the SUV vehicle in the New York–New Jersey region.

The tires were shipped by CANTIRE, Ltd. and installed in DROF–AG's plant facility in Germany. In addition, DROF–UK PLC manufactured and shipped certain auto parts for installation to DROF–AG's German plant. After reviewing accident reports prepared by local law enforcement authorities and the U.S. insurance company, the lawyers for the injured parties determined that the tires were faulty and the blowout attributable to negligent design and manufacture of the tread in the tires. The tires were manufactured by CANTIRE, Ltd., headquartered in Niagara, Canada. The SUV was manufactured by DROF AG, a German–UK joint venture, which is headquartered in Badenberg, Germany. The tires were assembled and installed by DROF–UK PLC in its plant facility in Ipswich, United Kingdom. VUSCO, L.L.C., the distributor, and DROF AG have a forum selection clause in their contract designating the choice of forum as the courts of the Netherlands. There is also a forum selection clause in the contract between VUSCO and CANTIRE which provides that the venue for all disputes that may result from orders for the tires should be in the court of competent jurisdiction in England.

Both the U.S. and UK parties consult with attorneys and solicitors in their respective countries. Counsel are requested to provide legal opinions as to the pros and cons of filing suit in the various countries where the auto manufacturer and tire company are headquartered and principally doing business. U.S. counsel are also engaged to consider whether suit can properly be maintained against CANTIRE, DROF AG, DROF–UK PLC, AND VUSCO on a personal jurisdiction theory sustainable under due process concepts. The UK parties are advised by their solicitors that there exist alternative forums in the United States and various European countries where the SUV was manufactured and/or assembled and they are advised of the advantages and disadvantages of suing in each location.

All of the injured parties decide to go forward with the suit in New Jersey and to name as defendants CANTIRE, DROF AG, DROF UK, PLC, AND VUSCO.

SECTION II.   FOCUS OF CONSIDERATION

Under the facts presented in the problem, the U.S. and UK plaintiffs to the product liability action have selected the United States as the forum to litigate the dispute. Have they made the right choice?

SECTION III.   READINGS, QUESTIONS AND COMMENTS

RUSSELL J. WEINTRAUB, THE UNITED STATES AS A MAGNET FORUM AND WHAT, IF ANYTHING, TO DO ABOUT IT

The Regulation of Forum Selection
Fourteenth Sokol Colloquium.
International Dispute Resolution 213.
Transnational Publishers 1997.

With a few exceptions, such as defamation actions, the United States is the plaintiff's forum of choice, and especially for wrongful death and personal injury suits. "Forum shopping" for the site of litigation most favorable to the plaintiff is not a pejorative term, but is part of the attorney's duty to the client. Even within the European Union, average awards differ greatly from country to country, and lawyers seek the forum that will yield the highest recovery * * *. Plaintiffs flock to United States courts for two elementary reasons–higher recoveries and lower barriers to suit. Higher recoveries are facilitated by four features of American law: trial by jury, choice-of-law rules, liability rules, and pretrial discovery. Barriers to suit are lowered by the contingent fee and the "American rule" that a losing plaintiff is not liable for the defendant's attorney's fee * * *. The most important reason why the United States is a magnet forum is that the trier of fact will be a jury that is 'prone to award fabulous damages.' There are several explanations for this phenomenon other than a desire to do good with someone else's money. The award is keyed to high U.S. living standards. The jury is aware that expenses and a large contingent fee will be deducted before the plaintiff receives the first dollar. Moreover, the social safety net in the United States is hung low and is full of holes. A seriously injured plaintiff is likely to have to rely on tort recovery to replace lost earnings and for medical treatment.

Whatever the reason, U.S. juries are likely to award more money for various categories of damages than juries or courts in other countries. Moreover, a peculiarity of conflict-of-laws doctrine reinforces the effect of an American jury on foreign claims. If the court decides that foreign law applies to the injury abroad, foreign "heads" of damages will apply. Heads of damages refer to the various items that the award may include, such as pain and suffering, loss of services, and punitive damages. The amount of money to be awarded under these heads is, however, determined by the procedures and practices of the forum. Suppose, for example, suit is brought in the United States for injuries suffered in Scotland and that the judge has ruled that Scottish law, including Scottish measures of damages, applies. The jury will award what they think is appropriate for the plaintiff's pain, and the fact that the award is three times the highest award ever made by a Scottish jury for this item of damage is irrelevant. If foreign law applies, so will a statutory cap on damages, as part of the foreign substantive law. There is some authority that a U.S. court will respect a judge-made cap on damages, such as a declaration by the foreign country's highest court that a particular sum is the "upper limit" on recovery for pain and suffering. Absent such specific limits on recovery, the general level of awards in the foreign jurisdiction is irrelevant, even though the forum is purporting to apply foreign law * * *. Moreover, the fact that an American jury award will exceed recovery in the foreign country where the plaintiff was injured influences the settlement value of the case. Under what has become known as the "mid-Atlantic formula," claims of foreign plaintiffs are being settled in amounts above what could have been obtained where the injury occurred. The excess is proportionate to the likelihood that the cases could have been litigated to a judgment in an American court * * *.

United States liability and choice-of-law rules work together to attract foreign plaintiffs. Although American liability rules, such as strict products liability, are spreading abroad, and although "tort reform" is proceeding state to state in the United States, it is still probable that U.S. law, when compared with foreign law, will be more likely to create liability and provide for more generous recovery than will foreign law. This feature of U.S. law would not benefit foreign plaintiffs if it were not also true that U.S. choice-of-law rules are more likely than foreign rules to select U.S. law as applicable to injuries abroad. * * * Most U.S. jurisdictions have abandoned the place-of-wrong rule for selecting the law applicable to torts. Whether the new approach is labeled "interest analysis," or "most significant relationship," or another phrase, it will choose law in a way designed to give maximum effect to the policies underlying conflicting rules in the jurisdictions that have contacts with the parties and the transaction. Suppose, for example, a foreign plaintiff is injured abroad by a product manufactured by a U.S. company in the United States, and that recovery is available under U.S. law but not under foreign law. Although there is a split of authority on the issue, a U.S. court is more likely than a foreign court to be beguiled into applying U.S. law on the ground that this will deter negligent manufacture in the United States and that the foreign country will not mind if its resident is the subject of this magnanimity * * *.

In U.S. courts, more extensive pretrial discovery is available than in any other country, even other common law countries. An opinion by the House of Lords describes American practice as follows:

> [T]he complaint is accompanied, or immediately followed, by a request to the defendants for pre-trial discovery which bears little resemblance to the kind of discovery that is available in English civil actions. It is characterized by [i]ts breath, the variety of methods, oral and written, that it makes available for a wide-roving search for any information that might be helpful to the case of the party seeking discovery, the enormous expense, irrecoverable in any award of costs to a successful defendant, in which it may involve parties from whom discovery is sought, and its potentiality for oppressive use by plaintiffs. British Airways Ltd. v. Laker Airways Ltd., (1985) App. Cas. 58, 78 (H.L. 1984).

Even for domestic U.S. litigation, there has been much talk, but little action, concerning reform in the administration of justice. Jury trial has been reviled and praised. The U.S. Supreme Court has ruled that if juries are permitted to assess punitive damages, they must be given specific guidelines concerning when and how this may be done and the size of the award must be subject to meaningful review by trial and appellate judges. Periodically there are calls to rein in "Rambo" trial tactics, including abuse of discovery by plaintiff and defense counsel to harass opponents. There are frequent proposals for the loser to pay the opponents' attorney's fee. So far there has been little effect and it is uncertain whether, in the light of the opposing political forces that these issues unleash, significant change can be expected.

PART A.   FORUM SELECTION CLAUSES

The following case emphasizes how courts favor forum selection clauses, even when they appear to have been imposed upon a party rather than negotiated. *The Bremen v. Zapata Off–Shore Co.*, is a 1972 U.S. Supreme Court decision. Earlier, the Court addressed forum selection in *Wilko v. Swan*, 346 U.S. 427, 74 S.Ct. 182, 98 L.Ed. 168 (1953), where the Court agreed with the federal district court's rejection of a forum selection clause. The clause provided for arbitration but the district court favored the intent of the applicable legislation (Securities Act of 1933) to forbid waivers of rights of investors protected by the law over the right of parties to choose "prompt, economical and adequate solutions of controversies through arbitration." But *The Bremen*, much like two other later Supreme Court cases enforcing agreements to arbitrate, *Scherk v. Alberto–Culver Co.*, 417 U.S. 506, 94 S.Ct. 2449, 41 L.Ed.2d 270 (1974), and *Mitsubishi Corp. v. Soler Chrylser–Plymouth, Inc.*, 473 U.S. 614, 105 S.Ct. 3346, 87 L.Ed.2d 444 (1985), ruled in favor of forum selection clauses where the transactions were international.

BREMEN v. ZAPATA OFF–SHORE CO.

Supreme Court of the United States, 1972.
407 U.S. 1, 92 S.Ct. 1907, 32 L.Ed.2d 513.

MR. CHIEF JUSTICE BURGER delivered the opinion of the Court.

We granted certiorari to review a judgment declining to enforce a forum-selection clause governing disputes arising under an international towage contract between petitioners and respondent. The circuits have differed in their approach to such clauses.

In November 1967, respondent Zapata, a Houston-based American corporation, contracted with petitioner Unterweser, a German corporation, to tow Zapata's ocean-going, self-elevating drilling rig *Chaparral* from Louisiana to a point off Ravenna, Italy, in the Adriatic Sea, where Zapata had agreed to drill certain wells.

Zapata had solicited bids for the towage, and several companies including Unterweser had responded. Unterweser was the low bidder and Zapata requested it to submit a contract, which it did. The contract submitted by Unterweser contained the following provision, which is at issue in this case:

> Any dispute arising must be treated before the London Court of Justice.

In addition the contract contained two clauses purporting to exculpate Unterweser from liability for damages to the towed barge.[1]

After reviewing the contract and making several changes, but without any alteration in the forum-selection or exculpatory clauses, a Zapata vice president executed the contract and forwarded it to Unterweser in Germany, where Unterweser accepted the changes, and the contract became effective.

On January 5, 1968, Unterweser's deep sea tug *Bremen* departed Venice, Louisiana, with the *Chaparral* in tow bound for Italy. On January 9, while the flotilla was in international waters in the middle of the Gulf of Mexico, a severe storm arose. The sharp roll of the *Chapporal* in Gulf waters caused its elevator legs, which had been raised for the voyage, to break off and fall into the sea, seriously damaging the *Chapparal*. In this emergency situation Zapata instructed the *Bremen* to tow its damaged rig to Tampa, Florida, the nearest port of refuge.

On January 12, Zapata, ignoring its contract promise to litigate "any dispute arising" in the English courts, commenced a suit in admiralty in the United States District Court at Tampa, seeking $3,500,000 damages against Unterweser *in personam* and the *Bremen in rem*, alleging negligent towage and breach of contract.[2] Unterweser responded by invoking the forum clause of the towage contract, and moved to dismiss for lack of jurisdiction or on *forum non conveniens* grounds, or in the alternative to stay the action pending submission of the dispute to the "London Court of Justice". Shortly thereafter, in February, before the District Court had ruled on its motion to stay or dismiss the United States action, Unterweser commenced an action against Zapata seeking damages for breach of the towage contract in the High Court of Justice in London, as the contract provided. Zapata appeared in that court to contest jurisdiction, but its challenge was rejected, the English courts holding that the contractual forum provision

---

1. The General Towage Conditions of the contract included the following:

'1. ... (Unterweser and its) masters and crews are not responsible for defaults and/or errors in the navigation of the tow.

'2. ... b) Damages suffered by the towed object are in any case for account of its Owners.'

In addition, the contract provided that any insurance of the Chaparral was to be 'for account of Zapata. Unterweser's ini-

tial telegraphic bid had also offered to 'arrange insurance coverage towage risk for rig if desired.' As Zapata had chosen to be self-insured on all its rigs, the loss in this was not compensated by insurance.

2. The Bremen was arrested by a United States marshal acting pursuant to Zapata's complaint immediately upon her arrival in Tampa. The tug was subsequently released when Unterweser furnished security in the amount of $3,500,000.

conferred jurisdiction.[3]

In the meantime, Unterweser was faced with a dilemma in the pending action in the United States court at Tampa. The six-month period for filing action to limit its liability to Zapata and other potential claimants was about to expire,[4] but the United States District Court in Tampa had not yet ruled on Unterweser's motion to dismiss or stay Zapata's action. On July 2, 1968, confronted with difficult alternatives, Unterweser filed an action to limit its liability in the District Court in Tampa. That court entered the customary injunction against proceedings outside the limitation court, and Zapata refiled its initial claim in the limitation action.[5]

It was only at this juncture, on July 29, after the six-month period for filing the limitation action had run, that the District Court denied Unterweser's January motion to dismiss or stay Zapata's initial action. In denying the motion, that court relied on the prior decision of the Court of Appeals in *Carbon Black Export Inc.* v. *The Monrosa*, 254 F.2d 297 (CA5 1958), cert. dismissed, 359 U.S. 180, 79 S.Ct. 710, 3 L.Ed.2d 723 (1959). In that case the Court of Appeals had held a forum-selection clause unenforceable, reiterating the traditional view of many American courts that "agreements in advance of controversy whose object is to oust the jurisdiction of the courts are contrary to public policy and will not be enforced."[6] 254 F.2d at 300–301. Apparently concluding that it was bound by the *Carbon Black* case, the District Court gave the forum-selection clause little, if any, weight. Instead, the court treated the motion to dismiss under normal forum non conveniens doctrine applicable in the absence of such a clause, citing *Gulf Oil Corp.* v. *Gilbert*, 330 U.S. 501, 67 S.Ct. 839, 91 L.Ed. 1055 (1947). Under that doctrine, "unless the balance is strongly in favor of the defendant, the plaintiff's

---

3. Zapata appeared specially and moved to set aside service of process outside the country. Justice Karminski of the High Court of Justice denied the motion on the ground the contractual choice-of-forum provision conferred jurisdiction and would be enforced, absent a factual showing it would not be "fair and right" to do so. He did not believe Zapata had made such a showing, and held that it should be required to "stick to (its) bargain." The Court of Appeal dismissed an appeal on the ground that Justice Karminski had properly applied the English rule.

4. 46 U.S.C. §§ 183, 185. See generally *G. Gilmore & C. Black, Admiralty*, § 10–15 (1957). Under admiralty law, a defendant vessel owner, in certain circumstances, can obtain a court order limiting its liability to the value of the vessel and its gear and cargo. The proceeding is known as a "limitations action."

5. In its limitation complaint, Unterweser stated it "reserve(d) all rights" under

its previous motion to dismiss or stay Zapata's action, and reasserted that the High Court of Justice was the proper forum for determining the entire controversy, including its own right to limited liability, in accord with the contractual forum clause. Unterweser later counterclaimed, setting forth the same contractual cause of action as in its English action and a further cause of action for salvage arising out of the Bremen's services following the casualty. In its counterclaim, Unterweser again asserted that the High Court of Justice in London was the proper forum for determining all aspects of the controversy, including its counterclaim.

6. The *Carbon Black* court went on to say that it was, in any event, unnecessary for it to reject the more liberal position taken in *Wm. H. Muller & Co.* v. *Swedish American Line Ltd.*, 224 F.2d 806 (CA2), cert. denied, 350 U.S. 903, 76 S.Ct. 182, 100 L.Ed. 793 (1955), because the case before it had a greater nexus with the United States than that in *Muller*.

choice of forum should rarely be disturbed." Id., at 508, 67 S.Ct., at 843. The District Court concluded: "the balance of conveniences here is not strongly in favor of (Unterweser) and (Zapata's) choice of forum should not be disturbed."

On appeal, a divided panel of the Court of Appeals affirmed, and on rehearing *en banc* the panel opinion was adopted, with six of the 14 *en banc* judges dissenting. As had the District Court, the majority rested on the *Carbon Black* decision, concluding that "at the very least" that case stood for the proposition that a forum-selection clause "will not be enforced unless the selected state would provide a more convenient forum than the state in which suit is brought." From that premise the Court of Appeals proceeded to conclude that, apart from the forum-selection clause, the District Court did not abuse its discretion in refusing to decline jurisdiction on the basis of *forum non conveniens*. It noted that (1) the flotilla never "escaped the Fifth Circuit's mare nostrum, and the casualty occurred in close proximity to the district court"; (2) a considerable number of potential witnesses, including Zapata crewmen, resided in the Gulf Coast area; (3) preparation for the voyage and inspection and repair work had been performed in the Gulf area; (4) the testimony of the *Bremen* crew was available by way of deposition; (5) England had no interest in or contact with the controversy other than the forum-selection clause. The Court of Appeals majority further noted that Zapata was a United States citizen and "[t]he discretion of the district court to remand the case to a foreign forum was consequently limited"—especially since it appeared likely that the English courts would enforce the exculpatory clauses.[7] In the Court of Appeals' view, enforcement of such clauses would be contrary to public policy in American courts. Therefore, "[t]he district court was entitled to consider that remanding Zapata to a foreign forum, with no practical contact with the controversy, could raise a bar to recovery by a United States citizen which its own convenient courts would not countenance."[8]

We hold, with the six dissenting members of the Court of Appeals, that far too little weight and effect were given to the forum clause in resolving this controversy. For at least two decades we have witnessed an expansion of overseas commercial activities by business enterprises based in the United States. The barrier of distance that once tended to confine a business concern to a modest territory no longer does so. Here we see an American company with special expertise contracting with a

---

7. The record contains an undisputed affidavit of a British solicitor stating an opinion that the exculpatory clauses of the contract would be held "prima facie valid and enforceable" against Zapata in any action maintained in England in which Zapata alleged that defaults or errors in Unterweser's tow caused the casualty and damage to the Chaparral. In addition, it is not disputed that while the limitation fund in the District Court in Tampa amounts to $1,390,000, the limitation fund in England would be only slightly in excess of $80,000 under English law.

8. The Court of Appeals also indicated in passing that even if it took the view that choice-of-forum clauses were enforceable unless "unreasonable" it was "doubtful" that enforcement would be proper here because the exculpatory clauses would deny Zapata relief to which it was "entitled" and because England was "seriously inconvenient" for trial of the action.

foreign company to tow a complex machine thousands of miles across seas and oceans. The expansion of American business and industry will hardly be encouraged if, notwithstanding solemn contracts, we insist on a parochial concept that all disputes must be resolved under our laws and in our courts. Absent a contract forum, the considerations relied on by the Court of Appeals would be persuasive reasons for holding an American forum convenient in the traditional sense, but in an era of expanding world trade and commerce, the absolute aspects of the doctrine of the *Carbon Black* case have little place and would be a heavy hand indeed on the future development of international commercial dealings by Americans. We cannot have trade and commerce in world markets and international waters exclusively on our terms, governed by our laws, and resolved in our courts.

Forum selection clauses have historically not been favored by American courts. Many courts, federal and state, have declined to enforce such clauses on the ground that they were "contrary to public policy," or that their effect was to "oust the jurisdiction" of the court. Although this view apparently still has considerable acceptance, other courts are tending to adopt a more hospitable attitude toward forum-selection clauses. This view, advanced in the well-reasoned dissenting opinion in the instant case, is that such clauses are prima facie valid and should be enforced unless enforcement is shown by the resisting party to be 'unreasonable' under the circumstances. This approach is substantially that followed in other common-law countries including England. It is the view advanced by noted scholars and that adopted by the Restatement of the Conflict of Laws. It accords with ancient concepts of freedom of contract and reflects an appreciation of the expanding horizons of American contractors who seek business in all parts of the world. Not surprisingly, foreign businessmen prefer, as do we, to have disputes resolved in their own courts, but if that choice is not available, then in a neutral forum with expertise in the subject matter. Plainly, the courts of England meet the standards of neutrality and long experience in admiralty litigation. The choice of that forum was made in an arm's-length negotiation by experienced and sophisticated businessmen, and absent some compelling and countervailing reason it should be honored by the parties and enforced by the courts.

The argument that such clauses are improper because they tend to "oust" a court of jurisdiction is hardly more than a vestigial legal fiction. It appears to rest at core on historical judicial resistance to any attempt to reduce the power and business of a particular court and has little place in an era when all courts are overloaded and when businesses once essentially local now operate in world markets. It reflects something of a provincial attitude regarding the fairness of other tribunals. No one seriously contends in this case that the forum-selection clause "ousted" the District Court of jurisdiction over Zapata's action. The threshold question is whether that court should have exercised its jurisdiction to do more than give effect to the agreement, by specifically enforcing the forum clause.

There are compelling reasons why a freely negotiated private international agreement, unaffected by fraud, undue influence, or overweening bargaining power,[9] such as that involved should be given full effect. In this case, for example, we are concerned with a far from routine transaction between companies of two different nations contemplating the tow of an extremely costly piece of equipment from Louisiana across the Gulf of Mexico and the Atlantic Ocean, through the Mediterranean Sea to its final destination in the Adriatic Sea. In the course of its voyage, it was to traverse the waters of many jurisdictions. The *Chaparral* could have been damaged at any point along the route, and there were countless possible ports of refuge. That the accident occurred in the Gulf of Mexico and the barge was towed to Tampa in an emergency were mere fortuities. It cannot be doubted for a moment that the parties sought to provide for a neutral forum for the resolution of any disputes arising during the tow. Manifestly much uncertainty and possibly great inconvenience to both parties could arise if a suit could be maintained in any jurisdiction in which an accident might occur or if jurisdiction were left to any place where the *Bremen* or Unterweser might happen to be found. The elimination of all such uncertainties by agreeing in advance on a forum acceptable to both parties is an indispensable element in international trade, commerce, and contracting. There is strong evidence that the forum clause was a vital part of the agreement,[10] and it would be unrealistic to think that the parties did not conduct their negotiations, including fixing the monetary terms, with the consequences of the forum clause figuring prominently in their calculations. Under these circumstances, as Justice Karminski reasoned in sustaining jurisdiction over Zapata in the High Court of Justice, "(t)he force of an agreement for litigation in this country, freely entered into between two competent parties, seems to me to be very powerful."

Thus, in the light of present-day commercial realities and expanding international trade we conclude that the forum clause should control absent a strong showing that it should be set aside. Although their

---

9. The record here refutes any notion of overweening bargaining power. Judge Wisdom, dissenting, in the Court of Appeals noted:

"Zapata has neither presented evidence of nor alleged fraud on undue bargain power in the agreement. Unterweser was only one of several companies bidding on the project. No evidence contradicts its Managing Director's affidavit that it specified English courts 'in an effort to meet Zapata Off–Shore Company half way.' Zapata's Vice President has declared by affidavit that no specific negotiations concerning the forum clause took place. But this was not simply a form contract with boilerplate language that Zapata had no power to alter. The towing of an oil rig across the Atlantic was a new business. Zapata did make alterations to the contract submitted by Unterweser. the forum clause could hardly be ignored. It is the final sentence of the agreement, immediately preceding the date and the parties' signatures...."

10. Zapata has denied specifically discussing the forum clause with Unterweser, but, as Judge Wisdom pointed out, Zapata made numerous changes in the contract without altering the forum clause, which could hardly have escaped its attention. Zapata is clearly not unsophisticated in such matters. The contract of its wholly owned subsidiary with an Italian corporation covering the contemplated drilling operations in the Adriatic Sea provided that all disputes were to be settled by arbitration in London under English law, and contained broad exculpatory clauses.

opinions are not altogether explicit, it seems reasonably clear that the District Court and the Court of Appeals placed the burden on Unterweser to show that London would be a more convenient forum than Tampa, although the contract expressly resolved that issue. The correct approach would have been to enforce the forum clause specifically unless Zapata could clearly show that enforcement would be unreasonable and unjust, or that the clause was invalid for such reasons as fraud or overreaching. Accordingly, the case must be remanded for reconsideration.

We note, however, that there is nothing in the record presently before us that would support a refusal to enforce the forum clause. The Court of Appeals suggested that enforcement would be contrary to the public policy of the forum because of the prospect that the English courts would enforce the clauses of the towage contract purporting to exculpate Unterweser from liability for damages to the *Chaparral*. A contractual choice-of-forum clause should be held unenforceable if enforcement would contravene a strong public policy of the forum in which suit is brought, whether declared by statute or by judicial decision.

This case involves a freely negotiated international commercial transaction between a German and an American corporation for towage of a vessel from the Gulf of Mexico to the Adriatic Sea. As noted, selection of a London forum was clearly a reasonable effort to bring vital certainty to this international transaction and to provide a neutral forum experienced and capable in the resolution of admiralty litigation. Whatever "inconvenience" Zapata would suffer by being forced to litigate in the contractual forum as it agreed to do was clearly foreseeable at the time of contracting. In such circumstances it should be incumbent on the party seeking to escape his contract to show that trial in the contractual forum will be so gravely difficult and inconvenient that he will for all practical purposes be deprived of his day in court. Absent that, there is no basis for concluding that it would be unfair, unjust, or unreasonable to hold that party to his bargain.

In the course of its ruling on Unterweser's second motion to stay the proceedings in Tampa, the District Court did make a conclusory finding that the balance of convenience was "strongly" in favor of litigation in Tampa. However, as previously noted, in making that finding the court erroneously placed the burden of proof on Unterweser to show that the balance of convenience was strongly in its favor. Moreover, the finding falls far short of a conclusion that Zapata would be effectively deprived of its day in court should it be forced to litigate in London. Indeed, it cannot even be assumed that it would be placed to the expense of transporting its witnesses to London. It is not unusual for important issues in international admiralty cases to be dealt with by deposition. Both the District Court and the Court of Appeals majority appeared satisfied that Unterweser could receive a fair hearing in Tampa by using deposition testimony of its witnesses from distant places, and there is no reason to conclude that Zapata could not use deposition testimony to equal advantage if forced to litigate in London as it bound itself to do. Nevertheless, to allow Zapata opportunity to carry its heavy burden of showing not only that the balance of convenience is strongly in favor of trial in Tampa (that is, that it will be far more inconvenient for Zapata to litigate in London than it will be for Unterweser to litigate in Tampa), but also that a London trial will be so manifestly and gravely inconvenient to Zapata that it will be effectively deprived of a meaningful day in court, we remand for further proceedings.

The judgment of the Court of Appeals is vacated and the case is remanded for further proceedings consistent with this opinion.

Vacated and remanded.

MR. JUSTICE DOUGLAS, dissenting.

Respondent is a citizen of this country. Moreover, if it were remitted to the English court, its substantive rights would be adversely affected. Exculpatory provisions in the towage control provide (1) that petitioners, the masters and the crews "are not responsible for defaults and/or errors in the navigation of the tow" and (2) that "(d)amages suffered by the towed object are in any case for account of its Owners."

Under our decision in *Dixilyn Drilling Corp. v. Crescent Towing & Salvage Co.*, "a contract which exempts the tower from liability for its own negligence" is not enforceable, though there is evidence in the present record that it is enforceable in England.

Moreover, the casualty occurred close to the District Court, a number of potential witnesses, including respondent's crewmen, reside in that area, and the inspection and repair work were done there. The testimony of the tower's crewmen, residing in Germany, is already available by way of depositions taken in the proceedings.

All in all, the District Court judge exercised his discretion wisely in enjoining petitioners from pursuing the litigation in England.[11]

HAROLD MAIER, THE U.S. SUPREME COURT AND THE "USER–FRIENDLY" FORUM SELECTION CLAUSE: THE EFFECT OF CARNIVAL CRUISE LINES ON INTERNATIONAL CONTRACTS

The Regulation of Forum Selection
Fourteenth Sokol Colloquium
International Dispute Resolution
Transnational Publishers 1997.

Since the early 1970s, the U.S. Supreme Court has adopted a "user-friendly" view of forum selection clauses in international contracts. The importance of establishing certainty of forum to resolve disputes arising

---

11. It is said that because these parties specifically agreed to litigate their disputes before the London Court of Justice, the District Court, absent "unreasonable" circumstances, should have honored that choice by declining to exercise its jurisdiction. The forum-selection clause, however, is part and parcel of the exculpatory provision in the towing agreement which, as mentioned in the text, is not enforceable in American courts. Judges in this country have traditionally been hostile to attempts to circumvent the public policy against exculpatory agreements.

in international business matters is the informing principle of these decisions. International entrepreneurs need such certainty. Enforcement of an agreement by the parties designating a forum guarantees that there will be at least one-and, perhaps, only one–venue in which a dispute will be settled. The theory is that giving effect to the parties' forum selection permits them to try a cause in a legal milieu acceptable to all and to avoid the prejudice, real or perceived, that might result if the cause were tried in the home courts or tribunals of any one of the parties to the transaction.

Furthermore, the ability to rely upon the enforcement of a forum selection agreement eliminates preliminary litigation over judicial or arbitral jurisdiction and thereby necessarily facilitates settlement before actual litigation begins. The functional propensities of the selected forum necessarily enter into the decision by the parties about acceptable terms of settlement. Such considerations include the size of awards in similar previous cases, the rules about admissibility of evidence, the number of cases on the selected forum's calendar and, therefore, the likely delay before an award might be handed down, and the probable competence of the decision makers.

Designating a forum also identifies the legal rules, including the choice-of-law rules, that are likely to govern the case if governing law has not already been selected in the contract. More important, selecting a forum also selects the local attitudes and mores that are the sociolegal context in which the decision maker will interpret the facts and the meaning and applicability of relevant legal rules. Furthermore, enforcement of such clauses would redound to the benefit of all U.S. citizens engaged in international commercial activities because foreign parties to such contracts could rely on litigating in the forum selected during negotiations without fear that their mutual expectations might be frustrated by a recalcitrant party successfully seeking the succor of U.S. courts.

The considerations above make it clear that the policies that support giving effect to a forum selected by international entrepreneurs necessarily presumes that the contracting parties have actually consented to the forum selected. This is important for at least two reasons. First, a jointly selected forum necessarily reflects the consent of the parties and, thus, that selection is as legitimately enforceable as any other contract term. Barring some showing that such consent was obtained by the stronger over the weaker party as a result of unequal bargaining power or that enforcement of the forum selection clause would effectively deny one party its day in court, the U.S. courts will enforce the forum selection in the contract. To protect against unfairness to parties making such forum selections, the U.S. Supreme Court established these important procedural safeguards to guarantee effectively that the forum chosen would not be so unreasonable with respect to any party as to violate fundamental principles of fairness.

The Supreme Court reiterated these principles in a series of international contract cases decided between 1972 and 1985, applying them to contracts selecting arbitral forums as well. These cases reaffirmed the dual themes of commercial utility and fundamental fairness as informing principles of decision. These considerations clearly overrode any lingering concern that giving effect to a forum selection clause might improperly "oust" the otherwise legitimate jurisdictional authority of a court in the United States. In these cases, an important justification for upholding the forum selection clause was that the parties had openly and freely bargained for the venue selected. That selection was, therefore, part of the business transaction giving rise to the substantive rights and duties that would be the subject of any later litigation. Furthermore, as long as the bargaining process occurred between parties of equal bargaining power and business acumen, the forum selected necessarily met any fairness concerns that might otherwise be created by enforcing a forum selection, especially if the forum selected would not have been otherwise available under the limitations of the due process clause.

In the light of this intellectual history justifying and limiting the enforcement of forum selection clauses, it is not surprising that *Carnival Cruise Lines, Inc. v. Shute* caused considerable consternation among academic publicists and practitioners alike. In that case, the Supreme Court required a Washington resident, injured in a fall on defendant's cruise ship, to sue in a Florida forum selected in the nonnegotiable fine print on the back of a steamship ticket issued by a Florida corporation but purchased in Washington state from a travel agent. The Court enforced the clause despite the plaintiff's claim, upheld by the Ninth Circuit, that the injuries for which her suit sought compensation seriously hindered her ability to prosecute her case in that forum, on the grounds that it was not supported by the record from the District Court.

Both the rationale and the constitutional principles supporting the existing Supreme Court jurisprudence with respect to forum selection clauses suggested a result exactly opposite to that reached by the *Carnival* Court. Critics of the case noted not only the hardships created for the plaintiff but that the Supreme Court appeared to ignore the policies informing most of its modern case law upholding forum selection clauses.

* * *

This special concern for considering the needs of the international system when determining results in private international cases is neither new to U.S. jurisprudence nor confined to cases involving the enforceability of forum selection clauses. The international systemic values reflected in the concepts of comity, international judicial cooperation and needs of international commerce have long been an important consideration in U.S. private transnational legal cases. These decisions do not reflect an altruistic or philosophical devotion to maintenance of an international legal system, but rather effectuate pragmatic U.S. interests in the development of an international regime within which transnational commercial intercourse can take place effectively. To the extent that the United States exercises self-restraint in the imposition of its own law and values on relationships among its nationals and those of other nations, it permits each participant in the transnational commercial system to maximize its own values while recognizing the importance of coordinating the exercise of concurrent prescriptive and enforcement authority to that end. In this sense, emphasizing the importance of reliable forum-selection agreements to private participants in the transnational commercial system recognizes that municipal courts, as well as national executives and legislatures, participate in the process of reciprocal tolerance and limited response that identifies the share perceptions necessary for an effective system of transnational commercial intercourse. Such a system necessarily removes as many unnecessary national roadblocks as possible to facilitate private transnational trading activity. Permitting transnational traders to negotiate their own arrangements for dispute settlement and to enforce the results of those negotiations subject only to minimum requirements of fairness under general transnational standards is essential to encourage that "mutual forbearance" in the application of parochial legal norms that is essential to effectuate the "interacting interests of the United States and of foreign countries" in creating a smoothly functional transnational trading system.

Transnational system considerations hold an important place in decisions in transnational cases before U.S. courts. Judge Learned Hand warned against irresponsible treatment of foreign-based agreements as unlawful under U.S. antitrust statutes because of the international complications that would arise from any wholesale attempt to punish all effects such agreements might have on U.S. trade and commerce without regard to the intent with which they were being carried out. The Supreme Court has refused to apply the National Labor Relations Act to foreign crews on foreign flag vessels on the grounds that short-term substantive advantages that might flow to U.S. workers from such decisions would not compensate for the longer-term advantages of restraining the exercise of jurisdiction in order to nurture a legal regime that would permit the effective operation and development of international maritime commerce. Some opinions in securities fraud cases argued that there was a systemic interest in developing a worldwide climate encouraging the prosecution of securities fraud by many nations, thus improving the reliability of transnational securities transactions. Some cases dealing with the principle of sovereign immunity and with the act of state doctrine emphasized the systemic values inherent in avoiding judicial interference with the otherwise legitimate acts of foreign sovereigns, even when those acts affected private individuals. The opinion in *Banco Nacional de Cuba v. Sabbatino* argued, in part, that judicial abstention from deciding the validity of a taking by a foreign government would serve both the interests of the United States and that of the "community of nations as a whole in the International sphere." In light of this history, there appears to be no doubt that the Supreme Court's emphasis on systemic values in its opinions in *The Bremen*,

Scherk and *Mitsubishi* is fully supported by precedent and good sense. The same cannot be said of its decision in *Carnival Cruise Lines*.

Carnival Cruise Lines includes only one of the elements that inform the decisions in . . . earlier Supreme Court cases. The sole basis for the Court's decision appears to be that the nature of the business in which the cruise line is engaged makes enforcement of the forum selection clause especially important. Without such a clause, the cruise line could well be subjected to multiple suits in many countries in the event of an accident that produced several plaintiffs. . . . In *Carnival*, the Court emphasized that it was especially important for a cruise line to [be] able to select a single forum in which it might be sued in order to avoid multiple suits in many forums, arising out of the same occurrence. In the event of a high-seas collision or a general malfunction, it is quite clear that, without the forum selection clause, Carnival Cruise Lines might well find itself defending suits in several U.S. states and foreign countries. Such a situation might well arise with respect to any international mass transit carrier.

* * *

This emphasis on the nature of the business in connection with which the forum was selected is not dissimilar from the emphasis on the needs of international business persons emphasized in [earlier cases]. Therefore, one implication of *Carnival Cruise Lines* might well be that the Court's failure to enforce the *Bremen* safeguards in *Carnival* increases the likelihood of the successful enforcement of choice-of-forum clauses in international contracts, even when the *Bremen* safeguards have not been met. In other words, if the special needs of the business activity in question in *Carnival Cruise*—a noninternational case—take precedence over the need to protect the weaker party as they clearly did in that case, any but the most egregiously unfair forum–selection clause in an international contract will likely be enforced in a U.S. court. . . . Whatever the ultimate effect of the *Carnival* case on the enforceability of forum selection clauses appearing in purely domestic contracts, there seems to be no doubt that the Court has accepted the proposition that effective U.S. participation in international commerce requires enforcement of forum selection clauses in international contracts. Second, when a conflict arises between protecting a weaker party to an international contract from being haled to a difficult forum and enforcing the forum selection, only an especially strong demonstration that the forum selected is unfair to the protesting party will support U.S. courts' refusal to enforce such a forum selection clause.

PART B.   ARBITRATION CLAUSES

In the alternative to forum selection clauses, which may name courts of particular jurisdictions, many international commercial contracts include arbitration clauses to submit disputes to arbitration rather than litigation. The use of arbitration as the means of resolving international disputes is discussed separately in Chapter 10. The Supreme Court noted in *Scherk v. Alberto–Culver*, 417 U.S. 506, 510, 94 S.Ct. 2449, 41 L.Ed.2d 270 (1974), that an "agreement to arbitrate before a specified tribunal is, in effect, a specialized kind of forum selection clause that posits not only the situs of the suit but also the procedure to be used in resolving the dispute." The Court further noted that arbitration clauses promoted orderliness in international business transactions and obviated the risk that the dispute might be submitted to a forum hostile to the interests of one of the parties. In *Mitsubishi Motors Corp. v. Soler Chrysler–Plymouth*, 473 U.S. 614, 105 S.Ct. 3346, 87 L.Ed.2d 444 (1985), the Supreme Court extended these same policy reasons in an international context in compelling enforcement of arbitration agreements which covered statutory claims, such as antitrust claims under the Sherman Act.

WILLIAM W. PARK, THE RELATIVE RELIABILITY OF ARBITRATION AGREEMENTS AND COURT SELECTION CLAUSES

The Regulation of Forum Selection
Fourteenth Sokol Colloquium.
International Dispute Resolution 3
Transnational Publishers 1997.

Failure to distinguish among different adjudicatory environments and alternatives has obscured much of the debate about forum selection both in the United States and abroad. Like Dr. Johnson's proverbial cow, a forum selection clause can be quite a good thing in some contexts, while in other circumstances it may be no more welcome than a cow tramping through a vegetable patch. Moreover, the type of forum selection clause that works effectively in one situation may in other circumstances turn out to be inadequate.

In the broad field of international business transactions, for example, arbitration and court selection mechanisms level the playing field in resolving disputes between companies from different countries and cultures. In the garden of domestic transactions, however, a forum selection clause can become an instrument of oppression, inserted into the fine print of a standard form contract to designate a court or an arbitral tribunal predisposed in favor of the dominant party.

Context-related contrasts of a different nature present themselves when one compares the relative reliability of arbitration agreements and court-selection clauses, the two principal forum selection mechanisms. In a domestic transaction, American business managers normally expect, and often find, that submitting a claim to a court will provide a greater level of predictability than arbitration. When the adversary is foreign, however, commercial actors can often enhance the reliability of contract adjudication through abandoning recourse to judges, substituting instead arbitration under the rules of a neutral institution and subject to the New York Convention's treaty-based enforcement regime.

As a preliminary matter, one should be clear about what the relevant differences between court selection and arbitration are not. Despite the practitioners and scholars who wax eloquent about arbitration's high speed and low cost, arbitral proceedings in the real world are rarely either quicker or cheaper than court actions. Whether arbitration commends itself as speedy and cost efficient depends entirely on the factual configuration of each transaction.

Arbitration justifies itself in a cross-border business context principally as a tool to minimize the real or imagined dangers of litigation abroad: a mechanism to reduce the risk of ending up before a biased foreign judge who will apply unfamiliar procedures in a strange language. It is not so much that business managers "choose" to submit controversies to arbitrators, as that arbitration imposes itself on an international transaction for want of any better way to resolve a conflict between parties whose different cultures create a high degree of mutual suspicion toward each other's judicial system.

Few attorneys, however, seem to give much attention to the relative merits of arbitration in contrast to court selection. When lawyers in Boston learn that I teach a course on international business transactions, they often share with me the details of a cross-border venture in which they spent a considerable amount of their own time and the client's money negotiating a well-crafted contract with a foreign buyer, seller, or licensee. But when asked about the forum selection provision, not many of them can explain why they chose particular courts or arbitration rules. It is as if they assumed the contract would enforce itself automatically.

Such failure to consider adequately the selection of those individuals or institutions that will interpret a contract may not make much of a difference in a domestic context, where language and procedural alternatives in litigation are relatively minimal. In an international transaction, however, foreign litigation can be both dramatically different and dramatically disagreeable.

* * *

Under the rules of an arbitral institution (such as the International Chamber of Commerce or the London Court of International Arbitration) the parties to an international contract can level by the playing field by providing for an arbitral tribunal in a mutually accessible country, chaired by someone of a nationality different from the parties, with proceedings in English or some other common language, and according to procedural rules that give neither side an unfair advantage.

In addition, the New York Arbitration Convention provides for the agreement and award to be enforced in approximately one hundred [ed. note 133] countries. Under the Convention courts must refer the parties to arbitration when a dispute is covered by a valid arbitration clause, and must recognize and enforce the resulting award. Recognition and enforcement might include attachment of assets if the claimant wins.

When the defendant wins the arbitration, the award's *res judicata* effect under the Convention would normally preclude recognition of any inconsistent judgment with respect to the merits of the dispute.

Questions and Comments

1.   Were *Scherk* (1974) and *Mitsubishi* (1985) influenced by *The Bremen* (1972)? Did *The Bremen* successfully separate acceptance of a forum selection clause from a *forum non conveniens* discussion? Did the court mean that too little weight was given to forum selection clauses in all litigation, or especially in international litigation? Is Chief Justice Burger saying that all forum selection clauses must be enforced? Is the fact that the selected foreign tribunal may apply the protective U.S. law of significance? But what if there is also a choice of law provision that designates a law that does not provide protection at all close to that provided under U.S. law?

2.   In *The Bremen* the Court held that a forum selection provision controls "absent a strong showing that it should be set aside." Did *Zapata* make any such attempt? What circumstances might exist in a case like *The Bremen* that might allow making "a strong showing" that the forum clause should be set aside? See *Carvalho v. Hull, Blyth (Angola) Ltd.,* [1979] 1 W.L.R. 1228 (party unwilling to return to Angola because of alleged threats to his and his family's lives where nation was undergoing a revolution that had already resulted in significant limits on due process).

3.   Would a dispute arising out of a transaction based on an allegation of fraud render the forum selection clause unenforceable? In *Leslie v. Lloyd's of London*, 1995 WL 661090 (S.D.Tex.1995), the court denied a motion to enforce *Lloyd's* forum selection clause where plaintiff was induced to accept the clause by fraud and overreaching.

4.   The Court in *Bremen* referred to a "freely negotiated international commercial transaction." It made a similar comment in *Scherk.* Does the *Carnival Cruise Lines, Inc. v. Schute,* 499 U.S. 585, 111 S.Ct. 1522, 113 L.Ed. 622 (1991), decision reject that language and extend permissible forum selection clauses into the realm of adhesion contracts? In *Carnival Cruise Lines,* the Schutes sued the line in federal court in the state of Washington for a fall suffered by Mrs. Schute in international waters on a cruise out of Los Angeles. Their tickets had a clause selecting Florida courts (where Carnival Cruise has its principal offices). The clause was in small print with many other clauses and had not been freely negotiated. The Ninth Circuit held that the clause would not be enforced both because it had not been freely negotiated and because the Schutes could not "physically and financially" pursue litigation in Florida. The Supreme Court reversed in a much debated decision, even though it conceded that such a clause is never negotiated. It was held to be an enforceable clause because the company was reasonable in attempting to limit the fora where it could be sued and that such limitation allowed the company to offer cruises at lower costs to the passengers. Additionally, Florida was not a remote forum as in *The Bremen.* The Court was influenced by its opinion that Carnival Cruise Lines was not seeking to discourage passengers from pursuing legitimate claims. But in doing so were they imposing an unfair burden on many potential plaintiffs?

Would the court have reached the same result had the ticket been purchased by a foreigner, for example a Japanese tourist who flew to California to begin the tour?

5. The dissent of Mr. Justice Douglas expresses a view he raised again in *Scherk*, protection of rights of U.S. citizens arising from U.S. legislation. In several cases involving the securities laws where Douglas dissented, the essence of his view was later the basis of the majority opinion. See, e.g., *Reliance Electric Co. v. Emerson Electric Co.*, 404 U.S. 418, 92 S.Ct. 596, 30 L.Ed.2d 575 (1972)(Douglas as part of the majority in interpreting § 16(b) of the Securities Exchange Act of 1934). Do you think that will prove true with *The Bremen* and *Scherk*? Is Douglas correct when he characterizes this case as involving a negligence exculpatory clause, which the law disfavors? The Court of Appeals thought enforcement of the forum clause would be contrary to public policy because it would result in England enforcing the contracts exculpatory clause. The Supreme Court majority agreed that public policy contravention would be reason for nonenforcement of the forum clause, but would not invalidate the forum clause unless convinced that such action would "significantly encourage" negligent conduct with the United States. Is there any justification for an exculpatory clause?

6. Are tort claims normally within the range of disputes arising out of forum selection clauses? If so, which of the parties to the product liability action may raise the forum selection clause as a defense to the subject action or subsequent contribution and/or indemnity claim? The subject facts include a forum selection clause between the distributor and automobile manufacturer. There is no reference to a similar clause between the plaintiff-purchaser and any of the defendants. (A forum selection clause would most likely not be part of a standard automobile sales contract). Assume that the car was leased by plaintiff from a company in Canada and driven to New Jersey where the accident occurred. Assume there is a clause in the lease which provides as follows: "All disputes that may arise from the leasing of this automobile must be instituted before the courts of Ontario, Canada, to the exclusion of the courts of any other state or country." Would this clause be enforced by a court in the United States?

7. We have learned from the *Bremen* decision that such clauses are prima facie valid and should be enforced unless enforcement is shown by the resisting party to be "unreasonable" under the circumstances. Examples of "unreasonableness" would be where "enforcement would contravene a strong public policy of the forum in which the suit is brought" or when "the chosen forum is seriously inconvenient for the trial of the action." 407 U.S. at 16. In *Shell v. R.W. Sturge, Ltd.*, 55 F.3d 1227 (6th Cir.1995), the court of appeals stated that public policy would be violated if plaintiff were deprived of any remedy or treated unfairly by enforcement of the forum selection clause. Does the home forum have a strong public interest in the subject case? Under the second prong of the *Bremen* test, would the Canadian forum in question qualify as "seriously inconvenient"? In *Carnival Cruise Lines*, the Supreme Court enforced a forum selection clause on a cruise passenger's ticket because the plaintiff, from Washington State, was unable to overcome the heavy burden articulated in *Bremen* that the litigation of the dispute in Florida would be so inconvenient as to be unreasonable. The Court held that Florida was not a "remote alien forum" that would seriously inconvenience

the passenger. What type of evidence of inconvenience is needed to satisfy this factor? Should a U.S. court assume inconvenience when reviewing forum selection clauses involving non—U.S. forums? In this connection, the Ninth Circuit in *Spradlin v. Lear Siegler Management Services Co.*, 926 F.2d 865 (9th Cir.1991), enforced a forum selection clause between two U.S. parties because of the plaintiff's failure to demonstrate inconvenience to resolve their dispute in Saudi Arabia. The Court of Appeals cited the absence of such evidence as travel costs, availability of counsel in Saudi Arabia, location of witnesses or the financial ability to bear such costs and inconvenience. In *Leslie v. Lloyd's of London,* 1995 WL 661090 (S.D.Tex.1995), the court denied a motion to enforce Lloyd's forum selection clause where plaintiff was induced to accept the clause by fraud and overreaching.

8. We know from the Weintraub article and other references that the United States is a magnet forum. If you represented any of the parties, would you attempt to include a forum selection clause in the international transaction specifying the U.S. forum? Which parties? Note that in Problem 3.1 there is a forum selection clause between VUSCO and DROF–AG which designates the choice of forum as the courts of Netherlands. Why would the parties specify a "neutral" forum? Is it safe to assume that parties to international transactions prefer to choose the home forum because of procedural familiarity and other advantages? Clearly, designation of the forum is an important part of the bargaining process in the negotiation of the international transaction. From a U.S. perspective, would our courts question the selection of a neutral forum? Is there any evidence presented in Problem 3.1 which indicates that a U.S. court might not enforce the choice of forum designated by the parties? Would there be an advantage to any of the parties to a forum selection clause specifying any of the EU countries as the choice of forum? Chapter 7 discusses recognition and enforcement of judgments in foreign courts. The EU countries are signatories to two multilateral enforcement of judgment conventions (Brussels and Lugano). The United States is not a party to any bilateral or multilateral treaties in this area. Under the provisions of the Brussels Convention, a judgment in one signatory country is enforceable in another. Can you provide examples from the subject problem where this might be a critical advantage to any of the parties?

9. Question 6 above assumes the existence of a forum selection clause between the plaintiff—purchaser and the defendants. Would an arbitration clause be preferable to a forum selection clause? The Park article gives a comparison of these two dispute resolution mechanisms. How would you assess arbitration versus litigation of the subject problem? What are some of the distinctive features of the U.S. legal system that make litigation of a product liability action so attractive? What aspects of arbitration seem preferable? Remember the special features of the arbitration process. Many countries are signatories to the United Nations Convention on the Recognition and Enforcement of Foreign Arbitral Awards ("the New York Convention"). The Federal Arbitration Act provides for liberal enforcement of an agreement to arbitrate or of an award under the New York Convention provided the corresponding jurisdiction is a convention member and enforces U.S. awards reciprocally. Compare the enforcement of judgment risks and issues that might be faced by plaintiff if the dispute were litigated with

plaintiff's ability to enforce any arbitral award entered concerning the product liability action in this problem?

PROBLEM 3.2 PERSONAL JURISDICTION OVER CANADIAN (CANTIRE), UK (DROF UK), AND GERMAN (DROF AG) DEFENDANTS

SECTION I. THE SETTING

As described in Problem 3.1, both the U.S. and UK plaintiffs, decide to bring the lawsuit in federal district court in New Jersey where the automobile accident occurred. U.S. plaintiffs are residents of the state of New Jersey. Plaintiffs name as defendants CANTIRE, Ltd., the tire manufacturer headquartered in Niagara, Canada, DROF AG and DROF UK, the jointly held UK/German automobile manufacturer, and VUSCO, L.L.C. the U.S. distributor which sells the automobile in the New York—New Jersey region. A cross-claim for contribution and indemnity is filed by VUSCO against DROF AG and DROF UK alleging that due to faulty design and manufacturing, the manufacturer should be held solely responsible for the accident and resulting injuries.

Fearing the worst in terms of a potential adverse outcome and huge monetary exposure, DROF AG, DROF UK and VUSCO enter into settlement negotiations with the U.S. and UK plaintiffs. CANTIRE, Ltd. refuses to discuss settlement, believing that it can avoid any lawsuit in the United States on jurisdictional grounds.

Additional claims for contribution and indemnity are instituted by DROF AG, DROF UK and VUSCO against CANTIRE, Ltd. seeking reimbursement of any settlement funds paid and contending that the tires were defective and were the cause of the accident.

Assume that the outstanding claims in need of resolution are: (1) the original claims; (2) the cross-claim for contribution and indemnity filed by VUSCO against DROF AG and DROF UK; and (3) the action for contribution and indemnity filed by DROF AG, DROF UK and VUSCO against CANTIRE, Ltd. Aside from contesting jurisdiction, defendants CANTIRE Ltd., DROF AG and DROF UK plan to rely on their respective forum selection clauses with VUSCO.

SECTION II. FOCUS OF CONSIDERATION

The focus is to explore whether the foreign defendants are subject to in personam jurisdiction in New Jersey pursuant to the state long-arm statute and whether the exercise of jurisdiction over these parties is consistent with the state and federal requirements of due process. Under the U.S. Constitution, state court jurisdiction is limited by the Fourteenth Amendment, and the scope of federal jurisdiction is limited by the due process clause of the Fifth Amendment.

SECTION III.   READINGS, QUESTIONS AND COMMENTS

PART A.   INTRODUCTION

In order to establish jurisdiction over foreign defendants, the U.S. court must possess both subject matter and *in personam* jurisdiction. See *In re Tuli*.[1] The same jurisdictional principles and due process limits apply to foreign defendants as to domestic defendants in the United States. This Problem deals with one of the two categories of jurisdiction, *in personam* jurisdiction, or jurisdiction to adjudicate as that term is used in the Restatement (Third) of Foreign Relations Law. The other category of jurisdiction, subject matter jurisdiction or jurisdiction to prescribe, is discussed in Problem 4.

For *in personam* jurisdiction, the court must determine whether the provisions of the state's long-arm statute have been satisfied consistent with constitutional limits of due process. In *International Shoe Co. v. Washington*,[2] the Supreme Court held that due process required that the requisite "minimum contacts" with the forum exist such that the exercise of jurisdiction "does not offend traditional notions of fair play and substantial justice." In *International Shoe*, the minimum contacts test was applied to a domestic corporation, not a foreign one, and the issue concerned jurisdiction based on claims arising out of the activity in the forum state. Nevertheless, the *International Shoe* standard remains applicable to both foreign and domestic corporations.

Since *International Shoe*, U.S. courts have increasingly analyzed *in personam* jurisdiction in the context of international commercial litigation. This expansion in the consideration of activity-based jurisdiction can be attributed to the growth of international commerce. *See World–Wide Volkswagen Corp. v. Woodson*.[3] This Problem covers many of the cross-border issues in resolving questions of *in personam* jurisdiction. This includes the presence of parties injured by products manufactured abroad but sold in the United States and those involved in the manufacture, sale and distribution of the product to plaintiffs in the United States. In product liability cases, it is common to have multiple suits or claims for contribution and indemnity against those involved in the chain of distribution of the product. This was the situation in *Asahi Metal Indus. Co. v. Superior Court of Cal.*[4] and numerous other reported cases have been considered in that context. The problem lies in identifying those parties in the chain of distribution whose conduct towards the forum constitutes "minimum contrats" sufficient for due process purposes.

While *World–Wide Volkswagen* did not involve cross-border issues, the Court's "minimum contacts" analysis factored into numerous subse-

---

1.   172 F.3d 707, 712 (9th Cir.1999).

2.   326 U.S. 310, 66 S.Ct. 154, 90 L.Ed. 95 (1945).

3.   444 U.S. 286, 100 S.Ct. 580, 62 L.Ed.2d 490 (1980).

4.   480 U.S. 102, 107 S.Ct. 1026, 94 L.Ed.2d 92 (1987).

quent international cases. Jurisdiction to adjudicate is covered in the Restatement (Third) of Foreign Relations Law as follows:

RESTATEMENT, FOREIGN RELATIONS LAW (THIRD)(1987)

§ 421, (1) A state may exercise jurisdiction through its courts to adjudicate with respect to a person or thing if the relationship of the state to the person or thing is such as to make the exercise of jurisdiction reasonable.

(2) In general, a state's exercise of jurisdiction to adjudicate with respect to a person or thing is reasonable if, at the time jurisdiction is asserted:

(a) the person or thing is present in the territory of the state, other than transitorily;

(b) the person, if a natural person, is domiciled in the state;

(c) the person, if a natural person, is resident in the state;

(d) the person, if a natural person, is a national of the state;

(e) the person, if a corporation or comparable juridical person, is organized pursuant to the law of the state;

(f) a ship, aircraft or other vehicle to which the adjudication relates is registered under the laws of the state;

(g) the person, whether natural or juridical, has consented to the exercise of jurisdiction;

(h) the person, whether natural or juridical, regularly carries on business in the state;

(i) the person, whether natural or juridical, had carried on activity in the state, but only in respect of such activity;

(j) the person, whether natural or juridical, had carried on outside the state an activity having a substantial, direct, and foreseeable effect within the state, but only in respect of such activity; or

(k) the thing that is the subject of adjudication is owned, possessed, or used in the state, but only in respect of a claim reasonably connected with that thing.

(3) A defense of lack of jurisdiction is generally waived by any appearance by or on behalf of a person or thing (whether as plaintiff, defendant, or third party), if the appearance is for a purpose that does not include a challenge to the exercise of jurisdiction.

Comment:

a. Jurisdiction to adjudicate and jurisdiction to prescribe: This section applies the principle of reasonableness to limit the exercise of jurisdiction to adjudicate, as § 403 does with respect to jurisdiction to prescribe. The standards of reasonableness under the two sections, however, are not the same. The fact that an exercise of jurisdiction to adjudicate in given circumstances is reasonable does not mean that the forum state has jurisdiction to prescribe in respect to the subject matter of the action. Conversely, there may be circumstances in which a state has jurisdiction to prescribe but jurisdiction to adjudicate is absent or doubtful. For the relation of jurisdiction to adjudicate to jurisdiction to enforce, see Introductory Note to Chapter 3 of this Part.

b. Civil and criminal jurisdiction: In principle, this section applies to the exercise of criminal as well as to civil jurisdiction. It does not apply to adjudication of family law controversies. For discussion of such controversies in connection with recognition of foreign judgments, see §§ 484–86. For judicial jurisdiction of criminal actions in the United States, see § 422.

c. Enumerated links discrete, not cumulative: In contrast with the factors for evaluating jurisdiction to prescribe, § 403(2), which are cumulative and illustrative, the links set forth in Subsection (2) of this section are independent; each is sufficient to support the state's jurisdiction to adjudicate. In general, the exercise of jurisdiction based on other links is not reasonable.

d. Factors applicable at time of assertion of jurisdiction: The criteria set forth in Subsection (2) are ordinarily applicable as of the time jurisdiction is asserted, i.e., when the action is commenced. Whether domicile or residence at a time prior to commencement of the action is sufficient to support jurisdiction under this section is not certain.

e. Transitory presence: "Tag" jurisdiction, i.e., jurisdiction based on service of process on a person only transitorily in the territory of the state, is not generally acceptable under international law. "Presence" in Subsection (2)(a) is satisfied by a less extended stay than is required to constitute residence, but it does not include merely transitory presence, such as while changing planes at an airport, coming on shore from a cruise ship, or a few days' sojourn unconnected with the activity giving rise to the claim.

f. Jurisdiction of State of United States: International law addresses the exercise of jurisdiction by a state; it does not concern itself with the allocation of jurisdiction among domestic courts within a state for example, between national and local courts in a federal system.

In the United States, the criteria for determining the reasonableness of an exercise of jurisdiction to adjudicate by State courts are generally similar to those for federal courts, but they are applied on a local (State) rather than a national basis. Thus, the courts of a State of the United States may exercise jurisdiction to adjudicate pursuant to paragraphs (b) and (c) of Subsection (2) only if the person in question has his domicile or residence in that State; pursuant to paragraphs (h), (i), and (j) only if the business or activity is carried out or has effect in that State; and pursuant to paragraph (k) only if the thing is situated in that State. Jurisdiction to adjudicate on the basis of United States nationality or citizenship in accordance with Subsection (2)(d) may be exercised by State courts pursuant to federal statute; whether they can do so on the authority of the State alone has not been determined. It may not be unreasonable for a State to exercise jurisdiction to adjudicate on the basis of State citizenship in a limited category of cases.

g. Appearance: In most legal systems, appearance in a proceeding, whether as plaintiff, defendant, or intervenor, is deemed to waive the defense of lack of jurisdiction, unless the appearance has as its purpose (or one of its purposes) a challenge to the court's jurisdiction. This rule applies in State as well as federal courts of the United States, but a petition to remove an action from a State to a federal court does not constitute an appearance. Participation in an action as amicus curiae does not constitute an appearance.

h.   Forum selection clauses: A provision in a contract that the courts or a designated court of a state shall have jurisdiction over disputes arising out of or related to the contract generally confers on the chosen forum jurisdiction over such disputes, even if the defendant is not otherwise amenable to suit in that state. If the agreement provides, or is interpreted as providing, that the forum selected is exclusive, an action brought elsewhere will generally be dismissed, unless the plaintiff shows that the chosen forum is no longer available or could not be expected to grant him a fair hearing. A claim that the contract itself was not validly concluded or is otherwise defective generally does not defeat a forum selection clause unless the clause itself is tainted with fraud; the prevailing view is that such challenges to the contract should be made in the chosen forum. For the comparable rule concerning agreements to arbitrate, see § 488, Reporters' Note 1. For the rule that a judgment rendered by a court other than the one chosen by the parties may be denied recognition, see § 482(2)(f) and Comment h to that section.

i.   Actions based on presence of property: Under Subsection (2)(k), it is reasonable for a State to adjudicate a possessory action in respect of a thing owned, possessed, or present in the State, or any other action in respect of that thing or of claims related to it. A State may not exercise general jurisdiction over a person on the ground that the defendant owns property in the State, but may exercise jurisdiction on that ground to enforce a judgment entitled to recognition and enforcement. See § 481, Comment h. Judgments against nonresidents rendered on the basis of presence of property only are generally not recognized by courts of other states.

PART B.   SPECIFIC VERSUS GENERAL JURISDICTION

In the due process analysis, the court is faced with the distinction between general jurisdiction and specific jurisdiction. General jurisdiction permits a court to adjudicate any claim against a defendant, if that defendant has sufficiently "continuous and systematic" contacts with the forum. Specific jurisdiction permits only the adjudication of claims that are related to or arise out of a defendant's contacts with the forum state.[5] Specific jurisdiction may be exercised when the activities of a defendant that relate to the plaintiff's suit have sufficient minimum contacts with the forum to satisfy the due process standard set forth in *International Shoe* and subsequent cases.[6] The importance of these distinctions in the international context has been noted as follows:

5. *See Helicopteros Nacionales de Colombia, S.A. v. Hall*, 466 U.S. 408, 104 S.Ct. 1868, 80 L.Ed.2d 404 (1984).

6. *See Aristech Chemical International Limited v. Acrylic Fabricators Limited*, 138 F.3d 624, 627 (6th Cir.1998).

Many have argued that the Court should adopt a higher or lower jurisdictional standard with respect to alien defendants for various policy reasons, including the promotion of international trade or the fear that low standards could bring reprisals against U.S. corporations in foreign forums. Although many cases involving foreign defendants are based on the application of specific jurisdiction, the distinction is important because at some point the defendant's activities in a forum will rise above a specific level and provide general jurisdiction over the defendant. The line between general and specific jurisdiction is obviously not a bright one, and the question will require a case-by-case analysis of the particular statutory grant of jurisdiction and the facts of each case.[7]

HELICOPTEROS NACIONALES DE COLOMBIA, S.A. v. HALL

United States Supreme Court, 1984.
466 U.S. 408, 104 S.Ct. 1868, 80 L.Ed.2d 404.

JUSTICE BLACKMUN delivered the opinion of the Court.

We granted certiorari in this case to decide whether the Supreme Court of Texas correctly ruled that the contacts of a foreign corporation with the State of Texas were sufficient to allow a Texas state court to assert jurisdiction over the corporation in a cause of action not arising out of or related to the corporation's activities within the State.

I

Petitioner Helicopteros Nacionales de Colombia, S.A. (Helicol), is a Colombian corporation with its principal place of business in the city of Bogota in that country. It is engaged in the business of providing helicopter transportation for oil and construction companies in South America. On January 26, 1976, a helicopter owned by Helicol crashed in Peru. Four United States citizens were among those who lost their lives in the accident. Respondents are the survivors and representatives of the four decedents.

At the time of the crash, respondents decedents were employed by Consorcio, a Peruvian consortium, and were working on a pipeline in Peru. Consorcio is the alter ego of a joint venture named Williams–Sedco–Horn (WSH). The venture had its headquarters in Houston, Tex. Consorcio had been formed to enable the venturers to enter into a contract with Petro Peru, the Peruvian state-owned oil company. Consorcio was to construct a pipeline for Petro Peru running from the interior of Peru westward to the Pacific Ocean. Peruvian law forbade construction of the pipeline by any non-Peruvian entity.

---

7. See David Epstein, Jeffrey L. Snyder & Charles S. Baldwin, IV, International Lit- igation, at 6–22.

Consorcio/WSH needed helicopters to move personnel, materials, and equipment into and out of the construction area. In 1974, upon request of Consorcio/WSH, the chief executive officer of Helicol, Francisco Restrepo, flew to the United States and conferred in Houston with representatives of the three joint venturers. At that meeting, there was a discussion of prices, availability, working conditions, fuel, supplies, and housing. Restrepo represented that Helicol could have the first helicopter on the job in 15 days. The Consorcio/WSH representatives decided to accept the contract proposed by Restrepo. Helicol began performing before the agreement was formally signed in Peru on November 11, 1974. The contract was written in Spanish on official government stationery and provided that the residence of all the parties would be Lima, Peru. It further stated that controversies arising out of the contract would be submitted to the jurisdiction of Peruvian courts. In addition, it provided that Consorcio/WSH would make payments to Helicol's account with the Bank of America in New York City.

Aside from the negotiation session in Houston between Restrepo and the representatives of Consorcio/WSH, Helicol had other contacts with Texas. During the years 1970–1977, it purchased helicopters (approximately 80% of its fleet), spare parts, and accessories for more than $4 million from Bell Helicopter Company in Fort Worth. In that period, Helicol sent prospective pilots to Fort Worth for training and to ferry the aircraft to South America. It also sent management and maintenance personnel to visit Bell Helicopter in Fort Worth during the same period in order to receive "plant familiarization" and for technical consultation. Helicol received into its New York City and Panama City, Fla., bank accounts over $5 million in payments from Consorcio/WSH drawn upon First City National Bank of Houston.

Beyond the foregoing, there have been no other business contacts between Helicol and the State of Texas. Helicol never has been authorized to do business in Texas and never has had an agent for the service of process within the State. It never has performed helicopter operations in Texas or sold any product that reached Texas, never solicited business in Texas, never signed any contract in Texas, never had any employee based there, and never recruited an employee in Texas. In addition, Helicol never has owned real or personal property in Texas and never has maintained an office or establishment there. Helicol has maintained no records in Texas and has no shareholders in that State. None of the respondents or their decedents were domiciled in Texas, but all of the decedents were hired in Houston by Consorcio/WSH to work on the Petro Peru pipeline project.

Respondents instituted wrongful-death actions in the District Court of Harris County, Tex., against Consorcio/WSH, Bell Helicopter Company, and Helicol. Helicol filed special appearances and moved to dismiss the actions for lack of *in personam* jurisdiction over it. The motion was denied. After a consolidated jury trial, judgment was entered against Helicol on a jury verdict of $1,141,200 in favor of respondents.

The Texas Court of Civil Appeals, Houston, First District, reversed the judgment of the District Court, holding that *in personam* jurisdiction over Helicol was lacking. The Supreme Court of Texas, with three justices dissenting, initially affirmed the judgment of the Court of Civil Appeals. Seven months later, however, on motion for rehearing, the court withdrew its prior opinions and, again with three justices dissenting, reversed the judgment of the intermediate court. In ruling that the Texas courts had *in personam* jurisdiction, the Texas Supreme Court first held that the State's long-arm statute reaches as far as the Due Process Clause of the Fourteenth Amendment permits. Thus, the only question remaining for the court to decide was whether it was consistent with the Due Process Clause for Texas courts to assert *in personam* jurisdiction over Helicol. Ibid.

II

The Due Process Clause of the Fourteenth Amendment operates to limit the power of a State to assert *in personam* jurisdiction over a nonresident defendant. *Pennoyer v. Neff*, 95 U.S. 714, 24 L.Ed. 565 (1878). Due process requirements are satisfied when *in personam* jurisdiction is asserted over a nonresident corporate defendant that has "certain minimum contacts with [the forum] such that the maintenance of the suit does not offend 'traditional notions of fair play and substantial justice.'" *International Shoe Co. v. Washington*, 326 U.S. 310, 316, 66 S.Ct. 154, 158, 90 L.Ed. 95 (1945), quoting *Milliken v. Meyer*, 311 U.S. 457, 463, 61 S.Ct. 339, 342, 85 L.Ed. 278 (1940). When a controversy is related to or "arises out of" a defendant's contacts with the forum, the Court has said that a "relationship among the defendant, the forum, and the litigation" is the essential foundation of *in personam* jurisdiction. *Shaffer v. Heitner*, 433 U.S. 186, 204, 97 S.Ct. 2569, 2579, 53 L.Ed.2d 683 (1977).

Even when the cause of action does not arise out of or relate to the foreign corporation's activities in the forum State, due process is not offended by a State's subjecting the corporation to its *in personam* jurisdiction when there are sufficient contacts between the State and the foreign corporation. *Perkins v. Benguet Consolidated Mining Co.*, 342 U.S. 437, 72 S.Ct. 413, 96 L.Ed. 485 (1952); see *Keeton v. Hustler Magazine, Inc.*, 465 U.S. 770, 779–780, 104 S.Ct. 1473, 1480–1481, 79 L.Ed.2d 790 (1984). In Perkins, the Court addressed a situation in which state courts had asserted general jurisdiction over a defendant foreign corporation. During the Japanese occupation of the Philippine Islands, the president and general manager of a Philippine mining corporation maintained an office in Ohio from which he conducted activities on behalf of the company. He kept company files and held directors' meetings in the office, carried on correspondence relating to the business, distributed salary checks drawn on two active Ohio bank accounts, engaged an Ohio bank to act as transfer agent, and supervised policies dealing with the rehabilitation of the corporation's properties in the Philippines. In short, the foreign corporation, through its president, "ha[d] been carrying on in Ohio a continuous and systematic, but limited, part of its general business," and the exercise of general jurisdiction over the Philippine corporation by an Ohio court was "reasonable and just." 342 U.S., at 438, 445, 72 S.Ct., at 414, 418.

All parties to the present case concede that respondents' claims against Helicol did not "arise out of," and are not related to, Helicol's activities within Texas. We thus must explore the nature of Helicol's contacts with the State of Texas to determine whether they constitute the kind of continuous and systematic general business contacts the Court found to exist in Perkins. We hold that they do not.

It is undisputed that Helicol does not have a place of business in Texas and never has been licensed to do business in the State. Basically, Helicol's contacts with Texas consisted of sending its chief executive officer to Houston for a contract-negotiation session; accepting into its New York bank account checks drawn on a Houston bank; purchasing helicopters, equipment, and training services from Bell Helicopter for substantial sums; and sending personnel to Bell's facilities in Fort Worth for training.

The one trip to Houston by Helicol's chief executive officer for the purpose of negotiating the transportation-services contract with Consorcio/WSH cannot be described or regarded as a contact of a "continuous and systematic" nature, as Perkins described it ... and thus cannot support an assertion of *in personam* jurisdiction over Helicol by a Texas court. Similarly, Helicol's acceptance from Consorcio/WSH of checks drawn on a Texas bank is of negligible significance for purposes of determining whether Helicol had sufficient contacts in Texas. There is no indication that Helicol ever requested that the checks be drawn on a Texas bank or that there was any negotiation between Helicol and Consorcio/WSH with respect to the location or identity of the bank on which checks would be drawn. Common sense and everyday experience suggest that, absent unusual circumstances, the bank on which a check is drawn is generally of little consequence to the payee and is a matter left to the discretion of the drawer. Such unilateral activity of another party or a third person is not an appropriate consideration when determining whether a defendant has sufficient contacts with a forum State to justify an assertion of jurisdiction

The Texas Supreme Court focused on the purchases and the related training trips in finding contacts sufficient to support an assertion of jurisdiction. We do not agree with that assessment, for the Court's opinion in *Rosenberg Bros. & Co. v. Curtis Brown Co.*, 260 U.S. 516, 43 S.Ct. 170, 67 L.Ed. 372 (1923), makes clear that purchases and related trips, standing alone, are not a sufficient basis for a State's assertion of jurisdiction.

The defendant in *Rosenberg* was a small retailer in Tulsa, Okla., who dealt in men's clothing and furnishings. It never had applied for a license to do business in New York, nor had it at any time authorized suit to be brought against it there. It never had an established place of business in New York and never regularly carried on business in that State. Its only connection with New York was that it purchased from New York wholesalers a large portion of the merchandise sold in its Tulsa store. The purchases sometimes were made by correspondence and sometimes through visits to New York by an officer of the defendant. The Court concluded: "Visits on such business, even if occurring at regular intervals, would not warrant the inference that the corporation was present within the jurisdiction of [New York]."

This Court in *International Shoe* acknowledged and did not repudiate its holding in *Rosenberg*. In accordance with Rosenberg, we hold that mere purchases, even if occurring at regular intervals, are not enough to warrant a State's assertion of *in personam jurisdiction* over a nonresident corporation in a cause of action not related to those purchase transactions. Nor can we conclude that the fact that Helicol sent personnel into Texas for training in connection with the purchase of helicopters and equipment in that State in any way enhanced the nature of Helicol's contacts with Texas. The training was a part of the package of goods and services purchased by Helicol from Bell Helicopter. The brief presence of Helicol employees in Texas for the purpose of attending the training sessions is no more a significant contact than were the trips to New York made by the buyer for the retail store in Rosenberg. See also *Kulko v. California Superior Court*, 436 U.S. at 93, 98 S.Ct. at 1697 (basing California jurisdiction on 3–day and 1–day of stopovers in that State "would make a mockery of" due process limitations on assertion of personal jurisdiction).

III

We hold that Helicol's contacts with the State of Texas were insufficient to satisfy the requirements of the Due Process Clause of the Fourteenth Amendment. Accordingly, we reverse the judgment of the Supreme Court of Texas.

It is so ordered.

PART C.   LONG–ARM STATUTES

Problem 3.2 deals with a "minimum contacts" analysis involving a product liability action in which a product manufactured by non-resident defendants allegedly injured the party-plaintiffs in the United States. Based on a specific jurisdiction inquiry, does the state long-arm statute authorize *in personam* jurisdiction over the non-resident defendants in the forum state? There are several types of long-arm statutes. The Virginia Code, for example, provides for specific jurisdiction over any defendant based on enumerated acts which took place within the forum or tortuous acts committed outside which cause injury in the Commonwealth of Virginia. Virginia Code 8.01–328.1(A)(1) permits the exercise of personal jurisdiction in Virginia over entities "transacting any business in this Commonwealth." Virginia Code 8.01–328.1(A)(4) permits the exercise of personal jurisdiction in Virginia over entities "causing tortuous injury in this Commonwealth by an act or omission outside this

Commonwealth if [if the defendant] regularly does or solicits business, or engages in any other persistent course of conduct, or derives substantial revenue from goods used or consumed or services rendered, in this Commonwealth."

In this type of long-arm statute, the court must first determine whether the claim asserted against the defendant comes within the enumerated factors and then whether defendant's contacts satisfy minimum contacts and due process requirements.

RZS HOLDINGS AVV v. PDVSA PETROLEOS S.A.

United States District Court, E.D. Virginia, 2003.
293 F.Supp.2d 645.

Defendant Banesco contends that its alleged contacts with the Commonwealth of Virginia-the sending of four fax communications to RZS in Virginia, the posting of a Spanish-language website marketing a Visa card to Venezuelan residents, and the existence of CITGO service stations in Virginia from which Banesco indirectly derives revenues are not sufficient to establish personal jurisdiction under either the Virginia long-arm ... or constitutional due process requirements. RZS counters that such contacts authorize personal jurisdiction ...

It is well-settled that a resolution of a personal jurisdiction challenge by a non-resident defendant requires a two-step inquiry. First, a court must assess whether the defendant is subject to jurisdiction under the Virginia long-arm statute given the nature of the cause of action and defendant's contacts with the Commonwealth. Second, a court must determine whether personal jurisdiction comports with due process-that is, whether the exercise of jurisdiction under the long-arm statute exceeds the constitutional grasp. [citations omitted]. This two-step analysis, applied here, compels the conclusion that neither the requirements of Virginia's long-arm statute nor constitutional due process are met with respect to the assertion of personal jurisdiction over Banesco.

RZS asserts that personal jurisdiction is appropriate under two provisions of the Virginia long-arm statute (1) Virginia Code 8.01–328.1(A)(1) which permits the exercise of personal jurisdiction in Virginia over entities "transacting any business in this Commonwealth" and (2) Virginia Code 8.01–328.1(A)(4), which permits the exercise of personal jurisdiction in Virginia over entities "causing tortuous injury in this Commonwealth by an act or omission outside this Commonwealth if the defendant regularly does or solicits business, or engages in any other persistent course of conduct, or derives substantial revenue from goods used or consumed or services rendered, on this Commonwealth."

Banesco's alleged contacts with Virginia are not sufficient to conclude that it "transact[s] business" in Virginia and is thus subject to personal jurisdiction under 8.01–328.1(A)(1). To begin with, it is undisputed that Banesco has no facilities or presence in Virginia. It maintains no offices in Virginia, nor indeed anywhere in the United States. It does not employ individuals in Virginia, own any assets here, or provide banking services to clients in Virginia. For its contention that Banesco "transacted business" in Virginia, RZS can point only to four fax communications to RZS. Yet, these faxes will not suffice for it is clear that "mere phone calls and letters, and arguably fax communications, in furtherance of a transaction are insufficient to form a basis for personal jurisdiction" [citations omitted]. Nor is it enough to show that Banesco maintains a website offering a Visa card to Venezuelan residents that may be accessed in Virginia. Where, as here, Banesco's website advertised its Visa card only to Venezuelan residents, there is no basis for jurisdiction. A website provides a basis for jurisdiction only if, as has not been shown here, the website's creator "(1) directs electronic activity into the State, (2) with the manifested intent of engaging in business or other interactions within the State, and (3) that activity creates, in a person within the State, a potential cause of action cognizable in the State's courts."

Plaintiff's principal argument to the contrary is that one of the faxes sent to RZS in Virginia or the posting of the website is sufficient to provide a basis for personal jurisdiction because Virginia's long-arm statute is a "single act" statute. This is a misunderstanding of the character of the Virginia long-arm statute. While a single act can furnish the basis for personal jurisdiction under the statute, that act must be more substantial than the faxes or website here at issue. To conclude otherwise "would convert the long-arm statute from a 'single' statute to a 'single act of any kind or nature whatsoever' statute, a result neither intended by the General Assembly, nor permitted by the statutory language."

Plaintiff's jurisdictional argument does not rest solely on the transacting business provision of the long-arm statute. Also relied on in this regard is Virginia Code 8.01–328.1(A)(4) which provides for personal jurisdiction where the defendant has caused tortious injury in Virginia by an act or omission outside Virginia provided that plaintiff can show that defendant (i) "regularly does or solicits business" in Virginia, (ii) "engages in any other persistent course of conduct" in Virginia, or (iii) "derives substantial revenue from goods used or consumed or services rendered" in Virginia. Va.Code 8.01–328.1(A)(4). [citations omitted]. Assuming without deciding that plaintiff can establish that the defendant caused tortious injury in Virginia, it is pellucidly clear that plaintiff cannot establish the additional statutory requirements. Plaintiff's contention that Banesco earns substantial revenue indirectly through payments it receives from CITGO, which operates service stations in Virginia, is meritless.

In sum, therefore, plaintiff has not shown that the grasp of Virginia's long-arm statute reaches Banesco in this case. While this is sufficient to end the analysis, it is nonetheless useful to address whether due process would be violated were the statute construed to reach Banesco in this case.

To determine whether a court's exercise of personal jurisdiction comports with due process, it is necessary to assess "whether the defendant purposefully established 'minimum contacts' in the forum state," ... such as the maintenance of the suit does not offend 'traditional notions of fair play and substantial justice.' ... Thus, the plaintiff must show that the defendant purposely directed his activities at residents of the forum, and that the plaintiff's claim arises out of the defendant's forum-related activities ... This test is designed to ensure that the defendant is not haled into a jurisdiction solely as a result of random, fortuitous, or attenuated contacts... That is, the defendant's contacts in Virginia must be such that he should reasonably anticipate being haled into court there...

These principles compel the conclusion that Banesco's contacts with Virginia are insufficient under the due process clause. Just as the four fax transmissions to plaintiff in Virginia and the posting of a website directed to Venezuelans are inadequate to meet the requirements of the "transacting business" provision of the long-arm statute, they are inadequate to show that Banesco purposefully directed its activities to Virginia. These contacts do not show, as due process requires, that Banesco has purposely availed [itself] of the privilege of conducting activities within the forum state, thus invoking the benefits and protections of its laws. Furthermore, plaintiff's claims arise out of its contract with defendant PDVSA and PDVSA's arrangement with Banesco and Commerzbank regarding the letter of credit, and not out of defendant's forum-related activities. Finally, given the nature of defendant's contacts in Virginia, it is not reasonable to conclude that defendant should have anticipated being sued in Virginia.

Based on the foregoing, Banesco's contacts with the Commonwealth of Virginia do not fall within the grasp of Virginia's long-arm statute. Moreover, even if they did, Banesco's contacts are insufficient under the due process clause. Accordingly, Banesco's motion to dismiss for lack of personal jurisdiction must be denied.

PART D. "MINIMUM CONTACTS" ANALYSIS

Since *International Shoe*, courts have analyzed a host of factual circumstances in determining what constitutes "minimum contacts" and when the exercise of jurisdiction is consistent with constitutional requirements of reasonableness. No precise formula has emerged despite the Supreme Court's numerous attempts to identify the "minimum contacts" required to establish personal jurisdiction. "The application of the rule will vary with the quality and nature of the defendant's activity, but it is essential in each case that there be some act by which the defendant purposefully avails itself of the privilege of conducting activities within the forum State, thus invoking the benefits and protections of its laws."[8]

---

8. *Hanson v. Denckla,* 357 U.S. 235, 253, 78 S.Ct. 1228, 2 L.Ed.2d 1283 (1958).

If "minimum contacts" have been established between the defendant and the forum, these "contacts may be considered in light of other factors to determine whether the assertion of personal jurisdiction would comport with traditional notions of 'fair play and substantial justice.' ".[9] In determining reasonableness in the context of international litigation, the Supreme Court has recognized that "[t]he unique burdens placed upon one who must defend oneself in a foreign legal system should have significant weight in assessing the reasonableness of stretching the long arm of personal jurisdiction over national borders."[10]

Comment on Product Liability Cases

Determination of judicial jurisdiction in product liability cases necessarily requires examination of forum-related contacts under the "stream of commerce" theory as determined by the Supreme Court in *World–Wide Volkswagen v. Woodson*, and the standard of reasonableness as a separate consideration. In *World–Wide Volkswagen* and in the subsequent *Asahi* case, the Supreme Court did not develop a clear standard of "purposeful direction" under the "stream of commerce" test. Due to the Supreme Court's lack of consensus, federal and state courts have split on what activities of the defendant will satisfy the "minimum contacts" requirement and whether the "stream of commerce" test should be applied to the subject controversy. We will see from the case discussions, *infra*, that the "stream of commerce" test is applied primarily in tort cases in light of the forum state's interest in protecting its citizens in product liability and other tort cases. Regardless of the test employed for determining personal jurisdiction, the focus in product liability cases will be on whether sale of the product was purposefully directed to the forum by activities of the manufacturer or whether there was "reasonable awareness" that the product would be sold in the forum through the chain of distribution of the product.

WORLD–WIDE VOLKSWAGEN CORP. v. WOODSON

United States Supreme Court, 1980.
444 U.S. 286, 100 S.Ct. 559, 62 L.Ed.2d 490.

MR. JUSTICE WHITE delivered the opinion of the Court.

The issue before us is whether, consistently with the Due Process Clause of the Fourteenth Amendment, an Oklahoma court may exercise *in personam jurisdiction* over a nonresident automobile retailer and its wholesale distributor in a products-liability action, when the defendants' only connection with Oklahoma is the fact that an automobile sold in New York to New York residents became involved in an accident in Oklahoma.

Applying these principles to the case at hand, we find in the record before us a total absence of those affiliating circumstances that are a

9. *Burger King v. Rudzewicz*, 471 U.S. 462, 476, 105 S.Ct. 2174, 85 L.Ed.2d 528 (1985); *International Shoe Co. v. Washington*, 326 U.S. 310, 320, 66 S.Ct. 154, 90 L.Ed. 95 (1945); *World–Wide Volkswagen Corp. v. Woodson*, 444 U.S. 286, 292, 100 S.Ct. 580, 62 L.Ed.2d 490 (1980).

10. *Asahi Metal Industry v. Superior Court of California*, 480 U.S. 102, 114, 107 S.Ct. 1026, 94 L.Ed.2d 92 (1987).

necessary predicate to any exercise of state-court jurisdiction. Petitioners carry on no activity whatsoever in Oklahoma. They close no sales and perform no services there. They avail themselves of none of the privileges and benefits of Oklahoma law. They solicit no business there either through salespersons or through advertising reasonably calculated to reach the State. Nor does the record show that they regularly sell cars at wholesale or retail to Oklahoma customers or residents or that they indirectly, through others, serve or seek to serve the Oklahoma market. In short, respondents seek to base jurisdiction on one, isolated occurrence and whatever inferences can be drawn therefrom: the fortuitous circumstance that a single Audi automobile, sold in New York to New York residents, happened to suffer an accident while passing through Oklahoma.

It is argued, however, that because an automobile is mobile by its very design and purpose it was "foreseeable" that the Robinsons' Audi would cause injury in Oklahoma. Yet "foreseeability" alone has never been a sufficient benchmark for personal jurisdiction under the Due Process Clause. In *Hanson v. Denckla, supra*, it was no doubt foreseeable that the settlor of a Delaware trust would subsequently move to Florida and seek to exercise a power of appointment there; yet we held that Florida courts could not constitutionally exercise jurisdiction over a Delaware trustee that had no other contacts with the forum State. In *Kulko v. California Superior Court*, 436 U.S. 84, 98 S.Ct. 1690, 56 L.Ed.2d 132 (1978), it was surely "foreseeable" that a divorced wife would move to California from New York, the domicile of the marriage, and that a minor daughter would live with the mother. Yet we held that California could not exercise jurisdiction in a child-support action over the former husband who had remained in New York.

This is not to say, of course, that foreseeability is wholly irrelevant. But the foreseeability that is critical to due process analysis is not the mere likelihood that a product will find its way into the forum State. Rather, it is that the defendant's conduct and connection with the forum State are such that he should reasonably anticipate being haled into court there. The Due Process Clause, by ensuring the "orderly administration of the laws," *International Shoe Co. v. Washington*, 326 U.S., at 319, 66 S.Ct., at 159, gives a degree of predictability to the legal system that allows potential defendants to structure their primary conduct with some minimum assurance as to where that conduct will and will not render them liable to suit.

When a corporation "purposefully avails itself of the privilege of conducting activities within the forum State," *Hanson v. Denckla*, 357 U.S., at 253, 78 S.Ct., at 1240, it has clear notice that it is subject to suit there, and can act to alleviate the risk of burdensome litigation by procuring insurance, passing the expected costs on to customers, or, if the risks are too great, severing its connection with the State. Hence if the sale of a product of a manufacturer or distributor such as Audi or Volkswagen is not simply an isolated occurrence, but arises from the efforts of the manufacturer or distributor to serve directly or indirectly, the market for its product in other States, it is not unreasonable to subject it to suit in one of those States if its allegedly defective merchandise has there been the source of injury to its owner or to others. The forum State does not exceed its powers under the Due Process Clause if it asserts personal jurisdiction over a corporation that delivers its products into the stream of commerce with the expectation that they will be purchased by consumers in the forum State.

But there is no such or similar basis for Oklahoma jurisdiction over World–Wide or Seaway in this case. Seaway's sales are made in Massena, N. Y. World–Wide's market, although substantially larger, is limited to dealers in New York, New Jersey, and Connecticut. There is no evidence of record that any automobiles distributed by World–Wide are sold to retail customers outside this tristate area. It is foreseeable that the purchasers of automobiles sold by World–Wide and Seaway may take them to Oklahoma. But the mere "unilateral activity of those who claim some relationship with a nonresident defendant cannot satisfy the requirement of contact with the forum State." *Hanson v. Denckla, supra*, at 253, 78 S.Ct., at 1239–1240.

In a variant on the previous argument, it is contended that jurisdiction can be supported by the fact that petitioners earn substantial revenue from goods used in Oklahoma. The Oklahoma Supreme Court so found, drawing the inference that because one automobile sold by petitioners had been used in Oklahoma, others might have been used there also. While this inference seems less than compelling on the facts of the instant case, we need not question the court's factual findings in order to reject its reasoning.

This argument seems to make the point that the purchase of automobiles in New York, from which the petitioners earn substantial revenue, would not occur *but for* the fact that the automobiles are capable of use in distant States like Oklahoma. Respondents observe that the very purpose of an automobile is to travel, and that travel of automobiles sold by petitioners is facilitated by an extensive chain of Volkswagen service centers throughout the country, including some in Oklahoma. However, financial benefits accruing to the defendant from a collateral relation to the forum State will not support jurisdiction if they do not stem from a constitutionally cognizable contact with that State. In our view, whatever marginal revenues petitioners may receive by virtue of the fact that their products are capable of use in Oklahoma is far too attenuated a contact to justify that State's exercise of in personam jurisdiction over them.

Because we find that petitioners have no "contacts, ties, or relations" with the State of Oklahoma, *International Shoe Co. v. Washington, supra*, 326 U.S., at 319, 66 S.Ct., at 159, the judgment of the Supreme Court of Oklahoma is Reversed.

.   .   .

ASAHI METAL INDUS. CO. v. SUPERIOR
COURT OF CALIFORNIA

United States Supreme Court, 1987.
480 U.S. 102, 107 S.Ct. 1026, 94 L.Ed.2d 92.

[Japanese manufacturer of valve stems for motorcycle tire assemblies sold worldwide sought to quash summons upon it from California Superior Court in products liability action arising from motorcycle accident.]

The "substantial connection" between the defendant and the forum State necessary for a finding of minimum contacts must come about by *an action of the defendant purposefully directed toward the forum State. Burger King, supra,* 471 U.S., at 476, 105 S.Ct., at 2184. The placement of a product into the stream of commerce, without more, is not an act of the defendant purposefully directed toward the forum State. Additional conduct of the defendant may indicate an intent or purpose to serve the market in the forum State, for example, designing the product for the market in the forum State, advertising in the forum State, establishing channels for providing regular advice to customers in the forum State, or marketing the product through a distributor who has agreed to serve as the sales agent in the forum State. But a defendant's awareness that the stream of commerce may or will sweep the product into the forum State does not convert the mere act of placing the product into the stream into an act purposefully directed toward the forum State.

Assuming, arguendo, that respondents have established Asahi's awareness that some of the valves sold to Cheng Shin [Taiwan tire company] would be incorporated into tire tubes sold in California, respondents have not demonstrated any action by Asahi to purposefully avail itself of the California market. Asahi does not do business in California. It has no office, agents, employees, or property in California. It does not advertise or otherwise solicit business in California. It did not create, control, or employ the distribution system that brought its valves to California. There is no evidence that Asahi designed its product in anticipation of sales in California. On the basis of these facts, the exertion of personal jurisdiction over Asahi by the Superior Court of California exceeds the limits of due process.

We have previously explained that the determination of the reasonableness of the exercise of jurisdiction in each case will depend on an evaluation of several factors. A court must consider the burden on the defendant, the interests of the forum State, and the plaintiff's interest in obtaining relief. It must also weigh in its determination "the interstate judicial system's interest in obtaining the most efficient resolution of controversies; and the shared interest of the several States in furthering fundamental substantive social policies." *World–Wide Volkswagen.*

A consideration of these factors in the present case clearly reveals the unreasonableness of the assertion of jurisdiction over Asahi, even apart from the question of the placement of goods in the stream of commerce. Certainly the burden on the defendant in this case is severe. Asahi has been commanded by the Supreme Court of California not only to traverse the distance between Asahi's headquarters in Japan and the Superior Court of California in and for the County of Solano, but also to submit its dispute with Cheng Shin to a foreign nation's judicial system. The unique burdens placed upon one who must defend oneself in a foreign legal system should have significant weight in assessing the reasonableness of stretching the long arm of personal jurisdiction over national borders.

When minimum contacts have been established, often the interests of the plaintiff and the forum in the exercise of jurisdiction will justify even the serious burdens placed on the alien defendant. In the present case, however, the interests of the plaintiff and the forum in California's assertion of jurisdiction over Asahi are slight. All that remains is a claim for indemnification asserted by Cheng Shin, a Taiwanese corporation, against Asahi. The transaction on which the indemnification claim is based took place in Taiwan; Asahi's components were shipped from Japan to Taiwan. Cheng Shin has not demonstrated that it is more convenient for it to litigate its indemnification claim against Asahi in California rather than in Taiwan or Japan.

Because the plaintiff is not a California resident, California's legitimate interests in the dispute have considerably diminished. The Supreme Court of California argued that the State had an interest in "protecting its consumers by ensuring that foreign manufacturers comply with the state's safety standards." The State Supreme Court's definition of California's interest, however, was overly broad. The dispute between Cheng Shin and Asahi is primarily about indemnification rather than safety standards. Moreover, it is not at all clear at this point that California law should govern the question whether a Japanese corporation should indemnify a Taiwanese corporation on the basis of a sale made in Taiwan and a shipment of goods from Japan to Taiwan. The possibility of being haled into a California court as a result of an accident involving Asahi's components undoubtedly creates an additional deterrent to the manufacture of unsafe components; however, similar pressures will be placed on Asahi by the purchasers of its components as long as those who use Asahi components in their final products, and sell those products in California, are subject to the application of California tort law.

World–Wide Volkswagen also admonished courts to take into consideration the interests of the "several States," in addition to the forum State, in the efficient judicial resolution of the dispute and the advancement of substantive policies. In the present case, this advice calls for a court to consider the procedural and substantive policies of other nations whose interests are affected by the assertion of jurisdiction by the California court. The procedural and substantive interests of other nations in a state court's assertion of jurisdiction over an alien defendant will differ from case to case. In every case, however, those interests, as well as the Federal interest in Government's foreign relations policies, will be best served by a careful inquiry into the reasonableness of the assertion of jurisdiction in the particular case, and an unwillingness to find the serious burdens on an alien defendant outweighed by minimal interests on the part of the plaintiff or the forum State. "Great care and reserve should be exercised when extending our notions of personal jurisdiction into the international field." *United States v. First National City Bank*, 379 U.S. 378, 404, 85 S.Ct. 528, 542, 13 L.Ed.2d 365 (1965) (Harlan, J., dissenting).

Considering the international context, the heavy burden on the alien defendant, and the slight interests of the plaintiff and the forum State, the exercise of personal jurisdiction by a California court over Asahi in this instance would be unreasonable and unfair.

III

Because the facts of this case do not establish minimum contacts such that the exercise of personal jurisdiction is consistent with fair play and substantial justice, the judgment of the Supreme Court of California is reversed, and the case is remanded for further proceedings not inconsistent with this opinion.

It is so ordered.

PART E.   POST–*ASAHI* DEVELOPMENTS

DOUGLAS ULENE, JURISDICTION: PERSONAL JURISDICTION OVER ALIEN CORPORATIONS— ASAHI METAL INDUSTRY CO. v. SUPERIOR COURT OF CALIFORNIA

29 Harv. J. Int'l L. 207 (1988).

The sharp fragmentation of the Court in *Asahi* has obscured the content of the minimum contacts doctrine. Until such time as the issue is resolved by a majority of the Justices, lower courts are seemingly free to experiment with the constitutional standard on a case-by-case basis.

Those decisions which adopt Justice O'Connor's position, requiring conduct beyond the mere placement of an item in the stream of commerce, will severely restrict a state's ability to exercise personal jurisdiction over foreign defendants. Such a result, however, runs counter to the rationale behind the expansion of state court jurisdiction under *International Shoe*. On the other hand, Justice Brennan's interpretation of the minimum contacts standard threatens to impose additional burdens on the already overcrowded court systems of the United States. In an age when manufacturers increasingly rely on others for the production of component parts, Justice O'Connor's due process standard recognizes the need to contain litigation within manageable limits. Indeed, much of the appeal of Justice O'Connor's approach stems from its institutionalization of a means for controlling litigation—the exclusion of parties whose contacts with the forum state are attenuated. Until a majority of the Court agrees on a reformulation of the minimum contacts doctrine, however, *Asahi* indicates that courts may rely solely on the reasonableness test in determining whether the exercise of personal jurisdiction violates due process.

The Court's determination that California's assertion of *in personam* jurisdiction over *Asahi* was unreasonable cannot, however, be read as providing blanket immunity to foreign manufacturers of component parts. Had Gary Zurcher [injured motorcycle rider] named Asahi as a defendant in his products liability action, California's interest in the exercise of long-arm jurisdiction would have been significantly greater, and the Court would have been hard-pressed to declare the exercise of *in personam* jurisdiction over the Japanese company "unreasonable and unfair." Instead, the Court addressed the issue in the context of a third-party cross-claim by an alien defendant seeking indemnification. The Justices were thus able to rest their determination largely on the basis of California's attenuated interest in the adjudication of the dispute. The Court's opinion in Asahi, however, gives scant guidance to judges who must make such determinations in other cases. Thus, while the Justices all agreed that personal jurisdiction could not be exercised over Asahi, the Court was unable to articulate a constitutional standard against which long-arm jurisdiction over alien defendants should be measured. The formal articulation of this standard must await a future decision of the Court and may then only appear as a subtext in a new elaboration of the minimum contacts doctrine.

The historical developments noted in *McGee*, of course, have only accelerated in the generation since that case was decided. This reasoning would appear to apply a fortiori to the rapid expansion of international trade in recent years.

The balance reached by the Court in assessing the reasonableness of long-arm jurisdiction virtually precludes the adjudication of indemnification claims by alien manufacturers against their suppliers in U.S. courts. The Court, in effect, has declared that there is no legitimate interest superior to the burden on the alien defendant of having to litigate such a claim in a U.S. court.

Questions and Comments

1. In *RZS Holdings AVV v. PDVSA PETROLEOS, supra,* the District Court noted that many states had collapsed the traditional two-part personal jurisdiction analysis—compliance with the requirements of Virginia's long-arm statute and constitutional due process—into a single inquiry into whether jurisdiction would comport with due process. Nonetheless, the court observed that it was possible that a defendant's contacts could meet the requirements of due process, yet escape the "literal grasp" of the long-arm statute. Thus, it deemed it appropriate in that case to proceed with the two-part analysis. It is of obvious importance to conform a personal jurisdiction analysis in the forum jurisdiction in strict conformity with due process requirements recognized by state law.

2. What standard should be applied by U.S. courts to determine whether the requisite minimum contacts exist? Although there was consensus among the Justices in *Asahi* that under the *International Shoe* test there was no jurisdiction over Asahi, the Court failed to reach a consensus on the standard for establishing minimum contacts. Thus, there is presently no uniform standard on how minimum contacts should be factored into the "stream of commerce" analysis. In the plurality opinion in *Asahi*, Justice O'Connor found that the "stream of commerce" theory alone was insufficient for purposes of establishing jurisdiction. In *World–Wide Volkswagen*, the Court had previously "rejected the assertion that a consumer's unilateral act of bringing the defendant's product into the forum State was a sufficient constitutional basis for personal jurisdiction over the defendant." 480 U.S. at 109. For a finding of minimum contacts, the *Asahi* Court formulation required a "substantial connection" that arises from "an action of the defendant purposefully directed toward the forum State." 480 U.S. at 112. Under Justice O'Connor's purposeful direction standard, there must be placement of a product into the stream of commerce plus "additional conduct of the defendant" indicating "an intent or purpose to serve the market in the forum state." *Id.* This standard was described as follows:

> The placement of a product into the stream of commerce, without more, is not an act of the defendant purposefully directed toward the forum State. Additional conduct of the defendant may indicate an intent or purpose to serve the market in the forum state, for example, designing the product for the market in the forum State, advertising in the forum State, establishing channels for providing regular advice to customers, or marketing the product through a distributor who has agreed to serve as the sales agent in the forum State. But a defendant's awareness that the stream of commerce may or will sweep the product into the forum State does not convert the mere act of placing the product into the stream into an act purposefully directed toward the forum state. *Id.*

Justice Brennan's opinion focused on the stream of commerce theory and found no additional conduct necessary to support jurisdiction. This approach was described as follows:

> I see no need for such a showing, however. The stream of commerce refers not to unpredictable currents or eddies, but to the regular and anticipated flow of products from manufacture to distribution to retail sale. As long as a participant in this process is aware that the final product is being marketed in the forum State, the possibility of a lawsuit there cannot come as a surprise. Nor will the litigation present a burden for which there is not corresponding benefit. A defendant who has placed goods in the stream of commerce benefits economically from the retail sale of the final product in the forum State, and indirectly benefits from the State's laws that regulate and facilitate commercial activity. *Id.* at 117.

3. What is the status of the "stream of commerce" theory after *Asahi*? Due to the Supreme Court's lack of consensus, lower courts have split on what actions of the defendant will satisfy minimum contacts and whether additional conduct purposefully directed at the forum state is necessary to assert personal jurisdiction under the stream of commerce theory. Lower

courts have tended to avoid taking a position on the current status of the "stream of commerce" theory and attempted, when possible, to decide the case on the basis of the facts of record. *See Hershey Pasta Group v. Vitelli–Elvea Co., Inc.*, 921 F.Supp. 1344, 1347 (M.D.Pa.1996).

4.   The Court of Appeals decision in *Kernan v. Kurz–Hastings, Inc.*, 175 F.3d 236 (2d Cir.1999), illustrates how many courts have typically analyzed "stream of commerce" in a product liability situation. In *Kernan*, an injured worker brought a product liability action against a seller of a hot stamping press. The seller filed a third-party complaint for contribution and indemnity against the employer and the foreign manufacturer of the press. The manufacturer's motion to dismiss for lack of personal jurisdiction was denied by the district court. The case presented the question of whether a New York court had personal jurisdiction over a foreign manufacturer whose machine allegedly injured plaintiff in circumstances where the manufacturer's distributor in Pennsylvania sold the machine to plaintiff's employer in New York. The Court of Appeals stated that the district court must conduct a two-part inquiry when considering a motion to dismiss for lack of personal jurisdiction. First, the plaintiff must show that the defendant is amenable to service of process under the forum state's laws; and second, it must assess whether the court's assertion of jurisdiction under these laws comports with the requirements of due process. Under the New York long-arm statute, the issue was whether the manufacturer should have had "reasonable expectations" that its actions would have consequences in New York. The Court of Appeals rejected "forseeability" alone that the product would find its way into New York as insufficient to satisfy due process and added that "forseeability" would need to be coupled with evidence of a purposeful New York affiliation, such as an effort to directly or indirectly serve the New York market. Long-arm jurisdiction was found to exist based upon the exclusive sales agreement between the manufacturer and the defendant distributor and evidence that the manufacturer had general knowledge that the distributor would resell the product in Pennsylvania and throughout the United States. Next, the court determined that the manufacturer had sufficient minimum contacts with New York to support the exercise of jurisdiction and that the assertion of jurisdiction was reasonable under the circumstances. In distinguishing *World–Wide Volkswagen*, the court held that the manufacturer had attempted to "to serve, directly or indirectly, the market for its product" through the exclusive sales agreement with the distributor. The court avoided adoption of any particular "stream of commerce" standard discussed in *Asahi* by stating that the exclusive sales agreement constituted the type of purposeful action sufficient to satisfy minimum contacts under either the plurality opinion or concurring opinion of Justice Brennan.

The court then considered five "reasonableness" factors in its due process analysis. In this connection, no unique burden was found to exist on defendant in having to defend the action in New York and, in any event, did not overcome the distributor's threshold showing of minimum contacts. The court determined, however, that the burden factor tipped in defendant's favor. Secondly, New York's interest in the dispute was strong since the person injured was a New York resident and New York product liability and negligence law applied in this case. Consideration was then given to the interests of the plaintiff in obtaining convenient and effective relief. The court stated that if New York could not exercise personal jurisdiction over the manufacturer in the third-party action, a separate suit would have to be filed relitigating the issues in another forum. In addition, the court was persuaded by the distributor's argument that the distributor lacked the technical expertise possessed by the manufacturer that was necessary to defend the issues of design or manufacturing defects in the New York action. The court of appeals further considered the factor of efficient administration of justice. It was noted that in evaluating this factor, the court generally considered where the witnesses and evidence were located. Finding in favor of the distributor on this factor, it noted that the machine was located in New York, which was the site of the accident. Although the design and manufacturing processes took place in Japan where the product was manufactured, this evidence relating to these processes was likely to be documentary in nature. The court of appeals concluded that exercising personal jurisdiction over the manufacturer would not offend "traditional notions of fair play and substantial justice."

5. In this Problem, if DROF AG, the manufacturer, had placed its product in the stream of commerce, with the knowledge that a significant number of automobiles would regularly be distributed in the forum state, and with some intent to derive a benefit (i.e., profits) from VUSCO, the distributor, would the "stream of commerce" plus "additional conduct" requirement be satisfied? What kind of evidence would be necessary to show some knowledge by DROF AG that its automobiles were destined for New Jersey? What kind of evidence is necessary to show sufficient "additional conduct" on the part of DROF AG to indicate an intent or purpose to serve the market in the forum state? Do the traditional earmarks for doing business in the forum state have to be present, i.e., maintenance of an office, bank accounts, marketing of products in the forum state or advertising there? What about DROF AG's relationship to VUSCO? Suppose DROF AG had no control over its distribution or marketing and its interest in the product ceases when the goods leave the assembly plant in the foreign country, i.e., an F.O.B. arrangement? Is the volume of sales of the automobile in the destination forum relevant? Is there a relationship between significant sales activity of DROF AG's product to customers in a given state and intentional marketing toward that state?

6. Should the court consider the hazardous nature of the product in the context of a product liability action as noted by Justice Stevens in *Asahi*? Should the court focus on whether a product was sold in a defective condition that was unreasonably dangerous to the consumer? What is the relevance of the distribution agreement between the manufacturer and the distributor? Suppose there is an exclusive distribution agreement to sell the product nationwide? Courts have held that retaining the services of a nationwide distributor evidences an intent to market the product in all the states. *See Tobin v. Astra Pharmaceutical Products, Inc.*, 993 F.2d 528, 544 (6th Cir.1993). What if the distributor of the automobiles distributes to a tristate or regional area? In *Vandelune v. 4B Elevator Components Unlimited*, 148 F.3d 943, 948 (8th Cir.1998),the Court of Appeals stated that when a foreign manufacturer "pours its products" into a regional distribution with the expectation that the distribution will penetrate a discrete, multi-state trade area, the manufacturer has "purposefully reaped the benefits" of the

laws of each State in that trade area for due process purposes. Must there be a showing of direct marketing in the forum? Is it significant to show that the product was designed for the U.S. market? What kind of specifications would be relevant? *See Travelers Indemnity Co. v. TEC America, Inc.*, 909 F.Supp. 249, 252–253 (M.D.Pa.1995).

7.   The action for contribution and indemnity filed by the auto manufacturer and the distributor against the tire company remains for consideration. What is the extent of liability of a component manufacturer under the "stream of commerce" theory? In *Volkswagenwerk v. Klippan*, 611 P.2d 498 (Sup.Ct. Alaska 1980), a judgment was entered against a German manufacturer of automobiles and its wholly-owned subsidiary importer in a personal injury action. In a subsequent action, the manufacturer and its importer brought suit for contribution and indemnity against the German manufacturer of seat belt systems and its parent corporation. The court ruled that the component manufacturer had established sufficient minimum contacts with the state, by deliberately placing their seat belt system in the general stream of commerce, satisfying due process standards for personal jurisdiction. The component manufacturer had sold millions of seat belt assemblies for incorporation into automobiles it knew were destined for purchase by consumers throughout the United States. Alaska law required installation of seat belts in all automobiles sold in the state during the model year of the car involved in the accident. Moreover, defendant represented in a label sewn on the belt involved in the accident that its systems were approved for sale in all states and complied with national safety standards. Thus, the court found that defendant had reason to believe that its seat belts could be sold and distributed in that particular state and did not limit the sale or marketing of the seat belts in the United States.

8.   In a post-*Asahi* case, *Felix v. Bomoro Kommanditgesellschaft*, 196 Cal.App.3d 106, 241 Cal.Rptr. 670 (1987), the California Court of Appeal reached a different conclusion than in *Klippan* under the "forseeability" test as to personal jurisdiction over a component manufacturer in a product liability action. This action was brought against defendant, a West German corporation, based on an alleged design defect in a door latch assembly which allegedly caused decedent to be thrown from the automobile during the accident. Other defendants included the manufacturer of the vehicle in which decedent was riding, the domestic subsidiary and the importer. The trial court granted defendant's motion to quash service of process and dismissed the complaint against the component manufacturer, finding that plaintiff had failed to carry his burden of establishing sufficient contacts between the foreign corporation and California to warrant the exercise of personal jurisdiction. The court cited that it would be unjust to require the component manufacturer to defend itself against the suit in California, where the corporation was not licensed in California, had not done any business there, and had not solicited, advertised, or otherwise sought to serve any particular market there. The appellate court affirmed the trial court's dismissal.

9.   In *Klippan*, the facts showed that the manufacturer had specially designed and/or modified its seat belt product to satisfy U.S. safety standards which was sufficient for contacts purposes to satisfy personal jurisdiction in the forum state. No such facts are shown in the *Bomoro* case which was

decided after *Asahi*. The decision noted in this respect that the component parts were designed by *Bomoro* according to Volkswagen's specifications. 196 Cal.App.3d at 116. Does this finding necessarily establish a lack of substantial connection between Bomoro and the forum state? Suppose that Volkswagen had special design specifications for the tires manufactured for sale and distribution in the United States? Would the reasonableness test have been satisfied if plaintiff in *Bomoro* had shown as the plaintiff did in *Klippan* that special design modifications had been made to the product for sale in the United States? Does the *Bomoro* decision satisfy you that the same contacts standard is being equally applied to both the manufacturer of the product and the component manufacturer? Would it matter in this analysis if the component manufacturer made special modifications to the product to conform to U.S. safety standards pursuant to the manufacturer's dictates?

10.   Based on the facts as presented in this Problem, should the court find personal jurisdiction over CANTIRE, LTD.? What "additional conduct" on the part of CANTIRE would be required to establish jurisdiction?

11.   Would personal jurisdiction exist over DROF AG and DROF UK if the automobile accident had occurred outside of the forum? What contacts or presence in the forum might persuade the court to find personal jurisdiction even though the cause of action arose elsewhere? Suppose there is evidence showing that DROF, AG has had substantial sales of the SUV in the forum for a number of years, and engaged in extensive advertising and marketing activities there. Could plaintiff sustain a theory of general or specific jurisdiction based on the nature of the contacts between the defendant and the forum? In *The Myth of General Jurisdiction*, 101 Harv.L.Rev. 610 (1988), Professor Twitchell states that courts have increasingly turned to the concepts of general and specific jurisdiction as a way of analyzing personal jurisdiction problems. General jurisdiction is described by Professor Twitchell as "dispute-blind", based on affiliations between the forum and one of the parties without regard to the nature of the dispute. Specific jurisdiction is defined as "dispute-specific", based only on affiliations between the forum and the controversy. Professor Twitchell argues that the courts have confused the meaning and application of the terms, particularly in cases where the nature of the dispute is only tenuously related to the defendant's contacts with the forum. In her view, courts have used general jurisdiction analysis to avoid deciding whether the relationship between the defendant's contacts and the cause of action was sufficient to support specific jurisdiction over the particular claim.

12.   Under the hypothetical facts in this Problem, would a showing that DROF AG benefitted economically from its sales and marketing activities in the forum support a specific jurisdiction theory where the cause of action arises outside of the forum? Is DROF AG's presence in the jurisdiction sufficient to support general jurisdiction? Does the State of New Jersey have a sufficient interest in providing a forum for its injured residents? How should the court evaluate that interest as compared to the interests of the place of injury?

PROBLEM 3.3   VEIL PIERCING TO OBTAIN PERSONAL JURISDICTION OVER A FOREIGN PARENT OF A UNITED STATES SUBSIDIARY

SECTION I.   THE SETTING

The litigation described in Problem 3.0–3.1 includes suits in the United States against CANTIRE, Ltd., the tire manufacturer in Canada, DROF AG, the SUV manufacturer in Germany, and DROF–UK, PLC, the assembly plant in the UK. The foreign companies all believe that any responsibility for the injuries is exclusively that of the U.S. auto distributor, VUSCO. DROF AG has admitted:

1.   That it owns 100 percent of the shares of the U.S. distributor, VUSCO,

2.   That the 11 members of the board of directors of VUSCO were appointed by the board of directors of DROF AG,

3.   That there is one director common to the boards of both DROF AG and VUSCO,

4.   That four other directors of VUSCO are employees (but not directors) of DROF AG, including DROF AG's Chief Operating Officer, the Vice–President for International Operations, the Vice–President & Counsel, and the Regional Asst. Vice–President for North America,

5.   That the current President of VUSCO was previously Regional Asst. Vice–President for Europe for DROF AG, Ltd., and Director (President) of DROF AG of Asia, and was appointed to the VUSCO position by the DROF AG board,

6.   That DROF AG maintains a single master bank account for DROF AG and all subsidiaries in the Deutschebank in Frankfurt, but with carefully maintained separate books in the home office for each subsidiary,

7.   That the law department at the home office of DROF AG provides occasional services to the subsidiary that are not always billed to the VUSCO account,

8.   That employee pensions for officers of the DROF AG "family" of corporations (including VUSCO) are held under a single contract with a London insurance firm,

9.   That the door of the VUSCO office in the United States states "VUSCO, L.L.C., a subsidiary of DROF AG," and that the letters of each company are the same size,

10.   That there have been occasions when an employee of DROF AG was "transferred" to VUSCO and used some DROF AG stationery until new VUSCO stationery was printed, and

11.   That there are other linkages between the parent DROF AG, VUSCO and other subsidiaries.

DROF AG has moved in each personal injury suit brought in state and federal courts in the United States to dismiss the action for lack of personal jurisdiction. You may act either as counsel for one or more of the plaintiffs in any of these suits, or as counsel for DROF AG.

SECTION II.   FOCUS OF CONSIDERATION

Problem 3.2 discussed issues of personal jurisdiction over foreign entities based on minimum contacts and due process. This problem considers another way in which jurisdiction might be obtained over the foreign entities.

Students most likely have been introduced to veil piercing in the basic course on corporation law. A brief review of that concept should be helpful. It is a frequently litigated issue; veil piercing cases are the second most numerous cases in corporation law after issues of long arm jurisdiction over foreign corporations. But these cases deal with veil piercing to hold the parent corporation liable for obligations of the subsidiary. After reviewing the substantive law that applies in such cases, we will turn to considering whether the same rules apply when the request to pierce a corporate veil is at the pretrial stage, for the purpose of obtaining jurisdiction over the parent where the subsidiary is more clearly subject to jurisdiction. Is the standard less demanding in veil piercing for jurisdiction because the conclusion is only that there is jurisdiction, not that the parent is liable on the substantive charges? A further question is does it make any difference when there is jurisdiction over what is likely to be a U.S. state-chartered corporation (a subsidiary), and a parent corporation not from a sister state but from a foreign nation?

An attempt to pierce a corporate veil occurs in two different areas of corporate structure. One situation is where there is an attempt to pierce the veil of what is usually a close corporation in order to reach the assumed to be greater personal assets of individual shareholders. The other is where the attempt is to pierce the veil of a subsidiary to reach the assumed to be greater assets of the parent corporation. A court might seem more inclined to hold another legal entity liable—the parent as liable for obligations of it's subsidiary—then to hold individual shareholders liable without benefit of the limitation they expected to have from choosing to incorporate. But the rules and decisions of veil piercing do not appear to favor veil piercing to reach a parent corporation over veil piercing to reach an individual. When we turn to the topic of this problem, we will consider only cases where there is a parent-subsidiary relationship, and especially where the subsidiary is domestic and the parent foreign. The basic course on corporation law probably addressed situations where the parent and subsidiary were both domestic entities, and often entities incorporated in the same state. This problem adds a new dimension, a foreign entity is involved.

The parent-subsidiary relationship is important. Often a veil piercing decision begins by the court affirming the legislatively sanctioned benefits of limited liability and making it clear that to pierce the corporate veil should not easily be accomplished. But on the other hand, the parent corporation may not create or use a subsidiary for "improper" purposes. The parent may not create or manage the operation of its subsidiary for an *unlawful* purpose, such as to engage in an unlawful securities scheme. Additionally, it may not create or manage the operation of a subsidiary for *fraudulent* purposes, such as to defraud insurance policyholders. For some time a few jurisdictions thought that there must be either fraud or illegal activity to pierce a corporate veil. But that is not the usual rule. A veil may also be pierced where the parent has created or has been operating the subsidiary for an *improper purpose* or has been engaged in *other misconduct* than fraud or illegal activities. The courts have been wrestling with the meaning of these words for decades. But we at least commence our consideration of veil piercing with the idea that "having" a subsidiary, including wholly owning the subsidiary, is itself insufficient to pierce a corporate veil and impose liability upon the parent.

Many veil piercing cases, domestic or international, address situations where there is no specific misconduct by the parent, but the plaintiff wishes to imply such wrong by showing that there are many common or linking relationships between the parent and the subsidiary that allegedly establish that the parent controls the subsidiary. That should not be surprising because the parent owns the subsidiary and has not only the right to manage the subsidiary but may also be said to have a responsibility to do so as its owner. The focus often becomes on whether the control of the subsidiary by the parent is so total and absolute that the subsidiary is considered the "mere alter ego" of the parent. But that should not eliminate the need to find something that is wrong, because a subsidiary is by definition owned and therefore controlled by the parent.

When common linkages between the parent and subsidiary are discussed, there are several such links invariably noted that are little more than common characteristics of nearly every parent-subsidiary relationship. The parent's board of directors, representing the corporation, will have the responsibility to appoint the board of directors of the subsidiary. That appointment will usually include persons who are officers and/or even directors of the parent. For example, a successful vice-president of the parent Volkswagen company in Germany might be asked to become the president of the Volkswagen subsidiary in the United States. Several if not all of the principal officers of the subsidiary may view their role as a long-term employee of the parent with occasional assignments to be officers and directors of the company's foreign subsidiaries. That by itself should not result in a veil piercing; it cannot, without more, be said to constitute misconduct.

Another common practice in the past few decades has been for international enterprises that have numerous subsidiaries to consolidate their finances in one bank account, especially for the parts of the enterprise that are in the same country. If the books of the enterprise show a separation of the usual assets and liabilities so that the financial condition of each subsidiary is disclosed, such practice should not be condemned as misconduct with the consequence being veil piercing. The same result may apply to the whole enterprise having a common medical plan, or pension plan, or vacation plan. If the veil is to be pierced it must be for more than common features that do not disclose any misconduct.

As the common features between a parent and subsidiary increase, some argue that the two should be considered one under a much discussed theory of "enterprise liability." That is a theory promoted by some academics that has gained little attention, however, in U.S. courts. The courts consistently hold that there must be more—there must be some illegal action, fraudulent action, or other misconduct, in order for the veil to be pierced. Such conclusion may be an appellate decision, reversing what are often jury conclusions based on little proof of misconduct and significant jury sympathy of "easy pickins" in a parent's often deep pocket. In the area we will address in this problem, there will be no jury to convince; veil piercing to achieve jurisdiction, or to provide service of process, is a pretrial decision of a judge. What may be important to consider is whether the multiple corporations each has a different function, such as manufacturing, distribution or sales. If each corporation does all the functions of the others, a court may wonder why the separate structure is necessary. But if the separateness deals with different corporate entities for different countries, that may be sufficient reason to reject veil piercing. Other areas likely to be discussed are whether the subsidiary was adequately capitalized, whether the formalities of conducting separate corporations such as meetings and records were fulfilled, and how the parent held out the subsidiary—as a subsidiary or as a branch or division. This is an important area and the stakes are high. The subsidiary may have adequate capitalization but not sufficient liquid assets to pay a very large judgment.

In the problem we face, we are not asking whether or not a court will pierce a veil to determine the substantive liability of the parent, but whether or not a court will rule in a pre-trial motion to pierce the veil to obtain jurisdiction over a parent that is abroad. If the veil is not pierced the case may proceed against the subsidiary, but without the parent before the court the court may not find it to be liable for a judgment. Should veil piercing for jurisdiction thus be granted where the linkage to the parent and the way in which the parent-subsidiary structure was created or operated would be considered insufficient for substantive liability?

SECTION III.   READINGS, QUESTIONS AND COMMENTS

Comment on the Issue of Jurisdiction and the Multinational Enterprise

The U.S. Supreme Court in 1925 in *Cannon Manufacturing Co. v. Cudahy Packing Co.,* 267 U.S. 333, 45 S.Ct. 250, 69 L.Ed. 634 (1925), rejected the idea that service on a wholly-owned Alabama subsidiary provided jurisdiction over the Maine parent. The Court found the Alabama subsidiary to be a "distinct corporate entity," and the separation "though perhaps merely formal, was real." Most lower courts in the first decades after the decision interpreted *Cannon* to limit jurisdiction on veil piercing to when there was something more than control or domination by the parent. If *Cannon* was a due process holding, is it not influenced by subsequent developments in due process theory? That would seem to modify *Cannon's* strictness. The elastic language of due process has led some courts to speak in terms of "undue degree of control", or "complete control", when addressing jurisdiction by veil piercing. The Supreme Court seems to have moderated *Cannon* in *United States v. Scophony Corp. of America*, 333 U.S. 795, 68 S.Ct. 855, 92 L.Ed. 1091 (1948), allowing jurisdiction where there is significant direct control by the parent of the operations of the subsidiary.

Since *Scophony* in 1948 the courts have been unable to develop a clear theory of veil piercing to establish jurisdiction. *Gallagher v. Mazda Motor of America,* addresses veil piercing of Mazda Motor of America to reach the parent Mazda Motor Corp. of Japan. The case is helpful in outlining three lines of cases in imputing jurisdictional contacts of a subsidiary to a parent, but leading to a law that is unclear. One line holds true to *Cannon* and starts with a rather strong premise that creating separate corporations and respecting and observing their distinctiveness negates imputing jurisdiction over the parent. The *Cannon* line has a considerable following, as the citations in *Gallagher* disclose. Some cases, noting respect for *Cannon,* have developed the *Scophony* moderation to shift the focus to the extent of control exerted by the parent over the general operations of the subsidiary. That is the second line of cases *Gallagher* identifies, and includes among our readings the post-*Gallagher* decisions of *Clark v. Matsushita, Brooks v. Bacardi Rum Corp.,* and *Rose v. Continental,* as well as having support in the Restatement extract. Although not cited in any of these second line of cases, *Color Systems v. Meteor Photo Reprographic Systems* seems to follow their view. Or is it more aligned with the third group, citing with approval the *Hargrave v. Fibreboard Corp.* decision? The third line of cases, that *Gallagher* approves and joins, allows imputing jurisdiction to the parent "when the subsidiary is engaged in functions that, but for the existence of the subsidiary, the parent would have to undertake." Following that theory *Gallagher* joins *Bulova Watch Co. v. Hattori* and *Hargrave v. Fibreboard Corp.*

Personal jurisdiction over a parent may also be based on agency when the subsidiary is considered the agent of the parent. Common law agency principles are sometimes applied to cases to allow jurisdiction over a parent, or principal. But the cases often focus less on the actual rules of agency and more on general assumptions raised from the relationship. See *CutCo Indus.,*

Inc. v. Naughton, 806 F.2d 361 (2d Cir.1986). This is consistent with the use of veil piercing, where courts tend to apply a less strict definition of alter ego for jurisdiction than for liability.

RESTATEMENT, CONFLICTS OF LAW (SECOND) (1971)

§ 52, Comment b

Judicial jurisdiction over a subsidiary corporation will ... give the state judicial jurisdiction over the parent corporation if the parent so controls and dominates the subsidiary as in effect to disregard the latter's independent corporate existence.

CLARK v. MATSUSHITA ELECTRIC INDUSTRIAL COMPANY, LTD.

United States District Court, Middle District of Pennsylvania, 1993.
811 F.Supp. 1061.

RAMBO, CHIEF JUDGE.

Before the court is the motion of defendant Matsushita Electric Industrial Company, Ltd. ("MEI") to dismiss it as a party in this case due to an alleged lack of personal jurisdiction. * * *

The captioned action arises out of personal injuries to Jina Clark, daughter of plaintiffs James and Lori Clark. The injuries were caused by a kerosene heater manufactured by MEI and distributed in the United States by DESA International ("DESA").

Based on this accident, Plaintiffs filed three separate actions in the Court of Common Pleas of York County, Pennsylvania against DESA, MEI, and Matsushita Electric Company of America ("MECA"), respectively. All three actions were removed to this court and consolidated into the captioned action.

Defendant MEI is a corporation incorporated and doing business in Japan. Among the goods MEI manufactures are electronic products, including those marketed in the United States under the brand names Panasonic, Quasar, and Technics, and home appliances, including kerosene heaters such as the one at issue in this case. MEI engages in no direct marketing or sales of its goods in the Commonwealth of Pennsylvania. However, its subsidiaries, including MECA, do market MEI products in the United States.

MECA, a wholly-owned subsidiary of MEI, is incorporated in Delaware and has its principal place of business in New Jersey. MECA distributes various products manufactured by MEI, including Quasar, Panasonic, and Technics name-brands. It has had a registered office in Pennsylvania since 1969.

DESA is a Kentucky corporation and is the admitted distributor of the subject kerosene heater.

Prior to the removal and consolidation of the other two actions into the captioned action, MEI filed a motion to dismiss alleging lack of personal jurisdiction over MEI and insufficiency of process and service of process with respect to MEI. This court deferred a decision on the personal jurisdiction issue pending limited discovery on the matter, but proceeded to address the service and process issues. In a memorandum dated July 31, 1992, this court found that service of process and the process itself were adequate and denied MEI's motion to dismiss on those grounds. MEI filed a motion for reconsideration of that order or, in the alternative, for an interlocutory appeal pursuant to 28 U.S.C. § 1292(d). Since the filing of the motion for reconsideration, discovery with respect to personal jurisdiction has been completed and briefs on the issue have been filed.

* * *

In this case, Plaintiffs have not specified whether they seek specific or general jurisdiction over Defendant MEI. Instead, Plaintiffs have made a blanket assertion that jurisdiction with respect to MEI is proper based on the contacts of MEI and its subsidiaries with the forum. Those alleged contacts are:

1) MECA has maintained a registered office in Philadelphia, Pennsylvania since 1969 and continues to do so.

2) MECA is a wholly owned subsidiary of MEI which sells Panasonic, Quasar, and Technics branded products.

3) MEI has admitted that it sells products bearing the Panasonic, Quasar and Technics brand to MECA which subsequently distributes the products in the United States. Because MEI named no other distributors of such products, "the clear inference ... is that MECA is the exclusive distributor of those brand names in the United States."

4) MEI has admitted that "we assume that products purchased from MEI were ultimately sold to consumers in the Commonwealth of Pennsylvania."

5) MEI has a "close nexus with MECA" and an "awareness of [MEI's] extensive American distribution network," as evidenced by the following facts:

1. The CEO of MECA, Akiya Imura, also serves on the Board of Directors of [MEI].

2. The Financial Highlights of [MEI's] 1992 Annual Report lump together [MEI] and all subsidiaries including MECA.

3. [MEI] maintains a Panasonic research lab in New Jersey which "spearheads [MEI's] research in developing technologies *for the U.S. market*" (emphasis added).

4. [MEI] is marketing flat screen televisions in North America.

5. Sales figures throughout the 1992 Annual Report are consistently reported in Japanese Yen and U.S. Dollars, including for home appliances (e.g., kerosene heaters), with increased sales. 6.

[MEI] in 1990 acquired MCA, Inc., which includes Universal Studios, a major U.S. film producer.

* * *

In the captioned case, Plaintiffs' argument for jurisdiction over MEI relies primarily on the Pennsylvania activities and contacts of its subsidiary, MECA. If proven, MECA's contacts with Pennsylvania, including a registered office in the state since 1969 and extensive marketing of Panasonic, Quasar, and Technics electronics goods undoubtedly subject *MECA* to jurisdiction in this state. However, *MECA* has not challenged personal jurisdiction in this case.

On the other hand, the acts or contacts of MECA, a corporate entity distinct from MEI, are not necessarily attributable to MEI. Mere ownership by a parent corporation of a subsidiary present in the forum state will not automatically subject the parent to personal jurisdiction in that forum.

* * *

* * * A subsidiary is an "alter ego" of its parent corporation if domination and control by the parent renders the subsidiary its mere instrumentality. In that instance, the parent corporation may be subject to personal jurisdiction in the forum, since it is doing business within the state under the facade of the subsidiary.

The agency and alter ego inquiries center on control: "The significant factor in this inquiry is the degree of control that the [parent corporation] retains over the [subsidiary]." However, there is no record evidence indicating a degree of control that would make MECA a mere agent or instrumentality of MEI.

First, for a subsidiary to be considered the alter ego of a parent corporation, "the degree of control exercised by the parent must be greater than normally would be associated with common ownership and directorship. Absent a showing of such control, subsidiaries, even if wholly-owned, are presumed separate and distinct entities from their parent corporations. *Cannon Mfg. Co. v. Cudahy Packing Co.*, 267 U.S. 333, 45 S.Ct. 250, 69 L.Ed. 634 (1925). The mere ownership of a subsidiary, even one hundred percent ownership, is not sufficient to assert that a subsidiary is the alter ego or agent of its parent corporation. Thus, MEI's one hundred percent ownership of MECA establishes neither an alter ego nor an agency relationship.[5]

5. This court recognizes that several courts have not followed the *Cannon* alter-ego test. *See, e.g., Zenith Radio Corp. v. Matsushita Electric Industrial Co.,* 402 F.Supp. 262 (E.D.Pa.1975); *Allen Organ Co. v. Kawai Musical Instruments Mfg. Co.,* 593 F.Supp. 107 (E.D.Pa.1984). This court previously declined to apply the *Zenith* and *Allen Organ* approaches in a situation analogous to this case, *Savin,* 661 F.Supp. at 468, and declines to do so now. First, *Zenith* was an antitrust case and the caselaw the *Zenith* court applied to distinguish *Cannon* was specific to the antitrust context. The *Zenith* approach appropriately is limited to the antitrust context. Second, *Allen Organ* relied on the stream of commerce theory to support its assertion of jurisdiction over a foreign manufacturer. The validity of that theory is dubious after its rejection by a

Second, the fact that MECA's chairman, Akiya Imura, is a member of MEI's Board of Directors alone does not establish control of MECA by MEI. Common officers and directors may be evidence that one corporation is the alter-ego of another, but they are not necessarily conclusive on the issue. * * *

* * *

Evidence that MECA may be an exclusive United States distributor of certain electronics products manufactured by MEI is also insufficient to show that MECA is the mere agent or alter ego of MEI.

* * *

The two remaining factors relevant to general jurisdiction also weigh against an assertion of general jurisdiction over MEI. First, there is no evidence that the subsidiary, MECA, played any part in the manufacture or sale of the heater here. Though Plaintiffs have alleged that MECA may have manufactured or distributed the heater, they have presented absolutely no evidence to substantiate it. The burden is clearly on Plaintiffs to establish such a connection by sworn affidavits or other competent evidence. * * *

Finally, there is no evidence that the independence of the separate corporate entities was disregarded. For instance, Plaintiffs have presented no evidence that MECA did not maintain separate corporate records, hold separate corporate meetings, or file its own tax forms. * * *

Plaintiffs have failed to show that MECA is merely an agent/alter ego of MEI rather than an independent entity. Therefore, if MEI is subject to general jurisdiction, it must be because of MEI's own contacts with Pennsylvania, in contrast to those of its subsidiary MECA.

The direct MEI contacts cited by Plaintiffs are too scant and attenuated to permit the assertion of general jurisdiction over MEI by this court. Those contacts include: (1) the fact that MEI "assumes" that certain of its products are ultimately sold in Pennsylvania; (2) MEI has a subsidiary which is incorporated in New Jersey which "develops technologies for the U.S. market;" (3) MEI has an ownership interest in MCA, Inc., which in turn owns Universal Studios, a major U.S. film producer; (4) MEI markets flat screen televisions in North America; and (5) MEI reports sales figures in Japanese yen and U.S. dollars.

First, under the principles discussed above, the mere fact that MEI "assumes" or knows that its products are likely to end up in Pennsylvania is not sufficient to find personal jurisdiction.

Second, the fact that an MEI subsidiary conducts research and targets products for the United States market is largely irrelevant, absent a clear showing of control of the subsidiary by the parent corporation, and a showing that MEI "purposefully directed" the re-

four justice plurality of the United States   107 S.Ct. at 1032.
Supreme Court in *Asahi,* 480 U.S. at 112,

search at Pennsylvania residents or consumers. The same is true with respect to MEI's ownership interest in MCA, Inc., and through MCA, of Universal Studios.

Similarly, absent a showing that such products are marketed in Pennsylvania or targeted at Pennsylvania residents, the fact that MEI allegedly markets flat-screen televisions in North America is largely irrelevant. * * * In any event, beyond a single statement from MEI's annual report, Plaintiffs have presented no relevant data for this court to utilize in assessing MEI's contacts with United States or Pennsylvania markets.

Finally, the fact that MEI reports its sales figures in both Japanese yen and United States dollars is wholly irrelevant. In a world-wide economy in which capital travels relatively freely between nations and markets, it is not at all surprising that sales figures are reported in currencies other than the national currency of the corporation.

Thus, there is insufficient basis to assert general jurisdiction over MEI. Because there is also no basis for the assertion of specific jurisdiction over MEI, MEI will be dismissed as a party to this action.

BROOKS v. BACARDI RUM CORP.

United States District Court, E.D. Pennsylvania, 1996.
943 F.Supp. 559.

JOYNER, District Judge.

Plaintiff Yvette Brooks has brought this diversity action against Defendant Bacardi Rum Corporation ("Bacardi") pursuant to 28 U.S.C. § 1332. This lawsuit arises out of an incident occurring on August 18, 1994 in which plaintiff fell while touring defendant's premises in San Juan, Puerto Rico.

Defendant has filed a motion to dismiss Ms. Brooks' complaint for lack of personal jurisdiction pursuant to Fed.R.Civ.P. 12(b)(2), and for failure to state a claim upon which relief may be granted, pursuant to Fed.R.Civ.P. 12(b)(6). Defendant has also filed a motion to dismiss a subsequent amended complaint filed by plaintiff. This memorandum resolves these motions.

Plaintiff Yvette Brooks was a tourist in San Juan, Puerto Rico in August 1994. While touring Puerto Rico, Ms. Brooks went on a tour of the Bacardi Rum Factory located in San Juan. While on the tour, Ms. Brooks slipped and fell on Bacardi's premises and was injured.

Defendant Bacardi Rum Corporation is a Delaware corporation with its principal place of business in San Juan, Puerto Rico. In support of its motion to dismiss, defendant has attached an affidavit from ... the secretary and general counsel of Bacardi–Martini USA ("Bacardi USA"). In his affidavit, Mr. Wilson avers that Bacardi USA is a Delaware corporation with its principal place of business in Miami. Mr. Wilson further states that Bacardi sells its products to Bacardi USA and Bacardi

International Limited, a Bermuda Corporation. Bacardi USA then sells Bacardi products to U.S. customers, including the Pennsylvania Liquor Control Board. Bacardi USA does all the advertising for Bacardi Rum products in the U.S. and, according to Mr. Wilson, Bacardi does not do business in the U.S. at all or have any contacts with this country.

In response, plaintiff has stated that Bacardi should be subject to personal jurisdiction because it conducts business in Pennsylvania through its "various subsidiaries and subdivisions." Plaintiff has not offered any proof such as affidavits or other evidence in support of its claim. Nor has plaintiff even alleged any other facts than the above-quoted sentence to show why this court should assert jurisdiction over Bacardi. If plaintiff is arguing that Bacardi USA is the alter ego of Bacardi, plaintiff has the burden of proving that fact. ... If plaintiff is arguing that the conduct of Bacardi's subsidiaries should be imputed to Bacardi for purposes of a personal jurisdiction analysis, plaintiff also has the burden of proving that it would be appropriate in this case. ... In fact, plaintiff must meet at least one of three tests in order to successfully show that the contacts of Bacardi's subsidiary must be considered by this court in determining if there is a sufficient basis to assert personal jurisdiction over Bacardi.

The first test would require plaintiff to show that the independence of the two entities has been disregarded. *Gallagher v. Mazda Motor of America*, 781 F.Supp. 1079, 1085 (E.D.Pa.1992); *Reverse Vending Assoc. v. Tomra Sys., Inc.*, 655 F.Supp. 1122, 1128 (E.D.Pa.1987); *Clark v. Matsushita Elec. Indus.*, 811 F.Supp 1061, 1068 (M.D.Pa.1993). The second test would require plaintiff to show that the parent company exercises such total control over the subsidiary, that both companies should be considered one company for purposes of a jurisdictional analysis. Gallagher, 781 F.Supp. at 1084. Under the third test, plaintiff must prove that the subsidiary performs important functions which the parent would otherwise have to perform itself. Id.

In this case, plaintiff Brooks has not alleged any of the above. She has not even alleged the exact relationship of Bacardi to Bacardi–USA. It could be that plaintiff's statement that Bacardi distributes its products through its subsidiaries and subdivisions in the U.S. was an attempt to show that Bacardi's U.S. subsidiaries perform indispensable functions for Bacardi. Plaintiff could have then intended to argue that we should therefore assert personal jurisdiction over Bacardi based on its subsidiary's contacts. Nevertheless, plaintiff has not alleged facts that would show that Bacardi's U.S. subsidiaries perform indispensable functions for it, nor has she even stated clearly that that is her theory. Furthermore, she has not given us any facts about Bacardi USA's Pennsylvania contacts. We therefore find that plaintiff has failed to meet her burden on this issue. Accordingly, Defendant Bacardi's motion to dismiss the complaint is granted for lack of personal jurisdiction, ...

ROSE v. CONTINENTAL AKTIENGESELLSCHAFT (AG)

United States District Court, Eastern District of Pennsylvania, 2001.
2001 WL 236738.

WALDMAN.

This is a product liability action arising from an automobile accident. Plaintiff Erik Johnson and Kenneth Rose were traveling in a BMW automobile in Germany when the tread separated from a tire which caused Mr. Johnson to lose control of the vehicle. According to an insurance report, the tire in question was manufactured by Continental Aktiengesellschaft ("Continental"). Plaintiffs asserted product liability claims against Continental, its American subsidiary Continental General Tire, Inc. ("Tire"), Bayerische Motorenwerke Aktiengesellschaft ("BMW"), and BMW of North America.[1]

Presently before the court is defendant Continental's motion to dismiss for lack of personal jurisdiction, or alternatively for forum non conveniens. Plaintiffs counter that Continental has the requisite forum contacts if not directly, then through three of its subsidiaries: Tire, Contitech North America, Inc. ("Contitech") and Continental Teves, Inc. ("Teves").

* * *

Plaintiffs contend ... that the contacts of Contitech, Tire and Teves should also be attributed to Continental for the purpose of personal jurisdiction.

"Generally, a foreign corporation is not subject to the jurisdiction of the forum state merely because of its ownership of the shares of stock of a subsidiary doing business in that state." *Lucas v. Gulf & Western Indus., Inc.,* 666 F.2d 800, 805–06 (3d Cir.1981) (internal quotations omitted). *See also Clark,* 811 F.Supp. at 1067 (even one hundred percent ownership is not sufficient); *Gallagher v. Mazda Motor of Am., Inc.,* 781 F.Supp. 1079, 1083 (E.D.Pa.1992). A foreign corporation may be subject to personal jurisdiction based on its ownership of stock in a subsidiary doing business in Pennsylvania only if one entity is the alter ego of the other, the entities disregarded corporate independence or one corporation exercised pervasive control over the other. *See Lewis–Ugdah v. HBE Corp.,* 2000 WL 1780233 (E.D.Pa. Dec.1, 2000); *Brooks v. Bacardi Rum Corp.,* 943 F.Supp. 559, 562 (E.D.Pa.1996).

That the companies may have a close relationship or may coordinate and cooperate, however, is not sufficient to impute forum contacts. *See Katz v. Princess Hotels Int'l, Inc.,* 839 F.Supp. 406, 410–11 (E.D.La. 1993); *Hopper v. Ford Motor Co.,* 837 F.Supp. 840, 844 (S.D.Tex.1993).

---

1. BMW of North America was dismissed as a party defendant by stipulation of December 14, 2000. Tire was dismissed as a party defendant by stipulation of April 6, 2000.

That a parent may be interested in and involved with a subsidiary is quite normal and does not demonstrate untoward control. *See Craig v. Lake Asbestos of Quebec, Ltd.*, 843 F.2d 145, 152 (3d Cir.1988). While relevant, overlapping boards of directors and common officers also are not enough to impute the contacts of one entity to another. *See Visual Sec. Concepts, Inc. v. KTV, Inc.*, 102 F.Supp.2d 601, 606 (E.D.Pa.2000); *Clark*, 811 F.Supp. at 1068; *Dutoit v. Strategic Minerals Corp.*, 735 F.Supp. 169 (E.D.Pa.1990), *aff'd*, 922 F.2d 830 (3d Cir.1990); *Dickson v. The Hertz Corp.*, 559 F.Supp. 1169, 1174 (D.Vi.1983).

Plaintiffs rely on the inclusion in Continental's consolidated annual report of financial information on its subsidiaries; the listing on Continental's internet site of information about its subsidiaries; Continental's ownership of 80% of Tire's stock; the presence of one Tire board member and one Contitech board member on Continental's board; the presence on Continental's board of one employee member from Teves; and, sales by Tire, purportedly the exclusive distributor of Continental products in the United States, of Continental products in Pennsylvania. These factors are insufficient to make the requisite showing for imputation of forum contacts for purposes of personal jurisdiction. This is particularly so when considered in view of the requirement of German law that Continental issue consolidated annual reports and the uncontroverted averment of Johannes Suttmeyer that Tire is the exclusive United States distributor only of Continental replacement tires, while it sells Continental original equipment tires to many automobile manufacturers.

It is also uncontroverted that Contitech sells products made by a distinct subsidiary and not Continental brand products, and that only 5–10% of Tire's sales are of Continental products. Tire, Teves and Contitech each maintain its own accounting and corporate formalities. Also, Tire was a separate corporate entity for over fifty years before it was purchased by Continental. *See B.L. Poe v. Babcock Int'l, PLC*, 662 F.Supp. 4, 7 (M.D.Pa.1985) (that subsidiary was separate corporate entity prior to acquisition by parent weighs against attribution). There has been no showing or suggestion that any of the subsidiaries are undercapitalized.

* * *

ACCORDINGLY, IT IS HEREBY ORDERED that said Motion is GRANTED and defendant Continental Aktiengesellschaft is DISMISSED as a party defendant for lack of personal jurisdiction.

COLOR SYSTEMS, INC. v. METEOR PHOTO REPROGRAPHIC SYSTEMS, INC.

United States District Court, District of Columbia, 1987.
1987 WL 11085.

GASCH, DISTRICT JUDGE.

* * * Plaintiff's complaint names as defendants Meteor–Siegen Apparatebau Paul Schmeck GmbH ("Meteor–Siegen"), incorporated in the

Federal Republic of Germany ("West Germany"), Meteor Photo Reprographic Systems, Inc. ("Meteor P.R.S."), incorporated in Delaware, several officers of these corporations, and Eastman–Kodak Company.

The defendants move the Court to reduce the number of defendants and to narrow the issues in the instant case. Defendants Meteor–Siegen, Muennich, Kuebler and Doody all question the Court's jurisdiction over them. * * *

This dispute originated in 1983 when Meteor–Siegen initiated a program to enter the color copying machine market in the United States. One of the first American companies to purchase Meteor's products was Technical Equipment Marketing and Sales, Inc. ("TEMSI"), a photographic equipment and supply company owned by Edward Blacketor and his son, Everly. TEMSI claims to have exclusively distributed the copiers in the District of Columbia, Maryland, and Virginia. A harbinger of future calamity was that no written contract memorialized this agreement. It is noteworthy that the Blacketors' relationship with Meteor–Siegen arose only after the West German company approached TEMSI. Shortly thereafter, in 1983, Meteor–Siegen formed Meteor P.R.S., a wholly owned American subsidiary incorporated in Delaware with its principal place of business in Irving, Texas. The stated purpose of this corporation was to market Meteor–Siegen's color copiers in the United States. After the creation of Meteor P.R.S., Meteor–Siegen ceased to function in its own name in North America.

Sometime between late 1983 and the middle of 1984, the Blacketors decided that they could better market Meteor copiers if they created a separate corporate entity specializing in the sale and service of such copiers. The Blacketors assert that on Meteor's recommendation, they created a separate corporation. To carry out their plan, the Blacketors hired Daniel Magarian in October of 1984 to "explore the possibility" of creating a new corporation. In December of the same year, Magarian traveled to Meteor P.R.S.'s headquarters in Irving, Texas, to discuss the details of initiating such a venture. Magarian claims that the defendants demanded that he commit himself and the Blacketors to the establishment of a new corporation before he left Texas. The defendants neither admit nor deny this conduct. They simply state that in early 1985, the Blacketors advised Meteor P.R.S. that a new dealership was to be created for the sole purpose of selling Meteor color copying equipment in the Washington, D.C. area.

Color Systems was formed at the outset of 1985. During that year the corporation engaged in a flurry of activity to prepare itself to act as a dealer of Meteor products. * * *

From the time of its incorporation, Color Systems had no contact with Meteor-Siegen other than the occasional borrowing of a West German technician. Even more striking, Color Systems still had no written contract with any of the defendants. The only documentary evidence of any weight is a Letter of Intent ostensibly signed in October of 1985. The letter sets out the tentative parameters of a grant to Color

Systems of an exclusive right to sell Meteor–Siegen color copiers in the Washington, D.C. metropolitan area. By its own terms, the document is not legally binding. On its face, it expires on December 31, 1985, if no definitive agreement is entered into on or before that date. No written agreement was ever executed by the parties.

The year 1985 was also marked by a spirit of cooperation between Color Systems and the Meteor group. Meteor P.R.S. agreed to defer its right to payment for nearly one year on two color copiers in Color Systems' possession. Further, Meteor agreed to reimburse Color Systems for one-half of any expenditure the latter might make to have brochures printed depicting Meteor products. The brochures were ultimately produced at a cost of $30,000. Finally, Meteor P.R.S. and Color Systems shared a booth at the Federal Office Systems Exposition in March of 1985. These instances of cooperation are cited by Color Systems for the proposition that Meteor was aware of, and a participant in, the creation of Color Systems. Meteor does not deny that it was aware of Color Systems' efforts. It is defendants' position that they simply never pledged any contractual support or assistance to Color Systems' venture.

In January of 1986, Meteor P.R.S. announced to Color Systems that Eastman-Kodak Company was to be the exclusive Meteor dealer for North America. Color Systems claims to have had 28 serious equipment purchases pending at that time, guaranteeing revenue of nearly $2 million.

* * *

Corporate defendant Meteor–Siegen and individual defendants Muennich, Kuebler, and Doody all claim that the Court does not have personal jurisdiction over them. The Court agrees in part and holds that it does not have *in personam* jurisdiction over defendants Muennich and Kuebler.

* * *

Defendants' affidavits state that Meteor–Siegen is incorporated in West Germany, is not authorized to do business in the District of Columbia, and maintains no office or employees in the District of Columbia. Nevertheless, Color Systems claims that Meteor-Siegen sent representatives to the District of Columbia to assist in at least one sale and "regularly" sent its Technical Service Manager to assist with installations of new copiers. * * * There is an absence of any evidence which might corroborate plaintiff's claims. These few incursions into the District of Columbia, even if they occurred, do not provide the kind of continuous and systematic activity required to establish minimum contacts with the forum state. *See International Shoe Co., see also Helicopteros Nacionales de Columbia, S.A. v. Hall.*

The plaintiff argues alternatively that Meteor P.R.S. is merely an alter ego of Meteor–Siegen. In fact, personal jurisdiction may be exerted over a parent corporation by virtue of its subsidiary's activities if the subsidiary is a mere alter ego or agent of the parent corporation. *See*

Hargrave v. Fibreboard Corp. [710 F.2d 1154 (5th Cir.1983)]. In such cases, the foreign parent will be found to be transacting business in the forum state through the activities of its subsidiary. Thus, the Court must determine whether Meteor P.R.S. is a mere alter ego of Meteor–Siegen.

To answer this question, the Court must first ascertain the nature and degree of control necessary to find that a subsidiary is an alter ego in the District of Columbia. In *Cannon Mfg. Co. v. Cudahy Packing Co.*, the Supreme Court upheld the validity of a parent-subsidiary relationship where "[t]he corporate separation, though perhaps merely formal, was real. It was not pure fiction." In *Cannon,* the parent possessed the entire capital stock of the subsidiary and dominated it completely. Nonetheless, the Court found it sufficient that each corporation maintained separate books and otherwise observed the formalities of corporate separateness.

Although *Cannon* remains good law, courts today probe more deeply the question of whether a corporate separation is "pure fiction." In *I.A.M. Nat'l Pension Fund v. Wakefield Indus.*, 699 F.2d 1254 (D.C.Cir. 1983), the United States Court of Appeals for the District of Columbia Circuit had little trouble arriving at the conclusion that a parent and subsidiary were not really separate entities where the parent assumed the subsidiary's obligations and managed its assets out of its home office. The Court did not ask whether corporate formalities were maintained. Accordingly, it allowed service of process on the parent to reach its subsidiary. Likewise, in *Vuitch v. Furr,* 482 A.2d 811 (D.C.1984), the District of Columbia Court of Appeals approved a liberal approach for determining whether one corporation is an alter ego of another. The Court cited the oft-quoted analysis of Justice Cardozo:

> the relationship between parents and subsidiary corporations is one that is still enveloped in the mist of metaphor.... We say at times that the corporate entity will be ignored when the parent corporation operates a business through a subsidiary which is characterized as an 'alias' or a 'dummy' ... the essential term is to be defined in the act of operation. Dominion may be so complete, interference so obtrusive, that by the general rules of agency the parent will be a principal and the subsidiary an agent. Where control is less than this, we are remitted to the test of honesty and justice ... [the court must seek to prevent] a perversion of the privilege to do business in a corporate form.' (citing to *Berkey v. Third Ave. R.R.,* 244 N.Y. 84, 94–95; 155 N.E. 58, 61 (1926)).

Although these decisions provide a license to reach beyond the *Cannon* decision to determine whether Meteor P.R.S. is a sham subsidiary, they do not provide a very useful technique for the job.

Useful guidance was introduced in this jurisdiction in *Chrysler Corp. v. General Motors Corp.,* 589 F.Supp. 1182 (D.D.C.1984). Citing to a District Court opinion from Pennsylvania, the *Chrysler* Court held the following factors relevant:

the performance by the subsidiary or affiliate of business activities in a district, for example, sales and servicings, that in a less elaborate corporate scheme the absent corporation would perform directly by its own branch offices or agents. Another is a partnership in world-wide business competition between the absent corporation and the corporation that is present in a district. A third factor is the capacity of the absent corporation to influence decisions of the subsidiary or affiliate that might have antitrust consequences. Controlling stock ownership and interlocking directorates are, of course, indices of such a capacity. Yet another factor is the part that the subsidiary or affiliated corporation plays in the over-all business activity of the absent corporation. A fifth factor is the existence of an integrated sales system involving manufacturing, trading and sales corporations. A related factor is the status of the subsidiary or affiliate as a marketing arm of the absent corporation. A seventh factor is the use by the subsidiary or affiliate of a trademark owned by the parent. The transfer of personnel back and forth between the absent corporation and its subsidiary or affiliate is another factor that a court may properly consider. So is the presentation of a common marketing image by the related corporations. This is especially true when those corporations hold themselves out to the public as a single entity that is conveniently departmentalized either nationally or worldwide. Yet another factor is the granting of an exclusive distributorship by the absent corporation to its subsidiary or affiliate. (citing to *Zenith Radio Corp. v. Matsushita Elec. Indus. Co., Ltd.*, 402 F.Supp. 262 (E.D.Pa.1975)).

* * *

Consistent with *Chrysler's* teachings, the Court examines the activities of Meteor P.R.S., Meteor–Siegen's wholly-owned subsidiary. Muennich and Kuebler are the joint managers of the parent corporation; they also comprise two-thirds of the Board of Directors of the subsidiary. Thus, the directorates interlock. Further, Jochen Muennich is the President of Meteor P.R.S.

Meteor–Siegen created Meteor P.R.S. to function as a marketing arm in the United States. Until the deal with Kodak was consummated, Meteor P.R.S. was the exclusive distributor and service representative of Meteor–Siegen in this country. This function was carried out by the parent corporation before Meteor P.R.S.'s creation. It may fairly be said that the two corporations function as an integrated whole. Meteor–Siegen manufactures copy machines and Meteor P.R.S. distributes them to retailers in its designated market. The two corporations thus compete in a worldwide enterprise in competition with other copier producers. Toward this end they use a single logo, presenting a common marketing image.

Finally, Meteor P.R.S. has little individual identity. Although once functioning as Meteor–Siegen's sole marketing arm in the United States, the plaintiff claims that Kodak's exclusive North American distributorship makes the subsidiary unnecessary. The defendants vigorously dispute this fact and claim that Meteor P.R.S. is still a dynamic corporate entity which continues to sell "other product lines." However, the defendants' claims are undermined by a communication sent by Meteor P.R.S. to its customers after the signing of the Kodak agreement. The message reads,

> we have decided to further enhance our image by taking on the identity of our parent organization, METEOR–SIEGEN. So, our letterhead bears a new name as well as a new phone number. Now when you call our new number, you will be answered with our new name: "Hello METEOR–SIEGEN."

At the very least, this document demonstrates that Meteor P.R.S.'s function was lessened following the Kodak agreement.

In sum, application of the *Chrysler* factors persuade the Court that Meteor P.R.S. is merely the alter ego of Meteor–Siegen. Accordingly, the Court will exert jurisdiction over Meteor–Siegen.

GALLAGHER v. MAZDA MOTOR OF AMERICA, INC.

United States District Court, E.D. Pennsylvania, 1992.
781 F.Supp. 1079.

CAHN, DISTRICT JUDGE.

On January 1, 1990, John and Judith Gallagher, husband and wife, were traveling with their four children, Gabriella, Yolanda, Laura and Dewi, in their 1989 Mazda MPV motor vehicle when they were involved in an accident. As a result of the accident, Judith, Gabriella and Yolanda were killed, and John, Laura and Dewi were injured. This suit has been brought by John, in his individual capacity and in his capacity as representative for the other Gallagher plaintiffs, against Mazda Motor of America, Inc. ["Mazda of America"] and Mazda Motor Corp. ["Mazda of Japan"]. Mazda of Japan has moved, pursuant to Fed.R.Civ.P. 12(b)(4) and Fed.R.Civ.P. 12(b)(5) to dismiss, or, in the alternative, to quash the plaintiffs' service of process.[1]

* * *

Although the parties will have little trouble deciding what evidence must be presented in order to establish that the Irvine, California post office box belongs to Mazda of Japan, the law is currently unclear as to when the jurisdictional contacts of a subsidiary may be imputed to the parent corporation. In order to provide guidance to the parties, the court will set forth the requirements for imputing such contacts.

While it is clear that the bare parent/subsidiary relationship does not allow a court to impute the jurisdictional contacts of the subsidiary to the parent, *see Wasden*, 131 F.R.D. at 209; *McClenon*, 726 F.Supp. at 826; *Meyers*, 711 F.Supp. at 1004, there are, in essence, three lines of

---

1. The service of process issue in this case is discussed in Problem 3.4.

cases dealing with when imputing jurisdictional contacts is proper. The first line of cases follows *Cannon Manufacturing Co. v. Cudahy Packing Co.*, 267 U.S. 333, 335–37, 45 S.Ct. 250, 250–52, 69 L.Ed. 634 (1925), and holds that, so long as both the parent and subsidiary corporations observe and respect the corporate form, the jurisdictional contacts of the subsidiary will not be imputed to the parent. *See Southmark Corp. v. Life Investors, Inc.*, 851 F.2d 763, 773–74 (5th Cir.1988); *I.A.M. National Pension Fund v. Wakefield Industries*, 699 F.2d 1254, 1258–59 (D.C.Cir. 1983); *Leach Co. v. General Sani–Can Manufacturing Corp.*, 393 F.2d 183, 186 (7th Cir.1968); *Savin Corp. v. Heritage Copy Products, Inc.*, 661 F.Supp. 463, 467–68 (M.D.Pa.1987); *Indian Coffee Corp. v. Procter & Gamble Co.*, 482 F.Supp. 1098, 1104 (W.D.Pa.1980), aff'd in part on other grounds, 752 F.2d 891 (3d Cir.), cert. denied, 474 U.S. 863, 106 S.Ct. 180, 88 L.Ed.2d 150 (1985).

The other two lines of cases set a lower threshold for imputing the jurisdictional contacts of a subsidiary to the parent corporation. One line of cases holds that contacts should be imputed when the parent corporation exercises total control over the affairs and activities of the subsidiary, and can therefore be said to be the subsidiary's alter ego. *See Patent Incentives, Inc. v. Seiko Epson Corp.*, 1988 Westlaw 92460 at *6 (D.N.J. September 6, 1988), aff'd, 878 F.2d 1446 (Fed.Cir.1989) (table); *Omega Homes, Inc. v. Citicorp Acceptance Co.*, 656 F.Supp. 393, 399 (W.D.Va. 1987); *Colcord v. Armstrong World Industries, Inc.*, 1985 Westlaw 17481 at *3 (D.Colo. May 13, 1985) ("the notion of a separate corporate existence of a parent and subsidiary will not be recognized where one corporation is so organized and controlled, and its business conducted in such a manner, as to make it merely an agency, instrumentality, adjunct, or alter ego of another corporation.... By the same reasoning, the acts of the subsidiary may be imputed to the parent for purposes of personal jurisdiction.") (citations omitted); *Akzona Inc. v. E.I. Du Pont De Nemours & Co.*, 607 F.Supp. 227, 237 (D.Del.1984) ("In order to find that a subsidiary is the alter ego or instrumentality of the parent, the Plaintiff must prove: 'control by the parent to such a degree that the subsidiary has become its mere instrumentality.' ") (citations omitted); *Lavrov v. NCR Corp.*, 591 F.Supp. 102, 109 (S.D. Ohio 1984); *S & S Industries, Inc. v. Nakamura–Tome Precision Industries Co., Ltd.*, 93 F.R.D. 564, 568–69 (D.Minn.1982). *Cf. Key v. Liquid Energy Corp.*, 906 F.2d 500, 503 (10th Cir.1990) (discussing the liability of a corporate parent for acts of a subsidiary in a tort context).

The other line of cases holds that contacts should be imputed when the subsidiary was either established for, or is engaged in, activities that, but for the existence of the subsidiary, the parent would have to undertake itself. See *Mirrow v. Club Med, Inc.*, 118 F.R.D. 418, 419–20 (E.D.Pa.1986) ("Also important is the fact that in marketing the vacation packages, Club Med Sales performs a function that Club Med itself would otherwise have to perform.... Here, Club Med Sales effectively operates as the sales department in the United States for Club Med. This allocation of functions implies that the two entities work in concert.

Such a relationship between parent and subsidiary helps to illustrate that the subsidiary 'is merely the incorporated department of its parent.' ") (Pollak, J.) (citations omitted); *Allen Organ Co.*, 593 F.Supp. at 111–12 (imputing contacts of a wholly owned subsidiary whose sole function was to distribute the parent's products); *Bulova Watch Co., Inc. v. K. Hattori & Co., Ltd.*, 508 F.Supp. 1322, 1342 (E.D.N.Y.1981) ("There are undoubtedly special reasons [the defendant] has chosen to operate in this country by means of incorporated subsidiaries. But these subsidiaries almost by definition are doing for their parent what their parent would otherwise have to do on its own. The question to ask is not whether the American subsidiaries can formally accept orders for their parent, but rather whether, in the truest sense, the subsidiaries presence substitutes for the presence of the parent.") (Weinstein, C.J.); *K.J. Schwartzbaum, Inc. v. Evans, Inc.*, 44 F.R.D. 589, 590–91 (S.D.N.Y.1968) ("where a corporation has a wholly-owned subsidiary performing services which would ordinarily be performed by its own service employees, or where its subsidiary exists for the purpose of making product purchases which otherwise would be made by purchasing agents of defendant corporation, the parent company should not be allowed to hide behind the corporate fiction but, rather, should be required to submit to the jurisdiction of the court located in that District in which the parent corporation, for all intents and purposes, transacts its business.") (citations omitted).

The court is persuaded that the last line of cases is the correct one, and that the jurisdictional contacts of a subsidiary corporation should be imputed to the corporate parent when the subsidiary corporation is engaged in functions that, but for the existence of the subsidiary, the parent would have to undertake.[10] If the subsidiary is engaged in activities that are vital to the survival or the success of the parent corporation, the parent will undoubtedly receive notice of any papers served on the subsidiary. Due process will therefore be fulfilled since the party to the lawsuit will know that it has been sued, and that it must mount a defense or suffer the consequences.

The court is also convinced that the parent corporation can truly be said to have "contacts" with a jurisdiction when it has chosen, for its own purposes, to make these contacts through a subsidiary. See *Bellomo v. Pennsylvania Life Co.*, 488 F.Supp. 744, 746 (S.D.N.Y.1980) ("Where,

---

10. The court's inquiry into whether the subsidiary is simply a substitute for the parent is, in the words of Chief Judge Weinstein, a pragmatic one. *See Bulova Watch Co.*, 508 F.Supp. at 1335. Naturally, a party is free to argue that the factors favored by the second line of cases, such as the overlap between members of the board of the subsidiary and the parent, are some evidence that the subsidiary is engaged in activities that the parent would otherwise perform. It would seem, however, that the most persuasive evidence of such a "proxy" relationship would consist of an analysis of the symbios-is between the corporate functions, combined with proof that, not only does the parent own 100% of the subsidiary, but that the subsidiary does 100% of its business with the parent. In such a case, the subsidiary would appear to be a mere "front" for the parent, established at the behest of accountants or tax experts. *See Akzona*, 607 F.Supp. at 239, citing *Bulova*, 508 F.Supp. at 1343 (where a subsidiary markets the products of the parent, and when the subsidiary has no independent manufacturing capacity, jurisdictional contacts are properly imputed).

on the other hand, the subsidiaries are created by the parent, for tax or corporate finance purposes, to carry on business on its behalf, there is no basis for distinguishing between the business of the parent and the business of the subsidiaries. There is a presumption, in effect, that the parent is sufficiently involved in the operation of the subsidiaries to become subject to jurisdiction.'') (footnote omitted).

Put another way, if a parent uses a subsidiary to do what it otherwise would have done itself, it has purposely availed itself of the privilege of doing business in the forum. Jurisdiction over the parent is therefore proper. *See Shaffer v. Heitner*, 433 U.S. 186, 215–16, 97 S.Ct. 2569, 2585–86, 53 L.Ed.2d 683 (1977); *Hanson v. Denckla*, 357 U.S. 235, 253, 78 S.Ct. 1228, 1239, 2 L.Ed.2d 1283 (1958); *Weight v. Kawasaki Motors Corp.*, U.S.A., 604 F.Supp. 968, 970 (E.D.Va.1985). This contrasts to the case of a holding company. In such a case, the subsidiary is not performing a function that the parent would otherwise have had to perform itself (the holding company could simply hold another type of subsidiary). In such a case, imputing jurisdictional contacts would be improper. *See Savin*, 661 F.Supp. at 471; *Akzona*, 607 F.Supp. at 229, 237.

As it has already been noted, the court will hold a hearing at which time the plaintiff may attempt to establish the facts necessary to impute the jurisdictional contacts of Mazda of America to Mazda of Japan. . . . The plaintiff will . . . be allowed sixty days for discovery limited to the relationship between Mazda of Japan and Mazda of America. At the close of that period, the court will schedule a hearing at which the plaintiff may attempt to prove either that the Irvine, California post office box is that of Mazda of Japan, or that the jurisdictional contacts of Mazda of America should be imputed to Mazda of Japan, and that service on Mazda of Japan has therefore been effectuated through service on Mazda of America.

BULOVA WATCH COMPANY, INC.
v. K. HATTORI & CO., LTD.

United States District Court, Eastern District of New York, 1981.
508 F.Supp. 1322.

Weinstein, Chief Judge.

This motion to dismiss for lack of personal jurisdiction presents a classic problem in adjudicating claims against a multinational corporation using subsidiaries to penetrate the American market. Under current doctrine, to be subject to personal jurisdiction by a state, the parent must 1) itself be present because it is doing business in the state; or, 2) under a "long arm" concept, have conducted specific activities out of which the cause of action arose either in the state or outside the state with foreseeable substantial effects in the state; in addition, exercise of judicial power over the person of defendant must not offend our notions of fairness.

Largely for reasons of historical and conceptual development, the doing business concept treats a defendant corporation as if it were present for all purposes in any kind of a suit to the same extent as a real person living and working here would be. The long arm alternative was designed to be used only in limited situations in which an outsider has a transient impact on activities in the state and it applies only to claims arising from that narrow contact.

Multinational activities such as those before us present a factual pattern that sometimes does not quite fit into either of the two tidy conceptual categories reflected in N.Y. CPLR 301 and 302. Here the foreign parent corporation may be considered to be doing business under 301 for limited purposes during the period of penetration of the American market before its subsidiaries have matured to relatively full independence. The implications of this view are that the foreign parent may be deemed to be present for the purpose of expanding into a new market by setting up subsidiaries and dealing with competition, while it may not be doing business for the purposes of day-to-day commercial activity such as dealing in watches, cars or sealing wax e. g., when a suit is based upon negligent operation of a car operated by an employee of a locally organized subsidiary. Similarly, while not within the strict limits of the 302 long arm provision, the parent's actions might be sufficiently within the CPLR's penumbra so that the combination of 301 and 302 read together covers the particular claims asserted and long arm personal jurisdiction lies. None of this would violate any constitutional requirements.

We do not suggest that the present jurisdictional bases be eliminated a proposal for the legislature rather than a trial court in any event. Nor do we ignore traditional indicia utilized to measure parent-subsidiary control for jurisdictional purposes. Rather, we note that in this as in so many other areas of the law, stuffing new and complex factual patterns into absolutely rigid legal cubbyholes often results in distortion of the facts. Some give in the categories is desirable lest the law lose touch with the real world.

To any layman it would seem absurd that our courts could not obtain jurisdiction over a billion dollar multinational which is exploiting the critical New York and American markets to keep its home production going at a huge volume and profit. This perception must have a bearing on our evaluation of fairness. The law ignores the common sense of a situation at the peril of becoming irrelevant as an institution.

* * *

A common sense appraisal of economic relationships is often more useful than prior cases based on situations different in detail. We tend to come closer to the mark when we examine a business relationship from the practical viewpoint of businessmen rather than through the distorting lens of a legal conceptual framework established in an earlier era. In the multidimensional complexity of real life a two dimensional straight line provides a misleading boundary. A court cannot simply "isolate each contact of the defendant with New York and say that each such contact does not constitute the doing of business." Rather it must look to the "cumulative significance" of all activities of a foreign corporation within the state in order to determine whether the corporation is doing business within the state for jurisdictional purposes. * * *

* * *

II. FACTS

A. *Parties*

Plaintiff Bulova Watch Co., Inc. charges K. Hattori & Co., Ltd. and individual defendants Moriya, Segal, Murphy, Waldman and others with unfair competition and disparagement and with engaging in a conspiracy to raid plaintiff's marketing staff in order to appropriate plaintiff's trade secrets.

Bulova is a New York corporation with its principal place of business in Flushing, New York. It manufactures and sells watches and claims to have the largest direct sales marketing system in the watch business.

Hattori is a company incorporated under the laws of Japan with its principal offices in Tokyo. It owns all the stock of Seiko Corporation of America (SCA), a New York corporation. SCA owns all the stock of Seiko Time Corp., Pulsar Time, Inc., and SPD Precision, Inc., all New York corporations. Hattori contracts in Japan for the manufacture of its watches and sells them under the Seiko, Pulsar and other brand names to its three American sub-subsidiaries. * * * A very substantial amount of its total revenue is derived from exports of watches and timepieces, the United States being its largest foreign market. * * *

Hattori sells products to distributors in over one hundred countries around the world. Wholly-owned subsidiaries of Hattori handle distribution of Hattori's products in about ten of those countries, including the United States. In the rest, or the great majority of the countries in which Hattori's products are sold, sales are made by Hattori or its subsidiaries to independent distributors who conduct their own advertising and other marketing activities and maintain their own repair centers pursuant to agreement or arrangements with Hattori. Hattori has never directly marketed its products in any country except Japan.

* * *

From 1967 to 1971, and again from 1975 to July, 1979, Moriya was assigned by Hattori to New York. During the period when the events complained of occurred he was president and director of SCA and its corporate predecessor, sole director of Pulsar Time and SPD Precision, director of Seiko Time, an officer of two other of Seiko's American distributors and a director of a third. While in New York, Moriya held the following positions with Hattori: Deputy Manager and Manager, International Marketing Department and Manager, Personnel Department. Moriya's immediate superior was Reijiro Hattori, Chairman of SCA and second-in-command at Hattori.

At the date of the filing of the complaint Moriya was a director of Hattori, to which he was elected upon his return from his American assignment. After this action was started he was named Chairman of SCA and apparently he did not resign his position as its president upon his return to Tokyo until sometime after the complaint was filed.

* * *

B. *Allegations*

Between July and December of 1978, six members of Bulova's staff three regional sales managers and three more senior executive personnel left Bulova to join either a Seiko subsidiary or a Seiko distributor. During December, 1978 four Bulova salesmen joined SPD Precision's Pulsar division which in January, 1979 was separately incorporated as Pulsar Time, Inc. Sometime during 1979 a number of Bulova salesmen were hired by Pulsar Time. What sharply divides plaintiff from defendant is the question of whether these hirings were the result of a conspiracy among defendants to appropriate Bulova's trade secrets and marketing system and to damage Bulova and destroy its business and reputation.

Plaintiff alleges that Hattori and Moriya decided during 1978 to market a new line of watches, Pulsar, a trademark that was acquired by Seiko Time in September, 1978. Plaintiff also alleges that the decision was taken by Hattori and Moriya to organize a clock division of Seiko Time. Seiko watches had been marketed through fifteen Seiko regional distributors, but the Pulsar watches were to be marketed directly to retail outlets. To accomplish this, a direct sales network had to be put quickly into place. It is contended that as part of the plan Moriya hired Schwartz, who had been vice-president and director of marketing at Bulova, to head the Pulsar operation.

In the beginning of October, Schwartz and Moriya met to discuss the Pulsar marketing strategy and Schwartz recommended that Moriya hire Cohen as director of sales. Meetings were held between Cohen and Schwartz, and Cohen was offered employment at SPD Precision with the view to directing Pulsar sales. Moriya, Cohen and Schwartz decided that a sales force of twenty would be required for the first year, 1979, and Cohen was told not to "divulge the name of his new employer" for one month. He recommended the hiring of Waldman, a Bulova regional sales manager. In early December of 1978, Waldman met with Cohen and Schwartz in New York, and the next day Waldman left Bulova to join Pulsar as field sales manager. In order to implement the goal of hiring twenty salesmen by January 1, 1979, the three ex-Bulova employees actively solicited other Bulova employees.

* * *

During December, special letters were drafted to be signed by Bulova salesmen joining SPD Precision, Pulsar's parent. The letters stated that the employees would not use any Bulova trade secrets and that SPD Precision was not interested in such secrets. It is plaintiff's theory that singling out Bulova personnel for use of these apparently self-serving letters suggests awareness of the impropriety of hiring such personnel.

* * *

Bulova contends that the concerted action of Hattori, Moriya and the other individual defendants caused serious dislocation and disruption at Bulova's corporate headquarters. The departure of six high level employees is alleged to have damaged sales throughout the country and in New York, and to have contributed substantially to a decrease in sales of some $18 million.

C. Moriya's Crucial Role

Moriya joined Hattori in Japan in 1954 after finishing his schooling. He has never worked for any employer aside from Hattori or its American subsidiaries. As already noted, during the course of his employment with the American subsidiaries he simultaneously held the Hattori positions of Deputy Manager and Manager of the International Division and Manager of the Personnel Department. Nonetheless, defendants assert that while in the United States "he performed services for the United States subsidiaries and none for Hattori." The court has not been able to see its way to reading the undisputed facts in such an unusual fashion. Common sense, which need not be banished from our reckoning, dictates the conclusion that while in the United States Moriya loyally performed substantial services for Hattori.

Moriya was no mere liaison officer, and his assignment by Hattori was far from casual. * * * Moriya understood that his assignment was undertaken to further the interests of Hattori and he admitted that he endeavored to carry out this task. Although he was employed by the Hattori subsidiaries he would not deny that he considered Mr. Unno of Hattori his superior.

* * * Even if we did not need to view the record in a light favorable to plaintiff, there could be no doubt who Moriya's true master was. It is beyond cavil that the establishment of a major presence in the American market is of critical importance to a firm like Hattori. * * * Moriya was directly responsible for formulating and implementing that strategy, and at all times his primary allegiance was to Hattori.

* * *

III. Jurisdiction Over K. Hattori & Co., Ltd.

* * *

CPLR 301 permits the exercise of such jurisdiction over "persons, property, or status as might have been exercised heretofore." It confers personal jurisdiction over unlicensed foreign corporations that are "doing business" in New York.

The definition of "doing business" has been variously stated, but the common denominator is that the corporation is operating within the state "not occasionally or casually, but with a fair measure of permanence and continuity."

It is no longer a matter of doubt that a foreign corporation can do business in New York through its employees, or through independent agents.

Equally settled is the concept that a corporation may be amenable to New York personal jurisdiction when the systematic activities of a subsidiary in this state may fairly be attributed to the parent. * * *

The parent-subsidiary relationship has not in itself been treated as sufficient to establish personal jurisdiction over the foreign parent. Some additional factor has been needed. Such circumstances include direct and indirect control of the local distributor, treating the subsidiary as an "incorporated division," as an agent or as both. One scholarly analysis suggests that the cases should be read as treating the principal and subsidiary as one for jurisdictional purposes where parent and subsidiary are part of a "single economic entity." See, generally, Wellborn, Subsidiary Corporations in New York: When is Mere Ownership Enough to Establish Jurisdiction over the Parent, 22 Buffalo L.Rev. 681 (1973) (criticizing the need to show more than "mere ownership").

The two tests that have been utilized in determining the closeness of the economic connection both look to realities rather than to formal relationships. The parent corporations will be found to be present in New York: "First, if the relationship between the foreign parents and local subsidiaries gives rise to a 'valid inference' of an agency relationship;" and second, "if control by the parent of the subsidiary is 'so complete that the subsidiary is, in fact, merely a department of the parent'".

Although the "agency" and "mere department" theories of jurisdiction are stated as separate principles, it should be clear from the mass of cases dealing with this problem that a line cannot be simply drawn between the two. The apparently distinct notions are metonyms for a jurisdictional balancing assessing the fairness of requiring an out-of-state party to defend itself in New York when it derives benefits from in-state activities. The factors to be weighed include the significance of the New York business to the defendant's overall activities.

* * *

The test of whether a foreign corporation does business here has been said to be a "simple pragmatic" one, but the problem with that classic formulation is that simplicity and pragmatism are, more often than not, mutually exclusive. Thus, it would often be a simple solution to find for a defendant on the basis of the relatively immaculate formal separation it has engineered between itself and its subsidiaries. But the pragmatic command of CPLR 301 emphatically rejects such niceties of etiquette. The realities and not the formalities must be dealt with.

* * *

An important question in assessing presence for jurisdictional purposes is whether a multinational has reached a state in its evolution when it can be said that its sales and marketing subsidiaries truly have a "life of their own." * * *

5. *Application of Law to Facts*

Moving defendants place great stock in the formal separation of Hattori from its 100% directly-owned subsidiary and its 100% indirectly-owned subsidiaries. They state that the subsidiaries do not receive loans from the parent, that they generally buy from the parent by letter of credit posted with a Japanese bank abroad, that they do their own advertising (although at times they participate in promotions organized by Hattori), and that the parent has no bank account, office or phone listing in New York, is not licensed to do business here, does not assign its "salaried employees" to New York, and is not involved in the personnel policies or the hiring of personnel by its New York subsidiaries.

Plaintiff, on the other hand, points to the complete stock ownership by the parent and additionally draws our attention to the interchange and overlap of directors and officers between parent and subsidiaries, to the fact that intercompany loans are made to other Hattori subsidiaries and are assertedly available, if needed, to the New York subsidiaries, that the financial statements of the New York subsidiaries are consolidated in Hattori's reports filed under the securities and exchange law of Japan, and that unrealized profits and losses arising from sales among the consolidated companies are eliminated in the financial statements. It also relies upon certain advertising materials produced by Hattori and distributed by the public relations firm of the New York subsidiaries that refer to Hattori's "marketing offices in ... New York" and an "international network of designated distributors ... supervised by the Tokyo headquarters."

It would be helpful were the law to provide some grand jurisdictional ledger sheets upon which formal points such as these could be assigned weights and totted up. That is not possible in our real world where so much depends on nuances, on a sense of interrelationships and on a realistic appraisal of subtle economic and power connections. Real rather than formal relationships must be considered.

* * * What is involved here is a series of relatively young sales and marketing subsidiaries abroad, whose purpose is to market a single product timepieces. * * * The use of the wholly-owned subsidiary form her reflects the desire for "unambiguous control" over sales and marketing subsidiaries to insure uniform quality and promotion of the product sold.

Hattori and its American subsidiaries do maintain some independence about as much as the egg and vegetables in a western omelette. * * *

* * * Hattori is a highly effective export manufacturer and not a fully developed multinational. * * * Large and sophisticated as it may be, it is very much the hub of a wheel with many spokes. It is appropriate, therefore, to look to the center of the wheel in Japan when the spokes violate substantive rights in other countries.

Defendant would have the court accept the notion that none of Moriya's work was done for the benefit of Hattori. The metaphoric fiction by which the parent and child corporation are treated as separate is here carried too far. * * *

What is decisive is that at the time this complaint was filed, Hattori, through its American subsidiaries, continued to engage in the market penetration and expansion that are its corporate raison d'etre and that are the grounds underlying this action. We have no doubt about the validity of an "inference as to the broad scope of the agency" linking Hattori to the activities of its subsidiaries in New York.

* * *

* * * The New York subsidiaries are the means by which Hattori has established and seeks to maintain its base in the country that is its single largest export market. The subsidiaries do for the parent everything that the parent would have to do if it were here directly. * * *

* * *

Our holding that the activities of Hattori's subsidiaries allow the court to take jurisdiction of Hattori is buttressed by the fact that the cause of action alleged here is integrally related to the doing of business by Hattori within the state. * * *

A court might well find substantial unfairness were it to drag a foreign parent into court to defend itself against actions completely unrelated to the subsidiary corporation's purposive activities on behalf of its parent. The holding in this case is simply that while a subsidiary establishes and expands a parent's market position then, so long as that activity is being conducted, and with respect to those activities furthering the parent's ends, the parent is doing business in New York. This is particularly true as to activities directly related to primary steps taken to ensure a place for its subsidiaries, as where action is taken to raid an established competitor's personnel in penetrating the American market.

B. Long Arm Jurisdiction, N.Y. CPLR 302

1. The Law

Plaintiff has also made a sufficient jurisdictional showing to support personal jurisdiction over Hattori under CPLR 302. * * *

* * *

* * * Here, as in the case of CPLR 301, courts look to the realities rather than the formalities of agency to decide whether business has been transacted through an agent.

* * *

* * * Planning and establishing significant new product lines and implementing a marketing strategy that entailed the hiring of established salespeople constitute the transaction of business out of which the present complaint arises. As to this business there is a strong showing that Hattori was informed. When actions of relatively minor significance might subject a foreign party to the jurisdiction of a New York court, it would be anomalous if the systematic and sustained planning for establishing and expanding the New York business of a billion dollar multinational did not. There is jurisdiction under CPLR 302(a)(1).

Similar considerations support finding jurisdiction over Hattori under CPLR 302(a)(2) as well.* * *

Questions and Comments

1.   Why would the plaintiff seek to obtain *jurisdiction* by veil piercing if there is little likelihood that *liability* will be obtained by veil piercing? How should the plaintiff argue the jurisdiction issue—identical to arguing the liability issue?

2.   Using your corporate knowledge of veil piercing for liability, would the veil be pierced in this Problem? For what reasons? Do you need to know more about the relationship between the parent and subsidiary? In each of the above extracted cases we need to try to identify the courts reasons for piercing the veil for jurisdiction purposes (or for declining to do so), to determine if the courts are developing a veil piercing jurisprudence that differs from veil piercing for substantive liability. Remember that in none of these cases is the plaintiff at this stage arguing veil piercing for liability. They are arguing veil piercing only to establish jurisdiction. That of course may lead to discovery and perhaps evidence that allows a veil piercing for liability argument.

3.   In most cases in the United States that address veil piercing there is no international issue. The parent and subsidiary are both from states within the United States. Does it make any difference that in our Problem the parent is from one country and the subsidiary is from another? Should the law of veil piercing of the parent's nation or the subsidiary's nation be the applicable law? What if the court concludes that it is the law of the parent's nation but the parent is the foreign entity and there is no veil piercing law in that nation? Does the court then apply the law of the U.S. subsidiary?

4.   Should we discount *Cannon* because it is a U.S. parent–U.S. subsidiary case, not a foreign parent-U.S. subsidiary case? Doesn't the *Scophony* case limit *Cannon*?

5.   Consider Restatement § 52 Comment b. Does this add anything? Does it support *Cannon*? Is it outdated, filled with the same fuzzy and elastic

words such as "so controls and dominates" and "disregard" that Cardozo warned us about in *Berkey v. Third Avenue Ry.*, 244 N.Y. 84, 94, 155 N.E. 58, 61 (1926), *cert. denied*, 244 N.Y. 602, 155 N.E. 914 (1927)?

6. *Clark* and *Color Systems*, which reach opposite conclusions, both refer to *Hargrave v. Fibreboard Corp.*, 710 F.2d 1154 (5th Cir. 1983). *Hargrave* involved asbestos injury claims by former employees of K & M, a Pennsylvania company incorporated in 1892, acquired during the 1930s by T & N (U.K.), and operated as a wholly-owned subsidiary from 1938 until 1962, when it was sold to a third party. The deep pocket appeared to be the English company T & N, over which the plaintiffs claimed jurisdiction. The district court allowed jurisdiction on an alter ego theory because it "exercised general guidance and retained the necessary authority" over K & M. On appeal, the circuit court cited *Cannon* and acknowledged that a foreign parent is not ordinarily subject to jurisdiction of a forum state merely because of the parent-subsidiary relationship. But the circuit court jurisprudence had begun to "demand proof of control by the parent over the internal business operations and affairs of the subsidiary in order to fuse the two for jurisdictional purposes." The control must be "greater than that normally associated with common ownership and directorship." The court found considerable control in the form of "complete authority" by T & N "over general policy decisions" at K & M, "including selection of product lines, hiring and firing of K & M officers, and approval of sizeable capital investments." But it was not enough—the court found the day-to-day and operational decisions to have remained with K & M. Although it noted that "only a prima facie showing was required on a jurisdiction motion," and that it was appropriate to apply a "less stringent standard for alter ego jurisdiction than for alter ego liability," T & N did little more than exercise a policy-making authority that is appropriate for a sole shareholder. How does *Color Systems* differ? Was T & N doing anything more than what a sole shareholder of a small corporation would be expected to do? Why should the rule be different when the sole shareholder is a large corporation? The *Hargrave* court noted that due process would have to be met but that it was unnecessary to consider due process in view of its alter ego ruling. Would due process requirements have been met because T & N acquired the U.S. entity, or must there be more?

7. What is absent in *Clark* that would justify finding jurisdiction as in *Color Systems*? Does the *Clark* court reject the reasoning of *Color Systems*? Does *Clark* apply alter ego liability standards to determine alter ego jurisdiction standards? Does *Clark* confuse or intentionally merge due process minimum contact elements with alter ego issues?

8. *Brooks v. Bacardi* restates the Gallagher three lines of decisions and gives them "test" status. Because the plaintiff failed to allege any of the requirements of any of the three "tests", nor even the "exact relationship" of Bacardi to Barcardi–USA, the case was dismissed. How did the plaintiff appear to view the Barcardi entities and does the relatively sparse structure the case mentions show enough to impute jurisdiction under any of the three lines of decisions?

9. The *Rose* decision, by citing *Clark* and *Gallagher,* may be merging the second and third lines of decisions, but its reference to *Gallagher* proves

to be more a citation for reference to a classification of *Ross* under the *Gallagher* scheme, then to adopt *Gallagher's* preference for the third line. Are the linkages between the parent and subsidiary, as the court concludes, insufficient to impute jurisdiction? Considering the links separately or in the aggregate? Rose then turns to comparing the roles of the parent and subsidiary, and concludes that they are quite different. Is that an application of the third line of reasoning? A correct application?

10. In *Color Systems* the court asserts jurisdiction over the German parent Meteor–Siegen. Would it have undertaken the same analysis were the case to have involved veil piercing for liability purposes? How important is it that Meteor–Siegen formerly operated in the United States but then formed the U.S. subsidiary Meteor P.R.S. to be its exclusive business entity in the United States? Does *Color Systems* say it is applying *Cannon* but then ignore it? Note the court's reference to the eight *Chrysler* decision factors that it considers in determining jurisdiction. Are these the same as the factors used in a traditional veil piercing case for substantive liability? Which factors should be given most weight? Do they differ from the factors in our hypothetical fact situation dealing with DROF AG and VUSCO? Doesn't the fact that this is a case involving parent and subsidiary corporations in two different nations influence the decision? The court noted that the two corporations functioned as an "integrated whole" in "a worldwide enterprise in competition with other copier producers." Isn't this *enterprise theory*, that Professor Blumberg has so eloquently advocated for over the years? See Phillip I. Blumberg, The Law of Corporate Groups (1987).

11. While *Gallagher* is useful in discussing the three lines of decisions, it also addresses a real fact situation. Adopting the third line of decisions, imputing jurisdiction should be limited to where "the subsidiary was either established for, or is engaged in, activities that, but for the existence of the subsidiary, the parent would have to undertake itself." What if a corporation manufactures cars. It is critical to its survival that they be sold. The company might choose to contract with an existing distributorship, or enter the sales area itself. If it creates a marketing subsidiary that owns automobile dealerships, under the third line of decisions isn't the subsidiary engaged in something that the parent would have to do in the absence of the subsidiary? Companies such as fast food enterprises often change their marketing from company owned to franchised stores. If it chooses company owned stores is it forever condemned by the third line of reasoning? The *Gallagher* court does not decide the issue, but orders a hearing. Were you representing the Mazda parent would you be worried? Note that the hearing is also to consider imputing service on the subsidiary to be service on the parent, an issue to be considered in problem 3.4 with the reading of *Volkswagenwerk, A.G. v. Schlunk*.

12. Does the *Bulova Watch v. Hattori* decision allow the "fairness" issue to override the forms of corporate organization? As the court noted, "the law ignores the common sense of a situation at the peril of becoming irrelevant as an institution." *Hattori* at 1327. Is this consistent with the comment of Oliver Wendell Holmes that "the life of the law is experience, not logic"? The *Hattori* decision discusses at length the evolution of a multinational corporation and how different stages may impose different liabilities. Is it a control decision—holding that so much of what the parent's

subsidiaries did was directed by the parent that jurisdiction (if not liability, not at issue in this decision) was justified? Was there something unique (or uniquely Japanese) about Moriya's service to Hattori that he could never escape in reality being a Hattori employee?

13. How is our hypothetical case resolved under each of the three lines of reasoning?

14. Under a different theory, the parent/subsidiary relationship being evaluated under principal/agency norms, how would such theory apply to DROF AG and VUSCO? In one of the more expansive rulings on agency, a New York state court allowed jurisdiction over Hilton Hotels (U.K.) Ltd., a British corporation, because of the relationship of providing services from New York by the Hilton Reservations Service to the London Hilton where the plaintiff was injured. *Frummer v. Hilton Hotels Int'l, Inc.*, 19 N.Y.2d 533, 227 N.E.2d 851, 281 N.Y.S.2d 41, *cert. denied*, 389 U.S. 923, 88 S.Ct. 241, 19 L.Ed.2d 266 (1967) . The Hilton Reservation Service was a subsidiary of Hilton (U.K.). "Significant and pivotal" was the acceptance and confirmation of room reservations in New York for London. However, the plaintiff had not used the reservation service to book the London hotel and thus *Frummer* is not a *specific* jurisdiction case. The court also referred to the "considerable benefits" received from the service and noted that the London Hilton "may not be heard to complain." Would the court have ruled the same had the plaintiff been from Kenya with no contact with the New York agent? A dissent in *Frummer* rejected extending jurisdiction of the New York Court "over a foreign corporation simply because of its relationship with subsidiary or affiliated corporations of a parent corporation." The dissent thought the court "grossly" extended the doing business rule "well beyond the existing principles or precedents." What are the "policy and commercial considerations" that concerned the dissenting judge? A Georgia federal district court applied a similarly broad test to allow jurisdiction over a Dutch parent on the basis of agency for acts of a U.S. subsidiary. *Cartwright v. Fokker Aircraft U.S.A., Inc.*, 713 F.Supp. 389 (N.D.Ga.1988). Would it have mattered if the plaintiff had not been a U.S. resident, but rather another Dutch company, or a Spanish passenger on a flight in Spain? Neither *Frummer* nor *Cartwright* contains a very careful discussion of the alleged agency relationship. Do not all parent-subsidiary relationships meet the agency test? Is agency appropriate for determining jurisdiction? If so, is it any less appropriate for determining substantive liability? If The New York Hilton Reservations Service had not been a subsidiary but separately owned by private investors there might still be an agency relationship. But sufficient to justify a similar ruling?

15. If veil piercing is found, the issues of jurisdiction discussed in Problem 3.2 might be viewed differently. No longer is there a question of fairness and minimum contacts with regard to a distinct foreign corporate entity. Because piercing the corporate veil effectively merges the parent and subsidiary, minimum contacts should be present and fairness easier to

establish. Another area is affected by veil piercing, service of process. If the veil is pierced, the part of the entity in the United States, whether parent or subsidiary, may be the location for service over the entire entity. Since service is made in the United States, the provisions of the Hague Convention on the Service Abroad of Judicial and Extrajudicial Document in Civil or Commercial Matters are not applicable. That issue is considered in Problem 3.4.

16.   All of the decisions extracted and discussed in this problem are from the federal courts. Is veil piercing a question of state or federal law? The federal courts have been developing a common law of veil piercing where issues relate to such federal statutes as CERCLA. Should the courts be referring to state law as the source of law in the cases we have discussed? There are very few references to state court decisions in any of the six cases we have included.

17.   Should the cases that have addressed U.S. subsidiaries and foreign parents have discussed the international issue—should the existence of a cross-border parent/subsidiary make any difference? Are courts that are developing the theory of imputing jurisdiction (and service) creating fictions in order to reach foreign parents?

PROBLEM 3.4   SERVICE OF PROCESS ON FOREIGN DEFENDANTS

SECTION I.   THE SETTING

Party-plaintiffs to the product liability action described in Problem 3.1 need to effectuate proper service of process on all named defendants. They are advised that it is better to be cautious where foreign defendants are involved inasmuch as service of process in a sovereign nation must conform to the laws of the particular country involved. CANTIRE, Ltd., the tire manufacturer, is headquartered in Canada. DROF, AG, the SUV manufacturer, is headquartered in Germany, and DROF–UK, PLC, which manufactured and shipped certain auto parts to DROF–AG in Germany. All of these countries are signatories to the Hague Service Convention. At the same time, plaintiffs are not anxious to incur special costs, especially translation expenses, in serving process abroad. They consult with their counsel on the least expensive and most efficient method possible for service on the automobile manufacturer in Germany. Plaintiffs inform their counsel that they have reason to believe one of the defendant automobile manufacturer's top executives will be in the United States in the near future. "We'll arrange to slap a summons and complaint on him as soon as he gets off the plane. Nothing beats that in terms of costs and efficiency," plaintiff's counsel advises.

To be extra cautious, counsel recommends other methods of service of process on the German defendant, DROF, AG. In order to minimize costs, they decide on the following strategy. They had earlier discovered that VUSCO, the marketing distributor in New Jersey is 100 percent owned and controlled by the German parent company, DROF, AG.

Counsel advises that for service purposes and under the New Jersey long-arm statute, they can treat the domestic subsidiary as the alter ego or agent of the German parent company and use the substituted service provisions under state law in serving the subsidiary by mail. As an alternative method, counsel advises that they can separately serve the non-resident parent company in Germany via the New Jersey Secretary of State as provided under the long-arm statute. The state official is responsible for promptly transmitting the documents to the foreign defendant in Germany. Plaintiffs notify counsel that if that procedure is to be utilized, they do not wish to incur any costs in translating the summons, complaint and accompanying exhibits into German. They feel certain that officials in company headquarters will quickly review the documents in an untranslated form. In any event, they fully expect the CEO to brief company officials when he is "slapped with the summons and complaint" in the United States.

Plaintiffs' counsel further researches the appropriate method of service on the defendant tire maker in Canada. Canada, also a signatory to the Hague Service Convention, has not taken a reservation under the service by mail provision of Article 10 of the treaty. Plaintiffs' counsel decides to avoid the fee imposed by the Canadian central authority when the documents are transmitted to that office for service and instead mails a copy of the summons and complaint directly to defendant's company headquarters in Canada.

As Problem 3.2 indicates, a new lawsuit for contribution and indemnity is brought in New Jersey federal district court by the auto manufacturer and the distributors against the Canadian tire maker. Since plaintiffs know the new lawsuit is no big surprise to the tire maker, they too wish to use abbreviated methods of serving defendant in Canada in order to save costs and avoid delays. Plaintiffs' counsel decides to utilize the "waiver of service" provisions of Rule 4(d) of the Federal Rules of Civil Procedure. Under this procedure, plaintiff notifies defendant of the action and requests that defendant waive service of the summons. As explained in the Advisory Committee Notes, the purpose of Rule 4(d) was to avoid unnecessary costs of serving the summons. After studying this provision, plaintiffs' counsel concludes that the waiver rule has equal validity to both domestic and foreign defendants located outside of the United States and mails the complaint to defendant in Canada with return receipt requesting acknowledgment of service.

SECTION II. FOCUS OF CONSIDERATION

To be effective, service of process must comply with the law of the forum. The party seeking service of process may have various options of serving the defendant in the home forum or abroad. We need to determine the best method of effecting service in terms of acquiring valid jurisdiction over the foreign defendant in a U.S. court and enforcing any subsequent U.S. judgment abroad.

SECTION III.   READINGS, QUESTIONS AND COMMENTS

PART A.   STATE LAW SERVICE OF PROCESS PROVISIONS

The product liability action described in Problem 3.1 was filed in U.S. federal district court in the State of New Jersey. The following provisions of New Jersey state law are relevant in determining how to effect service upon foreign corporations. Compliance with state "long arm" jurisdictional requirements is necessary in order to acquire personal jurisdiction over foreign companies which have a "presence" in the state but may not be physically located there. In that situation the plaintiff would be required to follow the state law provisions governing substituted or constructive service.

RULES GOVERNING THE STATE OF NEW JERSEY—RULE 4:4. PROCESS

4:4.   Summons; Personal Service; In Personam Jurisdiction Service of summons, writs and complaints shall be made as follows:

(a) Primary Method of Obtaining in Personam Jurisdiction. The primary method of obtaining in personam jurisdiction over a defendant in this State is causing the summons and complaint to be personally served within this State pursuant to R.4:4–3, as follows: . . .

(6) Upon a corporation, by serving a copy of the summons and complaint in the manner prescribed by paragraph (a)(1) of this rule on any officer, director, trustee or managing or general agent, or any person authorized by appointment or by law to receive service of process on behalf of the corporation, or on a person at the registered office of the corporation in charge thereof, or, if service cannot be made on any of those persons, then on a person at the principal place of business of the corporation in this State in charge thereof, or if there is no place of business in this State, then on any employee of the corporation within this State acting in the discharge of his or her duties, provided, however, that a foreign corporation may be served only as herein prescribed subject to due process of law; . . .

(b) Obtaining In Personam Jurisdiction by Substituted or Constructive Service.

(1) *By Mail or Personal Service Outside the State.* If it appears by affidavit satisfying the requirements of R. 4:4–5(c)(2) that despite diligent effort and inquiry personal service cannot be made in accordance with paragraph (a) of this rule, then, consistent with due process of law, in personam jurisdiction may be obtained over any defendant as follows:

(A) personal service in a state of the United States or the District of Columbia, in the same manner as if service were made within this State, except that service shall be made by a public official having authority to serve civil process in the jurisdiction in which the service is made or by a person qualified to practice law in this State or in the jurisdiction in which service is made or by a person specially appointed by the court for that purpose; or

(B) personal service outside the territorial jurisdiction of the United States, in accordance with any governing international treaty or convention to the extent required thereby, and if none, in the same manner as if service were made within the United States, except that service shall be made by a person specially appointed by the court for that purpose; or

(C) mailing a copy of the summons and complaint by registered or certified mail, return receipt requested, and, simultaneously, by ordinary mail to: (i) a competent individual of the age of 14 or over, addressed to the individual's dwelling house or usual place of abode; (ii) a minor under the age of 14 or an incompetent, addressed to the person or persons on whom service is authorized by paragraphs (a)(2) and (a)(3) of this rule; (iii) a corporation, partnership or unincorporated association that is subject to suit under a recognized name, addressed to a registered agent for service, or to its principal place of business, or to its registered office. Mail may be addressed to a post office box in lieu of a street address only as provided by R. 1:5–2.

(2) *As Provided by Law.* Any defendant may be served as provided by law.

(3) *By Court Order.* If service can be made by any of the modes provided by this rule, no court order shall be necessary. If service cannot be made by any of the modes provided by this rule, any defendant may be served as provided by court order, consistent with due process of law.

(c) Optional Mailed Service. Where personal service is required to be made pursuant to paragraph (a) of this rule, service, in lieu of personal service, may be made by registered, certified or ordinary mail, provided, however, that such service shall be effective for obtaining in personam jurisdiction only if the defendant answers the complaint or otherwise appears in response thereto. If defendant does not answer or appear within 60 days following mailed service, service shall be made as is otherwise prescribed by this rule, and the time prescribed by R. 4:4–1 for issuance of the summons shall then begin to run anew....

PART B.   FEDERAL SERVICE OF PROCESS REQUIREMENTS

Comment on Link to Personal Jurisdiction

Omni Capital Int'l v. Wolff, 484 U.S. 97, 108 S.Ct. 404, 98 L.Ed.2d 415 (1987), discusses the link between service of process and personal jurisdiction. A rule of thumb is that "minimum contacts" or other jurisdictional test plus valid service of process equals personal jurisdiction. The *Omni* case led to correcting a gap in establishing personal jurisdiction in cases involving claims arising under federal law where the defendant was not subject to the jurisdiction of any state. The "national contacts" jurisdiction set forth in Rule 4(k)(2) provides: "[i]f the exercise of jurisdiction is consistent with the Constitution of the United States, serving a summons or filing a waiver of service is also effective, with respect to claims arising under federal law, to establish personal jurisdiction over the person of any defendant who is not subject to the jurisdiction of the courts of general jurisdiction of any state."

The Advisory Committee Notes to the 1993 Amendments to Rule 4 (k) (2) comment as follows:

> This paragraph corrects a gap in the enforcement of federal law. Under the former rule, a problem was presented when the defendant was a non-resident of the United States having contacts with the United States sufficient to justify the application of United States law and to satisfy federal standards of forum selection, but having insufficient contact with any single state to support jurisdiction under state long-arm legislation or meet the requirements of the Fourteenth Amendment limitation on state court territorial jurisdiction. In such cases, the defendant was shielded from the enforcement of federal law by the fortuity of a favorable limitation on the power of state courts, which was incorporated into the federal practice by the former rule. In this respect, the revision responds to the suggestion of the Supreme Court made in *Omni Capital Int'l v. Wolff.*

OMNI CAPITAL INT'L v. WOLFF

Supreme Court of the United States, 1987.
484 U.S. 97, 108 S.Ct. 404, 98 L.Ed.2d 415.

Omni argues that the jurisdictional limits that Art. III of the Constitution places on the federal courts relate to subject-matter jurisdiction only. In this view, although Art. III § 1 leaves it to Congress to "ordain and establish" inferior federal courts, the only limits on those courts, once established, in the exercise of personal jurisdiction, relate to due process. Thus, *Omni* contends, the District Court may exercise personal jurisdiction over Wolff and Gourlay if the Due Process Clause of the Fifth Amendment does not forbid it.

Omni's argument that Art. III does not itself limit a court's personal jurisdiction is correct. "The requirement that a court have personal jurisdiction flows not from Art. III, but from the Due Process Clause.... It represents a restriction on judicial power not as a matter of sovereignty, but as a matter of individual liberty." *Insurance Corp. of Ireland v. Compagnie des Bauxites de Guinee*, 456 U.S. 694, 702, 102 S.Ct. 2099, 2104, 72 L.Ed.2d 492 (1982). *Omni's* argument fails, however, because there are other prerequisites to a federal court's exercise of personal jurisdiction.

Before a federal court may exercise personal jurisdiction over a defendant, the procedural requirement of service of summons must be satisfied. "[S]ervice of summons is the procedure by which a court having venue and jurisdiction of the subject matter of the suit asserts jurisdiction over the person of the party served." *Mississippi Publishing*

Corp. v. Murphree, 326 U.S. 438, 444–445, 66 S.Ct. 242, 245–246, 90 L.Ed. 185 (1946). Thus, before a court may exercise personal jurisdiction over a defendant, there must be more than notice to the defendant and a constitutionally sufficient relationship between the defendant and the forum. There also must be a basis for the defendant's amenability to service of summons. Absent consent, this means there must be authorization for service of summons on the defendant. . . .

The dissenters in the Court of Appeals argued that even if authorization to serve process is necessary and cannot be found in Rule 4(e), the federal courts should act to fill the "interstices in the law inadvertently left by legislative enactment" by creating their own rule authorizing service of process in this litigation. We decline to embark on that adventure.

As an initial matter, it is unclear at this time whether it is open to us to fashion a rule authorizing service of process. At common law, a court lacked authority to issue process outside its district, and Congress made this same restriction the general rule when it enacted the Judiciary Act of Sept. 24, 1789, § 11, 1 Stat. 79. Thus, specific legislative authorization of extraterritorial service of summons was required for a court to exercise personal jurisdiction over a person outside the district. Even were we to conclude that the bases for the rule … are no longer valid, we would not necessarily have the power to create service-of-process rules. We would have to decide that the provisions of Rules 4(e) and 4(f), in authorizing service in certain circumstances, were not intended to prohibit service in all other circumstances. We would also have to find adequate authority for common-law rulemaking. We need not decide these questions, however, since we would not fashion a rule for service in this litigation even if we had the power to do so.

We would consider it unwise for a court to make its own rule authorizing service of summons. It seems likely that Congress has been acting on the assumption that federal courts cannot add to the scope of service of summons Congress has authorized. This Court in the past repeatedly has stated that a legislative grant of authority is necessary. Indeed, as the dissent in the Court of Appeals conceded, "the weight of authority, both in the cases and in the commentary," considers statutory authorization necessary to a federal court's service of summons.

The strength of this longstanding assumption, and the network of statutory enactments and judicial decisions tied to it, argue strongly against devising common-law service of process provisions at this late date for at least two reasons. First, since Congress concededly has the power to limit service of process, circumspection is called for in going beyond what Congress has authorized. Second, as statutes and rules have always provided the measures for service, courts are inappropriate forums for deciding whether to extend them. Legislative rulemaking better ensures proper consideration of a service rule's ramifications with the pre-existing structure and is more likely to lead to consistent application.

Nothing about this case impels us to a different conclusion. If we do not create a rule here, the only harm to federal interests is the inability of a private litigant to bring a CEA [Commodity Exchange Act] action in the United States against an alien defendant who is not within the reach of the state long-arm statute. Since the CEA authorizes broader service of process in other enforcement actions, aliens cannot consider themselves immune from the Act's provisions. Also, a British court may be willing to enforce the CEA itself, if *Omni* brings suit against Wolff and Gourlay there.

We are not blind to the consequences of the inability to serve process on Wolff and Gourlay. A narrowly tailored service of process provision, authorizing service on an alien in a federal-question case when the alien is not amenable to service under the applicable state long-arm statute, might well serve the ends of the CEA and other federal statutes. It is not for the federal courts, however, to create such a rule as a matter of common law. That responsibility, in our view, better rests with those who propose the Federal Rules of Civil Procedure and with Congress.

IV

In summary, the District Court may not exercise jurisdiction over Wolff and Gourlay without authorization to serve process. That authorization is not found in either the CEA or the Louisiana long-arm statute to which we look under Rule 4(e). We reject the suggestion that we should create a common-law rule authorizing service of process, since we would consider that action unwise, even were it within our power.

The judgment of the Court of Appeals is affirmed.

National Contacts Analysis

Courts employ various tests in evaluating due process under a national contacts examination. While applying similar due process standards as with a minimum contacts analysis, courts focus more on national interests in furthering the policies of the laws under which the party is suing.

PINKER v. ROCHE HOLDINGS LTD.

United States Court of Appeals, Third Circuit 2002.
292 F.3d 361.

[This case involved an action under the Federal Securities Act]...

In determining whether a court may exercise personal jurisdiction we examine the relationship among the defendant, the forum, and the litigation... Here, where the plaintiff's cause of action is related to or arises out of the defendant's contacts with the forum, the court is said to exercise specific jurisdiction... In federal court, the exercise of specific jurisdiction must satisfy the requirements of the Due Process Clause of the Fifth Amendment... In particular, specific jurisdiction may be exercised only when the defendant has constitutionally sufficient minimum contacts with the forum, and where subjecting the defendant to the court's jurisdiction comports with traditional notions of fair play and substantial justice . . .

In a case such as this, where the plaintiff's claim is based on a federal statute authorizing nationwide service of process, *see* Section 27 of the 1934 Securities Act, 15 U.S.C. § 78aa, this Court has suggested in dicta that the relevant forum for analyzing the extent of the defendant's contacts is the United States as a whole. For instance, we [have] recognized the constitutional validity of national contacts as a jurisdictional base where a statute provides for nationwide service of process or service wherever defendant is "doing business" or "may be found." We [have] considered the aggregation of the national contacts of an alien defendant neither unfair nor unreasonable under the Fifth Amendment in light of the fact that a federal court sits as a unit of the national government and, therefore, the territorial limitations that apply to the exercise of state court jurisdiction-or, for that matter, federal jurisdiction in diversity cases are inapposite.

Where Congress has spoken by authorizing nationwide service of process, therefore, as it has in the Securities Act, the jurisdiction of a federal court need not be confined by the defendant's contacts with the state in which the federal court sits. Following this reasoning, the district courts within this Circuit have repeatedly held that a national contacts analysis is appropriate when appraising personal jurisdiction in a case arising under a federal statute that contains a nationwide service of process provision. [citations omitted] An assessment of personal jurisdiction under a statutory provision authorizing nationwide service of process necessitates an inquiry into the defendant's contacts with the *national* forum. We too are persuaded by the reasoning of our prior opinions on the subject, and, consistent with several of our sister courts of appeals, hold that a federal court's personal jurisdiction may be assessed on the basis of the defendant's national contacts when the plaintiff's claim rests on a federal statute authorizing nationwide service of process [citations omitted].

We have reasoned that in assessing the sufficiency of a defendant's contacts with the forum, a court should look at the extent to which the defendant availed himself of the privileges of American law and the extent to which he could reasonably anticipate being involved in litigation in the United States. . . In assessing whether a commercial entity has availed itself of the privileges of a forum's laws, jurisdiction is proper if the defendant has taken action purposefully directed toward the forum State.

Once minimum contacts have been established, we assess whether the exercise of personal jurisdiction is consistent with traditional notions of fair play and substantial justice. In the context of state courts, the Supreme Court has stated that this inquiry requires evaluating the burden on the defendant, the forum State's interest in adjudicating the dispute, the plaintiff's interest in obtaining convenient and effective relief, the interstate judicial system's interest in obtaining the most effective resolution of controversies, and the shared interests of the several States in furthering fundamental substantive social policies. In the federal court context, the inquiry will be slightly different, taking less account of federalism concerns, and focusing more on the national interest in furthering the policies of the law(s) under which the plaintiff is suing.

FEDERAL RULES OF CIVIL PROCEDURE

Rule 4 of the Federal Rules of Civil Procedure sets forth the methods of service and other procedural requirements for the establishment of jurisdiction over foreign parties to litigation in U.S. courts. In order to determine the proper method of service, the proper source of federal jurisdiction must be ascertained. As previously stated, Rule 4(k) applies to cases based on federal question jurisdiction under 28 U.S.C. § 1331. This rule authorizes the use of federal long-arm jurisdiction in situations where defendants cannot be served under any state law but who can be constitutionally subjected to the jurisdiction of the federal court. Federal court jurisdiction may also be founded on diversity of citizenship pursuant to 28 U.S.C. § 1332. In these cases, Rules 4(e) and (h) provide that state law service rules apply to service upon individuals and corporations, both foreign and domestic, within a judicial district of the United States.

Rule 4(f) provides for alternative means of service upon individuals in a foreign country. Some courts have determined that the Hague Service Convention permits service by mail on defendants in countries that have not objected under Article 10(a). Other courts have additionally required affirmative authorization under Rule 4(f) for the service method chosen by plaintiff. In *Brockmeyer v. May,* the Ninth Circuit Court of Appeals examined Rule 4(f) and found that no provision authorized international service by ordinary mail without prior court approval. The Court of Appeals determined that without explicit authority under Rule 4(f), there was no basis for international mail service even though it found mail service to be permissible under Article 10(a).

BROCKMEYER v. MAY

United States Court of Appeals, Ninth Circuit, 2004.
383 F.3d 798.

Article 10(a) does not itself affirmatively authorize international mail service. It merely provides that the Convention "shall not interfere with" the "freedom" to use postal channels if the "State of destination" does not object to their use. As the Rapporteur for the Convention wrote in explaining Article 10(a), "It should be stressed that in permitting the utilization of postal channels, the draft convention did not intend to pass on the validity of this mode of transmission under the law of the forum state: *in order for the postal channel to be utilized, it is necessary that it be authorized by the law of the forum state.*" . . .

In other words, we must look outside the Hague Convention for affirmative authorization of the international mail service that is merely not forbidden by Article 10(a). Any affirmative authorization of service by international mail, and any requirements as to how that service is to be accomplished, must come from the law of the forum in which the suit is filed.

Federal Rule of Civil Procedure 4(h)(2) directs that service on a foreign corporation, if done outside of the United States, shall be effected "in any manner prescribed for individuals by subdivision [4](f) except personal delivery as provided in paragraph (2)(C)(1) thereof," unless a waiver of service has been obtained and filed. No waiver of service under Rule 4(d) was obtained in this case. To determine whether service of process was proper, we therefore look to Federal Rule of Civil Procedure 4(f). As will be seen, no part of Rule 4(f), authorizes service by ordinary international first class mail.

* * *

Because it is undisputed in this case that the plaintiffs neither effected service under the Hague Convention or other international agreement in accordance with Rule 4(f)(1), nor effected service by registered mail by the clerk of the court in accordance with the requirements of Rule 4(f)(2)(C)(ii), nor obtained a court order in accordance with Rule 4(f)(3), the only remaining section on which plaintiffs can conceivably rely is Rule 4(f)(2)(A). Rule 4(f)(2)(A)...affirmatively authorizes service by means used in the receiving country for service in an action in its courts of general jurisdiction. As we read Rule 4(f)(2)(A), such means do not include service by international mail... The district court held that service was proper because the United Kingdom provides service for domestic suits in that country by both ordinary and registered post. A number of factors counsel against reading Rule 4(f)(2)(A) to authorize service by international mail, however.

First, the common understanding of Rule 4(f)(2)(A) is that it is limited to personal service ... Another reason to read Rule 4(f)(2)(A) not to authorize service by international mail is the explicit mention of international registered mail in Rule 4(f)(2)(C)(ii), considered above, and the absence of any such mention in Rule 4(f)(2)(A)... A further reason to read Rule 4(f)(2)(A) not to authorize service on foreign defendants by international mail to England and, in particular, by ordinary international first class mail-is found in an exchange between the British government and the United States Department of State in 1991, in which the British objected to a ... proposal [which] eventually became what is now Rule 4(d), authorizing a plaintiff to request a waiver of service.

* * *

The objection of the British government to the proposed rule makes sense only if the British government understood Rule 4(f) not to permit service by ordinary, international first class mail against a defendant in

England. This is so because if Rule 4(f)(2)(A) had authorized service by international first class mail, a plaintiff would never need to send a request for waiver of service by international first class mail. The plaintiff would simply effect service by international first class mail.

* * *

[W]e hold that any service by mail in this case was required to be performed in accordance with the requirements of Rule 4(f). Service by international mail is affirmatively authorized by Rule 4(f)(2)(C)(ii), which requires that service by sent by the clerk of the court, using a form of mail requiring a signed receipt. Service by international mail is also affirmatively authorized by Rule 4(f)(3), which requires that the mailing procedure have been specifically directed by the district court. Service by international mail is not otherwise affirmatively authorized by Rule 4(f). Plaintiffs neither followed the procedure prescribed in Rule 4(f)(2)(C)(ii) nor sought the approval of the district court under Rule 4(f)(3). They simply dropped the complaint and summons in a mailbox in Los Angeles, to be delivered by ordinary, international first class mail. There is no affirmative authorization for such service in Rule 4(f). The attempted service was therefore ineffective, and the default judgment . . . cannot stand.

REVERSED AND REMANDED, with instructions to vacate the judgment.

PART C.   MULTILATERAL SERVICE CONVENTIONS

Multilateral agreements, such as the Hague Service Convention and the Inter–American Convention on Letters Rogatory and Additional Protocol thereto [both are included in the Documents Supplement] prescribe methods of service abroad of judicial documents in civil and commercial cases. The Hague Service Convention is the principal treaty in the area and has been the subject of considerable discussion and debate concerning its role in U.S. litigation. There are currently 44 signatories to the convention. Before proceeding with service in the foreign country, the party serving should determine whether the country involved is a signatory to the Hague Service Convention. The reservations and declarations of the country where service is to be made should be reviewed in order to determine the terms and conditions agreed on by that country. As previously discussed, in order to acquire valid personal jurisdiction over foreign parties "doing business" in the United States, there must be adherence to state "long arm" jurisdictional requirements. Use of state "long arm" statutes for service purposes may well implicate service of process requirements in international treaties, such as the Hague Service Convention. In this connection, Rule 4(f) of the Federal Rules of Civil Procedure, which sets forth alternative means of service upon individuals in a foreign country, provides for service of process "by any internationally agreed means" such as the Hague Service Convention.

The Hague Service Convention provides mandatory procedures for service of documents abroad. Thus, Article 1 provides that the convention "shall apply in all cases, in civil or commercial matters, where there is occasion to transmit a judicial or extrajudicial document for service abroad." Problem 3.4, which discusses issues arising in U.S. litigation when foreign-based evidence is to be obtained, discusses the exclusivity issue in connection with the Hague Evidence Convention, the multilateral treaty in the evidence area. The mandatory nature of the Hague Service Convention is in sharp contrast to the non-exclusive nature of the Hague Evidence Convention as interpreted by the Supreme Court in *Societe Nationale Industrielle Aerospatiale v. United States Dist. Court*, 482 U.S. 522, 107 S.Ct. 2542, 96 L.Ed.2d 461 (1987). In *Aerospatiale* the Court interpreted the Hague Evidence Convention as providing only optional methods for litigants to gather evidence from foreign nationals of signatory countries. The mandatory language of Article 1 of the Hague Service Convention applies whenever the service takes place within another nation's borders. The question arose in the *Schlunk* case, *infra,* as to the applicability of the Hague Service Convention where service is made pursuant to procedures under domestic and local law. In *Schlunk,* the Court held that the Hague Service Convention did not apply when process was served on the foreign corporation's "alter ego," which under state law was the foreign corporation's involuntary agent for service of process.

VOLKSWAGENWERK, A.G. v. SCHLUNK

Supreme Court of the United States, 1988.
486 U.S. 694, 108 S.Ct. 2104, 100 L.Ed.2d 722.

JUSTICE O'CONNOR delivered the opinion of the Court.

This case involves an attempt to serve process on a foreign corporation by serving its domestic subsidiary which, under state law, is the foreign corporation's involuntary agent for service of process. We must decide whether such service is compatible with the [Hague Service Convention].

I

The parents of respondent Herwig Schlunk were killed in an automobile accident in 1983. Schlunk filed a wrongful death action on their behalf in the Circuit Court of Cook County, Illinois. Schlunk alleged that Volkswagen of America, Inc. (VWoA), had designed and sold the automobile that his parents were driving, and that defects in the automobile caused or contributed to their deaths. Schlunk also alleged that the driver of the other automobile involved in the collision was negligent; Schlunk has since obtained a default judgment against that person, who is no longer a party to this lawsuit. Schlunk successfully served his complaint on VWoA, and VWoA filed an answer denying that it had designed or assembled the automobile in question. Schlunk then amended the complaint to add as a defendant Volkswagen Aktiengesellschaft

(VWAG), which is the petitioner here. VWAG, a corporation established under the laws of the Federal Republic of Germany, has its place of business in that country. VWoA is a wholly owned subsidiary of VWAG. Schlunk attempted to serve his amended complaint on VWAG by serving VWoA as VWAG's agent.

VWAG filed a special and limited appearance for the purpose of quashing service. VWAG asserted that it could be served only in accordance with the Hague Service Convention, and that Schlunk had not complied with the Convention's requirements. The Circuit Court denied VWAG's motion. It first observed that VWoA is registered to do business in Illinois and has a registered agent for receipt of process in Illinois. The court then reasoned that VWoA and VWAG are so closely related that VWoA is VWAG's agent for service of process as a matter of law, notwithstanding VWAG's failure or refusal to appoint VWoA formally as an agent. The court relied on the facts that VWoA is a wholly owned subsidiary of VWAG, that a majority of the members of the board of directors of VWoA are members of the board of VWAG, and that VWoA is by contract the exclusive importer and distributor of VWAG products sold in the United States. The court concluded that, because service was accomplished within the United States, the Hague Service Convention did not apply.

The Circuit Court certified two questions to the Appellate Court of Illinois. For reasons similar to those given by the Circuit Court, the Appellate Court determined that VWoA is VWAG's agent for service of process under Illinois law, and that the service of process in this case did not violate the Hague Service Convention. After the Supreme Court of Illinois denied VWAG leave to appeal, VWAG petitioned this Court for a writ of certiorari to review the Appellate Court's interpretation of the Hague Service Convention. We granted certiorari to address this issue, which has given rise to disagreement among the lower courts.

II

The Hague Service Convention is a multilateral treaty that was formulated in 1964 by the Tenth Session of the Hague Conference of Private International Law. The Convention revised parts of the Hague Conventions on Civil Procedure of 1905 and 1954. The revision was intended to provide a simpler way to serve process abroad, to assure that defendants sued in foreign jurisdictions would receive actual and timely notice of suit, and to facilitate proof of service abroad. Representatives of all 23 countries that were members of the Conference approved the Convention without reservation. Thirty-two countries, including the United States and the Federal Republic of Germany, have ratified or acceded to the Convention.

The primary innovation of the Convention is that it requires each state to establish a central authority to receive requests for service of documents from other countries. Once a central authority receives a request in the proper form, it must serve the documents by a method prescribed by the internal law of the receiving state or by a method designated by the requester and compatible with that law. The central authority must then provide a certificate of service that conforms to a specified model. A state also may consent to methods of service within its boundaries other than a request to its central authority. The remaining provisions of the Convention that are relevant here limit the circumstances in which a default judgment may be entered against a defendant who had to be served abroad and did not appear, and provide some means for relief from such a judgment.

Article 1 defines the scope of the Convention, which is the subject of controversy in this case. It says: "The present Convention shall apply in all cases, in civil or commercial matters, where there is occasion to transmit a judicial or extrajudicial document for service abroad." This language is mandatory, as we acknowledged last Term in *Societe Nationale Industrielle Aerospatiale v. United States District Court*, 482 U.S. 522, 534, n. 15 (1987). By virtue of the Supremacy Clause, U.S. Const., Art. VI, the Convention pre-empts inconsistent methods of service prescribed by state law in all cases to which it applies. *Schlunk* does not purport to have served his complaint on VWAG in accordance with the Convention. Therefore, if service of process in this case falls within Article 1 of the Convention, the trial court should have granted VWAG's motion to quash.

When interpreting a treaty, we "begin 'with the text of the treaty and the context in which the written words are used.'" *Societe Nationale, supra,* at 534 (*quoting Air France v. Saks*, 470 U.S. 392, 397 (1985)). Other general rules of construction may be brought to bear on difficult or ambiguous passages. "'Treaties are construed more liberally than private agreements, and to ascertain their meaning we may look beyond the written words to the history of the treaty, the negotiations, and the practical construction adopted by the parties.'" *Air France v. Saks, supra,* at 396.

The Convention does not specify the circumstances in which there is "occasion to transmit" a complaint "for service abroad." But at least the term "service of process" has a well-established technical meaning. Service of process refers to a formal delivery of documents that is legally sufficient to charge the defendant with notice of a pending action. The legal sufficiency of a formal delivery of documents must be measured against some standard. The Convention does not prescribe a standard, so we almost necessarily must refer to the internal law of the forum state. If the internal law of the forum state defines the applicable method of serving process as requiring the transmittal of documents abroad, then the Hague Service Convention applies.

The negotiating history supports our view that Article 1 refers to service of process in the technical sense. The committee that prepared the preliminary draft deliberately used a form of the term "notification" (formal notice), instead of the more neutral term "remise" (delivery), when it drafted Article 1. Then, in the course of the debates, the negotiators made the language even more exact. The preliminary draft of Article 1 said that the present Convention shall apply in all cases in which there are grounds *to transmit or to give formal notice of* a judicial or extrajudicial document in a civil or commercial matter to a person staying abroad. To be more precise, the delegates decided to add a form of the juridical term "signification" (service), which has a narrower meaning than "notification" in some countries, such as France, and the identical meaning in others, such as the United States. The delegates also criticized the language of the preliminary draft because it suggested that the Convention could apply to transmissions abroad that do not culminate in service. The final text of Article 1, eliminates this possibility and applies only to documents transmitted for service abroad. The final report (*Rapport Explicatif*) confirms that the Convention does not use more general terms, such as delivery or transmission, to define its scope because it applies only when there is both transmission of a document from the requesting state to the receiving state, and service upon the person for whom it is intended.

The negotiating history of the Convention also indicates that whether there is service abroad must be determined by reference to the law of the forum state. The preliminary draft said that the Convention would apply "where there are grounds" to transmit a judicial document to a person staying abroad. The committee that prepared the preliminary draft realized that this implied that the forum's internal law would govern whether service implicated the Convention. The reporter expressed regret about this solution because it would decrease the obligatory force of the Convention. Nevertheless, the delegates did not change the meaning of Article 1 in this respect.

The Yugoslavian delegate offered a proposal to amend Article 1 to make explicit that service abroad is defined according to the law of the state that is requesting service of process. The delegate from the Netherlands supported him. The German delegate approved of the proposal in principle, although he thought it would require a corresponding reference to the significance of the law of the state receiving the service of process, and that this full explanation would be too complicated. The President opined that there was a choice to be made between the phrase used by the preliminary draft, "where grounds exist," and the Yugoslavian proposal to modify it with the phrase, "according to the law of the requesting state." This prompted the Yugoslavian delegate to declare that the difference was immaterial, because the phrase "where grounds exist" necessarily refers to the law of the forum. The French delegate added that, in his view, the law of the forum in turn is equivalent to the law of the requesting state. At that point, the President recommended entrusting the problem to the drafting committee.

The drafting committee then composed the version of Article 1 that ultimately was adopted, which says that the Convention applies "where there is occasion" to transmit a judicial document for service abroad. After this revision, the reporter again explained that one must leave to the requesting state the task of defining when a document must be served abroad; that this solution was a consequence of the unavailability of an objective test; and that while it decreases the obligatory force of the Convention, it does provide clarity. The inference we draw from this history is that the Yugoslavian proposal was rejected because it was superfluous, not because it was inaccurate, and that "service abroad" has the same meaning in the final version of the Convention as it had in the preliminary draft.

VWAG protests that it is inconsistent with the purpose of the Convention to interpret it as applying only when the internal law of the forum requires service abroad. One of the two stated objectives of the Convention is "to create appropriate means to ensure that judicial and extrajudicial documents to be served abroad shall be brought to the notice of the addressee in sufficient time." 20 U.S.T., at 362. The Convention cannot assure adequate notice, VWAG argues, if the forum's internal law determines whether it applies. VWAG warns that countries could circumvent the Convention by defining methods of service of process that do not require transmission of documents abroad. Indeed, VWAG contends that one such method of service already exists and that it troubled the Conference: *notification au parquet*.

Notification au parquet permits service of process on a foreign defendant by the deposit of documents with a designated local official. Although the official generally is supposed to transmit the documents abroad to the defendant, the statute of limitations begins to run from the time that the official receives the documents, and there allegedly is no sanction for failure to transmit them. At the time of the 10th Conference, France, the Netherlands, Greece, Belgium, and Italy utilized some type of *notification au parquet*.

There is no question but that the Conference wanted to eliminate *notification au parquet*. It included in the Convention two provisions that address the problem. Article 15 says that a judgment may not be entered unless a foreign defendant received adequate and timely notice of the lawsuit. Article 16 provides means whereby a defendant who did not receive such notice may seek relief from a judgment that has become final. Like Article 1, however, Articles 15 and 16 apply only when documents must be transmitted abroad for the purpose of service. VWAG argues that, if this determination is made according to the internal law of the forum state, the Convention will fail to eliminate variants of *notification au parquet* that do not expressly require transmittal of documents to foreign defendants. Yet such methods of service of process are the least likely to provide a defendant with actual notice.

The parties make conflicting representations about whether foreign laws authorizing *notification au parquet* command the transmittal of documents for service abroad within the meaning of the Convention. The final report is itself somewhat equivocal. It says that, although the strict language of Article 1 might raise a question as to whether the Convention regulates *notification au parquet,* the understanding of the drafting Commission, based on the debates, is that the Convention would apply.

Although this statement might affect our decision as to whether the Convention applies to *notification au parquet,* an issue we do not resolve today, there is no comparable evidence in the negotiating history that the Convention was meant to apply to substituted service on a subsidiary like VWoA, which clearly does not require service abroad under the forum's internal law. Hence neither the language of the Convention nor the negotiating history contradicts our interpretation of the Convention, according to which the internal law of the forum is presumed to determine whether there is occasion for service abroad.

Nor are we persuaded that the general purposes of the Convention require a different conclusion. One important objective of the Convention is to provide means to facilitate service of process abroad. Thus the first stated purpose of the Convention is "to create" appropriate means for service abroad, and the second stated purpose is "to improve the organization of mutual judicial assistance for that purpose by simplifying and expediting the procedure." By requiring each state to establish a central authority to assist in the service of process, the Convention implements this enabling function. Nothing in our decision today interferes with this requirement.

VWAG correctly maintains that the Convention also aims to ensure that there will be adequate notice in cases in which there is occasion to serve process abroad. Thus compliance with the Convention is mandatory in all cases to which it applies, and Articles 15 and 16 provide an indirect sanction against those who ignore it. Our interpretation of the Convention does not necessarily advance this particular objective, inasmuch as it makes recourse to the Convention's means of service dependent on the forum's internal law. But we do not think that this country, or any other country, will draft its internal laws deliberately so as to circumvent the Convention in cases in which it would be appropriate to transmit judicial documents for service abroad. For example, there has been no question in this country of excepting foreign nationals from the protection of our Due Process Clause. Under that Clause, foreign nationals are assured of either personal service, which typically will require service abroad and trigger the Convention, or substituted service that provides "notice reasonably calculated, under all the circumstances, to apprise interested parties of the pendency of the action and afford them an opportunity to present their objections." *Mullane v. Central Hanover Bank & Trust Co.,* 339 U.S. 306, 314 (1950).

Furthermore, nothing that we say today prevents compliance with the Convention even when the internal law of the forum does not so require. The Convention provides simple and certain means by which to serve process on a foreign national. Those who eschew its procedures risk discovering that the forum's internal law required transmittal of documents for service abroad, and that the Convention therefore provided the exclusive means of valid service. In addition, parties that comply with the Convention ultimately may find it easier to enforce their judgments abroad. For these reasons, we anticipate that parties may resort to the Convention voluntarily, even in cases that fall outside the scope of its mandatory application.

III

In this case, the Illinois long-arm statute authorized Schlunk to serve VWAG by substituted service on VWoA, without sending documents to Germany. VWAG has not petitioned for review of the Illinois Appellate Court's holding that service was proper as a matter of Illinois law. VWAG contends, however, that service on VWAG was not complete until VWoA transmitted the complaint to VWAG in Germany. According to VWAG, this transmission constituted service abroad under the Hague Service Convention.

VWAG explains that, as a practical matter, VWoA was certain to transmit the complaint to Germany to notify VWAG of the litigation. Indeed, as a legal matter, the Due Process Clause requires every method of service to provide "notice reasonably calculated, under all the circumstances, to apprise interested parties of the pendency of the action and afford them an opportunity to present their objections." *Mullane v. Central Hanover Bank & Trust Co., supra*, at 314. VWAG argues that, because of this notice requirement, every case involving service on a foreign national will present an "occasion to transmit a judicial ... document for service abroad" within the meaning of Article 1. VWAG emphasizes that in this case, the Appellate Court upheld service only after determining that "the relationship between VWAG and VWoA is so close that it is certain that VWAG 'was fully apprised of the pendency of the action' by delivery of the summons to VWoA."

We reject this argument. Where service on a domestic agent is valid and complete under both state law and the Due Process Clause, our inquiry ends and the Convention has no further implications. Whatever internal, private communications take place between the agent and a foreign principal are beyond the concerns of this case. The only transmittal to which the Convention applies is a transmittal abroad that is required as a necessary part of service. And, contrary to VWAG's assertion, the Due Process Clause does not require an official transmittal of documents abroad every time there is service on a foreign national. Applying this analysis, we conclude that this case does not present an occasion to transmit a judicial document for service abroad within the meaning of Article 1. Therefore the Hague Service Convention does not apply, and service was proper. The judgment of the Appellate Court is *Affirmed*.

. . .

Comment on Service by Mail Under the Hague Service Convention

Article 10 includes the authority to serve persons abroad directly by mail. Many member states, however, have made declarations or reservations prohibiting service by mail in their jurisdictions. Courts have been divided over whether the word "send" in article 10 (a) was intended to mean "service". This problem became particularly acute with respect to service by mail under the Hague Service Convention in Japan. The *Bankston v. Toyota Motor Corp.* case below represents one line of authority which found that Article 10, at least with respect to Japan, was not intended to authorize the use of mail as an effective means of service. Other courts have concluded that the word "send" in Article 10(a) was intended to mean "service" and the use of "send" was attributable to "careless drafting." Lower courts continue to be divided over the Article 10 issue reaching conflicting rulings as to the validity of service by mail even as to the same country. This issue raises the risk of using service procedures which may not be recognized in the foreign country.

BANKSTON v. TOYOTA MOTOR CORP.

United States Court of Appeals, Eighth Circuit, 1989.
889 F.2d 172.

The crucial article for this discussion is Article 10, under which appellants herein purportedly attempted to serve process upon Toyota by registered mail. Article 10 provides in relevant part:

Provided the State of destination does not object, the present Convention shall not interfere

with—

(a) the freedom to send judicial documents, by postal channels, directly to persons abroad,

(b) the freedom of judicial officers, officials or other competent persons of the State of origin to effect service of judicial documents directly through the judicial officers, officials or other competent persons of the State of destination,

(c) the freedom of any person interested in a judicial proceeding to effect service of judicial documents directly through the judicial officers, officials or other competent persons of the State of destination.

Japan has objected to subparagraphs (b) and (c), but not to subparagraph (a). The issue before this court is whether subparagraph (a) permits service on a Japanese defendant by direct mail.

In recent years, two distinct lines of Article 10(a) interpretation have arisen. Some courts have ruled that Article 10(a) permits service of process by mail directly to the defendant without the necessity of resorting to the central authority, and without the necessity of translating the documents into the official language of the nation where the documents are to be served.

In general, these courts reason that since the purported purpose of the Hague Convention is to facilitate service abroad, the reference to " 'the freedom to send judicial documents by postal channels, directly to persons abroad' would be superfluous unless it was related to the sending of such documents for the propose of service." *Ackermann v. Levine*, 788 F.2d 830, 839 (2d Cir.1986). These courts have further found that the use of the "send" rather than "service" in Article 10(a) "must be attributed to careless drafting."

The second line of interpretation, advocated by Toyota, is that the word "send" in Article 10(a) is not the equivalent of "service of process." The word "service" is specifically used in other sections of the Convention, including subsections (b) and (c) of Article 10. If the drafters of the Convention had meant for subparagraph (a) to provide an additional manner of service of judicial documents, they would have used the word "service." Subscribers to this interpretation maintain that Article 10(a) merely provides a method of sending subsequent documents after service of process has been obtained by means of the central authority.

We find this second line of authority to be more persuasive. It is a "familiar canon of statutory construction that the starting point for interpreting a statute is the language of the statute itself. Absent a clearly expressed legislative intention to the contrary, that language must ordinarily be regarded as conclusive." *Consumer Prod. Safety Comm'n v. GTE Sylvania, Inc.*, 447 U.S. 102, 108, 100 S.Ct. 2051, 2056, 64 L.Ed.2d 766 (1980). In addition, where a legislative body "includes particular language in one section of a statute but omits it in another section of the same Act, it is generally presumed that [the legislative body] acts intentionally and purposely in the disparate inclusion or exclusion." *Russello v. United States*, 464 U.S. 16, 23, 104 S.Ct. 296, 300, 78 L.Ed.2d 17 (1983). In *Suzuki Motor Co. v. Superior Court*, 249 Cal.Rptr. at 379, the court found that because service of process by registered mail was not permitted under Japanese law, it was "extremely unlikely" that Japan's failure to object to Article 10(a) was intended to authorize the use of registered mail as an effective mode of service of process, particularly in light of the fact that Japan had specifically objected to the much more formal modes of service by Japanese officials which were available in Article 10(b) and (c).

We conclude that sending a copy of a summons and complaint by registered mail to a defendant in a foreign country is not a method of service of process permitted by the Hague [Service] Convention. We affirm the judgment of the district court and remand this case with directions that appellants be given a reasonable time from the date of this Order in which to effectuate service of process over appellee Toyota Motor Corporation in compliance with the terms of the Hague [Service] Convention.

JOHN R. GIBSON, CIRCUIT JUDGE, concurring:

I concur in the court's opinion today in every respect. The court correctly interprets the Hague Convention. I write separately only to express nagging concerns I have about the practical effect of our opinion. Automobiles are subject to a plethora of regulations requiring particular equipment and detailed warnings. Should an automobile manufactured in Japan carry a disclosure that, if litigation ensures from its purchase and use, service of process on the Japanese manufacturer can only be obtained under the Hague Convention? Should the purchaser also be informed that this special service of process will cost $800 to $900, as we are told, and must include a translation of the suit papers in Japanese? These decisions we must leave to others. I write only to express my discomfort with the practical effect of Toyota's insistence on strict compliance with the letter of the Hague Convention. C.A. 8 (Ark.) 1989.

Questions and Comments

1. The service of process contemplated in this Problem on the German manufacturing company officer traveling to the United States is referred to as "tag jurisdiction." Under U.S. practice service of process on an individual defendant while he or she is physically within the forum state can provide an adequate basis of general jurisdiction, even if his or her presence is transitory. *See Burnham v. Super. Ct. of Cal.,* 495 U.S. 604, 110 S.Ct. 2105, 109 L.Ed.2d 631 (1990). It is debatable whether "tag jurisdiction" constitutes an acceptable basis of jurisdiction as applied to service on foreign corporations. *See MBM Fisheries v. Bollinger Mach. Shop & Shipyard, Inc.,* 60 Wash.App. 414, 804 P.2d 627 (1991). *But see, American–European Art Assoc., Inc. v. Moquay,* 1995 WL 317321 (S.D.N.Y.1995). This procedure would undoubtedly be rejected by foreign courts as a proper basis of personal jurisdiction under concepts of foreign judicial sovereignty and foreign jurisprudence. This is significant should enforcement be sought abroad of a judgment.

2. If the foreign country is a signatory to the Hague Service Convention, the party serving should study the declarations and reservations agreed to by that country in order to determine the proper method of service. Under the convention, Germany has not agreed to the use of service by mail pursuant to Article 10 and has imposed a translation requirement pursuant to Article 5. Germany is one of the civil law countries that regards service of process and obtaining evidence as an exercise of its judicial sovereignty. Under these circumstances, would it be a wise course of action for plaintiffs to consider abbreviated service procedures? Would your response be different if the defendant German manufacturer had an "alter ego" company doing business in the State of New Jersey? Neither Canada nor the United Kingdom have taken any declarations or reservations under Article 10. What would be the most effective argument to challenge service by mail to either one of these countries? Note that Article 19 of the Convention provides that "[t]o the extent that the internal law of a contracting State permits methods of transmission, other than those provided for in the preceding articles, of documents coming from abroad, for service within its territory, the present Convention shall not affect such provisions." Does this provision shift the burden to the plaintiff to require that the service method chosen be explicitly authorized by the foreign forum?

3. In the action for contribution and indemnity in Problem 3.1–1, the German manufacturing company seeks service on the Canadian tire maker under the "waiver of summons" procedures in Rule 4(d). The Advisory Committee Notes to the 1993 Amendment to Rule 4(d) comment as follows: "The aims of the provision are to eliminate the costs of service of a summons

on many parties and to foster cooperation among adversaries and counsel. The rule operates to impose upon the defendant those costs that could have been avoided if the defendant had cooperated reasonably in the manner prescribed. This device is useful in dealing with defendants who are furtive, who resided in places not easily reached by process servers, or who are outside the United States and can be served only at substantial and unnecessary expense. Illustratively, there is no useful purpose achieved by requiring a plaintiff to comply with all formalities of service in a foreign country, including costs of translation, when suing a defendant manufacturer, fluent in English, whose products are widely distributed in the United States." Under the facts presented, suppose the defendant Canadian tire maker refuses to acknowledge service under the Rule 4(d) procedures. Given foreign sensitivities in the area of international judicial assistance, does "waiver of summons" under Rule 4(d) constitute effective service on foreign parties? Where "waiver" procedures are used, does the foreign party have a good defense if enforcement of the U.S. judgment is sought abroad?

4.   Is it ever prudent to bypass Hague Service Convention procedures to save costs and avoid delays? Are there situations where abbreviated or questionable methods might be justified? Suppose the U.S. court is anxious to move the case forward and the certificate of service has not yet been returned by the foreign central authority. Is defendant warranted in seeking dismissal of the case for lack of personal jurisdiction? Rule 4(m) of the Federal Rules of Civil Procedure does not apply to service abroad the 120 day time limit for domestic service.

5.   In *Schlunk* the Supreme Court affirmed the mandatory nature of the Hague Service Convention "when it applies." Under the facts in *Schlunk*, exceptions to its application may exist under state law, such as, for example, when process is served on the foreign corporation's "alter ego," which under state law was the foreign corporation's involuntary agent for service of process. This Problem states that plaintiffs seek, as an alternate means, to serve the defendant German automobile manufacturer through its subsidiary marketing agent under the New Jersey long-arm statute for substituted service. Rule 4:4–4 (a) (6) of the New Jersey statute provides for service on a corporate defendant in the state via service on its general or specially designated agent, "provided, however, that a foreign corporation may be served only as herein prescribed subject to due process of law." How far should the *Schlunk* exception be applied for the domestic subsidiary to be an agent for service purposes?

6.   The service by mail issue has given rise to a related issue under substituted service provisions under state law. Under the laws of many states, substituted or constructive service on non-resident corporations is to be made upon certain local officials, usually the state Secretary of State. Under these provisions, this official is usually required to transmit the papers abroad in order to complete service of process unless the service is deemed to be complete when made on that official. Would the re-transmission of the service documents implicate the provisions of the Hague Service Convention if the foreign country is a signatory to the convention?

7.   Where would a party requesting service in a case filed in U.S. court look for information on service of process in foreign countries. Whether or

not service is made pursuant to local procedure or treaty, the litigant will need to know the laws and procedures of the foreign country involved. In ascertaining foreign laws on this subject, the party-plaintiff can contact the Office of American Citizens Services of the Department of State and the Office of International Judicial Assistance which is a part of the Civil Division of the Department of Justice.

8. Rule 4(f)(3) is a catch-all provision enabling courts to devise alternate methods of service not prohibited by international agreement, which are responsive to the unique facts of the case. Plaintiffs are required to obtain prior court approval for the alternative methods of serving process. Courts have authorized a variety of methods under Rule 4(f)(3) including not only ordinary mail and e-mail but also publication and telex. Is a service of process issue created when service effected by court-directed means violates foreign law?

9. Federal venue provisions may affect the determination of jurisdiction over foreign parties under a national contacts analysis. In *In re Automotive Refinishing Paint Antitrust Litigation,* 358 F.3d 288, 296–298 (3d Cir.2004), the Third Circuit Court of Appeals decided that satisfaction of the Clayton Act's nationwide service provision with respect to foreign parties was sufficient to establish personal jurisdiction independent of any assessment under the Act's special venue provision. However, other courts have determined that the exercise of personal jurisdiction under a national contacts analysis is dependent on satisfaction of federal venue provisions. *See GTE New Media Services, Inc. v. BellSouth Corp.,* 199 F.3d 1343 (D.C. Cir. 2000); *Daniel v. American Board of Emergency Medicine,* 428 F.3d 408 (2d Cir. 2005).

PROBLEM 3.5   DEPOSITIONS AND DISCOVERY IN CANADA, GERMANY AND ENGLAND

SECTION I.   THE SETTING

The litigation described in these problems involves a product liability suit in the United States District Court against CANTIRE, Ltd., the Canadian tire maker company and DROF, AG, the SUV manufacturer in Germany, and DROF–UK, PLC, the auto parts provider, in the UK. The various defendants named in the United States litigation are fearful in general about American pretrial discovery with which they have had little experience or exposure.

The U.S. and UK plaintiffs seek discovery in connection with the U.S. action. They wish to stipulate pursuant to Rule 29 of the Federal Rules of Civil Procedure to obtaining discovery against the foreign defendants. The various defendants who are contesting personal jurisdiction of the U.S. courts over them do not wish to stipulate to a discovery plan while their motion to dismiss is pending and, in any event, have raised various objections to the discovery proceeding under the U.S. pretrial system. They allege that obtaining foreign evidence should be governed by the Hague Evidence Convention and/or the laws and procedures of their country and not by U.S. procedures. The German defendant contends that producing documents relating to the manufacture of the automobile would violate Article 23 of the Hague Evidence Convention which restricts the pretrial production of documents as well as German law relating to trade secrets.

As to the German car manufacturer, the U.S. and UK plaintiffs seek depositions from current and former employees and officials of the company on German soil as to certain elements of manufactured components of the automobile. Plaintiffs also seek documents concerning production of the automobile which are located at the plant headquarters in Germany. They also seek to depose a German scientist, who has conducted studies as to the safety of the automobile and who may be useful as an expert witness. Similar depositions are sought from current and former employees from the UK automobile manufacturer who are located in the UK and from employees of the defendant tire manufacturer in Canada. Plaintiffs' attorneys are also considering depositions via telephone pursuant to Rule 39(b)(7) of the Federal Rules of Civil Procedure. If plaintiffs' attorneys have to travel to other countries to take the depositions, they would like to add to the stipulation that the depositions be video-taped for future use in the U.S. proceeding.

Defendants have consulted with their U.S. lawyers as well as counsel in their own countries. They have formulated a number of objections to plaintiffs' proposed discovery plan which will be raised in the discovery conference which has been scheduled pursuant to Rule 26(f) of the Federal Rules of Civil Procedure. If no agreement can be reached, defendants are considering filing a motion for a protective order pursuant to Rule 26(c) objecting to plaintiffs' discovery. In advising your client, you may act either as counsel for one or more of the plaintiffs to the U.S. action, or as counsel for any of the foreign defendant companies.

SECTION II.   FOCUS OF CONSIDERATION

The issues in this problem explore options and procedures for obtaining foreign-based evidence for use in U.S. courts. Parties seeking foreign-based evidence tend to rely on the broad range of discovery available under U.S. state and federal rules. Are there special rules which govern foreign evidence gathering? In exploring this issue, we need to consider a number of factors. Obtaining foreign evidence provides an interesting contrast to the problems previously considered in Problem 3.4 in connection with service of process. As with service of process, the procedural variations for obtaining evidence between the U.S. legal system and civil law systems are considerable. It is important to remember that U.S. pretrial discovery practice is unique and has no counterpart under other legal systems—even in other common law countries. Similar to the service of process area, which is governed by the Hague Service Convention, there is one multilateral treaty—the Hague Evidence Convention—which dominates the playing field. Unlike the Hague Service Convention, however, the evidence convention is not exclusive and only supplements state and federal rules concerning the production of evidence. Does this mean that U.S. courts will not accommodate foreign interests and apply special rules and procedures? Not necessarily. We need to also examine the type of evidence requests and special discovery issues which may give rise to valid defenses and application of foreign law and procedures.

Portions of the Hague Evidence Convention are essential for an understanding of this Problem. They are included in the Documents Supplement.

SECTION III. READINGS, QUESTIONS AND COMMENTS

PART A. FOREIGN ATTITUDES AND PROCEDURES

Confronted with broad U.S. discovery requests, foreign parties often raise defenses under applicable treaties and pursuant to procedural requirements under foreign law. In seeking to obtain evidence in foreign countries, it is important for U.S. attorneys to be aware of foreign law restrictions in this area as well as the consequences of conducting unauthorized acts on foreign soil. In this connection, the French "blocking" statute, (Art. 1A of the French Penal Code No. 80–538) provides in France that "subject to treaties or international agreements and applicable laws and regulations, it is prohibited for any party to request, seek or disclose, in writing, orally or otherwise, economic, commercial, industrial, financial or technical documents or information leading to the constitution of evidence with a view to foreign judicial or administrative proceedings or in connection therewith." Article 273 of the Swiss Criminal Code criminalizes the act of revealing Swiss manufacturing or business secrets to a public or private foreign authority or its agent.

DAVID EPSTEIN, JEFFREY L. SNYDER & CHARLES S. BALDWIN IV, INTERNATIONAL LITIGATION

Transnational Publishers, 3d ed. 2003.

A United States court may order a foreign national, subject to the court's jurisdiction, to produce evidence located abroad. However, such orders may conflict with different notions of gathering evidence in foreign nations. The evidentiary procedures of most civil law countries restrict a litigant's authority to collect evidence. This is totally different from procedures for gathering evidence in common law countries such as the United States, where discovery is largely in the hands of the parties and not the courts.

In civil law countries, the gathering of evidence by the courts is described as an exercise of "judicial sovereignty." Consequently, if a foreign person attempts to perform the act of obtaining evidence in a civil law country, it may be unauthorized, unless the governmental authorities participate or give their consent. For example, foreign attorneys attempting to secure a deposition or examine property in a civil law country might violate penal proscriptions of that country. This would be true, for example, under certain laws of France and Switzerland. This would also include unauthorized interviews of witnesses on foreign territory. In addition, many civil law countries object to a foreigner's taking evidence from a willing witness unless the proceeding takes place before a foreign consul authorized to take evidence. America lawyers should carefully examine the effect of foreign criminal law when engaging in extraterritorial discovery.

Certain U.S. discovery procedures are not commonly accepted in civil law countries. In this connection, the scope of United States discovery orders is unparalleled even in comparison with other common law jurisdictions such as the United Kingdom. The standard of relevance under Rule 26 of the Federal Rules of Civil Procedure is broad and permits discovery that is "reasonably calculated to lead to the discovery of admissible evidence." Thus, the use of pretrial discovery allows discovery of documents and other evidence that may not necessarily be used at trial. Also, the evidence-gathering in this country is conducted by the parties themselves, rather than the court.

Civil law countries have shown a wide-spread misunderstanding of the term "pretrial" discovery and the U.S. discovery system in general. This stems from confusion as to whether "pretrial" means "prior to the institution of suit" and the meaning of that term as used in the Hague Evidence Convention. Likewise, other countries, including English Commonwealth jurisdictions, object to "fishing expeditions," and the production of unlimited numbers of documents.

There is notable hostility in civil law countries to U.S. pretrial discovery of documents. In this connection, Article 23 of the Hague Evidence Convention permits a contracting state to declare that it will not execute a letter of request issued "for the purpose of obtaining pretrial discovery of documents as known in Common Law countries." Most of the signatory states to the Hague Evidence Convention have executed declarations under Article 23 of the Convention restricting, in whole or in part, pretrial discovery of documents.[1]

Countries that have made no declaration under Article 23 include: Barbados, the Czech Republic, Israel, the Slovak Republic and the United States. Others have made "limited" reservations where the documents sought have been specifically identified in the request. These include China, Cyprus, Estonia, Finland, France, Mexico, the Netherlands, Norway, Singapore, and the United Kingdom. The Article 23 reservations of Argentina, Australia, Denmark, Germany, Italy, Luxembourg, Monaco, Poland, Portugal, South Africa, Spain, and Sweden state that these countries will not execute letters of request for pretrial discovery purposes.

PART B.   GATHERING EVIDENCE IN CIVIL LAW COUNTRIES

When compulsory evidence is obtained in a foreign country, the laws and procedures of the host country control. Thus, even when discovery is

---

1. David Epstein, *Obtaining Evidence from Foreign Parties*, Course Handbook on   International Business Litigation & Arbitration 281 (PLI 2003).

permitted to proceed in a civil law country, the scope and type of evidence normally expected from an American-style deposition might be restricted due to the applicable foreign procedures. In civil-law countries, the searching out of evidence for use at trial is generally a function of the judge and not the parties. It is the judge who has the initial authority to determine the witnesses to question, the questions to ask, and the documents to be produced. Moreover, the judge would have the absolute discretion to control the scope of oral examination and the extent of discovery.

Ordinarily, a U.S. attorney will not be permitted to participate in such a proceeding. An attorney in the host country may attend the proceeding but full participation of counsel might not be allowed. For example, Germany permits attorneys to attend depositions and engage in cross-examination of a witness "under the control of the requested judge." The judge usually questions the witness and there is no oath-taking requirement. In some cases, the judge may permit the foreign attorney to put additional questions to the witness.

In addition, many civil law countries do not utilize the services of court reporters or provide verbatim transcripts. The presiding judge may dictate his recollection of witnesses' responses in summary form. The foreign state's procedures might also limit or foreclose cross-examination. The scope of foreign privilege might also prove to be broader under the letter of request procedure than under U.S. law. Finally, in some cases, official translations might be required for each piece of paper involved. This could add considerable cost to the litigants employing such procedures.[2]

PART C. HAGUE EVIDENCE CONVENTION

The Hague Evidence Convention on the Taking of Evidence Abroad in Civil or Commercial Matters,[3] is a multilateral treaty which prescribes methods of obtaining evidence abroad in civil and commercial transnational disputes. It is intended to alleviate the procedural obstacles encountered when litigants seek evidence in a foreign country that has a different legal system and evidence-gathering methods. The Convention, which was ratified by the United States, is in force between the United States and approximately 40 countries. The Convention is intended to encourage evidence-gathering methods that are both "tolerable" in the state of execution and "utilizable" in the forum of the state of origin where the action is pending.

The text of the convention provides as follows:

The States signatory to the present Convention,

Desiring to facilitate the transmission and execution of Letters of Request and to further the accommodation of the different methods which they use for this purpose.

---

2. *Id.* at 282.   **3.** 23 U.S.T. 2555.

Desiring to improve mutual judicial co-operation in civil or commercial matters.

Have resolved to conclude a Convention to this effect and have agreed upon the following provisions.

GENIRA TRADE & FINANCE INC. v. REFCO CAPITAL MARKETS LTD.

UK Court of Appeal (Civil Division 2001).

Once again time and money is being spent in the English courts over Letters Rogatory requesting the English court to order the production of documents and oral deposition from third parties to litigation in the United States of America. That time and money would be unnecessary, if those seeking the request from the United States Court appreciated the differences between the attitude of the United States Courts to the making of discovery orders against nonparties, and the attitude of the English court to the making of such orders. The United Kingdom, when becoming parties to the Hague convention concluded in 1970, registered a reservation pursuant to Article 23 which became enshrined in the Evidence (Proceedings in Other Jurisdictions) Act 1975 making it clear that discovery against non-parties was something the English court would not provide because it simply was not part of its procedure. It is only that Act which gives the English Court the jurisdiction to make orders to assist foreign courts. A number of authorities of the House of Lords since the coming into force of that Act have emphasized the position. But still much time is taken up in our courts trying to give effect to Letters of Request, problems in relation to which could have been avoided if proper steps had been taken to bring to the attention of the foreign court the constraints under which the English court operates. . . .

The Relevant Provisions of the Act.

(1) Subject to the provisions of this section, the High Court, the Court of Session and the High Court of Justice in Northern Ireland shall each have power, on any such application as is mentioned in section 1 above, by order to make such provision for obtaining evidence in the part of the United Kingdom in which it exercises jurisdiction as may appear to the court to be appropriate for the purpose of giving effect to the request in pursuance of which the application is made; and any such order may require a person specified therein to take such steps as the court may consider appropriate for that purpose.

* * *

(3) An order under this section shall not require any particular steps to be taken unless they are steps which can be required to be taken by way of obtaining evidence for the purpose of civil proceedings in the court making the order (whether or not proceedings of the same description as those to which the application for the order relates); but this

subsection shall not preclude the making of an order requiring a person to give testimony (either orally or in writing) otherwise than on oath where this is asked for by the requiring court.

(4) An order under this section shall not require a person

(a) to state what documents relevant to the proceedings to which the application for the order relates are or have been in his possession, custody or power; or

(b) to produce any documents other than particular documents specified in the order as being documents appearing to the court making the order to be, or to be likely to be, in his possession, custody or power.

THE PRINCIPLES

The first principle is of course that we should afford foreign courts all the assistance we can [sic] in Lord Dennings often quoted phrase [sic] It is the duty and the pleasure of the English courts to do all it can to assist the foreign court, just as it would expect the foreign court to help it in like circumstances. (see *Lord Denning MR in RTZ v Westinghouse* [1978] A.C. 547 at 560).

Second, the jurisdiction to make the order is statutory. Such an order shall not require any particular steps to be taken unless they are steps which can be required to be taken by way of obtaining evidence for the purposes of civil proceedings in the English court (section 2(3)). It is that provision which precludes the English court from making orders for the taking of oral depositions from a non-party simply as part of the discovery exercise which takes place under the United States procedure (see *Lord Diplock in RTZ v Westinghouse* at p.634). The position is clearer still so far as documents are concerned. (see section 2(4) above).

Third, the fact that Letters of Request may have been issued for the purpose of obtaining discovery or pre-trial depositions which fall foul of the above does not mean that the English court has no jurisdiction to attempt to give effect to the same (see most recently *Golden Eagle Refinery v Associated International Insurance COT 19th February 1998*). The court, so far as documents are concerned, can by application of the blue pencil identify particular documents, and so far as oral testimony is concerned make it subject to terms that for example the examination of witnesses shall be for the purpose only of eliciting and recording testimony appropriate to be given at trial and that no question may be asked of the witness that in the opinion of the examiner is not a question of the nature that could properly be asked by counsel examining a witness-in-chief at a trial before the High Court of England and Wales. Those were the terms on the basis of which the Court of Appeal in the *Golden Eagle* Case upheld the orders for examination of witnesses.

REASONS FOR REFUSING PERMISSION

There cannot be any doubt that the Letters of Request originally issued were for pre-trial discovery both so far as documents were concerned and so far as taking depositions from the witnesses were concerned.

It is extremely doubtful whether the attempt by Refco to salvage the position, so far as the documents were concerned, by requesting a different schedule of documents was permissible. A request to the court in effect to substitute such a schedule now compendious as far as all witnesses were concerned and taking the place of four extensive exhibits by operation of the blue-pencil technique would seem to us extremely difficult. We were indeed quite unconvinced by Mr Steinfelds attempts to demonstrate that on examination of the exhibits the court could somehow spell out a request for the particular classes of documents now described in the new schedule.

It would be quite impossible to attempt some further blue-pencil exercise to try and identify exact documents because there is no evidence to identify particular documents as existing, and indeed no suggestion was made that the English court should do so. We were informed, it is fair to say, of one draft document which had been identified by RM in his deposition in New York, which the Banks had searched for and which they could not find. It would appear that Refco will obtain this document in any event from RM pursuant to the settlement reached.

Finally, in any event, the request is not simply to take evidence about the fees or commission charged on a particular business with which the action is concerned. The request is in very broad form. We do not think it should be the function of this court to redraft Letters of Request where there are serious doubts about the admissibility of the evidence. That is particularly so where it does not appear that the New York court has considered precisely what evidence is being sought for the trial, or its likely weight if it were obtained.

Accordingly this is a case where it seems to us clear that the order so far as the Banks were concerned was rightly set aside by the judge. This is a case where if further Letters of Request are to be made they should only be made after further consideration by the New York court.

––––––

Does the Hague Evidence Convention operate exclusive of domestic law procedures, such as state or federal rules, or is it optional? The "exclusivity" issue was resolved by the Supreme Court in *Societe Nationale Industrielle Aerospatiale v. United States Dist. Court*, 482 U.S. 522 (1987). The Court rejected any interpretation of the Convention as exclusive. The Court concluded that the Convention was intended as a permissive supplement and not a mandatory replacement for other means of obtaining evidence located abroad, such as state or federal rules of civil procedure. Nor did the Court adopt any "first use" of convention procedures whenever discovery was sought from a foreign litigant. Moreover, the Court declined to articulate any specific comity test on use of convention procedures other than proposing that there be "prior scrutiny in each case of the particular facts, sovereign interests, and likelihood that resort to those procedures will prove effective." The concurring opinion recognized a general presumption requiring that courts resort first to the convention, unless utilization of the convention would be futile or unhelpful. The concurring opinion suggested that in attempting to reconcile a conflict between domestic and foreign law, a court "should perform a tripartite analyses that considers the foreign interests, the interests of the United States, and the mutual interests of all nations in a smoothly functioning international legal regime." The absence of any fixed comity criteria in the majority opinion has provided little guidance to lower courts in how to reconcile conflicts between domestic and foreign law in this area. As a result, the majority of lower courts have simply applied applicable state or federal rules and avoided use of convention procedures, even on a "first use" basis.

SOCIETE NATIONALE INDUSTRIELLE AEROSPATIALE v. UNITED STATES DISTRICT COURT

Supreme Court of the United States, 1987.
482 U.S. 522, 107 S.Ct. 2542, 96 L.Ed.2d 461.

JUSTICE STEVENS delivered the opinion of the Court.

The United States, the Republic of France, and 15 other Nations have acceded to the Hague Convention on the Taking of Evidence Abroad in Civil or Commercial Matters, opened for signature, Mar. 18, 1970, 23 U.S.T. 2555, T.I.A.S. No. 7444. This Convention—sometimes referred to as the "Hague Convention" or the "Evidence Convention"—prescribes certain procedures by which a judicial authority in one contracting state may request evidence located in another contracting state. The question presented in this case concerns the extent to which a federal district court must employ the procedures set forth in the Convention when litigants seek answers to interrogatories, the production of documents, and admissions from a French adversary over whom the court has personal jurisdiction.

The two petitioners are corporations owned by the Republic of France. They are engaged in the business of designing, manufacturing, and marketing aircraft. One of their planes, the "Rallye," was allegedly advertised in American aviation publications as "the World's safest and most economical STOL plane." On August 19, 1980, a Rallye crashed in Iowa, injuring the pilot and a passenger. Dennis Jones, John George, and Rosa George brought separate suits based upon this accident in the United States District Court for the Southern District of Iowa, alleging that petitioners had manufactured and sold a defective plane and that they were guilty of negligence and breach of warranty. Petitioners answered the complaints, apparently without questioning the jurisdiction of the District Court. With the parties' consent, the cases were consolidated and referred to a Magistrate. See 28 U.S.C. § 636(c)(1).

Initial discovery was conducted by both sides pursuant to the Federal Rules of Civil Procedure without objection. When plaintiffs served a second request for the production of documents pursuant to Rule 34, a set of interrogatories pursuant to Rule 33, and requests for admission pursuant to Rule 36, however, petitioners filed a motion for a protective order. The motion alleged that because petitioners are "French corporations, and the discovery sought can only be found in a foreign state, namely France," the Hague Convention dictated the exclusive procedures that must be followed for pretrial discovery. In addition, the motion stated that under French penal law, the petitioners could not respond to discovery requests that did not comply with the Convention.

The Magistrate denied the motion insofar as it related to answering interrogatories, producing documents, and making admissions. After reviewing the relevant cases, the Magistrate explained:

> To permit the Hague Evidence Convention to override the Federal Rules of Civil Procedure would frustrate the courts' interests, which particularly arise in products liability cases, in protecting United States citizens from harmful products and in compensating them for injuries arising from use of such products.

In the District Court and the Court of Appeals, petitioners contended that the Hague Evidence Convention "provides the exclusive and mandatory procedures for obtaining documents and information located within the territory of a foreign signatory." We are satisfied that the Court of Appeals correctly rejected this extreme position. We believe it is foreclosed by the plain language of the Convention. Before discussing the text of the Convention, however, we briefly review its history.

[handwritten margin note: French's arg.]

The Hague Conference on Private International Law, an association of sovereign states, has been conducting periodic sessions since 1893. The United States participated in those sessions as an observer in 1956 and 1960, and as a member beginning in 1964 pursuant to congressional authorization. In that year Congress amended the Judicial Code to grant foreign litigants, without any requirement of reciprocity, special assistance in obtaining evidence in the United States. In 1965 the Hague Conference adopted a Convention on the Service Abroad of Judicial and Extrajudicial Documents in Civil or Commercial Matters (Service Convention), 20 U.S.T. 361, T.I.A.S. No. 6638, to which the Senate gave its advice and consent in 1967. The favorable response to the Service Convention, coupled with the longstanding interest of American lawyers in improving procedures for obtaining evidence abroad, motivated the United States to take the initiative in proposing that an evidence convention be adopted. The Conference organized a special commission to prepare the draft convention, and the draft was approved without a dissenting vote on October 26, 1968. It was signed on behalf of the United States in 1970 and ratified by a unanimous vote of the Senate in 1972. The Convention's purpose was to establish a system for obtaining evidence located abroad that would be "tolerable" to the state executing the request and would produce evidence "utilizable" in the requesting state.

In arguing their entitlement to a protective order, petitioners correctly assert that both the discovery rules set forth in the Federal Rules of Civil Procedure and the Hague Convention are the law of the United States. This observation, however, does not dispose of the question before us; we must analyze the interaction between these two bodies of federal law. Initially, we note that at least four different interpretations of the relationship between the federal discovery rules and the Hague Convention are possible. Two of these interpretations assume that the Hague Convention by its terms dictates the extent to which it supplants normal discovery rules. First, the Hague Convention might be read as requiring its use to the exclusion of any other discovery procedures whenever evidence located abroad is sought for use in an American court. Second, the Hague Convention might be interpreted to require first, but not exclusive, use of its procedures. Two other interpretations assume that international comity, rather than the obligations created by the treaty, should guide judicial resort to the Hague Convention. Third, then, the Convention might be viewed as establishing a supplemental set of discovery procedures, strictly optional under treaty law, to which concerns of comity nevertheless require first resort by American courts in all cases. Fourth, the treaty may be viewed as an undertaking among sovereigns to facilitate discovery to which an American court should resort when it deems that course of action appropriate, after considering the situations of the parties before it as well as the interests of the concerned foreign state.

We reject the first two of the possible interpretations as inconsistent with the language and negotiating history of the Hague Convention. The preamble of the Convention specifies its purpose "to facilitate the transmission and execution of Letters of Request" and to "improve mutual judicial co-operation in civil or commercial matters." The preamble does not speak in mandatory terms which would purport to describe the procedures for all permissible transnational discovery and exclude all other existing practices. The text of the Evidence Convention itself does not modify the law of any contracting state, require any contracting state to use the Convention procedures, either in requesting evidence or in responding to such requests, or compel any contracting state to change its own evidence-gathering procedures.

Two of the Articles in chapter III, entitled "General Clauses," buttress our conclusion that the Convention was intended as a permissive supplement, not a pre-emptive replacement, for other means of obtaining evidence located abroad. Article 23 expressly authorizes a contracting state to declare that it will not execute any letter of request in aid of pretrial discovery of documents in a common-law country. Surely, if the Convention had been intended to replace completely the broad discovery powers that the common-law courts in the United States previously exercised over foreign litigants subject to their jurisdiction, it would have been most anomalous for the common-law contracting parties to agree to Article 23, which enables a contracting party to revoke its consent to the treaty's procedures for pretrial discovery. In the absence of explicit textual support, we are unable to accept the hypothesis that the common-law contracting states abjured recourse to all pre-existing discovery procedures at the same time that they accepted the possibility that a contracting party could unilaterally abrogate even the Convention's procedures. Moreover, Article 27 plainly states that the Convention does not prevent a contracting state from using more liberal methods of rendering evidence than those authorized by the Convention. Thus, the text of the Evidence Convention, as well as the history of its proposal and ratification by the United States, unambiguously supports the conclusion that it was intended to establish optional procedures that would facilitate the taking of evidence abroad.

American courts, in supervising pretrial proceedings, should exercise special vigilance to protect foreign litigants from the danger that unnecessary, or unduly burdensome, discovery may place them in a disadvantageous position. Judicial supervision of discovery should always seek to minimize its costs and inconvenience and to prevent improper uses of discovery requests. When it is necessary to seek evidence abroad, however, the district court must supervise pretrial proceedings particularly closely to prevent discovery abuses. For example, the additional cost of transportation of documents or witnesses to or from foreign locations may increase the danger that discovery may be sought for the improper purpose of motivating settlement, rather than finding relevant and probative evidence. Objections to "abusive" discovery that foreign litigants advance should therefore receive the most careful consideration. In addition, we have long recognized the demands of comity in suits involving foreign states, either as parties or as sovereigns with a coordinate interest in the litigation. See *Hilton v. Guyot,* 159 U.S. 113 (1895). American courts should therefore take care to demonstrate due respect for any special problem confronted by the foreign litigant on account of its nationality or the location of its operations, and for any sovereign interest expressed by a foreign state. We do not articulate specific rules to guide this delicate task of adjudication.

Accordingly, the judgment of the Court of Appeals is vacated and the case is remanded for further proceedings consistent with this opinion.

PART D.   POST–AEROSPATIALE CASES

Most of the post-*Aerospatiale* cases place the burden of proof on the foreign party defendant to show why, under one of the tests in *Aerospatiale* or other comity analysis, the Hague Convention or foreign law procedures should apply.[4] The foreign party may have difficulty in convincing a court in the United States that resort to Hague Convention or foreign law procedures would prove to be effective. This is attributable to the fact that the evidentiary procedures of most civil law countries restrict a litigant's authority to collect the evidence. In civil

---

4. *See e.g., Haynes v. Kleinwefers,* 119 F.R.D. 335 (E.D.N.Y.1988).

law countries, the gathering of evidence by the courts may constitute an exercise of "judicial sovereignty." Under this concept, a foreign party's attempts to perform the act of obtaining evidence in a civil law country without government consent, may be unauthorized. It is the judge, and not the party, who collects the evidence, calls the witnesses and asks the questions. In addition, the U.S. party may be able to show that the type of discovery, notably pretrial production of documents, is not recognized or restricted in the foreign country where the evidence is sought. Article 23 of the Hague Evidence Convention, which allows signatories to restrict the pretrial production of documents, is often cited as a barrier to effective discovery under convention procedures. In this connection, Germany has a full Article 23 reservation under the convention and Canada and the United Kingdom have limited restrictions with respect to document production as well. Given these procedural variances, the party objecting to discovery under U.S. procedures needs to make a strong case under applicable comity tests that foreign law should be followed.[5]

HUSA v. LABORATORIES SERVIER

New Jersey Superior Court, 1999.
326 N.J.Super. 150, 740 A.2d 1092.

The opinion of the court was delivered by D'ANNUNZIO, J.A.D.

This is a personal injury action against Les Laboratoires Servier (LS), a French pharmaceutical corporation, and other defendants. Plaintiff's respondents, Debra and Thomas McKeown, sought to take the depositions of three individuals living in France who either had or have high-ranking employment with LS. LS moved for an order requiring use of the Convention on the Taking of Evidence Abroad in Civil or Commercial Matters (Convention), 28 U.S.C.A. § 1781. We granted LS leave to appeal from a trial court ruling that declined to apply the Convention. We now reverse.

Thirty nations have acceded to the Convention, including the United States and France. One of its stated purposes is "to improve mutual judicial cooperation in civil or commercial matters." The Convention's core mechanism is the "Letter of Request." Article 1 provides that "a judicial authority of a Contracting State may, in accordance with the provisions of the law of that State, request the competent authority of another Contracting State, by means of a Letter of Request, to obtain evidence, or to perform some other judicial act." A Letter may be used only to obtain evidence "for use in judicial proceedings commenced or contemplated." Article 2 of the Convention requires each Contracting State to designate a Central Authority "to receive Letters of Request ... and to transmit them to the authority competent to execute them." Article 2. The Convention is particularly pertinent in this case because of a French "blocking statute." French Penal Law No. 80–538 provides:

5. David Epstein, *Obtaining Evidence from Foreign Parties, Course Handbook on*   *International Business Litigation & Arbitration* 290 (PLI 2003).

Subject to international treaties or agreements and laws and regulations in force, it is forbidden for any person to request, seek or communicate, in writing, orally or in any other form, documents or information of an economic, commercial, industrial, financial or technical nature leading to the constitution of evidence with a view to foreign judicial or administrative procedures or in the context of such procedures.

. . . .

Without prejudice to such heavier penalties as are provided by law, any violation of the provisions of [this] law shall be punished by imprisonment of from two to six months and/or a fine of from 10,000 to 120,000 francs.

Justice Blackmun [in *Aerospatiale*], writing for the four dissenting justices, criticized the majority's "case-by-case inquiry for determining whether to use Convention procedures and its failure to provide lower courts with any meaningful guidance for carrying out that inquiry." 482 U.S. at 549, 107 S.Ct. at 2558, 96 L.Ed.2d at 487. The dissent "would apply a general presumption that, in most cases, courts should resort first to the Convention." We are, of course, bound by the majority's construction of the Convention in Aerospatiale. Thus, we deem it to be an optional method of evidence gathering. In the present case, however, the choice is between the Convention and New Jersey procedural and substantive law. Consequently, we perceive no conflict with federal supremacy, if, in exercising the option to resort to the Convention, we are more generous in our use of the Convention's procedures than the United States' courts. Moreover, because the present litigation is in a state court, we are not concerned with issues regarding the distribution of power among the three branches of the federal government.

The Supreme Court in *Aerospatiale* noted that the United States took "the initiative in proposing that an evidence convention be adopted." 482 U.S. at 530, 107 S.Ct. at 2548, 96 L.Ed.2d at 475. The Convention was supported by the American Bar Association, the Judicial Conference of the United States and the National Conference of Commissions on Uniform State Laws. The Court acknowledged that the United States Secretary of State recommended the Convention to the President because

The substantial increase in litigation with foreign aspects arising, in part, from the unparalleled expansion of international trade and travel in recent decades had intensified the need for an effective international agreement to set up a model system to bridge differences between the common law and civil law approaches to the taking of evidence abroad.

Since the Senate ratified the Convention in 1972, international trade and transactions have increased substantially, and litigation in New Jersey involving foreign parties is common. New Jersey courts should utilize international agreements which facilitate the conduct of cross-border litigation in the absence of demonstrable prejudice to legitimate interests. Implementation of the Convention will demonstrate our cosmopolitan approach to litigation arising out of the global economy and our sensitivity to the concerns of our trading partners. Though the French "blocking statute" cannot control an American court's exercise "of the power to order a party subject to its jurisdiction to produce evidence," *Aerospatiale, supra* 482 U.S. at 544 n. 29, 107 S.Ct. at 2556, 96 L.Ed.2d at 484, the "blocking statute" is a cogent expression of French concerns which should be accommodated, when possible. As a result, our courts and litigants may harvest reciprocal benefits when in need of the cooperation of foreign tribunals to gather evidence from persons or entities not subject to the jurisdiction of our courts, or in the enforcement of judgments.

We agree with the observation of Chief Judge Munson in *Hudson v. Pfauter*, 117 F.R.D. 33 (N.D.N.Y.1987), first post-*Aerospatiale* decision]:[a]

> It appears that the major obstacle to the effective use of Convention procedures by litigants and the courts is the fact that we are less familiar with those procedures than with the discovery provisions of the Federal Rules. Consequently, use of Convention procedures will, at least initially, result in greater expenditures of time and money for attorneys pursuing causes of action against foreign parties on behalf of their clients and could require an increased commitment of judicial resources. Nonetheless, these inconveniences alone do not outweigh the important purposes served by the Hague Convention. Further, as judges and lawyers become more familiar with the discovery rules of the Convention, it is quite possible that its procedures will prove just as effective and cost-efficient as those of the Federal Rules. To assume that the "American" rules are superior to those procedures agreed upon by the signatories of the Hague Convention without first seeing how effective Convention procedures will be in practice would reflect the same parochial biases that the Convention was designed to overcome.

JENIA IONTCHEVA, SOVEREIGNTY ON OUR TERMS
110 Yale L.J. 885 (2001).*

In an era of economic globalization, U.S. judges must increasingly consider the international consequences of their decisions, even when those decisions are purely procedural or managerial. A salient example of the need for such consideration is the dispute over the procedures for conducting discovery of evidence located abroad: U.S. judges have been eager to employ the Federal Rules of Civil Procedure when ordering discovery, while foreign nations and defendants have insisted that the United States comply with its treaty obligations and employ the Hague Evidence Convention. In a recent decision, *In re Vitamins Antitrust*

---

a. Applying Justice Blackmun's tripartite analysis, the court determined that the Convention should be applied in the first instance to the discovery involved.

* Reprinted with permission of the Yale Law Journal.

Litigation, the District Court for the District of Columbia intervened in this debate by ordering that the Federal Rules be used not only for discovery on the merits, but also for discovery necessary to resolve a dispute over the court's jurisdiction. The court extended a questionable line of precedents that displaced the Hague Convention in the management of discovery in federal courts.

The extension of *Aerospatiale* to jurisdictional discovery is plagued by a logical inconsistency underlying all orders for discovery at the pre-jurisdiction stage. In the absence of an established link between the defendant and the forum, the court has no authorization to exercise its power over that defendant. As the Supreme Court has declared more than once, "[w]ithout jurisdiction the court cannot proceed at all in any cause." Jurisdiction is power to declare the law, and when it ceases to exist, the only function remaining to the court is that of announcing the fact and dismissing the cause. The power to order jurisdictional discovery is a concession to pragmatism. If the court did not possess such power, a defendant could thwart the process by challenging jurisdiction and then withholding the evidence needed to resolve the jurisdictional question. These pragmatic justifications do not, however, overcome the fact that the court's legitimacy in issuing discovery orders is tenuous. If "jurisdiction is power," then pre-jurisdiction lies at the threshold between power and powerlessness. Fundamental considerations of fairness and due process demand that the court proceed with caution in imposing its rules upon a defendant who might not have reasonably foreseen being brought before it. Fairness considerations become even more central when the defendant is a foreign party who owes no allegiance to the forum and is unfamiliar with the mandates of the forum's legal system. As the Supreme Court noted in *Asahi Metal Industry v. Superior Court,* "[t]he unique burdens placed upon one who must defend oneself in a foreign legal system should have significant weight in assessing the reasonableness of stretching the long arm of personal jurisdiction over national borders."

Extraterritorial discovery also affects the sovereign interests of the defendants' home states. Private parties conducting discovery abroad, with the permission of the U.S. court, assume a function that in civil-law countries is reserved to the judiciary. These countries believe that U.S. court orders authorizing discovery in their territory interfere with their judicial sovereignty. American jurisprudence recognizes that undue expansion of a court's personal jurisdiction raises sovereignty concerns. As the Supreme Court declared in *World–Wide Volkswagen Corp. v. Woodson,* the minimum contacts test not only protects the defendant against the burdens of litigating in a distant forum, but also "acts to ensure that the States through their courts, do not reach beyond the limits imposed on them by their status as coequal sovereigns in a federal system." In *Asahi,* the Court found that concerns about interfering with a foreign forum's sovereignty are more pressing in the international context and declared that sovereign interests would be "best served by a careful inquiry into the reasonableness of the assertion of jurisdiction in the particular case." The Court emphasized that "[g]reat care and reserve should be exercised when extending our notions of personal jurisdiction into the international field."

The Restatement (Third) of Foreign Relations Law also calls for reasonableness in the exercise of jurisdiction, as mandated by both U.S. and international law. After listing traditional grounds for jurisdiction, such as territoriality and nationality, the Restatement clarifies that "an exercise of jurisdiction on one of the bases . . . is nonetheless unlawful if it is unreasonable. [This principle] is established in United States law, and has emerged as a principle of international law as well." Reasonableness hinges on factors such as the firmness of the link between the defendant and the forum, the importance of the regulations to the regulating state, the potential for conflict with regulations by another state, and, importantly, the extent to which the regulation is consistent with the traditions of the international system. This last consideration— consistency with the traditions of the international system—is notably absent from the *Vitamins* opinion, and the sovereignty interests of the home states are reduced to the interest in protecting their citizens from abusive discovery. The failure to give effect to the Hague Convention in federal courts also violates treaty obligations undertaken by the United States in signing and ratifying the agreement. It is arguable that *Aerospatiale* itself was such a violation: The holding that the Convention did not provide a mandatory framework for conducting extraterritorial discovery was not shared by all parties to the treaty *Aerospatiale*, however, preserved a role for the Convention in cases of jurisdictional discovery and discovery directed to nonparties. The *Vitamins* court's extension of that holding, on the other hand, deprives the Convention of any practical significance in U.S. courts and effectively nullifies the executive's decision to sign and Congress's choice to ratify the Convention. Furthermore, it is inconsistent with the primacy accorded to treaties under both U.S. and international law.

In resolving questions of jurisdictional discovery, balancing the values of international treaties against the Federal Rules is neither a prudent nor a legitimate course for courts to take. The Hague Convention adequately protects the plaintiffs' and United States' interests in obtaining discovery. Unlike a decision on jurisdiction, the application of the Hague Convention is not outcome-determinative, but rather concerns the choice of a method for arriving at the jurisdictional question. The plaintiff is not denied her day in court—only ordered to employ internationally accepted procedures to gather evidence on her jurisdictional claims. On the other hand, the reluctance to employ the Hague Convention produces significant negative consequences both for U.S. foreign relations and for the international system as a whole. To outsiders, the interest "balancing" conducted by the *Vitamins* court appears more like "the assertion of the primacy of United States interests in the guise of applying an international jurisdictional rule of reason." While it purports to be balanced and fair, the *Vitamins* court sends quite a different message to the outside world: In a world with no supreme sovereign, we will take sovereignty by judicial fiat and assert it fully whenever pragmatic concerns motivate us and our power over a defendant with property or interests in the United States allows us. The court's balancing insinuates that sovereignty matters only insofar as it is American sovereignty.

Such a message has far-reaching international consequences. First, it invites antagonism and defensive reactions by the countries most likely to be affected by the ruling: the closest U.S. trading partners. These reactions might take the form of foreign countries' liberally extending their laws and procedures to U.S. parties who have only tenuous links to their jurisdiction. More generally, the antagonism incited by the extraterritorial application of U.S. discovery rules might result in unwillingness by foreign countries to compromise their values in other areas and hurt wider U.S. interests in the international arena. It might also jeopardize valuable efforts—often spearheaded by the United States—to reach international agreements on jurisdiction and procedure. The unilateral extension of U.S. laws across borders might also tarnish the image of the U.S. judiciary and lead to the increased use of international arbitration to settle disputes—a process that, like the Hague Convention, usually relies on a mix of civil-law and common-law procedures for gathering evidence, but that, unlike the Convention, is subject to very little supervision by national courts. All of these considerations weigh in favor of applying the rules of the Hague Convention on a first-resort basis when jurisdiction is contested. An even better way to ensure the uniform application of this standard would be to revive efforts to codify the *Aerospatiale* minority opinion, calling for first resort to the Hague Convention, at least in cases of jurisdictional discovery. District courts have proven unable to apply the balancing test consistently and clearly, and the limited opportunity to appeal rulings on discovery has exacerbated this tendency. Codification would be very useful in ensuring a more predictable and coherent application of the Convention.

The use of the Hague Convention rules might result in a somewhat less rapid resolution of jurisdictional disputes, but to quote Justice Blackmun's dissent in *Aerospatiale*, "unless the costs become prohibitive, saving time and money is not such a high priority in discovery that some additional burden cannot be tolerated in the interest of international goodwill." The strong negative reactions by foreign states to U.S. court orders for discovery on their territory have clearly indicated that international goodwill might be endangered by an aggressive approach to the regulation of extraterritorial discovery. When jurisdiction is contested, forum-centric regulation of discovery abroad becomes all the more unpalatable, as it conflicts with "traditional notions of fair play and substantive justice" and with international norms of reasonableness in the exercise of jurisdiction. It is therefore imperative that higher courts or legislators temper the assertiveness of district courts in the regulation of international jurisdictional discovery before the district courts' scattered decisions coalesce into a body of precedent carrying its own force.

PART E.   BALANCING OF U.S./FOREIGN INTERESTS

What criteria should be employed in balancing the respective U.S./foreign interests involved in the discovery request? In *Aerospatiale* the Court refused to specify a fixed comity test to guide lower courts in making such inquiries. As the Court stated: "(w)e therefore decline to hold as a blanket matter that comity requires resort to Hague Evidence Convention procedures without prior scrutiny in each case of the particular facts, sovereign interests, and likelihood that resort to those procedures will prove effective." 482 U.S. at 544. The Court considered as relevant to any comity analysis in the foreign discovery area, the factors set forth in Section 442 of the Restatement (Third) of Foreign Relations Law of the United States.

(1) the importance to the ... litigation of the documents or other information requested;

(2) the degree of specificity of the request;

(3) whether the information originated in the United States;

(4) the availability of alternative means of securing the information; and

(5) the extent to which noncompliance with the request would undermine important interests of the United States, or compliance with the request would undermine important interests of the state where the information is located.

*Id.*at 544.

ALFADDA v. FENN

United States District Court, Eastern District of New York, 1993.
149 F.R.D. 28.

The opinion was delivered by United States Magistrate Katz.

[This is an action for alleged violations of federal securities law in stock offering. The representative of the defendant corporations sought a protective order claiming that he was prohibited by Swiss secrecy laws from revealing the information sought].

At his deposition, [defendant] Radwan refused to answer certain questions on the grounds that he was prohibited from revealing the information sought by Swiss secrecy laws. Radwan claimed that he had recently been advised by counsel in Switzerland, that he could be subject to severe penalties under Swiss law if he revealed such information. Although this issue was raised for the first time during Radwan's deposition, and at that time Radwan's United States counsel was unable to explain the precise nature of the Swiss secrecy objections raised, the Court, over plaintiffs' objection, granted defendant time to seek a protective order in relation to the withheld information, assuming United States counsel could reasonably justify such a motion.

Radwan claims that he is prohibited from responding to the above-listed inquiries by a variety of Swiss laws, and has submitted opinions from experts in Swiss law to that effect. Plaintiffs claim that the Swiss laws invoked by Radwan are not implicated in this case, and they too have submitted expert opinion letters to this effect. The Swiss laws at issue are: (1) Article 162 of the Swiss Criminal Code; (2) Article 273 of the Swiss Criminal Code; (3) Article 28 of the Swiss Civil Code; and (4) Article 47 of the Swiss Federal Banking Act.

The following discussion of Swiss law is essentially a summary of the opinions expressed by the experts for the parties in this case. As this summary will demonstrate, the parties in this case have significantly divergent views as to the scope and proper interpretation of Swiss law, and they have not submitted controlling Swiss authority to the Court in support of their respective positions. In the few instances where it has been possible to cite independent authority regarding the scope of these Swiss laws, reference has been made to United States caselaw and law review articles which discuss the Swiss statute in issue.

It is undisputed that this Court has the power to require Radwan to answer the questions posed by plaintiffs' counsel at the deposition, even if to do so would require Radwan to violate Swiss law. *See Societe Nationale Industrielle Aerospatiale v. United States District Court,* 482 U.S. 522, 529 n. 4, 107 S.Ct. 2542, 2546 n. 4, 96 L.Ed.2d 461 (1987); *SEC v. Banca Della Svizzera Italiana,* 92 F.R.D. 111, 116 (S.D.N.Y.1981). The question is whether the Court should exercise its discretion to issue the protective order sought by Radwan. *See Minpeco,* 116 F.R.D. at 520; Compagnie Francaise D'Assurance Pour Le Commerce Exterieur v. Phillips Petroleum Co., *105 F.R.D. 16, 28 (S.D.N.Y.1984). In deciding the propriety of ordering disclosures prohibited by the law of a foreign nation, the Court should consider: (1) the competing interests of the nations whose laws are in conflict; (2) the hardship of compliance on the party or witness from whom discovery is sought; (3) the importance to the litigation of the information sought; and (4) the good faith of the party resisting discovery ...*

In addition, it is worth remembering that the party relying on foreign law bears the burden of demonstrating that such law actually bars the production or testimony at issue. *See United States v. Vetco, Inc.,* 691 F.2d 1281, 1289 (9th Cir.1981); *Roberts v. Heim,* 130 F.R.D. 430, 436 (N.D.Cal.1990). In order to meet that burden, the party resisting discovery must provide the Court with information of sufficient particularity and specificity to allow the Court to determine whether the discovery sought is indeed prohibited by foreign law. *See Compagnie Francaise,* 105 F.R.D. at 24–25; *State of Ohio v. Arthur Andersen & Co.,* 570 F.2d 1370, 1374 (10th Cir.1978). Similarly, under Rule 26(c), Fed. R.Civ.P., a party seeking a protective order must demonstrate "good cause" for issuance of the order. This requires specific and particular demonstrations of fact, not stereotyped or conclusory statements. *See, e.g., Gelb v. AT & T,* 813 F.Supp. 1022, 1034 (S.D.N.Y.1993); *Waltzer v. Connor,* No. 83–8806, 1985 WL 2522 (S.D.N.Y. September 12, 1985); 8 C. Wright & A. Miller, Federal Practice and Procedure, § 2035 at 264–65

(1970); *Cf. Gulf Oil v. Bernard,* 452 U.S. 89, 102 n. 16, 101 S.Ct. 2193, 2201 n. 16, 68 L.Ed.2d 693 (1981).

[handwritten margin note: U.S. interests]

The United States has a strong national interest in the enforcement of its securities fraud laws, which are one basis of liability in this action. *See, e.g., Fleck v. E.F. Hutton,* 891 F.2d 1047, 1051 (2d Cir.1989); *Epifano v. Boardroom Business Products,* 130 F.R.D. 295, 298 (S.D.N.Y. 1990); *Alfadda v. Fenn,* No. 89–6217, Memorandum and Order, dated January 29, 1993 (McKenna, J.) ("January 1993 District Court Order"), at 5, 1993 WL 33445. That interest is significant, despite the fact that a case is not a criminal or civil enforcement action, because private rights of action under RICO and the securities laws "have the effect-intended by Congress-of enforcing the law by means of 'private attorney generals.' ... In fact, it is difficult to imagine a private commercial lawsuit which could be more infused with public interest." *Minpeco,* 116 F.R.D. at 523. The United States also has an interest in the full and fair adjudication of matters before its courts, which is only possible through complete discovery. *Id.; Compagnie Francaise,* 105 F.R.D. at 30.

[handwritten margin note: Swiss interests]

The strength of the Swiss national interest in this case is less certain. Obviously, as a general matter, Switzerland has a strong interest in enforcement of its secrecy laws. *See Minpeco,* 116 F.R.D. at 524–25. Nonetheless, two considerations cut against the Swiss interest here. First, "when foreign governments ... have considered their vital national interest threatened, they have not hesitated to make known their objections...." *See U.S. v. First National City Bank,* 396 F.2d 897, 904 (2d Cir.1968). Consequently, a foreign government's failure to express a view that the disclosure at issue threatens its national interests militates against a finding that strong national interests of the foreign country are at stake. *See Minpeco,* 116 F.R.D. at 525; January 1993 District Court Order at 4–5; *SEC v. Banca Della Svizzera Italiana,* 92 F.R.D. 111, 117–18 (S.D.N.Y.1981). In this case, Switzerland, despite an opportunity to do so, has not expressed any view nor attempted to intervene in any manner to prevent disclosure of the information plaintiffs seek. The letter from M. Peter, Deputy General Attorney of the Swiss Confederation ("Peter Letter"), submitted by defendants, is not the expression of a view regarding this motion. The letter merely clarifies the requirements of Swiss law, but makes no attempt to apply the law to the facts of this case. Accordingly, the Peter Letter cannot be considered an intervention by the Swiss government or the expression of that government's views on this case. In fact, the letter makes clear that, to the extent that Swiss sovereignty interests are at stake, it is the Ministry of Foreign Affairs from whom a viewpoint as *amicus curiae* should be sought. That has not been done.

Second, as discussed further *infra,* the applicability of the Swiss secrecy laws to the facts involved in the instant motion is not at all clear. Unlike *Minpeco,* 116 F.R.D. at 525, where all the experts agreed that Art. 47 prohibited the disclosures in question, there is a significant dispute in this case between the parties' experts as to whether any Swiss law prohibits disclosure of the information sought by plaintiffs. To the extent that Swiss law is not truly implicated, Switzerland clearly does not have any interest in preventing the disputed discovery.

* * *

[The Court further balanced the respective interests of the parties submitted in various expert opinions under the following factors: 1) hardship to the parties; 2) importance of information sought; and 3) defendants' good faith in not producing the requested information].

Defendant Radwan's experts have expressed different views about the proper scope of Swiss law. However, even accepting as true Radwan's assertions regarding the proper interpretation of the Swiss laws at issue, Radwan has still failed to make a factual showing sufficient to establish that Swiss secrecy laws protect the information sought and expose him to penalties if he responds to plaintiffs' questions.

Defendant Radwan and his experts have themselves asserted somewhat inconsistent bases for the applicability of Swiss secrecy law ... Few of these factual assumptions regarding the companies about which information is sought and their relationships with Radwan are supported by competent evidence. Nor is it clear that the information plaintiffs seek is encompassed by the prohibitions of Swiss law ....

In sum, even were I to adopt completely the views of Radwan's experts regarding the scope of Swiss law, Radwan would still have failed to carry his burden of demonstrating the applicability of those laws to the specific information sought. Consequently, I cannot conclude either that Switzerland has a strong national interest in preventing the discovery at issue, or that Radwan faces a serious threat of hardship should he be required to provide plaintiffs the information they seek.

Finally, there is no escaping the fact that Radwan, SEIC and AIC are primary defendants in this action. While some courts have been hesitant to require a non-party witness, who is an innocent source of information and a stranger to the litigation, to be forced to undergo hardship for the sake of discovery, any potential hardship faced by a primary defendant in litigation may be weighed less heavily by the court. *See Minpeco,* 116 F.R.D. at 526–27.

It is conceded that the information sought is relevant to the plaintiffs' claim regarding the diversion of proceeds from the 1984 SEIC offering. Defendant suggests, however, that the information is "remote from the main issues." I do not agree. One of plaintiffs' primary claims is that Radwan diverted the proceeds of the 1984 SEIC offering through companies within his ownership or control and for the benefit of himself and others of his choosing. As the Court's December Order made clear, the management and ownership of the entities appearing on SEIC's Share Ledger, and their involvement in the various transactions listed there, are directly relevant to plaintiffs' case. Defendants did not appeal that Order.

Further, Radwan has not obtained waivers of confidentiality from any of the parties about whom plaintiffs seek information. Accordingly, unlike the situation in *Minpeco,* 116 F.R.D. at 529, this is not a case in which it can be said that the discovery plaintiffs seek has reduced importance in light of other discovery provided pursuant to waivers.

Finally, the importance of Mr. Radwan's testimony on the subjects at issue is greatly increased by the fact that he may prove to be the only source of much of this information. Documents which might provide some of the information sought at Radwan's deposition, and whose production was required by the Court's December Order, are now claimed by defendants to be missing ... The claimed disappearance of these documents makes Radwan's testimony that much more critical to plaintiffs' ability to obtain full discovery.

Plaintiffs contend that Mr. Radwan has acted in bad faith in interposing Swiss secrecy objections to discovery. Plaintiffs refer to what they consider to be a long pattern of obstruction and bad faith by Radwan in the conduct of discovery. In addition to the missing documents discussed above, plaintiffs also point out that Radwan's secrecy objection was raised in an untimely fashion, after other objections to the 30(b)(6) Notices had been argued and overruled. Plaintiffs argue that Swiss secrecy laws are in no way implicated here because none of the companies are Swiss, none of the information sought qualifies as commercial or business secrets, and none of the disclosures will take place in Switzerland ...

As evidence of good faith, Mr. Radwan points out his prudent decision to consult with Swiss counsel, his actions in reliance on such advice and his attempts, although unsuccessful, to secure waivers of secrecy rights from the parties involved Radwan also suggests that the volume of discovery already produced is indicative of his good faith participation in the discovery process.

Mr. Radwan's decision to consult with Swiss counsel about his Swiss secrecy obligations the week before his deposition is hardly evidence of good faith. Radwan has long been aware of the existence of Swiss secrecy laws, and has been aware of the subjects to be covered at this deposition since October 1992. He has been represented by counsel in this case since its inception. While I am not prepared to conclude that his raising of this issue at the deposition was "bad faith", the eleventh-hour timing of the objection and the inability of United States counsel to support the objection when raised, other than by reference to his client's claims of consultation with another attorney, is troubling.

Mr. Radwan's attempt to secure secrecy waivers, if genuine, is indeed evidence of good faith. Mr. Radwan claims that, in light of the fact that all of the confidentiality requirements at issue may be waived by consent of the "owners" of the protected information, he sought consent from the management of SMEE and Dalia, the Swiss fiduciary of AIC, and the Swiss fiduciary of SIIC, to his providing the information sought by plaintiffs, but that he was denied consent. Nevertheless, no company or person (or representative acting on its behalf) has submitted an affidavit indicating that its interests are threatened by disclosure of this information or that it does not consent to its disclosure. There is some evidence, however, that Mr. Radwan either owns or manages some or all of the companies at issue, and he has not denied that fact. Thus, he may himself be able to consent to the disclosure of all, or at least part, of the information the plaintiffs seek. Compounding these circumstances is the fact that, unlike the defendant in *Minpeco,* 116 F.R.D. at 527, Radwan has not submitted a categorical affirmation that no information regarding his own activities or ownership interests is being withheld on the grounds of Swiss secrecy. In light of these facts, there is reason to believe that Radwan may be protecting his own interests, not others, by invocation of the Swiss secrecy laws.

I consider the above evidence of good or bad faith inconclusive. In the end, however, it is Mr. Radwan who has the burden of proving his clear entitlement to a protective order. Mr. Radwan is an American citizen living in France. None of the companies he was asked about or on whose behalf he appeared to testify are Swiss. These companies appear to have had interlocking ownership interests and Mr. Radwan appears to have owned or managed many, if not all of them. There has been no evidence that the beneficial owners of these companies are Swiss. Although he was given the benefit of the doubt at his deposition, having had additional time to support his assertion of secrecy he has submitted equivocal and unconvincing evidence that he is entitled to the protection of Swiss secrecy laws, that Switzerland has a substantial interest in preventing the disclosure of the evidence sought, or that he will face real hardship if the information is disclosed. Balanced against that is the relevance of the information sought, the strong United States' interest in the enforcement of its securities and racketeering laws and the existence of a confidentiality order which limits the dissemination of the information and decreases the likelihood of injury to Mr. Radwan because of his disclosures. Accordingly, I conclude that a protective order should not be issued in this case.

CONCLUSION

For the foregoing reasons, defendant Jamal Radwan's motion for a protective order is denied.

Questions and Comments

1. Under this Problem, the U.S. court may request the parties to stipulate to a discovery plan which accommodates both U.S. and foreign interests. Is that feasible considering the wide-spread misunderstanding of the term "pretrial discovery" in other countries and the U.S. discovery system in general? Rule 29 of the Federal Rules of Civil Procedure states that the parties may, by written stipulation, provide that depositions" be taken before any person, at any time or place, upon any notice, and in any manner." Depositions by voluntary agreement between the parties provide the most effective means of taking testimony abroad since the participation of the foreign government is not required and the testimony can be taken in a manner compatible with U.S. discovery and evidentiary standards. If the

witness will not cooperate voluntarily, the testimony must be compelled by letters of request (letters rogatory) or by treaty means. If the witness is a "party" as defined in Rule 30(b)(6) of the Federal Rules of Civil Procedure, or similar state rules, there is a reasonable basis for reaching voluntary agreement for the taking of the evidence. If a party witness refuses to voluntarily cooperate, under *Aerospatiale* that person could be compelled to return to the United States to be deposed. On the other hand, where there is no in personam jurisdiction over witnesses, such as third party witnesses, expert witnesses, etc., compulsory means will be used in most cases in obtaining the evidence.

2. In determining the most effective strategy, counsel for the party seeking discovery should develop a checklist addressing the following factors: 1) the type of discovery involved? 2) is the deponent a party or a non-party witness? 3) is the deposition voluntary or compulsory? 4) are U.S.-style depositions before the U.S. consul permitted under the laws of the country where the witness resides? 5) is the discovery being sought under the Hague Evidence Convention or traditional letters of request (letters rogatory)? 6) whether document production requests can be limited in order to satisfy applicable foreign procedures. With such a checklist, counsel for the U.S. party will have a better idea of the areas that may present special discovery problems to the foreign party. At the same time, counsel for both of the parties will be able to identify special discovery issues which may need judicial supervision or resolution.

3. As the U.S. party, what are the advantages to stipulating to a discovery plan? Disadvantages? What are the pros and cons from the perspective of the foreign party? Remember the Supreme Court's dictum in the *Aerospatiale* decision that supervision of pretrial discovery is committed to the discretion of the trial court. As the *Husa* case illustrates, the foreign party may be able to persuade the trial court to apply Hague Evidence Convention procedures on a first use basis. It is in the interest of both the U.S. and foreign party to stipulate to a discovery plan that is reasonable and fair. This is the most effective means to obtain evidence for pretrial and trial purposes. If U.S. procedures are contested, the court may apply a balancing test to determine whether the foreign discovery should be produced at all. See Section 442 of the Restatement (Third) of Foreign Relations Law. The cited cases and articles accompanying this problem illustrate pro forum bias and the tendency of U.S. courts to apply state and federal procedures to foreign-based discovery. Each case and each set of discovery requests are different. U.S. parties should avoid requests that are unduly burdensome and oppressive to the foreign party. At the same time, the foreign party should avoid blanket refusals to comply with reasonable discovery requests. Where complex discovery requests are involved, compliance with foreign law and procedures may be unavoidable. For example, if countless numbers of witnesses and documents are located in other countries, it may be useless for the U.S. party to seek court orders that all of the discovery take place in the United States. What law would govern the taking of evidence on foreign soil? In many discovery situations, it may be necessary for the U.S. party to comply with foreign law, even where the U.S. rules may technically apply to the evidence request.

4.   The U.S. and UK plaintiffs may wish to conduct foreign discovery on issues relating to defendants' pending motion to dismiss for lack of personal jurisdiction. In *In re Vitamins Antitrust Litigation*, 120 F. Supp. 2d 45 (D.D.C.2000), the district court rejected application of any first use of the Hague Evidence Convention procedures to discovery requests concerning threshold personal jurisdiction issues as to foreign defendants. In criticizing this decision, the extract from the Yale Law Journal Note, *Sovereignty on our Terms*, states that extraterritorial discovery on pre-jurisdiction issues raises sensitive sovereignty concerns. Did the district court in applying the U.S. rules to jurisdictional discovery issues properly assess international comity concerns in foreign evidence gathering as noted in the *Aerospatiale* decision? Under the majority opinion analysis, does this type of discovery request present "special problems" requiring the court's "special vigilance to protect foreign litigants"? Does the result in *Vitamins* comport with the comity analysis in the concurring opinion in *Aerospatiale* which states that a court in reconciling the conflicts of law "should perform a tripartite analyses that considers the foreign interests, the interests of the United States, and the mutual interests of all nations in smoothly functioning international legal regime"? Should the *Aerospatiale* rationale apply to cases where jurisdiction over the foreign party has not yet been determined?

5.   Under the Hague Evidence Convention, there are three alternative methods for obtaining evidence in other countries. First, a litigant may request the court where the action is pending to transmit a letter of request to the central authority in the country where the evidence is to be obtained. The central authority transmits the request to the appropriate foreign court, which conducts an evidentiary proceeding under procedures of the foreign country. Under the second procedure, the litigant may request that the evidence be taken before a diplomatic or consular officer in the country where the action is pending. The Convention provides that a contracting state may reserve the right not to allow the taking of evidence before a diplomatic or consular officer. Under the third method, the litigant may request that a specially appointed commissioner take evidence in the foreign country. See Rule 28(b) of the Federal Rules of Civil Procedure which authorizes use of these procedures for the taking of depositions in foreign countries. Rule 28(b) provides: "(e)vidence obtained in response to a letter of request need not be excluded merely because it is not a verbatim transcript, because the testimony was not taken under oath, or because of any similar departure from the requirements for depositions taken within the United States under these rules." Of the three procedures, the letter of request is the most useful. It is the only method which applies to compulsory evidentiary proceedings. The other two methods are subject to limitation in the convention and many countries have taken a variety of exceptions regarding the use of these procedures. The reservations and declarations of signatories to the convention should be studied before deciding on the procedures for obtaining the evidence. See Martindale–Hubbell Int'l Law Digest, pp. 1C 15–26.

6.   Based on the facts presented in this Chapter, what discovery would likely be obtained by compulsory means in the foreign countries where the evidence is located? What evidence might be available on a voluntary basis? Remember that foreign law and procedure would govern evidence to be

obtained on foreign soil and would vary from country to country. For example, obtaining evidence in Germany would implicate judicial sovereignty concerns. This would generally result in the use of compulsory, rather than voluntary means, of gathering evidence there. In addition, Germany has taken an Article 23 reservation as to the production of documents. Common law countries, such as Canada and the United Kingdom, have less restrictive evidence gathering procedures which allow for U.S. style deposition procedures pursuant to court order. As reflected in *Genira Trade & Finance Inc. v. Refco Capital Markets Ltd.*, production of documents is available on a restricted basis provided the request establishes the documents are needed for trial purposes. Under UK practice, however, discovery requests for documents are not obtainable from third-party witnesses. The State Department web-site for international judicial assistance (http://travel.state.gov/) has information on foreign law and procedure which might be useful in deciding on appropriate evidence gathering procedures to be followed in the country where the evidence is located.

7. In civil law countries, the searching out of evidence for use at trial is generally a function of the judge and not the parties. At an evidence-taking proceeding, the judge usually questions the witness and there is no oath-taking requirement. Full participation of counsel might not be allowed to examine or cross-examine the witness. Should U.S. counsel seek authorization from the foreign judge to be present and participate in the proceeding? U.S. counsel should be familiar with certain provisions of the Hague Evidence Convention which might be helpful in the letter of request situation where compulsory evidence is requested. Article 3 provides that the request shall specify "any special method or procedure" to be followed by the executing authority. This provision should be read together with Article 9, which provides that the executing authority shall apply its own law as to the methods and procedures to be followed unless the requesting authority requests that special methods or procedures be followed. Under Article 9, the judicial authority executing the request need not observe any special methods or procedures if they are incompatible with internal law in the state of execution. U.S. parties may request that examination and cross-examination of the witness by counsel be allowed. However, executing authorities in civil law countries may refuse to substitute this procedure in place of the usual method of examination by the judge. Article 7 provides that the requesting authority shall, if it so desires, be informed of the time and place of the proceedings so that the parties, and their attorneys, may be present. It may be necessary in these situations to engage foreign counsel to be present at the evidence-taking proceeding.

8. How should the German party defend against production of the documents relating to the manufacture of the automobile? As stated in the problem, Germany has taken a reservation pursuant to Article 23 of the convention which restricts use of the treaty for obtaining pretrial production of documents. Under the rationale in *Haynes v. Kleinwefers*, most U.S. courts would employ applicable state or federal rules to obtain the documents. In *Haynes*, the district court refused to employ convention procedures in light of Germany's Article 23 declaration. A better defense for the German party might be that production of the documents would violate German trade secrecy. See discussion in *Alfadda v. Fenn, supra.*

9. Suppose the German defendant showed that compliance would subject its employees to criminal penalties under German law. Would the courts tend to view this factor as controlling? See discussion in *Alfadda v. Fenn, supra*. The law is unsettled concerning when the balancing test favors enforcement of U.S. discovery orders. However, some U.S. courts have shown a reluctance to order the foreign party to violate foreign law. *See e.g.,United States v. First Nat'l Bank of Chicago*, 699 F.2d 341 (7th Cir. 1983); *Cochran Consulting, Inc. v. Uwatec USA, Inc.*, 102 F.3d 1224 (Fed. Cir.1996).

10. Who qualifies as "party" witnesses under the Federal Rules of Civil Procedure? See Rules 30(b)(6). What procedures are available for taking depositions and obtaining production of documents in Germany, the United Kingdom and Canada as to those witnesses? As to "non-party" witnesses?

11. What are the advantages of working out a discovery plan with the opposing side? Is it wise litigation strategy in all situations to compel U.S. pretrial discovery against foreign parties? See *Cochran Consulting* case. In what situations would the conduct of discovery be controlled by foreign law?

12. The Office of American Citizens Services of the Department of State provides assistance to U.S. litigants in obtaining evidence abroad. That office provides information pertaining to the laws and procedures of a particular country for taking depositions of willing witnesses, compelling the testimony of an unwilling witness, and obtaining documentary and physical evidence. Country-by-country listings can be obtained from the State Department's web site (http.www.travel.state.gov). Voluntary testimony can usually be taken before U.S. consular officers. The web site has information with respect to those countries which prohibit consular depositions and those countries which restrict these depositions depending on whether the deponent is a U.S. citizen, host country national, or third country national. Information is further provided as to the use of special methods for taking depositions, such as telephone depositions and audio-visual means. As stated in the problem, will plaintiffs' attorneys be able to use these procedures in all of the countries where evidence is located? Use of these special methods in civil law countries, such as Germany and Switzerland, may implicate judicial sovereignty concerns. For purposes of Rule 30 (b)(7) of the Federal Rules of Civil Procedure, the place of conducting the telephone deposition is considered to be "at the place where the deponent is to answer questions." Under Rule 28(b)(3), which specifies procedures for conducting foreign depositions, the oath is to be administered "in the place where the examination is held." Oath-taking is not recognized in civil law countries. Would administering an oath to a witness in Germany in connection with a telephone deposition from the United States serve to invalidate the deposition? Does Rule 29, which allows the parties to stipulate to taking the deposition "in any manner" provide a solution? Can audio-visual equipment be transported to the designated country for the purpose of recording the deposition? State Department guidance is necessary in this area in order to avoid possible confiscation by foreign authorities of the equipment involved.

M 3.6 CANADIAN DEFENDANT IN U.S. CTION COMMENCES PARALLEL CEEDING IN CANADA. GERMAN DEFENDANTS IN U.S. ACTION SEEK –SUIT INJUNCTION IN ENGLISH COURT AGAINST U.S. AND ENGLISH PLAINTIFFS. PLAINTIFFS IN U.S. ACTION SEEK ANTI–ANTI–SUIT INJUNCTION IN U.S. COURT AGAINST GERMAN AND UK DEFENDANTS

SECTION I. THE SETTING

The U.S. and UK injured parties have all commenced litigation in U.S. courts against CANTIRE, Ltd. , the tire manufacturer in Canada; DROF, AG, the SUV manufacturer in Germany; and DROF–UK, PLC, the assembly plant in the UK. They have also sued the U.S. distributor, but that is domestic litigation not considered in these materials.

Two months after the U.S. suits were filed CANTIRE took two actions. First, it filed a suit in a court in Ontario, Canada. The Canadian suit was against the plaintiffs in the U.S. suit, and asked the court to rule (1) that the Canadian company was not negligent in the manufacture of the tires, and (2) that the Canadian courts would not enforce a judgment in the U.S. court because of lack of personal jurisdiction over CANTIRE. The case also included DROF AG as a defendant, and a Malaysian rubber supplier. The second action taken by CANTIRE was in the U.S. court proceeding, where it moved to stay the proceedings because of the "parallel" Canadian action.

The U.S. and UK injured parties, now defendants in the Canadian action, ask the Canadian court to dismiss the action because of the proceeding in the United States that was initiated prior to the initiation of the action in Canada.

At the same time, DROF AG and DROF–UK initiated an action in the High Court in London requesting a permanent injunction against the U.S. and UK plaintiffs from proceeding in any U.S. court and additionally in any courts other than UK courts.

A week later the U.S. and UK plaintiffs in the U.S. case requested that the U.S. court issue a permanent injunction against DROF AG and DROF UK from seeking injunctions in other nations' courts, referring specifically to the request in the High Court in London.

SECTION II. FOCUS OF CONSIDERATION

This problem first considers in Part A. parallel proceedings, raising a question regarding whether they really are parallel. And if they are, why not let them both proceed? The discussion then focuses on the more contentious areas of the anti-suit and anti-anti-suit injunctions in Part

B, and on some associated issues in Part C, such as ripeness of injunctive relief. All three parts deal with parallel proceedings but Part B addresses the more contentious area. One might further deal with anti-anti-anti-suit injunctions, etc., but the general idea is gained without going past Part B.

These injunctions sometimes lead to unpleasant if not disparaging judicial comments about another nation's legal system, such as foreign court criticism of the use by the other nation of juries, extensive discovery, punitive damages and contingent fee arrangements, making reference to "vexatious" or "oppressive" litigation. Such discussions seem to leave the idea of *comity* on the shelf. The litigation flowing from our hypothetical is becoming increasingly complex because of the national borders. The differences in comparison to litigation that is exclusively domestic should be apparent by now. The litigation outlined above is complex, and there are a number of possible conclusions to which the various suits may lead.

SECTION III.   READINGS, QUESTIONS AND COMMENTS

Not infrequently the same issues give rise to the initiation of litigation in two different nations. When one party sues in what it believes is the most favorable forum, the defendant may react not solely by defending and perhaps a counterclaim, but additionally or alternatively by commencing a proceeding in a court in another nation believed to be more favorable to its interests. That creates what are usually called *parallel proceedings*. The simple solution would be for all courts to recognize a rule that is based on the first to file. That is a race to the courthouse rule. But that simple solution does not always work. One court may reject the first to file view in favor of another theory. That court might wish to balance interests and attempt to determine which nation has the greater interest in resolving the controversy. The court may focus on comity, that not so very clearly defined doctrine of the golden rule—do unto others as you wish them to do unto you.

One important observation is that there is not necessarily only one forum that is an *appropriate* or *proper* forum to resolve a controversy between parties from different nations. The same can be said about the possibility of two or more different states within a country being appropriate forums, but the international dimension raises more complex issues because the laws are more likely to differ between two nations than between two states or provinces.

Perhaps the most common form of parallel proceeding occurs when a party from one nation sues in its own courts a party from another nation who in turn initiates a suit in its own nation's court. Thus the injured American sues the English auto company in the United States and soon thereafter the English auto company reacts by suing the injured American in an English court. But in our hypothetical there are also English nationals injured in the accident in New Jersey. If they alone sue the English auto company in a U.S. court, there is a suit with exclusively English parties, both plaintiffs and defendant. The defendant may believe that the English courts are the proper courts to resolve controversies involving English citizens and entities, even though the accident occurred in the United States. Our hypothetical is more complex. There are English and American plaintiffs, and Canadian, English and German defendants. If the U.S. courts are an appropriate or proper forum, why should a suit commenced in England dealing with the same issues proceed? But what if the English defendant sues only the English plaintiff in an English court, asking the court to issue an injunction requiring the English plaintiff in the U.S. action to withdraw from that action and pursue any claim against the English defendant in the U.S. action in English courts? That is what has become known as an anti-suit injunction, and is the principal focus of the latter portion of this problem. What makes the situation all the more interesting is that when the English plaintiff in the U.S. action hears of the filing of the anti-suit injunction in the English court by the English defendant in the U.S. action, the English plaintiff in the U.S. action may ask the U.S. court to issue an anti-anti-suit injunction, prohibiting the English defendant from initiating or pursuing the anti-suit request in the English court. Where does it all end? The end may not yet be in sight.

The cases addressing parallel proceedings and anti-suit injunctions do not seem to produce very adequate rules. Perhaps the legislatures might be a better place to deal with these issues. But some legislatures, including the U.S. Congress, seem inclined to nationalism and favoring their own courts. Might the matter be assisted by the executive branches? The experience of the executive branches of the United States and England in failing to agree to a solution to concerns about antitrust litigation initiated in the United States against English defendants does not bode well for executive resolution. The courts may have to resolve the issue by default.

In our hypothetical there were choices for the litigation forum, as discussed in Problem 3.1, and one of those was an English court. We assume that the U.S. court asserts personal jurisdiction over the foreign defendants, discussed in Problem 3.2 and Problem 3.3, and that proper service of process has been made, discussed in Problem 3.4. Now we turn to issues arising beyond the choice of forum, the issue of jurisdiction and proper service of process.

PART A. PARALLEL PROCEEDINGS

DAVID EPSTEIN, JEFFREY L. SNYDER & CHARLES S. BALDWIN, INTERNATIONAL LITIGATION

§ 5–37 (2002).

Because parties to international transactions are often located in different jurisdictions, when a dispute arises, there exists the possibility of litigation on the same subject matter occurring in each jurisdiction. Such concurrent litigation is known as "parallel proceedings." It has been observed:

> Three possible responses exist when proceedings, asserting the same claims, are pending before both a domestic and a foreign court:
>
> (1) stay or dismiss the domestic action;
>
> (2) enjoin the parties from proceeding in the foreign forum (referred to as an anti-suit injunction); or
>
> (3) allow both suits to proceed simultaneously, with the likely attendant race to judgment.
>
> Thus the question of strategy is where to fight one's battles—here, there, or both places. Louise Ellen Teitz, *International Litigation, I. Parallel Proceedings: Treading Carefully*, 32 Int'l Law. 223 (1998).
>
> Litigation concerning parallel proceedings commonly arises either (1) on a motion of a party to stay or dismiss the domestic action; or (2) on a motion of a party to enjoin the foreign proceeding.* * *
>
> These motions frequently require a Court to pass upon the nature of the foreign proceedings and their adequacy. Sensitive issues of international relations and comity may, therefore, be present. The U.S. Supreme Court has not yet articulated the standard for determining whether to stay or dismiss an action in deference to as foreign proceeding. U.S. Courts which have addressed the issue have considered a number of factors, including:
>
> (1) adequacy of relief available in alternative forum;
>
> (2) issue of fairness to and convenience of parties, counsel, and witnesses;
>
> (3) the possibility of prejudice to any of the parties; and
>
> (4) the temporal sequence of filing the actions. *Caspian Investments, Ltd. v. Vicom Holdings, Ltd.*, 770 F.Supp. 880, 884 (S.D.N.Y. 1991).

* * *

Two principal factors have been cited as causes of parallel proceedings: lack of a multilateral convention to which the United States is a party on the enforcement of foreign judgments and vexatious litigation. Lack of a U.S. Convention leads to parallel proceedings because it is uncertain whether a U.S. judgment will be enforced or whether a foreign judgment will be enforced in the United States. Faced with such uncertainty, parties may pursue actions in multiple jurisdictions. Vexatious litigation leads to parallel proceedings where parties file multiple actions or pursue separate actions for perceived strategic reasons, which may include questionable tactics of increasing the cost of the dispute or subjecting the opponent to proceedings in a distant place. Of course, parallel proceedings are not necessarily improper. A party may have well-founded, good faith reasons for filing a separate action on a common subject matter. These reasons may include, among many others, a substantial question regarding the personal or subject matter jurisdiction of a tribunal or concerning the corruption or bias of a tribunal in a state hostile to U.S. interests.

DRAGON CAPITAL PARTNERS L.P. v. MERRILL LYNCH CAPITAL SERVICES INC.

United States District Court, Southern District of New York, 1997.
949 F.Supp. 1123.

[The plaintiff Dragon Capital Partners is a limited partnership investment fund formed in the Cayman Islands. The defendants are a global investment banking firm incorporated in Delaware with their principal places of business in New York City. The case involved a suit for damages for wrongful liquidation of accounts by Merrill Lynch. Unlike the more common situation of parallel litigation where the parties are reversed in the two cases, plaintiff in the first action is the defendant in the second action and the defendant in the first is the plaintiff in the second, in *Dragon Capital* the limited partnership Dragon Capital Partners is the plaintiff in each case and Merrill Lynch is the sole defendant in one case (Hong Kong) and one of four defendants in the second case (New York).]

BATTS, DISTRICT JUDGE.

Courts have the inherent power to stay or dismiss an action based on the pendency of a related proceeding in a foreign jurisdiction. However, the Court recognizes that its discretion is not boundless, and is limited by its obligation to exercise jurisdiction. While the United States Supreme Court has not yet articulated the standard for determining whether to stay or dismiss an action in deference to a foreign proceeding, courts tend to weigh a number of factors in their determination* * *.

Neither the parties nor the issues in this action are identical to those addressed in the Hong Kong Action. While the Hong Kong Complaint was filed solely against ML Capital, the New York Complaint before this Court has named three additional ML entities as Defendants. While the Hong Kong Action focuses on the first liquidation of the Quanto Options, the New York Complaint addresses the fact that ML Capital has not yet remitted to Dragon the proceeds of the final liquidation; in addition, the New York Complaint delves into both transactions in more detail.

However, neither the addition of defendants nor the expansion of claims is dispositive to the disposition of this motion. Courts have repeatedly ruled that "parties and issues need not be identical in order for one action to be stayed or dismissed in deference to an earlier action."

Furthermore, those issues in the instant action that were not previously raised, could in fact now be addressed in the Hong Kong action, by applying for leave to amend the pleadings. Under Hong Kong's legal system, even after the close of pleadings, parties may amend their pleadings with leave of the court or consent of the parties, regardless of whether new causes of action are added to the action. The Hong Kong Rules of the Supreme Court, provide that, subject to the discretion of the court to prevent joinder, if it would embarrass or delay a trial or otherwise be inconvenient, persons may be joined together in one action as defendants with the leave of the court or where:

>   i) if separate actions were brought against each of them some common questions of law or fact would arise in all the actions; and

>   ii) all rights to relief claimed in the action are in respect of or arise out of the same transaction or series of transactions.

If the additional defendants were not joined in the existing Hong Kong action, the Plaintiff could bring additional actions against them in Hong Kong, after which, subject to the provisions of the Hong Kong Rules of the Supreme Court, the Hong Kong Court could consolidate all actions. However, these issues are not problematic as ML Capital has agreed to both amendment of the Hong Kong pleadings and addition of the three additional ML entities not already named in Hong Kong. And, all Defendants have agreed to submit to Hong Kong jurisdiction as well as to accept service of process there.

Courts in the Second Circuit have traditionally accorded weight to the temporal sequence of actions pending in two jurisdictions. When the foreign action is pending rather than decided, priority generally goes to the first suit filed. In this case, Plaintiff filed its complaint in Hong Kong almost one and a half years before initiating the instant suit. Courts have, in the past, deferred to foreign actions that had been filed closer in time to the pending matter than the time period which elapsed in this case. Regardless of the parties' disagreements as to the extent of completed discovery, it is clear that the Hong Kong action "has proceeded beyond an initial stage." Complaints as well as Answers have been filed, and a Summons for Costs was not only adjudicated but also preliminarily contested. In addition, deference to the first suit filed has been held to be particularly appropriate where, as here, the Plaintiff commenced the initial suit.

In this action, it appears that neither the Plaintiff nor the Defendants would be prejudiced by the resolution of this dispute in Hong Kong. Although none of the parties are citizens of Hong Kong, all have engaged in business in that forum and cannot expect to evade its court's jurisdiction.

Plaintiff chose to file its original complaint in Hong Kong. The law is clear that when a Plaintiff invokes the laws of a particular jurisdiction, it cannot then repudiate the courts of that jurisdiction as unable to afford justice to its claims.

The Plaintiff argues that the Defendants are bound by a forum selection clause in the disputed ISDA Master Agreement. While the Plaintiff has denied being bound by such an agreement, it alleges that the Defendants' contrary insistence on the validity of such a document recommends conducting the trial of this case in New York. Even though this Court will not address the merits of any claims surrounding the ISDA Agreement, Plaintiff's argument lacks merit. First, Plaintiff can not rely on an agreement that it disputes. Second, even if the Defendants were bound by the ISDA Agreement, a forum selection clause would now be moot as the Plaintiff originally chose to bring suit in Hong Kong. Third, even if the forum selection clause were still valid, it could be superseded by a strong argument in favor of deference to a foreign action. Fourth, the ISDA provision on Governing Law and Jurisdiction does not mandate that this action be brought in New York. In part, the provision states that the ISDA Agreement is governed by New York's law and a Hong Kong Court could therefore satisfy the clause by applying New York law. The remainder of the ISDA provision, addresses jurisdiction only and does not mandate that an action be filed in the Southern District. For these reasons, this Court holds that neither the Plaintiff nor the Defendants would be prejudiced by dismissal of this action.

* * * [T]his concern alone does not warrant allowing this case to continue in this jurisdiction. It appears that the Hong Kong Court would in fact serve as an adequate forum for the adjudication of these parties' claims.

First, courts in this Circuit have deferred to foreign jurisdictions, even if claims asserted by a party in the United States were recognized by the foreign jurisdiction as similar rather than identical causes of action. In this case, it is significant that Hong Kong is a "sister common law jurisdiction with procedures akin to our own." It appears that the Plaintiff could raise its common law claims for relief under existing Hong Kong law. It has also been determined that the Plaintiff could initiate causes of action for fraud, deceit or misrepresentation, in lieu of the statutory causes of action it is pursuing in this forum. While Plaintiff's Hong Kong counsel notes that the Hong Kong Court "would have no authority to provide the full range of remedies available under United States law," the task of this Court is to ensure that Plaintiff will have access to adequate relief, rather than to determine which forum would provide Plaintiff with the greatest relief.

Second, in deferring to foreign jurisdictions, courts in this Circuit have not felt impeded by "the mere fact that a foreign court may have to apply United States law to some of the claims before it." Here, it is doubtful that the Hong Kong Court would either be unwilling or unable to address the parties' substantive rights, if appropriate, under the twelve causes of action arising under United States law, where alternate relief was not available in Hong Kong.

Finally, judicial efficiency weighs in favor of deferring to the foreign action. The Hong Kong courts are already familiar with the facts in this case and the suit has already proceeded sufficiently in the foreign forum.

In reaching this decision the Court of course relies on the Defendants' representations that they will submit to jurisdiction and service of process in Hong Kong, as well as agree to the amendment of pleadings and joinder of parties in that action.

The Defendants' motion for dismissal pursuant to the doctrines of deference to foreign proceedings and forum non conveniens is GRANTED.

Questions and Comments

1. Why in our case have so many suits been initiated and motions made on what seem to be the same facts? After the first filing in the United States by the U.S. and U.K. parties against CANTIRE, DROF AG, and DROF UK PLC, what led counsel for the defendants to file the suits in Canada and the UK? Were these the best choices to follow in representing their clients? What are the reasons for parallel proceedings? Concurrent jurisdiction opens the door to multiple suits. Because the plaintiff who files the first suit often forum shops, the defendant may disagree with the selection of the store. Additionally, if a prospective judgment in nation A will not likely be enforced in nation B where the defendant has assets, the suit might be commenced in nation B. That may cause the defendant to initiate suit in nation A and attempt to have the suit in nation B stopped.

2. Why shouldn't the rule be that parallel proceedings should proceed simultaneously until there is a judgment in one case that might be argued as *res judicata* in the other? See *Laker Airways, Ltd. v. Sabena, Belgian World Airlines*, 731 F.2d 909, 926 (D.C. Cir. 1984). Might this rule lead to two simultaneous and inconsistent judgments? See *EFCO Corp. v. Aluma Systems USA*, 983 F.Supp. 816, 824 (S.D. Iowa 1997).

3. Many courts seem to turn to domestic cases and doctrine to resolve parallel litigation involving suits initiated in two different *nations*. Should the presence of an international dimension affect the applicable rules? If so, what is added by the international dimension to the litigation?

4. Might the U.S. court in our hypothetical issue a stay as at least a temporary resolution of the problem? It does not amount to a negation of the court's perceived duty to go forward if it has jurisdiction. A U.S. federal district court granted a stay in a proceeding initiated in Missouri where a parallel proceeding had been commenced some three years earlier in Kuwait. The court stated:

> "[A]n order merely staying the action does not constitute abnegation of judicial duty. On the contrary, it is a wise and productive discharge of it. There is only postponement of decision for its best fruition." Federal courts do have the power, based on abstention principles, to stay actions for damages.... [D]ue to the dissimilarity of the parties, the convenience of the present forum and the likelihood of dismissal of at least a portion of the foreign action, the Court finds that a stay pending the outcome of the litigation in Kuwait is also appropriate. *Abdullah Sayid Rajab Al–Rifai & Sons W.L.L. v. McDonnell Douglas Foreign Sales Corp.*, 988 F.Supp. 1285 (E.D. Mo. 1997), citing *Quackenbush v. Allstate Ins. Co.*, 517 U.S. 706, 116 S.Ct. 1712, 135 L.Ed.2d 1 (1996).

Are the factors the *McDonnell* court considered the same as those noted in the Epstein, Snyder and Baldwin extract, from the *Caspian* decision? The latter factors seem to apply to either a dismissal or a stay. But doesn't the *McDonnell* extract seem to suggest that the factors should be less strict for a stay?

5. Does the *Dragon* case follow the factors in either *McDonnell Douglas* or *Caspian* as discussed above? Having a fairly representative list of factors, and using the reasoning of the *Dragon* decision, consider each factor in determining whether a stay should be issued to CANTIRE in the U.S. cases in the hypothetical?

PART B. ANTI–SUIT AND ANTI–ANTI–SUIT INJUNCTIONS

DAVID EPSTEIN, JEFFREY L. SNYDER & CHARLES S. BALDWIN, INTERNATIONAL LITIGATION

§ 5–37 (2002).

* * * [A]n anti-suit injunction refers to the order of a domestic court purporting to stay or enjoin parties from proceeding with an action in a foreign forum.[a] As an anti-suit injunction necessarily involves a direct intrusion on the judicial process of another sovereign nation, it is proper in only extraordinary circumstances. The Second Circuit has announced five factors to consider:

(1) whether a policy of the enjoining forum is being frustrated;

(2) whether the maintenance of the action is vexatious;

(3) whether the court's jurisdiction is threatened;

(4) whether there are other equitable considerations; and

(5) the delay, inconvenience, expense, and race to judgment that would result if the injunction is not granted. *China Trade & Development Corp. v. M/V Choong Yong*, 837 F.2d 33, 36–37 (2d Cir. 1987).

The enforceability and effect of an anti-suit injunction may be uncertain as a tribunal may rebuff the attempted intrusion by an alien court.

The Saga of Sir Freddie Laker

LORD DIPLOCK. My Lords, of these conjoined appeals, two are brought in civil actions in which the British Airways Board (B.A.) and British Caledonian Airways Ltd. (B.C.) respectively are plaintiffs. With these I propose to deal first; the third appeal is brought in an application for judicial review. All three appeals form part of the aftermath of the relatively brief incursion into the ranks of airlines operating scheduled services between the United Kingdom and the

---

a. A court may not enjoin a foreign action. It may only enjoin parties from specific conduct.

United States of America, that was made by Sir Freddie Laker operating through a company, Laker Airways Ltd., incorporated in Jersey but with its principal office in London and transacting business there and elsewhere in the United Kingdom and in the United States. To this company, and the other companies through which Sir Freddie operated scheduled air services across the North Atlantic and the liquidators of those companies, I shall refer, collectively and individually, as "Laker."

Laker's attempts to break into the market for the provision of scheduled air services between places in the United Kingdom and places in the United States of America (which, under the Chicago Convention of 1944, required the consent of the governments of both countries) achieved success in 1977 when it became an airline designated by the United Kingdom to operate a scheduled service on the New York–London route.... The other designated British airline was B.A. Its status as sole designated British airline for the New York–London route was of long standing. Progressively, at intervals between 1977 and its subsequent financial collapse in February 1982, Laker also became a designated British airline for [other U.K.-U.S,. routes.]

The other airlines operating scheduled services across the North Atlantic between the United States and the United Kingdom and other destinations in Western Europe, including B.A. and B.C., were members of the International Air Transport Association ("I.A.T.A."). Between airlines that are members of I.A.T.A. ("I.A.T.A. airlines") there exist elaborate arrangements for co-operation, involving through-bookings for carriage by different airlines, interchangeability of tickets, co-ordination of time tables, uniform fares for various classes of travel providing differing standards of amenity and the like, with which air travellers are familiar. They are made possible by I.A.T.A.'s operating a clearing house for the adjustment of accounts between member airlines resulting from the carrying out of such collaborative agreements.

Laker, upon becoming a designated British airline for the New York–London route, did not become a member of I.A.T.A. It did not conform to the I.A.T.A. fare structure or participate in any of its arrangements for collaboration between I.A.T.A. airlines. Instead, it challenged the whole I.A.T.A. system by instituting a low-cost, no frills "skytrain" service in each direction at one-way fares which covered carriage only and, at the beginning, were little more than one-third of the price of the one-way fare then being charged for travel by I.A.T.A. airlines in the class that offered the lowest standard of amenities. This policy, which I will refer to for convenience as "the Skytrain policy," was extended by Laker to each of the new routes between the United Kingdom and the United States for which Laker progressively became a designated British airline. It was so successful in attracting passengers that by the time of its collapse, in February 1982, Laker was carrying one-seventh of all passengers by air across the Atlantic between the United Kingdom and the United States.

It may well be that the low fares charged under the Skytrain policy created a demand for air passages from persons who would not otherwise have contemplated transatlantic travel at all; but it appeared to the I.A.T.A. airlines operating transatlantic routes that fares so much less than the uniform standard fares charged by them under current I.A.T.A. agreements were calculated to attract, and to divert to Laker, passengers who would otherwise have travelled by I.A.T.A. airlines not only to destinations in the United Kingdom itself but to ultimate destinations in other Western European countries to which easy and frequent on-carriage was available to and from London. One of the most important factors in the profitability of operating a passenger airline is the payload, viz. the proportion of the total available seats which on an average it is able to fill. To meet what they regarded as the threat to the maintenance of payloads to which they were exposed by the lower fares charged by Laker under the Skytrain policy, the I.A.T.A. airlines introduced fares substantially lower than their uniform standard fares for the lowest class of travel, and approximately matching those charged by Laker. These new cheap fares were available on "stand-by" terms, depending on the availability of a seat, or were subject to compliance with requirements as to advanced booking; but, it is alleged by Laker, they were inclusive of "in-flight" amenities, for which extra charges were made under Laker's Skytrain policy, and entitled the passenger to other advantages resulting from the availability of collaborative arrangements with other I.A.T.A. airlines in consequence of their being parties to the various I.A.T.A. agreements.

By the beginning of 1982, Laker's finances had become overstretched, and disaster struck. The causes for this are not, in my view, a matter for your Lordships. Attempts at a rescue operation for re-financing Laker were made, but to no avail. The causes for their failure are also not a matter for your Lordships. On 5 February 1982 Laker ceased trading and on 17 February it went into liquidation in Jersey.

The above is from *British Airways Board v. Laker Airways, Ltd.*, [1984] 3 W.L.R. 413, [1985] A.C. 58 (House of Lords). Airlines strongly protected their rates through I.A.T.A., and much disliked the newcomer Laker who offered the public much lower fares on his "Skytrain." The airlines blocked his entry to the market for more than a half-dozen years. Skytrain was very successful. The foreign airlines did not accept Laker's presence without a fight. It was a fight that turned dirty. Laker alleged that the airlines did much more than Lord Diplock notes. Laker believed that the airlines acted together to threaten banks to not make loans to the new airline. That sounded like antitrust violations. Unable to gain needed financing, combined with rising fuel prices and too rapid expansion, Laker Airways ultimately collapsed.

In liquidation, Laker Airlines in November, 1982, filed suit in U.S. federal district court in the District of Columbia against several of the I.A.T.A. carriers, including British Airways, British Caledonian, Lufthansa, Swissair, TWA, Pan American and KLM, and also the aircraft manufacturer McDonnell Douglas. Laker asked for treble and punitive damages of more than $1 billion, and requested the production of a very extensive list of documents and answers to interrogatories.

British Airways responded in January, 1983, by requesting the High Court in London to enjoin Laker from continuing its suit against British Airways in the United States. Soon other European defendants (British Caledonian, Lufthansa and Swissair) joined in the High Court suit. Immediately Laker asked the U.S. court for an injunction restraining the remaining defendants (Pan American, TWA and McDonnell Douglas from the United States, and KLM and Sabena from Europe) from participating in the High Court suit. The court granted a TRO and set a hearing date.

The High Court granted an interim order (anti-suit) enjoining Laker from any further steps against British Airways and British Caledonian in the U.S. suit. The judge further scheduled a March 21st hearing for a permanent injunction. On March 7th the U.S. court issued an anti-anti-suit injunction against Pan American, TWA, McDonnell Douglas, KLM and Sabena, restraining them from joining the High Court proceedings. *Laker Airways, Ltd. v. Pan American World Airways*, 559 F.Supp. 1124 (D.D.C. 1983). The U.S. district court judge noted his regret at having to resort to such an injunction but believed that the High Court interfered with the U.S. proceeding in violation of comity. His order was appealed by the foreign airlines KLM and Sabena, but not by the U.S. entities.

In May the High Court held that the relief requested by British Airways and British Caledonian was not justified, but maintained the interim injunction pending appeal. *British Airways Board v. Laker Airways, Ltd.*, [1983] 3 W.L.R. 545, [1984] Q.B. 142. The Court of Appeal in London reversed the decision and issued a permanent injunction preventing Laker from any proceedings in the United States against British Airways or British Caledonian. *British Airways Board v. Laker Airways Ltd.*, [1983] 3 W.L.R. 544 (C.A.) The court was influenced by the then recent issuance of an order by the Secretary of Trade and Industry under the British Protection of Trading Interests Act 1980, prohibiting the two British airlines from complying with any U.S. court orders relating to antitrust measures. In view of that order the Court of Appeals believed that the case was "untriable" in the United States and if pursued would result in a denial of justice to the British airlines.

While the decision of the appeal to the House of Lords was pending the U.S. Circuit Court of Appeals for D.C. ruled 2–1 upholding the district court's injunction. *Laker Airways Ltd. v. Sabena, Belgian World Airlines*, 731 F.2d 909 (D.C.Cir. 1984). It was a strongly worded decision but without comments derogatory of the British legal system. The decision did note the differences in approach toward anticompetitive and restrictive business practices. Four months later the House of Lords, in the decision from which Lord Diplock's comments above are taken, rejected the Court of Appeals decision, principally because the British airlines had not established that their rights were infringed by having to proceed in the United States and that what Laker had done was not unconscionable.

Next Laker requested and obtained an injunction in the U.S. district court against British Airways and British Caledonian similar to the one against the other defendants. The judge angrily noted the "tenacity of these defendants in seeking a resolution of this lawsuit everywhere but in the appropriate legal forum" and added to the injunction a prohibition against seeking help outside the courts, such as in the British Parliament. *Laker Airways Ltd. v. Pan American World Airways, Inc.*, 604 F.Supp. 280, 285 (D.D.C. 1984). The British government began to reject requests from U.S. carriers to reduce fares and threatened to denounce the air services agreement between the United States and the United Kingdom enacted in 1977. Finally, in July, 1985, a settlement was announced. Sir Freddie Laker would receive $8 million and Laker Airlines creditors would receive $48 million. The lawyers for Laker received an additional $8 million. The CEO of British Airways offered the usual statement that the settlement was not an admission of guilt. The matter was over. The case law from the Laker saga remains important. There was some strong language, but not as strong as in some subsequent cases when the English judges labeled some characteristics of the U.S. legal system as oppressive. See, e.g., *Simon Engineering PLC v. Butte Mining PLC*, [1996] 1 Lloyd's Rep. 104.

GENERAL ELECTRIC CO. v. DEUTZ, AG

United States Court of Appeals, Third Circuit, 2001.
270 F.3d 144.

[The General Electric Company sued Deutz, the German corporation that guaranteed the obligations of its subsidiary, Moteren–Werke Mannheim, AG, that had agreed to design diesel locomotive engines for GE's manufacture. GE filed suit against Deutz in a U.S. federal district court in Pennsylvania, for breach of contract in December ,1998, after Deutz failed to provide additional needed funding for the venture. Deutz moved to dismiss for lack of personal jurisdiction or alternatively to compel international arbitration as it claimed the contract required. Deutz also initiated ICC arbitration proceedings. The district court held that jurisdiction over Deutz existed and that the contract did not unambiguously bring Deutz within the arbitration provisions. Before the arbitration panel issued any decision, in April, 2000, Deutz petitioned the High Court in London to enjoin GE from pursuing the proceedings in Pennsylvania. The High Court refused to issue an anti-suit injunction. In July the Pennsylvania district court enjoined Deutz from further action before the London High Court. In November, the arbitration panel held that arbitration was not required under the contract. Deutz appealed all the orders of the federal district court.]

WEIS, CIRCUIT JUDGE

We are persuaded that none of the bases relied upon by the District Court supports the issuance of an injunction in this case, and will discuss each of them in turn.

First, *res judicata* or claim preclusion[5] is designed to avoid piecemeal litigation of claims arising from the same events. The determination of whether two suits are based on the same cause of action turns on the essential similarity of the underlying events giving rise to the various legal claims. Generally speaking, claim preclusion or *res judicata* requires a final judgment on the merits in a prior suit involving the same parties or their privies, and a subsequent suit based on the same cause of action.

Res judicata is commonly, and properly, pleaded as an affirmative defense in a second suit arising out of the same injury. Only in aggravated circumstances may the court presiding over the first case anticipate the second by entering an injunction against initiation of further proceedings; the tendency to issue such injunctions should almost always be avoided. The judicial consensus is ably summarized by Wright and Miller in their treatise:

> "However tempting it may be for a court to conclude that it is in the best position to assess the preclusive effects of its own judgments, application of preclusion principles requires familiarity not only with the first judgment but also with the subsequent proceedings. The first court should not lightly usurp the jurisdiction of another court to dispose of pending litigation."

18 Charles A. Wright, Arthur R. Miller & Edward H. Cooper, *Fed. Prac. & Proc.* § 4405, at 41–42 (1981).

In the case before us, only the interlocutory orders finding personal jurisdiction and dismissing Deutz's arbitration request have been entered. General Electric's claims against Deutz for damages have not been resolved. Although the order denying arbitration was appealable, Deutz had not yet taken an appeal at the time the District Court entered its injunction.

* * *

"Anticipatory" injunctions, issued before the subsequent suit is under way, are to be used in the rarest of circumstances on the domestic front. In view of the international reach of the injunction, the District Court should have left the *res judicata* effect of its order to the determination of the other forum. The District Court's determination that its order was sufficient for *res judicata* purposes would not neces-

---

5. Courts and commentators have used varying terminology, often referred to collectively as "*res judicata*," in discussing the preclusive effects of prior adjudication. Today, however, *res judicata* is sometimes used to represent two distinct preclusion concepts, "issue preclusion" and "claim preclusion." While the former refers to the effect of a judgment in foreclosing further adjudication of a matter actually decided, claim preclusion prohibits litigants from pursuing a matter that has not previously been litigated but which should have been advanced in an earlier suit.

sarily be binding on English courts. The circumstances here were not so aggravated as to justify interference with the jurisdiction of the courts of another sovereign state, and there is no indication that the English courts would have prevented General Electric from arguing the *res judicata* effect of the February 28, 2000 order.

General Electric argues that if Deutz had not been so restrained, it might have destroyed the District Court's jurisdiction by securing an order from the High Court compelling arbitration. The record, however, reveals little basis for such qualms. Deutz petitioned the High Court two months after the District Court had dismissed the arbitration request, and the High Court declined to issue an injunction restraining General Electric from proceeding in the federal court, voicing serious doubts about the strength of Deutz's position. Thus, the District Court knew before it enjoined Deutz that the High Court had shown no inclination to disagree with the non-arbitrability ruling.

Similarly ill-founded is General Electric's assertion that the sanctity of the jury verdict would be jeopardized by permitting Deutz to repair once again to the High Court in London. Although the jury unquestionably has a more important role in the American jurisprudential system than in that of any other nation, its verdict is neither infallible nor immune from judicial scrutiny.

We have been cited to no authority that endorses enjoining proceedings in a foreign court on the grounds that an American jury verdict might be called into question. Indeed, in denying Deutz's application, the High Court took pains to mention that the findings of fact had been made by a jury. There is little reason to believe that the High Court would give any less deference to the jury's role as fact-finder if the issue were presented a second time.

In parallel litigation, the issue of comity is an important and omnipresent factor. Although it is a consideration in federal and state litigation, it assumes even more significance in international proceedings. The Supreme Court has described comity as "the recognition which one nation allows within its territory to the legislative, executive or judicial acts of another nation, having due regard both to international duty and convenience, and to the rights of its own citizens or of other persons who are under the protection of its laws." *Hilton v. Guyot*, 159 U.S. 113, 164, 16 S.Ct. 139, 40 L.Ed. 95 (1895); . . .

The Court of Appeals for the D.C. Circuit has described comity as a "complex and elusive concept," the deference a domestic court should pay to the actions of a foreign government, not otherwise binding on the forum. *Laker Airways Ltd. v. Sabena, Belgian World Airlines*, 731 F.2d 909, 937 (D.C.Cir.1984). The primary reason for giving effect to the rulings of foreign tribunals is that such recognition factors international cooperation and encourages reciprocity. Thus, comity promotes predictability and stability in legal expectations, two critical components of successful international commercial enterprises. It also encourages the rule of law, which is especially important because as trade expands across international borders, the necessity for cooperation among nations increases as well.

The Supreme Court has taken to task American courts that have demonstrated unduly narrow attitudes in this area:

> "The expansion of American business and industry will hardly be encouraged if, notwithstanding solemn contracts, we insist on a parochial concept that all disputes must be resolved under our laws and in our courts.... We cannot have trade and commerce in world markets and international waters on our terms, governed by our laws, and resolved in our courts." *THE BREMEN v. Zapata Off–Shore Co.*, 407 U.S. 1, 9, 92 S.Ct. 1907, 32 L.Ed.2d 513 (1972).

In another case emphasizing world economic interdependence, the Court of Appeals for the Sixth Circuit noted that the proper exercise of comity demonstrates confidence in the foreign court's ability to adjudicate a dispute fairly and efficiently. *Gau Shan Co., Ltd. v. Bankers Trust Co.*, 956 F.2d 1349, 1355 (6th Cir.1992). Failure to accord such deference invites similar disrespect for our judicial proceedings. Reciprocity and cooperation are worthy goals of comity.

The federal Courts of Appeals have not established a uniform rule for determining when injunctions on foreign litigation are justified. Two standards, it appears, have developed. Courts following the "liberal" or "lax" standard will issue an injunction where policy in the enjoining forum is frustrated, the foreign proceeding would be vexatious or would threaten a domestic court's *in rem* or *quasi in rem* jurisdiction or other equitable considerations, and finally, where allowing the foreign proceedings to continue would result in delay. The Courts of Appeals for the Fifth, Seventh, and Ninth Circuits generally apply this standard.

By contrast, the Second, Sixth and District of Columbia Circuits use a more restrictive approach, rarely permitting injunctions against foreign proceedings. These courts approve enjoining foreign parallel proceedings only to protect jurisdiction or an important public policy. Vexatiousness and inconvenience to the parties carry far less weight.... Our Court is among those that resort to the more restrictive standard.... Our jurisprudence thus reflects a serious concern for comity. This Court may properly be aligned with those that have adopted a strict approach when injunctive relief against foreign judicial proceedings is sought. Although it recognized our adherence to that restrictive standard, the District Court in this case invoked the threat to jurisdiction and violation of public policy factors to justify the injunction. As we noted earlier, the evidence supporting application of these factors was extremely weak, and any doubts to the contrary should have been put to rest by the High Court's judgment, issued before the injunction was granted.

The High Court's Justice Thomas commented with respect to General Electric's request for an injunction, then pending in the District Court:

"He [the district judge] will no doubt take into account ... that he, as a judge of the United States Court, is being asked to exercise extraordinary extra-territorial jurisdiction over an arbitral tribunal sitting in London within the jurisdiction of this Court. He will no doubt pay high regard to issues of comity, just as this Court has paid high regard to issues of comity in relation to the decisions made by him."

At another point in his judgment, concluding that there was no serious issue of arbitrability, Justice Thomas observed, "It seems to me very difficult to see on what basis this Court should intervene in a proceeding so far advanced in the United States, where that particular issue has already been determined against Deutz."

Assuming *arguendo* that the District Court's order denying arbitration can constitute a ruling that is final for *res judicata* purposes before its disposition on appeal, it does not follow that there is a sufficient basis for enjoining the proceedings in the English courts. This is not an aggravated case that calls for extraordinary intervention, nor is it sufficient that the ruling of the arbitral panel might have jeopardized the District Court's jurisdiction.

We do, of course, have a considerable advantage over the District Court, because the ICC Panel has now agreed that the case was not arbitrable. Although that decision colors our ruling, it does not weaken our conclusion, arrived at independently, that the District Court lacked sufficient grounds to grant the injunction. We are also confident that there was no serious threat to an important public policy because of the happenstance that essential fact finding in the District Court was performed by a jury rather than by the judge.

The Order granting the injunction will be reversed. In all other respects, we will affirm the Orders of the District Court.

KAEPA, INC. v. ACHILLES CORP.

United States Court of Appeals, Fifth Circuit, 1996.
76 F.3d 624.

WIENER, CIRCUIT JUDGE:

This case arises out of a contractual dispute between two sophisticated, private corporations: Kaepa, an American company which manufactures athletic shoes; and Achilles, a Japanese business enterprise with annual sales that approximate one billion dollars. In April 1993, the two companies entered into a distributorship agreement whereby Achilles obtained exclusive rights to market Kaepa's footwear in Japan. The distributorship agreement expressly provided that Texas law and the English language would govern its interpretation, that it would be enforceable in San Antonio, Texas, and that Achilles consented to the jurisdiction of the Texas courts.

Kaepa grew increasingly dissatisfied with Achilles's performance under the contract. Accordingly, in July of 1994, Kaepa filed suit in

Texas state court, alleging (1) fraud and negligent misrepresentation by Achilles to induce Kaepa to enter into the distributorship agreement, and (2) breach of contract by Achilles. Thereafter, Achilles removed the action to federal district court, and the parties began a laborious discovery process which to date has resulted in the production of tens of thousands of documents. In February 1995, after appearing in the Texas action, removing the case to federal court, and engaging in comprehensive discovery, Achilles brought its own action in Japan, alleging mirror-image claims: (1) fraud by Kaepa to induce Achilles to enter into the distributorship agreement, and (2) breach of contract by Kaepa.

Back in Texas, Kaepa promptly filed a motion asking the district court to enjoin Achilles from prosecuting its suit in Japan (motion for an antisuit injunction). Achilles in turn moved to dismiss the federal court action on the ground of forum non conveniens. The district court denied Achilles's motion to dismiss and granted Kaepa's motion to enjoin, ordering Achilles to refrain from litigating the Japanese action and to file all of its counterclaims with the district court. Achilles timely appealed the grant of the antisuit injunction.

Achilles's primary argument is that the district court failed to give proper deference to principles of international comity when it granted Kaepa's motion for an antisuit injunction. * * * Under this deferential standard, findings of fact are upheld unless clearly erroneous, whereas legal conclusions " 'are subject to broad review and will be reversed if incorrect.' "

* * * The circuits differ * * * on the proper legal standard to employ when determining whether that injunctive power should be exercised. We have addressed the propriety of an antisuit injunction on two prior occasions, in *In re Unterweser Reederei Gmbh*[7] and *Bethell v. Peace*.[8] Emphasizing in both cases the need to prevent vexatious or oppressive litigation, we concluded that a district court does not abuse its discretion by issuing an antisuit injunction when it has determined "that allowing simultaneous prosecution of the same action in a foreign forum thousands of miles away would result in 'inequitable hardship' and 'tend to frustrate and delay the speedy and efficient determination of the cause.' "[9] The Seventh and the Ninth Circuits have either adopted or "incline[d] toward" this approach, but other circuits have employed a standard that elevates principles of international comity to the virtual exclusion of essentially all other considerations.

Achilles urges us to give greater deference to comity and apply the latter, more restrictive standard. We note preliminarily that, even though the standard espoused in *Unterweser* and *Bethell* focuses on the potentially vexatious nature of foreign litigation, it by no means excludes

---

7. *Unterweser*, 428 F.2d 888.

8. *Bethell*, 441 F.2d 495.

9. *Unterweser*, 428 F.2d at 890, 896 (noting as well that antisuit injunctions have been granted when foreign litigation would (1) frustrate a policy of the forum issuing the injunction; (2) be vexatious or oppressive; (3) threaten the issuing court's in rem or quasi in rem jurisdiction; or (4) prejudice other equitable considerations);* * *

the consideration of principles of comity. We decline, however, to require a district court to genuflect before a vague and omnipotent notion of comity every time that it must decide whether to enjoin a foreign action.

In the instant case, for example, it simply cannot be said that the grant of the antisuit injunction actually threatens relations between the United States and Japan. First, no public international issue is implicated by the case.... Second, the dispute has been long and firmly ensconced within the confines of the United States judicial system: Achilles consented to jurisdiction in Texas; stipulated that Texas law and the English language would govern any dispute; appeared in an action brought in Texas; removed that action to a federal court in Texas; engaged in extensive discovery pursuant to the directives of the federal court; and only then, with the federal action moving steadily toward trial, brought identical claims in Japan. Under these circumstances, we cannot conclude that the district court's grant of an antisuit injunction in any way trampled on notions of comity.

On the contrary, the facts detailed above strongly support the conclusion that the prosecution of the Japanese action would entail "an absurd duplication of effort" and would result in unwarranted inconvenience, expense, and vexation. Achilles's belated ploy of filing as putative plaintiff in Japan the very same claims against Kaepa that Kaepa had filed as plaintiff against Achilles smacks of cynicism, harassment, and delay. Accordingly, we hold that the district court did not abuse its discretion by granting Kaepa's motion for an antisuit injunction.

GARZA, CIRCUIT JUDGE, dissenting:

... I write to emphasize ... that under concurrent jurisdiction, "parallel proceedings on the same in personam claim should ordinarily be allowed to proceed simultaneously, at least until a judgment is reached in one which can be pled as res judicata in the other." The filing of a second parallel action in another jurisdiction does not necessarily conflict with or prevent the first court from exercising its legitimate concurrent jurisdiction.

The issuance of an antisuit injunction runs directly counter to this principle of tolerating parallel proceedings. An antisuit injunction "conveys the message ... that the issuing court has so little confidence in the foreign court's ability to adjudicate a given dispute fairly and efficiently that it is unwilling even to allow the possibility." It makes no difference that in formal terms the injunction is only addressed to the parties. The antisuit injunction operates to restrict the foreign court's ability to exercise its jurisdiction as effectively as if it were addressed to the foreign court itself. Enjoining the parties from litigating in a foreign court will necessarily compromise the principles of comity, and may lead to undesirable consequences. For example, the foreign court may react by issuing a similar injunction, thereby preventing any party from obtaining a remedy. The foreign court may also be less inclined to enforce a judgment by our courts. The refusal to enforce a foreign judgment, however, is less offensive than acting to prevent the foreign court from hearing the matter in the first place.

Antisuit injunctions intended to carve out exclusive jurisdiction may also have unintended, widespread effects on international commerce. Without "an atmosphere of cooperation and reciprocity between nations," the ability to predict future consequences of international transactions will inevitably suffer. To operate effectively and efficiently, international markets require a degree of predictability which can only be harmed by antisuit injunctions and the resulting breakdown of cooperation and reciprocity between courts of different nations. The attempt to exercise exclusive jurisdiction over international economic affairs is essentially an intrusion into the realm of international economic policy that should appropriately be left to our legislature and the treaty making process. As the court in *Laker Airways* stated, "Absent an explicit directive from Congress, this court has neither the authority nor the institutional resources to weigh the policy and political factors that must be evaluated when resolving competing claims of jurisdiction. In contrast, diplomatic and executive channels are, by definition, designed to exchange, negotiate, and reconcile the problems which accompany the realization of national interests within the sphere of international association."

The majority appears to require an affirmative showing that the granting of an antisuit injunction in this case would immediately and concretely affect adversely the relations between the United States and Japan. Unless there is evidence that this antisuit injunction would "actually threaten" the relations between the two countries, the majority is comfortable to assume otherwise. * * *Insisting on evidence of immediate and concrete harm, in the form of a diplomatic protest or otherwise, is both unrealistic and shortsighted. As with most transnational relations, the potential harm to international comity caused by the issuance of a specific antisuit injunction will be as difficult to predict, as it will be to remedy. It is precisely this troubling uncertainty, and the recognition that our courts are ill equipped to weigh these types of international policy considerations, that cautions us to make the respectful deference underlying international comity the rule rather than the exception.

... [T]he majority appears to rely primarily on the duplicative nature of the Japanese suit and the resulting "unwarranted inconvenience, expense, and vexation." The inconvenience, expense and vexation, however, are factors likely to be present whenever there is an exercise of concurrent jurisdiction by a foreign court. The majority's standard can be understood to hold, therefore, that "a duplication of the parties and issues, alone, is sufficient to justify a foreign antisuit injunction." ...

By focusing on the potential hardship to Kaepa of having to litigate in two forums, the majority applies an analysis that is more appropriately brought to bear in the context of a motion to dismiss for forum non conveniens. Considerations that are appropriate in deciding whether to decline jurisdiction are not as persuasive when deciding whether to deprive another court of jurisdiction. ... A dismissal on grounds of forum non conveniens by either court in this case would satisfy the majority's concern with avoiding hardship to the parties, without harming the interests of international comity. The district court is not in a position, however, to make the forum non conveniens determination on behalf of the Japanese court. In light of the important interests of international comity, the decision by a United States court to deprive a foreign court of jurisdiction must be supported by far weightier factors than would otherwise justify that court's decision to decline its own jurisdiction on forum non conveniens grounds.

Accordingly, I believe that the standard followed by the Second, Sixth, and D.C. Circuits more satisfactorily respects the principle of concurrent jurisdiction and safeguards the important interests of international comity. Under this stricter standard, a district court should look to only two factors in determining whether to issue an antisuit injunction: (1) whether the foreign action threatens the jurisdiction of the district court; and (2) whether the foreign action was an attempt to evade important public policies of the district court. Neither of these factors are present in this case. Because neither factor supports the issuance of an antisuit injunction in this case, I believe the district court abused its discretion by enjoining Achilles from prosecuting an action filed in Japan. Accordingly, I respectfully dissent.

Questions and Comments

1. The *Saga of Sir Freddie Laker* could make up an entire course on international litigation. The case has a special place in jurisprudence because it is one of the first to develop anti-suit injunction theory. Jurisdiction over airlines is relatively easy in each of the nations where the defendant airlines have regular service. The UK High Court certainly has jurisdiction over Laker, British Airways and British Caledonian, and also those foreign airlines that serve the British market. But it might not have jurisdiction over McDonnell Douglas. That would not seem to matter, a main focus of the English litigation was on *airlines*, not *airplanes*. The Laker cases do not give us any very clear law, but they confirm the use of anti-suit and anti-anti-suit injunctions and lead us to more recent decisions that help tell us when the use of those injunctions is allowed. Or do they? *Deutz* and *Kaepa* may help, or merely muddy the waters.

2. The Third Circuit in the *Deutz* decision first commented that using the better approach of international comity it would only issue an injunction (1) if *res judicata* applied, or (2) if "the foreign proceeding threatened the Court's jurisdiction ... or a strong public policy." 270 F.3d at 157. When it more thoroughly focused on comity, 270 F.3d 159–162, did it apply these standards? With regard to *res judicata*, wasn't the district court's injunction sufficient to anticipate its final decision? There had been a jury verdict in the federal district court decision, that the contract did not mandate arbitration. Isn't that *res judicata*?

3.   The jury verdict is not given any special sanctity by the circuit court. But the circuit court did mention that the English High Court noted that findings of fact had been made by a jury. The jury is of course important in England for criminal and a few civil trials. Would a civil law tradition nation court have commented in the same manner as did the English High Court?

4.   The *Deutz* circuit court's comity discussion helps to express the idea of comity, but does the decision really assist in establishing a predictable rule of application? Would the court be as inclined to apply comity to rulings of a Guatemalan court, or a Nigerian court, where "corrupt" may be an apt label for the judicial system? Is it fair and correct to suggest that most decisions applying comity refer to decisions of nations with a perceived well developed legal system, and a perceived low index of judicial corruption?

5.   The *Deutz* court notes the split among circuits. *Deutz* is considered among the courts following the "restrictive" view, granting injunctions infrequently. The next case, *Kaepa*, presents the "liberal" or "lax" standard. Is the difference that the liberal courts reject the concept of comity? The *Deutz* opinion does state that "Our jurisprudence thus reflects a serious concern for comity." Isn't this an issue begging for acceptance by the Supreme Court? Would the present Supreme Court be likely to handle the issue of comity with sensitivity? Has the Supreme Court handled international cases very effectively? Cases with international issues that have been strongly criticized include *Asahi Metal Industry Co., Ltd. v. Superior Court of California,* 480 U.S. 102, 107 S.Ct. 1026, 94 L.Ed.2d 92 (1987)(jurisdiction-discussed in Problem 3.2), *Société Nationale Industrielle Aerospatiale v. United States District Court,* 482 U.S. 522, 107 S.Ct. 2542, 96 L.Ed.2d 461 (1987) (taking of evidence abroad—discussed in Problem 3.5); *United States v. Alvarez–Machain,* 504 U.S. 655, 112 S.Ct. 2188, 119 L.Ed.2d 441 (1992) (extradition).

6.   What if the High Court in the U.K. Deutz litigation had granted the anti-suit injunction, commenting that the U.S. legal system is oppressive because it allows contingent fees, punitive and treble damages, high costs not recoverable by the winning party, and long delays? Some U.K. courts have been quite explicit in discussing the nature of another nation's legal system when discussing what the English call the "natural" or "proper" forum. For example in referring to the U.K. forum as proper when considered in conflict with U.S. courts, U.K. courts have criticized U.S. contingent fees, punitive damages, use of a jury in civil trials, expense of litigation, and extensive discovery. See, e.g., *Simon Engineering,* [1996] 1 Lloyd's Rep. 104.

7.   The *Kaepa* case facts deal with Japan, as opposed to Germany and the UK in *Deutz*. It is thus hard to suggest that the case differs because of different notions of comity towards the different nations' legal systems involved in these two cases. Is *Kaepa* easier from the perspective of similar parallel proceedings? Would the better tactic have been to ask the Japanese court for a stay? Is the case brought in the High Court in our hypothetical a mirror-image claim?. In our hypothetical DROF AG and DROF UK have sued the two plaintiffs. Presumably, the request for an anti-suit injunction preventing the U.S. and UK parties from proceeding in any actions means those actions brought in the United States.

8.   Achilles, the defendant in *Kaepa,* argues that the district court failed to give adequate consideration to comity. Does the Circuit Court do any better? Do you agree, as the Circuit Court notes, that "other circuits have employed a standard that elevates principles of international comity to the virtual exclusion of essentially all other considerations?" Doesn't comity incorporate within it other considerations, such as *res judicata?*

9.   The *Kaepa* court discounts two factors that might suggest restraint. First, that the case might have public international law implications. Second, that it is not a case where similar claims were brought nearly *simultaneously*. With regard to the first, doesn't the court's view mean that anti-suit injunctions are fair game in all private litigation? With regard to the second, is the court merely adopting a first to file view? Was the case in the United States really "long and firmly ensconced within the confines of the United States judicial system?" Should the fact that Achilles appeared in Texas, consented to jurisdiction and actively engaged in discovery be more important? Does that mean that Achilles should not have appeared at all?

10.   Does Achilles' filing "smack of cynicism, harassment, and delay?"

11.   The dissent in *Kaepa* begins with a discussion of comity. Is it more in line with the *Deutz* decision's discussion? Is the dissent trying to define comity without making it a legal obligation?. The dissent believes that the majority was correct in its view that the court has power over persons within its jurisdiction. But does that not beg the question? We assume that in these cases there is dual jurisdiction, and are trying to find some solution to the problems of having cases proceed in two jurisdictions. The dissent suggests that refusing to enforce a foreign judgment is less offensive than use of an anti-suit injunction. Do you agree?

12.   Does the dissent agree with the majority that private commercial disputes seem to justify the use of anti-suit injunctions where suits involving questions of public international law do not? It may be interesting to explore how the legislature or executive might help reduce the friction caused by anti-suit injunctions.

13.   The dissent suggests that a *forum non conveniens* dismissal might be the better solution? But does Japan recognize such theory? And what if both courts denied a *forum non conveniens* motion?

14.   Does the *Kaepa* dissent offer a rule any different than the "other" circuit courts, that have adopted the "restrictive" view?

PART C.   PARALLEL PROCEEDINGS: CONSTITUTIONAL ISSUES AND RIPENESS

The Yahoo! decision illustrates the use of parallel proceedings in a relatively new area—cyberspace. Control over the transfer of information raises First Amendments issues. An aggrieved party in the United States might wait for a final foreign judgment to be rendered and challenge the judgment when and if it is brought to the United States for enforcement. But the U.S. party may prefer not to wait, as in Yahoo!, and initiate litigation in the United States to enjoin any future such foreign judgment, or for a declaration that the U.S. did not engage in the challenged conduct. The district court in Yahoo! Focused almost exclusively on the First Amendment issue, while the 9th Circuit Court, in a very divided en banc decision, was less certain about the constitutional issue.

YAHOO!, INC. v. LA LIGUE CONTRE LE RACISME ET L'ANTISEMITISME

United States District Court, Northern District of California, 2001.
169 F.Supp.2d 1181.

Fogel, District Judge.

Defendants * * *, citizens of France, are non-profit organizations dedicated to eliminating anti-Semitism. Plaintiff Yahoo!, Inc. * * * is a [Delaware] corporation * * *. Yahoo! is an Internet service provider that operates various Internet websites and services * * *. Yahoo! services ending in the suffix, ".com," without an associated country code as a prefix or extension * * * use the English language and target users who are residents of, utilize servers based in and operate under the laws of the United States. Yahoo! subsidiary corporations operate regional Yahoo! sites and services in twenty other nations, including, for example, Yahoo! France * * *. Each of these regional web sites contains the host nation's unique two-letter code * * * (e.g., Yahoo! France is found at *http://www.yahoo.fr*). Yahoo!'s regional sites use the local region's primary language, target the local citizenry, and operate under local laws.

Yahoo! provides a variety of means by which people from all over the world can communicate and interact with one another over the Internet. * * * Any computer user * * * is able to post materials on many of these Yahoo! sites, which * * * are instantly accessible by anyone who logs on * * *. Yahoo!'s auction site allows anyone to post an item for sale and solicit bids from any computer user * * * around the globe. * * * Yahoo! is never a party to a transaction, and the buyer and seller are responsible for arranging * * * payment and shipment * * *. Yahoo! monitors the transaction through limited regulation by prohibiting particular items from being sold (such as stolen goods, body parts, prescription and illegal drugs, weapons, and goods violating U.S. copyright laws or the Iranian and Cuban embargos) * * *. Yahoo! informs auction sellers that they must comply with Yahoo!'s policies and may not offer items to buyers in jurisdictions in which the sale of such item violates the jurisdiction's applicable laws. Yahoo! does not actively regulate the content of each posting, and individuals are able to post, and have in fact posted, highly offensive matter, including Nazi-related propaganda and Third Reich memorabilia, on Yahoo!'s auction sites.

* * * LICRA sent a "cease and desist" letter to Yahoo!'s * * * informing Yahoo! that the sale of Nazi and Third Reich related goods through its auction services violates French law. * * * Defendants subsequently * * *filed a civil complaint against Yahoo! in * * * Paris. The French Court found that approximately 1,000 Nazi and Third Reich related objects * * * were being offered for sale on Yahoo.com's auction site. * * * [T]he French Court concluded that the Yahoo.com auction

site violates * * * the French Criminal Code, which prohibits exhibition of Nazi propaganda and artifacts for sale. * * * [T]he French Court entered an order requiring Yahoo! to (1) eliminate French citizens' access to any material on the Yahoo.com auction site that offers for sale any Nazi objects, relics, insignia, emblems, and flags; (2) eliminate French citizens' access to web pages on Yahoo.com displaying text, extracts, or quotations from *Mein Kampf* and *Protocol of the Elders of Zion;* (3) post a warning to French citizens on Yahoo.fr that any search through Yahoo.com may lead to sites containing material prohibited by * * * the French Criminal Code, and that such viewing of the prohibited material may result in legal action against the Internet user; (4) remove from all browser directories accessible in the French Republic index headings entitled "negationists" and from all hypertext links the equation of "negationists" under the heading "Holocaust". * * * The order concludes:

> We order the Company YAHOO! Inc. to take all necessary measures to dissuade and render impossible any access via Yahoo.com to the Nazi artifact auction service and to any other site or service that may be construed as constituting an apology for Nazism or a contesting of Nazi crimes. High Court of Paris, May 22, 2000, Interim Court Order No. 00/05308, 00/05309 * * *

Yahoo! asked the French Court to reconsider the terms of the order, claiming that although it easily could post the required warning on Yahoo.fr, compliance with the order's requirements with respect to Yahoo.com was technologically impossible. The French Court * * * "reaffirmed" its order * * *. The French Court ordered Yahoo! to comply with the * * * order within three (3) months or face a penalty of 100,000 Francs (approximately U.S. $13,300) for each day of non-compliance. The French Court also provided that penalties assessed against Yahoo! Inc. may not be collected from Yahoo! France. * * *

Yahoo! subsequently posted the required warning and prohibited postings * * * from appearing on Yahoo.fr. Yahoo! also amended the auction policy of Yahoo.com to prohibit individuals from auctioning:

> Any item that promotes, glorifies, or is directly associated with groups or individuals known principally for hateful or violent positions or acts, such as Nazis or the Ku Klux Klan. Official government-issue stamps and coins are not prohibited under this policy. Expressive media, such as books and films, may be subject to more permissive standards as determined by Yahoo! in its sole discretion.

Yahoo! claims * * * it cannot comply with the French order without banning Nazi-related material from Yahoo.com altogether. Yahoo! contends that such a ban would infringe impermissibly upon its rights under the First Amendment * * *. Accordingly, Yahoo! filed a complaint in this Court seeking a declaratory judgment that the French Court's orders are neither cognizable nor enforceable under the laws of the United States.

What is at issue here is whether it is consistent with the Constitution and laws of the United States for another nation to regulate speech by a United States resident within the United States on the basis that such speech can be accessed by Internet users in that nation. * * * [T]he implications of this question go far beyond the facts of this case. The modern world is home to widely varied cultures with radically divergent value systems. There is little doubt that Internet users in the United States routinely engage in speech that violates, for example, China's laws against religious expression, the laws of various nations against advocacy of gender equality or homosexuality, or even the United Kingdom's restrictions on freedom of the press. * * * The Court has stated that it must and will decide this case in accordance with the Constitution and laws of the United States. * * * [I]t necessarily adopts certain value judgments embedded in those enactments, including the fundamental judgment * * * that it is preferable to permit the non-violent expression of offensive viewpoints rather than to impose viewpoint-based governmental regulation upon speech. The government and people of France have made a different judgment * * *.

* * *

The French order prohibits the sale or display of items based on their association with a particular political organization and bans the display of websites based on the authors' viewpoint with respect to the Holocaust and anti-Semitism. A United States court constitutionally could not make such an order. The First Amendment does not permit the government to engage in viewpoint-based regulation of speech absent a compelling governmental interest, such as averting a clear and present danger of imminent violence. In addition, the French Court's mandate that Yahoo! "take all necessary measures to dissuade and render impossible any access via Yahoo.com to the Nazi artifact auction service and to any other site or service that may be construed as constituting an apology for Nazism or a contesting of Nazi crimes" is far too general and imprecise to survive the strict scrutiny required by the First Amendment. The phrase, "and any other site or service that *may be construed* as an apology for Nazism or a contesting of Nazi crimes" fails to provide Yahoo! with a sufficiently definite warning as to what is proscribed. Phrases such as "all necessary measures" and "render impossible" instruct Yahoo! to undertake efforts that will impermissibly chill and perhaps even censor protected speech. "The loss of First Amendment freedoms, for even minimal periods of time, unquestionably constitutes irreparable injury."

* * * The extent to which the United States, or any state, honors the judicial decrees of foreign nations is a matter of choice, governed by "the comity of nations." *Hilton v. Guyot,* 159 U.S. 113, 163, 16 S.Ct. 139, 40 L.Ed. 95 (1895). * * * United States courts generally recognize foreign judgments and decrees unless enforcement would be prejudicial or contrary to the country's interests. *Somportex Ltd. v. Philadelphia*

Chewing Gum Corp., ... Laker Airways v. Sabena Belgian World Airlines, ...

* * * What makes this case uniquely challenging is that the Internet in effect allows one to speak in more than one place at the same time. Although France has the sovereign right to regulate what speech is permissible in France, this Court may not enforce a foreign order that violates the protections of the United States Constitution by chilling protected speech that occurs simultaneously within our borders. *See, e.g., Matusevitch v. Telnikoff,* 877 F.Supp. 1, 4 (D.D.C.1995) (declining to enforce British libel judgment because British libel standards "deprive the plaintiff of his constitutional rights"); *Bachchan v. India Abroad Publications, Inc.,* 154 Misc.2d 228, 585 N.Y.S.2d 661 (Sup.Ct.1992) (declining to enforce a British libel judgment because of its "chilling effect" on the First Amendment); ... The reason for limiting comity in this area is sound. "The protection to free speech and the press embodied in [the First] amendment would be seriously jeopardized by the entry of foreign judgments granted pursuant to standards deemed appropriate in [another country] but considered antithetical to the protections afforded the press by the U.S. Constitution." *Bachchan,* 585 N.Y.S.2d at 665. Absent a body of law that establishes international standards with respect to speech on the Internet and an appropriate treaty or legislation addressing enforcement of such standards to speech originating within the United States, the principle of comity is outweighed by the Court's obligation to uphold the First Amendment.

* * *

Yahoo! seeks a declaration from this Court that the First Amendment precludes enforcement within the United States of a French order intended to regulate the content of its speech over the Internet. * * * Defendants have failed to show the existence of a genuine issue of material fact or to identify any such issue the existence of which could be shown through further discovery. Accordingly, the motion for summary judgment will be granted.

YAHOO! INC. v. LA LIGUE CONTRE LE RACISME ET L'ANTISEMITISME

United States Court of Appeals, Ninth Circuit, 2006.
433 F.3d 1199.

A majority of the en banc court concludes that the district court had personal jurisdiction over the defendants. Of that majority, three judges conclude that the action should be dismissed for lack of ripeness. Five judges conclude that the case is ripe for adjudication. The three remaining judges conclude that the action should be dismissed because the district court lacked personal jurisdiction over the defendants.

FLETCHER, with whom SCHROEDER and GOULD, join as to the entire opinion, and with whom HAWKINS, FISHER, PAEZ, CLIFTON and BEA, join as to Parts I and II. [Part I was background and Part II personal jurisdiction. Part III was ripeness.]:

The district court held that the exercise of personal jurisdiction over LICRA and UEJF was proper, that the dispute was ripe, that abstention was unnecessary, and that the French orders are not enforceable in the United States because such enforcement would violate the First Amendment. The district court did not reach the question whether the orders are recognizable. LICRA and UEJF appeal only the personal jurisdiction, ripeness, and abstention holdings. A majority of the en banc panel holds, as explained in Part II, that the district court properly exercised personal jurisdiction. . . . A plurality of the panel concludes, as explained in Part III, that the case is not ripe. . . . We do not reach the abstention question.

* * *

The French court has not imposed any penalty on Yahoo! for violations of the May 22 or November 20 orders. Nor has either LICRA or UEJF returned to the French court to seek the imposition of a penalty. Both organizations affirmatively represent to us that they have no intention of doing so if Yahoo! maintains its current level of compliance. Yet neither organization is willing to ask the French court to vacate its orders. As LICRA and UEJF's counsel made clear at oral argument, "My clients will not give up the right to go to France and enforce the French judgment against Yahoo! in France if they revert to their old ways and violate French law."

* * *

* * * [W]e agree with the district court that the effect of the French court's orders on Yahoo! is sufficient to create a case or controversy within the meaning of Article III. However, we disagree with the district court's conclusion that there is prudential ripeness. In its current form, this case presents the sort of "[p]roblems of prematurity and abstractness" that counsel against reaching the First Amendment question that Yahoo! insists is presented by this case. In determining whether a case satisfies prudential requirements for ripeness, we consider two factors: "the fitness of the issues for judicial decision," and "the hardship to the parties of withholding court consideration."

Whether a dispute is sufficiently ripe to be fit for judicial decision depends not only on the state of the factual record. It depends also on the substantive legal question to be decided. If the legal question is straightforward, relatively little factual development may be necessary. . . . By contrast, if the legal question depends on numerous factors for its resolution, extensive factual development may be necessary.

* * * The legal question presented by this case is whether the two interim orders of the French court are enforceable in this country. These orders, by their explicit terms, require only that Yahoo! restrict access by Internet users located in France. The orders say nothing whatsoever about restricting access by Internet users in the United States. We are asked to decide whether enforcement of these interim orders would be "repugnant" to California public policy.

In a typical enforcement case, the party in whose favor the foreign judgment was granted comes to an American court affirmatively seeking enforcement. . . . However, this is not the typical case, for the successful plaintiffs in the French court do not seek enforcement. Rather, Yahoo!, the unsuccessful defendant in France, seeks a declaratory judgment that the French court's interim orders are unenforceable anywhere in this country.

* * *

Under the repugnancy standard, American courts sometimes enforce judgments that conflict with American public policy or are based on foreign law that differs substantially from American state or federal law. See, e.g., In re Hashim, 213 F.3d 1169, 1172 (9th Cir.2000) (reversing bankruptcy court's refusal to enforce English court's award of $10 million in costs against debtors whose assets had been frozen by Saddam Hussein); Milhoux v. Linder, 902 P.2d 856, 861–62 (Colo.Ct.App.1995) (affirming recognition of Belgian judgment as a matter of comity, even though it was based on a 30–year Belgian statute of limitations). Inconsistency with American law is not necessarily enough to prevent recognition and enforcement of a foreign judgment in the United States. The foreign judgment must be, in addition, repugnant to public policy.

With the suit in its current state, it is difficult to know whether enforcement of the French court's interim orders would be repugnant to California public policy. The first difficulty is evident. As indicated by the label "interim," the French court contemplated that it might enter later orders. We cannot know whether it might modify these "interim" orders before any attempt is made to enforce them in the United States. A second, more important, difficulty is that we do not know whether the French court would hold that Yahoo! is now violating its two interim orders. After the French court entered the orders, Yahoo! voluntarily changed its policy to comply with them, at least to some extent. There is some reason to believe that the French court will not insist on full and literal compliance with its interim orders, and that Yahoo!'s changed policy may amount to sufficient compliance.

LICRA and UEJF insist that Yahoo! has now, in their words, "substantially complied" with the French court's orders. We take this to be a statement that, in their view, Yahoo! has complied "in large measure" with the orders. For its part, however, Yahoo! insists that it continues to be in serious violation of the orders. The district court did not hold that Yahoo! is in violation, substantial or otherwise, of the French court's orders. It wrote only that Yahoo! does not "appear" to be in full compliance with the French court's order with respect to its auction site, and that various anti-semitic sites continue to be accessible through yahoo.com. There is only one court that can authoritatively tell us whether Yahoo! has now complied "in large measure" with the French court's interim orders. That is, of course, the French court.

To the extent that we are uncertain about whether Yahoo! has complied "in large measure" with the French court's orders, the responsibility for that uncertainty can be laid at Yahoo!'s door. * * * Because we do not know whether Yahoo! has complied "in large measure" with the French court's orders, we cannot know what effect, if any, compliance with the French court's orders would have on Yahoo!'s protected speech-related activities.

In its briefing to this court, Yahoo! contends that restricting access by French Internet users in a manner sufficient to satisfy the French court would in some unspecified fashion require Yahoo! simultaneously to restrict access by Internet users in the United States. This may or may not be true. It is almost certainly not true if Yahoo! is now complying "in large measure" with the French court's orders, for in that event the French court will almost certainly hold that no further compliance is necessary.... However, it is possible, as Yahoo! contends, that it has not complied "in large measure" with the French court orders, and that the French court would require further compliance. It is also possible, as Yahoo! contends, that further compliance might have the necessary consequence of requiring Yahoo! to restrict access by American Internet users....

The possible—but at this point highly speculative—impact of further compliance with the French court's orders on access by American users would be highly relevant to the question whether enforcement of the orders would be repugnant to California public policy. But we cannot get to that question without knowing whether the French court would find that Yahoo! has already complied "in large measure," for only on a finding of current noncompliance would the issue of further compliance, and possible impact on American users, arise.

Without a finding that further compliance with the French court's orders would necessarily result in restrictions on access by users in the United States, the only question in this case is whether California public policy and the First Amendment require unrestricted access by Internet users in France. In other words, the only question would involve a determination whether the First Amendment has extraterritorial application. The extent of First Amendment protection of speech accessible solely by those outside the United States is a difficult and, to some degree, unresolved issue. We are thus uncertain about whether, or in what form, a First Amendment question might be presented to us. If the French court were to hold that Yahoo!'s voluntary change of policy has already brought it into compliance with its interim orders "in large measure," no First Amendment question would be presented at all. Further, if the French court were to require additional compliance with respect to users in France, but that additional compliance would not require any restriction on access by users in the United States, Yahoo! would only be asserting a right to extraterritorial application of the First Amendment. Finally, if the French court were to require additional compliance with respect to users in France, and that additional compliance would have the necessary consequence of restricting access by users in the United States, Yahoo! would have both a domestic and an extraterritorial First Amendment argument. The legal analysis of these different questions is different, and the answers are likely to be different as well.

We next consider "the hardship to the parties of withholding court consideration." As discussed above, we believe that Yahoo! has suffered sufficient harm to justify (though not by a wide margin) the exercise of personal jurisdiction over LICRA and UEJF. The threshold requirement for hardship for purposes of personal jurisdiction, however, is not necessarily the same as the threshold for purposes of prudential ripeness. Particularly where, as here, there are substantial uncertainties bearing on the legal analysis to be performed, there is a high threshold requirement for hardship. Yahoo! contends that it will suffer real hardship if we do not decide its suit at this time. Yahoo! makes essentially two arguments. First, it argues that the potential monetary penalty under the French court's orders is mounting every day, and that the enforcement of a penalty against it here could be extremely onerous. Second, it argues that the French court's orders substantially limit speech that is protected by the First Amendment. * * * In sum, it is extremely unlikely that any penalty, if assessed, could ever be enforced against Yahoo! in the United States. Further, First Amendment harm may not exist at all, given the possibility that Yahoo! has now "in large measure" complied with the French court's orders through its voluntary actions, unrelated to the orders. Alternatively, if Yahoo! has not "in large measure" complied with the orders, its violation lies in the fact that it has insufficiently restricted access to anti-semitic materials by Internet users located in France. There is some possibility that in further restricting access to these French users, Yahoo! might have to restrict access by American users. But this possibility is, at this point, highly speculative. This level of harm is not sufficient to overcome the factual uncertainty bearing on the legal question presented and thereby to render this suit ripe.

The dissent addressed to the question of ripeness makes two principal contentions. First, it contends that the French court's interim orders are unconstitutional on their face, and that further factual development is therefore not needed. Second, it contends that if any further factual development is necessary, we should remand to the district court for that purpose. * * * If it were true that the French court's orders by their terms require Yahoo! to block access by users in the United States, this would be a different and much easier case. In that event, we would be inclined to agree with the dissent. But this is not the case. The French court's orders, by their terms, require only that Yahoo! restrict access by users in France....

... The dissent argues that we should remand to the district court to determine whether this is a necessary consequence. But we cannot obtain this determination merely by remanding to the district court. Before the district court can engage in useful factfinding, it must know whether (or to what extent) Yahoo! has already sufficiently complied with the French court's interim orders.

... [T]he essential initial step is to find out from the French court whether Yahoo! has complied "in large measure" with its orders, and, if not, what further compliance is required. Until we know that, the district court cannot perform any useful factfinding on the question of whether a necessary consequence of compliance with the French court's orders will be to restrict access by Internet users in the United States.

Yahoo! wants a decision providing broad First Amendment protection for speech and speech-related activities on the Internet that might violate the laws or offend the sensibilities of other countries. As currently framed, however, Yahoo!'s suit comes perilously close to a request for a forbidden advisory opinion. There was a live dispute when Yahoo! first filed suit in federal district court, but Yahoo! soon thereafter voluntarily changed its policy to comply, at least in part, with the commands of the French court's interim orders. This change in policy may or may not have mooted Yahoo!'s federal suit, but it has at least come close. Unless and until Yahoo! changes its policy again, and thereby more clearly violates the French court's orders, it is unclear how much is now actually in dispute.

When the votes of the three judges who conclude that the suit is unripe are combined with the votes of the three dissenting judges who conclude that there is no personal jurisdiction over LICRA and UEJF, there are six votes to dismiss Yahoo!'s suit. We therefore REVERSE and REMAND to the district court with instructions to dismiss without prejudice.

Questions and Comments

1. The Yahoo litigation involving parallel proceedings in French and U.S. courts is especially important because it involves cyberspace. The issue of jurisdiction over the Internet is far from settled throughout the world. Australian courts in *Dow Jones & Co. v. Gutnick*, [2002] HCA 56 (10 Dec 2002)(www.hcourt.gov.au) have asserted jurisdiction over Dow Jones for a Barron's Magazine article published in the United States and also carried on Barron's website. The website is accessible from anywhere in the world. Of some 550,000 paid subscribers to the website, several hundred live in Victoria, the home of Gutnick and his business headquarters. See Jon Hart, Internet Libel Suit Against Dow Jones Permitted to Proceed in Australian Courts, www.dlalaw.com. The Google organizational structure seems to place it at greater risk than Yahoo! It has more substantial subsidiaries in foreign nations. Might not Google wish to reorganize in view of Yahoo!'s experience? See Jason Krause, Casting A Wide Net, 88 ABA Journal, November 2002, at 20; Paul Schiff Berman, The Globalization of Jurisdiction, 151 U.Penn. L.Rev. 311 (2002).

2. What if the French order had been more specific, including only item (1) "eliminating French citizens' access to any material on the Yahoo.com auction that offers for sale any Nazi objects, relics, insignia, emblems, and flags?" Nothing about which the French complained seemed to be current promotion of a policy of the extermination of all Jewish persons throughout the world. What if such a website was available?

3. The Constitutional discussion came within the consideration of ripeness. Is it an issue of ripeness? Is the Court's extraterritorial extension of the First Amendment supported by sound reasoning?

4. The personal jurisdiction portion of the Circuit Court's decision (a majority believed there was personal jurisdiction) has been discussed in Problem 3.2. Five of eleven of the Circuit Court believed that the case was ripe for decision, in support of the conclusion of the District Court. But the three that believed the case should be dismissed for lack of ripeness joined with the three that believed that there was no personal jurisdiction gave a plurality resulting in reversal and remanding. Where does this leave us?

5. The Circuit Court did not address abstention. The District Court stated:

> Defendants * * * argue that this Court should abstain from deciding the instant case because Yahoo! simply is unhappy with the outcome of the French litigation and is trying to obtain a more favorable result here. Indeed, abstention is an appropriate remedy for international forum-shopping. In *Supermicro Computer, Inc. v. Digitechnic, S.A.,* 145 F.Supp.2d 1147 (N.D.Cal.2001), a California manufacturer was sued by a corporate customer in France for selling a defective product. The California company sought a declaratory judgment in the United States that its products were not defective, that the French customer's misuse of the product caused the product to fail, and that if the California company was at fault, only limited legal remedies were available. The court concluded that the purpose of the action for declaratory relief was to avoid an unfavorable result in the French courts. It noted that the action was not filed until a year after the French proceedings began, that the French proceedings were still ongoing, and that the French defendants had no intent to sue in the United States. It concluded that the declaratory relief action clearly was "litigation involving the same parties and the same disputed transaction."

In view of the Circuit's opinion, how might it have ruled on abstention?

6. How should the U.S. court rule in our hypothetical in view of the above discussions? Is there additional information needed to make such a ruling? How do you act if you are the U.S. attorney for the UK plaintiffs and the High Court in the UK had granted the defendants in the U.S. action (DROF AG and DROF–UK) the anti-suit injunction? Does it serve any purpose to get the anti-anti-suit injunction?

7. What if a member of the British Parliament, in response to the U.S. court's granting an anti-anti-suit injunction, following the Laker experience, that prohibited the UK defendants in the U.S. action from taking any actions, including seeking legislative assistance, filed a bill to relieve the DROF AF AND DROF–UK PLC of any responsibility in the event of a decision in favor of the plaintiffs the United States?

8. The *Bachchan* and *Telnikoff* decisions referred to near the end of the district court Yahoo! extract are included in Problem 6.1 on bringing a foreign judgment to the United States for recognition and enforcement. Whether it is enforcing a foreign judgment or addressing a request to enjoin parties from litigating abroad, U.S. First Amendment rights often appear to

trump considerations of comity or interest balancing. For a more recent decision *see Sarl Louis Feraud Int'l v. Viewfinder Inc.*, 406 F.Supp.2d 274 (S.D.N.Y. 2005).

PROBLEM 3.7   PRE–TRIAL PROVISIONAL, PROTECTIVE MEASURES

SECTION I. THE SETTING

At the very beginning of making decisions such as the choice of forum, the plaintiffs should anticipate the entire course of the litigation to consider whether a favorable judgment might be collected. However willing the courts of another nation may be to recognize and enforce a foreign judgment, a favorable judgment may be a hollow victory if there are no assets upon which to execute the judgment. While the plaintiffs may believe that the various defendants have assets that are reachable, that may not be the case. CANTIRE may not have the assets of Bridgestone/Firestone, and DROF AG may not have the assets of Daimler–Benz. VUSCO, the U.S. distributor, may have few assets if it does not have title to the vehicles that it distributes. Assuming that it is not clear how extensive the assets are of each defendant, we return to the initial considerations of counsel for the plaintiffs and address the issue of some form of pre-trial provisional measure whereby the plaintiffs may identify and prohibit the transfer of assets of the defendants.

Assume some additional facts. An article in the New York Times arts section discussed the extensive American art collection owned by VUSCO, located in its corporate offices in New York City and on loan to the art museums at both Stanford University in California and Oxford in England, both universities from which VUSCO's CEO and founder graduated. DROF UK has physical assets in England and maintains a substantial Euro account in Deutsche Bank in Frankfurt. The plaintiffs' lawyers have further discovered that DROF AG entered the auto financing and insurance business a dozen years ago. Both are undertaken by wholly owned subsidiaries, DROF CREDIT, LLC and DROF INSURANCE LLC, chartered and headquartered in Hamilton, Bermuda. Some investigations have disclosed that both of the Bermuda subsidiaries have been extremely profitable and have large bank accounts in Bermuda and accounts receivables in several countries, including the United States. That may be important, because, upon investigation, DROF AG appears to have more liabilities than assets in Germany. Recent newspaper articles have talked about it being an acquisition target of Porsche.

SECTION II. FOCUS OF CONSIDERATION

When the four plaintiffs sue VUSCO in the federal district court in New Jersey, they would like to attach whatever property VUSCO has, including the art collections in California and Oxford. They would also like to prevent DROF UK from moving any of its assets from the Deutsche Bank in Frankfurt, and to both tie-up the bank accounts in Bermuda and locate and block the accounts receivable in the United

States. Your role is to advise them on the laws applicable to pre-trial attachment and whether those laws have extraterritorial reach. VUSCO will oppose the attachment of the art, as may the museums in California and especially Oxford. DROF UK will object to any attempt by a U.S. court to extend its laws extraterritorially and control DROF UK's assets in Germany and Bermuda. Deutsche Bank in Germany may also object to any possible U.S. court order affecting Euro accounts in the Frankfurt bank.

The reasoning behind the rules of attachment of a nation may be influenced by the rules of jurisdiction. Problems 5.1 and 5.2 address some of the distinctions between U.S. jurisdictional norms and those of other nations, specifically the United Kingdom and Germany, with the influence of European Union law, and Japan. This problem attempts to focus on the specific rules of attachment, leaving jurisdiction to the later problems.

SECTION III. READINGS, QUESTIONS AND COMMENTS

PART A. PRE–TRIAL PROVISIONAL PROTECTIVE MEASURES IN THE UNITED STATES

Over the past century, property as a basis for jurisdiction has developed as an important theory, encouraged by the strictness of personal jurisdiction elaborated in *Pennoyer v. Neff* in 1877,[1] and perhaps reaching an apogee of broadness of scope in *Harris v. Balk* in 1905.[2] Real property, bank accounts and even claims a defendant had against a third party, if within the jurisdiction of the court, could be the property that provided jurisdiction over a non-resident, whether or not the property related to the cause of action. But any judgment recovery based on this *quasi in rem* jurisdiction could not be in excess of the value of the attached property. The judgment had little value abroad since it was not entitled to full faith and credit in other nations. The two paths of jurisdiction, property based and personal jurisdiction that were winding an uncertain course through the courts, would not endure. In the 1977 *Shaffer v. Heitner* decision,[3] the Supreme Court nearly closed the door to *in rem* jurisdiction, requiring any assertion of jurisdiction to meet the standards of minimum contacts and due process first established in *International Shoe*.[4] Jurisdiction would thus be measured by a single standard. This brings us to pre-trial provisional relief. Justice Marshall in *Shaffer* stated that "a State in which property is located should have jurisdiction to attach that property, by use of proper procedures, as security for a judgment being sought in a forum where litigation can be maintained consistently with *International Shoe*."[5] That is a very limited form of relief, tied to the forum for the principal case. We are concerned

---

1. 95 U.S. 714, 24 L.Ed. 565.

2. 198 U.S. 215, 25 S.Ct. 625, 49 L.Ed. 1023.

3. 433 U.S. 186, 97 S.Ct. 2569, 53 L.Ed.2d 683.

4. *International Shoe Co. v. State of Washington*, 326 U.S. 310, 66 S.Ct. 154, 90 L.Ed. 95 (1945).

5. 433 U.S. at 210, 97 S.Ct. at 2583.

with a much broader possibility, provisional relief against property outside the United States, and, while not at issue in our hypothetical, would a U.S. court respect a provisional relief order of a foreign court directed to property in the United States?

In view of *Shaffer,* our plaintiffs are most unlikely to be able to proceed directly against the art of VUSCO located in California, but may enforce a judgment obtained in New Jersey in California. The plaintiffs, consequently, may wish to attach the California property to assure that it is not removed during the New Jersey proceedings. Another intention of the plaintiffs is to secure any debts that various U.S. distributors of DROF AG or DROF UK owe the foreign companies. A judgment against DROF AG or DROF UK in New Jersey may be enforced against those debts, and perhaps they may be attached. But what about a judgment obtained in Germany by the plaintiffs against DROF AG, or in England against DROF UK? Could that judgment be enforced in Michigan against a distributor who owed a debt to DROF AG or DROF UK, respectively. If the foreign judgment were brought to the United States and a court ordered the attachment pending its decision on enforcing the foreign judgment there should be little problem satisfying a U.S. enforcement judgment against the attached assets. But what if the German or English court issued some form of pre-trial provisional ruling that ordered the Michigan debtor not to pay or otherwise transfer funds representing the amount of the debt? Would a Michigan court respect that order?

DAVID EPSTEIN, JEFFREY L. SNYDER & CHARLES S. BALDWIN, IV, INTERNATIONAL LITIGATION

3d ed. 1998, Supp. 2002.

If there is jurisdiction over a dispute in the courts of two or more countries, an important consideration in selecting the right forum is the location in which sufficient assets exist to satisfy the judgment. This is a crucial factor since enforcement of the judgment in a foreign jurisdiction-may be problematic and subject to varying conditions and exceptions. If assets are located in more than one jurisdiction, a further element to be considered is the availability of preliminary remedies to maintain the status quo during the pendency of the litigation, such as preliminary injunctive relief and preliminary attachments. These are important remedies, especially where there is a threat of asset flight out of the jurisdiction prior to final adjudication of the dispute.

The issue has arisen as to whether a United States District Court has the power to issue a preliminary injunction in order to protect a potential future damages remedy, even if the usual requirements for obtaining preliminary equitable relief have been met. In *De Beers Consol. Mines v. United States*[24] the government sought to enjoin future antitrust violations by De Beers. The government did not seek a prelimi-

---

24. 325 U.S. 212 (1945).

nary injunction to protect any potential future damages remedy to which it might become entitled. Instead, the government sought to preserve a source of funds against which it could later threaten a contempt sanction as a practical means of enforcing whatever injunction might be granted. The Court held that the preliminary injunction was inappropriate inasmuch as it "deal[t] with a matter wholly outside the issues in the suit."[25] In this connection, the Court stated as follows:

> To sustain the (preliminary injunction) would create a precedent of sweeping effect. This suit ... is not to be distinguished from any other suit in equity. What applies to it applies to all such. Every suitor who resorts to chancery for any sort of relief by injunction may, on a mere statement of belief that the defendant can easily make away with or transport his money or goods, impose an injunction on him, indefinite in duration, disabling him to use so much of his funds or property as the court deems necessary for security or compliance with its possible decree. And, if so, it is difficult to see why a plaintiff in any action for a personal judgment in tort or contract may not, also, apply to the chancellor for a so-called injunction sequestering his opponent's assets pending recovery and satisfaction of a judgment in such a law action. No relief of this character has been thought justified in the long history of equity jurisprudence.[26]

In *United States v. First Nat'l City Bank*,[27] the government sought to collect taxes allegedly owed to it by a foreign corporation. Pending personal service on the foreign corporation, the government sought a preliminary injunction ordering the bank to freeze the taxpayer's accounts in its foreign branches. The Court distinguished *De Beers Consol. Mines*, and held that in the instant suit there was property which would be "the subject of the provisions of any final decree in the cause." In approving the injunction, the Court stated as follows:

> The temporary injunction issued ... seems to us to be eminently appropriate to prevent further dissipation of assets ... If such relief were beyond the authority of the District Court, foreign taxpayers facing jeopardy assessments might either transfer assets abroad or dissipate those in foreign accounts under control of American institutions before personal service on the foreign taxpayer could be made. Such a scheme was underfoot here, the affidavits aver. Unlike *De Beers* ..., there is here property which would be "the subject of the provisions of any final decree in the cause." ... We conclude that this temporary injunction is "a reasonable measure to preserve the status quo. ..."[29]

The Court agreed that *De Beers* was inapplicable because the trial court in that case could award only injunctive relief whereas in *First Nat'l* the judgment sought was monetary relief.

25. Id. at 220.

26. Id.

27. 379 U.S. 378 (1965).

29. Id. at 385.

In subsequent decisions, federal courts of appeals have issued conflicting holdings with respect to the propriety of the issuance of preliminary injunctive relief in order to protect a potential future damages remedy.

GEORGE A. BERMANN, TRANSNATIONAL LITIGATION IN A NUTSHELL

Chapter 9, Transnational Provisional Relief (2003).

Just as transnational litigation may occasion a need for cross-border service and cross-border evidence-gathering, so it may occasion a need for transnational provisional relief. The same purposes that are served by provisional relief in domestic litigation (e.g. ensuring the adequacy of an eventual judgment, preserving the *status quo* pending the litigation) may be served by provisional relief in transnational cases. The difficulty that arises of course is that, in order for relief in transnational cases to be adequate, it may have to exert extraterritorial effects, which may in turn render it objectionable to the affected foreign States. Indeed the very prospect of objections may cause US courts to decline to order transnational provisional relief in the first place, even in situations in which, in entirely domestic cases, they ordinarily would.

Conversely, US courts should expect that from time to time foreign courts, in the context of the transnational litigation before them, will order measures of provisional relief having consequences of some sort in the US. These may be most pronounced when a US court is called upon actually to "enforce" a measure of provisional relief that a foreign court has ordered. Extraterritorial measure may elicit a range of responses in the courts of the country.

US courts in domestic litigation regularly entertain, and grant, applications for provisional relief when equitable circumstances so suggest. There may be a need to protect persons or property from irreparable harm while litigation on the merits is pending, and there may be other reasons to preserve the status quo in the period before judgment is rendered. More specifically, there may be a need to secure a probable judgment. The prime instruments are preliminary injunctions and attachment

As for preliminary injunctions, the Federal Rules do not prescribe a standard for their issuance. While Rule 65 addresses requirements of notice duration, form and security, it leaves the question of whether and when a preliminary injunction should issue to the discretion of the courts and traditional equity principles. * * * As for attachments, Rule 64 of the Federal Rules authorizes a federal court to issue such an order if the law of the state where the court sits permits In New York (CPLR, sec. 6201), for example, an applicant for an attachment must demonstrate an entitlement, at least in part, to a money judgment against one or more defendant, and also show one of several circumstances, including (a) that the defendant is a non-domiciliary and non-resident, or a foreign corporation not qualified to do business in the state, or (b) that the defendant will assign or remove property from the state with intent to defraud creditors or frustrate the enforcement of an eventual judgment in plaintiff's favor. Generally, then, an applicant must show that it has a good chance of prevailing on the merits and that there is a likelihood that the defendant will dispose of its assets before the eventual judgment can be executed.

In this chapter, we assume that the same general considerations that would in principle justify an order of provisional relief in domestic cases before US courts will be deemed to justify it in transnational cases. We therefore focus on the extent to which the transnational character of the case or of the relief sought might make a difference.

US practice in this area has undoubtedly been influenced by the practice of UK courts, notably the so-called *"Mareva* injunction," [the *Mareva* decision is extracted below] ... A *Mareva* injunction is an order restraining a party from removing or disposing of assets found within the jurisdiction, regardless of whether those assets relate to the underlying cause of action. Typically, no notice to the opposing party is required and the injunction will be issued on an *ex parte* basis. The practice of issuing *Mareva* injunctions has been extended so as even to reach assets outside the jurisdiction, provided their owner is otherwise subject to the jurisdiction of the court. *Babanaft Int'l Co. SA v. Bassatne* (Ct.App. 1988); *Republic of Haiti v. Duvalier* (Ct.App.1988).

The UK Court of Appeal explored the "extraterritorial" application of *Mareva* injunctions in greater depth in the case of *Derby & Co. Ltd. v. Weldon (I)* (Ct.App.1988)[associated case extracted below]. While conceding that a world-wide injunction (and an ancillary order to disclose the location of world-wide assets) is a drastic and potentially oppressive remedy to be granted only in exceptional circumstances, it found such circumstances to be present in that case. These included the fact that the defendants' assets in the UK were wholly insufficient to satisfy an eventual judgment and that the defendants were very likely to dispose of their foreign assets in anticipation of an adverse judgment.

Republic of the Philippines v. Marcos (9th Cir. 1988), is a high-profile example drawn from US practice. This was a suit by the Republic of the Philippines against its former president, his wife and others under RICO and pendent state law claims, arising out of the defendants' alleged investment in the US of fraudulently obtained moneys. The plaintiff sought and was granted a preliminary injunction barring the defendants from disposing of any assets, except as needed to pay their attorneys' fees and meet their normal living expenses. The order targeted assets located not only in the US, but also in the UK and Switzerland. The Court of Appeals sustained the district court's order in view of the likelihood of success on the merits and the risk of irreparable injury. To defeat the argument that the order was impermissibly extraterritorial, the court underscored that the defendants were before the court and that the injunction operated entirely *in personam,* rather than against the overseas assets *in rem*. The Court did not invoke any particular provision of federal law, including the Federal Rules, but rather its inherent equitable power to issue provisional remedies ancillary to its authority to provide final equitable relief.

The *Marcos* case was not unprecedented. In *United States v. First Nat'l City Bank* (S.Ct.1965), an action by the US against a Uruguyan corporation for income taxes owed, the Court had sustained a federal court order enjoining a New York bank from transferring any assets of the corporation held in the bank's Montevideo branch. The Court deemed the branch to be within the court's jurisdiction due to the close control exercised over it by the bank's New York office. Courts in subsequent cases have restricted a party's free use of overseas assets, where the circumstances are found to justify that remedy. *Reebok Int'l, Ltd. v. Marnatech Enterp.,* Inc. (9th Cir.1992); *SEC v. International Swiss Invs. Corp.* (9th Cir.1990); *In re Feit & Drexler, Inc.* (2d Cir.1985).

This growing practice has recently been curtailed, at least in the federal courts, by the Supreme Court's ruling in *Grupo Mexicano de Desarrollo, S.A. v. Alliance Bond Fund* (S.Ct.1999)[next reading below], . . . Some state courts, in determining the availability of an injunctive remedy under these circumstances have followed the majority's view in *Grupo Mexicano*. See e.g., *Credit Agricole Indosuez v. Rossiyskiy Kredit Bank* (N.Y.2000).

In the past, some courts have exercised their injunctive powers to order a party before the court to "repatriate" foreign assets, thereby enabling their attachment. See. e.g., *Inter-Regional Financial Group, Inc. v. Hashemi* (2d Cir.1977). The availability of such a remedy in federal court and certain state courts after *Grupo Mexicano* may be severely curtailed. Presumably, the availability of local attachments under Rule 64 will continue to depend on state law.

PROVISIONAL RELIEF IN AID OF ENFORCING A FOREIGN JUDGMENT

In its decision in *Shaffer v. Heitner,* the Supreme Court suggested that "a State in which property is located should have jurisdiction to attach that property, by use of proper procedures, as security for a judgment being sought in a forum where the litigation can be maintained consistently with [the requirements of due process]." On occasion, US courts have indeed shown a willingness to exercise attachment jurisdiction in aid of execution of a future foreign judgment at the request of party to the foreign proceeding, in much the same way as they do in aid of the eventual execution of a sister state judgment. See, e.g., *Cameco Indus., Inc. v. Mayatrac, S.A.* (D.Md.1992); *Barclays Bank, S.A. v. Tsakos* (D.C.App.1988).

While the practice of issuing attachment orders over local property to help secure an eventual foreign court judgment may not be particularly well developed in the US, there appears to be no formal bar to doing so. There is certainly no bar as between states of the European Union, whose Regulation 44/2001 (art. 31) on jurisdiction and judgments, build-

ing upon the prior Brussels Convention (art. 24) on that subject, expressly provides that a court lacking jurisdiction to decide the merits of a case
may nevertheless entertain a request for provisional relief pending a
decision. on the merits by a competent court in another EU Member
State. Needless to emphasize, the fact that there is authority to afford
relief of this sort does not mean that this authority will be exercised in
any given case. As with provisional relief generally, the decision is
considered to be a highly discretionary one.

The likelihood of enforcement in the US may be enhanced if the
foreign court has itself awarded provisional relief, and the party benefit-
ting from it then, so to speak, seeks "enforcement" of the order in the
US. This is not unimaginable since foreign courts, like US courts, do
award provisional relief in appropriate circumstances in domestic and
transnational litigation alike. When a litigant before a foreign court
seeks to have such an order of provisional relief enforced in the US, we
find ourselves very close to the situation examined in the next chapter,
viz. efforts by a party prevailing in overseas litigation to have the
resulting judgment enforced in the US. The principal difference-which
flows from the very nature of provisional relief-is that the order does not
reflect a final judgment on the merits (as in the standard enforcement of
judgments situation), but rather an interim measure that the foreign
court has seen fit, for reasons of justice or utility, to order during the
pendency of the litigation. In fact, the instances in which foreign orders
of provisional relief are sought to be enforced as such in the US are
remarkably few. If they are ordered, there remains a serious question as
to whether a US will be willing to enforce them.

Sometimes it is difficult even to determine whether a party to
foreign litigation is seeking enforcement of a foreign order of provisional
relief or rather a new order "extending" the scope of the previous one.
In *Pilkington Bros. PLC v. AFG Indus. Inc.* (D.Del.1984), a UK company
that had won an *ex parte* interim injunction against a US company from
a UK court then sought parallel provisional relief from a US court.
Characterizing the request as seeking enforcement of the UK injunction
in the US, the court nevertheless declined the request, chiefly on the
ground that the UK order was purely interlocutory and had not been
based on a full consideration of the merits of the underlying dispute, but
also because of the awkwardness of coordinating parallel orders of two
courts over time. To the same effect, see *Cliffs-Neddrill Turnkey Int'l
Oranjestad v. M/T Rich Duke* (D.Del.1990). Other courts have been
much more hospitable to interlocutory foreign court orders. See, e.g.,
Nahar v. Nahar (Fla.Dist.Ct.App.1995), where a Florida court enforced
an Aruban court order requiring a decedent's Florida bank accounts to
be transferred to Aruba for disposition in accordance with Dutch law.
The court declined to distinguish sharply, for enforcement purposes,
between final and interlocutory orders of foreign courts.

Among the *Pilkington* court's stated reasons for declining to issue
the requested injunction was that doing so might be seen as intruding in
a matter before the UK courts in violation of principles of international

comity. To the extent that comity is in issue, it may be reasonable to assume that the outcome of a request could vary according to whether it emanates from a litigant in a foreign court or from the foreign court itself. In *de Pacanins v. Pacanins* (Fla.App.1995), a Florida appellate court reversed a trial court's ruling denying a request from a Venezuelan court to freeze funds in Florida belonging to the Venezuelan defendant, pending the outcome of the main action. It ruled that compelling public policy considerations might require a relaxation of the general rule against enforcing non-final orders of foreign courts. The same court had previously taken such a step. *Cardenas v. Solis* (Fla.App. 1990).

In bankruptcy cases, federal law specifically authorizes preliminary relief in aid of foreign judicial proceedings. 11 U.S.C.A. sec. 304 permits a foreign trustee or other representative in bankruptcy to commence an ancillary action in US court so as to ensure that domestic US creditors do not pursue or execute on US assets belonging to the bankrupt entity, pending the outcome of the foreign proceeding. * * *

GRUPO MEXICANO de DESARROLLO, S.A. v. ALLIANCE BOND FUND, INC.

Supreme Court of the United States, 1999.
527 U.S. 308, 119 S.Ct. 1961, 144 L.Ed.2d 319.

SCALIA, J., delivered the opinion for a unanimous Court with respect to Part II, and the opinion of the Court with respect to Parts I, III, and IV, in which REHNQUIST, C. J., and O'CONNOR, KENNEDY, and THOMAS, JJ., joined. GINSBURG, J., filed an opinion concurring in part and dissenting in part, in which STEVENS, SOUTER, and BREYER, JJ., joined.

This case presents the question whether, in an action for money damages, a United States District Court has the power to issue a preliminary injunction preventing the defendant from transferring assets in which no lien or equitable interest is claimed.

I.

[A Mexican holding company, Grupo Mexicano de Desarrollo, S.A. (Desarrollo), issued $250 million of unsecured, guaranteed notes. Several U.S. investment funds purchased some $75 million of the notes. The notes were payable in New York. Desarrollo became an investor in a toll road construction program sponsored by the Government of Mexico. Economic problems in Mexico resulted in severe losses for the toll road concessionaries, and Desarrollo could not pay interest on its notes. The investment funds sued in the U.S. District Court for the Southern District of New York, alleging that Desarrollo was at risk of, if not already in, insolvency, and was dissipating its most significant asset (toll road notes) and furthermore was preferring its Mexican creditors, and that such actions would "frustrate any judgement" respondents could obtain. The District Court preliminarily enjoined petitioners "from dissipating, disbursing, transferring, conveying, encumbering or otherwise distributing or affecting any [petitioner's] right to, interest in, title to or right to receive or retain, any of the [assets]." The Second Circuit affirmed and the Supreme Court granted certiorari.]

* * *

III

We turn ... to ... whether the District Court had authority to issue the preliminary injunction ... pursuant to Federal Rule of Civil Procedure 65. The Judiciary Act of 1789 conferred on the federal courts jurisdiction over "all suits ... in equity." We have long held that "[t]he 'jurisdiction' thus conferred ... is an authority to administer in equity suits the principles of the system of judicial remedies which had been devised and was being administered by the English Court of Chancery at the time of the separation of the two countries." "Substantially, then, the equity jurisdiction of the federal courts is the jurisdiction in equity exercised by the High Court of Chancery in England at the time of the adoption of the Constitution and the enactment of the original Judiciary Act, 1789 ." A. Dobie, Handbook of Federal Jurisdiction and Procedure 660 (1928). "[T]he substantive prerequisites for obtaining an equitable remedy as well as the general availability of injunctive relief are not altered by [Rule 65] and depend on traditional principles of equity jurisdiction." Wright, Miller, & Kane, Federal Practice and Procedure § 2941, p. 31 (2d ed.1995). We must ask, therefore, whether the relief respondents requested here was traditionally accorded by courts of equity.

Respondents do not even argue this point. The United States as amicus curiae, however, contends that the preliminary injunction issued in this case is analogous to the relief obtained in the equitable action known as a "creditor's bill." This remedy was used (among other purposes) to permit a judgment creditor to discover the debtor's assets, to reach equitable interests not subject to execution at law, and to set aside fraudulent conveyances. It was well established, however, that, as a general rule, a creditor's bill could be brought only by a creditor who had already obtained a judgment establishing the debt. The rule requiring a judgment was a product, not just of the procedural requirement that remedies at law had to be exhausted before equitable remedies could be pursued, but also of the substantive rule that a general creditor (one without a judgment) had no cognizable interest, either at law or in equity, in the property of his debtor, and therefore could not interfere with the debtor's use of that property. As stated by Chancellor Kent: "The reason of the rule seems to be, that until the creditor has established his title, he has no right to interfere, and it would lead to an unnecessary, and, perhaps, a fruitless and oppressive interruption of the exercise of the debtor's rights." Wiggins v. Armstrong, 2 Johns. Ch. 144, 145–146 (N.Y.1816).

The United States asserts that there were exceptions to the general rule requiring a judgment. The existence and scope of these exceptions is by no means clear.... Particularly in the absence of any discussion of this point by the lower courts, we are not inclined to speculate upon the existence or applicability to this case of any exceptions, and follow the well-established general rule that a judgment establishing the debt was necessary before a court of equity would interfere with the debtor's use of his property. Justice GINSBURG [in the dissent] concedes that federal equity courts have traditionally rejected the type of provisional relief granted in this case. She invokes, however, "the grand aims of equity," and asserts a general power to grant relief whenever legal remedies are not "practical and efficient," unless there is a statute to the contrary. This expansive view of equity must be rejected. Joseph Story's famous treatise reflects what we consider the proper rule, both with regard to the general role of equity in our "government of laws, not of men," and with regard to its application in the very case before us:

> "Mr. Justice Blackstone has taken considerable pains to refute this doctrine. 'It is said,' he remarks, 'that it is the business of a Court of Equity, in England, to abate the rigor of the common law. But no such power is contended for. Hard was the case of bond creditors, whose debtor devised away his real estate.... But a Court of Equity can give no relief....' ..." 1 Commentaries on Equity Jurisprudence § 12, pp. 14–15 (1836).

We do not question the proposition that equity is flexible; but in the federal system, at least, that flexibility is confined within the broad boundaries of traditional equitable relief. To accord a type of relief that has never been available before-and especially (as here) a type of relief that has been specifically disclaimed by longstanding judicial precedent-is to invoke a "default rule," not of flexibility but of omnipotence. When there are indeed new conditions that might call for a wrenching departure from past practice, Congress is in a much better position than we both to perceive them and to design the appropriate remedy. Despite Justice GINSBURG's allusion to the "increasing complexities of modern business relations," and to the bygone "age of slow-moving capital and comparatively immobile wealth," we suspect there is absolutely nothing new about debtors' trying to avoid paying their debts, or seeking to favor some creditors over others—or even about their seeking to achieve these ends through "sophisticated ... strategies," The law of fraudulent conveyances and bankruptcy was developed to prevent such conduct; an equitable power to restrict a debtor's use of his unencumbered property before judgment was not.

Respondents argue (supported by the United States) that the merger of law and equity changed the rule that a general creditor could not interfere with the debtor's use of his property. But the merger did not alter substantive rights.

* * *

As further support for the proposition that the relief accorded here was unknown to traditional equity practice, it is instructive that the English Court of Chancery, from which the First Congress borrowed in conferring equitable powers on the federal courts, did not provide an injunctive remedy such as this until 1975. In that year, the Court of Appeal decided *Mareva Compania Naviera S.A. v. International Bulkcarriers S.A.*, 2 Lloyd's Rep. 509. *Mareva* ... relied on a statute giving courts the authority to grant an interlocutory injunction " 'in all cases in which it shall appear to the court to be just or convenient,' " 2 Lloyd's Rep., at 510 (quoting Judicature Act **1973 of 1925, Law Reports 1925(2), 15 & 16 Geo. V, ch. 49, § 45). It held (in the words of Lord Denning) that "[i]f it appears that the debt is due and owing-and there is a danger that the debtor may dispose of his assets so as to defeat it before judgment-the Court has jurisdiction in a proper case to grant an interlocutory judgment so as to prevent him [sic] disposing of those assets." 2 Lloyd's Rep., at 510. The *Mareva* injunction has now been confirmed by statute. See Supreme Court Act of 1981, § 37, 11 Halsbury's Statutes 966, 1001 (1991 reissue) ... Commentators have emphasized that the adoption of *Mareva* injunctions was a dramatic departure from prior practice.

The parties debate whether *Mareva* was based on statutory authority or on inherent equitable power. Regardless of the answer to this question, it is indisputable that the English courts of equity did not actually exercise this power until 1975, and that federal courts in this country have traditionally applied the principle that courts of equity will not, as a general matter, interfere with the debtor's disposition of his property at the instance of a nonjudgment creditor. We think it incompatible with our traditionally cautious approach to equitable powers, which leaves any substantial expansion of past practice to Congress, to decree the elimination of this significant protection for debtors.

IV

The parties and amici discuss various arguments for and against creating the preliminary injunctive remedy at issue in this case. The United States suggests that the factors supporting such a remedy include "simplicity and uniformity of procedure; preservation of the court's ability to render a judgment that will prove enforceable; prevention of inequitable conduct on the part of defendants; avoiding disparities between defendants that have assets within the jurisdiction (which would be subject to pre-judgment attachment 'at law') and those that do not; avoiding the necessity for plaintiffs to locate a forum in which the defendant has substantial assets; and, in an age of easy global mobility of capital, preserving the attractiveness of the United States as a center for financial transactions."

But there are weighty considerations on the other side as well, the most significant of which is the historical principle that before judgment (or its equivalent) an unsecured creditor has no rights at law or in equity in the property of his debtor....

The requirement that the creditor obtain a prior judgment is a fundamental protection in debtor-creditor law-rendered all the more important in our federal system by the debtor's right to a jury trial on the legal claim. There are other factors which likewise give us pause: The remedy sought here could render Federal Rule of Civil Procedure 64, which authorizes use of state prejudgment remedies, a virtual irrelevance. Why go through the trouble of complying with local attachment and garnishment statutes when this all-purpose prejudgment injunction is available? More importantly, by adding, through judicial fiat, a new and powerful weapon to the creditor's arsenal, the new rule could radically alter the balance between debtor's and creditor's rights which has been developed over centuries through many laws-including those relating to bankruptcy, fraudulent conveyances, and preferences. Because any rational creditor would want to protect his investment, such a remedy might induce creditors to engage in a "race to the courthouse" in cases involving insolvent or near-insolvent debtors, which might prove financially fatal to the struggling debtor. (In this case, we might observe, the respondents did not represent all of the holders of the Notes; they were an active few who sought to benefit at the expense of the other noteholders as well as [Desarrollo's] other creditors). It is significant that, in England, use of the *Mareva* injunction has expanded rapidly. "Since 1975, the English courts have awarded *Mareva* injunctions to freeze assets in an ever-increasing set of circumstances both within and beyond the commercial setting to an ever-expanding number of plaintiffs." Wasserman at 339. As early as 1984, one observer stated that "[t]here are now a steady flow of such applications to our Courts which have been estimated to exceed one thousand per month." Shenton, *Attachments and Other Interim Court Remedies in Support of Arbitration*, 1984 Int'l Bus. Law. 101, 104.

We do not decide which side has the better of these arguments. We set them forth only to demonstrate that resolving them in this forum is incompatible with the democratic and self-deprecating judgment we have long since made: that the equitable powers conferred by the Judiciary Act of 1789 did not include the power to create remedies previously unknown to equity jurisprudence. Even when sitting as a court in equity, we have no authority to craft a "nuclear weapon" of the law like the one advocated here. Joseph Story made the point many years ago:

> "If, indeed, a Court of Equity in England did possess the unbounded jurisdiction, which has been thus generally ascribed to it, of correcting, controlling, moderating, and even superceding the law, and of enforcing all the rights, as well as charities, arising from natural law and justice, and of freeing itself from all regard to former rules and precedents, it would be the most gigantic in its sway, and the most formidable instrument of arbitrary power, that could well be devised. It would literally place the whole rights and property of the community under the arbitrary will of the Judge, acting, if you please, arbitrio boni judicis, and it may be, ex aequo et bono, according to his own notions and conscience; but still acting with a despotic and sovereign authority. A Court of Chancery might then well deserve the spirited rebuke of Seldon; 'For law we have a

measure, and know what to trust to-Equity is according to the conscience of him, that is Chancellor; and as that is larger, or narrower, so is Equity. T is all one, as if they should make the standard for the measure the Chancellor's foot. What an uncertain measure would this be? One Chancellor has a long foot; another a short foot; a third an indifferent foot. It is the same thing with the Chancellor's conscience.'" 1 Commentaries on Equity Jurisprudence § 19, at 21.

The debate concerning this formidable power over debtors should be conducted and resolved where such issues belong in our democracy: in the Congress.

* * *

Because such a remedy was historically unavailable from a court of equity, we hold that the District Court had no authority to issue a preliminary injunction preventing petitioners from disposing of their assets pending adjudication of respondents' contract claim for money damages. We reverse the judgment of the Second Circuit and remand the case for further proceedings consistent with this opinion.

Justice GINSBURG, with whom Justice STEVENS, Justice SOUTER, and Justice BREYER join, concurring in part and dissenting in part.

* * * The Court holds the District Court's preliminary freeze order impermissible principally because injunctions of this kind were not "traditionally accorded by courts of equity" at the time the Constitution was adopted. In my view, the Court relies on an unjustifiably static conception of equity jurisdiction. From the beginning, we have defined the scope of federal equity in relation to the principles of equity existing at the separation of this country from England; we have never limited federal equity jurisdiction to the specific practices and remedies of the pre-Revolutionary Chancellor. Since our earliest cases, we have valued the adaptable character of federal equitable power. ...We have also recognized that equity must evolve over time, "in order to meet the requirements of every case, and to satisfy the needs of a progressive social condition in which new primary rights and duties are constantly arising and new kinds of wrongs are constantly committed." *Union Pacific R. Co. v. Chicago, R.I. & P.R. Co.*, 163 U.S. 564, 601, 16 S.Ct. 1173, 41 L.Ed. 265 (1896).... A dynamic equity jurisprudence is of special importance in the commercial law context. As we observed more than a century ago: "It must not be forgotten that in the increasing complexities of modern business relations equitable remedies have necessarily and steadily been expanded, and no inflexible rule has been permitted to circumscribe them." On this understanding of equity's character, we have upheld diverse injunctions that would have been beyond the contemplation of the 18th-century Chancellor.

Compared to many contemporary adaptations of equitable remedies, the preliminary injunction Alliance sought in this case was a modest measure. In operation, moreover, the preliminary injunction to freeze assets *pendente lite* may be a less heavy-handed remedy than prejudgment attachment, which deprives the defendant of possession and use of the seized property.

I do not question that equity courts traditionally have not issued preliminary injunctions stopping a party sued for an unsecured debt from disposing of assets pending adjudication. But it is one thing to recognize that equity courts typically did not provide this relief, quite another to conclude that, therefore, the remedy was beyond equity's capacity. I would not draw such a conclusion.

Chancery may have refused to issue injunctions of this sort simply because they were not needed to secure a just result in an age of slow-moving capital and comparatively immobile wealth. By turning away cases that the law courts could deal with adequately, the Chancellor acted to reduce the tension inevitable when justice was divided between two discrete systems. But as the facts of this case so plainly show, for creditors situated as Alliance is, the remedy at law is worthless absent the provisional relief in equity's arsenal. Moreover, increasingly sophisticated foreign-haven judgment proofing strategies, coupled with technology that permits the nearly instantaneous transfer of assets abroad, suggests that defendants may succeed in avoiding meritorious claims in ways unimaginable before the merger of law and equity. I am not ready to say a responsible Chancellor today would deny Alliance relief on the ground that prior case law is unsupportive.

The development of *Mareva* injunctions in England after 1975 supports the view of the lower courts in this case, a view to which I adhere.... Although the cases reveal some uncertainty regarding *Mareva* 's jurisdictional basis, the better-reasoned and more recent decisions ground *Mareva* in equity's traditional power to remedy the "abuse" of legal process by defendants and the "injustice" that would result from defendants "making themselves judgment-proof" by disposing of their assets during the pendency of litigation.

* * *

The Court worries that permitting preliminary injunctions to freeze assets would allow creditors, " 'on a mere statement of belief that the defendant can easily make away with or transport his money or goods, [to] impose an injunction on him, indefinite in duration, disabling him to use so much of his funds or property as the court deems necessary for security or compliance with its possible decree.' " Given the strong showings a creditor would be required to make to gain the provisional remedy, and the safeguards on which the debtor could insist, I agree with the Second Circuit "that this 'parade of horribles' [would] not come to pass." 143 F.3d 688, 696 (1998).

Under standards governing preliminary injunctive relief generally, a plaintiff must show a likelihood of success on the merits and irreparable injury in the absence of an injunction. Plaintiffs with questionable claims would not meet the likelihood of success criterion. The irreparable injury requirement would not be met by unsubstantiated allegations that a defendant may dissipate assets. As the Court of Appeals recognized, provisional freeze orders would be appropriate in damages actions only upon a finding that, without the freeze, "the movant would be unable to collect [a money] judgment." The preliminary asset-freeze order, in short, would rank and operate as an extraordinary remedy.

Federal Rule of Civil Procedure 65(c), moreover, requires a preliminary injunction applicant to post a bond "in such sum as the court deems proper, for the payment of such costs and damages as may be incurred or suffered by any party who is found to have been wrongfully enjoined." As an essential condition for a preliminary freeze order, a district court could demand sufficient security to ensure a remedy for wrongly enjoined defendants. Furthermore, it would be incumbent on a district court to "match the scope of its injunction to the most probable size of the likely judgment," thereby sparing the defendant from undue hardship.

The protections in place guard against any routine or arbitrary imposition of a preliminary freeze order designed to stop the dissipation of assets that would render a court's judgment worthless. The case we face should be paradigmatic. There was no question that [Desarrollo's] debt to Alliance was due and owing. And the short span-less than four months-between preliminary injunction and summary judgment shows that the temporary restraint on [Desarrollo] did not linger beyond the time necessary for a fair and final adjudication in a busy but efficiently operated court. Absent immediate judicial action, Alliance would have been left with a multimillion dollar judgment on which it could collect not a penny. In my view, the District Court properly invoked its equitable power to avoid that manifestly unjust result and to protect its ability to render an enforceable final judgment.

* * *

Contrary to the Court's suggestion, this case involves no judicial usurpation of Congress' authority. Congress, of course, can instruct the federal courts to issue preliminary injunctions freezing assets pending final judgment, or instruct them not to, and the courts must heed Congress' command. Indeed, Congress has restricted the equity jurisdiction of federal courts in a variety of contexts.

The Legislature, however, has said nothing about preliminary freeze orders. The relevant question, therefore, is whether, absent congressional direction, the general equitable powers of the federal courts permit relief of the kind fashioned by the District Court. I would find the default rule in the grand aims of equity. Where, as here, legal remedies are not "practical and efficient," the federal courts must rely on their "flexible jurisdiction in equity ... to protect all rights and do justice to all concerned," *Rubber Co. v. Goodyear*, 9 Wall. 805, 807 (1870). No countervailing precedent or principle holds the federal courts powerless to prevent a defendant from dissipating assets, to the destruction of a plaintiff's claim, during the course of judicial proceedings. Accordingly, I would affirm the judgment of the Court of Appeals and uphold the District Court's preliminary injunction.

Questions and Comments

1. The plaintiffs' suit in federal court in New Jersey may lead to a judgment that may be enforced in other states under full faith and credit principles, but, as the materials in Chapter 5 will relate, it is less certain that a U.S. judgment will be enforced abroad, whether in Bermuda, the UK or Germany. VUSCO may be ordered by the New Jersey court not to dispose of the art on loan to Stanford and Oxford, and DROF UK, if jurisdiction is determined to exist in the U.S. court, may be ordered not to move funds from the Germany bank, nor to remove assets from its Bermuda subsidiaries. When the U.S. court protective order addresses assets outside the United States, the extraterritorial effect of the order must be considered. In view of the readings how will the U.S. court rule? Can *De Beers* and *First Nat'l*, discussed in the Epstein, Snyder & Baldwin extract, be distinguished? Note that Epstein and his coauthors make a very important point in that the choice of forum should include consideration of obtaining pre-trial provisional relief. If there is a choice of forum clause it might be a forum without such available relief. In Problem 4.1 this issue should be revived.

2. Bermann's discussion of Rules 64 and 65 shows that the plaintiffs will have to establish several things, such as entitlement to a money judgment. The plaintiffs will also have to establish that the defendants are neither domiciled nor resident in the United States, which is not true of VUSCO but seems to be true of the DROF entities. It will also have to shown that the defendant is likely to assign or remove property *from the state* with intent to defraud creditors or the enforcement of a judgment. But that means property in the United States, not in Bermuda, the UK or Germany. Does that mean the plaintiffs ought to commence some kind of action in one or more of those nations, rather than relying on a decree of the U.S. court?

3. Bermann's notes the *Mareva* injunction of the UK and its progeny, discussed more in Part B. The U.S. *Marcos* case shows that targeting assets abroad, specifically in the UK and Switzerland, might work by ignoring the Federal Rules and turning to "inherent equitable power" of the courts. Would our case have a chance under such a viewpoint—we are not in the somewhat adventuresome 9th Circuit? But Bermann closes noting the reduction of the use of the *Marcos* decision theory.

4. Part of Bermanns' extract covers U.S. aid in foreign proceedings, which may help when a request is made in a U.S. court for a order with extraterritorial effect. Do any of the cases he discusses help the plaintiffs in our case?

5. The 1999 *Groupo Mexicano* 5–4 decision of the Supreme Court is the foundation for present law. It is based on Federal Rule 65, rather than inherent equitable powers. Was Federal Rule 65 enacted to freeze equity relief at the time of the Constitution or at the time Rule 65 was adopted? Does the case close the door to our plaintiffs? Should Rule 65 be amended to allow injunctions as advocated by the dissent?

6. Do you prefer the reasoning of the dissent in *Groupo Mexicano* both as to the use of equitable power and its application in the case? Is the Court majority, as Justice Ginsberg suggests in her dissent, oblivious of economic changes and the need to have protective relief based on a more "dynamic equity jurisprudence?" Is her concern that this is another decision that looks to the conditions that existed at the time the Constitution was adopted? Isn't the concept of equity fairness in dealing with the matter before the court, after all equity developed to deal with the unflexible common law?

7. What if the Oxford museum has contracted with a new museum in Dubai to exchange some art for six months—could a U.S. order limit such action? Should it make any difference to the court whether the requested action orders the non-resident party to act affirmatively or negatively? Is it less intrusive to order the Oxford museum not to dispose of or in any way transfer any art that is on loan from VUSCO, than to order the museum to make an inventory of all the art it has owned by VUSCO? *See Amey v. Colebrook Guar. Sav. Bank*, 92 F.2d 62 (2d Cir. 1937), *cert. denied* 302 U.S. 750, 58 S.Ct. 271, 82 L.Ed. 580 (1937)(distinction criticized).

8. Judicial orders related to foreign real property are given only in exceptional circumstances. It is clear that any such order cannot be enforced abroad, but the situs court might honor such a decree under the doctrine of comity. But the U.S. court presumably has jurisdiction over the party who owns the foreign land. Would a U.S. court order a party before the court who owns land in Canada on the border with the United States, to stop using harmful fertilizer on the Canadian land. that washed into a stream that entered the United States and provided drinking water to a small U.S. town? What if Canada had taken the position that the fertilizer was not harmful and was appropriate for farming?

9. *See, e.g.*, Shenton, *Attachments and Other Interim Court Remedies in Support of Arbitration*, 1984 Int'l Bus. Law. 101, 104.

PART B. PRE–TRIAL PROVISIONAL PROTECTIVE MEASURES IN THE UNITED KINGDOM AND BERMUDA: THE MAREVA INJUNCTION

The *Mareva* injunction, and the later *Anton Piller* order (preventing a party, often one violating a copyright, from transferring infringing material) have been adopted in many common law nations of the British Commonwealth, including Bermuda.

MAREVA COMPANIA NAVIERA S.A. v. INTERNATIONAL BULKCARRIERS S.A.

U.K. Court of Appeal.
[1975] 2 Lloyd's L.Rep 509.

LORD DENNING, M.R.: The plaintiffs, Mareva Compania Naviera S.A., are shipowners who owned the vessel Mareva. They let it to the defendants, International Bulkcarriers S.A., on a time charter for a trip out to the Far East and back. The vessel was to be put at the disposal of the defendants at Rotterdam. Hire was payable half monthly in advance and the rate was 3,850 dollars a day from the time of delivery. The vessel was duly delivered to the defendants on May 12, 1975. The defendants sub-chartered it. They let it on a voyage charter to the President of India. Freight was payable under that voyage charter: 90 per cent. was to be paid against the documents and the 10 per cent. later.

Under that voyage charter the vessel was loaded at Bordeaux on May 29, 1975, with a cargo of fertilizer consigned to India. The Indian High Commission, in accordance with the obligations under the voyage charter, paid 90 per cent. of the freight. But paid it to a bank in London. It was paid out to the Bank of Bilbao in London to the credit of the time charterers. The total sum which the India High Commission paid into the bank was £174,000. Out of that the time charterers paid to the shipowners, the plaintiffs, the first two instalments of the half monthly hire. They paid those instalments by credit transferred to the shipown-ers. The third was due on June 12, 1975; but the time charterers failed to pay it. They could easily have done it, of course, by making a credit transfer in favour of the shipowners. But they did not do it. Telexes passed which make it quite plain that the time charterers were unable to pay. They said they were not able to fulfil any part of their obligations under the charter, and they had no alternative but to stop trading. Their efforts to obtain further financial support had been fruitless.

Whereupon the owners of the vessel treated the defendants' conduct as a repudiation of the charter. They issued a writ on June 20. They claimed the unpaid hire which comes to 30,800 U.S. dollars and damages for the repudiation. The total will be very large. They have served the writ on agents here, and they have applied also for service out of the jurisdiction. But meanwhile they believe that there is a grave danger that these moneys in the bank in London will disappear. So they have applied for an injunction to restrain the disposal of those moneys which are now in the bank. They rely on the recent case of *Nippon Yusen Kaisha v. Karageorgis*, [1975] 2 Lloyd's Rep. 137. Mr. Justice Donaldson felt some doubt about that decision because we were not referred to *Lister v. Stubbs*, [1890] 45 Ch.D. 1. There are observations in that case to the effect that the Court has no jurisdiction to protect a creditor before he gets judgment.

Mr. Justice Donaldson felt that he was bound by *Lister v. Stubbs* and that he had no power to grant an injunction. But, in deference to the recent case, he did grant an injunction, but only until 17 00 today (June 23, 1975), on the understanding that by that time this Court would be able to reconsider the position.

Now Mr. Rix has been very helpful. He has drawn our attention not only to *Lister v. Stubbs* but also to s. 45 of the Judicature Act, which repeats s. 25 (8) of the Judicature Act, 1875. It says: A mandamus or an injunction may be granted or a receiver appointed by an interlocutory order of the court in all cases in which it shall appear to the court to be just or convenient. In *Beddow v. Beddow*, (1878) 9 Ch.D. 89, Sir George Jessel, the then Master of the Rolls, gave a very wide interpretation to that section. He said: I have unlimited power to grant an injunction in any case where it would be right or just to do so.

There is only one qualification to be made. The Court will not grant an injunction to protect a person who has no legal or equitable right whatever.... But, subject to that qualification, the statute gives a wide general power to the Courts. It is well summarized in Halsbury's Laws of England, vol. 21, 3rd ed., p. 348, par. 729:

> ... now, therefore, whenever a right, which can be asserted either at law or in equity, does exist, then, whatever the previous practice may have been, the Court is enabled by virtue of this provision, in a proper case, to grant an injunction to protect that right.

In my opinion that principle applies to a creditor who has a right to be paid the debt owing to him, even before he has established his right by getting judgment for it. If it appears that the debt is due and owing—and there is a danger that the debtor may dispose of his assets so as to defeat it before judgment—the Court has jurisdiction in a proper case to grant an interlocutory judgment so as to prevent him disposing of those assets. It seems to me that this is a proper case for the exercise of this jurisdiction. There is money in a bank in London which stands in the name of these time charterers. The time charterers have control of it. They may at any time dispose of it or remove it out of this country. If they do so, the shipowners may never get their charter hire. The ship is now on the high seas. It has passed Cape Town on its way to India. It will complete the voyage and the cargo discharged. and the shipowners may not get their charter hire at all. In face of this danger, I think this Court ought to grant an injunction to restrain the defendants from disposing of these moneys now in the bank in London until the trial or judgment in this action. If the defendants have any grievance about it when they hear of it, they can apply to discharge it. But meanwhile the plaintiffs should be protected. It is only just and right that this Court should grant an injunction. I would therefore continue the injunction.

Lord Justice Roskill:

I agree that this injunction should be extended until judgment in the action or until further order. * * * If the defendants were represented, it would no doubt be said on their behalf that the decision of this Court in *Lister v. Stubbs* precludes this Court, not as a matter of jurisdiction but as a matter of practice from granting this injunction.

Indeed it is right to say that, as far as my own experience in the Commercial Court is concerned, an injunction in this form has in the past from time to time been applied for but has been consistently refused. This Court should not, therefore, on an ex parte interlocutory application be too ready to disturb the practice of the past save for good reasons. But on the facts of this case, there are * * *good reasons for granting this injunction.* * *

* * *If therefore this Court does not interfere by injunction, it is apparent that the plaintiffs will suffer a grave injustice which this Court has power to help avoid—the injustice being that the ship will have to continue on her voyage to India and perhaps—as is not unknown in Indian ports—wait a long time there for discharge without remuneration while the defendants will be able to dissipate that £174,000.

* * *

There is or may be a legal or perhaps equitable right which the owners may be entitled to have protected by the Court. The full extent and nature of that right has long been a controversial matter which may have to be resolved hereafter and I therefore say no more about it. For those rather narrow reasons I should continue this injunction until judgment or further order. It is open to the defendants to apply to discharge the injunction or to apply for a stay under the arbitration clause at any time if they are so advised. I agree with the order proposed by my Lord.

Lord Justice Ormrod:

I agree. In my judgment the plaintiffs here have a very strong case on the merits. We have not heard any argument from the other side because it is an ex parte application. In these circumstances I would reserve my own views until I have heard argument from the other side if any such argument is put forward. But in the absence of any such argument, in my view this injunction should be continued.

[Authors note: The injunction worked, the defendants never applied to challenge it. A judgment was issued and the funds in the bank were used to pay the judgment. Another *Mareva* injunction was issued in *Rasu v. Perusahaan ("Pertamina")*, [1978] QB 644. This time the defendants appeared but failed to convince Lord Denning and the court that the injunction was improper. But two months later, in *The Siskina*, while the Court of Appeal granted a *Mareva* injunction, [1977] 2 Lloyd's Rep. 230, the House of Lords reversed, [1979] A.C. 210, in what Lord Denning later wrote was his greatest disappointment in being reversed. Lord Denning, the Due Process of Law 141 (1980). The House of Lords did not overrule the *Mareva* in principle, but thought the Court of Appeal had extended it too far, and rebuked Lord Denning for doing so. But Parliament soon affirmed the injunction, in the Supreme Court Act 1981, in which § 37(3) states: "The power of the High Court ... to grant interlocutory injunction restraining a party to any proceedings from removing from the jurisdiction of the High Court, or otherwise dealing with, assets located within that jurisdiction shall be exercisable in cases where that party is, as well as in cases where he is not, domiciled, resident or present within that jurisdiction." As the next decision relates, the scope of the *Mareva* injunction is yet to be fully determined.]

DERBY & CO. LTD. AND OTHERS
v. WELDON AND OTHERS[6]

U.K. Court of Appeal.
[1989] 2 W.L.R. 412.

LORD DONALDSON OF LYMINGTON M.R.

* * * The action first came before this court in July 1988 when the plaintiffs successfully appealed against the refusal of Mervyn Davies J. to grant *Mareva* relief on a worldwide basis against the first two defendants (Mr. Anthony Weldon and Mr. Ian Jay): *Derby & Co. Ltd. v. Weldon* [1990] Ch. Cas. No. 37. In so far as this court then decided any matters of law, its decision of course binds us. I refer to this judgment by May, Parker and Nicholls L.JJ. as *Derby v. Weldon (No. 1)*. The present appeal is by the fourth defendant, C.M.L. Holding S.A. of Luxembourg (referred to in argument and hereafter in this judgment as "C.M.I." in order to distinguish it from the plaintiff Cocoa Merchants Ltd.). C.M.I. appeals against orders by Sir Nicolas Browne–Wilkinson V.-C. on 4 and 7 November 1988 as amended by a further order on 11 November 1988 granting a worldwide *Mareva* injunction, appointing a receiver of the assets of C.M.I. and a disclosure order. The plaintiffs cross-appeal against the refusal of the Vice–Chancellor to continue a worldwide *Mareva* injunction granted ex parte against the third defendant, Milco Corporation of Panama, ("Milco") and his refusal to appoint a receiver of its assets and to order disclosure of its assets. * * *

The issues confronting this court have been simplified ... by four concessions which have very sensibly been made (for the purposes of the appeal only) on behalf of C.M.I. and Milco.... They are: (a) that the first defendant (Mr. Weldon) and the second defendant (Mr. Jay) might be likely to dissipate their own assets so as not to be available to satisfy any judgment against them in this action; (b) that Mr. Weldon and Mr. Jay are to be assumed to exercise a high degree of control over C.M.I. and Milco; (c) that, in view of (a) and (b) above, C.M.I. and Milco might be likely to dissipate their assets so as not to be available to satisfy any judgment against them or either of them in this action, and (d) that C.M.I. and Milco might at trial be found liable to some one or other of the plaintiffs in respect of the claims (referred to in specified paragraphs of the amended statement of claim) and that the approximate amount of the judgment against C.M.I. or Milco could with interest be as much as £25 million.

Three issues arise, namely: (1) whether, and if so in what circumstances and on what terms, a pre-judgment *Mareva* injunction should be granted against a foreign defendant who has no assets within the jurisdiction of the court; (2) whether, and if so in what circumstances

---

6. The portions of this case that discuss   below.
the European Union are extracted in Part C

and on what terms, a receiver of the assets of such a foreign defendant should be appointed before judgment for purposes similar to those served by a *Mareva* injunction; (3) whether, and if so in what circumstances and on what terms, such a foreign defendant should be required to disclose the nature, value and whereabouts of his assets.

The fundamental principle underlying this jurisdiction is that, within the limits of its powers, no court should permit a defendant to take action designed to ensure that subsequent orders of the court are rendered less effective than would otherwise be the case. On the other hand, it is not its purpose to prevent a defendant carrying on business in the ordinary way or, if an individual, living his life normally pending the determination of the dispute, nor to impede him in any way in defending himself against the claim. Nor is it its purpose to place the plaintiff in the position of a secured creditor. In a word, whilst one of the hazards facing a plaintiff in litigation is that, come the day of judgment, it may not be possible for him to obtain satisfaction of that judgment fully or at all, the court should not permit the defendant artificially to create such a situation. * * *

* * * We live in a time of rapidly growing commercial and financial sophistication and it behooves the courts to adapt their practices to meet the current wiles of those defendants who are prepared to devote as much energy to making themselves immune to the courts' orders as to resisting the making of such orders on the merits of their case. * * * I would add that a failure or refusal to grant an injunction in any particular case is an exercise of discretion which cannot, as such, provide a precedent binding upon another court concerned with another case, save in so far as that refusal is based upon basic principle applicable in both such cases.

* * * In my judgment, the key requirement for any *Mareva* injunction, whether or not it extends to foreign assets, is that it shall accord with the rationale upon which *Mareva* relief has been based in the past. That rationale, legitimate purpose and fundamental principle I have already stated, namely, that no court should permit a defendant to take action designed to frustrate subsequent orders of the court. If for the achievement of this purpose it is necessary to make orders concerning foreign assets, such orders should be made, subject, of course, to ordinary principles of international law. When the Vice–Chancellor said that special circumstances had to be present to justify such an exceptional order, I do not understand him to have been saying more than that the court should not go further than necessity dictates, that in the first instance it should look to assets within the jurisdiction and that in the majority of cases there will be no justification for looking to foreign assets.

* * * The reality is, I think, that it is only recently that litigants have sought extra-territorial relief and that the courts have had to consider whether to grant it and upon what conditions. During the last year it has been granted in the three cases to which the Vice–Chancellor

referred, namely, *Babanaft International Co. S.A. v. Bassatne* [1990] Ch. 13; Republic of Haiti v. Duvalier [1990] 1 Q.B. 202 and *Derby v. Weldon (No. 1)* [1990] Ch. 48. Mr. Bompas seeks to distinguish the *Babanaft* case upon the grounds that the injunction was granted in aid of execution of an existing judgment. This I accept as a distinction in that the court will have less hesitation in taking measures in support of a judgment creditor than it would in support of a potential judgment creditor. The decision in the *Duvalier* case he seeks to distinguish upon the grounds that it was a tracing case and that the funds were under the control of an agent resident within the jurisdiction. This is certainly a distinction in fact, although I am not sure that it is one of principle. *Derby v. Weldon (No. 1)* he seeks to distinguish upon the ground that the defendants had assets within the jurisdiction, but, for the reasons which I have already given, I do not consider this to be a distinction in principle. There remains one other authority to which I should refer. This is the decision of the House of Lords in *South Carolina Insurance Co. v. Assurantie Maatschappij "De Zeven Provincien" N.V.* [1987] A.C. 24. Mr. Bompas relied upon it for the general proposition that the jurisdiction of the court under section 37(1) of the Act of 1981 was "circumscribed by judicial authority dating back many years:". It followed, so he said, that there was no scope for a new and extended use of the power. I do not accept this submission for at least two reasons. First, Lord Brandon said in terms that the jurisdiction in relation to *Mareva* injunctions was an exception to the principle that its exercise was circumscribed by judicial authority. * * * Second, the House was not considering a case which involved *Mareva* injunctions.

Once the suggested distinction based upon the absence of any assets within the jurisdiction is rejected, the short answer to the submission that the court cannot, or alternatively should not, grant a *Mareva* injunction extending to the overseas assets of C.M.I. is provided by *Derby v. Weldon (No. 1)* [1990] Ch. Cas. No. 37. This is binding authority for the proposition that the court can grant such an injunction in the circumstances of this case and persuasive authority for doing so. * * *

Enforceability of the injunctions

[As the V.-C.] said, "nothing brings the law into greater disrepute than the making of orders which cannot be enforced. The maxim 'equity does not act in vain' is a very sound one." It was suggested in argument that, on the authorities, the maxim referred not to enforceability but to the making of orders with which it was impossible to comply, * * *. Courts assume, rightly, that those who are subject to its jurisdiction will obey its orders: * * *. It is only if there is doubt about whether the order will be obeyed and if, should that occur, no real sanction would exist, that the court should refrain from making an order which the justice of the case requires.

* * *

When it came to Milco, which is incorporated in Panama, but no doubt like most Panamanian companies has its base of operations elsewhere, the Vice-Chancellor said that "there is no evidence before me that either a *Mareva* order or any eventual judgment can be enforced against Milco in Panama even if it has any assets." This involves two considerations—lack of assets and Panamanian enforcement. So far as lack of assets is concerned, there was evidence that, until recently Milco had very considerable assets. Whether they have indeed gone elsewhere and how and why they have disappeared will be a matter of some interest to the plaintiffs if they become judgment creditors of Milco, and I do not think that any alleged and unproved lack of assets should be regarded as a bar to the making of the order. * * * I think that it is a mistake to spend time considering whether English orders and judgments can be enforced against Panamanian companies in Panama. Whilst that is not perhaps the last forum to be considered in the context of such enforcement, it is certainly not the first. If in due time the plaintiffs are concerned to enforce a judgment against Milco, they will be resorting to the jurisdiction where its assets, if any, happen to be. In the event the Vice–Chancellor refused to make any order against Milco, but made an order against C.M.I. calling for the disclosure of assets of its subsidiary Dumaine and subsidiaries of that subsidiary, which includes Milco. For my part, for the reasons which I have given, I would make no distinction between C.M.I. and Milco in relation to the grant of a *Mareva* injunction.

The impact of international law

Considerations of comity require the courts of this country to refrain from making orders which infringe the exclusive jurisdiction of the courts of other countries. A *Mareva* injunction operates solely in personam and does not normally offend this principle in any way. I will revert to this aspect when considering the appointment of a receiver.

Court orders only bind those to whom they are addressed. However, it is a serious contempt of court, punishable as such, for anyone to interfere with or impede the administration of justice. This occurs if someone, knowing of the terms of the court order, assists in the breach of that order by the person to whom it is addressed. All this is common sense and works well so long as the "aider and abettor" is wholly within the jurisdiction of the court or wholly outside it. If he is wholly within the jurisdiction of the court there is no problem whatsoever. If he is wholly outside the jurisdiction of the court, he is either not to be regarded as being in contempt or it would involve an excess of jurisdiction to seek to punish him for that contempt. Unfortunately, juridical persons, notably banks, operate across frontiers. A foreign bank may have a branch within the jurisdiction and so be subject to the English courts. An English bank may have branches abroad and be asked by a defendant to take action at such a branch which will constitute a breach by the defendant of the court's order. Is action by the foreign bank to be regarded as contempt, although it would not be so regarded but for the probably irrelevant fact that it happens to have an English branch? Is action by the foreign branch of an English bank to be regarded as contempt, when other banks in the area are free to comply with the defendant's instructions?

All this was considered in the Babanaft appeal * * * and gave rise to what is known as the *"Babanaft* proviso" which was included in the order made by the Vice–Chancellor. This is not in fact the proviso adopted by the Court of Appeal in the *Babanaft* case itself, but was its preferred solution. As applied by the Vice–Chancellor to the circumstances of the application before him, it read:

"(a) No person other than * * * [C.M.I.] and any officer and any agent appointed by power of attorney of [C.M.I.] and any individual resident in England and Wales who has notice of this paragraph shall as regards acts done or to be done outside England and Wales be affected by the terms of this paragraph or concerned to inquire whether any instruction given by or on behalf of [C.M.I.] or anyone else, whether acting on behalf of [C.M.I.] or otherwise, is or may be a breach of this paragraph save to the extent that this paragraph is declared enforceable by or is otherwise enforced by an order of a court outside England and Wales and then only within the jurisdiction of that other court; . . ."

The express reason for including such a proviso was that *Mareva* injunctions "have an in rem effect on third parties" and that *"Mareva* injunctions have a direct effect on third parties who are notified of them and hold assets comprised in the order:" per Kerr L.J. in the *Babanaft* case, . . . I know what was meant, but I am not sure that it is possible to have an "in rem effect" upon persons whether natural or juridical and a *Mareva* injunction does not have any in rem effect on the assets themselves or the defendant's title to them. Nor does such an injunction have a direct effect on third parties. The injunction (a) restrains those to whom it is directed from exercising what would otherwise be their rights and (b) indirectly affects the rights of some, but not all, third parties to give effect to instructions from those directly bound by the order to do or concur in the doing of acts which are prohibited by the order. Whether any particular third party is indirectly affected, depends upon whether that person is subject to the jurisdiction of the English courts.

I have no doubt of the practical need for some proviso, because in its absence banks operating abroad do not know where they stand and foreign banks without any branch in England who are thus outside the jurisdiction of the English courts may take, and have indeed taken, offence at being, as they see it, "ordered about" by the English courts. All this is recorded in the judgment of Kerr L.J. in the *Babanaft* case. However I am not sure that the *Babanaft* proviso is the right answer to this dilemma. The first objection is that it treats natural persons differently from juridical persons. Why should an English merchant bank which is a partnership, if such there still be, and carries on business abroad as well as in this country be treated differently from a company, yet the proviso does not apply to "any individual resident in England." The second objection is that it places an English corporate bank in a very difficult position. It may know of the injunction and wish to support the court in its efforts to prevent the defendant from frustrating the due course of justice, but the proviso deprives it of the one justification which it would otherwise have for refusing to comply with his instructions.

* * *

What should be done? I should prefer a proviso on the following lines:

"Provided that, in so far as this order purports to have any extraterritorial effect, no person shall be affected thereby or concerned with the terms thereof until it shall be declared enforceable or be enforced by a foreign court and then it shall only affect them to the extent of such declaration or enforcement unless they are: (a) a person to whom this order is addressed or an officer of or an agent appointed by a power of attorney of such a person or (b) persons who are subject to the jurisdiction of this court and (i) have been given written notice of this order at their residence or place of business within the jurisdiction, and (ii) are able to prevent acts or omissions outside the jurisdiction of this court which assist in the breach of the terms of this order." This seems to me to meet any charge that the court is seeking to exercise an exorbitant jurisdiction, to be even handed as between natural and juridical persons and to avoid any argument based upon circularity.

By an order made on 7 November 1988 as amended by a further order made on 11 November, the Vice–Chancellor appointed a receiver of the assets of C.M.I. and ordered the two individual defendants and C.M.I. to do all in their power to vest these assets in the receiver. This order was subject to a *Babanaft* proviso covering the position of third parties and to a special proviso that no steps should be taken to enforce the vesting of the assets until after the courts of Luxembourg should have declared his order enforceable or otherwise enforced it. Finally the receiver was instructed to allow C.M.I. to defend this action independently of him.

Extraterritoriality

Panama is not a party to the European Judgments Convention or to any agreement to which effect would be given under the Foreign Judgments (Reciprocal Enforcement) Act 1933. There would therefore be problems in enforcing the orders of the English courts in Panama. However, I do not think that this should be regarded as an absolute bar to the appointment of a receiver of its assets. What really matters is the extent to which the receiver could effectively carry out his task, whatever that might be. In the instant case it would be to preserve any assets of Milco. He would be assisted by the sanction that, absent co-operation, Milco would not be allowed to defend the action. He would also be able to make use of the European Judgments Convention if, as seems not unlikely, any assets of Milco were situated in countries which were parties to that Convention. In the circumstances I see no reason why Milco should be treated differently from C.M.I. Once it is decided that a receiver should be appointed of all Milco's assets, it follows that Milco should be required to reveal the nature, value and whereabouts of those assets. It is not therefore necessary to consider whether it would be right to order such disclosure if no other relief were to be granted against Milco.

I would vary the orders in relation to C.M.I. by deleting the proviso in the *Mareva* injunction and * * * in the receivership order substituting in each case the following proviso: "Provided that, in so far as this order purports to have any effect outside England and Wales, no person shall be affected by it or concerned with the terms of it until it shall have been declared enforceable or shall have been recognised or registered or enforced by a foreign court (and then it shall only affect such person to the extent of such declaration or recognition or registration or enforcement) unless that person is; (a) a person to whom this order is addressed or an officer or an agent appointed by power of attorney of such a person, or (b) a person who is subject to the jurisdiction of this court and who: (i) has been given written notice of this order at his or its residence or place of business within the jurisdiction; and (ii) is able to prevent acts or omissions outside the jurisdiction of this court which assist in the breach of the terms of this order." I would make orders in relation to Milco in the same terms mutatis mutandis as those in relation to C.M.I.

Neill L.J.

I have had the advantage of reading in draft the judgment of Lord Donaldson of Lymington M.R. I agree with it and with the orders which Lord Donaldson proposes. * * *

It may be open to argument in some future case that in certain circumstances a discovery order can be made with a wider ambit than the *Mareva* injunction to which it is ancillary. * * * I remain of the opinion * * * that the discovery order, if made at all, should not go further than the injunction. * * * I do not find it necessary in this case to consider further whether, and, if so, in what circumstances, there may be exceptions to this general rule. I would only urge that in this field the court should scrutinise very carefully any submission that its powers are circumscribed more narrowly than the justice of the case demands. In the course of this appeal some reference was made to the fact that assets, like the Cheshire cat, may disappear unexpectedly. It is also to be remembered that modern technology and the ingenuity of its beneficiaries may enable assets to depart at a speed which can make any feline powers of evanescence appear to be sluggish by comparison.

Butler-Sloss L.J.

I agree with the judgments of Lord Donaldson of Lymington M.R. and Neill L.J.

Questions and Comments

1. While the English courts are debating the contours of pretrial protective relief, the U.S. courts have not even approved what was accom-

plished by the limited, original *Mareva* injunction. Do the three Court of Appeal justices agree as to the justification for granting the injunction? Looking back at the U.S. Supreme Court decision in *Groupo Mexicano*, both the majority and dissent referred to the *Mareva* injunction of the United Kingdom. Why would they refer to it if it has no influence on their decision?

2. The second English decision, *Derby v. Weldon*, was in the courts many times, to the frustration of some of the judges to whom it was assigned. Would the decision encourage the plaintiffs to request of a UK court in London that DROF UK disclose its assets in the Deutsche Bank and make no transfers of such assets, and that Oxford retain all art work on loan from VUSCO, and evaluate the value of the art and disclose any other locations it believes VUSCO has loaned art? If the UK court asserts jurisdiction over VUSCO, CANTIRE, and DROF AG as well as DROF UK, might the plaintiffs obtain a far reaching injunction over assets in other countries, including assets in Bermuda of the DROF AG subsidiaries? What limitations on injunctions would be likely in view of the *Derby* decision? How would the *Babanaft* proviso affect the court's ruling?

3 Considering the broader relief available in the United Kingdom, wouldn't the four plaintiffs in our case, especially the two UK nationals, to choose a UK forum for the principal litigation, not just to seek provisional relief in the event of a judgment in the U.S. court?

4. In addition to Lord Denning's Due Process of Law, he discusses both the *Mareva* injunction and *Anton Pillar* order in Denning, The Closing Chapter, 225, 235 (1983). *See also* M. Hetherington (ed.), Mareva Injunctions 1 (1983), Wasserman, *Equity Renewed: Preliminary Injunctions to Secure Potential Money Judgments*, 67 Wash. L. Rev. 257, 337 (1992) (Mareva "revolutionized English practice"); R. Ough & W. Flenley, The Mareva Injunction and Anton Piller Order: Practice and Precedents xi (2d ed.1993)("nuclear weapo[n] of the law"). An Anton Pillar order removes any privilege against self-incrimination in civil proceedings pertaining to intellectual property, essentially allowing intellectual property owners to obtain an order sequestering pirated copies of movies, DVDs, etc.

PART C.   ATTACHMENT IN THE EUROPEAN UNION

Article 31 of the Brussels Regulation (Article 24 of the earlier Brussels Convention) states:

> **Article 31**. Application may be made to the courts of a Member State for such provisional, including protective, measures as may be available under the law of that State, even if, under this Regulation, the courts of another Member State have jurisdiction as to the substance of the matter.

This Regulation does not specifically cover an order by a court of one EU state that has extraterritorial affect. The readings begin with more of the above *Derby* decision of the U.K. Court of Appeal, this time the portion of the decision that refers to the EU Convention (and thus Regulation)

DERBY & CO. LTD. AND OTHERS
v. WELDON AND OTHERS[7]

U.K. Court of Appeal.
[1989] 2 W.L.R. 412.

LORD DONALDSON OF LYMINGTON M.R.

This consideration led the Vice–Chancellor to examine the extent to which a Mareva injunction could be enforced against C.M.I. in Luxembourg, which is a party to the European Convention on Jurisdiction and the Enforcement of Judgments in Civil and Commercial Matters to which this country gave effect by the Civil Jurisdiction and Judgments Act 1982. This certainly is deserving of examination but, in the context of the grant of the Mareva injunction, I think that a sufficient sanction exists in the fact that, in the event of disobedience, the court could bar the defendant's right to defend. This is not a consequence which it could contemplate lightly as it would become a fugitive from a final judgment given against it without its explanations having been heard and which might well be enforced against it by other courts. It may be that C.M.I. is inherently law-abiding or that some such consideration has occurred to it, but it is certainly the fact that it has co-operated fully with the receiver appointed by the Vice–Chancellor, has made some disclosure of its assets and began to do so before the Luxembourg court made an order enforcing that of the Vice–Chancellor.

I have no doubt of the practical need for some proviso, because in its absence banks operating abroad do not know where they stand and foreign banks without any branch in England who are thus outside the jurisdiction of the English courts may take, and have indeed taken, offence at being, as they see it, ordered about by the English courts. All this is recorded in the judgment of Kerr L.J. in *Babanaft*. However I am not sure that the *Babanaft* proviso is the right answer to this dilemma.

* * *

The third objection I record without expressing any view on its validity. It is that an order which includes this proviso has ex facie no extraterritorial effect and so is not of a character enabling it to be recognised under the European Judgments Convention and enforced abroad thereunder. In other words, the proviso has a circular effect. This is apparently being argued in the Luxembourg Court of Appeal following an order for the recognition and enforcement of the Vice–Chancellor's order by the Luxembourg Court of first instance

The main action is proceeding in this country. We are therefore not concerned with the powers referred to in article 24 which enable the courts in one Convention country to make interlocutory orders in aid of

---

7. The portions of this case that discuss   below.
the European Union are extracted in Part C

actions which are proceeding in another Convention country. At a later stage of the action, however, it may be necessary to look further at the way the present orders are enforced by registration or otherwise both in Convention countries and elsewhere. It is to be remembered that a Mareva injunction is a remedy which takes effect in personam and may have characteristics which are unfamiliar in some jurisdictions overseas.

Sir Nicolas Browne–Wilkinson V.-C. posed the question of whether it was right for the court to appoint a receiver of assets outside the jurisdiction belonging to a company which had no residence in this country. He answered it by saying:

> I have grave doubts whether, in the absence of proper evidence of Luxembourg law, I would have been prepared to appoint a receiver. It seems to me that the court should not appoint receivers over non-residents in relation to assets which are not within the jurisdiction of this court, unless satisfied that the local court either of residence or of the situation of the assets will act in aid of the English court in enforcing it. That is why the evidence of Luxembourg law is, to my mind, important in this case.

> The evidence of Luxembourg law is not in any way full at this stage but, broadly, it appears to be this. Under the 1968 European Judgments Convention which is incorporated in English law in the Civil Jurisdiction and Judgments Act 1982, article 24 provides under the rubric 'Provisional, including protective, measures' as follows: Application may be made to the courts of a contracting state for such provisional, including protective, measures as may be available under the law of that state, even if, under this Convention, the courts of another contracting state have jurisdiction as to the substance of the matter.

> Under article 24, therefore, it is proper for this court to make protective orders of the kind such as in *Mareva* relief or in aid of *Mareva* relief, which can be enforced under the Convention in the other Convention countries including Luxembourg. The evidence before me suggests that the Luxembourg court will probably enforce any order that I make for the appointment of a receiver. The exact working out of such order and the manner in which the effect of the English order is reproduced under Luxembourg law may give rise to trouble. But the basic position, as I understand the evidence before me, is that if the order properly falls within article 24 (as it does), the Luxembourg court will enforce it.

> I am not seeking by this order in any way to make an order encroaching on the jurisdiction of the Luxembourg court. I will require the insertion in the order of a proviso modelled on the proviso in the *Babanaft* case . . .

> Accordingly, the order I propose to make today will not be directly enforceable within Luxembourg save to the extent that the Luxembourg court itself thinks it proper so to do in a case falling within article 24.

I think that there may have been some confusion between the objects and effects of article 24 on the one hand and article 25 et seq. on the other. The Convention in no way affects the powers of the courts of state A which is properly seised of the substance of the dispute. However, it provides for the courts of another contracting state, state B, to assist in two quite different ways. First, in articles 25 et seq. it provides a code for the recognition and enforcement of the orders of the courts of state A by the courts of state B. Second, in article 24, it authorises the courts of state B to entertain a direct application for protective orders in support of the primary proceedings before the courts of state A. In the instant case the Vice–Chancellor seems, rightly as events have shown, to have contemplated that the Luxembourg courts would be invited to recognise and enforce his orders, i.e., would act under article 25 et seq. and not under article 24.

* * * In this situation I do not understand why the order that the assets vest in the receiver should only take effect if and when the order was recognised by the Luxembourg courts. True it is that C.M.I. is a Luxembourg company, but it is a party to the action and can properly be ordered to deal with its assets in accordance with the orders of this court, regardless of whether the order is recognised and enforced in Luxembourg. The only effect of non-recognition would be to remove one of the potential sanctions for disobedience.

I would affirm the orders of the Vice–Chancellor in relation to the receivership of the assets of C.M.I., subject only to (a) amending the *Babanaft* proviso in the terms which I have already indicated and (b) deleting the proviso that the order requiring C.M.I. and the two individual defendants to vest the assets in the receiver should only take effect if the order was recognised by the Luxembourg courts.

Questions and Comments

1. DROF AG may raise EC issues under the European Convention. Would the UK Courts ruling that it might make under *Derby* with regard to non-EU nations have to be modified with regard to application in Germany? Is the "modified" *Babanaft* provision preferred by Lord Donaldson very different from that applicable outside the EU?

2. Does the discussion at this point suggest that plaintiffs ought to be thinking about some action in Canada, the UK and/or Bermuda?

3. The EU approach to protective measures is discussed in Peter Kaye, *Extraterritorial Mareva Orders and the Relevance of Enforceability*, C.J.Q. 1990, 9 (JAN), 12–16; Lawrence Collins, *The Territorial Reach of Mareva Injunctions*, L.Q.R.1989, 105 (APR.) 262.

Chapter 4

FOREIGN PLAINTIFF/U.S. DEFENDANT

INTRODUCTION 4.0   FOREIGN PLAINTIFFS SUING U.S. DEFENDANTS IN U.S. COURTS

The United States is an attractive forum for foreign plaintiffs with claims against U.S. persons, whether individuals or corporations. The late Lord Denning, as Master of the Rolls of the Court of Appeal of England, stated that "As a moth is drawn to the light, so is a litigant drawn to the United States."[1] He was correct. Many foreigners, especially from poorer countries, view the United States as a nation of unlimited riches. The U.S. legal system has not discouraged that perception. With plaintiffs' attorneys ready with contingent fee contracts, and the prospect of punitive as well as pain and suffering damages, why should foreign plaintiffs want to stay home and litigate in domestic courts? Furthermore, it is likely to be much easier to obtain personal jurisdiction over a U.S. defendant in the United States than abroad.

In the following five problems, the same hypothetical will be used to address different, but interrelated issues. But the topic of each problem cannot be considered entirely separate. One important lesson for each party is to plan case strategy from the very beginning, considering the implications of each of these issues, as well as such additional issues as the possibility of recognition and enforcement of foreign judgments.

Problem 4.1 includes much opportunity to plan strategy. It is the choice of forum made by the plaintiff. Because there are often multiple forums with the legal capacity or jurisdiction to litigate the issues, the choice of forum is usually where the plaintiff believes it has the greatest advantage. In our hypothetical, each plaintiff must ask "Should the litigation be commenced in the United States, or Mexico, or some other location, such as Germany, or England or Japan?" This problem does not deal with situations where there are forum selection clauses in an agreement; that was covered in Problem 3.1. This problem rather

---

1. *Smith Kline & French Laboratories Ltd. v. Bloch* [1983] 2 All E.R. 72 (Ct. App.).

addresses what factors cause plaintiffs' counsel to choose a particular forum. What are the most important legal and non-legal factors the plaintiffs should consider in deciding where they will commence the litigation? The strategy *must* consider the legal implications of each choice. If plaintiffs choose Japan because some of the ingredients of Sollate™ come from Japan, will the Japanese courts dismiss the action because Japan is an inappropriate forum, or because there is no direct link between the injuries and the Japanese supplier, or for some other reason in Japanese law? We will learn some new language used in other nations, especially the U.K., such as which is the "proper" forum. We also see that other nations view characteristics of the U.S. legal system with disfavor. And we will address some ethical issues in forum shopping.

Once the plaintiff has chosen the forum and filed suit, the defendant will have to respond. There are various responses to the plaintiff's choice of a forum. The defendant may argue that the choice was improper or that there is a more appropriate forum. An improper choice might be where the plaintiff chose a court that does not have personal jurisdiction (i.e., insufficient contacts with the forum), or lacks subject matter jurisdiction, an issue explored in Problem 4.2. However, even if a plaintiff's choice is proper on jurisdictional grounds, the defendant may still be able to challenge that choice on grounds that the chosen forum is inconvenient for the action pursuant to the doctrine of *forum non conveniens*. This issue is explored in Problem 4.3. The defendant also may raise a question of removal within the United States, which may precede a motion to dismiss under *forum non conveniens*. For example, if the injured Mexican parties initiated suit in a U.S. state court considered exceptionally sympathetic to plaintiffs, GROWFAST might consider first removing the matter to federal court in that same state, and then to a federal court in a different location that has a more favorable record for the final *coup de grâce*—dismissal on grounds of *forum non conveniens* under the theory that Mexico is the more appropriate forum for the litigation.

Problem 4.2 turns to subject matter jurisdiction. The rules are very different for contract and tort cases. Very often a *contract* has links with more than one country and subject matter jurisdiction is relatively easy, because more than one country is justified in concluding that there are sufficient links to find subject matter jurisdiction. Problem 4.2 involves some contract linkages to both the United States and Mexico. For the tort claims, however, exactly where did the tort occur? In Mexico where the explosion occurred? Or perhaps in the United States or Germany where the Sollate™ was made. Or maybe in England or Japan, if the suppliers prepared and shipped unsafe ingredients. Some countries encourage litigation in their courts. For example, courts in England assert subject matter jurisdiction on rather tenuous grounds, especially for commercial litigation, when compared with courts in the United States or Mexico, for example. The English seem to believe that their courts are the fairest of them all. England has allowed jurisdiction on a contract for the sale of coffee from a Belgian seller to a Spanish buyer because the parties used English as the language for the contract and the fact that coffee prices were listed on the London coffee exchange. The United States requires more substantive contacts, as does Mexico and most of the rest of the world. Additionally, defendants' motions based on *forum non conveniens* or choice of law may influence a court's thinking as it addresses a challenge to subject matter jurisdiction. If there is subject matter jurisdiction in more than one jurisdiction, the issue of parallel proceedings, considered in problem 3.6, again arises.

Problem 4.3 considers *forum non conveniens*, the idea of dismissal by the forum in which the suit is commenced because it is an inconvenient forum, or actually because there is a *more* convenient forum elsewhere. Since the case in this problem was initiated in the United States, the U.S. court was clearly the choice of the plaintiff. Shouldn't that choice be respected if there is jurisdiction? If another forum is to be considered, which factors will the court consider and give more weight to—public interest factors or private interest factors? Making a motion to dismiss for *forum non conveniens* reasons involves some strategy by the defendant. Will control over the case be lost if it is moved abroad? Perhaps the lawyers for the U.S. defendant prefer not to move it abroad because they may lose significant fees. What if the defendant's lawyers believe the plaintiffs could not afford to litigate in the foreign court or that the case would take? Do these questions raise ethical issues? There are some challenges being made to *forum non conveniens*, and we consider those in England, the European Union, and parts of Latin America.

Problem 4.4 assumes the cases are going forward in the U.S. courts. What law will a U.S. court apply? A U.S. judge probably feels more comfortable applying the law of the forum—U.S. law. But the judge may be persuaded that the applicable law in our hypothetical problem is that of Mexico, or perhaps the law of Germany, or Japan, or England. Does a U.S. judge "know" foreign law as that judge is deemed to know U.S. law? When must an assertion that a particular law ought to be applied be made, and how is it made? There are very different issues to consider in these cases, other than those we would address if the cases involved the law of different states in the United States.

The final Problem 4.5 assumes that the court has chosen an applicable law, in this case the law of Mexico. The problem addresses how Mexican law will be applied, and includes a brief introduction to a civil law nation's law. While a U.S. lawyer for the plaintiffs or defendants would certainly associate with a lawyer with knowledge of Mexican law, the former must understand some of the fundamental characteristics of the Mexican legal system.

PROBLEM 4.1   CHOICE OF FORUM: EXPLOSION IN MEXICAN SUBSIDIARY OF U.S. PESTICIDE MANUFACTURER

SECTION I.   THE SETTING

GROWFAST CHEMICALS, INC. ("GROWFAST") is a Delaware chartered corporation with principal administrative offices in Tampa, Florida. It is wholly-owned by U.S. shareholders. It has manufacturing facilities in several states, including Florida and Texas. It also has wholly-owned subsidiaries in Canada ("GROWCAN, LTD."), Mexico ("GROWMEX, S.A."), and Germany ("GROWGER, GmbH"). GROW-FAST manufactures many different pesticides and fungicides used by commercial growers of ornamental plants. One of the fungicides is Sollate™. For nearly two decades Sollate™ has been used extensively by commercial and home growers of many different tropical plants. It has long been considered the only successful fungicide to control several harmful fungi. Some of the ingredients in Sollate™ come from companies (unaffiliated with GROWFAST) located in England and Japan.

A serious accident occurred at the GROWMEX, S.A., plant in Veracruz. While transferring Sollate™ concentrate into vats for dilution and packaging, under the supervision of both Mexican (Veracruz residents and Mexican citizens) employees and two technicians (U.S. citizens and residents of Tampa) "on loan" from GROWFAST in Tampa, an unexplained explosion occurred. One of the U.S. technicians and 35 Mexican employees were killed. Dozens of other employees who were Veracruz area residents and Mexican citizens suffered serious injuries. The smoke from the explosion drifted over Veracruz and adjacent towns, causing serious burns to several hundred more people, including a number of foreign tourists from different states in the United States and from several European countries. Several victims and relatives of decedents are considering initiating lawsuits based on a variety of torts.

The estates of the deceased U.S. technician the 35 Mexican employees who were killed, the injured employees, and the injured persons in the area (including the foreign tourists), might bring suit in Mexico or the United States, against GROWMEX and/or GROWFAST. Where are these parties likely to bring suit, and for what reasons? Assuming suits are brought in the United States, there are further choices. Should they be brought in federal or state court? We know GROWFAST has manufacturing facilities in Florida and Texas. It has administrative offices in Tampa and is chartered in Delaware. Within each of these states there will be proper venue questions.[1] These are questions that may have been

---

1. Alien plaintiffs may have more problems with venue than domestic plaintiffs. The Alien Venue Statute, 28 U.S.C. § 1391(d), provides for suits *against* aliens, not suits *by* aliens. *See, The Alien Venue Statute: An Historical Analysis of Federal* *Venue Provisions and Alien Right,* 3 N.Y.U.J. Int'l & Comp. L. 307 (1982). An alien plaintiff usually has no domestic residence, and may thus only bring suit where the claim arose or where the defendant resides.

addressed in the introductory course in civil procedure. Because Mexico is also a federal system, there may be a similar question regarding litigation in either federal or state court.

Although GROWFAST believes that the explosion was the fault of Mexican employees of GROWMEX who disobeyed instructions given by the U.S. parent and the technicians, it also believes that the two companies in England and Japan that supplied some of the ingredients to manufacture the Sollate™ may be wholly or partly responsible for the explosion and damages. However, both of those companies have denied any responsibility. GROWFAST, nevertheless, is prepared to bring both of these foreign companies into the litigation, whether by joining them in suits filed in the United States, or by initiating separate suits in the United States , England or Japan for indemnity, contribution and breach of contract for supplying a defective product.

You were introduced to forum selection clauses in Problem 3.1, where a U.S. plaintiff sued a foreign manufacturer of tires whose tire tread separated and caused an accident in the United States. Choice of forum agreements are common where there is a contract, and may extend to tort actions linked to the contract. In our hypothetical fact situation there are no forum selection clauses designating Mexican or U.S. courts for injuries from plant accidents. Certainly, the non-employee persons who were injured (nearby residents and tourists) will not be subject to any forum selection clauses. The employees of GROWMEX and GROWFAST, however, might have been required to agree in their employment contracts to arbitration of injury claims. Although U.S. workers' compensation schemes would probably not apply to any of the potential plaintiffs other than the two U.S. "on-loan" employees of GROWFAST, the Mexican Social Security system and related labor laws provide for a compulsory scheme for addressing injuries to workers in the GROWMEX plant. The amount is not so high to discourage GROWFAST from its attempt to move the litigation to Mexico or have Mexican law apply. Would a Mexican court facing a suit by a GROWMEX employee against GROWMEX enforce an arbitration provision that stipulated that any liability resulting from the employment relationship would be the exclusive responsibility of GROWMEX and GROWFAST would be excused from liability, and that called for the *arbitration* of any dispute arising from the employment relationship? Would such a provision limit the employees' rights under the Mexican labor code or other Mexican law?

SECTION II. FOCUS OF CONSIDERATION

Carrying on business in another country may give rise to choice of forum and choice of law issues when there is a breach of contract or accident. In the GROWFAST situation, there are both potential contract and tort claims. Those claims create very different considerations. In Mexico, commercial contracts are governed by the federal code, but torts are governed by the separate civil codes of each state. But if the tort occurred on federal land, such as a national highway, the federal civil code would apply in lieu of the state civil code. Because both Mexico and the United States have adopted as treaty law the United Nations

Convention on Contracts for the International Sale of Goods ("CISG"), substantive contract law is essentially harmonized where the CISG is applicable.[2] Mexican tort law, in contrast to contract law, is very different from U.S. tort law. Chapter Four focuses on tort issues, and is intended to make readers aware of the principal issues facing foreign plaintiffs and U.S. defendants in tort litigation in the United States. It builds upon the issues in Chapter Three immediately preceding, which addressed a similar task when U.S. parties sue foreign defendants in U.S. courts. One point may become clear immediately, choice of forum and choice of law issues are often complex, no matter who is suing whom. Choosing where to initiate a suit requires knowledge about many of the legal rules in each of the possible forums. Further, counsel must think the litigation through from start to finish. Obviously, counsel for plaintiffs and for defendants have very different objectives.

The plaintiffs who were non-employee "persons in the area", including the tourists, would not be subject to any forum selection clause. That is also very likely the case with regard to the Mexican and U.S. employees of GROWMEX and GROWFAST. In any event, that will be assumed to be the case for this part of the discussion.

SECTION III.   READINGS, QUESTIONS AND COMMENTS

The first two readings involve a case study from which this problem was developed in 1995. It involved a different situation. The explosion did not occur in a Mexican subsidiary of GROWFAST, but in a Mexican company neither owned nor controlled by GROWFAST. The Juenger article discusses generally the idea of forum shopping. The Republic of Bolivia and Kinney decisions illustrate the frustration of some courts with forum shopping, and the English decisions reflect upon forum shopping when it involves English forums that may be viewed as the "proper" forum.

A SERIOUS ACCIDENT OCCURS IN THE MEXICAN PLANT: PROBLEMS OF CORPORATE AND PRODUCT LIABILITY

4 U.S.-Mexico Law Journal 125 (1996).

Moderator: Michael W. Gordon[al] Panel Members: Keith Harvey,[aal] M.E. Occhialino,[aaal] Boris Kozolchyk[aaaal], and Ignacio Gomez Palacio[aaaaal]

2. The CISG is generally applicable to contracts for the international sale of goods where the contract is silent on choice of law or, less frequently, expressly names the CISG.

al. Chesterfield Smith Professor of Law, University of Florida College of Law, Gainesville, Florida.

aal. Partner Davis & Harvey, Dallas, Texas.

aaal. Professor of Law, University of New Mexico School of Law.

aaaal. Director and President, National Law Center for Inter–American Free Trade, Tucson, Arizona.

aaaaal. Of Counsel, Jauregui, Navarrete, Nader y Rojas, S.C. Mexico, D.F.

After several years of successful association between GROWFAST and AGRICOLAS S.A. de C.V., a serious accident occurred at the AGRICOLAS plant in Monterrey. [GROWFAST is incorporated in Delaware, has principal offices in Kansas and a plant in Texas.]While transferring Sollate™ concentrate into vats for dilution and packaging, supervised by both AGRICOLAS employees and two technicians "on loan" from GROWFAST, an unexplained explosion occurred. Three supervisory persons and 35 other employees were killed. Serious injury was caused to dozens of other employees. The chemical laden smoke from the explosion drifted over parts of Monterrey and adjacent towns. By the time it had dissipated, it had caused serious burns to several hundred more people, including a number of foreigners. The foreigners included two U.S. citizens vacationing in Mexico. Lawsuits are being considered by Mexicans, the two United States citizens, and four Europeans. [These facts are quite similar to those in the hypothetical in this problem. The most significant difference is that in this casebooks problems the Mexican GROWMEX is a wholly owned subsidiary of GROWFAST, while in the above extract discussion AGRICOLAS is a Mexican contractual distributor of GROWFAST. The materials address the differences.]

THE DISCUSSION

Michael Gordon: As an attorney representing some of the potential plaintiffs, what are your thoughts as to where you would want to bring your suit?

Keith Harvey: The plaintiffs of course would be the U.S. citizens, the Mexican workers at the plant and the Europeans. But what about that poor Mexican corporation AGRICOLAS that was destroyed by that defective product produced in the United States? I thought they might be a good plaintiff as well, especially under Texas product liability law which gives an indemnification provision for sellers of a defective product.

Gordon: Lic. Gomez–Palacio, would you encourage the Mexican plaintiffs to stay home and sue in Mexico if several of the Mexicans came to you in Mexico, or would you encourage them to travel to another forum?

Ignacio Gomez–Palacio: First of all, we know that, in a case like this, American courts would award more compensation, and second, the defendant here is an American corporation. I would advise my client to sue in the United States. The way American judges think is important. What law will be applicable is something else. This is a very crucial issue because generally speaking it is believed that Mexican tort law is a bad law for the plaintiffs to use because the damages awarded will be rather small. My experience indicates that the Mexican law applied by an American judge and a Mexican judge may be entirely different because the backgrounds of each of the judges are entirely different. For example, Mexico's law refers to el daño moral, "moral damages." Mexican law does not allow punitive damages. Formerly, "moral damages" had a limit. However, by amendment to the Civil Code of the Federal District, this cap was removed. The judges now feel rather free to impose higher awards. If a person had $1,000 damages in the hospital, and the person may have lost an arm, a Mexican judge would feel very generous if they awarded $5,000. You put this "moral damage" concept in the hands of an American judge and he may throw everything into the moral damages and grant an award of half a million dollars. So, the same law may be applied quite differently in one place than the other.

M.E. Occhialino: There would be jurisdiction in the state courts of both Kansas and Delaware, and also in Kansas or Delaware federal courts. In this fact pattern, then, there are at least six U.S. forums that are available. The plaintiff's difficult task is to choose the one of those six places that will lead to the most favorable result. Assuming that all jurisdictional requirements are met, the plaintiff's attorney would then ask which of these six different forums would apply law most favorable to the plaintiffs.

Gordon: [Kansas, Texas and Delaware state and federal courts all may have jurisdiction.] If you were assured of having U.S. law applied, it would certainly seem better as plaintiff's lawyer to choose Delaware if Delaware had a record of higher punitive damages than Kansas and Texas. If Kansas or Texas were more likely to apply Mexican law, then you wouldn't want to go there as the plaintiff.

Occhialino: That's a fair statement. Choosing among the courts of three American states doesn't necessarily tell us that law will apply or what American law will apply. Many people think of the United States as a single entity; one country with one body of law. In fact, each state has it's own often different body of tort law. In addition each state has it's own system for choosing whether to apply it's own tort law or that of another state or country. The latter are found in the states choice of law principles. Each state can either apply its own law or the law of another state or a foreign country.... So, plaintiffs would pick which state to sue in and, in part, that would depend upon which law that state would apply. It is not only a question of Mexico versus the United States but the attorney would also have to be concerned about the substantive laws of Delaware, Texas and Kansas, as well as each state's choice of law rules.

Gordon: Nowhere do the facts suggest that AGRICOLAS, is owned or controlled by GROWFAST. It is a Mexican corporation; it has an entirely separate board of directors; it is chartered in Mexico; it simply has a distributorship contract with the GROWFAST company. So how can we possibly bring suit against GROWFAST? It could be argued that the accident was caused by AGRICOLAS.

Harvey: GROWFAST, of course, will be the target defendant of the Americans that were injured, as well as the European and probably the Mexican citizens because I am sure some American lawyers would try to recruit them as clients. In thinking about the possible defendants other than GROWFAST, I considered the independent Mexican company, AGRICOLAS. But what was AGRICOLAS doing? GROWFAST sent the product to Mexico. AGRICOLAS then took the product, put it in vats to dilute it, and then put it in the containers to sell it. Then there was a mysterious explosion. Who caused this? So I thought that AGRICOLAS too may have a cause of action against GROWFAST because they have damages to their plant; they may be sued in Mexico or in the United States. The most logical thing for AGRICOLAS to do is go to the United States where they could sue GROWFAST under the doctrine of strict liability or some other causes of action.

Gordon: If we change the facts a little and make the party in Mexico not AGRICOLAS but a wholly owned subsidiary of GROWFAST, then we have the opportunity to try the Mexican enterprise under the doctrine of strict liability.

Harvey: I think you would have a better case all across the board.

Occhialino: Your fact pattern as written is very subtle. It states that the product blew up during the process of dilution, but it doesn't say that the product blew up because of any defect in the product as opposed to the way it was being handled by AGRICOLAS at the time. If improper handling, rather than a defective product, was the cause, American concepts of strict product liability might not apply. Product liability law requires a defect. Possibly the product was fine, but the way it was handled was not. The facts * * * suggest as well that there were two GROWFAST employees who were present, but they were on loan to AGRICOLAS. This would suggest that they might have been under the control of AGRICOLAS. Therefore, under American law the manufacturer, GROWFAST, may not be liable for their conduct at the time. This scenario suggests that GROWFAST might not be liable at all and that only AGRICOLAS would be liable. This would be disastrous for plaintiffs because: (1) they couldn't sue AGRICOLAS in the United States anywhere due to the lack of personal jurisdiction; and (2) according to our panelists, Mexican law may not be very favorable to them in Mexico.

Gordon: Assuming you are not going to be able to bring this case in the United States but will have to bring it in Mexico, in what state in Mexico will you bring it. It could be brought in Monterrey, Nuevo Leon, where AGRICOLAS has its plant. But could it be brought in the Federal District and how would you get jurisdiction over GROWFAST there?

Gomez–Palacio: If this accident occurred in Monterrey, I would agree that the Civil Code of the State of Nuevo Leon would apply unless it could be considered of a federal nature, in which case, the Civil Code of the Federal District might apply. For example, accidents occurring on the ocean beaches are governed by federal law because a strip of land twenty meters in from the highest tide is federal land. Thus, a swimming pool which is within twenty meters of the ocean is actually on federal territory. The principle is that *locus regit actum*, the place governs the act.

Mark P. Lang: What I hear from you is that we should tell our clients that they should get down on their knees and give thanks if they are sued in Mexico because the award of damages will be so low that the check will fly in the mail after the judgment and there will never need be a collection proceeding filed in this country. However, in the event some enterprising plaintiff's attorney like Mr. Harvey or myself would get those clients and sue in Texas, we would certainly sue on alternative counts and claim negligent failure to warn, and even sue the corporate officers for gross negligence and breach of contract and request a jury trial, and so on and so forth, negligent failure to properly supervise, negligent retention of attorneys, alter ego, joint and several liability. So GROWFAST would be in deep trouble if it were sued in Texas. I know, I've been there.

Trujillo: It is my understanding that U.S. courts and particularly federal courts are fairly deferential to litigation that has commenced in a foreign jurisdiction. Would it be possible for the U.S. corporation, feeling the threat of litigation in the United States, to commence litigation in Mexico, and by that means divert jurisdiction to Mexico?

Occhialino: Although it is unlikely to be successful, there is such a mechanism in the United States. At least theoretically, GROWFAST might choose not to be the defendant but to become the plaintiff by filing a declaratory judgment action seeking a declaration of non-liability before the injured persons sue GROWFAST. Declaratory judgments are available in most states and in the federal courts. The corporation would seek a declaration of non-liability to whomever it is that they have hurt. In that way GROWFAST would be able to pick the time, the place, and if they do it right, also pick the law that will be applicable by picking the right place in which to file the declaratory judgment action. However, several American cases have ruled that it is improper to use the declaratory judgment act if the party filing the action is really a potential personal injury defendant who is likely to be sued soon, and who is merely trying to turn itself into a plaintiff. So in theory there is an American device. In practice the cases are not very favorably disposed to the use of the device in these circumstances. I do not know whether such a procedure is recognized in Mexico.

Lang: Could a prospective Mexican defendant sue in Mexico in order to establish jurisdiction in Mexico when he has injured an American corporation by defrauding it? Assume that the Mexican party begins a lawsuit in Mexico under some pretense in order to prevent the U.S. corporation from establishing jurisdiction over this defendant to claim treble damages or some other type of compensation that is available in the U.S. I think many of the federal courts and even the state courts, would be deferential to the suit that has begun in Mexico already. I think it's possible for a Mexican defendant to do that.

Harvey: In Texas, a plea of abatement is permitted by which an action in the courts of Texas may be delayed or stopped until a pending action in another jurisdiction has been resolved. If a procedure exists in Mexico for somebody who would be a defendant to actually become a plaintiff, such a person might be able to file a plea of abatement in Texas on the ground that there is a pending proceeding in Mexico, and everything else ought to stop. This might prevent people from using the American courts with very favorable choice of law principles.

Gordon: Is there any way in Mexico for GROWFAST to start a suit immediately, asking a Mexican court to declare that it is not GROW-FAST's fault?

Gomez–Palacio: I must confess ignorance there. I think it is a matter of procedural law and I'm not familiar. I would establish a big doubt, though.

Alvin Garcia: What about *res judicata* and collateral estoppel? Would a judgment in Mexico, preclude litigation by the same parties in the United States? Would a judgment from the United States stop litigation in Mexico?

Occhialino: Let me rephrase your question: If there were a Mexican judgment and it made certain findings and there was subsequent American litigation, would the findings of the Mexican court be binding so that re-litigation would not be permitted in the American court? That question would normally be answered affirmatively under constitutional principles requiring one of giving full faith and credit to the judgments of another state, but since Mexico, rather than a state, is the first forum, full faith and credit is not required; at best it would be a question of comity. And under comity principles, an American court could either say the Mexican court has already found "X" to be true so we don't have to re-litigate it, or it could choose not to. So there is a lot more deference in an American court to not give collateral estoppel or *res judicata* impact to a foreign country judgment. I don't know how a Mexican court would deal with the question of an earlier American judgment.

M.E. OCCHIALINO, REPRESENTING MEXICAN CLIENTS IN U.S. COURTS IN CLAIMS OF LIABILITY IN INDUSTRIAL ACCIDENTS

4 U.S.-Mexico L.J. 147 (1996).

* * *The lawyer who represents only U.S. citizens will plan the litigation differently from the lawyer who represents the Mexican nationals and the Europeans instead of, or in addition to, the U.S. citizens.

If the lawyer now represents only one or a few persons, the lawyer should explore the possibility of expanding the client base to include everyone who was injured. This would make the lawsuit more efficient, allowing more thorough representation because the costs would be shared among more clients and the greater judgment available with multiple plaintiffs might justify higher expenditures for investigation, planning, legal research and hiring of expert witnesses.* * * The lawyer might consider choosing a forum for the litigation in part based upon which forums provide for class actions and have rules making class actions relatively easy to use.

The U.S. lawyer who lacks knowledge of the jurisdictional and substantive laws of Mexico must first learn the rudiments of Mexican law,* * * A review only of library sources almost certainly would not suffice. After becoming familiar with the basic principles of Mexican law, the U.S. lawyer would want to retain a lawyer who practices law in Mexico to provide a detailed evaluation of relevant Mexican law.

The U.S. lawyer typically would begin analysis by determining the maximum number of forums that would be available in which to bring the lawsuit. For an U.S. lawyer, the forum-availability question requires consideration of the following: 1) Jurisdiction of the subject matter; 2) Jurisdiction over the person of the defendant(s); 3) Proper venue; and 4) Problems of service of process. The lawyer would survey the law of every state of the United States that had any connection with the transactions or the potential defendants to see how many of them could meet the four requirements and qualify as proper forums for the litigation. The lawyer would analyze separately whether U.S. federal courts had jurisdiction to hear the case. Finally, the lawyer would ask the consulting Mexican attorney to do the equivalent analysis to determine the maximum number of forums in Mexico in which the lawsuit could be brought.

Consideration of possible forums includes not only an analysis of the place where the plaintiffs can obtain jurisdiction, but also whether the defendant would be able to veto the plaintiffs' choice of any of these available forums through the use of procedural rules allowing defendants to dismiss or move a case brought by plaintiffs in any of these forums. These "defendant-veto" procedures include: 1) Motion for change of venue; 2) Motion to dismiss for *forum non conveniens*; and 3) Removal of the action to federal court if the lawsuit is brought in a state court. At this point, the goal is simply to identify all the places where the action could be brought and where the defendant could not frustrate the plaintiff's choice of forum.* * *

FRIEDRICH K. JUENGER, FORUM SHOPPING, DOMESTIC AND INTERNATIONAL

63 Tul. L. Rev. 553 (1989).

My topic has a bad name. As a rule, counsel, judges, and academicians employ the term "forum shopping" to reproach a litigant who, in their opinion, unfairly exploits jurisdictional or venue rules to affect the outcome of a lawsuit. But in spite of the phrase's pejorative connotation, forum shopping remains popular. Without much exaggeration, Judge

Skelly Wright called it "a national legal pastime.' * * * Whatever opprobrium some legal minds may attach to it, counsel's jockeying for position is not universally condemned. Then Justice Rehnquist, for one, sanguinely countenanced the "litigation strategy of countless plaintiffs who seek a forum with favorable substantive or procedural rules or sympathetic local populations."

* * *

American counsels' forum-shopping expertise has benefitted alien as well as domestic clients. The bulk of reported international cases involve foreign torts litigated in this country, where contingency fees are lawful and juries notoriously generous—features that appeal to victims irrespective of their residence or citizenship.

A striking example of the American judicial systems' attraction as a tort haven is the litigation following the crash near Paris of a DC–10 owned by a Turkish airline. The plane, en route from Paris to London, plunged into the forest of Ermenonville shortly after takeoff, killing 330 passengers from 5 continents and the 13–member Turkish crew. The widow of an English victim retained a New York firm, which filed a complaint in a federal court in Los Angeles fifteen days after the accident. Seminars conducted by American experts on aviation cases persuaded English solicitors to send their clients' cases to the United States, and the relatives of victims from other nations followed suit. To escape the Warsaw Convention's notoriously low damages ceiling[61] and jurisdictional limitations,[62] the plaintiffs' attorneys recast the plane crash as a products liability suit. Their primary targets were the manufacturer of the aircraft, McDonnell Douglas, and its subcontractor, General Dynamics. Actions filed in various states, primarily New York and California, were consolidated by the Judicial Panel on Multidistrict Litigation. Ultimately more than eleven hundred plaintiffs from all over the world appeared in a Los Angeles federal courtroom.

The United States District Court for the Central District of California offered procedures far superior to those available in France, England, and Japan—not to mention Turkey—for litigating a complex products liability case. American-style pretrial discovery, in particular, is largely unknown in civil-law countries. Even compared to English law, the discovery possibilities afforded by the Federal Rules of Civil Procedure are much broader. In the Paris air crash case, discovery was conducted for over a year, and it proved to be damning to the defendants. After McDonnell Douglas' motion to dismiss on forum non conveniens grounds was denied, the defendants saw the handwriting on the wall and agreed not to contest liability. The only major issue left was the amount of

---

61. The maximum amount recoverable at the time was $20,000 per passenger. * * *

62. * * * An action for damages must be brought, at the option of the plaintiff, in the territory of one of the High Contracting Parties, either before the court of the domicile of the carrier or of his principal place of business, or where he has a place of business through which the contract has been made, or before the court at the place of destination. Art.28(1). This provision would have precluded suit in the United States.

damages. The first—and only—jury verdict, rendered in favor of the two orphaned infant daughters of an English couple, awarded one and one-half million dollars, almost forty times the maximum amount recoverable under the Warsaw Convention. That figure provided a benchmark for settling the other cases.

This example shows why, in Lord Denning's words, 'as a moth is drawn to the light, so is a litigant drawn to the United States.' Not that the Master of Rolls relished this country's drawing power. On the contrary, he not only enjoined some moths from flying here, but his observations about American personal injury lawyers fall considerably short of flattery.[76] The House of Lords, in contrast, tends to look more benignly at those who seek a more generous justice in the United States. It lifted an antisuit injunction against Sir Freddy Laker who, victimized by British Airways, sought antitrust relief in an American federal court. Lord Denning's disparaging observations notwithstanding, the English court of last resort permitted a Portuguese seaman injured in England to gamble for higher stakes in Texas, even though he had already brought suit in England, where he had also collected interim payments. But even on the English judiciary's highest rungs, patience with the games plaintiffs play is not unlimited. Thus, the Privy Council held that Brunei plaintiffs could be enjoined from suing a French company in a Texas state court for a helicopter crash in Brunei.[79]

More important than such foreign attempts to keep the moths away from the light is our own Supreme Court's inhospitable attitude toward aliens. In Piper Aircraft Co. v. Reyno the Court held that the forum non conveniens doctrine barred Scottish plaintiffs from access to United States justice. * * * As Justice Marshall recognized, this decision presents an opportunity for "reverse forum-shopping," of which numerous products liability defendants have since availed themselves successfully. In consequence, foreign victims, deprived of a day in an American court, no longer enjoy the measure of protection from shoddy products to which United States residents are accustomed. Nor is the Supreme Court's gloss on the hoary forum non conveniens doctrine limited to products liability claimants. This powerful anti-forum-shopping tool is available to any American concern sued by foreigners* * *. Some aliens, however, should be able to overcome this hurdle by suing in a state that* * *disfavors the doctrine. * * *

Compared to the United States Supreme Court, some foreign tribunals positively welcome forum shoppers. This is true even of the English courts, which have adopted the forum non conveniens doctrine and which have discretion to deny writs to summon defendants who cannot be served in England. Nonetheless, their attitude toward foreign suitors is, on the whole, much more accommodating than that of our judiciary. As Lord Denning once boasted:

76. See Castanho v. Brown & Root (U.K.) Ltd., [1980] 3 All E.R. 72, 81, 83 (H.L.) (Lord Denning, dissenting), aff'd, 1981 A.C. 557 (1980).

79. Societe Nationale Industrielle Aerospatiale v. Lee Kui Jak, 1987 A.C. 871 (P.C.).

No one who comes to these courts asking for justice should come in vain. . . . This right to come here is not confined to Englishmen. It extends to any friendly foreigner. He can seek the aid of our courts if he desires to do so. You may call this 'forum-shopping' if you please, but if the forum is England, it is a good place to shop in, both for the quality of the goods and the speed of service.[89]

Although the House of Lords disavowed these jingoistic remarks, English judges are far less concerned than our Supreme Court about burdening themselves with lawsuits brought by aliens. On the contrary, as one reads in a standard English conflict of laws treatise, "there is a public interest in allowing trial in England of what are, in essence, foreign actions. When foreigners litigate in England this forms a valuable invisible export, and confirms judicial pride in the English legal system."

Lured by the "quality of the goods and the speed of service" (no pun intended), Americans have not hesitated to forum shop on the scepter'd isle. Take, for instance, The Independent, which was an action brought by Du Pont in the English Commercial Court against products liability insurers four days after an Illinois jury awarded several million dollars of compensatory and punitive damages for an injury caused by the company's anti-coagulant drug Coumadin. For good measure, Du Pont requested an antisuit injunction to restrain the insurers from proceeding in Illinois; the insurers in turn moved to stay the English proceedings. Each side resisted litigation on its home ground because Illinois law disfavors coverage for punitive damages, while English law allows it.
* * *

* * *

* * * [S]ome nations provide a full range of goods and services to foreigners. This is true, in particular, of the Federal Republic of Germany, which attracts aliens by means of an exorbitant jurisdictional basis. Section 23 of the West German Code of Civil Procedure authorizes suits against any nonresident who owns assets in West Germany. It is irrelevant whether the cause of action has any contact with the Federal Republic, nor does the value of the defendant's assets matter. * * *

* * *

The Federal Republic offers several additional advantages to American parties who can surmount the language barrier. As in England, justice is relatively quick, there is no jury to confound the facts, and the loser pays the court costs as well as the winner's attorneys fees. Moreover, unlike Great Britain, the Federal Republic does not temper its jurisdictional exorbitance by forum non conveniens dismissais. * * * Like the English, the Germans do not seem to mind offering their juridical wares for export. * * *

89. The Atlantic Star, [1973] 1 Q.B. 364, 381–82.

Although they have played the game for some time and are steeped in the practice of seizing jurisdictional opportunities here and abroad, Americans are not the only forum shoppers. Others have learned the technique, and our expression "forum shopping" has enriched Europe's legal vocabulary. * * * Not all of the personal injury suits brought in the United States by aliens were necessarily engineered by American attorneys; some may have found their way here because of spreading awareness among foreign counsel that tort victims fare better here than at home.

To watch the forum shoppers' antics may be mildly amusing, but can anything be learned from it? I believe that even this impressionistic account suggests several lessons. First of all, not all forum shopping merits condemnation.* * * [C]an anyone blame the solicitors who retained American attorneys, instead of the barristers with whom they normally deal, to litigate the Paris air-crash cases? Far from doing anything legally or morally reprehensible, the solicitors simply served their clients well. Moreover, shifting the suits to the United States promoted the cause of international justice by neutralizing the absurdly low recovery limits imposed by the Warsaw Convention.

The first lesson, then, is not to let a disparaging term becloud our thinking. Lord Simon of Glaisdale said it well:

> 'Forum-shopping' is a dirty word; but it is only a pejorative way of saying that, if you offer a plaintiff a choice of jurisdictions, he will naturally choose the one in which he thinks his case can be most favourably presented: this should be a matter neither for surprise nor for indignation.[132]

To be sure, some of the things forum shoppers do may provoke indignation. The reaction of a federal district court judge, for instance, to members of the bar who had flown to India shortly after the Bhopal disaster with calling cards in their pockets, is not surprising. But this extreme case of international ambulance-chasing did at least alert the Indian Government to the need to pursue the victims' claims aggressively. Although the actions brought in the United States were dismissed on forum non conveniens grounds, the American foreplay probably helped establish an acceptable framework for recovery.[135] Thus, forum shopping can promote important substantive policies, such as the protection of those injured by transnational activities.* * *

Second, looking at the world from the practitioners' point of view, they cannot afford simply to deplore the lack of a universal set of legal standards. Counsel must be aware that the jurisdictional overlap, the "homeward trend" in the conflict of laws, and differing practices create a risk that afflicts all international transactions. Members of the bar who advise clients on such transactions must appreciate that international

132. The Atlantic Star, 1974 A.C. 436, 471.

135. Galanter, When Legal Worlds Collide: Reflections on Bhopal, the Good Lawyer, and the American Law School, 36 J. Legal Educ. 292, 309–10 (1986).

risk and hedge against it through arbitration and forum-selection clauses. Nevertheless, lawyers should also be aware of the opportunities presented by the pluralism of legal cultures. This is as true of litigation as it is of planning, for seeking out tax havens and flags of convenience is not the only task faced by the international practitioner. When a relationship becomes litigious, failure to select an advantageous forum may amount to malpractice, for attorneys owe a duty to vindicate their clients' rights wherever they can expect the best results. That proposition ought to be obvious, and so it would be but for the nasty phrase "forum shopping," which suggests that those who represent their clients' interests effectively commit a breach of professional etiquette.

Finally, the phenomenon of forum shopping can help scholars gain insights into the proper role of the conflict of laws. Commentators have often assumed that the primary reason for selecting a particular forum is the desire to garner favorable conflicts and substantive law rules. To be sure, in some instances that is the plaintiff's principal or exclusive motivation. Examples are Keeton v. Hustler Magazine, Inc.[140] and the actions brought in the United States by French governmental entities, enterprises, and individuals for the catastrophic oil spill that fouled the coast of Brittany after the Amoco Cadiz hit the rocks.[141] In Keeton, the plaintiff had already seen her action time-barred in another state, and in Amoco Cadiz the alien plaintiffs sued in this country, rather than at home, to escape the liability limits of the International Convention on Civil Liability for Oil Pollution Damage, which France, but not the United States, had ratified.

In the Paris air crash litigation, however, the American venue was chosen for entirely different reasons. France, where at least some of the plaintiffs might have sued, imposed strict liability for accidents caused by defective products even before the recent European Communities Council Directive required it. Moreover, unlike California and most American states, France grants the relatives of persons killed in an accident damages for pain and suffering. Thus, at first glance, France would seem to offer the best prospects for recovery. However, there are no French specialists in products liability and air crash litigation, nor does France permit American-style discovery or contingent fees that compensate counsel for the time and money necessary to litigate complex and highly technical cases. Above all, France does not provide for jury trials of civil matters, and no French judge would award damages as high as those commonly granted by Los Angeles jurors.

Clearly, in the Paris air crash case the choice to sue in the United States was dictated by procedural and practical considerations rather than conflicts or substantive rules. In fact, choice of law played hardly any role in selecting the forum: the plaintiff's attorneys researched the pertinent principles only after the suits had been filed. Similarly, in the

---

140. 465 U.S. 770 (1984).

141. In re Oil Spill by the Amoco Cadiz off the Coast of France, 1984 AMC 2123 (N.D. Ill. 1984).

Rhine pollution case, if substantive and conflicts rules did matter, their significance paled in comparison to geographical and societal realities. As a knowledgeable English author put it:

> [I]t is likely that the true causes of forum shopping are to be found elsewhere than in the divergencies of the rules of private international law. The plaintiff usually shops in the forum with which he is most familiar or in which he gains the greatest procedural advantage or puts the defendant to the greatest procedural disadvantage.[150]

Several other factors are also pertinent to an informed choice. They include the forum's reputation for fairness (or pro-plaintiff bias), the efficacy and speed of judicial proceedings, the quality of available counsel, and something Henry de Vries used to call the "legal climate." That climate varies from country to country, and may even vary, within a given state or nation, from one place to the next. As World–Wide Volkswagen illustrates, differences in the favor juratorum may warrant taking a case to the Supreme Court for the sole purpose of assuring that it will be tried in a city rather than a suburb.

These realities inevitably pose a question that * * * ought to be of interest to conflicts scholars. If forum shopping is prompted, in large measure, by reasons other than the diversity of substantive and choice-of-law rules, which is the purpose of the conflict of laws? It cannot ever attain the illusory goal of uniform decisions. Nor can the conflict of laws * * * effectively vindicate "governmental interests," for those interests as well are at the forum shopper's mercy. Of course, one possible objective remains for our discipline: like all others, it could serve the ends of substantial justice. If so, we need rules and approaches that differ from those that are currently in vogue. Watching forum shoppers ply their trade should make us think about the possibility of such a reorientation. Only to the extent that we can design choice-of-law rules that are attuned to the exigencies of interstate and international justice, can forum shopping ever become obsolete.

REPUBLIC OF BOLIVIA v. PHILIP MORRIS COMPANIES

United States District Court, Southern District of Texas, 1999.
39 F.Supp.2d 1008.

KENT, DISTRICT JUDGE.

Plaintiff, the Republic of Bolivia, brings this action to recover from numerous tobacco companies various health care costs it allegedly incurred in treating illnesses its residents suffered as a result of tobacco use. This action was originally filed in the District Court of Brazoria County, Texas, 239th Judicial District, and removed to this Court * * * For the following reasons, the Court exercises its authority and discre-

---

150. Collins, Contractual Obligations— The EEC Preliminary Draft Convention on Private International Law, 25 Int'l & Comp. L. Q. 35, 36 (1976).

tion * * * to *sua sponte* **TRANSFER** this case to the United States District Court for the District of Columbia.

This is one of at least six similar actions brought by foreign governments in various courts throughout the United States. The governments of Guatemala, Panama, Nicaragua, Thailand, Venezuela, and Bolivia have filed suit in the geographically diverse locales of Washington, D.C., Puerto Rico, Texas, Louisiana, and Florida, in both state and federal courts. Why none of these countries seems to have a court system their own governments have confidence in is a mystery to this Court. Moreover, given the tremendous number of United States jurisdictions encompassing fascinating and exotic places, the Court can hardly imagine why the Republic of Bolivia elected to file suit in the veritable hinterlands of Brazoria County, Texas. The Court seriously doubts whether Brazoria County has ever seen a live Bolivian ... even on the Discovery Channel. Though only here by removal, this humble Court by the sea is certainly flattered by what must be the worldwide renown of rural Texas courts for dispensing justice with unparalleled fairness and alacrity, apparently in common discussion even on the mountain peaks of Bolivia! Still, the Court would be remiss in accepting an obligation for which it truly does not have the necessary resources. Only one judge presides in the Galveston Division—which currently has before it over seven hundred cases and annual civil filings exceeding such number— and that judge is presently burdened with a significant personal situation which diminishes its ability to always give the attention it would like to all of its daunting docket obligations, despite genuinely heroic efforts to do so. And, while Galveston is indeed an international seaport, the capacity of this Court to address the complex and sophisticated issues of international law and foreign relations presented by this case is dwarfed by that of its esteemed colleagues in the District of Columbia who deftly address such awesome tasks as a matter of course. Indeed, this Court, while doing its very best to address the more prosaic matters routinely before it, cannot think of a Bench better versed and more capable of handling precisely this type of case, which requires a high level of expertise in international matters * * * Such a Bench, well-populated with genuinely renowned intellects, can certainly better bear and share the burden of multidistrict litigation than this single judge division, where the judge moves his lips when he reads....

* * * [I]t is the Court's opinion that the District of Columbia, located in this Nation's capital, is a much more logical venue for the parties and witnesses in this action because, among other things, Plaintiff has an embassy in Washington, D.C., and thus a physical presence and governmental representatives there, whereas there isn't even a Bolivian restaurant anywhere near here! Although the jurisdiction of this Court boasts no similar foreign offices, a somewhat dated globe is within its possession. While the Court does not therefrom profess to understand all of the political subtleties of the geographical transmogrifications ongoing in Eastern Europe, the Court is virtually certain that Bolivia is not within the four counties over which this Court presides,

even though the words Bolivia and Brazoria are a lot alike and caused some real, initial confusion until the Court conferred with its law clerks. Thus, it is readily apparent, even from an outdated globe such as that possessed by this Court, that Bolivia, a hemisphere away, ain't in south-central Texas, and that, at the very least, the District of Columbia is a more appropriate venue (though Bolivia isn't located there either). Furthermore, as this Judicial District bears no significant relationship to any of the matters at issue, and the judge of this Court simply loves cigars, the Plaintiff can be expected to suffer neither harm nor prejudice by a transfer to Washington, D.C., a Bench better able to rise to the smoky challenges presented by this case, despite the alleged and historic presence there of countless "smoke-filled" rooms. Consequently, for the convenience of parties and witnesses, and in the interest of justice, this case is hereby **TRANSFERRED** to the United States District Court for the District of Columbia.

KINNEY SYSTEM, INC. v. CONTINENTAL INSURANCE COMPANY

Supreme Court of Florida, 1996.
674 So.2d 86.

KOGAN, JUSTICE

* * * Commentators generally have noted a growing trend in private international law of attempting to file suit in an American state even for injuries or breaches that occurred on foreign soil.[3] There is already evidence the practice is growing to abusive levels in Florida. * * * Nothing in our law establishes a policy that Florida must be a courthouse for the world, nor that the taxpayers of this state must pay to resolve disputes utterly unconnected with this state's interest. * * * The use of Florida courts to police activities even in the remotest parts of the globe is not a purpose for which our judiciary was created. Florida courts exist to judge matters with significant impact upon Florida's interests, especially in light of the fact that the taxpayers of this state pay for the operation of its judiciary. Nothing in our Constitution compels the taxpayers to spend their money even for the rankest forum shopping by out-of-state interests.

SMITH KLINE & FRENCH LABORATORIES LTD. AND OTHERS v. BLOCH

[1983] 2 All E.R. 72 (Ct.App.).

LORD DENNING M.R.

As a moth is drawn to the light, so is a litigant drawn to the United States. If he can only get his case into their courts, he stands to win a

---

3. American states are attractive compared to some foreign nations because of more liberal discovery rules, a perception of more generous juries, and the ability to obtain lawyers on a contingent-fee basis.

fortune. At no cost to himself; and at no risk of having to pay anything to the other side. The lawyers there will conduct the case "on spec" as we say, or on a "contingency fee" as they say. The lawyers will charge the litigant nothing for their services but instead they will take 40 per cent. of the damages, if they win the case in court, or out of court on a settlement. If they lose, the litigant will have nothing to pay to the other side. The courts in the United States have no such costs deterrent as we have. There is also in the United States a right to trial by jury. These are prone to award fabulous damages. They are notoriously sympathetic and know that the lawyers will take their 40 per cent. before the plaintiff gets anything. All this means that the defendant can be readily forced into a settlement. The plaintiff holds all the cards. If you wish to know how it is all done, you should read Castanho v. Brown & Root (U.K) Ltd. [1980] 1 W.L.R. 833; [1981] A.C. 557. There a Portuguese sailor was badly injured at Great Yarmouth in England. It was an American ship. He started an action in England but was persuaded by American lawyers to take proceedings in the United States. I was against it: see [1980] 1 W.L.R. 833, 849–858. But when it got to the House of Lords they allowed the litigant to go ahead in the United States: see [1981] A.C. 557. His American lawyers won a huge settlement to the profit of the litigant and of course for themselves as well. You should also read Piper Aircraft Co. v. Reyno (1981) 454 U.S. 235 decided on December 8, 1981, by the Supreme Court of the United States. A small commercial aircraft crashed in Scotland, killing all six Scottish people on it. The propellers had been manufactured in the United States. The widows and children were persuaded by lawyers in the United States to bring proceedings there against the manufacturers of the propellers, alleging that they were faulty. No doubt the lawyers had their eyes on the heavy damages and their contingency fees. The Supreme Court of the United States refused to allow the proceedings to continue in the United States. They should have been brought in Scotland which was the only appropriate forum.

Now we have another case of that ilk. Dr. Maurice Bloch lives in England. He has a complaint against an English company. He says that they broke their contract with him. It was an English contract governed by English law. The obvious place where it should be tried is in England. Yet he has gone to American lawyers and they have found an excuse for bringing it in the United States. It is because the English company were a wholly-owned subsidiary of an American corporation. So the American lawyers for Dr. Bloch have brought an action in the United States courts against the English subsidiary and their American parent, hoping, no doubt, to get a good settlement out of it—both for themselves and Dr. Bloch—at no cost to him.

Now here is the twist in the story. The English company and their American parent wish to stop the proceedings in the United States courts. They want to nip them in the bud. They have applied to the United States courts to stop them. But with no success so far there. An American judge has made an order allowing Dr. Bloch to go ahead with the proceedings in the United States court. Having been thus rebuffed in America, the English subsidiary (and now their Americans parent) have applied to the English court. They ask us to issue an injunction against Dr. Bloch to restrain him from proceeding in the United States. They say that he is quite at liberty to sue them in England if he is so advised—in which case they will defend themselves. But he should not be allowed to go on in the United States. I may say that, even in England, Dr. Bloch is "sitting pretty" anyway. He has got legal aid with the result that all his costs here will be paid by the legal aid fund. * * *

He had been in touch with English solicitors as far back as 1976, but they foresaw difficulties in litigation in England. So he turned to American lawyers. They advised him to bring an action in the United States—both against the English subsidiary and the American parent. He instituted it on May 16, 1980. He is quite frank about his reasons:

> there were financial considerations in that litigation in this country would undoubtedly involve me in substantial expense; on the other hand, if American lawyers agreed to take on my case, they would be prepared to do so in accordance with American legal practice for a contingency fee so that they would be remunerated out of any damages which I might recover.

To my mind this claim of Dr. Bloch against the American parent is a device, adopted by American lawyers, so as to get the case into the United States courts—where they will get contingency fees and force a settlement. Such a device ought not to be allowed to succeed. I trust that our courts on both sides of the Atlantic will not allow it. It often happens that a plaintiff is entitled to bring proceedings in two or more jurisdictions. Sometimes it is said that the choice is his. He can choose whichever of them suits him best. If he can get more damages in one than he can in the other, then good luck to him. Let him go there. If he will be met by a time bar in one and not in the other, let him go to the one where he is not barred. If it is more convenient for the plaintiff in one than it is for the defendant, then the plaintiff can choose. You need not spin a coin between the two contestants. It always comes down in favour of the plaintiff—so it is said—unless the defendant can prove that it would work an injustice to him. Once a plaintiff institutes an action in accordance with this prior claim of his, then no court in a rival jurisdiction should grant an injunction to prevent the plaintiff from exercising and pursuing his action to its determination. This is the only way, it is said, to avoid unseemly conflict and to ensure comity.

The basis of all this reasoning has now been removed. In England by the House of Lords in MacShannon v. Rockware Glass Ltd. [1978] A.C. 795. In the United States by the Supreme Court in Piper Aircraft Co. v. Reyno, 454 U.S. 235. The plaintiff has no longer an inborn right to choose his own forum. He no longer wins the toss on every throw. The decision rests with the courts. No matter which jurisdiction is invoked, the court must hold the balance between the plaintiff and the defendant. It must take into account the relative advantages and disadvantages to each of them; not only the juridical advantages and disadvantages, but also the personal conveniences and inconveniences; not only the private interests of the parties but also the public interests involved. The court decides according to which way the balance comes down. This was the approach of the House of Lords in MacShannon v. Rockware Glass Ltd., where it was much to the juridical advantage of the plaintiff to bring his action in England where he would get higher damages, but the natural forum was Scotland. It was in the public interest that a Scottish case should be tried in Scotland. So he was bound to go to Scotland. His action in England was stayed. It was also the approach of the Supreme Court of the United States in Piper Aircraft Co. v. Reyno where it was much to the juridical advantage of the plaintiffs that they should sue in Pennsylvania where they would get higher damages and the lawyers would get contingency fees. But the public interest was against trial in the United States. If claims such as these aircraft claims were all to be brought in the United States, it would involve far too great a commitment of judicial time and resources. Scotland was the natural forum. The public interest favoured Scotland. So the trial should take place there.

By contrast, in Castanho v. Brown & Root (U.K.) Ltd. [1981] A.C. 557 the plaintiff had an undisputed claim for damages against a Texan based group of companies. The only question at issue was quantum. The plaintiff had a legitimate advantage in suing in Texas where he could get such damages as a Texan court thought appropriate. Although I took the other view, the House of Lords held that the balance came down clearly in the plaintiff's favour. Seeing that England is the natural and proper forum for any proceedings that Dr. Maurice Bloch is advised to bring, I would grant and injunction against him personally to stop him from going on with any proceedings in the United States. I would grant it at the instance not only of the English subsidiary but also of the American parent. Seeing that both are being harassed in the United States courts, both should be able to come to these courts to stop it. The like is the position with regard to the trustees.

I would thus . . . dismiss the appeal.

CASTANHO v. BROWN AND ROOT (U.K.) LTD. AND ANOTHER

[1980] 1 W.L.R. 833 (C.A.).

LORD DENNING M.R.

"A Texas-style claim is big business." That is how the newspaper put it. The managers of the business are two attorneys of Houston, Texas. They keep a look-out for men injured on the North Sea oil rigs. The worse a man is injured, the better for business. Especially when he has been rendered a quadriplegic and his employers have no answer to his claim. Their look-out man tells the Texan attorneys. They come across to England. They see the injured man and say to him: "Do not bring your action in England or Scotland. You will only get £150,000 there. Let us bring it in Texas. We can get you £2,500,000 in Texas." If he agrees, they get him to sign a power of attorney which provides for their reward. Under it the attorneys are to get 40 per cent.of any damages recovered. That is £1,200,000 for themselves. Big business indeed!

In our present case, however, the Texan attorneys struck a snag. Their look-out man was too late. The injured man had already gone to solicitors in England before the Texan attorneys got to know of it. His English solicitors had already started an action for him against his employers. They had succeeded so well that they had already obtained from the English court orders for interim payments amounting to £27,250. He had spent that sum on buying land and putting a house on it. How were the Texan lawyers to overcome that snag? Could they legitimately start an action in Texas when the English proceedings had got so far?

They devised a plan. They said to the English solicitors: "Let us arrange things together. You drop the action in England and let us help one another in an action in Texas. We will ourselves pay back the £27,250 out of our own pocket. We will pay him his salary and everything. We will pay you all your proper costs for the actual work you do. We will recoup it out of the £ 2,500,000 we get in Texas." So they would get their 40 per cent. The English solicitors would get their proper costs. A clever plan indeed. But will it work? That is the question in this case.

A motor vessel called the American Moon was engaged in carrying supplies to oil rigs in the North Sea. On February 11, 1977, she was lying at Great Yarmouth in Norfolk. One of her crew was the plaintiff Inocencio Castanho, a Portuguese. He was transferring oil from a drum to a tank—by a pipe with compressed air. A valve flew off and went into his neck. It penetrated his spinal cord. He was completely paralysed in his arms and legs—a quadriplegic. He is completely dependent on others for everything. Both by day and night.

He was in Stoke Mandeville hospital for nine months ... The employers treated him very well. They continued to pay him his full salary of $690 a month. They arranged for members of his family to visit him from Portugal. They paid all their expenses. Their representative visited him regularly once a month to see to his welfare. After nine months, the doctors thought it would be better for him to be with his wife and family in Portugal. So his employers arranged for a specially fitted plane to take him back to Portugal. They also provided special equipment at his home in Portugal—so as to enable him to get about. Their representative in Lisbon visited him at his home—so as to do all they could for him and his family. His wife has been very good. She is doing everything for him. The only thing outstanding is the amount of compensation to be paid to him.

Soon after the accident, his wife and brother came to see him at Stoke Mandeville. They asked the Portuguese consulate to find a solicitor for him to claim compensation. The Portuguese consulate suggested

B. M. Birnberg & Co. ("Birnbergs"), solicitors, of London. They were instructed on May 4, 1977. They got into touch with the employers' solicitors, Clyde & Co. ("Clydes") of London. No doubt Clydes were aware of the Texas-style claims made by some injured men. So they were glad the proceedings were started in England rather than America. They did everything they could to keep them in England. They said they would willingly make an interim payment on account. This was arranged and everything done properly. A writ was issued in September 1977. An order by consent was made on March 22, 1978, for £7,250 to be paid as an interim payment. A statement of claim was delivered on March 28, 1978. But no defence was delivered at that time. It was deferred by consent till later.

The Texans came on the scene in June 1978. Someone told them of the accident to the plaintiff. They did not know his address in Portugal. So they wrote to Stoke Mandeville and got them to forward it to him. Then things moved rapidly. No expense was spared. The Texan lawyers were ready to pay out large sums themselves out of their own pocket— without security—because of the 40 per cent. contingency fee opening up before them. They were ready to cast their bread upon the waters in the expectancy of the £1,200,000 fee which would be theirs.

One of their top men, Bob Chaffin (he had been named in the newspapers), went to Portugal to see the plaintiff. Bob Chaffin was closely associated with the firm of Benton Musslewhite Inc. of Houston, Texas. Bob Chaffin pressed the plaintiff to let their firm take over the claim. He succeeded so far that on July 3, 1978, their firm, Benton Musslewhite, sent the plaintiff a power of attorney to sign authorising them to institute proceedings in Texas. They told him to sign it where marked "X" and to return it to them.

The plaintiff seems to have been a little uncertain. He did not sign the power of attorney at that time. Instead, in August 1978, he got in touch with the employers' representative in Lisbon. He told him "he would like the case to rest with the people (in London) who are handling it." This made the Texan lawyers very concerned. They had not got the power of attorney back signed by the plaintiff. So they took quick action. Early in September 1978 Mr. Benton Musslewhite himself went over to Portugal. He saw the plaintiff and told him the advantage of proceeding in the United States. He then went from Portugal over to London and saw Mrs. Margaret Bowden, the managing clerk from Birnbergs. He told her how American law operated. He told her that, if they were permitted to sue in the United States, they would make advance payments to the plaintiff so as to cover all his needs: and that they were confident of success: and that they would expect the damages to come up to $5,000,000. Mrs. Bowden was impressed and asked him to send her his credentials. He did so. He went back and sent her a batch of papers showing the successes which Benton Musslewhite and Bob Chaffin had achieved in the cases they had handled: and in addition a draft claim which they proposed to file on behalf of the plaintiff in the American court.

This was followed up by another visit to England by Mr. Benton Musslewhite in December 1978. He had meetings again with Mrs. Margaret Bowden: and also with counsel, Mr. Melville Williams. It was then decided that the American lawyers should be instructed to pursue a claim in the United States of America where the potential damages were very much greater. Counsel advised that "the English action should proceed, though not to judgment, as this would be a bar to the American action," that Birnbergs should co-operate with the American lawyers in the interests of the plaintiff, but should only get their proper costs. Benton Musslewhite were to pay the English lawyers their proper costs for work done, charged in the ordinary way, win or lose.

That decision was duly implemented. So much so that on January 31, 1979, Mrs. Bowden herself visited the plaintiff at his home in Portugal, taking with her various papers including a power of attorney in Portuguese for him to sign in favour of Benton Musslewhite—prepared by Benton Musslewhite.

The power of attorney in Portuguese was executed in the plaintiff's hamlet of Varzim. By it the plaintiff conferred on Benton Musslewhite exclusive powers to represent him judicially in the United States: and promised to pay them, if settled out of court, one third part of the moneys received: and 40 per cent. if the petition were filed in the court. Any expenses that were incurred on behalf of the plaintiff were to come out of the sums he received. If he got nothing, he had to pay nothing. There was an express clause that: "It is understood that the process initiated in England will not be concluded prior to the decision in the United States." The object of that provision was, no doubt, to keep the English proceedings alive in case the American proceedings were unsuccessful.

The power of attorney also contained a provision by which Benton Musslewhite agreed to pay the plaintiff his salary—if the employers stopped paying it: and also agreed to repay any amounts received by the plaintiff by way of interim payments in the English proceedings: also any extra cost necessary to complete the house, etc. in Portugal. All these payments were no doubt being made by Benton Musslewhite out of their own pocket—in view of the large contingency fee which they hoped to receive in due course.

To English eyes that power of attorney was champertous in the extreme. The Texan lawyers were maintaining the proceedings in the United States—laying out large sums in support of it—and stipulating in return for 40 per cent. of the damages received: if they lost, they were to get nothing. And the English lawyers were helping them—going out to Portugal to get the power of attorney signed—and so forth. If such an agreement was made in regard to English proceedings, it would be invalid as contrary to public policy. But I would assume that it was not invalid by the law of the United States.

* * *

SHAW L.J.

* * * The plaintiff is a Portuguese subject. This fact is not without significance since it makes him a foreigner equally in England and in the United States of America.

* * * The plaintiff had been approached by the American lawyers ... The practice of exacting payment on a contingency basis for legal services is not only foreign to English concepts but is viewed here with positive disapproval. None the less it does not behoove English legal institutions, whether solicitors or the Bar or the judiciary, to adopt a lofty, let alone a pious, attitude in regard to the contingency system. It is accepted by the legal institutions of the United States and they are entitled not only to hold to their views on the matter but to apply them in practice, as they regularly do. It is no business of ours, and we must allow that they know theirs.

* * * The plaintiff in the federal court of Texas is a Portuguese subject; he is unlikely, especially having regard to his physical state, ever to be in England. His American lawyers are in duty bound to act in his best interests in pursuing the action in Texas. They must regard an order of an English court which forbids them to do their professional duty in America as an unwarranted and ridiculous charade. They too are outside the jurisdiction.... This is a case about money, not morality. I see no warrant for the injunction and I would discharge it. In my judgment the appeal should be allowed in its entirety.

Questions and Comments

1. Forum shopping by plaintiffs' counsel in most cases is simply good lawyering—trying to initiate the suit in a forum where there is jurisdiction and favorable characteristics such as contingent fees or punitive damages. But when it involves adding parties to gain jurisdiction that have no legitimate linkage to the litigation, or when an attorney representing several of the injured parties in our hypothetical filed four individual, separate and duplicate lawsuits within 30 minutes of each other against GROWFAST in a Texas court, and withdrew three actions and amended the fourth to include all the clients after it was assigned to a judge deemed by the lawyer to be the most favorable to his clients, isn't there an ethical issue that might result in sanctions against the attorney? That kind of practice actually occurred in Texas and the attorney was sanctioned $250,000. Where might counsel for each of the respective parties in the hypothetical bring suit and why? What if you represent all the parties from all the various countries? Would you use one or multiple forums?

2. Most of the potential Mexican plaintiffs probably have not had contact with a U.S. attorney. The initial choice of where to file their suits may thus be in the hands of a Mexican attorney, unless U.S. lawyers have flocked to Mexico in search of clients. It is important to note that there is a professional responsibility question regarding U.S. lawyers entering Mexico to sign up plaintiffs for suits in the United States. Bhopal, India, was overrun by U.S. lawyers after the Union Carbide plant explosion. The

comment of Mark Lang in the panel discussion reading suggests that U.S. lawyers "would get those clients and sue in Texas." Lord Denning speaks disparagingly of such practice in the UK *Castanho* decision. Will a Mexican attorney talking to the Mexican plaintiffs be likely to recommend litigation in the United States where that attorney may have little or no participation or fee? Might the Mexican attorney turn over Mexican clients to a U.S. attorney for a percentage of the U.S. attorney's contingent fee? Mexican lawyer Gomez–Palacio believes the United States would be the better choice to bring the suits. Is his reasoning sound?

3. The defendant obviously does not have the choice of where to initiate the litigation. But the defendant will analyze a plaintiff's choice and may respond in several ways. The defendant could move to dismiss for lack of jurisdiction or for reasons of *forum non conveniens*. The defendants might also seek to consolidate the case with litigation pending elsewhere, or seek class certification under Rule 23 of the U.S. federal or state rules of civil procedure. Why and why not might Rule 23 class certification appeal to a defendant? To a plaintiff? One option for GROWFAST is not to appear at all if it is only sued in Mexico. Is that good advice? If GROWMEX has few assets, GROWFAST may be willing to forfeit them to satisfy a Mexican judgment. If there is a Mexican judgment against GROWMEX only, any attempt to have that Mexican judgment recognized and enforced in the United States would be futile if GROWMEX has no assets in the United States.[4] But what if the judgment in Mexico is also against GROWFAST? Might GROWFAST succeed in a U.S. court judgment enforcement proceeding by arguing that there was no personal jurisdiction in Mexico over GROWFAST, only over GROWMEX? Would a U.S. court respect a Mexican decision that pierced the corporate veil of GROWMEX to reach GROW-FAST? These issues will be further explored in the next few problems.

4. Notice how different the situation is where GROWFAST does business in Mexico by way of a distributor, AGRICOLAS, and where it does business by way of a wholly-owned subsidiary, GROWMEX. For example, Harvey notes that AGRICOLAS, the distributor, might have a cause of action against GROWFAST. The subsidiary GROWMEX in our hypothetical will not sue GROWFAST, the parent. What are the key differences affecting the plaintiffs' choice of forum, given these circumstances? Do you agree with Harvey's comment that by replacing AGRICOLAS with GROWMEX there is a better chance for each plaintiff? Why? If only AGRICOLAS is likely to be liable when GROWFAST has chosen to use a distributor rather than a subsidiary, is it better for business to use distributors rather than to establish subsidiaries?

5. Professor Occhialino makes it clear that the plaintiffs' choice of forum does not only involve choosing the country in which to proceed; the plaintiffs must also consider in which courts within Mexico or which courts within the United States to file suit. In Mexico, the courts in Veracruz are arguably the most apparent choice. What if GROWMEX has a business office in Mexico City? Would that allow suit in the Federal District? If so, that will involve some analysis of choice of law, considered in Problem 4.4.

---

4. Enforcement of foreign judgments is the subject of Problem 6.1.

6. Occhialino in his separate article stresses that plaintiffs should consider applicable law issues as to all possible fora—both the United States and Mexico. For this the plaintiffs will likely need assistance from a Mexican attorney. Do the answers look the same when Mexican law is considered? Some of the panel commentary should help in answering the question, as should some of the readings in Problem 4.4.

7. Trujillo raises an interesting option—for GROWFAST to initiate suit in Mexico to divert the case from the United States. What would the cause of action be, and who would the defendants be? Could the defendants try to move the case back to the United States under *forum non conveniens*? Occhialino notes the possibility of GROWFAST seeking a declaratory judgment of non-liability in a U.S. court. If that is possible, which is the better choice? What if GROWMEX sued a supplier in Europe and sought to consolidate?

8. Lang raises the possibility of a Mexican defendant distributor, as opposed to a subsidiary, commencing suit in Mexico if it defrauded GROWFAST by such acts as selling the Sollate™ concentrate secretly and substituting a poor product to make the final pesticide. By commencing suit in Mexico the Mexican defendant distributor might or might not avoid being sued by GROWFAST in the United States where greater damages are available. Would GROWMEX bring such a suit? Harvey discusses the comparable plea in abatement in the United States (Texas) that is relevant to these issues.

9. Occhialino works through the various subjects that a lawyer must consider before making any move, including choice of forum, subject matter and personal jurisdiction, venue, service of process, choice of law and enforcement of judgments. Note how he emphasizes the need to know Mexican law to consider properly most of these issues. At what point would you contact a Mexican lawyer, or an expert on Mexican law, in the United States? How will you find one upon whom you can rely? Does the internet make lawyers and legal advice more accessible?

10. Is the experience that Juenger describes, especially the DC–10 crash near Paris, anything more than lawyers acting properly by selecting the best forum for their clients? Forum shopping is an important part of being a successful international lawyer if it means selecting the best forum for your client's interests. The problem seems to be where to draw the line—when do the actions of the lawyers go beyond aggressive and ethical representation of the client? Comment 1 above notes when the line seems to be crossed. Was the line crossed in the Paris air crash? Do you agree with Juenger that bringing the suit in the United States promoted the "cause of international justice by neutralizing the absurdly low recovery limits imposed by the Warsaw Convention"?

11. Does the disparagement of the U.S. tort system by Lord Denning noted by Juenger make what the Paris air crash lawyers did constitute improper or illegal forum shopping? What is it about the U.S. tort system that might make an English judge assist English nationals escape from being defendants before U.S. courts? Would Denning criticize a U.K. citizen and resident who was a plaintiff in the Paris air crash case from participating in the suit in the United States, where they might receive and take back to England a very large judgment? Note the U.K. Privy Council decision in the

case involving a Brunei plaintiff suing a French company in a Texas court. *Société Nationale Industrielle Aérospatiale v. Lee Kui Jak,* [1987] A.C. 871. In *Amoco v. TGTLI* the High Court in London granted an antisuit injunction in favor of Amoco/Phillips (both UK) against Enron's (USA) pursuing a suit in Texas against the two UK entities. Problem 3.5 addressed antisuit injunctions, where the choice of forum of the plaintiff is challenged in English courts, not because there is no jurisdiction (Problems 3.2 and 4.2), or because the forum is inadequate (Problem 4.3), but because the U.S. forum is not **the** "proper" forum, or because it is a "vexatious and oppressive" forum.

12.   Juenger refers to an "inhospitable attitude toward aliens" by the U.S. Supreme Court, by reference to *forum non conveniens* decisions. The *Piper* case he refers to is included in Problem 4.3. Why would a court show such an attitude towards any of the foreigners in the GROWFAST litigation? Is inhospitability a euphemism for the presence of sound criteria for dismissal?

13.   The United States is not the only Shangri-la for forum shoppers. Juenger notes the English justification for a kind of national solicitation of foreign litigation with minimal contacts to England. Why is it that England is "less concerned . . . about burdening themselves with lawsuits brought by aliens" than the U.S. courts? That may not be surprising in view of the former extensive British Empire and the patronizing attitude towards members of those nations to which England brought "enlightened" rule. But it is not clear that the welcome mat is still out–some courts such as the English Commercial Court within the High Court have serious backlogs of cases.

14.   Forum shopping is also allowed in some European nations, as Juenger illustrates. Asset based jurisdiction in Germany and Austria has been criticized, largely because it encourages forum shopping. Juenger's comments are interesting, instead of U.S. style forum shopping based largely on the potential high judgments, in Europe it is a preference for a forum that does not have a jury ("confounds the facts") and where the loser pays all the costs. Is there any real difference between U.S. and European forum shopping?

15.   Juenger alludes to, and others have focused upon, the avoidance or ignorance of conflicts of law rules by lawyers and courts involved in forum shopping. Juenger notes some instances where conflicts rules were used, and others, such as the Paris air crash, where other non conflicts factors were more important, such as the absence of French specialists in products liability, limited discovery, absence of juries and low damages. One suggestion is that all courts apply a *lex fori* rule, without interest balancing exceptions that muddy the waters as much as the law has to date. The argument suggests that if there is jurisdiction, it therefore must be partly based on linkages with the forum and they ought to be enough to justify application of the *lex fori*. But won't some court start the exception process over again by finding that where the interests of the forum are much less significant than the interests of the foreign nation, under the concept of comity the foreign nation should hear the case, or at least its law should be applied?

16. The *Republic of Bolivia* and *Kinney System* cases illustrate some judicial frustration at foreign plaintiffs' forum shopping. Why did the defendant in the *Republic of Bolivia* not ask to have the case dismissed on *forum non conveniens* grounds at the very beginning in the Texas state court, rather than first requesting removal to the federal district court in Texas and then asking that court to remove the case to Washington, D.C.? Do you suppose that once the case is removed to Washington, there will be a motion filed to dismiss for *forum non conveniens* reasons? That may be better answered after studying Problem 4.3.

17. *Kinney System* was issued just as the Florida legislature was about to consider changes to the statutory law to accomplish what the Florida Supreme Court did alone. Florida thus joined another favorite forum shopping center—Texas—in allowing dismissal on *forum non conveniens* grounds. But apparently it is taking Florida plaintiffs' attorneys a long time to read or understand the *Kinney System* decision, the shopping sprees continued after *Kinney System*.

18. Lord Denning always believed that England was the most proper place to receive justice, and certainly disliked many characteristics of the U.S. legal system, and especially the way lawyers use that system. How do you counter his comments? Does Justice Shaw in *Castanho* rebut Lord Denning's comments because the plaintiff is not English and there is little link to England? The accident did occur at an English port (Norfolk) and the injured plaintiff spent nine months in an English hospital. Isn't that a sufficient link?

19. The above materials have focused on tort claims. The GROWFAST hypothetical, however, could lead to contract litigation as well. For example, assume that several years ago the Sollate™ that was delivered throughout Latin America contained some chemicals that were poisonous to plants. The result was that many Latin American commercial growers lost their entire stocks of ornamental plants. The Sollate™ that caused the damage was purchased using standard documentary transactions, and each transaction included provisions that the goods were sold "as is, with all faults," and that the contract was governed "by the law of the state of Florida." The name GROWFAST appeared on the invoices. GROWFAST believes that it bears no direct liability, however, because the Sollate™ was both mixed improperly and misapplied by the growers in Mexico, and therefore that only GROWMEX, and/or the growers, are responsible. Furthermore, if it were responsible, GROWFAST believes that *force majeure* should be applied to excuse GROWFAST from any responsibility because the explosion was really an "Act of God." Or maybe *caveat emptor* applies?

The Latin American growers who have lost plants will face some of the same issues discussed in this chapter. They will have to decide whether to bring suit in their country or in a foreign forum such as the United States. The reasons guiding such a decision may be quite different. Contingent fees and punitive damages are most common in U.S. tort litigation, which is an advantage to the plaintiffs. The law regarding damages from breach of contract obligations is more likely to be similar in both nations. Indeed, both Mexico and the United States are parties to the Convention on Contracts for the International Sale of Goods ("CISG").[5] Thus, the substantive contract law in the two countries may be similar, although the courts of the two countries may view the CISG provisions differently. In the case of contracts, the parties are likely to have considered and chosen the applicable law, and possibly the applicable forum. They may have chosen arbitration. There will be some similar questions of personal jurisdiction, but the question of subject matter jurisdiction will differ. Quite likely there will be sufficient connection with each forum to justify subject matter jurisdiction. A motion for dismissal under the *forum non conveniens* doctrine is far less likely to be attempted in a contract dispute; such motions have nearly become the patrimony of tort rather than contract litigation. Questions regarding the application of foreign law may also come into play, but contract law may have fewer variations than tort law, and also as noted the parties may both be signatories to the CISG. In Mexico, commercial contracts are governed by the federal commercial code (Codigo Comercio). But for torts, each Mexican state has its own civil code, plus there is both a civil code for the federal district and a federal civil code.

PROBLEM 4.2   SUBJECT MATTER JURISDICTION—PLACE OF INJURY/ PLACE OF MANUFACTURE

SECTION I.   THE SETTING

The reasons why a plaintiff chooses a specific forum were discussed in Problem 4.1, which tends to assume that the plaintiffs have chosen a forum that has jurisdiction. Problems 3.2 and 3.3 considered some issues of personal jurisdiction. A U.S. court must have both subject matter and personal jurisdiction to go forward. This problem focuses on what cases courts will or must accept. It is *subject matter* jurisdiction. What is the scope of a specific court's subject matter jurisdiction, or where do the outermost limits of a court's jurisdiction lie? We should reemphasize that in civil law tradition nations jurisdiction does not have the same personal/subject-matter division as in the United States and other common law tradition nations. In our hypothetical, there are a number of suits that plaintiffs' attorneys might file in the United States. They include:

1.   Estates of 35 Mexican employees and one U.S. technician killed in the explosion, dozens of Mexican employees and nearby residents and tourists from the United States and Europe injured in the explosion versus GROWFAST in *state* courts in Delaware, Florida and Texas, and possibly in other states.

2.   Same estates and persons versus GROWFAST in *federal* courts in Delaware, Florida and Texas, and possibly in other states.

3.   GROWFAST versus the English and Japanese ingredient suppliers in state courts in Florida and Texas, and possibly in other states.

---

5.   United Nations Convention on Contracts for the International Sale of Goods (1980), contracted to by more than 60 nations, including Canada, Mexico, Germany and the United States, but not including Japan or the United Kingdom.

4. GROWFAST versus same defendants in federal courts in Florida and Texas, and possibly in other states.

The "possibly in other states" may depend on the presence of defendants in the "other" states. But for the purposes of this problem, the potential suits in Delaware, Florida and Texas will provide the basis for a discussion of the principal issues of subject matter jurisdiction. By the addition of a few special facts in Part D jurisdiction is extended by the introduction of some special laws, such as the Alien Tort Claims Act. Just how far these special laws may or should extend subject matter jurisdiction again raises the "outer limits" issue noted first above.

SECTION II. FOCUS OF CONSIDERATION

The division into personal jurisdiction and subject matter jurisdiction has roots in the U.S. Constitution. *Subject matter jurisdiction* asks whether the U.S. Constitution or statutes empower U.S. courts to hear a particular form of dispute. *Personal jurisdiction* asks whether, in addition to the court's empowerment over the subject matter, the court has jurisdiction over the defendant. Assuming the answer to both inquiries is in favor of jurisdiction, a further inquiry might be made in international litigation as to whether any rules of international law impose limitations on the court's exercise of jurisdiction. That might be stated in two ways. One, possessing subject matter and personal jurisdiction, should the court go forward in view of such doctrines as comity? Two, should the court include in its consideration of whether personal jurisdiction actually exists, the balancing of interests of the nations involved? The first approach says the court has jurisdiction but might be best not to exercise it. The second approach incorporates the appropriateness of exercising jurisdiction within the determination of whether jurisdiction it even exists.

Part A considers some issues of state court jurisdiction, including removal to federal court. Part B addresses federal court jurisdiction. Part C specially addresses the extraterritorial reach of subject matter jurisdiction, and lastly, Part D focuses on the Alien Tort Statute (often called the Alien Tort Claims Act or ATCA), and the Torture Victim Protection Act, statutes that have increasingly been used in civil litigation alleging sometimes quite creative violations of international law.

Restatement §§ 402 and 403 and their associated comments, and both the Alien Tort Claims Act and Torture Victim Protection Act, may be helpful to an understanding of this problem. They are included in the Documents Supplement.

SECTION III. READINGS, QUESTIONS AND COMMENTS

Problem 3.2 focused on personal or *in personam* jurisdiction. It is called *jurisdiction to adjudicate* using the language of the Restatement (Third) of Foreign Relations Law (included in the Documents Supplement) principally in Art. 421. The Restatement refers to what is more commonly known of as subject matter jurisdiction as *jurisdiction to prescribe,* in articles 402 and 403. In Article 401 b., the restatement notes that the term *subject matter jurisdiction* is not used in the Restatement. Most jurists appear to prefer viewing subject matter jurisdiction as the power of a court to hear specific matters, regardless of who may be before the court, without reference to the Restatement. Often jurists refer to *legislative jurisdiction* to mean the power of a legislature to establish laws without necessarily designating specific courts to apply such law.

Although the Restatement is not statutory law, it is sometimes influential in judicial decisions. As in Problem 3.2, the Restatement is a good place to start, with the caveat that the Restatement is not itself legislation, but addresses a subject that is principally *legislation* in source, plus some additional sources such as administrative rules and regulations. The Restatement is especially useful because it tends to push U.S. jurisdiction to the edge of reality. Its provisions are not at all universally accepted; they tend to be controversial and part of a sphere of law that is undergoing constant questioning and debate. The Restatement is more the law academics might draft than the law legislators and judges have actually crafted. But it contains a huge investment of careful and considerate thought, and however aspirational it is to some, it speaks the truth to others.

Questions and Comments about the Restatement

1.   Our hypothetical cases are mostly tort actions. Under Restatement § 402 is there any basis for jurisdiction to prescribe over the kind of tort actions likely to be brought?

2.   Restatement § 402 Comment b. discusses overlapping jurisdiction, such as where both territorial and nationality links exist. Does it attempt to determine which of two or more possible bases of jurisdiction is the preferred?

3.   Does the "effects" principle of Restatement § 402 comment d. apply to our hypothetical? The Restatement suggests that for such jurisdiction a "reasonableness" test be applied. Would it apply to the acts in Japan and England?

4.   Do either the "protective" or "passive personality" principles of Restatement § 402 Comments f. and g. apply to our hypothetical?

5.   Restatement § 403 outlines some *limitations* on subject matter jurisdiction. Do any of them seem to apply to our hypothetical? The first limitation is when such exercise of jurisdiction would be *unreasonable.* What does that mean? Reasonableness was discussed in question 3. above. The Restatement mentions eight "relevant factors" to consider. Do any apply?

PART A.   STATE COURT JURISDICTION

DAVID EPSTEIN, JEFFREY L. SNYDER & CHARLES S. BALDWIN, IV, INTERNATIONAL LITIGATION*
5–6, 6–9 (2002).

Although the lion's share of international litigation in the United States occurs in federal court, state courts provide an alternate forum in many instances. State courts are empowered by legislation to hear various actions and, unless federal courts have been given exclusive jurisdiction over a particular cause of action, many suits may be originally brought in state courts and litigated there. As one commentator has noted:

> In addition to a significant difference between federal and state in personam jurisdiction, ... there is a fundamental difference in *subject matter jurisdiction*. Federal courts constituted under Article III of the Constitution are limited to the subject matter jurisdiction embodied in that provision. In contrast, state courts of "general jurisdiction" are free to entertain any suit unless forbidden by state constitution or statute or* * *by an act of Congress. It is significant that, generally, the areas of jurisdiction enumerated in article III are not made exclusively federal by operation of the Constitution. Broadly speaking, aside from admiralty cases, state courts have concurrent jurisdiction unless forbidden by Congress. Congressional prohibition is the exception rather than the rule.[3]

Typically, international litigation in a state court is pursued in actions in torts, family law, or employment law. Some international commercial disputes, however, are also pursued in state courts.

The basis for the exercise of U.S. state court jurisdiction under international law is described in the Restatement (Third) of Foreign Relations Law [referring to § 402, cmt. k., reporter's note 5].

If suit is commenced in state court, a foreign defendant has a right of removal to federal district court under 28 U.S.C.A. § 1441(a) and (b). Subsections (a) and (b) provide, in pertinent part:

> (a) Except as otherwise expressly provided by Act of Congress, any civil action brought in a State court of which the district courts have original jurisdiction, may be removed by the defendant or the defendants, to the district court of the United States for the district and division embracing the place where such action is pending.

> (b) Any civil action of which the district courts have original jurisdiction founded on a claim or right arising under the Constitution, treaties or laws of the United States shall be removable without regard to the citizenship or residence of the parties. Any other such

---

* Reprinted with permission of Transnational Publishers, Inc.

3. Graham C. Lilly, *Jurisdiction Over Domestic and Alien Defendants*, 69 Va. L. Rev. 85, 123, n.142 (1983).

action shall be removable only if none of the parties in interest properly joined and served as defendants is a citizen of the State in which the action is brought.

The procedures for removal are contained in section 1446, including the time limits for filing a notice of removal. The removability of actions is a function of whether the federal district courts have original jurisdiction over such actions.* * *

Removal of Actions to Federal Court

Cases involving foreign defendants that are originally brought in state court are often removed to federal court. Removal of actions is governed by 28 U.S.C. § 1441, which provides, generally, that any action that could originally have been brought in federal court may be removed if brought in state court. Removal does not operate as a waiver of objections to the assertion of personal jurisdiction; objections are preserved and may operate in the federal forum.

In *Ruhrgas, AG v. Marathon Oil Co.,* the U.S. Supreme Court considered whether a federal court must first decide whether it has subject matter jurisdiction over a case removed from state court before determining whether it should exercise personal jurisdiction. The dispute in *Ruhrgas* stemmed from a venture to produce gas in the North Sea. Marathon Oil Co. sued Ruhrgas in Texas state court, asserting state-law claims of fraud, tortuous interference with prospective business relations, breach of fiduciary duty, and civil conspiracy.

Ruhrgas removed the case to the federal District Court, asserting three bases for federal jurisdiction: diversity of citizenship under 28 U.S.C.A. § 1332, on the theory that another party (Marathon Petroleum Norge) had been fraudulently joined; federal question, because Marathon's claims raised questions of international relations under 28 U.S.C.A. § 1331; and 9 U.S.C.A. § 205, which authorizes removal of cases relating to international arbitration agreements. Ruhrgas moved to dismiss the complaint for lack of personal jurisdiction. Marathon moved to remand the case to the state court for lack of federal subject-matter jurisdiction.

The District Court granted Ruhrgas' motion to dismiss for lack of personal jurisdiction. The Texas long arm statute authorized personal jurisdiction to the extent permitted by the due process clause of the U.S. Constitution. The District Court, however, found Ruhrgas' contacts with Texas insufficient to support personal jurisdiction.

The Fifth Circuit, en banc, vacated the District Court's decision and remanded the case, ruling that, in removed cases, district courts must decide issues of subject matter jurisdiction first, and then determine personal jurisdiction issues only if subject matter jurisdiction is found to exist. The Fifth Circuit limited its holding to removed cases, finding the procedure it outlined necessary to prevent federal courts from usurping the jurisdiction of state courts.

A unanimous Supreme Court reversed the Fifth Circuit and remanded the case. The Court held that in cases removed from state court to federal court, as in cases originating in federal court, there is no unyielding jurisdictional hierarchy requiring the federal court to adjudicate subject matter jurisdiction before considering a challenge to personal jurisdiction. The Court ruled:

> The Fifth Circuit erred in according absolute priority to the subject-matter jurisdiction requirement on the ground that it is nonwaivable and delimits federal court power, while restrictions on a court's jurisdiction over the person are waivable and protect individual rights. Although the character of the two jurisdictional bedrocks unquestionably differs, the distinctions do not mean that subject-matter jurisdiction is ever and always the more "fundamental." Personal jurisdiction, too, is an essential element of district court jurisdiction, without which the court is powerless to proceed to an adjudication.

The Court noted, however, that "in most instances, subject-matter jurisdiction will involve no arduous inquiry, and both expedition and sensitivity to state courts' coequal stature should impel the federal court to dispose of that issue first."

Questions and Comments

1. What states may enact as laws is limited largely by the federal Constitution, treaties and U.S. laws that preempt state legislative action. State constitutions may of course limit state legislative action, but state court limitations remain mostly federally imposed. In one sense state court subject matter jurisdiction is therefore what is left after the federal Constitution, treaties and federal law have reserved specific matters for the federal courts. Nevertheless, state courts remain free to hear many international cases. But there is another danger lurking for a matter properly brought in state court, there may be federal laws allowing such matter to be removed to federal court.

2. As the Epstein, Snyder and Baldwin reading indicates, international tort actions are commonly filed in state courts. Do the state courts have subject matter jurisdiction in such cases, or have the federal courts preempted the area of international litigation? If preemption has not limited the filing to federal court, why would any of the plaintiffs in the hypothetical file a suit in a state court? Further suggesting the use of federal courts is the general perception that federal courts are more favorable to, or more sympathetic with, or more tolerant of, foreign parties, or that federal courts are simply more sophisticated than state courts.

3. The reading further notes that the typical international litigation in a state court involves torts, family law and employment law, and some commercial cases. If international commercial cases are more commonly commenced in federal court, why is that true?

4. Are any of the actions in the hypothetical likely to be preempted by federal law, or forbidden or severely limited by state law?

5. Assuming that any of the actions are initiated in state court, what would cause the defendants to attempt to remove the cases to federal court? Do they have a statutory right to such removal?

6. In *Ruhrgas, AG v. Marathon Oil Co.*, discussed in the reading, the Supreme Court considered whether a case transferred to a federal court from a state court required the federal court to first consider whether it has subject matter jurisdiction, and only thereafter consider personal jurisdiction. Should it really matter which consideration occurs first? If the decision had been upheld, the matter could not have proceeded in federal court for lack of personal jurisdiction. But couldn't it be again initiated in state court with hope of a different personal jurisdiction decision? Can a court rule against both personal and subject matter jurisdiction? Might the court not conclude that there is no subject matter jurisdiction for one of the pleaded reasons and then add that the matter could not go forward anyway because there is no personal jurisdiction?

PART B.   FEDERAL COURT JURISDICTION

DAVID EPSTEIN, JEFFREY L. SNYDER & CHARLES S. BALDWIN, IV, INTERNATIONAL LITIGATION*
5–8 (2002).

Foreign parties frequently prefer U.S. federal court over U.S. state court. Foreign parties may perceive that the national character of the federal courts facilitates impartiality and that federal judges may be more sophisticated concerning commercial and international disputes.[10] The jurisdiction of the federal courts, however, is limited and delineated by Article III of the Constitution and federal law. If a specific jurisdictional grant is not present, the judicial power is absent. Consequently, the first step in analyzing any federal jurisdiction issue is identifying the specific jurisdictional grant. All federal jurisdictional authority starts with the Constitution. It provides broad categories of jurisdictional authority under which Congress provides specific legislation authorizing particular cases. Section 2 of Article III provides, in pertinent part:

> The judicial Power shall extend to all Cases, in Law and Equity arising under this Constitution, the Laws of the United States, and Treaties made, or which shall be made, under their Authority;—to all Cases affecting Ambassadors, other public Ministers and Consuls;—to all Cases of admiralty and maritime Jurisdiction;—to Controversies to which the United States shall be a Party;—to Controversies between two or more States;—between a State and Citizens of another State;—between citizens of different States;—between Citizens of the same State claiming lands under Grants of different States, and between a State, or the Citizens thereof, and foreign States, Citizens, or Subjects.

* Reprinted with permission of Transnational Publishers, Inc.

10. See 2d Circuit Bars Suits by "Offshore" Corporations, NAT'L L.J., Mon., Aug. 25, 1997, at B9 (suggesting federal court bias of foreign litigants).

If the Constitution contains a grant of jurisdictional power encompassing a particular type of action (e.g., federal question, diversity) then the next step is generally to identify a specific statutory grant of jurisdiction. As the Supreme Court has stated: "the subject matter jurisdiction of the lower federal courts is determined by Congress, 'in the exact degree and character which to Congress may seem proper for the public good.' "[12]

For instance, Congress has specifically authorized federal court jurisdiction over diversity actions in 28 U.S.C.A. § 1332. Section 1332(a)(2) provides for "alienage jurisdiction," or jurisdiction to hear civil cases between citizens of a state or states and of foreign states (assuming the in-excess-of-$75,000.00 amount in controversy requirement is met). Recent cases have dealt with certain issues which may arise in determining alien citizenship.[13] Section 1332(a)(3) provides that jurisdiction exists where there is diversity of citizenship between domestic U.S. parties and where foreign citizens are additional parties to either or both sides of the action.[14] Section 1332(c)(1) states that "a corporation shall be deemed to be a citizen of any State by which it has been incorporated and of the State where it has its principal place of business . . . ."[15] * * *

In addition to the Constitution, federal statutes, and treaties, federal common law has also been held to supply federal-question jurisdiction under 28 U.S.C.A. § 1331. Courts have found federal-question jurisdiction to exist with regard to issues of international relations even when the Plaintiff's complaint alleges only state law.

In an action over a state law claim, even if the federal court finds lack of jurisdiction based on diversity of citizenship, it may be possible to pursue the claim on the grounds of pendent jurisdiction, when a related federal claim can be asserted. Pendent jurisdiction over state claims exists when the federal claim is sufficient to confer federal jurisdiction, and there is a common nucleus of operative fact between the state and federal claim. The ultimate lack of merit of the federal claim does not mean that pendent jurisdiction cannot attach; the federal claim must be devoid of merit and frivolous in order to divest the court of pendent jurisdiction. The court may retain jurisdiction even if the federal claims

---

12. Carry v. Curtis, 44 U.S. (3 How.) 236, 245 (1845).

13. *See* Foy v. Schantz, 108 F.3d 1347 (11th Cir. 1997) (official permanent resident status required to avoid categorization as alien and mere intent to permanently reside in U.S. is insufficient); Singh v. Daimler–Benz, A.G., 9 F.3d 303 (3d Cir. 1993) (complete diversity of citizenship among parties Plaintiff and Defendant is not required for jurisdiction as long as U.S. citizen is in action); Lloyds Bank v. Norkin, 817 F. Supp. 414 (S.D.N.Y. 1993) (contra; requiring complete diversity of citizenship); Saadeh v. Farouki, 107 F.3d 52 (D.C. Cir. 1997)(intent of 1988 amendment to

§ 1332(a) was to deny jurisdiction in actions between citizen of state and permanent resident alien of same state).

14. Dresser Industries, Inc. v. Underwriters at Lloyds of London, 106 F.3d 494 (3d Cir.1997) (diversity jurisdiction exists in suit by New York citizen against California citizen and French citizen).

15. One court has concluded "that for diversity purposes a corporation incorporated in the United States with its principal place of business abroad is solely a citizen of its 'State' of incorporation." Torres v. Southern Peru Copper Corp., 113 F.3d 540 (5th Cir. 1997).

over which it had original jurisdiction are dismissed. The decision to retain jurisdiction over state law claims is within the district court's discretion, weighing factors such as economy, convenience, fairness, and comity.

Because federal courts exercising diversity jurisdiction must apply state law, some international cases require the federal courts to apply state law on particular issues. For instance, in *Clarkson Co., Ltd. v. Shaheen*,[24] a federal court in New York was faced with a suit by a Canadian trustee in bankruptcy, appointed by a Canadian court, to obtain records located in the New York offices of bankrupt corporations. The trustee sought an order obtaining access to the records. The district court granted access, and the defendant appealed, bringing a collateral attack on the Canadian bankruptcy proceeding. The Second Circuit, in rejecting the challenge, applied the New York law of international comity. Under this doctrine "New York courts recognize the statutory title of an alien trustee in bankruptcy, as long as the foreign court had jurisdiction over the bankrupt and the foreign proceeding has not resulted in injustice to New York citizens, prejudice to creditors' New York statutory remedies, or violation of the laws or public policy of the state." The *Clarkson* case illustrates the application of a state law doctrine of international deference applied in a diversity suit in federal court. Counsel must be prepared for the application of state law, even in cases brought in federal court involving international issues.

CRESSWELL v. SULLIVAN & CROMWELL

United States Court of Appeals, Second Circuit, 1990.
922 F.2d 60.

KEARSE, CIRCUIT JUDGE:

This case has its roots in Bache's 1981–1982 offering in Europe of certain financial instruments (the "Spreads") based on the price differential between two types of futures contracts. [The suit was brought by foreign investors against Bache, a U.S. securities firm, and Sullivan & Cromwell, a U.S. law firm that represented Bache. Three of the large group of plaintiffs were U.S. residents domiciled abroad.]* * *

FEDERAL JURISDICTION

The complaint asserted two bases of subject matter jurisdiction: (1) diversity of citizenship "except as to [three named plaintiffs]," and (2) jurisdiction "ancillary and pendent to [Cresswell I] ... and to the existence of Federal questions arising under the Commodity Exchange Act, and Federal Rules of Civil Procedure.* * * For the reasons below, we conclude that there is neither diversity jurisdiction nor federal question jurisdiction under the provisions relied on by plaintiffs.* * *

The federal diversity statute, to the extent pertinent here, gives the district courts jurisdiction (a) over cases between "citizens of different

---

24. 544 F.2d 624 (2d Cir. 1976).

States," and (b) over cases between "citizens of a State" and "citizens or subjects of a foreign State." [28 U.S.C.A. § 1332] It is well established that for a case to come within this statute there must be complete diversity and that diversity is not complete if any plaintiff is a citizen of the same state as any defendant. United States citizens who are domiciled abroad are neither citizens of any state of the United States nor citizens or subjects of a foreign state, and § 1332(a) does not provide that the courts have jurisdiction over a suit to which such persons are parties. Though we are unclear as to Congress's rationale for not granting United States citizens domiciled abroad rights parallel to those it accords to foreign nationals, the language of § 1332(a) is specific and requires the conclusion that a suit by or against United States citizens domiciled abroad may not be premised on diversity.

According to the complaint, though most of the plaintiffs are citizens of foreign countries, three plaintiffs are United States citizens who permanently reside abroad. Under the above principles, therefore, since not all of the plaintiffs are entitled to sue in federal court based on the diversity statute, plaintiffs may not maintain this suit on the basis of diversity.

In response to our raising this issue, plaintiffs have suggested that the three plaintiffs who are United States citizens residing abroad might be dropped from the suit. Though there is authority for permitting the dismissal of claims against nondiverse defendants in order to cure a defect in diversity jurisdiction, the dismissal of the three nonqualifying plaintiffs in the present case may not provide a cure, because S & C has advised the Court that several of its own partners are United States citizens who reside abroad and that at least one of them has maintained his primary residence in France for more than a decade. Plaintiffs have not challenged S & C's representation, and indeed, the complaint itself suggests that two of S & C's partners may be domiciled in foreign countries. If in fact any of S & C's foreign-residing United States citizen partners are domiciled abroad, a diversity suit could not be brought against them individually; in that circumstance, since for diversity purposes a partnership is deemed to take on the citizenship of each of its partners, a suit against S & C could not be premised on diversity.

JOSEPH MULLER CORPORATION ZURICH v. SOCIETE ANONYME de GERANCE et D'ARMEMENT

United States Court of Appeals, Second Circuit, 1971.
451 F.2d 727.

PER CURIAM:

Joseph Muller Corporation Zurich, a Swiss corporation, brought two separate but related actions in the District Court for the Southern District of New York against Societe Anonyme de Gerance et D'Armement (SAGA), a French corporation, and other defendants. In the first action, Joseph Muller charged SAGA and another defendant with breach of a charter party agreement to transport certain chemical commodities from the United States to Europe and failure to honor Joseph Muller's exercise of an allegedly irrevocable option to extend the charter party agreement. In the second action, Joseph Muller charged SAGA and other defendants with conspiring to fix prices for and with the monopolization of the transportation of various chemical commodities. On motions by SAGA to dismiss both actions for lack of subject matter jurisdiction because of a Franco–Swiss treaty requiring that suits between nationals of France and Switzerland be brought in the courts of the defendant's nation, the District Court deemed the issue in the case of both suits to be "plaintiff's legal capacity to sue defendant in the United States."

* * *

While considerations of international comity would suggest that— given the policy expressed in the Franco–Swiss treaty—United States courts should decline to exercise jurisdiction over a purely private action such as the contract suit here at issue, particularly when the contracts were entered into and were to be performed largely outside the United States, we need not rest our decision on that ground. The pleadings in that suit fail to reveal any basis of federal jurisdiction. Joseph Muller's complaint asserted jurisdiction based upon diversity of citizenship. But as the pleadings clearly show, all parties are aliens, and neither the constitutional nor statutory grants of jurisdiction include such a suit. Although we have given consideration to the doctrine of pendent jurisdiction, we have concluded that this would not be an appropriate case for doing so, since the actions are based on different facts, are of entirely different types, and would not ordinarily be tried in one judicial proceeding.

Questions and Comments

1. Are the foreign perceptions of the U.S. judiciary noted by Epstein, Snyder and Baldwin justified? Are judges in your state sitting in the federal courts "better" than judges sitting in state courts? Are judges in the federal district courts of New York or Washington, D.C., "better" than the federal district court judges in Mississippi or Oregon or Vermont? How does this affect international litigation?

2. Is the U.S. view of subject matter jurisdiction similar to that in other federations, such as Germany or Mexico?

3. Article III, § 2, is the basic governing provision in the Constitution. That section clearly notes judicial power in what we know as diversity cases. The Congress has built upon that as Epstein, Snyder and Baldwin discuss. But diversity is complex. Persons may be citizens of one nation, be domiciled in a second and resident in a third. Shouldn't diversity be based upon citizenship and not domicile or residence? See 28 U.S.C.A. § 1332(a). Are there thus stateless persons that may bar diversity?

4. If in our hypothetical all the injured parties and the estates of all the deceased parties brought suit in a U.S. federal district court in Tampa,

would there be any problem with diversity? Could a suit be fashioned by some of the plaintiffs against GROWFAST that would survive diversity?

5. Do you agree with *Cresswell* that dropping the claims of the three U.S. citizens domiciled abroad would not have provided diversity? The case illustrates a problem with multinational partnerships. Sullivan & Cromwell may be thought of as a U.S. law firm, but the case discloses that it has partners located abroad that are foreign citizens. If one applies the aggregate theory to the partnership, it seems to have a multi-national character. That may prevent diversity from existing, perhaps to its benefit as a defendant.

Note that a suit may be correctable by dropping certain plaintiffs or defendants.

Do you feel the same way about your answer to 4 above in view of *Cresswell* (the U.S. technician and U.S. tourists having been dropped from the suit)?

6. Should the diversity rule be based on citizenship, domicile or residency? Why not consider U.S. citizens domiciled or resident abroad to be U.S. citizens for diversity rather than displaced persons? What is residency— spending three months in the French office to learn a little about its operations? Is that domicile if the person intends to do everything possible to stay in France? The court mentions persons who "permanently reside abroad." What about the definition of domicile as where you hang your heart? What if all those "permanently residing abroad" intend someday to return to the homes they continue to own in the United States?

7. What do you recommend with regard to diversity jurisdiction to the law firm that has signed up all the estates and injured parties in the hypothetical? What if the U.S. parties are dropped as possible plaintiffs, but one injured Mexican citizen (not GROWFAST employee) had returned to the town to visit her parents from her home in Florida, where she has resided with her husband and two children for eight years?

8. Did the court in *Joseph Muller* get comity right? It didn't need to do so since it had a basis to rule against subject matter jurisdiction—the absence of any basis for federal jurisdiction. None of the parties were U.S. citizens, or domiciliaries, or residents, or whatever is required.

PART C.   EXTRATERRITORIALITY OF U.S. LAWS

Although Chapter 3 addressed situations where there is a U.S. plaintiff and a foreign defendant, and this Chapter 4 addresses situations where there is a foreign plaintiff and U.S. defendant, this Part covers one of the former situations because it is a natural progression of the GROWFAST litigation initiated by foreigners in the United States (shifting the blame back in the stream of commerce to England or Japan), and it is an issue of subject matter jurisdiction. Thus we assume that GROWFAST files suit in the United States federal district court in Tampa against the Japanese and English suppliers. The suit is based on contractual liability because GROWFAST believes the purchased ingredients were not suitable and not as ordered. The suit is also brought on anti-trust grounds claiming the Japanese and English suppliers conspired to fix the prices at which they sold the ingredients to GROW-

FAST. Among other responses, the defendants challenge subject matter jurisdiction.

DAVID EPSTEIN, JEFFREY L. SNYDER & CHARLES S. BALDWIN, IV, INTERNATIONAL LITIGATION

5–12 (3d ed. 1998, Supp. 2002).

Some international litigation may involve a suit brought over conduct of a defendant overseas on the grounds that the conduct is proscribed or regulated by a U.S. statute. The issue then arises whether the court can exercise its subject matter jurisdiction based on the statute. As a general rule, the answer is no, based on the doctrine known as the presumption against extraterritoriality. The Supreme Court recently reminded us that "it is a longstanding principle of American law that legislation of Congress, unless a contrary intent appears, is meant to apply only within the territorial jurisdiction of the United States."[27] The presumption serves to protect against unintended clashes between our laws and those of other nations which would result in international discord. Moreover, the presumption recognizes that Congress is primarily concerned with domestic conditions when it legislates. * * *

The act of Congress will not apply to conduct occurring outside the United States unless the affirmative intention of Congress is clearly expressed in the statute. In *Kollinas v. D & G Marine Maintenance,*[30] the court interpreted *Aramco* as holding that a court may consider the specific language of a statute and other indicia of Congressional intent—including legislative history and administrative interpretations—to determine if the presumption against extraterritoriality has been overcome. In *Environmental Defense Fund v. Massey,*[34] the court enumerated three distinct categories of cases in which the presumption does not apply: (1) where the regulated conduct occurs within the United States; (2) where Congress clearly intended to extend the scope of a statute to conduct occurring within foreign nations; and (3) where the failure to extend the scope of the statute to a foreign setting will result in "adverse effects" in the United States. * * *

MICHAEL WALLACE GORDON, UNITED STATES EXTRATERRITORIAL SUBJECT MATTER JURISDICTION IN SECURITIES FRAUD LITIGATION

10 Fla. J. Int'l L. 487 (1996).

* * * The . . . extraterritorial application of laws has developed in the United States principally in the federal circuit courts of appeal, with only occasional but important rulings from the Supreme Court. This judicial development of the law has been influenced, not always helpful-

---

27. EEOC v. Arabian American Oil Co. (Aramco), 499 U.S. 244 (1991), *quoting* Foley Bros., Inc. v. Folardo, 336 U.S. 281 (1949).

30. 29 F.3d 67, 70–75 (2d Cir. 1994).

34. 986 F.2d 528, 531 (D.C. Cir. 1993).

ly, by the two * * * Restatements of Foreign Relations Law produced by the American Law Institute (ALI). Sections of the Restatements have been important to the development of the conduct and effects tests, when courts have searched for a way to express the uncertain congressional intent regarding whether U.S. laws have extraterritorial reach. But other sections of the Restatement have proven ineffective and even a hinderance to the resolution of international disputes. These include the interest balancing or comparative interests theory provisions, which have their source less in what the courts or Congress have said than in what the drafters of the Restatement thought the law should be. Their creation has contributed to considerable confusion as to what courts ought to do. While the courts have ignored interest balancing for the most part, its advocates continue to promote it as the best solution to international conflict.

This author agrees with the advocates of interest balancing that it may be the ideal solution, but believes it is unworkable and unpredictable, and in practice has proven inconsistent in application. Interest balancing had its moment of glory in antitrust litigation, but it has not proven its merit in other areas * * *. Efforts to promote interest balancing might be better spent attempting to assist the development of positive rules regarding what quality and quantity of conduct and what effects in the United States justify the application of extraterritorial jurisdiction * * * Furthermore, foreign courts seeking to interpret international law, especially international comity, do not consider the Restatement to be anything more than what it is, a U.S. view of the world as interest balancing advocates in the United States would like it to be. It has limited relevance in the resolution of international disputes in foreign or international forums.

* * *

Both the initial antitrust laws and the initial securities fraud laws in the United States were enacted to address domestic problems. The Sherman Antitrust Act of 1898 was intended to reduce the anticompetitive conduct of the various "trusts" of the late nineteenth century, which were harming competition in the United States. The Act was not drafted to reach any then existing foreign conduct causing anticompetitive effects in the United States, but it does refer to "trade or commerce . . . with foreign nations."

Although the first major test of the reach of the Act abroad was the *American Banana Co. v. United Fruit Co.* decision in 1910,[31] Justice Oliver Wendell Holmes' territorial based limitations of the Act did not long survive. These limitations were based on a rigid conflict of laws theory that the law of the place of the act determines both the existence and the extent of an obligation. Even if conflict of laws principles were the proper approach to resolve the current lack of clarity over the extraterritorial application of laws, the rigid conflicts views that pre-

31. 213 U.S. 347 (1909).

vailed in the first half of the century were moderated in subsequent decisions and legislative amendments in the antitrust field. * * *

The first important challenge to territorial based limits on extraterritorial application of domestic law was the 1945 *United States v. Aluminum Co. of America* (Alcoa) decision, where the Second Circuit Court of Appeals introduced the "effects" test.[34] This test interpreted the Sherman Antitrust Act language as applicable to conduct that is wholly or partly foreign, and where that conduct is intended to and does have an effect in the United States. As becomes evident in subsequent antitrust cases, * * * "conduct" and "effects" as the basis for jurisdiction carry the debate into more complex dimensions than where the limits on jurisdiction stop at the water's edge or the border under the territorial approach. As long as conduct and effects (or conduct or effects) remain unburdened by a complex interest balancing test, they retain some predictability.

Thirty-one years passed before the next significant case law development in the evolution of subject matter jurisdiction in antitrust law. * * * In the interim, Professor Kingman Brewster suggested in 1958 that judges should consider, when determining liability or relief in antitrust cases, a list of factors representing the interests of each affected nation.[38] This list would be amended and altered by successive supporters of Brewster's work. More importantly, the use of the list would extend beyond the suggestion for consideration to determine liability or relief to whether there should be subject matter jurisdiction, or whether the court should go forward after determining that there is jurisdiction.

One of the first uses of a list to consider different national interests appeared in 1965 in the Restatement (Second) of Foreign Relations Law of the United States. This list was intended by the Restatement drafters to limit enforcement jurisdiction. * * * [It was further developed in the Third Restatement (1987).] * * * The provision of the Third Restatement that is important to this [discussion] is its basis for jurisdiction to prescribe, which includes "conduct outside its territory that has or is intended to have substantial effect within its territory." Left without further clarification, this provision would allow [case law] development of a theory with far greater predictability than the confusion created by the Third Restatement's section 403, which lists eight limitations on jurisdiction. This list includes three more factors than the Second Restatement * * *. The Third Restatement also considers the section 403 interest balancing test applicable to specific problems of antitrust and securities regulation. Section 403 has not been well received by the courts in either area of litigation.

Midway between the adoption of the Second * * * and Third Restatement, the often adventuresome Ninth Circuit * * *, in 1976, ad-

---

34. 148 F.2d 416, 416 (2d Cir. 1945).

38. Kingman Brewster, Antitrust and American Business Abroad 446 (1958) * * *.

dressed an antitrust case where conduct had occurred outside the United States but the alleged effect was within the United States.[56] In *Timberlane Lumber Co. v. Bank of America*, the Ninth Circuit, departing from the Second Circuit, viewed the direct and substantial effects test introduced in Alcoa as inadequate because it failed "to consider other nations' interests ... [or] take into account the full nature of the relationship between the actors and this country."

* * * While *Timberlane* may have pleased jurists who support § 403 of the Restatement, it contributed to the development of inconsistent views among the various federal circuits. Although the Ninth Circuit's interest balancing theory has been accepted in several circuits, it has been questioned or ignored in others. *Timberlane's* value was diminished by the enactment in 1982 of the Foreign Trade Antitrust Improvement Act (FTAIA). The FTAIA, which seems largely ignored by those scholars and judges who are determined to develop interest balancing theory, provided that the challenged conduct in export commerce or wholly foreign conduct must have a "direct, substantial, and reasonably foreseeable effect" on U.S. domestic commerce, or on the trade of a person who is engaged in export commerce.

* * * There seems to be a reluctance to accept the idea that the FTAIA replaced the *Timberlane* decision's unpredictable rule with a more specific and predictable, but perhaps less ideal and aspirational rule. Although the opportunity was presented, the FTAIA did not address interest balancing theory specifically or international comity generally.

The impact of the FTAIA beyond its specific application to export trade rests in the logic of the assumption that the "direct, substantial and foreseeable" effect language is the norm for any extraterritorial application of the antitrust law. That of course does not preclude a court from (1) finding such effect to exist as a result of foreign conduct, and (2) refusing to go forward under principles of international comity. This process seemed to be an alternative until the Supreme Court in the 1993 *Hartford Fire Insurance* decision severely restricted comity usage.[66] While that Supreme Court decision postdated the 1976 *Timberlane* decision by seventeen years, other cases in the interim illustrated the increasing isolation of extensive interest balancing under international comity and the diminishing value of attempting to draft interest balancing guidelines.

One of the more forceful rejections of interest balancing came in the 1984 Laker Airways antitrust litigation.[67] The Laker Airways litigation first involved a suit brought in the United States by U.K.-chartered

---

56. 549 F.2d 597 (9th Cir. 1976), on remand, 574 F. Supp. 1453 (N.D.Cal. 1983), aff'd, 749 F.2d 1378 (9th Cir. 1984), cert. denied, 472 U.S. 1032 (1985).

66. Hartford Fire Insurance, 509 U.S. at 798–99.

67. The principal decision in the United States is Laker Airways, 731 F.2d at 909, which also contains a lengthy discussion of international comity. The principal decision in England is British Airways Bd. v. Laker Airways, Ltd., [1984] 1 Q.B. 142, [1985] 1 App. Cas. 58.

Laker Airways against several U.S. and foreign airlines, including British Airways and British Caledonian, which were both chartered in the United Kingdom. The complaint alleged predatory pricing on Laker routes, secret commissions to travel agents to not book flights on Laker Airways, and attempts to prevent Laker Airways from receiving loans.

The D.C. Circuit followed the effects test. The court rejected interest balancing and suggested that the approach "is unsuitable when courts are forced to choose between a domestic law which is designed to protect domestic interests, and a foreign law which is calculated to thwart the implementation of the domestic law in order to protect foreign interests allegedly threatened by the objectives of the domestic law." Courts increasingly are faced with interpreting legislative expressions of strongly expressed domestic interests that effectively nullify judicial interest balancing.

The U.S. *Laker Airways* decision would seem to leave few if any domestic legislative statutes * * * outside its scope, since every legislative enactment seems to be based on some "domestic interest." The more difficult determination is what constitutes a foreign nation's expression of an intention to "thwart the implementation of the domestic law in order to protect foreign interests." The U.S. *Laker Airways* decision nevertheless suggests that whether or not there is such foreign legislation, interest balancing is inappropriate.

Another significant group of antitrust cases that rejected interest balancing after *Timberlane* involved the uranium antitrust litigation.[75] The Westinghouse company sold nuclear power plants to numerous power companies in the United States and abroad. To assure these sales, Westinghouse also contracted to provide uranium for long terms at rates that soon thereafter proved to be so far below the increasing market price that Westinghouse could not fulfill its agreements. As one defense to breach of contract claims, Westinghouse argued that there was an international uranium suppliers cartel: therefore, Westinghouse was relieved of performance under frustration of contract theory. In attempts to establish the cartel theory by obtaining evidence abroad, much of which was frozen by blocking statutes, a Federal District Court in Illinois rejected the Second Restatement's interest balancing approach, stating that "[a]side from the fact that the judiciary has little expertise, or perhaps even authority, to evaluate the economic and social policies of a foreign country, such a balancing test is inherently unworkable in this case."[77]

Laker Airways and *In re Uranium* were two of the most complex international antitrust litigations of the past two decades. These early 1980s experiences seemed to have had little effect on the development of section 403 of the 1987 Third Restatement.[78] They underline the fact

---

75. In re Uranium Antitrust Litigation, 617 F.2d 1248 (7th Cir. 1980).

77. Uranium Antitrust Litig., 480 F. Supp. at 1148.

78. See Third Restatement, supra note 9, § 403 reporter's notes (citing several of the Uranium and Laker decisions, but making no reference to the comments in those

that the interest balancing theory of section 403 is an interesting exercise at most, that is, a benign theoretical blip on the intellectual continuum of academe, essentially useless as a dispute resolution assist for resolving the most important international litigation that had occurred over the past decades.

The attempt of the Third Restatement in 1987 to supply principles for resolving complex litigation involving the extraterritorial application of U.S. law received its most serious shock six years later in *Hartford Fire Insurance*.[79] The case has been criticized for failing to apply the "reasonableness" test of section 403 of the Third Restatement,[80] accused of misunderstanding the Restatement,[81] and praised for having buried the purported test.[82] The latter two views have been challenged.[83]

HARTFORD FIRE INSURANCE CO. v. CALIFORNIA

United States Supreme Court, 1993.
509 U.S. 764, 113 S.Ct. 2891, 125 L.Ed.2d 612.

SOUTER, J., announced the judgment of the Court and delivered the opinion for a unanimous Court with respect to Parts I and II–A, the opinion of the Court with respect to Parts III and IV, in which REHNQUIST, C.J., and WHITE, BLACKMUN, and STEVENS, JJ., joined, and an opinion concurring in the judgment with respect to Part II–B, in which WHITE, BLACKMUN, and STEVENS, JJ., joined. SCALIA, J., delivered the opinion of the Court with respect to Part I, in which REHNQUIST, C.J., and O'CONNOR, KENNEDY, and THOMAS, JJ., joined, and a dissenting opinion with respect to Part II, in which O'CONNOR, KENNEDY, and THOMAS, JJ., joined.

cases rejecting interest balancing). Although the notes to section 415 on jurisdiction to legislate in antitrust matters refer both to *Timberlane* and its sole important follower, *Mannington Mills*, nowhere do they refer to the Laker decisions, the Uranium litigation, or federal circuits that had not accepted the ideas of *Timberlane* and *Mannington Mills*.

79. Hartford Fire Ins., 509 U.S. at 764.

80. See David G. Gill, Note, Hartford Fire Insurance Co. v. California, 88 Am. J. Int'l L. 109, 114 (1994). Gill further criticizes what he views as the court's failure to consider the fact that a case involving private plaintiffs should be analyzed differently than one involving a government plaintiff. Id. In Hartford Fire Insurance the plaintiffs were both private and government.

81. Andreas F. Lowenfeld, Conflict, Balancing of Interests, and the Exercise of Jurisprudence to Prescribe: Reflections on the Insurance Antitrust Case, 89 Am. J.

Int'l L. 42, 50 (1995). Professor Lowenfeld, who helped prepare the brief for the losing side, attempts to elevate the Restatement to the level of "Aristotle, the Bible, the Koran, the American Constitution, and other authorities" in his defense of § 403 and explanation of how the majority got it wrong.

82. Phillip R. Trimble, The Supreme Court and International Law: The Demise of Restatement Section 403, Editorial Comment, 89 Am. J. Int'l L. 53, 57 (1995).

83. Larry Kramer, Extraterritorial Application of American Law After the Insurance Antitrust Case: A Reply to Professors Lowenfeld and Trimble, 89 Am. J. Int'l L. 750 (1995). Professor Kramer suggested that the Court, in its first opinion on the application of the Sherman Antitrust Act to conduct abroad with intended effects in the United States, overlooked its earlier EEOC v. Arabian American Oil Co. opinion, which established a general principle of territorial jurisdiction for all U.S. federal laws in the absence of contrary intent.

The Sherman Act makes every contract, combination, or conspiracy in unreasonable restraint of interstate or foreign commerce illegal ... The plaintiffs (respondents here) allege that both domestic and foreign defendants (petitioners here) violated the Sherman Act by engaging in various conspiracies to affect the American insurance market. A * * * group of foreign defendants argues that the principle of international comity requires the District Court to refrain from exercising jurisdiction over certain claims against it. We hold that * * * the principle of international comity does not preclude District Court jurisdiction over the foreign conduct alleged.

I

According to the complaints, the object of the conspiracies was to force certain primary insurers (insurers who sell insurance directly to consumers) to change the terms of their standard CGL [commercial general liability] insurance policies to conform with the policies the defendant insurers wanted to sell. * * *

First, most primary insurers rely on certain outside support services for the type of insurance coverage they wish to sell. * * * Second, primary insurers themselves usually purchase insurance to cover a portion of the risk they assume from the consumer. This so-called "reinsurance" may serve at least two purposes, protecting the primary insurer from catastrophic loss, and allowing the primary insurer to sell more insurance than its own financial capacity might otherwise permit. * * * Many of the defendants here are reinsurers or reinsurance brokers, or play some other specialized role in the reinsurance business * * *.

Dissatisfied with this state of affairs, the defendants began to take other steps to force a change in the terms of coverage of CGL insurance generally available, steps that, the plaintiffs allege, implemented a series of conspiracies in violation of the Sherman Act.

* * *

Nineteen States and a number of private plaintiffs filed 36 complaints against the insurers involved in this course of events, charging that the conspiracies described above violated the Sherman Act.... [T]he defendants moved to dismiss for failure to state a cause of action, or, in the alternative, for summary judgment. * * * The District Court ... dismissed the three claims that named only certain London-based defendants, invoking international comity and *Timberlane Lumber Co. v. Bank of America, N.T. & S.A.*, 549 F.2d 597 (1976). The Court of Appeals reversed. * * * First, it held, the foreign reinsurers were beyond the regulatory jurisdiction of the States; ... [A]s to the three claims brought solely against foreign defendants, the court applied its *Timberlane* analysis, but concluded that the principle of international comity was no bar to exercising Sherman Act jurisdiction.

We granted certiorari * * *. We now affirm in part, reverse in part, and remand.

* * *

At the outset, we note that the District Court undoubtedly had jurisdiction of these Sherman Act claims, as the London reinsurers apparently concede. See Tr. of Oral Arg. 37 ("Our position is not that the Sherman Act does not apply in the sense that a minimal basis for the exercise of jurisdiction doesn't exist here. Our position is that there are certain circumstances, and that this is one of them, in which the interests of another State are sufficient that the exercise of that jurisdiction should be restrained"). Although the proposition was perhaps not always free from doubt, see *American Banana Co. v. United Fruit Co.,* 213 U.S. 347, 29 S.Ct. 511, 53 L.Ed. 826 (1909), it is well established by now that the Sherman Act applies to foreign conduct that was meant to produce and did in fact produce some substantial effect in the United States. Such is the conduct alleged here * * *.

According to the London reinsurers, the District Court should have declined to exercise such jurisdiction under the principle of international comity. The Court of Appeals agreed that courts should look to that principle in deciding whether to exercise jurisdiction under the Sherman Act. This availed the London reinsurers nothing, however. To be sure, the Court of Appeals believed that "application of [American] antitrust laws to the London reinsurance market 'would lead to significant conflict with English law and policy,'" and that "[s]uch a conflict, unless outweighed by other factors, would by itself be reason to decline exercise of jurisdiction." But other factors, in the court's view, including the London reinsurers' express purpose to affect United States commerce and the substantial nature of the effect produced, outweighed the supposed conflict and required the exercise of jurisdiction in this litigation.

When it enacted the FTAIA [Foreign Trade Antitrust Improvements Act] Congress expressed no view on the question whether a court with Sherman Act jurisdiction should ever decline to exercise such jurisdiction on grounds of international comity. * * * We need not decide that question here, however, for even assuming that in a proper case a court may decline to exercise Sherman Act jurisdiction over foreign conduct (or, as Justice SCALIA would put it, may conclude by the employment of comity analysis in the first instance that there is no jurisdiction), international comity would not counsel against exercising jurisdiction in the circumstances alleged here.

The only substantial question in this litigation is whether "there is in fact a true conflict between domestic and foreign law." The London reinsurers contend that applying the Act to their conduct would conflict significantly with British law, and the British Government, appearing before us as *amicus curiae,* concurs. They assert that Parliament has established a comprehensive regulatory regime over the London reinsurance market and that the conduct alleged here was perfectly consistent with British law and policy. But this is not to state a conflict. "[T]he fact that conduct is lawful in the state in which it took place will not, of itself, bar application of the United States antitrust laws," even where the foreign state has a strong policy to permit or encourage such conduct. Restatement (Third) Foreign Relations Law § 415, Comment j. No conflict exists, for these purposes, "where a person subject to regulation by two states can comply with the laws of both." Since the London reinsurers do not argue that British law requires them to act in some fashion prohibited by the law of the United States, or claim that their compliance with the laws of both countries is otherwise impossible, we see no conflict with British law. We have no need in this litigation to address other considerations that might inform a decision to refrain from the exercise of jurisdiction on grounds of international comity.

JUSTICE SCALIA delivered * * * a dissenting opinion with respect to Part II.

Petitioners, various British corporations and other British subjects, argue that certain of the claims against them constitute an inappropriate extraterritorial application of the Sherman Act. It is important to distinguish two distinct questions raised by this petition: whether the District Court had jurisdiction, and whether the Sherman Act reaches the extraterritorial conduct alleged here. On the first question, I believe that the District Court had subject-matter jurisdiction over the Sherman Act claims against all the defendants (personal jurisdiction is not contested). Respondents asserted nonfrivolous claims under the Sherman Act, and 28 U.S.C. § 1331 vests district courts with subject-matter jurisdiction over cases "arising under" federal statutes. As precedents such as *Lauritzen v. Larsen,* 345 U.S. 571, 73 S.Ct. 921, 97 L.Ed. 1254 (1953), make clear, that is sufficient to establish the District Court's jurisdiction over these claims. * * *

The second question—the extraterritorial reach of the Sherman Act—has nothing to do with the jurisdiction of the courts. It is a question of substantive law turning on whether, in enacting the Sherman Act, Congress asserted regulatory power over the challenged conduct. See *EEOC v. Arabian American Oil Co.,* 499 U.S. 244, 248, 111 S.Ct. 1227, 1230, 113 L.Ed.2d 274 (1991)("It is our task to determine whether Congress intended the protections of Title VII to apply to United States citizens employed by American employers outside of the United States"). If a plaintiff fails to prevail on this issue, the court does not dismiss the claim for want of subject-matter jurisdiction—want of power to adjudicate; rather, it decides the claim, ruling on the merits that the plaintiff has failed to state a cause of action under the relevant statute.

There is, however, a type of "jurisdiction" relevant to determining the extraterritorial reach of a statute; it is known as "legislative jurisdiction," or "jurisdiction to prescribe," This refers to "the authority of a state to make its law applicable to persons or activities," and is quite a separate matter from "jurisdiction to adjudicate," There is no doubt, of course, that Congress possesses legislative jurisdiction over the acts alleged in this complaint: Congress has broad power under Article I, § 8, cl. 3, "[t]o regulate Commerce with foreign Nations," and this Court has repeatedly upheld its power to make laws applicable to persons or activities beyond our territorial boundaries where United States interests are affected. But the question in this litigation is whether, and to what extent, Congress *has* exercised that undoubted legislative jurisdiction in enacting the Sherman Act.

Two canons of statutory construction are relevant in this inquiry. The first is the "longstanding principle of American law 'that legislation of Congress, unless a contrary intent appears, is meant to apply only within the territorial jurisdiction of the United States.'" Applying that canon in *Aramco*, we held that the version of Title VII of the Civil Rights Act of 1964 then in force did not extend outside the territory of the United States even though the statute contained broad provisions extending its prohibitions to, for example, "'any activity, business, or industry in commerce.'" We held such "boilerplate language" to be an insufficient indication to override the presumption against extraterritoriality. The Sherman Act contains similar "boilerplate language," and if the question were not governed by precedent, it would be worth considering whether that presumption controls the outcome here. We have, however, found the presumption to be overcome with respect to our antitrust laws; it is now well established that the Sherman Act applies extraterritorially.

But if the presumption against extraterritoriality has been overcome or is otherwise inapplicable, a second canon of statutory construction becomes relevant: "[A]n act of congress ought never to be construed to violate the law of nations if any other possible construction remains." *Murray v. Schooner Charming Betsy*, (Marshall, C.J.). This canon is "wholly independent" of the presumption against extraterritoriality. It is relevant to determining the substantive reach of a statute because "the law of nations," or customary international law, includes limitations on a nation's exercise of its jurisdiction to prescribe. Though it clearly has constitutional authority to do so, Congress is generally presumed not to have exceeded those customary international-law limits on jurisdiction to prescribe. Consistent with that presumption, this and other courts have frequently recognized that, even where the presumption against extraterritoriality does not apply, statutes should not be interpreted to regulate foreign persons or conduct if that regulation would conflict with principles of international law.

* * *

More recent lower court precedent has also tempered the extraterritorial application of the Sherman Act with considerations of "international comity." The "comity" they refer to is not the comity of courts, whereby judges decline to exercise jurisdiction over matters more appropriately adjudged elsewhere, but rather what might be termed "prescriptive comity": the respect sovereign nations afford each other by limiting the reach of their laws. That comity is exercised by legislatures when they enact laws, and courts assume it has been exercised when they come to interpreting the scope of laws their legislatures have enacted. It is a traditional component of choice-of-law theory. Comity in this sense includes the choice-of-law principles that, "in the absence of contrary congressional direction," are assumed to be incorporated into our substantive laws having extraterritorial reach. Considering comity in this way is just part of determining whether the Sherman Act prohibits the conduct at issue.

In sum, the practice of using international law to limit the extraterritorial reach of statutes is firmly established in our jurisprudence. In proceeding to apply that practice to the present cases, I shall rely on the Restatement (Third) for the relevant principles of international law. Its standards appear fairly supported in the decisions of this Court construing international choice-of-law principles and in the decisions of other federal courts, especially *Timberlane*. Whether the Restatement precisely reflects international law in every detail matters little here, as I believe this litigation would be resolved the same way under virtually any conceivable test that takes account of foreign regulatory interests.

Under the Restatement, a nation having some "basis" for jurisdiction to prescribe law should nonetheless refrain from exercising that jurisdiction "with respect to a person or activity having connections with another state when the exercise of such jurisdiction is unreasonable." Restatement (Third) § 403(1). The "reasonableness" inquiry turns on a number of factors including, but not limited to: "the extent to which the activity takes place within the territory [of the regulating state]," *id.*, § 403(2)(a); "the connections, such as nationality, residence, or economic activity, between the regulating state and the person principally responsible for the activity to be regulated," *id.*, § 403(2)(b); "the character of the activity to be regulated, the importance of regulation to the regulating state, the extent to which other states regulate such activities, and the degree to which the desirability of such regulation is generally accepted," *id.*, § 403(2)(c); "the extent to which another state may have an interest in regulating the activity," *id.*, § 403(2)(g); and "the likelihood of conflict with regulation by another state," *id.*, § 403(2)(h). Rarely would these factors point more clearly against application of United States law. The activity relevant to the counts at issue here took place primarily in the United Kingdom, and the defendants in these counts are British corporations and British subjects having their principal place of business or residence outside the United States. Great Britain has established a comprehensive regulatory scheme governing the London reinsurance markets, and clearly has a heavy "interest in regulating the activity." * * * I think it unimaginable that an assertion of legislative jurisdiction by the United States would be considered reasonable, and therefore it is inappropriate to assume, in the absence of statutory indication to the contrary, that Congress has made such an assertion.

It is evident from what I have said that the Court's comity analysis, which proceeds as though the issue is whether the courts should "decline to exercise ... jurisdiction," rather than whether the Sherman Act covers this conduct, is simply misdirected. I do not at all agree, moreover, with the Court's conclusion that the issue of the substantive scope of the Sherman Act is not in the cases. To be sure, the parties did not make a clear distinction between adjudicative jurisdiction and the scope of the statute. Parties often do not, as we have observed (and have declined to punish with procedural default) before. It is not realistic, and also not helpful, to pretend that the only really relevant issue in this litigation is not before us. In any event, if one erroneously chooses, as the Court does, to make adjudicative jurisdiction (or, more precisely, abstention) the vehicle for taking account of the needs of prescriptive comity, the Court still gets it wrong. It concludes that no "true conflict" counseling nonapplication of United States law (or rather, as it thinks, United States judicial jurisdiction) exists unless compliance with United States law would constitute a *violation* of another country's law. That breathtakingly broad proposition, which contradicts the many cases discussed earlier, will bring the Sherman Act and other laws into sharp and unnecessary conflict with the legitimate interests of other countries—particularly our closest trading partners.

In the sense in which the term "conflic[t]" was used in *Lauritzen,* * * * there is clearly a conflict in this litigation. The petitioners here * * * were not compelled by any foreign law to take their allegedly wrongful actions, but that no more precludes a conflict-of-laws analysis here than it did there. Where applicable foreign and domestic law provide different substantive rules of decision to govern the parties' dispute, a conflict-of-laws analysis is necessary.

Literally the *only* support that the Court adduces for its position is § 403 of the Restatement (Third)—or more precisely Comment *e* to that provision, which states:

> Subsection (3) [which says that a State should defer to another state if that State's interest is clearly greater] applies only when one state requires what another prohibits, or where compliance with the regulations of two states exercising jurisdiction consistently with this section is otherwise impossible. It does not apply where a person subject to regulation by two states can comply with the laws of both....

The Court has completely misinterpreted this provision. Subsection (3) of * * * comes into play only after subsection (1) * * * has been complied with—*i.e.,* after it has been determined that the exercise of jurisdiction by *both* of the two States is not "unreasonable." That prior question is answered by applying the factors (*inter alia*) set forth in subsection (2) * * *, that is, precisely the factors that I have discussed in text and that the Court rejects.

Questions and Comments

1. As the Esptein, Snyder and Baldwin extract noted, the Supreme Court in *EEOC v. Arabian American Oil Co.* seemed to establish a rule that U.S. laws apply only within the United States "unless a contrary intent appears." Was that rule applied in *Hartford Fire Insurance Co.?* Justice Souter, writing for the majority in *Hartford Fire Insurance*, made no reference to *Aramco,* leading Professor Kramer to call it "sloppy opinion writing." Larry Kramer, Extraterritorial Application of American Law After the Insurance Antitrust Case: A Reply to Professors Lowenfeld and Trimble, 89 Am. J. Int'l L. 750 (1995). Does the language of the Sherman Act show a clear intent that the law is to apply extraterritorially? If it does not show a clear intent, does that mean the reversal of all the case law since Alcoa and a limitation of extraterritoriality in antitrust litigation to the language of the Foreign Trade Antitrust Improvement Act, discussed in Gordon?

2. The *Environmental Defense Fund* decision of the D.C. Circuit, mentioned by Epstein, Snyder & Baldwin, suggests that extraterritorial application of U.S. law is permissible when "the failure to extend the scope of the statute to a foreign setting will result in 'adverse effects' in the United States." Is that consistent with *Hartford Fire Insurance*? With the Restatement?

3. If you applied interest balancing theory to our case of GROWFAST versus the English and Japanese companies, what would be important factors to consider?

4. If the court concludes that the acts of the English and Japanese defendants were intended to and did cause effects in the United States, what might be their defense?

5. The Ninth Circuit has continued its use of the *Timberlane* test in spite of *Hartford Fire Insurance*. See *Metro Industries, Inc. v. Sammi Corp.*, 82 F.3d 839 (9th Cir. 1996), cert. denied, 519 U.S. 868, 117 S.Ct. 181, 136 L.Ed.2d 120 (1996). But other circuits have not followed the Ninth. In *United States v. Nippon Paper Industries Co.*, 109 F.3d 1 (1st Cir. 1997), cert. denied, 522 U.S. 1044, 118 S.Ct. 685, 139 L.Ed.2d 632 (1998), the First Circuit found *Hartford Fire Insurance* to have reigned in the expansion of the scope of comity.

6. *Hartford Fire Insurance* also involved a defense under the McCarran–Ferguson Act exemption from regulation of insurance that is regulated by state law. It involved primarily a domestic issue, but with international overtones because the "state" regulation in this case was English. Justice Scalia thought that there was only "slight" interest on the part of the United States in regulating the English defendant's conduct. Should that depend on whether English regulation extends to anticompetitive conduct by insurance companies?

7. Does Justice Scalia incorrectly merge jurisdiction to prescribe and legislative jurisdiction?

PART D. THE ALIEN TORT STATUTE

Further investigation into the "accident" at the GROWFAST plant in Mexico has disclosed that it was caused by a terrorist group in Mexico.

One of the group, wealthy Juan Hernandez who funded the activities, has been found and detained in the United States. He has been arrested and additionally sued by the estates of the deceased Mexican employees and all the injured Mexican and U.S. employees in federal court in the United States. The suit is based on the Alien Tort Statute (often called the Alien Tort Claims Act or ATCA), 28 U.S.C.A. § 1350, and Torture Victim Protection Act (TVPA), 28 U.S.C. § 1350 (Supp. V 1993). Prior to the *1980 Filártiga* decision, jurisdiction under the ATCA had been upheld only twice (in about two dozen attempts) in the nearly two hundred years of its existence. Two things are clear. First, the ATCA was not enacted as a means to address human rights issues. Second, beginning with *Filártiga,* the ATCA has become one of the main methods of addressing human rights issues. Since *Filártiga* the ATCA has been used extensively, its limitations influencing the adoption of the 1994 Torture Victim Protection Act (TVPA) and 1996 amendments to the Foreign Sovereign Immunities Act (FSIA). The U.S. Supreme Court addressed the ATCA in *Sosa v. Alvarez Machian.*

DAVID EPSTEIN, JEFFREY L. SNYDER & CHARLES S. BALDWIN, IV, INTERNATIONAL LITIGATION*
5–15 (3d ed. 1998).

The principal exception to the general rule, that U.S. courts do not have jurisdiction over suits whose parties and subject matter are wholly foreign, is the Alien Tort Statute, 28 U.S.C.A. § 1350. The Statute provides:

> The district courts shall have original jurisdiction of any civil action by an alien for a tort only, committed in violation of the law of nations or a treaty of the United States.

The Statute, therefore, provides a private right of action concerning violations of (i) *jus cogens* (internationally recognized norms) or (ii) of a treaty of the United States. The Statute was originally enacted in 1789 to allow U.S. courts to redress acts of piracy but has been seldom invoked.[49] The requirement under provision (i) that the violation be of "the law of nations" is extremely restrictive and, until recently, few cases met such standard.

Jurisdiction under the Alien Tort Statute was recently expanded by the Second Circuit in *Kadic v. Karadzic.* Suit in *Karadzic* was brought by Croat and Muslim citizens of Bosnia–Herzegovina against defendant Radovan Karadzic, leader of a non-internationally recognized Bosnian–Serb republic within Bosnia–Herzegovina. Plaintiffs complained of acts by troops under Karadzic's command, including, among others, rape, torture, and execution. Karadzic was personally served with process

---

* Reprinted with permission of Transnational Publishers, Inc.

49. See Kadic v. Karadzic, 70 F.3d 232 (2d Cir. 1995), *reh'g denied,* 74 F.3d 377, *cert. denied,* 116 S. Ct. 2524 (1996) (examining legislative history and prior court decisions regarding Statute).

while visiting in New York as an invitee of the United Nations. The Second Circuit ruled that the Alien Tort Statute conferred jurisdiction for violations of the law of nations committed by those not acting under the authority of a recognized state and that such violations include genocide, war crimes, and crimes against humanity. The Court further observed that the content of the law of nations must be judged, "not as it was in 1789, but as it has evolved and exists among the nations of the world today."

It should be noted, however, that the jurisdictional standard under the Alien Tort Statute remains extremely high. Current law only supports jurisdiction where the acts involved were violative of fundamental human rights as codified by international Convention. As the *Filartiga* Court observed:

> the mere fact that every nations' municipal law may prohibit theft does not incorporate "the Eighth Commandment, 'Thou Shalt not steal' ... [into] the law of nations. It is only where the nations of the world have demonstrated that the wrong is of mutual, and not merely several, concern, by means of express international accords, that a wrong generally recognized becomes an international law violation within the meaning of the statute.

The Alien Tort Statute has been found to confer jurisdiction over corporations, as well as over individuals. Commercial/property torts and air crash disasters have not provided jurisdiction under the Alien Tort Statute.

It may also be noted that the second provision of the Alien Tort Statute, concerning violation of a treaty of the United States, has been rarely invoked. As with the first provision of the Alien Tort Statute, the treaty provision is extremely narrow. As one court observed, the Statute applies only to those treaty provisions that create a "tort" action by their violation and not to all violations of a U.S. Treaty.

FILARTIGA v. PENA–IRALA

United States Court of Appeals, Second Circuit, 1980.
630 F.2d 876.

[The plaintiffs were the parents of a 17 year old son Joselito Filártiga who was kidnaped and tortured to death in 1976 by Pena–Irala, Inspector General of Police in Asunción, Paraguay, where the events occurred and where all parties were nationals. Joselito's father was long an opponent of Paraguay's president Stroessner. Filártiga initiated a criminal action in Paraguay for his son's murder, and he was arrested and threatened. His lawyer was disbarred. No one was ever convicted in Paraguay for the boy's death. Filártiga's daughter Dolly entered the United States in 1978 asking for political asylum. Pena entered the United States in 1978 under a visitor's visa, and remained after the visa expired. Dolly Filátiga learned of Pena's presence and initiated suit for wrongful death serving Pena. The Penas were arrested by U.S. immigration officials (INS), and ultimately deported, the Filártiga's losing attempts to keep Pena in the United States. The civil suit claimed general federal question subject matter jurisdiction on several grounds, ultimately principally under the ATCA. The complaint was dismissed by the federal district court on jurisdictional grounds, narrowly interpreting the law of nations as excluding treatment by a foreign nation of its own citizens.]

KAUFMAN, CIRCUIT JUDGE:

. . . [T]he First Congress established original district court jurisdiction over "all causes where an alien sues for a tort only (committed) in violation of the law of nations." Judiciary Act of 1789. Construing this rarely-invoked provision, we hold that deliberate torture perpetrated under color of official authority violates universally accepted norms of the international law of human rights, regardless of the nationality of the parties. Thus, whenever an alleged torturer is found and served with process by an alien within our borders, § 1350 provides federal jurisdiction. Accordingly, we reverse the judgment of the district court dismissing the complaint for want of federal jurisdiction.

II

Appellants rest their principal argument in support of federal jurisdiction upon the Alien Tort Statute. In light of the universal condemnation of torture in numerous international agreements, and the renunciation of torture as an instrument of official policy by virtually all of the nations of the world (in principle if not in practice), we find that an act of torture committed by a state official against one held in detention violates established norms of the international law of human rights, and hence the law of nations.

The Supreme Court has enumerated the appropriate sources of international law. The law of nations "may be ascertained by consulting the works of jurists, writing professedly on public law; or by the general usage and practice of nations; or by judicial decisions recognizing and enforcing that law." *United States v. Smith*, 18 U.S. (5 Wheat.) 153, 160–61, 5 L.Ed. 57 (1820). The *Smith* Court discovered among the works of Lord Bacon, Grotius, Bochard and other commentators a genuine consensus that rendered the crime "sufficiently and constitutionally defined."

The *Paquete Habana*, 175 U.S. 677, 20 S.Ct. 290, 44 L.Ed. 320 (1900), reaffirmed that

> where there is no treaty, and no controlling executive or legislative act or judicial decision, resort must be had to the customs and usages of civilized nations; and, as evidence of these, to the works of jurists and commentators, who by years of labor, research and experience, have made themselves peculiarly well acquainted with the subjects of which they treat. Such works are resorted to by judicial tribunals, not for the speculations of their authors concern-

ing what the law ought to be, but for trustworthy evidence of what the law really is.

Modern international sources confirm the propriety of this approach.

* * *

The requirement that a rule command the "general assent of civilized nations" to become binding upon them all is a stringent one. Were this not so, the courts of one nation might feel free to impose idiosyncratic legal rules upon others, in the name of applying international law. * * *

[A]lthough there is no universal agreement as to the precise extent of the "human rights and fundamental freedoms" guaranteed to all by the [U.N.]Charter, there is at present no dissent from the view that the guaranties include, at a bare minimum, the right to be free from torture. * * *

Having examined the sources from which customary international law is derived the usage of nations, judicial opinions and the works of jurists we conclude that official torture is now prohibited by the law of nations. * * * Accordingly, we must conclude that the dictum in *Dreyfus v. von Finck* to the effect that "violations of international law do not occur when the aggrieved parties are nationals of the acting state," is clearly out of tune with the current usage and practice of international law. * * * While the ultimate scope of those rights will be a subject for continuing refinement and elaboration, we hold that the right to be free from torture is now among them. We therefore turn to the question whether the other requirements for jurisdiction are met.

III

Appellee submits that even if the tort alleged is a violation of modern international law, federal jurisdiction may not be exercised consistent with the dictates of Article III of the Constitution. The claim is without merit. Common law courts of general jurisdiction regularly adjudicate transitory tort claims between individuals over whom they exercise personal jurisdiction, wherever the tort occurred. Moreover, as part of an articulated scheme of federal control over external affairs, Congress provided, in the first Judiciary Act, § 9(b), 1 Stat. 73, 77 (1789), for federal jurisdiction over suits by aliens where principles of international law are in issue. The constitutional basis for the Alien Tort Statute is the law of nations, which has always been part of the federal common law.

It is not extraordinary for a court to adjudicate a tort claim arising outside of its territorial jurisdiction. A state or nation has a legitimate interest in the orderly resolution of disputes among those within its borders, and where the lex loci delicti commissi is applied, it is an expression of comity to give effect to the laws of the state where the wrong occurred. Thus, Lord Mansfield in *Mostyn v. Fabrigas*, 1 Cowp.

161 (1774), quoted in *McKenna v. Fisk*, 42 U.S. (1 How.) 241, 248, 11 L.Ed. 117 (1843) said:

> (I)f A becomes indebted to B, or commits a tort upon his person or upon his personal property in Paris, an action in either case may be maintained against A in England, if he is there found.... (A)s to transitory actions, there is not a colour of doubt but that any action which is transitory may be laid in any county in England, though the matter arises beyond the seas.

Mostyn came into our law as the original basis for state court jurisdiction over out-of-state torts and it has not lost its force in suits to recover for a wrongful death occurring upon foreign soil, as long as the conduct complained of was unlawful where performed. Here, where in personam jurisdiction has been obtained over the defendant, the parties agree that the acts alleged would violate Paraguayan law, and the policies of the forum are consistent with the foreign law, state court jurisdiction would be proper. Indeed, appellees conceded as much at oral argument.

Recalling that *Mostyn* was freshly decided at the time the Constitution was ratified, we proceed to consider whether the First Congress acted constitutionally in vesting jurisdiction over "foreign suits," * * *. A case properly "aris(es) under the ... laws of the United States" for Article III purposes if grounded upon statutes enacted by Congress or upon the common law of the United States. The law of nations forms an integral part of the common law, and a review of the history surrounding the adoption of the Constitution demonstrates that it became a part of the common law of the United States upon the adoption of the Constitution. Therefore, the enactment of the Alien Tort Statute was authorized by Article III. * * *

As ratified, the judiciary article contained no express reference to cases arising under the law of nations. Indeed, the only express reference to that body of law is contained in Article I, sec. 8, cl. 10, which grants to the Congress the power to "define and punish ... offenses against the law of nations." Appellees seize upon this circumstance and advance the proposition that the law of nations forms a part of the laws of the United States only to the extent that Congress has acted to define it. This extravagant claim is amply refuted by the numerous decisions applying rules of international law uncodified in any act of Congress * * * and we reject it today. As John Jay wrote in The Federalist No. 3, at 22 (1 Bourne ed. 1901), "Under the national government, treaties and articles of treaties, as well as the laws of nations, will always be expounded in one sense and executed in the same manner, whereas adjudications on the same points and questions in the thirteen states will not always accord or be consistent." Federal jurisdiction over cases involving international law is clear.

Thus, it was hardly a radical initiative for Chief Justice Marshall to state in *The Nereide*, 13 U.S. (9 Cranch) 388, 422, 3 L.Ed. 769 (1815), that in the absence of a congressional enactment, United States courts are "bound by the law of nations, which is a part of the law of the land."

These words were echoed in *The Paquete Habana*, 175 U.S. at 700, 20 S.Ct. at 299: "(i)nternational law is part of our law, and must be ascertained and administered by the courts of justice of appropriate jurisdiction, as often as questions of right depending upon it are duly presented for their determination."

* * *

Although the Alien Tort Statute has rarely been the basis for jurisdiction during its long history, in light of the foregoing discussion, there can be little doubt that this action is properly brought in federal court.[22] This is undeniably an action by an alien, for a tort only, committed in violation of the law of nations. The paucity of suits successfully maintained under the section is readily attributable to the statute's requirement of alleging a "violation of the law of nations" (emphasis supplied) at the jurisdictional threshold. Courts have, accordingly, engaged in a more searching preliminary review of the merits than is required, for example, under the more flexible "arising under" formulation. Thus, the narrowing construction that the Alien Tort Statute has previously received reflects the fact that earlier cases did not involve such well-established, universally recognized norms of international law that are here at issue.

Since federal jurisdiction may properly be exercised over the Filártigas' claim, the action must be remanded for further proceedings. Appellee Pena, however, advances several additional points that lie beyond the scope of our holding on jurisdiction. Both to emphasize the boundaries of our holding, and to clarify some of the issues reserved for the district court on remand, we will address these contentions briefly.

IV

Pena argues that the customary law of nations, as reflected in treaties and declarations that are not self-executing, should not be applied as rules of decision in this case. In doing so, he confuses the question of federal jurisdiction under the Alien Tort Statute, which requires consideration of the law of nations, with the issue of the choice of law to be applied, which will be addressed at a later stage in the proceedings. The two issues are distinct. Our holding on subject matter jurisdiction decides only whether Congress intended to confer judicial power, and whether it is authorized to do so by Article III. The choice of law inquiry is a much broader one, primarily concerned with fairness, consequently, it looks to wholly different considerations.

Finally, we have already stated that we do not reach the critical question of forum non conveniens, since it was not considered below. In closing, however, we note that the foreign relations implications of this and other issues the district court will be required to adjudicate on

---

22. We recognize that our reasoning might also sustain jurisdiction under the general federal question provision, 28 U.S.C. § 1331. We prefer, however, to rest our decision upon the Alien Tort Statute, in light of that provision's close coincidence with the jurisdictional facts presented in this case.

remand underscores the wisdom of the First Congress in vesting jurisdiction over such claims in the federal district courts through the Alien Tort Statute. Questions of this nature are fraught with implications for the nation as a whole, and therefore should not be left to the potentially varying adjudications of the courts of the fifty states. * * *

SOSA v. ALVAREZ–MACHAIN

United States Supreme Court, 2004.
542 U.S. 692, 124 S.Ct. 2739, 159 L.Ed.2d 718.

JUSTICE SOUTER delivered the opinion of the Court.

In 1985, an agent of the Drug Enforcement Administration (DEA), Enrique Camarena–Salazar, was captured on assignment in Mexico and taken to a house in Guadalajara, where he was tortured over the course of a 2–day interrogation, then murdered. ... DEA officials ... came to believe that respondent Humberto Alvarez–Machain (Alvarez), a Mexican physician, was present at the house and acted to prolong the agent's life in order to extend the interrogation and torture. In 1990, a federal grand jury indicted Alvarez for the torture and murder of Camarena–Salazar, and the United States District Court for the Central District of California issued a warrant for his arrest. The DEA asked the Mexican Government for help in getting Alvarez into the United States, but when the requests and negotiations proved fruitless, the DEA approved a plan to hire Mexican nationals to seize Alvarez and bring him to the United States for trial. As so planned, a group of Mexicans, including petitioner Jose Francisco Sosa, abducted Alvarez from his house, held him overnight in a motel, and brought him by private plane to El Paso, Texas, where he was arrested by federal officers.

Once in American custody, Alvarez moved to dismiss the indictment on the ground that his seizure was "outrageous governmental conduct," and violated the extradition treaty between the United States and Mexico. The District Court agreed, the Ninth Circuit affirmed, and we reversed, holding that the fact of Alvarez's forcible seizure did not affect the jurisdiction of a federal court. The case was tried in 1992, and ended at the close of the Government's case, when the District Court granted Alvarez's motion for a judgment of acquittal.

In 1993, after returning to Mexico, Alvarez began the civil action before us here. He sued Sosa, Mexican citizen and DEA operative Antonio Garate–Bustamante, five unnamed Mexican civilians, the United States, and four DEA agents. So far as it matters here, Alvarez sought damages from the United States under the FTCA, alleging false arrest, and from Sosa under the ATS. The District Court granted the Government's motion to dismiss the FTCA claim, but awarded summary judgment and $25,000 in damages to Alvarez on the ATS claim. A three-judge panel of the Ninth Circuit then affirmed the ATS judgment, but reversed the dismissal of the FTCA claim. A divided en banc court came to the same conclusion. As for the ATS claim, the court called on its own precedent, "that [the ATS] not only provides federal courts with subject matter jurisdiction, but also creates a cause of action for an alleged violation of the law of nations." The Circuit then relied upon what it called the "clear and universally recognized norm prohibiting arbitrary arrest and detention," to support the conclusion that Alvarez's arrest amounted to a tort in violation of international law.

We granted certiorari ... to clarify the scope of both the FTCA and the ATS. We now reverse in each.

III

... Sosa ... argues (as does the United States supporting him) that there is no relief under the ATS because the statute does no more than vest federal courts with jurisdiction, neither creating nor authorizing the courts to recognize any particular right of action without further congressional action. Although we agree the statute is in terms only jurisdictional, we think that at the time of enactment the jurisdiction enabled federal courts to hear claims in a very limited category defined by the law of nations and recognized at common law. We do not believe, however, that the limited, implicit sanction to entertain the handful of international law cum common law claims understood in 1789 should be taken as authority to recognize the right of action asserted by Alvarez here.

Judge Friendly called the ATS a "legal Lohengrin, ... no one seems to know whence it came," and for over 170 years after its enactment it provided jurisdiction in only one case.

The parties and amici here advance radically different historical interpretations of this terse provision. Alvarez says that the ATS was intended not simply as a jurisdictional grant, but as authority for the creation of a new cause of action for torts in violation of international law. We think that reading is implausible. As enacted in 1789, the ATS gave the district courts "cognizance" of certain causes of action, and the term bespoke a grant of jurisdiction, not power to mold substantive law. * * * we think the statute was intended as jurisdictional in the sense of addressing the power of the courts to entertain cases concerned with a certain subject. But holding the ATS jurisdictional raises a new question, this one about the interaction between the ATS at the time of its enactment and the ambient law of the era. Sosa would have it that the ATS was stillborn because there could be no claim for relief without a further statute expressly authorizing adoption of causes of action. Amici professors of federal jurisdiction and legal history take a different tack, that federal courts could entertain claims once the jurisdictional grant was on the books, because torts in violation of the law of nations would have been recognized within the common law of the time. We think history and practice give the edge to this latter position. * * *

[T]he history does tend to support two propositions. First, there is every reason to suppose that the First Congress did not pass the ATS as a jurisdictional convenience to be placed on the shelf for use by a future Congress or state legislature that might, someday, authorize the creation of causes of action or itself decide to make some element of the law of nations actionable for the benefit of foreigners. The anxieties of the preconstitutional period cannot be ignored easily enough to think that the statute was not meant to have a practical effect. Consider ... that the First Congress was attentive enough to the law of nations to recognize certain offenses expressly as criminal, including the three mentioned by Blackstone. It would have been passing strange for ... this very Congress to vest federal courts expressly with jurisdiction to entertain civil causes brought by aliens alleging violations of the law of nations, but to no effect whatever until the Congress should take further action. There is too much in the historical record to believe that Congress would have enacted the ATS only to leave it lying fallow indefinitely.

The second inference to be drawn from the history is that Congress intended the ATS to furnish jurisdiction for a relatively modest set of actions alleging violations of the law of nations. Uppermost in the legislative mind appears to have been offenses against ambassadors, violations of safe conduct were probably understood to be actionable, and individual actions arising out of prize captures and piracy may well have also been contemplated. But the common law appears to have understood only those three of the hybrid variety as definite and actionable, or at any rate, to have assumed only a very limited set of claims. As Blackstone had put it, "offences against this law [of nations] are principally incident to whole states or nations," and not individuals seeking relief in court.

The sparse contemporaneous cases and legal materials referring to the ATS tend to confirm both inferences, that some, but few, torts in violation of the law of nations were understood to be within the common law. * * *

In sum, although the ATS is a jurisdictional statute creating no new causes of action, the reasonable inference from the historical materials is that the statute was intended to have practical effect the moment it became law. The jurisdictional grant is best read as having been enacted on the understanding that the common law would provide a cause of action for the modest number of international law violations with a potential for personal liability at the time.

IV

* * * [T]here are good reasons for a restrained conception of the discretion a federal court should exercise in considering a new cause of action of this kind. Accordingly, we think courts should require any claim based on the present-day law of nations to rest on a norm of international character accepted by the civilized world and defined with a specificity comparable to the features of the 18th-century paradigms we have recognized. This requirement is fatal to Alvarez's claim.

A series of reasons argue for judicial caution when considering the kinds of individual claims that might implement the jurisdiction conferred by the early statute. First, the prevailing conception of the common law has changed since 1789 in a way that counsels restraint in judicially applying internationally generated norms. * * *

Second, along with, and in part driven by, that conceptual development in understanding common law has come an equally significant rethinking of the role of the federal courts in making it. Erie R. Co. v. Tompkins, was the watershed in which we denied the existence of any federal "general" common law.... [A]lthough we have even assumed competence to make judicial rules of decision of particular importance to foreign relations, such as the act of state doctrine, the general practice has been to look for legislative guidance before exercising innovative authority over substantive law. It would be remarkable to take a more aggressive role in exercising a jurisdiction that remained largely in shadow for much of the prior two centuries.

Third, this Court has recently and repeatedly said that a decision to create a private right of action is one better left to legislative judgment in the great majority of cases. The creation of a private right of action raises issues beyond the mere consideration whether underlying primary conduct should be allowed or not, entailing, for example, a decision to permit enforcement without the check imposed by prosecutorial discretion. Accordingly, even when Congress has made it clear by statute that a rule applies to purely domestic conduct, we are reluctant to infer intent to provide a private cause of action where the statute does not supply one expressly. While the absence of congressional action addressing private rights of action under an international norm is more equivocal than its failure to provide such a right when it creates a statute, the possible collateral consequences of making international rules privately actionable argue for judicial caution.

Fourth, the subject of those collateral consequences is itself a reason for a high bar to new private causes of action for violating international law, for the potential implications for the foreign relations of the United States of recognizing such causes should make courts particularly wary of impinging on the discretion of the Legislative and Executive Branches in managing foreign affairs.* * * Since many attempts by federal courts to craft remedies for the violation of new norms of international law would raise risks of adverse foreign policy consequences, they should be undertaken, if at all, with great caution.

The fifth reason is particularly important in light of the first four. We have no congressional mandate to seek out and define new and debatable violations of the law of nations, and modern indications of congressional understanding of the judicial role in the field have not affirmatively encouraged greater judicial creativity.

* * * All Members of the Court agree that § 1350 is only jurisdictional. We also agree, or at least Justice SCALIA does not dispute, that the jurisdiction was originally understood to be available to enforce a small number of international norms that a federal court could properly recognize as within the common law enforceable without further statuto-

ry authority. Justice Scalia concludes, however, that two subsequent developments should be understood to preclude federal courts from recognizing any further international norms as judicially enforceable today, absent further congressional action. As described before, we now tend to understand common law not as a discoverable reflection of universal reason but, in a positivistic way, as a product of human choice. And we now adhere to a conception of limited judicial power first expressed in reorienting federal diversity jurisdiction, that federal courts have no authority to derive "general" common law.

Whereas Justice SCALIA sees these developments as sufficient to close the door to further independent judicial recognition of actionable international norms, other considerations persuade us that the judicial power should be exercised on the understanding that the door is still ajar subject to vigilant doorkeeping, and thus open to a narrow class of international norms today. * * * For two centuries we have affirmed that the domestic law of the United States recognizes the law of nations. It would take some explaining to say now that federal courts must avert their gaze entirely from any international norm intended to protect individuals.

While we agree with Justice SCALIA to the point that we would welcome any congressional guidance in exercising jurisdiction with such obvious potential to affect foreign relations, nothing Congress has done is a reason for us to shut the door to the law of nations entirely. It is enough to say that Congress may do that at any time (explicitly, or implicitly by treaties or statutes that occupy the field), just as it may modify or cancel any judicial decision so far as it rests on recognizing an international norm as such.

We must still, however, derive a standard or set of standards for assessing the particular claim Alvarez raises, and for this action it suffices to look to the historical antecedents. * * *

To begin with, Alvarez cites two well-known international agreements that, despite their moral authority, have little utility under the standard set out in this opinion. He says that his abduction by Sosa was an "arbitrary arrest" within the meaning of the Universal Declaration of Human Rights. And he traces the rule against arbitrary arrest not only to the Declaration, but also to article nine of the International Covenant on Civil and Political Rights, to which the United States is a party, and to various other conventions to which it is not. But the Declaration does not of its own force impose obligations as a matter of international law. * * * And, although the Covenant does bind the United States as a matter of international law, the United States ratified the Covenant on the express understanding that it was not self-executing and so did not itself create obligations enforceable in the federal courts. Accordingly, Alvarez cannot say that the Declaration and Covenant themselves establish the relevant and applicable rule of international law. He instead attempts to show that prohibition of arbitrary arrest has attained the status of binding customary international law.

Alvarez thus invokes a general prohibition of "arbitrary" detention defined as officially sanctioned action exceeding positive authorization to detain under the domestic law of some government, regardless of the circumstances. Whether or not this is an accurate reading of the Covenant, Alvarez cites little authority that a rule so broad has the status of a binding customary norm today. He certainly cites nothing to justify the federal courts in taking his broad rule as the predicate for a federal lawsuit, for its implications would be breathtaking. His rule would support a cause of action in federal court for any arrest, anywhere in the world, unauthorized by the law of the jurisdiction in which it took place, and would create a cause of action for any seizure of an alien in violation of the Fourth Amendment, supplanting the actions under Rev. Stat. § 1979, 42 U.S.C. § 1983, and Bivens v. Six Unknown Fed. Narcotics Agents, 403 U.S. 388, 91 S.Ct. 1999, 29 L.Ed.2d 619 (1971), that now provide damages remedies for such violations. It would create an action in federal court for arrests by state officers who simply exceed their authority; and for the violation of any limit that the law of any country might place on the authority of its own officers to arrest. And all of this assumes that Alvarez could establish that Sosa was acting on behalf of a government when he made the arrest, for otherwise he would need a rule broader still.* * *Whatever may be said for the broad principle Alvarez advances, in the present, imperfect world, it expresses an aspiration that exceeds any binding customary rule having the specificity we require. Creating a private cause of action to further that aspiration would go beyond any residual common law discretion we think it appropriate to exercise. It is enough to hold that a single illegal detention of less than a day, followed by the transfer of custody to lawful authorities and a prompt arraignment, violates no norm of customary international law so well defined as to support the creation of a federal remedy. * * *

The judgment of the Court of Appeals is Reversed.

Questions and Comments

1. The motion to dismiss on jurisdiction having been denied, the Filártiga case was remanded and the Filártigas received a default judgment for $385,364 in compensatory damages, plus $10 million punitive damages. Realizing that Chapter 8 on state immunity in this casebook is yet to come, could the suit have been brought against the government of Paraguay? A judgment against Paraguay might be collected. A judgment of $187 million was rendered in 1997 against the government of Cuba for shooting down two civilian airplanes. *Alejandre v. Republic of Cuba*, 996 F.Supp. 1239 (S.D. Fla. 1997) Some has been collected. *Alejandre v. Republic of Cuba*, 42 F.Supp.2d 1317 (S.D.Fla. 1999).

Dozens of cases have followed *Filártiga* under the Alien Tort Claims Act, at least until the *Sosa v. Alvarez–Machain* decision. Potential defendants would seem to be warned by these cases to avoid traveling to the United States, much less attempting to emigrate. Cases filed subsequent to

Filártiga establish an expansion of the previously infrequent use of the Alien Tort Claims Act.

2. Did the *Filártiga* court effectively deal with the argument that written laws prohibiting torture in many areas of the world exist in nations where they are commonly ignored?

3. At the time of the decision, there was a draft of the subsequently adopted Torture Victim Protection Act. 28 U.S.C.A. § 1350. Might that have influenced the court? What more does the TVPA add that is not covered in the ATCA?

4. Could the Filártigas have brought suit in state court? Had the suit been initiated in state court, could it have been removed by the defendant to federal court?

5. *Sosa v. Alvarez–Machain* provides Supreme Court confirmation that the ATCA is both jurisdictional and provides the basis for the substantive claim. Did *Sosa* change any of the opinion rendered in *Filártiga*?

6. ATCA cases have been brought against environmental wrongs and abuse of women. See, e.g., *Beanal v. Freeport–McMoran, Inc.,* 197 F.3d 161 (5th Cir. 1999); *Ford v. Garcia*, 289 F.3d 1283 (11th Cir. 2002), cert. denied, 537 U.S. 1147, 123 S.Ct. 868, 154 L.Ed.2d 849 (2003). The ATCA is thoroughly considered in *Tel-Oren v. Libyan Arab Republic,* 726 F.2d 774 (D.C.Cir. 1984), cert. denied, 470 U.S. 1003, 105 S.Ct. 1354, 84 L.Ed.2d 377 (1985). For a discussion of the ATCA, *see, e.g.,* Anne–Marie Burley, The Alien Tort Statute and the Judiciary Act of 1789: A Badge of Honor, 83 Am.J. Int'l L. 461 (1989); Kenneth C. Randall, Federal Jurisdiction over International Claims: Inquiries into the Alien Tort Statute, 18 N.Y.U. J. L. & Pol. 1 (1985); Jean–Marie Simon, The Alien Tort Claims Act: Justice or Show Trials?, 11 B.U. Int'l L.J. 1 (1993); Joseph Modeste Sweeney, A Tort Only in Violation of the Law of Nations, 18 Hastings Int'l & Comp. L. Rev. 445 (1995).

7. Why was the Alien Tort Statute limited to aliens and why was it applicable only to torts? The answer is not clear. What is clear is that the recent use of the ATCA in human rights cases was not envisioned in 1789 when the Act was passed. Another question is whether the statute provides only a basis for jurisdiction, or additionally includes a basis for liability?

8. *Doe v. Unocal* established the possibility for corporation liability for participation in human rights abuses abroad. *Doe* was a class action under the ATCA, RICO, and federal question jurisdiction brought by Burmese nationals. 963 F.Supp. 880 (C.D. Cal. 1997)(motion to dismiss); 110 F.Supp. 2d 1294 (C.D. Cal. 2000)(summary judgment). The plaintiffs claimed that Unocal paid the Burma military junta to provide security and labor for the construction of a pipeline in Burma, knowing that the workers may have been forced labor. The federal district court granted summary judgment to Unocal because there was no establishment that Unocal attempted to employ forced or slave labor. The federal circuit court reversed that determination, finding sufficient allegations for a ATCA claim, and that an issue of fact existed regarding Unocal's aiding and abetting Myanmar's military in the use of forced labor, murder and rape. 395 F.3d 932 (9th Cir. 2002)(rehearing ordered in 2003).

9. What source of international law seemed to be the most convincing to the courts?

10. There is an intersection of the ATCA with the Foreign Sovereign Immunities Act (FSIA), the subject of Chapter Eight, and also with head-of-state immunity. Human rights cases often involve challenges to foreign governments and their officials. Invariably a defense of sovereign and/or head-of-state immunity is raised. An important point to carry to the discussions of Chapter Eight is that the FSIA is the exclusive basis of subject matter jurisdiction over foreign states. In 1996, the FSIA was amended to add § 1605(a)(7) that denies immunity to foreign states for personal injury caused by torture, extra-judicial killing, aircraft sabotage, hostage taking if the acts are engaged in by an official of the state acting within the scope of employment. But the claimant or victim must be a U.S. national, thus avoiding increasing the United States as a forum of choice for foreigners. The foreign state in question also has to have been designated by the United States as a state sponsor of terrorism. Is it appropriate to tamper with the FSIA to remove immunity from states that sponsor terrorism? The FSIA has been subject to amendments in 1996, 1998 and 2000.

11. The 1994 Torture Victim Protection Act (TVPA 28 U.S.C.A. § 1350) addressed a limitation of the ATCA. The ATCA allowed only claims by aliens. The TVPA allows claims to be brought by both aliens and citizens against some defined defendants and where there is personal jurisdiction. There are thus three jurisdictional bases for actions against foreign persons that have some human rights scope. But a money judgment in a U.S. court that cannot be satisfied may have nominal value in achieving the broader goal of reducing human rights violations. But not all such judgments remain unsatisfied. When the judgment of $49.9 million compensatory and $137.7 million punitive was rendered against Cuba for shooting down two civilian aircraft off the Cuban coast remained uncollected despite attempts by the plaintiffs to execute on debts owed Cuba by U.S. based communications companies (mainly for telephone services), *Alejandre v. Republic of Cuba,* 42 F.Supp. 2d 1317 (S.D.Fla. 1999); *Alejandre v. Telefonica Larga Distancia de Puerto Rico,* 183 F.3d 1277 (11th Cir. 1999), Congress enacted legislation offering some compensation to the Cuban claimants and several others, including the recipients of $247.5 million in damages against Iran, *Flatow v. Islamic Republic of Iran,* 999 F.Supp. 1 (D.D.C. 1998), from blocked assets. Was it appropriate to remove these blocked funds from the President's arsenal of negotiating factors for ultimate reestablishment of relations with Cuba? What about other claimants who filed claims against Cuba in the 1960s under the Foreign Claims Commission's procedures, and have long expected to share in the blocked assets? Why should the families of the downed pilots have priority? Does this all reflect badly upon the *Filártiga* decision and its aftermath?

12. A further criticism of the TVPA is its retroactive application. See *Alvarez-Machain v. United States,* 107 F.3d 696 (9th Cir. 1996), *cert. denied,* 522 U.S. 814, 118 S.Ct. 60, 139 L.Ed.2d 23 (1997). There is a ten year statute of limitations in the TVPA that has been ruled subject to "equitable" tolling. See *Hilao v. Estate of Marcos,* 103 F.3d 767 (9th Cir. 1996).

13.　Do the plaintiffs in our hypothetical have a valid cause of action under the ATCA? Who would be the defendant(s)? What part of the ATCA is most likely to create a problem for the plaintiffs?

PROBLEM 4.3　DEFENDANT MOVES TO DISMISS FOR *FORUM NON CONVENIENS*

SECTION I.　THE SETTING

The defendants' lawyers in each of the suits initiated in the United States are considering preparing motions to dismiss the actions under the doctrine of *forum non conveniens*. They must give thought to two areas. First, as a matter of strategy should they try to dismiss the suits under *forum non conveniens?* Second, if they decide to submit such motions, what will they have to establish to succeed? If a *forum non conveniens* motion is submitted, the plaintiffs' lawyers will have to think of arguments to keep the matter before the U.S. forum. You may represent the defendants in considering both whether or not to file such a motion, and if you decide to file the motion, what you must establish to succeed. Or you may represent the plaintiffs and prepare to challenge the motion, arguing that the United States is the better forum. As noted in the facts in Problem 4.1, among the plaintiffs in the various suits in the United States are citizens and residents of the United States, Mexico, and several European countries.

SECTION II.　FOCUS OF CONSIDERATION

Forum non conveniens provides a method for removing the case from its present location, where there is both subject matter and personal jurisdiction to what is, for various reasons, a "better", or more "appropriate", or more "convenient" forum.[1] It provides a check on what might be considered forum shopping by plaintiffs' attorneys, applicable usually when plaintiffs from foreign nations bring suit in the United States. It is a doctrine now well established in the United States, evolving from somewhat difficult to trace roots[2] going back to some Scottish cases.[3] The theory was adopted as part of both English and

---

1.　The jurisdiction issue, especially personal jurisdiction, may not have yet been decided. See #22 in the Questions and Comments at the end of Part A.

2.　*American Dredging Co. v. Miller,* 510 U.S. 443, 114 S.Ct. 981, 127 L.Ed.2d 285 (1994) ("origins of the doctrine in Anglo–American law are murky").

3.　See, e.g., Alexander Reus, *Judicial Discretion: A Comparative View of the Doctrine of Forum Non Conveniens in the United States, the United Kingdom, and Germany,* 16 Loy. L.A. Int'l & Comp. L.J. 455 (1994); Robert Braucher, *The Inconvenient Federal Forum,* 60 Harv.L.Rev. 908 (1947);

Edward L. Barrett, Jr., *The Doctrine of Forum Non Conveniens,* 35 Cal. L. Rev. 380, 387 n.35 (1947); Paxton Blair, *The Doctrine of Forum Non Conveniens in Anglo–American Law,* 29 Colum. L. Rev 1 (1929) (Blair, a New York practitioner, urged the use of *forum non conveniens* to help clear crowded court dockets). The Scottish origins may date to the 17th century, although the term *forum non conveniens* does not appear until the 19th century. See *Vernor v. Elvies,* 6 Dict. of Dec. 4788 (1610) (Scot.); *Col. Brog's Heir v . . . .* 6 Dict. of Dec. 4816 (1639) (Scot.). England adopted

American law in the last half of the 19th and first half of the 20th century.[4] It is not a well developed theory in most nations, especially on the continent. It was not known in Roman law, nor in the *jus commune* that developed in Europe in the first millennium.[5]

In Part A the *forum non conveniens* jurisprudence in the United States is considered. Part B shifts to the UK and EU positions, which provide a very interesting contrast to the U.S. decisions, at least partly because of civil law tradition notions of jurisdiction. Part C concludes with a challenge to *forum non conveniens* from Latin America.

SECTION III.   READINGS, QUESTIONS AND COMMENTS

PART A.   FORUM NON CONVENIENS IN UNITED STATES COURTS

Forum non conveniens' comparatively rapid development and current prominence in the United States is attributable to the attractiveness of U.S. courts as a forum for civil litigation. Because so many cases based on alleged torts occurring abroad are brought in the United States due to the relatively efficient and impartial legal system, abundance of competent plaintiffs' counsel, and the possibility of high damage awards and contingent fees, almost any suit initiated by a *foreign* plaintiff in the United States is immediately suspect. No longer is there a tendency to defer to a foreign plaintiff's choice of a U.S. forum.

If the defendants choose not to move to dismiss under *forum non conveniens*, the matter will proceed in the U.S. court. The defendants may believe they retain better control over the proceeding than when it is dismissed under *forum non conveniens*. Dismissal means the case will or may be commenced in the more convenient foreign forum.[6] Local counsel in the foreign nation will have to be selected and probably supervised by U.S. counsel for the defendant and, where applicable, the defendant's in-house corporate counsel. More than likely the foreign court will apply its own domestic law rather than U.S. law. As law firms merge and form associations with foreign firms, some of these problems diminish. If the U.S. lawyers for the defendants have a foreign "branch," they may be more comfortable with turning the matter over to the foreign lawyers.

If the matter remains in a U.S. court, the defendant's lawyers may diminish their concern about a large judgment including punitive damages *if* the court rules that the foreign law is applicable. The court may

the theory in the last century. See *Logan v. Bank of Scotland* [1906] 1 K.B. 141.

4. *The Abidin Daver* [1984] A.C. 398 (U.K.); *Gulf Oil Corp. v. Gilbert*, 330 U.S. 501, 67 S.Ct. 839, 91 L.Ed. 1055 (1947). Some early 19th century cases dismissed suits in U.S. courts brought by foreign plaintiffs, usually admiralty actions dismissed for reasons of comity or judicial abstention. Late 19th century decisions in some New York courts rejected tort claims by foreigners asserted in New York courts, but without using the name *forum non conveniens*.

5. Joseph Henry Beale, *The Jurisdiction of Courts Over Foreigners*, 26 Harv. L. Rev. 193, 293 (1913).

6. The *Piper* case, included in the Readings, was never initiated in Scotland after dismissal in the United States.

make that decision as part of the *forum non conveniens* consideration. The laws of most other nations do not provide for punitive damages, and usually not for pain and suffering. But there may be new concepts of damages in the applicable foreign nation, such as moral damages, that might allow a large award.

No *forum non conveniens* motion should be made until the defendants have researched two questions. The first is "what law will apply?" and the second is "if the applicable law is a foreign law will that law be more favorable to the defendants than U.S. law?" It would be unwise to move to dismiss on *forum non conveniens* grounds only to have the plaintiffs initiate the case in a nation where the defendant has less chance of winning, and where potential damages are greater. But if that were the case, why would the plaintiff have first chosen to initiate the suit in the United States? Because a U.S. court may be influenced in its *forum non conveniens* decision on what law will apply if the matter remains in the United States, the defendants should want to learn something about the foreign law. For example, if the case involves antitrust issues, does the foreign law provide for treble damages?[7]

The law of *forum non conveniens* is evolving as a matter of judicial discretion rather than a rule. It differs among states within the United States. Some states have been reluctant to adopt a *forum non conveniens* rule, because special interests (especially personal injury lawyers) want the litigation and the contingent fees its generates. Texas and Florida, however, within the past dozen years have changed previously restrictive views to adopt a *forum non conveniens* rule. The Texas legislature adopted the doctrine with the support of large corporations with facilities in Texas.[8] The Florida Supreme Court adopted the doctrine overruling the earlier restrictive view.[9] The federal position was first stated in *Gulf Oil Corp. v. Gilbert*,[10] a case without international dimensions. But two subsequent cases, *Piper* and *Bhopal*, both in the readings, involve accidents occurring abroad and cases initiated in the United States by foreign plaintiffs.

DAVID EPSTEIN, JEFFREY L. SNYDER & CHARLES S. BALDWIN, IV, INTERNATIONAL LITIGATION*
§ 5–07 (3d ed. 1998, Supp. 2002).

It is the defendant's responsibility to assert a motion to dismiss on forum non conveniens grounds within a reasonable time after the facts

---

7. Most civil law nations reject treble damages, but some, such as Panama, include treble damages in their antitrust laws.

8. Texas Civil Practice and Remedies Code § 71.051 (1993). The adoption followed adverse reaction by corporations with some presence in Texas to *Dow Chemical Co. v. Castro Alfaro*, 786 S.W.2d 674 (Tex. 1990), *cert. denied*, 498 U.S. 1024, 111 S.Ct. 671, 112 L.Ed.2d 663 (1991).

9. *Kinney System, Inc. v. Continental Insurance Co.*, 674 So.2d 86 (Fla. 1996), adopting the federal standard and overruling *Houston v. Caldwell*, 359 So.2d 858 (Fla. 1978).

10. 330 U.S. 501, 67 S.Ct. 839, 91 L.Ed. 1055 (1947).

* Reprinted with the permission of Transnational Publishers, Inc.

or circumstances which serve as the basis for a motion have developed and have become known or reasonably knowable to defendant. The court must give deference to plaintiff's choice of forum, so the moving defendant must establish that private and public interests weigh heavily on the side of holding trial in foreign forum.

The analysis proceeds in two steps. First, a defendant must demonstrate the existence of an adequate alternative forum. If that threshold requirement is met, the court must then weigh the relevant private factors of convenience and judicial efficiency and public factors of community interest as well as burden, and the conflict of laws issues, as set forth in Gilbert. However, the foreign plaintiff's choice of forum will be given less deference than the local plaintiff's choice of forum, as it may not be reasonable to assume that the plaintiff's choice was convenient.

The trial court has broad discretion in deciding a motion to dismiss based on forum non conveniens. On appeal, trial court decisions can be reversed only if discretion was abused.

DOUGLAS W. DUNHAM & ERIC F. GLADBACH, FORUM NON CONVENIENS AND FOREIGN PLAINTIFFS IN THE 1990s

24 Brooklyn J. Int'l L. 665 (1999)*

Courts applying the doctrine of forum non conveniens in the 1990s have almost invariably begun their analyses by looking to the United States Supreme Court's seminal opinions that have set forth the basic criteria for deciding whether to grant a motion to dismiss based on the grounds of forum non conveniens. In these opinions, the Court has made clear that the doctrine of forum non conveniens is designed to be flexible and adaptive, which necessitates determinations on an ad hoc and fact-intensive basis. Indeed, several years ago, the Supreme Court explained that forum non conveniens makes "uniformity and predictability of outcome almost impossible" due to the "discretionary nature of the doctrine, combined with the multifariousness of the factors relevant to its application."[9]

Koster v. Lumbermens Mutual Casualty Co.[10] involved a derivative action brought by a policyholder living in New York against a company that was incorporated in Illinois and had its principal place of business in Illinois. The Supreme Court affirmed the lower courts' dismissal of the action on the grounds that New York was an inconvenient forum because Illinois was the center of the dispute. The Supreme Court emphasized that "the ultimate inquiry is where trial will best serve the convenience of the parties and the ends of justice." The Court made clear that, although a plaintiff's choice of a home forum in bringing suit

---

* Reprinted with the permission of the Brooklyn Journal of International Law.

9. American Dredging Co. v. Miller, 510 U.S. 443, 455 (1994).

10. 330 U.S. 518 (1947).

is generally entitled to great deference, the presumption in favor of respecting such a choice may be overcome by a "clear showing" that either "(1) establish(es) such oppressiveness and vexation to a defendant as to be out of all proportion to plaintiff's convenience, which may be shown to be slight or nonexistent, or (2) make(s) trial in the chosen forum inappropriate because of considerations affecting the court's own administrative and legal problems."

The Supreme Court provided additional guidance in the companion case of *Gulf Oil Corp. v. Gilbert.*[16] In that action, the Court affirmed the lower court's dismissal of a tort action that was filed in New York when all of the relevant events took place in Virginia, which was also where the plaintiff resided, and where the defendant conducted business. In so ruling, the Court reiterated its general belief that "unless the balance is strongly in favor of the defendant, the plaintiff's choice of forum should rarely be disturbed." Nonetheless, the Court stressed the fundamental principle underlying forum non conveniens that a trial court may, in its discretion, refuse to exercise jurisdiction over a case, even though jurisdiction is authorized by a venue statute.

Gulf Oil divided the relevant factors to be considered in a forum non conveniens inquiry into matters involving either private interests or the public interest. Matters involving private interests included "the relative ease of access to sources of proof; availability of compulsory process for attendance of unwilling, and the cost of obtaining attendance of willing, witnesses; possibility of view of premises, if view would be appropriate to the action; and all other practical problems that make trial of a case easy, expeditious and inexpensive." As to public interest factors, the Court identified a number of court-related considerations. These considerations included administrative difficulties based on a congested court docket, the burdens of imposing jury duty on members of a community that has no relation to the litigation, the interest in having "localized controversies decided at home," and the desirability of having a diversity case tried in the same forum as the state law to be applied.

The Court's opinions in both *Koster* and *Gulf Oil* recognize the general principle that the plaintiff's choice of forum should rarely be disturbed. However, this presumption in favor of the plaintiff's choice may be overcome by a showing that the relevant private and public interest factors clearly outweigh the deference to be afforded to plaintiff's selected forum. * * *

PIPER AIRCRAFT CO. v. REYNO

Supreme Court of the United States, 1981.
454 U.S. 235, 102 S.Ct. 252, 70 L.Ed.2d 419.

[A small airplane crashed in the highlands of Scotland. The pilot was new to commercial flying and was probably flying too low. He was killed, along with the five passengers. All who died were Scottish nationals and

---

16.   330 U.S. 501 (1947).

residents. The plane was registered in Great Britain. The company that owned the plane and the air taxi company from which the decedents chartered the plane were Scottish. But there were links to the United States. The plane was made by the Piper Aircraft Company at its plant in Pennsylvania. The propellers were made by Hartzell Propeller, Inc., in Ohio. Suit was initiated in state court in California by Reyno, secretary to the plaintiffs' attorney. Reyno was appointed by a California probate court as administratrix of the estates of the deceased passengers. The case was first transferred to federal court in California and then transferred to Pennsylvania under 28 U.S.C. § 1404(a) because Hartzell Propeller was not subject to personal jurisdiction in California. Hartzell was subject to Pennsylvania jurisdiction. The defendants next filed a motion to dismiss for *forum non conveniens* reasons. The district court dismissed the case, finding the connections with Scotland to be "overwhelming" and giving little weight to the plaintiffs' choice.[11] The court gave some weight to public interest factors such as the U.S. court's unfamiliarity with Scottish law, and the likelihood of high expenses in bringing the action in the United States. The case was appealed to the Third Circuit, which reversed.[12] The court thought the district court abused its discretion in applying *Gulf Oil,* especially by the little weight given to the plaintiffs' choice. The court also found it inappropriate to dismiss such a motion whenever the law of the foreign forum was less favorable to the plaintiff. The court disagreed with the suggested application of Scottish law, finding Pennsylvania and Ohio law to reduce public factors in favor of removal because of the difficulty in applying Scottish law. The Supreme Court granted certiorari.]

Justice Marshall delivered the opinion of the Court.

. . . . A preliminary report . . . suggested that mechanical failure in the plane or the propeller was responsible. At Hartzell's request, this report was reviewed. * * *. The Review Board found no evidence of defective equipment and indicated that pilot error may have contributed to the accident. The pilot, who had obtained his commercial pilot's license only three months earlier, was flying over high ground at an altitude considerably lower than the minimum height required by his company's operations manual.

* * * Reyno candidly admits that the action against Piper and Hartzell was filed in the United States because its laws regarding liability, capacity to sue, and damages are more favorable to her position than are those of Scotland. Scottish law does not recognize strict liability in tort. Moreover, it permits wrongful-death actions only when brought by a decedent's relatives. The relatives may sue only for "loss of support and society."

* * *

11. Reyno v. Piper Aircraft Co., 479 F. Supp. 727 (M.D. Pa. 1979).

12. 630 F.2d 149 (3d Cir. 1980).

The Court of Appeals erred in holding that plaintiffs may defeat a motion to dismiss on the ground of *forum non conveniens* merely by showing that the substantive law that would be applied in the alternative forum is less favorable to the plaintiffs than that of the present forum. The possibility of a change in substantive law should ordinarily not be given conclusive or even substantial weight in the *forum non conveniens* inquiry.

* * * [B]y holding that the central focus of the *forum non conveniens* inquiry is convenience, *Gilbert* implicitly recognized that dismissal may not be barred solely because of the possibility of an unfavorable change in law. Under *Gilbert*, dismissal will ordinarily be appropriate where trial in the plaintiff's chosen forum imposes a heavy burden on the defendant or the court, and where the plaintiff is unable to offer any specific reasons of convenience supporting his choice. If substantial weight were given to the possibility of an unfavorable change in law, however, dismissal might be barred even where trial in the chosen forum was plainly inconvenient.

The Court of Appeals' decision is inconsistent with this Court's earlier *forum non conveniens* decisions in another respect. Those decisions have repeatedly emphasized the need to retain flexibility. In *Gilbert*, the Court refused to identify specific circumstances "which will justify or require either grant or denial of remedy." Similarly, in *Koster*, the Court rejected the contention that where a trial would involve inquiry into the internal affairs of a foreign corporation, dismissal was always appropriate. "That is one, but only one, factor which may show convenience." * * * If central emphasis were placed on any one factor, the *forum non conveniens* doctrine would lose much of the very flexibility that makes it so valuable.

In fact, if conclusive or substantial weight were given to the possibility of a change in law, the *forum non conveniens* doctrine would become virtually useless. Jurisdiction and venue requirements are often easily satisfied. As a result, many plaintiffs are able to choose from among several forums. Ordinarily, these plaintiffs will select that forum whose choice-of-law rules are most advantageous. Thus, if the possibility of an unfavorable change in substantive law is given substantial weight in the *forum non conveniens* inquiry, dismissal would rarely be proper. * * *

The Court of Appeals' approach is not only inconsistent with the purpose of the *forum non conveniens* doctrine, but also poses substantial practical problems. If the possibility of a change in law were given substantial weight, deciding motions to dismiss on the ground of *forum non conveniens* would become quite difficult. Choice-of-law analysis would become extremely important, and the courts would frequently be required to interpret the law of foreign jurisdictions. First, the trial court would have to determine what law would apply if the case were tried in the chosen forum, and what law would apply if the case were tried in the alternative forum. It would then have to compare the rights, remedies, and procedures available under the law that would be applied in each forum. Dismissal would be appropriate only if the court concluded that the law applied by the alternative forum is as favorable to the plaintiff as that of the chosen forum. The doctrine of *forum non conveniens*, however, is designed in part to help courts avoid conducting complex exercises in comparative law. As we stated in *Gilbert*, the public interest factors point towards dismissal where the court would be required to "untangle problems in conflict of laws, and in law foreign to itself."

Upholding the decision of the Court of Appeals would result in other practical problems. At least where the foreign plaintiff named an American manufacturer as defendant,[17] a court could not dismiss the case on grounds of *forum non conveniens* where dismissal might lead to an unfavorable change in law. The American courts, which are already extremely attractive to foreign plaintiffs, would become even more attractive. The flow of litigation into the United States would increase and further congest already crowded courts. * * *

We do not hold that the possibility of an unfavorable change in law should *never* be a relevant consideration in a *forum non conveniens* inquiry. Of course, if the remedy provided by the alternative forum is so clearly inadequate or unsatisfactory that it is no remedy at all, the unfavorable change in law may be given substantial weight; the district court may conclude that dismissal would not be in the interests of justice.[22] In these cases, however, the remedies that would be provided by the Scottish courts do not fall within this category. Although the relatives of the decedents may not be able to rely on a strict liability theory, and although their potential damages award may be smaller, there is no danger that they will be deprived of any remedy or treated unfairly.

III

The Court of Appeals also erred in rejecting the District Court's *Gilbert* analysis. The Court of Appeals stated that more weight should have been given to the plaintiff's choice of forum, and criticized the District Court's analysis of the private and public interests. However, the District Court's decision regarding the deference due plaintiff's choice of forum was appropriate. Furthermore, we do not believe that

17. In fact, the defendant might not even have to be American. A foreign plaintiff seeking damages for an accident that occurred abroad might be able to obtain service of process on a foreign defendant who does business in the United States. Under the Court of Appeals' holding, dismissal would be barred if the law in the alternative forum were less favorable to the plaintiff—even though there is absolutely no nexus between the subject matter of the litigation and the United States

22. At the outset of any *forum non conveniens* inquiry, the court must determine whether there exists an alternative forum. Ordinarily, this requirement will be satisfied when the defendant is "amenable to process" in the other jurisdiction. In rare circumstances, however, where the remedy offered by the other forum is clearly unsatisfactory, the other forum may not be an adequate alternative, and the initial requirement may not be satisfied. Thus, for example, dismissal would not be appropriate where the alternative forum does not permit litigation of the subject matter of the dispute.

the District Court abused its discretion in weighing the private and public interests.

The District Court acknowledged that there is ordinarily a strong presumption in favor of the plaintiff's choice of forum, which may be overcome only when the private and public interest factors clearly point towards trial in the alternative forum. It held, however, that the presumption applies with less force when the plaintiff or real parties in interest are foreign.

The District Court's distinction between resident or citizen plaintiffs and foreign plaintiffs is fully justified. In *Koster*, the Court indicated that a plaintiff's choice of forum is entitled to greater deference when the plaintiff has chosen the home forum. When the home forum has been chosen, it is reasonable to assume that this choice is convenient. When the plaintiff is foreign, however, this assumption is much less reasonable. Because the central purpose of any *forum non conveniens* inquiry is to ensure that the trial is convenient, a foreign plaintiff's choice deserves less deference.

The *forum non conveniens* determination is committed to the sound discretion of the trial court. It may be reversed only when there has been a clear abuse of discretion; where the court has considered all relevant public and private interest factors, and where its balancing of these factors is reasonable, its decision deserves substantial deference. Here, the Court of Appeals expressly acknowledged that the standard of review was one of abuse of discretion. In examining the District Court's analysis of the public and private interests, however, the Court of Appeals seems to have lost sight of this rule, and substituted its own judgment for that of the District Court.

In analyzing the private interest factors, the District Court stated that the connections with Scotland are "overwhelming." This characterization may be somewhat exaggerated. Particularly with respect to the question of relative ease of access to sources of proof, the private interests point in both directions. As respondent emphasizes, records concerning the design, manufacture, and testing of the propeller and plane are located in the United States. She would have greater access to sources of proof relevant to her strict liability and negligence theories if trial were held here. However, the District Court did not act unreasonably in concluding that fewer evidentiary problems would be posed if the trial were held in Scotland. A large proportion of the relevant evidence is located in Great Britain.

The Court of Appeals found that the problems of proof could not be given any weight because Piper and Hartzell failed to describe with specificity the evidence they would not be able to obtain if trial were held in the United States. It suggested that defendants seeking *forum non conveniens* dismissal must submit affidavits identifying the witnesses they would call and the testimony these witnesses would provide if the trial were held in the alternative forum. Such detail is not necessary. Piper and Hartzell have moved for dismissal precisely because many crucial witnesses are located beyond the reach of compulsory process, and thus are difficult to identify or interview. Requiring extensive investigation would defeat the purpose of their motion. Of course, defendants must provide enough information to enable the District Court to balance the parties' interests. Our examination of the record convinces us that sufficient information was provided here. Both Piper and Hartzell submitted affidavits describing the evidentiary problems they would face if the trial were held in the United States.

The District Court correctly concluded that the problems posed by the inability to implead potential third-party defendants clearly supported holding the trial in Scotland. Joinder of the pilot's estate, Air Navigation, and McDonald is crucial to the presentation of petitioners' defense. If Piper and Hartzell can show that the accident was caused not by a design defect, but rather by the negligence of the pilot, the plane's owners, or the charter company, they will be relieved of all liability. It is true, of course, that if Hartzell and Piper were found liable after a trial in the United States, they could institute an action for indemnity or contribution against these parties in Scotland. It would be far more convenient, however, to resolve all claims in one trial. The Court of Appeals rejected this argument. Forcing petitioners to rely on actions for indemnity or contributions would be "burdensome" but not "unfair." Finding that trial in the plaintiff's chosen forum would be burdensome, however, is sufficient to support dismissal on grounds of *forum non conveniens.*

The District Court's review of the factors relating to the public interest was also reasonable. On the basis of its choice-of-law analysis, it concluded that if the case were tried in the Middle District of Pennsylvania, Pennsylvania law would apply to Piper and Scottish law to Hartzell. It stated that a trial involving two sets of laws would be confusing to the jury. It also noted its own lack of familiarity with Scottish law. Consideration of these problems was clearly appropriate under *Gilbert* ; in that case we explicitly held that the need to apply foreign law pointed towards dismissal. The Court of Appeals found that the District Court's choice-of-law analysis was incorrect, and that American law would apply to both Hartzell and Piper. Thus, lack of familiarity with foreign law would not be a problem. Even if the Court of Appeals' conclusion is correct, however, all other public interest factors favored trial in Scotland.

Scotland has a very strong interest in this litigation. The accident occurred in its airspace. All of the decedents were Scottish. Apart from Piper and Hartzell, all potential plaintiffs and defendants are either Scottish or English. As we stated in *Gilbert*, there is "a local interest in having localized controversies decided at home." Respondent argues that American citizens have an interest in ensuring that American manufacturers are deterred from producing defective products, and that additional deterrence might be obtained if Piper and Hartzell were tried in the United States, where they could be sued on the basis of both negligence and strict liability. However, the incremental deterrence that would be gained if this trial were held in an American court is likely to be insignificant. The American interest in this accident is simply not sufficient to justify the enormous commitment of judicial time and resources that would inevitably be required if the case were to be tried here.

The Court of Appeals erred in holding that the possibility of an unfavorable change in law bars dismissal on the ground of *forum non conveniens*. It also erred in rejecting the District Court's *Gilbert* analysis. The District Court properly decided that the presumption in favor of the respondent's forum choice applied with less than maximum force because the real parties in interest are foreign. It did not act unreasonably in deciding that the private interests pointed towards trial in Scotland. Nor did it act unreasonably in deciding that the public interests favored trial in Scotland. Thus, the judgment of the Court of Appeals is *Reversed*.

IN RE UNION CARBIDE CORPORATION GAS PLANT DISASTER AT BHOPAL, INDIA IN DECEMBER, 1984

United States Court of Appeals, Second Circuit, 1987.
809 F.2d 195.

[Lethal gas was released from a chemical plant operated by Union Carbide India Limited (UCIL). It was majority owned by the Union Carbide Corporation (UCC) in the United States, with minority percentages held by the Indian government and some 23,500 Indian citizens. The gas was blown by winds over parts of the city. More than 2,000 died and more than 200,000 were injured. U.S. plaintiffs attorneys flocked to India with contingent fee contracts in hand. Some 145 class actions were soon filed in the United States, soon consolidated to be heard in the Southern District of New York. Another 6,500 actions were initiated in India against UCIL, the State of Madhya and Municipality of Bhopal, and the government of India. These actions were consolidated in the District Court in Bhopal. The Indian Parliament soon passed the Bhopal Gas Leak Disaster Act, granting the Indian government the exclusive right to represent the victims in litigation in India or elsewhere. The government took over the actions in India and the United States. UCC filed a motion to dismiss for *forum non conveniens*. Federal district court judge Keenan turned to the *Gulf Oil* and *Piper Aircraft* decisions, noting that as foreign plaintiffs they were not entitled to the deference to their choice of forum that would be accorded to U.S. plaintiffs. Judge Keenan reviewed considerable affidavit testimony regarding India's law and legal system, and found that, despite some disadvantages, it provided an "adequate alternative forum." He granted the motion to dismiss, but subject to three conditions:

1. UCC must consent to the jurisdiction of the courts of India and waive defenses based on the statute of limitations;

2.   UCC must agree to satisfy any judgment by an Indian court and upheld on appeal provided the judgment met "minimal requirements of due process" under United States standards; and

3.   UCC must agree to allow discovery under the Federal Rules of Civil Procedure of the United States.

UCC accepted the conditions, but reserving the right and having full intention to appeal. The appeal, the decision of which appears below, began with an unusually long presentation of characteristics of India's legal system, gathered from Judge Keenan's decision. The extract of the case begins with part of those remarks.]

MANSFIELD, CIRCUIT JUDGE:

The Indian judiciary was found by the [district] court to be a developed, independent and progressive one, which has demonstrated its capability of circumventing long delays and backlogs prevalent in the Indian courts' handling of ordinary cases by devising special expediting procedures in extraordinary cases, such as by directing its High Court to hear them on a daily basis, appointing special tribunals to handle them, and assigning daily hearing duties to a single judge. He [Judge Keenan] found that Indian courts have competently dealt with complex technological issues. Since the Bhopal Act provides that the case may be treated speedily, effectively and to the best advantage of the claimants, and since the Union of India represents the claimants, the prosecution of the claims is expected to be adequately staffed by the Attorney General or Solicitor General of India.

The tort law of India, which is derived from common law and British precedent, was found to be suitable for resolution of legal issues arising in cases involving highly complex technology. Moreover, Indian courts would be in a superior position to construe and apply applicable Indian laws and standards than would courts of the United States. * * * The absence in India of a class action procedure comparable to that in federal courts here was found not to deprive the plaintiffs of a remedy, in view of existing Indian legal authorization for "representative" suits, * * * which would permit an Indian court to create representative classes. Judge Keenan further found that the absence of juries and contingent fee arrangements in India would not deprive the claimants of an adequate remedy.

In two areas bearing upon the adequacy of the Indian forum the district court decided to impose somewhat unusual conditions on the transfer of the American cases to India. One condition dealt with pre-trial discovery. Indian courts, following the British pattern, permit parties to have pre-trial discovery of each other through written interrogatories, liberal inspection of documents and requests for admissions. Non-party witnesses can be interviewed and summoned to appear at trial or to produce documents. * * * Witnesses unable to appear at trial are sometimes permitted to give evidence by means of affidavits. * * * Discovery in India, however, as in Britain, is limited to evidence that may be admitted at trial. Litigants are not permitted to engage in wide-ranging discovery, which allows inquiry into any unprivileged matter that could reasonably lead to the discovery of admissible evidence.

Judge Keenan, concluding that the Indian system might limit the victims' access to sources of proof, directed that dismissal of the actions on grounds of *forum non conveniens* must be conditioned on UCC's consent to discovery of it in accordance with the Federal Rules of Civil Procedure after the cases were transferred to India. He added, "While the Court feels that it would be fair to bind the plaintiffs to American discovery rules, too, it has no authority to do so."

Another condition imposed by the district court upon dismissal on grounds of *forum non conveniens* dealt with the enforceability in the United States of any judgment rendered by an Indian court in the cases. Judge Keenan, expressing the view that an Indian judgment might possibly not be enforceable in the United States, provided in his order that UCC must "agree to satisfy any judgment rendered by an Indian court, and if applicable, upheld by an appellate court in that country, where such judgment and affirmance comport with the minimal requirements of due process."

As the district court found, the record shows that the private interests of the respective parties weigh heavily in favor of dismissal on grounds of *forum non conveniens*. The many witnesses and sources of proof are almost entirely located in India, where the accident occurred, and could not be compelled to appear for trial in the United States. The Bhopal plant at the time of the accident was operated by some 193 Indian nationals, including the managers of seven operating units employed by the Agricultural Products Division of UCIL, who reported to Indian Works Managers in Bhopal. The plant was maintained by seven functional departments employing over 200 more Indian nationals. UCIL kept at the plant daily, weekly and monthly records of plant operations and records of maintenance as well as records of the plant's Quality Control, Purchasing and Stores branches, all operated by Indian employees. The great majority of documents bearing on the design, safety, start-up and operation of the plant, as well as the safety training of the plant's employees, is located in India. Proof to be offered at trial would be derived from interviews of these witnesses in India and study of the records located there to determine whether the accident was caused by negligence on the part of the management or employees in the operation of the plant, by fault in its design, or by sabotage. In short, India has greater ease of access to the proof than does the United States.

The plaintiffs seek to prove that the accident was caused by negligence on the part of UCC in originally contributing to the design of the plant and its provision for storage of excessive amounts of the gas at the plant. As Judge Keenan found, however, UCC's participation was limited and its involvement in plant operations terminated long before the accident. Under 1973 agreements negotiated at arm's-length with UCIL, UCC did provide a summary "process design package" for construction of the plant and the services of some of its technicians to monitor the progress of UCIL in detailing the design and erecting the plant. However, the UOI controlled the terms of the agreements and precluded UCC from exercising any authority to "detail design, erect and commission the plant," which was done independently over the period from 1972 to 1980 by UCIL process design engineers who supervised, among many others, some 55 to 60 Indian engineers employed by the Bombay engineering firm of Humphreys and Glasgow. The preliminary process design information furnished by UCC could not have been used to construct the plant. Construction required the detailed process design and engineering data prepared by hundreds of Indian engineers, process designers and sub-contractors. During the ten years spent constructing the plant, its design and configuration underwent many changes.

The vital parts of the Bhopal plant, including its storage tank, monitoring instrumentation, and vent gas scrubber, were manufactured by Indians in India. Although some 40 UCIL employees were given some safety training at UCC's plant in West Virginia, they represented a small fraction of the Bhopal plant's employees. The vast majority of plant employees were selected and trained by UCIL in Bhopal. The manual for start-up of the Bhopal plant was prepared by Indians employed by UCIL.

In short, the plant has been constructed and managed by Indians in India. No Americans were employed at the plant at the time of the accident. In the five years from 1980 to 1984, although more than 1,000 Indians were employed at the plant, only one American was employed there and he left in 1982. No Americans visited the plant for more than one year prior to the accident, and during the 5–year period before the accident the communications between the plant and the United States were almost non-existent.

The vast majority of material witnesses and documentary proof bearing on causation of and liability for the accident is located in India, not the United States, and would be more accessible to an Indian court than to a U.S. court. The records are almost entirely in Hindi or other Indian languages, understandable to an Indian court without translation. The witnesses for the most part do not speak English but Indian languages understood by an Indian court but not by an American court. These witnesses could be required to appear in an Indian court but not in a court of the United States. Although witnesses in the United States could not be subpoenaed to appear in India, they are comparatively few in number and most are employed by UCC which, as a party, would produce them in India, with lower overall transportation costs than if the parties were to attempt to bring hundreds of Indian witnesses to the United States. Lastly, Judge Keenan properly concluded that an Indian court would be in a better position to direct and supervise a viewing of the Bhopal plant, which was sealed after the accident. * * *

India's interest is increased by the fact that it has for years treated UCIL as an Indian national, subjecting it to intensive regulations and governmental supervision of the construction, development and operation of the Bhopal plant, its emissions, water and air pollution, and safety precautions. Numerous Indian government officials have regularly conducted on-site inspections of the plant and approved its machinery and equipment, including its facilities for storage of the lethal methyl isocyanate gas that escaped and caused the disaster giving rise to the claims. Thus India has considered the plant to be an Indian one and the disaster to be an Indian problem. It therefore has a deep interest in ensuring compliance with its safety standards. Moreover, plaintiffs have conceded that in view of India's strong interest and its greater contacts with the plant, its operations, its employees, and the victims of the accident, the law of India, as the place where the tort occurred, will undoubtedly govern. In contrast, the American interests are relatively minor. Indeed, a long trial of the 145 cases here would unduly burden an already overburdened court, involving both jury hardship and heavy expense. It would face the court with numerous practical difficulties, including the almost impossible task of attempting to understand extensive relevant Indian regulations published in a foreign language and the slow process of receiving testimony of scores of witnesses through interpreters.

Having made the foregoing findings, Judge Keenan dismissed the actions against UCC on grounds of *forum non conveniens* upon the conditions indicated above, after obtaining UCC's consent to those conditions subject to its right to appeal the order. * * * Having reviewed Judge Keenan's detailed decision, in which he thoroughly considered the comparative adequacy of the forums and the public and private interests involved, we are satisfied that there was no abuse of discretion in his granting dismissal of the action. On the contrary, it might reasonably be concluded that it would have been an abuse of discretion to deny a *forum non conveniens* dismissal.

Plaintiffs' principal contentions in favor of retention of the cases by the district court are that deference to the plaintiffs' choice of forum has been inadequate, that the Indian courts are insufficiently equipped for the task, that UCC has its principal place of business here, that the most probative evidence regarding negligence and causation is to be found here, that federal courts are much better equipped through experience and procedures to handle such complex actions efficiently than are Indian courts, and that a transfer of the cases to India will jeopardize a $350 million settlement being negotiated by plaintiffs' counsel. All of these arguments, however, must be rejected.

Little or no deference can be paid to the plaintiffs' choice of a United States forum when all but a few of the 200,000 plaintiffs are Indian citizens located in India who, according to the UOI, have revoked the authorizations of American counsel to represent them here and have substituted the UOI, which now prefers Indian courts. The finding of our district court, after exhaustive analysis of the evidence, that the Indian courts provide a reasonably adequate alternative forum cannot be labeled clearly erroneous or an abuse of discretion.

The emphasis placed by plaintiffs on UCC's having its domicile here, where personal jurisdiction over it exists, is robbed of significance by its consent to Indian jurisdiction. Plaintiffs' contention that the most crucial and probative evidence is located in the United States is simply not in accord with the record or the district court's findings. * * *

The conditions imposed by the district court upon its *forum non conveniens* dismissal stand on a different footing. * * * The first condition, that UCC consent to the Indian court's personal jurisdiction over it and waive the statute of limitations as a defense, are not unusual and have been imposed in numerous cases where the foreign court would not provide an adequate alternative in the absence of such a condition. The remaining two conditions, however, pose problems. In requiring that UCC consent to enforceability of an Indian judgment against it, the district court proceeded at least in part on the erroneous assumption that, absent such a requirement, the plaintiffs, if they should succeed in obtaining an Indian judgment against UCC, might not be able to enforce it against UCC in the United States. The law, however, is to the contrary. Under New York law, which governs actions brought in New York to enforce foreign judgments, a foreign-country judgment that is final, conclusive and enforceable where rendered must be recognized and will be enforced as "conclusive between the parties to the extent that it grants or denies recovery of a sum of money" except that it is not deemed to be conclusive if:

> 1. the judgment was rendered under a system which does not provide impartial tribunals or procedures compatible with the requirements of due process of law;

> 2. the foreign court did not have personal jurisdiction over the defendant.

Although [New York law] further provides that under certain specified conditions a foreign country judgment need not be recognized, none of these conditions would apply to the present cases except for the possibility of failure to provide UCC with sufficient notice of proceedings or the existence of fraud in obtaining the judgment, which do not presently exist but conceivably could occur in the future.

UCC contends that Indian courts, while providing an adequate alternative forum, do not observe due process standards that would be required as a matter of course in this country. As evidence of this apprehension it points to the haste with which the Indian court in Bhopal issued a temporary order freezing its assets throughout the world and the possibility of serious prejudice to it if the UOI is permitted to have the double and conflicting status of both plaintiff and co-defendant in the Indian court proceedings. It argues that we should protect it against such denial of due process by authorizing Judge Keenan to retain the authority, after *forum non conveniens* dismissal of the cases here, to monitor the Indian court proceedings and be available on call to rectify in some undefined way any abuses of UCC's right to due process as they might occur in India. UCC's proposed remedy is not only impractical but evidences an abysmal ignorance of basic jurisdictional principles, so much so that it borders on the frivolous. The district court's jurisdiction is limited to proceedings before it in this country. Once it dismisses those proceedings on grounds of *forum non conveniens* it ceases to have any further jurisdiction over the matter unless and until a proceeding may some day be brought to enforce here a final and conclusive Indian money judgment. Nor could we, even if we attempted to retain some sort of supervisory jurisdiction, impose our due process requirements upon Indian courts, which are governed by their laws, not ours. The concept of shared jurisdictions is both illusory and unrealistic. The parties cannot simultaneously submit to both jurisdictions the resolution of the pre-trial and trial issues when there is only one consolidated case pending in one court. Any denial by the Indian courts of due process can be raised by UCC as a defense to the plaintiffs' later attempt to enforce a resulting judgment against UCC in this country.

We are concerned, however, that as it is written the district court's requirement that UCC consent to the enforcement of a final Indian judgment, which was imposed on the erroneous assumption that such a judgment might not otherwise be enforceable in the United States, may create misunderstandings and problems of construction. Although the order's provision that the judgment "comport with the *minimal* requirements of due process" (emphasis supplied) probably is intended to refer to "due process" as used in the New York Foreign Country Money Judgments Law and others like it, there is the risk that it may also be interpreted as providing for a lesser standard than we would otherwise require. Since the court's condition with respect to enforceability of any final Indian judgment is predicated on an erroneous legal assumption and its "due process" language is ambiguous, and since the district court's purpose is fully served by New York's statute providing for recognition of foreign-country money judgments, it was error to impose this condition upon the parties.

We also believe that the district court erred in requiring UCC to consent (which UCC did under protest and subject to its right of appeal) to broad discovery of it by the plaintiffs under the Federal Rules of Civil Procedure when UCC is confined to the more limited discovery authorized under Indian law. We recognize that under some circumstances, such as when a moving defendant unconditionally consents thereto or no undiscovered evidence of consequence is believed to be under the control of a plaintiff or co-defendant, it may be appropriate to condition a *forum non conveniens* dismissal on the moving defendant's submission to discovery under the Federal Rules without requiring reciprocal discovery by it of the plaintiff. Basic justice dictates that both sides be treated equally, with each having equal access to the evidence in the possession or under the control of the other. Application of this fundamental principle in the present case is especially appropriate since the UOI, as the sovereign government of India, is expected to be a party to the Indian litigation, possibly on both sides.

For these reasons we direct that the condition with respect to the discovery of UCC under the Federal Rules of Civil Procedure be deleted without prejudice to the right of the parties to have reciprocal discovery of each other on equal terms under the Federal Rules, subject to such approval as may be required of the Indian court in which the case will be pending. If, for instance, Indian authorities will permit mutual discovery pursuant to the Federal Rules, the district court's order, as modified in accordance with this opinion, should not be construed to bar such procedure. In the absence of such a court-sanctioned agreement, however, the parties will be limited by the applicable discovery rules of the Indian court in which the claims will be pending.

As so modified the district court's order is affirmed.

Questions and Comments

1. Does the theory of *forum non conveniens* make any sense? When a motion to dismiss is granted, the court has rejected the forum choice of the plaintiff. Shouldn't the plaintiff's choice always be the deciding factor where there are alternative forums? Should it be the deciding factor if the plaintiff is a U.S. citizen (or resident) and the defendant a U.S. citizen (individual or entity)? What about when the plaintiff is a U.S. citizen and the defendant is foreign, as in the problems in Chapter 3? Epstein, Snyder and Baldwin note a different level of deference to a plaintiff's choice of forum depending on whether the plaintiff is a U.S. national as opposed to a foreign national. Does the law distinguish between the plaintiff as a *citizen* as opposed to a *resident* of the United States? What if one of the Mexican citizens injured by the explosion was a legal resident of Texas visiting his family in Veracruz. Does forum shopping by foreign plaintiffs cause courts to diminish the deference to the plaintiff's choice, especially when the chosen forum is a location where juries are perceived to be very generous? What if an American lawyer went to Veracruz, held a press conference and met with the families of injured and deceased Mexicans injured in the GROWMEX explosion. Should that influence the *forum non conveniens* decision after that lawyer has returned and filled suit in the United States representing a number of the persons contacted in Mexico? See *In re Bridgestone/Firestone, Inc.*, 305 F.Supp.2d 927 (S.D.Ind. 2004)(Mexican accidents), *vacated and remanded* 420 F.3d 702 (7th Cir. 2005). Compare *In re Bridgestone/Firestone, Inc.*, 190 F.Supp.2d 1125 (S.D. Ind. 2002)(Colombian and Venezuelan accidents).

In the GROWFAST litigation, the plaintiffs include some U.S. citizens and some foreigners. How does this affect the decision? Could only the suits of the foreigners be dismissed? What if GROWFAST is able to join the English and Japanese companies as defendants? The extract from the panel discussion shows the importance of having some U.S. citizens as plaintiffs.

2. If the plaintiffs' choice is given some weight, what are the other factors to consider? Should they all be given the same weight? How does the court allocate weight? Is "justice" a reasonable factor to consider? See, e.g., *Mendes Junior Int'l Co. v. Banco do Brasil, S.A.*, 15 F.Supp.2d 332 (S.D.N.Y. 1998). How do you weigh the factors in GROWFAST? Or perhaps what are the factors that a court will likely consider?

3. What reasons might lead the defendants' attorneys to recommend retaining the matter in the U.S. courts and not filing a motion to dismiss for *forum non conveniens* reasons? How strong an argument is retention of control by counsel if there is a 50–50 chance of losing in the U.S. court and incurring pain and suffering and/or punitive damages? What if the chance of losing is only 10% but damages in the United States might be $100 million, but not more than $100,000–200,000 in the foreign nation? Should a court consider the relative damages amounts in the alternate jurisdictions? How do these thoughts apply to GROWFAST?

4. Does *forum non conveniens* clash with judicial abstention? Justice Black, dissenting in *Gulf Oil*, thought the court had abdicated jurisdiction that had been conferred upon it by Congress. The *Koster* and *Gulf Oil* decisions are domestic cases that set the stage for the *Piper Aircraft* and subsequent decisions, such as the *Bhopal* litigation. In *Gulf Oil* the Supreme Court said it "wisely" declined to provide an exhaustive list of factors to consider in a *forum non conveniens* decision. Was that really "wise?" Wouldn't a list have assisted the *Piper Aircraft* and other cases? Would preparation of our list for GROWFAST have been easier had *Piper Aircraft* and *Bhopal* developed a list? Although *Gulf Oil* did not develop a clear list of factors, the discussion of private and public interest factors played a part, as it has in *Piper* and subsequent decisions. Are those factors easily identified in *Piper*?

5. In *Piper*, the plaintiffs initiated the case in California state court.[13] What was the connection with California? The plane was manufactured in Kansas and the propeller was manufactured in Ohio. Weren't the families of the decedents clever to have thought of California, or perhaps they had clever attorneys? In view of the conclusion, was there a better choice for the plaintiffs? What about a state court in Ohio? Or a court in the south of Texas, which state at the time did not accept the *forum non conveniens* doctrine? Were the choices made by our plaintiffs in Problem 4.1 wiser than the plaintiffs' choice in *Piper*?

6. Why did the defendants wait until the case had been transferred to Pennsylvania before filing their motion to dismiss under *forum non conveniens*? Could that motion not have been filed in California, where there were very tenuous connections favoring retention? Was Pennsylvania a sound choice for the defendants seeking removal? Had the GROWFAST plaintiffs brought suit in the south of Texas, should the defendant GROWFAST have moved to dismiss and moved to transfer to federal court, next moved to transfer to Tampa, and finally moved to dismiss?

28 U.S.C. § 1404(a) governs federal district *forum non conveniens* transfers within the United States. It is not used in international litigation, where the common law applies. But it may be applicable to the first stage if a case in federal court in Texas is moved to Washington, D.C., and then to a foreign nation. The analysis under § 1404(a) is similar to that under common law. *See Van Dusen v. Barrack*, 376 U.S. 612, 84 S.Ct. 805, 11 L.Ed.2d 945 (1964).

---

13. Reyno filed another suit in Scotland against the estate of the pilot, the owner of the airplane, and the air taxi service that operated the airplane. That influenced the district court's decision, partly because of the risk of conflicting decisions. Might that filing also have influenced the U.S. Supreme Court's decision?

7.   The Third Circuit in *Piper* found removal inappropriate when the foreign law was less favorable than that chosen by the plaintiff. Since it may be assumed that a plaintiff would always choose the most favorable law, doesn't that position repudiate the whole concept of *forum non conveniens*? What was less favorable about Scottish law? How do we learn whether the Mexican law is less favorable that U.S. law for the GROWFAST litigation? Is it for the same reasons the law was viewed as less favorable in Scotland in *Piper Aircraft*? What if the foreign forum provides no remedy at all? Is that the same as the U.S. providing damages that might reach tens of millions while the foreign forum might allow at most $15,000–20,000 in damages?

8.   The Supreme Court was faced with very different views on *forum non conveniens* by the two courts below. Did the Court totally reject the Third Circuit's view that the case should not be removed where the law of the foreign state is less favorable? How does this affect the GROWFAST litigation? What specific statutory or constitutional authority did the Court cite in its holding?

9.   The Court was concerned that the Third Circuit's view would require the court to conduct a choice of law determination and have to compare rights, remedies and procedures available under each law. Isn't that required for a choice of law decision anyway, after the court decides to retain the case? Rejecting the motion to dismiss does not also mean that the applicable law will be the law of the U.S. forum.

10.   The Court also was concerned that the Third Circuit's view would lead to excessive court congestion in the United States. Isn't that a matter for the legislature to address, not the courts?

11.   Footnote 17 in *Piper* notes the paradox that exists if the defendant as well as the plaintiff were not American and the Circuit Court's view were applied—dismissal would not be allowed if the law of the defendant's nation was less favorable even though both parties were from that nation and there was no connection relating the litigation subject matter and the United States. What if the Mexican plaintiffs brought suit in the United States solely against GROWMEX—would a *forum non conveniens* motion to dismiss be granted? What about a motion to dismiss for lack of personal or subject matter jurisdiction?

12.   Are not Piper and Hartzell engaged in reverse forum shopping by trying to move the matter to Scotland, where the law is more favorable to them?

13.   Is there sufficient reasoning in Parts I and II of *Piper*, as three justices thought, to reach the majority's conclusion, without the discussion in Part III?

14.   The Third Circuit in the *Bhopal* case clearly was impressed with the thorough analysis by Judge Keenan of the private and public interests. Do you have any quarrel with the Third Circuit's analysis, other than with the conditions that Judge Keenan imposed upon Union Carbide to gain dismissal. Was there as thorough an analysis in *Piper*? Two reasons foreign plaintiffs suing large U.S. corporations choose a U.S. forum are contingent fee arrangements with U.S. attorneys and punitive damages. But some nations are adopting a form of contingent fee; the United Kingdom has a

"conditional fee" arrangement which increases the fee, but does not link it to the judgment. Damage theory is also changing in many foreign nations, but not yet so as to allow damages anywhere close to those permitted in the United States. Why did the courts in *Piper* and *Bhopal* not discuss remedies available in Scotland and India in more depth? Do you believe a U.S. judge would want to know about remedies available in Mexico in the GROWFAST litigation?

15. Were the plaintiffs in *Piper* and *Bhopal* to have brought suit in Scotland and India, respectively, would there have been problems of asserting jurisdiction over Piper and Hartzell in Scotland, and UCC in India? The High Court in India was fully prepared to do so. See *Union Carbide Corporation v. Union of India*, Madhya Pradesh High Court, April 4, 1988. What if the UCC board of directors, all U.S. citizens, were meeting in Madhya Pradesh when the disaster occurred and they were all killed? Might the court have allowed their suit to continue in the United States, but dismissed the suit by the Indian government? Is GROWFAST subject to personal jurisdiction in Mexico? What if Mexico enacted legislation similar to that in India and assumed control of the plaintiffs role in the litigation?

16. In *Piper* all the parties killed in the crash were Scottish. Would it have made any difference had one passenger, or the pilot, been a U.S. citizen and resident? Or if all the decedents had been Americans?

17. Should the consequences of the *Piper* and *Bhopal* decisions be considered in future cases? The plaintiffs in *Piper* applied for legal aid in Scotland. It was never granted and the suit has never progressed. In *Bhopal*, the Indian government settled with UCC for $470 million, after several proceedings in India following a High Court order than UCC make an interim payment of $350 million before the matter proceed to trial. The plaintiffs had sought $3 billion. Can you at all predict what is likely to happen if the motion to dismiss is granted in GROWFAST? A Texas law professor collected data on 55 personal injury and 30 commercial cases between *Gilbert* and the end of 1984 (a period of about 37 years) that were dismissed on *forum non conveniens* grounds. The study showed that only one of the personal injury cases and two of the commercial cases ever actually reached the trial stage in the foreign court. See Gary B. Born, International Civil Litigation in United States Courts, 308 at n. 73 (3d ed 1996). Should these results make any difference? Would you present them to the court were you representing the plaintiffs?

18. One reason a U.S. court may not grant a *forum non conveniens* motion to dismiss is that the foreign nation's courts do not have a legal system that can reasonably assure a fair trial. Courts are reluctant to characterize a legal system so harshly. What would have to be established to so succeed in blocking removal? Can you outline an argument for the GROWFAST plaintiffs that the Mexican legal system is so inadequate that the case should not be sent there?

19. The conditions imposed by Judge Keenan in *Bhopal* included first a requirement that UCC submit to the jurisdiction of the Indian court. That has been a condition in several cases. If UCC could successfully avoid personal jurisdiction in India, is it fair to say that the Indian courts are an available forum? As to waiving any statute of limitations argument, that too

seems reasonable. But the other conditions seemed more radical and were unacceptable to the Third Circuit. The second condition, that UCC comply with any final judgment rendered in India, seems to conflict with New York's enforcement of judgment provisions. May these provisions be waived? The third condition, that involved discovery and the application of U.S. rules, showed that Judge Keenan was not willing to fully set UCC free of U.S. law. Why wasn't Judge Keenan concerned with UCC's probable inability to obtain similar discovery in India? Could Judge Keenan have ruled differently to achieve the result he wanted? Are there any conditions that might be imposed in the GROWFAST litigation that would be acceptable under the *Bhopal* reasoning?

20.   What law should the New York federal court apply? New York law of *forum non conveniens* under the *Erie R. Co. v. Tomkins* decision?

21.   India admitted that its legal system had deficiencies in dealing with tort litigation. In view of such admission, would that same U.S. court be reluctant to enforce a tort judgment from an Indian court? For a decision of the U.S. federal district court for the Southern District of Florida, see *Eastman Kodak Co. v. Kavlin*, 978 F.Supp. 1078 (S.D. Fla. 1997). The court was convinced by expert testimony that the Bolivian civil justice system was seriously corrupt, refusing to send a case to Bolivia on a *forum non conveniens* motion to dismiss.

22.   The Supreme Court rarely addressed *forum non conveniens* after *Piper* until it ruled in 2007 in *Sinochem Int'l Co. Ltd. v. Malaysia Int'l Shipping Corp.*, ___ U.S. ___, 127 S.Ct. 1184, 167 L.Ed.2d 15 (2007), that a federal district court was not required to first establish jurisdiction before dismissing a suit on *forum non conveniens* grounds. The decision resolved a split among circuits. But the Court viewed the case as "a textbook" case for immediate *forum non conveniens* dismissal. The Court additionally suggested that where "a court can readily determine that it lacks jurisdiction over the cause or the defendant, the proper course would be to dismiss on that ground." How does this affect strategy for the defendants in pretrial challenges? Does it favor defendants or plaintiffs?

PART B.   FORUM NON CONVENIENS IN THE UK AND EU

LUBBE AND OTHERS v. CAPE PLC

[2000] 2 Lloyd's Rep. 383 (H.L.).

[More than 3000 plaintiffs claimed to have contracted asbestos related diseases while working in or living near various wholly owned subsidiaries of the defendant Cape Asbestos Co. Ltd., a corporation chartered in England. . . . The case was initiated in the High Court in London. The defendant moved for dismissal for *forum non conveniens* reasons. The High Court judge ruled that:

> everything pointed towards South Africa as the natural forum for the trial of the action and that there was no pressing circumstance which would justify him in deciding that the interests of justice required a trial in this country instead of the natural forum in South Africa. 2 Lloyd's Rep. at 387.

The plaintiffs appealed and the Court of Appeal held that the High Court failed to give weight to the fact that the claim of negligence was made against the parent defendant as opposed to the subsidiaries in South Africa, and because the only reason the defendant could be sued in South Africa was because of its agreement to such a condition in a prior court hearing. The Court of Appeal held that the defendant did not establish that South Africa was "clearly and distinctly the more appropriate forum." After further proceedings in the various actions in both the High Court and Court of Appeal, . . . the matter came to the House of Lords when it gave leave to appeal.]

LORD BINGHAM OF CORNHILL:

My Lords, the central issue between the plaintiffs and the defendant in these interlocutory appeals is whether proceedings brought by the plaintiffs against the defendant should be tried in this country or in South Africa. * * *

I have already referred to the high repute in which the South African Courts are held. There is also in South Africa a legal profession with high standards and a tradition of public service, though I do not suggest that lawyers in South Africa, any more than those anywhere else, can be expected to act on a large scale without prospects of remuneration. * * * Moreover, given the accessibility to the wealth of scientific, technical and medical evidence available in this context, I am confident that it could be made available in a South African Court, to the extent required to achieve a proper consideration of the plaintiffs' cases. The action would by no means be novel or speculative. * * *

. . . In *Spiliada* it was stated: " . . . The basic principle is that a stay will only be granted on the ground of forum non conveniens where the Court is satisfied that there is some other available forum, having competent jurisdiction, which is the appropriate forum for the trial of the action, i.e. in which the case may be tried more suitably for the interests of all the parties and the ends of justice." [*Spiliada Maritime Corporation v Cansulex Ltd* [1987], AC 460.] In applying this principle the Court's first task is to consider whether the defendant who seeks a stay is able to discharge the burden resting upon him now just to show that England is not the natural or appropriate forum for the trial but to establish that there is another available forum which is clearly or distinctly more appropriate than the English forum. In this way, proper regard is had to the fact that jurisdiction has been founded in England as of right. At this first stage of the inquiry the Court will consider what factors there are which point in the direction of another forum. If the Court concludes at that stage that there is no other available forum which is clearly more appropriate for the trial of the action, that is likely to be the end of the matter. But if the Court concludes at that stage that there is some other available forum which prima facie is more appropriate for the trial of the action it will ordinarily grant a stay unless the plaintiff can show that there are circumstances by reason of which justice requires that a stay should nevertheless not be granted. In this second stage the Court will concentrate its attention not only on factors connecting the proceedings with the foreign or the English forum, but on whether the plaintiff will obtain justice in the foreign jurisdiction. The plaintiff will not ordinarily discharge the burden lying upon him by showing that he will enjoy procedural advantages, or a higher scale of damages or more generous rules of limitation if he sues in England; generally speaking, the plaintiff must take a foreign forum as he finds it, even if it is in some respects less advantageous to him than the English forum. It is only if the plaintiff can establish that substantial justice will not be done in the appropriate forum that a stay will be refused. This is not an easy condition for a plaintiff to satisfy, and it is not necessarily enough to show that legal aid is available in this country but not in the more appropriate foreign forum. * * *

The issues in the present cases fall into two segments. The first segment concerns the responsibility of the defendant as a parent company for ensuring the observance of proper standards of health and safety by its overseas subsidiaries. Resolution of this issue will be likely to involve an inquiry into what part the defendant played in controlling the operations of the group, what its directors and employees knew or ought to have known, what action was taken and not taken, whether the defendant owed a duty of care to employees of group companies overseas and whether, if so, that duty was broken. Much of the evidence material to this inquiry would, in the ordinary way, be documentary and much of it would be found in the offices of the parent company, including minutes of meetings, reports by directors and employees on visits overseas and correspondence.

The second segment of the cases involves the personal injury issues relevant to each individual: diagnosis, prognosis, causation (including the contribution made to a plaintiff's condition by any sources of contamination for which the defendant was not responsible) and special damage. Investigation of these issues would necessarily involve the evidence and medical examination of each plaintiff and an inquiry into the conditions in which that plaintiff worked or lived and the period for which he did so. Where the claim is made on behalf of a deceased person, the inquiry would be essentially the same, although probably more difficult.

In his review of the *Lubbe* case, which was alone before him, Mr. Kallipetis [High Court] considered that the convenience of trying the personal injury issues in South Africa outweighed any benefit there might be in trying the parent company responsibility issue here. That was in my opinion a tenable though not an inevitable conclusion on the case as then presented. * * * I question whether the first Court of Appeal was justified in disturbing Mr. Kallipetis' conclusion and substituting its own. But its own assessment of the balance between the parent company responsibility issue and the personal injury issues is not shown to be unreasonable or wrong. On the case as then presented there was room for the view that South Africa was not shown to be a clearly more appropriate forum. This is a field in which differing conclusions can be reached by different tribunals without either being susceptible to legal challenge. The jurisdiction to stay is liable to be perverted if parties litigate the issue at different levels of the judicial hierarchy in the hope of persuading a higher Court to strike a different balance in the factors pointing for and against a foreign forum.

The emergence of over 3000 new plaintiffs following the decision of the first Court of Appeal had an obvious and significant effect on the balance of the proceedings. While the parent company responsibility issue remained very much what it had always been, the personal injury issues assumed very much greater significance. To investigate, prepare and resolve these issues, in relation to each of the plaintiffs, would plainly involve a careful, detailed and cumbersome factual inquiry and, at least potentially, a very large body of expert evidence. In this changed situation Mr. Justice Buckley, applying the first stage of the *Spiliada* test, regarded South Africa as clearly the more appropriate forum for trial of the group action and the second Court of Appeal agreed. Both Courts were in my view plainly correct. The enhanced significance of the personal injury issues tipped the balance very clearly in favour of South Africa at the first stage of the *Spiliada* exercise, and no effective criticism has been made of that conclusion. The brunt of the plaintiffs' argument on these appeals to the House has been directed not against the decisions of Mr. Justice Buckley and the second Court of Appeal on the first stage of the *Spiliada* test but against their conclusion that the plaintiffs had not shown that substantial justice would not be done in the more appropriate South African forum.

Funding

The plaintiffs submitted that legal aid in South Africa had been withdrawn for personal injury claims, that there was no reasonable likelihood of any lawyer or group of lawyers being able or willing to fund proceedings of this weight and complexity under the contingency fee arrangements permitted in South Africa since April, 1999.... The defendant roundly challenged these assertions. Reliance was placed on the facts that the plaintiffs had not applied for legal aid in South Africa before its withdrawal and had made no determined effort to obtain funding in South Africa. Even if legal aid was no longer available in South Africa, contingency fee agreements were now permissible.... If contingency fee arrangements could not be made in South Africa because South African Counsel and attorneys did not judge the claims to have a reasonable prospect of success, that did not involve a denial of justice to the plaintiffs. * * *

Other material before the House makes plain that before this decision [curtailing legal aid in South Africa] the Legal Aid Board had experienced a period of extreme financial stringency. * * * [T]here is no convincing evidence to suggest that legal aid might be made available in South Africa to fund this potentially protracted and expensive litigation. * * *

The South African Contingency Fees Act (1997) sanctioned a new regime similar (although not identical) to that governing conditional fees in this country. It enables Counsel and attorneys to undertake work for plaintiffs on the basis that if the claim is successful they will receive a fee in excess of that ordinarily chargeable, and that they receive nothing if the claim fails. This regime does not apply to the fees of expert witnesses, who may not be engaged on the basis that they are paid only if the plaintiff by whom they are called is successful. The defendant referred to an affidavit sworn by very experienced South African Counsel who deposed:

> In my view, if a firm of attorneys with a reasonable infrastructure is of the view that the claims of the present Plaintiffs are good, this would mean that the firm would be able to earn very substantial sums of money by way of fees. At the same time, one should not lose sight of the fact that this case is likely to have a very high profile and that the Plaintiffs' attorney/s would be accorded a great deal of positive publicity in the media.... There is every reason to believe that there would be no shortage of firms of attorneys who would be desirous of taking on such a case if they believed that it had good prospects of success.

Accordingly, if there are attorneys in South Africa who are as positive about the prospects of success as [the plaintiffs' solicitor] is, I feel sure that there will be no lack of attorneys in South Africa prepared to represent these plaintiffs under Contingency Fee arrangements. This very general assertion of belief by a member of the Bar was flatly contradicted by a number of other equally distinguished Counsel who provided sworn statements to the plaintiffs, and Counsel for the defendant indicated that he placed no reliance on it. More significantly, it received no support from any practising attorney, and it would be attorneys who would be required, if these proceedings were undertaken for the plaintiffs on a contingency fee basis, to finance the investigation of the claims, the obtaining and calling of evidence and the conduct of the trial during a period which would inevitably last for months and, very much more probably, years. The clear, strong and unchallenged view of the attorneys who provided statements to the plaintiffs was that no firm of South African attorneys with expertise in this field had the means or would undertake the risk of conducting these proceedings on a contingency fee basis. . . .

If these proceedings were stayed in favour of the more appropriate forum in South Africa the probability is that the plaintiffs would have no means of obtaining the professional representation and the expert evidence which would be essential if these claims were to be justly decided. This would amount to a denial of justice. In the special and unusual circumstances of these proceedings, lack of the means, in South Africa, to prosecute these claims to a conclusion provides a compelling ground . . . for refusing to stay the proceedings here. * * *

In England, there has been a vast amount of litigation by victims of asbestos dust without resort to group actions. Whether by a form of group action or otherwise, I have no doubt that the High Court of South Africa will be able to devise and adopt suitable procedures for the efficient despatch of business such as this. None of the evidence or submissions on behalf of the plaintiffs suggests any significant obstacle to that efficient despatch by the Court of cases before it. I do, however, think that the absence, as yet, of developed procedures for handling group actions in South Africa reinforces the submissions made by the plaintiffs on the funding issue. It is one thing to embark on and fund a heavy group action where the procedures governing the conduct of the proceedings are known to and understood by experienced Judges and practitioners. It may be quite another where the exercise is novel and untried. There must then be an increased likelihood of interlocutory decisions which are contentious, with the likelihood of appeals and delay. It cannot be assumed that all Judges will respond to this new procedural challenge in the same innovative spirit. The exercise of jurisdiction by the South African High Court through separate territorial divisions, while not a potent obstacle in itself, could contribute to delay, uncertainty and cost. The procedural novelty of these proceedings, if pursued in South Africa, must in my view act as a further disincentive to any person or body considering whether or not to finance the proceedings. * * *

Public interest

Both the plaintiffs and the defendant placed reliance on public interest considerations as strengthening their contentions that these proceedings should be tried in the forum for which they respectively contended. I agree with my noble and learned friend Lord Hope of Craighead, for the reasons which he gives, that public interest considerations not related to the private interests of the parties and the ends of justice have no bearing on the decision which the Court has to make. Where a catastrophe has occurred in a particular place, the facts that numerous victims live in that place, that the relevant evidence is to be found there and that site inspections are most conveniently and inexpensively carried out there will provide factors connecting any ensuing litigation with the Court exercising jurisdiction in that place. * * *

Conclusion

I would dismiss the defendant's appeal against the decision of the first Court of Appeal. * * *

Lord HOPE OF CRAIGHEAD [agreeing that the appeal should be dismissed]:

In my opinion the principles on which the doctrine of forum non conveniens rest leave no room for considerations of public interest or public policy which cannot be related to the private interests of any of the parties or the ends of justice in the case which is before the Court. * * *

I would * * * decline to follow those Judges in the United States who would decide issues as to where a case ought to be tried on broad grounds of public policy: see Union Carbide Corporation Gas Plant Disaster at Bhopal, and Piper Aircraft Co. v. Reyno. * * * [T]he Court is not equipped to conduct the kind of inquiry and assessment of the international as well as the domestic implications that would be needed if it were to follow that approach. However tempting it may be to give effect to concerns about the expense and inconvenience to the administration of justice of litigating actions such as these in this country on the one hand or in South Africa on the other, the argument must be resolved upon an examination of their effect upon the interests of the parties who are before the Court and securing the ends of justice in their case.* * *

OWUSU v. JACKSON

Case C–281/02, 2005 E.C.R. I–1383.

[Owusu was a U.K. domiciled British national who suffered a very serious accident while swimming during a holiday in Jamaica, leaving him tetraplegic. Owusu sued both Jackson (who let Owusu a villa) and several Jamaican companies in tort in the High Court in London. Jackson and several other defendants raised *forum non conveniens* in a motion to stay in favor of the Jamaican courts. The High Court refused to stay and the Court of Appeal referred to the European Court the question of the mandatory nature of Article 2 of the Brussels Convention, in the context of the application of *forum non conveniens* in favor of the courts of a non-Contracting State, when one of the defendants is domiciled in a Contracting State.]

THE COURT (Grand Chamber) * * *

24. Nothing in the wording of Article 2 of the Brussels Convention suggests that the application of the general rule of jurisdiction laid down by that article solely on the basis of the defendant's domicile in a Contracting State is subject to the condition that there should be a legal relationship involving a number of Contracting States. * * *

37. It must be observed, first, that Article 2 of the Brussels Convention is mandatory in nature and that, according to its terms, there can be no derogation from the principle it lays down except in the cases expressly provided for by the Convention. It is common ground that no exception on the basis of the forum non conveniens doctrine was provided for by the authors of the Convention, . . .

38. Respect for the principle of legal certainty, which is one of the objectives of the Brussels Convention, would not be fully guaranteed if the court having jurisdiction under the Convention had to be allowed to apply the forum non conveniens doctrine.

39. According to its preamble, the Brussels Convention is intended to strengthen in the Community the legal protection of persons established therein, by laying down common rules on jurisdiction to guarantee

certainty as to the allocation of jurisdiction among the various national courts before which proceedings in a particular case may be brought.

40. The Court has thus held that the principle of legal certainty requires, in particular, that the jurisdictional rules which derogate from the general rule laid down in Article 2 of the Brussels Convention should be interpreted in such a way as to enable a normally well-informed defendant reasonably to foresee before which courts, other than those of the State in which he is domiciled, he may be sued.

41. Application of the forum non conveniens doctrine, which allows the court seised a wide discretion as regards the question whether a foreign court would be a more appropriate forum for the trial of an action, is liable to undermine the predictability of the rules of jurisdiction laid down by the Brussels Convention ... and consequently to undermine the principle of legal certainty, which is the basis of the Convention.

42. The legal protection of persons established in the Community would also be undermined. First, a defendant, who is generally better placed to conduct his defence before the courts of his domicile, would not be able, in circumstances such as those of the main proceedings, reasonably to foresee before which other court he may be sued. Second, where a plea is raised on the basis that a foreign court is a more appropriate forum to try the action, it is for the claimant to establish that he will not be able to obtain justice before that foreign court or, if the court seised decides to allow the plea, that the foreign court has in fact no jurisdiction to try the action or that the claimant does not, in practice, have access to effective justice before that court, irrespective of the cost entailed by the bringing of a fresh action before a court of another State and the prolongation of the procedural time-limits.

43. Moreover, allowing forum non conveniens in the context of the Brussels Convention would be likely to affect the uniform application of the rules of jurisdiction contained therein in so far as that doctrine is recognised only in a limited number of Contracting States, whereas the objective of the Brussels Convention is precisely to lay down common rules to the exclusion of derogating national rules.

44. The defendants in the main proceedings emphasise the negative consequences which would result in practice from the obligation the English courts would then be under to try this case, inter alia as regards the expense of the proceedings, the possibility of recovering their costs in England if the claimant's action is dismissed, the logistical difficulties resulting from the geographical distance, the need to assess the merits of the case according to Jamaican standards, the enforceability in Jamaica of a default judgment and the impossibility of enforcing cross-claims against the other defendants.

45. In that regard, genuine as those difficulties may be, suffice it to observe that such considerations, which are precisely those which may be taken into account when forum non conveniens is considered, are not such as to call into question the mandatory nature of the fundamental

rule of jurisdiction contained in Article 2 of the Brussels Convention, for the reasons set out above. * * *

On those grounds, the Court (Grand Chamber) rules as follows:

The Convention ... precludes a court of a Contracting State from declining the jurisdiction ... on the ground that a court of a non-Contracting State would be a more appropriate forum for the trial of the action even if the jurisdiction of no other Contracting State is in issue or the proceedings have no connecting factors to any other Contracting State.

Questions and Comments

1. How does the English approach to the factors to be considered in a *forum non conveniens* analysis differ from that in the United States? Are the principles applied in the English court the same as in the United States, and are they given similar weight? Is an English court reluctant to move a matter unless there is a "clearly" more appropriate forum? How much weight should be placed on the availability of legal aid? England has been trying to reduce legal aid in civil matters because of the enormous cost.

2. Are Lord Bingham's comments about the quality of South African legal services in *Lubbe* supported with reasons, or are they more a courteous assumption based on comity? Would you expect a U.S. judge to make comments about the Mexican legal system that roughly parallel those made by Lord Bingham about the South African legal system?

3. The English court quite nicely divides some of the discussion into considering all the amount of evidence located in England, and then separately the amount located in South Africa. Should that be weighed without considering the *accessibility* of the evidence in the other country under discovery rules? Note also that the English Court of Appeal and House of Lords have great respect for the judges in the court or courts below them, but not necessarily below the High Court. That leads to a reluctance to disturb a decision where the judge has discretion. That is clearly the case of *forum non conveniens*- abuse of discretion is not easy to establish on appeal.

4. Lord Hope's comments, concurred in by Lord Bingham, focus on private and public interest factors, specifically citing and rejecting the U.S. *Piper* and *Bhopal* decisions. Are their reasons sound? Cannot many or most public interest factors be characterized as private interest factors? Does the court distinguish between the desirability and the capacity of the court to consider public interest factors? Are there any special public interest factors in the GROWFAST litigation? Could they be characterized as private interest factors?

5. How can one not agree with the EU view that *forum non conveniens* does not provide adequate predictability when Lord Bingham in Lubbe stated: "This is a field in which differing conclusions can be reached by different tribunals without either being susceptible to legal challenge?

6. The *Owusu* decision has created considerable opposition in England. Do you agree with its comments on protecting legal certainty and predictability? At what expense does that come? The impact of *Owusu* may be

significant if the English courts abandon *forum non conveniens*. Other Commonwealth nations pay careful attention to *forum non conveniens* developments in English courts. Might they begin to look to U.S. courts?

7. The European Court additionally stated that "the fundamental objective pursued by the Convention ... was to ensure the free movement of judgments between Contracting States." How would limiting the application of the Convention/Regulation to contracting states impede any "fundamental objective?"

PART C.   A CHALLENGE FROM LATIN AMERICA

MICHAEL W. GORDON, FORUM NON CONVENIENS MISCONSTRUED: A RESPONSE TO HENRY SAINT DAHL

38 Inter–American L.R. 141 (2006).

PARLATINO MOVEMENT: A CALL TO THE NORTH YET UNHEARD

Little known in the United States, Parlatino is an acronym for Latin American Parliament. It is not a law-making parliament, but an organization of some members of some Latin American legislatures. It is clearly a group of legislators committed to assisting their nationals in responding to the frequent *forum non conveniens* dismissals in U.S. courts. The organization seems to have been a reaction to the final dismissal in the long-running *Delgado* case.[190] Soon after the lower court decision in *Delgado*, Parlatino challenged *forum non conveniens* by drafting a brief Model Law on International Jurisdiction and Applicable Law to Tort Liability in 1998.... The law reads:

> Art. 1. National and international jurisdiction. The petition that is validly filed, according to both legal systems, in the defendant's domiciliary court, extinguishes national jurisdiction. The latter is only reborn if the plaintiff non-suits of his foreign petition and files a new petition in the country, in a completely free and spontaneous way.

> Art. 2. International tort liability. Damages. In cases of international tort liability, the national court may, at the plaintiff's request, apply to damages and to the pecuniary sanctions related to such damages, the relevant standards and amounts of the pertinent foreign law.

The model law was intended to clarify "certain rules on international jurisdiction." ... [S]everal legislatures of Parlatino members' nations have enacted laws based upon or drawing from the Parlatino Model Law.... The proposed provisions have no relevance to U.S. courts' jurisdiction, including motions to dismiss for any reason recognized in the United States. Furthermore, the comments by Parlatino are confusing in that they attempt to give the plaintiff's choice of forum greater weight than do the laws of that chosen foreign forum. They seek to "strengthen[ ]" the choice made by the plaintiff. Parlatino suggests that

---

190.   890 F.Supp. 1324 (S.D.Tex. 1995), *aff'd*, 231 F.3d 165 (5th Cir. 2000).

its proposed law would allow a plaintiff to choose a foreign forum that meets the norms of the Bustamante Code and that the foreign "judge will not be able to close the doors of the [foreign] court on him as, for instance, has been happening with the theory of *forum non conveniens*." Since none of the Parlatino nations recognizes the doctrine of *forum non conveniens*, the reference to foreclosure can only refer to the United States, or other foreign courts recognizing that theory. But it is not the parliaments of other nations that open or close the doors to the U.S. courts. That U.S. judges alone have discretion to decide *forum non conveniens*-based motions to dismiss is undeniably correct. They may dismiss cases for many other reasons such as failure to state a cause of action or absence of subject matter jurisdiction. This represents a discretionary authority that most civil law system judges do not fully share. But failure to possess an authority to dismiss a case under one nation's legal procedure is not reason to impose that view on another nation.

Parlatino has been careful not to extinguish fully home-nation jurisdiction of a plaintiff when it first files abroad.... The model law allows one of its beneficiaries who has been dismissed abroad, ... to file an action in the home court, as long as he does so in a "completely free and spontaneous way." If a suit has been dismissed from a U.S. court under *forum non conveniens*, the foreign plaintiff is "completely free" to decide what to do next. Dahl believes this foreign plaintiff is coerced and compelled to file at home. In actuality, the plaintiff may propose settlement negotiations with the other parties who were the defendants in the dismissed suits, appeal the dismissal to a higher state or federal court in the United States, file a suit in any other country, including but not necessarily his own, or do absolutely nothing. The plaintiff is also entitled to return to the United States in the event his own forum proves to be unavailable.... One wonders how Dahl would view a U.S. court that, upon dismissing an action on *forum non conveniens* grounds, hypothetically stated: "This ruling only dismisses this action. It does not compel, order or suggest any future action by the plaintiff. Any further suit filed by the foreign plaintiff at home or in any other jurisdiction, any settlement action, or any agreement to arbitrate is considered by this court to be done in a 'completely free and spontaneous way.'"

Dahl ends his article with the suggestion that these laws do not really change the existing law, but only clarify long standing law based on the Bustamante Code. I believe the experience of the several nations that have adopted laws with Parlatino Model Law characteristics belie this supposition. U.S. courts have struggled at times with the meaning of these laws. That is largely because the subject foreign nation's laws of jurisdiction have always provided for alternative forms of jurisdiction. All of these nations provide for jurisdiction over a tort where the tortuous act occurred, in addition to a provision for jurisdiction in the domicile of the defendant. Thus there has always been a choice of jurisdiction for the plaintiff. But before Parlatino, foreign plaintiffs were arguing that these traditional laws of jurisdiction accomplished the same goal that

Parlatino would seek more aggressively. Essentially they claimed that the plaintiff's choice to file in the location of the foreign defendant carried with it a mandate to that foreign court to both accept jurisdiction and proceed to trial. Courts were obviously suspicious of such arguments. In one of the early dibromochlorpropane (DBCP) pesticide cases, *Patrickson v. Dole Food Company*,[211] the Hawaiian federal district court dismissed cases after considering claims that the laws of Costa Rica, Ecuador, Guatemala and Panama, terminated jurisdiction in those countries when a case arising from the same facts was initiated in the United States. The *Patrickson* decision was not kind to the plaintiff's arguments and found the foreign courts in each case to be available. The Parlatino Model Law was completed in January1998, a few months before the *Patrickson* decision.

Guatemalan law was quite unlike the Model Law, but specifically attempted to nullify *forum non conveniens* by declaring it to be "unacceptable and invalid" in Article 1 of the Guatemalan Law for the Defense of Procedural Rights of Nationals and Residents. But Article 3 gave judges authority to resume jurisdiction after a *forum non conveniens* dismissal "to avoid procedural abandonment of the Guatemalan nationals and residents." Ecuador had also addressed the issue by enacting Law 55. Dahl referred to Guatemalan and Ecuadorian law in his article as the examples of laws that did not change previous law. But even though they attempted to nullify *forum non conveniens*, they were rejected by the Hawaiian federal district court in *Patrickson* as justification to retain the cases. The court had less trouble with the laws of Panama and Costa Rica, which had no such *forum non conveniens* provisions.

While the future is difficult to predict, as I suspect Dahl would agree, we undoubtedly follow different paths leading to where we believe the law will evolve. Dahl thinks U.S. courts will respond positively to the enactment of the kind of law Parlatino has promoted. In contrast, I believe that when U.S. courts are aware of the motivation behind these forum shopping support laws, and especially the escape routes that make these laws selective depending upon the motivations of the foreign plaintiffs, *forum non conveniens* will continue to be the basis to dismiss most of these actions. Of course there could be legislation enacted to address these issues. Drawing from the efforts of Parlatino it might state that forum shopping in U.S. courts by foreigners is a threat to the overburdened capacity of U.S. courts to render fair process to parties who have not forum shopped. In such a case the U.S. court would not dismiss the action on *forum non conveniens* grounds; the court would simply not have subject matter jurisdiction to hear the matter. The court would make one inquiry: is the plaintiff's claim one which, assuming the principal defendants are domestic, gives rise to a cause of action that is recognized in the majority of nations with legal systems that provide due process? How many foreign plaintiffs would then insist that their gov-

211. Civil Action No. 97–01516 (D.Haw. 1998).

ernments develop viable judicial systems to deal with these cases? Such U.S. legislation is unlikely to be adopted, however. The more predictable response to the concept of the Parlatino movement is that courts will raise the level or alter the focus of inquiry to why the foreign plaintiff is forum shopping in the United States. Courts have already begun both to make strong statements about excessive forum shopping and its impacts....

... I sense that when courts are properly briefed on the background and motivation of these laws the courts will be more inclined to reject the forum shopping motive of these foreign plaintiffs seeking legal asylum from their nations' laws than to accept the application of interpretations of the Bustamante Code as applicable in U.S. courts.... With the greatest reluctance, the U.S. may be inclined to give up its reputation as the world's best place to forum shop. Lord Denning's flame is out—the moths should use their night radar to fly home.

ECUADOR LAW 55

January 27, 1998.

Article 1. Articles 27, 28, 29, and 30 of the Code of Civil Procedure, notwithstanding the literal language of their text, shall be interpreted to the effect that, in dealing with concurrent international jurisdiction, a plaintiff will be able to freely elect between filing its complaint in Ecuador or abroad, with the exception of those cases in which the law expressly requires that the matter must be decided exclusively by Ecuador judges, such as the divorce of an Ecuadorian national married in Ecuador. In the event a complaint is filed outside Ecuador, national jurisdiction is terminated, as is the jurisdiction of Ecuadorean judges in the matter.

Questions and Comments

1. Several of the less developed nations of Latin America have enacted laws following Parlatino and similar to that of Ecuador. Guatemala adopted a law that states "the theory called 'Forum Non Conveniens' is declared unacceptable and invalid, when it intervenes to prevent the continuation of a lawsuit in the domiciliary courts of the defendant." Other nations with similar laws include Costa Rica and Panama. In Ecuador, Law 55 was promoted by a group of plaintiffs who had first initiated suit in Florida and lost a defendant's motion to dismiss under *forum non conveniens*. The plaintiffs used political influence to have Law 55 enacted. They filed the suits in Ecuador and asked for their dismissal. It was granted and they went back to the Florida court claiming that Ecuador was not an available forum. The judge declined their demands and again dismissed the case. Should the reason be because they sought the enactment of the law and therefore themselves made the forum unavailable, because they filed the cases and then asked for their dismissal, because they might have waived the effect of Law 55 by not requesting dismissal, or for other reasons? How should such a law be treated in a U.S. court when the parties have not been the promoters

of the law and when there is no ability to waive its effect? Mexico has not adopted a Law 55 type law. Would you recommend it do so? Would it help the plaintiffs in GROWFAST?

PROBLEM 4.4   DEFENDANT MOVES TO APPLY FOREIGN LAW

SECTION I.   THE SETTING

We assume for this problem that the cases remain in U.S. courts. Motions to dismiss for improper forum, lack of jurisdiction, or *forum non conveniens* were either not filed or were rejected. The various U.S. courts must now determine the applicable law. We know from basic civil procedure that the courts will apply the procedural law of the forum. But the judges must also decide which substantive law to apply, including the law of damages.

SECTION II.   FOCUS OF CONSIDERATION

In a case in the United States that involves an issue that crosses *state* borders, the court must determine the applicable law. Were the explosion to have occurred in a GROWFAST plant in Oregon and were the injured and the deceased persons all U.S. citizens and residents of various states, the law of Oregon might apply, or the law of one of the other states where GROWFAST is doing business, or perhaps the law of one of the states of residency of the injured or deceased parties. There may be differences in the tort law of those states, but for the most part the legal claims are likely to be similar as to liability. There may be some differences in damages, particularly punitive or exemplary damages, however, since some states are placing caps on tort damage awards. The laws of compensatory damages are likely to be similar.

Our problem crosses national rather than state borders, and thus the methodology of choosing the applicable law may differ. What clearly differs is the nature of the substantive law of two different nations, especially, as in our problem, when one is a common law tradition nation and other a civil law tradition nation. The differences in tort law and damages will be shown to be very different in Mexico and the United States. In problems 4.1 and 4.2, we considered the choice of forum and subject matter jurisdiction that led us to determine where the suits would likely be filed, in federal courts or in state courts and in which states. The federal or state courts in Florida or Texas were thought to be the most likely, but not exclusive, forums that would be chosen by the plaintiffs. The choice of law decision made by the court is very important to the parties. If we assume that much larger damage awards are rendered when U.S. law is applied, the plaintiffs will argue for the application of U.S. law. The defendants will want Mexican law to be applied, or even the law of France or Germany or Japan or England, or any other European country that is home to an injured tourist in Mexico. If Mexican law is chosen and the possible damages are very low, the defendants may offer to settle with an offer that may approach the highest possible damages in order to avoid litigation expenses.

Were contract rather than tort actions involved, such as in an action by GROWFAST against a Japanese supplier, choice of law would also be important. But nations are harmonizing substantive contract law, reflected in the widespread enactment of the Convention on Contracts for the International Sale of Goods (CISG). Furthermore, contract damages are more uniform internationally than tort damages. Many of the choices faced below in the tort hypothetical will nevertheless have to be faced in international contract litigation.

What are the unique features of choice of law and proof of foreign law in an international case? There are several questions that have some order but often are interlinked. They include:

1.   May a court of one nation apply the law of another nation? This raises a fundamental question about the legal authorization or capacity of a court to apply the law of another nation. Although many nations prohibited any application of foreign law in decades past, the more modern approach is to adopt policies that permit the application of foreign law. Legal authority to apply foreign law does not mean that a court will do so. In many nations, including Mexico, it is very unlikely that a court will apply foreign law.

2.   Will the court recognize a contractual provision that designates foreign law? Must the chosen law have any link to the parties and/or issues?

3.   Who raises the issue of foreign law? If it is not raised by one of the parties may or must the judge initiate a choice of law analysis?

4.   When must a request to apply foreign law be made? For example might it be included as part of a request to dismiss on *forum non conveniens* grounds? One concern a court may have with denying such a motion is that it might have to apply foreign law.

5.   How is the request made? Is there a formal motion procedure, or might it arise as part of the discussion of another issue, such as a challenge to a forum choice or a *forum non conveniens* dismissal request?

6.   What rules are applicable to determine the choice of law? Is *lex loci delicti* the most appropriate basis for the choice? Or interest balancing? Or most significant contacts? What are the sources of those rules?

7.   Once a foreign law is determined to be the applicable law, what sources are allowed to establish that law? Is such process a question of law or fact?

8.   Is the judge deemed to know foreign law as a U.S. judge is deemed to know U.S. law? Does proof of *foreign* law as a question of law differ significantly from proof of *U.S.* law as a question of law?

9. How does one select experts and does the expert have any role different than when testifying on domestic law?

In Part A, we will consider whether it is necessary to apply foreign law when the parties have not so requested. Also, without determining which law will apply, we consider such issues as when a request for the application of foreign law should be made and its proper form. In Part B, we assume the court is willing or feels compelled to determine the applicable choice of law and, without yet looking at the substance of a specific foreign law, consider both the way in which courts approach choice of law, and some of the tasks facing counsel and the court in proving foreign law. Finally, Part C briefly considers some of the possible sources of law. In the following Problem 4.5, we proceed with the assumption that the court has chosen foreign law, specifically Mexican law, and we consider the various applicable sources and provisions of the applicable foreign law. It is obviously difficult to fully separate the various stages discussed in problems 4.4 and 4.5, but making some distinction of issues between the choice and application of foreign law issues may assist understanding this important area.

SECTION III.   READINGS, QUESTIONS AND COMMENTS

PART A.   CHOICE OF LAW: WHAT RULES DETERMINE THE PROPER CHOICE AND MUST THE COURT APPLY FOREIGN LAW IF THE PARTIES DO NOT REQUEST ITS APPLICATION?

Several variations may arise in a given case. First, there may be a choice of law provision that the court accepts, whether the court is compelled to do so by law or it exercises judicial discretion. Second, what must the court do when the facts of the dispute appear to call for the possible application of foreign law but none of the parties requests such application? Third, foreign law is requested by a party and the court turns to the applicable choice of law rules to make the determination. We address the second and third, including when and how a party must request the application of foreign law.

ROGER J. MINER, THE RECEPTION OF FOREIGN LAW IN THE U.S. FEDERAL COURTS*

American Journal of Comparative Law 581 (1995).

* * *

Our haste to avoid confrontation with foreign law leads us into some strange decisions. For example, a panel of my court some years back held as follows:

> While ... a court is still permitted to apply foreign law even if not requested by a party, we believe that the law of the forum may be applied here, where the parties did not at trial take the position that

plaintiffs were required to prove their claims under Vietnamese law, even though the forum's choice of law rule would have called for application of foreign law.[5]

It is strange indeed for a court to consciously apply the wrong law, based on the position taken by the parties, while acknowledging a discretionary authority to apply the right law. Such an approach with regard to questions of domestic law would be highly unusual.

The decision that I used as my example, *Vishipco Line v. Chase Manhattan Bank*, was spawned by an action brought by Vietnamese corporations and individuals to recover funds deposited in the Saigon branch of the Chase Manhattan Bank. The bank had closed the branch following the Communist takeover and argued that it was not obligated to make good on the deposits for a number of reasons. In another bizarre twist in that opinion, Vietnamese law was applied to Chase's affirmative defenses. The panel reasoned as follows: "While Chase invoked foreign law ... with respect to its own affirmative defenses only, neither party invoked foreign law with respect to Chase's basic obligations to its depositors...." That case still is cited as precedent by the district courts in this circuit for the proposition that forum law should be applied where the parties do not provide the court with the appropriate foreign law. Just last year, a district court in the Southern District was confronted with claims that revolved around a contract providing that any disputes regarding its terms would be governed by Malaysian law. Citing the *Vishipco* case, the district court noted the failure of the parties to provide it with the applicable Malaysian legal principles, "deem[ed] the parties to have acquiesced in the application of local law and hence look[ed] to pertinent authority within the forum."[7]

The failure of the parties to establish foreign law also results in the application of the law of the forum in many other circuits. My own view of the matter is that a court has the affirmative obligation to seek out the applicable foreign law whether the parties have established that law or not. Let me be clear about any disagreements that I might have with some of the decisions made by panels of my court in regard to the reception of foreign law. Like all other judges of the court, I am bound by the precedent created by the panels.* * *

We do have a federal rule, of course, that requires a party who intends to raise an issue concerning the law of a foreign country to give notice of that intention through pleadings or other reasonable written notice. I refer, of course, to Rule 44.1 of the Rules of Civil Procedure* * * This clearly provides the federal courts with a tremendous amount of flexibility in ascertaining foreign law. It is just too bad that they do not use it! Rule 44.1, originally adopted in 1966, concludes with a very important sentence and it is this: "The court's determination shall be treated as a ruling on a question of law." * * *

5. Vishipco Line v. Chase Manhattan Bank, N.A., 660 F.2d 854, 860 (2d Cir. 1981), cert. denied, 459 U.S. 976 (1982).

7. Kleartex (U.S.A.), Inc. v. Kleartex SDN BHD, 1994 WL 733688, at * 15 n.5 (S.D.N.Y. June 9, 1994).

It appears that some federal courts still have not gotten the word and continue to impose upon the parties a factual burden of proof of foreign law. In a case decided in the Southern District just two years ago, the court held that "[f]oreign law is a question of fact which must be proved."[15] The court observed that affidavits of experts on Polish law were unsatisfactory and decided that a hearing would be required to decide the issues. Although the court certainly was entitled to take testimony, its decision on Polish law ultimately would be a legal one, not a factual one. One commentator has opined that foreign law implicates a mixture of fact and law under Rule 44.1. He has characterized foreign law as "a tertium genus, a third category, between fact and law."[16] I disagree and see the decision as purely one of law. Because I have this view, I think that it becomes the duty of the court to find and apply the relevant foreign law as soon as it becomes apparent to the court that foreign law governs.

* * *

I think that the Seventh Circuit Court of Appeals had it right when it stated that, in determining questions of foreign law, both trial and appellate courts must research and analyze the law independently.[21] * * * The court quoted with approval in the course of its decision this statement by a commentator: " 'All too often counsel will do an inadequate job of researching and presenting foreign law or will attempt to prove it in such a partisan fashion that the court is obliged to go beyond their offerings.' "[22] While I am in agreement with the idea that the courts must do their own analysis, I do not agree that the work of the attorneys often is inadequate. In most cases, the foreign law is completely and fairly presented on all sides, and the court can proceed to do its job. I once wrote an opinion for a panel of our court that revolved around the Ecuadorian Law of Guaranty and found the foreign law well and fully presented.[23] * * * In fact, our federal courts have shown a commendable ability to get their hands around foreign law when fully briefed on the issues.* * *

In most of the foreign law cases that I have participated in, the affidavits of experts have been supplied, along with copies of pertinent laws and codes. These have proved sufficient to allow me to make up my own mind about the applicable foreign law after completing any research that I have considered necessary. Foreign law experts come from many places. * * * Although the opinions differ, * * * affidavits are straightforward and helpful.

15. Weiss v. Glemp, 792 F. Supp. 215, 229 (S.D.N.Y. 1992).

16. Sass, "Foreign Law in Federal Courts," 29 Am. J. Comp. L. 97, 98 (1981).

21. Twohy v. First Nat'l Bank of Chicago, 758 F.2d 1185, 1193 (7th Cir. 1985); see also Grand Entertainment Group, Ltd. v. Star Media Sales, Inc., 988 F.2d 476, 488—89 (3rd Cir. 1993).

22. 758 F.2d at 1193 (quoting Wright & Miller, supra n. 8, § 2444).

23. Indasu Int'l, C.A. v. Citibank, N.A., 861 F.2d 375 (2d Cir. 1988).

I do not agree with those who consider an expert automatically suspect because he or she is retained by one side or the other.[31] If we think that we are getting some "junk" foreign law from an expert, we can take a leaf from the book given to us by the Supreme Court in *Daubert v. Merrell Dow Pharmaceuticals*.[32] In that case, it was determined that a federal judge should act as a gatekeeper in deciding whether to admit scientific evidence. I think that a federal judge can also act as a gatekeeper in deciding whether to accept the foreign law opinion of an expert. Testimony will sometimes be required to determine whether an expert's opinion is reliable or relevant. I am not greatly enamored of taking testimony from a foreign law expert, however, and think that it would be necessary only in a rare case.

It seems to me that the federal courts should make more use of court-appointed experts in all kinds of cases where an expert opinion would be helpful. I think that in close questions of foreign law, where experts engaged by the parties are in serious disagreement, the court should appoint its own expert in an effort to close the gap. Rule 706 of the Federal Rules of Evidence provides that "[t]he court may on its own or on the motion of any party enter an order to show cause why expert witnesses should not be appointed, and may request the parties to submit nominations." The issue for the expert may be clarified at a pretrial conference and the expert's findings must be provided to the parties, who may depose or cross-examine the expert. The compensation of the court-appointed expert must be paid "by the parties in such proportion and at such time as the court directs, and thereafter charged in like manner as costs."

The use of a court-appointed expert is a highly desirable tool for ascertaining the governing foreign law * * * The elaborate system provided by Rule 706 for testing the opinion of a court-appointed expert means that we are pretty sure of getting the foreign law right in a case where such an opinion is given. It does not by any means, however, divest us of our independent duty of research, for the responsibility of arriving at a correct decision is ours and ours alone. Expert opinion, whether from the parties or from a court-appointed expert is only one way for us to get there. And get there we must, without applying the law of the forum when it does not apply, without utilizing fictitious presumptions, without regarding the search for foreign law as an arcane enterprise whose mysteries we cannot fathom, and without evading the responsibility that every court in this nation has—to find the law and apply it.

The logical consequence of this view from the bench is our need for a reliable source of competent expertise to which judges may refer and to which they may in appropriate instances direct counsel. The American Foreign Law Association, an organization whose members include many

---

31. See, e.g., Merryman, "Foreign Law as a Problem," 19 Stan. J. Int'l L. 151, 157 (1983).

32. 113 S.Ct. 2786 (1993).

of the foremost foreign law experts in our nation, is well-suited to help in this effort. Following the lead of or perhaps joining with many of the academic members of the American Society of Comparative Law, who have joined together in the American Academy of Foreign Law, the Association could pool and publicize members' foreign-law expertise, together with educational background, professional experience, and present affiliations. Disseminated to the federal trial and appellate courts, and to those members of the bar engaged in international practice, this information would help assure a warmer reception for foreign law in the federal courts.

* * *

DAVID EPSTEIN, JEFFREY L. SNYDER & CHARLES S. BALDWIN, IV, INTERNATIONAL LITIGATION

§§ 9.01–9.02 (3d ed. 2002).

9.01 INTRODUCTION

Any party intending to rely on foreign law as part of the proof of its case must be familiar with the requirement of Rule 44.1 of the Federal Rules of Civil Procedure. That rule provides as follows:

> A party who intends to raise an issue concerning the law of a foreign country shall give notice in his pleadings or other reasonable written notice. The court, in determining foreign law, may consider any relevant material or source, including testimony, whether or not submitted by a party or admissible under the Federal Rules of Evidence. The court's determination shall be treated as a ruling on a question of law.

Rule 44.1, which was adopted in 1966, is an endeavor to furnish the federal courts with a uniform and effective procedure for raising and determining an issue concerning the law of a foreign country. Prior to 1966, foreign law questions were regarded as questions of fact which had to be proved as such. Treating foreign law considerations as a question of fact meant that foreign law issues had to be raised in the pleadings and proven in accordance with the rules of evidence. It further encouraged courts to regard juries as the appropriate body to ascertain questions of foreign law, thus limiting appellate review of determinations of foreign law. Even under the more liberal standards of Rule 44.1, however, it is essential that parties, while preparing for litigation, first consider whether they intend to rely on foreign law as part of their case and then determine how they intend to prove foreign law in accordance with the requirements of Rule 44.1

9.02 REASONABLE NOTICE

Rule 44.1 provides that a "party who intends to raise an issue concerning the law of a foreign country shall give notice in his pleadings or other reasonable written notice." The notes of the Advisory Committee on Rules state:

> In some situations the pertinence of foreign law is apparent from the outset; accordingly the necessary investigation of that law will have been accomplished by the party at the pleading stage, and the notice can be given conveniently in the pleadings.

The pleader, however, does not have to commit to the application of foreign law before pretrial discovery. In *Grice v. Mowinckels,*[4] defendant filed a Rule 12(b)(6) motion to dismiss on the ground that plaintiff had failed to allege whether foreign law was applicable and hence the complaint failed to state a claim upon which relief could be granted. The court stated that while the purpose of Rule 44.1 was to avoid surprise, it would be unfair to require plaintiff, in order to survive a Rule 12(b)(6) motion, to set out in its complaint the identity and substance of the applicable law involved. Similarly, where defendant raised the applicability of foreign law in a motion to dismiss, the district court in *Hodson v. A. H. Robins Co., Inc.,*[6] stated as follows:

> Certainly there is no risk of surprise present in the cases, for it is the defendants who have raised the question of the relevance of British law. . . . [w]here the applicability of foreign law is not obvious at the outset and is a matter of some contention among the parties, the "reasonable written notice," if required at all under Rule 44.1, may come at any time sufficient to give the court and the defendants adequate notice of the need to research the foreign rules.

Where a party is provided with ample opportunity to present its own position as to the applicability of foreign law in the suit, however, it cannot be heard to complain that it lacked reasonable notice under Rule 44.1.

Any form of notice is sufficient provided there is no issue of "unfair surprise." Although foreign law materials may be considered at any time, a party should submit such evidence as early in the proceeding as possible, preferably in the district court and not at the appellate stage. In this connection it has been held that plaintiffs waived their right to rely on foreign law because the issue was not raised for the first time until the plaintiffs' motion for reconsideration.[10] Some courts have held that if a party fails to give reasonable written notice in the district court, it is precluded from raising the issue of foreign law on appeal.[11] Other courts have held that, absent special circumstances, the parties should present issues of foreign law in their appellate briefs at the latest.[12] Similarly, where a party fails to raise a foreign law issue prior to the issuance of a

---

4. 477 F. Supp. 365 (S.D. Ala. 1979).

6. 528 F. Supp. 809 (E.D. Va. 1981), aff'd, 715 F.2d 142 (4th Cir. 1983).

10. Frietsch v. Refco, Inc., 56 F.3d 825, 828 (7th Cir. 1995).

11. *See* Ruff v. St. Paul Mercury Ins. Co., 393 F.2d 500, 502 (2d Cir. 1968).

12. *See* Stuart v. United States, 813 F.2d 243, 251 (9th Cir. 1987), *rev'd on other grounds,* 489 U.S. 353 (1988).

final order, it may have waived the foreign law issue on remand of the case to the trial court.[13]

STUART v. UNITED STATES

United States Court of Appeals, Ninth Circuit, 1987.
813 F.2d 243.

BOOCHEVER, CIRCUIT JUDGE.

* * * We note with concern that the government has made similar late submissions of foreign law material in at least two other reported cases of this type. ... We realize that we may consider foreign law materials at any time, whether or not submitted by a party, and that late submissions often have been considered in cases interpreting treaties. ... We decline to consider these. The purpose of Rule 44.1's notice requirement is to avoid unfairly surprising opposing parties. Fed. R.Civ.P. 44.1 advisory committee's notes. Our task is certainly easier if a party who intends to raise an issue of foreign law does so as early as possible. Submission of such materials in the district court may well have the salutary effect of avoiding the delay encountered in Appeals. Absent special circumstances, parties should present issues of foreign law in their appellant briefs at the latest. The excerpts submitted to us arrived without exact citations as to their source or their present validity. In fairness to the taxpayers and in order to encourage early submission of such material in the future, we decided the good faith issue on the briefs and oral argument. The government may submit the additional material upon remand, if necessary. At that time the taxpayers will have adequate opportunity to respond.

REVERSED AND REMANDED

TWOHY v. FIRST NATIONAL BANK OF CHICAGO

United States Court of Appeals, Seventh Circuit, 1985.
758 F.2d 1185.

CUMMINGS, CHIEF JUDGE

Philip Twohy, the majority shareholder and principal of Bevco Baleares, S.A. (hereinafter "Bevco"), a Spanish corporation, brought suit ... against the defendant, First National Bank of Chicago (hereinafter "First Chicago" or "the Bank"), a national banking association with its principal place of business in Chicago, Illinois. Plaintiff's claims arise out of a series of events involving an alleged loan transaction with the defendant that was to facilitate an expansion of Bevco's business in Spain to Mallorca and the Canary Islands. ... Twohy charged breach of contract and counts of fraud, misrepresentation and libel.

* * *

13. Thyssen Steel Co. v. M/V Kavo Yerakas, 911 F. Supp. 263, 267–268 (S.D. Tex. 1996).

Judge Leighton in his July 1 Judgment Order found that "all parties agree that the law of Spain controls [the action] * * *." At a June 3, 1983, hearing he stated that "[e]vidently everybody agrees that the law of Spain controls," and asked both parties' counsel, "Is that correct?" Plaintiff's counsel, Ronald Szopa of the firm of Mitchell, Russell & Kelly, replied affirmatively. Furthermore, plaintiff acted at all times consistently with the position taken at the June 3 hearing. Twohy filed counter-affidavits of Spanish law experts pursuant to Fed.R.Civ.P. 44.1, seeking to contradict defendant's memorandum of law and the affidavits of its foreign law experts. Plaintiff also failed to contend at any time prior to judgment that Spanish law was inapplicable or that any other law governed the alleged contract dispute and injury arising out of it.

In plaintiff's motion to amend, Twohy asserted that his counsel's stipulation that Spanish law governed the case was incorrect and inadvertent, that plaintiff intended to bring the action at all times under the laws of the United States and that the attorney making the stipulation was acting only as his local counsel at the time and was unfamiliar with the legal issues of the case.... Judge Leighton correctly rejected these arguments. The court characterized Twohy's use of the term "local counsel" to describe the law firm of Mitchell, Russell & Kelly as "misleading" and noted both the firm's status as plaintiff's only counsel of record and the absence of any indication that its authority was limited in any way during the early stages of litigation. The court further observed that plaintiff litigated the Spanish law questions raised by defendant and "never so much as suggested that any other law might apply." ... Here, the law of Spain bears a reasonable relationship to the alleged transaction and injury in question and does not violate public policy nor call into question the court's subject matter jurisdiction. * * * [I]t would be a waste of the court's resources and an inequity to allow plaintiff to return to the district court and attempt to show that some other law should govern this action and perhaps escape his stipulation.

Questions and Comments

1. Judge Roger J. Miner is a highly respected federal court judge of the United States Court of Appeals for the Second Circuit. That is an important circuit (encompassing New York state and an extensive case load) for the development of the law affecting international contracts and torts. Miner's comments address whether a court has an obligation to apply foreign law when choice of law rules point to foreign law, even if the parties have not requested the application of foreign law. Why does Miner believe that "foreign law has not been welcomed by our federal courts"? Miner seems to believe that a court has an *obligation* to apply foreign law even if none of the parties requests its application. However, the *Vishipco Line* decision of the Second Circuit seems to suggest that the law of the forum should be applied where the parties do not suggest any foreign law. Why? If Miner is correct, should the court instruct the parties to present evidence of the foreign law or should the court on its own undertake an investigation into the foreign law? Do Epstein, Snyder & Baldwin present a different view of *Vishipco Line* in

their second extract in Part B? The Third Circuit has recently reaffirmed its view that courts have no duty to determine foreign law and when the parties do not prove foreign law the court will apply the forum's law. *Ferrostaal, Inc. v. M/V Sea Phoenix*, 447 F.3d 212 (3d Cir. 2006).

2. Miner introduces us to Rule 44.1. What does Miner mean by suggesting that Rule 44.1 provides a latitude of flexibility that is not used? Is Rule 44.1 as flexible as he suggests?

3. One of Miner's concerns is the confusion regarding the proof of foreign law as a question of fact or of law. He says it is a question of law for the court. See *Grupo Protexa, S.A. v. All American Marine Slip*, 20 F.3d 1224 (3d Cir. 1994). That being the case, how does the proof of foreign law differ from the proof of U.S. law?

4. Is Miner taking on too much responsibility by his position that *judges* must research the foreign law? Will his view lead lower court judges to merely acknowledge the possibility of the application of some foreign law before stating that U.S. law applies, solely to avoid being overruled by circuit court judges such as Miner because they failed to even consider applying foreign law?

5. Do you agree with Miner that an expert is not automatically suspect because the expert was retained by one of the parties? If Miner's view is incorrect, should all experts on foreign law retained by the parties be rejected? Wouldn't that view have to be applied to all experts, not just experts on foreign law?

6. Miner favors the use of court appointed experts. Do you see any problems with his position? Many prominent academics frequently serve as experts on various issues of foreign law. In most cases the expert "appears" in court only by way of an affidavit. But the expert may also have consulted with the party on some strategy of the case, such as which foreign law to argue in favor of, and how damages differ under different choices of law. An expert appointed by the court would not discuss strategy. Or might not the court want to know *why* the party is urging the application of a particular foreign law, as well as know the substance of that law?

7. The Epstein, Snyder & Baldwin extract emphasizes the need for counsel to research the state rules of civil procedure when the matter is in state court. Since many of the states have adopted rules similar to the Federal Rules of Civil Procedure, however, Rule 44.1 may mirror the state rule. What did the adoption of Rule 44.1 accomplish? Some of our cases may be initiated in or removed to federal court, thus making Rule 44.1 the applicable procedural rule. Why would the defendant wish to remove a case from state to federal court? Sometimes a matter is removed from state to federal court because a subsequent motion to dismiss on *forum non conveniens* reasons may be better received. That has been discussed in Problem 4.2.

8. One of the first requirements of Rule 44.1 is that a party wishing to raise an issue of foreign law must give notice of such intention. How does a party do that? What are the consequences if the defendant GROWFAST fails to provide reasonable notice that it intends to raise the issue of the applicability of foreign (probably Mexican) law in a U.S. court?

9. When is the last time that reasonable notice may be given by GROWFAST? What if GROWFAST has successively seen the court deny GROWFAST's separate motions to dismiss for reasons of improper forum, jurisdiction and *forum non conveniens*? Can GROWFAST then move that the court rule that Mexican law apply, or must it have come as part of a previous motion to dismiss? What if GROWFAST does not raise the issue at trial and U.S. law is applied? May the applicability of Mexican law be raised on appeal?

10. *Stuart v. United States* deals with late submissions. Is the decision inconsistent with Judge Miner's view of the flexibility of Rule 44.1?

11. The *Twohy* decision, extracted in two locations in this Problem, and also in Problem 4.5, illustrates how the use of foreign law arises in practice at the pre-trial stage. The *Twohy* court found that the stipulated Spanish law had a reasonable relationship to the alleged transaction and injury in question. Would you try to use the same kind of experts in our cases as were used in *Twohy*? Should the court allow the use of counter-affidavits, and counter-counter-affidavits and so on? Why was no authority other that the actual statutes presented?

PART B.   CHOICE OF THE APPLICABLE LAW RULES

The court must choose the applicable law. The conflicts rules applied to make that decision will almost certainly be the rules of the forum. Just how will the court make that decision if GROWFAST moves to apply the law of Mexico? The Supreme Court has briefly referred to choice of law, such as in *Asahi Metal Indus. Co. v. Superior Court of California* (extract in Problem 3.2 on personal jurisdiction) where the Court stated "Moreover, it is not at all clear at this point that California law should govern the question whether a Japanese corporation should indemnify a Taiwanese corporation on the basis of a sale made in Taiwan and a shipment of goods from Japan to Taiwan." Another question that has recently been discussed is the choice of international law as the applicable law. More recently than *Asahi*, the Supreme Court 2004 decision in *Sosa v. Alvarez–Machain* (extract in Problem 4.2, Part D on subject matter jurisdiction, addressing the Alien Tort Statute), led a federal district court to comment as follows:

IN RE AGENT ORANGE PRODUCT LIABILITY LITIGATION

United States District Court, Eastern District of New York, 2005.
373 F.Supp.2d 7.

Vietnamese nonprofit group and individual Vietnamese nationals brought product liability action against chemical companies under Alien Tort Statute (ATS), alleging personal injury and property damage, in violation of federal, state, and international law, caused by use of toxic herbicides manufactured by the companies and sold to the United States for use during Vietnam War. Companies moved to dismiss or for partial summary judgment.

* * *

The Court of Appeals for the Second Circuit has avoided reaching the conflicts of law question of applicability of international law rather than that of the forum. * * * While its analysis is not crystal clear, *Sosa v. Alvarez–Machain,* the *Sosa* court specifically rejected state choice of law rules in denying applicability of the headquarters doctrine because "current flexibility" in choice of law methodology [of the states or foreign countries] would sometimes lead to a result inconsistent with federal policy.

The Court of Appeals for the Ninth Circuit's analysis of choice of law in international law cases was instructive. *See Doe I v. Unocal Corp.* It declared:

> Unocal urges us to apply not international law, but the law of the state where the underlying events occurred, i.e., Myanmar. Where, as in the present case, only *jus cogens* violations are alleged—i.e., violations of norms of international law that are binding on nations even if they do not agree to them—it may, however, be preferable to apply international law rather than the law of any particular state, such as the state where the underlying events occurred or the forum state. The reason is that, by definition, the law of any particular state is either identical to the *jus cogens* norms of international law, or it is invalid. . . .
>
> Application of international law—rather than the law of Myanmar, California state law, or our federal common law—is also favored by a consideration of the factors listed in the Restatement (Second) of Conflict of Laws § 6 (1969). First, "the needs of the . . . international system[ ]" are better served by applying international rather than national law. Second, "the relevant policies of the forum" cannot be ascertained by referring . . . to one out-of-circuit decision which happens to favor federal common law and ignoring other decisions which have favored other law, including international law. Third, regarding "the protection of justified expectations," the "certainty, predictability and uniformity of result," and the "ease in the determination and application of the law to be applied," we note that the standard we adopt today from an admittedly recent case nevertheless goes back at least to the Nuremberg trials and is similar to that to the Restatement (Second) of Torts. Finally, "the basic polic[y] underlying the particular field of law" is to provide tort remedies for violations of international law. This goal is furthered by the application of international law, even when the international law in question is criminal law but is similar to domestic tort law. . . .

Courts are not precluded from referring to appropriate state or national law for analogies to fill in procedural-and even substantive-gaps left in international law as it is shaped so it can be enforced in a reasonable way.

A good place to start in trying to identify the rules of choice of law is the Restatement of Conflict of Laws, referred to above in *In Re Agent Orange* above. The Restatement commences with rules applicable in a very different context, choice of law involving two different sister states, and choice of law where a state and one or more foreign nations are involved. The Restatement suggests that in the latter situation "there may be factors ... which call for a result different from that which would be reached in an interstate case." § 10. It then notes some differences in the two varieties of cases—interstate and international—but makes no attempt at stating applicable choice of law rules in the international context. Epstein, Baldwin and Snyder provide more help, and several case extracts show the development of quite different views.

DAVID EPSTEIN, JEFFREY L. SNYDER & CHARLES S. BALDWIN, IV, INTERNATIONAL LITIGATION

§§ 9.05–9.06 (3d ed. 2002).

9.05 CHOICE OF LAW CONSIDERATIONS

Choice of law is distinguishable from pleading and proof of foreign law. Even before the practitioner is faced with the determination of how to plead and prove foreign law, he must first determine whether foreign law or the law of the forum applies to the case. This is essentially a conflict of laws exercise and may be governed by choice of law rules of the forum. Traditional conflict of laws rules for contracts and torts have been reexamined and replaced in many states by more flexible contemporary standards. In preparing the case the attorney should be familiar with local choice of law rules applicable to each substantive issue.

What are the consequences of a party's failure to provide evidence of foreign law where local choice of law rules provide that the case is governed by foreign law? This was one of the issues presented in *Vishipco Line v. Chase Manhattan Bank,*[45] which involved the bank's failure to honor plaintiff's certificate of deposit contracts after closing its branch in Vietnam. The court of appeals determined that the outcome of this issue depended on whether the forum's choice of law rules were mandatory rather than permissive. The court of appeals cited the movement away from the "vested rights" theory and mandatory application of the forum's choice of law rules toward the adoption of a discretionary rule. It was noted that, while under Rule 44.1 a court is still permitted to apply foreign law even if not requested to do so by a party, Rule 44.1 would allow the application of the law of the forum, where the parties had not asserted at trial that the foreign law applied with respect to underlying obligations involved on the part of the defendant. The law of the forum applied despite the fact that the forum's choice of law rules

---

45. 660 F.2d 854, 838 n.7 (2d Cir. 1981), *cert. denied,* 459 U.S. 976 (1982).

called for the application of foreign law. The mandatory/permissive nature of choice of law rules should first be analyzed in determining whether plaintiff's claims may be dismissed under the standards of Rule 44.1 for failure to provide evidence of foreign law.

An example of a modern approach to conflicts of laws analysis is *Liew v. Official Receiver & Liquidator.*[52] The issue on appeal involved whether the district court had applied the proper choice of law in evaluating the validity of an assignment of contract rights against a banking institution. Since jurisdiction was based on diversity, the district court applied the choice of law rules of California, where the action was brought. The court of appeals summarized this approach, the "governmental interest" analysis, as follows:

(1) To examine the substantive law relating to assignments in Singapore and in California, to determine if the laws in the two jurisdictions differ as applied to this assignment transaction;

(2) If they do differ, then to determine whether both jurisdictions have an interest in having their laws applied. If only one jurisdiction has such an interest, then we do not have a "true conflict" and we apply the law of that jurisdiction;

(3) If there is a "true conflict" then we proceed, under the "comparative impairment" approach, to determine which jurisdiction's interest would be more impaired if its policy were subordinated to the policy of the other. The conflict should be resolved by applying the law of the jurisdiction whose interest would be more impaired if its laws were not applied.

In applying this analysis, the district court previously found that the law of the forum should apply since the receiver, the party seeking the application of foreign law, had made no actual showing of Singapore's interest in having its law applied, or of how such an interest would be impaired by California law However, the court of appeals ruled that under the governmental interest approach in California, the burden was not placed on the party relying on foreign law and the receiver had satisfactorily raised the issue of foreign law and advanced policy reasons for its application.* * *

§ 9.06　CHOICE OF LAW RULES

In a diversity case, a federal district court will look to the law of the forum, including its choice-of-law provisions. This applies to both the substantive law as well as the conflict of laws rules of the forum. A choice of law analysis depends upon the particular issue involved and may lead to varying applications of domestic or foreign law in a single case. One commentator observed:

there is at least one point on which there seems to be general agreement in the United States. This is that choice of the applicable law should frequently depend upon the issue involved. The search in

---

52.　685 F.2d 1192, 1195 (9th Cir. 1982).

these instances is not for the state whose law will be applicable to govern all issues in a case; rather it is for the rule of law that can most appropriately be applied to govern the particular issue. As a result, situations do arise where the court must decide whether it should apply the rules of different states to determine different issues in a single case.[62]

The "pick and choose" approach is evident in choice of law rules which recognize the law of the state having the "greatest interest or more significant relationship to the transaction and the parties." Under the pick and choose analysis, a variety of factors are considered, including the interest of the foreign state; the relevant policies of the forum; the protection of justified expectations; the basic policies underlying the particular field of law, certainty, predictability and uniformity of result; and ease in the determination and application of the law to be applied.

The Restatement (Second) of Conflict of Laws generally applies to foreign conflicts as well as interstate conflicts, although "[t]here may . . . be factors in a particular international case which call for a result different from that which would be reached in an interstate case." However, in applying relevant factors under a "significant state interest" analysis, courts may reach different results in resolving similar international conflicts issues. In a case involving an aircraft accident, *Ciprari v. Servicos Aereos Cruzeiro*,[66] the district court applied Brazilian law which limited the liability of the Brazilian air carrier. The court determined under the local choice of law rule that Brazil's interest in the limitation of damages was greater and more direct then New York's. However, in a personal injury case, *Panicotto v. Sociedade de Safaris de Mocambigue, S.A.R.L.*,[68] the district court, distinguishing *Ciprari,* refused to apply the law of Mozambique which limited liability for travel accidents. The court determined that the foreign law was unreasonable and contrary to Illinois public policy and that, unlike *Ciprari,* there was no "exceptional national concern" which justified its application.

Finally, in *McDaniel v. Petroleum Helicopters, Inc.*,[70] the court of appeals reversed the lower court, which refused to apply Colombian law restricting the amount recoverable for loss of love and affection in wrongful death cases. Analyzing the case under the state's lex loci rule, the court of appeals refused to apply any public policy exception against enforcement of the foreign law in *Pancotto* and *Ciprari* also illustrate the need to isolate the substantive legal issues for choice of law analysis since both involved multiple issues, including liability and measure of damages.

A further consideration under a typical choice of law analysis is whether the law to be applied is procedural or substantive. As previously

---

62. Reese, *Depacage: A Common Phenomenon in Choice of Law, 73* Colum. L. Rev. 58 (1973).

66. 245 F. Supp. 819, 823 (S.D.N.Y. 1965), *aff'd,* 359 F.2d 855 (2d Cir. 1966).

68. 422 F. Supp. 405 (N.D. Ill. 1976).

70. 455 F.2d 137, 140 (5th Cir. 1972).

stated, in diversity cases, a federal court applies the substantive law of the state in which it sits. In many cases the procedural/substantive distinction is not a critical problem in deciding whether to apply local law or foreign law. However, a difficult issue in terms of procedure versus substance is whether local or foreign statutes of limitations should be applied under a choice of law analysis. The basic choice of law rule is that statutes of limitations are procedural in nature. Thus, the statute of limitations of the forum will usually apply, even though the course of action may be governed by the law of the foreign jurisdiction.

An exception to the application of the forum's statute of limitations is recognized where the foreign cause of action is created by statute. In general, courts will follow a foreign prescriptive period if the time period within which suit is to be brought is contained in the statute which creates the right or otherwise conditions the right of action. A majority of courts have held that where the foreign limitation period is based on the assertion of the statutorily created right, it is a matter of substantive as distinguished from procedural law. Courts following the choice of law approach have stated that if the time element in the foreign law is devoted "specifically" to the right sought to be enforced, the foreign limitation period is substantive rather than procedural.

CIPRARI v. SERVICOS AEREOS CRUZEIRO, S.A. (CRUZEIRO)

United States District Court for the Southern District of New York, 1965.
245 F.Supp. 819.

WYATT, DISTRICT JUDGE.

The motion raises the single question whether as a matter of New York law (which clearly must here be followed by this Court) the Brazilian limitation of liability is valid in an action in New York. Put in a different way: would the Court of Appeals of New York apply in the case at bar the principle laid down for the first cause of action in Kilberg v. Northeast Airlines, Inc., 9 N.Y.2d 34, 211 N.Y.S.2d 133, 172 N.E.2d 526 (1961)?

Plaintiff is 38 years old. He is a citizen of the United States and since October 1962 has been resident and domiciled in New York. He has been employed as a Sales Engineer by Honeywell, Inc., a large, publicly owned Delaware corporation which makes and sells control, regulator, and other equipment. The principal place of business of Honeywell is in Minneapolis, Minnesota but it does business over most, if not all, of the United States. It has subsidiaries which do business in foreign countries, including Honeywell Controles Ltda. in Brazil.

Defendant Cruzeiro is a Brazilian corporation, wholly owned by residents and nationals of Brazil. It is a commercial air carrier, flying scheduled flights on routes principally in Brazil; it has some flights to four neighboring South American countries. It has no flights to or from any of the States of this country. It does not itself sell any tickets in this country. It does not advertise here and it has no ticket office here. Cruzeiro is, however, a member of a large group of air carriers which by agreement issue tickets good over the lines of other members. Some members of this group, such as Pan–American World Airways, Inc., have ticket offices in New York and thus it would be possible for a person, through some other air carrier such as Pan American, to buy a ticket in New York good over the lines of Cruzeiro.

In January 1963, plaintiff made a business trip to Brazil. He bought in New York a ticket to Rio do Janeiro from Pan–American and arrived in Rio on a Pan–American plane on January 15, 1963. He evidently had no plans up to that time to go to Sao Paulo, Brazil. When he arrived in Rio, however, he was told by an employee of Honeywell (or Honeywell Controles Ltda.) working in Brazil that he (plaintiff) and the other employee were required at once to go on a business trip to Sao Paulo. There are regular flights by Cruzeiro between Rio and Sao Paulo. On the day of plaintiff's arrival in Rip-January 15, 1963–he and the other employee bought tickets from Cruzeiro for a flight to Sao Paulo. The ticket was entirely in Portuguese and on the reverse contained, among other things, the following (in English translation):

> Contractual conditions. The present transportation is governed by the Brazilian Air Code and other legislation pertinent to the matter. * * *'

Plaintiff does not understand Portuguese. No English translation was given him of the ticket, nor was his attention directed to any of its terms. Plaintiff made no attempt to find out the terms. Whether his companion, who had been working in Brazil, understood Portuguese, does not appear. Plaintiff and his fellow employee left Rio on Cruzeiro's flight 403 at 2:20 in the afternoon of January 15, 1963. The plane had been made in the United States. During the landing at Sao Paulo at about 4:05 the same afternoon, the plane crashed and plaintiff sustained severe injuries. While plaintiff was receiving medical treatment in Brazil, Cruzeiro paid for such treatment much more than 100,000 cruzeiros. Plaintiff was released from the hospital in Brazil and returned to New York. Plaintiff has made claim under the Workmen's Compensation Law of New York ...

The problem begins with *Kilberg v. Northeast Airlines, Inc.*, 9 N.Y.2d 34 (1961). Edward Kilberg, a resident (domiciliary) of New York, bought a ticket in New York from defendant for a flight to Nantucket, boarded in New York a plane of defendant for that flight and was killed when the plane crashed in Massachusetts. Jack Kilberg, as administrator of Edward's estate, sued Northeast ... in negligence under a Massachusetts wrongful death statute.... [Four of the Judges in what was technically dicta stated that recovery for the full amount of damages could be had on the first cause of action despite the limit of $15,000 specified in the Massachusetts wrongful death statute. This result was reached by following the classic choice of law rule and looking to the law of Massachusetts (the place of the tort) as the source of the right but rejecting as contrary to New York public policy the damage limit in the Massachusetts statute; it was also stated that in view of the strong public policy of New York, the measure of damages could be treated as a 'procedural or remedial question' governed by New York law. Judge Fuld declined to express any opinion except as to [a separate] second (contract) cause of action. Judges Froessel any Van Voorhis (like Judge Fuld) felt that no question should be reached except that of the second cause of action but they expressed complete disagreement with the majority views on the first cause of action.

The next year came *Davenport v. Webb*, 11 N.Y.2d 392 (1962), where prejudgment interest, allowed by the law of New York, was not allowed where the judgment was in a New York action, where decedents were New York residents, but where the wrongful death occurred in Maryland and under Maryland law prejudgment interest was not allowed. This seems a retreat from the broad language of Kilberg that measure of damages was procedural and governed by New York law.

Then came *Babcock v. Jackson*, 12 N.Y.2d 473 (1963) where five of the judges agreed to abandon the classic choice of law rule that the law of the place of the tort invariably governed. There was substituted as a rule of New York law that in tort cases controlling effect will be given 'to the law of the jurisdiction which, because of its relationship or contact with the occurrence or the parties has the greatest concern with the specific issue raised in the litigation'. Babcock and Jackson were both residents of New York. They went in an automobile of Jackson on a trip over a weekend to Ontario. The trip thus began and was to have ended in New York. The car had been licensed, insured and garaged in New York. While Jackson was driving in Ontario, he lost control of the car, it crashed into a stone wall and Babcock was injured. When they returned to New York, Babcock sued Jackson in a New York court. The lower courts dismissed the action by applying the law of Ontario which denies any liability by a host driver of an automobile to a guest passenger. The Court of Appeals reversed, ruling that the law of New York was applicable (although Ontario was the place of the tort) because the 'contacts' and 'interests' of New York as to 'the issue presented' made it clear 'that the concern of New York is unquestionably the greater and more direct' than that of Ontario. The issue was whether a host driver is liable for negligence to his guest passenger. New York law as a matter of policy imposes such liability and no reason appeared for substituting Ontario law in a case 'affecting New York residents and arising out of the operation of a New York based automobile'. The policy of the denial by Ontario of such liability is to prevent collusive claims against insurance companies but this policy was directed at preventing such claims 'against Ontario defendants and their insurance carriers, not New York defendants and their insurance carriers'. Judge Van Voorhis and Judge Scileppi dissented on the ground that the established rule applying the law of the place of the tort should not be changed.

The last New York decision to be considered is that recently (July 9, 1965) handed down by the Court of Appeals in *Dym v. Gordon*, 209

N.E.2d 792. Dym and Gordon were both residents (domiciliaries) of New York. Gordon owned an automobile which was licensed, insured and regularly based (garaged) in New York. Gordon drove his automobile to Boulder, Colorado where he enrolled as a summer student at the University of Colorado. Dym went separately and without any prearrangement with Gordon to Boulder where she also became a summer student. On August 11, 1959 Dym drove with Gordon in his automobile, they intending to ride from Boulder to Longmont, another town in Colorado. On the trip, there was a collision between the car driven by Gordon and another car. Dym suffered injuries and after both returned to their homes in New York, she sued Gordon in New York on the theory that his negligence caused or contributed to her injuries. Colorado has a statute which denies liability by a host driver to a guest passenger except for 'negligence consisting of a willful and wanton disregard of the rights of others'. It was conceded that if this statute applied Dym could not recover because the negligence of Gordon was 'ordinary negligence'. A bare majority of the Court of Appeals (Judges Dye, Burke, Van Voorhis and Scileppi) held that the law of Colorado applied. The minority (Chief Judge Desmond and Judges Fuld and Bergan) believed that New York law should apply. The majority professed to follow *Babcock v. Jackson* (in which Judge Van Voorhis and Judge Scileppi had dissented) but to find factual distinctions. In *Babcock*, only New York residents were involved in the accident; in *Dym*, there was a collision and the other car presumably was Colorado based and contained a Colorado resident or residents. The host-guest relationship was formed in New York in *Babcock* but in Colorado in *Dym*. The New Yorkers were in transit in Babcock whereas in *Dym* they 'had come to rest' in Colorado and 'had thus chosen to live their daily lives under the protective arm of Colorado law'. The accident in *Dym* 'arose out of Colorado based activity' and thus the place of the accident was not 'fortuitous'. The majority also referred to the public policy of Colorado expressed by its statute as resting on three factors: protection against fraudulent (collusive) claims, prevention of suits by ungrateful guests, and establishment of a priority for injured persons in other cars against the negligent driver.

In the light of these decided cases, it seems reasonably clear to me that at least a majority of the New York Court of Appeals, and probably all of the judges of that Court, would apply the law of Brazil, including that part of Brazilian law limiting damages against an air carrier, to the case at bar. Because of its relationship (geographical and otherwise) to the accident in the case at bar and to defendant as a Brazilian air carrier, Brazil 'has the greatest concern with the specific issue raised in the litigation', namely, the issue of limitation of liability. The contract between plaintiff and defendant was made in Brazil. The flight began in Brazil, was to end there, and did end there. (It has been suggested that where the relationship arises and the trip originates and ends in the same state, the law of that state will in every case be applied by the New York Courts.) At no time was defendant's plane over or even near New York. Plaintiff 'had come to rest' in Brazil even though his onward journey to Sao Paulo (not planned beforehand) began on the day of his arrival. The trip being made by plaintiff was occasioned by activities in Brazil-the operations of Honeywell's Brazilian subsidiary and plaintiff's participation in Brazil in those operations. That the place of the accident was Brazil was thus in no sense 'fortuitous'. Defendant is not a New York corporation; it is a thoroughly Brazilian corporation, owned by Brazilians, and conducts only very limited activities in New York. While it has been held liable to suit here, its activities in New York relate entirely to the purchase of materials and not to the solicitation or even the encouragement of passenger business. Unlike Northeast (defendant in the *Kilberg* action), Cruzeiro (defendant here) does not deal with the public in New York and of course never dealt with plaintiff in New York. While plaintiff is a resident of New York, there is no likelihood of his becoming a public charge to affect the policy of this State; the accident in suit occurred in the course of his employment and he is covered by the Workmen's Compensation Law of New York. His employer is not a New York corporation. This is not a wrongful death case; the public policy of New York to which the majority in *Kilberg* referred was a public policy applicable to wrongful death cases. In any event, a public policy of New York does not appear to survive as a factor in choice of law after the *Babcock* and *Dym* decisions. Nothing has been submitted as to the Brazilian policy behind the statutory limitation of the liability of a Brazilian air carrier, but it is reasonable to suppose, as it has been judicially declared, that the statute is based on 'Brazil's concern for the financial integrity of her local airlines' and was enacted 'with a view toward protecting * * * an infant industry of extraordinary public and national importance'. In the same opinion it is stated that a national airline to Brazil 'is an object of concern in terms of national policy' and that the success of such an airline is to Brazil 'a matter not only of pride and commercial well-being, but perhaps even of national security'.What the case at bar comes down to is that the only relationship or contact of New York is the fact that plaintiff is a resident of New York. Surely this is not enough, standing alone, to warrant the application of New York law to the issue of measure of damages. It has been suggested that if the forum state has no interest in the application of its law while the state of the place of the conduct and injury does have such an interest, the law of the latter state should be applied. New York seems to have no interest here. This is not a wrongful death action. The New York Workmen's Compensation Law covers plaintiff. Such law must embody the policy of New York so far as he is concerned and so far as concerns the prevention of his dependents from becoming public charges.

But if New York does have an interest in the application of its law because of the residence here of plaintiff, the contrary interest of Brazil in the issue involved (limitation of damages) seems clearly 'the greater and more direct', 'the strongest interest in the resolution of the particular issue presented'. For the reasons set out, the conclusion is that the law of Brazil as to the measure of damages must be applied.

RASKIN v. ALLISON

Court of Appeals, Kansas, 2002.
30 Kan.App.2d 1240, 57 P.3d 30.

PADDOCK, S.J.

This is an interlocutory appeal by the plaintiffs from the partial summary judgment granted to defendants on a choice-of-law question. The trial court found the substantive law of Mexico would govern the claims in this personal injury action where the injuries occurred in Mexico although all parties were Kansas residents. We affirm.

The facts are brief and uncontroverted. Kaley Raskin and Jenna Turnbaugh, both minors, received personal injuries resulting from a collision of the water craft they occupied and a water craft operated by Chad Leathers in the ocean waters off Cabo San Lucas, Mexico. Kaley's and Jenna's parents filed this action individually and as next friends to their minor daughters against Ken and Karen Allison individually and as guardians ad litem for their minor son and stepson, Chad Leathers. Plaintiffs' claims were framed on the theories of negligence and negligent entrustment.

Here, plaintiffs do not dispute the injuries were sustained in Mexican waters and that under the rule of *lex loci delicti,* Mexican law would normally control. However, plaintiffs argue the rule should not apply in this case because (1) all the parties are residents of Kansas, (2) Kansas has never invoked the rule in a case where a foreign country's law would apply, and (3) the rule of comity requires that Kansas protect its own residents and apply Kansas law. Plaintiffs argue that because all the parties are Kansas residents, Kansas has the greater interest in applying its substantive law; therefore, the case should be governed by Kansas law. However, the Kansas Supreme Court has repeatedly applied the law of the place of the injury, even when all the parties were residents of Kansas. In each of those cases, the law of the place of injury was less favorable to the plaintiffs than Kansas law. * * *

Plaintiffs also contend that because Kansas courts have never applied the *lex loci delicti* rule to apply the law of a foreign country, the rule should be rejected in this case. Plaintiffs are correct in asserting that neither of the Kansas appellate courts have applied the law of a foreign country in a tort case. This court, however, recently applied Canadian law in a contract case where the contract was made in Canada by applying the rule of *lex loci contractus.* Plaintiffs have not cited compelling authority that the rule of *lex loci delicti* does not apply in cases involving foreign countries. Kansas follows traditional choice of law principles largely reflected in the original Restatement of Conflict of Laws (1934). We have no hesitation in finding that the *lex loci delicti* rule would apply in tort cases notwithstanding the injuries were incurred in a foreign country. Finally, plaintiffs challenge the *lex loci delicti* rule by arguing principles of comity mitigate against applying Mexican law.

Plaintiffs are wide of the mark by trying to distinguish comity principles from choice-of-law principles. Choice-of-law principles, essentially, are rules defining when a court will extend comity to the laws of another state. Both principles are inextricably joined. * * *

While the court is not required to apply Mexico's law under principles of comity, the *lex loci delicti* rule is well established under Kansas law and there is no indication that Kansas intends to abandon the rule. For example, the Supreme Court rejected the analytical approach which allows the forum court to apply the law of the jurisdiction most intimately concerned with the outcome of the particular litigation.

Actually, the thread that weaves through all of the plaintiffs' arguments is that damage limitations purportedly contained in Mexico's law are contrary to Kansas public policy and should not be enforced by Kansas courts. Plaintiffs seem to argue that public policy is defined by Kansas legislative enactments and since the Kansas Legislature had not enacted statutes with damage limitations similar to those in Mexico, Mexican laws are therefore contrary to Kansas public policy. Plaintiffs cite no authority establishing what damage limitations exist in Mexico. However, a recent case cited by defendants appeared to support the conclusion that Mexico recognizes that contributory negligence is a complete defense in a tort claim. *Spinozzi v. ITT Sheraton Corp.* 174 F.3d 842, 844 (7th Cir.1999). Also, Mexican law apparently limits recovery of damages in tort cases to the amount of the injured party's medical and rehabilitative expense and lost wages at the minimum wage rate. See *Hernandez v. Burger,* 102 Cal.App.3d 795, 799, 162 Cal.Rptr. 564 (1980). Plaintiffs assert these damage limitations in their brief.

Kansas cases consistently hold that a Kansas court will not apply the law of another state to a claim if that other state's law is contrary to Kansas public policy.* * * [The Supreme] Court invalidated a contractual choice-of law provision finding that its reference to New York law was contrary to "strong public policy" in Kansas and would not be enforced. In its discussion, the Supreme Court held that a "strong public policy" is one " 'so thoroughly established as a state of public mind so united and so definite and fixed that its existence is not subject to any substantial doubt. " * * * The * * * court found a strong public policy in the fact that the incorporation of New York law into the contract between a Kansas resident and a securities broker evaded Kansas' securities law prohibiting the sale of unregistered securities. None of these cases appear to set forth a public policy exception as broad as plaintiffs are arguing here. Kansas appears to be following the prevailing view that the public policy exception in conflict of law theory should be narrowly limited. As previously noted, the plaintiffs here appear to contend that if the law of another jurisdiction is different than Kansas law, it is contrary to Kansas public policy.

The Kansas Supreme Court has repeatedly upheld the application of the law of other states in tort cases even when those laws impose a higher burden of proof on plaintiffs *before* they can recover damages. The

Supreme Court has even upheld the application of another State's wrongful death statute even though that statute excluded some types of damages allowed under Kansas law. Thus, Kansas cases indicate the "public policy" exception in the choice-of-law context is limited and generally not triggered because of limitations on damages or higher burdens of proof. Finally, plaintiffs cannot seriously contend that the application of Mexican law is unfair when they voluntarily vacationed there. As the Tenth Circuit once stated:

> It is a firmly established principle of American jurisprudence that the laws of one state have no extra-territorial effect in another state. The forum state will give effect to foreign law as long as the foreign law is not repugnant to the moral sense of the community. The mere fact that the law of the foreign state differs from the law of the state in which recognition is sought is not enough to make the foreign law inapplicable.... Indeed, this Court is reminded of the oft-para-phrased advice of St. Ambrose, Catholic bishop of Milan in the fourth century, to St. Augustine. 'When you are at Rome, live in the Roman style; when you are elsewhere, live as they do elsewhere.' *Brennan v. University of Kansas,* 451 F.2d 1287, 1289–90 (10th Cir.1971).

The record before the court fails to establish a sound basis to refuse to apply Mexican law in this case based on the public policy exception. The limitations on damages allegedly contained in Mexican law do not appear to violate a "strong public policy" as defined by prior Kansas Supreme Court decisions. The trial court correctly determined that the substantive law of Mexico would govern the claims in this personal injury action. AFFIRMED

TWOHY v. FIRST NATIONAL BANK OF CHICAGO

United States Court of Appeals, Seventh Circuit, 1985.
758 F.2d 1185.

CUMMINGS, CHIEF JUDGE.

Twohy argues that the district court erroneously based its decision to dismiss upon conflicting affidavits of expert witnesses regarding foreign law and that it abused its discretion by refusing to amend the judgment and allow the filing of an amended complaint without a finding that undue prejudice would result to the defendant. For the reasons set forth below, we affirm. * * *

First Chicago filed a "Motion for Judgment on the Pleaded Defenses" ... reiterating the defenses raised in its answer. In support of the motion, the Bank attached the affidavits of Rolf K. Zion, an Assistant Vice-President of First Chicago stationed in Spain, and of James A. Baker, an attorney licensed to practice law in Illinois and Spain and an expert in Spanish law. ... The Baker affidavit opined that under Spanish conflict of law rules, Spanish law would govern the action and that under Spanish law "based upon affiant's background and his knowledge of and experience with the law of Spain * * *, a shareholder, such as the plaintiff, has no right to proceed in contract, tort or libel on the alleged contract and alleged transaction of the corporation of which he is a shareholder'', or in other words Twohy ''has no standing to bring this complaint for the remedies alleged as a matter of law''... .The Baker affidavit contains no citations to authority of any kind to support the opinions contained therein. Plaintiff filed his answer to the motion for judgment ..., and asserted that there was a genuine issue of material fact which precluded the entry of judgment on the pleadings. ...

The district court initially denied defendant's ... motion ..., but submitted a motion for a more particularized statement of the fraud and libel allegations. The court concluded that ''there remain unresolved issues of fact'' in the case. ... * * * First Chicago filed a motion for reconsideration of the November 23 denial order.... The motion raised no new arguments but took issue with Judge Leighton's claim that unresolved questions of fact remained in the case. As to the court's assertion that plaintiff could prove he personally contracted with defendant, First Chicago responded that plaintiff in his individual capacity only could assert an action for recovery of a broker's or finder's fee (but had not done so) and that plaintiff as a shareholder simply could not recover under Spanish law for injury and damages asserted in the complaint—injury to and harm suffered by the shareholder's corporation.... In support of the motion for reconsideration, defendant filed a supplemental affidavit of Mr. Baker which stated that under Spanish law, Twohy, acting in his individual capacity, could not enter into a contract on behalf of Bevco and that even if Twohy had established an agency relationship with Bevco, any action arising out of the contract would belong solely to the corporation.

Plaintiff responded to the motion for reconsideration by filing the joint counter-affidavits of Antonio de Fortuny y Maynés and Valentín Molins Altarriba, licensed Spanish attorneys. The affidavits discussed issues of jurisdiction, venue, nationality, and citizenship of the parties and asserted that plaintiff Twohy had in fact stated a valid ''personal action'' (''acción personal'') under Spanish law. The affidavits conceded that ''between Mr. Twohy and the First National Bank of Chicago there was no contract'' and asserted that plaintiff's claims were based on Spanish civil law, Article 1902 of Chapter 2cd, which states: ''The person that by action or omission causes damages to another party with fault or negligence, is obliged to repair the damage * * * ''... . The affidavits also pointed out that under Spanish Civil Law, Article 1903 of the same Chapter, the acts of representatives of a person, such as directors and employees, may give rise to liability for that person under Article 1902. No authority apart from the statutes was cited in the affidavits to serve as a basis for Twohy's suit.

Defendant filed further supplemental affidavits of Mr. Baker and of Mr. Francisco J. Iglesias, another Spanish law expert, with its reply memorandum in support of the motion to reconsider. The memorandum and affidavits pointed out that the plaintiff's affidavits of Fortuny y Maynés and Molins focused solely on the liability of defendant and failed to address the so-called "standing" issue of whether Twohy was a proper plaintiff to bring the suit. First Chicago also contested the Fortuny y Maynés and Molins discussion of venue, jurisdiction and other matters. ... Finally, plaintiff filed further counter-affidavits of Fortuny y Maynés and Molins and reasserted that Twohy had commenced a valid personal claim under Article 1902 of Spanish civil law. . . .

The trial court reconsidered its order ... and ... granted defendant's motion for judgment on the pleaded defenses. * * * Plaintiff appeals both the dismissal of the case and the denial of his motion to amend the judgment.

The district court was correct in determining that the substantive law of Spain governed the action and that, as a matter of Spanish law, plaintiff failed to state a claim upon which relief could be granted.

Questions and Comments

1. Considering the *In re Agent Orange* decision, what is the international law that might be applied in our hyopothetical?

2. Before a court begins to receive foreign law, and address many of the questions above, it must determine that foreign law is the applicable law. The second extract of Epstein, Snyder & Baldwin (¶ ¶ 9.05–9.06) may help in making that determination in our cases. The early view, still preferred by some courts, is based on territoriality. It holds that the applicable law should be the law of the place where the tort occurred—the *lex loci delicti*. But many courts have questioned that view, and have adopted other justifications. They include interest analysis in one of its many variations, and public policy of the forum. What would be the different interests used in an interest analysis case? Is the court really capable of performing an adequate interest analysis? Perhaps an American court can identify U.S. interests, but can it properly identify Mexican interests? Should GROWFAST attempt to show that Mexico has an interest in having its law applied? Is there an interest in Mexico in *limiting* the damages received by its citizens? Should it ask assistance from Mexico? What public policy might demand that U.S. law be applied? Would interest analysis be any different in a contract case?

3. The final two paragraphs of the Epstein, Snyder & Baldwin extract note the choice of law issue as applied to procedural versus substantive issues. As the authors note, a statute of limitations is often considered procedural. Very often where a motion to dismiss for *forum non conveniens* reasons is granted, a condition is that the defendants do not raise a statute of limitations argument in the foreign forum. The U.S. court is essentially saying that if the statute of limitations has not run in the United States, the defendants should not be able to have the case moved to the foreign nation and then dismissed under that nation's statute of limitations. But the foreign nation's court might raise the issue itself and decline to proceed. Could the U.S. court reassert jurisdiction in that event?

Causing considerable debate is the question whether the law of *damages* should be considered substantive or procedural. Is it appropriate to apply substantive Mexican law to determine responsibility and then U.S. law of damages? See *Victor v. Sperry*, 163 Cal.App.2d 518, 329 P.2d 728 (1958)("measure of damages is inseparably connected to the cause of action and cannot be severed therefrom.") See also *Hurtado v. Superior Court*, 35 Cal.App.3d 176, 110 Cal.Rptr. 591 (1973)(applying Mexican law, but not rejecting *Victor*).

4.   Might the *Ciprari* decision change the above analysis?

5.   The *Raskin* decision shows that use of *lex loci delicti* is not dead, at least in Kansas. In our hypothetical *lex loci delicti* seems to point to Mexican law, or does it?

6.   The *Twohy* decision, in the second extract, notes that all the parties agreed to the application of Spanish law. It is not clear that they did. Would you have recommended that the parties consider what the law states in each possible choice of law country? It seems that Twohy's lawyer (or successor appellate lawyer) later changed his mind and did not want Spanish law to apply. Why? The court did explain briefly that Spanish law was appropriate. Does it make an analysis acceptable to your understanding of the choice of law process? The *Twohy* court finds the research and analysis of foreign law to be inadequate. Why? Does the court consequently place more emphasis on U.S. law and an assumption that Spanish law is "probably" the same?

PART C.   SOURCES OF FOREIGN LAW

DAVID EPSTEIN, JEFFREY L. SNYDER & CHARLES S. BALDWIN, IV, INTERNATIONAL LITIGATION

§ 9.03 (3d ed. 2002).

§ 9.03   MATERIAL THE COURT MAY CONSIDER

Rule 44.1 permits the court, in determining foreign law, to consider any relevant material or source, including testimony, without regard to whether the material considered would be admissible under the rules of evidence. This liberal standard of proof is intended to make the process of determining foreign law identical, to the extent possible, with the methods of ascertaining domestic law. Thus, the court is free to accept any material presented by the parties, including extracts from foreign written sources and written or oral expert testimony, and to give whatever probative value, in the court's opinion, is deserved. Moreover, a determination of foreign law in a related case does not preclude a court in a separate proceeding from considering the same issue of foreign law under Rule 44.1 in light of both evidence admitted and the court's own research and interpretation. Since, under Rule 44.1, foreign law sources are exempt from the hearsay rule, courts may consider such materials as affidavits, briefs and arguments of counsel, and opinion letters. In considering "any relevant material or source ... whether or not submitted by a party" under Rule 44.1, a court has the choice of conducting its own research or insisting that counsel fully engage in this task. According to the advisory committee note to Rule 44.1:

> In further recognition of the peculiar nature of the issue of foreign law, the new rule provides that in determining this law the court is not limited by material presented by the parties; it may engage in its own research and consider any relevant material thus found. The court may have at its disposal better foreign law materials than counsel have presented, or may wish to reexamine and amplify material that has been presented by counsel in partisan fashion or in insufficient detail. On the other hand, the court is free to insist on a complete presentation by counsel.[22]

Expert testimony is not a necessity in establishing foreign law, and a court may reach different conclusions based on an individual examination of foreign legal authorities. In *Chantier Naval Voisin v. M/Y Daybreak*,[24] the district court stated that while it could accept evidence submitted by the parties regarding the substance of the foreign law, it was not bound by the testimony of the expert witnesses presented. In that case, the court rejected the testimony of plaintiffs expert witness and made its own investigation concerning the foreign law involved.
* * *

The use of affidavits or other written statements to present expert testimony on foreign law is more common than oral testimony in federal courts. Generally, translated copies of the relevant foreign law upon which the expert relies are attached to the affidavit?

The case of *Bing v. Halstead*,[29] illustrates the use of written affidavits to prove foreign law. In that case, plaintiff, a New York citizen who resided in Costa Rica, sued defendant for damages for intentional infliction of emotional distress. Defendant moved for summary judgment on the ground that Costa Rican law, which the court decided should determine the right to recover, did not recognize such a tort. Both plaintiff and defendant submitted affidavits from Costa Rican attorneys reciting the foreign law based on decisions from Costa Rican courts, including an analysis of relevant portions of the criminal code. On the basis of the written submissions of the foreign law question, the court entered summary judgment for the defendant. *Bing v. Halstead* illustrates the relative ease with which courts can resolve disputes of foreign law in summary judgment situations under Rule 44.1.

The best method of proving foreign law (i.e, by documents or foreign law experts) undoubtedly depends on the availability of foreign law sources and the nature of the foreign law issue to be addressed. Although the assistance of foreign law experts is often essential, the need to use them in every case has been questioned. As such, experts are not required to meet any special qualifications, and federal courts are not

22. 39 F.R.D. 69, 117 (1966).

24. 677 F. Supp. 1563, 1567 (S.D. Fla. 1988).

29. 495 F. Supp. 517, 522 (S.D.N.Y. 1980).

bound by their testimony and may reject their conclusions. Some authorities have urged that parties brief and argue the foreign law in the same manner as with domestic law and that the use of documentary authorities (translated copies of judicial decisions, etc.) may be more effective than the oral testimony of a foreign law expert.

UNITED STATES v. MITCHELL

United States Court of Appeals, Fourth Circuit, 1993.
985 F.2d 1275.

MURNAGHAN, CIRCUIT JUDGE:

* * * The government alleged in Count 8 that in September of 1987, Mitchell transported the hides and horns of a Punjab urial (wild sheep) and a Chinkara gazelle out of Pakistan and into the United States knowing that the animals had been taken, possessed or transported in violation of Pakistani law. The superseding indictment identified two laws of Pakistan prohibiting the unlicensed hunting, possession or export of such animal trophies: the Pakistani Imports and Exports (Control) Act of 1950 and the Punjab Wildlife Act of 1974.

The government moved the district court to make a determination of foreign law under Federal Rule of Criminal Procedure 26.1, and both parties offered memoranda and affidavits to support their readings of the Pakistani laws. After a hearing on the matter, the district court held that a personal baggage exception in the Imports and Exports Act's Control Order of 1987 permitted Mitchell's unlicensed export of the animal hides from Pakistan. It held the Punjab Wildlife Act invalid to the extent that it regulated exports across provincial borders, because the Pakistani Constitution reserved such powers to the federal government. Accordingly, the district court dismissed Count 8, and subsequently denied the government's motion for reconsideration of the ruling, which was accompanied by new affidavits concerning the interpretation of the Act.

The determination of foreign law is a question of law to be established by any relevant source, whether or not submitted by a party or admissible under the Federal Rules of Evidence. ... The broad discretion afforded a court in considering evidence to determine foreign law derives from the general unavailability of foreign legal materials, and the frequent need for expert assistance in understanding and applying the materials. In determining questions of foreign law, courts have turned to a wide variety of sources including affidavits and expert testimony from an Australian Federal Judge, *United States v. Molt*, 599 F.2d 1217, 1220 (3rd Cir.1979), a Peruvian Minister of Agriculture, *United States v. 2,507 Live Canary Winged Parakeets*, 689 F.Supp. 1106, 1009 (S.D.Fla.1988), and a South African attorney, *United States v. Taitz*, 130 F.R.D. 442, 446 n. 2 (S.D.Cal.1990); certified translations of Bolivian Supreme Decrees, *United States v. 3,210 Crusted Sides of Caiman Crocodilus Yacare*, 636 F.Supp. 1281, 1285 (S.D.Fla.1986); foreign case law, *United States v. Peterson*, 812 F.2d 486, 491 (9th Cir.1987); a student note in a Philippine

Law Review, *id.;* information obtained by a law clerk in a telephone conversation with the Hong Kong Trade Office and presented ex parte to the court, *United States v. Hing Shair Chan,* 680 F.Supp. 521, 524 (E.D.N.Y.1988); and the court's "own independent research and analysis" of a Yugoslavian law. *Kalmich v. Bruno,* 553 F.2d 549, 552 (7th Cir.), *cert. denied,* 434 U.S. 940, 98 S.Ct. 432, 54 L.Ed.2d 300 (1977).

Interpretation of the Pakistani laws in question presents some difficulty, because, although the legal system of Pakistan is based on common-law, similar in many respects to American law, neither party produced any cases bearing on the laws. Instead, the parties produced affidavits, letters, telexes, and documents obtained from Pakistani government officials and lawyers, and a legal expert on Pakistani law from the Library of Congress, in an attempt to establish the official position of the Pakistani government on the interpretation of the laws in question. We review the evidence presented *de novo* . . . .

The government submitted the sworn affidavit of the Inspector General for Forests in the Ministry of Agriculture for the Government of Pakistan (who is also the Secretary of the National Council for Conservation of Wildlife in Pakistan), an expert on Pakistan law from the Library of Congress, official communiques from the American Embassy in Islamabad, Pakistan and the Pakistani Embassy in Washington D.C., and a Fifth Circuit court opinion that had previously addressed the Import and Export law, . . . Mitchell, for his part, submitted a letter from a Pakistani Senator, a statement from a Joint Secretary of the Ministry of Commerce, the sworn affidavit of an attorney in active practice in Pakistan, and a letter from the Minister of Wildlife for the Sindh Province.

Not surprisingly, those affidavits and letters present conflicting views of the interpretation of the Import and Export Act, as well as of the constitutionality of the Punjabi Wildlife Act, and fail to establish, to this court's satisfaction, a definitive answer as to the official Pakistani interpretation of the laws. Perhaps, as is the case with many of our own laws, a consensus has not yet been reached in Pakistan. Yet we are charged with determining the best reading of the laws. In doing so we have considered all of the evidence brought by the parties, have drawn upon the canons of statutory construction with which we interpret our own laws, and have examined the policies that appear to underlie the Pakistani laws in question. We reject the government's argument that some of Mitchell's affidavits should not have been considered because they were unsworn as well as Mitchell's contention that the additional evidence produced by the government with its motion for reconsideration should not be considered because it was produced after the court below had made its determination. * * *

REVERSED AND REMANDED WITH INSTRUCTIONS

Questions and Comments

1.   Epstein, Snyder & Baldwin in ¶ 9.03 discuss materials the court may consider. Does Rule 44.1 address this issue? Is the *Mitchell* case consistent with the extracts of Miner and Epstein et al.? Should the court have demanded cases from Pakistan? After all, it notes that Pakistan is in the common law tradition group of nations where cases establish legal precedent?

2.   The readings illustrate that courts will consider a wide variety of sources of foreign law. What would be the best sources the parties might use in our case to prove Mexican law? Would you submit to the court the chapter in the following Problem 4.5 by Professor Vargas on Mexican Tort Law? Should affidavits or opinion letters explaining Mexican law be from Mexican experts or U.S. persons with knowledge of Mexican law? What benefits or burdens might each class of expert bring? What if the court is not satisfied with the evidence offered by the two parties as to the nature of Mexican law?

PROBLEM 4.5   PROOF OF FOREIGN LAW

SECTION I.   THE SETTING

The setting remains the same as in the previous problem. The court in the United States has decided that Mexican law is the applicable law.

SECTION II.   FOCUS OF CONSIDERATION

To illustrate how foreign law is applied, we return to the *Twohy* case that was discussed in the previous problem, which we considered for choice of law. Now we will read its subsequent ruling on the application of Spanish law. Then we turn to the application of Mexican law, with some questions about which Mexican law, such as whether to apply Mexican federal law or the law of one of Mexico's 30 states?

SECTION III.   READINGS, QUESTIONS AND COMMENTS

U.S. counsel who are not bilingual have several sources of Mexican law that will assist in understanding that legal system. That does not lessen the need to have an expert on Mexican law work on the case, but it will allow the U.S. lawyer to be better able to understand the Mexican lawyer who is describing how his law will impact the case.

An excellent recent volume on the Mexican legal system is Mexican Law by Stephen Zamora, José Ramón Cossío, Leonel Pereznieto, José Roldán-Xopa & David Lopez (2005). It is especially good for understanding such areas as constitutional challenges (*amparo*). Used along with a four volume set by Jorge A. Vargas, A Treatise for Legal Practitioners and International Investors (West Group 1998), consisting of edited materials on specific subjects, including Mexican law of tort (extracontractual responsibility), U.S. counsel should have little trouble understanding our neighbor-to-the-south's very different system.

Additionally, important to know are the specific Mexican code provisions that may apply in the case, including the basic rules of responsibility, damages, prescription (statute of limitations), and jurisdiction. There are useful translations of the Mexican Civil and Commercial Codes into English. See Vargas, Mexican Civil Code Annotated (West 2005), and Vargas, Mexican Commercial Code Annotated (West 2005). Additionally helpful is Gerardo Solís and Raúl Gasteazoro, Spanish–English / English–Spanish Law Dictionary (West Group 1992), that includes brief definitions of certain legal topics, such as prescripción (limitations) and simulación (deceit), and Vargas, Mexican Legal Dictionary and Desk Reference, West 2003.

One significant development has occurred since the 1998 publication of the first two extracts below. As Vargas describes, each state in Mexico has a civil code and another exists entitled the Civil Code for the Federal District in Ordinary Matters and for the Entire Republic in Federal Matters. There was considerable debate in Mexico about the definition of "Federal Matters." That debate indeed continues in determining whether an issue involves federal or state law. In 2000, this latter code was essentially split into two separate civil codes. One is a civil code for the Federal District, an area including metropolitan Mexico City that is roughly comparable to Washington, D.C. A second code was created that is a Federal Civil Code. Its scope is not yet fully known, but it appears that it has become the model looked to by states when considering amendments to state civil codes. The Federal Civil Code might have applicability to our case, if some significant federal linkage were proven.[1] But the likelihood is that the state civil code of Veracruz will apply in our case. The state civil codes are not very different than the federal civil code, but in time that may change. When the authors and discussants below refer to the "Federal Civil Code" they are referring to the old code, essentially as it applied to federal matters anywhere in the Republic. That is now the role of the new Federal Civil Code.

Essential to the resolution of this problem are the selected provisions of the Mexican Civil Code in the Documents Supplement.

TWOHY v. FIRST NATIONAL BANK OF CHICAGO

United States Court of Appeals, Seventh Circuit, 1985.
758 F.2d 1185.

CUMMINGS, CHIEF JUDGE.

Determination of Spanish Law

The district court correctly determined the substance of Spanish law and held that it required dismissal of plaintiff's complaint. In his decision to dismiss, Judge Leighton focused on an inadequacy of the complaint raised several times by defendant and its foreign law experts. * * *

The question which remains is whether the district court was correct in determining that under Spanish law plaintiff could not main-

---

1. In contrast to U.S. law, a vehicle accident on a Mexican federal highway brings into play federal law, but a similar accident just off the highway on a state road would be subject to the state civil code.

tain an action for injury to a corporation solely on the basis of his status as shareholder of the corporation. Our review under the appropriate standard convinces us that the lower court's determination was correct, although we cannot fully endorse the court's method of reaching its conclusion.

As noted previously, both parties submitted a series of affidavits of foreign law experts concerning issues of Spanish law relevant to the case, including the issue of a shareholder's right to sue. Plaintiff's experts, however, never directly responded to the defendant's challenge to Twohy's individual right to maintain an action. The Fortuny y Maynés and Molins affidavits, stating that an action exists under Spanish civil law providing that "The person that by action or omission causes damages to another party with fault or negligence, is obliged to repair the damage * * * ", merely beg the question, as does the citation to Spanish law providing that acts of representatives of a person may subject that person to liability * * *.

* * *

Distinguished commentators have noted the benefits, and at times necessity, of independent research and analysis by courts on questions of foreign law: ...

> All too often counsel will do an inadequate job of researching and presenting foreign law or will attempt to prove it in such a partisan fashion that the court is obliged to go beyond their offerings. * * * [I]t must be remembered that one of the policies inherent in Rule 44.1 is that whenever possible issues of foreign law should be resolved on their merits and on the basis of a full evaluation of the available materials. To effectuate this policy, the court is obliged to take an active role in the process of ascertaining foreign law.

9 C. Wright & A. Miller, [Federal Practice & Procedure] at § 2444, p. 408. The inadequacy in research referred to above unfortunately is present in the instant case. Defendant's experts, attorneys practicing in Spain, opined from their personal knowledge that plaintiff's action is barred under Spanish law because, as is the rule in common law, shareholders of Spanish corporations may not sue for third party harms to the corporation in which they hold stock. Something more concrete might have been expected of defendant, and plaintiff has been quick to point out the lack of discussion of substantive law within and the conclusory nature of defendant's affidavits. Plaintiff's experts have fared no better in this matter, however, in view of their above-noted failure even to address the issue. Nor are we convinced that the district court fully met its duty to ascertain foreign law under Rule 44.1, although we recognize that investigating Spanish law on the relevant issue presents no simple task. Nothing in Rule 44.1 strictly requires a district judge to engage in private research. ... Under these circumstances, however, it would have been appropriate for the court to demand a more "complete

presentation by counsel" on the issue, as is suggested in the Advisory Committee's Note to Rule 44.1. . . .

The lower court's investigation of foreign law appears to have been limited to the district judge's understanding that Spanish law did not differ from the law of Illinois on the question of a shareholder's right to sue for a third party breach of a corporate contract:

> And it is amazing when you look at it, how similar are the laws of the various countries—that is the civilized countries—of the world.

* * *

* * * It is fundamental. The law of Spain, the civil law, the common law—one person cannot sue for injury to another person. The court was correct in not dismissing plaintiff's claim merely because Twohy had failed to establish relevant controlling Spanish law since:

> The rare case in which there is a failure of proof * * * [of foreign law] would be an especially unappealing case for holding that the party whose claim or defense is based on foreign law must lose because this would be a case in which the foreign law could not be ascertained despite the diligent efforts of both counsel and the trial judge. It simply is not fair to bar a party from recovering when neither his attorney nor the court is able to conjure up the content of governing law.

9 C. Wright & A. Miller, *supra,* at § 2447, p. 416.

Under the circumstances, if the district court had decided not to request a more detailed presentation by counsel, before plaintiff's complaint properly could be dismissed, Rule 44.1 required a deeper inquiry into the law of Spain than that undertaken by the court below. Nevertheless, we are convinced that Spanish law does not permit plaintiff Twohy's action against First Chicago.

Under general principles of United States corporate law, as well as under Illinois law, a stockholder of a corporation has no personal or individual right of action against third persons for damages that result indirectly to the stockholder because of an injury to the corporation. . . . Our inquiry, however, must focus on whether, as defendant's experts suggest, the law of Spain utilizes the same general rule regarding stockholder actions and whether similar or broader exceptions to the rule exist under Spanish law.

Comparative law studies of shareholder rights and shareholder suits indicate that the American rule barring shareholder damages actions arising out of corporate transactions with third parties has universal application among Western nations: . . . A major comparative law treatise describes the "non-interference rule" as follows:

> The shareholder normally can only sue for damages other than that incurred by him because of the fact that the corporation has been hurt. The decrease in value in his shares is normally no[t a] sufficient basis for an individual cause of action.

XIII INTERNATIONAL ENCYCLOPEDIA OF COMPARATIVE LAW—BUSINESS AND PRIVATE ORGANIZATIONS 4–256 (A. Conard ed. 1973). Spain is not cited as an exception to this general rule in either of the above works. The law of the United States is singled out as allowing the most significant encroachment upon the general "non-interference rule." . . . The Spanish system of civil law, in contrast, appears to follow the "non-interference rule" quite strictly.

The Spanish corporation, or "sociedad anónima" (S.A.) (more correctly referred to in English as a "joint stock company"), is "similar in all major respects to a United States corporation." PRICE WATER-HOUSE, DOING BUSINESS IN SPAIN 31 (1980). See Arthur Andersen & Co., Tax and Trade Guide—Spain 36–37 (2d ed. 1972). Translations of the Spanish Code of Commerce and the Law for Joint Stock Companies of July 17, 1951 (the basic law governing Spanish joint stock companies), confirm this point and indicate that shareholders in a joint stock company enjoy very limited rights regarding management of the company. Article 116, Section One, Title One, Book Two of the Code of Commerce provides that each commercial company (including a sociedad anónima) "will have juridical personality in all its acts and contracts." 20 Commercial Laws of the World, Commercial Laws of Spain 31 (1970). Article 39 of the Law for Joint Stock Companies of July 17, 1951, enumerates the rights of shareholders: the sharing in the profits and capital on liquidation, the right of preference in subscribing to new issues of stock of their corporation, the right of voting at stockholders' meetings, summoning a general stockholders' meeting under certain circumstances, challenging resolutions of the stockholders when their actions are contrary to law or damaging to the interests of the corporation's stockholders or to the corporation, leaving the company when the latter effects a change in its corporate purposes, and the right to hold directors liable for their actions. 20 Commercial Laws of Spain, . . . No right to sue third parties on the basis of corporate contracts or corporate transactions appears among these rights.

Another treatise reveals, however, that under the Law of July 17, 1951, a stockholder of a joint stock company enjoys "standing to sue in place of the real party in interest" with respect to certain corporate contracts. Miguel y Alonso, *Access to Justice in Spanish Law* in I ACCESS TO JUSTICE, A WORLD SURVEY (Book 2) 880 (M. Cappelletti & B. Garth eds. 1978). The exceptions allow "[c]ertain persons or entities who would not have had standing to bring an action * * * the right to do so because they are considered affected by the outcome of the dispute." *Id.* The first exception allows a stockholder or administrator of a corporation to challenge illegal and void corporate agreements. The second exception, more akin to an American stockholder's derivative suit, allows a stockholder's action to invalidate corporate agreements that violate the articles of incorporation or those which impair the interests of the company to the benefit of one or more stockholders. *Id.*

Plaintiff's suit does not fall within either of these two exceptions to the non-interference rule. More importantly, the treatise's description of these special standing situations as departures from the normal rule strongly indicates that Spanish law does not recognize a suit of the type plaintiff brought before the district court. Plaintiff failed to state a cognizable claim under Spanish law.

* * * The judgment of the district court is AFFIRMED.

JORGE A. VARGAS, MEXICAN LAW*
Ch. 21 (West Group 1998).

INTRODUCTION

Unlike the United States, the principles governing tort law in Mexico have remained schematic, archaic and uninteresting for legal practitioners. When an injury occurs, Mexicans rely on a non-confrontational arrangement, instead of the more litigious avenue so common in the U.S. Mexican culture dictates that the tortfeasor is to provide the necessary assistance to the victim, covering the resulting medical and hospital expenses, and all material deterioration suffered by the victim's property, as well as any lost wages and any incapacities as calculated in the Federal Labor Act. The Mexican legal system does not allow punitive damages or compensation for pain and suffering. "Inexcusable negligence" by the plaintiff bars recovery.

Under Mexican law, tortious acts are governed by two separate types of legislation: (1) the Civil Code, and (2) the Federal Labor Act. As the Civil Code is hardly equipped to solve the issues raised by extracontractual liability cases, the Mexican legislature chose to assimilate the cases to occupational injuries regulated under Title IX of the Federal Labor Act. This allows civil judges some amount of discretion in deciding cases. As a result, many personal injury cases generated in Mexico are being filed by Americans before U.S. courts, to be governed by U.S. law, rather than the applicable Mexican law in a Mexican court, especially when one considers that the economic compensation provided by Mexican law is so modest when compared to that allowed under U.S. law.

Does Mexico have Tort Law as part of its legal system?

No. Unlike the United States, Mexico has not developed what may be considered a specialized and technically advanced tort law. * * * this kind of liability is defined as "extra-contractual liability" and is regulated by Articles 1910–1934 of the Federal Civil Code.

What are Mexico's Civil Law principles which govern extra-contractual liability cases?

Mexico adheres to the principle that whoever causes a damage or injury to another as a result of acting illegally or against good customs is obligated to repair it. However, if the defendant can prove that the

---

* Reprinted with the permission of the West Group.

damage or injury occurred as a direct consequence of the fault or inexplicable negligence of the victim, the defendant is then freed from any liability. In other words, the victim's contributory negligence operates as a total bar to recovery. This principle is found in Article 1910 of the Federal Civil Code and duplicated in each of the other 31 State codes.

How is the victim's economic compensation calculated under Mexican law?

The Mexican civil code provides that the compensation will consist of, at the election of the injured party, (a) the restoration of the status previously existing (when this is possible) or (b) in the payment of damages and losses. In order to calculate the corresponding damages and losses, the civil code refers to a special formulation contained in Mexico's Federal Labor Act. Since Mexico's tort law is so schematic, the Mexican legislator equated the injuries suffered by victim of a tortious act with a laborer who suffers an injury at work. Thus, depending on the type and seriousness of injury (whether it causes death or a specific type of disability), the Federal Labor Act stipulates the amount of compensation which is due in each individual case.

Does Mexico have compensation for pain and suffering and punitive damages?

No. Under Mexican law, the economic compensation resulting from tortious acts basically consists of: (a) medical and surgical assistance; (b) rehabilitation; (c) hospitalization, when needed; (d) medicines and other curative materials; (e) prosthetic and orthopedic devices; (f) lost wages; and (g) the economic indemnification provided by the Federal Labor Act. In cases of death, in addition to the indemnification, a two-month salary payment towards funeral expenses is also required.

Does Mexico recognize corporate liability?

Yes. Mexican Civil Law contemplates specific cases whereby Mexican legal entities may be liable for tortious acts committed by their employees or workers in the performance of their functions, unless they can prove that the damage or injury in question is not the consequence of any fault or negligence on their part.

Personal Injuries to Tourists

* * *

Unfortunately, many * * * tourists suffer personal injuries while visiting Mexico and are otherwise exposed to vehicular or other incidents which affect their well-being and personal possessions. These incidents sometimes result in major physical problems or, in some cases, even death.

Three Hypotheticals of Tort Cases in Mexico

A.   The Alina Allen Case.

* * * Alina Allen * * * works as a banking manager in Atlanta. She traveled as a tourist to Acapulco where she was planning to stay for a couple of weeks. During her stay at a beautiful hotel at Caleta beach, she returned to her hotel room in the early hours of the morning after having a few "Margaritas" and learning to dance "La Macarena" at a local disco. Since the hotel elevator was not working due to a power outage triggered by a strong tropical storm, Alina decided to use the stairway to go to her second floor suite overlooking Caleta beach. After climbing up five short sections of the staircase in the darkness, Alina lost her step and fell down the stairs fracturing her pelvis and an arm. She remained there, unconscious, for several hours until the early morning shift of hotel employees arrived at 5 a.m. to sweep the staircase. The hotel employees carried her downstairs where they waited for 45 minutes for an ambulance to take her to a local hospital.

B.   The Craig Curtiss Case.

Craig Curtiss exchanged his Colorado condominium to go to Can Cún for a couple of weeks. Tall and athletic, Craig had loved to dive since his college days, when he was a member of the University of Colorado diving team. After graduating from this university with a degree in business, Craig worked for five years as an accounting manager in a large corporation. He made all his traveling and lodging arrangements through a Colorado travel agency. After flying for several hours in a highly-packed and noisy charter airplane, Craig finally arrived in Can Cún. He never thought that going through Mexican immigration and customs in the small, hot and overcrowded airport was going to take him two hours. Craig could not wait to go swimming when he finally saw the large and beautiful swimming pool at the condominium where his timeshare was located. After resting for a while and drinking two bottles of the best Mexican beer, he decided to go swimming. He went directly to the closest diving platform and dove into the swimming pool. This is all he can remember. A few hours later, after a delicate and costly emergency operation, Craig woke up in a Can Cún hospital, with a serious fracture at the base of his neck. He almost fainted when he was told that the water in the swimming pool in the place where he dove was only two feet deep. Craig is quadriplegic today.

C.   The Mary Moore Case.

Mary Moore had been a nurse at the Medical Memorial Hospital at La Jolla, California. After enjoying a long weekend in Ensenada, Baja California, she decided to head back home after dinner. Driving her 1996 convertible, Mary left Ensenada around 8 p.m. While driving through the small town of Rosarito on September 15, at around 10:30 p.m., Mary realized the entire town was celebrating "El Grito," a big national fiesta to commemorate Mexico's initiation of its independence in 1810. People were singing and dancing in the streets and before Mary could do anything, two teenage boys ran in front of her car. Mary's car hit them, throwing them several feet. As a result of the collision, one teenager was gravely injured, and the other broke both legs. Both were taken by ambulance to a local hospital while Mary was detained and interrogated by a Mexican Highway Patrol officer at the place of the accident. Soon after a local police car arrived, Mary was taken to the Rosarito Police Department where her statement was taken by a bilingual public prosecutor. As a result of this accident, one teenager died and the other must use a wheelchair for the rest of his life.

Tort Law Cases are Not for Mexican Attorneys

Whereas a U.S. legal practitioner would not hesitate to take any of the cases described [above] to a U.S. court, confident that well-established principles of tort law would be applied to render a decision, from a Mexican attorney's viewpoint, the legal approach regarding these cases is radically different. First of all, no reputable law firm in Mexico handles personal injury cases resulting from a tortious act. This lack of professional interest may be explained from four different angles: Cultural, economic, legal and professional. When a tortious act takes place in Mexico, say in a hotel, store or restaurant, the affected corporation is expected to take care of the basic expenses. Mexican culture dictates that the corporation in question is to provide the necessary assistance to the victim, covering the resulting medical and hospital expenses, with the understanding that the victim will be satisfied with this treatment and abstain from pursuing a judicial remedy. Mexicans rely more on this non-confrontational, civilized arrangement, instead of choosing the more aggressive litigious avenue which is so common in the United States. From an economic viewpoint, the compensation provided by the Civil Code in tort cases is relatively modest, especially when it is considered that pain and suffering, as well as punitive damages (and the considerable amounts of money invariably associated with them), are unknown in Mexico's legal system.

From a professional standpoint, it seems that given the simplicity of the system currently used in Mexico, the generalized perception among the legal community is that economic recovery in personal injury cases derived from tortious acts does not require the professional services of an attorney. Rather, this task appears better suited for a legal technician, such as a paralegal, although Mexico has not yet developed this category. This may explain why attorneys in Mexico, instead of developing a practice in tort law, perceive themselves as called upon to render legal services on more elevated planes or in cases which are more legally challenging or profitable.

Mexican Damages and Losses

The four concepts are embraced by two larger fundamental civil law notions: damages *(Danos)* and losses *(Perjuicios)*.

Mexico's Federal Civil Code defines "damages" as "the loss or deterioration suffered by property through failure to fulfill an obligation." "Losses" is defined as "the deprivation of any lawful gain which should have been obtained from the fulfillment of the obligation." In order to recover, both damages and losses "must be the immediate direct consequence" of the tortious act.

Today, under Mexico City standards, for example, the compensation mandated by Article 1915 of the Federal Civil Code to be given to the family of the victim who died as a result of a tortious act amounts to only some $15,000 U.S. dollars. Determining the compensation which is due to a victim of a tortious injury is more of an accounting exercise rather than an intellectual analysis of a complicated legal transaction. Basically, the victim's compensation consists of: medical expenses and hospitalization; lost wages; material deterioration suffered by the victim's property; and the privation of a legal gain which should have been obtained by the victim.

As a result of these considerations, the bulk of personal injury cases generated in Mexico are being filed principally by Americans before U.S. courts to be governed by U.S. law, rather than being initiated in a Mexican court in accordance with the applicable law of that country.

Tort Law is an Incipient but Developing Area of Mexican Law

In sum, Mexico's legal system is not conceptually equipped with the legal principles or doctrines, nor with the technical standards and varied legal scope, found in the tort law practiced in common law countries, particularly in the United States. This assertion may be easily understood considering that tort law is a common law institution. Moreover, this dynamic area of U.S. law is of a recent origin, having experienced an unprecedented growth over the last century. As reported by specialists, prior to 1859 a U.S. treatise on "torts" simply did not exist.

From a theoretical perspective, Mexico, unlike the United States, has not constructed a legal doctrine to explain the functions, goals and justifications of tort law, or to describe the evolutions of tort concepts and remedies mainly because of socioeconomic reasons. Consequently, standards of conduct, proof of negligence, the concept of duty and the different degrees of negligence are notions alien to Mexican legal thinking. The same criterion applies to the well-known U.S. defenses to negligence liability, such as contributory negligence, comparative negligence, assumption of risk, mitigation of damages and statutes of limitations and repose, which are also clearly absent from Mexico's domestic legislation.

MEXICAN LAW GOVERNING TORTIOUS ACTS

In General

Under the Civil Law of Mexico, there are three different types of liability: (1) contractual liability; (2) "objective liability;" and (3) the so-called "extracontractual liability."

Second, the Mexican notion of "objective liability" closely resembles the notion of strict liability for a U.S. practitioner. Objective liability results from the commission of an illegal act which was precipitated by the use of mechanisms or inherently dangerous equipment or apparatus, animals and tangible things, regardless of the existence of fault or

> If a person employs mechanisms, instruments, equipment or substances which by themselves are dangerous, or because of the speed they develop, their explosive nature and inflammable characteristics, or by the intensity of the electric current, or similar causes, he is liable for the damage or injuries they cause even though he is using them licitly, *unless he can prove that the damage was caused by the fault or inexcusable negligence of the victim.*

Third, Articles 1910–1934 of the Federal Civil Code apply to "extracontractual liability," statutorily defined as the liability that derives from illicit acts (i.e., *De las obligaciones que nacen de los actos ilícitos*). This form of liability is not derived from a contractual relationship, * * * Whereas contractual liability fords its source in a given contract and materializes when that contract is breached, or when a specific contractual obligation is not fulfilled, extracontractual liability exists even in the absence of any contractual relationship or legal link between the parties. Accordingly, it may be said that extracontractual civil liability stems from the will of the drafters of the Civil Code.

* * *

The Civil Code

The Civil Code is at the center of Mexico's civil practice and litigation. Under the larger category of obligations, this code governs all matters in the civil legal realm, ranging from the civil status of individuals, family law, assets, possession and property, to successions, wills, inheritances and, in particular, contracts. Tortious acts appear under the category of: "Obligations which arise from illegal acts," commonly referred to as "Extra-contractual liability." There are two different kinds of civil codes in Mexico.

The Federal Civil Code

The Federal Civil Code applies to the Federal District (Mexico City) in ordinary matters and to the entire nation in federal matters. * * * Articles 1910–1934 of the Federal Civil Code (and the corresponding articles in the respective state codes) govern the civil liability generated by tortious acts under Mexican law, including. (a) "Fault liability" *(Responsabilidad por culpa);* (b) "Objective or absolute liability" *(Responsabilidad objetiva o absoluta); (c)* the economic compensation resulting from damages and losses; and (d) vicarious liability.

The State Civil Codes of the 31 Mexican States

The Republic of Mexico is composed of 31 States, each of which has its own Constitution and Civil code. * * * Each state code governs civil law questions which take place within its territory. In general, each of these codes is a replica of the Federal Civil Code, with few and insignificant changes. The basic principle regarding tortious acts and the corresponding liability and compensation, is governed by the principles contained in the civil code of the state where the tortious act took place.

Applicability of Federal Law or State Law

One of the choice of law questions most commonly asked by U.S. legal practitioners regarding a tort law case that occurred in the Republic of Mexico (but which is now being litigated in a U.S. court) is whether the case should be governed by the Federal Civil Code or by the Civil Code of the State where the tortious act took place.

Mexico adheres to the principle of "Limited Territorialism" contained in Article 12 of the Federal Civil Code, which provides:

> *Mexican laws apply to all persons within the Republic, as well as to acts and events which take place within its territory or under its jurisdiction, including those persons [whether Mexicans or foreigners] who have submitted themselves to said laws,* except when these laws provide for the application of a (given) foreign law or depending, further, on what is provided in the treaties and conventions to which Mexico is a party.

* * * Accordingly, in the hypothetical cases of Alma Allen, the Atlanta tourist visiting * * * Acapulco, located in * * * Guerrero, the case should be decided by the provisions of the Civil Code of the State of Guerrero. Applying the same principle, the Mary Moore case should be decided by the law of the State of Baja California, since the accident took place in that * * * state.

However, the case of Craig Curtiss departs from the application of is the principle of "Limited territorialism." The State of Quintana Roo is the only state in Mexico that contains this provision:

> The effects of legal transactions *(negocios juridicos)* entered into abroad which should be executed in the territory of the State [of Quintana Roo], *shall be governed by the federal laws.*

This Quintana Roo provision must be construed in conjunction with Article 13 of the Federal Civil Code, which establishes the rules that determine the application of foreign law in Mexico. Paragraph V of the article provides that "the legal effects of acts and contracts shall be governed by the law of the place where they should be executed, save when the parties had validly chosen the applicability of another law." Under Mexican law, this choice of law principle, known as *Lex loci executionis* or, the law of the place where the legal transaction or contract is to be executed, is the law that governs the case.

* * * Curtiss made all his traveling and lodging arrangements through, a Denver, Colorado, travel agency where he lived. Since these contractual arrangements were to produce its effects in Can Cún, Mexico, where Mr. Curtiss was going to have his vacation, under Article 13 (V) of the Federal Civil Code the legal effects of these contracts are to be governed by the law of the State of Quintana Roo. However, this

principle, which remains legally valid throughout the Republic of Mexico, does not apply to the State of Quintana Roo because of Article 15 of its Code, which provides that contracts entered into outside Mexico, say in Denver, Colorado, but which should be executed in the State of Quintana Roo, *"shall be governed by the federal laws."* Accordingly, the Curtiss case is governed by the pertinent provisions of the Federal Civil Code. Articles 1910 through 1934, placed under the title of "Obligations which arise from Illegal Acts," provide the substantive federal law applicable to the Curtiss case.

A few legal precisions may be needed at this time. First, it should be made clear that, in its Civil Code, * * * Quintana Roo includes several substantive law principles that closely parallel those of the Federal Civil Code. However, these state law principles apply only to acts and legal transactions that have been entered into "in any part of the Republic [of Mexico]" but which should be executed in the State of Quintana Roo. Second, the Civil Code of the State of Quintana Roo has been more recently formulated and adopted than that of any other Mexican State. Enacted in 1974, almost half a century *after* the Federal Civil Code was promulgated, it is evident that the State Legislature adopted a policy that clearly departs from the principle of "Limited Territorialism" prevalent in the other 30 civil codes in Mexico.

It seems that the local legislature's intention was to apply the federal laws of Mexico when foreigners entered into legal transactions outside Mexico but the effects of these transactions were to be executed, enforced, implemented or caused their effects in Quintana Roo. However, when the same transactions are entered into in any State of the Republic of Mexico, including the State of Quintana Roo, those transactions should be governed by the law of Quintana Roo. This distinction appears to have been made based on the legislature's assumption that in the latter case, the transactions are conducted by Mexican nationals and not by foreigners.

Lastly, it should be mentioned that, from a substantive viewpoint, there is a drastic difference between Article 1910 of the Federal Civil Code, which represents the most fundamental principle of Mexican tort law, and Article 87 of the Civil Code of the State of Quintana Roo. Whereas Article 1910 of the Federal Civil Code provides a complete bar to the Plaintiff's recovery when the resulting damage or injury "was caused as a consequence of the fault or inexcusable negligence of the victim," Article 87 of the Quintana Roo code simply provides:

> Any act of a person, which does not constitute a crime *(Delito),* executed by fault or negligence, whether unintentional or intentional, which causes damage to another in his/her person or in his/her assets, *obligates his/her author to repair the damage and to give an indemnity for the losses (Perjuicios),* in conformity with the provisions of this code.

In Article 15, the legislature of the State of Quintana Roo, unlike the Federal Civil Code, created a double standard, one for foreigners (especially U.S. citizens), and another for Mexican nationals. Foreigners are to be subject to the federal law whereas Mexicans are subject to Quintana Roo law. The standard applied to foreigners tended to favor the local tourism industry (hotels, in particular) by including negligence as a tort cause of action. If the foreign plaintiff was contributorily negligent, the local hotel in Quintana Roo could bar any recovery, as the resulting "damage was caused as a consequence of the fault or inexcusable negligence of the victim." On the other hand, the standard created for Mexican nationals gives them an almost automatic cause of action for "Extracontractual liability" (similar to U.S. tort law), obliging the author of the tortious act to repair the damage and to indemnify for any losses.

Federal Civil Law Provisions Governing "Extracontractual Liability" Cases

Following the ideas advanced by French and Spanish doctrinarians, Mexican specialists consider that the source of extracontractual liability derives from illegal enrichment, illegal acts and a created risk.

"Fault liability" occurs when an individual or a legal entity commits an illegal act by fault that causes damage or inflicts injury to another individual. Articles 1910 and 1913 of the Federal Civil Code govern this kind of liability. In this case, the tortfeasor is liable because of his/her fault or negligence.

Articles 1910 and 1915 of the Federal Civil Code establish the two most fundamental principles that govern extracontractual liability cases (i.e., tortious acts) in Mexico. [Article 110 states:]

> He who acting illegally or against good customs causes damage to another, is obliged to repair it, unless he proves that the damage occurred in consequence of the fault or inexplicable negligence of the victim.

Pursuant to this article, "fault or inexplicable negligence of the victim" provides a complete bar to the plaintiff's recovery. From the viewpoint of a U.S. legal practitioner, this bar results from the plaintiff's comparative contributory negligence. [Article 1915 states:]

> The repair of the damage shall consist, at the election of the injured party, in the restoration of the status previously existing, when this is possible, or in the payment of damages and losses.

> When the damage is caused to persons and produces death, total permanent, partial permanent, total temporary or partial temporary incapacity, the amount of the indemnity shall be determined by the Federal Labor Act *(Ley Federal del Trabajo)*. To calculate the appropriate indemnity one shall take as the base four times the minimum daily salary which is the highest in force in the region and shall be multiplied by the number of days indicated in the Federal

Labor Law for each of the incapacities mentioned. In case of death, the indemnity shall correspond to the heirs of the victim.[a]

The indemnity credits, when the victim is a salaried person, are not transferable and shall be covered preferably in one exhibit, save agreement between the parties. . . . .

Mexican jurists agree that reparation of the damage is directed at placing the victim in the situation that existed before the occurrence of the tortious act. Only when this is not possible, or when the act causes a corporal or moral injury, does the resulting obligation convert into the payment of an indemnity to compensate for the material or moral damage inflicted to the victims. This indemnity should cover both damages and losses, as defined by the Federal Civil Code in Articles 2108 and 2109. Thus, the notion of civil liability includes not only the duty to repair or restitute for the damage caused but also the obligation to pay an indemnity, derived as a consequence of an illegal act or a created risk, which is typical of extracontractual liability. To calculate the damages and losses, the Federal Civil Code expressly refers this question to the pertinent legal principles contained in Mexico's Federal Labor Act.

The Federal Labor Act—Generally

In Mexico, the notion of civil liability is instantly associated with a contractual relationship. This is logical when one considers that, under Mexican civil law, a contract is the only legal avenue for creating, transferring, modifying or extinguishing obligations In a sense, this provision establishes the most fundamental principle that governs civil liability in Mexico.

Accordingly, any civil liability derived from a different legal source, such as a tortious act, where no contract is in place, is only addressed in a cursory manner by the Federal Civil Code. For example, whereas the Code devotes close to 1,200 sections to obligations and contracts, and the corresponding civil liabilities associated with them, only 25 sections address civil liabilities from illegal acts. This explains the need confronted by the drafters of the Federal Civil Code to find more detailed legal principles elsewhere within the Mexican legal system to supplement the sparse provisions in this code. That supplementary legislation, as mandated by Article 1915 of the Federal Civil Code, is the Federal Labor Act.

As the Federal Civil Code is not equipped with the degree of legislative detail needed to solve the issues raised by extracontractual liability cases, the Mexican legislature chose to assimilate these cases to occupational injuries, industrial accidents and occupational diseases as regulated by Title IX of the Federal Labor Act. Given the few extracontractual liability cases decided by civil courts in Mexico, it is not entirely clear to what degree civil judges apply the provisions of the Federal Labor Act. Unquestionably, civil judges apply the basic principles enu-

---

a. The "minimum daily salary" is set by commissions at the federal level. The level for a commission's area depends upon the costs of living in that area. Thus the amount is higher along the northern border than in some rural interior areas.

merated by the Federal Labor Act. However, the same degree of certainty does not exist with respect to the factual or technical details that may be present in a civil case, allowing judges to exercise some discretion. Occasionally, the application of Federal Labor Act provisions to extracontractual liability cases poses serious challenges and difficulties to civil courts. This is especially evident when one considers that these two sets of rules were formulated to address two different legal areas.

* * *

The Federal Labor Act—Labor Incapacities

Occupational accidents and occupational diseases (known in Mexico as labor risks or *Riesgos de Trabajo*) may produce four different results: (1) temporary incapacity; (2) partial permanent incapacity; (3) total permanent incapacity; and (4) death.

When any of these incapacities occur, the employer is obligated to pay an indemnity to the worker according to the amounts established by the Federal Labor Act.

1.   Temporary Incapacity.

Temporary incapacity is the loss of faculties, which partially or totally impedes a person from performing his/her work for some time. In this case, the employer is obligated to pay the worker an indemnity consisting of his/her full salary during the period of time he/she is unable to work. Payments start from the very first day of incapacity. If the incapacity persists after three months, the worker or the employer may request a special examination and opinion of whether the worker should continue under the same medical treatment or proceed to declare the worker's permanent incapacity, with the corresponding indemnity. These examinations may be repeated every three months.

2.   Partial Permanent Incapacity.

Partial permanent incapacity is the diminution of faculties suffered by a person in his/her working capacity on a permanent basis. In this case, the indemnity consists of the percentage established by the "Table of Incapacities," which forms a part of the Federal Labor Act, calculated as if the incapacity had been a total permanent incapacity. The percentage in question is established by the Labor Court, taking into consideration the worker's age, the seriousness of the incapacity and the ability to perform other paying jobs similar to his/her profession or trade. The FLA provides that the employer is not obligated to pay an amount larger than the one established for the total permanent incapacity, even when more than two incapacities are present.

3.   Total Permanent Incapacity.

Total permanent incapacity is the loss of faculties suffered by a person which prevents him/her from performing any job for the rest of his/her life. In this case, the indemnity consists of an amount equivalent to 1,095 days of salary.

4. Death.

In the case of death, the indemnification comprises two months of salary for funeral expenses and 730 days of salary, without deducting the indemnification received by the worker during the time of his/her temporal incapacity.

The Federal Labor Act—Workers' Labor Rights

A worker who suffers a labor risk has the right to: medical and surgical assistance; rehabilitation; hospitalization, when required; medication; the necessary prosthetic and orthopedic devices; and the indemnification established by the Federal Labor Act.

The Federal Labor Act—Liability Exceptions That Benefit the Employer

The employer is excepted from the obligations established in Article 487 of the Federal Law Act in the following cases: (a) if the accident occurred while the worker was under the influence of alcohol; or (b) any narcotic or drug; (c) if the injury suffered by the worker was intentional; and (d) if the incapacity results from a fight or attempted suicide. In any event, the employer is obligated to provide first medical services and transport the worker to his/her domicile or to a medical center.

The employer is not freed from his/her obligation when the accident occurs as a result of the worker's imprudence or negligence, or the imprudence or negligence of another worker or a third party. Furthermore, in cases involving "inexcusable fault of the employer," the worker's indemnity may be increased up to twenty five percent (25%) at the discretion of the Labor Court. * * *

APPLICATION OF MEXICAN LAW TO SPECIFIC TORT CASES

In General

Mexican Civil Law predicates that civil liability is the obligation that any person has to repair the damages and to compensate for the losses caused to another individual as a consequence of the tortfeasor's acting illegally or against good customs, or as a result of the involvement of inanimate objects or animals. It is said that civil liability constitutes the application of the pertinent legal precept to repair a damage. Although the language of the Federal Civil Code (and the corresponding State codes) refers only to "damage" in the singular, under Mexican law this concept should be construed broadly, including physical and moral injuries, as well as losses.

The All or Nothing Principle

In general, Mexico adheres to the "all or nothing principle," which the United States used to apply three to four decades ago. According to this principle, applied in Mexico in conformity with Article 1910 of the Federal Civil Code (and the 31 respective State codes), when an individual "causes damage" to another, the tortfeasor is liable and should compensate the victim. However, if the damage was caused as a result of "the fault or inexcusable negligence of the victim" (and this can be proven in a Mexican court), then there is no cause of action under Mexican Civil Law, the tortfeasor is not liable and he/she does not have to pay anything to the victim. In other words, the victim's contributory negligence operates as a "total bar" to the tortfeasor's liability.

Applying this principle to the three hypotheticals given earlier, some of the consequences may be as follows: In the *Alina Allen* case, the defendant hotel may indicate, for example, that Alina was drunk and her injuries resulted from her own fault and negligence. Further, Alina crossed the barrier placed by the hotel employees at the base of the stairway that alerted guests not to climb to their suites because the stairways were dark and slippery due to the power outage and rain left by the tropical storm. In the *Craig Curtiss* case, Craig was so anxious to go swimming that he did not pay attention to the signs posted in English and Spanish around the swimming pool indicating the water depth in different parts of the pool. And in the case of *Mary Moore,* according to the report produced by the Rosarito Highway Patrol, the two teenagers were intoxicated and had failed to heed the traffic light indicating that pedestrians must wait.

Absence of a Standard of Negligence or Fault

It may be surprising for legal practitioners in the U.S. or Canada to learn that Mexico does not have any legal standards applicable to negligence or fault. Moreover, the Mexican legal system has not produced a statutory definition of "negligence" or "fault," nor any explicit legislative distinctions between "negligence" and "inexcusable negligence." Regarding these legal notions, the Supreme Court, the highest judicial court in Mexico, has rendered these rather succinct *Jurisprudencias:*

> CIVIL LIABILITY. INEXCUSABLE NEGLIGENCE OF THE VICTIM. The existence of fault or inexcusable negligence *must be appreciated by the judge according to the circumstances of the specific case.* Amparo directo 1924/69 (July 2, 1973).

With respect to the notion of "Good customs," to which Article 1910 of the Federal Civil Code alludes, in another *jurisprudencia,* the Supreme Court wrote:—

> GOOD CUSTOMS. Good customs constitute a concept which authors seek to define in a precise manner. They have reached this conclusion: anything that hurts morality is contrary to good customs, and jurisprudence has slowly considered that there is a criterion of morality in society and that the social environment is the source of good customs. Therefore, *it is not necessary to give a precise definition of good customs because no legislature is going to*

do this but leave it to the wisdom of the courts. Amparo civil directo 476/54 (October 25, 1954).

Since very few cases resulting from tortious actions are decided by trial courts * * * in Mexico, not to mention those rare cases that reach the appellate court level, it is understandable that, rather than enacting domestic legislation on this matter, Mexico has opted for the more practical avenue of allowing judges to use their ample discretion in deciding these rather unusual cases.

Quantification of Damages and Losses Under Mexican Civil Law

As enunciated by Article 1915, the fundamental principle of the Federal Civil Code provides that the repair of damages consist, at the election of the injured party, of the restoration of their prior status, when possible, or the payment of damages and losses.

The reparation of damages would not result in the re-establishment of the *status quo ante* when applied to any of the three hypotheticals given at the beginning of this chapter * * *. Legally, this makes it necessary to shift the reparation or indemnity to the payment of damages and losses, as defined by Articles 2108 and 2109 of the Federal Civil Code, respectively. In general, "damages" may be equated to "out-of-pocket expenses." * * *

* * *

Specific Application to the Three Hypotheticals.

Hypothetical A.

From a purely Mexican law viewpoint, Alina Allen would receive: (1) her complete salary, multiplied by four, during the 90 days that she was "temporarily incapacitated," pursuant to Article 1915 of the Federal Civil Code and the Federal Labor Act. Assuming her salary was $36,000 a year, she would receive $36,000 for the three months she missed work. In addition, Alina's expenses for hospitalization (15 days/$15,000), surgical work ($10,000), rehabilitation ($5,000) and medication ($3,000) would be paid. In Mexico, these expenses are paid directly by the tortfeasor. Grand total: $69,000.

Hypothetical B.

Since Craig became a quadriplegic, the seriousness of the injury caused him to have a "total permanent incapacity," as defined by Article 495 of the Federal Labor Act. Craig had a $48,000 annual salary, amounting to some $133 per day. This salary is multiplied four times and then multiplied again by the 1,095 days mandated by Article 494 of the Federal Labor Act, totaling $582,540. Craig's expenses for hospitalization (15 days/$15,000), surgical work ($10,000), rehabilitation ($5,000), medication ($5,000) and an adequate wheelchair ($25,000) totals $60,000. Grand total: $642,540.

Hypothetical C.

Mary is obligated to pay the hospitalization and medical expenses of both victims. For the teenager whose legs were broken, these expenses amounted to $13,500. For the teenager who died, these expenses amounted to $12,500. In addition, Mary has to indemnify the family of this teenager. Assuming that the teenager's daily salary was $5.00, multiplied by four and then by 750 days, the total is $15,000. In the case of the worker's death, the indemnity also includes a two-month salary for funeral expenses, amounting to $300. Grand total: $41,300.

It is evident that the Mexican legal system, contrary to ours, does not recognize punitive damages, or compensation for pain and suffering and emotional distress. Although the Federal Civil Code, in Article 1916, refers to "moral damages," this legal notion applies only to the injury caused to a person's "feelings, affections, beliefs, honor, decorum, reputation, privacy, image and physical appearance," or how that person "is perceived in the opinion of others." For this reason, moral damages in Mexico are construed now as "non-physical damages" or "defamatory injuries."

Moral damages is a legal notion that has been recently added to Mexico's Civil Law. It tends to be associated with libel and defamation, as well as with injuries resulting from the use of "mechanisms, instruments, equipment and substances," as enunciated by Article 1913 of the Federal Civil Code in cases involving the so-called "objective liability." So far, very few legal actions have been filed in Mexico based on this novel concept.

Joint and Vicarious Liability

The Federal Civil Code contains several provisions imposing joint liability, as well as vicarious liability. Vicarious liability encompasses cases involving master craftsmen, managers and owners of commercial establishments, owners of animals or buildings and heads of households. In Mexico, most attorneys and judges are unfamiliar with the special meaning given in the U.S. to the legal expressions "vicarious liability" and "respondeat superior."

In regard to *joint liability*, the principle enunciated in Article 1917 of the Federal Civil Code is quite clear: Those individuals who have jointly caused damage to another person are jointly and severally liable to the victim for the corresponding indemnity, in accordance with the applicable civil code provisions.

In turn, corporations and other legal entities *(Personas morales)* are liable for the damages and losses caused by their lawful representatives in the performance of their duties. Employers and owners *(Patrons y dueños)* of commercial legal entities are liable for the damages and losses caused by their workers or dependents in the performance of their duties. Consistent with the principle enunciated in Article 1910, this provision establishes that liability will not attach if the employers and owners prove that the damage is not attributable to any fault or negligence on their part. Lastly, hotel owners and innkeepers are liable for damages and injuries caused by their employees in the performance of their duties.

All of the provisions of the Federal Civil Code are written in a simple and concise language. This legislative technique allows Mexican judges to exercise ample discretion when applying them to specific but rare cases.

A SERIOUS ACCIDENT OCCURS IN THE MEXICAN PLANT: PROBLEMS OF CORPORATE AND PRODUCT LIABILITY*

4 United States–Mexico Law Journal 125 (1996).

Moderator: Michael W. Gordon,[1] Panel Members: Keith Harvey,[2] M.E. Occhialino,[3] Boris Kozolchyk[4], and Ignacio Gomez–Palacio[5]

THE PROBLEM

After several years of successful association between GROWFAST and AGRICOLAS, S.A. de C.V., a serious accident occurred at the AGRICOLAS plant in Monterrey. While transferring Sollate concentrate into vats for dilution and packaging, supervised by both AGRICOLAS employees and two technicians "on loan" from GROWFAST, an unexplained explosion occurred. Three supervisory persons and 35 other employees were killed. Serious injury was caused to dozens of other employees. The chemical laden smoke from the explosion drifted over parts of Monterrey and adjacent towns. By the time it had dissipated, it had caused serious burns to several hundred more people, including a number of foreigners. The foreigners included two United States citizens vacationing in Mexico. Lawsuits are being considered by Mexicans, the two United States citizens, and four Europeans.

THE DISCUSSION

* * *

Boris Kozolchyk: My feeling is that the application of Mexican law by the U.S. court may prevent a healthy recovery. This is not a case of strict liability; it is a case of product liability. As far as I know, there is no cause of action under Mexican law for an injured party to sue a remote manufacturer or vendor, unless the plaintiff is in privity of contract with the defendant or can prove the manufacturer's or the

---

* Reprinted with permission of the U.S.—Mexico Law Journal.

1. Chesterfield Smith Professor of Law, University of Florida College of Law.

2. Partner, Davis & Harvey, Dallas, Texas.

3. Professor of Law, University of New Mexico School of Law.

4. Director and President, National Law Center for Inter–American Free Trade, Tucson, Arizona.

5. Of Counsel, Jauregui, Navarrete, Nader y Rojas, S.C. Mexico, D.F.

vendor's negligence. Product liability is a distinctly U.S. concept which emerged from the fall of Prosser's famous "citadel" which separated tort and contract law. Despite its continued use, commentators and courts continue to question it from a conceptual and public policy standpoint. Mexican law does have a doctrine of strict liability, but not of product liability. Under Mexico's strict liability, the *defendant* is normally *the user* (whether owner, agent or bailee) of an inherently dangerous mechanism, instrument, apparatus or substance who, with his use, injures the *plaintiff.*[9]

Strict liability has been used in Mexico predominantly by the victims of vehicular, industrial or hotel accidents in actions against drivers, trucking companies or hotel owners. In these strict liability lawsuits, defendants can raise the defenses of the victims' fault or inexcusable negligence, or the occurrence of a fortuitous event or force majeure.[11] The product liability cause of action, then, simply does not fit the Mexican strict liability mold. Nonetheless, assuming *arguendo* that it does, the cause of action on product liability would still have to get over the hurdle of inadequate compensation by U.S. standards. The amount recovered under Mexican law are set forth in workmens compensation tables for loss of the victim's life or limb. The amount recovered under these tables are quite low by U.S. personal injury damage standards. It is true that Mexican law allows for the recovery of "moral damages," but judging from Mexican judicial decisions and doctrinal comments these are also quite modest in nature. Thus, it is my opinion that a product liability cause of action is unavailable under Mexican law and that defendant's motion for summary judgment, based upon such an allegation, would dispose of the complaint before an American court. If the cause of action were for strict liability, the amount recovered under Mexican law, including moral damages, would be insignificant by U.S. standards.

Gomez-Palacio: It is my understanding of the facts that an explosion happened in this Mexican company while AGRICOLAS was bottling the pesticide. I'm not too sure we are talking about what I understand to be product liability. There are three types of liabilities under Mexico's Civil Code: (1) contractual liability (2) extra-contractual liability and (3) objective liability.[14] Contractual liability arises through breach of obligations under the contract. That clearly is not applicable. But the other two, extra-contractual and objective liability may be applicable. Extra-contractual liability arises due to the performance of an illegal act or an act *contra buenos costumbres*, "against good customs."[15] This may not be applicable in this case, because AGRICOLAS was not engaged in an illegal act, the company was just bottling this pesticide. Objective liability arises due to the use of mechanisms, instruments, apparatus or

9. C.C.D.F. art. 1913.

11. See B. Kozolchyk and M. Ziontz, A Negligence Action in Mexico: An Introduction to the Application of Mexican Law in the United States, 7 Ariz. J. Int'l. & Comp. Law, 1 at 27–30. Id. at 33–35.

14. C.C.D.F. art. 1910, 1913.

15. C.C.D.F. art. 1910.

substances which are dangerous in themselves or by reason of their velocity, explosive or inflammable nature, strength of the electrical current they conduct or other analogous causes. This terminology may vary from state to state and some are broader than others. In any event there was recognition of objective liability by the legislature as industry began to develop in this century. Objective liability was recognized because modern industrial mechanisms created risks of doing injury without fault.

However, in the case of both extra-contractual and objective liability, the defendant is not liable if the damage occurs as a consequence of the fault or inexcusable negligence of the victim. Under the facts of this case, people who were injured appear to have been outside the factory. So I believe there would be a cause of action under objective liability.

Kozolchyk: I think that the interpretation that would lead to liability would have to be based upon the *per se* dangerousness of the vehicle or the process of manufacture. Translating Article 1913 literally, "When a person makes use of mechanisms, instruments, apparatuses or substances dangerous in themselves or by reason of their velocity or the explosive or inflammable nature of the object itself, or by the electric current that they conduct, they are responsible for the damage which is caused...." The Article seems to be looking to inherently dangerous objects. In that enumeration, trucks and automobiles have been held to be such inherently dangerous objects. This may be a basis for claiming liability under these facts, but my feeling is that if somebody is asked to give testimony under Mexican law as to whether or not there is in the Mexican law a doctrine of product liability, where negligence doesn't count, where there is no assumption of the risk, and where there is no contributory negligence, a cause of action somewhere between contract and tort, the answer would have to be no. That kind of a cause of action, *per se*, does not exist.

We have different interpretations of one of the crucial provisions here, Article 1913 of the Mexican Civil Code. I read Article 1913 to say that when a person makes use of dangerous mechanisms or instrumentalities, that person becomes the target defendant. It would not be because of a doctrine of product liability. Under Article 1913, it is not the party who manufactured the dangerous mechanism or instrumentality who may be liable, but the person who harms someone by making use of it. That's the way I read it. I believe that Lic. Gomez–Palacio reads Article 1913 more broadly.

Gomez-Palacio: I believe that our difference is limited to the breadth of meaning to be applied to "dangerous mechanisms, instruments and substances." I agree that Article 1913 does not extend to the manufacturer of such "dangerous mechanisms;" it extends only to the person who makes use of them.

Harvey: I find it intriguing that we have a debate right here among our Mexican law experts about what is the Mexican law. An American judge, asked to apply Mexican law, is probably going to be a little bit disquieted by the thought that it may be difficult to determine what Mexican law is. If that judge had the alternative, would he probably go with the good old safe "what the judge knows" law of the forum? I wonder if we could talk about proof of foreign law in American courts.

Gomez-Palacio: I think conflicting expert opinions will always be possible in an American court. Defendant and plaintiff are going to bring their own experts. I've been in cases where there have been twenty expert opinions. Of course it is always difficult to apply foreign law for any court in the world.

The only area that gets a little closer to product liability is the statute on consumer protection.[17] But I must say that I have signed a legal opinion saying that in my opinion, a swimming pool is a dangerous thing that would fall within the doctrine of objective liability. This case involved a swimming pool at a hotel in Mexico owned by an international hotel chain. As I mentioned before there are certain state codes that are more ample, broader, and that is the case of the code of Quintana Roo which was a code that was issued thinking about the tourists in Quintana Roo.

Gordon: A similar problem occurred in a case on which I worked with one of our large battery companies. A U.S. court was being asked to apply Mexican law, and the court wanted to assure itself that there was a cause of action under Mexican law and a possibility of some damages being awarded under Mexican law. The court did not want to recognize that Mexican law applies, and then learn that there's no cause of action under Mexican law. It's a little bit like the courts not being willing to remove a case under the doctrine of *forum non conveniens*, unless there is an agreement that jurisdiction will be accepted in the other area. This occurred in the *Bhopal* case, where one of the conditions of the court was that the company accept the jurisdiction of India. It is not just a matter of determining the applicable law; the court may want to know what lies downstream.

*   *   *

Gordon: In purely domestic parent-subsidiary cases in the United States where there is piercing of the corporate veil, there are relatively few cases where the court doesn't require a finding of some kind of wrongful conduct on the part of the parent corporation. It's usually where the parent has used the subsidiary illegally, fraudulently or there is some other kind of misuse. The great fear, of course, is that somebody is going to recognize enterprise liability and that suggests that, if you have a parent and a subsidiary, there ought to be unity and there ought to be liability.

I don't find the courts talking much about enterprise liability in the United States, the area where I do most of my consulting work for large

---

17. Ley Federal de Proteccion al Consu-   (D.O. December 24, 1994).
midor, Federal Consumer Protection Law,

U.S. corporations, and we've never had that raised, by opposing counsel. The defendant corporation doesn't want to raise enterprise liability, of course, and then have to defend against it. Yet we are beginning to hear enterprise liability referred to in the multinational enterprise context. Do you think we are likely to see a development of that in the transnational context?

Harvey: In Texas, the corporate entity is respected and piercing the corporate veil is very difficult. However, in tort cases there has been a little movement in that direction, e.g., in the *Hornsby* case[20] and the *Western Horizontal Drilling, Inc.* case.[21] These cases deal with different approaches to finding individuals liable either for their own negligence or by the way their business is structured through the piercing of the corporate veil by way of the *alter ego* theory. The facts of the case before us lend themselves to another common law theory used by courts in Texas to pierce the corporate veil namely, the single business enterprise theory.[22] Under this theory, one business can be made liable for the debts (and I would extend that principle to include tortious or negligent acts) of another.

Gordon: We find the same thing with experts in the U.S. I was asked to respond in a case where there were two plaintiffs' and two defendants' expert affidavits with regard to whether punitive damages are permissible because the law doesn't say anything about them. Two lawyers had said they were totally inconsistent with civil law and the other two lawyers had said since they are not expressly excluded in the civil code, therefore it would be in the power of the court to grant punitive damages. I agreed with the first and went back into some of the history of the development of punitive damages, and the court agreed with that side. But it certainly isn't surprising that we get very, very different views on the law.

Allan Van Fleet: If this were a consignment arrangement where the title was held by the party in the United States, GROWFAST, and title

---

20. Leitch v. Hornsby, 885 S.W.2d 243, 252 (Tex.App.1994) (The appeals court upheld a jury's finding of an officer and agent's personal liability for their own negligence. The piercing of the corporate veil was deemed not necessary unless the individual's negligence is merely derivative of the corporation's negligence).

21. In Western Horizontal Drilling, Inc. v. Jonnet Energy Corp., 11 F.3d 65, 66 (5th Cir.1994) the Court referred to the Texas Supreme Court decision in Castleberry v. Branscum, 721 S.W. 2d 270, 272 (Tex. 1986) (which defined the concept of alter ego as when "a corporation is organized and operated as a mere tool or business conduit of another corporation").

22. The single business enterprise theory was defined in Paramount Petroleum Corp. v. Taylor Rental Center, 712 S.W.2d 534, 536 (Tex. App. 1986), as "... when

corporations are not operated as separate entities but rather integrate their resources to achieve a common business purpose, each constituent corporation may be held liable for debts incurred in pursuit of that business." In determining whether two or more corporations have not been maintained as separate entities, courts in Texas have typically considered the following factors: (1) common employees; (2) common offices; (3) centralized accounting; (4) payment of wages by one corporation to another corporation's employees; (5) common business name; (6) services rendered by the employees of one corporation on behalf of another corporation; (7) undocumented transfers of funds between corporations; and (8) unclear allocation of profits and losses between corporations.

didn't pass until the buyer, AGRICOLAS, purchased the explosive substances, wouldn't there be liability on the part of GROWFAST under the Mexican code, Article 1932(I)? Article 1932(I) says, "the proprietors shall equally be responsible for damage caused: (I) By the explosion of machines or by the combustion of explosive substances;...."

Gordon: It happened in a building.

Kozolchyk: I believe that the provision in Article 1932 refers back to Article 1931, which concerns the responsibilities of owners of a building. They're not talking about other ownership of the movable property or personalty, the explosive substances.

Gordon: The provision of Article 1929 refers to responsibility of owners of animals, so I'm not so sure that there is a reference in 1932 to 1931.

Kozolchyk: But 1929 refers specifically to the "owner of an animal," *(el dueno de un animal)* unlike the reference to "the proprietors" *(los proprietarios)* in Article 1932.

John Stephenson: Let me change the facts a little bit. What if GROWFAST sells these products to AGRICOLAS by selling them, FOB, from the factory in either Texas or some other U.S. location, so that GROWFAST has no connection to Mexico, other than selling products in the United States to a distributor from Mexico. Suppose the distribution agreement requires title to transfer in the United States. Does that affect the results?

Occhialino: From my perspective, the answer wouldn't be different so long as there was a defect in the product as it left the manufacturer's hands in the United States. I think a Texas Court would apply Texas strict products liability, if the product was manufactured in Texas. On the other hand, if the problem is not a defect created by the manufacturer, but by the way the product was handled by the Mexican company in Mexico, there may be no substantive liability under American law. A person is not liable for the negligence of an independent distributor. The corporate setup under which the product was distributed then could make a significant difference.

Gordon: Would your view change if GROWFAST had no idea who the purchaser was or where the goods would be taken?

Occhialino: That would be important for purposes of personal jurisdiction if a Mexican court were trying to assert jurisdiction and GROWFAST opposed Mexico's jurisdiction by saying, it didn't know the product would end up there. I don't think it would affect a Texas court's choice of law. I do think it would affect a Mexican court's jurisdiction if Mexico has jurisdiction principles like the United States that focus on foreseeability that you might be sued in the forum.

Gordon: Whose choice of law rules will be applied by a court in the United States? Whose choice of law rules will be applied by a court in Mexico? Could we look for a moment at the source of this law?

Occhialino: In the United States all fifty states are free, within the bounds of the constitutional provisions of full faith and credit and due process, to choose the choice of law system that they would prefer. There are two basic choice of law systems: traditional, as reflected in the First Restatement,[27] which is very rule-oriented; and the Second Restatement,[28] which requires a more "significant relationship" or "contacts approach." Every American state is free to use either one of those systems or any of the many variations of these two that also exist. There are professors who become famous by getting their name on a slight variation of one of the two basic choice of law systems. There is no single choice of law system that must be applied in each state in the United States. There could have been, I suppose, but the U.S. Supreme Court held that, when a federal court is sitting as a diversity jurisdiction court, instead of having a single federal system of choice of law to apply the federal courts are bound to follow the choice of law system of the state in which the federal court sits.[29] So even if you file a product liability claim in a federal court, you don't get a single federal choice of law principle applied by all federal courts. A federal court in Delaware applies state of Delaware principles of choice of law, and a Texas federal court applies state of Texas principles. The big challenge for an American lawyer trying to choose a forum is to find a forum that: (1) has jurisdiction, and (2) has a choice of law system that will point to the product liability law most favorable to the plaintiffs.

Gordon: Would a Texas court have recognized a contractual provision that Texas law ought to apply in the sales of these products to AGRICOLAS?

Occhialino: That is a difficult question because in our hypothetical bystanders are suing rather than parties to the contract itself. I'm not sure that a choice of law clause in a contract between GROWFAST and AGRICOLAS would be relevant to a personal injury action by third persons who aren't parties to that contract.

Gordon: What if AGRICOLAS itself were suing GROWFAST?

Occhialino: The contractual provision probably would be recognized. Choice of law clauses in contracts are an antidote to the vague choice of law systems that operate in the absence of a contractual provision. The principles of choice of law that are applied in the United States are so vague and so ambiguous that, absent a choice of law clause, this very ambiguity means that good lawyering can make a difference. When one says that the law of the place of the most significant relationship applies, one has said almost nothing. Then the lawyering begins. It is the power of lawyers to shape the policies of the different governments that are involved and the fairness arguments for the parties and then, after making excellent technical arguments, to touch the judge's sense of

---

27. RESTATEMENT OF CONFLICT OF LAWS (1934).

28. RESTATEMENT (SECOND) OF CONFLICT OF LAWS (1971).

29. Klaxon Co. v. Stentor Elec. Mfg. Co., 313 U.S. 487 (1941).

justice. In this case the question really is; "Does a Texas federal judge want to hurt an American corporation with a large presence in Texas by choosing an applicable law that will give large damages and easy rules of liability when for the most part, non-American and non-Texan plaintiffs are suing?" In my view, it probably would come down to that. But it would take fifty pages of briefing on pure law before we got to the real issue.

Gordon: If the contract had a provision that Mexican law applied, or that Texas law applied if the matter went to a Mexican court either because it was initiated before a Mexican court or after a *forum non conveniens* argument, would the Mexican court recognize the choice made in the contract? And, assuming no choice had been made in the contract, how would the Mexican court decide? Do they apply a "significant relationship" principle in determining what law is applicable?

Gomez-Palacio: I believe we would say that there is no choice of law situation. If AGRICOLAS bottled the product in the wrong way, there was an illicit act. There are three distinct principles of liability, and one of them is contractual liability. There you have a choice of law. But in objective liability, which is an accident, then you just go to see whether according to the rules of the code that Mexican law applies. And Article 12 of the Mexican Civil Code says that Mexican laws are applicable to all persons who are in the Republic.

* * *

Gordon: Please look at the damage provisions for a minute because certainly that seems critical as to where you are going to initiate your suit. The plaintiffs' counsel are going to look at Delaware, Kansas, Texas, and Mexico and find where they are most likely to get a judgment of the highest possible damages, and then argue that state's law ought to apply. We are all assuming that Mexican damages aren't going to be very high, though Lic. Gomez-Palacio suggested that under moral damages concepts, damages might go as high as a half million dollars for each plaintiff.[38]

Gomez-Palacio: In Mexico, there are two kinds of damages, physical and moral damages. Physical damage is an amount based on the Federal Labor Law depending on the damage caused.[39] And whatever the Federal Labor Law states, the amount is multiplied by 4 and you have your physical damage. For example, Article 480 of the labor law covers total permanent incapacity. Article 479 covers partial permanent incapacity. In the case of total permanent incapacity, the Federal Labor Law recognizes that you have to obtain the "highest minimum daily salary applicable in the area." For example, minimum salary in a given area in Mexico right now is 4 dollars a day. So you multiply that by 4 and that gives you 16 dollars. And then the Federal Labor Law will recognize for total permanent incapacity 1,095 days, which you multiply by 16 dollars.

38. C.C.D.F.art. 1916.   **39.** C.C.D.F. art. 1915.

As a matter of fact, it comes out to $16,420 for total permanent incapacity. That is the physical damages. There used to be a cap on moral damages, which was two thirds of the physical damages. You would take the $16,420, plus two thirds for moral damage. The Federal District Code was amended years ago. The amendment consisted of abolishing a cap for the moral damages.[41] It is open now; the judge can just consider whatever amount he feels is proper. What are moral damages? Article 1916 of the Civil Code covers damage to the feelings, affections, beliefs, appearance, honor, reputation, private life, physical aspects or the reactions of others to him or her. It refers to the profession of the injured person and recognizes the fact that, depending on his or her profession and income, the damages may be larger in the United States. Now the judge has a free hand because a price is put upon "honor." Well, how much is it worth? For example, one testicle, how much will it affect your feelings? Here, the judge has an absolute free hand with no cap situation. However, due to our traditions, the Mexican judge who is used to applying a cap for moral damages is not going to feel that he is as free as an American judge using this very same standard of moral damages. Punitive damages are still not applicable in Mexico. If a twelve-year old girl scout with a grade school education suffered total permanent incapacity, what would a judge in the United States grant for moral damages? Ten or twenty thousand dollars? A jury would probably award even higher damages in the United States. The application of the Mexican law in an American court may be far more favorable to plaintiffs than it is in Mexico.

Gordon: Why did you say initially that the labor law would apply? I thought the injured parties bringing the civil action were not employees of GROWFAST or AGRICOLAS?

Gomez-Palacio: The civil code specifically refers the judge to the Federal Labor Code.[44] It says, "When damage is caused to persons and results in death, total or permanent incapacity, partial permanent, total temporary or partial temporary incapacity, the amount of damages shall be determined according to the provisions established by the Federal Labor Law."[45] To calculate the appropriate indemnity one should take as a base four times the "highest minimum daily salary."

Gordon: Why would you rely on the Federal District Code if the accident took place in Monterrey? Why wouldn't you look to the Civil Code of the State of Nuevo Leon?

Gomez-Palacio: If the accident occurred in Nuevo Leon, one would rely on the Code of that state. But most of the civil codes follow the Code of the Federal District.

---

41. The previous version of the C.C.D.F article 1916 capped the moral damages at one third of the total recovery the limit was removed on December 31, 1982. See C.C.D.F. art. 1916 bis D.O. (Dec. 31, 1982).

44. C.C.D.F. art. 1915.

45. Ley Federal de Trabajo (Federal Labor Law) [L.F.T.] art. 495.

Gordon: But since the amendments to the Federal District Code, some states may not have made comparable amendments to the moral damage provision.

Kozolchyk: The Mexican system of tort compensation is predicated basically on a public law approach to the problem, not a private law approach as in the United States. It is as if to say that the business of the person who has been affected, the victim of the tort, is everybody's business. The concept is much closer to criminal law in conception than it is to tort law in conception. And this is why what you have is basically workmen's compensation tables applied to the accident because it's everybody's problem. It's part of way to resolve a situation in a social fashion, and that's number one. If you add up what an engineer in Mexico would have earned over 25–35 years of productive life as an engineer, it could be two or three million dollars. That is not a consideration under the workmen's compensation table. It seeks the status quo ante to bring the victim to where he was at the time the accident occurred, as if the accident had not occurred. That is the rationale behind this way of compensation. When I first reviewed moral damages under Mexican law, I reviewed the legislative history. What seemed to have motivated it at first was basically trying to inject some rationale for libel and slander into the compensation. This is why they talked about honor.

Gordon: It seems to me that it is not yet determined how judges are going to interpret this authority to impose unlimited damages in the long run. I feel very uncomfortable in telling people that they absolutely do not have to worry about any large judgment in Mexico, in view of the open-ended moral damage provision. It wouldn't surprise me if we do see larger awards in the future.

Kozolchyk: The last time I looked up "danos morales" (moral damages) in Mexico's Semanario Judicial de la Federacion (whose rough equivalent in the United States would be the Supreme Court Reporter of West's National Reporter System) at the National Law Center for Inter–American Free Trade database, Mexican courts were awarding, uniformly, very small amounts for moral damages.

Questions and Comments

1. Are there any lessons from *Twohy* to consider as we begin to apply Mexican law to our hypothetical?

2. Perhaps the most important sentence in the Vargas extract is that "Mexico has not developed what may be considered a specialized and technically advanced tort law." How would you respond to a letter from the GROWFAST in-house legal counsel that asked several dozen specific and detailed questions, drafted based upon considerable experience with tort litigation in the United States, about how Mexico addresses these issues?

3. What law will apply to the cases in the United States, Mexican state or federal law? Is there any chance that the Civil Code for the Federal

District would apply? Or the Federal Civil Code? Does it really make much difference whether the civil code for Veracruz or the Federal District or the Federal Code applies?

4.   Vargas brings into the discussion the Federal Labor Act. Would that apply in our case?

5.   May the injured parties be awarded damages for pain and suffering? Punitive damages? Just what damages are available?

6.   Does GROWFAST really need to worry about moral damages? Do you suppose Mexican courts award moral damages in the peso equivalent of millions of dollars?

7.   Working through the three tourists cases illustrates the likely outcomes in these typical torts. Are they encouraging to the plaintiffs if the court has ruled that Mexican law applies?

8.   There are some Mexican attorneys that are becoming well established in civil litigation. But they do not have the expectations of a U.S. attorney signing clients to contingent fee contracts. Such contracts are not allowed. Mexican lawyers are paid by the hour or by a negotiated fee, but not a percentage of a settlement or judgment.

9.   Should GROWFAST argue that Mexican plaintiffs, who will take their judgments back to Mexico, should not be awarded more than what is proper under Mexican law because that undermines the whole Mexican legal theory of torts and compensation?

10.   Contributory negligence may help GROWFAST. Or will it? What if the product of GROWFAST is inherently dangerous? Isn't objective liability the same in Mexico as in the United States? Would the contributory negligence rule significantly affect plaintiffs' counsel's choice of forum? Why should it? See Vargas' discussion of § 1910 of the Civil Code.

11.   How is fault defined in Mexican law?

12.   Sitting as a judge in the U.S. court with the hypothetical cases before you, would you apply Mexican law now that you know more about it?

13.   The panel discussants in the second extract all seem to believe that the plaintiffs are better off if the U.S. court applies U.S. law. What is their essentially common position based on?

14.   Gordon mentions veil piercing and enterprise liability. Problem 3.3 discussed veil piercing in the context of jurisdiction, not substantive liability. Mexico and essentially all civil law tradition nations do not recognize the theory of "piercing the corporate veil", but it may be assumed that all of these nations disallow the use of a corporate entity by individuals for illegal or fraudulent purposes. Many nations have provisions in the civil code allowing a cause of action where a person has abused the exercise of a right. Does that not mean the exercise of the right to form and operate a business entity? Notwithstanding such a cause based on existing provisions, an adventuresome civil law nation court might create a veil piercing theory, as has Argentina, referring to a group of linked corporations as a *conjunto economico* or economic unit. It is most likely that such a theory would be applied to cases involving bankruptcy.

Do you believe that a U.S. court would pierce the veil in our case for liability purposes, drawing on your corporations classes and the introduction to veil piercing in Problem 3.3? The commonalities expressed in footnote 22 of the extract are usually not alone sufficient to pierce the veil—what is the wrongful conduct of GROWFAST that a court amy additionally require?

15. The brief dialogue of Van Fleet, Gordon and Kozolchyk about Articles 1929, 1931 and 1932 touch upon the origins of civil law tradition tort liability in the French civil code section establishing liability of an owner for his "things". Things in 1804 meant little more than animals. Some nations have changed their codes over the decades very little, allowing courts to expand the meaning of "things" to machines and even buildings. There is almost always debate in these nations regarding the meaning of this language.

16. Stephenson and Occhialino break the link between GROWFAST and the Mexican user to have the latter a purchaser from a distributor. Thus no privity would exist. But that may not affect the application of the strict liability provision of Mexican law—if the fault occurred at the GROWFAST facility.

17. The discussion turns to contract law and choice of law. Often there is a provision in a contract stipulating that the law of a particular nation will apply. But Occhialino suggests a court might not accept such a provision where GROWFAST attempts to apply it to personal injury flowing from such a contract. Why? Since GROWMEX is the purchaser does that mean that its injured employees would be subject to a choice of law provision in the sales contract?

Part Three

LITIGATION INITIATED
OUTSIDE THE UNITED
STATES

Chapter 5

ACTIONS IN FOREIGN COURTS

PROBLEM 5.1 JURISDICTION: A U.S. CORPORATION INITIATES LITIGATION IN A FOREIGN COURT AGAINST A LOCAL DEFENDANT

SECTION I. THE SETTING

This problem deals with issues raised when a lawsuit is considered in order to get relief from a transaction gone bad. The issues are similar to those for tort claims, but begin with a business relationship between the ultimate plaintiff and defendant. Decisions at the outset of litigation often affect rights asserted later, including how and whether any resulting judgment may be satisfied if the defendant has insufficient assets in the country in which the court is located.

Your client is Celsius Manufacturing, Inc. (Celsius), a Delaware corporation with its principal place of business in Pittsburgh, Pennsylvania. Celsius manufactures induction molding devices (IMDs) used in the further manufacture of plastic products. In October 2007, Celsius demonstrated its IMDs at a trade fair in London, where a purchasing agent for Plastic Maker GmbH ("Plastic Maker"), of Hamburg, Germany, became interested in the product. At the trade fair, Plastic Maker submitted a purchase order to Celsius, offering to purchase 1,000 IMDs at $400 per unit, "terms c.i.f. London," to be shipped in January 2008. The President of Celsius responded while she was still in London with a letter in which she acknowledged receipt of the purchase order and accepted all the terms and conditions of the offer. Neither the purchase order form nor the letter of acceptance contained either a choice of law or a choice of forum clause.

The 1,000 IMDs were shipped on open account on January 6, 2008, and arrived in London on January 28, where they were unloaded to a warehouse owned and operated by Plastic Maker. Plastic Maker had intended to redistribute the IMDs to its facilities in Germany, The Netherlands, and Spain. Upon receipt of the IMDs, Plastic Maker informed Celsius that the IMDs did not conform to the quality of IMDs demonstrated at the London trade fair and that Plastic Maker was rejecting them. Plastic Maker informed Celsius that it was holding the IMDs at the Plastic Maker warehouse in London, awaiting further instructions concerning return or disposal of the IMDs.

On a recent trip to Europe, Celsius engineers stopped in London and inspected the IMDs that were shipped to Plastic Maker. Those engineers have explained to you that the IMDs shipped to Plastic Maker did in fact conform to the contract requirements and were consistent with the IMDs demonstrated at the London trade fair. You have received opinions confirming this from English experts. Moreover, the Celsius engineers have reported that the IMDs were stored by Plastic Maker in a location that left them open to rain and as a result the IMDs have been damaged. While repair may be possible if the IMDs are returned to Celsius, there would be substantial cost in repairing them.

Celsius has asked you to bring suit against Plastic Maker to collect the contract price of the IMDs plus interest and other losses due to the breach by Plastic Maker. Celsius has also asked that, should a contract action not be successful, you file an alternative tort claim for damage to the IMDs through Plastic Maker's negligence.

SECTION II. FOCUS OF CONSIDERATION

This problem involves a contract action in which a U.S. plaintiff is ready to bring suit against a foreign defendant. The client would likely prefer suit in a U.S. court, but that should depend on your analysis of the legal issues involved. A good starting point is whether there is jurisdiction to sue in a U.S. court. You already know that, even if the relevant state long-arm statute would provide for jurisdiction as the result of a contract to be performed in part (through manufacture of goods) in a U.S. state, this is a transaction that indicates no activity on the part of the German defendant in the United States. Thus, the requisite minimum contacts may not exist for suit in a U.S. court, and there is no consent to jurisdiction through contract terms. The next step is then to determine whether there is jurisdiction under German law to sue in Germany, or (in the alternative) whether there might be jurisdiction to sue in London.

As we shall see in the materials below, jurisdiction in a foreign court can be affected by more than just national law, and may require resort to treaties or regional legal instruments. Ultimately, wherever suit is brought, attention must be given to the collection of any resulting judgment. A judgment easily obtained in one jurisdiction, but not subject to recognition and enforcement in another, will be worthless if the judgment creditor has no assets in the rendering jurisdiction from which the judgment can be satisfied.

At some point it will be necessary to consider the following issues:

     (1) jurisdiction in a U.S. court

     (2) jurisdiction in a U.K. court

(3) jurisdiction in a German court ¹⁄₂

(4) location of property from which the judgment may be collected ⌐

(5) rules on recognition and enforcement of the resulting judgment

At this time you are to address only issues 1–3.

The Brussels Regulation and Rule 6.20 of the Civil Procedure Rules (CPR) of the Supreme Court of England and Wales are essential to an understanding of this problem. They are contained in the Documents Supplement.

SECTION III.   READINGS, QUESTIONS AND COMMENTS

PART A.   FORUM SHOPPING I: JURISDICTION IN THE UNITED STATES (AN OPPORTUNITY FOR REVIEW)

Most U.S. plaintiffs will want to sue in a U.S. court if that is possible. It is possible only if jurisdiction exists in the court in which the action would be filed. You should at this point review the analysis of jurisdictional issues raised by Problem 5.1 in state or federal court in Pennsylvania, the plaintiff's place of business. You should also consider what that decision would mean in terms of procedure for service of process, taking of evidence, trial, and ultimately the enforcement of any resulting judgment. The material covering these issues is found in other chapters of this book. We here focus on actions in foreign courts. Thus, even if you decide that jurisdiction exists in a Pennsylvania court, consideration should be given to the alternative of bringing the action in a foreign court. This involves the process of forum shopping to determine where best to initiate litigation.

PART B.   GENERAL ISSUES IN THE CONSIDERATION OF FOREIGN LAW AND FOREIGN LITIGATION

Forum shopping necessarily involves consideration of the law of multiple jurisdictions. This raises the question of the propriety of a lawyer advising a client on the law outside of the jurisdiction in which that lawyer is admitted to practice. Can a Pennsylvania lawyer advise a client on U.K. or German law? Can a Pennsylvania lawyer represent a client in court in either of those jurisdictions? Even if she could legally do so, should she? Questions of multijurisdictional practice are relevant to the issues raised in Problem 5.1 and deserve some consideration at this point.

PART C.   FORUM SHOPPING II: JURISDICTION IN THE UNITED KINGDOM

The facts in Problem 5.1 include conduct by both of the parties in the United Kingdom. In addition, there may be reasons (language, applicable law, etc.) that favor bringing the action in a U.K. court. This requires consideration of U.K. rules on jurisdiction. The first system of jurisdiction existing in the U.K. is that provided in European Union Regulation 44/2001 (Dec. 22, 2000), which came into effect on March 1, 2002. The Regulation applies to civil and commercial matters where a defendant is domiciled in an EU Member State. The U.K. claims special status under the Regulation, not having fully acquiesced in the Treaty of Amsterdam amendments to the European Convention Treaty that transferred competence for judicial cooperation matters from the Member States to the Community institutions. Nonetheless, in the Civil Jurisdiction and Judgments Order 2001, the U.K. conformed its basic jurisdictional rules to those found in the Regulation. For defendants domiciled outside the European Union, the traditional rules of jurisdiction apply in U.K. courts. These rules make judicial competence of the court dependent on service of a claim form on the defendant. Such service can occur if the defendant is present within the jurisdiction, if the defendant submits to jurisdiction by consent, or if the courts authorize service out of the jurisdiction under CPR 6.20.

Council Regulation (EC) No 44/2001 of 22 December 2000 on jurisdiction and the recognition and enforcement of judgments in civil and commercial matters, Official Journal of the European Communities L 12/1 (16 Jan. 2001)

You should read carefully the "Brussels Regulation," which is available in the Documents Supplement. Consider especially the rules on jurisdiction, how those rules apply to cases involving a defendant domiciled in an EU Member State, how those rules apply (or do not apply) to a defendant not domiciled in an EU Member State, and what those rules mean to a U.S. plaintiff considering an action against a defendant domiciled in an EU Member State.

The UK Civil Jurisdiction and Judgments Order 2001

On December 11, 2001, the United Kingdom revised its rules on jurisdiction over defendants domiciled in the United Kingdom, adopting rules that parallel those found in the Brussels Regulation. This is the Civil Jurisdiction and Judgments Order 2001. Like the Brussels Regulation, it became effective on March 1, 2002, and contains Schedule 4, which provides "Rules for Allocation of Jurisdiction within U.K." Since those rules apply only to U.K. defendants, they are not otherwise relevant to this problem.

Civil Procedure Rule (CPR) 6.20 of the Rules of the Supreme Court of England and Wales

You should read carefully CPR 6.20 of the Rules of the Supreme Court of England and Wales, which is available in the Documents Supplement. CPR 6.20 provides the rules for jurisdiction over foreign parties not domiciled in European Union Member States with whom no treaty on jurisdiction exists. The rules of CPR 6.20 reflect the U.K. emphasis on the relationship between service and jurisdiction. Consider the language of CPR 6.20 and how it applies to the questions raised in Problem 5.1.

Questions and Comments

1. The "general" rule of jurisdiction under the Brussels Regulation is found in Article 2, which provides that a defendant may be sued at its place of domicile. For a legal person, Article 60 provides that domicile is where the corporation has its "(a) statutory seat, or (b) central administration, or (c) principal place of business." Can suit be brought against Plastic Maker in Problem 5.1 based on Article 2 of the Brussels Regulation? Compare the Article 2 rule on general jurisdiction to U.S. concepts of general jurisdiction discussed in earlier chapters.

2. The German defendant is domiciled within the European Union. Thus, the Brussels Regulation applies. Does jurisdiction exist in a U.K. court under the provisions of the Regulation? See Article 5(1) of the Regulation. What is the place of performance of the contract? The price-delivery term calls for shipment "c.i.f. London." This is a standard price-delivery term in international commerce, often governed by the "Incoterms" prepared by the International Chamber of Commerce. It should be used only when the goods will be loaded into a sea-going vessel in the traditional fashion, and makes the seller responsible for loading the goods on the vessel at the port of shipment, paying all necessary export charges, and paying for the cost of freight and insurance. Risk of loss passes to the buyer under a c.i.f. contract when the goods are loaded "over the rail" onto the carrier, and the seller not only carries no more risk of loss after this time, but the sellers's obligations are then all completed upon delivery of the documents required by the transaction (including the bill of lading from the ship's master which becomes the document of title). This all normally occurs at the place of shipment, not the place of destination. Thus, a c.i.f. contract is a "shipment contract." The seller's obligations regarding the goods are completed upon delivery to the carrier. Does this affect the jurisdictional analysis when considering whether suit may be brought in a court in London? To what extent should the price-delivery term affect the jurisdictional analysis, if at all? Consider Article 5(1) of the Brussels Regulation. Where in Problem 5.1 is the "place of performance of the obligation in question" under Article 5(1)(a)? If the suit is on the payment obligation, what is the meaning of Article 5(1)(b) in terms of where suit may be brought? Does jurisdiction exist in the United Kingdom for a contract action against Plastic Maker under Article 5(1) of the Brussels Regulation? See Ronald A. Brand, *CISG Article 31: When Substantive Law Rules Affect Jurisdictional Results*, 25 J.L. Com. 181 (2005).

3. The facts of Problem 5.1 indicate that Plastic Maker owns and operates a warehouse in London. Does this make any difference in our analysis of jurisdiction? Does jurisdiction exist in the United Kingdom for a contract action against Plastic Maker under Article 5(5) of the Brussels Regulation?

4. The facts of Problem 5.1 also indicate that the IMDs have been damaged due to the negligence of Plastic Maker. If Celsius would fail on the contract claim, would it have jurisdiction to bring a tort action in the United Kingdom? Consider whether jurisdiction exists in the United Kingdom for a

tort action against Plastic Maker under Article 5(3) of the Brussels Regulation.

5. Suppose CPR 6.20 applied in Problem 5.1. Would the jurisdictional analysis be the same? If not, is there a clear rationale for the difference? What provisions of CPR 6.20 would govern, and how do they compare with the Brussels Regulation?

6. In planning the litigation for Problem 5.1, assuming a judgment is obtained against Plastic Maker in a United Kingdom court, will the enforcement of that judgment be any different than it might be for a judgment from a U.S. court? If the defendant's assets are all in Germany, what is the value of a judgment from a U.K. court? Consider Chapter III of the Brussels Regulation. How does it work in conjunction with Chapter II? These are questions to keep in mind for later discussion in Chapters 6 and 7.

7. Would you recommend that Celsius bring a lawsuit in the United Kingdom against Plastic Maker? Are there any questions you might want to discuss with U.K. counsel before making a final decision? If so, what are those questions?

PART D. FORUM SHOPPING III: JURISDICTION IN GERMANY

Comment on the Brussels Regulation and Its Effect on the Jurisdictional Issue

Article 220 of the Rome Treaty of 1957 (now Article 293 of the European Community Treaty) specifically directed the original Member States of the European Economic Community to enter into negotiations to simplify formalities governing reciprocal recognition and enforcement of judgments.[1] This process began in 1959, resulting in the completion of the Brussels Convention in 1968.[2] That Convention was amended to provide for the accession of each new Member State in the Community. With the completion of the Treaty of Amsterdam in 1997, competence for matters of judicial cooperation shifted from the Member States to the Community institutions (Commission, Council of Ministers, and Parliament), and this resulted in the conversion of the Brussels Convention to internal European Community legislation in the form of the Brussels Regulation.[3] Germany is a

---

1. Article 220 included a direction to simplify the recognition and enforcement of arbitration awards. The Brussels Convention deals only with court judgments. A separate Community treaty on arbitration awards has been unnecessary due to the existence of the New York Arbitration Convention, to which over eighty states are party. Convention on the Recognition and Enforcement of Foreign Arbitral Awards, *done* June 10, 1958, 21 U.S.T. 2517, 330 U.N.T.S. 38.

2. *See, e.g.,* Alan Dashwood, Richard J. Hacon & Robin C.A. White, A Guide to the Civil Jurisdiction and Judgments Convention 3–5 (1986).

3. Council Regulation (EC) No 44/2001 of 22 Dec. 2000 on jurisdiction and the recognition and enforcement of judgments in civil and commercial matters, O.J. L12/1 (2001) ("Brussels Regulation") (entered into force on March 1, 2002). The Regulation replaced the Brussels Convention that had been the most successful example of regional judicial cooperation in history in the areas of jurisdiction and enforcement of judgments. European Convention on Jurisdiction and Enforcement of Judgments in Civil and Commercial Matters, done at Brussels, Sept. 27, 1968, 41 O.J. Eur. Comm. (C 27/1) (Jan. 26, 1998) (consolidated and updated version of the 1968 Conven-

Member State of the European Union. Thus, the Brussels Regulation is in effect in Germany, and must be considered when litigation involves a defendant from an EU Member State.

RONALD A. BRAND, CURRENT PROBLEMS, COMMON GROUND, AND FIRST PRINCIPLES: RESTRUCTURING THE PRELIMINARY DRAFT CONVENTION TEXT

A Global Law of Jurisdiction and Judgments: Lessons from the Hague Convention 75, 89–91 (John J. Barcelo III and Kevin M. Clermont, eds., 2002).*

[In reading the following excerpt, keep in mind that decisions interpreting the Brussels Convention provide authority as well for interpretation of the Brussels Regulation which has replaced the Convention.]

Article 2 of the Brussels Regulation provides for jurisdiction in the courts of the state in which the defendant is domiciled. In the Brussels context, Article 2 jurisdiction is referred to as the rule of "general" jurisdiction, with other rules (including the tort provision of Article 5(3)), referred to as rules of "special" jurisdiction.

Pursuant to Article 2 of the Convention, persons domiciled in a Contracting State are, subject to the provisions of the Convention, 'whatever their nationality, to be sued in the courts of that State'. Section 2 of Title II of the Convention, however, provides for 'special jurisdictions', by virtue of which a defendant domiciled in a Contracting State may be sued in another Contracting State .....[4]

The principle laid down in the Convention is that jurisdiction is vested in the courts of the State of the defendant's domicile and that the jurisdiction provided for in [the "special jurisdiction" articles are] exception[s] to that principle.[5]

[T]he 'special jurisdictions' enumerated in Articles 5 and 6 of the Convention constitute derogations from the principle that jurisdiction is vested in the courts of the State where the defendant is domiciled and as such must be interpreted restrictively.[6]

Thus, in *Kalfelis v. Schröder*, the European Court held that, in an action in both tort (Article 5(3)), and contract (Article 5(1)), "a court which has jurisdiction under Article 5(3) over an action in so far as it is based on tort or delict does not have jurisdiction over that action in so far as it is not so based." The existence of tort jurisdiction in the German courts over a Luxembourg defendant did not bring with it the existence of contract jurisdiction over the same defendant resulting from the same set of facts.

tion and the Protocol of 1971, following the 1996 accession of the Republic of Austria, the Republic of Finland and the Kingdom of Sweden) ("Brussels Convention").

* Copyright 2002 Kluwer Law International. Reproduced with permission.

4. Case 189/87, Kalfelis v. Schröder, 1988 E.C.R. 5565, 5583, ¶ 7.

5. *Id*. at 5583, ¶ 8.

6. *Id*. at 5585, ¶ 19.

The restrictive interpretation of special jurisdiction provisions of the Brussels Convention was also a part of the decision in the *Shevill* case, when the Court stated that the Article 5(3) tort rule of jurisdiction, as interpreted in *Bier* to provide a two-pronged choice to the plaintiff,

> is based on the existence of a particularly close connecting factor between the dispute and the courts other than those of the State of the defendant's domicile which justifies the attribution of jurisdiction to those courts for reasons relating to the sound administration of justice and the efficacious conduct of the proceedings.[7]

Thus, the Court emphasized the court/claim nexus that is the foundation of the "special" jurisdiction rules of the Brussels Convention.

Three rules of interpretation under the Brussels Convention are thus clearly established:

> (1) Article 2 jurisdiction is more "general" than the rules of special jurisdiction;

> (2) the special jurisdiction rules (Articles 5–16) are to be narrowly interpreted; and

> (3) the rules of special jurisdiction are based on a "close connecting factor between the dispute and the courts."

These rules generate several observations about a convention that mixes jurisdictional rules based on different relationships to the court. First, it is instructive that the "general" rule of jurisdiction focuses on the court/defendant nexus, but that so many problems have arisen from the court/claim nexus that underlies the subsidiary "special" rules of jurisdiction. The *Bier–Dumez–Shevill* line of cases indicates the difficulties the European Court has had with the interpretation of the Article 5(3) rule that provides jurisdiction in the "place where the harmful event occurred." Even more difficult problems have resulted from the court/claim nexus found in the Article 5(1) Brussels Convention rule that jurisdiction in a contract case lies in the courts of the "place of performance of the obligation in question."[8]

---

7. Case C–68/93, *Shevill v. Presse Alliance*, S.A., 1995 E.C.R. I–415, I–459, ¶ 19.

8. *See, e.g.*, Case C–420/97, Leathertex Divisione Sintetici SpA v. Bodetex BVBA, 1999 E.C.R. I–6747, ¶ 40 ("the same court does not ... have jurisdiction to hear the whole of an action founded on two obligations of equal rank arising from the same contract when, according to the conflict rules of the State where that court is situated, one of those obligations is to be performed in that State and the other in another Contracting State"); Case 266/85, *Shenavai v. Kreischer*, 1987 E.C.R. 239, ¶ 20 ("the obligation to be taken into consideration in a dispute concerning proceedings for the recovery of fees commenced by an architect commissioned to draw up plans for the building of houses is the contractual obligation which forms the actual basis of legal proceedings"); Case 133/81, *Ivenel v. Schwab*, 1982 E.C.R. 1891 (in an employment contract, the obligation to be taken into consideration is that which characterized the contract and was normally the obligation to carry out work); Case 13/76, *De Bloos v. Bouyer*, 1976 E.C.R. 1497 (the important obligation was the obligation on which the plaintiff's action was based); and Case 12/76, *Tessili v. Dunlop*, 1976 E.C.R. 1473 (the location of the place of performance of a contract is to be determined pursuant to the law governing the obligation at issue).

Two other results of the European Court's jurisprudence under Article 5(3) add to the problems created by a focus on a court/claim connection. The first is "the hostility of the Convention towards the attribution of jurisdiction to the courts of the plaintiff's domicile."[9] The second is the assumption that the "scheme and objectives of the Convention"[10] (including (1) the structure of Article 2 jurisdiction in the courts of the state of the defendant's domicile and (2) the special jurisdiction rules based on a court/claim nexus), result in a presumption against a proliferation of forums.[11]

In the *Dumez* case, the European Court acknowledged concerns with rules that lead to jurisdiction in the plaintiff's home state:

> [T]he hostility of the Convention towards the attribution of jurisdiction to the courts of the plaintiff's domicile was demonstrated by the fact that the second paragraph of article 3 precluded the application of national provisions attributing jurisdiction to such courts for proceedings against defendants domiciled in the territory of a contracting state.[12]

———

For a deeper understanding of the provisions of the Brussels Regulation, the following cases are useful in considering some of the more basic issues as noted. While some of these cases involve European Court of Justice interpretation of the Brussels Convention (the predecessor to the Brussels Regulation), they remain good law in considering the Regulation.

COLOR DRACK GMBH v. LEXX INTERNATIONAL VERTRIEBS GMBH

Case C–386/05, [2007] E.C.R. I–3699.

Judgment

1.   This reference for a preliminary ruling concerns the interpretation of the first indent of Article 5(1)(b) of Council Regulation (EC) No 44/2001 of 22 December 2000 on jurisdiction and the recognition and enforcement of judgments in civil and commercial matters (OJ 2001 L 12, p. 1).

2.   According to recital 2 in the preamble to Regulation No 44/2001, "[p]rovisions to unify the rules of conflict of jurisdiction in civil and commercial matters and to simplify the formalities with a view to rapid

---

9. Dumez France v. Hessische Landesbank, 1990 E.C.R. I–49, I–79, ¶ 16.

10. Kalfelis v. Schroder, 1988 E.C.R. at 5585, ¶ 16.

11. "[T]he Convention provides a collection of rules which are designed *inter alia* to avoid the occurrence, in civil and commercial matters, of concurrent litigation in two or more Member States and which, in the interests of legal certainty and for the benefit of the parties, confer jurisdiction upon the national court territorially best qualified to determine a dispute." Case 38/81, Effer Spa v. Kantner, 1982 E.C.R. 825, 834, ¶ 6.

12. *Dumez*, 1990 E.C.R. I–79, ¶ 16.

and simple recognition and enforcement of judgments from Member States bound by this Regulation are essential."

3. Recital 11 in the preamble to Regulation No 44/2001 states: "[t]he rules of jurisdiction must be highly predictable and founded on the principle that jurisdiction is generally based on the defendant's domicile and jurisdiction must always be available on this ground save in a few well-defined situations in which the subject-matter of the litigation or the autonomy of the parties warrants a different linking factor."

4. The rules on jurisdiction laid down by Regulation No 44/2001 are set out in Chapter II thereof, consisting of Articles 2 to 31.

5. Article 2(1) of Regulation No 44/2001, which forms part of Chapter II, Section 1, entitled "General provisions", states:

Subject to this Regulation, persons domiciled in a Member State shall, whatever their nationality, be sued in the courts of that Member State.

6. Article 3(1) which appears in the same section, provides:

Persons domiciled in a Member State may be sued in the courts of another Member State only by virtue of the rules set out in Sections 2 to 7 of this Chapter.

7. Article 5, which appears in Section 2, entitled "Special jurisdiction", of Chapter II of Regulation No 44/2001, provides:

A person domiciled in a Member State may, in another Member State, be sued:

(1)(a) in matters relating to a contract, in the courts for the place of performance of the obligation in question;

(b) for the purpose of this provision and unless otherwise agreed, the place of performance of the obligation in question shall be:

— in the case of the sale of goods, the place in a Member State where, under the contract, the goods were delivered or should have been delivered,

— in the case of the provision of services, the place in a Member State where, under the contract, the services were provided or should have been provided,

(c) if Article 5(b) does not apply then Article 5(a) applies;

The dispute in the main proceedings and the question referred for a preliminary ruling

8. This reference for a preliminary ruling has been submitted in the context of proceedings between Color Drack GmbH (Color Drack), a company established in Schwarzach (Austria), and Lexx International Vertriebs GmbH (Lexx'), a company established in Nuremberg (Germany), concerning the performance of a contract for the sale of goods, under which Lexx undertook to deliver goods to various retailers of Color

Drack in Austria, inter alia in the area of the registered office of Color Drack, which undertook to pay the price of those goods.

9. The dispute concerns in particular the non-performance of the obligation to which Lexx was subject under the contract to take back unsold goods and to reimburse the price to Color Drack.

10. By reason of that non-performance, on 10 May 2004 Color Drack brought an action for payment against Lexx before the Bezirks-gericht St Johann im Pongau (Austria) within whose jurisdiction its registered office is located. That court accepted jurisdiction on the basis of the first indent of Article 5(1)(b) of Regulation No 44/2001.

11. Lexx appealed to the Landesgericht Salzburg (Austria), which set aside that judgment on the ground that the first instance court did not have jurisdiction. The appeal court took the view that a single linking place, as provided for in the first indent of Article 5(1)(b) of Regulation No 44/2001 for all claims arising from a contract for the sale of goods, could not be determined where there were several places of delivery.

12. Color Drack appealed against the decision of the Landesgericht Salzburg, to the Oberster Gerichtshof, which considers that an interpre-tation of the first indent of Article 5(1)(b) of Regulation No 44/2001 is necessary in order to resolve the question of the jurisdiction of the Austrian court first seised.

13. The Oberster Gerichtshof notes that that provision specifies a single linking place for all claims arising out of a contract for the sale of goods, that is to say the place of delivery, and that that provision, which lays down a rule of special jurisdiction, must in principle be given a restrictive interpretation. In those circumstances, the Oberster Geri-chtshof asks whether the court first seised on the basis of that provision has jurisdiction since, in this case, the goods were delivered not only in the area of that court's jurisdiction but at different places in the Member State concerned.

14. The Oberster Gerichtshof therefore decided to stay the pro-ceedings and to refer the following question to the Court:

> Is Article 5(1)(b) of [Regulation No 44/2001] to be interpreted as meaning that a seller of goods domiciled in one Member State who, as agreed, has delivered the goods to the purchaser, domiciled in another Member State, at various places within that other Member State, can be sued by the purchaser regarding a claim under the contract relating to all the (part) deliveries—if need be, at the plaintiff's choice—before the court of one of those places (of per-formance)?

The question referred for a preliminary ruling

15. By its question, the national court is essentially asking whether the first indent of Article 5(1)(b) of Regulation No 44/2001 applies in the case of a sale of goods involving several places of delivery within a single Member State and, if so, whether, where the claim relates to all those

deliveries, the plaintiff may sue the defendant in the court for the place of delivery of its choice.

16. As a preliminary point, it must be stated that the considerations that follow apply solely to the case where there are several places of delivery within a single Member State and are without prejudice to the answer to be given where there are several places of delivery in a number of Member States.

17. First of all, it should be noted that the wording of the first indent of Article 5(1)(b) of Regulation No 44/2001 does not by itself enable an answer to be given to the question referred since it does not refer expressly to a case such as that to which the question relates.

18. Consequently, the first indent of Article 5(1)(b) of Regulation No 44/2001 must be interpreted in the light of the origins, objectives and scheme of that regulation (see, to that effect, Case C103/05 Reisch Montage [2006] ECR I6827, paragraph 29, and Case C283/05 ASML [2006] ECR I0000, paragraph 22).

19. In that regard, it is clear from recitals 2 and 11 in its preamble that Regulation No 44/2001 seeks to unify the rules of conflict of jurisdiction in civil and commercial matters by way of rules of jurisdiction which are highly predictable.

20. In that context, the regulation seeks to strengthen the legal protection of persons established in the Community, by enabling the plaintiff to identify easily the court in which he may sue and the defendant reasonably to foresee before which court he may be sued (see Reisch Montage, paragraphs 24 and 25).

21. To that end the rules of jurisdiction set out in Regulation No 44/2001 are founded on the principle that jurisdiction is generally based on the defendant's domicile, as provided for in Article 2 thereof, complemented by the rules of special jurisdiction (see Reisch Montage, paragraph 22).

22. Thus, the rule that jurisdiction is generally based on the defendant's domicile is complemented, in Article 5(1), by a rule of special jurisdiction in matters relating to a contract. The reason for that rule, which reflects an objective of proximity, is the existence of a close link between the contract and the court called upon to hear and determine the case.

23. Under that rule the defendant may also be sued in the court for the place of performance of the obligation in question, since that court is presumed to have a close link to the contract.

24. In order to reinforce the primary objective of unification of the rules of jurisdiction whilst ensuring their predictability, Regulation No 44/2001 defines that criterion of a link autonomously in the case of the sale of goods.

25. Pursuant to the first indent of Article 5(1)(b) of that regulation, the place of performance of the obligation in question is the place in

a Member State where, under the contract, the goods were delivered or should have been delivered.

26.   In the context of Regulation No 44/2001, contrary to Lexx's submissions, that rule of special jurisdiction in matters relating to a contract establishes the place of delivery as the autonomous linking factor to apply to all claims founded on one and the same contract for the sale of goods rather than merely to the claims founded on the obligation of delivery itself.

27.   It is in the light of those considerations that it must be determined whether, where there are several places of delivery in a single Member State, the first indent of Article 5(1)(b) of Regulation No 44/2001 applies and, if so, whether, where the claim relates to all the deliveries, the plaintiff may sue the defendant in the courts for the place of delivery of its choice.

28.   First of all, the first indent of Article 5(1)(b) of the regulation must be regarded as applying whether there is one place of delivery or several.

29.   By providing for a single court to have jurisdiction and a single linking factor, the Community legislature did not intend generally to exclude cases where a number of courts may have jurisdiction nor those where the existence of that linking factor can be established in different places.

30.   The first indent of Article 5(1)(b) of Regulation No 44/2001, determining both international and local jurisdiction, seeks to unify the rules of conflict of jurisdiction and, accordingly, to designate the court having jurisdiction directly, without reference to the domestic rules of the Member States.

31.   In that regard, an answer in the affirmative to the question whether the provision under consideration applies where there are several places of delivery within a single Member State does not call into question the objectives of the rules on the international jurisdiction of the courts of the Member States set out in that regulation.

32.   Firstly, the applicability of the first indent of Article 5(1)(b) of Regulation No 44/2001 where there are several places of delivery within a single Member State complies with the regulation's objective of predictability.

33.   In that case, the parties to the contract can easily and reasonably foresee before which Member State's courts they can bring their dispute.

34.   Secondly, the applicability of the first indent of Article 5(1)(b) of Regulation No 44/2001 where there are several places of delivery within a single Member State also complies with the objective of proximity underlying the rules of special jurisdiction in matters relating to a contract.

35. Where there are several places of delivery within a single Member State, that objective of proximity is met since, in application of the provision under consideration, it will in any event be the courts of that Member State which will have jurisdiction to hear the case.

36. Consequently, the first indent of Article 5(1)(b) of Regulation No 44/2001 is applicable where there are several places of delivery within a single Member State.

37. However, it cannot be inferred from the applicability of the first indent of Article 5(1)(b) of Regulation No 44/2001 in circumstances such as those of the main proceedings that that provision necessarily confers concurrent jurisdiction on a court for any place where goods were or should have been delivered.

38. With regard, secondly, to the question whether, where there are several places of delivery within a single Member State and the claim relates to all those deliveries, the plaintiff may sue the defendant in the court for the place of delivery of its choice on the basis of the first indent of Article 5(1)(b) of Regulation No 44/2001, it is necessary to point out that one court must have jurisdiction to hear all the claims arising out of the contract.

39. In that regard, it is appropriate to take into consideration the origins of the provision under consideration. By that provision, the Community legislature intended, in respect of sales contracts, expressly to break with the earlier solution under which the place of performance was determined, for each of the obligations in question, in accordance with the private international rules of the court seised of the dispute. By designating autonomously as the place of performance' the place where the obligation which characterises the contract is to be performed, the Community legislature sought to centralise at its place of performance jurisdiction over disputes concerning all the contractual obligations and to determine sole jurisdiction for all claims arising out of the contract.

40. In that regard it is necessary to take account of the fact that the special jurisdiction under the first indent of Article 5(1)(b) of Regulation No 44/2001 is warranted, in principle, by the existence of a particularly close linking factor between the contract and the court called upon to hear the litigation, with a view to the efficient organisation of the proceedings. It follows that, where there are several places of delivery of the goods, place of delivery' must be understood, for the purposes of application of the provision under consideration, as the place with the closest linking factor between the contract and the court having jurisdiction. In such a case, the point of closest linking factor will, as a general rule, be at the place of the principal delivery, which must be determined on the basis of economic criteria.

41. To that end, it is for the national court seised to determine whether it has jurisdiction in the light of the evidence submitted to it.

42. If it is not possible to determine the principal place of delivery, each of the places of delivery has a sufficiently close link of proximity to

the material elements of the dispute and, accordingly, a significant link as regards jurisdiction. In such a case, the plaintiff may sue the defendant in the court for the place of delivery of its choice on the basis of the first indent of Article 5(1)(b) of Regulation No 44/2001.

43.   Giving the plaintiff such a choice enables it easily to identify the courts in which it may sue and the defendant reasonably to foresee in which courts it may be sued.

44.   That conclusion cannot be called into question by the fact that the defendant cannot foresee the particular court of that Member State in which it may be sued; it is sufficiently protected since it can only be sued, in application of the provision under consideration, where there are several places of performance in a single Member State, in the courts of that Member State for the place where a delivery has been made.

45.   In the light of all the foregoing considerations, the answer to the question referred must be that the first indent of Article 5(1)(b) of Regulation No 44/2001 applies where there are several places of delivery within a single Member State. In such a case, the court having jurisdiction to hear all the claims based on the contract for the sale of goods is that for the principal place of delivery, which must be determined on the basis of economic criteria. In the absence of determining factors for establishing the principal place of delivery, the applicant may sue the plaintiff in the court for the place of delivery of its choice.

COSTS

46.   Since these proceedings are, for the parties to the main proceedings, a step in the action pending before the national court, the decision on costs is a matter for that court. Costs incurred in submitting observations to the Court, other than the costs of those parties, are not recoverable.

RULING

On those grounds, the Court (Fourth Chamber) hereby rules:

The first indent of Article 5(1)(b) of Council Regulation (EC) No 44/2001 of 22 December 2000 on jurisdiction and the recognition and enforcement of judgments in civil and commercial matters must be interpreted as applying where there are several places of delivery within a single Member State. In such a case, the court having jurisdiction to hear all the claims based on the contract for the sale of goods is that for the principal place of delivery, which must be determined on the basis of economic criteria. In the absence of determining factors for establishing the principal place of delivery, the plaintiff may sue the defendant in the court for the place of delivery of its choice.

BIER v. MINES DE POTASSE D'ALSACE

Case No. 21/76, 1976 E.C.R. 1741.

1.   By judgment of February 1976, which reached the Court Registry on the following 2 March, the Gerechtshof (Appeal Court) of the Hague has referred a question, pursuant to the Protocol on 3 June 1971 on the interpretation of the Convention of 27 September 1968 on Jurisdiction and the Enforcement of Judgments in Civil and Commercial Matters (hereinafter called "the Convention"), on the interpretation of Article 5(3) of the said Convention.

2.   It appears from the judgment making the reference that at the present stage the main action, which has come before the Gerechtshof by way of appeal, concerns the jurisdiction of the court of first instance at Rotterdam, an in general, of the Netherlands courts, to entertain an action brought by an undertaking engaged in horticulture, established within the area for which the court before which the action was first brought has jurisdiction, and by the Reinwater Foundation, which exists to promote the improvement of the quality of the water in the Rhine Basin, against Mines de Potasse d'Alsace, established at Mulhouse (France), concerning the pollution of the waters of the Rhine by the discharge of saline waste from the operations of the defendant into that inland waterway.

3.   It appears from the file that as regards irrigation the horticultural business of first-named appellant depends mainly on the waters of the Rhine, the high salt content of which, according to the said appellant, causes damage to its plantations and obliges it to take expensive measures in order to limit that damage.

4.   The appellants consider that the excessive salinization of the Rhine is due principally to the massive discharges carried out by Mines de Potasse d'Alsace and they declare that it is for that reason that they have chosen to bring an action for the purposes of establishing the liability of that undertaking.

5.   By judgment delivered on 12 May 1975, the court at Rotterdam held that it had no jurisdiction to entertain the action, taking the view that under Article 5(3) of the Convention the claim did not come within its jurisdiction but under that of the French court for the area in which the discharge at issue took place.

6.   Bier and Reinwater brought an appeal against that judgment before the Gerechtshof, The Hague, which subsequently referred the following question to the Court:

"Are the words 'the place where the harmful event occurred', appearing in the text of Article 5(3) of the Convention on Jurisdiction and the Enforcement of Judgments in Civil and Commercial

Matters, concluded at Brussels on 27 September 1968, to be understood as meaning 'the place where the damage occurred (the place where the damage took place or became apparent)' or rather 'the place where the event having the damage as its sequel occurred (the place where the act was not performed)'?''

7. Article 5 of the Convention provides "A person domiciled in a Contracting State may, in another Contracting State, be sued: . . . (3) in matters relating to tort, delict, or quasi-delict, in the courts for the place where the harmful event occurred."

8. That provision must be interpreted in the context of the scheme of conferment of jurisdiction which forms the subject-matter of Title II of the Convention.

9. That scheme is based on a general rule, laid down by Article 2, that the courts of the State in which the defendant is domiciled shall have jurisdiction.

10. However, Article 5 makes provision in a number of cases for a special jurisdiction, which the plaintiff may opt to choose.

11. This freedom of choice was introduced having regard to the existence, in certain clearly defined situations, of a particularly close connecting factor between a dispute and the court which may be called upon to hear it, with a view to the efficacious conduct of the proceedings.

12. Thus in matters of tort, delict or quasi-delict Article 5(3) allows the plaintiff to bring his case before the courts for "the place where the harmful event occurred."

13. In the context of the Convention, the meaning of that expression is unclear when the place of the event which is at the origin of the damage is situated in a State other than the one in which the place where the damage occurred is situated, as is the case inter alia with atmospheric or water pollution beyond the frontiers of a State.

14. The form of words "place where the harmful event occurred", used in all the language versions of the Convention, leaves open to question whether, in the situation described, it is necessary, in determining jurisdiction, to choose as the connecting factor the place of the event giving rise to the damage, or the place where the damage occurred, or to accept that the plaintiff has an option between the one and the other of those two connecting factors.

15. As regards this, it is well to point out that the place of the event giving rise to the damage no less than the place where the damage occurred can, depending on the case, constitute a significant connecting factor form the point of view of jurisdiction.

16. Liability in tort, delict or quasi-delict can only arise provided that a causal [connection] can be established between the damage and the event in which that damage originates.

17. Taking into account the close [connection] between the component parts of every sort of liability, it does not appear appropriate to opt

for one of the two connecting factors mentioned to the exclusion of the other, since each of them can, depending on the circumstances, be particularly helpful from the point of view of the evidence and of the conduct of the proceedings.

18. To exclude on option appears all the more undesirable in that, by its comprehensive form of words, Article 5(3) of the Convention covers a wide diversity of kinds of liability.

19. Thus the meaning of the expression "place where the harmful event occurred" in Article 5(3) must be established in such a way as to acknowledge that the plaintiff has an option to commence proceedings either at the place where the damage occurred or the place of the event giving rise to it.

20. This conclusion is supported by the consideration, first, that to decide in favour only of the place of the event giving rise to the damage would, in an appreciable number of cases, cause confusion between the heads of jurisdiction laid down by Articles 2 and 5(3) of the Convention, so that the latter provision would, to that extent, lose its effectiveness.

21. Secondly, a decision in favour only of the place where the damage occurred would, in cases where the place of the event giving rise to the damage does not coincide with the domicile of the person liable, have the effect of excluding a helpful connecting factor with the jurisdiction of a court particularly near to the cause of the damage.

22. Moreover, it appears from a comparison of the national legislative provisions and national case-law on the distribution of jurisdiction—both as regards internal relationships, as between courts for different areas, and in international relationships—that, albeit by differing legal techniques, a place is found for both of the two connecting factors here considered and that in several States they are accepted concurrently.

23. In these circumstances, the interpretation stated above has the advantage of avoiding any upheaval in the solutions worked out in the various national systems of law, since it looks to unification, in conformity with Article 5(3) of the Convention, by way of a systemization of solutions which, as to their principle, have already been established in most of the States concerned.

24. Thus it should be answered that where the place of the happening of the event which may give rise to liability in tort, delict or quasi-delict and the place where that event results in damage are not identical, the expression "place where the harmful event occurred", in Article 5(3) of the Convention, must be understood as being intended to cover both the place where the damage occurred and the place of the event giving rise to it.

25. The result is that the defendant may be sued, at the option of the plaintiff, either in the courts for the place where the damage occurred or in the courts for the place of the event which gives rise to and is at the origin of that damage.

Costs

26. The costs incurred by the Government of the French Republic, the Government of the Kingdom of the Netherlands and the Commission of the European Communities, which have submitted observations to the Court, are not recoverable.

27. As these proceedings are, so far as the parties to the main action are concerned, a step in the action pending before the Gerechtshof, The Hague, the decision on costs is a matter for that court.

On those grounds THE COURT in answer to the question referred to it by the Gerechtshof, The Hague, by judgment of 27 February 1976, hereby rules:

> Where the place of the happening of the event which may give rise to liability in tort, delict or quasi-delict and the place where that event results in damage are not identical, the expression 'place where the harmful event occurred', in Article 5(3) of the Convention of 27 September 1968 on Jurisdiction and the Enforcement of Judgments in Civil and Commercial Matters, must be understood as being intended to cover both the place where the damage occurred and the place of the event giving rise to it.

The result is that the defendant may be sued, at the option of the plaintiff, either in the courts for the place where the damage occurred or in the courts for the place of the event which gives rise to and is at the origin of that damage.

Questions and Comments

1. As you read the Brussels Regulation, note particularly that the order of its Articles is not the order in which you must necessarily consider them when reviewing a case. While the Article 2 "general" rule of jurisdiction is basic to the Regulation, it is trumped by a number of other provisions. The result is that proper analytical order (*i.e.,* the order in which provisions of the Regulation "trump" other provisions) is (1) exclusive jurisdiction (Article 22), (2) jurisdiction in consumer, insurance and employment contracts (Articles 8–21), (3) choice of court clauses (Articles 23–24), (4) general jurisdiction (Article 2), and then (5) special jurisdiction (Articles 5–6). Our problem does not involve any of the first three categories of jurisdiction, leaving the focus on Articles 2 and 5.

2. The following is a brief discussion of some of the leading cases interpreting the Brussels Regulation:

(a) On the scope of the Convention as applying to "civil and commercial matters: Case No. 29/76, *LTU Lufttransportunternehmen GmbH & Co. KG v. Eurocontrol,* 1976 E.C.R. 1541 (holding that "[i]n the interpretation of the concept 'civil and commercial matters' for the purposes of the application of the Convention . . ., in particular Title III thereof, reference must not be made to the law of one of the States concerned but, first, to the objectives and scheme of the Convention and, secondly, to the general principles which stem from the corpus of the national legal systems," and that "[a] judgment given in an action between a public authority and a person governed by private law, in which the public authority has acted in the exercise of its powers, is excluded from the area of application of the Convention.").

(b) On the exclusive jurisdiction rules of the Convention: Case No. 241/83, *Rösler v. Rottwinkel*, 1985–1 E.C.R. 99 (holding that Article 16(1) of the Convention (Article 22(1) of the Regulation) meant that the state in which real property was located had jurisdiction over all matters regarding that property, even if the dispute involved two parties from another state who had engaged in a contract for short-term vacation rental of the property; a holding that was changed by amendment to the Convention, continued in Article 22(1) of the Regulation for cases in which the landlord and tenant on short-term rentals are domiciled in the same Member State).

(c) On choice of court agreements: Case No. 150/80, *Elefanten Schuh GmbH v. Jacqmain*, 1981 E.C.R. 1671 (holding that "legislation of a Contracting State may not allow the validity of an agreement conferring jurisdiction to be called into question solely on the ground that the language used is not that prescribed by that legislation," and interpreting what is now Article 24 of the Regulation to clearly allow a special appearance to challenge jurisdiction, without that appearance constituting an agreement to jurisdiction even where an initial response on the merits is filed).

(d) On jurisdiction in the State of an agency: Case No. 218/86, *SAR Schotte GmbH v. Parfums Rothschild SARL*, 1987–11 E.C.R. 4905 (holding that the jurisdictional rule of Article 5(5) of the Convention (now found in the same Article of the Regulation) establishes jurisdiction over a corporation from another Member State when in the forum state that corporation "maintains no dependent branch, agency or other establishment in another Contracting State but nevertheless pursues its activities there through an independent company with the same name and identical management which negotiates and conducts business in its name and which it uses as an extension of itself.").

(e) On the limits of jurisdiction for multiple causes of action: Case 189/87, *Kalfelis v. Schröder*, 1988 E.C.R. 5565, 5585, ¶ 19 (holding that, in an action in both tort (Article 5(3)), and contract (Article 5(1)), "a court which has jurisdiction under Article 5(3) over an action in so far as it is based on tort or delict does not have jurisdiction over that action in so far as it is not so based."), and Case C–420/97, *Leathertex Divisione Sintetici SpA v. Bodetex BVBA*, 1999 E.C.R. I–06747, ¶ 40 ("the same court does not ... have jurisdiction to hear the whole of an action founded on two obligations of equal rank arising from the same contract when, according to the conflict rules of the State where that court is situated, one of those obligations is to be performed in that State and the other in another Contracting State.").

3. Does jurisdiction exist in Germany for an action against Plastic Maker under Article 2 of the Brussels Regulation?

4. Does jurisdiction exist in Germany for a contract action against Plastic Maker under either Article 5(1) or 5(5) of the Brussels Regulation?

5.   If you decide to bring the contract claim against Plastic Maker in the United Kingdom, can the alternative tort claim also be brought there under Article 5(3) of the Brussels Regulation? What impact does the existence of two types of claims have on the jurisdictional system set up in the Regulation? How does this compare to jurisdictional rules in the United States? Is one system better than the other, or are they just different?

6.   Much of the world has followed the civil law model of continental Europe in terms of jurisdictional practice. Thus, the United States is rather alone in (1) the idea that jurisdiction is a constitutional issue, and (2) the related idea that jurisdiction relates in the end to the court's relationship with the defendant (most rules other than the general rule of jurisdiction in civil law systems consider primarily the relationship between the court and the claim, rather than the relationship between the court and the defendant). For the results of a multilateral effort to create common rules on some aspects of jurisdiction and the recognition and enforcement of judgments, see the 2005 Hague Convention on Choice of Court Agreements in the Documents Supplement.

7.   A full discussion of recognition and enforcement of judgments is left for Chapters 6 and 7 of this book. At this point, however, you should begin to think about this issue. Do the rules found in Chapter III of the Brussels Regulation have any impact on the decision on where to file a contract action against Plastic Maker?

PROBLEM 5.2   JURISDICTION: A FOREIGN PLAINTIFF BRINGS SUIT IN ITS OWN COUNTRY AGAINST A U.S. CORPORATION

SECTION I.   THE SETTING

The facts for this Problem parallel the facts in Problem 5.1, but contain some important differences.

Celsius Manufacturing, Inc. (Celsius), a Delaware corporation, has its principal place of business in Pittsburgh, Pennsylvania. Celsius manufactures induction molding devices (IMDs) used in the further manufacture of plastic products. In October 2007, Celsius demonstrated its IMDs at a trade fair in London, where a purchasing agent for Plastic Maker GmbH ("Plastic Maker"), of Munich, Germany, became interested in the product. At the trade fair, Plastic Maker submitted a purchase order to Celsius, offering to purchase 1,000 IMDs at $400 per unit, "terms c.i.f. London," to be shipped in January 2008. The President of Celsius responded while she was still in London with a letter in which she acknowledged receipt of the purchase order and accepted all the terms and conditions of the offer. Neither the purchase order form nor the letter of acceptance contained either a choice of law or a choice of forum clause.

Plastic Maker wired Celsius the entire $400,000 purchase price on January 3, 2008, and the IMDs were shipped on January 6, 2008 and arrived in London on January 28, where they were unloaded to a warehouse owned and operated by Plastic Maker. Plastic Maker had intended to redistribute the IMDs to its facilities in Germany, The Netherlands, and Spain. Upon receipt of the IMDs, Plastic Maker informed Celsius that the IMDs did not conform to the quality of the product demonstrated at the London trade fair and that Plastic Maker was rejecting them. Plastic Maker informed Celsius that it was holding the IMDs at Plastic Maker's London warehouse, awaiting further instructions concerning their return or disposal.

All experts who have been contacted on the matter agree that the goods are in fact non-conforming, and unsuitable for the use intended by Plastic Maker. Plastic Maker is ready to sue for breach of contract, demanding return of the purchase price, on the basis of this non-conformity of the goods. Plastic Maker has found substitute goods at a cost of $500,000, and also intends to sue for the added cost of obtaining replacement goods.

SECTION II. FOCUS OF CONSIDERATION

This problem involves a contract action in which a German plaintiff is ready to bring suit against a U.S. defendant. Based on earlier chapters of this book, you know there would be general jurisdiction in state or federal courts in Pennsylvania. It is likely, however, that the plaintiff would prefer suit in a German court. Thus, the first question is whether there is jurisdiction to sue in a German court. Like Problem 5.1, this situation involves a contract relationship established in England between U.S. and German parties. The U.S. defendant is not domiciled in Germany, so the basic civil law rule of general jurisdiction does not apply. Germany has no due process analysis similar to that in the United States, so general jurisdiction cannot be established by some sort of "minimum contacts" or "doing business" analysis. The facts indicate no activity of the U.S. defendant in Germany. Thus, if U.S. rules of jurisdiction were to apply, it would seem that jurisdiction would not exist in Germany. But the German rules of jurisdiction are not the same as those in the United States, and assumptions based on knowledge only of U.S. law will not suffice.

While the defendant in this action is "domiciled" in the United States, and not in a European Union Member State, the Brussels Regulation may nevertheless have application. This occurs not in the jurisdictional rules, however, but in the rules on recognition and enforcement. Thus, it will be important to be aware from the outset of concerns regarding the location of any assets of the U.S. defendant that ultimately may be available for purposes of enforcement of the judgment. Jurisdictional rules in Germany have important implications for the enforcement of any resulting judgment in both Europe and the United States.

The Brussels Regulation is essential to an understanding of the Problem. It is included in the Documents Supplement.

SECTION III. READINGS, QUESTIONS AND COMMENTS

PART A. JURISDICTION IN A GERMAN COURT

Jurisdiction in German courts is governed by the Zivilprozessordnung (the ZPO or German Code of Civil Procedure). The following excerpt, though published in 1982, remains valuable in describing the jurisdictional provisions of the ZPO. While the German Law of Civil Procedure Reform Act entered into force on January 1, 2002, the basic rules of jurisdiction remain the same.

CHRISTOF VON DRYANDER, JURISDICTION IN CIVIL AND COMMERCIAL MATTERS UNDER THE GERMAN CODE OF CIVIL PROCEDURE

16 International Lawyer 671–692 (1982).*

A discussion of the rules of jurisdiction in other countries serves two distinct purposes.[1] The first lies in the value of analyzing and comparing the views of other communities for the advancement of one's own legal system. This aspect is of primary concern to lawmakers, and in a common law system like the United States to courts, too. The second purpose is of immediate practical relevance and thus of special interest to lawyers and other practitioners that are concerned with the legal aspects of international business operations. This purpose is to facilitate the protection of American individuals, companies, and interests abroad by helping acquire a basic understanding of the principles under which foreign courts assume jurisdiction to decide international controversies.[3] Such an understanding is valuable not only in dealing with actual proceedings before foreign courts, but also in designing means by which to avoid such proceedings, e.g., arbitration and choice of forum clauses.

BASIC CHARACTERISTICS

Before discussing the individual bases for jurisdiction in the German Code of Civil Procedure (*Zivilprozessordnung*, ZPO), the main differences between the American and the German concept of jurisdiction

---

1. This paper uses the word *jurisdiction* to describe the *power* of a state to entertain an action through its judicial tribunals that is not entirely local in character. In this meaning *jurisdiction* corresponds to the German term (*Internationale Zustaendigkeit*). Often *jurisdiction* is also used in respect to the power of a *court;* the power of individual courts, however, is more appropriately described by the word *competence.* In yet other contexts *jurisdiction* refers to the power of a state to perform acts in the territory of another state, or the power of a state to apply its laws to cases involving a foreign element. *See* Akehurst, *Jurisdiction in International Law,* 46 BRIT. Y.B. INT'L L. 147 (1972/73).

3. In international litigation the place of litigation often predetermines the substantive outcome of the case. The forum generally applies not only its own procedural law, but also its own conflict of laws rules. This makes it likely that the dispute will be adjudicated under the forum's substantive law as well, either on the assumption that the substantive laws of the involved countries are identical, or as a matter of choice of law. The tendency of U.S. Courts to apply U.S. substantive law is outlined in REESE AND ROSENBERG, CONFLICT OF LAWS, CASES AND MATERIALS, 440 *et seq.* (7th ed. 1978).

should be pointed out. While Germany, like the United States, has a federal structure with a federal government and individual states (*Laender*), issues of jurisdiction only arise in proceedings that involve international rather than interstate elements. This is due to compared to the United States, the more limited power and lesser autonomy of the states in Germany. There, the states enjoy no jurisdictional power of their own, and therefore cannot create their own system of courts and rules of civil procedure. In Germany there is only one system of courts of general jurisdiction, and all the courts thereunder apply the rules of the federal Code of Civil Procedure regardless of the courts' respective location. Under the Code the allocation of cases among the various courts in different states is carried out by venue provisions.[6] Further, because jurisdiction in Germany does not concern the relationship between the federal government and the several states, there is no need for constitutional limitations on the exercise of jurisdiction. Thus, rather than having a single standard to determine the permissible reach of a jurisdictional basis, German courts derive limitations on the exercise of judicial power from individual statutory interpretation.

A further significant difference between the German and the American concept of jurisdiction lies in the structure of specific jurisdictional bases. In Germany, like in most civil law countries, the dichotomy of *in rem, quasi in rem,* and *in personam* jurisdiction is unknown. While the German Code of Civil Procedure provides some bases for *in rem* jurisdiction, assertion of jurisdiction generally is personal jurisdiction. This, however, should not be equated with a more limited reach of judicial power. On the contrary, German courts assume personal jurisdiction in some fact situations that under American law would fall under *quasi in rem* jurisdiction.

A further noteworthy distinction between German and American jurisdictional methodology is the irrelevance of method and place of service for the exercise of jurisdiction in Germany. Under the German Code of Civil Procedure the only function of service of process is to give notice to the defendant. The separation of jurisdiction from service is rooted in the adherence to territoriality as the underlying principle of jurisdiction in Germany. This concept has two implications. First, jurisdiction is never based on a procedural step alone, such as service of a summons. It is invariably founded on a relationship or contract that connects the parties or their acts with the forum. Therefore, objective territorial ties, not citizenship, underlie the individual bases for jurisdiction of the ZPO. Second, because of the interaction between territorial competence and jurisdictional power, the locally competent court also has jurisdiction over the parties. Accordingly, the German Code of Civil Procedure dispenses with separate rules for jurisdiction and venue. The Code simply merges jurisdictional rules in venue provisions.

---

6. The ZPO does not contain special jurisdictional provisions. Rather the locally competent court is considered also to have jurisdiction . . . . .

Lastly, considerable differences between the two countries exist with respect to the consequences of lack of jurisdiction. In the United States, the rule appears to be settled that the judgment of a court lacking jurisdiction is open to collateral attack even in the rendering state. Germany and other civil law countries agree with the United States that the judgment of a court not having jurisdiction may be refused recognition in other countries, yet in the rendering state such judgment is final and not subject to collateral attack once the time for an appeal has run out. This is true regardless of whether the issue of jurisdiction was litigated.

The Individual Bases for Jurisdiction

The ZPO draws a distinction between places of general jurisdiction (*allgemeine Gerichtsstaende*) and places of special jurisdiction (*besondere Gerichtsstaende*). The two fora differ from each other in that any kind of action may be brought in the court at the place of general jurisdiction while only actions for pecuniary claims (*vermoegensrechtliche Ansprueche*) may be brought in the court at the place of special jurisdiction, and then only in particular circumstances. General jurisdiction over natural persons exists where the defendant is domiciled. General jurisdiction over legal persons and other entities is usually obtained at the place of their seat. * * * Among the more important bases for special jurisdiction are the places of residence, the place of branch, the place of location of property, the place of performance, and the place of commission of a tort.

A.   Jurisdiction over Commercial Enterprises: ZPO sections 17(1) and 21(1)

* * * Section 17(1)[35] embodies the place of general jurisdiction over defendants that although not natural persons, are capable of being a party in court. While judicial practice has not often focused on this section of the Code, the provision is nonetheless of great practical import. A problem that deserves special attention is the definition of the word *seat* ("sitz"). With respect to corporations the articles of association establish the place of the seat. Usually, they must choose as seat one of the following three places: the location where the management is situated, the location where the corporation maintains an establishment, or the location where the administration is conducted.

ZPO section 21(1),[39] the place of branch establishment (*Niederlassung*), enlarges the scope of jurisdiction over natural and legal persons

---

35. The text of the section is as follows:

For actions against municipalities, corporations, and those companies, associations, societies, foundations, institutions and estates capable of being sued, the court of the district within which the seat is located, has jurisdiction. Absent special circumstances, the seat is the place where the administration is conducted.

39. The provision reads as follows:

Actions against persons or entities which for the operation of a plant, trade or other business maintain a branch establishment, from which contracts are directly entered into, can be brought at the place of such branch, establishment for all claims related to the business activities conducted there.

and other entities referred to in ZPO section 17(1). The provision is of particular importance for foreign exporters and investors, for it indicates how far they may expand their local business activities without subjecting themselves to jurisdiction. From time to time, judicial attention has focused on the words *branch establishment*. The term encompasses not only branches registered in the commercial register, but also other places of business that simultaneously display the following features: some continuity in the established premises, more than mere short term purpose, and some independence of the local part of the management. The last aspect, the independence or autonomy of the branch is manifested by the authority to enter independently and directly into contracts. Viewing these requirements together one may say that warehouses, inventories, receiving stations, sales representatives, or agencies, without more, do not render a business venture subject to suit at their respective location.

The forum of branch, as made plain by the language of the provision, will not entertain all kinds of claims. In order to sue a commercial enterprise at the location of its branch, the claim must be related to the business activity carried out through the branch. * * *

B. *Forum of* Location of Property: *ZPO Section 23*

This provision[48] embodies two independent bases of special jurisdiction. The first, the place of jurisdiction for actions *in rem,* does not pose specific problems. It is widely used in jurisdictions outside Germany, including the United States. Our attention therefore focuses on the second basis of jurisdiction under ZPO section 23. This part of the provision contains the most interesting, but also the most controversial jurisdictional basis of the ZPO. It grants *in personam* jurisdiction over absent alien defendants on the basis of property within the district of the forum. In contrast to American *quasi-in rem* jurisdiction, the property found within the district need not even be attached to ground jurisdiction; nor is a judgment rendered on the basis of ZPO section 23 limited to the value of the property situated within the district. Literally applied, the provision leads to extreme results, as the following example may illustrate: an American traveler forgets his slippers in a hotel in Heidelberg. On the basis of this property he is sued for a debt of 100,000 German marks before the district court (*Landergericht*) in Heidelberg. This example vividly illustrates what a sharp weapon ZPO section 23 can be. * * *[52]

---

48. ZPO § 23:

For actions asserting pecuniary claims against a person who has no domicile within the country, the court of the district within which this person has property, or within which the subject of the action is situated, has jurisdiction. Claims shall be deemed to be situated at the domicile of the debtor, and if the claims are secured, also the place where the security is situated.

52. Due to the mutual enforcement obligation under Article 26 of the European Convention, the judgment would also be enforceable against property located in any other member state of the Common Market.

It would seem that such an extraordinary basis of jurisdiction would be unique in the laws of international jurisdiction. On the contrary, the provision not only survived some hundred years of German civil procedure, but also was followed by several other countries.[53] Interestingly, the very same countries that rely on property as basis for jurisdiction over aliens have considerably limited recognition of judgments rendered on that basis among themselves.

* * *

To the American jurist, *forum non conveniens* may appear to be a way out of the dilemma caused by ZPO section 23. Yet German jurisprudence adheres strictly to the principle that once jurisdiction is conferred upon a court pursuant to ZPO that court must adjudicate the matter. * * *

Another route to limit the application of ZPO section 23 to actions with which * * * Germany has a valid concern, would have been to apply the provision only to plaintiffs that are domiciled in the country. This issue was addressed by the court of appeals (*Kammergericht*) in Berlin in 1914. * * * The court ... held that the plaintiff could invoke ZPO section 23 regardless of his nationality or domicile. * * *

* * *

C. *Forum of the Place of Performance: ZPO Section 29*[88]

While the reach of this provision is also extensive, it is not considered exorbitant in the jurisdictional terminology. Many European states claim jurisdiction when either the place of contracting, or the place of performance is located within their territory. Italy even provides both bases. In the United States, on the other hand, the place of contracting or performance alone—while not unimportant—generally is not sufficient to ground jurisdiction.

Between the member states of the Common Market, Article 5(1) of the European Convention which also makes the place of performance a basis for jurisdiction has largely suspended ZPO section 29. As a result, much of the international litigation that previously occurred under section 29 is now adjudicated pursuant to Article 5(1).

Under ZPO section 29, the crucial issue is the determination of the place of performance. For this purpose, the contract is not viewed as a single unit with only one single place of performance; rather, the concept refers to the specific contractual obligation in dispute. In a contractual relationship there are thus several different places of performance, e.g., the place of performance for the seller's obligation to deliver goods and

---

53. *E.g.* by Greece, Japan, Denmark, Austria and some Swiss cantons.

88. The section provides:

For actions for declaratory judgment concerning the existence or nonexistence of a contract, actions for specific performance or rescission of a contract, and actions for damages for breach of contract, the court of the district within which the disputed obligation is to be performed, shall have jurisdiction.

the place of performance for the buyer's obligation to pay the purchase price. Courts, in ascertaining the procedural issue of where the place of performance is, often must resolve substantive questions because under German law the question of where an obligation is to be performed is one of the substantive law that applies to the performance of the contract. * * *

* * *

D. Forum of Commission of a Tort: ZPO Section 32[105]

* * *

Under ZPO section 32, the [U.S. *World-Wide Volkswagen*] case would have come out the opposite way, despite the similar language of the underlying jurisdictional provisions. A German court would have pointed out that the place of the event (here: the sale of the allegedly defectively manufactured Audi automobile) and the place where the violation of the protected interest occurred (here: Oklahoma as the place of injury) are not the same. Therefore, under German law, plaintiffs could bring suit, at their option, either at the place of sale or at the place of injury. Under section 32, amenability to suit of the seller of chattels would, in fact, travel with the chattel, a notion vigorously rejected by the U.S. Supreme Court. In other words, while the approach of the U.S. Supreme Court focuses on the seller, in particular whether he sells in the forum state or otherwise establishes sufficient contacts, ZPO Section 32 focuses on the product itself. This distinction may display its full import mainly in distributorship agreements and other resale agreements whenever the manufacturer does not know to whom and in which jurisdiction the intermediate purchaser will resell.

CONCLUSION

The above discussion of the principal bases of jurisdiction in Germany has shown a jurisdictional concept which, on the whole, asserts judicial power over a broader range of international activities than the jurisdictional concept of the United States. In that, Germany finds itself largely in accordance with most of the other civil law countries which in some form or other also use exorbitant bases of jurisdiction mainly in order to protect their own nationals. Therefore, if the views of foreign jurisdictions should be one criterion in applying U.S. rules of jurisdiction to international disputes U.S. courts certainly have not reached the limits of what international harmony and comity would deem permissible.

DOMICILIARIES

On the other hand, the rigidity of the German jurisdictional concept and its obvious lack of concern for international implications must not

---

105. The provision reads: For actions in tort the court of the district within which the tortious act was committed has jurisdiction.

be equated with less fairness *vis-à-vis* alien litigants. After all, German jurisdictional provisions provide a high degree of predictability and certainty; and this seems to be of particular importance in the field of jurisdiction.

PETER F. SCHLOSSER, LECTURES ON CIVIL–LAW LITIGATION SYSTEMS AND AMERICAN COOPERATION WITH THOSE SYSTEMS

45 U. Kan. L. Rev. 9, 19–20, 22–23 (1996).*

* * *

. . . [T]he distinction between jurisdiction and venue is little developed in Europe. Justice Holmes' "power concept" as the basis for jurisdiction, is foreign to civil-law systems. Except for Switzerland, uniform codes of civil procedure are in force in all European states. These uniform codes are not like the United States Uniform Commercial Code. European states are either unitarian, with uniform law over all the territory, or they are federal. Civil procedure is a matter of federal law everywhere except Switzerland. All the codes include provisions on what is called "territorial competence." If, in an international case, no court is found to be competent by reason of territory, that is because international competency is lacking. Territorial competence is mostly derived from the fact that the courts of the state in question also have international competency. In some states, as for example in Austria, there is an additional requirement that the case must be related to the state of the court addressed. Only in very few respects is international competence dealt with in a different way than local competence. In Germany, for example, decisions on local competence cannot be appealed. In contrast, decisions on the issue of whether any competence can be found in Germany can be appealed.

The lack of distinction between jurisdiction and venue has some very important and characteristic implications. Jurisdiction and service of process are totally disassociated from each other in civil-law countries. It is inconceivable to base jurisdiction on the mere fact that a document is served upon the defendant. It is true that in civil-law countries it is possible to serve process upon the defendant at any place where he may be found. But this event is without any significance for the jurisdiction of the court.

* * *

But, however service is accomplished, it has nothing to do with establishing jurisdiction. If the defendant does not enter any appearance, the court has to verify, on its own motion, whether or not it has jurisdiction. The plaintiff must provide sufficient evidence for the facts on which he wants to base the jurisdiction of the court. On the other hand, a court having jurisdiction is not prevented from exercising it by

* Reprinted with permission.

the mere fact that service of process may turn out to be impossible. In Germany, as a last resort, service of process may be realized by publishing the document initiating proceedings in a newspaper and simultaneously putting it on the court's official board. In France, and in many other countries, service may be made with an official whose normal function is public prosecution ("signification au parquet").

Because there is no civil-law concept of jurisdiction fundamentally distinct from venue, nothing exists in civil-law countries which could properly be called a long-arm statute. A European court has jurisdiction over categories of lawsuits and other kinds of proceedings instituted against categories of persons as defined by the respective provisions in the state's code of civil procedure.

A German court, for example, must enforce a judgment of any other German court by garnishments if the debtor has his residence within the court's district. If enforcement is to be made by an entry into the land register, any German judgment must be enforced by the court in the district of which the respective piece of land is located. No registration for enforcement is required.

As far as jurisdiction for normal lawsuits is concerned, a long-lasting tradition distinguishes between specific jurisdiction and general jurisdiction. Today, this distinction is also known in the United States, but this is only due to a recent development. The Supreme Court of the United States did not adopt this distinction before its well-known decision in *Shaffer v. Heitner*.

In civil-law countries this distinction is as old as the codes of civil procedure. General jurisdiction is based only on the defendant's permanent residence. As far as specific jurisdiction is concerned, there are many particularities in the numerous codes of civil procedure of the various civil-law countries. Where a tort occurs is recognized almost everywhere as a good venue for lawsuits arising out of it. Very often there is also a basis for specific jurisdiction for matters relating to a contract. Doing business in a particular jurisdiction does not figure among the bases for specific jurisdiction, let alone of general jurisdiction. There must be an actual branch or other establishment of the foreign debtor in the respective country. Only recently have consumers and employees very often enjoyed the privilege of a basis for specific jurisdiction at their own permanent residence.

On the European continent, no rule against ousting the jurisdiction of the court has ever existed. The liberal European tradition allowed practically unlimited freedom to agree upon which court or courts would have jurisdiction. But for two decades there has been a strong movement in Europe to invalidate such agreements in contracts to which a consumer is a party.

No doctrine of forum non conveniens has ever been developed in civil-law countries. A court having jurisdiction is committed to exercise it, because it is a public service entrusted to it by statute. A German or French judge would find it very awkward if he had any discretionary power to decline jurisdiction. When the United Kingdom negotiated for accession to the Brussels Convention, it was made clear to them by express terms that they ought to be under an obligation to exercise all jurisdiction they would have under the Convention.

* * *

All civil-law systems have provisions creating jurisdiction over defendants neither residing within the jurisdiction nor having sufficient contact with the court's district that would normally allow specific jurisdiction to be exercised. All these provisions may be characterized as provisions discriminating against foreigners. Only very recently have Europeans started to discuss whether these provisions conform to due process standards. Switzerland, however, has a longer tradition in this respect. Pursuant to article 59 of the Swiss constitution, a Swiss national can only be sued in the courts of his own canton. Put into American legal terms, the Swiss constitution prohibits long-arm statutes. Yet, this constitutional provision is protective only of Swiss nationals. The Swiss are very distrustful of persons residing abroad. Considering the time when the Swiss constitution came into force, this is very understandable. To be compelled to sue somebody abroad was very cumbersome and often useless. Hence, they have developed a kind of quasi-in-rem jurisdiction, which, however, will be restricted by 1997 to claims with a sufficient relationship to Switzerland.

French law provides that every Frenchman can sue his opponent in France if the underlying legal relationship has a contractual nature. In Germany, Austria, and some Scandinavian countries, any person not residing within the court's jurisdiction can be sued in that court if his or her assets are located in that jurisdiction. The lawsuit need not be related to these assets. According to case law, minimal assets may be sufficient. For example, in Sweden, a hotel guest forgot his umbrella in the room he had rented. This was found to be a sufficient ground to assume jurisdiction over him. Since that time, such provisions have been called umbrella provisions.

The most ridiculous case in this respect was decided in Germany. In previous legal proceedings, a German plaintiff had lost a case instituted against a foreigner. The consequence was, under the German system allocating the cost of the proceedings, that the foreigner had a claim against the German plaintiff to be reimbursed for his expenses, including lawyer's fees. The foreigner's claim was held to be located at the residence of the German plaintiff in Germany. The foreign defendant thus had assets in Germany. This was found to constitute sufficient grounds to assume jurisdiction over the foreigner in a second lawsuit, which was entirely unrelated to the first one. The German provision does not only protect German nationals or people residing in Germany. In the aftermath of the Iranian Revolution, United States and British banks were able to sue the Iranian National Oil Company in Germany for more than $100,000,000 because both banks had bank accounts in Germany.

In 1992, the German Federal Court decided that due process considerations were a compelling reason to restrict the scope of this provision. This had been proposed for a decade by legal theorists. According to the German Federal Court, jurisdiction is lacking if the case is not in any way related to Germany. Regrettably, the court seems to be in favor of the proposition that the lawsuit is related to Germany if the plaintiff is a resident of Germany. I am convinced, however, that the court will go further and decide that the underlying legal relationship must also be related to Germany.

Case law discussing other aspects of due process and jurisdiction is lacking in civil-law countries.

Questions and Comments

1. Assume that Celsius has sent representatives to Germany to demonstrate their product and to negotiate the sale to Plastic Maker, as well as to other potential buyers. Assume also that as part of this process, Celsius established a bank account in Munich, in which there is a balance of about 3,000 Euros. Does this change the jurisdictional analysis?

2. The von Dryander article above includes a discussion of Article 23 of the German Zivilprozessordnung (Code of Civil Procedure). What are the implications of that provision given the changes in the facts? Here again is that provision:

> For complaints asserting pecuniary claims against a person who has no domicile within the country, the court of the district within which this person has property, or within which is found the object claimed by the complaint, has jurisdiction. In the case of claims the debtor's domicile is considered the place where the property is located, and when the claim is secured, the place where the security is located is also considered.

Now suppose the buyer is French rather than German, but that all other facts remain the same. Can Celsius be sued in France? Consider Art. 14 of the French Civil Code, which provides as follows:

> An alien, even not residing in France, may be summoned before the French courts for the fulfillment of obligations contracted by him in France toward a French person; he may be brought before the French courts for obligations contracted by him in a foreign country toward a French person.

3. What are the bases of jurisdiction in Germany that Celsius should be most concerned about? Obviously, a U.S. lawyer is not qualified to make a final decision on these issues of German law. Given the information you now have, what questions might you have for a German lawyer? How might you best go about finding German counsel in order to pursue these questions and to engage local counsel for litigation if that is necessary? Given that the basic rules of jurisdiction are the same as the fundamental rules of the Brussels Regulation, is there jurisdiction in Germany over Celsius for an action in contract?

4. Article 23 of the German Code of Civil Procedure and Article 14 of the French Civil Code are considered "exorbitant" bases of jurisdiction.

Thus, pursuant to Article 3(2) and Annex I of the Brussels Regulation, these bases of jurisdiction are not available for use against defendants domiciled in other Member States of the European Union. They remain available, however, against defendants not domiciled in the European Union, including defendants from the United States. This is made explicit in Article 4(1) of the Brussels Regulation. This discrimination is further enhanced by Article 4(2) of the Regulation, which makes these bases of jurisdiction available against non-EU defendants to any EU national domiciled in the Member State in which the jurisdictional basis exists. Thus, for example, a German national domiciled in Paris could sue a U.S. defendant in a French court under Article 14 of the French Civil Code. Moreover, as a result of Articles 33 and 38 of the Regulation, once judgment is obtained as a result of such exorbitant jurisdictional rules, the judgment must be recognized in all other Member States of the EU. The result is a substantial extension of the effect of such exorbitant bases of jurisdiction against defendants not domiciled within the European Union. Whether this is simply a nice problem for academic discussion, or a practical problem of significant proportion is not yet clear. Whether reported cases of its application exist may be a much different matter than the impact the condition may have on planning considerations. Given the exacerbation of exorbitant jurisdiction effected by the Brussels Regulation, can you think of any way that a U.S. party to litigation in Europe might try to counter this situation?

5. Consider again the United Kingdom Civil Procedure Rule 6.20 from the Problem 5.1. materials. Suppose Plastic Maker brought suit in the UK against Celsius on the facts of Problem 5.2. Would there be jurisdiction in the UK courts for such an action?

PART B. JURISDICTION IN A JAPANESE COURT

Assume for the purposes of this section of the discussion that Plastic Maker is a Japanese corporation, headquartered in Tokyo, and that all German aspects of the facts are now connected instead with Japan. Given the facts of Problem 5.2, can you advise Celsius on some of the basic questions about possibilities for suit in Japan?

GOTO v. MALAYSIA AIRLINE

35 Minshū (No. 7) 1224 (Supreme Court, Oct. 16, 1981),
translated in 26 Japanese Annual of International
Law 122 (1983).*

STATUTORY REFERENCES

Code of Civil Procedure:

Article 4

(1) The general forum of a juridical person or any other association or foundation shall be determined by the place of its principal office or principal place of business, or in case there is no office or place of business, by the domicile of the principal person in charge of its affairs.

. . .

* Reprinted here as amended by John O. Haley with permission.

(3) In regard to the general forum of a foreign association or foundation, the provisions of paragraph 1 shall apply to the office, place of business or person in charge of its affairs in Japan.

Hōrei (Law Concerning the Application of laws in General):

Article 7

(1) As regards the formation and effect of a juristic act, the question as to the law of which country is to govern shall be determined by the intention of the parties.

(2) In case the intention of the parties is uncertain, the law of the place where the act is done shall govern.

Decree

1. The appeal is dismissed [Decision below affirmed.]
2. The cost of appeal shall be borne by the appellant.

Reasons

In their Grounds for Appeal Nos. 1 and 2(1) and (2), Yasuomi Hayashida and Toshihiko Kashiwagi, counsel for the appellant, argue as follows: the court below reversed the judgement of the court of the first instance which dismissed the lawsuit on the ground that it was not subject to Japanese jurisdiction; however, in doing so, the court below erred in the interpretation and application of Article 4, paragraph 3 and Article 5 of the Code of Civil Procedure and, accordingly, the court below did not provide sufficient reasons for its judgement.

This case involves claims for damages by Japanese nationals against a foreign corporation. The appellees allege as follows: on December 4, 1977, Tomio Goto made a contract of air transport with the appellant in the Federation of Malaysia; in accordance with the contract, he boarded a plane operated by the appellant from Penang to Kuala Lumpur; the plane crashed in Johore Bahrn in Malaysia on the same day and he died in that accident; therefore, the appellant shall be liable for payment of 40,454,442 Yen to Tomio Goto as compensation for damages caused by the crash of the plane which constitutes the appellant's breach of the air transport contract; the appellees Michiko Goto (his wife), Yukiko Goto and Takayuki Goto (his children) succeeded to his rights in proportion to their shares in the succession, which are one-third each; accordingly, each appellee demands the appellant to pay 13,330,000 Yen for the above damages.

In general, adjudicatory jurisdiction (*saiban kankatsuken*) is exercised as an effect of the national sovereignty, and the scope of adjudicatory jurisdiction is in principle co-extensive with the scope of the national sovereignty. Consequently, if a defendant is a foreign corporation with a main office abroad, it is ordinarily beyond the adjudicatory jurisdiction of Japan, unless it is willing to subject itself to Japanese jurisdiction. Nevertheless, as an exception, a defendant can be subjected to the adjudicatory jurisdiction of Japan, whatever its nationality may be or wherever it may be located, if the case relates to Japan or if the defendant has some legal nexus with Japan. With respect to the limits of such an exception, we have no statutes expressly prescribing international adjudicatory jurisdiction, no treaties that apply, nor any well-defined, generally recognized rules of international law. Under these circumstances, it is reasonable to determine international adjudicatory jurisdiction in accordance with the principles of *jōri*, which require that fairness between parties be maintained and an appropriate and speedy trial be secured. In accordance with these principles of *jōri*, a defendant may be appropriately subjected to the jurisdiction of Japan when the requirements of the provisions for domestic territorial jurisdiction (*tochi kankatsuken*) set out in the Code of Civil Procedure are satisfied, for example, when the defendant's domicile (article 2), if a juridical person or other association, office or place of business (article 4), the place of performance (article 5), the location of the defendant's property (article 8), the place of tort (article 15), or such other place for trial (*saiban-seki*) as set forth in the Code of Civil Procedure is located in Japan.

In accordance with the findings of the court below, the appellant is a Malaysian corporation which is established under the Company Law of the Federation of Malaysia and has its head office in that country. The appellant has appointed Gyokusho Cho as its representative in Japan and has established a place of business in Tokyo. On these premises, the appellant shall be reasonably subjected to the jurisdiction of Japan, even though it is a foreign corporation that has its head office abroad. Therefore, we affirm the decision of the court below which held that a Japanese court has jurisdiction over this case. The judgment of the court below is not erroneous as the appellant argues. We cannot accept the appellant's argument which criticizes the judgement below from a point of view different from our above-stated view.

. . .

Presiding Justice Tadayoshi Kinoshita
Justice Kazuo Kurimoto
Justice Yasuyoshi Shiono
Justice Goichi Miyazaki

The Japanese Code of Civil Procedure was revised on June 26, 1996. Consider the following basic provisions:

Article 4. (Jurisdiction by general forum)

1. A suit shall be subject to the jurisdiction of the court governing the place of the defendant's general forum.

2. The general forum of a person shall be determined by such person's domicile, or by the place of residence when there is no domicile in Japan or the domicile is unknown, or by the last domicile when there is no place of residence in Japan or the place of residence is unknown.

3. When an ambassador or minister envoy, or any other Japanese citizen who, being in a foreign nation, enjoys immunity from the jurisdic-

tion of such foreign nation, has no general forum in accordance with the provisions of the preceding paragraph, such person's general forum shall be in the place prescribed by the Rules of the Supreme Court. [Rules of Civil Procedure (Minji Sosho Kisoku) Article 6 designates such place as the Chiyoda Ward of Tokyo.]

4. The general forum of a juridical person or any other association or foundation shall be determined by the location of its principal office or principal place of business, or when there is no such office or place of business, by the domicile of the representative or principal person in charge of its affairs.

5. Notwithstanding the provisions of the preceding paragraph, the general forum of a foreign association or foundation shall be determined by the location of its principal office or principal place of business in Japan, or when there is no such office or place of business in Japan, by the domicile of the representative or principal person in charge of its affairs in Japan.

6. The general forum of the State shall be determined by the location of the government office that shall represent the State in the suit.

Article 5. (Jurisdiction of suit concerning property right, etc.)

A suit prescribed by either of the following items may be filed before the court governing the place designated by the respective applicable items:

i.   a suit concerning a property right—the place of performance of the obligation; [+ The actual term used in statute "zaisanken" literally means property right. It includes in practice generally such rights as contract rights, rights to claim for damages, intellectual property rights, and proprietary rights.]

ii.   a suit for the purpose of claiming monetary payment of bills or checks—the place for payment of the bills or checks;

iii.   a suit against a member of a ship's crew and which concerns a property right—the place of the ship's registry;

iv.   a suit against a person who has no domicile (in cases where the suit is filed against a juridical person, office or place of business; hereinafter in this item the same shall apply) in Japan or whose domicile is unknown and which concerns a property right—the place where the subject matter of the claim, the subject matter of the security therefor, or any of the defendant's property which may be attached is located;

v.   a suit against a person maintaining an office or place of business and which concerns the affairs of such office or place of business—the place where the office or place of business is located;

vi.   a suit against a ship-owner or any other person using a ship and which concerns the ship or voyage—the place of the ship's registry;

vii.   a suit based on an obligation-right against a ship or any other obligation-right secured by a ship—the place where the ship is located;

viii.   a suit concerning a company or any other association or foundation and which is prescribed as follows

a. a suit by a company or other association against a member of such organization or a person who was a member, or a suit by a member against a member or a person who was a member, or a suit by a person who was a member against a member, and which is based on membership status:

b. a suit by an association or a foundation against an officer or a person who was an officer, and which is based on official status:

c. a suit by a company against a promoter or a person who was a promoter, or an inspector or a person who was an inspector, and which is based on the status of the promoter or inspector:

d. a suit by an obligee of a company or other association against a member or a person who was a member of such organization, and which is based on membership status:—the place of the general forum of the association or the foundation;

ix. a suit relating to a tort—the place of the tort;

x. a suit for damages based on a collision of ships or any other accident at sea—the place where the damaged ship first arrived;

xi. a suit relating to salvage—the place where the salvage was effected or the place where the salvaged ship first arrived;

xii. a suit relating to immovables—the place where the immovable is located;

xiii. a suit relating to a registration—the place where such registration is to be made;

xiv. a suit relating to an inheritance right or legal share, or a suit relating to a legacy or any other act that shall take effect upon death—the place of the decedent's general forum at the time of commencement of succession;

xv. insofar as it does not come within the provisions of the preceding item, a suit relating to an obligation-right against a decedent's estate, or other encumbrance upon the estate (provided the whole or a part of the decedent's estate exists in the district of the court governing the place prescribed by the preceding item)—the place prescribed by the preceding item.[1]

JOHN O. HALEY, THE ADJUDICATORY JURISDICTION OF JAPANESE COURTS IN TRANSNATIONAL LITIGATION

Law and Justice in a Multistate World: Essays in Honor of Arthur T. von Mehren 706–719 (James A.R. Nafziger & Symeon C. Symeonides, eds. 2002).*

* * *

THE CONTEXT

The judgment in *Goto v. Malaysia Airline* was the first post-war Supreme Court statement on the issue of whether and on what grounds

---

1. Translation from DOING BUSINESS IN JAPAN, App. 6A (Matthew Bender & Company, Inc. 2007).

the adjudicatory jurisdiction of Japanese courts extends to actions against a non-Japanese defendant arising out of events that occur outside of Japan. * * * The case involved a claim for damages brought by the surviving spouse and two children of Tomio Goto, who had died in a Malaysia Airline crash in Johore Bahrn, Malaysia, on December 4, 1977. The action was filed in the Nagoya District Court, which dismissed the action on the grounds that Japanese courts lacked adjudicatory jurisdiction over the airline company in this case. On appeal, the Nagoya High Court reversed and remanded the case to the Nagoya District Court for trial on the merits. The defendant airline appealed to the Supreme Court. The Court affirmed the Nagoya High Court's judgment, allowing the plaintiffs to sue the airline company for compensatory damages in Japan.

Seventeen years later, on January 1, 1998, Japan's long-anticipated revised Code of Civil Procedure finally came into force after a two-year hiatus after its enactment and official promulgation in 1996 to allow the Supreme Court time to develop and issue supplementary rules. The revised code, however, made few substantive changes in Japanese civil procedure. The underlying aim of the revision and its principal contribution was to rewrite the old code, an artifact of formal 19th century linguistic conventions, in contemporary language, thereby making the code more accessible to the public. The new code did not make any substantive change in the provisions on jurisdiction. The provisions on adjudicatory jurisdiction (*kankatsu*) included in the 1890 Code of Civil Procedure (*Minji soshōhō*, Law No. 29, 1890) were based largely on German law. They have now survived, with scant modification, all subsequent revisions. Nor did the 1996 revision add any special provisions on international adjudicatory jurisdiction, despite efforts to add at least *lis alibi pendens* provisions to allow courts to stay actions in cases of parallel litigation where suits between the same parties and addressing the same claims have been filed and are being litigated abroad. * * *

As in other civil law systems, the Japanese rules for adjudicatory jurisdiction are more akin to common law rules of venue in that they allocate in territorial terms the adjudicatory jurisdiction for all courts within Japan. For readers unfamiliar with civil procedure in civil law systems, it should also be emphasized that all private law cases are what a common lawyer would classify as *in personam* actions. The exercise of adjudicatory jurisdiction in private law is always the equivalent of an exercise of personal jurisdiction. The notion of *in rem* or *quasi in rem* jurisdiction does not exist. In all cases, the judgments apply to the parties. * * * Unlike the common law approach, in civil law systems, jurisdiction is not conceived as a question of the authority and potentially coercive power of the courts over the parties or object of the lawsuit. It relates solely to the competence of the court to adjudicate-to find facts, determine the applicable legal rules and principles and issue a judgment that is binding on the parties and, in cases involving a determination of property rights, the world at large. The physical presence of the defendant in the forum is not required, nor, as a result, is service of process a requirement for jurisdiction, although to proceed with a lawsuit, a summons and some form of notice to the defendant is separately required. It might also be noted that the common law doctrine of *forum non conveniens,* at least as separate from a determination of adjudicatory jurisdiction, is also an alien notion in most civil law systems.

The rules divide into two categories: general forum rules and special forum rules. With respect to the former, lawsuits are in principle to be adjudicated by the courts for the district of the defendant's general forum, which is determined by the defendant's domicile (*jūsho*) or, in the case of a defendant without domicile in Japan or unknown domicile, by residence (kyosho). Consequently, unless permitted under a particular special forum rule or case law, no Japanese court has adjudicatory competence in lawsuits filed against natural persons who have neither domicile nor residence in Japan. For companies and other juridical persons, the general forum rules provide for adjudicatory jurisdiction in the district of their principal office or place of business. In the absence of either, a juridical person's general forum is determined by the domicile of the principal person in charge of its affairs. Likewise, the Code explicitly provides that the general forum of a foreign company, association or foundation is its principal office or place of business in Japan, or the Japanese domicile or residence of the person in charge of its business in Japan.

Most special forum rules in the Code are quite specific. For example * * * suits by a corporation, shareholders or creditors against shareholder, directors, executive officers, incorporators or auditors of a company are to be adjudicated by the court for the district in which the company's general forum is located. * * *

Three special forum rules have potentially quite broad application. First, pecuniary actions (*zaisanken-jō no uttae*), including contract actions, may be adjudicated by the court in the district where the obligation (ordinarily contract) is to be performed (1996 Code, art.5[1]). Tort claims (*fuhkiōKōi no uttae*) are to be adjudicated where ... the tort was committed, which has been construed to be either where the injury or the tortious act occurred (1996 Code, art. 5[9]). And, third, a provision based on Article 23 of the German Code of Civil Procedure allows suits against parties without a general forum in Japan to be brought in the court for any district where the subject-matter of the claim, the property subject to a security interest or other attachable property is located (1996 Code, art. 5[4]).

A fourth special forum rule deserves mention. Current Article 7 (Article 21 of the 1890 Code) provides for the adjudicatory jurisdiction despite the lack of an applicable special forum rule or a general forum for all parties, in cases of joint liability. Thus, the provision permits the exercise of jurisdiction over a party with no general forum within the judicial district to be sued for alleged joint liability with a party that satisfies the general forum requirements. In such a case, the claim to be litigated need not be an event or transaction with sufficient relation to Japan to satisfy one or more of the other special forum rules. As noted below, there is at least one district court judgment affirming an exercise of adjudicatory jurisdiction in such a case arising out of an airline accident in Spain where one of the defendants was a domestic Spanish airline without business presence in Japan.

The applicability of Article 7 and the Code's other adjudicatory jurisdiction rules in lawsuits in which at least one of the parties does not reside or have "domicile" or a place of business in Japan, or the conduct or transactions giving rise to the lawsuit have occurred outside of the territorial limits of Japan—the question *Goto v. Malaysia Airline* is thought to have answered—had divided Japanese scholars since the end of World War II. The majority of post-war Japanese scholars had long grappled with the issue of when and why it might be appropriate in such cases to apply the rules on jurisdiction of the Code. They had divided into two groups. Private international law scholars tended to agree with the view introduced into the literature in 1949 by Professor Sueo Ikehara that sought to identify a set of universally applicable principles to guide the courts. Japanese law lacked, in their view, any positive law rules directly applicable to what they labeled as "international" lawsuits (*kokusai soshō*). They considered the provisions on jurisdiction in the Code to have been designed solely for "domestic" litigation. Thus, to determine whether an exercise of adjudicatory jurisdiction would be appropriate in cases involving non-Japanese parties or events occurring outside of Japan, these scholars argued, the courts should look to *jōri*.

The late Dan Henderson described *jōri* as an expression of the Japanese notion of "common sense" or "reason." The first use of the term in modern Japanese law was a Great Council of State decree issued in 1875, two years after the establishment of Japan's first modern court. The decree provided for the application of *jōri* by the courts in the absence of applicable positive law or custom. Writing in 1933, Kotaro Tanaka characterized *jōri* as equivalent to the European concept of "natural reason" and the German "*natur de sache*." By the early 1940s, *jōri* was generally regarded as a conceptual fount of undefined, gap-filling principles. In other words, *jōri* serves as a readily available conceptual device that judges are able to use to justify outcomes at variance with the logic of legislated or other forms of positive law rules. *Jōri*,i viewed as a source of law, functioned as a device to legitimate judge-made rules.

For Ikehara, *jōri* served as a reflection of generally accepted, just and reasonable bases for jurisdiction. In the case of adjudicatory jurisdiction, resort to *jōri* would thus allow judges to fashion the rules that they believe to be appropriate without also having to justify judicial law making overriding an extensive corpus of legislated rules. The courts could also use *jōri* more narrowly to develop supplementary, gap-filling rules.

For many Japanese private international law scholars and perhaps some judges, *jōri* was a very attractive device. If the application of the Code rules did not seem appropriate, it enabled judges to articulate and apply contrary rules or principles. If indeed the case did fall between the cracks of the Code rules, *jōri* enabled judges to justify the creation of new, supplementary, gap-filling rules without application of existing Code rules. Yet in cases where judges approved the application of the Code rules, they could rationalize their application by reasoning that they conform to the principles of *jōri*. The consequence of such an approach was to enhance the law-making authority of the courts and, perhaps more telling, the influence of private law scholars who could then define the principles of *jōri*.

Comprising a second group of scholars were mostly civil procedure specialists, who argued that, for lack of any alternative, by "reverse inference" the provisions of the Code should be applied. Usually cited as the seminal article reflecting this point of view is the 1942 work of Professor Hidefumi Egawa. One of the first Japanese scholars to address this issue of the adjudicatory jurisdiction of Japanese courts in transnational litigation, Egawa noted that Japan lacked any provisions for lawsuits involving non-Japanese parties but concluded that the courts should apply whatever Code rules would otherwise be applicable, adding there was no reason for Japan not to follow the example of Germany and France inasmuch as Japanese law was so similar.

The Egawa suggestion taken to its logical conclusion—and stated more bluntly than any Japanese civil procedure scholar might wish—has as much appeal to comparative law scholars as the Ikehara approach has for international law scholars. It enhances their role and influence. If Code provisions only apply by analogy, but the rules of Japanese civil procedure are deemed to be inextricably enmeshed within a community or tradition of shared principles and approaches, then it makes sense for judges to look to that community or within that tradition for norms to aid in deciding how best to interpret and to apply, even by analogy, the Code's rules. Hence comparative scholarship on civil procedure in continental Europe, especially Germany, becomes essential. And who best to carry out such research, and thereby influence the judges applying the rules, but scholars specializing in comparative civil procedure.

In the end, both groups agreed that the Code provisions were designed for "domestic" lawsuits and did not apply directly in cases of "international" litigation. The two approaches thus reached, in practice, essentially the same conclusion. As University of Tokyo Professor Kazunori Ishiguro has observed, except for theoretical justifications, the views of the two groups did not fundamentally differ—the Code provisions applied but only indirectly and, therefore, were subject to judicially created exceptions. Ishiguro indeed argues vigorously in favor of their common point of departure—that Japan has no directly applicable positive law rules for international adjudicatory jurisdiction. The Code rules therefore apply only by necessity and only insofar as they are appropriate under the particular facts of the case to be adjudicated. Ishiguro emphasizes the shared view, dismissing as trivial the differences between the two camps. Whether the results are rationalized as an application of *jōri* or "reverse inference" has little if any significance, he argues, beyond the rarified world of scholarly discourse. Such differences indeed matter less for Ishiguro—one of the best known and certainly among the most prolific contemporary private international and comparative civil procedure scholars in Japan.

Combining expertise as a private international lawyer and comparativist, Ishiguro, in a recent work, hints at a significant potential benefit of the conventional approaches. So long as the courts are not fully constrained by Code rules and can find in either *jōri* or continental European law more appropriate choices in "transnational" litigation, recent American and European developments, in particular the 1968 Brussels convention, could be a source of norms for Japan. Thus, the convention's prohibition of "exorbitant" jurisdiction under Article 3, expressed positively in terms of the interest of the plaintiff in having a claim adjudicated in Japan and a reasonable nexus between Japan and the defendant or the claim, could be imported into Japanese law via either the Ikehara or the Egawa view.

In the early 1970s, Yasuhiro Fujita, a young Japanese attorney then teaching at the University of Washington in Seattle, took issue with both groups. In a pair of articles in *Hanrei Times*, one of Japan's leading legal periodicals, Fujita rejected the conventional dichotomy between international and domestic adjudicatory jurisdiction, arguing that the Code applied to all lawsuits brought in Japan. He maintained the Code's rules on jurisdiction already accounted for the nationality, domicile or residence of the parties as well as the *situs* of the conduct or transaction that gave rise to the lawsuit. The rules of the Code were, according to Fujita, as applicable to "international" litigation as to any domestic lawsuit.

As Fujita emphasizes in his most recent challenge to the prevailing views, including the Supreme Court, the Code deals explicitly with the competence of courts to adjudicate actions involving aliens and foreign enterprise as well as conduct and transactions that occur outside of Japan. Fujita is equally insistent in pointing out the historical context in which the first Code was drafted and enacted. The 1890 Code was enacted as a major component of Japan's legal transformation in the late 19th century. One of the aims behind its enactment was to end as quickly as possible the exercise of extraterritorial jurisdiction in Japan by the European powers and the United States. The promulgation of 1890 Code was thus used to justify successfully the renegotiation of these treaties and the elimination of the consular courts. All sides considered

Japan's newly created judicial system and the adjudicatory procedures established under the Code to be adequate for litigation in Japan involving European and American nationals as parties. Moreover, Fujita adds, during the pre-war period judges and legal scholars alike took for granted the application of the Code in cases involving foreign nationals and international transactions. In support, Fujita cites a leading decision of the Great Court of Cassation (*Daishin'in*), pre-war Japan's highest court for civil and criminal appeals. He also quotes, at length, from the minutes of the 1923 Civil Procedure Code Revision Committee deliberations of January 17 on the provisions for adjudicatory jurisdiction with respect to "westerners" and foreign companies. To assert that the Code was not intended to cover transnational litigation, Fujita persuasively argues, one must ignore the express language of the Code, its history, as well as the prevailing pre-war consensus.

Goto v. Malaysia Airline dealt with all of these questions in a single paragraph, worth quoting here in its entirety:

> In general, adjudicatory jurisdiction (*saiban kankatsu*) is exercised as an effect of national sovereignty, and the scope of adjudicatory jurisdiction is in principle co-extensive with the scope of national sovereignty. Consequently, if a defendant is a foreign corporation with a main office abroad, it is ordinarily beyond the adjudicatory jurisdiction of Japan, unless it is willing to subject itself to Japanese jurisdiction. Nevertheless, as an exception, a defendant can be subjected to the adjudicatory jurisdiction of Japan, whatever its nationality may be or wherever it may be located, if the case relates to Japan or if the defendant has some legal nexus with Japan. With respect to the limits of such exceptions, we have no statutes expressly prescribing international adjudicatory jurisdiction, no treaties that apply, nor any well-defined, generally recognized rules of international law. Under these circumstances, it is reasonable to determine international adjudicatory jurisdiction in accordance with the principles of *jōri*, which require that fairness between the parties be maintained and an appropriate and speedy trial be secured. In accordance with these principles of *jōri*, a defendant may be appropriately subjected to the jurisdiction of Japan when the requirements of the provisions for domestic territorial jurisdiction (*tochi kankatsuken*) set out in the [1890] Code of Civil Procedure are satisfied, for example, when the defendant's domicile (article 2), if a juridical person or other association, office or place of business (article 4), the place performance (article 5), the location the defendant's property (article 8), the place of tort (article 15) or any other place for trial (*saiban-seki*) set forth in the Code of Civil Procedure is located in Japan.

The justices begin by deferring to the shared feature of the conventional academic approaches. They accept the standard post-war view separating "international" from "domestic" litigation, and then note that Japanese positive law, as well as private international law, both fail to provide a set of applicable rules for "international" litigation. Echoing words used by Ikehara three decades earlier, they refer to *jōri* as a source of norms to guide the courts to ensure that any exercise of adjudicatory jurisdiction is fair to the parties and reasonable. Then, as if speaking on behalf of the civil procedure scholars, they agree that in the absence of rules in Japanese positive law or international treaty or convention, it is reasonable for the courts to apply the rules for "domestic" litigation. Despite this deference to both sides of the scholars' debate, as Sophia University Professor and, like Fujita, practicing attorney Hideyuki Kobayashi pointed out in a highly regarded commentary on the case, the justices avoid both the formulation preferred by international private law scholars based on the identification of universally accepted principles of jurisdiction, as well as the characterization preferred by civil procedure scholars that the Code provisions apply only indirectly by analogy.

In the end, the justices side with Fujita. As Fujita had argued, they apply the Code's provisions directly, accepting, via the application of *jōri*, Fujita's conclusion that the Code rules should be viewed as rules for transnational litigation. From the language of the opinion, the justices have equated *jōri* with the Code's provisions. Also missing, as noted by Kobayashi, are the common formulations for justifying judicially crafted exceptions to legislated rules, such as "in principle" [*gensoku to shite*] or as required by "special circumstances" [*tokudan no jijō*], both stock phrases in Japanese judgments. The opinion thus on its face allows scant, if any, basis for accommodation in situations where the direct application of the Code provisions might be regarded as inappropriate.

The Legacy

Since 1981, the Supreme Court has decided appeals in only two subsequent cases in which the international adjudicatory jurisdiction of Japanese courts has been at issue. Both also petty bench decisions, they were decided after the 1996 Code had been enacted but before it came into force. The decision in the first case—*Kono v. Kono*[20]—was handed down on June 24, 1996. The second case—*K.K. Family v. Miyahara*[21]— was decided a year and a half later in November 1997, less than two months before the revised code went into effect. The continuity of code law may be considered an enthymeme of both decisions.

The first of the two decisions involved a divorce action brought in Japan by a Japanese national who had been living for several years in Germany. He had married in the former Democratic Republic of Germany in 1982. A daughter was born in 1984, and in 1988 the family moved to West Berlin. A year later the couple separated. The daughter remained with her father, who brought her to Japan in April 1989. On July 8, 1989, the wife filed for divorce in Berlin. The husband did not appear and the German court entered a default judgment that became

---

20. 51 Minshū 1451 (Sup. Ct., 2nd P.B., June 21, 1996), *translated in* 40 Japanese Annual of International Law 333 (1997).

21. Hanrei Jiho (No. 1626) 74 (Sup. Ct., 3rd P.B., Nov. 11, 1997), *translated in* 41 Japanese Annual of International Law 117 (1998).

final in February 1990. The German judgment affirmed the divorce and awarded parental authority to the wife. Meanwhile, in a parallel action, on July 26, 1989, the husband had filed for divorce in Japan. The Urawa District Court initially dismissed the case for lack of jurisdiction inasmuch as the wife had never resided in Japan. On appeal, however, the Tokyo High Court reversed and granted jurisdiction. The wife appealed to the Supreme Court.

The five justices admitted that ordinarily the courts would not have jurisdiction in cases where the defendant did not have domicile or reside in Japan, (but whose whereabouts was known), but, under the peculiar circumstances of the case, they deemed the hardship the husband would have in returning to Germany and attempting to obtain a separate German divorce to justify the exercise of jurisdiction in the case.

The second action was brought by a small firm in Japan that had contracted with a Japanese expatriate who had been living in Frankfurt, Germany since the mid 1960s, to purchase used cars in Europe and arrange for them to be shipped to Japan for resale by the plaintiff. The plaintiff had deposited nearly 92 million yen (approximately U.S. $750,000) with a German bank to be used by the defendant to cover the anticipated costs of the first several shipments, but doubts regarding the defendant's trustworthiness prompted the plaintiff to modify the arrangements to provide for payments by letter of credit to be made after the automobiles were purchased and shipped. The plaintiff demanded the return of all remaining funds—almost 25 million yen (approximately U.S. $210,000). The defendant refused the request, causing the plaintiff to sue for the funds in Japan.

The court upheld both lower court decisions dismissing the actions for lack of adjudicatory jurisdiction. In the first case, the defendant had no general forum in Japan under the special statute for adjudication of domestic relations cases, the provisions for adjudicatory jurisdiction in which parallel those in the Code, nor in the second case did the court find any applicable general or special forum rule under the Code. The justices refused to construe the transaction to include Japan as the place for performance. The outcomes in both cases, in their view, were just and reasonable. Nonetheless, *K.K. Family v. Miyahara* did modify the approach articulated in *Goto v. Malaysia Airline*.

* * *

The Cases

A review of lower court decisions from 1981 though 1999 reveals that, despite an occasional exception, judges initially followed the *Goto v. Malaysia Airline* approach articulating the prevailing scholarly view (*gakusetsu*) on the lack of provisions for international litigation and the applicability of *jōri* but, as Fujita argued, applying the Code directly. However, even in the first cases judges began to add the well-worn rubric of "unless required by special circumstances" [*tokudan no jōri*] and often made no explicit reference to *jōri*. They simply applied the

Code provisions as the applicable rules, while expressly reserving authority to override the Code if required by "special circumstances" to avoid an unjust or unreasonable result. By the late 1990s, as Professor Kobayashi observes, this had become the prevailing approach in district court decisions. Using this language to justify the dismissal of the action in *K. K. Family v. Miyahara*, the five justices of Third Petty Bench have thus approved a modification of *Goto v. Malaysia Airline* that lower courts, especially the Tokyo District Court, had initiated several years before. As modified *Goto v. Malaysia* now fully accommodates the Fujita argument to the prevailing scholarly views that sought to allow lower court judges some potential for flexibility. Yet, since 1997, no court has exercised that authority; the holdings in all cases since *K. K. Family v. Miyahara* conform to the Code rules.

Except cases involving divorce or other family relationships, the courts have not, to my knowledge, in any reported case since *Goto v. Malaysia Airline* exercised jurisdiction without an express finding of facts that supports the application of a general or special forum rule. And even before 1997, only rarely did the courts refuse to exercise jurisdiction where they determined a basis for jurisdiction under the Code exists under the facts of the case. In effect, therefore, they have reserved an authority that they very rarely use and may not need.

In all but six of 46 reported decisions in cases in which the parties contested and the court had to determine the basis for adjudicatory jurisdiction, the court either dismissed the action, expressly noting the lack of any basis for jurisdiction under any of the general or special forum rules of the Code or upheld its adjudicatory jurisdiction over the case, noting the applicability of one or more of the Code provisions. Of the six remaining cases, two involved divorce actions in which the court accepted adjudicatory jurisdiction with express reference to principles of *jōri* to overcome the lack of any applicable provision in the Code. In only four cases—one, a parallel action for a defensive declaration of non-liability and the remaining three, tort claims—the court dismissed the action despite acknowledgment of at least a colorable claim that the defendant had a general forum in Japan or that the special forum rule for torts—the place where the tort was committed or the injury occurred—or both applied.

The most recent of the four cases—the 1991 Tokyo District Court decision in *Masaki Bussan K. K. v. Nanka Seimen Company*—was the second of two declaratory judgment actions brought to confirm the lack of liability of a Japanese manufacturer in related products liability actions brought in the United States. The first suit was filed against an employee of the purchaser of a noodle-making machine manufactured by the Japanese firm. The second Japanese suit was brought against Nanka Seimen, a third party that had gratuitously provided the buyer with information about the machinery received from the seller and joined as a defendant in the U.S. products liability action. In a second U.S. suit, Nanka Seimen sought indemnification from the Japanese manufacturer in the event of being held liable in the products liability suit. The

Japanese declaratory action against Nanka Seimen was thus a defensive parallel action. The court expressly found that Nanka Seimen did not have a general forum in Japan but that Japan could properly [be] deemed the place of the tort under the Code. The court concluded, however, that under the exceptional circumstances [*tokudan no jijō*] of the case, the court should decline to exercise jurisdiction.

A year earlier, in 1990, the Tokyo District Court had dismissed another case despite an acknowledged basis for adjudicatory jurisdiction. In that decision—*R.W. Starge & Company v. King Kong Li*—the judges may perhaps have doubted the validity of claimed applicability of a special forum rule and may have preferred not to decide that issue and instead justify their denial of jurisdiction on the grounds of "unreasonableness" of adjudicating the case in Japan. In any event, the basis for jurisdiction under the Code was *de minimis*. The plaintiff in the case was an English underwriter with its principal office in Hong Kong. It brought the action for the yen equivalent of U.K. £210,000 in damages against King Kong Li, an ethnic Chinese with English citizenship domiciled in Hong Kong. The claim arose from the theft of a rare Ming dynasty porcelain plate, insured by Lloyds and reinsured by the plaintiff, from a hotel room in London as a result of the defendant's alleged negligence. Although a basis for adjudicatory jurisdiction might have existed under the joint liability and consolidated claims provisions of Article 21 of the 1890 Code (1996 Code, arts.7 and 38) inasmuch as the plaintiff had joined Mr. Li's employer, which did have a general forum in Japan. The district court nevertheless dismissed the claim against Li, stating that to adjudicate the case in Japan would not be fair or reasonable. In a separate action, the plaintiff recovered its loss from Li's employer, Dainido K. K.

The case should be also be compared to *Inoue v. ABIANCO Airlines*. Adjudicatory jurisdiction was upheld in that decision. The case involved a damage action against a domestic Spanish airline company in connection with an accident that occurred at the Badajos Airport, Spain, between an airplane operated by ABIANCO and an Iberian Airlines plane in which the Japanese plaintiffs were passengers by virtue of the Code's consolidated claims provisions. The obvious difference is that, in the *Inoue* case, the plaintiffs were Japanese nationals.

In the other cases, however, the basis under the Code for adjudicatory jurisdiction was manifest. The courts dismissed the actions in both, expressly conceding that adjudicatory jurisdiction could be justified under the Code rules. The decisions in these two cases are, I submit, exceptional. A close examination reveals factors that persuaded the courts in both that adjudication in Japan was less appropriate than elsewhere. In effect, the courts in both cases transformed the *Goto v. Malaysia Airline* decision into an approach that allows Japanese judges to dismiss actions where an alternative forum already exists in which the plaintiff's interests can be fully protected.

Greenlines Shipping Co., Ltd. v. California First Bank involved a damage action brought against a California bank with an office in Japan based on an alleged tort committed outside of Japan; however, the bank had a general forum in Japan and the injury could be said to have occurred at least in part in Japan. The court nevertheless dismissed the case on the grounds that exercise of adjudicatory jurisdiction would be inappropriate under the principles of *jōri*. The case arose out of an acrimonious California divorce in which the wife claimed ownership to funds for an account under a separate name. Although the bank had received notice that the account was being contested, it subsequently remitted the funds as requested by the account holder to an account in its Tokyo branch. The wife then sought to enforce her claim, causing a vessel chartered by the plaintiff to be arrested in a California port. The plaintiff brought the suit in Japan to recover for the alleged tort committed by the bank in improperly remitting the funds.

Similarly, in *Mukoda v. The Boeing Company*, the court emphasized that Boeing maintained an office in Japan and could be sued in Japan based on the general forum provisions of the Code. The case involved tort claims by the successors and family of Kuniko Mukoda, a well-known writer, who had died in an airplane accident in Taiwan. In dismissing the action, however, the court explained that it was following the lead of a court in the U.S. that had declined to exercise jurisdiction in favor of adjudication of the claims in Taiwan based on the U.S. common law *forum non conveniens* doctrine. The plaintiffs appealed the Tokyo High Court, but a settlement was reached before the appeal was adjudicated.

Of all four of the cases *R.W. Starge & Company v. King Kong Li* seems to be the easiest to explain. The facts only barely provided grounds for adjudicatory jurisdiction under the Code. It involved a non-resident plaintiff and individual defendant, neither of whom had any connection with Japan. Inasmuch as the argument for jurisdiction rested under the facts on a solid claim of joint liability with a defendant with a general forum in Japan, the court had little choice under a strict application of Code rules. To dismiss, the court had to find refuge in the "special circumstances" of the case—to no one's real dismay. As noted, Li's employer in the companion case was subsequently found to be liable. In contrast, in *Greenlines Shipping Co., Ltd. v. California First Bank* at least the defendant, unlike Mr. Li, did have a general forum in Japan. However, neither the plaintiff nor its claim against the defendant had any significant relationship to Japan. Were the courts to exercise jurisdiction under the Code in either case, Japanese adjudicatory jurisdiction would be deemed to extend to any suit against any party so long as even *a de minimis* basis for jurisdiction existed under the Code even where litigation over the claim could or was actually available in another action, either in Japan or elsewhere. Both cases thus draw a line. The claim, or the parties, or both should have some meaningful nexus with Japan, but that nexus is to be defined by the Code rules. The resort to "special circumstances" is thus essentially prophylactic, to be used only sparingly on a case by case basis to prevent manifestly inappropriate exercises of jurisdiction in cases with only *a de minimis* basis under the Code. Such cases are rare. Few non-Japanese plaintiffs sue in Japan to enforce claims unrelated to Japan when alternative fora are available.

The judges deciding *Masaki Bussan K. K. v. Nanka Seimen Company* and *Mukoda v. The Boeing Company* seemed to have had a more ambitious agenda. Both cases involved claims by Japanese nationals domiciled in Japan in actions where the basis for jurisdiction under the Code and case law was manifest. The former is the only case in which a Japanese court has dismissed an action brought by a Japanese national because of parallel litigation abroad. At the time the case was decided some were arguing, as noted, that the revised Code include permissive *lis alibi pendens* provisions to allow Japanese courts to stay parallel proceedings filed subsequently in Japan. Indeed, the judges deciding the case expressly acknowledged that they sought to create some limits to parallel litigation in Japan. The judgment thus illustrates the capacity of Japanese courts to create such doctrines through decisional law. But the decision cannot be considered to be viable as case law today. The holding in *Masaki Bussan K. K.* was effectively rejected in the legislative process and subsequent cases in which the courts have in fact adjudicated defensive actions to confirm the non-liability of Japanese defendants in response to parallel tort and contract actions abroad. Moreover, the courts have been able quite successfully to screen out unwarranted parallel actions on the basis of the Code provisions themselves.

Mukoda v. The Boeing Company can similarly be viewed as an attempt to create new case law—in this case, an approach analogous to the American *forum non conveniens* doctrine. On this question as well, several influential scholars had urged reform. As noted by Ishiguro, who opposes the adoption of an approach that gives the courts so much discretion, the approach used in *Mukoda* parallels developments in German law; to read into *jōri* or "special circumstances" principles the courts could use to deny jurisdiction despite a basis under the Code. However, no court has since accepted the invitation. Most telling is *Goto v. Malaysia Airline* itself. And prior cases leave little room for any case law development in that direction. The 1987 decision in *Inoue v. ABIAN-CO Airlines* has been noted previously. A more recent decision with an opposing result was the 1987 case against Korean Airlines arising out of the downing of the Korean Airlines' commercial flight by a Soviet fighter in 1983. The court agreed to adjudicate the claims in that case despite the fact that the plaintiffs had filed similar actions in both Canada and the United States.

CONCLUSION

Since *Goto v. Malaysia Airline* Japan's judges have developed what appears to be a widespread consensus on the limits of their adjudicatory jurisdiction in transnational litigation. In effect, the Fujita view prevails with a caveat. With the notable exception of actions involving the family court and domestic relations, subject to separate procedural rules and case law, in all other civil litigation the rules of the Code of Civil Procedure apply and define the court's jurisdiction. The courts thus do not exercise jurisdiction unless the requirements of the general forum, or special forum rules, or both are satisfied. In the rare case where only *de minimus* grounds for jurisdiction exist, where there is little if any other nexus with Japan by the parties or the cause of action, and relief appears to be available to the plaintiff in another forum, Japanese courts have, and may again, refuse to adjudicate, pointing to such "special circumstances" to support their denial.

Questions and Comments

1. Given the *Malaysia Airlines* case and the discussion by Professor Haley, do you think there would be jurisdiction in Japan over Celsius based on the revised facts? What questions might you have for a Japanese lawyer? How might you best go about finding Japanese counsel in order to pursue these questions and to engage local counsel for litigation if that is necessary?

2. What are the similarities between jurisdiction over foreign defendants in Japan and in Germany? What are the differences? Given this comparison, what advice might you give U.S. businesses facing potential litigation in either of these countries? How would that advice compare with advice to a foreign business facing potential litigation in the United States?

3. Consider the discussion of the concept of *jōri*, in *Goto v. Malaysia Airline* and in the Haley comment. How is that concept similar to or different from the concept of reasonableness applied by the U.S. Supreme Court in applying the Due Process Clauses to questions of jurisdiction over a foreign defendant? If they differ, which is the better approach in a global business environment?

PART C.   U.S. JUDICIAL ASSISTANCE IN FOREIGN PROCEEDINGS

DAVID EPSTEIN, JEFFREY L. SNYDER, & CHARLES S. BALDWIN, IV, INTERNATIONAL LITIGATION: A GUIDE TO JURISDICTION, PRACTICE, AND STRATEGY
10.13–10.15 (3d ed. 2000).*

§ 10.13   PROVIDING INTERNATIONAL JUDICIAL ASSISTANCE TO FOREIGN COURTS

Litigants in foreign countries which are parties to the Hague Evidence Convention may obtain evidence in the United States pursuant to the treaty procedures. Usually, the letter of request is transmitted from the requesting court or the foreign central authority directly to the United States Central Authority. Hague Evidence Convention, Art. 2. The Central Authority in the United States for processing letters of

* Reprinted with permission of Transnational Publishers, Inc.

request in civil and commercial matters is the Civil Division of the Department of Justice. After reviewing the request, the Department of Justice transmits the letter of request for execution to the United States Attorney for the judicial district in which the witness resides or in which the evidence is located.

Federal courts provide international judicial assistance to foreign courts pursuant to 28 U.S.C. § 1782. The statute provides, in pertinent part, as follows:

§ 1782. Assistance to foreign and international tribunals and to litigants before such tribunals.

(a) The district court of the district in which a person resides or is found may order him to give his testimony or statement or to produce a document or other thing for use in a proceeding in a foreign or international tribunal. The order may be made pursuant to a letter rogatory issued, or request made, by a foreign or international tribunal or upon the application of any interested person ...

A person may not be compelled to give his testimony or statement or to produce a document or other thing in violation of any legally applicable privilege.

(b) This chapter does not preclude a person within the States from voluntarily giving his testimony or statement, or producing a document or other thing, for use in a proceeding in a foreign or international tribunal before any person and in any manner acceptable to him.

The Justice Department's Civil Division acts as the transmitting office for letters of request received pursuant to 28 U.S.C. § 1782 from foreign countries which are not signatories to the Hague Convention. The letters of request are processed in the same manner as letters of request under the Hague Evidence Convention, i.e., to the appropriate United States attorney's office.

Under 28 U.S.C. § 1781, the Department of State has the power to receive letters rogatory from foreign or international tribunals and to forward them to appropriate courts or officials in the United States for execution. Requests are received from foreign countries pursuant to section 1781 which require, as part of their judicial procedures, that letters rogatory be transmitted via diplomatic channels. Letters rogatory which are referred to the Department of Justice through diplomatic channels under section 1781(a)(1) are honored on the basis of international comity. Requests received under the Hague Evidence Convention are executed as United States treaty obligations. The Department of State forwards all letters of request to the Department of Justice for execution.

[Effective June 1, 2003, Process Forwarding International (PFI), a private organization, entered into a five year contract with the U.S. Department of Justice to perform the duties as Central Authority. Thus, those duties are managed by PFI for purposes of The Hague Service

Convention, the Inter–American Convention on Letters Rogatory, and for letters rogatory from non-convention countries.]

Once the request is transmitted to the appropriate United States Attorney, that office is encouraged, whenever possible, to obtain a witness' testimony through voluntary cooperation. *See* 28 U.S.C.A. § 1782(b) (1997). This is because in the United States, as opposed to the practice in civil law countries, district court judges do not themselves examine witnesses as part of their judicial function. If a witness agrees, the testimony is furnished in affidavit form and no court order is required. This voluntary procedure, authorized under section 1782(b), is used in the majority of cases. In order to conform to procedures in civil law countries, U.S. Attorneys do not use court stenographers or prepare verbatim transcripts unless requested to do so by the requesting court. The transcript and all pertinent documents, together with bills for any fees or expenses, are forwarded to the Department of Justice for return to the requesting country.

If the witness refuses to cooperate voluntarily, or when documents cannot be obtained without a subpoena, application may be made to the district court for an order under section 1782(a) compelling the witness to appear or compelling the production of documents or other things. Applications for such orders are made ex parte. The order usually designates as "commissioner" a U.S. Magistrate or the Assistant U.S. Attorney. The commissioner subpoenas the witness and advises the witness of the nature of the proceedings and any applicable rights and privileges. It should be noted that under section 1782(a), a person may not be compelled to give testimony in violation of any legally applicable privilege. Article 11 of the Hague Evidence Convention similarly provides that the person examined may claim a privilege not to give the evidence under the law of the state of execution or under the law of the state of origin. Art. 11. The requesting party should specify the privilege under the law of the state of origin in the Letter of Request and, for convenience of the witness, attach translated copies of the privilege to the request. The commissioner records the witness' answers to the questions and certifies the transcript.

§ 10.14 DEFENSES TO REQUESTS FOR JUDICIAL ASSISTANCE TO FOREIGN COURTS

A party against whom the requested information is to be used has standing to challenge the validity of the request on the theory that it is not authorized by or exceeds section 1782's provisions. For example, it has been held that requests for international judicial assistance pursuant to section 1782 are an incorrect vehicle to enforce a foreign judgment. This statute has been interpreted to apply to criminal as well as civil proceedings. Under section 1782, testimony may be taken in compliance with foreign practice and procedure and used against the witness in that proceeding. If the court fails to prescribe the procedure, the provisions of the Federal Rules of Civil Procedure are to be followed, regardless of whether the foreign proceeding is civil or criminal in nature.

Section 1782 authorizes wide latitude to courts to provide assistance to foreign courts, but does not require discovery assistance. *Intel Corp. v. Advanced Micro Devices, Inc.*, 124 S.Ct. 2466 (2004). In *Intel* the Supreme Court extended the definition of "for use in foreign or international tribunals" to foreign administrative and quasi-judicial proceedings. The Supreme Court recognized the broad range of discovery authorized under Section 1782. In this connection, the Court determined that discovery assistance was not limited for use in foreign proceedings that are "pending" or "imminent", but may be provided where the proceeding is "within reasonable contemplation." Finally, a party to a foreign proceeding cannot use Section 1782 to obtain documents held by a person outside of the United States.

§ 10.15   WHO MAY REQUEST INTERNATIONAL JUDICIAL ASSISTANCE IN U.S. COURTS

Section 1782 authorizes an "interested person" as well as a foreign tribunal to request judicial assistance. The request can be made on behalf of foreign officials or actual litigants. In *Intel* the Court emphasized that the definition of "interested person" was not limited to parties but included those with an interest in obtaining judicial assistance.

Section 1782 is freely available to persons seeking international judicial assistance and is not dependent upon a finding of reciprocity in the foreign procedure prior to issuance of the discovery order requested by a foreign litigant. Nor is issuance of the order by the district court pursuant to section 1782 predicated upon the ultimate admissibility of evidence in the foreign jurisdiction. In *Intel*, the Supreme Court interpreted Section 1782 as not containing a "discoverability" requirement–a requirement that no Section 1782 order could be granted unless the material sought would be discoverable in the foreign jurisdiction in which it was to be used. Under this reasoning, a United States party involved in litigation in a foreign country with limited pretrial discovery would be placed at a substantial disadvantage vis-à-vis the foreign party who has gained access to unlimited discovery under section 1782. These courts have further reasoned that foreign litigants may not use section 1782 to circumvent foreign law and procedure.

The district court is not required to grant a Section 1782 discovery application. In *Intel*, the Court noted that relevant factors that bear consideration in ruling on a 1782 request include whether the person from whom discovery is sought is a participant in the foreign proceeding. The Court noted that non-participants in the foreign proceeding usually have greater need for judicial assistance since foreign courts could order parties to produce evidence. Courts may also consider the nature and character of the foreign tribunal as well as the receptivity of the foreign government or the court to the judicial assistance sought. Other pertinent considerations include whether the request conceals an attempt to circumvent foreign proof-gathering restrictions in the foreign country or is unduly intrusive or burdensome.

Requests for assistance under section 1782 incorporate by reference the scope of discovery permitted by the Federal Rules of Civil Procedure. Thus, assistance may be denied where the information sought was "unreasonably cumulative" under Rule 26(b)(2) of the Federal Rules of Civil Procedure.

INTEL CORPORATION v. ADVANCED MICRO DEVICES, INC.

United States Supreme Court, 2004.
542 U.S. 241, 124 S.Ct. 2466, 159 L.Ed.2d 355.

Justice Ginsburg delivered the opinion of the Court.

This case concerns the authority of federal district courts to assist in the production of evidence for use in a foreign or international tribunal. In the matter before us, respondent Advanced Micro Devices, Inc. filed an antitrust complaint against petitioner Intel Corporation (Intel) with the Directorate–General for Competition (DG–Competition) of the Commission of the European Communities (European Commission or Commission). In pursuit of that complaint, AMD applied to the United States District Court for the Northern District of California, invoking 28 U.S.C. 1782(a), for an order requiring Intel to produce potentially relevant documents. Section 1782(a) provides that a federal district court "may order" a person "resid[ing]" or "found" in the district to give testimony or produce documents "for use in a proceeding in a foreign or international tribunal ... upon the application of any interested person."

Concluding that 1782(a) did not authorize the requested discovery, the District Court denied AMD's application. The Court of Appeals for the Ninth Circuit reversed that determination and remanded the case, instructing the District Court to rule on the merits of AMD's application. In accord with the Court of Appeals, we hold that the District Court had authority under 1782(a) to entertain AMD's discovery request. The statute, we rule, does not categorically bar the assistance AMD seeks: (1) A complainant before the European Commission, such as AMD, qualifies as an "interested person" within 1782(a)'s compass: (2) the Commission is a 1782(a) "tribunal" when it acts as a first instance decisionmaker; (3) the "proceeding" for which discovery is sought under 1782(a) must be in reasonable contemplation, but need not be "pending" or "imminent"; and (4) 1782(a) contains no threshold requirement that evidence sought from a federal district court would be discoverable under the law governing the foreign proceeding. We caution, however, that 1782(a) authorizes, but does not require, a federal district court to provide judicial assistance to foreign or international tribunals or to "interested 'person[s]' " in proceedings abroad. Whether such assistance is appropriate in this case is a question yet unresolved. To guide the district Court on remand, we suggest considerations relevant to the disposition of that question.

* * *

AMD's complaint alleged that Intel, in violation of European competition law, had abused its dominant position in the European market through loyalty rebates, exclusive purchasing agreements with manufacturers and retailers, price discrimination, and standard–setting cartels

... After the DG–Competition declined to seek judicial assistance in the United States, AMD, pursuant to 1782(a), petitioned the District Court for the Northern District of California for an order directing Intel to produce documents discovered [in connection with other litigation in the U.S.]. AMD asserted that it sought the materials in connection with the complaint it had filed with the European Commission.

* * *

We take up next the foreign-discoverability rule on which lower courts have divided: Does 1782(a) categorically bar a district court from ordering production of documents when the foreign tribunal or the "interested person" would not be able to obtain the documents if they were located in the foreign jurisdiction?

We note at the outset, and count it significant, that 1782 expressly shields privileged material: "A person may not be compelled to give his testimony or statement or to produce a document or other thing in violation of any legally applicable privilege." ... Beyond shielding material safeguarded by an applicable privilege, however, nothing in the text of 1782 limits a district court's production-order authority to materials that could be discovered in the foreign jurisdiction if the materials were located there. "If Congress had intended to impose such a sweeping restriction on the district court's discretion, at a time when it was enacting liberalizing amendments to the statute, it would have included statutory language to that effect." [citations omitted].

Nor does 1782(a)'s legislative history suggest that Congress intended to impose a blanket foreign-discoverability rule on the provision of assistance under 1782(a). The Senate Report observes in this regard that 1782(a) "leaves the issuance of an appropriate order to the discretion of the court which, in proper cases, may refuse to issue an order or may impose conditions it deems desirable." S.Rep. No. 1580, at 7, U.S.Code Cong. & Admin.News 1964, pp. 3782, 3788.

Intel raises two policy concerns in support of a foreign-discoverability limitation on 1782(a) aid—avoiding offense to foreign governments, and maintaining parity between litigants ... While comity and parity concerns may be important as touchstones for a district court's exercise of discretion in particular cases, they do not permit our insertion of a generally applicable foreign-discoverability rule into the text of 1782(a).

We question whether foreign governments would in fact be offended by a domestic prescription permitting, but not requiring, judicial assistance. A foreign nation may limit discovery within its domain for reasons peculiar to its own legal practices, culture, or traditions—reasons that do not necessarily signal objection to aid from United States federal courts ... When the foreign tribunal would readily accept relevant information discovered in the United States, application of a foreign-discoverability rule would be senseless. The rule in that situation would serve only to thwart 1782(a)'s objective to assist foreign tribunals in obtaining relevant information that the tribunals may find useful but, for reasons having no bearing on international comity, they cannot obtain under their own laws.

Concerns about maintaining parity among adversaries in litigation likewise do not provide a sound basis for a cross-the-board foreign discoverability rule. When information is sought by an "interested person," a district could condition relief upon that person's reciprocal exchange of information ... Moreover, the foreign tribunal can place conditions on its acceptance of the information to maintain whatever measure of parity it concludes is appropriate.

We also reject Intel's suggestion that a 1782(a) applicant must show that United States law would allow discovery in domestic litigation analogous to the foreign proceeding... Section 1782 is a provision for assistance to tribunals abroad. It does not direct United States courts to engage in comparative analysis to determine whether analogous proceedings exist here. Comparisons of that order can be fraught with danger. For example, we have in the United States no close analogue to the European Commission regime under which AMD is not free to mount its own case in the Court of First Instance or the European Court of Justice, but can participate only as complainant, an "interested person," in Commission-steered proceedings ...

... [T]he judgment of the Court of Appeals for the Ninth Circuit is *Affirmed*.

Questions and Comments

1. What kinds of judicial assistance may be requested if an action is filed against Celsius in the United Kingdom, Germany, or Japan? How might Celsius prepare for the possibilities? Will they be able to challenge any requests successfully?

2. The above materials indicate that the United States is quite liberal in providing assistance to courts in other countries. Should this be the case? Should the U.S. provide such assistance without by treaty requiring reciprocity in the other country?

3. Several courts subsequent to the Supreme Court's decision in *Intel* have extended the scope of Section 1782 to include foreign arbitral proceedings. In *In re Roz Trading Ltd.*, 469 F.Supp.2d 1221 (N.D.Ga. 2006), the court determined that an international commercial arbitral body in Austria was a "tribunal" within the meaning of Section 1782. The court relied on comments from *Intel*, in which the Court, quoting from a law review article, stated that "the term 'tribunal' included investigating magistrates, and administrative and *arbitral tribunals*." [Italics added]. The court concluded in *Roz Trading* that the arbitral body was a "first instance decision-maker similar to the quasi-judicial EU Commission involved in *Intel*" and hence should be given the same status as a tribunal under the Supreme Court's rationale. Cases decided prior to *Intel* have rejected the application of 1782 to foreign arbitral proceedings. See *National Broadcasting Co., Inc. v. Bear Stearns & Co.*, 165 F.3d 184 (2d Cir. 1999); *Republic of Kazakhstan v. Biedermann*, 168 F.3d 880 (5th Cir. 1999). Should foreign arbitral proceedings be considered as tribunals of "first instance" decision making similar to litigation proceedings? Does this interpretation affect present practice and procedure for evidence-gathering under the Federal Arbitration Act?

4. The Court in *Intel* emphasized the lower courts' broad discretion to grant or reject Section 1782 applications and impose necessary conditions on

any exercise of their authority. The Court noted that the need for assistance was generally greater as to non-parties than parties to the foreign proceeding. According to the Court in *Intel* the District Court should also take into account the nature of the foreign tribunal, the character of the foreign proceeding, and the receptivity of the foreign court or government to U.S. judicial assistance. On remand in *Intel,* the court denied assistance on the ground that none of the factors noted by the Court in determining the Section 1782 request had been satisfied. *Advanced Micro Devices v. Intel Corp.,* 2004 WL 2282320 (N.D.Cal.). In *Schmitz v. Bernstein Liebhard & Lifshitz, LLP,* 376 F.3d 79 (2d Cir. 2004), the Court of Appeals for the Second Circuit, in affirming denial of the request, emphasized the German government's opposition to the request on grounds that the information sought would impede an ongoing criminal investigation in the foreign country.

Part Four

RECOGNITION AND ENFORCEMENT OF FOREIGN JUDGMENTS

Chapter 6

RECOGNITION AND ENFORCEMENT OF FOREIGN JUDGMENTS IN THE UNITED STATES

PROBLEM 6.1   BRINGING THE PROBLEM 5.2 GERMAN JUDGMENT TO THE UNITED STATES

SECTION I.   THE SETTING

The basic facts in this Problem are the same as those in Problem 5.2:

Celsius Manufacturing, Inc. (Celsius), a Delaware corporation, has its principal place of business in Pittsburgh, Pennsylvania. Celsius manufactures induction molding devices (IMDs) used in the further manufacture of plastic products. In October 2007, Celsius demonstrated its IMDs at a trade fair in London, where a purchasing agent for Plastic Maker GmbH ("Plastic Maker"), of Munich, Germany, became interested in the product. At the trade fair, Plastic Maker submitted a purchase order to Celsius, offering to purchase 1,000 IMDs at $400 per unit, "terms c.i.f. London," to be shipped in January 2008. The President of Celsius responded while she was still in London with a letter in which she acknowledged receipt of the purchase order and accepted all the terms and conditions of the offer. Neither the purchase order form nor the letter of acceptance contained either a choice of law or a choice of forum clause.

Plastic Maker wired Celsius the entire $400,000 purchase price on January 3, 2008, and the IMDs were shipped on January 6, 2008 and arrived in London on January 28, where they were unloaded to a warehouse owned and operated by Plastic Maker. Plastic Maker had intended to redistribute the IMDs to its facilities in Germany, The Netherlands, and Spain. Upon receipt of the IMDs, Plastic Maker informed Celsius that the IMDs did not conform to the quality of the product demonstrated at the London trade fair and that Plastic Maker was rejecting them. Plastic Maker informed Celsius that it was holding the IMDs at Plastic Maker's London warehouse, awaiting further instructions concerning their return or disposal.

All experts who have been contacted on the matter agree that the goods are in fact non-conforming, and unsuitable for the use intended by Plastic Maker. Plastic Maker is ready to sue for breach of contract, demanding return of the purchase price, on the basis of this nonconformity of the goods. Plastic Maker has found substitute goods at a cost of $500,000, and also intends to sue for the added cost of obtaining replacement goods.

Variation 1:

Assume further that Plastic Maker has brought suit in Germany and that the German court has duly granted judgment against Celsius. Celsius has no assets in Germany. All of its assets are in Pennsylvania.

Variation 2:

There have been published allegations by both Celsius and Plastic Maker in the trade press in Germany and the United States in which they each challenge the veracity and fair dealing of the other. Suppose also that in Plastic Maker's German contract action against Celsius, Plastic Maker alleged libel and obtained a judgment including 200,000 Euros damages on the libel claim.

SECTION II. FOCUS OF CONSIDERATION

The problem now is to determine the value of the judgment generated by the German litigation. This will depend on the ability of the German plaintiff to enforce the judgment in the United States, where the defendant has assets.

SECTION III. READINGS, QUESTIONS AND COMMENTS

PART A. SISTER STATE JUDGMENTS: THE FULL FAITH AND CREDIT CLAUSE

Article IV of the U.S. Constitution provides that, "Full Faith and Credit shall be given in each State to the public Acts, Records, and judicial Proceedings of every other State...." One result of this provision is a common market for judgments within the United States, allowing a judgment from one U.S. state to be taken and enforced rather easily in any other U.S. state. As the Supreme Court stated in *Underwriters National Assurance Co. v. North Carolina Guaranty Assn.*, 455 U.S. 691, 703–04, 102 S.Ct. 1357, 71 L.Ed.2d 558 (1982),

> The concept of full faith and credit is central to our system of jurisprudence. Ours is a union of States, each having its own judicial system capable of adjudicating the rights and responsibilities of the parties brought before it. Given this structure, there is always a risk that two or more States will exercise their power over the same case or controversy, with the uncertainty, confusion, and delay that

necessarily accompany relitigation of the same issue . . . . . [I]n order to fulfill this constitutional mandate, "the judgment of a state court should have the same credit, validity, and effect, in every other court of the United States, which it had in the state where it was pronounced."

The Full Faith and Credit clause precludes any inquiry into the merits of the cause of action, the logic or consistency of the decision, or the validity of the legal principles on which the judgment is based.[1] While a second court may refuse recognition if the originating court lacked jurisdiction, the principles of issue preclusion inherent in the Full Faith and Credit clause apply to questions of jurisdiction as well as to other issues. Thus, if the originating court ruled that it had jurisdiction, that ruling is given full faith and credit by the recognizing court.

Even though the language of the Full Faith and Credit clause states that each "State" shall accord full faith and credit to the acts of each other "State," the clause has been applied to encompass recognition within the entire state-federal system.[2] Thus, a judgment rendered in any state or federal court in the United States is entitled to full recognition in any other state or federal court in the United States.

PART B. THE COMITY APPROACH TO ENFORCEMENT OF FOREIGN NATION JUDGMENTS

The Full Faith and Credit clause of the U.S. Constitution does *not* apply to foreign nation judgments. Nor is the matter governed by treaty or federal statute. Thus, the enforcement of judgments in the United States traditionally has been governed by state common law, now replaced in a majority of the states by a uniform act, the Uniform Foreign Money–Judgments Recognition Act, 13 U.L.A. 263 (1986). Even under the uniform act, two Supreme Court cases serve to define this area. In the 1895 case of *Hilton v. Guyot*, 159 U.S. 113, 16 S.Ct. 139, 40 L.Ed. 95 (1895), a French plaintiff sought enforcement of a French judgment against a U.S. defendant. Justice Gray's opinion for the Court established the comity analysis that continues to provide the foundation for judgment recognition practice in the United States.

HILTON v. GUYOT

Supreme Court of the United States, 1895.
159 U.S. 113, 16 S.Ct. 139, 40 L.Ed. 95.

[An action was brought in the Circuit Court for the Southern District of New York by the liquidator and the surviving members of a French firm against two U.S. citizens who had been trading as partners. The plaintiffs had recovered a judgment in the French courts upon which nearly $200,000 remained unpaid. Defendants' answer denied that they were

---

1. Jack H. Friedenthal, Mary Kay Kane & Arthur R. Miller, Civil Procedure 708–713 (4th ed. 2005).

2. *See* Stephen B. Burbank, *Interjurisdictional Preclusion, Full Faith and Credit and Federal Common Law: A General Approach*, 71 Cornell L. Rev. 733 (1986).

indebted to plaintiffs and asserted that the French judgment was procured by fraud. Defendants also filed a bill in equity to enjoin the prosecution of the action. The plaintiffs prevailed in both cases and defendants, by writ of error and appeal, brought the case to the Supreme Court.]

MR. JUSTICE GRAY, after stating the case, delivered the opinion of the court

* * *

International law, in its widest and most comprehensive sense,—including not only questions of right between nations, governed by what has been appropriately called the "law of nations," but also questions arising under what is usually called "private international law," or the "conflict of laws," and concerning the rights of persons within the territory and dominion of one nation, by reason of acts, private or public, done within the dominions of another nation,—is part of our law, and must be ascertained and administered by the courts of justice as often as such questions are presented in litigation between man and man, duly submitted to their determination.

The most certain guide, no doubt, for the decision of such questions is a treaty or a statute of this country. But when, as is the case here, there is no written law upon the subject, the duty still rests upon the judicial tribunals of ascertaining and declaring what the law is, whenever it becomes necessary to do so, in order to determine the rights of parties to suits regularly brought before them. In doing this, the courts must obtain such aid as they can from judicial decisions, from the works of jurists and commentators, and from the acts and usages of civilized nations.

* * *

No law has any effect, of its own force, beyond the limits of the sovereignty from which its authority is derived. The extent to which the law of one nation, as put in force within its territory, whether by executive order, by legislative act, or by judicial decree, shall be allowed to operate within the dominion of another nation, depends upon what our greatest jurists have been content to call "the comity of nations." Although the phrase has been often criticized, no satisfactory substitute has been suggested.

"Comity," in the legal sense, is neither a matter of absolute obligation, on the one hand, nor of mere courtesy and good will, upon the other. But it is the recognition which one nation allows within its territory to the legislative, executive, or judicial acts of another nation, having due regard both to international duty and convenience, and to the rights of its own citizens, or of other persons who are under the protection of its laws * * *.

Chief Justice Taney, * * * speaking for this court, while Mr. Justice Story was a member of it, and largely adopting his words, said * * *

"The comity thus extended to other nations is no impeachment of sovereignty. It is the voluntary act of the nation by which it is offered, and is inadmissible when contrary to its policy, or prejudicial to its interests. But it contributes so largely to promote justice between individuals, and to produce a friendly intercourse between the sovereignties to which they belong, that courts of justice have continually acted upon it as a part of the voluntary law of nations." "It is not the comity of the courts, but the comity of the nation, which is administered and ascertained in the same way, and guided by the same reasoning, by which all other principles of municipal law are ascertained and guided." *Bank v. Earle* (1839) 13 Pet. 519, 589; Story, Confl. Laws, § 38 * * *.

In order to appreciate the weight of the various authorities cited at the bar, it is important to distinguish different kinds of judgments. Every foreign judgment, of whatever nature, in order to be entitled to any effect, must have been rendered by a court having jurisdiction of the cause, and upon regular proceedings, and due notice. In alluding to different kinds of judgments, therefore, such jurisdiction, proceedings, and notice will be assumed. It will also be assumed that they are untainted by fraud, the effect of which will be considered later.

A judgment in rem, adjudicating the title to a ship or other movable property within the custody of the court, is treated as valid everywhere * * *.

Other judgments, not strictly in rem, under which a person has been compelled to pay money, are so far conclusive that the justice of the payment cannot be impeached in another country, so as to compel him to pay it again. For instance, a judgment in foreign attachment is conclusive, as between the parties, of the right to the property or money attached. * * *

Other foreign judgments which have been held conclusive of the matter adjudged were judgments discharging obligations contracted in the foreign country between citizens or residents thereof. * * *

The extraterritorial effect of judgments in personam, at law, or in equity may differ, according to the parties to the cause. A judgment of that kind between two citizens or residents of the country, and thereby subject to the jurisdiction in which it is rendered, may be held conclusive as between them everywhere. So, if a foreigner invokes the jurisdiction by bringing an action against a citizen, both may be held bound by a judgment in favor of either; and if a citizen sues a foreigner, and judgment is rendered in favor of the latter, both may be held equally bound. * * *

The effect to which a judgment, purely executory, rendered in favor of a citizen or resident of the country, in a suit there brought by him against a foreigner, may be entitled in an action thereon against the latter in his own country, as is the case now before us, presents a more difficult question, upon which there has been some diversity of opinion. * * *

The English cases [discussed in the omitted portion] have been stated with the more particularity and detail, because they directly bear upon the question, what was the English law, being then our own law, before the Declaration of Independence? They demonstrate that by that law, as generally understood, and as declared by Hardwicke, Mansfield, Buller, Camden, Eyre, and Ellenborough, and doubted by Kenyon only, a judgment recovered in a foreign country for a sum of money, when sued upon in England, was only prima facie evidence of the demand, and subject to be examined and impeached. * * *

The law upon this subject as understood in the United States at the time of their separation from the mother country was clearly set forth by Chief Justice Parsons, speaking for the supreme judicial court of Massachusetts, in 1813, and by Mr. Justice Story in his Commentaries on the Constitution of the United States, published in 1833. Both those eminent jurists declared that by the law of England the general rule was that foreign judgments were only prima facie evidence of the matter which they purported to decide; and that by the common law, before the American Revolution, all the courts of the several colonies and states were deemed foreign to each other, and consequently judgments rendered by any one of them were considered as foreign judgments, and their merits re-examinable in another colony, not only as to the jurisdiction of the court which pronounced them, but also as to the merits of the controversy, to the extent to which they were understood to be re-examinable in England. * * *

It was because of that condition of the law, as between the American colonies and states, that the United States, at the very beginning of their existence as a nation, ordained that full faith and credit should be given to the judgments of one of the states of the Union in the courts of another of those states. * * *

From this review of the authorities, it clearly appears that, at the time of the separation of this country from England, the general rule was fully established that foreign judgments in personam were prima facie evidence only, and not conclusive of the merits of the controversy between the parties. But the extent and limits of the application of that rule do not appear to have been much discussed, or defined with any approach to exactness, in England or America, until the matter was taken up by Chancellor Kent and by Mr. Justice Story. * * *

Mr. Justice Story, in his Commentaries on the Conflict of Laws, first published in 1834, after reviewing many English authorities, said: "The present inclination of the English courts seems to be to sustain the conclusiveness of foreign judgments,"—to which, in the second edition, in 1841, he added: 'Although, certainly, there yet remains no inconsiderable diversity of opinion among the learned judges of the different tribunals." * * *

He then proceeded to state his own view of the subject, on principle, saying: "It is, indeed, very difficult to perceive what could be done if a different doctrine were maintainable to the full extent of opening all the evidence and merits of the cause anew on a suit upon the foreign judgment. Some of the witnesses may be since dead; some of the vouchers may be lost or destroyed. The merits of the cause, as formerly before the court upon the whole evidence, may have been decidedly in favor of the judgment; upon a partial possession of the original evidence, they may now appear otherwise. Suppose a case purely sounding in damages, such as an action for an assault, for slander, for conversion of property, for a malicious prosecution, or for a criminal conversation; is the defendant to be at liberty to retry the whole merits, and to make out, if he can, a new case upon new evidence? Or is the court to review the former decision, like a court of appeal, upon the old evidence? In a case of covenant, or of debt, or of a breach of contract, are all the circumstances to be re-examined anew? If they are, by what laws and rules of evidence and principles of justice is the validity of the original judgment to be tried? Is the court to open the judgment, and to proceed ex aequo et bono? Or is it to administer strict law, and stand to the doctrines of the local administration of justice? Is it to act upon the rules of evidence acknowledged in its own jurisprudence, or upon those of the foreign jurisprudence? These and many more questions might be put to show the intrinsic difficulties of the subject. Indeed, the rule that the judgment is to be prima facie evidence for the plaintiff would be a mere delusion if the defendant might still question it by opening all or any of the original merits on his side; for, under such circumstances, it would be equivalent to granting a new trial. It is easy to understand that the defendant may be at liberty to impeach the original justice of the judgment by showing that the court had no jurisdiction, or that he never had any notice of the suit, or that it was procured by fraud, or that upon its face it is founded in mistake, or that it is irregular and bad by the local law, fori rei judicatae. To such an extent the doctrine is intelligible and practicable. Beyond this, the right to impugn the judgment is in legal effect the right to retry the merits of the original cause at large, and to put the defendant upon proving those merits." * * *

In view of all the authorities upon the subject, and of the trend of judicial opinion in this country and in England, following the lead of Kent and Story, we are satisfied that where there has been opportunity for a full and fair trial abroad before a court of competent jurisdiction, conducting the trial upon regular proceedings, after due citation or voluntary appearance of the defendant, and under a system of jurisprudence likely to secure an impartial administration of justice between the citizens of its own country and those of other countries, and there is nothing to show either prejudice in the court, or in the system of laws under which it was sitting, or fraud in procuring the judgment, or any other special reason why the comity of this nation should not allow it full effect, the merits of the case should not, in an action brought in this country upon the judgment, be tried afresh, as on a new trial or an appeal, upon the mere assertion of the party that the judgment was erroneous in law or in fact. The defendants, therefore, cannot be permitted, upon that general ground, to contest the validity or the effect of the judgment sued on.

But they have sought to impeach that judgment upon several other grounds, which require separate consideration.

It is objected that the appearance and litigation of the defendants in the French tribunals were not voluntary, but by legal compulsion, and, therefore, that the French courts never acquired such jurisdiction over the defendants that they should be held bound by the judgment. * * *

The present case is not one of a person traveling through or casually found in a foreign country. The defendants, although they were not citizens or residents of France, but were citizens and residents of the state of New York, and their principal place of business was in the city of New York, yet had a storehouse and an agent in Paris, and were accustomed to purchase large quantities of goods there, although they did not make sales in France. Under such circumstances, evidence that their sole object in appearing and carrying on the litigation in the French courts was to prevent property in their storehouse at Paris, belonging to them, and within the jurisdiction, but not in the custody, of those courts, from being taken in satisfaction of any judgment that might be recovered against them, would not, according to our law, show that those courts did not acquire jurisdiction of the persons of the defendants.

It is next objected that in those courts one of the plaintiffs was permitted to testify not under oath, and was not subjected to cross-examination by the opposite party, and that the defendants were therefore deprived of safeguards which are by our law considered essential to secure honesty and to detect fraud in a witness; and also that documents and papers were admitted in evidence, with which the defendants had no connection, and which would not be admissible under our own system of jurisprudence. But it having been shown by the plaintiffs, and hardly denied by the defendants, that the practice followed and the method of examining witnesses were according to the laws of France, we are not prepared to hold that the fact that the procedure in these respects differed from that of our own courts is, of itself, a sufficient ground for impeaching the foreign judgment. * * *

There is no doubt that both in this country, as appears by the authorities already cited, and in England, a foreign judgment may be impeached for fraud. * * *

It has often, indeed, been declared by this court that the fraud which entitles a party to impeach the judgment of one of our own tribunals must be fraud extrinsic to the matter tried in the cause, and not merely consist in false and fraudulent documents or testimony submitted to that tribunal, and the truth of which was contested before it and passed upon by it. * * *

But it is now established in England, by well-considered and strongly-reasoned decisions of the court of appeal, that foreign judgments may be impeached, if procured by false and fraudulent representations and testimony of the plaintiff, even if the same question of fraud was presented to and decided by the foreign court. * * *

But whether those decisions can be followed in regard to foreign judgments, consistently with our own decisions as to impeaching domestic judgments for fraud, it is unnecessary in this case to determine, because there is a distinct and independent ground upon which we are satisfied that the comity of our nation does not require us to give conclusive effect to the judgments of the courts of France; and that ground is the want of reciprocity, on the part of France, as to the effect to be given to the judgments of this and other foreign countries. * * *

The defendants, in their answer, cited the above provisions of the statutes of France, and alleged, and at the trial offered to prove, that by the construction given to these statutes by the judicial tribunals of France, when the judgments of tribunals of foreign countries against the citizens of France are sued upon in the courts of France, the merits of the controversies upon which those judgments are based are examined anew, unless a treaty to the contrary effect exists between the republic of France and the country in which such judgment is obtained (which is not the case between the republic of France and the United States), and that the tribunals of the republic of France give no force and effect, within the jurisdiction of that country, to the judgments duly rendered by courts of competent jurisdiction of the United States against citizens of France after proper personal service of the process of those courts has been made thereon in this country. We are of opinion that this evidence should have been admitted. . . . By the law of France, settled by a series of uniform decisions of the court of cassation, the highest judicial tribunal, for more than half a century, no foreign judgment can be rendered executory in France without a review of the judgment au fond (to the bottom), including the whole merits of the cause of action on which the judgment rests. * * *

[Here the opinion provides an elaborate discussion of the law of other nations, concluding that the general practice was to require reciprocity in the recognition of foreign judgments.]

It appears, therefore, that there is hardly a civilized nation on either continent which, by its general law, allows conclusive effect to an executory foreign judgment for the recovery of money. In France and in a few smaller states—Norway, Portugal, Greece, Monaco, and Haiti—the merits of the controversy are reviewed, as of course, allowing to the foreign judgment, at the most, no more effect than of being prima facie evidence of the justice of the claim. In the great majority of the countries on the continent of Europe,—in Belgium, Holland, Denmark, Sweden, Germany, in many cantons of Switzerland, in Russia and Poland, in Roumania, in Austria and Hungary (perhaps in Italy), and in Spain,—as well as in Egypt, in Mexico, and in a great part of South America, the judgment rendered in a foreign country is allowed the same effect only as the courts of that country allow to the judgments of the country in which the judgment in question is sought to be executed.

The prediction of Mr. Justice Story in section 618 of his Commentaries on the Conflict of Laws, already cited, has thus been fulfilled, and the rule of reciprocity has worked itself firmly into the structure of international jurisprudence.

The reasonable, if not the necessary, conclusion appears to us to be that judgments rendered in France, or in any other foreign country, by the laws of which our own judgments are reviewable upon the merits, are not entitled to full credit and conclusive effect when sued upon in this country, but are prima facie evidence only of the justice of the plaintiffs' claim.

In holding such a judgment, for want of reciprocity, not to be conclusive evidence of the merits of the claim, we do not proceed upon any theory of retaliation upon one person by reason of injustice done to another, but upon the broad ground that international law is founded upon mutuality and reciprocity, and that by the principles of international law recognized in most civilized nations, and by the comity of our own country, which it is our judicial duty to known and to declare, the judgment is not entitled to be considered conclusive.

By our law, at the time of the adoption of the constitution, a foreign judgment was considered as prima facie evidence, and not conclusive. There is no statute of the United States, and no treaty of the United States with France, or with any other nation, which has changed that law, or has made any provision upon the subject. It is not to be supposed that, if any statute or treaty had been or should be made, it would recognize as conclusive the judgments of any country, which did not give like effect to our own judgments. In the absence of statute or treaty, it appears to us equally unwarrantable to assume that the comity of the United States requires anything more.

If we should hold this judgment to be conclusive, we should allow it an effect to which, supposing the defendants' offers to be sustained by actual proof, it would, in the absence of a special treaty, be entitled in hardly any other country in Christendom, except the country in which it was rendered. * * *

[Both cases were reversed and the cause remanded for a new trial.]

Comment on *Hilton* in State Courts and Lower Federal Courts

The result in *Hilton v. Guyot* is today significantly affected by the Supreme Court's later decision in *Erie R.R. v. Tompkins*, 304 U.S. 64, 58 S.Ct. 817, 82 L.Ed. 1188 (1938). In *Erie*, the Court denied the existence of a general federal common law, and held that federal courts are to look to state common law (as well as state statutory law) to determine the substantive law applicable in diversity cases. This has been uniformly interpreted to mean that state law governs the recognition and enforcement of judgments in U.S. federal courts. Thus, U.S. law on this issue is a mix of state court decisions, federal court decisions interpreting or projecting state law, and statutes that present a relatively uniform set of rules developed largely from Justice Gray's comity analysis in *Hilton v. Guyot*. The following case is a good example of this process when the state law applicable in an action brought in federal district court for enforcement of a foreign judgment does not include an applicable statute.

SOMPORTEX LTD. v. PHILADELPHIA CHEWING GUM CORP.

United States Court of Appeals, Third Circuit, 1971.
453 F.2d 435, *cert. denied*, 405 U.S. 1017, 92 S.Ct. 1294, 31 L.Ed.2d 479 (1972).

ALDISERT, CIRCUIT JUDGE.

Several interesting questions are presented in this appeal from the district court's order granting summary judgment to enforce a default judgment entered by an English court. To resolve them, a complete recitation of the procedural history of this case is necessary.

This case has its genesis in a transaction between appellant, Philadelphia Chewing Gum Corporation, and Somportex Limited, a British corporation, which was to merchandise appellant's wares in Great Britain under the trade name "Tarzan Bubble Gum." According to the facts as alleged by appellant, there was a proposal which involved the participation of Brewster Leeds and Co., Inc., and M. S. International, Inc., third-party defendants in the court below. Brewster made certain arrangements with Somportex to furnish gum manufactured by Philadelphia; M. S. International, as agent for the licensor of the trade name "Tarzan," was to furnish the African name to the American gum to be sold in England. For reasons not relevant to our limited inquiry, the transaction never reached fruition.

Somportex filed an action against Philadelphia for breach of contract in the Queen's Bench Division of the High Court of England. Notice of the issuance of a Writ of Summons was served, in accordance with the rules and with the leave of the High Court, upon Philadelphia at its registered address in Havertown, Pennsylvania, on May 15, 1967. The extraterritorial service was based on the English version of long-arm statutes utilized by many American states.[3] Philadelphia then consulted

---

3. The English Statute provides:

(f) if the action begun by the Writ is brought against a Defendant not domiciled or ordinarily resident in Scotland to enforce, rescind, dissolve, annul or otherwise affect a contract, or to recover damages or obtain other relief in respect of the breach of a contract, being (in either case) a contract which—

(i) was made within the jurisdiction, or

(ii) was made by or through an Agent trading or residing within the Jurisdiction on behalf of a principal

trading or residing out of the jurisdiction, or

(iii) is by the terms, or by implication, governed by the English law;

(g) If the action begun by the Writ is brought against a Defendant not domiciled or ordinarily resident in Scotland or Northern Ireland, in respect of a breach committed within the Jurisdiction of a contract made within or out of Jurisdiction, and irrespective of the fact, if such be the case, that the breach was preceded or accompanied by a breach committed out of the Jurisdiction that rendered im-a firm of English solicitors, who, by letter of July 14, 1967, advised its Pennsylvania lawyers:

> I have arranged with the Solicitors for Somportex Limited that they will let me have a copy of their Affidavit and exhibits to that Affidavit which supported their application to serve out of the Jurisdiction. Subject to the contents of the Affidavit, and any further information that can be provided by Philadelphia Chewing Gum Corporation after we have had the opportunity of seeing the Affidavit, it may be possible to make an application to the Court for an Order setting the Writ aside. But for such an application to be successful we will have to show that on the facts the matter does not fall within the provision of (f) and (g) [of the long-arm statute, note 1, *supra*] referred to above. In the meantime we will enter a conditional Appearance to the Writ in behalf of Philadelphia Chewing Gum Corporation in order to preserve the status quo.

On August 9, 1967, the English solicitors entered a "conditional appearance to the Writ" and filed a motion to set aside the Writ of Summons. At a hearing before a Master on November 13, 1967, the solicitors appeared and disclosed that Philadelphia had elected not to proceed with the summons or to contest the jurisdiction of the English Court, but instead intended to obtain leave of court to withdraw appearance of counsel. The Master then dismissed Philadelphia's summons to set aside plaintiff's Writ of Summons. Four days later, the solicitors sought to withdraw their appearance as counsel for Philadelphia, contending that it was a conditional appearance only. On November 27, 1967, after a Master granted the motion, Somportex appealed. The appeal was denied after hearing before a single judge, but the Court of Appeal, reversing the decision of the Master, held that the appearance was unconditional and that the submission to the jurisdiction by Philadelphia was, therefore, effective. But the court let stand "the original order which was made by the master on Nov. 13 dismissing the application to set aside. The writ therefore will stand. On the other hand, if the American company would wish to appeal from the order of Nov. 13, I see no reason why the time should not be extended and they can argue that matter out at a later stage if they should so wish."

possible the performance of so much of the Contract as ought to have been performed within the Jurisdiction;

Cf. the Pennsylvania Statute authorizing service on a foreign corporation, which provides:

> For the purpose of determining jurisdiction of courts within this Commonwealth, the doing by any corporation in this Commonwealth of a series of similar acts for the purpose of thereby realizing pecuniary benefit or otherwise accomplishing an object, or doing a single act in this Commonwealth for such purpose, with the intention of thereby initiating a series of such acts, shall constitute "doing business". For the purposes of this subsection the shipping of merchandise directly or indirectly into or through this Commonwealth shall be considered the doing of such an act in this Commonwealth.

15 PA. STAT. ANN. § 2011, subd. C.

Pennsylvania decisional law has generously interpreted its long-arm statute. See state cases summarized in *Siders v. Upper Mississippi Towing Corp.*, 423 F.2d 535 (3d Cir.1970).

Thereafter, Philadelphia made a calculated decision: it decided to do nothing. It neither asked for an extension of time nor attempted in any way to proceed with an appeal from the Master's order dismissing its application to set aside the Writ. Instead, it directed its English solicitors to withdraw from the case. There being no appeal, the Master's order became final.

Somportex then filed a Statement of Claim which was duly served in accordance with English Court rules. In addition, by separate letter, it informed Philadelphia of the significance and effect of the pleading, the procedural posture of the case, and its intended course of action.

Philadelphia persisted in its course of inaction; it failed to file a defense. Somportex obtained a default judgment against it in the Queen's Bench Division of the High Court of Justice in England for the sum of £39,562.10 (approximately $94,000.00). The award reflected some $45,000.00 for loss of profit; $46,000.00 for loss of good will and $2,500.00 for costs, including attorneys' fees.

Thereafter, Somportex filed a diversity action in the court below, seeking to enforce the foreign judgment, and attached to the complaint a certified transcript of the English proceeding. The district court granted two motions which gave rise to this appeal: it dismissed the third-party complaints for failure to state a proper claim and it granted plaintiff's motion for summary judgment, F.R.C.P. 56(a).

* * *

Appellant presents a cluster of contentions supporting its major thesis that we should not extend hospitality to the English judgment. First, it contends, and we agree, that because our jurisdiction is based solely on diversity, "the law to be applied . . . is the law of the state," in this case, Pennsylvania law. *Erie R. Co. v. Tompkins* * * *

Pennsylvania distinguishes between judgments obtained in the courts of her sister states, which are entitled to full faith and credit, and those of foreign courts, which are subject to principles of comity. *In re Christoff's Estate*, 411 Pa. 419, 192 A.2d 737, *cert. denied*, 375 U.S. 965, 84 S.Ct. 483, 11 L.Ed. 2d 414 (1964).

Comity is a recognition which one nation extends within its own territory to the legislative, executive, or judicial acts of another. It is not a rule of law, but one of practice, convenience, and expediency. Although more than mere courtesy and accommodation, comity does not achieve the force of an imperative or obligation. Rather, it is a nation's expression of understanding which demonstrates due regard both to international duty and convenience and to the rights of persons protected by its own laws. Comity should be withheld only when its acceptance would be contrary or prejudicial to the interest of the nation called upon to give it effect.[17]

17. In *Hilton v. Guyot*, 159 U.S. 113, 16 S.Ct. 139, 40 L.Ed. 95 (1895), the Supreme Court spoke of the likelihood of reciprocity as a condition precedent to the recognition

Thus, the court in *Christoff*, acknowledged the governing standard enunciated in *Hilton v. Guyot*:

> When an action is brought in a court of this country by a citizen of a foreign country against one of our own citizens ... and the foreign judgment appears to have been rendered by a competent court, having jurisdiction of the cause and of the parties and upon due allegations and proofs, and opportunity to defend against them, and its proceedings are according to the course of a civilized jurisprudence, and are stated in a clear and formal record, the judgment is prima facie evidence, at least, of the truth of the matter adjudged; and it should be held conclusive upon the merits tried in the foreign court, unless some special ground is shown for impeaching the judgment, as by showing that it was affected by fraud or prejudice, or that by the principles of international law, and by the comity of our own country, it should not be given full credit and effect. It is by this standard, therefore, that appellant's arguments must be measured.

Appellant's contention that the district court failed to make an independent examination of the factual and legal basis of the jurisdiction of the English Court at once argues too much and says too little. The reality is that the court did examine the legal basis of asserted jurisdiction and decided the issue adversely to appellant.

Indeed, we do not believe it was necessary for the court below to reach the question of whether the factual complex of the contractual dispute permitted extraterritorial service under the English long-arm statute. In its opinion denying leave of defense counsel to withdraw, the Court of Appeal specifically gave Philadelphia the opportunity to have the factual issue tested before the courts; moreover, Philadelphia was allocated additional time to do just that. Lord Denning said: "... They can argue that matter out at a later stage if they should so wish." Three months went by with no activity forthcoming and then, as described by the district court, "[d]uring this three month period, defendant changed its strategy and, not wishing to do anything which might result in its submitting to the English Court's jurisdiction, decided to withdraw its appearance altogether." Under these circumstances, we hold that defendant cannot choose its forum to test the factual basis of jurisdiction. It

of comity. The doctrine has received no more than desultory acknowledgement. *Direction der Disconto–Gesellschaft v. United States Steel Corp.*, 300 F. 741, 747 (S.D.N.Y. 1924); *see also Banco Nacional de Cuba v. Sabbatino*, 376 U.S. 398, 411, 84 S.Ct. 923, 11 L.Ed.2d 804 (1964) (dictum). It has been rejected by the courts of New York, *Johnston v. Compagnie Generale Transatlantique*, 242 N.Y. 381, 152 N.E. 121 (N.Y. 1926), and by statute in California. See Reese, *The Status in this Country of Judgments Rendered Abroad*, 50 Col. L. Rev. 783, 790–93 (1950).

We agree with the district court that this issue of the enforceability of foreign judgments has not frequently been litigated in Pennsylvania, and the Court has not been cited to, nor has independent examination revealed any Pennsylvania cases which even intimate that a finding of reciprocity is an essential precondition to their enforcing a foreign judgment.

Somportex Limited v. Philadelphia Chewing Gum Corp., 318 F.Supp. 161, 168 (E.D.Pa. 1970).

was given, and it waived, the opportunity of making the adequate presentation in the English Court.

Additionally, appellant attacks the English practice wherein a conditional appearance attacking jurisdiction may, by court decision, be converted into an unconditional one. It cannot effectively argue that this practice constitutes "some special ground ... for impeaching the judgment," as to render the English judgment unwelcome in Pennsylvania under principles of international law and comity because it was obtained by procedures contrary or prejudicial to the host state. The English practice in this respect is identical to that set forth in both the Federal and Pennsylvania rules of civil procedure. F.R.C.P. 12(b)(2) provides the vehicle for attacking jurisdiction over the person, and, in *Orange Theatre Corp. v. Rayherstz Amusement Corp.*, 139 F.2d 871, 874 (3d Cir.1944), we said that Rule 12 "has abolished for the federal courts the age-old distinction between general and special appearances." * * * A challenge to jurisdiction must be asserted there by a preliminary objection raising a question of jurisdiction. * * *

Thus, we will not disturb the English Court's adjudication. That the English judgment was obtained by appellant's default instead of through an adversary proceeding does not dilute its efficacy. In the absence of fraud or collusion, a default judgment is as conclusive an adjudication between the parties as when rendered after answer and complete contest in the open courtroom. * * * The polestar is whether a reasonable method of notification is employed and reasonable opportunity to be heard is afforded to the person affected. * * *

English law permits recovery, as compensatory damages in breach of contract, of items reflecting loss of good will and costs, including attorneys' fees. These two items formed substantial portions of the English judgment. Because they are not recoverable under Pennsylvania law, appellant would have the foreign judgment declared unenforceable because it constitutes an " ... action on the foreign claim [which] could not have been maintained because contrary to the public policy of the forum," citing Restatement, Conflict of Laws, § 445.[24] We are satisfied with the district court's disposition of this argument:

> The Court finds that ... while Pennsylvania may not agree that these elements should be included in damages for breach of contract, the variance with Pennsylvania law is not such that the enforcement "tends clearly to injure the public health, the public morals, the public confidence in the purity of the administration of the law, or to

---

24. The limited scope of public policy as a controlling principle of Pennsylvania jurisprudence was underscored by Justice Stern in *Mamlin v. Genoe*, 340 Pa. 320, 325, 17 A.2d 407, 409 (1941):

"It is only when a given policy is so obviously for or against the public health, safety, morals or welfare that there is a virtual unanimity of opinion in regard to it, that a court may constitute itself the voice of the community in so declaring.... Familiar illustrations are those involving unreasonable restraints of marriage or of trade, collusive arrangements for obtaining divorces, suppression of bids for public contracts, interference with freedom of conscience or religion.... Only in the clearest cases, therefore, may a court make an alleged public policy the basis of judicial decision."

undermine that sense of security for individual rights, whether of personal liberty or of private property, which any citizen ought to feel, is against public policy." *Goodyear v. Brown*, 155 Pa. 514, 518, 26 A. 665, 666 (1893).

Finally, appellant contends that since "it maintains no office or employee in England and transacts no business within the country" there were no insufficient contacts there to meet the due process tests of *International Shoe*. It argues that, at best, "the only contact Philadelphia had with England was the negotiations allegedly conducted by an independent New York exporter by letter, telephone and telegram to sell Philadelphia's products in England." In *Hanson v. Denckla*, Chief Justice Warren said: "The application of [the requirement of contact] rule will vary with the quality and nature of the defendant's activity, but it is essential in each case that there be some act by which the defendant purposely avails itself of the privilege of conducting business within the forum State, thus invoking the benefits and protection of its laws." We have concluded that whether the New York exporter was an independent contractor or Philadelphia's agent was a matter to be resolved by the English Court. For the purpose of the constitutional argument, we must assume the proper agency relationship. So construed, we find his activity would constitute the "quality and nature of the defendant's activity" similar to that of the defendant in *McGee v. International Life Ins. Co.*, there held to satisfy due process requirements.

For the reasons heretofore rehearsed we will not disturb the English Court's adjudication of jurisdiction; we have deemed as irrelevant the default nature of the judgment; we have concluded that the English compensatory damage items do not offend Pennsylvania public policy; and hold that the English procedure comports with our standards of due process.

In sum, we find that the English proceedings met all the tests enunciated in *Christoff*. We are not persuaded that appellant met its burden of showing that the British "decree is so palpably tainted by fraud or prejudice as to outrage our sense of justice, or [that] the process of the foreign tribunal was invoked to achieve a result contrary to our laws of public policy or to circumvent our laws or public policy."

The judgment of the district court will be affirmed.

Comment on the Restatement of Foreign Relations Law §§ 481 and 482

In 1986, the American Law Institute adopted the Restatement (Third) of Foreign Relations Law, summarizing the common law rule on recognition and enforcement of foreign judgments in two sections:

§ 481.   Recognition and Enforcement of Foreign Judgments

(1) Except as provided in § 482, a final judgment of a court of a foreign state granting or denying recovery of a sum of money, establishing or confirming the status of a person, or determining interests in

property, is conclusive between the parties, and is entitled to recognition in courts in the United States.

(2) A judgment entitled to recognition under Subsection (1) may be enforced by any party or its successor or assigns against any other party, its successors or assigns, in accordance with the procedure for enforcement of judgments applicable where enforcement is sought.

§ 482.   Grounds for Nonrecognition of Foreign Judgments.

(1) A court in the United States may not recognize a judgment of the court of a foreign state if:

(a) the judgment was rendered under a judicial system that does not provide impartial tribunals or procedures compatible with due process of law; or

(b) the court that rendered the judgment did not have jurisdiction over the defendant in accordance with the law of the rendering state and with rules set forth in § 421 [outlining analysis under traditional U.S. Due Process standards].

(2) A court in the United States need not recognize a judgment of a court of a foreign state if:

(a) the court that rendered the judgment did not have jurisdiction of the subject matter of the action;

(b) the defendant did not receive notice of the proceedings in sufficient time to enable him to defend;

(c) the judgment was obtained by fraud;

(d) the cause of action on which the judgment was based, or the judgment itself, is repugnant to the public policy of the United States or of the State where recognition is sought;

(e) the judgment conflicts with another final judgment that is entitled to recognition; or

(f) the proceeding in the foreign court was contrary to an agreement between the parties to submit the controversy on which the judgment is based to another forum.

Comment on the Uniform Foreign Money–Judgments Recognition Act

The Uniform Foreign Money–Judgments Recognition Act was completed by the National Conference of Commissioners on Uniform State Laws in August of 1962 and approved by the American Bar Association in February 1963. As of late 2003, thirty-one states, plus the District of Columbia and the Virgin Islands, had adopted some version of the Uniform Act. The Act "applies to any foreign judgment that is final and conclusive and enforceable where rendered even though an appeal therefrom is pending or it is subject to appeal." Section 2. Section 3 of the Act makes any such judgment "conclusive between the parties to the extent that it grants or denies recovery of a sum of money." Section 4 then sets out three mandatory defenses to recognition and six discretionary defenses to recognition. When no defense to recognition is available, or a discretionary defense is denied, the foreign judgment is then "enforceable in the same manner as the judgment of a sister state which is entitled to full faith and credit." Section 3. In states that have enacted the Uniform Enforcement of Foreign Judgments Act,[25] enforcement is accomplished in the administrative manner provided in that Act. Section 4 of the Act becomes particularly important with its list of grounds for non-recognition of a foreign judgment, listing both mandatory and discretionary grounds for non-recognition. You should consult that provision in the Documents Supplement, along with the other provisions of the Recognition Act, as well as the Uniform Enforcement of Foreign Judgments Act.

In July 2005, the National Conference of Commissioners on Uniform State Laws approved and recommended for enactment in all the states a new Uniform Foreign–Country Money Judgments Recognition Act.[26] Rather than produce a simple amendment of the 1962 Uniform Foreign Money–Judgments Recognition Act, it was decided to produce an entirely new Act. While the 2005 Act follows the 1962 Act very closely, it makes at least six important changes:[27]

1) Section 2 provides significant revision of the definitions provisions, choosing the term "foreign country" over the previous use of "foreign State."[28] This should remove the confusion that sometimes arises between the 1962 Recognition Act and the Uniform Enforcement of Foreign Judgments Act, which applies to sister state judgments.[29]

2) Section 3 includes an expanded set of provisions dealing with scope of the Act, and adds an explicit rule on burden of proof. The scope provision limits the act to judgments that grant or deny "recovery of a sum of money" that are "final, conclusive, and enforceable" "under the law of the foreign country where rendered,"[30] and explicitly excludes from its scope judgments for taxes or penalties and judgments in domestic relations matters.[31] For the first time, the Act makes explicit that the "party seeking recognition

---

25. 13 U.L.A. 149 (1964 Revised Act) (1986) [hereinafter Enforcement Act]. The Enforcement Act applies only to "a judgment, decree, or order of a court of the United States or of any other court which is entitled to full faith and credit" in the enforcing state. *Id.* § 1. The Recognition Act applies only to judgments of "any governmental unit other than the United States, or any state, district, commonwealth, territory, insular possession thereof, or the Panama Canal Zone, the Trust Territory of the Pacific Islands, or the Ryukyu Islands." Recognition Act § 1, *supra* note 7. Unfortunately, courts applying the acts have not always acknowledged this distinction. *See, e.g.,* Stevens v. Superior Court for County of Los Angeles, 28 Cal.App.3d 1, 104 Cal.Rptr. 369 (1972), applying the Rec-

ognition Act to an Oklahoma action on appeal and allowing a stay pending appeal.

26. National Conference of Commissioners on Uniform State Laws, Uniform Foreign–Country Money Judgments Recognition Act, *available at* http://www.nccusl.org/ Update/ActSearchResults.aspx [hereinafter 2005 Recognition Act].

27. *See id.,* Prefatory Note.

28. *Id.* § 2.

29. *See supra* notes 26–90 and accompanying text.

30. 2005 Recognition Act, *supra* note 97, § 3(a).

31. *Id.* § 3(b).

of a foreign-country judgment has the burden of establishing that [the Act] applies to the foreign-country judgment."[32]

3) Section 6 provides specific rules of procedure for recognition of a judgment, making clear that an action must be filed seeking recognition of a foreign judgment,[33] and that defensive recognition of a foreign judgment may be "raised by counterclaim, cross-claim, or affirmative defense."[34]

4) Section 9 establishes a specific 15 year statute of limitations applicable to bringing claims for recognition, measured "from the date that the foreign-country judgment became effective in the foreign country."[35]

5) Section 4(d) establishes the rule regarding burden of proof for raising and proving grounds for non-recognition, providing that the "party resisting recognition of a foreign-country judgment has the burden of establishing that a ground for nonrecognition ... exists."[36]

6) Most importantly, Section 4 adds new grounds for non-recognition of a judgment. The public policy ground in the 1962 Recognition Act provided for non-recognition only if "the [cause of action] [claim for relief] on which the judgment is based is repugnant to the public policy of this state." In the 2005 Recognition Act, the language provides that a judgment need not be recognized if "the judgment or the [cause of action] [claim for relief] on which the judgment is based is repugnant to the public policy of this state or of the United States."[37] This adds breadth to the provision both in terms of the matter which can offend public policy and the source of the policy that may be offended. Section 4(b) is further expanded in the 2005 Act through authorization of non-recognition if "the judgment was rendered in circumstances that raise substantial doubt about the integrity of the rendering court with respect to the judgment,"[38] or if "the specific proceeding in the foreign court leading to the judgment was not compatible with the requirements of due process of law."[39]

Finally, it is significant to note what the 2005 Act did not do. It did not institute a reciprocity requirement,[40] with the drafters deciding "that the approach of the 1962 Act continues to be the wisest course with regard to this issue."[41] By January 2008, the 2005 Recognition Act had been

---

32. *Id.* § 3(c).

33. *Id.* § 6(a).

34. *Id.* § 6(b).

35. *Id.* § 9.

36. *Id.* § 4(d).

37. *Id.* § 4(c)(3).

38. *Id.* § 4(c)(7). This ground for non-recognition is a significant change to the 1962 Recognition Act, which provided for non-recognition only if the entire legal system could be challenged as not impartial. *See* Society of Lloyd's v. Turner, 303 F.3d 325, 330 (5th Cir. 2002).

39. *Id.* § 4(c).

40. *See supra* notes 77–82 and accompanying text.

41. 2005 Recognition Act, *supra* note 97, Prefatory Note.

enacted in California, Idaho, and Nevada.[42] In the questions below, consider whether the replacement of the 1962 Recognition Act by the 2005 Recognition Act would result in any differences.

Questions and Comments

1. Suppose that jurisdiction is available over Celsius in two different U.S. states, one of which has adopted the Uniform Foreign Money–Judgments Recognition Act, and one of which has not. If you are advising Plastic Maker in bringing the action for enforcement of the German judgment, does the availability of the Uniform Act in one state make a difference in your decision about where to bring the enforcement action? Would you bring the action in state or federal court?

2. Will the German judgment in favor of Plastic Maker be enforceable in Pennsylvania? Pennsylvania enacted the Uniform Foreign Money–Judgments Recognition Act in 1990 (subsequent to the *Somportex* decision). Do any of the grounds for non-recognition in Article 4 of the Act apply to the German judgment? Did the German court have personal and subject matter jurisdiction in accordance with Pennsylvania law? What arguments would you make on behalf of each of Celsius and Plastic Maker if the judgment is brought to Pennsylvania for recognition and enforcement?

3. Compare the provisions of the Uniform Foreign Money–Judgments Recognition Act in the Documents Supplement with the common law applied in both *Hilton v. Guyot* and *Somportex* and the Restatement provisions. Is the Uniform Act consistent with the common law as stated in the cases and the Restatement? What has happened to the reciprocity requirement that was important to the holding in *Hilton*? It is not in either the Restatement or the Uniform Act, but was added as a discretionary requirement in at least six states, and a mandatory requirement in two others, when those states adopted the Act. *See* Fla. Stat. Ann. § 55.605(g) (West Supp. 2003) (discretionary); N.C. Gen. Stat. § 1C–1804(b)(7) (2001) (discretionary); Idaho Code § 10–1404(g) (Michie 1998) (discretionary); Tex. Civ. Prac. & Rem. Code Ann. § 36.005(b)(7) (Vernon 1995) (discretionary); Ohio Rev. Code Ann. § 2329.92(B) (West 1994) (discretionary); Me. Rev. Stat. Ann. tit. 14, § (West 1964) (discretionary); Ga. Code Ann. § 9–12–114(10) (2002) (mandatory); Mass. Gen. Laws Ann. ch. 235, § 23A (West 2000) (mandatory). New Hampshire has a reciprocity requirement, but only for Canadian judgments. N.H. Rev. Stat. Ann. § 524–A (1997). What would be the rationale for and against adoption of a reciprocity requirement?

4. *Somportex* makes it clear that federal courts look to state law for the rules on enforcement of foreign judgments under *Erie Ry. Co. v. Tompkins*. Is this an issue that should be dealt with by separate rule in each U.S. state, or should it be federalized? If it should be federalized, what is the best approach to accomplishing this change?

5. The Uniform Foreign Money–Judgments Recognition Act provides in § 3 that "a foreign judgment meeting the requirements of section 2 is

---

42. *See* http://www.nccusl.org/Update/ ufcmjra.asp. uniformact_factsheets/uniformacts-fs-

conclusive between the parties" and "enforceable in the same manner as the judgment of a sister state which is entitled to full faith and credit." The manner of enforcement is not dealt with in the Recognition Act, but in most states is found in the separate Uniform Enforcement of Foreign Judgments Act. The Enforcement Act use of "foreign" refers to sister state judgments, rather than foreign state judgments. Thus, § 3 of the Recognition Act effectively provides for sister state treatment for enforcement purposes, which is then defined in the Enforcement Act. Review the provisions of the Enforcement Act found in the Documents Supplement. Assuming recognition is appropriate under the Recognition Act, how will Plastic Maker accomplish enforcement of its judgment in Pennsylvania (which has enacted the Enforcement Act)?

6.   Note the discussion in *Hilton* of the fact that the case involved a French plaintiff against an American defendant. Justice Gray suggests that if the judgment for which enforcement was being sought was in favor of a French plaintiff against a French defendant the result would have been different. Is this distinction of any importance under the Recognition Act? Why or why not? Suppose the German judgment we are dealing with is against a German defendant, rather than a U.S. defendant, and that the German defendant has assets in a U.S. state. Would that make the recognition and enforcement process any different? Should it?

7.   What are the essential elements of fair procedure ("impartial tribunals or procedures compatible with due process of law") as defined in *Hilton*? When should a judgment be denied recognition because it comes from a state that does not provide impartial tribunals? Can a judgment from a developed, Western European nation ever be denied recognition on such a basis?

8.   Should the determination of "impartial" tribunal and other Uniform Act requirements be on a country-by-country basis, a tribunal-by-tribunal basis, or a judgment-by-judgment basis? Who is best situated to make such a determination? A state or federal court trial judge? Should this be a diplomatic decision made by the State Department as representative of the executive branch?

9.   Restatement § 483 states that U.S. courts are "not required to recognize or to enforce judgments for the collection of taxes, fines or penalties rendered by the courts of other states." Why should U.S. courts enforce foreign civil judgments but not foreign tax or penal judgments?

10.   Should the same full faith and credit consideration given to sister state judgments in the United States be granted to foreign judgments? The United States Constitution, through the interstate commerce clause, the full faith and credit clause, and other provisions, creates a common market within the United States. Does this process justify treating judgments from outside the United States differently from judgments from within the United States? Does the Brussels Regulation in Europe effectively create the same results as the full faith and credit clause in the U.S. Constitution? What are the differences?

11.   Now is a good time to take a look at the United Nations Convention on the Recognition and Enforcement of Foreign Arbitral Awards (the New York Convention) in the Documents Supplement. How does the exis-

tence of such a convention dealing with arbitration affect dispute resolution decisions? When a party can plan a choice of forum clause, the existence of the arbitration convention means that choosing arbitration will make enforcement of the resulting award more likely—and more convenient in terms of procedure—than enforcement of a court judgment. The United States has no similar convention regarding enforcement of court judgments with any nation.

12.   Should ease of enforcing an arbitral award render arbitration the preferred method of international dispute resolution? What other considerations may guide the choice between litigation in national courts and arbitration or some other form of alternative dispute settlement?

13.   Much is made (even in this book) of Lord Denning's admonition that a plaintiff is drawn to U.S. courts like a moth to a flame. This is worth some reconsideration, especially in contract cases. The *Somportex* decision provides a good example of why this is so. In *Somportex*, the Third Circuit enforced an English judgment for $93,500 that included about $45,000 for loss of profit, $46,000 for loss of good will, and $2,500 for costs, including attorney fees. Judge Aldisert notes that damages for loss of good will and compensation for attorney fees would not have been available if the case had been brought in a state or federal court in Pennsylvania. This means that a Pennsylvania judgment on the same matter would have been for only $45,000. Thus, the judgment received in an English court was for more than twice the amount that would have been received in a U.S. court. Perhaps the moths should consider a few more flames before making hasty judgments about the U.S. legal system that may not hold up in practice. Similarly, foreign defendants might reconsider their aversion to U.S. courts, at least in contract cases.

14.   Sections 2 and 3 of the Recognition Act provide for recognition when the foreign judgment is "final, conclusive, and enforceable where rendered." Even a local or sister state judgment is not "enforceable" if a post-judgment settlement has been reached and replaces the judgment between the parties. *See, e.g., Coane v. Girard Trust Co.*, 182 Md. 577, 583, 35 A.2d 449, 452 (1944). The court in *Guinness PLC v. Ward*, 955 F.2d 875, 886 (4th Cir.1992) suggested in dicta that a post-judgment settlement constituting an accord and satisfaction or a substituted contract would leave the foreign judgment no longer "enforceable where rendered," and thus not entitled to recognition under the Act. Although a judgment subject to appeal may be a final judgment for purposes of the Act, § 6 of the Recognition Act provides that a U.S. court may stay recognition until the foreign appeal has run its course.

15.   The *Somportex* case involved a default judgment. Judge Aldisert's opinion concludes that recognition should be no different for a default judgment than for a judgment based on a contested trial. Do you agree with this conclusion? Should there be any limits on recognition of default judgments? What would be the implications of a rule that denied recognition to default judgments?

16.   The lists of grounds for non-recognition in the Restatement and the Uniform Act are very similar. Consider the following situations in regard

to each of these grounds and how they might affect the situation in Problem 5.2:

(a) *Lack of impartial tribunals.* Can it be argued that a German judgment should not be recognized because it was "rendered under a system which does not provide impartial tribunals or procedures compatible with the requirements of due process of law?" If such an argument is made, must the claimed defect arise from the specific judgment, the court that rendered it, or the entire German legal system? *See, Dresdner Bank AG v. Haque,* 161 F.Supp.2d 259 (S.D.N.Y.2001), noting plaintiff's (apparently uncontested) assertion that the German court system "has been found to provide impartial tribunals or procedures compatible with the requirements of due process of law;" and *Society of Lloyd's v. Ashenden,* 233 F.3d 473 (7th Cir.2000) (en banc), rejecting the claim that a judgment from England could be challenged on this ground.

(b) *Lack of personal jurisdiction.* The German court may have had jurisdiction under its own laws, but would not have had jurisdiction "over the defendant" if U.S. concepts of due process had been applied by that court. Should the judgment be recognized if the defendant can argue that personal jurisdiction did not meet the *International Shoe–World–Wide Volkswagen–Asahi* line of cases from the U.S. Supreme Court? The prevailing view is that, even if the rendering court had jurisdiction under the laws of its own state, a court in the United States asked to recognize a foreign judgment should scrutinize the basis for asserting jurisdiction in the light of American concepts of jurisdiction to adjudicate. RESTATEMENT (THIRD) FOREIGN RELATIONS LAW § 482 cmt. c (1986). *See, e.g., Koster v. Automark Industries, Inc.,* 640 F.2d 77 (7th Cir.1981); *Mercandino v. Devoe & Raynolds, Inc.,* 181 N.J.Super. 105, 436 A.2d 942 (1981); *Compagnie du Port de Rio de Janeiro v. Mead Morrison Mfg. Co.,* 19 F.2d 163, 166–67 (D.Me.1927); *Davidson & Co. v. Allen,* 89 Nev. 126, 508 P.2d 6, 7–8 (1973); *Jackson v. Stelco Employees' Credit Union Limited,* 203 So.2d 669 (Fla.1967). Thus, U.S. courts apply U.S. concepts of due process rather than looking to similar concepts applicable in the foreign jurisdiction. *See, e.g., Hunt v. BP Exploration Co. (Libya) Ltd.,* 492 F.Supp. 885, 895 (N.D.Tex.1980); *Royal Bank of Canada v. Trentham Corp.,* 491 F.Supp. 404, 406 (S.D. Tex. 1980), *rev'd on other grounds,* 665 F.2d 515 (5th Cir.1981); *Cherun v. Frishman,* 236 F.Supp. 292, 296 (D.D.C. 1964); *Boivin v. Talcott,* 102 F.Supp. 979, 981 (N.D. Ohio 1951); *Compagnie du Port de Rio de Janeiro v. Mead Morrison Mfg. Co.,* 19 F.2d 163, 166–67 (D. Me. 1927); *Davidson & Co. Ltd. v. Allen,* 89 Nev. 126, 508 P.2d 6, 7–8 (1973); *Rzeszotarski v. Rzeszotarski,* 296 A.2d 431, 437 (D.C.Ct.App.1972). Given the expansive nature of this doctrine in determining whether jurisdiction exists, most courts have found compliance with U.S. due process requirements in the granting of foreign judgments. *See, e.g., Somportex v. Philadelphia Chewing Gum Corp.,* 453 F.2d 435 (3d Cir.1971), *cert. denied,* 405 U.S. 1017, 92 S.Ct. 1294, 31 L.Ed.2d 479 (1972), where a contract negotiated with an English company by letter, telex and telephone was considered to be sufficient to create minimum contacts with the English forum. *But see, De La Mata v. American Life Ins. Co.,* 771 F.Supp. 1375, 1386–88

(D.Del.1991), where the court refused recognition of a Brazilian judgment on due process grounds when service on the American defendant was by service on a *former* agent and the defendant had actual knowledge of the proceeding only after default judgment had been granted. Nonetheless, the procedures required in foreign adjudications in order to comply with due process requirements need not be identical to those employed in American courts. They need only be "compatible with the requirements of due process of law." *See, e.g., Ingersoll Milling Machine Co. v. Granger*, 833 F.2d 680, 686 (7th Cir.1987). "[A] mere difference in the procedural system is not a sufficient basis for non-recognition. A case of serious injustice must be involved." UNIFORM FOREIGN MONEY-JUDGMENTS RECOGNITION ACT § 4 comment, 13 U.L.A. 268 (1986). *See Panama Processes v. Cities Service Co.*, 796 P.2d 276, 285 (Okla.1990) (differences in procedure not grounds for denial of enforcement of Brazilian judgment where "in Brazil (1) no witnesses of any party may be subpoenaed, (2) testimony of corporate employees is inadmissible, (3) there is no available process for requiring testimony of indispensable U.S. witnesses; (4) there is no right of cross-examination, and (5) the parties may neither conduct pre-trial discovery nor subpoena documents").

(c) *Lack of subject matter jurisdiction.* "[J]urisdiction of the rendering court over the subject matter is normally presumed, and an inquiry into possible lack of competence is initiated only on the basis of a credible challenge by the judgment debtor or by another person resisting recognition or enforcement." RESTATEMENT (THIRD) FOREIGN RELATIONS LAW § 482 cmt. a (1986).

(d) *Lack of proper notice and opportunity to respond.* Suppose the notice to Celsius was served in German and not in English, and that it was not transmitted in accordance with the rules of the Hague Service Convention. Would that be grounds for denial of recognition of the resulting judgment? How much time is necessary to satisfy the requirement that there be an opportunity to respond and be heard? Does a default judgment not satisfy this requirement? *See, e.g., Tahan v. Hodgson*, 662 F.2d 862 (D.C.Cir.1981) (personal service in Israel was sufficient when suit papers were prepared in Hebrew, even though defendant did not read Hebrew); *De La Mata v. American Life Ins. Co.*, 771 F.Supp. 1375, 1386–88 (D.Del.1991) (service on Brazilian national who was a *former* agent of American defendant was insufficient where defendant had actual notice of proceedings only after default judgment was granted); *Boivin v. Talcott*, 102 F.Supp. 979 (N.D.Ohio 1951) (service under foreign service of process statute which only required notice by publication held insufficient to satisfy due process requirements necessary to give foreign court personal jurisdiction); *Hager v. Hager*, 1 Ill.App.3d 1047, 274 N.E.2d 157, 160–161 (1971) (personal service insufficient when complaint was served without summons showing appearance date). Suppose service met the German procedural rules, but would be constitutionally defective in the United States? Evaluation of "proper service" by the courts has focused both on compliance with the foreign country's statutory notice provisions and on constitutional concerns requiring adequate notice of the proceedings. *See, e.g., Tahan v. Hodgson*, 662 F.2d 862 (D.C.Cir.1981) (though Israeli procedure was inconsistent with Federal Rules calling for giving of a second notice at least three days prior to hearing and application for entry of default judgment, it was unrealistic for U.S. to require all foreign judicial systems to adhere to Federal Rules).

(e) *Fraud.* A foreign judgment generally can be impeached only for extrinsic fraud, which deprives the aggrieved party of an adequate opportunity to present the case to the court. *See United States v. Throckmorton*, 98 U.S. (8 Otto) 61, 65, 25 L.Ed. 93 (1878); *Laufer v. Westminster Brokers, Ltd.*, 532 A.2d 130 (D.C.App.1987). A judgment cannot be impeached for intrinsic fraud, which involves matters passed upon by the original court, such as the veracity of testimony and the authenticity of documents. *See, e.g., Mackay v. McAlexander*, 268 F.2d 35, 39 (9th Cir.1959) (fraud in obtaining a Canadian naturalization decree by false statements not grounds for denial of recognition). *See also Laufer v. Westminster Brokers, Ltd.*, 532 A.2d 130, 133–34 (D.C.App.1987); *Harrison v. Triplex Gold Mines*, 33 F.2d 667, 671–72 (1st Cir.1929); *The W. Talbot Dodge*, 15 F.2d 459, 462 (S.D.N.Y.1926); *Tamimi v. Tamimi*, 38 A.D.2d 197, 328 N.Y.S.2d 477 (1972). The RESTATEMENT (SECOND) JUDGMENTS § 68 and § 70 cmt. c (1982), rejects the intrinsic/extrinsic distinction. In *Hilton v. Guyot*, the Supreme Court noted that certain allegations of fraud were intrinsic fraud, and that extrinsic fraud was generally required to impeach domestic judgments, but did not decide whether intrinsic fraud was sufficient to impeach a foreign judgment. 159 U.S. 113, 207–10, 16 S.Ct. 139, 40 L.Ed. 95 (1895). Section 4(b)(2) of the Uniform Foreign Money–Judgments Recognition Act allows discretionary non-recognition for judgments "obtained by fraud," without specifying whether extrinsic fraud is necessary. 13 U.L.A. 268 (1986).

(f) *Public policy.* United States courts uniformly declare themselves not required to recognize or enforce a foreign judgment that contravenes state public policy. *See, e.g., Somportex Ltd. v. Philadelphia Chewing Gum Corp.*, 453 F.2d 435, 443 (3d Cir.1971), *cert. denied*, 405 U.S. 1017, 92 S.Ct. 1294, 31 L.Ed.2d 479 (1972); *Adamsen v. Adamsen*, 151 Conn. 172, 195 A.2d 418 (1963); *Yoder v. Yoder*, 24 Ohio App.2d 71, 263 N.E.2d 913 (1970); *Gutierrez v. Collins*, 583 S.W.2d 312, 322 (Tex.1979). Such a declaration, however, seldom leads to a denial of recognition or enforcement. A judgment is necessarily offensive to public policy when it "tends clearly to injure the public health, the public morals, the public confidence in the purity of the administration of the law, or to undermine that sense of security for individual rights, whether of personal liberty, or of private property, which any citizen ought to feel, is against public policy." *Somportex Ltd. v. Philadelphia Chewing Gum Corp.*, 453 F.2d 435, 443 (3d Cir.1971), *cert. denied*, 405 U.S. 1017, 92 S.Ct. 1294, 31 L.Ed.2d 479 (1972), *quoting Goodyear v. Brown*, 155 Pa. 514, 26 A. 665, 666 (1893). *See also Southwest Livestock and Trucking Co., Inc. v. Ramon*, 169 F.3d 317 (5th Cir.1999) (Mexican judgment on promissory note calling for 52% interest did not violate Texas public policy represented in state usury act); *Ricart v. Pan American World Airways, Inc.*, 1990 WL 236080 (D.D.C.1990) (damages awarded by Dominican court enforced even though liability to deported passenger was for action taken in obedience to immigration authorities); *Gutierrez v. Collins*, 583 S.W.2d 312, 321–22 (Tex.1979) (the laws of a foreign nation do not violate the public policy of Texas unless they are "inimical to good morals, natural justice, or the general interests of the citizens of this state").

The public policy basis for non-recognition has recently become the source of denials of recognition based on the failure of the originating court to apply principles consistent with the U.S. Constitution. This is discussed further below.

(g) *Conflicting judgments.* A foreign judgment may conflict with either a sister state judgment or with another foreign judgment. Although U.S. courts have at times recognized the later of two inconsistent foreign judgments, they may also recognize the earlier one. RESTATE-MENT (THIRD) FOREIGN RELATIONS LAW § 482 cmt. g (1986). When a foreign judgment is otherwise entitled to recognition but conflicts with an earlier sister state judgment, there is no requirement of automatic preference for the sister state judgment. *Id. See Ackerman v. Ackerman*, 517 F.Supp. 614, 623–26 (S.D.N.Y.1981), *aff'd*, 676 F.2d 898 (2d Cir. 1982) (indicating that a later foreign judgment would be enforced notwithstanding a conflict with an earlier sister state judgment entitled to full faith and credit).

(h) *Judgments contrary to choice of forum clauses.* The U.S. Supreme Court articulated a strong policy in favor of choice of forum clauses in *The Bremen v. Zapata Off–Shore Co.*, 407 U.S. 1, 92 S.Ct. 1907, 32 L.Ed.2d 513 (1972). Consistent with this position, judgments obtained in an effort to evade jurisdiction in the forum originally selected by the parties are not likely to be enforced.

(i) *Tag jurisdiction and reverse forum non conveniens.* Section 4 of the Recognition Act authorizes refusal of recognition where the judgment is "rendered in a foreign country on the basis only of personal service," and the U.S. enforcing court "believes the original action should have been dismissed by the court in the foreign country on grounds of forum non conveniens." This exception is both discretionary and limited. It is available only when personal jurisdiction is based solely on personal service. Is this an acknowledgment that tag jurisdiction (jurisdiction based solely on the transient presence of the defendant in the forum state at the time of service of process) is somehow exorbitant? Does a state statute with this provision conflict with the policies enunciated by the Supreme Court in *Burnham v. Superior Court of California*, 495 U.S. 604, 110 S.Ct. 2105, 109 L.Ed.2d 631 (1990), which upheld the exercise of tag jurisdiction by California courts?

PART C. PUBLIC POLICY AND CONSTITUTIONAL ISSUES IN THE RECOGNITION OF JUDGMENTS

Recent cases have applied the public policy ground to deny recognition to English libel judgments on the basis that the English procedure was inconsistent with U.S. Constitutional standards. Consider these decisions and their impact on the future of judgments enforcement in the United States.

BACHCHAN v. INDIA ABROAD PUBLICATIONS INC.

New York Supreme Court, 1992.
154 Misc.2d 228, 585 N.Y.S.2d 661.

[An Indian plaintiff sued a New York defendant in the High Court of Justice in London, alleging defamation resulting from a story written in London and wired by the defendant to a news service in India. The publication in Indian and New York newspapers received some distribution in the United Kingdom. After an English jury awarded £40,000 in damages, plus attorney fees, the plaintiff sought to enforce the judgment in New York.]

SHIRLEY FINGERHOOD, JUSTICE:

Entry of the judgment is opposed on the ground that it was imposed without the safeguards for freedom of speech and the press required by the First Amendment of the US Constitution and NY Constitution, article I, § 8. Defendant asks this court to reject the judgment as repugnant to public policy, a ground for nonrecognition of foreign judgments under CPLR 5304 (b) (4).

* * *

It is plaintiff's position that the public policy exception to the rule that foreign judgments are afforded comity is narrow and inapplicable here. He asserts that this court should not reexamine the claim for which the judgment was awarded to determine whether it would be culpable under United States precedents. Pointing to CPLR 5304 (b) (4)'s reference to "cause[s] of action" rather than judgments, he argues that libel causes of action are cognizable in New York. If that paragraph is deemed to refer to judgments as well as causes of action, plaintiff asks this court to exercise its discretion to recognize the judgment in view of the common antecedents of the law of Great Britain and that of the United States.

It is doubtful whether this court has discretion to enforce the judgment if the action in which it was rendered failed to comport with the constitutional standards for adjudicating libel claims. In his commentary on CPLR 5304, David D. Siegel notes that one of the grounds for nonrecognition of a foreign judgment in subdivision (b), a lack of fair notice in sufficient time to enable a defendant to defend, "goes to the roots of due process." . . . . For that reason, he suggests that a refusal to recognize a foreign country judgment for lack of fair notice may be constitutionally mandatory, rather than, as subdivision (b) would have it, discretionary . . . . . Similarly, if, as claimed by defendant, the public policy to which the foreign judgment is repugnant is embodied in the First Amendment of the US Constitution or the free speech guarantee of the NY Constitution, the refusal to recognize the judgment should be, and it is deemed to be, "constitutionally mandatory." Accordingly, the libel law applied by the High Court of Justice in London in granting judgment to plaintiff will be reviewed to ascertain whether its provisions meet the safeguards for the press which have been enunciated by the courts of this country.

. . . .

Under English law, any published statement which adversely affects a person's reputation, or the respect in which that person is held, is *prima facie* defamatory. (See Justice Otten's instructions to the jury deciding Bachchan's action.) Plaintiffs' only burden is to establish that the words complained of refer to them, were published by the defendant, and bear a defamatory meaning. If, as in the present case, statements of fact are concerned, they are presumed to be false and the defendant must plead justification for the issue of truth to be brought before the jury. An unsuccessful defense of justification may result in the award of aggravated damages. For, in the language of Lord Hailsham of the House of Lords in *Broome v. Cassell & Co.* "Quite obviously, the award must include factors for injury. . . . the absence of apology, or the reaffirmation of the truth of the matter complained of . . ."

English law does not distinguish between private persons and those who are public figures or are involved in matters of public concern. None are required to prove falsity of the libel or fault on the part of the defendant. No plaintiff is required to prove that a media defendant intentionally or negligently disregarded proper journalistic standards in order to prevail.

The defendant has the burden of proving not only truth but also of establishing entitlement to the qualified privilege for newspaper publications and broadcasters provided by the 1952 Defamation Act Section 7(3) where "the matter published is . . . of public concern *and* . . . its publication . . . is . . . for the public benefit."

As stated by Mr. Gray, plaintiff's barrister, "[t]he difference between the American and English jurisdictions essentially comes down to where the burden of proof lies. . . ."

Defendant argues that the defamation law of England fails to meet the constitutional standards required in the United States because plaintiff, a friend of the late prime minister of India Rajiv Ghandi and the brother and manager of a movie star and former member of Parliament, is a public figure. In *New York Times Co. v. Sullivan,* 376 U.S. 254, 279–280, 84 S.Ct. 710, 726, 11 L.Ed.2d 686 (1964), the Supreme Court of the United States ruled that in order to recover damages for defamation a public official must prove by clear and convincing evidence that the defendant published the allegedly defamatory statement with " 'actual malice'—that is, with knowledge that it was false or with reckless disregard of whether it was false or not." That burden of proof was placed on public figures who sued media defendants in *Curtis Publishing Co. v. Butts,* 388 U.S. 130, 87 S.Ct. 1975, 18 L.Ed.2d 1094 (1967).

However, it seems neither necessary nor appropriate to decide whether plaintiff, an Indian national residing in England or Switzerland, is a public figure. Instead, the procedures of the English Court will be compared to those which according to decisions of the United States Supreme Court are constitutionally mandated for suits by private persons complaining of press publications of public concern.

In *Gertz v. Robert Welch, Inc.,* 418 U.S. 323, 347, 94 S.Ct. 2997, 3010, 41 L.Ed.2d 789 (1974) the Court held that a private figure could not recover damages for defamation without showing that a media defendant was at fault, leaving the individual States to "define for themselves the appropriate standard of liability for a publisher or broadcaster of defamatory falsehood injurious to a private individual."

* * *

It is obvious that defendant's publication relates to a matter of public concern. The affidavits and documents submitted by both parties reveal that the wire service report was related to an international scandal which touched major players in Indian politics and was reported in India, Sweden, the United States, England and elsewhere in the world. Consider the revelation of Mr. Zaiwalla, who had the conduct of the action resulting in the English judgment, that it was given priority over other defamation actions waiting to be tried because "the Indian General Election was imminent and the Bofars affairs and the plaintiff's long-time family friendship with Mr. Rajiv Gandhi, the former prime minister of India * * * and leader of the main opposition party * * * were being used as electoral weapons in India." Mr. Justice Otten, in his instructions, referred to the political context of the story by suggesting to the jury that it "ignore the complexities" of the Indian politics and political parties which were the background of the news stories.

Placing the burden of proving truth upon media defendants who publish speech of public concern has been held unconstitutional because fear of liability may deter such speech.

> Because such a 'chilling' effect would be antithetical to the First Amendment's protection of true speech on matters of public concern, we believe that a private-figure plaintiff must bear the burden of showing that the speech at issue is false before recovering damages for defamation from a media defendant. To do otherwise could 'only result in a deterrence of speech which the Constitution makes free.' (citation omitted) *Philadelphia Newspapers, Inc. v. Hepps.*

The "chilling" effect is no different where liability results from enforcement in the United States of a foreign judgment obtained where the burden of proving truth is upon media defendants. Accordingly, the failure of Bachchan to prove falsity in the High Court of Justice in England makes his judgment unenforceable here.

There is, of course, another reason why enforcement of the English judgment would violate the First Amendment: in England, plaintiff was not required to and did not meet the "less forbidding" constitutional requirement that a private figure show that a media defendant was at fault.

New York's standard for liability in actions brought by private persons against the press is set forth in *Chapadeau v. Utica Observer–Dispatch,* "[W]here the content of the article is arguably within the sphere of legitimate public concern, which is reasonably related to matters warranting public exposition, the party defamed may recover; however, to warrant such recovery he must establish, by a preponderance of the evidence, that the publisher acted in a grossly irresponsible manner without due consideration for the standards of information gathering and dissemination ordinarily followed by responsible parties."

As stated above, the English courts do not require plaintiff to prove that a press defendant was at fault in any degree. Bachchan certainly did not establish, as required by *Chapadeau,* that defendant was grossly irresponsible, a difficult task, where defendant disseminates another's news report.

It is true that England and the United States share many common law principles of law. Nevertheless, a significant difference between the two jurisdictions lies in England's lack of an equivalent to the First Amendment to the United States Constitution. The protection to free speech and the press embodied in that amendment would be seriously jeopardized by the entry of foreign libel judgments granted pursuant to standards deemed appropriate in England but considered antithetical to the protections afforded the press by the U.S. Constitution.

For the above stated reasons, the motion for summary judgment in lieu of complaint is denied.

TELNIKOFF v. MATUSEVITCH

Maryland Court of Appeal, 1997.
347 Md. 561, 702 A.2d 230, *aff'd* (table), 159 F.3d 636 (D.C.Cir.1998).

[In this case, the American defendant lived in England at the time of the alleged libel. After the Federal District Court for the District of Columbia granted the defendant's motion for summary judgment and refused to enforce the English judgment (*Matusevitch v. Telnikoff,* 877 F.Supp. 1 (D.D.C. 1995)), the case was appealed to the D.C. Circuit Court of Appeals, which upheld the refusal of recognition and enforcement. *Matusevitch v. Telnikoff,* 1998 U.S. App. LEXIS 10628 (unpublished opinion listed in table at 159 F.3d 636) (D.C.Cir.1998). Before rendering its decision, however, the Federal Court of Appeals asked the Maryland Court of Appeals whether recognition would violate Maryland public policy. Thus, the principal decision is that of the Maryland Court of Appeals.

Vladimir Matusevitch, a Maryland resident born in Belarus, had worked at various times for Radio Free Europe/Radio Liberty. Vladimir Telnikoff, an English citizen born in Leningrad was a freelance writer and broadcaster for the British Broadcasting Corporation (BBC). On February 13, 1984, an article written by Telnikoff and published in the London *Daily Telegraph* criticized the methods the BBC employed to recruit the persons who broadcasted to Russia for RFE/Radio Liberty. On February 18, the *Daily Telegraph* published a letter in reply from Matusevitch, taking issue with Telnikoff's article, which included the following sentence: "Mr. Telnikoff is stressing his racialist recipe by claiming that no matter how high the standards and integrity 'of ethnically alien' people Russian staff might be, they should be dismissed. I am certain the *Daily Telegraph* would reject any article with similar suggestions of lack of racial purity of the writer in any normal section of the British media." A published reply by Telnikoff requested an apology. When Matusevitch did not apologize, Telnikoff filed a libel action in the High Court of Justice, Queen's Bench Division, in London. An initial default judgment against Matusevitch in the amount of £ 65,000 was set aside by the High Court of Justice, finding the letter to constitute "fair comment" under English law. At the second trial, the High Court of Justice granted Matusevitch's motion for a judgment as a matter of law, holding that a "reasonable jury" would find the letter to be fair comment. This was affirmed by the Court of Appeal, but reversed by the House of Lords. On remand a jury verdict of £ 240,000 was returned in favor of Telnikoff. This is the judgment brought to the United States for recognition and enforcement.]

ELDRIDGE, JUDGE

* * *

The question before us is whether Telnikoff's English libel judgment is based upon principles which are so contrary to Maryland's public policy concerning freedom of the press and defamation actions that recognition of the judgment should be denied.

* * *

While we shall rest our decision in this case upon the non-constitutional ground of Maryland public policy, nonetheless, in ascertaining that public policy, it is appropriate to examine and rely upon the history, policies, and requirements of the First Amendment and Article 40 of the Declaration of Rights. In determining non-constitutional principles of law, courts often rely upon the policies and requirements reflected in constitutional provisions.

* * *

American and Maryland history reflects a public policy in favor of a much broader and more protective freedom of the press than ever provided for under English law.

* * *

The contrast between English standards governing defamation actions and the present Maryland standards is striking. For the most part,

English defamation actions are governed by principles which are unchanged from the earlier common law period.

Thus, under English defamation law, it is unnecessary for the plaintiff to establish fault, either in the form of conscious wrongdoing or negligence. The state of mind or conduct of the defendant is irrelevant. * * *

Moreover, under English law, defamatory statements are presumed to be false unless a defendant proves them to be true. * * *

In England, a qualified privilege can be overcome without establishing that the defendant actually knew that the publication was false or acted with reckless disregard of whether it was false or not. It can be overcome by proof of "spite or ill-will or some other wrong or improper motive." Peter F. Carter–Ruck, Libel and Slander 137 (1073). English law authorizes punitive or exemplary damages under numerous circumstances in defamation actions; unlike Maryland law, they are not limited to cases in which there was actual knowledge of the falsehood or reckless disregard as to truth or falsity. Furthermore, as one scholar has pointed out, *id*, at 172,

> [i]n practice only one sum is awarded and it is impossible to tell to what extent the damages awarded in any particular case were intended to be compensatory and to what extent exemplary or punitive. The very high damages awarded in recent years in actions against newspapers can only be explained on the basis that the sums awarded reflect the juries' opinion of the defendants' conduct."

English defamation law presumes that a statement is one of fact, and the burden is on the defendant to prove "fair comment." According to one English writer (Carter–Ruck),

> [f]or the defence of fair comment to succeed it must be proved that the subject matter of the comment is a matter of legitimate public interest; that the facts upon which the comment is based are true; and that the comment is fair in the sense that it is relevant to the facts and in the sense that it is the expression of the honest opinion of the writer or speaker.

Proof of malice, in the sense of ill-will, spite, etc., "will vitiate fair comment as a defense event though in all other respects the comment fulfills the qualifications which the law stipulates." In addition, "the malice of one defendant will destroy the defence for all the defendants and each defendant is not entitled to have his case considered separately." Moreover, as the opinion of the House of Lords in the present controversy shows, a statement is not evaluated in the context of the publication to which it responds. Context appears to be eliminated from a court's determination of whether a statement is considered fact or comment.

Finally, English defamation law flatly rejects the principles set forth in *New York Times Co. v. Sullivan, supra,* and *Gertz v. Robert Welch, Inc.* The basic rules are the same regardless of whether the plaintiff is a public official, public figure, or a private person, regardless of whether the alleged defamatory statement involves a matter of public concern, and regardless of the defendant's status. As Professor Smolla has observed (Rodney A. Smolla, Law of Defamation),

> British law recognizes no special protection for defamation actions arising from critiques of public figures or public officials, routinely imposing large damages awards in cases involving what American courts would characterize as core political discourse.

* * *

A comparison of English and present Maryland defamation law does not simply disclose a difference in one or two legal principles. Instead, present Maryland defamation law is totally different from English defamation law in virtually every significant respect. Moreover, the differences are rooted in historic and fundamental public policy differences concerning freedom of the press and speech.

* * *

The principles governing defamation actions under English law, which were applied to Telnikoff's libel suit, are so contrary to Maryland defamation law, and to the policy of freedom of the press underlying Maryland law, that Telnikoff's judgment should be denied recognition under principles of comity. In the language of the Uniform Foreign–Money Judgments Recognition Act, § 10–704(b)(2) of the Courts and Judicial Proceedings Article, Telnikoff's English "cause of action on which the judgment is based is repugnant to the public policy of the State...."

* * *

[R]ecognition of English defamation judgments could well lead to wholesale circumvention of fundamental public policy in Maryland and the rest of the country. With respect to the sharp differences between English and American defamation law, Professor Smolla has observed:

> This striking disparity between American and British libel law has led to a curious recent phenomenon, a sort of balance of trade deficit in libel litigation: Prominent persons who receive bad press in publications distributed primarily in the United States now often choose to file their libel suits in England. London has become an international libel capital. Plaintiffs with the wherewithal to do so now often choose to file suit in Britain in order to exploit Britain's strict libel laws, even when the plaintiffs and the publication have little connection to that country.

* * *

"At the heart of the First Amendment," as well as Article 40 of the Maryland Declaration of Rights and Maryland public policy, "is the recognition of the fundamental importance of the free flow of ideas and opinions on matters of public interest and concern." *Hustler Magazine v.*

Falwell, 485 U.S. at 50. The importance of that free flow of ideas and opinions on matters of public concern precludes Maryland recognition of Telnikoff's English libel judgment.

Questions and Comments

1. Did U.S. concepts of First Amendment freedom of the press influence the courts' decisions in these two cases? Should such national considerations be the basis for denial of recognition and enforcement of a judgment from another country? Might a foreign money judgment impinge upon other freedoms in the United States? What about the remaining Amendments in the Bill of Rights?

2. *Bachchan* and *Telnikoff* demonstrate that defects in foreign proceedings that would rise to a constitutional level if the case had originated in the United States trigger the public policy ground for non-recognition of the resulting judgment. In *Bachchan*, the New York court, relying heavily on the Practice Commentaries to the New York Civil Practice Law and Rules, noted that public policy usually is a discretionary ground for non-recognition, but went on to state that "if ... the public policy to which the foreign judgment is repugnant is embodied in" the Constitution, "the refusal to recognize the judgment should be, and it is deemed to be, 'constitutionally mandatory.' " *Bachchan v. India Abroad Publications Inc.*, 154 Misc.2d 228, 585 N.Y.S.2d 661, 662 (N.Y.Sup.Ct.1992) (quoting from Siegel, Practice Commentaries, McKINNEY'S CONS. LAWS OF N.Y., Book 7B, C.P.L.R. C5304:1). While the *Bachchan* case determined such non-recognition to be mandatory when the issue was a violation of First Amendment protections, it did so in reliance on commentary dealing with due process concepts. This implies that the same mandatory non-recognition would result if the defect in the originating foreign court is a denial of due process.

3. In May of 2005, the American Law Institute (ALI) approved the *Recognition and Enforcement of Foreign Judgments: Analysis and Proposed Federal Statute.* The proposed statute would make the recognition and enforcement of foreign judgments subject to a single federal law. That law would differ from the 1964 and 2005 NCCUSL Uniform Recognition Acts. It would be broader in scope, not being limited only to money judgments. The 2005 Uniform Act excludes from its scope judgments for taxes, fines, penalties, and domestic relations matters. 2005 Recognition Act, *supra* note 97, § 3(b). Thus, unlike the ALI proposed statute, it does not disturb the traditional rule that a U.S. court will not recognize and enforce a foreign tax or penal judgment. *See, e.g.*, Her Majesty the Queen in Right of the Province of British Columbia v. Gilbertson, 597 F.2d 1161 (9th Cir. 1979) (refusing enforcement of a British Columbia judgment for a logging tax against a U.S. citizen). Unlike the Uniform Acts, the ALI statute specifically allows the recognition and enforcement of tax and penal judgments, as well as declaratory judgments and injunctions. Like the 2005 Recognition Act, the ALI statute generally places the burden of proof of a ground for non-recognition clearly on the party resisting recognition or enforcement, but changes this rule for jurisdictional challenges to default judgments and challenges to the validity of a choice of court agreement. The ALI proposed statute also treats grounds for non-recognition differently than do the Recognition Acts. Where-

as Section 4 of the Acts make failure to provide a system of impartial tribunals, personal jurisdiction, and subject matter jurisdiction mandatory grounds for non-recognition, with other grounds being discretionary, section 5 of the ALI statute provides for mandatory non-recognition upon proof of any of the following grounds:

1) the judgment comes from a system that "does not provide impartial tribunals or procedures compatible with fundamental principles of fairness" (§ 5(a)(I));

2) "the judgment was rendered in circumstances that raise substantial and justifiable doubt about the integrity of the rendering court with respect to the judgment in question";

3) the judgment resulted from jurisdiction deemed unacceptable under section 6 of the statute (§ 5(a)(iii));

4) the judgment resulted from improper notice to the defendant (§ 5(a)(iv));

5) "the judgment was obtained by fraud" that deprived the party from having "an adequate opportunity to present its case" (§ 5(a)(v));

6) "the judgment or the claim on which the judgment is based is repugnant to the public policy of the United States, or to the public policy of a particular state" (§ 5(a)(vi)); or

7) the judgment was obtained "contrary to an agreement under which the dispute was to be determined exclusively in another forum" (§ 5(b)(i)).

One of the more significant differences between the Uniform Acts and the ALI statute was also one of the more debated issues during the ALI process. Section 7 of the statute provides a reciprocity requirement, preventing recognition or enforcement in a U.S. court of a judgment from a country that would not recognize a comparable judgment from a court in the United States.

It is not hard to justify unification under the interstate and foreign commerce powers of Congress. But it may be harder to decide what should be included in such a statute. The Reporters for the ALI Project originally suggested that the result in the *Telnikoff* case was not appropriate, and that "libel ... contained in a letter from one resident of England published in an English newspaper alleged to defame another resident of England ... would not seem [to sufficiently engage] American interests ... to over come the narrow limits of the public policy defense." ALI, International Jurisdiction and Judgments Project 60–61 (Discussion Draft of March 29, 2002). The Reporters further suggested that in balancing "the public policy in favor of free speech against the public policy in favor of recognition and enforcement of foreign judgments" a court should "not appraise the foreign judgment by the specialized constitutional standards of U.S. libel law as it has developed in recent years." Is this a correct balancing of arguably conflicting public policies? If one policy has Constitutional foundations, can another policy (with no Constitutional basis) so easily be found to win out in the event of a conflict? Is there a "public policy" in favor of recognition of foreign judgments that deserves consideration under the Uniform Foreign Money–Judgments Recognition Act analysis under § 4(b)(3)? If a policy outside the

Act that has Constitutional roots cannot outweigh the policy behind the Act itself, what policy can result in denial of recognition under § 4(b)(3)?

4. Consider Variation 2 to Problem 6.1, in which there have been published allegations by both Celsius and Plastic Maker in which they challenge the veracity and fair dealing of the other. Suppose also that in Plastic Maker's German contract action against Celsius, variation 2 applies and Plastic Maker alleged libel and obtained a judgment including 200,000 Euros in damages on the libel claim. Would that make a difference in an enforcement action in a U.S. court? Should it? Suppose the suit by Plastic Maker was in a U.K. court, and a judgment including damages for libel has been awarded. How would that affect enforcement in the United States?

5. Two cases have developed the analysis in *Bachchan* and *Telnikoff* beyond defamation claims. In Sarl Louis Feraud Int'l v. Viewfinder, Inc., 489 F.3d 474 (2d Cir. 2007), the Federal District Court had held that a French judgment for copyright violation against a defendant who had placed images of fashion shows on the internet was not entitled to recognition because it violated First Amendment concerns implicated in the U.S. copyright doctrine of fair use. The Court of Appeal sent the matter back to the District Court for further analysis of the level of protection of both the rights of French fashion designers and of fashion photographers in order to create a more complete record of interests that fall under the U.S. First Amendment. In *Yahoo! Inc. v. La Ligue Contre le Racisme*, 433 F.3d 1199 (9th Cir. 2006), a mixed decision of an *en banc* court dismissed an action seeking a declaratory judgment that two interim orders by a French court were not entitled to recognition. The French orders prohibited Yahoo! Inc. from allowing its internet subscribers to advertise Nazi memorabilia for sale on the internet. This was challenged as a violation of public policy reflected in the First Amendment.

6. On May 1, 2008, the Governor of New York signed into law the "Libel Terrorism Protection Act," which amended section 5304(a) of the New York Civil Practice Law and Rules (New York's version of the 1962 Uniform Money-Judgments Recognition Act) by adding a new ground for non-recognition of a foreign judgment as follows:

§ 5304   Grounds for non-recognition

(a) No recognition. A foreign country judgment is not conclusive if:

....

8. The cause of action resulted in a defamation judgment obtained in a jurisdiction outside the United States, unless the court before the matter is brought sitting in this state first determines that the defamation law applied in the foreign court's adjudication provided at least as much protection for freedom of speech and press in that case as would be provided by both the United States and New York constitutions.

Chapter 7

RECOGNITION AND ENFORCE-
MENT OF U.S. JUDGMENTS
IN FOREIGN COURTS

PROBLEM 7.1   U.S. JUDGMENT AGAINST
CANADIAN, UK AND GERMAN
DEFENDANTS TAKEN TO FOREIGN
COURT FOR ENFORCEMENT

SECTION I.   THE SETTING

The following facts in Problem 3.2, which develops the facts of Problem 3.1, apply to this problem and should be reviewed:

Plaintiffs are two U.S. citizens residing in the State of New Jersey and two UK citizens. While traveling in their 1999 SUV through New Jersey on a sightseeing trip to view "on location" scenes in a popular TV series, they experienced a sudden blowout causing the car to roll over, resulting in severe medical injuries and emotional trauma to the U.S. parties and to their U.K. friends, who were sitting in the rear of the vehicle. The SUV was originally purchased by the U.S. plaintiffs from VUSCO, a distributor which held a distribution franchise for the SUV vehicle in the New York–New Jersey region.

After reviewing accident reports prepared by local law enforcement authorities and the U.S. insurance company, the lawyers for the injured parties determined that the tires were faulty and the blowout attributable to negligent design and manufacture of the tread in the tires. The tires were manufactured by CANTIRE, Ltd., headquartered in Niagara, Canada. The SUV was manufactured by DROF AG, a German–UK joint venture, which is headquartered in Badenberg, Germany. The tires were assembled and installed by DROF–UK PLC in its plant facility in Ipswich, United Kingdom. VUSCO, L.L.C., the distributor, and DROF AG have a forum selection clause in their contract designating the choice of forum as the courts of the Netherlands. There is also a forum selection clause in the contract between VUSCO and CANTIRE which provides that the venue for all disputes that may result from orders for the tires should be in the court of competent jurisdiction in England.

All of the injured parties decide to go forward with the suit in New Jersey and to name as defendants CANTIRE, DROF AG, DROF-UK PLC, and VUSCO. A cross-claim is filed by VUSCO against DROF AG, alleging liability as a result of faulty design and manufacture.

Additional claims for contribution and indemnity are instituted by DROF AG and the VUSCO against the CANTIRE contending that the tires were defective and the cause of the accident. Aside from contesting jurisdiction, CANTIRE plans to rely on the forum selection clause in the contract with DROF AG.

Assume that no settlement is reached between any of the parties and that a money judgment is rendered in a Federal District Court in New Jersey against CANTIRE, DROF AG, and DROF-UK PLC, listing all three as jointly and severally liable for all damages. The judgment awarded the plaintiffs $50,000 for lost wages, $125,000 for past medical expenses, $75,000 for future medical expenses, and $400,000 in punitive damages (based on a finding of intentionally reckless conduct). The judgment as entered includes acknowledgment that 40% of all amounts are to be paid to the plaintiff's attorneys as compensation for their fees.

SECTION II.   FOCUS OF CONSIDERATION

This problem raises the question of recognition and enforcement of a U.S. judgment in foreign courts (the reverse of the issues considered in Chapter 6). Several issues must be considered at the outset. First, in what countries do the defendants have assets sufficient to satisfy the judgment? If more than one of the defendants have assets in the same country, and that country's laws are favorable to enforcement, then that is where the next proceeding should be initiated. If each of the three defendants has assets only in its home country, then it is important to consider the fact that liability is joint and several and the country in which enforcement will be most easily accomplished. If each defendant's liability is separate, then collection on the judgment may require enforcement proceedings in all three jurisdictions.

Obviously, all questions regarding foreign law cannot be answered in detail by a U.S. lawyer and local counsel will be necessary. Some understanding of the differences in recognition and enforcement practice is useful, however, and in fact necessary to an informed decision regarding additional proceedings. In fact, these are issues that should have been considered at the outset when determining where to bring the initial action, and what procedures to use for service of process, discovery, and other matters.

SECTION III.   READINGS, QUESTIONS AND COMMENTS

The ideal condition for taking a judgment from one country to another exists when the two countries involved are parties to a treaty on reciprocal recognition and enforcement of judgments. Numerous such bilateral treaties exist throughout the world, and the European Union has developed the Brussels Convention (now the Brussels Regulation and the best example of such relationships on a multilateral basis). Importantly, however, the United States is not a party to any bilateral or multilateral treaty dealing generally with recognition and enforcement of judgments. While negotiations have been underway at the Hague Conference on Private International Law for just such a multilateral convention, they have not yet achieved the desired results, and recognition of U.S. judgments in other countries remains a matter of local law in the country in which enforcement is sought.

PART A.   RECOGNITION AND ENFORCEMENT IN CANADA

In Canada, like in the United States, recognition of judgments generally is a matter of provincial law. Also like the United States, Canadian law regarding foreign matters often develops from the law dealing with inter-provincial relationships. Thus, the starting point in Canada in considering the recognition of foreign judgments is a case involving the respect one province should accord to a judgment from another province. The *Morguard* case below provides the foundation for the development of Canadian law. The *Ivey* case following it indicates the way in which *Morguard* has been applied particularly to judgments from the United States.

MORGUARD INVESTMENTS LTD. v. DE SAVOYE

Canadian Supreme Court, 1990.
52 B.C.L.R. (2d) 160, 76 D.L.R.4th 256, [1990] 3 S.C.R. 1077.

The judgment of the court was delivered by *La Forest J.*:

This appeal . . . concerns the recognition to be given by the courts in one province to a judgment of the courts in another province in a personal action brought in the latter province at a time when the defendant did not live there. Specifically, the appeal deals with judgments granted in foreclosure proceedings for deficiencies on sale of mortgaged property.

The respondents, Morguard Investments Limited and Credit Foncier Trust Company, became mortgagees of land in Alberta in 1978. The appellant, Douglas De Savoye, who then resided in Alberta, was originally guarantor but later took title to the land and assumed the obligation of mortgagor. Shortly afterwards he moved to British Columbia, and he has not resided or carried on business in Alberta since. The mortgages fell into default and the respondents brought action in Alberta. The appellant was served with process in the action by double registered mail addressed to his home in British Columbia pursuant to orders for service by the Alberta court in accordance with the rules for service outside its jurisdiction. There are rules to the same effect in British Columbia.

The appellant took no steps to appear or to defend the action. There was no clause in the mortgage by which he agreed to submit to the jurisdiction of the Alberta court, and he did not attorn to its jurisdiction.

FACTS

The respondents obtained judgments nisi in the foreclosure action. At the expiry of the redemption period, they obtained "Rice orders" against the appellant. Under these orders, a judicial sale of the mortgaged properties to the respondents took place and judgment was entered against the appellant for the deficiencies between the value of the property and the amount owing on the mortgages. The respondents then each commenced a separate action in the British Columbia Supreme Court to enforce the Alberta judgment for the deficiencies. Judgment was granted to the respondents by the Supreme Court in a decision which was upheld on appeal to the British Columbia Court of Appeal. The appellant then sought and was granted leave to appeal to this court,

* * *

THE ENGLISH BACKGROUND

No one denies the Alberta court's jurisdiction to entertain the action and enforce it there if it can. It would be surprising if they did. It concerns a transaction entered into in Alberta by individuals who were resident in Alberta at the time of the transaction, and involves land situate in that province. Though the defendant appellant was outside Alberta at the time the action was brought and judgment given, the Alberta rules for service outside the jurisdiction permitted him to be served in British Columbia. These rules are similar to those in other provinces, and specifically British Columbia. The validity of such rules does not appear to have been subjected to much questioning, a matter to which I shall, however, return.

The issue, then, as already mentioned, is simply whether a personal judgment validly given in Alberta against an absent defendant may be enforced in British Columbia, where he now resides.

The law on the matter has remained remarkably constant for many years. It originated in England during the 19th century and, while it has been subjected to considerable refinement, its general structure has not substantially changed. The two cases most commonly relied on, *Singh v. Faridkote (Rajah)*, [1894] A.C. 670 (P.C.) [Punjab], and *Emanuel v. Symon*, date from the turn of the century. I shall confine myself to a discussion of the latter because it is the more frequently cited.

In *Symon*, the defendant, while residing and carrying on business in Western Australia, entered into a partnership in 1895 for the working of a gold mine situated in the colony and owned by the partnership. He later ceased to carry on business there, and moved permanently to England in 1899. Two years later, other members of the partnership brought an action in the colony for the dissolution of the partnership, sale of the mine, and an accounting. The writ was served on the defendant in England, but he took no step to defend the action. The colonial court decreed a dissolution of the partnership and sale of the mine, and in taking the accounts found a sum due from the partnership.

The plaintiffs paid the sum and brought action in England to recover the portion which they alleged was owed by the defendant. Channell J. gave judgment for the plaintiffs, but a unanimous Court of Appeal reversed the judgment.

Buckley L.J.'s summary of the law in that case bears a remarkable resemblance to a code and has been cited repeatedly ever since. He stated,

> In actions in personam there are five cases in which the Courts of this country will enforce a foreign judgment: (1.) Where the defendant is a subject of the foreign country in which the judgment has been obtained; (2.) where he was resident in the foreign country when the action began; (3.) where the defendant in the character of plaintiff has selected the forum in which he is afterwards sued; (4.) where he has voluntarily appeared; and (5.) where he has contracted to submit himself to the forum in which the judgment was obtained.

Though the first of these propositions may now be open to doubt, Buckley's statement of the law, with one qualification to be noted, otherwise accurately represents the common law in England to this day.

* * *

The Canadian Background

In Canada, the courts have until recent years unanimously accepted the authority of *Emanuel v. Symon*, supra, in dealing with the recognition of foreign judgments. This was, of course, inevitable so far as foreign judgments were concerned until 1949, when appeals to the Privy Council were abolished. But the approach was not confined to foreign judgments. It was extended to judgments of other provinces, which for the purposes of the rules of private international law are considered "foreign" countries. There is thus a plethora of cases throughout Canada where two persons have entered into a contract in one province, frequently when both were resident there at the time, but have found it impossible to enforce a judgment given in that province because the defendant had moved to another province when the action was brought * * * Essentially, then, recognition by the courts of one province of a personal judgment against a defendant given in another province is dependent on the defendant's presence at the time of the action in the province where the judgment was given, unless the defendant in some way submits to the jurisdiction of the court giving the judgment.

Soon after the decision in *Travers v. Holley*, supra, however, Professor Gilbert D. Kennedy began to argue for the extension of the "reciprocity" approach, adopted in that case, to personal actions, at least in the case of judgments given in other provinces. A British Columbia case, *Archambault v. Solloway*, * * * Wilson J. of the British Columbia Supreme Court * * * found the jurisdictional reciprocity approach "highly persuasive" and failed to apply it solely because Quebec (where the judgment sought to be enforced had been given) gave effect to a foreign judgment only after an inquiry on its merits. It was therefore not comparable to the effect given to foreign judgments in cases where these are recognized in common law provinces. Subsequently, Professor Castel joined Kennedy in arguing for the adoption of the reciprocity approach.

Until 1987, however, no case appears to have adopted that position. But in that year Gow Co. Ct. J., in a forceful judgment, applied the reciprocity approach to an in personam action, in *Marcotte v. Megson,* * * *.

* * *

ANALYSIS

The common law regarding the recognition and enforcement of foreign judgments is firmly anchored in the principle of territoriality as interpreted and applied by the English courts in the 19th century. This principle reflects the fact, one of the basic tenets of international law, that sovereign states have exclusive jurisdiction in their own territory. As a concomitant to this, states are hesitant to exercise jurisdiction over matters that may take place in the territory of other states. Jurisdiction being territorial, it follows that a state's law has no binding effect outside its jurisdiction. Great Britain, and specifically its courts, applied that doctrine more rigorously than other states. The English approach, we saw, was unthinkingly adopted by the courts of this country, even in relation to judgments given in sister provinces.

* * *

In any event, the English rules seem to me to fly in the face of the obvious intention of the Constitution to create a single country. This presupposes a basic goal of stability and unity where many aspects of life are not confined to one jurisdiction. A common citizenship ensured the mobility of Canadians across provincial lines, a position reinforced today by s. 6 of the Canadian Charter of Rights and Freedoms. * * * In particular, significant steps were taken to foster economic integration. One of the central features of the constitutional arrangements incorporated in the Constitution Act, 1867, was the creation of a common market. Barriers to interprovincial trade were removed by s. 121. Generally, trade and commerce between the provinces was seen to be a matter of concern to the country as a whole. * * *

These arrangements themselves speak to the strong need for the enforcement throughout the country of judgments given in one province. But that is not all. The Canadian judicial structure is so arranged that any concerns about differential quality of justice among the provinces can have no real foundation. All superior court judges—who also have superintending control over other provincial courts and tribunals—are appointed and paid by the federal authorities. And all are subject to final review by the Supreme Court of Canada, which can determine when the courts of one province have appropriately exercised jurisdiction in an action and the circumstances under which the courts of another province should recognize such judgments. Any danger resulting from unfair procedure is further avoided by sub-constitutional factors, such as for example the fact that Canadian lawyers adhere to the same code of ethics throughout Canada. In fact, since *Black v. Law Soc. of Alta.*, *supra*, we have seen a proliferation of interprovincial law firms.

These various constitutional and sub-constitutional arrangements and practices make unnecessary a "full faith and credit" clause such as exists in other federations, such as the United States and Australia. The existence of these clauses, however, does indicate that a régime of mutual recognition of judgments across the country is inherent in a federation. Indeed, the European Economic Community has determined that such a feature flows naturally from a common market, even without political integration. To that end its members have entered into the 1968 Convention on Jurisdiction and Enforcement of Judgments in Civil and Commercial Matters.

The integrating character of our constitutional arrangements as they apply to interprovincial mobility is such that some writers have suggested that a "full faith and credit" clause must be read into the Constitution and that the federal Parliament is, under the "Peace, Order and good Government" clause, empowered to legislate respecting the recognition and enforcement of judgments throughout Canada. The present case was not, however, argued on that basis, and I need not go that far. For present purposes it is sufficient to say that, in my view, the application of the underlying principles of comity and private international law must be adapted to the situations where they are applied, and that in a federation this implies a fuller and more generous acceptance of the judgments of the courts of other constituent units of the federation. In short, the rules of comity or private international law as they apply between the provinces must be shaped to conform to the federal structure of the Constitution.

This court has, in other areas of the law having extraterritorial implications, recognized the need for adapting the law to the exigencies of a federation. * * *

A similar approach should, in my view, be adopted in relation to the recognition and enforcement of judgments within Canada. As I see it, the courts in one province should give full faith and credit, to use the language of the United States Constitution, to the judgments given by a court in another province or a territory, so long as that court has properly, or appropriately, exercised jurisdiction in the action. I referred earlier to the principles of order and fairness that should obtain in this area of the law. Both order and justice militate in favour of the security of transactions. It seems anarchic and unfair that a person should be able to avoid legal obligations arising in one province simply by moving to another province. Why should a plaintiff be compelled to begin an action in the province where the defendant now resides whatever the inconvenience and costs this may bring and whatever degree of connection the relevant transaction may have with another province? And why should the availability of local enforcement be the decisive element in the plaintiff's choice of forum?

These concerns, however, must be weighed against fairness to the defendant. I noted earlier that the taking of jurisdiction by a court in one province and its recognition in another must be viewed as correlatives, and I added that recognition in other provinces should be dependent on the fact that the court giving judgment "properly" or "appropriately" exercised jurisdiction. It may meet the demands of order and fairness to recognize a judgment given in a jurisdiction that had the greatest, or at least significant, contacts with the subject matter of the action. But it hardly accords with principles of order and fairness to permit a person to sue another in any jurisdiction, without regard to the contacts that jurisdiction may have to the defendant or the subject matter of the suit . . . . . Thus fairness to the defendant requires that the judgment be issued by a court acting through fair process and with properly-restrained jurisdiction.

As discussed, fair process is not an issue within the Canadian federation. The question that remains, then, is: When has a court exercised its jurisdiction appropriately for the purposes of recognition by a court in another province? This poses no difficulty where the court has acted on the basis of the accepted grounds traditionally accepted by courts as permitting the recognition and enforcement of foreign judgments—in the case of judgments in personam, where the defendant was within the jurisdiction at the time of the action or when he submitted to its judgment, whether by agreement of by attornment. In the first case, the court had jurisdiction over the person, and in the second case by virtue of the agreement. No injustice results.

The difficulty, of course, arises where, as here, the defendant was outside the jurisdiction of that court and he was served ex juris. To what extent may a court of a province properly exercise jurisdiction over a defendant in another province? The rules for service ex juris in all the provinces are broad—in some provinces, Nova Scotia and Prince Edward Island, very broad indeed. It is clear, however, that, if the courts of one province are to be expected to give effect to judgments given in another province, there must be some limits to the exercise of jurisdiction against persons outside the province.

It will be obvious from the manner in which I approach the problem that I do not see the "reciprocity approach" as providing an answer to the difficulty regarding in personam judgments, whatever utility it may have on the international plane. Even there, I am more comfortable with the approach taken by the House of Lords in *Indyka v. Indyka*, supra, where the question posed in a matrimonial case was whether there was a real and substantial connection between the petitioner and the country or territory exercising jurisdiction. I should observe, however, that in a case involving matrimonial status the subject matter of the action and the petitioner are obviously at the same place. That is not necessarily so of a personal action, where a nexus may have to be sought between the subject matter of the action and the territory where the action is brought.

A case in this court, *Moran v. Pyle Nat. (Can.) Ltd.*, [1975], though a tort action, is instructive as to the manner in which a court may properly exercise jurisdiction in actions in contracts as well. In that case, an electrician was fatally injured in Saskatchewan while removing a spent light bulb manufactured in Ontario by a company that neither carried on business nor held any property in Saskatchewan. The company sold all its products to distributors and none to consumers. It had no salesmen or agents in Saskatchewan. The electrician's wife and children brought action against the company under the Fatal Accidents Act of Saskatchewan, claiming that the company had been negligent in the manufacture of the light bulb and in failing to provide an adequate safety system to prevent unsafe bulbs from leaving the plant and being sold or used. On a chambers motion, the trial judge held that any negligence would have occurred in Ontario, and so the tort was committed out of Saskatchewan. However, he, granted special leave under a provision of the Queen's Bench Act to commence an action in Saskatchewan, and made an order allowing service of the statement of claim and a writ of summons in Ontario. The company successfully appealed to the Saskatchewan Court of Appeal, but the Court of Appeal's judgment was reversed by this court.

Dickson J. gave the reasons of the court. The location of a tort, he noted, was a matter of some difficulty. A plaintiff, he observed, could be sued on the theory that the court where the defendant happened to be had physical power over the defendant. But, he added, that suit could also be brought where the tort had been committed. Where the situs of the tort was, however, was not an easy question. One theory was that it was situated where the wrongful action took place (there, Ontario). Another would have it that it is the place where the damage occurred. But, as he noted:

> Logically, it would seem that if a tort is to be divided and one part occurs in state A and another in state B, the tort could reasonably for jurisdictional purposes be said to have occurred in both states or, on a more restrictive approach, in neither state. It is difficult to understand how it can properly be said to have occurred only in state A.

At the end of the day, he rejected any rigid or mechanical theory for determining the situs of the tort. Rather, he adopted "a more flexible, qualitative and quantitative test" [p. 407], posing the question, as had some English cases there cited, in terms of whether it was "inherently reasonable" [p. 408] for the action to be brought in a particular jurisdiction, or whether, to adopt another expression, there was a "real and substantial connection" between the jurisdiction and the wrong-doing. Dickson J. thus summarized his view:

> Generally speaking, in determining where a tort has been committed, it is unnecessary, and unwise, to have resort to any arbitrary set

of rules. The place of acting and the place of harm theories are too arbitrary and inflexible to be recognized in contemporary jurisprudence. In the *Distillers'* case and again in the *Cordova* case a real and substantial connection test was hinted at. Cheshire has suggested a test very similar to this; the author says that it would not be inappropriate to regard a tort as having occurred in any country substantially affected by the defendant's activities or its consequences and the law of which is likely to have been in the reasonable contemplation of the parties. Applying this test to a case of careless manufacture, the following rule can be formulated: where a foreign defendant carelessly manufactures a product in a foreign jurisdiction which enters into the normal channels of trade and he knows or ought to know both that as a result of his carelessness a consumer may well be injured and it is reasonably foreseeable that the product would be used or consumed where the plaintiff used or consumed it, then the forum in which the plaintiff suffered damage is entitled to exercise judicial jurisdiction over that foreign defendant. This rule recognizes the important interest a state has in injuries suffered by persons within its territory. It recognizes that the purpose of negligence as a tort is to protect against carelessly inflicted injury and thus that the predominating element is damage suffered. *By tendering his products in the market place directly or through normal distributive channels, a manufacturer ought to assume the burden of defending those products wherever they cause harm as long as the forum into which the manufacturer is taken is one that he reasonably ought to have had in his contemplation when he so tendered his goods. This is particularly true of dangerously defective goods placed in the interprovincial flow of commerce.* [emphasis added]

Before going on I should observe that, if this court thinks it inherently reasonable for a court to exercise jurisdiction under circumstances like those described, it would be odd indeed if it did not also consider it reasonable for the courts of another province to recognize and enforce that court's judgment. This is obvious from the fact that in *Moran* Dickson J. derived the reasonableness of his approach from the "normal distributive channels" of products [p. 409], and in particular the "interprovincial flow of commerce". If, as I stated, it is reasonable to support the exercise of jurisdiction in one province, it would seem equally reasonable that the judgment be recognized in other provinces. This is supported by the statement of Dickson J. in *Zingre* that comity is based on the common interest of both the jurisdiction giving judgment and the recognizing jurisdiction. Indeed, it is in the interest of the whole country, an interest recognized in the Constitution itself.

The above rationale is not, as I see it, limited to torts. It is interesting to observe the close parallel in the reasoning in *Moran* with that adopted by this court in dealing with jurisdiction for the purposes of the criminal law. In particular, barring express or implied agreement, the reasoning in *Moran* is obviously relevant to contracts; indeed, the same activity can often give rise to an action for breach of contract and one in negligence. As Professor Sharpe observes:

> It is inconsistent to permit jurisdiction in tort claims on the basis that the defendant should reasonably have foreseen that his goods would reach the plaintiff and cause damage within the jurisdiction and, on the other hand, to refuse service out of the jurisdiction in contractual actions where the defendant clearly knows that his goods are going to the foreign jurisdiction.

Turning to the present case, it is difficult to imagine a more reasonable place for the action for the deficiencies to take place than Alberta. As noted earlier, the property is situate there, and the contract was entered into there by parties then both resident in the province. Moreover, deficiency actions follow upon foreclosure proceedings, which should obviously take place in Alberta, and the action for the deficiencies cries out for consolidation with the foreclosure proceedings in some manner similar to a Rice order. A more "real and substantial" connection between the damages suffered and the jurisdiction can scarcely be imagined. In my view, the Alberta court had jurisdiction, and its judgment should be recognized and be enforceable in British Columbia.

I am aware, of course, that the possibility of being sued outside the province of his residence may pose a problem for a defendant. But that can occur in relation to actions in rem now. In any event, this consideration must be weighed against the fact that the plaintiff, under the English rules, may often find himself subjected to the inconvenience of having to pursue his debtor to another province, however just, efficient or convenient it may be to pursue an action where the contract took place or the damage occurred. It seems to me that the approach of permitting suit where there is a real and substantial connection with the action provides a reasonable balance between the rights of the parties. It affords some protection against being pursued in jurisdictions having little or no connection with the transaction or the parties. In a world where even the most familiar things we buy and sell originate or are manufactured elsewhere, and where people are constantly moving from province to province, it is simply anachronistic to uphold a "power theory" or a single situs for torts or contracts for the proper exercise of jurisdiction.

The private international law rule requiring substantial connection with the jurisdiction where the action took place is supported by the constitutional restriction of legislative power "in the province." As Guérin J. observed in *Dupont v. Taronga Holdings Ltd.*, [1987], "In the case of service outside of the issuing province, service ex juris must measure up to constitutional rules." The restriction to the province would certainly require at least minimal contact with the province, and there is authority for the view that the contact required by the Constitution for the purposes of territoriality is the same as required by the rule of private international law between sister provinces * * *.

I would dismiss the appeal with costs.

Appeal dismissed.

UNITED STATES OF AMERICA v. C. ROBERT IVEY, MAZIV INDUSTRIES, LTD.

Ontario Court of Justice, General Division, 1995.
[1995] 130 D.L.R. 4th 674, aff'd, 139 D.L.R. 4th 570.

[After cleaning up a waste disposal site north of Detroit, Michigan, the U.S. Environmental Protection Agency ("EPA") brought suit in Federal District Court in Michigan against the Canadian shareholders of the Michigan corporation (LDI) that had managed the waste disposal site, seeking reimbursement of the costs of that clean up under the Comprehensive Environmental Response, Compensation and Liability Act (CERCLA). Though Ivey contested jurisdiction in the U.S. court, this contest was unsuccessful, and the case resulted in summary judgment against Ivey and default judgment against two other corporate defendants (Maziv and Ineco), both of which were Ontario corporations owned by Ivey to which shares of LDI had been transferred. When the resulting judgment was not fully satisfied in the U.S., the United States government brought an action in Ontario to recover $4,594,763.70 remaining due.]

SHARPE J.:

The plaintiff United States of America brings this motion for summary judgment in an action to enforce two judgments it has obtained against the defendants in the United States District Court for the Eastern District of Michigan ("District Court"). The defendants, by way of a cross-motion, ask that the action be dismissed. The District Court judgments were obtained pursuant to the *Comprehensive Environmental Response, Compensation and Liability Act 1980* ("CERCLA"). The plaintiff sued for reimbursement of the cost of remedial measures undertaken by the Environmental Protection Agency ("EPA") in relation to a waste disposal site owned and operated by the defendants. The defendants did not defend the District Court actions, and resist enforcement of the judgments by this court on a number of grounds summarized in the four issues which follow.

* * *

JURISDICTION

The plaintiff submits that there are two grounds for finding that the District Court had jurisdiction that this court will recognize. First, they submit that the "real and substantial connection" test, established by the Supreme Court of Canada in *Morguard* should be applied. Second, and in the alternative, the plaintiff submits that although the defendants did not defend the District Court action on the merits, the unsuccessful motion brought by Ivey and Ineco to dismiss for want of jurisdiction provides a sufficient basis to hold that those parties attorned to the jurisdiction of the District Court.

REAL AND SUBSTANTIAL CONNECTION

The *Morguard* decision dealt specifically with the recognition and enforcement of a judgment of the courts of one province by the courts of another province. The Court held that the exigencies of modern life and commerce in the Canadian federation required a departure of the traditional and restrictive rules governing recognition and enforcement. Provided there was a "real and substantial connection" between the rendering province and the subject matter of the action, the judgment is entitled to recognition and enforcement throughout Canada.

The question of whether *Morguard* applies to the judgments of the courts of the United States and other foreign courts with legal regimes based upon principles compatible with Canadian concepts of justice has been addressed in a number of subsequent cases. The predominant view of these authorities is that the "real and substantial connection" test mandated by *Morguard* is appropriate. While there is no doubt that considerations relating specifically to Canadian federalism played an important role in the Supreme Court's decision in *Morguard*, principles of broader application were also at work. * * *

* * *

The Supreme Court of Canada has not hesitated to apply the comity principle, as enunciated in *Morguard*, in relation to truly foreign judgments in other areas of conflict of laws. In *Arrowmaster Inc. v. Unique Forming Ltd.* (1993), MacPherson J. described the rationale for applying *Morguard* to a United States judgment as follows:

> I think it fair to say that the overarching theme of La Forest J.'s reasons is the necessity and desirability, in a mobile society, for governments and courts to respect the orders made by courts of foreign jurisdictions with comparable legal systems, including substantive laws and rules of procedure. ... [T]he historical analysis in La Forest J.'s judgment, of both the United Kingdom and Canadian jurisprudence, and the doctrinal principles enunciated by the court are equally applicable, in my view, in a situation where the judgment has been rendered by a court in a foreign jurisdiction.

A similar rationale is expressed by the British Columbia Court of Appeal in *Moses v. Shore Boat Builders Ltd.* (1993), Cumming J.A.: "Modern rules of international law must accommodate the flow of wealth, skills and people across state lines and promote international commerce."

Morguard has been applied to non-Canadian judgments in several other cases.

* * *

The defendants rely on what appears to be the only reported decision which refuses to extend *Morguard* beyond the judgments of other Canadian courts, *Evans Dodd v. Gambin Associates* (1994). In that case, one of the first to be decided on the point, Sheard J. held that it would be inappropriate to defeat the defendant's reliance on the traditional rules and enforce a default judgment obtained in England. No evidence was offered here that the decision not to participate in the District Court action was made in reliance on the pre-*Morguard* rules, and, in any event, the summary judgment and default proceedings were taken after the release of the *Morguard* judgment.

In my view, the *Morguard* real and substantial connection test is applicable for reasons expressed by MacPherson J. in *Arrowmaster* and by the British Columbia Court of Appeal in *Moses*. In my view, the law would be seriously deficient and at odds with the reality of modern commercial life if it were possible for a resident of this province to actively engage in a business in the United States for a period of several years, but then shelter behind the borders of Ontario from answering to a claim for civil liability for harm caused by that activity.

APPLICATION TO THE REAL AND SUBSTANTIAL CONNECTION TEST

I have no hesitation in finding that with respect to all of the defendants, the real and substantial connection test is met. The defendants engaged in the waste disposal business in Michigan, and the cause of action arose within the jurisdiction of the District Court. Maziv and Ivey had a direct ownership interest in LDI, and Ivey was a principal officer of both corporations. Ivey regularly was present in Michigan to make decisions concerning the very environmental issues which gave rise to the plaintiff's claim. Ivey dealt with and appeared before environmental regulatory agencies on behalf of LDI. Ineco acquired its interest in the shares of LDI on the express understanding that it would assume any liability of Maziv. The findings of Judge Zatkoff on the issue of "long arm" jurisdiction, quoted above, may be cited as added support for this finding.

PENAL, REVENUE OR OTHER PUBLIC LAW

The defendants submit that the provisions of CERCLA which were the basis for the District Court judgment are "penal," "revenue," or "public" laws, and that, accordingly, this court should refuse enforcement.

PENAL LAWS

The scope of the category "penal" laws was defined by the Privy Council in *Huntington v. Antrill*, [1893] A.C. 150, at p. 156, as

> all suits in favour of the state for the recovery of pecuniary penalties for any violation of statutes for the protection of its revenue or other municipal laws, and to all judgments for such penalties.

In my view, the CERCLA provisions imposing liability against the defendants cannot be classified as penal in nature. In *United States v. Monsanto*, 858 F.2d 160 (4th Cir.1988), CERCLA was characterized as follows:

> CERCLA does not exact punishment. Rather it creates a reimbursement obligation on any person judicially determined responsible for the costs of remedying hazardous conditions at a waste disposal facility. The restitution of cleanup costs was not intended to operate, nor does it operate in fact, as a criminal penalty or a punitive deterrent.

The measure of recovery is directly tied to the cost of the required environmental cleanup. The court must be satisfied that the amounts it seeks to recover were actually expended in response to the environmental threat, and that those costs were incurred in the manner prescribed by CERCLA and the National Recovery Plan. While the nature of liability imposed may be unexpected, it is restitutionary in nature, and is not imposed with a view to punishment of the party responsible.

Revenue Laws

* * *

[I]t is for this court to characterize the nature of CERCLA for the purposes of these arguments. Revenue or tax law appears not to have been precisely defined for these purposes, but it is difficult to imagine how a claim for reimbursement of costs incurred as a result of the actionable conduct of the defendant could be viewed as a tax. In view of the fact that the damages claimed by the plaintiff were measured directly and precisely by the actual cost of removal and remedial measures, I see no basis for the argument the judgments are to enforce the revenue laws of the rendering jurisdiction.

Other Public Law

* * *

The principle of comity which underpins the recent pronouncements of the Supreme Court of Canada * * * should, in my view, inform the development of this area of the law. What is sought to be enforced here is a judgment requiring parties who engaged in an environmentally hazardous activity for profit to make good the cost actually incurred to eliminate that environmental hazard. There is clearly a public purpose at stake, but in my view, the presence of that public purpose does not defeat the plaintiff's case. Given the prevalence of regulatory schemes aimed at environmental protection and control in North America, considerations of comity strongly favour enforcement. In an area of law dealing with such obvious and significant trans-border issues, it is particularly appropriate for the forum court to give full faith and credit to the laws and judgments of neighbouring states. To the extent that the comity principle entails an element of reciprocity, it is significant to note that the courts of the United States enforce foreign judgments for environmental clean-up costs similar to those at issue in the case at bar.

Natural Justice

The defendants submit that the judgments sought to be enforced were obtained in a manner which violates the principles of natural justice. * * *

Acceptance of the argument that the imposition of strict liability or a relaxed burden of proof should render American judgments unenforceable in Canada would have far-reaching consequences. Rules of liability and the burden of proof are pre-eminently matters for the law of the foreign jurisdiction. I am aware of no authority for the proposition that a judgment rendered on the basis of a strict form of statutory liability will not be enforced. Moreover, the Ontario Environmental Protection Act (OEPA) imposes similarly strict liability in certain situations.

Public Policy

The defendants submit that given the severity of the CERCLA liability regime, both procedurally and substantively, it would be contrary to public policy for this court to enforce the judgments. This argument was supported by a comparison of CERCLA with OEPA, which, the defendants allege, does not suffer the same defects as CERCLA.

In my view, this argument fails for a number of reasons. First, most, if not all, of the arguments advanced here have already been dealt with under the natural justice defence. Second, while the public policy defence exists in theory, it has rarely been applied. * * * There is no authority of which I have been made aware that would allow it to be applied in the present case. It is plainly not the case that enforcement will be refused on the grounds that judgment sought to be enforced depends upon a law or basis of liability more strict or severe than the law of the forum. As noted by Lacourcière J.A. in *Boardwalk Regency Corp. v. Maalouf* (1992), "where foreign law is applicable, Canadian courts will generally apply that law even if the result may be contrary to domestic law." In the same case, Carthy J.A. emphasized "the care which courts must exercise in relying upon public policy as a ground for refusing enforcement." He went on to state:

> The common ground of all expressed reasons for imposing the doctrine of public policy is essential morality. This must be more than the morality of some persons and must run through the fabric of society to the extent that it is not consonant with our system of justice and general moral outlook to countenance the conduct, no matter how legal it may have been where it occurred.

* * *

CONCLUSION

The plaintiff has established that the District Court had jurisdiction to render the judgments sued upon, and I have found that none of the defences to enforcement of the District Court judgments are sustainable in law. Both parties moved for summary judgment, and there are no material facts in dispute which require a trial. The requirements under Rule 20 for summary judgment have been fully satisfied. Accordingly, there shall be judgment for the plaintiff for the amount in Canadian currency necessary to purchase (U.S.) $4,594,763.70, plus interest from the date of the judgments, July 18, 1991. I may be spoken to with respect to rate of interest and costs, if necessary.

Motion granted.

THE CANADIAN UNIFORM ENFORCEMENT OF FOREIGN JUDGMENTS ACT

In 2003, the Uniform Law Conference of Canada adopted a Uniform Enforcement of Foreign Judgments Act. That Act is reproduced in the Documents Supplement to this casebook. You should review its terms and consider whether and how its adoption would change the common law reflected in the preceding cases. As of early 2008, Saskatchewan was the only province to have enacted the Act.

Questions and Comments

1. How likely is it that the New Jersey judgment in Problem 7.1 against the Canadian defendant will be enforced in a Canadian court? What, if any, defenses might be raised to recognition and enforcement of the judgment? If they are raised, will any of them be successful? If you were counsel for the Canadian defendant, would you advise an aggressive position that resulted in spending time and expense in contesting an action for recognition and enforcement?

2. In *Morguard*, the review of English law, particularly the early quote from *Emanuel v. Symon,* indicates an approach that contrasts with what we have seen in the United States (and with what we will see below is the practice in Germany). Instead of listing grounds for refusal of recognition, the *Symon* quote lists instances where a foreign judgment is to be recognized. This raises a basic question of national approach to this issue. Is it best to presume recognition and provide exceptions, or to presume non-recognition and provide exceptions in the other direction? If you were to draft national law on the matter, which approach would be most appropriate? If you were to draft a multilateral treaty on the matter, which approach would be most appropriate?

3. The *Morguard* opinion also speaks of the creation of a Canadian "common market." To what extent is recognition of judgments a trade law matter? In other words, in a union of states or provinces where goods, services, capital, and people move freely across borders, is it necessary for judicial judgments to move freely across the same borders in order to remain consistent in terms of policy? Is this what the full faith and credit clause of the U.S. Constitution accomplishes? After noting that such an approach was

not argued in the *Morguard* case, Justice La Forest states that "the rules of comity or private international law as they apply between the provinces must be shaped to conform to the federal structure of the Constitution." To what extent does (or should) trade law shape arguments for the development of private international law dealing with recognition of judgments? Are those arguments limited in their application to cases internal to a federal state or an organization like the European Union? Or can lawyers in judgment enforcement cases draw upon trade law (aspects of the WTO, NAFTA, etc.) to strengthen their positions in private litigation? *See,* Ronald A. Brand, *Recognition of Foreign Judgments as a Trade Law Issue: The Economics of Private International Law*, in THE ECONOMIC ANALYSIS OF INTERNATIONAL LAW 592 (Jagdeep Bhandari & Alan O. Sykes, eds., 1998).

4. Justice La Forest suggests three approaches to recognition of foreign judgments in *Morguard*: (1) categorization of the types of cases that will result in recognition, (2) a "reciprocity approach" in which the recognizing court considers whether the basis for jurisdiction exercised by the originating court is also available in the recognizing jurisdiction, and (3) the "real and substantial connection" approach, which La Forest finds to more appropriately address issues of fairness to the defendant. Do you agree with La Forest that the third of these is the most appropriate? At base, it is a jurisdictional inquiry and has similarities to the "minimum contacts" analysis of jurisdiction by the U.S. Supreme Court in cases such as *International Shoe* and *World-Wide Volkswagen*. What are the similarities and differences between the U.S. minimum contacts approach to jurisdiction and the Canadian Supreme Court's "real and substantial connection" approach to recognition of judgments (and thus indirectly to jurisdiction)?

PART B.   RECOGNITION AND ENFORCEMENT IN GERMANY

In most civil law jurisdictions, enforcement of a foreign judgment in the absence of a treaty means that a new action must be brought on the judgment in order to obtain recognition, with the resulting local judgment of recognition being the one for which enforcement is sought. Most often, the prerequisites for judgment recognition and enforcement are found in the civil procedure code. This is the case in Germany.

THE GERMAN CODE OF CIVIL PROCEDURE (ZIVILPROZESSORDNUNG)

§ 328

(1) The judgment of a foreign court shall not be recognized:

1. if the courts of the State to which the foreign court belongs have no jurisdiction under German law;

2. if the documents instigating the proceedings were not served on the defendant in accordance with law or in such a timely manner that he could defend himself and he made no appearance and he pleads this fact;

3. if the judgment conflicts with a German judgment or with an earlier recognizable foreign judgment or if the proceeding underlying the foreign judgment conflicts with a German proceeding that began before the foreign proceeding;

4. if recognition of the judgment would lead to a result that would clearly conflict with essential principles of German law, in particular if recognition would conflict with the Basic Law (German Constitution);

5. if reciprocity is not guaranteed.

§ 722

(1) The judgment of a foreign court shall not be enforced except by virtue of a judgment for enforcement

(2) Jurisdiction to pronounce such a judgment for enforcement shall be exercised by the Amtsgericht (County Court) or Landgericht (District Court) respectively, having general jurisdiction over the debtor, or otherwise by the Amtsgericht or Landgericht respectively, before which an action may be brought against the debtor under § 723.

§ 723

(1) The judgment for enforcement shall be rendered without review of the merits of the case.

(2) The judgment for enforcement shall not be rendered until the judicial decision of the foreign court has become final and conclusive under the law applicable to that court. Nor shall it be rendered where recognition of the judgment is excluded under § 328.

INTRODUCTORY LAW TO THE GERMAN CIVIL CODE

Art. 40

* * *

(3) Claims under foreign law cannot be asserted as far as they

1. reach substantially beyond what is necessary to adequately compensate the victim,

2. Obviously pursue aims different from adequate compensation of the victim, or

3. Contravene conventions on civil responsibility entered into by the Federal Republic of Germany.

GERMANY ENFORCING FOREIGN JUDGMENTS IN THE UNITED STATES AND UNITED STATES JUDGMENTS ABROAD

111–113 (Ronald A. Brand, ed. 1992).*

(This chapter was written by Peter Chrocziel and Rolf Trittmann of the Frankfurt office of Bruckhaus Westrick Stegemann)

In considering enforcement of foreign judgments in Germany, one must consult both the German Code of Civil Procedure (Zivilprozessordnung, or "ZPO") and any applicable treaties or conventions. Germany, like other European countries, has different provisions for enforcing court judgments from countries such as the United States (which is not a party to any multilateral or bilateral treaty with Germany on the subject) and those from countries such as England (which is a party to various enforcement treaties with Germany, such as the Brussels Convention on Jurisdiction and Enforcement of Judgments of 1982).

The basic German Civil Code provisions concerning enforcement of U.S. judgments are § 328, and §§ 722 and 723 ZPO. Section 328 ZPO deals with the acknowledgement of a foreign judgment (so-called "automatic acknowledgment") without any further proceeding. Sections 722 and 723 ZPO govern the enforcement of a judgment, which makes a new procedure necessary. In order to obtain enforcement of a foreign judgment, the prerequisites for acknowledgment must first be fulfilled.

Section 723(1) stipulates that German courts will enforce foreign court judgments without examining the merits of the dispute. Under this provision, German courts, unlike their U.S. counterparts, generally do not consider the legal standards of the forum rendering the judgment in determining whether it should be enforced.

Prerequisites to Enforcement

Certain general requirements must be met for a German court to declare a foreign judgment enforceable. The foreign judgment must be enforceable in the state from which it originates; the German court has to have jurisdiction in order to declare enforceability; and the judgment may not have been previously satisfied.

Sections 723(2) and 328 ZPO set forth six exceptions to the general enforcement requirement of § 723(1).

First, the foreign judgment will not be enforced unless it is final. Unlike the situation in the United States, foreign judgments subject to appeal where rendered are not considered final in Germany.

Second, the foreign judgment must not be contrary to basic principles of German law, especially German constitutional rights. As in the United States, this public policy exception to enforcement does not extend to any judgment at variance with German law. It rather requires an obvious and fundamental contradiction of basic fairness or of the essential elements of the German legal system, such as a violation of due process principles or fraud in obtaining the judgment. Problems also may come up if the U.S. judgment includes punitive damages or was rendered after extensive pre-trial discovery in the U.S. proceeding.

Third, the foreign judgment must have been entered by a court having both personal jurisdiction over the judgment debtor, and subject matter jurisdiction over the dispute giving rise to the judgment. German courts will apply this requirement according to principles of German jurisdictional law alone and not look to the jurisdictional standards of the forum issuing the judgment.[7] As a practical matter, the jurisdictional

---

7. Although it is sometimes said that German courts will apply jurisdictional principles of "international law," they consider such principles to be an integral part

requirements will not pose a substantial hurdle to enforcement of most judgments of U.S. courts, because German jurisdictional requirements tend to be somewhat less rigorous than those of the United States. For example, German courts generally can assert personal jurisdiction over an individual based solely on the presence of the individual's property within Germany.[9]

Fourth, the German Code of Civil Procedure denies enforcement if the defendant was not involved in the foreign proceeding, but only if he did not receive timely service so that he had an opportunity to defend himself. The underlying danger of this requirement can be avoided if the judgment creditor, in bringing the original suit, effected service in the foreign forum through the mechanism of the Hague Convention on the Service Abroad of Judicial and Extrajudicial Documents in Civil or Commercial Matters.

Fifth, the German Code of Civil Procedure provides that a U.S. judgment cannot be enforced in Germany, "if reciprocity is not warranted." German courts have interpreted this requirement as limited to partial reciprocity—that is, the country whose judgment is being enforced would likely enforce a similar judgment of a German court—rather than a requirement that all German court judgments be enforced in the foreign jurisdiction. Presently, reciprocity generally exists between most U.S. states and Germany. Difficulties nevertheless may occur in regard to Mississippi, North Dakota and Oregon.

The *sixth* and final enforcement requirement of the German Code of Civil Procedure provides for non-recognition of foreign judgments that contradict an earlier judgment or proceeding. This acknowledges the basic principle of priority of judgments.

Enforcement Procedure

To enforce a U.S. judgment in Germany, the judgment creditor must initiate a German action on the judgment, requesting an enforcement order from the German court. Such action must be instituted within thirty years of the date that the foreign judgment became final. The action has to be filed either with the Amtsgericht (when the value of the matter in dispute is below DM 6000) or with the Landgericht (above DM 6000) and must be brought in a court with proper jurisdiction, usually where the defendant has his domicile or where assets of the defendant are located.

German courts will enforce foreign judgments rendered in "civil matters" (which in Germany includes commercial and labor disputes but excludes tax and penal judgments). Unlike U.S. courts, German courts

of the general German law of jurisdiction as set forth in the Code of Civil Procedure. In enforcing foreign judgments, German courts will look to this domestic law of jurisdiction to assess both whether the court rendering the judgment had jurisdiction and whether the German court itself has jurisdiction to enforce the judgment.

9. The Brussels Convention now precludes the application of such broad jurisdictional doctrines to nationals of other states party to the Convention.

will denominate their judgments in foreign currencies in appropriate circumstances. Moreover, insofar as a conversion is necessary, it is done at the date of enforcement—not the date of breach or judgment.

DECISION OF THE GERMAN FEDERAL COURT OF JUSTICE (BGH)

From June 4, 1992, Translation From 32 I.L.M. 1327 (1993).[2]*

THE FACTS

The Plaintiff wishes to enforce in the Federal Republic of Germany a US damages judgment. Both parties are citizens of the USA; the Defendant also has German citizenship. Both parties are resident in Stockton, California. In May, 1984, the Defendant who had been sentenced by an American court to imprisonment for sexual abuse of a minor, left the USA. Since that time, he has lived in Germany, where he owns property. The Plaintiff was awarded damages of US $750,260 against the Defendant in a judgment made by the Superior Court of the State of California in and for the County of San Joaquin (hereinafter known as: Superior Court) on 24 April, 1985. The judgment did not set out the facts of the case in any detail or the reasons for the decision. Nevertheless, it was apparent from the transcript of the court proceedings that the judgment was based on a sexual offence committed on the Plaintiff, who was, at the time of the offence, 14 years old and that the damages awarded to the Plaintiff were made up as follows: US $260 for past medical damages, US $100,000 in damages for future medical treatment, US $50,000 for the cost of placement of the Plaintiff, US $200,000 for anxiety, pain, suffering and general damages of that nature and US $400,000 for exemplary and punitive damages. The American lawyer acting for the Plaintiff was awarded 40% of all those monies which it obtained on the Plaintiff's behalf. The District Court (*Landgericht*) [Germany] decided that it was possible for an enforcement order to be issued in Germany in respect of the judgment made by the Superior Court, plus interest. Upon appeal from the Defendant, the Appellate Court (*Oberlandesgericht*) in Düsseldorf upheld the enforcement order in the amount of US $275,325; it rejected the rest of the petition. Both parties lodged an appeal against this judgment. The German Federal Court of Justice ("BGH") decided that exemplary and punitive damages in the amount of US $400,000 could not be enforced in Germany. All the other claims were recognised.

2. Officially reported in *Entscheidungen des Bundesgerichtshofes (Zivilsachen)* BGHZ 118, 312 (1993) (Case reference: IX ZR 149/91 Civil Division). Excerpts also reported in two leading legal periodicals: *Recht der Internationalen Wirtschaft* (RIW) 1993, 132 and *Neue Juristische Wochenschrift* (NJW) 1992, 3096. An appeal from the Appellate Court (*Oberlandesgericht* (OLG)) Düsseldorf (reported in RIW 1991, 594).

* Reproduced with permission from the September 1993 issue of International Legal Materials, © The American Society of International Law.

EXCERPTS FROM THE JUDGMENT:

"III.   ... 4. The arguments upon which the appellate court based its decision to reject a violation of the procedural ordre public in view of the other circumstances of the case before the Superior Court are.... free of errors in law.

[PRE-TRIAL DISCOVERY]

(a) The appellate court was particularly correct in asserting that the fact that the judgment of the Superior Court had been preceded by a summons to the Defendant to a "pre-trial discovery" does not preclude an enforcement order. The conduct of a procedure of this kind for the hearing of evidence between the time at which the petition is filed and the oral hearing ("trial") does not, in itself, under general party rule in the USA, constitute sufficient grounds for a violation of ordre public as defined by § 328, para. 1, sub-para. 4 of the ZPO.

The mere possibility that, amongst other things, this would result in an investigation which would be impermissible under German procedural law, does not fulfill the conditions of § 328, para. 1, sub-para. 4 of the ZPO. The requirement to concentrate on the basic values which must be protected goes beyond the—binding—individual regulations of German positive legislation. It is not just the principles of German procedural law which must be considered (for a dissenting opinion, see *Schütze, Deutsch-amerikanische Urteilsanerkennung*—hereinafter known as "Urteilsanerkennung", p. 169); the legal system as a whole, including the duties of disclosure under German substantive law, which could supersede foreign procedural regulations which have a comparable effect, also has to be taken into account. At this point, the decisive factor is whether or not the concrete outcome of the application of the foreign law, including any associated infringement, in contravention of international law, upon the sovereignty of the country of the court to which application has been made is, in itself, manifestly incompatible with the essential principles of German law established in this manner and with the value of judicial inquiry.

Nothing of the sort has been proven in this case. On the contrary, according to the uncontested assertions of the appellate court, the consequences of default linked by the Superior Court to the Defendant's failure to appear at the "pre-trial discovery" relate only to the facts upon which the claim is based, which facts were revealed by the criminal proceedings against the Defendant in the USA and which the Defendant has to date not contested. There is therefore no legal basis upon which to object to the fact that the appellate court accepted that the judgment of the Superior Court was not, in effect, based upon the "pre-trial discovery" procedure.

[AMERICAN RULE OF COSTS]

(b) Contrary to an interpretation put forward in some quarters (Schütze WM 1979, 1174, 1176), no general objection to the recognition of US civil judgments can be justified on the simple basis that such judgments do not, in principle, provide for reimbursement of costs to the successful party (Jestaedt RIW 1986, 95 f.). It is not unreasonable for a foreign defendant to enter into such proceedings, even if the costs which will have to be borne, which are, in all cases, considerable, are taken into consideration.

... the primary reason given for costs not being reimbursed pursuant to the "American rule of costs" is the need to make it more straightforward to gain access to the courts by reducing the risk in terms of costs (The American Law Institute, Enterprise Responsibility for Personal Injury Vol. II, p. 274 f.; Hommelsheim, ibid., p. 81 f., 155 f.). This also goes some way towards replacing the legal aid which is rarely available. Furthermore, the outcome of the trial is not seen as a sufficiently reliable criterion for justification of the standpoints adopted by the parties prior to the trial (The American Law Institute, ibid., p. 274; Fleming, The American Tort Process, p. 193, each with further evidence; Hommelsheim, ibid., p. 67 ff.).

In accordance with this, aspects of evaluation and of legal policy determine the various regulations concerning costs.

From a German point of view, the regular exclusion of reimbursement of costs in US civil actions does not infringe upon the civil constitutional fundamental rights of the parties or upon the basic principles of the rule of law. It is to be accepted. Cases of deliberate abuse should be countered with the general means provided for the purpose, provided the title in respect of which an enforcement order is to be issued is based upon such abuse.

Furthermore, the results of this application of the "American rule of costs" do not encumber the Defendant in the present case.

[RECIPROCITY WITH CALIFORNIA]

5. The parties are correct, under the presently applicable law, to proceed from the guarantee of reciprocity in relation to California (see Schütze, *Urteilsanerkennung*, p. 43 f. and JR 1986, 177 ff., 235; Geimer/Schütze [*Internationale Urteilsanerkennung*] Vol. I 2 § 246 p. 1917 f.; Martiny, Handbuch, Annotation 1534; Hoechst, *Produzenthaftung*, p. 123; Brenscheidt RIW/AWD 1976, 554, 556, 558, each with further evidence).

[LEVEL OF DAMAGES EXCESSIVE BY DOMESTIC CRITERIA]

IV. Where the appellate court assessed, on the basis of the requirements of substantive ordre public, the value of the damages awarded to the Plaintiff in respect of the material and non-material injury it suffered itself in the judgment of the Superior Court pursuant to § 723, para. 2, sentence 2 and § 328, para. 1, sub-para. 4 of the ZPO, there are no ostensible errors to the detriment of the Defendant in its statements.

The appellate court also rejected an infringement of substantive ordre public in relation to the fact that the Superior Court awarded the

Plaintiff damages of US $100,000 in respect of future psychological treatment and of a further US $50,000 for the associated future costs of placement, irrespective of whether or not the Plaintiff decides to undergo such medical treatment. It determined that the Superior Court, after hearing an expert, considered treatment of this kind, and the charges estimated for it, to be objectively necessary, and considered decisive the fact that, in exceptional cases, the German legal system permits compensation for "fictive" repair costs.

No objection can be raised, on legal grounds, to this conclusion. The appeal is quite correct in its assertion that, in German law on damages, the injured party is not, in the event of personal injury—unlike in the event of material damage (BGHZ 66, 239, 241 ff.[4])—given the opportunity to decide whether or not it wishes to use the sum of money required for production to repair the damage and that the injured party cannot, therefore, request damages in respect of "fictive" costs of treatment (BGHZ 97, 14, 18 ff.). In itself, however, this does not prevent the judgment of the Superior Court being recognised.

(a) §§ 249 ff. [Awards of Damages] of the German Civil Code, which are authoritative under German law, do not take precedence in this case over either Article 5 or over Article 38 of the Introductory Act of the German Civil Code (EGBGB) [concerning Conflict of Laws].

(bb) Article 38 of the EGBGB, pursuant to which claims against a German arising from a tort committed abroad cannot be asserted before German courts which go beyond those available under German law, also does not exclude an enforcement order ... Article 38—may not be interpreted to the effect that any foreign judgment against a German tortfeasor, under which damages are awarded to an injured party who is also German, which damages exceed those which would be payable under German law, constitutes a contravention of German ordre public and should not therefore be recognised. This principle is also followed by the adjudicating Senate [division of the Federal Court of Justice] in its issuance of enforcement orders in respect of foreign judgments, pursuant to § 722 and § 723 of the ZPO. In this respect, there are no differences of fact. Outside the scope of Article 5, sub-para. 3 of the EGÜbk [European Convention on the law applicable to contractual obligations of June 19, 1980], the injured party is also free to file a petition in the foreign tortious venue (§ 328, para. 1, sub-para. 1 of the ZPO). The legality of foreign judgments in respect of which enforcement orders are to be issued does not have to be verified, pursuant to Article 29 of the EGÜbk and to the general provisions of § 723, para. 1 of the ZPO.

(b) § 328, para. 1, sub-para. 4 of the ZPO does not prevent the recognition of the judgment on the basis of the claim for damages in this case. The fact that the German judge, if he had had to make a decision on the trial, would, by the application of binding German law, have come to a different conclusion to that reached by the foreign court, does not mean that a foreign judgment is incompatible with substantive ordre

4. BB 1977, p. 116.

public (compare Zöller/Geimer, ibid, § 328, Annotation 152, with further evidence). What is much more important is the question of whether the result of the application of foreign law conflicts so strongly with the fundamental concepts of the German regulations and with the notions of justice contained within them as to make it seem intolerable on the basis of domestic notions ("ordre public international"—BGHZ 50, 370, 375 f.; 75, 32, 43; BGH, judgment of 21 January, 1991—II ZR 50/90, NJW 1991, 1418, 1420). Accordingly, if foreign law provides for liability on the part of the owner of a motor vehicle, as well as on the part of the driver of that motor vehicle, beyond the level applicable in Germany, and also provides for payment of compensation by those individuals (BGHZ 88, 17, 25 f.), this is not an infringement of German law and order as defined by Article 27, sub-para. 1 of the EGÜbk; nor is it an infringement of German law and order if foreign law provides for an overall estimation of the value of damages where the liability for those damages has been ascertained (BGHZ 75, 167, 171 f.[5]).

Within the terms of § 328, para. 1, sub-para. 4 of the ZPO, it is acceptable under German law for an injured party to claim damages for medical expenses without actually intending, at the time in question, to undergo medical treatment. The divergent regulation within German law, which does not provide for any freedom to decide, is based above all upon the assumption that damages in respect of physical or mental injury which cannot be treated and which therefore ultimately has to be endured would in fact constitute compensation for the lasting impairment of health, in circumvention of § 253 of the BGB (BGHZ 97, 14, 19). As far as an infringement of law and order is concerned, it is immaterial whether or not the domestic and foreign laws are founded upon conflicting principles; the only decisive factor is whether or not the substantive result of the application of foreign law is undesirable (BGHZ 39, 173, 177, with further evidence).

It is on this basis that the Superior Court awarded the Plaintiff damages in respect of its medical costs; such damages could, in the same circumstances, have been paid under German law. In effect, the liability of the Defendant for these cannot be denounced as grossly unjust. The reason for the award of medical expenses in advance is that, pursuant to US law, the total possible damages for each claim must be awarded conclusively in a lump sum in a single trial (Fleming, ibid, p. 231; Kionka [Torts in a Nutshell], p. 354). If Californian law provides the injured party with the right to decide, not only on the integrity of its case, but also on that of its body or of its mental health, this does not affect adversely any position of the tortfeasor which requires protection; as far as the tortfeasor is concerned, even under German law the free will of its victim alone determines whether or not damages are to be paid in respect of medical costs. The different method of settlement of claims which is applied abroad does not affect German law and order to an

---

5. RIW/AWD 1979, p. 861.

intolerable extent, particularly as there is little likelihood of a considerable extension of domestic liability as a consequence of it.

[CONTINGENCY FEES]

The fact that, pursuant to the judgment of the Superior Court, the Plaintiff is required to pay over to its lawyer, as a contingency fee, 40% of all the money received, also does not prevent the recognition of the judgment.

An equivalent agreement with a German lawyer would, under German law, generally be null and void, pursuant to § 138, para. 1 [Transactions in Breach of Public Policy] of the BGB (compare BGHZ 34, 64, 70 ff.; Senate judgment of 31 October, 1991—IX ZR 303/90, WM 1992, 279, 281, with further evidence). This principle is not, however, sufficiently important for German notions of justice as to justify unrestricted validity in all cases world-wide. The BGH has, in respect of remuneration agreements between German and foreign lawyers pursuant to foreign law, which, pursuant to German material private international law, would be subject to verification of their compatibility with Article 30 of the former version of the EGBGB, determined that an agreement in relation to a contingency fee does not necessarily fail on the basis of ordre public (BGHZ 22, 162, 166; 44, 183, 190 f.[6]). Contrary to the case contained within BGHZ 51, 290, 293 ff.[7], in which a foreign lawyer—pursuant to § 183, para. 1 of the Federal Indemnification Law (BEG)—was granted the powers of a domestic lawyer, the contingency fee in this case arises from an agreement concluded abroad between a foreign party and its foreign lawyer for the conduct of an action abroad. If a foreign court enforces an agreement of this kind, pursuant to the law it applies, this fact does not constitute an intolerable infringement upon German law and order. The contractual relations all have to be developed abroad. All legal systems are free to determine the professional restrictions which they impose upon their own lawyers (see Martiny, Handbuch, Annotation 1111).

The Defendant in the damages trial is only affected if the contingency fee has a direct influence on the assessment of the damages awarded (likewise Zekoll, *Produkthaftpflichtrecht*, p. 118 f.). This has neither been proven nor disproven in the present case. Even if the compensatory damages awarded to the Plaintiff were generous, in view of the costs it had to bear, that fact would not, from a German point of view, constitute an unacceptable result; if the Plaintiff had taken action for damages against the Defendant in Germany, the Defendant would also have been required to indemnify the Plaintiff against its legal costs. As far as domestic ordre public is concerned, no objection can be raised if the injured party demands indemnity against its legal costs, as well as full compensation for the injury it has suffered. The question of how these individual costs have been calculated is not significant.

6. AWD 1965, p. 456.   **7.** AWD 1969, p. 543.

The level of the contingency fee awarded to the lawyer in the present case also does not prevent the recognition of the judgment. The Superior Court justified this contingency fee expressly on the basis of the complexity and of the difficulty of the prosecution. While, in BGHZ 44, 183, 190 f.7, the sum agreed was deducted from the damages won, with reference to the former version of Article 30 of the EGBGB, it is not possible to derive anything from that case in terms of substantiation as to what is to be understood as observation of ordre public, as defined by§ 328, para. 1, sub-para. 4 of the ZPO, for a case with a questionable foreign aspect such as the present one (for another opinion, see Stiefel/Sturner, ibid, p. 842). The level of the contingency fee is customary by American standards although it has to be borne in mind that, with this type of agreement, the American lawyer is required to advance the costs of the prosecution and therefore assumes the risk of legal and economic failure (see Zekoll, *Produkthaftpflichtrecht*, p. 121 f.). In the relationship between the Plaintiff and the lawyer, the quota in the judgment for which recognition is sought has been bindingly fixed, irrespective of whether there is any change to the relationship with the Defendant, which relationship is the sole matter in dispute.

It would be possible to apply the impediment to recognition which is contained within § 328, para. 1, sub-para. 4 to the Defendant's advantage if it were to have to pay, as "compensatory damages", a total sum which far exceeded that sum required to compensate the Plaintiff for the damage it had actually suffered, including an appropriate proportion of the costs. This makes it even less comprehensible why the Plaintiff's lawyers have, for several years, conducted a case which has a high amount in dispute and involves complicated foreign connections, without, as yet—as far as has been proven—receiving any fee.

[Punitive Damages]

V.   The appeal is successful, insofar as the judgment of the Superior Court upheld the Plaintiff's claim to "exemplary and punitive damages" in the amount of US $400,000. On this matter, the appeal court's interpretation was that an enforcement order could be issued only in respect of that sum required to cover legal costs; this sum is, however, subject to examination under ordre public. This would mean that instead of an amount of 40% of the damages award provided for by the judgment of the Superior Court, only an amount of 25% thereof could be recognised. A proportion amounting to US $55,065 of the "punitive damages" could then be recognised.

These statements are not sufficiently convincing to withstand the arguments put forward by the Defendant during the appeal. A US judgment awarding lump sum punitive damages of a not inconsiderable amount in addition to an award for damages for material and non-material injury cannot, as a rule, be held to be enforceable in Germany.

1.   "Punitive or exemplary damages" are, pursuant to the law in most individual states of the USA—including California—awarded as a

sum additional to that required to repair the damage caused, if the tortfeasor has, in aggravation of a general offence, behaved wilfully, maliciously, or negligently (Prosser [Handbook of the Law of Torts, 2nd Ed.], p. 9 f., with evidence; Ed. note in 70 Harvard Law Review, p. 517 ...). More recently, it has been sufficient for there to have been a conscious, negligent, overt contempt for public safety (... Madden, Products Liability 2nd ed., p. 317, 319; The American Law Institute, ibid, 248; Stiefel/Sturner, ibid, p. 835). The imposition of such damages is generally at the free discretion of the court (Prosser, ibid, p. 11, with evidence; Stoll in International Encyclopedia of Comparative Law Vol. XI Part 2—hereinafter known as "Encyclopedia"—Notes 8–107 on footnote 803 and opinion p. 102). The imposition of such damages serves up to four principal purposes (compare Prosser, ibid, p. 9, 20; ed. note in 70 Harvard Law Review 517, 520 ff.; Stoll, Encyclopedia, Notes 8–109 and opinion p. 101 ff., 113 ff ...).

The offender should be punished for its uncivilised conduct, if only to ensure that any possible acts of retribution on the part of the victim are prevented. In cases where the risk of having to pay compensation is not, in itself, sufficient to ensure an adequate change in behaviour, the offender and the general public should be deterred from indulging, in the future, in any conduct which may be detrimental to society. The injured party should be rewarded for the enforcement of law—and the associated improvement in general law and order—which is dependent upon its involvement. Finally, the victim should receive a supplement to the payment in respect of repair of damage, which might be considered to be inadequate; a lack of social security cover may be considered to form part of such an inadequacy (compare Zekoll, *Produkthaftpflichtrecht*, p. 40, 158; Sabella, ibid, p. 1187 f.); it is on this basis that compensation for the out-of-court costs of the Plaintiff (III 4 b, above), which are not automatically reimbursable, can be taken into consideration.

* * *

In American law, "punitive damages" are generally part of civil law, irrespective of the punitive and deterrent function they are intended to fulfil. . . .

* * *

The modern German system of civil law provides for compensation for damage only as the legal consequence of a tort (§§ 249 ff. of the BGB); it does not provide for enrichment of the injured party. * * *

* * *

Neither the judgment nor the transcript of the Superior Court, however, contain reliable information as to whether or not the "punitive damages" awarded are intended to cover all the legal costs incurred by the Plaintiff. The proportion of 40% awarded to its lawyer as remuneration applies to all sums of damages which are actually paid, irrespective of their legal classification. The sums paid in compensation for medical expenses and in damages for pain and suffering have not been calculated so precisely as to exclude the possibility of their already including an element in respect of costs. Consideration by a court—above all, by a jury—to award compensation for costs can, in the USA, lead to increased "compensatory damages."

* * *

If clear and comprehensible information is not provided by the foreign court itself, the German court which is responsible for the enforcement order is hampered in its efforts to ascertain the actual motives in each individual case. As has been stated (see 1, above), a US award of this nature can be based legitimately upon several different motives, which are treated individually or which are treated together with others, provided the award as a whole complies with the acknowledged principles of the foreign law (Stiefel/Stürner, ibid, p. 838, is relevant to this). In order to gain a more substantial view of the content of the judgment than that which is provided by the official reasoning for it, the domestic judge would, if possible, have to take the place of the foreign judge.

§ 723, para. 1 of the ZPO shows that the [German] judge is not entitled to do this. Any such reconsideration of a judgment would be based to a large extent upon conjecture and would therefore put the certainty of the law at risk.

* * *

US punitive damages are characterised by the elements of punishment and deterrent. Historically, it is upon these elements that punitive damages have been based; even today, these elements regularly play a part in the assessment of the damages. The increased allegation of fault is the sole crucial condition. The lesser emphasis placed upon its private interests illustrates the fact that the injured party does not have a legal claim. As, in addition, there is no ostensible general relationship between the sums to be determined and the damage suffered, the question of compensation is generally accorded less significance.

(e) On this basis, it is clearly incompatible with essential fundamental principles of German law for lump sum punitive damages of a not inconsiderable amount to be enforced in Germany.

* * *

Sanctions which are intended to be punitive or deterrent—i.e. to protect general law and order—are, however, in German interpretation of the law, part of the monopoly on punishment held by the state. The state exercises this monopoly in the public interest in a special procedure, in which on one hand the official investigation is intended to provide a better guarantee that the substantive decision is accurate, while on the other hand better protection is granted to the rights of the Defendant. From a local point of view, it would seem unacceptable to impose, in a civil judgment, payment of a considerable sum of money, which is not intended as compensation for damages, but is rather calculated essentially on the basis of the public interest and may be imposed in addition to a criminal punishment for the same offence.

In effect, this is what has happened in the present case. The damages imposed are higher than the total of all the sums awarded to compensate for the damage caused. Even the total legal fees payable would amount to only around one third of the "punitive damages". There is no evidence of any other damages for which compensation has to be paid. The effect of any enforcement on the Defendant would therefore be excessive.

(bb) The punitive damages imposed at the discretion of the court, which damages have no firm relationship with the damage suffered and some of which are extraordinarily high, have contributed to a sharp increase in the burden of damages on the economy as a whole, which burden has now reached the limit of the calculable and the insurable risk.

From a German point of view, the motives which are alien to civil law and the lack of adequately determined and reliable limitations in the event of recognition of judgments of this nature would be likely to go beyond all the domestic criteria for liability......

(cc) Enforcement in Germany is, therefore, in this respect, excluded. It is not necessary to determine whether enforcement of a damages award also contravenes German law and order on other grounds. In particular, there is no need to determine whether the conditions for the imposition of a judgment for punitive damages, which conditions are difficult to stipulate, and the amount of damages, are to be assessed on the basis of Article 103, para. 2 [Constitutional Rights in Court] of the Basic Law (GG) [German Constitution], or whether condemnation to the payment of damages, as well as to a criminal penalty, would, from a German point of view, be in violation of the prohibition of multiple punishment (Article 103, para. 3 of the GG).

VI. The fact that the judgment of the Superior Court cannot be enforced in Germany because it imposes punitive damages does not mean that the rest of the judgment cannot be recognised.

Contrary to the opinion expressed in the appeal, the fact that the matter at issue in the enforcement judgment consists not in the substantive claim upon which the foreign title is based, but is determined by the creditor's desire to make this title enforceable domestically, does not mean that a single decision has always to be made on the enforcement order for the entire sum awarded in a foreign payment judgment. In cases where a single foreign judgment upholds several, legally independent claims, each of these claims can be investigated individually, in order to see whether it complies with the conditions for recognition.

If not all the claims so comply, then lesser, partial recognition is possible; the Plaintiff does not have to take this into account in its petition. Pursuant to this, there are no grounds for objection to the fact that the appellate court subjected those sums shown in the judgment of the Superior Court for past and future medical costs or costs of placement, for immaterial damages and for "punitive damages" to a separate ordre public inspection.

According to the findings of the Senate, a decision does not have to be made as to whether partial recognition is also permissible in relation to a uniform material claim.

Questions and Comments

1. Based upon the 1992 Bundesgerichtshof decision, how likely is it that the New Jersey judgment in this Problem against the German defendant will be enforced in a German court? What, if any, defenses might the defendant raise to recognition and enforcement of the judgment? If they are raised, will any of them be successful? Would you advise the defendant to take an aggressive position and spend the resulting time and cost of contesting an action for recognition and enforcement?

2. One German court, asked to enforce a default judgment rendered in a U.S. federal district court in Wisconsin (including an award of punitive damages), denied recognition on the basis that the Wisconsin court did not have jurisdiction consistent with German law because the German defendant had no assets in Wisconsin and no other substantial relationship with the State of Wisconsin. The court rejected the argument that the relationship with the United States as a whole would have been sufficient to justify jurisdiction. *Oberlandesgericht Hamm*, Judgment of 4 June 1997, 1 U 2/96, *reported in* RIW, Heft 12, Internationales Wirtschaftsrecht at 139. Is this approach likely to have implications for enforcement of our New Jersey judgment?

3. Like courts dealing with recognition and enforcement of foreign judgments in the United States, the Bundesgerichtshof (German Supreme Court) generally determines that mere differences in procedures do not constitute grounds for denial of recognition based on public policy. Thus, differences in matters like allocation of attorney fees, pre-trial discovery, the method for dealing with future medical expenses, and the level of damages for pain and suffering are not sufficient to rise to the level of public policy for purposes of denial of recognition of the judgment. Punitive damages, on the other hand, are a different matter. Do you agree with the German court's analysis of these issues? Is the issue of punitive damages so different as to cross the public policy threshold? What is the difference that matters here? *See* Ronald A. Brand, *Punitive Damages and the Recognition of Judgments*, Netherlands Int'l L. Rev. 143 (1996).

4. ZPO § 328(1) parallels the U.S. approach by providing that a foreign judgment will be denied recognition if the foreign court did not have jurisdiction under German law. We have seen in Chapter 6 that U.S. courts will deny recognition if the foreign court from which the judgment originates did not have jurisdiction in accordance with the due process standards enunciated by the U.S. Supreme Court in *International Shoe*, *World-Wide Volkswagen* and related cases. Note that this raises issues to be dealt with at the time of filing the initial litigation, when jurisdiction rules of both the

court in which the case is filed and the court in which the judgment may need to be enforced must be considered. Considering the U.S. jurisdictional bases established in Chapter 3, and the German rules of jurisdiction considered in Chapter 5, what are the most likely problems that may be encountered when a New Jersey Federal Court judgment is taken to be enforced in a German court?

5. ZPO § 328(2) provides for non-recognition if the documents initiating the suit were not served upon the defendant (now judgment debtor) "in accordance with law." Consider again the *Schlunk* case excerpted in Chapter 3. There the U.S. Supreme Court determined that, under an Illinois statute providing that service upon an Illinois subsidiary was effective as service on the German parent corporation, there was no "occasion to transmit documents for service abroad" and thus the Hague Service Convention did not apply. The German government filed an *amicus* brief with the U.S. Supreme Court in the *Schlunk* case, taking a position contrary to this result. If service in accordance with the Illinois statute is considered sufficient by the U.S. Supreme Court, but the German government considers such service to violate the Hague Service Convention, how would you accomplish service of process in a case like *Schlunk* when you anticipate the need to enforce the resulting judgment in Germany? In terms of professional responsibility, should a lawyer ever rely solely on a statute like the Illinois statute that allows service on a local subsidiary to be effective service on a foreign parent corporation?

6. ZPO § 328(5) requires that the jurisdiction from which the foreign judgment issues provide reciprocity to German judgments. Thus, in the German court it will be necessary to prove that the U.S. court issuing the judgment for which recognition is sought would recognize and enforce a judgment from the German court. How might reciprocity be proved to the German court? Consider the portion of the 1992 Bundesgerichtshof decision dealing with this issue. If the state from which the U.S. judgment issues has enacted the Uniform Foreign Money–Judgments Recognition Act (UF-MJRA), proof of reciprocity may come simply from the example of the Act. If the judgment is from a U.S. state in which the Recognition Act is not the law, how would you prove reciprocity to the German court when seeking enforcement? Consider the *Somportex* case from Chapter 6 in this regard. That case was decided by a U.S. Federal Circuit Court of Appeals applying Pennsylvania law at a time before Pennsylvania had enacted the Recognition Act. How would you explain to a German court that reciprocity existed at that time for a judgment from the Federal District Court for the Eastern District of Pennsylvania? This would require an explanation that the Federal District Court would recognize a German judgment, which would further require an explanation of the *Erie* doctrine and why federal courts apply state law, and why in this type of case state law is often most evident in federal court decisions interpreting state law since diversity jurisdiction exists for purposes of the enforcement action. Do you now see another very good reason for states to adopt the Recognition Act, and for actions when the judgment may require enforcement abroad to be brought in states that have enacted that Act?

PROBLEM 7.2 ENFORCEMENT OF JUDGMENTS UNDER THE BRUSSELS REGULATION

SECTION I. THE SETTING

Consider again the facts in Problems 5.2 and 6.1:

Celsius Manufacturing, Inc. (Celsius), a Delaware corporation, has its principal place of business in Pittsburgh, Pennsylvania. Celsius manufactures induction molding devices (IMDs) used in the further manufacture of plastic products. In October 2007, Celsius demonstrated its IMDs at a trade fair in London, where a purchasing agent for a Plastic Maker, GmbH ("Plastic Maker"), of Munich, Germany, became interested in the product. At the trade fair, Plastic Maker submitted a purchase order to Celsius, offering to purchase 1,000 IMDs at $400 per unit, "terms c.i.f. London," to be shipped in January 2008. The President of Celsius responded while she was still in London with a letter in which she acknowledged receipt of the purchase order and accepted all the terms and conditions of the offer. Neither the purchase order form nor the letter of acceptance contained either a choice of law or a choice of forum clause.

Plastic Maker wired Celsius the entire $400,000 purchase price on January 3, 2008, and the IMDs were shipped on January 6, 2008 and arrived in London on January 28, where they were unloaded to a warehouse owned and operated by Plastic Maker. Plastic Maker had intended to redistribute the IMDs to its facilities in Germany, The Netherlands, and Spain. Upon receipt of the IMDs, Plastic Maker informed Celsius that the IMDs did not conform to the quality of the product demonstrated at the London trade fair and that Plastic Maker was rejecting them. Plastic Maker informed Celsius that it was holding the IMDs at Plastic Maker's London warehouse, awaiting further instructions concerning their return or disposal.

All experts who have been contacted on the matter agree that the goods are in fact non-conforming, and unsuitable for the use intended by Plastic Maker. Plastic Maker sued in Germany for breach of contract, demanding return of the purchase price, on the basis of this non-conformity of the goods. The German court has duly granted judgment against Celsius. Celsius has a bank account in Munich, with a current balance of 3,000 Euros. It has substantial assets in Dublin, Ireland, where it has established a manufacturing facility to serve the European market.

SECTION II. FOCUS OF CONSIDERATION

Now there is an option in enforcing the German judgment. In Chapter 6 we already considered taking it to the United States for enforcement. Now, however, we know that Celsius has assets in a European Union Member State (Ireland). This brings into play the recognition provisions of Chapter III of the Brussels Regulation, which are much different from the national law applicable when no treaty or other multilateral instrument is available. You should begin your analysis here by rereading the recognition and enforcement provisions of the Brussels Regulation.

The Brussels Regulation is essential to an understanding of this problem. It is included in the Documents Supplement.

SECTION III.   READINGS, QUESTIONS AND COMMENTS

PART A.   A RETURN TO THE BRUSSELS REGULATION

Comment on the Historical Background and Structure

In the European Community, the original six Member States first agreed in Article 220 (now Article 293) of the Rome Treaty to negotiate toward "the simplification of formalities governing the reciprocal recognition and enforcement of judgments of courts or tribunals and of arbitration awards."[1] This process began in 1959, resulting in the completion of the Brussels Convention in 1968. This process was extended to the European Free Trade Area (EFTA) states through the similar Lugano Convention,[2] and then revised when the Brussels Convention was formed into the Brussels Regulation as internal legislation of the European Community.[3]

Most recognition and enforcement treaties are "simple" treaties dealing only with the decision of the court asked to recognize a judgment from another jurisdiction. This follows the "indirect jurisdiction" approach exemplified by the Restatement and Uniform Recognition Act technique in the United States. The enforcing court does not question whether the court of origin properly exercised its own jurisdiction. Rather the jurisdictional analysis conducted by the enforcing court deals only with whether the court of origin exercised jurisdiction in a manner recognized as appropriate either by the recognizing state or in the applicable convention.

The Brussels Convention was an example of the more complex "double" treaty, providing rules of direct jurisdiction. Thus, rather than listing only the acceptable jurisdictional bases on which a recognizable judgment may be based, the Contracting States limited from the start the jurisdictional bases available in an action against a defendant domiciled in another Contracting State. These direct limits on jurisdiction are

---

1. TREATY ESTABLISHING THE EUROPEAN ECONOMIC COMMUNITY [EEC TREATY] art. 220.

2. European Communities–European Free Trade Association: Convention on Jurisdiction and Enforcement of Judgments in Civil and Commercial Matters, done at Lugano, September 16, 1988, O.J. Eur. Comm. (No. L 319) 9 (Nov. 25, 1988), *reprinted in* 28 INT'L LEGAL MATERIALS 620 (1989) [hereinafter "Lugano convention"]. In addition to the Member States of the European Community, the Lugano Convention includes as Contracting States the Member States of the European Free Trade Association (EFTA).

3. Council Regulation (EC) No 44/2001 of 22 Dec. 2000 on jurisdiction and the recognition and enforcement of judgments in civil and commercial matters, O.J. L12/1 (2001) ("Brussels Regulation") (entered into force on March 1, 2002).

now found in Chapter II of the Brussels Regulation. Chapter III covers issues of recognition and enforcement, providing the general rule in Article 32 that "[a] judgment given in a Member State shall be recognized in the other Member States without any special procedure being required."

Like the Restatement and Recognition Act approaches in the United States, the Brussels Regulation tempers the general rule of recognition with a list of defenses in Article 34 that justify non-recognition. A judgment "shall not be recognized," (1) if recognition would be contrary to public policy in the recognizing state; (2) where it is a default judgment given without service in sufficient time to allow preparation of a defense; (3) if the judgment is irreconcilable with a judgment in a dispute between the same parties in the recognizing state; (4) if the judgment necessarily went beyond the civil or commercial issue in dispute and required determination of a matter of status or legal capacity or rights in property arising out of a matrimonial relationship, wills or succession; or (5) if the judgment is irreconcilable with an earlier judgment from a non-Member State which is entitled to recognition and is on the same cause of action and between the same parties.

The relationship between the jurisdictional provisions of the Brussels Regulation and its provisions on recognition presents issues not found in a simple convention or Recognition Act-type approach that is based on indirect jurisdiction concepts. Article 3 and Annex I list jurisdictional provisions in the Member States determined by negotiation to be exorbitant, and provides that such bases for jurisdiction "shall not be applicable as against" persons domiciled in a Member State. The Regulation thus complements the acceptable list of appropriate jurisdictional bases with this list of exorbitant jurisdictional bases from which persons domiciled in a Member State are protected. Because exercise of an exorbitant jurisdictional basis against a domiciliary of another Member State is prohibited, no further provision is required to prevent the recognition of a judgment based on such jurisdiction. The Regulation thus addresses condemned bases for jurisdiction in a direct manner.

Articles 35(3) and 36 of the Regulation develop this structure further. Subject to narrow limitations, "the jurisdiction of the court in which the judgment was given may not be reviewed." A review of the substance of the original decision by the recognizing court is prohibited.

While a domiciliary of a European Union Member State cannot be sued in the courts of other Member States where the only source of jurisdiction is one of the Article 3 "exorbitant" bases of jurisdiction, under Article 4 a defendant not domiciled in a Member State remains subject to such grounds of jurisdiction. Thus, a judgment rendered against a defendant not domiciled in a Member State (*e.g.*, a U.S. defendant) is enforceable in all other Member States, even if rendered under jurisdictional grounds that all other Member States consider improper. Article 4 further exacerbates this problem by making national exorbitant jurisdiction provisions available to any plaintiff domiciled in a

Member State who asserts jurisdiction against a defendant not domiciled in a Member State.

Consider the following cases and what they say about the application and interpretation of Chapter III of the Brussels Regulation. Keep in mind that the numbering of the Articles of the Convention has now been changed in the Regulation.

HOFFMANN v. KRIEG

Case No. 145/86, 1988 E.C.R. 645.

1. By a judgment of 6 June 1986, which was received at the court on 13 June 1986, the Hoge Raad der Nederlanden referred to the court for a preliminary ruling under the protocol of 3 June 1971 on the interpretation by the Court of Justice of the convention of 27 September 1968 on jurisdiction and the enforcement of judgments in civil and commercial matters (hereinafter referred to as "the convention") five questions on the interpretation of a number of Articles contained in that convention.

2. The questions arose in the course of proceedings between h. L. M. Hoffman (hereinafter referred to as "the husband") and a. Krieg (hereinafter "the wife"), concerning the enforcement in the Netherlands of a judgment of the Amtsgericht (local court) Heidelberg, ordering the husband to make monthly maintenance payments to the wife.

3. It is apparent from the documents before the court that the parties to the main proceedings are German nationals who were married in 1950 and that, in 1978, the husband left the matrimonial home in the Federal Republic of Germany and settled in the Netherlands. On application by the wife, the husband was ordered by a Decision of the Amtsgericht, Heidelberg of 21 August 1979 to make maintenance payments to her as a separated spouse.

4. On the application of the husband, the Arrondissementsrechtbank (district court), Maastricht, granted a decree of divorce by a judgment of 1 May 1980 given in default, applying german law in accordance with Netherlands rules on the conflict of laws. On 19 August the divorce was entered in the civil register at the Hague whereupon in the Netherlands the marriage was dissolved. The decree of divorce, which falls outside the scope of the convention, had not been recognized in the Federal Republic of Germany at the time which the national court considers material for the purposes of the case.

5. On the application of the wife, The President of the Arrondissmentsrechtbank, Almelo, made an order on 29 July 1981 for the enforcement of the judgment of the Amtsgericht, Heidelberg, in accordance with Article 31 of the convention. In April 1982 notice of that enforcement order was served on the husband who did not appeal against the order.

6. On 28 February 1983 the wife obtained an attachment of the husband's earnings paid by his employer. The husband brought interloc-

utory proceedings before the Arrondissementsrechtbank, Almelo, in order to have the attachment order discharged, or at least suspended. He was successful at first instance but on appeal the Gerechtshof (regional court of appeal), Arnhem, dismissed his application. He appealed in cassation against that judgment to the Hoge Raad.

7. The Hoge Raad took the view that the Resolution of the dispute depended on the interpretation of a number of Articles in the convention and referred the following questions to the court for a preliminary ruling:

'1. Does the obligation imposed on the contracting states to recognize a judgment given in another contracting state (Article 26 of the Brussels convention) mean that such a judgment must be given the same effect in the other contracting states as it has under the law of the state in which it was given and does this mean that it is therefore enforceable in the same cases as in that state?

2. If question 1 is answered in the affirmative:

Must Articles 26 and 31 of the Brussels convention, read together, be interpreted as meaning that the obligation to recognize a judgment given in a contracting state requires that, because the judgment remains enforceable under the law of the state in which it was given, it is also enforceable in the same cases in the other contracting state?

3. If question 2 is answered in the affirmative:

In a case such as this, is it possible to plead that the German maintenance order is irreconcilable with the subsequent Netherlands decree of divorce or to plead public policy (Article 27 (1) and (3) of the Brussels convention)?

4. Does (the scheme of) the Brussels convention require acceptance of the rule that, if the party against whom enforcement is sought of a judgment given in another contracting state fails to plead, in the appeal against the order for enforcement of the judgment, matters of which he was aware before the end of the period referred to in the first paragraph of Article 36 of the Brussels convention and which preclude (further) enforcement of that judgment, he may no longer plead those matters in subsequent execution proceedings in which he is appealing against (continued) enforcement?

5. If question 4 is answered in the affirmative:

Does (the scheme of) the Brussels convention require it to be assumed that the court of the state in which an enforcement order is issued must apply of its own motion the rule referred to in the fourth question in subsequent execution proceedings, even if its own law makes no provision for the application of such a rule?'

8. Reference is made to the report for the hearing for a fuller account of the facts, the course of the procedure and the written

observations submitted to the court, which are mentioned or discussed hereinafter only in so far as is necessary for the reasoning of the court.

9. The national court's first question seeks, in essence, to establish whether a foreign judgment, which has been recognized pursuant to Article 26 of the convention, must in principle have the same effects in the state in which enforcement is sought as it does in the state in which judgment was given.

10. In that regard it should be recalled that the convention "seeks to facilitate as far as possible the free movement of judgments, and should be interpreted in this spirit". Recognition must therefore "have the result of conferring on judgments the authority and effectiveness accorded to them in the state in which they were given" (Jenard Report on the convention on jurisdiction and the enforcement of judgments in civil and commercial matters, Official Journal 1979, c 59, pp. 42 and 43).

11. It follows that the answer to be given to the national court's first question is that a foreign judgment which has been recognized by virtue of Article 26 of the convention must in principle have the same effects in the state in which enforcement is sought as it does in the state in which judgment was given.

12. In the circumstances of the main proceedings, as disclosed by the documents before the court, the national court's second question seeks, in essence, to establish whether a foreign judgment whose enforcement has been ordered in a contracting state pursuant to Article 31 of the convention must continue to be enforced in all cases in which it would still be enforceable in the state in which it was given even when, under the law of the state in which enforcement is sought, the judgment ceases to be enforceable for reasons which lie outside the scope of the convention.

13. In this instance, the judgment whose enforcement is at issue is one which orders a husband to make maintenance payments to his spouse by virtue of his obligations, arising out of the marriage, to support her. Such a judgment necessarily presupposes the existence of the matrimonial relationship.

14. Consideration should therefore be given to whether the dissolution of that matrimonial relationship by a decree of divorce granted by a court of the state in which the enforcement is sought can terminate the enforcement of the foreign judgment even when that judgment remains enforceable in the state in which it was given, the decree of divorce not having been recognized there.

15. In that connection it must be observed that indent (1) of the second paragraph of Article 1 of the convention provides that the convention does not apply inter alia to the status or legal capacity of natural persons. Moreover, it contains no rule requiring the court of the state in which enforcement is sought to make the effects of a national decree of divorce conditional on recognition of that decree in the state in which the foreign maintenance order is made.

16.   That is confirmed by Article 27 (4) of the convention, which excludes in principle the recognition of any foreign judgment involving a conflict with a rule—concerning inter alia the status of natural persons—of the private international law of the state in which the recognition is sought. That provision demonstrates that, as far as the status of natural persons is concerned, it is not the aim of the convention to derogate from the rules which apply under the domestic law of the court before which the action has been brought.

17.   It follows that the convention does not preclude the court of the state in which enforcement is sought from drawing the necessary inferences from a national decree of divorce when considering the enforcement of the foreign maintenance order.

18.   Thus the answer to be given to the national court is that a foreign judgment whose enforcement has been ordered in a contracting state pursuant to Article 31 of the convention and which remains enforceable in the state in which it was given must not continue to be enforced in the state where enforcement is sought when, under the law of the latter state, it ceases to be enforceable for reasons which lie outside the scope of the convention.

19.   The national court's third question seeks, in essence, to establish whether a foreign judgment ordering a person to make maintenance payments to his spouse by virtue of his conjugal obligations to support her is irreconcilable within the meaning of Article 27 (3) of the convention with a national judgment pronouncing the divorce of the spouses or, alternatively, whether such a foreign judgment is contrary to public policy in the state in which recognition is sought within the meaning of Article 27 (1).

20.   The provisions to be interpreted set out the grounds for not recognizing foreign judgments. Under the second paragraph of Article 34, an enforcement order may be refused for those same reasons.

21.   As far as the second part of the third question is concerned, it should be noted that, according to the scheme of the convention, use of the public-policy clause, which "ought to operate only in exceptional cases" (Jenard Report, cited above, at p. 44) is in any event precluded when, as here, the issue is whether a foreign judgment is compatible with a national judgment; the issue must be resolved on the basis of the specific provision under Article 27 (3), which envisages cases in which the foreign judgment is irreconcilable with a judgment given in a dispute between the same parties in the state in which enforcement is sought.

22.   In order to ascertain whether the two judgments are irreconcilable within the meaning of Article 27 (3), it should be examined whether they entail legal consequences that are mutually exclusive.

23.   It is apparent from the documents before the court that, in the present case, the order for enforcement of the foreign maintenance order was issued at a time when the national decree of divorce had already

been granted and had acquired the force of res judicata, and that the main proceedings are concerned with the period following the divorce.

24. That being so, the judgments at issue have legal consequences which are mutually exclusive. The foreign judgment, which necessarily presupposes the existence of the matrimonial relationship, would have to be enforced although that relationship has been dissolved by a judgment given in a dispute between the same parties in the state in which enforcement is sought.

25. The answer to be given to the third question submitted by the national court is therefore that a foreign judgment ordering a person to make maintenance payments to his spouse by virtue of his conjugal obligations to support her is irreconcilable within the meaning of Article 27 (3) of the convention with a national judgment pronouncing the divorce of the spouses.

26. The national court's fourth and fifth questions ask whether Article 36 of the convention must be interpreted as meaning that a party who has not appealed against the enforcement order in accordance with that provision is precluded, at the stage of the execution of the judgment, from relying on a valid argument which he could have raised in an appeal against the enforcement order, and whether that rule must be applied of their own motion by the courts of the state in which enforcement is sought.

27. In answering those questions it should first be pointed out that, in order to limit the requirements to which the enforcement of a judgment delivered in one contracting state may be subjected in another contracting state, the convention lays down a very simple procedure for the issue of the enforcement order, which may be withheld only on the grounds exhaustively set out in Articles 27 and 28. However, the convention merely regulates the procedure for obtaining an order for the enforcement of foreign enforceable instruments and does not deal with execution itself, which continues to be governed by the domestic law of the court in which execution is sought (judgment of 2 July 1985 in case 148/84 Deutsche Genossenschaftsbank v. Brasserie du Pecheur [1985] ECR 1981).

28. Consequently, a foreign judgment for which an enforcement order has been issued is executed in accordance with the procedural rules of the domestic law of the court in which execution is sought, including those on legal remedies.

29. However, the application, for the purposes of the execution of a judgment, of the procedural rules of the state in which enforcement is sought may not impair the effectiveness of the scheme of the convention as regards enforcement orders.

30. It follows that the legal remedies available under national law must be precluded when an appeal against the execution of a foreign judgment for which an enforcement order has been issued is lodged by the same person who could have appealed against the enforcement order

and is based on an argument which could have been raised in such an appeal. In those circumstances, to challenge the execution would be tantamount to again calling in question the enforcement order after the expiry of the strict time-limit laid down by the second paragraph of Article 36 of the convention, and would thereby render that provision ineffective.

31.   In view of the mandatory nature of the time-limit laid down by Article 36 of the convention, the national court must ensure that it is observed. It should therefore of its own motion dismiss as inadmissible an appeal lodged pursuant to national law when that appeal has the effect of circumventing that time-limit.

32.   Nevertheless, that rule, arising from the scheme of the convention, cannot apply when—as in this case—it would have the result of obliging the national court to ignore the effects of a national decree of divorce, which lies outside the scope of the convention, on the ground that the decree is not recognized in the state in which the foreign judgment whose enforcement is at issue was given.

33.   As was established in the context of the reply to the second question, the convention contains no rule compelling the courts of the state in which enforcement is sought to make the effects of a national decree of divorce conditional on recognition of that decree in the state in which a foreign maintenance order—falling within the scope of the convention—was made.

34.   Accordingly, the answer to be given to the national court's fourth and fifth questions is that Article 36 of the convention must be interpreted as meaning that a party who has not appealed against the enforcement order referred to in that provision is thereafter precluded, at the stage of the execution of the judgment, from relying on a valid ground which he could have pleaded in such an appeal against the enforcement order, and that that rule must be applied of their own motion by the courts of the state in which enforcement is sought. However, that rule does not apply when it has the result of obliging the national court to make the effects of a national judgment which lies outside the scope of the convention conditional on its recognition in the state in which the foreign judgment whose enforcement is at issue was given.

35.   The costs incurred by the government of the Federal Republic of Germany, the United Kingdom and the Commission of the European Communities, which have submitted observations to the court, are not recoverable. As these proceedings are, in so far as the parties to the main proceedings are concerned, in the nature of a step in the action pending before the national court, the Decision on costs is a matter for that court.

RULING

On those grounds, the court, in answer to the questions referred to it by the Hoge Raad by a judgment of 6 June 1986, hereby rules:

(1) A foreign judgment which has been recognized by virtue of Article 26 of the convention must in principle have the same effects in the state in which enforcement is sought as it does in the state in which the judgment was given;

(2) A foreign judgment whose enforcement has been ordered in a contracting state pursuant to Article 31 of the convention and which remains enforceable in the state in which it was given must not continue to be enforced in the state where enforcement is sought when, under the law of the latter state, it ceases to be enforceable for reasons which lie outside the scope of the convention;

(3) A foreign judgment ordering a person to make maintenance payments to his spouse by virtue of his conjugal obligations to support her is irreconcilable within the meaning of Article 27 (3) of the convention with a national judgment pronouncing the divorce of the spouses;

(4) Article 36 of the convention must be interpreted as meaning that a party who has not appealed against the enforcement order referred to in that provision is thereafter precluded, at the stage of the execution of the judgment, from relying on a valid ground which he could have pleaded in such an appeal against the enforcement order, and that that rule must be applied of their own motion by the courts of the state in which enforcement is sought. However, that rule does not apply when it has the result of obliging the national court to make the effects of a national judgment which lies outside the scope of the convention conditional on its recognition in the state in which the foreign judgment whose enforcement is at issue was given.

GAETANO VERDOLIVA v. J. M. VAN DER HOEVEN BV

Case C–3/05, [2006] E.C.R. I–1579.

1.   This reference for a preliminary ruling concerns the interpretation of Article 36 of the Convention of 27 September 1968 on Jurisdiction and the Enforcement of Judgments in Civil and Commercial Matters (OJ 1978 L 304, p. 36), as amended by the Convention of 9 October 1978 on the Accession of the Kingdom of Denmark, Ireland and the United Kingdom of Great Britain and Northern Ireland (OJ 1978 L 304, p. 1, and—amended version—p. 77), by the Convention of 25 October 1982 on the Accession of the Hellenic Republic (OJ 1982 L 388, p. 1) and by the Convention of 26 May 1989 on the Accession of the Kingdom of Spain and the Portuguese Republic (OJ 1989 L 285, p. 1) (the "Brussels Convention").

2.   The reference was made in the course of proceedings between Mr Verdoliva and J.M. Van der Hoeven BV (Van der Hoeven'), Banco di Sardegna and San Paolo IMI SpA, formerly Instituto San Paolo di Torino, concerning the enforcement, in Italy, of a judgment given by the Arrondissementsrechtsbank 'sGravenhage (Netherlands), ordering Mr Verdoliva to pay NLG 365 000 to Van der Hoeven.

3.   Under the first paragraph of Article 26 of the Brussels Convention, a judgment given in a Contracting State is to be recognised in the other Contracting States without any special procedure being required.

4.   Article 27(2) of the Convention provides that a judgment is not to be recognised where it was given in default of appearance, if the defendant was not duly served with the document which instituted the proceedings or with an equivalent document in sufficient time to enable him to arrange for his defence.

5.   According to the first paragraph of Article 31 of the Convention, a judgment given in a Contracting State and enforceable in that State is to be enforced in another Contracting State when, on the application of any interested party, it has been declared enforceable there.

6.   Under Article 34 of the Brussels Convention:

> The court applied to shall give its decision without delay; the party against whom enforcement is sought shall not at this stage of the proceedings be entitled to make any submissions on the application.

The application may be refused only for one of the reasons specified in Articles 27 and 28.

7.   Article 35 of the Convention requires the appropriate officer of the court to bring the decision given on the application to the notice of the applicant without delay, in accordance with the procedure laid down by the law of the State in which enforcement is sought.

8.   Article 36 of the Convention provides:

> If enforcement is authorised, the party against whom enforcement is sought may appeal against the decision within one month of service thereof.

> If that party is domiciled in a Contracting State other than that in which the decision authorising enforcement was given, the time for appealing shall be two months and shall run from the date of service, either on him in person or at his residence. No extension of time may be granted on account of distance.

9.   Article 40(1) of the Brussels Convention provides that the applicant may appeal if the application for enforcement is refused.

Italian procedural law

10.   Article 143 of the Italian Code of Civil Procedure (Codice di Procedura Civile, the CPC) provides that, if a person's place of residence or domicile are unknown, the bailiff is to effect service by lodging a copy of the document in the town hall of the last place of residence and attaching another copy to the notice board of the bailiff's office.

11.   Article 650 of the CPC provides that the addressee of an order for payment can also appeal against enforcement of the order, even after expiry of the period set by the order, provided that he proves that he had no notice of the order in sufficient time, owing inter alia to defective

service. However, such an appeal ceases to be admissible 10 days from the date of the first notice of enforcement.

The main proceedings and the questions referred for a preliminary ruling

12.   By judgment of 14 September 1993, the Arrondissements-rechtsbank 'sGravenhage ordered Mr Verdoliva to pay Van der Hoeven the sum of NLG 365 000, together with interest and incidental expenses.

13.   On 24 May 1994, the Corte d'appelo di Cagliari made an order authorising enforcement of that judgment in the Italian Republic and attachment of the amount owed by Mr Verdoliva in the sum of ILT 220 million.

14.   An initial attempt to serve the enforcement order at Mr Verdoliva's residence in Capoterra (Italy) was unsuccessful. According to the certificate of service dated 14 July 1994, Mr Verdoliva, while still registered in that area, had moved elsewhere more than a year previously.

15.   Service of the order was therefore effected a second time in accordance with Article 143 of the CPC. According to the certificate of service dated 27 July 1994, the bailiff lodged a copy of the order at the town hall in Capoterra and posted a second copy on his office notice board.

16.   Since Mr Verdoliva did not appeal against that order within 30 days of such service, Van der Hoeven proceeded to enforce the judgment against Mr Verdoliva by intervening in the enforcement procedure already initiated against him by Banco di Sardegna and San Paolo IMI SpA.

17.   By an application lodged on 4 December 1996 before the Tribunale civile di Cagliari (Italy), Mr Verdoliva appealed against enforcement on the grounds, first, that the enforcement order had not been served on him, and, secondly, that it had not been lodged at the Capoterra town hall and that, consequently, the certificate of service of 27 July 1994 was false.

18.   That appeal was dismissed by judgment of the Tribunale civile di Cagliari of 7 June 2002, on the ground, in particular, that it was time-barred. According to that court, it would be permissible, by analogy with Article 650 of the CPC, to appeal out of time where, on account of defective service, no notice of the enforcement order had been obtained in sufficient time. However, the period for lodging such an appeal could not, in any event, exceed 30 days from the date of the first enforcement document which brought that order to Mr Verdoliva's notice.

19.   Mr Verdoliva appealed against that judgment to the Corte d'appello di Cagliari, advancing the same arguments as at first instance and adding that service of the enforcement order was also invalid by reason of infringement of Article 143 of the CPC, as interpreted by the Corte suprema di cassazione (Italy). The bailiffs had neither carried out the necessary enquiries to determine whether the addressee was in fact

untraceable nor given an account of such enquiries in the certificate of service of 27 July 1994.

20. Taking the view that resolution of the dispute depended on the interpretation of Article 36 of the Brussels Convention, the Corte d'appello di Cagliari decided to stay proceedings and refer the following questions to the Court for a preliminary ruling:

(1) Does the Brussels Convention provide an independent definition of notice of procedural documents or is that term left to be defined by national rules?

(2) Can it be inferred from the rules of the Brussels Convention, and in particular from Article 36 thereof, that service of the enforcement order provided for in [that article] may be effected in a manner deemed equivalent to service?

(3) Does notice of the enforcement order, in cases of failure of, or defective, service, none the less cause time to run for the purposes of the time-limit laid down in that article? If not, is the Brussels Convention to be interpreted as limiting the ways in which notice of the enforcement order will be deemed to have been acquired?'

Concerning the questions referred

21. By its questions, which it is appropriate to examine together, the national court asks essentially whether, in cases of failure, or defective, service of the decision authorising enforcement, the mere fact that the party against whom enforcement is sought had notice of that decision is sufficient to cause time to run for the purposes of Article 36 of the Brussels Convention.

22. In that regard, it must be observed at the outset that the wording of Article 36 of the Brussels Convention does not by itself enable an answer to be given to the questions raised.

23. While that provision provides that the time-limit for appealing against the decision authorising enforcement begins to run from the day on which that decision is served, it does not define service and does not specify the manner in which it must be effected in order to be effective, except where the party against whom enforcement is sought is domiciled in a Contracting State other than that in which the decision authorising enforcement was given. Service in such a case is required to be effected either on him in person or at his residence before the time for appealing begins to run.

24. Further, Article 36 of the Brussels Convention does not, in contrast to Article 27(2) of that Convention, include any express condition for validity of service.

25. Accordingly, Article 36 of the Brussels Convention must be interpreted in the light of the scheme and aims of that Convention.

26. In relation to the aims of the Brussels Convention, it is clear from its preamble that it is intended to secure the simplification of formalities governing the reciprocal recognition and enforcement of

judgments of courts or tribunals. It is settled case-law that it is not, however, permissible to achieve that aim by undermining in any way the right to a fair hearing (see, in particular, Case 49/84 Debaecker and Plouvier [1985] ECR 1779, paragraph 10, and Case C–522/03 Scania Finance France [2005] ECR I–0000, paragraph 15).

27.   More particularly, as far as enforcement is concerned, the principal aim of the Convention is to facilitate, to the greatest possible extent, the free movement of judgments by providing for a simple and rapid enforcement procedure whilst giving the party against whom enforcement is sought an opportunity to lodge an appeal (see, in particular, Case 148/84 Deutsche Genossenschaftsbank [1985] ECR 1981, paragraph 16, and Case C–7/98 Krombach [2000] ECR I–1935, paragraph 19).

28.   In relation to the scheme established by the Brussels Convention for recognition and enforcement, it is appropriate to point out that, in addition to Article 36, other provisions of that Convention provide for the service on the defendant of documents or decisions.

29.   Accordingly, by virtue of Articles 27(2) and the second sentence of Article 34 of that Convention, a judgment given in default of appearance is not to be recognised or enforced in another Contracting State if the defendant was not duly served with the document which instituted the proceedings or with an equivalent document in sufficient time to enable him to arrange for his defence. In that context, the Court has held that a judgment given in default of appearance in a Contracting State must not be recognised in another Contracting State where the document which instituted the proceedings was not duly served on the defendant, even if the defendant subsequently had notice of the judgment and did not have recourse to the available legal remedies (Case C–305/88 Lancray [1990] ECR I–2725, paragraph 23, and Case C–123/91 Minalmet [1992] ECR I–5661, paragraph 21).

30.   Moreover, it must be observed that, under the scheme established by the Brussels Convention with regard to enforcement, the interests of the applicant and of the person against whom enforcement is sought are protected differently.

31.   Article 36 of the Convention provides, in relation to the party against whom enforcement is sought, for the use of a formal mechanism of service' of the decision authorising enforcement. Conversely, it follows from Article 35 of the Convention that the decision given on the application is required only to be brought to the notice' of the applicant.

32.   Further, according to Article 36 of the Brussels Convention, the party against whom enforcement is sought may appeal against the decision, according to whether or not he is domiciled in the Contracting State in which the decision authorising enforcement was given, within a time-limit of one or two months from the date of service of the decision. That time-limit is of a strict and mandatory nature (Case 145/86 Hoffmann [1988] ECR 645, paragraphs 30 and 31). Conversely, it follows from both the wording of Article 40(1) of that Convention and the Jenard Report on the Convention (OJ 1979 C 59, p. 1, 53), that an

applicant's right of appeal against a decision refusing the application for enforcement is not subject to any time-limit.

33.   In light of those considerations it must be established whether, in cases of failure of, or defective, service of the decision authorising enforcement, the mere fact that the person against whom enforcement is sought has notice of that decision suffices for the time-limit fixed in Article 36 of the Brussels Convention to begin to run.

34.   In that regard, it is common ground, first, as stated by the Advocate General at point 56 of her Opinion, that the requirement that the decision authorising enforcement be served has a dual function: on the one hand, it serves to protect the rights of the party against whom enforcement is sought and, on the other, it allows, in terms of evidence, the strict and mandatory time-limit for appealing provided for in Article 36 of the Brussels Convention to be calculated precisely.

35.   That double function, combined with the aim of simplification of the formalities to which enforcement of judicial decisions delivered in other Contracting States is subject, explains why the Brussels Convention, as is clear from paragraph 32 of this judgment, makes transmission of the decision authorising enforcement to the party against whom enforcement is sought subject to procedural requirements that are more stringent than those applicable to transmission of that same decision to the applicant.

36.   Secondly, it should be borne in mind that, if the sole issue were whether the document authorising enforcement came to the attention of the party against whom enforcement was sought, that could render the requirement of due service meaningless. Claimants would then be tempted to ignore the prescribed forms for due service (see, to that effect, in the context of Article 27(2) of the Brussels Convention, Lancray, paragraph 20).

37.   Moreover, that would make the exact calculation of the time-limit provided for in Article 36 of the Convention more difficult, thus thwarting the uniform application of the provisions of the Convention (see, to that effect, Lancray, paragraph 20).

38.   Therefore the reply to the questions put to the Court must be that Article 36 of the Brussels Convention is to be interpreted as requiring due service of the decision authorising enforcement, in accordance with the procedural rules of the Contracting State in which enforcement is sought, and therefore, in cases of failure of, or defective, service of the decision authorising enforcement, the mere fact that the party against whom enforcement is sought has notice of that decision is not sufficient to cause time to run for the purposes of the time-limit fixed in that article.

Costs

39.   Since these proceedings are, for the parties to the main proceedings, a step in the action pending before the national court, the decision on costs is a matter for that court. Costs incurred in submitting

observations to the Court, other than the costs of those parties, are not recoverable.

RULING

On those grounds, the Court (Second Chamber) hereby rules:

Article 36 of the Convention of 27 September 1968 on jurisdiction and the enforcement of judgments in civil and commercial matters, as amended by the Convention of 9 October 1978 on the accession of the Kingdom of Denmark, Ireland and the United Kingdom of Great Britain and Northern Ireland, the Convention of 25 October 1982 on the accession of the Republic of Greece and the Convention of 26 May 1989 on the accession of the Kingdom of Spain and the Portuguese Republic, is to be interpreted as requiring due service of the decision authorising enforcement in accordance with the procedural rules of the Contracting State in which enforcement is sought, and therefore, in cases of failure of, or defective, service of the decision authorising enforcement, the mere fact that the party against whom enforcement is sought has notice of that decision is not sufficient to cause time to run for the purposes of the time-limit fixed in that article.

Questions and Comments

1. What provisions of the Brussels Regulation must we be concerned with in this Problem in considering the action for recognition and enforcement of the German judgment in Irish courts? How will they affect the action? What is the likely outcome?

2. Should the Brussels Regulation be available for use by a party outside the European Union to enforce a judgment against a defendant from an EU Member State? What are the implications of its application in this manner? Should the Regulation be available to enforce a judgment against a defendant not domiciled in a Member State by a plaintiff who is domiciled in a Member State?

3. Are any of the bases for non-recognition of a judgment found in Article 34 potentially available in our enforcement action?

4. Compare the Brussels Regulation to both the U.S. Recognition Act system of judgment recognition and the national law of Germany. Which do you prefer? Why?

5. If the United States were to enter into a multilateral convention on jurisdiction and the recognition and enforcement of judgments would the Brussels Regulation serve as a good model from which to negotiate? Why or why not?

Part Five

LITIGATION INVOLVING A FOREIGN STATE

Chapter 8

FOREIGN STATE IMMUNITY

INTRODUCTION 8.0 THE BACKGROUND AND FUNDAMENTALS OF FOREIGN STATE IMMUNITY: A QUESTION OF JURISDICTION

In what circumstances, if any, should a private litigant be permitted to sue a foreign sovereign (read "King", hence "sovereign" immunity)? Historically, the answer was seldom.[1] This was known as the "absolute theory" of sovereign immunity; i.e., no one could sue a sovereign state without its consent. Concerns of international relations dictated the application by U.S. courts of the absolute theory of sovereign immunity; that is, U.S. courts held that they had no jurisdiction to entertain disputes against a foreign sovereign.

Imagine a hypothetical case, such as *10,000 Outraged Texans v. Mexico*, Eastern District of Texas (1845). As the following case illustrates, international comity[2] and the need for peaceful relations between sovereigns underly U.S. application of the absolute theory of sovereign immunity.

THE SCHOONER EXCHANGE v. MCFADDON

Supreme Court of the United States, 1812.
11 U.S. (7 Cranch) 116, 3 L.Ed. 287.

* * * The case was this—on the 24th of August, 1811, *John McFaddon & William Greetham*, of the State of Maryland, filed their libel in the District Court of the United States, for the District of Pennsylvania, against the *Schooner Exchange*, setting forth that they were her sole owners, on the 27th of October, 1809, when she sailed from Baltimore,

---

1. Suits were permitted for certain actions, such as those relating to inheritance/succession rights, gifts, real property, and certain maritime claims against a merchant vessel of a foreign state.

2. "Comity is a recognition which one nation extends within its own territory to the legislative, executive, or judicial acts of another. It is not a rule of law, but one of practice, convenience, and expediency. Although more than mere courtesy and accommodation, comity does not achieve the focus of an imperative or an obligation." Somportex, Ltd. v. Philadelphia Chewing Gum Corp., 453 F.2d 435, 440 (3d Cir. 1971).

bound to St. Sebastians, in Spain. That while lawfully and peaceably pursuing her voyage, she was on the 30th of December, 1810, violently and forcibly taken by certain persons, acting under the decrees and orders of NAPOLEON, *Emperor of the French,* out of the custody of the libellants, and of their captain and agent, and was disposed of by those persons, or some of them, in violation of the rights of the libellants, and of the law of nations in that behalf. * * * That no sentence or decree of condemnation had been pronounced against her, by any court of competent jurisdiction; but that the property of the libellants in her, remained unchanged and in full force. They therefore prayed the usual process of the court, to attach the vessel, and that she might be restored to them.

* * *

On the 20th of September, *Mr. Dallas,* the Attorney of the United States, for the District of Pennsylvania, appeared, and (at the instance of the executive department of the government of the United States, as it is understood,) filed a *suggestion,* to the following effect:

* * * That in as much as there exists between the United States of America and Napoleon, emperor of France and king of Italy, &c. &c. a state of peace and amity; the public vessels of his said Imperial and Royal Majesty, conforming to the law of nations, and laws of the said United States, may freely enter the ports and harbors of the said United States, and at pleasure depart therefrom without seizure, arrest, detention or molestation. * * * That [the vessel] having entered the said port from necessity, and not voluntarily; having procured the requisite refreshments and repairs, and having conformed in all things to the law of nations and the laws of the United States, was about to depart from the said port of Philadelphia, and to resume her voyage in the service of his said Imperial and Royal Majesty, when on the 24th of August, 1811, she was seized, arrested, and detained in pursuant of the process of attachment issued upon the prayer of the libellants. That the said public vessel had not, at any time, been violently and forcibly taken or captured from the libellants, their captain and agent on the high seas, as prize of war, or otherwise; but that if the said public vessel, belonging to his said Imperial and Royal Majesty as aforesaid, ever was a vessel navigating under the flag of the United States, and possessed by the libellants, citizens thereof, as in their libel is alleged, (which nevertheless, the said Attorney does not admit) the property of the libellants, in the said vessel was seized and divested, and the same became vested in his Imperial and Royal Majesty, within a port of his empire, or of a country occupied by his arms, out of the jurisdiction of the United States, and of any particular state of the United States, according to the decrees and laws of France, in such case provided. And the said Attorney submitting, whether, in consideration of the premises, the court will take cognizance of the cause, respectfully prays that the court will be pleased to order and decree, that the process of attachment, heretofore issued, be quashed; that the libel be dismissed with costs; and that the said public vessel, her tackle, &c. belonging to his said Imperial and Royal Majesty, be released, &c. * * *

MARSHALL, CH. J. DELIVERED THE OPINION OF THE COURT AS FOLLOWS:

This case involves the very delicate and important inquiry, whether an American citizen can assert, in an American court, a title to an armed national vessel, found within the waters of the United States.

* * *

In exploring an unbeaten path, with few, if any, aids from precedents or written law, the court has found it necessary to rely much on general principles, and on a train of reasoning, founded on cases in some degree analogous to this.

The jurisdiction of *courts* is a branch of that which is possessed by the nation as an independent sovereign power.

The jurisdiction of the nation within its own territory is necessarily exclusive and absolute. It is susceptible of no limitation not imposed by itself. Any restriction upon it, deriving validity from an external source, would imply a diminution of its sovereignty to the extent of the restriction, and an investment of that sovereignty to the same extent in that power which could impose such restriction.

All exceptions, therefore, to the full and complete power of a nation within its own territories, must be traced up to the consent of the nation itself. They can flow from no other legitimate source.

* * *

The world being composed of distinct sovereignties, possessing equal rights and equal independence, whose mutual benefit is promoted by intercourse with each other, and by an interchange of those good offices which humanity dictates and its wants require, all sovereigns have consented to a relaxation in practice, in cases under certain peculiar circumstances, of that absolute and complete jurisdiction within their respective territories which sovereignty confers.

This consent may, in some instances, be tested by common usage, and by common opinion, growing out of that usage.

* * *

This perfect equality and absolute independence of sovereigns, and this common interest impelling them to mutual intercourse, and an interchange of good offices with each other, have given rise to a class of cases in which every sovereign is understood to wave the exercise of a part of that complete exclusive territorial jurisdiction, which has been stated to be the attribute of every nation.

1st. One of these is admitted to be the exemption of the person of the sovereign from arrest or detention within a foreign territory.

If he enters that territory with the knowledge and license of its sovereign, that license, although containing no stipulation exempting his person from arrest, is universally understood to imply such stipulation.

Why has the whole civilized world concurred in this construction? The answer cannot be mistaken. A foreign sovereign is not understood as intending to subject himself to a jurisdiction incompatible with his dignity, and the dignity of his nation, and it is to avoid this subjection that the license has been obtained. The character to whom it is given, and the object for which it is granted, equally require that it should be construed to impart full security to the person who has obtained it. This security, however, need not be expressed; it is implied from the circumstances of the case.

* * *

2d. A second case, standing on the same principles with the first, is the immunity which all civilized nations allow to foreign ministers.

Whatever may be the principle on which this immunity is established, whether we consider him as in the place of the sovereign he represents, or by a political fiction suppose him to be extra-territorial, and, therefore, in point of law, not within the jurisdiction of the sovereign at whose Court he resides; still the immunity itself is granted by the governing power of the nation to which the minister is deputed. This fiction of exterritoriality could not be erected and supported against the will of the sovereign of the territory. He is supposed to assent to it.

This consent is not expressed. It is true that in some countries, and in this among others, a special law is enacted for the case. But the law obviously proceeds on the idea of prescribing the punishment of an act previously unlawful, not of granting to a foreign minister a privilege which he would not otherwise possess.

The assent of the sovereign to the very important and extensive exemptions from territorial jurisdiction which are admitted to attach to foreign ministers, is implied from the considerations that, without such exemption, every sovereign would hazard his own dignity by employing a public minister abroad. His minister would owe temporary and local allegiance to a foreign prince, and would be less competent to the objects of his mission. A sovereign committing the interests of his nation with a foreign power, to the care of a person whom he has selected for that purpose, cannot intend to subject his minister in any degree to that power; and, therefore, a consent to receive him, implies a consent that he shall possess those privileges which his principal intended he should retain—privileges which are essential to the dignity of his sovereign, and to the duties he is bound to perform.

In what cases a minister, by infracting the laws of the country in which he resides, may subject himself to other punishment than will be inflicted by his own sovereign, is an inquiry foreign to the present purpose. If his crimes be such as to render him amenable to the local jurisdiction, it must be because they forfeit the privileges annexed to his character; and the minister, by violating the conditions under which he was received as the representative of a foreign sovereign, has surrendered the immunities granted on those conditions; or, according to the true meaning of the original assent, has ceased to be entitled to them.

3d. A third case in which a sovereign is understood to cede a portion of his territorial jurisdiction is, where he allows the troops of a foreign prince to pass through his dominions.

In such case, without any express declaration waving jurisdiction over the army to which this right of passage has been granted, the sovereign who should attempt to exercise it would certainly be considered as violating his faith. By exercising it, the purpose for which the free passage was granted would be defeated, and a portion of the military force of a foreign independent nation would be diverted from those national objects and duties to which it was applicable, and would be withdrawn from the control of the sovereign whose power and whose safety might greatly depend on retaining the exclusive command and disposition of this force. The grant of a free passage therefore implies a waver of all jurisdiction over the troops during their passage, and permits the foreign general to use that discipline, and to inflict those punishments which the government of his army may require.

But if, without such express permit, an army should be led through the territories of a foreign prince, might the jurisdiction of the territory be rightfully exercised over the individuals composing this army?

Without doubt, a military force can never gain immunities of any other description than those which war gives, by entering a foreign territory against the will of its sovereign. But if his consent, instead of being expressed by a particular license, be expressed by a general declaration that foreign troops may pass through a specified tract of country, a distinction between such general permit and a particular license is not perceived. It would seem reasonable that every immunity which would be conferred by a special license, would be in like manner conferred by such general permit.

* * *

But the rule which is applicable to armies, does not appear to be equally applicable to ships of war entering the ports of a friendly power. The injury inseparable from the march of an army through an inhabited country, and the dangers often, indeed generally, attending it, do not ensue from admitting a ship of war, without special license, into a friendly port. A different rule therefore with respect to this species of military force has been generally adopted. If, for reasons of state, the ports of a nation generally, or any particular ports be closed against vessels of war generally, or the vessels of any particular nation, notice is usually given of such determination. If there be no prohibition, the ports of a friendly nation are considered as open to the public ships of all powers with whom it is at peace, and they are supposed to enter such ports and to remain in them while allowed to remain, under the protection of the government of the place.

* * *

Those treaties which provide for the admission and safe departure of public vessels entering a port from stress of weather, or other urgent cause, provide in like manner for the private vessels of the nation; and where public vessels enter a port under the general license which is implied merely from the absence of a prohibition, they are, it may be urged, in the same condition with merchant vessels entering the same port for the purposes of trade who cannot thereby claim any exemption from the jurisdiction of the country. It may be contended, certainly with much plausibility if not correctness, that the same rule, and same principle are applicable to public and private ships; and since it is admitted that private ships entering without special license become subject to the local jurisdiction, it is demanded on what authority an exception is made in favor of ships of war.

* * *

To the Court, it appears, that where, without treaty, the ports of a nation are open to the private and public ships of a friendly power, whose subjects have also liberty without special license, to enter the country for business or amusement, a clear distinction is to be drawn between the rights accorded to private individuals or private trading vessels, and those accorded to public armed ships which constitute a part of the military force of the nation.

* * *

When private individuals of one nation spread themselves through another as business or caprice may direct, mingling indiscriminately with the inhabitants of that other, or when merchant vessels enter for the purposes of trade, it would be obviously inconvenient and dangerous to society, and would subject the laws to continual infraction, and the government to degradation, if such individuals or merchants did not owe temporary and local allegiance, and were not amenable to the jurisdiction of the country. * * *

But in all respects different is the situation of a public armed ship. She constitutes a part of the military force of her nation; acts under the immediate and direct command of the sovereign; is employed by him in national objects. He has many and powerful motives for preventing those objects from being defeated by the interference of a foreign state. Such interference cannot take place without affecting his power and his dignity. The implied license therefore under which such vessel enters a friendly port, may reasonably be construed, and it seems to the Court, ought to be construed, as containing an exemption from the jurisdiction of the sovereign, within whose territory she claims the rites of hospitality.

* * *

It seems then to the Court, to be a principle of public law, that national ships of war, entering the port of a friendly power open for their reception, are to be considered as exempted by the consent of that power from its jurisdiction.

Without doubt, the sovereign of the place is capable of destroying this implication. He may claim and exercise jurisdiction either by employing force, or by subjecting such vessels to the ordinary tribunals. But until such power be exerted in a manner not to be misunderstood, the sovereign cannot be considered as having imparted to the ordinary tribunals a jurisdiction, which it would be a breach of faith to exercise. * * *

The principles which have been stated, will now be applied to the case at bar.

In the present state of the evidence and proceedings, the Exchange must be considered as a vessel, which was the property of the Libellants, whose claim is repelled by the fact, that she is now a national armed vessel, commissioned by, and in the service of the emperor of France. The evidence of this fact is not controverted. But it is contended, that it constitutes no bar to an enquiry into the validity of the title, by which the emperor holds this vessel. Every person, it is alleged, who is entitled to property brought within the jurisdiction of our Courts, has a right to assert his title in those Courts, unless there be some law taking his case out of the general rule. It is therefore said to be the right, and if it be the right, it is the duty of the Court, to enquire whether this title has been extinguished by an act, the validity of which is recognized by national or municipal law.

If the preceding reasoning be correct, the Exchange, being a public armed ship, in the service of a foreign sovereign, with whom the government of the United States is at peace, and having entered an American port open for her reception, on the terms on which ships of war are generally permitted to enter the ports of a friendly power, must be considered as having come into the American territory, under an implied promise, that while necessarily within it, and demeaning herself in a friendly manner, she should be exempt from the jurisdiction of the country.

If this opinion be correct, there seems to be a necessity for admitting that the fact might be disclosed to the Court by the suggestion of the Attorney for the United States.

I am directed to deliver it, as the opinion of the Court, that the sentence of the Circuit Court, reversing the sentence of the District Court, in the case of the Exchange be reversed, and that of the District Court, dismissing the libel, be affirmed.

———

In the early 1950s, U.S. policy began to shift from the "absolute" toward the "restrictive" theory of sovereign immunity. Under the restrictive theory, foreign states retain their traditional immunity for governmental acts, but are denied immunity for private or commercial acts.

LETTER FROM JACK B. TATE, ACTING LEGAL ADVISOR OF DEPARTMENT OF STATE, TO PHILLIP PERLMAN, ACTING U.S. ATTORNEY GENERAL (MAY 19, 1952)

reprinted in, 26 Dept. State Bull. 984 (1952), also reprinted in, *Alfred Dunhill of London, Inc. v. Republic of Cuba,* 425 U.S. 682, 712–15, app. 2, 96 S.Ct. 1854, 48 L.Ed.2d 301 (1976).

MY DEAR MR. ATTORNEY GENERAL:

The Department of State has for some time had under consideration the question whether the practice of the Government in granting immunity from suit to foreign governments made parties defendant in the courts of the United States without their consent should not be changed. The Department has now reached the conclusion that such immunity should no longer be granted in certain types of cases. In view of the obvious interest of your Department in this matter I should like to point out briefly some of the facts which influenced the Department's decision.

A study of the law of sovereign immunity reveals the existence of two conflicting concepts of sovereign immunity, each widely held and firmly established. According to the classical or absolute theory of sovereign immunity, a sovereign cannot, without his consent, be made a respondent in the courts of another sovereign. According to the newer or restrictive theory of sovereign immunity, the immunity of the sovereign is recognized with regard to sovereign or public acts (*jure imperii*) of a state, but not with respect to private acts (*jure gestionis*). There is agreement by proponents of both theories, supported by practice, that sovereign immunity should not be claimed or granted in actions with respect to real property (diplomatic and perhaps consular property excepted) or with respect to the disposition of the property of a deceased person even though a foreign sovereign is the beneficiary.

The classical or virtually absolute theory of sovereign immunity has generally been followed by the courts of the United States, the British Commonwealth, Czechoslovakia, Estonia, and probably Poland.

The decisions of the courts of Brazil, Chile, China, Hungary, Japan, Luxembourg, Norway, and Portugal may be deemed to support the classical theory of immunity if one or at most two old decisions anterior to the development of the restrictive theory may be considered sufficient on which to base a conclusion.

The position of the Netherlands, Sweden, and Argentina is less clear since although immunity has been granted in recent cases coming before the courts of those countries, the facts were such that immunity would have been granted under either the absolute or restrictive theory. However, constant references by the courts of these three countries to the distinction between public and private acts of the state, even though the distinction was not involved in the result of the case, may indicate an intention to leave the way open for a possible application of the restrictive theory of immunity if and when the occasion presents itself.

A trend to the restrictive theory is already evident in the Netherlands where the lower courts have started to apply that theory following a Supreme Court decision to the effect that immunity would have been applicable in the case under consideration under either theory.

The German courts, after a period of hesitation at the end of the nineteenth century have held to the classical theory, but it should be noted that the refusal of the Supreme Court in 1921 to yield to pressure by the lower courts for the newer theory was based on the view that that theory had not yet developed sufficiently to justify a change. in view of the growth of the restrictive theory since that time the German courts might take a different view today.

The newer or restrictive theory of sovereign immunity has always been supported by the courts of Belgium and Italy. It was adopted in turn by the courts of Egypt and of Switzerland. In addition, the courts of France, Austria, and Greece, which were traditionally supporters of the classical theory, reversed their position in the 20's to embrace the restrictive theory. Rumania, Peru, and possibly Denmark also appear to follow this theory.

Furthermore, it should be observed that in most of the countries still following the classical theory there is a school of influential writers favoring the restrictive theory and the views of writers, at least in civil law countries, are a major factor in the development of the law. Moreover, the leanings of the lower courts in civil law countries are more significant in shaping the law than they are in common law countries where the rule of precedent prevails and the trend in these lower courts is to the restrictive theory. Of related interest to this question is the fact that ten of the thirteen countries which have been classified above as supporters of the classical theory have ratified the Brussels Convention of 1926 under which immunity for government owned merchant vessels is waived. In addition the United States, which is not a party to the Convention, some years ago announced and has since followed, a policy of not claiming immunity for its public owned or operated merchant vessels. Keeping in mind the importance played by cases involving public vessels in the field of sovereign immunity, it is thus noteworthy that these ten countries (Brazil, Chile, Estonia, Germany, Hungary, Netherlands, Norway, Poland, Portugal, Sweden) and the United States have already relinquished by treaty or in practice an important part of the immunity which they claim under the classical theory.

It is thus evident that with the possible exception of the United Kingdom little support has been found except on the part of the Soviet Union and its satellites for continued full acceptance of the absolute theory of sovereign immunity. There are evidences that British authorities are aware of its deficiencies and ready for a change. The reasons which obviously motivate state trading countries in adhering to the theory with perhaps increasing rigidity are most persuasive that the United States should change its policy. Furthermore, the granting of sovereign immunity to foreign governments in the courts of the United States is most inconsistent with the action of the Government of the United States in subjecting itself to suit in these same courts in both contract and tort and with its long established policy of not claiming immunity in foreign jurisdictions for its merchant vessels. Finally, the Department feels that the widespread and increasing practice on the part of governments of engaging in commercial activities makes necessary a practice which will enable persons doing business with them to have their rights determined in the courts. For these reasons it will hereafter be the Department's policy to follow the restrictive theory of sovereign immunity in the consideration of requests of foreign governments for a grant of sovereign immunity. It is realized that a shift in policy by the executive cannot control the courts but it is felt that the courts are less likely to allow a plea of sovereign immunity where the executive has declined to do so. There have been indications that at least some Justices of the Supreme Court feel that in this matter courts should follow the branch of the Government charged with responsibility for the conduct of foreign relations. In order that your Department, which is charged with representing the interests of the Government before the courts, may be adequately informed it will be the Department's practice to advise you of all requests by foreign governments for the grant of immunity from suit and of the Department's action thereon.

For the Secretary of State: JACK B. TATE Acting Legal Adviser

The Tate Letter was not followed by the State Department in all instances. The State Department continued to act politically and in certain instances sent suggestions of immunity to the courts in cases clearly commercial. The State Department even developed a hearing process before it concerning suggestions of immunity. It took the FSIA to put an end to the political involvement of the State Department in immunity decisions, *see Vencedora Oceanica Navigacion v. Compagnie Nationale Algerienne De Navigation*, 730 F.2d 195, 198 (5th Cir.1984) ("With its accommodation of diplomatic and political concerns, the State Department often lacked consistency, measured in legal terms, in applying the restrictive theory of immunity. In response, the Departments of State and Justice proposed the FSIA to Congress").

The rationale for the restrictive theory was well-articulated by a British court, *Trendtex Trading Corp. v. Central Bank of Nigeria*, [1977] 2 W.L.R. 356, 386 (C.A.), *reprinted in* 16 I.L.M. 471, 498 (1977):

> Governments everywhere engage in activities which although incidental in one way or another to the business of government are in themselves essentially commercial in their nature. To apply a universal doctrine of sovereign immunity to such activities is much more likely to disserve than to conserve the comity of nations on the

preservation of which the doctrine is founded. It is no longer necessary or desirable that what are truly matters of trading rather than of sovereignty should be hedged about with special exonerations and fenced off from the processes of the law by the attribution of a perverse and inappropriate notion of sovereign dignity.

Restatement (Third) of Foreign Relations Law (herein Restatement) § 451 and comment (a) (1986 Main Vol.) (Immunity of Foreign State from Jurisdiction to Adjudicate: The Basic Rule).

> Under international law, a state or state instrumentality is immune from the jurisdiction of the courts of another state, except with respect to claims arising out of activities of the kind that may be carried on by private persons.

> Comment: a. Restrictive theory of immunity. The basic rule stated in this section reflects the restrictive theory of immunity, now accepted by nearly all non-Communist states, though they differ as to detail in its application. Under the restrictive theory, a state is immune from any exercise of judicial jurisdiction by another state in respect of claims arising out of governmental activities (*de jure imperii*); it is not immune from the exercise of such jurisdiction in respect of claims arising out of activities of a kind carried on by private persons (*de jure gestionis*), notably commercial activities. Under the restrictive theory, suits on claims arising out of nongovernmental activities are not precluded even if the activities took place outside the forum state. Under United States law, however, courts in the United States may exercise jurisdiction of claims arising out of such activities outside the United States only if they had effect in the United States.

Enter the Foreign Sovereign Immunities Act

In an effort to provide guidelines and to promote consistency in the treatment by U.S. courts of foreign immunity issues, Congress enacted the Foreign Sovereign Immunities Act in 1976.[3] The Foreign Sovereign Immunities Act,[4] dictates the specific circumstances in which U.S. courts have jurisdiction over disputes of private litigants against a foreign sovereign. The Act also sets forth the procedures to be followed, from service of process to execution upon a judgment. Analyzing a foreign sovereign immunities case, therefore, requires counsel to consider, in advance, the stages of the litigation process from start to finish.

The FSIA provides the exclusive basis for both personal and subject matter jurisdiction over a foreign state. Therefore, unless an exception to

3. *See generally* Report of the House Judiciary Committee, H.R. Rep. No. 1487, 94th Congress, 2d Sess. (1976), at 1, *reprinted in* 1976 U.S.C.C.A.N. 6604 (herein House Report) ("It was also designed to bring U.S. practice into conformity with that of most other nations by leaving sovereign immunity decisions exclusively to the courts, thereby discontinuing the practice of judicial deference to 'suggestions of immunity' from the Executive Branch").

4. The Foreign Sovereign Immunities Act of 1976, Pub. L. No. 94–583, 90 Stat. 2891 (1976), 28 U.S.C.A. §§ 1330, 1332(a)(2), (3), and (4), 1391(f), 1441(d), 1602–4611 (2001), *reprinted in*, 71 Am. J. Int'l L. 595 (1977).

sovereign immunity stated in the Act exists, the U.S. court lacks both subject matter jurisdiction and personal jurisdiction. Under the FSIA, therefore, immunity is not merely a defense, it goes to jurisdiction itself, the power of the court to adjudicate the action. The legislative history explains:

> A judgment dismissing the action for lack of jurisdiction because the foreign state is entitled to sovereign immunity would be determinative of the question of sovereign immunity. Thus, a private party, who lost on the question of jurisdiction, could not bring the same case in a state court claiming that the federal court's decision extended only to the question of federal jurisdiction and not to sovereign immunity. House Report at 13.

Read FSIA provisions 28 U.S.C.A. §§ 1602, 1604, 1605, 1607 and 1610 (reprinted in the Documents Supplement).

The FSIA requires counsel to identify and address early in an engagement, certainly prior to commencement of litigation, a number of critical issues including:

A.   Jurisdiction and exclusivity of FSIA;

B.   Whether an exception to immunity is applicable;

C.   Distinction between foreign state and agency or instrumentality;

D.   Service of process;

E.   Removal from state to federal court;

F.   Absence of jury;

G.   Limited availability of punitive damages;

H.   Venue; and

I.   Default and execution on judgments.

While the FSIA requires counsel to examine a number of issues, they may be approached in a logical, systematic fashion. The FSIA provides specific rules with respect to each. These issues are discussed *ad seriatim* in Problem 8.1.

Under the FSIA, U.S. federal and state courts lack jurisdiction to entertain claims against foreign states (including agencies and instrumentalities thereof), except in cases of:

a. Waiver [1605(a)(1)]. The foreign state has expressly or impliedly waived immunity. Examples would be where immunity is waived in a clause contained in a contract for goods or services; or where the state does not raise immunity as a defense to an action. Waiver is discussed in more detail in Problem 8.2 below.

b. Commercial Activity [1605(a)(2)]. The foreign state has participated in the marketplace and should not be immune where others are liable. The theory is that international commerce would suffer were states able to repudiate contracts and avoid their obligations. Who would sell to or buy from a foreign state? This exception to immunity, if not the most common, is certainly the most litigated.

c. Property taken in violation of international law [1605 (a) (3)]. The case concerns rights in property taken in violation of international law and the property or its proceeds are present in the United States; or the property or its proceeds are held by an agency or instrumentality which is engaged in a commercial activity in the United States. This exception is discussed in Problem 8.2 below.

d. U.S. Property acquired by succession or gift or immovable [1605(a)(4)]. The case concerns rights in property in the United States acquired by inheritance/succession or immovable property (real estate) in the United States. Policy concerns for free alienation of land and the need to establish title/ownership to real and personal property and to settle estates underlie this exception. This exception, therefore, reflects universal norms which operated even under the absolute theory of sovereign immunity. As noted in the Tate Letter, supra, "sovereign immunity should not be claimed or granted in actions with respect to real property (diplomatic and perhaps consular property excepted) or with respect to the disposition of the property of a deceased person even though a foreign sovereign is the beneficiary."

e. Tortious act or omission [1605(a)(5)]. The case is not encompassed by the commercial activity exception, but seeks money damages for personal injury, death, or property damage caused by a foreign official or employee in the United States in the scope of his employment. Accidents in the United States among foreign officials/employees and U.S. citizens are contemplated by this provision. It is important to note that this provision does not permit suits alleging harm arising from the performance or failure to perform a discretionary act. For instance, a foreign official could not be sued for making or refusing to make a discretionary, administrative decision. Immunity here is similar to immunity granted public officials in the United States for acts in the scope of their employment. This provision also expressly prohibits a number of tort claims against a foreign state. These are: malicious prosecution, abuse of process, libel, slander, misrepresentation, deceit, and interference with contract rights.

f. Arbitration [1605(a)(6)]. The case concerns an agreement to arbitrate (such as an action to compel arbitration or stay a proceeding pending arbitration) or enforcement of an arbitral award. Given the prevalence of international agreements regarding arbitration, most arbitration proceedings or awards would meet the specific criteria set forth in 1605(a)(6). Further, a waiver of immunity may be found where the State agreed to arbitrate or included such agreement in a contract. Counsel should check whether an arbitration provision was contained in the contract documents.

g.   *Terrorist Acts [1605 (a) (7)].* The FSIA was amended by the Antiterrorism and Effective Death Penalty Act of 1996, Pub. L. No. 104–132, 110 Stat. 1241, to waive immunity with respect to money damages claims against a foreign state for personal injury or death that was caused by an act of torture, extrajudicial killing, aircraft sabotage, hostage taking, or the provision of material support or resources for such an act.

h.   *Maritime Liens and Ship Mortgages [1605(b), (c), and (d)].* The FSIA essentially codifies maritime law in that commercial shipping activities of a foreign state do not have sovereign immunity. Strong practical and commercial concerns underlie this regime. Ships in foreign ports must be able to receive necessaries such as fuel, supplies and repairs. Merchants and workmen must be able to enforce their liens against the vessel for providing same. Further, practices and laws which have developed with respect to ship finance and mortgages should not be upset by sovereign immunity notions. The FSIA expressly exempts ship mortgages from immunity.

i.   *Counterclaims [1607].* The FSIA may not be a shield and a sword for a foreign state. Having asserted claims against a party, the party may counterclaim against the foreign state, provided the counterclaim concerns the subject matter of the state's claim or would be permissible under one of the foregoing exceptions to immunity. Further, the counterclaim must seek relief similar in nature and amount to the foreign state's claim. In essence, the foreign state, by bringing a claim, waives its immunity to the extent of the claim it asserts.

Questions and Comments

1.   Chief Justice Marshall in *The Schooner Exchange* stated that immunity was rooted in the "perfect equality and absolute independence of sovereigns." However, he also stated "that the sovereign power of the nation is alone competent to avenge wrongs committed by a sovereign, that the questions to which such wrongs give birth are rather questions of policy than law, that they are for diplomatic, rather than legal discussion...." The Court, consistent with this latter reasoning, apparently gave great weight to the U.S. Attorney's suggestion that the vessel be released. Is the underlying rationale of the case, and indeed of the sovereign immunity doctrine, based upon the theory of separation of powers, under which potentially embarrassing foreign affairs are the domain of the Executive Branch? Might there be and did the court in fact articulate other rationales for the doctrine? *See* Restatement (3rd) of Foreign Relations Law of the United States, Chapter 5, Subchapter A, Introductory Note; *c.f. Vencedora Oceanica Navigacion v. Compagnie Nationale Algerienne De Navigation,* 730 F.2d 195, 198 (5th Cir.1984) ("the underlying rationale of *Schooner* rested on the theory of separation of powers, under which potentially embarrassing foreign affairs were the domain of the Executive Branch"), *citing,* Restatement (2d) of Foreign Relations Law of the United States, § 1 (1965).

2. Could the Court have declined to hear *The Schooner Exchange* case on purely jurisdictional grounds? Bear in mind that the case essentially involved a claim by U.S. citizens to title to a vessel present in U.S. waters. Would not the Court have a strong interest in protecting such rights of U.S. citizens and discouraging, if the plaintiffs McFaddon & Greetham were correct, what was essentially a foreign nation's piracy of a U.S.-owned vessel?

3. *The Schooner Exchange* case involved a ship. Many early state immunity decisions involve vessels. Why?

4. Does the shift to the restrictive theory reflect increasing international commerce of sovereigns, changing notions of sovereignty or of "fairness", greater judicial activism, i.e., willingness to decide cases involving matters of foreign policy, or other considerations?

5. What considerations of foreign policy or other considerations are evidenced by the specific exceptions to immunity carved out by the FSIA? Does the FSIA reflect concerns that domestic judicial rulings not impede international relations and commerce?

6. Do the exceptions to sovereign immunity recognized in the FSIA reflect the needs of international commerce and financial markets?

PROBLEM 8.1 REMOVAL, JURISDICTION AND THE COMMERCIAL ACTIVITY EXCEPTION; SELECTED FSIA ISSUES AND PROCEDURE: U.S. COMPANY SELLS FURNITURE TO CHINESE GOVERNMENT–OWNED TRAVEL AGENCY. SUIT FOR FAILURE TO PAY COMMENCED IN CALIFORNIA STATE COURT

SECTION I. THE SETTING

Red Star Travel (Red Star) is a Chinese government-owned instrumentality which primarily promotes tourism in China from the United States and Europe. Using the internet, Red Star ordered 1,000 executive desks for $1,000 each. The Seller was Travel Desks International & Co. (TDI), a company organized and existing under the laws of California with its principal place of business in San Francisco. TDI timely shipped the desks to Red Star, free along side (FAS) Red Star's designated vessel berthed at the Port of San Francisco, but Red Star's check was dishonored by the Chinese bank upon which it was drawn. Red Star has not responded to TDI's demands for payment. There is no bona fide dispute about the receipt, suitability or merchantability of the desks.

SECTION II. FOCUS OF CONSIDERATION

With the adoption of the FSIA in 1977, the focus of sovereign immunity litigation shifted from the developing common law noted in the above Introduction 8.0 to an analysis of the various provisions of the FSIA, which is itself rapidly building a body of interpretive case law. The focus of this problem is on some of the frequently raised issues involving the interpretation of provisions of the FSIA.

Important to this problem are the following provisions of the FSIA: § 1603(a) definitions (foreign state); § 1604 Immunity of a foreign state from jurisdiction; § 1605(a)(b) & (d) general exceptions to the jurisdictional immunity of a foreign state; and § 1607 counterclaims. They are included in the Documents Supplement.

SECTION III.   READINGS, QUESTIONS AND COMMENTS

PART A.   JURISDICTION AND EXCLUSIVITY OF FSIA

ARGENTINE REPUBLIC v. AMERADA HESS SHIPPING CORP.

Supreme Court of the United States, 1989.
488 U.S. 428, 109 S.Ct. 683, 102 L.Ed.2d 818.

CHIEF JUSTICE REHNQUIST delivered the opinion of the Court.

Two Liberian corporations sued the Argentine Republic in a United States District Court to recover damages for a tort allegedly committed by its armed forces on the high seas in violation of international law. We hold that the District Court correctly dismissed the action, because the Foreign Sovereign Immunities Act of 1976 (FSIA), does not authorize jurisdiction over a foreign state in this situation.

Respondents alleged the following facts in their complaints. Respondent United Carriers, Inc., a Liberian corporation, chartered one of its oil tankers, the Hercules, to respondent Amerada Hess Shipping Corporation, also a Liberian corporation. The contract was executed in New York City. Amerada Hess used the Hercules to transport crude oil * * *.

By June 8, 1982, after a stop in Brazil, the Hercules was in international waters about 600 nautical miles from Argentina and 500 miles from the Falklands; she was outside the "war zones" designated by Britain and Argentina. At 12:15 Greenwich mean time, the ship's master made a routine report by radio to Argentine officials, providing the ship's name, international call sign, registry, position, course, speed, and voyage description. About 45 minutes later, an Argentine military aircraft began to circle the Hercules. The ship's master repeated his earlier message by radio to Argentine officials, who acknowledged receiving it. Six minutes later, without provocation, another Argentine military plane began to bomb the Hercules; the master immediately hoisted a white flag. A second bombing soon followed, and a third attack came about two hours later, when an Argentine jet struck the ship with an air-to-surface rocket. Disabled but not destroyed, the Hercules reversed course and sailed to Rio de Janeiro, the nearest safe port. At Rio de Janeiro, respondent United Carriers determined that the ship had suffered extensive deck and hull damage, and that an undetonated bomb remained lodged in her No. 2 tank. After an investigation by the Brazilian Navy, United Carriers decided that it would be too hazardous to remove the undetonated bomb, and on July 20, 1982, the Hercules was scuttled 250 miles off the Brazilian coast.

Following unsuccessful attempts to obtain relief in Argentina, respondents commenced this action in the United States District Court for the Southern District of New York for the damage that they sustained from the attack. United Carriers sought $10 million in damages for the loss of the ship; Amerada Hess sought $1.9 million in damages for the fuel that went down with the ship. Respondents alleged that petitioner's attack on the neutral Hercules violated international law. They invoked the District Court's jurisdiction under the Alien Tort Statute, which provides that "[t]he district courts shall have original jurisdiction of any civil action by an alien for a tort only, committed in violation of the law of nations or a treaty of the United States." Amerada Hess also brought suit under the general admiralty and maritime jurisdiction, and "the principle of universal jurisdiction, recognized in customary international law." The District Court dismissed both complaints for lack of subject-matter jurisdiction, ruling that respondents' suits were barred by the FSIA.

A divided panel of the United States Court of Appeals for the Second Circuit reversed. The Court of Appeals held that the District Court had jurisdiction under the Alien Tort Statute, because respondents' consolidated action was brought by Liberian corporations, it sounded in tort ("the bombing of a ship without justification"), and it asserted a violation of international law ("attacking a neutral ship in international waters, without proper cause for suspicion or investigation"). Viewing the Alien Tort Statute as "no more than a jurisdictional grant based on international law," the Court of Appeals said that "who is within" the scope of that grant is governed by "evolving standards of international law." The Court of Appeals reasoned that Congress' enactment of the FSIA was not meant to eliminate "existing remedies in United States courts for violations of international law" by foreign states under the Alien Tort Statute. The dissenting judge took the view that the FSIA precluded respondents' action. We granted certiorari, and now reverse.

We start from the settled proposition that the subject-matter jurisdiction of the lower federal courts is determined by Congress "in the exact degrees and character which to Congress may seem proper for the public good." In the FSIA, Congress added a new chapter 97 to Title 28 of the United States Code, 28 U.S.C. §§ 1602–1611, which is entitled "Jurisdictional Immunities of Foreign States." The FSIA also added § 1330(a) to Title 28; it provides that "[t]he district courts shall have original jurisdiction without regard to amount in controversy of any nonjury civil action against a foreign state ... as to any claim for relief in personam with respect to which the foreign state is not entitled to immunity under sections 1605–1607 of this title or under any applicable international agreement."

We think that the text and structure of the FSIA demonstrate Congress' intention that the FSIA be the sole basis for obtaining jurisdiction over a foreign state in our courts. Sections 1604 and 1330(a) work in tandem: § 1604 bars federal and state courts from exercising jurisdiction when a foreign state *is* entitled to immunity, and § 1330(a) confers jurisdiction on district courts to hear suits brought by United States citizens and by aliens when a foreign state is *not* entitled to immunity. As we said in *Verlinden,* the FSIA "must be applied by the district courts in every action against a foreign sovereign, since subject-matter jurisdiction in any such action depends on the existence of one of the specified exceptions to foreign sovereign immunity."

* * *

Congress had violations of international law by foreign states in mind when it enacted the FSIA. For example, the FSIA specifically denies foreign states immunity in suits "in which rights in property taken in violation of international law are in issue." Congress also rested the FSIA in part on its power under Art. I, § 8, cl. 10, of the Constitution "[t]o define and punish Piracies and Felonies committed on the high Seas, and Offenses against the Law of Nations." From Congress' decision to deny immunity to foreign states in the class of cases just mentioned, we draw the plain implication that immunity is granted in those cases involving alleged violations of international law that do not come within one of the FSIA's exceptions.

* * *

In light of the comprehensiveness of the statutory scheme in the FSIA, we doubt that even the most meticulous draftsman would have concluded that Congress also needed to amend *pro tanto* the Alien Tort Statute and presumably such other grants of subject-matter jurisdiction in Title 28 * * *. Congress provided in the FSIA that "[c]laims of foreign states to immunity should *henceforth* be decided by courts of the United States in conformity with the principles set forth in this chapter," and very likely it thought that should be sufficient. § 1602.

For similar reasons we are not persuaded by respondents' arguments based upon the rule of statutory construction under which repeals by implication are disfavored. This case does not involve two statutes that readily could be seen as supplementing one another, nor is it a case where a more general statute is claimed to have repealed by implication an earlier statute dealing with a narrower subject. We think that Congress' decision to deal comprehensively with the subject of foreign sovereign immunity in the FSIA, and the express provision in § 1604 that "a foreign state shall be immune from the jurisdiction of the courts of the United States and of the States except as provided in sections 1605–1607," preclude a construction of the Alien Tort Statute that permits the instant suit. The Alien Tort Statute by its terms does not distinguish among classes of defendants, and it of course has the same effect after the passage of the FSIA as before with respect to defendants other than foreign states.

Respondents also argue that the general admiralty and maritime jurisdiction, § 1333(1), provides a basis for obtaining jurisdiction over petitioner for violations of international law, notwithstanding the FSIA. But Congress dealt with the admiralty jurisdiction of the federal courts when it enacted the FSIA. Section 1605(b) expressly permits an *in personam* suit in admiralty to enforce a maritime lien against a vessel or cargo of a foreign state. Unless the present case is within § 1605(b) or another exception to the FSIA, the statute conferring general admiralty and maritime jurisdiction on the federal courts does not authorize the bringing of this action against petitioner.

Having determined that the FSIA provides the sole basis for obtaining jurisdiction over a foreign state in federal court, we turn to whether any of the exceptions enumerated in the Act apply here. * * * We agree with the District Court that none of the FSIA's exceptions applies on these facts.

Respondents assert that the FSIA exception for noncommercial torts, § 1605(a)(5), is most in point. * * * Section 1605(a)(5) is limited by its terms, however, to those cases in which the damage to or loss of property occurs *in the United States.* Congress' primary purpose in enacting § 1605(a)(5) was to eliminate a foreign state's immunity for traffic accidents and other torts committed in the United States, for which liability is imposed under domestic tort law.

In this case, the injury to respondents' ship occurred on the high seas some 5,000 miles off the nearest shores of the United States. Despite these telling facts, respondents nonetheless claim that the tortious attack on the Hercules occurred "in the United States." They point out that the FSIA defines "United States" as including all "territory and waters, continental and insular, subject to the jurisdiction of the United States," § 1603(c), and that their injury occurred on the high seas, which is within the admiralty jurisdiction of the United States. They reason, therefore, that "by statutory definition" petitioner's attack occurred in the United States.

We find this logic unpersuasive. We construe the modifying phrase "continental and insular" to restrict the definition of United States to the continental United States and those islands that are part of the United States or its possessions; any other reading would render this phrase nugatory. Likewise, the term "waters" in § 1603(c) cannot reasonably be read to cover all waters over which United States courts might exercise jurisdiction. When it desires to do so, Congress knows how to place the high seas within the jurisdictional reach of a statute. We thus apply "[t]he canon of construction which teaches that legislation of Congress, unless contrary intent appears, is meant to apply only within the territorial jurisdiction of the United States." Because respondents' injury unquestionably occurred well outside the 3–mile limit then in effect for the territorial waters of the United States, the exception for noncommercial torts cannot apply.

The result in this case is not altered by the fact that petitioner's alleged tort may have had effects in the United States. Respondents state, for example, that the Hercules was transporting oil intended for use in this country and that the loss of the ship disrupted contractual payments due in New York. Under the commercial activity exception to the FSIA, a foreign state may be liable for its commercial activities "outside the territory of the United States" having a "direct effect" inside the United States. But the noncommercial tort exception, upon which respondents rely, makes no mention of "territory outside the United States" or of "direct effects" in the United States. Congress' decision to use explicit language in § 1605(a)(2), and not to do so in § 1605(a)(5), indicates that the exception in § 1605(a)(5) covers only torts occurring within the territorial jurisdiction of the United States.

We also disagree with respondents' claim that certain international agreements entered into by petitioner and by the United States create an exception to the FSIA here. As noted, the FSIA was adopted "[s]ubject to international agreements to which the United States [was] a party at the time of [its] enactment." This exception applies when international agreements "expressly conflic[t]" with the immunity provisions of the FSIA, hardly the circumstances in this case. Respondents point to the Geneva Convention on the High Seas, and the Pan American Maritime Neutrality Convention. These conventions, however, only set forth substantive rules of conduct and state that compensation shall be paid for certain wrongs. They do not create private rights of action for foreign corporations to recover compensation from foreign states in United States courts. Nor do we see how a foreign state can waive its immunity under § 1605(a)(1) by signing an international agreement that contains no mention of a waiver of immunity to suit in United States courts or even the availability of a cause of action in the United States. We find similarly unpersuasive the argument of respondents and *Amicus Curiae* Republic of Liberia that the Treaty of Friendship, Commerce and Navigation, carves out an exception to the FSIA. Article I of this Treaty provides, in pertinent part, that the nationals of the United States and Liberia "shall enjoy freedom of access to the courts of justice of the other on conforming to the local laws." The FSIA is clearly one of the "local laws" to which respondents must "conform" before bringing suit in United States courts.

We hold that the FSIA provides the sole basis for obtaining jurisdiction over a foreign state in the courts of this country, and that none of the enumerated exceptions to the Act apply to the facts of this case. The judgment of the Court of Appeals is therefore

Reversed.

Questions and Comments

1. Does the FSIA apply to TDI's claims against Red Star in the Problem?

2. What, if any, exception(s) to immunity may apply to TDI's claims against Red Star?

PART B.   THE COMMERCIAL ACTIVITY EXCEPTION

Litigation has arisen about the definition of "commercial activity" for purposes of the commercial activity exception to sovereign immunity because the FSIA does not define precisely what acts are "commercial" (non-immune) versus governmental (immune). A guiding star that has emerged from the case law is whether a private actor in the marketplace could engage in the activity at issue. *See* § 1603(d) & (e) (definitions pertaining to commercial activity).

Even where the foreign state contracts concerning goods or services, it is critical that the contract at issue be of a type which a private party could have made. For instance, contracts involving the exploitation or exporting of natural resources, such as petroleum or animals, have been deemed to involve a uniquely sovereign function to which the FSIA commercial activity exception does not apply. *See International Ass'n of Machinists and Aerospace Workers (IAM) v. Organization of Petroleum Exporting Countries (OPEC),* 477 F.Supp. 553, 567–581 (C.D.Cal.1979), *aff'd on other grounds,* 649 F.2d 1354 (9th Cir.1981)("In determining whether the activities of the OPEC members are governmental or commercial in nature, the Court can and should examine the standards recognized under international law. The United Nations, with the concurrence of the United States, has repeatedly recognized the principle that a sovereign state has the sole power to control its natural resources. * * * there can be little question that establishing the terms and conditions for removal of natural resources from its territory, when done by a sovereign state, individually and separately, is a governmental activity"); *MOL, Inc. v. Peoples Republic of Bangladesh,* 736 F.2d 1326, 1328–29 (9th Cir.), *cert. denied,* 469 U.S. 1037, 105 S.Ct. 513, 83 L.Ed.2d 403 (1984) (commercial activity exception inapplicable to termination by Bangladesh of licensing contract to export rhesus monkeys, and noting that right to regulate natural resources is uniquely sovereign function).

REPUBLIC OF ARGENTINA v. WELTOVER, INC.

Supreme Court of the United States, 1992.
504 U.S. 607, 112 S.Ct. 2160, 119 L.Ed.2d 394.

JUSTICE SCALIA delivered the opinion of the Court.

This case requires us to decide whether the Republic of Argentina's default on certain bonds issued as part of a plan to stabilize its currency was an act taken "in connection with a commercial activity" that had a "direct effect in the United States" so as to subject Argentina to suit in an American court under the Foreign Sovereign Immunities Act of 1976.

Since Argentina's currency is not one of the mediums of exchange accepted on the international market, Argentine businesses engaging in foreign transactions must pay in United States dollars or some other internationally accepted currency. In the recent past, it was difficult for Argentine borrowers to obtain such funds, principally because of the instability of the Argentine currency. To address these problems, petitioners, the Republic of Argentina and its central bank, Banco Central (collectively Argentina), in 1981 instituted a foreign exchange insurance contract program (FEIC), under which Argentina effectively agreed to assume the risk of currency depreciation in cross-border transactions involving Argentine borrowers. This was accomplished by Argentina's agreeing to sell to domestic borrowers, in exchange for a contractually predetermined amount of local currency, the necessary United States dollars to repay their foreign debts when they matured, irrespective of intervening devaluations.

Unfortunately, Argentina did not possess sufficient reserves of United States dollars to cover the FEIC contracts as they became due in 1982. The Argentine Government thereupon adopted certain emergency measures, including refinancing of the FEIC-backed debts by issuing to the creditors government bonds. These bonds, called "Bonods," provide for payment of interest and principal in United States dollars; payment may be made through transfer on the London, Frankfurt, Zurich, or New York market, at the election of the creditor. Under this refinancing program, the foreign creditor had the option of either accepting the Bonods in satisfaction of the initial debt, thereby substituting the Argentine Government for the private debtor, or maintaining the debtor/creditor relationship with the private borrower and accepting the Argentine Government as guarantor.

When the Bonods began to mature in May 1986, Argentina concluded that it lacked sufficient foreign exchange to retire them. Pursuant to a Presidential Decree, Argentina unilaterally extended the time for payment and offered bondholders substitute instruments as a means of rescheduling the debts. Respondents, two Panamanian corporations and a Swiss bank who hold, collectively, $1.3 million of Bonods, refused to accept the rescheduling and insisted on full payment, specifying New York as the place where payment should be made. Argentina did not pay, and respondents then brought this breach-of-contract action in the United States District Court for the Southern District of New York, relying on the Foreign Sovereign Immunities Act of 1976 as the basis for jurisdiction. * * *

The Foreign Sovereign Immunities Act of 1976 (FSIA) establishes a comprehensive framework for determining whether a court in this country, state or federal, may exercise jurisdiction over a foreign state. Under the Act, a "foreign state *shall* be immune from the jurisdiction of the courts of the United States and of the States" unless one of several statutorily defined exceptions applies. § 1604 (emphasis added). The FSIA thus provides the "sole basis" for obtaining jurisdiction over a foreign sovereign in the United States. The most significant of the FSIA's exceptions—and the one at issue in this case—is the "commercial" exception of § 1605(a)(2), which provides that a foreign state is not immune from suit in any case

"in which the action is based upon a commercial activity carried on in the United States by the foreign state; or upon an act performed in the United States in connection with a commercial activity of the foreign state elsewhere; or upon an act outside the territory of the United States in connection with a commercial activity of the foreign state elsewhere and that act causes a direct effect in the United States."

In the proceedings below, respondents relied only on the third clause of § 1605(a)(2) to establish jurisdiction, and our analysis is therefore limited to considering whether this lawsuit is (1) "based ... upon an act outside the territory of the United States"; (2) that was taken "in connection with a commercial activity" of Argentina outside this country; and (3) that "cause[d] a direct effect in the United States." The complaint in this case alleges only one cause of action on behalf of each of the respondents, viz., a breach-of-contract claim based on Argentina's attempt to refinance the Bonods rather than to pay them according to their terms. The fact that the cause of action is in compliance with the first of the three requirements—that it is "based upon an act outside the territory of the United States" (presumably Argentina's unilateral extension)—is uncontested. The dispute pertains to whether the unilateral refinancing of the Bonods was taken "in connection with a commercial activity" of Argentina, and whether it had a "direct effect in the United States." We address these issues in turn.

A

Respondents and their *amicus,* the United States, contend that Argentina's issuance of, and continued liability under, the Bonods constitute a "commercial activity" and that the extension of the payment schedules was taken "in connection with" that activity. The latter point is obvious enough, and Argentina does not contest it; the key question is whether the activity is "commercial" under the FSIA.

* * *

This definition [of "commercial activity" in § 1603(d)], however, leaves the critical term "commercial" largely undefined: The first sentence [of § 1603(d)] simply establishes that the commercial nature of an activity does *not* depend upon whether it is a single act or a regular course of conduct; and the second sentence merely specifies what element of the conduct determines commerciality (*i.e.,* nature rather than purpose), but still without saying what "commercial" means. Fortunately, however, the FSIA was not written on a clean slate. As we have noted, the Act (and the commercial exception in particular) largely codifies the so-called "restrictive" theory of foreign sovereign immunity first endorsed by the State Department in 1952. The meaning of "commercial" is the meaning generally attached to that term under the restrictive theory at the time the statute was enacted.

This Court did not have occasion to discuss the scope or validity of the restrictive theory of sovereign immunity until our 1976 decision in *Alfred Dunhill of London, Inc. v. Republic of Cuba,* 425 U.S. 682, 96 S.Ct. 1854, 48 L.Ed.2d 301. Although the Court there was evenly divided on the question whether the "commercial" exception that applied in the foreign-sovereign-immunity context also limited the availability of an act-of-state defense, there was little disagreement over the general scope of the exception. The plurality noted that, after the State Department endorsed the restrictive theory of foreign sovereign immunity in 1952, the lower courts consistently held that foreign sovereigns were not immune from the jurisdiction of American courts in cases "arising out of purely commercial transactions." The plurality further recognized that the distinction between state sovereign acts, on the one hand, and state commercial and private acts, on the other, was not entirely novel to American law. The plurality stated that the restrictive theory of foreign sovereign immunity would not bar a suit based upon a foreign state's participation in the marketplace in the manner of a private citizen or corporation. A foreign state engaging in "commercial" activities "do[es] not exercise powers peculiar to sovereigns"; rather, it "exercise[s] only those powers that can also be exercised by private citizens." The dissenters did not disagree with this general description. Given that the FSIA was enacted less than six months after our decision in *Alfred Dunhill* was announced, we think the plurality's contemporaneous description of the then-prevailing restrictive theory of sovereign immunity is of significant assistance in construing the scope of the Act.

In accord with that description, we conclude that when a foreign government acts, not as regulator of a market, but in the manner of a private player within it, the foreign sovereign's actions are "commercial" within the meaning of the FSIA. Moreover, because the Act provides that the commercial character of an act is to be determined by reference to its "nature" rather than its "purpose," 28 U.S.C. § 1603(d), the question is not whether the foreign government is acting with a profit motive or instead with the aim of fulfilling uniquely sovereign objectives. Rather, the issue is whether the particular actions that the foreign state performs (whatever the motive behind them) are the *type* of actions by which a private party engages in "trade and traffic or commerce," Black's Law Dictionary 270 (6th ed. 1990). Thus, a foreign government's issuance of regulations limiting foreign currency exchange is a sovereign activity, because such authoritative control of commerce cannot be exercised by a private party; whereas a contract to buy army boots or even bullets is a "commercial" activity, because private companies can similarly use sales contracts to acquire goods.

The commercial character of the Bonods is confirmed by the fact that they are in almost all respects garden-variety debt instruments: They may be held by private parties; they are negotiable and may be traded on the international market (except in Argentina); and they promise a future stream of cash income. * * * There is, however, nothing distinctive about the state's assumption of debt (other than perhaps its purpose) that would cause it always to be classified as jure imperii. * * * Because the FSIA has now clearly established that the "nature" governs, we perceive no basis for concluding that the issuance of debt should be treated as categorically different from other activities of foreign states.

Argentina contends that, although the FSIA bars consideration of "purpose," a court must nonetheless fully consider the *context* of a transaction in order to determine whether it is "commercial." Accordingly, Argentina claims that the Court of Appeals erred by defining the relevant conduct in what Argentina considers an overly generalized, acontextual manner and by essentially adopting a *per se* rule that all "issuance of debt instruments" is "commercial." We have no occasion to consider such a *per se* rule, because it seems to us that even in full context, there is nothing about the issuance of these Bonods (except perhaps its purpose) that is not analogous to a private commercial transaction.

Argentina points to the fact that the transactions in which the Bonods were issued did not have the ordinary commercial consequence of raising capital or financing acquisitions. Assuming for the sake of argument that this is not an example of judging the commerciality of a transaction by its purpose, the ready answer is that private parties regularly issue bonds, not just to raise capital or to finance purchases, but also to refinance debt. * * *

Argentina argues that the Bonods differ from ordinary debt instruments in that they "were created by the Argentine Government to fulfill its obligations under a foreign exchange program designed to address a domestic credit crisis, and as a component of a program designed to control that nation's critical shortage of foreign exchange." In this regard, Argentina relies heavily on *De Sanchez v. Banco Central de Nicaragua,* 770 F.2d 1385 (1985), in which the Fifth Circuit took the view that "[o]ften, the essence of an act is defined by its purpose"; that unless "we can inquire into the purposes of such acts, we cannot determine their nature"; and that, in light of its purpose to control its reserves of foreign currency, Nicaragua's refusal to honor a check it had issued to cover a private bank debt was a sovereign act entitled to immunity. Indeed, Argentina asserts that the line between "nature" and "purpose" rests upon a "formalistic distinction [that] simply is neither useful nor warranted." We think this line of argument is squarely foreclosed by the language of the FSIA. However difficult it may be in some cases to separate "purpose" (*i.e.,* the *reason* why the foreign state engages in the activity) from "nature" (*i.e.,* the outward form of the conduct that the foreign state performs or agrees to perform), the statute unmistakably commands that to be done, 28 U.S.C. § 1603(d). We agree with the Court of Appeals that it is irrelevant *why* Argentina participated in the bond market in the manner of a private actor; it matters only that it did so. We conclude that Argentina's issuance of the Bonods was a "commercial activity" under the FSIA.

B

The remaining question is whether Argentina's unilateral rescheduling of the Bonods had a "direct effect" in the United States, 28 U.S.C.

§ 1605(a)(2). * * * Of course the generally applicable principle *de minimis non curat lex* ensures that jurisdiction may not be predicated on purely trivial effects in the United States. But we reject the suggestion that § 1605(a)(2) contains any unexpressed requirement of "substantiality" or "foreseeability." As the Court of Appeals recognized, an effect is "direct" if it follows "as an immediate consequence of the defendant's . . . activity."

* * *

We nonetheless have little difficulty concluding that Argentina's unilateral rescheduling of the maturity dates on the Bonods had a "direct effect" in the United States. Respondents had designated their accounts in New York as the place of payment, and Argentina made some interest payments into those accounts before announcing that it was rescheduling the payments. Because New York was thus the place of performance for Argentina's ultimate contractual obligations, the rescheduling of those obligations necessarily had a "direct effect" in the United States: Money that was supposed to have been delivered to a New York bank for deposit was not forthcoming.

* * *

We conclude that Argentina's issuance of the Bonods was a "commercial activity" under the FSIA; that its rescheduling of the maturity dates on those instruments was taken in connection with that commercial activity and had a "direct effect" in the United States; and that the District Court therefore properly asserted jurisdiction, under the FSIA, over the breach-of-contract claim based on that rescheduling. Accordingly, the judgment of the Court of Appeals is

Affirmed.

Questions and Comments

1. In *Republic of Argentina v. Weltover, Inc.*, the Supreme Court considered whether the issuance of bonds ("Bonods") by the Argentine government constituted a commercial activity under the FSIA. In reviewing the definition of commercial activity in the FSIA, the Court noted that it "leaves the critical term 'commercial' largely undefined." The first sentence of 1603(d) simply establishes that the commercial nature of an activity does not depend upon whether it is a single act or a regular course of conduct, and the second sentence merely specifies what element of the conduct determines commerciality (i.e., nature rather than purpose), but still without saying what "commercial" means. Were Congress to define the term "commercial", might Congress unwittingly extend (or fail to extend) the FSIA to conduct in a manner contrary to the FSIA's goals?

2. Would the immunity granted by the FSIA be greater if courts were to focus on the "purpose" of the commercial activity or on the "nature" of the commercial activity? The grant of immunity would be much broader were courts to focus on the "purpose" of an act, as, a foreign sovereign could

always argue that the purchase of the item, whether furniture, equipment, military hardware or funds was for some governmental, regulatory or military purpose. Courts, therefore, have focused on the "nature" of the act, *i.e.*, was it the type of commercial activity in which private parties could engage? *See International Ass'n of Machinists and Aerospace Workers (IAM) v. OPEC*, 649 F.2d 1354, 1357, fn. 6 (9th Cir. 1981), *cert. denied*, 454 U.S. 1163, 102 S.Ct. 1036, 71 L.Ed.2d 319 (1982):

> The categorization of activity as commercial or non-commercial is a source of controversy. Two different tests arose to determine the character of state activity. One focused on the purpose of the activity, the other on the nature of the activity. The purpose test, which asks whether the act in question was undertaken for sovereign ends, is subjective. The nature test, which focuses on the nature of the act itself, is objective. The purpose test grants broader immunity, since even the most commercial activity could have an underlying governmental purpose. For example, the purchase of furniture is objectively a commercial act. If the furniture is purchased for a state's embassy, however, under the purpose test, the act is sovereign and immunity applies. The problem with the purpose test is that the expectations of the furniture seller relying on the commercial appearance of activity would be frustrated if the foreign government could claim immunity and disclaim its obligation to pay. Only the objective test would protect the seller's reliance on the nature and appearance of the purchase as commercial activity subject to domestic laws.

PART C. THE THREE CLAUSES OF THE COMMERCIAL ACTIVITY EXCEPTION

1. *Clause 1: Commercial Activity in the United States*. Clause 1 of 1605(a)(2) concerns a commercial activity carried on in the United States by the foreign state. Such activity would include import-export transactions. *See* H.R. Rep. 94–1487 at 16–17 (House Report) (stating "import-export transactions involving sales to, or purchases from, concerns in the United States" are included within the conduct of the first clause of § 1605(a)(2) and defining commercial activity under § 1603(d) to include "a single contract, if of the same character as a contract which might be made by a private person"). Clause 1 is amplified by 1603(e): a "commercial activity carried on in the United States by a foreign state" means commercial activity carried on by such state and having substantial contact with the United States. For Clause 1 to apply, therefore, the nature of the claim must bear substantial contact, i.e., a "nexus" to the commercial activity carried on in the United States. *See Vencedora Oceanica Navigacion v. Compagnie Nationale Algerienne de Navigation*, 730 F.2d 195 (5th Cir. 1984) (dismissing action by petitioner vessel owner against instrumentality of Algerian government arising from loss of vessel overseas).

Comment

In *Vencedora* the court found that although the defendant had a continuing business contact with the United States, the action did not arise from such contact. Consequently, the court concluded that jurisdiction was not available under Clause 1 of section 1605(a)(2) because there was no "nexus" between the act at issue and the continuing business of the defendant in the United States. A court may be more likely to find such a nexus where the parties contracted in the United States for provision of goods or services. In *Honduras Aircraft Registry, Ltd. v. Government of Honduras*, 129 F.3d 543, *reh'g en banc denied*, 131 F.3d 157 (11th Cir.1997), the court found that Honduras had acted as a private party in the marketplace by contracting for the provision of goods and services in the U.S. to assist in implementing a Honduran civil aircraft registry. The court found that the underlying activities of providing know-how, training, resources, etc., were commercial in nature and of the type negotiable among private parties. The court observed that "[o]nly the 'nature' of the act, not the 'purpose' or 'motivation' for the act, is determinative.... [I]t is irrelevant that ... Honduras may have intended only to fulfill its unique sovereign objectives."

---

2.   *Clause 2: Commercial Activity Outside the United States*. Clause 2 of 1605(a)(2) concerns an act performed in the United States in connection with a commercial activity carried on outside the United States by the foreign state. The House Report explains that Clause 2 looks to conduct of the foreign state in the United States which relates either to a regular course of commercial conduct elsewhere or to a particular commercial transaction concluded or carried out in part elsewhere. Examples of this type of situation might include: a representation in the United States by an agent of a foreign state that leads to an action for restitution based on unjust enrichment; an act in the United States that violates U.S. securities laws or regulations; the wrongful discharge in the United States of an employee of the foreign state who has been employed in connection with a commercial activity carried on in some third country.

See Gilson v. Republic of Ireland, 682 F.2d 1022 (D.C. Cir. 1982) (finding Clause 2 of Section 1605(a)(2) applicable to claims of James K. Gilson, a mechanical engineer and American citizen and a resident of Massachusetts that defendants, instrumentalities of the Republic of Ireland, stole his expertise and equipment and made money from them).

In *Ohntrup v. Firearms Center, Inc.*, 516 F.Supp. 1281 (E.D.Pa. 1981), *aff'd*, 760 F.2d 259 (3d Cir. 1985), the court found jurisdiction under Clause 3 for an action involving injury in the United States resulting from a malfunctioning firearm manufactured by a Turkish government-owned firm. The injury was a substantial and foreseeable result of the defendant's actions because the sales agreement specifically envisioned sales in the United States. In contrast, the court in *Zernicek v. Brown & Root, Inc.,* 826 F.2d 415, 417 (5th Cir.1987), *cert. denied,* 484 U.S. 1043, 108 S.Ct. 775, 98 L.Ed.2d 862 (1988), construed Clause 3 and held that "the eventual effect in the United States of the personal injury or death of an American citizen while abroad is not direct within the meaning of the Act even if the foreign government agency might foresee that a U.S. citizen might be injured while traveling or working within its territory." Similarly, in *Four Corners Helicopters, Inc. v. Turbomeca,* 677 F.Supp. 1096 (D.Colo. 1988), the court held that the crash of an aircraft in Colorado did not constitute a "direct effect" for FSIA purposes where the foreign manufactured hull had been salvaged after a crash in Europe, transferred to the United States, fitted with a new engine, and sold to the plaintiff, all without the knowledge or participation of the defendant. The court found that the "complaint does not provide any basis for inferring the effect in this country was foreseeable or the immediate causal effect of an act of defendant ... or was substantial. If anything, it actually outlines the very intervening elements which preclude the inference of a 'direct effect' as that term has been judicially interpreted."

Questions and Comments

1. Does the conduct of Red Star constitute "commercial activity" for purposes of the commercial activity exception to sovereign immunity? More specifically, does Red Star's transacting commerce using TDI's website satisfy Clause 1 as a commercial act carried on in the United States? What factors are important to finding a Clause 1 exception? It was the clear legislative intent that Clause 1 would apply to import-export transactions. *See S & Davis Int'l, Inc. v. Yemen,* 218 F.3d 1292 (11th Cir.2000) (finding Clause 1 satisfied where instrumentality of Yemen breached contract to purchase grain from U.S. company).

2. Do the activities of Red Star constitute acts performed in the United States in connection with a commercial activity carried on outside the United States by the foreign state for purposes of Clause 2? What factors are important to finding a Clause 2 exception?

3. Do the activities of Red Star constitute acts outside the United States in connection with a commercial act of the foreign state outside the United States which act causes a direct effect in the United States for purposes of Clause 3? What factors are important to finding a Clause 3 exception?

PART D. SERVICE OF PROCESS

Assume some additional facts to Section I., The Setting. Suit is filed in state court, San Francisco against Red Star and Instrumentality. Process (summons and complaint) is served upon Red Star and Instrumentality by publication. Red Star and Instrumentality file a motion to dismiss—based upon the absence of personal jurisdiction for improper service of process and lack of personal and subject matter jurisdiction based upon sovereign immunity. Alternatively, Red Star and Instrumentality move the court to remove the case to federal court. In its motion,

Defendants assert that the desks were not purchased to run a travel agency but to staff a new Chinese ministry designed to deal with student dissidents by requiring them to perform bureaucratic office work. *See* § 1608 Service; time to answer; default.

The FSIA sets forth the exclusive means of service of process upon a foreign state. In order to properly serve a foreign state, agency or instrumentality, a party must follow strictly the hierarchy of methods stated in Section 1608. Note that different methods of service apply to states or to a political subdivision thereof under 1608 (a), as compared to the methods for agencies or instrumentalities under 1608 (b).

See Magness v. Russian Federation, 247 F.3d 609 (5th Cir. 2001) (finding service of process for FSIA purposes technically improper, where plaintiffs forwarded copies of their papers to the U.S. State Department and the Texas Secretary of State for service upon defendant but finding sufficient service where defendant had actual notice of lawsuit). The *Magness* court held that in "keeping with the plain language of the FSIA, we conclude that Congress intended to require strict compliance with section 1608(a) as to service upon foreign states and their political subdivisions", but also held that "substantial compliance—that is, actual notice of the suit and the consequences thereof—can be sufficient to satisfy the requirements of section 1608(b) as to service upon an agency or instrumentality of a foreign state."

Questions and Comments

1.   TDI's counsel should follow this analysis. Under § 1608(b)(1), was there any agreement, in the e-contract or otherwise, between a defendant and TDI for service? If not, then counsel would have proceeded to the first clause of § 1608(b)(2), and explored whether an officer or agent of the defendant was located in the United States for service. For example, had a defendant registered an agent with the California Secretary of State for service of process? Was an officer of the company (president, secretary, etc.) located in the United States? If not, counsel should have determined under the second clause of § 1608(b)(2) whether an international convention existed among the United States, China and Hong Kong for service of process. In fact, all three states were Parties to the Hague Convention on Service Abroad of Judicial and Extrajudicial Documents, 20 U.S.T. 361, T.I.A.S. No. 6638 (1969). Counsel, therefore, would have been required to attempt service under the Hague Convention provisions. Had there not been an international convention, counsel would have considered, in order, the methods stated in § 1608(b)(3)(A), (B), and (C).

Publication is not an authorized means of service under § 1608 or, generally, under the Hague Convention.

2.   One might check a variety of sources to determine whether the United States is a party to a particular convention on service. A starting point may be international litigation treatises which discuss the various conventions and their signatories. *See e.g.*, David Epstein, Jeffrey L. Snyder & Charles S. Baldwin, IV, International Litigation: A Guide to Jurisdiction,

Practice & Strategy, 3d ed., Appendix CH–1 (Transnational Publishers 2000) (comparative chart showing parties to selected private international law treaties). One may also contact the Department of State, Office of the Assistant Legal Adviser for Treaty Affairs or research the State Department/Government Printing Office publication Treaties in Force: A List of Treaties and Other International Agreements of the United States, which is also available on the State Department's website, www.state.gov at www. state.gov/www/global/legal_ affairs/tifindex.html.

3. Does service by publication comply or substantially comply with the FSIA requirements for service of process? Were TDI's counsel's methods of service of process by publication effective?

4. Does the FSIA contemplate that substantial compliance with its service provisions is sufficient to establish jurisdiction over foreign sovereigns? Were TDI's counsel's efforts sufficient under the FSIA? *See Magness v. Russian Federation*, 247 F.3d 609 (5th Cir.2001).

5. It is Defendants' position that acquiring the desks was an act of state security, not a commercial act. How does the court rule? (*See Argentina v. Weltover*, and § 1603(d) (test of commercial nature of activity is not whether purpose of activity was governmental but whether powers exercised could be exercised by private individuals)). It might also be noted that even if the activity is commercial in nature, it must still satisfy one of the three clauses of § 1605(a)(2).

PART E.   REMOVAL, USE OF A JURY, PUNITIVE DAMAGES, VENUE AND DEFAULT AND EXECUTION OF JUDGMENTS

Removal under the FSIA applies to all claims and parties to the action. The Act's legislative history, House Report at 32, states the rationale for unconditional removal:

> In view of the potential sensitivity of actions against foreign states and the importance of developing a uniform body of law in this area, it is important to give foreign states clear authority to remove to a Federal forum actions brought against them in the State courts. New subsection (d) of section 1441 permits the removal of any such action at the discretion of the foreign state, even if there are multiple defendants and some of these defendants desire not to remove the action or are citizens of the State in which the action is brought.

Questions and Comments

1. Can Red Star and Instrumentality remove TDI's claims from state court to federal court?

2. Can TDI's claims be tried to a jury? *See* § 1441(d). What foreign policy or other considerations might underlie this provision?

3. Can TDI obtain punitive damages on its claims? *See* § 1606. What policy considerations underlie this provision?

4. Why are foreign states treated differently with respect to punitive damages than agencies or instrumentalities?

5.   The four subsections of § 1391(f) (venue) provide separate rules for different types of defendants and actions under the FSIA. As to claims against foreign states or political subdivisions, venue is proper in both the District of Columbia under subsection (f)(4) and for commercial or tort actions in the appropriate forum under subsection (f)(1). As to claims against agencies/instrumentalities of foreign states, subsection (f)(3) provides that venue is proper only where the instrumentality is licensed to do or is doing business. Finally, in admiralty cases under § 1605(b), venue is proper only where the vessel or cargo is located. Assuming U.S. courts have jurisdiction of the matter under the FSIA, in what U.S. court may the action be brought? That is, where is venue proper?

6.   Because default judgments could be disruptive to amicable international relations, the FSIA imposes safeguards. The default provisions are set forth in § 1608(e). Before entering default, a court must determine whether it has jurisdiction over the matter; i.e., is an exception to immunity available under the FSIA? The burden of establishing the existence of jurisdiction through an exception to immunity rests with the court in the absence of an appearance by the foreign state, "even if the foreign state does not enter an appearance to assert an immunity defense, a district court must still determine that immunity is unavailable under the Act." *Verlinden B.V. v. Central Bank of Nigeria*, 461 U.S. 480, at 493 n.20, 103 S.Ct. 1962, 76 L.Ed.2d 81 (1983).

7.   Can a U.S. court grant a default judgment on TDI's claims? Why might the FSIA require "the claimant [to] establis[h] his claim or right to relief by evidence satisfactory to the court" for default to be entered, even when the foreign state fails to appear or to comply with the court's deadlines or procedures? How does this differ from court practice with respect to nonsovereign litigants?

8.   Property of a foreign state or agency or instrumentality in the United States may be subject to execution under §§ 1610(a) and (e) in eight circumstances, which generally track the immunity exceptions stated in § 1605. The FSIA, in codifying the restrictive theory of sovereign immunity, begins with the proposition that property in the United States of a foreign state, agency or instrumentality, is immune from execution to satisfy a judgment. *See* § 1609. Section 1610 then states certain limited circumstances in which property of a foreign state, agency or instrumentality can be subject to execution to satisfy a judgment.

Additional execution provisions are contained in § 1610(b), which section applies only to agencies and instrumentalities and not to foreign states. It provides that any property of the agency or instrumentality used for commercial activity in the U.S. may be subject to execution, not just property used in connection with the matter in dispute, as provided in § 1610(a). Therefore, for instance, an agency's or instrumentality's New York bank account might be executed upon, though the transaction, injury or events in dispute occurred in San Francisco, or even outside the United States. However, this provision applies only where the agency or instrumentality waived its execution immunity or where the judgment concerns certain specified actions brought under §§ 1605(a)(2), (3) or (5), or 1605(b).

9. What hurdles might exist in executing on a judgment against Red Star or Instrumentality? Can Instrumentality's property be subject to execution to satisfy a judgment?

10. Are the policies underlying the FSIA's treatment of claims against foreign sovereigns in § 1605 mirrored in the execution provisions of the FSIA in §§ 1610 and 1611?

PROBLEM 8.2 THE INTERNATIONAL LAW AND WAIVER EXCEPTIONS TO FOREIGN SOVEREIGN IMMUNITY; VENUE, AND ATTACHMENT/EXECUTION UNDER THE FSIA: U.S. OIL COMPANY CONCESSION EXPROPRIATED IN VENEZUELA

SECTION I. THE SETTING

The President of Venezuela has vigorously implemented a socialist, labor-oriented economic agenda. The Government has "nationalized", i.e., expropriated, facilities of several key industries, including the electric power, telecommunication, and petroleum industries. TexOil Co. (TOCO) is a multinational corporation, chartered in Delaware, with headquarters in Houston, Texas. For decades, TOCO has operated oil exploration, drilling and refining facilities in Venezuela and off the coast of Venezuela. In 1994, under a former Venezuelan President, the Government of Venezuela and TOCO entered into a twenty-five (25) years Agreement by which TOCO was granted the exclusive rights to explore, drill and refine petroleum products in certain areas of Venezuela, including off-shore. The Agreement required TOCO to pay royalties to Venezuela based on production of petroleum products. Further, the Agreement contained the following language:

> 85. Waiver of Immunity: Venezuela, a Sovereign State, does hereby waive all immunities and defenses arising solely by virtue of its sovereign status, including those conferred by any national or international law, statute, code, or common law, expressly including, without limitation, immunity under the U.S. Foreign Sovereign Immunities Act, 28 U.S.C.A. § 1330, et seq., or other similar laws, with respect to any lawful claim or counterclaim which TOCO may assert in a proceeding to enforce its rights hereunder. Further, Venezuela hereby waives the aforesaid immunities with respect to any lawful proceeding to enforce or collect a judgment or arbitral award rendered against it by a national court or tribunal of competent jurisdiction.

The current Venezuelan Legislature, controlled by the President's party, has passed legislation declaring that the President, by Executive Order, may elect to either ratify or repudiate any previous agreement between Venezuela and a foreign corporation pertaining to the exploitation of Venezuela's natural resources. Pursuant to this Act, the President of Venezuela, by Executive Order, has purported to terminate, among other agreements, the 1994 TOCO Agreement.

The Venezuelan national oil company (VOCO), subsequently has seized a TOCO oil refinery in Caracas. As compensation for the seizure, Venezuela promptly has tendered to TOCO a thirty-year maturity "Promissory Note" issued in the rapidly inflating Bolivar (currency of Venezuela), that is rapidly losing value against foreign hard currencies, such as the U.S. dollar. Immediately subsequent to the taking, TOCO stopped all payments to VOCO, including royalty payments for oil previously extracted and exported by TOCO.

TOCO has filed a complaint against Venezuela and VOCO for breach of contract and conversion of property in violation of international law in the United States district court for the Southern District of Texas, Houston Division. TOCO has alleged that Venezuela and VOCO have continued to operate the expropriated facilities to their financial gain and deprived TOCO of revenues to which it was entitled.

Venezuela and VOCO, in response, have filed a motion to dismiss the action on the bases that: 1) the court lacks jurisdiction over Venezuela and VOCO because of their sovereign immunity; 2) No exception to sovereign immunity applies, including because prompt, adequate and effective compensation was paid for the expropriation, so there was no taking under international law; 3) the 1994 TOCO Agreement, including its waiver of sovereign immunity clause, was terminated by Executive Order; 4) TOCO repudiated and breached the 1994 Agreement prior to commencement of the litigation by failing to pay required royalties; and 5) Venue is not proper in the Southern District of Texas, as Venezuela and VOCO have no assets there, are not licensed to conduct business there, and conduct no business there.

Venezuela and VOCO each maintain several bank accounts in New York City. Venezuela's accounts are used for governmental, including central banking, purposes. VOCO's accounts are used in furtherance of its activities in the petroleum business and related financing. Venezuela maintains a consulate in New York City. VOCO maintains an office in New York City which is used to support its petroleum business and financing activities.

You may argue the position of TOCO, Venezuela, or VOCO as to how the District court should rule on the motion to dismiss.

SECTION II.   FOCUS OF CONSIDERATION

Clearly, Venezuela is a sovereign state and the FSIA exclusively governs claims against it and its majority-owned instrumentality, VOCO. Counsel must first identify the exceptions to immunity under the FSIA which may be applicable. These are the waiver exception of § 1605(a)(1); the commercial activity exception of § 1605(a)(2); and the exception for property taken in violation of international law contained in § 1605(a)(3).

Counsel must then consider where venue is proper under § 1391(f). Finally, counsel must consider whether assets of Venezuela or VOCO may be executed upon to satisfy a judgment under §§ 1610 and 1611.

SECTION III. READINGS, QUESTIONS AND COMMENTS

PART A. WAIVER EXCEPTION TO SOVEREIGN IMMUNITY

DAVID EPSTEIN, JEFFREY L. SNYDER & CHARLES S. BALDWIN, IV, INTERNATIONAL LITIGATION
§ 7.05(2) (3d ed. 2002).*

Section 1605(a)(1) provides an exception to jurisdictional immunity if the foreign sovereign explicitly or implicitly waives its sovereign immunity. The section also provides that an explicit waiver may not be revoked unilaterally, but only according to its terms. In describing what it contemplated would qualify as an explicit waiver, Congress explained that:

> [a] foreign state may renounce its immunity by treaty, as has been done by the United States with respect to commercial and other activities in a series of treaties of friendship, commerce, and navigation, or a foreign state may waive its immunity in a contract with a private party.... Report of the House Judiciary Committee, H.R. Rep. No. 1487, 94th Cong., 2d Sess. at 18 (1976) (House Report). An example of an explicit waiver of immunity in a contract is that considered in *Proyecfin de Venezuela, S.A. v. Banco Industrial de Venezuela*, 760 F.2d 390, 393 (2d Cir.1985). Proyecfin, a privately owned Venezuelan development corporation, had entered into a loan agreement with a Venezuelan bank. The agreement included a "Supervisory Contract" which clearly stated that "the foregoing waiver of immunity shall have effect under and be construed in accordance with the United States Sovereign Immunities Act [of] 1976." A waiver this unambiguous is rarely litigated, and need not be so explicit to be considered effective. It is clear, however, that merely entering into a contract with a foreign state does not constitute an express waiver of immunity. As one court noted, the waiver must be an "intentional and knowing relinquishment of the legal right." *Castro v. Saudi Arabia*, 510 F. Supp. 309, 312 (W.D. Tex. 1980).

Under the FSIA, explicit waiver can also occur by virtue of provisions contained in an international agreement. For instance, in *Harris Corp. v. National Iranian Radio & Television,* 691 F.2d 1344, 1350–51 (11th Cir.1982), the court considered whether a clause in the Treaty of Amity, Economic Relations, and Consular Rights Between the United States and Iran operated as an explicit waiver of immunity. In pertinent part, the clause stated:

* Reprinted with permission of Transnational Publishers, Inc.

> No enterprise of either high contracting party, including corporations, associations, and government agencies and instrumentalities, which is publicly owned or controlled shall, if it engages in commercial, industrial, shipping or other business activities, within the territories of the other high contracting party, claim or enjoy for either itself or for its property, immunity therein from taxation, suit, execution or judgment or other liability in which privately owned and controlled enterprises are subject therein.

The court found this clause sufficient to constitute an explicit waiver of immunity by the defendant.

In contrast, in *O'Connell Machinery Co. v. M.V. Americana*, 734 F.2d 115, 117–18 (2d Cir.), *cert. denied*, 469 U.S. 1086 (1984), the Second Circuit refused to find an explicit waiver of immunity from prejudgment attachment pursuant to a Treaty of Friendship, Commerce and Navigation between the United States and Italy. The language used, in what are commonly called FCNs, was deemed to be too narrow to constitute an explicit waiver of immunity to prejudgment attachment. The words used in the Treaty, that the parties "shall [not] ... claim ... immunity ... from any other liability", were held not to be an express waiver of immunity under section 1605(a)(1). The court was particularly concerned with a perceived attempt on the part of the plaintiffs to obtain jurisdiction by means of a prejudgment attachment.

On the issue of prejudgment attachment and explicit waiver, it is important to note the court's finding that "prejudgment attachment is permitted only where the foreign state explicitly has waived its immunity...." A waiver of attachment may not be sufficient for purposes of jurisdiction; prudent counsel will seek to include both in any agreements with FSIA parties.

* * *

Section 1605(a)(1) also contemplates implicit waivers of sovereign immunity from jurisdiction. The legislative history specifies three situations in which a waiver of sovereign immunity may be implied. The House Report at 18 states:

> With respect to implicit waivers, the courts have found such waivers in cases where a foreign state has agreed to arbitration in another country or where a foreign state has agreed that the law of a particular country should govern a contract. An implicit waiver would also include a situation where a foreign state has filed a responsive pleading in an action without raising the defense of sovereign immunity.

Courts have been reluctant to find implicit waivers in circumstances other than those identified in the legislative history and absent definite and precise language, but have confronted actions involving allegations of all three forms of implicit waivers contemplated by Congress. The D.C. Circuit concluded that the case precedents are "virtually unanimous ... construing the implied waiver provisions narrowly" and ...

"implicit in § 1605(a)(1) is the requirement that the foreign state have intended to waive its sovereign immunity." *Creighton Ltd. v. Gov't of State of Qatar,* 181 F.3d 118, 122 (D.C.Cir.1999).

With respect to an implied waiver by virtue of an arbitration agreement, contracts with foreign states and instrumentalities often contain agreements stipulating that disputes arising from the transaction shall be submitted to arbitration. Because of the frequent use of arbitration clauses and strict construction of the implied waiver provision, courts have held that merely agreeing to arbitrate does not waive immunity. The *Creighton Ltd.* court found that Qatar did not implicitly waive immunity where Qatar merely agreed to arbitrate in France. If, however, Qatar had been a signatory to the New York Convention or other agreement with the U.S. to enforce foreign arbitral awards, an implied waiver of immunity may have been found.

In *Seetransport Wiking Trader Schiffarhtgesellschaft MBH & Co. v. Navimpex Centrala Navala,* 989 F.2d 572, 577–578 (2d Cir.1993), the court reasoned that "when a country becomes a signatory to the [New York Convention on Recognition and Enforcement of Foreign Arbitral Awards], by the very provisions of the Convention, the signatory state must have contemplated enforcement actions in other signatory states." The Court held that implicit waiver generally does not occur merely by entering into a contract naming a third country for arbitration or choosing which law applies; however, when arbitration had already occurred with knowledge the enforcement was possible, waiver occurred.

In *Maritime Int'l Nominees Estab. v. Republic of Guinea,* 693 F.2d 1094, 1100–04 (D.C.Cir.1982), *cert. denied,* 464 U.S. 815 (1984), a commercial contract between Maritime International and the Republic of Guinea stipulated that all disputes resulting from the contract would be settled by arbitration conducted by the International Center for the Settlement of Investment Disputes (ICSID). The plaintiff argued that designating the ICSID implicitly designated Washington, D.C., because ICSID is located in Washington, D.C. Despite ICSID's location in Washington, D.C., the court held that it was not foreseeable that traditional United States courts would become involved in dispute resolution. Plaintiff's contention that an implicit waiver of sovereign immunity by Guinea had occurred was therefore rejected.

The second form of implied waiver contemplated by Congress involves the designation of a particular law as governing any disputes arising from the contract. Such a recognition operates as an acceptance of the submission of the dispute to legal resolution, and may constitute an implied waiver of immunity. For instance, in *Marlowe v. Argentine Naval Comm'n,* 604 F.Supp. 703, 708–09 (D.D.C.1985), the court held that a choice of law clause constituted an implied waiver of immunity. In the agreement at issue, the choice of law clause provided that the contract "shall be governed by and construed in accordance with the laws of the District of Columbia." The court found that precedent on the issue was clear: "if the parties to a contract agree that the laws of one country will govern contractual interpretations, they have implicitly waived the defense of sovereign immunity."

The final form of implicit waiver of immunity contemplated by Congress involves an implicit waiver through a foreign sovereign defendant's participation in litigation without invoking immunity. House Report, at 18. At issue in such a case is whether responsive pleadings or an appearance in court constitutes waiver of sovereign immunity by a foreign defendant.

In *Canadian Overseas Ores, Ltd. v. Compania De Acero del Pacifico S.A.*, 727 F.2d 274, 277–78 (2d Cir.1984), the court was faced with the issue of whether the defendant had implicitly waived its immunity by failing to raise the defense until after it had filed several motions and participated in limited discovery. The court found that the defendant had not waived immunity because the motions were not pleadings as contemplated by Congress in designing the waiver provision, and certain types of participation do not automatically result in waiver. Similarly, in *Drexel Burnham Lambert v. Committee of Receivers*, 12 F.3d 317, 326 (2d Cir.1993), the court found that the defendant had not waived immunity by its participation in the litigation. The court held that the proper standard is that "the filing of a responsive pleading is the last chance to assert FSIA immunity if the defense has not been previously asserted."

Other cases have dealt with other forms of implicit waivers, including for example, whether an implicit waiver can result from participation in international agreements such as the United Nations Charter and the Helsinki Accords. In *Frolova v. Union of Soviet Socialist Republics*, 761 F.2d 370, 378 (7th Cir.1985), a U.S. citizen sought to recover damages from the Soviet Union stemming from the Soviet Union's refusal to allow plaintiff's husband to emigrate expeditiously. The plaintiff asserted that the Soviet Union's signing of the United Nations Charter and the Helsinki Accords constituted an implied waiver for purposes of the FSIA. The court, however, disagreed, stating that there was:

> absolutely no evidence from the language, structure or history of the agreements at issue that implies a waiver of the U.S.S.R.'s sovereign immunity. There is no basis for finding a waiver from the vague, general language of the agreements nor is there any reason to conclude that the nations that are parties to these agreements anticipated when signing them that American courts would be the means by which the documents' provisions would be enforced.... To the contrary ..., the countries that agreed to the United Nations Charter and the Helsinki Accords retained considerable discretion in implementing the provisions on which Frolova's suit is based....

The court in *Frolova* also noted that "[c]ourts have generally required convincing evidence that a treaty was intended to waive sovereign immunity before holding that a foreign state may be sued in this country." To this end, courts have failed to find an implied waiver where an instrumentality was endowed with the ability to sue and to be sued, merely entered into a contract, and participated in a foreign aid contract.

Questions and Comments

1. Why would a court, such as in *O'Connell Machinery Co. v. M.V. Americana*, 734 F.2d 115, 117–18 (2d Cir.), *cert. denied*, 469 U.S. 1086, 105 S.Ct. 591, 83 L.Ed.2d 701 (1984), be "particularly concerned" with a plaintiff's attempt to obtain jurisdiction by means of a prejudgment attachment?

2. In this Problem, was there an express, written waiver of immunity in the 1994 Agreement? Was VOCO a party to the waiver?

3. Does the Venezuela Executive Order purporting to terminate the 1994 Agreement affect the enforceability or validity of the waiver provision? Would it be advisable for counsel for TOCO to obtain letters or affidavits to the court from the U.S. Departments of State, Justice, Commerce, and other Executive Departments/Agencies, on whether the court should acknowledge as valid Venezuela's Executive Order purporting to terminate the 1994 Agreement?

4. What foreign policy concerns might the court consider in choosing whether or not to give legal effect to the Venezuela Executive Order?

5. Does the Venezuela allegation that TOCO breached the 1994 Agreement by failing to pay royalties affect the enforceability or validity of the waiver provision? Does that section cover the circumstances at hand; i.e., was the waiver withdrawn "in accordance with the terms of the waiver"?

6. Why might counsel for Venezuela/VOCO caution their client(s) against asserting a counterclaim for the royalties owed? *See* § 1607.

PART B. THE INTERNATIONAL LAW EXCEPTION TO IMMUNITY

Section 1605(a)(3) concerns the circumstance where property has been taken in violation of international law and that property or property exchanged for that property bear a commercial nexus to the United States. The FSIA does not define the term "taken." However, the legislative history makes clear that the phrase "taken in violation of international law" refers to "the nationalization or expropriation of property without payment of the prompt adequate and effective compensation required by international law," including "takings which are arbitrary or discriminatory in nature." House Report at 19. The term "taken" thus clearly refers to acts of a sovereign, not a private enterprise, that deprive a plaintiff of property without adequate compensation. *Zappia Middle East Const. Co., Ltd. v. Emirate of Abu Dhabi*, 215 F.3d 247 (2d Cir.2000); *accord Alfred Dunhill of London, Inc. v. Republic of Cuba*, 425 U.S. 682, 685, 96 S.Ct. 1854, 1857, 48 L.Ed.2d 301 (1976).

The international takings exception has been discussed in several cases.

SIDERMAN DE BLAKE v. ARGENTINA

United States Court of Appeals, Ninth Circuit, 1992.
965 F.2d 699.

FLETCHER, CIRCUIT JUDGE:

Susana Siderman de Blake and Jose, Lea, and Carlos Siderman (collectively, "the Sidermans") appeal the dismissal of their action against the Republic of Argentina and the Argentine Province of Tucuman (collectively, "Argentina"). The Sidermans' complaint alleged eighteen causes of action arising out of the torture of Jose Siderman and the expropriation of the Sidermans' property by Argentine military officials. The district court dismissed the expropriation claims on the basis of the act of state doctrine, but granted a default judgment to Jose and Lea Siderman on the torture claims. Argentina then entered its first appearance in the case and moved for relief from judgment on the ground that the Foreign Sovereign Immunities Act ("FSIA"), rendered it immune from the Sidermans' action. The district court granted the motion and vacated the default judgment. The Sidermans now appeal. We reverse and remand for further proceedings.

FACTS

The factual record, which consists only of the Sidermans' complaint and numerous declarations they submitted in support of their claims, tells a horrifying tale of the violent and brutal excesses of an anti-Semitic military junta that ruled Argentina. On March 24, 1976, the Argentine military overthrew the government of President Maria Estela Peron and seized the reins of power for itself, installing military leaders of the central government and the provincial governments of Argentina. That night, ten masked men carrying machine guns forcibly entered the home of Jose and Lea Siderman, husband and wife, in Tucuman Province, Argentina. The men, who were acting under the direction of the military governor of Tucuman, ransacked the home and locked Lea in the bathroom. They then blindfolded and shackled 65–year old Jose, dragged him out of his home, tossed him into a waiting car, and drove off to an unknown building. For seven days the men beat and tortured Jose. Among their tools of torture was an electric cattle prod, which they used to shock Jose until he fainted. As they tortured him, the men repeatedly shouted anti-Semitic epithets, calling him a "Jew Bastard" and a "Shitty Jew." They inflicted all of these cruelties upon Jose Siderman because of his Jewish faith.

At the end of this nightmarish week, his body badly bruised and his ribs broken, Jose was taken out of the building and driven to an isolated area, where the masked men tossed him out of the car. The men told Jose that if he and his family did not leave Tucuman and Argentina immediately, they would be killed. On the day of Jose's release, he and Lea fled to Buenos Aires in fear for their lives. Their son Carlos followed shortly thereafter, and the night Carlos left Tucuman, military authorities ransacked his home. In June 1976, Jose, Lea, and Carlos left Argentina for the United States, where they joined Susana Siderman de Blake. She is the daughter of Jose and Lea and is a United States citizen.

Before the hasty flight from Tucuman to Buenos Aires, Jose was forced to raise cash by selling at a steep discount part of his interest in 127,000 acres of land. Prior to their departure for the United States, the Sidermans also made arrangements for someone to oversee their family business, Inmobiliaria del Nor–Oeste, S.A. ("INOSA"), an Argentine corporation. Susana Siderman de Blake, Carlos Siderman and Lea Siderman each owned 33% of INOSA and Jose owned the remaining one percent. Its assets comprised numerous real estate holdings including a large hotel in Tucuman, the Hotel Gran Corona. * * *

After the Sidermans left Argentina for the United States, Argentine military officers renewed their persecution of Jose. They altered real property records in Tucuman to show that he had owned not 127,000, but 127, acres of land in the province. They then initiated a criminal action against him in Argentina, claiming that since he owned only 127 acres he had sold land that did not belong to him. Argentina sought the assistance of our courts in obtaining jurisdiction over his person, requesting via a letter rogatory that the Los Angeles Superior Court serve him with documents relating to the action. The court, unaware of Argentina's motives, complied with the request.

Soon thereafter, while he was travelling in Italy, Jose was arrested pursuant to an extradition request from Argentina to the Italian government. Argentina charged that Jose had fraudulently obtained the travel documents enabling him to leave Argentina in 1976. Jose was not permitted to leave Cremora, Italy, for seven months, and actually was imprisoned for 27 days, before an Italian Appeals Court finally held that Argentina's extradition request would not be honored, as it was politically motivated and founded on pretextual charges.

The Argentine military also pursued INOSA with vigor. In April 1977, INOSA was seized through a sham "judicial intervention," a proceeding in which property is put into receivership. The purported reasons for the intervention were that INOSA lacked a representative in Argentina and that INOSA had obtained excessive funds from a Tucuman provincial bank. Though these reasons were pretexts for persecuting the Sidermans because of their religion and profiting from their economic success, the Sidermans were unable to oppose the intervention because Argentine officials had imprisoned and killed the accountant to whom they had granted management powers over INOSA. In 1978, the Sidermans retained an attorney in Argentina and brought a derivative action in a Tucuman court in an effort to end the intervention. The court ordered that the intervention cease, and the order was upheld by the Supreme Court of Tucuman, but the order remains unenforced and the intervention has continued. Argentine military officials and INOSA's appointed receivers have extracted funds from INOSA, purchased various assets owned by INOSA at sharply discounted prices, and diverted INOSA's profits and revenues to themselves.

B.   INTERNATIONAL TAKINGS EXCEPTION

The Sidermans argue that their claims also fall within the international takings exception to the FSIA's rule of immunity. That exception provides that a foreign state is not immune in an action

> in which rights in property taken in violation of international law are in issue and [1] that property or any property exchanged for such property is present in the United States in connection with a commercial activity carried on in the United States by the foreign state; or [2] that property or any property exchanged for such property is owned or operated by an agency or instrumentality of the foreign state and that agency or instrumentality is engaged in a commercial activity in the United States. . . .

Though few courts have had the opportunity to consider the international takings exception, it is clear that Jose, Lea, and Carlos Siderman cannot assert a claim that comes within this exception. In *Chuidian v. Philippine Nat'l Bank*, 912 F.2d 1095, 1105 (9th Cir.1990), we held that the exception does not apply where the plaintiff is a citizen of the defendant country at the time of the expropriation, because "[e]xpropriation by a sovereign state of the property of its own nationals does not implicate settled principles of international law." However, Susana Siderman de Blake is eligible to invoke the international takings exception, and the Sidermans' allegations and evidence bring her claims within clause two of that exception.

Under that clause, the property at issue must have been taken in violation of international law. At the jurisdictional stage, we need not decide whether the taking actually violated international law; as long as a "claim is substantial and non-frivolous, it provides a sufficient basis for the exercise of our jurisdiction." *West v. Multibanco Comermex, S.A.*, 807 F.2d 820, 826 (9th Cir.), *cert. denied*, 482 U.S. 906, 107 S.Ct. 2483, 96 L.Ed.2d 375 (1987). In *West*, we described three requisites under international law for a valid taking. First, "[v]alid expropriations must always serve a public purpose." Second, "aliens [must] not be discriminated against or singled out for regulation by the state." Finally, "[a]n otherwise valid taking is illegal without the payment of just compensation." These well-established principles track the Restatement of Foreign Relations Law, which provides:

> A state is responsible under international law for injury resulting from:
>
> > (1) a taking by the state of the property of a national of another state that
> >
> > > (a) is not for a public purpose, or
> > >
> > > (b) is discriminatory, or

      (c) is not accompanied by provision for just compensation....

Restatement (Third) of the Foreign Relations Law of the United States § 712 (1987). The legislative history of the FSIA reveals a similar understanding of what constitutes a taking in violation of international law. *See* H.R.Rep. No. 1487, 94th Cong., 2d Sess. 19–20, reprinted in 1976 U.S.Code Cong. & Admin.News 6604, 6618 (taking violates international law if it is done "without payment of the prompt adequate and effective compensation required by international law" or is "arbitrary or discriminatory in nature"). If a taking violates any one of the aforementioned proscriptions, it violates international law.

    Susana Siderman de Blake's claim that Argentina violated the international law of expropriation is substantial and non-frivolous. The complaint alleges that Argentina officials seized INOSA for their personal profit and not for any public purpose. The complaint also alleges that Argentina seized INOSA because the Siderman family is Jewish—a discriminatory motivation based on ethnicity. See Restatement § 712 Comment f (noting that "taking that singles out aliens generally, or aliens of a particular nationality, or particular aliens, would violate international law"). Finally, none of the Sidermans has received any compensation for the seizure, let alone just compensation. As in *West*, we have no difficulty concluding that the Sidermans' complaint contains "substantial and non-frivolous" allegations that INOSA was taken in violation of international law.

    Beyond establishing that property has been taken in violation of international law, Susan Siderman de Blake must demonstrate that the expropriated property, or property exchanged for it, is owned or operated by an agency or instrumentality of Argentina and that the agency or instrumentality is engaged in commercial activity in the United States. The Sidermans' allegations establish that INOSA itself has become an agency or instrumentality of Argentina. * * * As an Argentine corporation, INOSA satisfies the first and third elements of the above definition, and the Sidermans' basic allegation that Argentina has expropriated INOSA suffices as an allegation that INOSA is now an "organ" of Argentina or Tucuman. The Sidermans' allegations thus satisfy the "agency or instrumentality" definition. The final requirement under clause two—that the agency or instrumentality must be engaged in a commercial activity in the United States—is also met. The Sidermans' allegations concerning Argentina's solicitation and entertainment of American guests at the Hotel Gran Corona and the hotel's acceptance of American credit cards and traveler's checks are sufficient at this stage of the proceedings to show that Argentina is engaged in a commercial activity in the United States. The Sidermans' allegations bring Susana Siderman de Blake's expropriation claims within clause two of the international takings exception.

    We hold that the Sidermans' complaint and declarations allege sufficient facts to bring their expropriation claims within both the commercial activity and international takings exceptions to the FSIA's grant of foreign sovereign immunity. We emphasize the preliminary nature of our holding; following further development of the factual record on remand, the district court ultimately must determine whether the FSIA exceptions do or do not apply to the expropriation claims. While the Sidermans have sustained their initial burden of alleging applicable exceptions to the FSIA, Argentina will have the opportunity on remand to challenge the evidence presented by the Sidermans and to present its own. Under the procedures our circuit has developed for considering jurisdiction under the FSIA, Argentina now bears the burden of proving by a preponderance of the evidence that none of the FSIA exceptions applies to the Sidermans' claims. To the extent that the jurisdictional facts are disputed on remand, the parties should be allowed to conduct discovery for the limited purpose of establishing jurisdictional facts before the claims can be dismissed.

REPUBLIC OF AUSTRIA et al.
v. MARIA V. ALTMANN

Supreme Court of the United States, 2004.
541 U.S. 677, 124 S.Ct. 2240, 159 L.Ed.2d 1.

JUSTICE STEVENS delivered the opinion of the Court.

In 1998 an Austrian journalist, granted access to the Austrian Gallery's archives, discovered evidence that certain valuable works in the Gallery's collection had not been donated by their rightful owners but had been seized by the Nazis or expropriated by the Austrian Republic after World War II. The journalist provided some of that evidence to respondent, who in turn filed this action to recover possession of six Gustav Klimt paintings. Prior to the Nazi invasion of Austria, the paintings had hung in the palatial Vienna home of respondent's uncle, Ferdinand Bloch–Bauer, a Czechoslovakian Jew and patron of the arts. Respondent claims ownership of the paintings under a will executed by her uncle after he fled Austria in 1938. She alleges that the Gallery obtained possession of the paintings through wrongful conduct in the years during and after World War II.

The defendants (petitioners here)-the Republic of Austria and the Austrian Gallery (Gallery), an instrumentality of the Republic-filed a motion to dismiss the complaint asserting, among other defenses, a claim of sovereign immunity. The District Court denied the motion, ... and the Court of Appeals affirmed.... We granted certiorari limited to the question whether the Foreign Sovereign Immunities Act of 1976 (FSIA or Act), ... which grants foreign states immunity from the jurisdiction of federal and state courts but expressly exempts certain cases, including "case[s] ... in which rights in property taken in violation of international law are in issue," § 1605(a)(3), applies to claims that, like respondent's, are based on conduct that occurred before the Act's enactment, and even before the United States adopted the so-called "restrictive theory" of sovereign immunity in 1952.

* * *

II

The complaint ... asserts that petitioners are not entitled to immunity under the FSIA because the Act's "expropriation exception," § 1605(a)(3), expressly exempts from immunity all cases involving "rights in property taken in violation of international law," provided the property has a commercial connection to the United States or the agency or instrumentality that owns the property is engaged in commercial activity here.

The provision reads:

"(a) A foreign state shall not be immune from the jurisdiction of courts of the United States or of the States in any case-

* * *

"(3) in which rights in property taken in violation of international law are in issue and that property or any property exchanged for such property is present in the United States in connection with a commercial activity carried on in the United States by the foreign state; or that property or any property exchanged for such property is owned or operated by an agency or instrumentality of the foreign state and that agency or instrumentality is engaged in a commercial activity in the United States."

Petitioners filed a motion to dismiss raising several defenses including a claim of sovereign immunity. Their immunity argument proceeded in two steps. First, they claimed that as of 1948, when much of their alleged wrongdoing took place, they would have enjoyed absolute immunity from suit in United States courts. Proceeding from this premise, petitioners next contended that nothing in the FSIA should be understood to divest them of that immunity retroactively.

III

Chief Justice Marshall's opinion in *Schooner Exchange v. McFaddon*, 7 Cranch 116, 3 L.Ed. 287 (1812), is generally viewed as the source of our foreign sovereign immunity jurisprudence. In that case, the libellants claimed to be the rightful owners of a French ship that had taken refuge in the port of Philadelphia. The Court first emphasized that the jurisdiction of the United States over persons and property within its territory "is susceptible of no limitation not imposed by itself," and thus foreign sovereigns have no right to immunity in our courts. Chief Justice Marshall went on to explain, however, that as a matter of comity, members of the international community had implicitly agreed to waive the exercise of jurisdiction over other sovereigns in certain classes of cases, such as those involving foreign ministers or the person of the sovereign. Accepting a suggestion advanced by the Executive Branch, the Chief Justice concluded that the implied waiver theory also served to exempt the Schooner Exchange—"a national armed vessel ... of the emperor of France"—from United States courts' jurisdiction. * * *

In accordance with Chief Justice Marshall's observation that foreign sovereign immunity is a matter of grace and comity rather than a constitutional requirement, this Court has "consistently ... deferred to the decisions of the political branches—in particular, those of the Executive Branch—on whether to take jurisdiction" over particular actions against foreign sovereigns and their instrumentalities. * * * Until 1952 the Executive Branch followed a policy of requesting immunity in all actions against friendly sovereigns. In that year, however, the State Department concluded that "immunity should no longer be granted in certain types of cases." In a letter to the Acting Attorney General, the Acting Legal Adviser for the Secretary of State, Jack B. Tate, explained that the Department would thereafter apply the "restrictive theory" of sovereign immunity:

> "A study of the law of sovereign immunity reveals the existence of two conflicting concepts of sovereign immunity, each widely held and firmly established. According to the classical or absolute theory of sovereign immunity, a sovereign cannot, without his consent, be made a respondent in the courts of another sovereign. According to the newer or restrictive theory of sovereign immunity, the immunity of the sovereign is recognized with regard to sovereign or public acts (*jure imperii*) of a state, but not with respect to private acts (*jure gestionis*). ...[I]t will hereafter be the Department's policy to follow the restrictive theory ... in the consideration of requests of foreign governments for a grant of sovereign immunity."

"[T]he responsibility fell to the courts to determine whether sovereign immunity existed, generally by reference to prior State Department decisions.... Thus, sovereign immunity determinations were made in two different branches, subject to a variety of factors, sometimes including diplomatic considerations. Not surprisingly, the governing standards were neither clear nor uniformly applied." * * *

In 1976 Congress sought to remedy these problems by enacting the FSIA, a comprehensive statute containing a "set of legal standards governing claims of immunity in every civil action against a foreign state or its political subdivisions, agencies, or instrumentalities." The Act "codifies, as a matter of federal law, the restrictive theory of sovereign immunity," and transfers primary responsibility for immunity determinations from the Executive to the Judicial Branch. The preamble states that "henceforth" both federal and state courts should decide claims of sovereign immunity in conformity with the Act's principles. 28 U.S.C. § 1602.

The Act itself grants federal courts jurisdiction over civil actions against foreign states,.... Finally, the Act carves out certain exceptions to its general grant of immunity, including the expropriation exception on which respondent's complaint relies. These exceptions are central to the Act's functioning: "At the threshold of every action in a district court against a foreign state, ... the court must satisfy itself that one of the exceptions applies," as "subject-matter jurisdiction in any such action depends" on that application.

* * *

V

This leaves only the question whether anything in the FSIA or the circumstances surrounding its enactment suggests that we should not apply it to petitioners' 1948 actions. Not only do we answer this question in the negative, but we find clear evidence that Congress intended the Act to apply to preenactment conduct.

To begin with, the preamble of the FSIA expresses Congress' understanding that the Act would apply to all postenactment claims of sovereign immunity. That section provides:

"*Claims* of foreign states to immunity should *henceforth* be decided by courts of the United States and of the States in conformity with the principles set forth in this chapter." 28 U.S.C. § 1602 (emphasis added).

[T]his language is unambiguous: Immunity *"claims"*—not actions protected by immunity, but assertions of immunity to suits arising from those actions—are the relevant conduct regulated by the Act; those claims are *"henceforth"* to be decided by the courts. As the District Court observed, this language suggests Congress intended courts to resolve all such claims "in conformity with the principles set forth" in the Act, regardless of when the underlying conduct occurred.

The dissent is quite right that " '[a] statement that a statute will become effective on a certain date does not even arguably suggest that it has any application to conduct that occurred at an earlier date.' " The provision of the FSIA to which this observation applies, however, is not the preamble but § 8, which states that the "Act shall take effect ninety days after the date of its enactment." The office of the word "henceforth" is to make the statute effective with respect to claims to immunity thereafter asserted. Notably, any such claim asserted immediately after the statute became effective would necessarily have related to conduct that took place at an earlier date.

The FSIA's overall structure strongly supports this conclusion. Many of the Act's provisions unquestionably apply to cases arising out of conduct that occurred before 1976. In *Dole Food Co. v. Patrickson*, 538 U.S. 468, 123 S.Ct. 1655, 155 L.Ed.2d 643 (2003), for example, we held that whether an entity qualifies as an "instrumentality" of a "foreign state" for purposes of the FSIA's grant of immunity depends on the relationship between the entity and the state at the time suit is brought rather than when the conduct occurred. In addition, *Verlinden*, which upheld against constitutional challenge 28 U.S.C. § 1330's grant of subject-matter jurisdiction, involved a dispute over a contract that predated the Act. 461 U.S., at 482–483, 497, 103 S.Ct. 1962. And there has never been any doubt that the Act's procedural provisions relating to venue, removal, execution, and attachment apply to all pending cases.

Thus, the FSIA's preamble indicates that it applies "henceforth," and its body includes numerous provisions that unquestionably apply to claims based on pre–1976 conduct. In this context, it would be anomalous to presume that an isolated provision (such as the expropriation exception on which respondent relies) is of purely prospective application absent any statutory language to that effect.

Finally, applying the FSIA to all pending cases regardless of when the underlying conduct occurred is most consistent with two of the Act's principal purposes: clarifying the rules that judges should apply in resolving sovereign immunity claims and eliminating political participation in the resolution of such claims. We have recognized that, to accomplish these purposes, Congress established a comprehensive framework for resolving any claim of sovereign immunity:

> "We think that the text and structure of the FSIA demonstrate Congress' intention that the FSIA be the sole basis for obtaining jurisdiction over a foreign state in our courts. Sections 1604 and 1330(a) work in tandem: § 1604 bars federal and state courts from exercising jurisdiction when a foreign state is entitled to immunity, and § 1330(a) confers jurisdiction on district courts to hear suits brought by United States citizens and by aliens when a foreign state is not entitled to immunity. As we said in *Verlinden*, the FSIA 'must be applied by the district courts in every action against a foreign sovereign, since subject-matter jurisdiction in any such action depends on the existence of one of the specified exceptions to foreign sovereign immunity.' " *Verlinden*, 461 U.S., at 493, 103 S.Ct. 1962.

The *Amerada Hess* respondents' claims concerned conduct that postdated the FSIA, so we had no occasion to consider the Act's retroactivity. Nevertheless, our observations about the FSIA's inclusiveness are relevant in this case: Quite obviously, Congress' purposes in enacting such a comprehensive jurisdictional scheme would be frustrated if, in postenactment cases concerning preenactment conduct, courts were to continue to follow the same ambiguous and politically charged " 'standards' " that the FSIA replaced.

We do not endorse the reasoning of the Court of Appeals. Indeed, we think it engaged in precisely the kind of detailed historical inquiry that the FSIA's clear guidelines were intended to obviate. Nevertheless, we affirm the panel's judgment because the Act ... clearly applies to conduct, like petitioners' alleged wrongdoing, that occurred prior to 1976 and, for that matter, prior to 1952 when the State Department adopted the restrictive theory of sovereign immunity.

* * *

Finally, while we reject the United States' recommendation to bar application of the FSIA to claims based on pre-enactment conduct, Brief for United States as Amicus Curiae, nothing in our holding prevents the State Department from filing statements of interest suggesting that courts decline to exercise jurisdiction in particular cases implicating foreign sovereign immunity.

The judgment of the Court of Appeals is affirmed.

It is so ordered.

Justice KENNEDY, with whom THE CHIEF JUSTICE and Justice THOMAS join, dissenting.

This is an important decision for interpreting the Foreign Sovereign Immunities Act of 1976 (FSIA or Act). As the Court's careful opinion illustrates, the case is difficult. In my respectful view, however, its decision is incorrect.

At the outset, here is a summary of my primary concerns with the majority opinion: To reach its conclusion the Court must weaken the reasoning and diminish the force of the rule against the retroactivity of statutes, a rule of fairness based on respect for expectations; the Court abruptly tells foreign nations this important principle of American law is unavailable to them in our courts; this is so despite the fact that treaties and agreements on the subject of expropriation have been reached against a background of the immunity principles the Court now rejects; as if to mitigate its harsh result, the Court adds that the Executive Branch has inherent power to intervene in cases like this; this, however, is inconsistent with the congressional purpose and design of the FSIA; the suggestion reintroduces, to an even greater degree than before, the same influences the FSIA sought to eliminate from sovereign immunity determinations; the Court's reasoning also implies a problematic answer to a separation-of-powers question that the case does not present and that should be avoided; the ultimate effect of the Court's inviting foreign nations to pressure the Executive is to risk inconsistent results for private citizens who sue, based on changes and nuances in foreign affairs, and to add prospective instability to the most sensitive area of foreign relations.

The majority's treatment of our retroactivity principles, its rejection of the considered congressional and Executive judgment behind the FSIA, and its questionable constitutional implications require this respectful dissent.

KALAMAZOO SPICE EXTRACTION CO. v. ETHIOPIA

United States Court of Appeals, Sixth Circuit, 1984.
729 F.2d 422.

[This case, which arose in the act of state, not FSIA, context, discussed the international standard for a taking without adequate compensation.]

KEITH, CIRCUIT JUDGE.

Appellant, Kalamazoo Spice Extraction Company (Kal–Spice) is an American corporation which, in a joint venture with Ethiopian citizens, established the Ethiopian Spice Extraction Company (ESESCO) in 1966, an Ethiopian based corporation. Kal–Spice owned approximately 80% of the shares of ESESCO. Kal–Spice also contributed capital, built a production facility, and trained ESESCO's staff, which consisted of Ethiopian citizens. Production began in 1970 after several years of preparation, construction and training.

The Provisional Military Government of Socialist Ethiopia (PMGSE) came to power in 1974. As part of its program to assure that Ethiopian industries would "be operated according to the philosophy of Ethiopian socialism", the PMGSE announced the seizure of "control of supervision and a majority shareholding" of a number of corporations, including ESESCO, in February 1975. As a result of the expropriation, Kal–Spice's ownership interest in ESESCO was reduced from 80% to approximately 39%.

In December 1975, the PMGSE established a Compensation Commission. The Commission's purpose was to compensate those claimants whose property had been expropriated. Kal–Spice claimed it was entitled to compensation of $11,000,000. In October 1981, the PMGSE offered Kal–Spice the equivalent of $450,000 in Ethiopian currency. Kal–Spice, however, has rejected the PMGSE's offer. The PMGSE contends that Kal–Spice should have accepted the offer because: 1) Kal–Spice retains an interest in ESESCO of approximately 40% and 2) Kal–Spice carried expropriation insurance based on a total investment in ESESCO of less than $1,000,000.

* * *

We do not agree with the district court's decision that the provision of the treaty requiring payment of prompt, just and effective compensation fails to provide a controlling legal standard. To the contrary, we find that this is a controlling legal standard in the area of international law. As the appellant and amici correctly point out, the term "prompt, just and effective compensation" and similar terms are found in many treaties where the United States and other nations are parties.

The 1953 United States–Ethiopia Treaty of Amity and Economic Relations is one of a series of treaties, also known as the FCN Treaties, between the United States and foreign nations negotiated after World War II. As the legislative history of these treaties indicates, they were adopted to protect American citizens and their interests abroad. Almost all of these treaties contain sections which provide for "prompt, adequate, and effective compensation", "just compensation", or similar language regarding compensation for expropriated property.

* * *

Banco Nacional de Cuba v. Chase Manhattan Bank, 658 F.2d 875 (2d Cir.1981), provides an example of the utility of the "prompt, just and effective compensation" standard that is employed in many treaties. In *Chase Manhattan Bank*, the Second Circuit was faced with the task of determining the value of Cuban branches of Chase Manhattan which had been expropriated by the Cuban revolutionary government. After examining several theories regarding the appropriate standard for the compensation of expropriated property, the court concluded Chase Manhattan Bank was entitled to the net asset value of the branches that were expropriated by the Cuban government.

We do not suggest, however, by our citation of *Chase Manhattan Bank*, that the district court in the present case is bound to use the same method employed in *Chase Manhattan Bank* for determining compensation, if any, to which Kal–Spice will be entitled. There are sufficient factual differences in the present case and *Chase Manhattan Bank*, e.g., nature of the property expropriated, status of the expropriated property, the facts surrounding the expropriation, etc., which may call for a different compensation standard. The citation to *Chase Manhattan Bank* is only for the purpose of illustrating the point that the standard of compensation provided for in the Treaty of Amity between Ethiopia and the United States can provide a basis for determining the extent of compensation to which Kal–Spice may be entitled.

Moreover, the Supreme Court's decision in *Sabbatino*, in addition to the *American International Group, Inc. v. Islamic Republic of Iran*, 493 F.Supp. 522 (D.D.C.1980), and *Chase Manhattan Bank* decisions, requires a reversal of the district court decision that the 1953 Treaty of Amity was too ambiguous to be susceptible to judicial interpretation. As the Supreme Court stated in *Sabbatino*:

> It should be apparent that the greater the degree of codification or consensus concerning a particular area of international law, the more appropriate it is for the judiciary to render decisions regarding it, since the courts can then focus on the application of an agreed principle to circumstances of fact rather than on the sensitive task of establishing a principle not inconsistent with the national interest or with international justice.

376 U.S. at 423, 84 S.Ct. at 937.

Numerous treaties employ the standard of compensation used in the 1953 Treaty of Amity between Ethiopia and the United States. Undoubtedly, the widespread use of this compensation standard is evidence that it is an agreed upon principle in international law.

VENCEDORA OCEANICA NAVIGACION, S.A. v. COMPAGNIE NATIONALE ALGERIENNE DE NAVIGATION (C.N.A.N.)

United States Court of Appeals, Fifth Circuit, 1984.
730 F.2d 195.

[Owner of vessel seized by Algerian government and subsequently wrecked in storm brought action against Algeria and its instrumentality in charge of that country's harbor and coastal tugs, alleging that they had tortiously deprived owner of its vessel.]

PER CURIAM:

* * * While it is not clear whether any property was "taken in violation of international law" here, the district court decided that this exception did not apply because defendants did not own or operate the vessel.

Vencedora argues that "own" or "operate" may mean "possess" or "control," and that CNAN owned or operated the vessel when it initially towed the vessel to Bejaia and later to the Port of Arzew. We disagree with this interpretation of the statutory language. Although no court has interpreted "owned or operated," the legislative history of the FSIA indicates that section 1605(a)(3) was intended to subject to United States jurisdiction any foreign agency or instrumentality that has nationalized or expropriated property without compensation, or that is using expropriated property taken by another branch of the state. * * * The vessel in this case thus would have been owned or operated under section 1605(a)(3) if CNAN or some Algerian agency had assumed control of the vessel and had used it to carry oil for the benefit of the Algerian government.

The record indicates that no act of CNAN resembled this scenario. That CNAN may have disobeyed Vencedora's request to tow the vessel to Palermo does not render the act of towing akin to owning or operating in the sense contemplated by Congress. Similarly, CNAN towed the vessel to the Port of Arzew only because it had been deemed a threat to safety in the first port. Finally, CNAN's seizure of the vessel for security falls short of ownership or operation.[16]

We also cannot conclude that the actions of the Republic of Algeria or any of its agencies triggered this exception. The only Algerian agency that possibly can be charged with ownership is the Maritime Administrative Authority, which began forfeiture proceedings against the vessel. Yet there is no question but that the Maritime Administrative Authority did not "engag[e] in commercial activity in the United States" as required by section 1605(a)(3). It follows that the district court did not err in concluding that the immunity exception in section 1605(a)(3) was inapplicable.

We conclude that the FSIA bars Vencedora's suit against CNAN and the Republic of Algeria, and that the district court correctly dismissed the case for lack of subject matter jurisdiction.

AFFIRMED.

Questions and Comments

1. Does the exception to immunity apply to Venezuela or to VOCO, considering §§ 1603(a), 1604 and 1605; specifically the waiver exception (§ 1605(a)(1)), the three clauses of the commercial activity exception

---

16. Moreover, there is no possibility that the vessel will be exchanged for property that will be owned or operated by CNAN. The Algerian Maritime Code provides that the proceeds from the sale of a wrecked vessel must be used for the "social protection of seamen."

(§ 1605(a)(2)), and the taking of property in violation of international law exception (§ 1605(a)(3))?

2. The international law exception of § 1605(a)(3) has two requirements as it applies to Venezuela, a foreign state: 1) "property [is] taken in violation of international law"; and 2) "that property or any property exchanged for such property is present in the United States in connection with a commercial activity carried on in the United States by the foreign state".

3. Was the conduct of Venezuela a taking in violation of international law? See Restatement (3rd) of Foreign Relations Law of the U.S., § 455, cmt. c (1987) ("The FSIA provides no guidance for determining whether a taking of property violates international law"). Considering the decisions above, does the "Promissory Note" offered by Venezuela constitute prompt, adequate and effective compensation for international law purposes?

4. While the *Kalamazoo* court found that the formulation of "prompt, just and effective compensation.... is a controlling legal standard in the area of international law", did the court's decision provide substantive guidance as to what the standard actually is?

5. Are there facts that suggest "that property or any property exchanged for such property is present in the United States in connection with a commercial activity carried on in the United States by [Venezuela]" (§ 1605(a)(3))?

6. As to VOCO, an instrumentality, the two requirements of § 1605(a)(3) are: 1) "property [is] taken in violation of international law"; and 2) "that property or any property exchanged for such property is owned or operated by an agency or instrumentality of the foreign state and that agency or instrumentality is engaged in a commercial activity in the United States." Does VOCO's conduct constitute a taking in violation of international law? Does VOCO own or operate the expropriated property in Venezuela and engage in commercial activity in the U.S.? For an agency or instrumentality, does it matter whether the expropriated property is located in the United States?

7. Why might the FSIA drafters have accorded different treatment of agencies or instrumentalities, as compared to that accorded to a foreign state?

8. By ruling that the Foreign Sovereign Immunities Act applies to all claims against a sovereign state, regardless of when the conduct at issue occurred, did the court in *Republic of Austria v. Altmann* open the flood gates to numerous claims involving Nazi-era takings or other historical acts of misconduct?

9. In *dicta*, the court observed that "nothing in our holding prevents the State Department from filing statements of interest suggesting that courts decline to exercise jurisdiction in particular cases implicating foreign sovereign immunity." Is the court's invitation for Executive Branch involvement in FSIA litigation contrary to the FSIA's stated intention of avoiding inconsistent court rulings based upon political recommendations from the Executive Branch? *See* Justice Kennedy dissent, *Republic of Austria v. Altmann*.

Comment on Venue and Arbitration

The FSIA makes express provision for venue. Consider one by one the venue clauses of § 1391(f)(1)–(4). The FSIA also contains an exception to immunity for arbitration. *See* § 1605(a)(6). An exception to immunity also applies to execution upon property to enforce an arbitral award. *See* § 1610(a)(6).

Questions and Comments

1.   Is venue in this Problem properly in the Southern District of Texas, Houston Division? If not, where might the action properly be brought?

2.   Assume the 1994 Venezuela–TOCO Agreement provided:

Any disputes which may arise between the parties concerning the entry, validity, meaning, enforcement, or effect of the Agreement shall be submitted exclusively to binding arbitration before the International Chamber of Commerce, Paris, France. Any award which may be entered by the arbitral tribunal may be enforced against a party by a national court of competent jurisdiction.

What, if any, significance would that provision have regarding Venezuela's and VOCO's motion to dismiss?

3.   What, if any, significance would paragraph 86 of the 1994 Agreement have regarding execution upon an arbitral award obtained against Venezuela or VOCO?

Comment on Torture and Terrorism Exceptions to Immunity

The FSIA makes express provision for tort claims concerning acts of torture and terrorism. The Antiterrorism and Effective Death Penalty Act of 1996, Pub. L. No. 104–132, Title II, § 221(a), Apr. 24, 1996, 110 Stat. 1241, added a new exception to sovereign immunity concerning certain terrorist acts carried out by official action of a foreign state. New section 1605(a)(7) provides that a foreign state is not immune from the jurisdiction of the courts of the United States where:

money damages are sought against a foreign state for personal injury or death that was caused by an act of torture, extrajudicial killing, aircraft sabotage, [or] hostage taking, or the provision of material support or resources ... for such an act if such act or provision of material support is engaged in by an official, employee, or agent of such foreign state while acting within the scope of his or her office, employment, or agency...

The Statute imposes, however, several limitations. The defendant-foreign state must be officially designed as a "state sponsor of terrorism" at the time the act complained of occurred or later so designated because of such act. Also, the claimant must have allowed reasonable opportunity for the foreign state to "arbitrate the claim in accordance with accepted international rules of arbitration," where the complained of act occurred in the foreign states' territory. Also the claimant must have been a U.S. national when the act occurred.

The Statute defines the terms "torture," "hostage taking," and "aircraft sabotage." § 1605(e)(1)–(3). The Statute also imposes a ten year limitation period. § 1605(f). Such limitation period, however, is subject to "equitable tolling, including the period during which the foreign state was immune from suit..." Additionally, discovery may be curtailed where the U.S. Attorney General certifies that the discovery would significantly interfere with a criminal investigation or national security operation. § 1605(g).

Questions and Comments

1. Does Section 1605(a)(7)'s limiting the torture and terrorism exceptions to immunity to claimants who were U.S. nationals when the act occurred substantially curtail the applicability of the exception? *See* Alien Tort Statute, 28 U.S.C.A. § 1350 ("The district courts shall have original jurisdiction of any civil action by an alien for a tort only, committed in violation of the law of nations, or a treaty of the United States"). *See also* Torture Victim Protection Act of 1991, Pub. L. 102–256, Mar. 12, 1992, 106 Stat. 73 (codified at 28 U.S.C. § 1350), reprinted in Documents Supplement: Sec. 2. (a) "Liability. An individual who, under actual or apparent authority, or color of law, of any foreign nation...

1. Subjects an individual to torture shall, in a civil action, be liable for damages to that individual; or

2. Subjects an individual to extrajudicial killing shall, in a civil action, be liable for damages to the individual's legal representative, or to any person who may be a claimant in an action for wrongful death."

PART C. WAIVER OF SOVEREIGN IMMUNITY FOR PURPOSES OF EXECUTION ON A JUDGMENT

A waiver of sovereign immunity for jurisdictional purposes (§ 1605(a)(1)) does NOT constitute a waiver of sovereign immunity for purposes of execution on a judgment (§§ 1610, 1611). The FSIA provides additional procedural hurdles with respect to execution on a judgment because of the peculiar, sensitive nature of foreign sovereign property located in the United States. Although a sovereign may consent to litigate a matter in the United States, the sovereign is not deemed to have consented for attachment or execution upon its property, which may be entirely unrelated to that matter. As above noted, prudent counsel drafting a commercial contract with a sovereign state will include express waivers of immunity as to jurisdiction AND as to execution on a judgment or arbitral award.

Waiver of immunity for purposes of execution on a judgment is discussed in the FSIA § 1609, § 1610(a)(1) & (b)(1), and § 1611. The following case poignantly demonstrates that a waiver of immunity is not a waiver of execution upon property.

HERCAIRE INT'L INC. v. ARGENTINA

United States Court of Appeals, Eleventh Circuit, 1987.
821 F.2d 559.

PITTMAN, SENIOR DISTRICT JUDGE:

* * * PROCEDURAL HISTORY

On June 9, 1983, Hercaire filed suit against Argentina for breach of contract, alleging that Argentina owed Hercaire $253,322.62, plus interest and costs, for Argentina's failure to pay for parts it bought from Hercaire. Argentina denied receiving the parts, and raised a counterclaim seeking $1.25 million for Hercaire's failure to supply the wing tanks to be used on Argentina's A–4 Skyhawk jets. Argentina later amended its counterclaim to allege that the wing tank dispute had been settled and that Hercaire was in breach of that settlement agreement by demanding a letter of credit in connection with the sale of an aircraft engine.

Argentina included the following language in its answer and counterclaim: Defendant, The Argentine Republic, hereby waives its sovereign immunity and that of its agencies exclusively to that in the above-entitled matter. This waiver relating to this action shall not be considered as a precedent for any other matters in this or any other Court in the United States in which The Argentine Republic or any of its agencies are involved and any of which it may invoke sovereign immunity in accordance with International Law. * * *

Aerolineas Argentinas (Aerolineas) appeals the orders of the district court which permitted Hercaire to seize a Boeing 727 owned by Aerolineas to satisfy the judgment against Argentina. On May 3, 1986, that aircraft was seized by U.S. Marshals as it landed at Miami International Airport. Aerolineas regained possession by posting a cash bond equal to twice the amount of the judgment. After a hearing, the court directed the Clerk to release $293,761.27 to the plaintiff in satisfaction of the judgment. * * *

Aerolineas Argentinas (Aerolineas) appeals the trial court's rulings which allowed Hercaire to seize a Boeing 727, owned by the appellant Aerolineas, in aid of execution of the judgment rendered against the Republic of Argentina. The critical question for this court is whether the assets of a foreign state's wholly-owned national airline are subject to execution to satisfy a judgment obtained against the foreign state, where the airline was neither a party to the litigation nor was in any way connected with the underlying transaction giving rise to the suit. For the reasons expressed below, we answer this question in the negative.

Our analysis of this question begins with the Foreign Sovereign Immunities Act of 1976. The FSIA provides the exclusive basis for federal court jurisdiction in civil actions against foreign states, their agencies and instrumentalities, and the circumstances under which judgments rendered against foreign states can be executed.... Under the framework established by Congress, the FSIA grants foreign states immunity from suit and from execution in U.S. courts, subject to certain specified exceptions. * * *

Among the specified circumstances under which a foreign state may be denied immunity from suit or execution is waiver. Thus, Section 1605(a)(1) provides that a foreign state may waive its immunity from suit "either explicitly or by implication." Section 1610 provides a similar exception with respect to immunity from execution. * * *

The dispute on this appeal is whether Argentina's express waiver of immunity for itself "and its agencies" operated to waive Aerolineas' immunity as well, and if not, whether the district court erred in ignoring Aerolineas' separate juridical existence.

The district court, in its Order Denying Release of Substitute Security, ... found that both Argentina and Aerolineas Argentinas implicitly waived immunity from execution under Sections 1610(a)(1) and 1610(b)(1). The district court also concluded that any presumption of separate juridical existence, ... was overcome by the fact that Argentina owns 100% of Aerolineas' stock. The district court did not address the applicability of Section 1610(a)(2) (commercial activity upon which the claim arose).

Hercaire argues that under Section 1610(a)(1), a foreign state's commercial property is subject to attachment in aid of execution if the foreign state has waived its immunity. Since under Section 1603(a) the definition of foreign state includes its political subdivisions, its agencies or instrumentalities, a waiver by the sovereign state itself operates to waive immunity for all its political subdivisions, agencies or instrumentalities. Put another way, since the immunity for agencies, instrumentalities or political subdivisions is derived from the sovereign state, once the sovereign loses its immunity through waiver, all derivative immunity is also waived.

Resolution of the waiver issue depends on the propriety of the district court's ruling on Aerolineas' separate juridical existence. If Aerolineas lacks separate status, then the Boeing 727 seized by the Marshals certainly is Argentina's commercial property found in the United States.

Aerolineas asserts that it is an instrumentality of Argentina and as such enjoys a "presumption of independent status." That presumption may be overcome only upon a showing that there has been some abuse of the corporate form. Aerolineas argues that the district court committed clear legal error in determining that, based on Argentina's 100% ownership of Aerolineas' stock, its corporate existence is, in effect, a sham.

Hercaire's argument fails to account for the policy considerations underlying the recognition of Aerolineas' separate juridical existence. As the *Bancec* Court noted

[g]overnment instrumentalities established as juridical entities distinct and independent from their sovereign should normally be treated as such. We find support for this conclusion in the legislative history of the FSIA. During its deliberations, Congress clearly expressed its intention that duly created instrumentalities of a foreign state are to be accorded a presumption of independent status. In its discussion of FSIA § 1610(b), the provision dealing with the circumstances under which a judgment creditor may execute upon the assets of an instrumentality of a foreign government, the House Report states:

> 'Section 1610(b) will not permit execution against the property of one agency or instrumentality to satisfy a judgment against another, unrelated agency or instrumentality. There are compelling reasons for this. If US law did not respect the separate juridical identities of different agencies or instrumentalities, it might encourage foreign jurisdictions to disregard the juridical divisions between different US corporations or between a US corporation and its independent subsidiary. However, a court might find that property held by one agency is really the property of another.' HR Rep No. 94–1487, pp 29–30 (1976) (citation omitted).

[*First National City Bank v. Banco Para El Comercio Exterior De Cuba (Bancec)*, 462 U.S. 611 at 626–28, 103 S.Ct. 2591 at 2600–01, 77 L. Ed. 2d 46 (1983)].

That discussion teaches two things. First, it states that Section 1610(b) is the provision governing execution of the assets of foreign instrumentalities. Second, it warns that the presumption of independent status is not to be lightly overcome. The *Bancec* Court listed two possible means for ignoring an instrumentality's separate juridical status. That status may be overcome "where a corporate entity is so extensively controlled by its owner that a relationship of principal and agent is created," or upon equitable principles, where to recognize the corporate entity "would work fraud or injustice." While that list is not meant to be exhaustive, we are offered "a conceptual framework for resolving" the issues at hand.

The district court was in error in holding that Argentina's 100% ownership of Aerolineas' stock was sufficient to overcome the presumption of separate juridical existence. In the present case there is no showing that Argentina exercises such extensive control over Aerolinas as to warrant a finding of principal and agent. Neither can we perceive any "fraud or injustice" which results from insulating Aerolineas' property from attachment in aid of execution of the judgment against Argentina. Having had no connection whatsoever with the underlying transaction which gives rise to Argentina's liability, it would be manifestly unfair to subject Aerolineas' assets to such attachment.

We recognize that this ruling makes Hercaire's task more difficult, but it must be remembered that the FSIA was not intended to eliminate sovereign immunity entirely, but merely to "remedy, in part," the "predicament of a plaintiff who has obtained a judgment against a foreign state." Prior to the FSIA, "a foreign state in our courts enjoy[ed] absolute immunity from execution, even in ordinary commercial litigation where commercial assets [were] available for satisfaction of a judgment."

Accordingly, we VACATE the district court's Order Denying Release of Substitute Security, and REMAND for further proceedings in accordance with this opinion.

Questions and Comments

1. Assuming the issues of immunity and venue are surmountable, and a valid judgment is obtained, first recourse must be had to the execution provisions of §§ 1610 and 1611. The analysis and conclusion reached by the court in Problem 8.1 regarding the validity of the 1994 Agreement jurisdictional immunity waiver clause would likely apply to the waiver of execution immunity. Put differently, if the action proceeded to judgment, the court would likely uphold the jurisdictional waiver clause and would find also a valid waiver of attachment/execution immunity. In paragraph 85 of the 1994 Agreement, Venezuela expressly "hereby waive[d] the aforesaid [sovereign] immunities with respect to any lawful proceeding to enforce or collect a judgment or arbitral award rendered against it by a national court or tribunal of competent jurisdiction."

However, § 1610(a)(1) and (2) only permit execution upon foreign state property in the U.S. used for a commercial purpose which must, further, be the property subject of the claims. Section 1610(a)(2) requires that "the property is or was used for the commercial activity upon which the claim is based".

Even absent a finding of waiver, § 1610(a)(3) permits attachment/execution concerning property taken in violation of international law. As concerns a foreign state, however, the property expropriated or property exchanged for it must be the property upon which attachment/execution is sought.

Section § 1610(b)(2) permits ANY property in the U.S. used in commercial activity of an agency or instrumentality to be attached/executed upon, whether or not the property is related to the claims at issue, where the claims concern, among other permitted claims, commercial activity and taking of property in violation of international law.

The *Hercaire* decision, 821 F.2d 559 (11th Cir.1987), cautions counsel that mere affiliation with a foreign state may not be enough to subject property to attachment/execution. In *Hercaire*, property of the wholly owned national airline, a Boeing 727, was not subject to execution to enforce a judgment against Argentina.

The principal difference in execution upon property of a foreign state and property of an agency/instrumentality is that, with certain specific exceptions, such as for arbitration awards under § 1610(a)(6) and terrorist acts under § 1605(a)(7), only the property of the foreign state at issue in the litigation may be attached/executed upon. Compare § 1610(a)(2) with

§ 1610(b)(2). In contrast, § 1610(b)(2) provides that ANY property in the U.S. used in commercial activity of an agency or instrumentality may be attached/executed upon in claims regarding § 1605(a)(2) [commercial activity], (3) [taking in violation of international law], (5) [tortious act/car accident], (7) [terrorism], or § 1605(b) [maritime lien], whether or not the property is related to the claims at issue. A further difference may be found in § 1611, which immunizes from execution foreign state central bank and military property.

2.　May the New York bank accounts of Venezuela or VOCO be attached or levied upon in aid of execution upon a judgment rendered by the district court? What is the significance, if any, of the waiver contained in the 1994 TOCO Agreement? What guidance or limitations do §§ 1610 and 1611(b) and *Hercaire Int'l Inc. v. Argentina* provide? Contrast the rules applicable to Venezuela and to VOCO.

3.　Under § 1611 property used for central bank and military purposes is protected from attachment/execution. Does the 1994 Agreement address those types of property?

PART D.　ATTACHMENT AND EXECUTION

DAVID EPSTEIN, JEFFREY L. SNYDER & CHARLES S. BALDWIN, IV, INTERNATIONAL LITIGATION
§ 7.17　3d ed. 2002.*

Once a judgment has been obtained, whether by default or on the merits, one of the most essential questions facing any attorney is how that judgment may be enforced. Under the FSIA, compared with attachment and execution in a non-FSIA context, special rules restrict the options available for attachment and execution. The attachment and execution provisions are some of the most important provisions of the FSIA, because they represent one of the most significant departures from pre-FSIA jurisprudence. The legislative history of the FSIA noted that the FSIA renders "unnecessary the practice of seizing and attaching the property of a foreign government for the purpose of obtaining jurisdiction," and seeks "to restrict [the] broad immunity from execution." House Report, at 8.

To implement the first of these purposes, section 1609 provides for the immunity of foreign state property from "attachment arrest and execution," unless one of the exceptions in sections 1610 or 1611 applies. This prohibits the attachment of property of a foreign state for the purpose of obtaining jurisdiction over it. § 1610(d)(2). To implement the second purpose, the FSIA commences with a presumption that the property of the foreign state and instrumentalities is immune from attachment and execution. From this general premise, Congress carved out various categories of property and made them susceptible to attachment and execution. In short, with the adoption of section 1610, Congress excepted from this immunity certain property of the foreign state,

* Reprinted with permission of Transnational Publishers, Inc.

and property of the agencies and instrumentalities of foreign states, under differing rules based on the commercial nature of the property. Next, in section 1611, the FSIA preserves the immunity of certain classes of property notwithstanding its possession of the requisite commercial nexus.

Turning to the heart of the FSIA's attachment and execution provisions, section 1610 is divided into five subsections. Subsection (a) provides seven exceptions to the general rule of immunity from attachment and execution for the property of states and instrumentalities that generally track the jurisdictional immunity provisions in section 1605 (i.e., waiver; commercial activity; expropriation; succession, gift, or immovable property; automobile or other casualty or liability insurance; enforcement of arbitral awards; and terrorist acts). If the property at issue falls into one of these categories, then the foreign state or its agency or instrumentality is not immune from attachment in aid of execution or satisfaction of a judgment, so long as the notice and time period provided for in subsection (c) have been satisfied.

Subsection (b) provides additional exceptions for certain property held by foreign instrumentalities engaged in commercial activity in the United States. If the instrumentality is engaged in a commercial activity, then any of its property is subject to execution if it has waived its immunity, or if the judgment is based on an action for which an exception to jurisdictional immunity was found under certain sections of 1605(a) or (b). As one commentator has described it:

> For these defendants, both the commercial use and the nexus to the claim in question are eliminated. Thus, so long as the agency or instrumentality is engaged in a commercial activity in the United States, any of its property can be executed upon if there has been an effective waiver, or if the defendant is found liable and not immune for a commercial act, a taking in violation of international law, a non-commercial tort, or for certain maritime claims. Joseph W. Dellapenna, Suing Foreign Governments and Their Corporations, Com. L. J. 298, 302 (Aug./Sep. 1980).

It is important to note that a waiver of immunity from attachment is insufficient to waive immunity from jurisdiction, and vice versa. Prudent counsel will seek to include both waivers in any agreements with sovereign parties.

Additionally, even if a waiver or other exception to immunity allows attachment, the FSIA permits attachment in the aid of execution, that is, only upon order of the court. § 1610(c). This provision mandates that the court be involved to ensure that notice has been provided of the judgment pursuant to section 1608(e) and that a reasonable time has elapsed following the entry of judgment.

Neither subsection 1610(a) nor (b) contain the tort exception to attachment and execution that is present in section 1605(a)(5). For this reason, waiver presents the only option for enforcement of a tort judgment obtained under the FSIA against property of the foreign state in the United States. *See De Letelier v. Republic of Chile*, 748 F.2d 790, 798 (2d Cir.1984) (admonishing Congress for failing to provide for collection against a foreign state of tort awards, essentially resulting in creation of "a right without a remedy"). However, section 1610(b)(2) expressly provides that the property of a foreign states' agency or instrumentality is subject to execution to enforce a tort award under section 1605(a)(5).

Where the claim is based upon a terrorist act, enforcement of a judgment under section 1605(a)(7) is facilitated by section 1610(a)(7). That section provides that property of the foreign state or its agency or instrumentality in the U.S. "used for commercial activity in the United States" may be attached and judgment thereupon executed. § 1610(a)(7), (b)(2).

Section 1610(d) provides that a foreign state's property used for a commercial activity in the U.S. is not immune from pre-judgment attachment if two conditions are met:

> (1) the foreign state has explicitly waived its immunity from attachment; and

> (2) the purpose of the attachment is to secure satisfaction of a judgment, and not to obtain jurisdiction.

Section 1610(e) allows vessel attachments in actions to foreclose a preferred mortgage.

The last attachment and execution provision, which overrides any exceptions in section 1610, covers those classes of property for which immunity is preserved, regardless of their commercial nature. Section 1611 of the FSIA outlines three types of property that are always entitled to immunity from execution, unless there has been a valid waiver. The first category is for property belonging to international organizations "designated by the President as being entitled to enjoy the privileges, exemptions, and immunities provided by the International Organizations Immunities Act." § 1611(a). The second category exempts property of "a foreign central bank or monetary authority held for its own account." § 1611(b)(1). The final category includes property that "is, or is intended to be, used in connection with a military activity and (A) is of a military character, or (B) is under the control of a military authority or defense agency." § 1611(b)(2).

Chapter 9

ACT OF STATE

INTRODUCTION 9.0   THE BACKGROUND AND FUNDAMENTALS OF ACT OF STATE: A QUESTION OF GOING FORWARD

THE DOCTRINE. The act of state doctrine is a judge-made rule of law that U.S. courts will not sit in judgment of the public acts of foreign governments concerning property or matters within the territory of the foreign sovereign. The Supreme Court in an 1897 decision, *Underhill v. Hernandez*, 168 U.S. 250, 252, 18 S.Ct. 83, 84, 42 L.Ed. 456, 457, stated:

> Every sovereign State is bound to respect the independence of every other sovereign State, and the courts of one country will not sit in judgment on the acts of the government of another done within its own territory. Redress of grievance by reason of such acts must be obtained through the means open to be availed of by sovereign powers as between themselves.

The act of state doctrine serves a gate-keeping function. It requires the court to determine whether a case which is otherwise justiciable should go forward where the validity of a foreign sovereign's acts within its own territory are called into question. Various justifications and definitions of the Act of state doctrine have been propounded.

THE BASES OF THE DOCTRINE

1.   **Upholding international comity and peaceful relations among sovereign states.** *Oetjen v. Central Leather Co.*, 246 U.S. 297, 303–04, 38 S.Ct. 309, 311, 62 L.Ed. 726 (1918) (act of state doctrine rests upon "the highest considerations of international comity and expediency" and "[t]o permit the validity of the acts of one sovereign State to be reexamined and perhaps condemned by the courts of another would very certainly 'imperil the amicable relations between governments and vex the peace of nations' ");

2.   **A special choice of law rule**. *Banco Nacional de Cuba v. Sabbatino*, 376 U.S. 398, 438, 84 S.Ct. 923, 11 L.Ed.2d 804 (1964) ("The act of state doctrine, however, although it shares with the immunity

doctrine a respect for sovereign states, concerns the limits for determining the validity of an otherwise applicable rule of law. It is plain that if a recognized government sued on a contract with a U.S. citizen, concededly legitimate by the locus of its making, performance, and most significant contacts, the forum would not apply its own substantive law of contracts. Since the act of state doctrine reflects the desirability of presuming the relevant transaction valid, the same result follows; the forum may not apply its local law regarding foreign expropriations");

3. **A matter of U.S. Constitutional separation of powers requiring Judicial Branch deference to the Executive Branch in the conduct of foreign relations**. *Sabbatino*, (stating that the doctrine reflects "the strong sense of the Judicial Branch that its engagement in the task of passing on the validity of foreign acts of state may hinder" the conduct of foreign affairs, and is "concerned with a basic choice regarding the competence and function of the Judiciary and the National Executive in ordering our relationships with other members of the international community");

4. **A rule of judicial abstention**. *Honduras Aircraft Registry, Ltd. v. Gov't of Honduras*, 129 F.3d 543, 550, *reh'g en banc denied*, 131 F.3d 157 (11th Cir.1997) (act of state doctrine limits, for prudential rather than jurisdictional reasons, the courts in this country from inquiring into the validity of a recognized foreign sovereign's public acts committed within its own territory).

REQUIREMENTS FOR THE DOCTRINE TO APPLY. Because of its requirements, U.S. courts only infrequently apply the doctrine. For the act of state doctrine to apply, the following elements must be present:

1. **Governmental Act**. A governmental act of a foreign sovereign is at issue; not the act of a foreign individual, nor a challenge in U.S. courts to the validity of a U.S. government act;

2. **Location of Act**. The property, tangible or intangible, at issue is located in the territory of the foreign sovereign or the act of a governmental character is done within the foreign state's own territory and applicable there; and

3. **Controlling Legal Principles**. There are no controlling legal provisions applicable to the dispute, such as might be contained in a treaty of friendship, commerce and navigation (FCN) between the U.S. and foreign sovereign or certain *jus cogens* norms of international law, such as flagrant human rights abuses.

The party seeking application of the act of state doctrine has the burden of proving these elements.

The modern statement of the Doctrine is included in the Restatement (3rd) of Foreign Relations Law of the U.S. § 443, and *Banco Nacional De Cuba v. Sabbatino*, 376 U.S. 398, 84 S.Ct. 923, 11 L.Ed.2d 804 (1964). Restatement (Third) of Foreign Relations Law of the U.S., § 443 ("In the absence of a treaty or other unambiguous agreement regarding controlling legal principles, courts in the United States will generally refrain from examining the validity of a taking by a foreign state of property within its own territory, or from sitting in judgment on other acts of a governmental character done by a foreign state within its own territory and applicable there.").

The Restatement (Third) of Foreign Relations Law, § 443, reporters' note 11, notes that:

[T]he doctrine of sovereign immunity is addressed essentially to the jurisdiction of the courts; the act of state doctrine is addressed to the permissible scope of inquiry by courts into particular issues presented.... Jurisdiction, including any defense of immunity, should be decided first; a determination that the defendant state is not entitled to immunity is not dispositive of applicability of the act of state doctrine.

The act of state doctrine should not be confused with the jurisdictional issue of Foreign State Immunity, discussed above in Chapter 8. As above stated, the threshold issue of U.S. court jurisdiction over matters involving a foreign sovereign is now determined under the Foreign Sovereign Immunities Act (FSIA). Even where the FSIA would permit a suit in U.S. court, however, the court may still decline to hear the case based upon the act of state doctrine. The Eleventh Circuit has observed:

[O]ur standard of review is different from that applied under the FSIA in the denial of the motion to dismiss. More is involved than accepting what the complaint alleges as true. The act of state doctrine does not limit courts' jurisdiction as the FSIA does, but it is flexibly designed to avoid judicial action in sensitive areas. *Honduras, supra*, 129 F.3d at 550.

Consider the Fifth Circuit's comments in *De Sanchez v. Banco Central De Nicaragua*, 770 F.2d 1385, 1389 (5th Cir.1985):

Unlike the act of state doctrine, sovereign immunity is not merely a defense on the merits—it is jurisdictional in nature. If sovereign immunity exists, then the court lacks both personal and subject matter jurisdiction to hear the case and must enter an order of dismissal.... In contrast, the act of state doctrine merely requires that a court, after exercising jurisdiction, decline to review certain issues—in particular, the validity or propriety of foreign acts of state.... Because sovereign immunity is jurisdictional and the act of state defense is not, we must consider sovereign immunity before reaching the act of state doctrine.

A court must, therefore, first consider whether an exception to immunity under the FSIA would permit suit against the foreign state, i.e., whether the court has jurisdiction; then the court must decide whether the act of state doctrine should be applied to bar the action from going forward. Unless the court first determines that it has jurisdiction under an exception to immunity stated under the FSIA, the court is prohibited from considering whether the act of state doctrine applies.

Unlike the FSIA, the "act of state doctrine is a judicial policy of restraint, [and its] application ... cannot be 'waived' by the foreign state." *See* Restatement, § 443, cmt. e.; *Dayton v. Czechoslovak Socialist Republic,* 834 F.2d 203, 206 (D.C.Cir.1987). "In cases in which a state or other party fails to appear or assert the act of state doctrine, the court may itself raise the applicability of the doctrine." Restatement, § 443, cmt. i. While a written jurisdictional waiver or forum selection clause in a contract with a foreign state would not be dispositive, it may influence the court that the policies underlying the application of the act of state doctrine are not applicable to the case. Restatement, § 443, cmt. e.

In terms of rules of civil procedure, a foreign state's motion to dismiss under the FSIA would be brought pursuant to Rule 12(b)(1) for lack of subject matter jurisdiction. A foreign state's motion to dismiss the action on the basis of the act of state doctrine would be a motion pursuant to Rule 12(b)(6) for failure to state a claim for which relief may be granted.

There are, of course, similarities between the doctrines of sovereign immunity and act of state. "Both the act of state doctrine and sovereign immunity are based on considerations of respect for the sovereign independence and equality of states, and on perceived limitations on the authority of domestic courts of one state to judge the activities of another state." Restatement, § 443, Reporters' Note 11.

EXCEPTIONS TO THE DOCTRINE. Because the act of state doctrine is judge-made, many of its exceptions are not codified and are, therefore, of uncertain applicability in a given case. The generally recognized exceptions to the act of state doctrine (i.e., where the court will permit the case to go forward) are:

1. **Treaty Exception**. The Supreme Court in *Banco Nacional de Cuba v. Sabbatino,* 376 U.S. 398, 428, 84 S.Ct. 923, 940, 11 L.Ed.2d 8804, 823–24 (1964), stated:

> [R]ather than laying down or reaffirming an inflexible and all-encompassing rule in this case, we decide only that the Judicial Branch will not examine the validity of a taking of property within its own territory by a foreign sovereign government, extant and recognized by this country at the time of suit, in the absence of a treaty or other unambiguous agreement regarding controlling legal principles. . . .

In *Kalamazoo Spice Extraction Co. v. Government of Socialist Ethiopia,* 729 F.2d 422, 427 (6th Cir.1984), the court held a Treaty of Amity to be a controlling legal standard in the area of international law. The court held that because the Treaty contained the common language contained in treaties of FCN requiring "prompt, just and effective compensation", the Treaty "can provide a basis for determining the extent of compensation to which Kal–Spice may be entitled."

2. *Bernstein* **Letter**. Because the act of state doctrine concerns international relations, a statement of the U.S. government's position in a given case may hold great sway over a court's decision whether to apply the doctrine. In certain cases, a letter from the U.S Department of State, Office of the Legal Adviser, has been requested. This type of letter is known as a "*Bernstein* Letter" as the practice arose in the case of *Bernstein v. N.V. Nederlandsche–Amerikaansche Stoomvaart–Maatschapij*, 210 F.2d 375 (2d Cir.1954). In that case the Plaintiff, Arnold Bernstein, sued in New York federal court to recover property taken from him by the government of Nazi Germany. A letter from the Acting Legal Advisor of the Department of State was sent to the court stating:

> The policy of the Executive, with respect to claims asserted in the United States for the restitution of identifiable property (or compensation in lieu thereof) lost through force, coercion, or duress as a result of Nazi persecution in Germany, is to relieve American courts from any restraint upon the exercise of their jurisdiction to pass upon the validity of the acts of Nazi officials.

Based upon this letter, the Second Circuit instructed the lower courts to "strik[e] out all restraints based on the inability of the courts to pass on acts of officials in Germany during the period in question." The practice has been summarized:

> It seems that if the State Department issues a letter requesting that the courts not review the validity of a particular act, such a letter will be highly persuasive if not binding.... If the State Department issues a letter stating that it has no objection on foreign relations grounds to adjudication of the validity of a given act of a foreign state, courts in the United States will make their own determination as to whether to apply the act of state doctrine, taking the view of the Executive Branch into account but not being bound by it. Restatement (Third) of Foreign Relations Law, § 443, reporters' note 8 (1986 Main Vol.).

3. **Counterclaim/Setoff**. Where the State Department has issued a Bernstein letter and the foreign State has brought an action in U.S. court, a defendant may assert a counterclaim against the foreign state up to the amount sought by the foreign state. *See also* § 1607 (counterclaim exception of FSIA).

In *Banco Nacional de Cuba v. Chase Manhattan Bank*, 658 F.2d 875 (2d Cir.1981), the Second Circuit observed:

> Where (1) the Executive Branch has provided a *Bernstein* letter advising the courts that it believes act of state doctrine need not be applied, (2) there is no showing that an adjudication of the claim will interfere with delicate foreign relations, and (3) the claim against the foreign sovereign is asserted by way of counterclaim and does not exceed the value of the sovereign's claim, adjudication of the counterclaim for expropriation of the defendant's property is not barred by the act of state doctrine.

4. **Commercial Act**. In *Alfred Dunhill of London, Inc. v. Cuba*, 425 U.S. 682, 704, 96 S.Ct. 1854, 1866, 48 L.Ed.2d 301 (1976), Justice White, writing for a plurality of only four Justices of the Court, analogized the act of state doctrine to sovereign immunity and reasoned that the act of state doctrine, like sovereign immunity, should not immunize foreign states when they have acted in a commercial capacity. In a dissent of four Justices, Justice Marshall observed that the various considerations underlying the act of state doctrine counsel against making the doctrine co-extensive with the doctrine of sovereign immunity.

Circuit courts appear to be skeptical whether there is a commercial act exception to the act of state doctrine. In *International Association of Machinists and Aerospace Workers, (IAM) v. OPEC*, 649 F.2d 1354 (9th Cir.1981), *cert. denied*, 454 U.S. 1163, 102 S.Ct. 1036, 71 L.Ed.2d 319 (1982), Judge Choy concluded that carving a broad commercial act exception would undercut the act of state doctrine's purpose to permit U.S. courts the flexibility to avoid, where appropriate, deciding politically sensitive cases involving sovereign prerogatives. The court, in essence, distinguished sovereign immunity from act of state by noting the sovereign immunity act focus on the *nature* of the act [i.e., whether a statutory exception exists under the FSIA] and the act of state focus on the *purpose* [i.e., sovereign prerogative] of the act. *See also, Braka v. Bancomer*, 762 F.2d 222, 225 (2d Cir.1985) ("We leave for another day consideration of the possible existence in this Circuit of a commercial exception to the act of state doctrine under *Dunhill*"); *Kalamazoo Spice Extraction Co. v. Ethiopia*, 729 F.2d 422, 425 (6th Cir.1984) (finding that while commercial act exception may exist by virtue of *Dunhill* ruling, the exception is "of doubtful precedential value"); *Clayco Petroleum Corp. v. Occidental Petroleum Corp.*, 712 F.2d 404, 408 (9th Cir.1983) ("we need not reach the question whether to adopt an exception to the act of state doctrine for purely commercial activity"), cert. denied, 464 U.S. 1040, 104 S.Ct. 703, 79 L.Ed.2d 168 (1984); *Honduras Aircraft Registry v. Government of Honduras*, 129 F.3d 543, 550 (11th Cir.1997) ("there is no commercial exception to the act of state doctrine as there is under the FSIA").

5. **Expropriation/Taking of Property in Violation of International Law**. As a result of the Supreme Court's decision in *Sabbatino*, in which the Court, applying the act of state doctrine, refused to review acts of the Cuban government in expropriating private property within its own territory in violation of international law, Congress passed legislation to limit the applicability of the act of state doctrine. The legislation provides:

> Notwithstanding any other provision of law, no court in the United States shall decline on the ground of the federal act of state doctrine to make a determination on the merits giving effect to the principles of international law in a case in which a claim of title or other right to property is asserted by any party including a foreign state (or a party claiming through such state) based upon (or traced through) a confiscation or other taking after January 1, 1959, by an act of that

state in violation of the principles of international law, including the principles of compensation and the other standards set out in this subsection: Provided, That this subparagraph shall not be applicable (1) in any case in which an act of a foreign state is not contrary to international law or with respect to a claim of title or other right to property acquired pursuant to an irrevocable letter of credit of not more than 180 days duration issued in good faith prior to the time of the confiscation or other taking, or (2) in any case with respect to which the President determines that application of the act of state doctrine is required in that particular case by the foreign policy interests of the United States and a suggestion to this effect is filed on his behalf in that case with the court. 22 U.S.C.A. § 2370(e)(2) (commonly known as the *Sabbatino* or Second *Hickenlooper* Amendment).

The legislation requires that a court examine the validity of a taking of property in violation of international law unless: (1) the President indicates that the examination could jeopardize foreign affairs; or (2) the taking is consistent with international law. "In the absence of a Presidential determination to the contrary, the act of state doctrine will not be applied in a case involving a claim of title or other right to property, when the claim is based on the assertion that a foreign state confiscated the property in violation of international law." Restatement, § 444.

6. **Human Rights Abuses**. Courts are unlikely to characterize human rights abuses as acts of state. The Second Circuit stated in *Kadic v. Karadzic*, 70 F.3d 232, 250 (2d Cir.1995), *reh'g denied*, 74 F.3d 377, *cert. denied*, 518 U.S. 1005, 116 S.Ct. 2524, 135 L.Ed.2d 1048 (1996):

> The act of state doctrine, under which courts generally refrain from judging the acts of a foreign state within its territory ... might be implicated in some cases arising under [28 U.S.C.A. § 1350 (Alien Tort Statute)]. However, we doubt that the acts of even a state official, taken in violation of a nation's fundamental law and wholly unratified by that nation's government, could properly be characterized as an act of state.

A number of human rights agreements define and protect human rights. Human rights abuses, therefore, can hardly be judicially recognized as a public, governmental act. Further, they may fall within the above discussed Treaty exception, because controlling legal principles exist with respect thereto.

7. **Arbitration**. Recognizing the potential conflict of the act of state doctrine with international agreements requiring the enforcement in U.S. courts of arbitration awards, Congress amended the Federal Arbitration Act in 1988 to add a new section on the act of state doctrine. The new section provides:

> Enforcement of arbitral agreements, confirmation of arbitral awards, and execution upon judgments based on orders confirming such awards shall not be refused on the basis of the act of state

doctrine. Pub. L. No. 100–669, 102 Stat. 3969 § 1 (1988) (codified at 9 U.S.C. § 15).

8. **Validity of Foreign Governmental Act Is Not Contested**. In *W.S. Kirkpatrick v. Environmental Tectonics*, 493 U.S. 400, 110 S.Ct. 701, 107 L.Ed.2d 816 (1990), the Supreme Court explained that "the act of state doctrine does not establish an exception for causes and controversies that may embarrass foreign governments, but merely requires that, in the process of deciding, the act of foreign governments taken within their own jurisdiction shall be deemed valid." In reaching this conclusion and in permitting the plaintiffs' claim to go forward, the unanimous Court held that the act of state doctrine does not bar a court in the United States from entertaining a cause of action that requires imputing to foreign officials an unlawful motivation (obtaining bribes) in the performance of an official act. The Court ruled that the "doctrine has no application to the present case because the validity of no foreign sovereign act is at issue."

In *Lamb v. Phillip Morris, Inc.*, 915 F.2d 1024 (6th Cir.1990), the U.S. Court of Appeals for the Sixth Circuit determined that the act of state doctrine did not bar an action by domestic tobacco growers against tobacco importers alleging violations of the federal antitrust law. The Court of Appeals held that the act of state doctrine did not bar the suit because the antitrust claims merely called into question the contracting parties' motivations and the resulting anti-competitive effects of their agreement, not the validity of any foreign sovereign act.

PROBLEM 9.1   ACT OF STATE AS A DEFENSE TO BREACH OF CONTRACT CLAIM

SECTION I.   THE SETTING

Assume that you are a federal district court judge who has been asked to decide whether to grant or deny the Rule 12(b)(6), Fed. R. Civ. P., motion of a foreign state party to dismiss the case pursuant to the act of state doctrine. Assume that an exception to immunity under the FSIA was found to permit jurisdiction over the plaintiff's claims against the foreign state. For purposes of this problem consider only the act of state issue.

The district court found as follows, after reviewing the complaint and briefs on the motions to dismiss:

> Plaintiff Travel Desks International & Co. ("TDI"), is a company organized and existing under the laws of the State of California with its principal place of business in San Francisco;

> Defendant Red Star Travel ("Red Star"), is a Chinese Government-owned instrumentality which primarily promotes tourism in China from the United States and Europe;

> Red Star's principal place of business is located in Beijing, China, although Red Star maintains offices in the United States and Europe;

Using the internet, Red Star ordered 1,000 executive desks for $1,000 each from TDI;

Red Star is alleged to have breached the contract by failing to make payment for the desks;

The conduct of Red Star was not sovereign, but was commercial in nature, notwithstanding Red Star's assertion that the desks were purchased for public, governmental uses;

The contract at issue, while electronic in nature, was consummated in the United States by TDI's receipt on its computers in the United States of Red Star's order and transmittal to Red Star of TDI's acknowledgment of same;

TDI appears to have fully performed the contract in the United States by delivering the goods, F.A.S. (free along side) to Red Star's designated vessel at the Port of San Francisco;

The chairs purchased by Red Star are used by the Chinese military at a base in Hong Kong;

The conduct of Red Star was commercial in nature such that an exception to immunity exists under the FSIA;

Red Star has asserted a motion to dismiss the case under the act of state doctrine, alleging that TDI's claim impermissibly interferes with Chinese internal sovereign acts and military affairs.

SECTION II.   FOCUS OF CONSIDERATION

The district court properly first analyzed whether an exception to immunity under the FSIA was available to permit the court subject matter jurisdiction over the plaintiff's claims against the foreign state. Having found jurisdiction based upon an FSIA exception to immunity, the district court then considered whether the act of state doctrine should be applied to bar the plaintiff's claims from going forward. Of course, if the district court had not found an FSIA exception applicable, that would have ended the litigation and the act of state doctrine would not have been considered.

For a proper act of act of state doctrine analysis, the court should:

1.   Apply the three step test discussed above for the act of state doctrine to be applicable:

   a.   Nature of Act (governmental act);

   b.   Location of Act (within foreign state's own territory and applicable there); and

   c.   No Controlling Legal Principles (treaty or *jus cogens* norms).

2.   Consider whether one of the eight exceptions to the act of state doctrine is present:

   a.   Treaty;

    b.   *Bernstein* letter;

    c.   Counterclaim/set-off;

    d.   Expropriation of property;

    e.   Human rights abuses;

    f.   Arbitration;

    g.   Validity of government act not contested; and

    h.   Commercial act (whether this exception exists is debated by courts, as discussed in 9.0 above).

SECTION III.   READINGS, QUESTIONS AND COMMENTS

W.S. KIRKPATRICK & CO., INC. v. ENVIRONMENTAL TECTONICS CORP., INT'L

Supreme Court of the United States, 1990.
493 U.S. 400, 110 S.Ct. 701, 107 L.Ed.2d 816.

JUSTICE SCALIA delivered the opinion of the Court.

The facts ... are as follows: In 1981, Harry Carpenter, who was then chairman of the board and chief executive officer of petitioner W.S. Kirkpatrick & Co., Inc. (Kirkpatrick), learned that the Republic of Nigeria was interested in contracting for the construction and equipment of an aeromedical center at [an] Air Force Base in Nigeria. It was agreed that, in the event the contract was awarded to Kirkpatrick, Kirkpatrick would pay to two Panamanian entities a "commission" equal to 20% of the contract price, which would in turn be given as a bribe to officials of the Nigerian Government. In accordance with this plan, the contract was awarded to petitioner Kirkpatrick.... All parties agree that Nigerian law prohibits both the payment and the receipt of bribes in connection with the award of a government contract.

Respondent Environmental Tectonics Corporation, International, an unsuccessful bidder for the Kaduna contract, learned of the 20% "commission" and brought the matter to the attention of the Nigerian Air Force and the United States Embassy in Lagos. Following an investigation by the Federal Bureau of Investigation, the United States Attorney for the District of New Jersey brought charges against both Kirkpatrick and Carpenter for violations of the Foreign Corrupt Practices Act of 1977, and both pleaded guilty.

Respondent then brought this civil action in the United States District Court for the District of New Jersey ... seeking damages.... The defendants moved to dismiss the complaint under Rule 12(b)(6) of the Federal Rules of Civil Procedure on the ground that the action was barred by the act of state doctrine.

The District Court concluded that the act of state doctrine applies "if the inquiry presented for judicial determination includes the motivation of a sovereign act which would result in embarrassment to the sovereign or constitute interference in the conduct of foreign policy of the United States."

The Court of Appeals for the Third Circuit reversed. Although agreeing with the District Court that "the award of a military procurement contract can be, in certain circumstances, a sufficiently formal expression of a government's public interests to trigger application" of the act of state doctrine, it found application of the doctrine unwarranted on the facts of this case. The Court of Appeals found particularly persuasive the letter to the District Court from the legal adviser to the Department of State, which had stated that in the opinion of the Department judicial inquiry into the purpose behind the act of a foreign sovereign would not produce the "unique embarrassment, and the particular interference with the conduct of foreign affairs, that may result from the judicial determination that a foreign sovereign's acts are invalid." The Court of Appeals acknowledged that "the Department's legal conclusions as to the reach of the act of state doctrine are not controlling on the courts," but concluded that "the Department's factual assessment of whether fulfillment of its responsibilities will be prejudiced by the course of civil litigation is entitled to substantial respect."

II

This Court's description of the jurisprudential foundation for the act of state doctrine has undergone some evolution over the years. We once viewed the doctrine as an expression of international law, resting upon "the highest considerations of international comity and expediency," *Oetjen v. Central Leather Co.* We have more recently described it, however, as a consequence of domestic separation of powers, reflecting "the strong sense of the Judicial Branch that its engagement in the task of passing on the validity of foreign acts of state may hinder" the conduct of foreign affairs, *Banco Nacional de Cuba v. Sabbatino.* Some Justices have suggested possible exceptions to application of the doctrine, where one or both of the foregoing policies would seemingly not be served: an exception, for example, for acts of state that consist of commercial transactions, since neither modern international comity nor the current position of our Executive Branch accorded sovereign immunity to such acts, see *Alfred Dunhill of London, Inc. v. Republic of Cuba.* (opinion of WHITE, J.); or an exception for cases in which the Executive Branch has represented that it has no objection to denying validity to the foreign sovereign act, since then the courts would be impeding no foreign policy goals, see *First National City Bank v. Banco Nacional de Cuba.* (opinion of REHNQUIST, J.).

The parties have argued at length about the applicability of these possible exceptions, and, more generally, about whether the purpose of the act of state doctrine would be furthered by its application in this case. We find it unnecessary, however, to pursue those inquiries, since the factual predicate for application of the act of state doctrine does not exist. Nothing in the present suit requires the Court to declare invalid, and thus ineffective as "a rule of decision for the courts of this country," the official act of a foreign sovereign.

In every case in which we have held the act of state doctrine applicable, the relief sought or the defense interposed would have required a court in the United States to declare invalid the official act of a foreign sovereign performed within its own territory. * * *

Petitioners point out, however, that the facts necessary to establish respondent's claim will also establish that the contract was unlawful. Specifically, they note that in order to prevail respondent must prove that petitioner Kirkpatrick made, and Nigerian officials received, payments that violate Nigerian law, which would, they assert, support a finding that the contract is invalid under Nigerian law. Assuming that to be true, it still does not suffice. The act of state doctrine is not some vague doctrine of abstention but a *"principle of decision binding on federal and state courts alike." Sabbatino* (emphasis added). As we said in *Ricaud,* [*v. American Metal Co.*, 246 U.S. 304, 38 S.Ct. 312, 62 L.Ed. 733 (1918)] "the act within its own boundaries of one sovereign State ... becomes ... a rule of decision for the courts of this country." Act of state issues only arise when a court *must decide*—that is, when the outcome of the case turns upon—the effect of official action by a foreign sovereign. When that question is not in the case, neither is the act of state doctrine. That is the situation here. Regardless of what the court's factual findings may suggest as to the legality of the Nigerian contract, its legality is simply not a question to be decided in the present suit, and there is thus no occasion to apply the rule of decision that the act of state doctrine requires.

Petitioners insist, however, that the policies underlying our act of state cases—international comity, respect for the sovereignty of foreign nations on their own territory, and the avoidance of embarrassment to the Executive Branch in its conduct of foreign relations—are implicated in the present case because, as the District Court found, a determination that Nigerian officials demanded and accepted a bribe "would impugn or question the nobility of a foreign nation's motivations," and would "result in embarrassment to the sovereign or constitute interference in the conduct of foreign policy of the United States." The United States, as *amicus curiae,* favors the same approach to the act of state doctrine, though disagreeing with petitioners as to the outcome it produces in the present case. We should not, the United States urges, "attach dispositive significance to the fact that this suit involves only the 'motivation' for, rather than the 'validity' of, a foreign sovereign act," and should eschew "any rigid formula for the resolution of act of state cases generally". In some future case, perhaps, "litigation ... based on alleged corruption in the award of contracts or other commercially oriented activities of foreign governments could sufficiently touch on 'national nerves' that the act of state doctrine or related principles of abstention would appropriately be found to bar the suit," and we should therefore resolve this case on the narrowest possible ground, viz., that the letter from the legal adviser to the District Court gives sufficient indication that, "in the setting of this case," the act of state doctrine poses no bar to adjudication.

These urgings are deceptively similar to what we said in *Sabbatino,* where we observed that sometimes, even though the validity of the act of a foreign sovereign within its own territory is called into question, the policies underlying the act of state doctrine may not justify its application. We suggested that a sort of balancing approach could be applied— the balance shifting against application of the doctrine, for example, if the government that committed the "challenged act of state" is no longer in existence. But what is appropriate in order to avoid unquestioning judicial acceptance of the acts of foreign sovereigns is not similarly appropriate for the quite opposite purpose of expanding judicial incapacities where such acts are not directly (or even indirectly) involved. It is one thing to suggest, as we have, that the policies underlying the act of state doctrine should be considered in deciding whether, despite the doctrine's technical availability, it should nonetheless not be invoked; it is something quite different to suggest that those underlying policies are a doctrine unto themselves, justifying expansion of the act of state doctrine (or, as the United States puts it, unspecified "related principles of abstention") into new and uncharted fields.

The short of the matter is this: Courts in the United States have the power, and ordinarily the obligation, to decide cases and controversies properly presented to them. The act of state doctrine does not establish an exception for cases and controversies that may embarrass foreign governments, but merely requires that, in the process of deciding, the acts of foreign sovereigns taken within their own jurisdictions shall be deemed valid. That doctrine has no application to the present case because the validity of no foreign sovereign act is at issue.

The judgment of the Court of Appeals for the Third Circuit is affirmed.

Questions and Comments

1. Should the act of state doctrine be applicable only where the Court must rule the foreign act to be invalid? Can you envision cases where the imputation of unlawful conduct to a foreign sovereign might justify application of the doctrine, though the Court is not required to declare the foreign act unlawful? Might the *Kirkpatrick* court have applied the doctrine had the Nigerian government been a party defendant to the lawsuit?

2. In *Kirkpatrick*, the Court stated that the "act of state doctrine does not establish an exception for cases and controversies that may embarrass foreign governments, but merely requires that, in the process of deciding, the acts of foreign sovereigns taken within their own jurisdictions shall be deemed valid." The Court also appears to have put great weight on the opinion of the U.S. Executive Branch that the case going forward would not embarrass the Executive in the conduct of foreign relations. Does this reasoning reflect an evolution of the doctrine from one that constitutes a special choice of law rule and avoids embarrassment to foreign states or

international notions of comity to one that avoids embarrassment to the U.S. Executive? Might that approach hinder international relations or the objectives of the act of state doctrine? The *Sabbatino* Court was careful not to limit the doctrine to Executive Branch guidance:

> It is suggested that if the act of state doctrine is applicable to violations of international law, it should only be so when the Executive Branch expressly stipulates that it does not wish the courts to pass on the question of validity. * * * Often the State Department will wish to refrain from taking an official position, particularly at a moment that would be dictated by the development of private litigation but might be inopportune diplomatically. Adverse domestic consequences might flow from an official stand which could be assuaged, if at all, only by revealing matters best kept secret. We do not now pass on the *Bernstein* exception, but even if it were deemed valid, its suggested extension is unwarranted.

3. Might there be many cases where a U.S. court would not consider the validity of a foreign sovereign act but may award damages for such act on the basis that, though valid in the foreign state, the act violates a litigant's rights under U.S. law? Might this exception swallow the rule?

4. Is the definition of the doctrine in Restatement § 443(1), which encompasses both a U.S. court's "examining the validity of a taking" and "sitting in judgment on other acts of a governmental character" broader than *Kirkpatrick* permits?

5. The *Kirkpatrick* Court declared that the act of state doctrine is "not some vague doctrine of abstention but a *'principle of decision* binding on federal and state courts alike' ''. Is this consistent with the doctrine's genesis as a discretionary self-limitation on judicial competence? *See Underhill v. Hernandez*, 168 U.S. 250, 252, 18 S.Ct. 83, 84, 42 L.Ed. 456, 457 (1897) ("Every sovereign State is bound to respect the independence of every other sovereign State, and the courts of one country will not sit in judgment on the acts of the government of another done within its own territory"); *Honduras Aircraft Registry, Ltd. v. Gov't of Honduras*, 129 F.3d 543, 550, *reh'g en banc denied*, 131 F.3d 157 (11th Cir. 1997) (act of state doctrine limits, for prudential rather than jurisdictional reasons, the courts in this country from inquiring into the validity of a recognized foreign sovereign's public acts committed within its own territory); *Liu v. Republic of China*, 892 F.2d 1419, 1432 (9th Cir. 1989), *cert. dismissed*, 497 U.S. 1058, 111 S.Ct. 27, 111 L.Ed.2d 840 (1990) ("The doctrine, today, is a flexible one designed to prevent judicial pronouncements on the legality of the acts of foreign states which could embarrass the Executive Branch in the conduct of foreign affairs").

6. The Restatement, § 443(2) notes that Congress can amend the act of state doctrine. Could Congress Constitutionally do so if the doctrine is really a "principle of decision" as *Kirkpatrick* suggests? Would such amendment raise Constitutional separation of powers issues or even federal versus state rights issues as to the doctrine's applicability to state courts?

7. Is the act of state doctrine more likely or less likely to be applied by courts as a result of the *Kirkpatrick* decision? That is, does *Kirkpatrick* expand or constrict the doctrine's applicability?

WALTER FULLER AIRCRAFT SALES, INC.
v. REPUBLIC OF THE PHILIPPINES

United States Court of Appeals, Fifth Circuit, 1992.
965 F.2d 1375.

KING, CIRCUIT JUDGE:

Shortly after the Marcos regime was ousted from the Philippines, the new government of Corazon Aquino created the Presidential Commission on Good Government (PCGG) to recover any ill-gotten gains of Marcos and his confederates. Using its power to sequester property, the PCGG obtained control of a Falcon 50 jet aircraft (the Falcon) that had been leased by a Philippine corporation with alleged ties to the former Marcos regime. The owner of the plane was Faysound, Ltd., a Hong Kong corporation. The PCGG ultimately sold the Falcon to an American corporation, Walter Fuller Aircraft Sales, Inc. (Fuller), which brought it to the United States. Faysound, distressed about the disposition of its property, brought an action against Fuller in federal district court in Arkansas to try title, and won.

This lawsuit arose out of the Arkansas proceedings. Fuller, claiming that the PCGG had promised in the deed of sale to defend any action brought by an adverse claimant to the Falcon, sued the PCGG and the Republic of the Philippines (Republic) in the United States District Court for the Northern District of Texas in an effort to recover the cost of defending Faysound's lawsuit. We * * * reject the defendants' argument that the act of state doctrine bars the suit.

The act of state doctrine serves to enhance the ability of the Executive Branch to engage in the conduct of foreign relations by preventing courts from judging foreign public acts. When determining whether the act of state doctrine limits adjudication in American courts, we look not only to the acts of the named defendants, "but [to] any governmental acts whose validity would be called into question by adjudication of the suit." The defendants assert that the act of state doctrine applies because resolution of this suit will call into question the Philippine government's grant of power to the PCGG to sequester and sell assets, the PCGG's official acts of sequestering and selling the Falcon, the Philippines Supreme Court's decision that the PCGG had no authority to sell the aircraft and that the proceeds of the sale should be placed in escrow until title is determined, and various other official acts. Furthermore, the defendants argue that, even if there is an exception to the act of state doctrine for the repudiation of commercial obligations, it is inapplicable here because the PCGG's commercial acts were traceable to sovereign acts.

We share none of the defendants' concerns about the effect of this lawsuit. The district court need not adjudicate the validity of any of the public acts authorizing the PCGG to sequester and sell assets in the course of determining whether the PCGG wrongfully repudiated its contractual obligation. Apart from the decision of the Philippines Supreme Court, all of the public acts cited by the defendants directly involve the creation and extent of the PCGG's authority to acquire and convey title. This lawsuit, however, has nothing to do with title to the aircraft, but is instead a damages action arising from a contract breach [i.e., the PCGG's failure to defend Fuller's title to the aircraft]. There is no connection here between any public acts and the PCGG's refusal to defend.

Moreover, finding a breach here would not call into question the decision of the Philippines Supreme Court, for that court has merely determined that the PCGG had no authority to sequester and sell the Falcon without permission from the Sandiganbayan [the special Phillippine court set up to adjudicate claims to property sequestered by the PCGG]. In short, all the public acts and decisions cited by the defendants may be valid and yet the PCGG still may have breached the contract. Although public acts lurk in the background, the act of state doctrine "does not preclude judicial resolution of all commercial consequences stemming from the occurrence of . . . public acts."

[The court therefore upheld the district court's finding that the act of state doctrine was inapplicable].

HONDURAS AIRCRAFT REGISTRY, LTD. v. GOVERNMENT OF HONDURAS

United States Court of Appeals, Eleventh Circuit, 1997.
129 F.3d 543.

WOOD, JR., SENIOR CIRCUIT JUDGE:

At first glance one may wonder how plaintiffs, a Honduran corporation and its subsidiary, a Bahamian corporation, can bring a suit against the defendants Government of Honduras in the Southern District of Florida. In fact, that is the issue we must decide in this case.

Two Miami-based businessmen with airline knowledge, one of whom had Honduran contacts, established [the Plaintiff] corporations to facilitate negotiating with Honduran officials the contract at issue in this appeal. In general, plaintiff companies' contract proposal was to upgrade and establish a modern civil aeronautics program for Honduras.

In 1994, the leadership of Honduras changed. In August of that year Honduras, without prior notice to plaintiff companies, abrogated the contract. Plaintiff companies then filed this suit against Honduras * * *.

Honduras seeks in the alternative [to seeking dismissal under the FSIA] to have the case dismissed under the act of state doctrine. Under this doctrine, Honduras argues, the courts of the United States should not pass on the validity of Honduras' alleged decision to terminate registration under the Honduran flag of aircraft processed by plaintiff companies. The act of state doctrine limits, for prudential rather than jurisdictional reasons, the courts in this country from inquiring into the validity of a recognized foreign sovereign's public acts committed within its own territory. The doctrine is fully discussed in *W.S. Kirkpatrick & Co., Inc. v. Environmental Tectonics Corp., Int'l*, where the Court explains that the policies underlying the doctrine are "international comity, respect for the sovereignty of foreign nations on their own territory, and the avoidance of embarrassment to the Executive Branch in its conduct of foreign affairs." The Ninth Circuit discussed the application of the doctrine in *Liu v. Republic of China*, and it reiterates that the burden of proving acts of state rests on the party asserting the application of the doctrine. Accepting jurisdiction of this issue, our standard of review is different from that applied under the FSIA in the denial of the motion to dismiss. More is involved than accepting what the complaint alleges as true. The act of state doctrine does not limit courts' jurisdiction as the FSIA does, but it is flexibly designed to avoid judicial action in sensitive areas.

The district court found Honduras' act of state doctrine argument to be without merit. The court discussed some of the underlying principles of the doctrine, but its reason for finding the doctrine inapplicable appears to be that this case involves a perceived commercial exception to the doctrine as under the FSIA. However, there is no commercial exception to the act of state doctrine as there is under the FSIA. The factors to be considered, as recited in *Kirkpatrick,* may sometimes overlap with the FSIA commercial exception, but a commercial exception alone is not enough. The district court may have been correct in holding the doctrine was no bar to this case, but whatever the result may be it must be reached only after consideration of the pertinent factors. On this issue, therefore, we must vacate the result reached and remand to the district court for further consideration under the controlling factors mentioned above.

The district court's decision as to the act of state doctrine it is VACATED and REMANDED for further consideration.

Questions and Comments

1. Does the act of state doctrine bar Travel Desks International & Co.'s (TDI's) claim against Red Star Travel (Red Star) for breach of contract from going forward?

2. Would the court in this Problem be called upon to question the act of a foreign sovereign? *See Walter Fuller Aircraft Sales, Inc.*, 965 F.2d at 1387–88. *See W. S. Kirkpatrick* (the "act of state doctrine has no application to the present case because the validity of no foreign sovereign act is at issue"); *Honduras Aircraft Registry* (stating that "act of state doctrine is flexibly designed to avoid judicial action in sensitive areas" and that "a commercial exception alone is not enough" to show an exception to the doctrine).

3. Does the act of state doctrine bar TDI's claims against Instrumentality for breach of contract and promissory estoppel (estopped to deny the existence of a contract) from going forward?

4. Where did the act occur: in Hong Kong from where the correspondence to TDI emanated and where the property is located; or in the United States where TDI received the written confirmation?

5. Are there controlling international legal principles? Might the court be influenced by the military usage of the property?

6. Is there an exception to the act of state doctrine available? Might a letter from the Executive Branch as to whether the Court's involvement would impinge on conduct of the Executive be helpful to the Court's decision whether to abstain under the act of state doctrine?

7. Procedurally, an act of state defense is typically asserted by the foreign sovereign in the context of a motion to dismiss the claim for lack of personal jurisdiction (Rule 12(b)(2), Fed. R. Civ. P. [or corresponding state rule of civil procedure]), insufficiency of process and service of process (Rules 12(b)(4) & (5)), and failure to state a claim for which relief can be granted (Rule 12(b)(6)). The defense is often asserted along with a foreign state immunity defense under the FSIA for lack of subject matter jurisdiction (Rule 12(b)(1)). The act of state doctrine may also be applied by the court *sua sponte*, where the court is concerned with the potential for embarrassing the Executive Branch. *Liu v. Republic of China*, 892 F.2d 1419 (9th Cir. 1989), *cert. dismissed*, 497 U.S. 1058, 111 S.Ct. 27, 111 L.Ed.2d 840 (1990) (considering application of doctrine *sua sponte* in case involving murder in the United States by a foreign official).

PROBLEM 9.2   ACT OF STATE AS A DEFENSE TO EXPROPRIATION CLAIM

SECTION I.   THE SETTING

The Venezuelan government expropriated property of a Texas corporation that had been operating in Venezuela under various concession and licensing contracts. As in the previous problem, we assume that an exception to the FSIA was found to exist and thus allowed jurisdiction over the foreign state. This problem addresses only the Act of State issues. Assume that you are the District Court Judge being asked to rule upon the Rule 12(b)(6), Fed. R. Civ. P., Motion of Defendant Venezuela to dismiss all claims of the Texas corporation.

The district court found as follows, after reviewing the complaint and briefs on the motions to dismiss:

> Plaintiff TexOil Co. (TOCO) is a multinational corporation, chartered in Delaware, with headquarters in Houston, Texas;

> Defendant Venezuela is a sovereign state, recognized as such by the U.S. Executive Branch;

> Defendant VOCO is an instrumentality of Venezuela;

> An agreement dated 1994 existed between TOCO and Venezuela (1994 Agreement) which granted TOCO certain licenses and rights with respect to the exploitation of Venezuela's petroleum resources;

Conferring licenses and rights for the exploitation of natural resources, such as petroleum, is a peculiarly sovereign function;

The Venezuelan Legislature duly passed legislation declaring that the President, by Executive Order, may elect to either ratify or repudiate any previous agreement between Venezuela and a foreign corporation pertaining to the exploitation of Venezuela's natural resources;

Pursuant to this Act, the President of Venezuela, by Executive Order, terminated, among other agreements, the 1994 Agreement;

The 1994 Agreement contained an express waiver of sovereign immunity;

Unlike sovereign immunity under the FSIA, the act of state doctrine rests upon judicial discretion and may not be waived;

Venezuela has "nationalized", i.e., expropriated, facilities of several key industries in Venezuela, including the electric power, telecommunication, and petroleum industries;

The properties taken have included those of Venezuelan nationals as well as foreign companies;

The properties were taken pursuant to a public policy of economic reform of the Government of Venezuela;

Pursuant to the Government policy, which included decrees of the Venezuela Legislative and Executive branches, Venezuela expropriated property of Plaintiff TOCO located in Venezuela, consisting of an oil refinery in Caracas;

The taking occurred subsequent to Venezuela's termination of the 1994 Agreement;

The taking occurred in areas of Venezuelan sovereignty and no property taken or property exchanged for it has been present in the U.S during the course of this litigation;

VOCO has operated the facilities since the expropriation;

As purported compensation for the seizure, Venezuela tendered to TOCO a thirty-year maturity "Promissory Note" issued in the rapidly inflating Bolivar (currency of Venezuela);

The Promissory Note does not constitute the prompt, adequate and effective compensation required by international law for the taking of property; and

In connection with its nationalization of TOCO facilities, the Venezuelan military engaged in acts of brutality and torture against certain TOCO employees who have since returned to the United States; TOCO and certain of its employees, parties to this lawsuit, assert claims against Venezuela arising from the employees' mistreatment at the hands of the Venezuelan military; and

The U.S. Executive Branch, while indicating that Venezuela is a sovereign state and that the court should give due consideration to such sovereign status, has taken no position whether the act of state doctrine is applicable to TOCO's claims.

SECTION II. FOCUS OF CONSIDERATION

As in Problem 9.1, the district court first analyzed whether an exception to immunity under the FSIA was available to permit the court subject matter jurisdiction over the plaintiff's claims against the foreign state. Having found jurisdiction based upon an FSIA exception to immunity, the district court then considered whether the act of state doctrine should be applied to bar the plaintiff's claims from going forward. Of, course, if the district had not found an FSIA exception applicable, that would have ended the litigation and the act of state doctrine would not have been considered.

For a proper act of act of state doctrine analysis, the court should:

    1. Apply the three step test discussed above for the act of state doctrine to be applicable:

        a. Nature of Act (governmental act);

        b. Location of Act (within foreign state's own territory and applicable there); and

        c. No Controlling Legal Principles (treaty or *jus cogens* norms).

    2. Consider whether one of the eight exceptions to the act of state doctrine is present:

        a. Treaty;

        b. *Bernstein* letter;

        c. Counterclaim/set-off;

        d. Expropriation of property;

        e. Human rights abuses;

        f. Arbitration;

        g. Validity of government act not contested; and

        h. Commercial act (whether this exception exists is debated by courts, as discussed in 9.0 above).

SECTION III. READINGS, QUESTIONS AND COMMENTS

BANCO NACIONAL DE CUBA v. SABBATINO

Supreme Court of the United States, 1964.
376 U.S. 398, 84 S.Ct. 923, 11 L.Ed.2d 804.

Mr. Justice Harlan delivered the opinion of the Court.

[Statement of Facts]

In February and July of 1960, respondent Farr, Whitlock & Co., an American commodity broker, contracted to purchase Cuban sugar, free alongside the steamer, from a wholly owned subsidiary of Compania Azucarera Vertientes–Camaguey de Cuba (C.A.V.), a corporation organized under Cuban law whose capital stock was owned principally by United States residents. Farr, Whitlock agreed to pay for the sugar in New York upon presentation of the shipping documents and a sight draft.

On July 6, 1960, the Congress of the United States amended the Sugar Act of 1948 to permit a presidentially directed reduction of the sugar quota for Cuba. On the same day President Eisenhower exercised the granted power. The day of the congressional enactment, the Cuban Council of Ministers adopted 'Law No. 851,' which characterized this reduction in the Cuban sugar quota as an act of 'aggression, for political purposes' on the part of the United States, justifying the taking of countermeasures by Cuba. The law gave the Cuban President and Prime Minister discretionary power to nationalize by forced expropriation property or enterprises in which American nationals had an interest. Although a system of compensation was formally provided, the possibility of payment under it may well be deemed illusory. Our State Department has described the Cuban law as 'manifestly in violation of those principles of international law which have long been accepted by the free countries of the West. It is in its essence discriminatory, arbitrary and confiscatory.'

Between August 6 and August 9, 1960, the sugar covered by the contract between Farr, Whitlock and C.A.V. was loaded, destined for Morocco, onto the S.S. Hornfels, which was standing offshore at the Cuban port of Jucaro (Santa Maria). On the day loading commenced, the Cuban President and Prime Minister, acting pursuant to Law No. 851, issued Executive Power Resolution No. 1. It provided for the compulsory expropriation of all property and enterprises, and of rights and interests arising therefrom, of certain listed companies, including C.A.V., wholly or principally owned by American nationals. The preamble reiterated the alleged injustice of the American reduction of the Cuban sugar quota and emphasized the importance of Cuba's serving as an example for other countries to follow 'in their struggle to free themselves from the brutal claws of Imperialism.' In consequence of the resolution, the consent of the Cuban Government was necessary before a ship carrying sugar of a named company could leave Cuban waters. In order to obtain this consent, Farr, Whitlock, on August 11, entered into contracts, identical to those it had made with C.A.V., with the Banco Para el Comercio Exterior de Cuba, an instrumentality of the Cuban Government. The S.S. Hornfels sailed for Morocco on August 12.

Banco Exterior assigned the bills of lading to petitioner, also an instrumentality of the Cuban Government, which instructed its agent in New York, Societe Generale, to deliver the bills and a sight draft in the sum of $175,250.69 to Farr, Whitlock in return for payment. Societe Generale's initial tender of the documents was refused by Farr, Whitlock, which on the same day was notified of C.A.V.'s claim that as rightful owner of the sugar it was entitled to the proceeds. In return for a promise not to turn the funds over to petitioner or its agent, C.A.V. agreed to indemnify Farr, Whitlock for any loss. Farr, Whitlock subsequently accepted the shipping documents, negotiated the bills of lading to its customer, and received payment for the sugar. It refused, however, to hand over the proceeds to Societe Generale. Shortly thereafter, Farr, Whitlock was served with an order of the New York Supreme Court, which had appointed Sabbatino as Temporary Receiver of C.A.V.'s New York assets, enjoining it from taking any action in regard to the money claimed by C.A.V. that might result in its removal from the State. Following this, Farr, Whitlock, pursuant to court order, transferred the funds to Sabbatino, to abide the event of a judicial determination as to their ownership.

Petitioner then instituted this action in the Federal District Court for the Southern District of New York. Alleging conversion of the bills of lading it sought to recover the proceeds thereof from Farr, Whitlock and to enjoin the receiver from exercising any dominion over such proceeds.

The question which brought this case here, and is now found to be the dispositive issue, is whether the so-called act of state doctrine serves to sustain petitioner's claims in this litigation. Such claims are ultimately founded on a decree of the Government of Cuba expropriating certain property, the right to the proceeds of which is here in controversy. The act of state doctrine in its traditional formulation precludes the courts of this country from inquiring into the validity of the public acts a recognized foreign sovereign power committed within its own territory.

* * *

The classic American statement of the act of state doctrine, which appears to have taken root in England as early as 1674, *Blad v. Bamfield*, 3 Swans. 604, 36 Eng.Rep. 992, and began to emerge in the jurisprudence of this country in the late eighteenth and early nineteenth centuries, * * * is found in *Underhill v. Hernandez*, 168 U.S. 250, p. 252, 18 S.Ct. 83, at p. 84, 42 L.Ed. 456, where Chief Justice Fuller said for a unanimous Court:

> 'Every sovereign state is bound to respect the independence of every other sovereign state, and the courts of one country will not sit in judgment on the acts of the government of another, done within its own territory. Redress of grievances by reason of such acts must be obtained through the means open to be availed of by sovereign powers as between themselves.'

Following this precept the Court in that case refused to inquire into acts of Hernandez, a revolutionary Venezuelan military commander whose government had been later recognized by the United States, which were made the basis of a damage action in this country by Underhill, an American citizen, who claimed that he had had unlawfully assaulted, coerced, and detained in Venezuela by Hernandez.

None of this Court's subsequent cases in which the act of state doctrine was directly or peripherally involved manifest any retreat from

Underhill. See *Oetjen v. Central Leather Co.*, 246 U.S. 297, 38 S.Ct. 309, 62 L.Ed. 726; *Ricaud v. American Metal Co.*, 246 U.S. 304, 38 S.Ct. 312, 62 L.Ed. 733. On the contrary in two of these cases, *Oetjen* and *Ricaud*, the doctrine as announced in Underhill was reaffirmed in unequivocal terms.

Oetjen involved a seizure of hides from a Mexican citizen as a military levy by General Villa, acting for the forces of General Carranza, whose government was recognized by this country subsequent to the trial but prior to decision by this Court. The hides were sold to a Texas corporation which shipped them to the United States and assigned them to defendant. As assignee of the original owner, plaintiff replevied the hides, claiming that they had been seized in violation of the Hague Conventions. In affirming a judgment for defendant, the Court suggested that the rules of the Conventions did not apply to civil war and that, even if they did, the relevant seizure was not in violation of them. Nevertheless, it chose to rest its decision on other grounds. It described the designation of the sovereign as a political question to be determined by the legislative and executive departments rather than the judicial department, invoked the established rule that such recognition operates retroactively to validate past acts, and found the basic tenet of *Underhill* to be applicable to the case before it.

> "The principle that the conduct of one independent government cannot be successfully questioned in the courts of another is as applicable to a case involving the title to property brought within the custody of a court, such as we have here, as it was held to be to the cases cited, in which claims for damages were based upon acts done in a foreign country, for its rests at last upon the highest considerations of international comity and expediency. To permit the validity of the acts of one sovereign state to be re examined and perhaps condemned by the courts of another would very certainly 'imperil the amicable relations between governments and vex the peace of nations.'"

In *Ricaud* the facts were similar—another general of the Carranza forces seized lead bullion as a military levy—except that the property taken belonged to an American citizen. The Court found *Underhill*, and *Oetjen* controlling. Commenting on the nature of the principle established by those cases, the opinion stated that the rule

> 'does not deprive the courts of jurisdiction once acquired over a case. It requires only that when it is made to appear that the foreign government has acted in a given way on the subject-matter of the litigation, the details of such action or the merit of the result cannot be questioned but must be accepted by our courts as a rule for their decision. To accept a ruling authority and to decide accordingly is not a surrender or abandonment of jurisdiction but is an exercise of it. It results that the title to the property in this case must be determined by the result of the action taken by the military authorities of Mexico * * *.'

To the same effect is the language of Mr. Justice Cardozo in the *Shapleigh* case, where, in commenting on the validity of a Mexican land expropriation, he said: "The question is not here whether the proceeding was so conducted as to be a wrong to our nationals under the doctrines of international law, though valid under the law of the situs of the land. For wrongs of that order the remedy to be followed is along the channels of diplomacy."

In deciding the present case the Court of Appeals relied in part upon an exception to the unqualified teachings of *Underhill, Oetjen,* and *Ricaud* which that court had earlier indicated. In *Bernstein v. Van Heyghen Freres Societe Anonyme,* suit was brought to recover from an assignee property allegedly taken, in effect, by the Nazi Government because plaintiff was Jewish. Recognizing the odious nature of this act of state, the court, through Judge Learned Hand, nonetheless refused to consider it invalid on that ground. Rather, it looked to see if the Executive had acted in any manner that would indicate that United States Courts should refuse to give effect to such a foreign decree. Finding no such evidence, the court sustained dismissal of the complaint. In a later case involving similar facts the same court again assumed examination of the German acts improper, *Bernstein v. N.V. Neder-landsche–Amerikaansche Stoomvaart–Maatschappij,* 2 Cir., 173 F.2d 71, but, quite evidently following the implications of Judge Hand's opinion in the earlier case, amended its mandate to permit evidence of alleged invalidity, subsequent to receipt by plaintiff's attorney of a letter from the Acting Legal Adviser to the State Department written for the purpose of relieving the court from any constraint upon the exercise of its jurisdiction to pass on that question.[18]

Preliminarily, we discuss the foundations on which we deem the act of state doctrine to rest, and more particularly the question of whether state or federal law governs its application in a federal diversity case.

We do not believe that this doctrine is compelled either by the inherent nature of sovereign authority, as some of the earlier decision seem to imply, or by some principle of international law. If a transaction takes place in one jurisdiction and the forum is in another, the forum does not by dismissing an action or by applying its own law purport to divest the first jurisdiction of its territorial sovereignty; it merely declines to adjudicate or makes applicable its own law to parties or property before it. The refusal of one country to enforce the penal laws of another is a typical example of an instance when a court will not

18. The letter stated: "1. This government has consistently opposed the forcible acts of dispossession of a discriminatory and confiscatory nature practiced by the Germans on the countries or peoples subject to their controls.

* * *

"3. The policy of the Executive, with respect to claims asserted in the United States for the restitution of identifiable property (or compensation in lieu thereof) lost through force, coercion, or duress as a result of Nazi persecution in Germany, is to relieve American courts from any restraint upon the exercise of their jurisdiction to pass upon the validity of the acts of Nazi officials." State Department Press Release, April 27, 1949, 20 Dept. State Bull. 592.

entertain a cause of action arising in another jurisdiction. While historic notions of sovereign authority do bear upon the wisdom or employing the act of state doctrine, they do not dictate its existence.

That international law does not require application of the doctrine is evidenced by the practice of nations. Most of the countries rendering decisions on the subject to follow the rule rigidly. No international arbitral or judicial decision discovered suggests that international law prescribes recognition of sovereign acts of foreign governments, and apparently no claim has ever been raised before an international tribunal that failure to apply the act of state doctrine constitutes a breach of international obligation. If international law does not prescribe use of the doctrine, neither does it forbid application of the rule even if it is claimed that the act of state in question violated international law. The traditional view of international law is that it establishes substantive principles for determining whether one country has wronged another. Because of its peculiar nation-to-nation character the usual method for an individual to seek relief is to exhaust local remedies and then repair to the executive authorities of his own state to persuade them to champion his claim in diplomacy or before an international tribunal. Although it is, of course, true that United States courts apply international law as a part of our own in appropriate circumstances, *The Paquete Habana,* the public law of nations can hardly dictate to a country which is in theory wronged how to treat that wrong within its domestic borders.

Despite the broad statement in *Oetjen* that "The conduct of the foreign relations of our government is committed by the Constitution to the executive and legislative * * * departments," it cannot of course be thought that "every case or controversy which touches foreign relations lies beyond judicial cognizance." *Baker v. Carr.* The text of the Constitution does not require the act of state doctrine; it does not irrevocably remove from the judiciary the capacity to review the validity of foreign acts of state.

The act of state doctrine does, however, have "constitutional" underpinnings. It arises out of the basic relationships between branches of government in a system of separation of powers. It concerns the competency of dissimilar institutions to make and implement particular kinds of decisions in the area of international relations. The doctrine as formulated in past decisions expresses the strong sense of the Judicial Branch that its engagement in the task of passing on the validity of foreign acts of state may hinder rather than further this country's pursuit of goals both for itself and for the community of nations as a whole in the international sphere. Whatever considerations are thought to predominate, it is plain that the problems involved are uniquely federal in nature. If federal authority, in this instance this Court, orders the field of judicial competence in this area for the federal courts, and the state courts are left free to formulate their own rules, the purposes behind the doctrine could be as effectively undermined as if there had been no federal pronouncement on the subject.

However, we are constrained to make it clear that an issue concerned with a basic choice regarding the competence and function of the Judiciary and the National Executive in ordering our relationships with other members of the international community must be treated exclusively as an aspect of federal law. * * * We conclude that the scope of the act of state doctrine must be determined according to federal law.

VI.

If the act of state doctrine is a principle of decision binding on federal and state courts alike but compelled by neither international law nor the Constitution, its continuing vitality depends on its capacity to reflect the proper distribution of functions between the judicial and political branches of the Government on matters bearing upon foreign affairs. It should be apparent that the greater the degree of codification or consensus concerning a particular area of international law, the more appropriate it is for the judiciary to render decisions regarding it, since the courts can then focus on the application of an agreed principle to circumstances of fact rather than on the sensitive task of establishing a principle not inconsistent with the national interest or with international justice. It is also evident that some aspects of international law touch much more sharply on national nerves than do others; the less important the implications of an issue are for our foreign relations, the weaker the justification for exclusivity in the political branches. The balance of relevant considerations may also be shifted if the government which perpetrated the challenged act of state is no longer in existence, as in the *Bernstein* case, for the political interest of this country may, as a result, be measurably altered. Therefore, rather than laying down or reaffirming an inflexible and all-encompassing rule in this case, we decide only that the (Judicial Branch) will not examine the validity of a taking of property within its own territory by a foreign sovereign government, extant and recognized by this country at the time of suit, in the absence of a treaty or other unambiguous agreement regarding controlling legal principles, even if the complaint alleges that the taking violates customary international law.

There are few if any issues in international law today on which opinion seems to be so divided as the limitations on a state's power to expropriate the property of aliens. There is, of course, authority, in international judicial and arbitral decisions, in the expressions of national governments, and among commentators for the view that a taking is improper under international law if it is not for a public purpose, is discriminatory, or is without provision for prompt, adequate, and effective compensation. However, Communist countries, although they have in fact provided a degree of compensation after diplomatic efforts, commonly recognize no obligation on the part of the taking country. Certain representatives of the newly independent and underdeveloped countries have questioned whether rules of state responsibility toward aliens can bind nations that have not consented to them and it is argued that the traditionally articulated standards governing expropriation of property reflect "imperialist" interests and are inappropriate to the circumstances of emergent states.

The disagreement as to relevant international law standards reflects an even more basic divergence between the national interests of capital importing and capital exporting nations and between the social ideologies of those countries that favor state control of a considerable portion of the means of production and those that adhere to a free enterprise system. It is difficult to imagine the courts of this country embarking on adjudication in an area which touches more sensitively the practical and ideological goals of the various members of the community of nations.

When we consider the prospect of the courts characterizing foreign expropriations, however justifiably, as invalid under international law and ineffective to pass title, the wisdom of the precedents is confirmed. While each of the leading cases in this Court may be argued to be distinguishable in its facts from this one * * * the plain implication of all these opinions is that the act of state doctrine is applicable even if international law has been violated.

The possible adverse consequences of a conclusion to the contrary of that implicit in these cases in highlighted by contrasting the practices of the political branch with the limitations of the judicial process in matters of this kind. Following an expropriation of any significance, the Executive engages in diplomacy aimed to assure that United States citizens who are harmed are compensated fairly. Representing all claimants of this country, it will often be able, either by bilateral or multilateral talks, by submission to the United Nations, or by the employment of economic and political sanctions, to achieve some degree of general redress. Judicial determinations of invalidity of title can, on the other hand, have only an occasional impact, since they depend on the fortuitous circumstance of the property in question being brought into this country. Such decisions would, if the acts involved were declared invalid, often be likely to give offense to the expropriating country; since the concept of territorial sovereignty is so deep seated, any state may resent the refusal of the courts of another sovereign to accord validity to acts within its territorial borders. Piecemeal dispositions of this sort involving the probability of affront to another state could seriously interfere with negotiations being carried on by the Executive Branch and might prevent or render less favorable the terms of an agreement that could otherwise be reached. Relations with third countries which have engaged in similar expropriations would not be immune from effect.

The dangers of such adjudication are present regardless of whether the State Department has, as it did in this case, asserted that the relevant act violated international law. If the Executive Branch has undertaken negotiations with an expropriating country, but has refrained from claims of violation of the law of nations, a determination to that effect by a court might be regarded as a serious insult, while a finding of compliance with international law would greatly strengthen the bargaining hand of the other state with consequent detriment to American interests.

* * *

It is suggested that if the act of state doctrine is applicable to violations of international law, it should only be so when the Executive Branch expressly stipulates that it does not wish the courts to pass on the question of validity. We should be slow to reject the representations of the Government that such a reversal of the *Bernstein* principle would work serious inroads on the maximum effectiveness of United States diplomacy. Often the State Department will wish to refrain from taking an official position, particularly at a moment that would be dictated by the development of private litigation but might be inopportune diplomatically. Adverse domestic consequences might flow from an official stand which could be assuaged, if at all, only by revealing matters best kept secret. We do not now pass on the *Bernstein* exception, but even if it were deemed valid, its suggested extension is unwarranted.

However offensive to the public policy of this country and its constituent States an expropriation of this kind may be, we conclude that both the national interest and progress toward the goal of establishing the rule of law among nations are best served by maintaining intact the act of state doctrine in this realm of its application.

Since the act of state doctrine proscribes a challenge to the validity of the Cuban expropriation decree in this case, any counterclaim based on asserted invalidity must fail. Whether a theory of conversion or breach of contract is the proper cause of action under New York law, the presumed validity of the expropriation is unaffected.

Judgment of Court of Appeals reversed and case remanded to the District Court.

Questions and Comments

1. What justifications and underpinnings for the act of state doctrine did the *Sabbatino* court advance? Should changing international norms affect the doctrine's contours, which the *Sabbatino* Court analyzed as generally unchanged since the doctrine's ancient announcement?

2. Was the act of state doctrine, as announced by *Sabbatino*, flexible and designed to avoid judicial interference with the Executive's conduct of foreign affairs, or rigid in its application?

3. The Sabbatino Court expressly stated two considerations which might influence a court's application of the act of state doctrine: (1) "It is also evident that some aspects of international law touch more sharply on national nerves than do others; the less important the implications of an issue are for our foreign relations, the weaker the justification for exclusivity in the political branches:" (2) "[T]he greater the degree of codification or consensus concerning a particular area of international law, the more appropriate it is for the judiciary to render decisions regarding it, since the

courts can then focus on the application of an agreed principle to circumstances of fact rather than on the sensitive task of establishing a principle not inconsistent with the natural interests or with international justice." *Banco Nacional de Cuba v. Sabbatino*, 376 U.S. at 428, 84 S.Ct. at 940, 11 L.Ed.2d at 823.

4. The *Sabbatino* Court was emphatic that the scope of the act of state doctrine must be determined as a matter of federal law because of the doctrine's potential to affect international relations. Is the Court's concern well founded in light of the fact that the act of state doctrine, as the Restatement § 443 makes clear, is subject to amendment by Congress? That is, Congress could correct by legislation any perceived misapplication of the doctrine by state courts. As the act of state doctrine is a discretionary, self-imposed limit by the judiciary on its own competence in certain cases, should not state courts be equally qualified as federal courts to develop common law on the doctrine? Would not a state court, having cognizance of the specific facts before it and international/political issues posed, be best qualified to consider the doctrine's applicability, without being bound by federal precedent based upon different facts and parties?

5. The *Sabbatino* Court declined to "pass on the *Bernstein* exception, but even if it were deemed valid, its suggested extension is unwarranted." Is it contradictory that a Court may decline to hear a case based on the act of state doctrine even when the Executive has indicated through a *Bernstein* letter that it does not perceive the action to impede the Executive's conduct of foreign affairs? Would not a *Bernstein* letter alleviate the concerns underpinning the act of state doctrine as announced in *Sabbatino*?

Conflicting views as to whether a commercial activity exception exists to the act of state doctrine are reflected in the following excerpts from *Alfred Dunhill of London, Inc. v. Republic of Cuba*, 425 U.S. 682, 96 S.Ct. 1854, 48 L.Ed.2d 301 (1976) and *International Assoc. of Machinists and Aerospace Workers, (IAM) v. OPEC*, 649 F.2d 1354 (9th Cir. 1981), *cert. denied*, 454 U.S. 1163, 102 S.Ct. 1036, 71 L.Ed.2d 319 (1982).

ALFRED DUNHILL OF LONDON, INC. v. REPUBLIC OF CUBA

Supreme Court of the United States, 1976.
425 U.S. 682, 96 S.Ct. 1854, 48 L.Ed.2d 301.

Mr. Justice White delivered the opinion of the Court.

The issue in this case is whether the failure of respondents to return to petitioner Alfred Dunhill of London, Inc. (Dunhill), funds mistakenly paid by Dunhill for cigars that had been sold to Dunhill by certain expropriated Cuban cigar businesses was an "act of state" by Cuba precluding an affirmative judgment against respondents.

* * *

III.

The major underpinning of the act of state doctrine is the policy of foreclosing court adjudications involving the legality of acts of foreign states on their own soil that might embarrass the Executive Branch of our Government in the conduct of our foreign relations. *Banco Nacional de Cuba v. Sabbatino*. But based on the presently expressed views of those who conduct our relations with foreign countries, we are in no sense compelled to recognize as an act of state the purely commercial conduct of foreign governments in order to avoid embarrassing conflicts with the Executive Branch. On the contrary, for the reasons to which we now turn, we fear that embarrassment and conflict would more [sic] likely ensue if we were to require that the repudiation of a foreign government's debts arising from its operation of a purely commercial business be recognized as an act of state and immunized from question in our courts.

Although it had other views in years gone by, in 1952, as evidenced by Appendix 2 (the Tate letter) attached to this opinion, the United States abandoned the absolute theory of sovereign immunity and embraced the restrictive view under which immunity in our courts should be granted only with respect to causes of action arising out of a foreign state's public or governmental actions and not with respect to those arising out of its commercial or proprietary actions. This has been the official policy of our Government since that time as the attached letter of November 26, 1975, confirms:

> "Moreover, since 1952, the Department of State has adhered to the position that the commercial and private activities of foreign states do not give rise to sovereign immunity. Implicit in this position is a determination that adjudications of commercial liability against foreign states do not impede the conduct of foreign relations, and that such adjudications are consistent with international law on sovereign immunity."

Repudiation of a commercial debt cannot, consistent with this restrictive approach to sovereign immunity, be treated as an act of state; for if it were, foreign governments, by merely repudiating the debt before or after its adjudication, would enjoy an immunity which our Government would not extend them under prevailing sovereign immunity principles in this country. This would undermine the policy supporting the restrictive view of immunity, which is to assure those engaging in commercial transactions with foreign sovereignties that their rights will be determined in the courts whenever possible.

* * *

Since that time, as we have said, the United States has adopted and adhered to the policy declining to extend sovereign immunity to the commercial dealings of foreign governments. It has based that policy in part on the fact that this approach has been accepted by a large and increasing number of foreign states in the international community; in part on the fact that the United States had already adopted a policy of consenting to be sued in foreign courts in connection with suits against its merchant vessels; and in part because the enormous increase in the extent to which foreign sovereigns had become involved in international trade made essential "a practice which will enable persons doing business with them to have their rights determined in the courts."

* * *

Participation by foreign sovereigns in the international commercial market has increased substantially in recent years. Cf. International Economic Report of the President 56 (1975). The potential injury to private businessmen and ultimately to international trade itself from a system in which some of the participants in the international market are not subject to the rule of law has therefore increased correspondingly. As noted above, courts of other countries have also recently adopted the restrictive theory of sovereign immunity. Of equal importance is the fact that subjecting foreign governments to the rule of law in their commercial dealings presents a much smaller risk of affronting their sovereignty than would an attempt to pass on the legality of their governmental acts. In their commercial capacities, foreign governments do not exercise powers peculiar to sovereigns. Instead, they exercise only those powers that can also be exercised by private citizens. Subjecting them in connection with such acts to the same rules of law that apply to private citizens is unlikely to touch very sharply on "national nerves."

* * *

Nothing in our national policy calls on us to recognize as an act of state a repudiation by Cuba of an obligation adjudicated in our courts and arising out of the operation of a commercial business by one of its instrumentalities. For all the reasons which led the Executive Branch to adopt the restrictive theory of sovereign immunity, we hold that the mere assertion of sovereignty as a defense to a claim arising out of purely commercial acts by a foreign sovereign is no more effective if given the label "Act of State" than if it is given the label "sovereign immunity." describing the act of state doctrine in the past we have said that it "precludes the courts of this country from inquiring into the validity of the Public acts a recognized foreign sovereign power committed within its own territory." *Banco Nacional de Cuba v. Sabbatino* (emphasis added), and that it applies to "acts done within their own States, in the exercise of Governmental authority." *Underhill v. Hernandez*. We decline to extend the act of state doctrine to acts committed by foreign sovereigns in the course of their purely commercial operations. Because the act relied on by respondents in this case was an act arising out of the conduct by Cuba's agents in the operation of cigar businesses for profit, the act was not an act of state.

Questions and Comments

1. The foregoing Part III of Justice White's opinion, pertaining to Act of State, was joined only by THE CHIEF JUSTICE, Mr. Justice POWELL, and Mr. Justice REHNQUIST. What reasons may have influenced other Justices not to join?

See footnote 18:

The dissent states that the doctrines of sovereign immunity and act of state are distinct the former conferring on a sovereign "exemption from suit by virtue of its status" and the latter "merely (telling) a court what law to apply to a case." It may be true that the one doctrine has been described in jurisdictional terms and the other in choice-of-law terms; and it may be that the doctrines point to different results in certain cases. It cannot be gainsaid, however, that the proper application of each involves a balancing of the injury to our foreign policy, the conduct of which is committed primarily to the Executive Branch, through judicial affronts to sovereign powers, compare *Mexico v. Hoffman* (sovereign immunity), with *Banco Nacional de Cuba v. Sabbatino* (act of state), against the injury to the private party, who is denied justice through judicial deference to a raw assertion of sovereignty, and a consequent injury to international trade. The State Department has concluded that in the commercial area the need for merchants "to have their rights determined in courts" outweighs any injury to foreign policy. This conclusion was reached in the context of the jurisdictional problem of sovereign immunity. We reach the same one in the choice-of-law context of the act of state doctrine.

Was the Dissent correct that the FSIA and Act of State analyses are indeed distinct?

2. Might the Plurality's holding have embraced economic considerations as well as legal considerations?

INTERNATIONAL ASS'N OF MACHINISTS AND AEROSPACE WORKERS (IAM) v. ORGANIZATION OF PETROLEUM EXPORTING COUNTRIES (OPEC)

United States Court of Appeals, Ninth Circuit, 1981.
649 F.2d 1354, *cert. denied*, 454 U.S. 1163, 102 S.Ct. 1036, 71 L.Ed.2d 319.

CHOY, CIRCUIT JUDGE:

I. Introduction

The members of the International Association of Machinists and Aerospace Workers (IAM) were disturbed by the high price of oil and petroleum-derived products in the United States. They believed the actions of the Organization of the Petroleum Exporting Countries, popularly known as OPEC, were the cause of this burden on the American public. Accordingly, IAM sued OPEC and its member nations in December of 1978, alleging that their price-setting activities violated United States anti-trust laws. IAM sought injunctive relief and damages. The district court entered a final judgment in favor of the defendants, holding that it lacked jurisdiction and that IAM had no valid anti-trust claim. We affirm the judgment of the district court on the alternate ground that, under the act of state doctrine, exercise of federal court jurisdiction in this case would be improper.

B. The Act of State Doctrine

The act of state doctrine declares that a United States court will not adjudicate a politically sensitive dispute which would require the court to judge the legality of the sovereign act of a foreign state. This doctrine was expressed by the Supreme Court in *Underhill v. Hernandez*:

> Every sovereign State is bound to respect the independence of every other sovereign State, and the courts of one country will not sit in judgment on the acts of the government of another done within its own territory.

The doctrine recognizes the institutional limitations of the courts and the peculiar requirements of successful foreign relations. To participate adeptly in the global community, the United States must speak with one voice and pursue a careful and deliberate foreign policy. The political branches of our government are able to consider the competing economic and political considerations and respond to the public will in order to carry on foreign relations in accordance with the best interests of the country as a whole. The courts, in contrast, focus on single disputes and make decisions on the basis of legal principles. The timing of our decisions is largely a result of our caseload and of the random tactical considerations which motivate parties to bring lawsuits and to seek delay or expedition. When the courts engage in piecemeal adjudication of the legality of the sovereign acts of states, they risk disruption of our country's international diplomacy. The executive may utilize protocol, economic sanction, compromise, delay, and persuasion to achieve international objectives. Ill-timed judicial decisions challenging the acts of foreign states could nullify these tools and embarrass the United States in the eyes of the world.

The act of state doctrine is similar to the political question doctrine in domestic law. It requires that the courts defer to the legislative and executive branches when those branches are better equipped to resolve a politically sensitive question. Like the political question doctrine, its applicability is not subject to clear definition. The courts balance various factors to determine whether the doctrine should apply.

While the act of state doctrine has no explicit source in our Constitution or statutes, it does have "constitutional underpinnings." *Banco Nacional de Cuba v. Sabbatino*. The Supreme Court has stated that the act of state doctrine arises out of the basic relationships between branches of government in a system of separation of powers The doctrine as formulated in past decisions expresses the strong sense of the Judicial Branch that its engagement in the task of passing on the validity of foreign acts of state may hinder rather than further this country's pursuit of goals both for itself and for the community of nations as a whole in the international sphere. *Id*.

The principle of separation of powers is central to our form of democratic government. Just as the courts have carefully guarded their primary role as interpreters of the Constitution and the laws of the United States, so have they recognized the primary role of the President and Congress in resolution of political conflict and the adoption of foreign policy. Compare *Marbury v. Madison*; *Baker v. Carr*; *Banco Nacional de Cuba v. Sabbatino*.

The doctrine of sovereign immunity is similar to the act of state doctrine in that it also represents the need to respect the sovereignty of foreign states. The two doctrines differ, however, in significant respects. The law of sovereign immunity goes to the jurisdiction of the court. The act of state doctrine is not jurisdictional. *Ricaud v. American Metal Co.* Rather, it is a prudential doctrine designed to avoid judicial action in sensitive areas. Sovereign immunity is a principle of international law, recognized in the United States by statute. It is the states themselves, as defendants, who may claim sovereign immunity. The act of state doctrine is a domestic legal principle, arising from the peculiar role of American courts. It recognizes not only the sovereignty of foreign states, but also the spheres of power of the co-equal branches of our government. Thus a private litigant may raise the act of state doctrine, even when no sovereign state is a party to the action. The act of state doctrine is apposite whenever the federal courts must question the legality of the sovereign acts of foreign states.

It has been suggested that the FSIA supersedes the act of state doctrine, or that the amorphous doctrine is limited by modern jurisprudence. We disagree.

Congress in enacting the FSIA recognized the distinction between sovereign immunity and the act of state doctrine. See, e. g., H.R.Rep. No.94–1487, 94th Cong., 2d Sess. 20 n.1, reprinted in (1976) U.S.Code Cong. & Ad.News 6619 n.1 ("The Committee has found it unnecessary to address the act of state doctrine in this legislation"); ... Immunities of Foreign States: Hearings on H.R.3493 Before the Subcomm. on Claims & Governmental Relations of the Committee on the Judiciary, 93d Cong., 1st Sess. 20 (1973) (the FSIA "in no way affects existing law concerning the extent to which the 'act of state' doctrine may be applicable in similar circumstances"). Indeed, because the act of state doctrine addresses concerns central to our system of government, the doctrine must necessarily remain a part of our jurisprudence unless and until such time as a radical change in the role of the courts occurs.

The act of state doctrine is not diluted by the commercial activity exception which limits the doctrine of sovereign immunity. While purely commercial[8] activity may not rise to the level of an act of state, certain seemingly commercial activity will trigger act of state considerations. As the district court noted, OPEC's "price-fixing" activity has a significant sovereign component. While the FSIA ignores the underlying purpose of a state's action, the act of state doctrine does not. This court has stated that the motivations of the sovereign must be examined for a public

---

8. In *Alfred Dunhill of London, Inc. v. Cuba*, the court held that purely commercial activity does not require judicial deference under the act of state doctrine. The *Dunhill* case suggested but did not decide the question of whether the act of state doctrine is subsumed by the doctrine of sovereign immunity. *Compare opinion* of Justice White, 425 U.S. 682, 705 at n.18, 96 S.Ct. 1854, 1866 at n.18, 48 L.Ed.2d 301, with Justice Marshall's dissent, at 725–728, *96 S.Ct. at 1875.*

interest basis. When the state qua state acts in the public interest, its
sovereignty is asserted. The courts must proceed cautiously to avoid an
affront to that sovereignty. Because the act of state doctrine and the
doctrine of sovereign immunity address different concerns and apply in
different circumstances, we find that the act of state doctrine remains
available when such caution is appropriate, regardless of any commercial
component of the activity involved.

* * *

The decision to deny access to judicial relief is not one we make
lightly.

There is no question that the availability of oil has become a
significant factor in international relations. The growing world energy
crisis has been judicially recognized in other cases. The record in this
case contains extensive documentation of the involvement of our executive and legislative branches with the oil question.... It is clear that
OPEC and its activities are carefully considered in the formulation of
American foreign policy.

The remedy IAM seeks is an injunction against the OPEC nations.
The possibility of insult to the OPEC states and of interference with the
efforts of the political branches to seek favorable relations with them is
apparent from the very nature of this action and the remedy sought.
While the case is formulated as an anti-trust action, the granting of any
relief would in effect amount to an order from a domestic court instructing a foreign sovereign to alter its chosen means of allocating and
profiting from its own valuable natural resources. On the other hand,
should the court hold that OPEC's actions are legal, this "would greatly
strengthen the bargaining hand" of the OPEC nations in the event that
Congress or the executive chooses to condemn OPEC's actions.

* * *

While conspiracies in restraint of trade are clearly illegal under
domestic law, the record reveals no international consensus condemning
cartels, royalties, and production agreements. The United States and
other nations have supported the principle of supreme state sovereignty
over natural resources. The OPEC nations themselves obviously will not
agree that their actions are illegal. We are reluctant to allow judicial
interference in an area so void of international consensus. An injunction
against OPEC's alleged price-fixing activity would require condemnation
of a cartel system which the community of nations has thus far been
unwilling to denounce. The admonition in *Sabbatino* that the courts
should consider the degree of codification and consensus in the area of
law is another indication that judicial action is inappropriate here.

The district court was understandably reluctant to proceed on the
complaint below and the act of state doctrine provides sound jurisprudential support for such reluctance. While the act of state doctrine does
not compel dismissal as a matter of course, in a case such as this where
the controlling issue is the legality of a sovereign act and where the only

remedy sought is barred by act of state considerations dismissal is appropriate.

IV. Conclusion

The act of state doctrine is applicable in this case. The courts should not enter at the will of litigants into a delicate area of foreign policy which the executive and legislative branches have chosen to approach with restraint. The issue of whether the FSIA allows jurisdiction in this case need not be decided, since a judicial remedy is inappropriate regardless of whether jurisdiction exists.

Questions and Comments

1. Why was the act of state doctrine applied in *IAM v. OPEC* to bar claims where it was previously ruled inapplicable by the Court in *Alfred Dunhill of London, Inc. v. Republic of Cuba*, 425 U.S. 682, 96 S.Ct. 1854, 48 L.Ed.2d 301 (1976)? Can *IAM v. OPEC* be distinguished from *Alfred Dunhill* on any factual grounds? Did the nature of the plaintiffs themselves, the desired legal remedy, or the government conduct at issue differ between the two cases?

2. Based upon the factors deemed significant by the courts in *Sabbatino*, *Alfred Dunhill* and *IAM v. OPEC*, is it fair to say that the application of the act of state doctrine may differ depending upon factors, including, without limitation, the complexity of the case; the number of parties; the number of transactions involved; the number of foreign governments involved; the degree of consensus in international law concerning the legality of the sovereign conduct; the nature of the legal remedies sought (monetary relief, injunctive relief, declaratory judgment, etc.); the prevailing U.S. political climate; the international political climate ("sensitivity" of the issue); how closely the conduct is aligned to commercial activities in which individual persons or entities could engage? Are there other factors which courts have or should consider?

Some factual differences are apparent between *IAM v. OPEC*, 649 F.2d 1354 (9th Cir. 1981) and *Alfred Dunhill of London, Inc. v. Republic of Cuba*, 425 U.S. 682, 96 S.Ct. 1854, 48 L.Ed.2d 301 (1976):

A. Nature of the Plaintiffs

    I. Plaintiff in *Alfred Dunhill* was a single company financially harmed by the unlawful expropriation by Cuba of cigars.

    II. Plaintiffs in *IAM v. OPEC* was an international association of machinists and aerospace workers whose harm was more tangential/further down the chain of proximate cause and whose members were likely damaged, if at all, in varying degrees.

B. The Desired Legal Remedy

    I. Plaintiff company in *Alfred Dunhill* sought monetary damages in a sum certain for funds mistakenly paid for cigars expropriated by the Cuban government.

II.   Rather than monetary damages, the Plaintiff in *IAM v. OPEC* sought the legal remedy of injunction against certain cartel price fixing activities of the various nations comprising OPEC.

C.   Government Conduct at Issue

I.   The government conduct at issue in *Alfred Dunhill* was unlawful expropriation of certain cigars.

II.   The conduct at issue in *IAM v. OPEC* concerned cartel and price fixing activities of a variety of nations. The *IAM v. OPEC* court specifically noted that there was little international consensus regarding the legality of such practices.

CLAYCO PETROLEUM CORP. v. OCCIDENTAL PETROLEUM CORP.

United States Court of Appeals, Ninth Circuit, 1983.
712 F.2d 404.

PER CURIAM.

This appeal arises from an antitrust suit filed by Clayco Petroleum Corporation against Occidental Petroleum Corporation charging Occidental with making secret payments to an official of Umm Al Qaywayn in order to obtain unlawfully an off-shore oil concession. The district court dismissed the action on the basis of the act of state doctrine. We affirm.

The crux of the complaint is that Occidental conspired to make and made secret payments in England and Switzerland totalling $417,000 to Sheikh Sultan bin Ahmed Muallah (Sultan), Umm Al Qaywayn's Petroleum Minister and son of its ruler, Sheikh Ahmed al Mualla (Ahmed). The complaint further alleges that only through these unlawful and anticompetitive actions did defendants secure the valuable off-shore oil concession. More specifically, plaintiffs allege that in September 1969, Ahmed agreed that Clayco would receive the concession, but instead, on November 18, 1969, he awarded the concession to defendant Occidental of Umm Al Qaywayn, Inc., Occidental Petroleum's subsidiary.

Plaintiffs allege that these $417,000 in payments plus "entertainment" expenses constituted bribes to induce Sultan and his father to award the concession to Occidental. Plaintiffs contend that Occidental, its subsidiary, and Dr. Hammer conspired to prevent competition and to deprive plaintiffs of the concession.

The district court granted defendants' motion to dismiss, based on the act of state doctrine. The court stated that an exercise of sovereignty—the award of the offshore oil concession—was implicated in the case, and that adjudication would interfere with United States foreign policy. The court noted that plaintiffs' obligation to prove that they were damaged by defendants' conduct would necessitate review of the ethical validity of the sovereign's conduct. The court also refused to apply a commercial exception to the act of state doctrine.

The appellants raise numerous challenges to the district court's application of the act of state doctrine. In essence, appellants argue first that this case is outside the purview of the act of state doctrine; and second, that the foreign sovereign action involved fits within "corruption" or "commercial" exceptions to the doctrine.

Sabbatino prescribed a flexible approach to the doctrine; the critical element is the potential for interference with our foreign relations. "[T]he less important the implications of an issue are for our foreign relations, the weaker the justification for exclusivity in the political branches.".

With this in mind, we address appellants' claim that the complained of actions in this case do not include a sovereign policy decision. We cannot agree. We acknowledge that without sovereign activity effectuating "public" rather than private interests, the act of state doctrine does not apply. *International Association of Machinists and Aerospace Workers (IAM) v. OPEC.* That test is met here. This case differs from those relied upon by appellants, in which sovereign activity merely formed the background to the dispute or in which the only governmental actions were the neutral application of the laws.

Appellants first contend that an exception for purely commercial acts should apply in this case. A plurality of the Supreme Court recognized an exception for purely commercial activity in *Alfred Dunhill of London, Inc. v. Republic of Cuba,* but only four Justices concurred in that section of the opinion. The *Dunhill* plurality emphasized that a commercial exception is appropriate in situations where governments are not exercising powers peculiar to sovereigns. Unlike the context *Dunhill* envisioned, the governmental action here could not have been taken by a private citizen. Granting a concession to exploit natural resources entails an exercise of powers peculiar to a sovereign.

The Ninth Circuit has not definitively ruled on the commercial exception. *Compare Northrup,* (alluding to existence of commercial exception), with *IAM v. OPEC,* (holding that presence of a "commercial component" does not create an exception). Because the rule espoused by the *Dunhill* plurality would not apply in any event, we need not reach the question whether to adopt an exception to the act of state doctrine for purely commercial activity.

For the reasons above, we hold that the act of state doctrine applies, and that appellants do not come within any exception to the doctrine. The decision of the trial court dismissing the action is therefore AFFIRMED.

KALAMAZOO SPICE EXTRACTION CO.
v. PROVISIONAL MILITARY GOV'T
OF SOCIALIST ETHIOPIA

United States Court of Appeals, Sixth Circuit, 1984.
729 F.2d 422.

[The Provisional Military Government of Ethiopia (PMGSE) expropriated in 1975 the Ethiopian Spice Extraction Company (ESESCO), which was a joint venture between an American corporation, Kalamazoo Spice Extraction Company (Kal–Spice), and Ethiopian citizens. Kal–Spice sued PMGSE for compensation in U.S. courts.]

Once the suit reached the United States District Court of the Western District of Michigan, the court decided that the act of state doctrine precluded adjudication of the claims against the PMGSE based on the expropriation of Kal–Spice's interests. The district court further held that the Treaty of Amity between the United States and Ethiopia was "so inherently general, doubtful, and susceptible of multiple interpretation" that it could not be applied by a United States court to satisfy the "treaty exception" to the act of state doctrine.

We disagree, and reverse and remand for the reasons set forth below.

The act of state doctrine is an exception to the general rule that a court of the United States, where appropriate jurisdictional standards are met, will decide cases before it by choosing the rules appropriate for decision from among various sources of law, including international law.

Justice Harlan, writing for the majority in *Sabbatino,* noted that the act of state doctrine has "constitutional underpinnings." These constitutional underpinnings, according to Justice Harlan, arise out of a recognition of the separation of powers doctrine and the fact that the executive branch is usually best equipped to deal with matters of foreign policy since this area often requires "political acts." Moreover, action by the judiciary while the executive branch is simultaneously acting upon the same matter could potentially be embarrassing or detrimental to those executive efforts.

However, after *Sabbatino,* the Court began to limit the breadth of the act of state doctrine and ruled that United States courts could be the proper forum for the adjudication of expropriation claims in certain circumstances. In *First National City Bank v. Banco Nacional de Cuba, (Citibank)* the Court ruled that expropriation claims may be heard as set-offs in some circumstances. A plurality of the Court in *Citibank* recognized the "*Bernstein* exception" as a basis for a court to exercise jurisdiction over the acts of a foreign sovereign committed within that sovereign's borders. The *Bernstein* exception consists of a letter from the United States Department of State advising a court that foreign relations considerations do not necessitate an application of the act of state doctrine.

A further narrowing of the act of state doctrine was the result in *Alfred Dunhill of London, Inc. v. Cuba.* The court held in *Dunhill* that immunity from the United States judiciary through the act of state doctrine was granted to foreign sovereigns for acts within their borders. However, in order for there to be act of state immunity, the act in question must be public and not commercial in nature. Justice White, writing for four of the justices, analogized the act of state doctrine with sovereign immunity and reasoned that the act of state doctrine, like sovereign immunity, should not immunize foreign sovereigns when they have acted in a commercial capacity.[3]

It is against this background of Supreme Court decisions that appellant Kal–Spice, as well as the United States Departments of State, Treasury, Justice, and the American Bar Association, as amici curiae, request that this Court recognize a "treaty exception" to the act of state doctrine. According to appellant and amici, the following language in *Sabbatino* provides the basis for a treaty exception:

> [T]he Judicial Branch will not examine the validity of a taking of property within its own territory by a foreign sovereign government, extant and recognized by this country at the time of suit, *in the absence of a treaty or other unambiguous agreement regarding controlling legal principles,* even if the complaint alleges that the taking violates customary international law (emphasis added).

This language and the existence of a treaty between the United States and Ethiopia asserts appellant and amici, requires a "treaty" exception to the rule that a United States court will not exercise jurisdiction over a foreign sovereign for an act done by that sovereign within its borders. The treaty in existence between the United States and Ethiopia is the 1953 Treaty of Amity and Economic Relations (Treaty of Amity). Article VIII, paragraph two of that treaty provides:

> Property of nationals and companies of either High Contracting Party, including interests in property, shall receive the most constant protection and security within the territories of the other High contracting party. *Such property shall not be taken except for a public purpose, nor shall it be taken without prompt payment of just and effective compensation* (emphasis added).

We do not agree with the district court's decision that the provision of the treaty requiring payment of prompt, just and effective compensation fails to provide a controlling legal standard. To the contrary, we find that this is a controlling legal standard in the area of international law. As the appellant and amici correctly point out, the term "prompt, just and effective compensation" and similar terms are found in many treaties where the United States and other nations are parties.

---

3. The decision in *Dunhill* that commercial acts of a sovereign would not be entitled to immunity under the act of state doctrine is known as the "commercial act exception". However, that exception, like the *Bernstein* exception, was recognized by only a plurality of the Court. Only Chief Justice Burger and Justices Powell and Rehnquist joined in Justice White's opinion creating the exception. Thus, this exception also seems to be of doubtful precedential value.

The 1953 United States–Ethiopia Treaty of Amity and Economic Relations is one of a series of treaties, also known as the FCN Treaties, between the United States and foreign nations negotiated after World War II. As the legislative history of these treaties indicates, they were adopted to protect American citizens and their interests abroad. Almost all of these treaties contain sections which provide for "prompt, adequate, and effective compensation", "just compensation", or similar language regarding compensation for expropriated property.

The United States District Court for the District of Columbia used a treaty to find a "treaty exception" in *American International Group, Inc. v. Islamic Republic of Iran*. There, several American insurance companies held investments in insurance companies doing business in Iran. After the Iranian revolution of 1979 the Iranian government nationalized the insurance industry, and did not compensate the American companies for their investments which had been expropriated. The American insurance companies subsequently brought suit seeking damages for the property that had been expropriated without compensation.

There is a striking similarity between the treaty in the present case and the one involved in *American International*. Both treaties contain similar provisions for compensation when property is expropriated by one of the nations that is a party to the treaty. Consequently, *American International* provides authoritative guidance to us on the use of the treaty exception, and illustrates the error of the district court's decision that the treaty in this case was too ambiguous to allow a court to exercise jurisdiction.

Banco Nacional de Cuba v. Chase Manhattan Bank, provides an example of the utility of the "prompt, just and effective compensation" standard that is employed in many treaties. In *Chase Manhattan Bank*, the Second Circuit was faced with the task of determining the value of Cuban branches of Chase Manhattan which had been expropriated by the Cuban revolutionary government. After examining several theories regarding the appropriate standard for the compensation of expropriated property, the court concluded Chase Manhattan Bank was entitled to the net asset value of the branches that were expropriated by the Cuban government.

Moreover, the Supreme Court's decision in *Sabbatino,* in addition to the *American International* and *Chase Manhattan Bank* decisions requires a reversal of the district court decision that the 1953 Treaty of Amity was too ambiguous to be susceptible to judicial interpretation. As the Supreme Court stated in *Sabbatino:*

It should be apparent that the greater the degree of codification or consensus concerning a particular area of international law, the more appropriate it is for the judiciary to render decisions regarding it, since the courts can then focus on the application of an *agreed principle* to circumstances of fact rather than on the sensitive task of establishing a principle not inconsistent with the national interest or with international justice.

Numerous treaties employ the standard of compensation used in the 1953 Treaty of Amity between Ethiopia and the United States. Undoubtedly, the widespread use of this compensation standard is evidence that it is an agreed upon principle in international law.

Nor will adjudication in this matter interfere with any efforts by the Executive branch to resolve this matter. In fact, the Executive branch has also intervened in this matter through the Departments of State, Treasury, and Justice who have filed a joint amicus brief urging that the 1953 Treaty of Amity makes the act of state doctrine inapplicable. Obviously, the Executive branch feels that an adjudication in this matter is appropriate.

Additionally, there is a great national interest to be served in this case, i.e., the recognition and execution of treaties that we enter into with foreign nations. Article VI of the Constitution provides that treaties made under the authority of the United States shall be the supreme law of the land. Accordingly, the Supreme Court has recognized that treaties, in certain circumstances, have the "force and effect of a legislative enactment." The failure of this court to recognize a properly executed treaty would indeed be an egregious error because of the position that treaties occupy in our body of laws.

Our decision that the 1953 Treaty of Amity makes the act of state doctrine inapplicable only begins this controversy. The district court must determine what rights, if any, the treaty confers upon Kal–Spice. We recognize that further proceedings will be an arduous task for all parties involved. However, proper briefing of this issue before the court should lead to the resolution of this dispute.

Accordingly, the decision of the district court dismissing [Kal–Spice] appellant's counterclaim is reversed and remanded for further proceedings not inconsistent with this opinion.

(The so-called *Sabbatino* or Second Hickenlooper Amendment)

22 U.S.C.A. § 2370(e)(2)

Notwithstanding any other provision of law, no court in the United States shall decline on the ground of the federal act of state doctrine to make a determination on the merits giving effect to the principles of international law in a case in which a claim of title or other right to property is asserted by any party including a foreign state (or a party claiming through such state) based upon (or traced through) a confiscation or other taking after January 1, 1959, by an act of that state in violation of the principles of international law, including the principles of compensation and the other standards set out in this subsection: Provided, That this subparagraph shall not be applicable (1) in any case in which an act of a foreign state is not contrary to international law or with respect to a claim of title or other right to property acquired pursuant to an irrevocable letter of credit of not more than 180 days duration issued in good faith prior to the time of the confiscation or other taking, or (2) in any case with respect to which the President determines that application of the act of state doctrine is required in that particular case by the foreign policy interests of the United States and a suggestion to this effect is filed on his behalf in that case with the court.

Comment on Expropriation Exception

Courts have split on whether the expropriated property, or property exchanged for it, must have found its way to the United States, or been within the United States at the time the action was commenced, for the *Sabbatino* or Second Hickenlooper amendment to apply. *See Banco Nacional de Cuba v. First Nat'l City Bank*, 431 F.2d 394 (2d Cir.1970), *rev'd on other grounds*, 406 U.S. 759, 92 S.Ct. 1808, 32 L.Ed.2d 466 (1972) (Amendment applies only where property comes within territorial jurisdiction of U.S.); *Hunt v. Coastal States Gas Producing Co.*, 583 S.W.2d 322 (Tex.), *cert. denied*, 444 U.S. 992, 100 S.Ct. 523, 62 L.Ed.2d 421 (1979) (same); *West v. Multibanco Comermex, S.A.*, 807 F.2d 820 (9th Cir.), *cert. denied*, 482 U.S. 906, 107 S.Ct. 2483, 96 L.Ed.2d 375 (1987) (Amendment permits court to consider claim of illegal expropriation occurring in Mexico); *Ramirez de Arellano v. Weinberger*, 745 F.2d 1500, 1541, n. 180 (D.C.Cir.1984) (rejecting dissent's suggestion that the word "property" in the Hickenlooper Amendment means invariably property located in the United States), *rev'd on other grounds*, 471 U.S. 1113, 105 S.Ct. 2353, 86 L.Ed.2d 255 (1985).

The Restatement § 444, cmt. e, analyzed the state of the law as of its 1987 date of publication as follows:

> The exception to the act of state doctrine embodied in the Second Hickenlooper Amendment has been held to be limited to actions asserting title to property before the court. Thus, if the plaintiff claims ownership of a vessel that has been taken by a foreign state and the vessel is at a port in the United States, the plaintiff may rely on the Amendment in asserting title before a court in the United States. A bill of lading of comparable document of title, and in some cases property in processed form (e.g., timber from a forest), may meet the requirements of the Amendment, but money said to represent proceeds from the sale of the property probably would not.... If the property in the United States is not related directly to the taking on which the claim is based, or if there is no property in the United States ..., the act of state doctrine may apply but the Amendment does not. In order for the [Second] Hickenlooper Amendment to apply, the plaintiff must allege and prove that the property that is the subject of the claim is in the United States or was there at the time that action was commenced. There is no requirement that the specific property remain before the court throughout the action. It is not necessary (and indeed it may sometimes not be possible ...) to attach the property or reduce it to possession, and it is apparently not necessary that the property remain within the United States throughout the pendency of the action.

The discretionary nature of the act of state doctrine should be noted. Put differently, a court presumably may still decline to apply the act of state doctrine in an expropriation case, even if the *Sabbatino*/Second Hickenlooper Amendment does not apply; e.g., the property at issue is not located in the U.S. Also, another exception may apply to the taking, such as where a *Bernstein* Letter is obtained or an arbitration provision exists.

Questions and Comments

1. Does the act of state doctrine bar the claims of TexOil Co. (TOCO) against Venezuela and Venezuela Oil Co. (VOCO) from going forward?

2. Is a foreign government act at issue in the Problem? *Clayco Petroleum, supra,* 712 F.2d at 408 ("[g]ranting a concession to exploit natural resources [e.g., oil] entails an exercise of powers peculiar to a sovereign"). Where did the act at issue occur? Is there a controlling principle of international law or treaty? *See Sabbatino, supra,* 84 S.Ct. at 940 ("the Judicial Branch will not examine the validity of a taking of property within its own territory by a foreign sovereign government, extant and recognized by this country at the time of suit, in the absence of a treaty or other unambiguous agreement regarding controlling legal principles. . . .").

3. Is there an exception to the act of state doctrine available? Would the expropriation exception to the act of state doctrine, as codified in the *Sabbatino*/Second Hickenlooper Amendment, apply? Is there property or property exchanged for that property in the U.S.? Would the subsequent operation of the facilities be a purely commercial matter or would the lawsuit, in effect, question the validity of the taking? *See Kirkpatrick,* 110 S.Ct. at 409–410 (act of state doctrine applies where validity of a foreign sovereign act is at issue).

4. While a party cannot waive applicability of the act of state doctrine, might the written waiver of sovereign immunity contained in the 1994 TOCO–Venezuela Agreement influence the court as to whether the act of state doctrine should apply? Is it significant that the 1994 Agreement was terminated prior to the taking? *See* Restatement, § 443, Comment e:

> . . . insofar as the act of state doctrine is designed to reflect respect for foreign states, indications of consent to adjudication by the courts of another state are highly relevant, though they are not conclusive, since the doctrine also reflects judicial deference to the Executive Branch of the United States and the courts' sense of their lack of competence. When a state has expressly subjected certain kinds of obligations to adjudication in the courts of another state, or to international arbitration, it may be said to have acknowledged that its acts with respect to those obligations take place in the international arena and are subject to international scrutiny; in such cases the justification for applying the act of state doctrine is significantly weaker.

5. Assume that a treaty of friendship, commerce and navigation (commonly known as an FCN treaty) exists between the U.S. and Venezuela. The treaty provides:

Property of nationals and companies of either Party shall not be expropriated within the territories of the other Party except for public purposes and reasons of social utility as defined by law, nor shall it be expropriated without prompt and just compensation. Such compensation shall be in an effectively realizable form and shall represent the full equivalent of the property taken; and adequate provision shall have been made at or prior to the time of the expropriation for determining and effecting such compensation.

How might the provisions of the FCN treaty affect the court's ruling as to whether the act of state doctrine should apply? *See Kalamazoo Spice.*

A longer extract of the following case, *Filartiga v. Pena–Irala*, has also been considered in Problem 4.2, to introduce students to the Alien Tort Claims Act and subject matter jurisdiction.

FILARTIGA v. PENA–IRALA

United States Court of Appeals, Second Circuit, 1980.
630 F.2d 876.

IRVING R. KAUFMAN, CIRCUIT JUDGE:

The appellants, plaintiffs below, are citizens of the Republic of Paraguay. Dr. Joel Filartiga, a physician, describes himself as a long-standing opponent of the government of President Alfredo Stroessner, which has held power in Paraguay since 1954. His daughter, Dolly Filartiga, arrived in the United States in 1978 under a visitor's visa, and has since applied for permanent political asylum. The Filartigas brought this action in the Eastern District of New York against Americo Norber-to Pena–Irala (Pena), also a citizen of Paraguay, for wrongfully causing the death of Dr. Filartiga's seventeen-year old son, Joelito.

The appellants contend that on March 29, 1976, Joelito Filartiga was kidnapped and tortured to death by Pena, who was then Inspector General of Police in Asuncion, Paraguay.

The Filartigas claim that Joelito was tortured and killed in retaliation for his father's political activities and beliefs.

Pena argues that "(i)f the conduct complained of is alleged to be the act of the Paraguayan government, the suit is barred by the Act of State doctrine." This argument was not advanced below, and is therefore not before us on this appeal. We note in passing, however, that we doubt whether action by a state official in violation of the Constitution and laws of the Republic of Paraguay, and wholly unratified by that nation's government, could properly be characterized as an act of state. Paraguay's renunciation of torture as a legitimate instrument of state policy, however, does not strip the tort of its character as an international law violation, if it in fact occurred under color of government authority. See Declaration on the Protection of All Persons from Being Subjected to Torture.

In the twentieth century the international community has come to recognize the common danger posed by the flagrant disregard of basic human rights and particularly the right to be free of torture. Spurred first by the Great War, and then the Second, civilized nations have banded together to prescribe acceptable norms of international behavior. From the ashes of the Second World War arose the United Nations Organization, amid hopes that an era of peace and cooperation had at last begun. Though many of these aspirations have remained elusive goals, that circumstance cannot diminish the true progress that has been made. In the modern age, humanitarian and practical considerations have combined to lead the nations of the world to recognize that respect for fundamental human rights is in their individual and collective interest. Among the rights universally proclaimed by all nations, as we have noted, is the right to be free of physical torture. Indeed, for purposes of civil liability, the torturer has become like the pirate and slave trader before him *hostis humani generis*, an enemy of all mankind. Our holding today, giving effect to a jurisdictional provision enacted by our First Congress, is a small but important step in the fulfillment of the ageless dream to free all people from brutal violence.

FILARTIGA v. PENA–IRALA

On Remand to the United States District Court,
Eastern District of New York, 1984.
577 F.Supp. 860.

NICKERSON, DISTRICT JUDGE:

Plaintiffs, Dolly M.E. and Dr. Joel Filartiga, citizens of Paraguay, brought this action against defendant Pena, also a Paraguayan citizen, and the former Inspector General of Police of Asuncion. They alleged that Pena tortured and murdered Joelito Filartiga, the seventeen year old brother and son, respectively, of plaintiffs, in retaliation for Dr. Filartiga's opposition to President Alfredo Stroessner's government.

The first [matter] is whether the court should abstain in deference to the so-called act of state doctrine. *See Banco Nacional de Cuba v. Sabbatino*. Were the government of Paraguay concerned that a judgment by the court as to the propriety of Pena's conduct would so offend that government as to affect adversely its relations with the United States, presumably Paraguay would have had the means so to advise the court.

In any event, the Court of Appeals held that the alleged acts constitute, by the "general assent of civilized nations," a "clear and unambiguous" violation of the law of nations. As the Supreme Court noted in discussing the act of state doctrine in the *Sabbatino* decision, "the greater the degree of codification or consensus concerning a particular area of international law, the more appropriate it is for the judiciary to render decisions regarding it." Where the principle of international law is as clear and universal as the Court of Appeals has found it to be, there is no reason to suppose that this court's assumption of jurisdiction would give justifiable offense to Paraguay.

Moreover, as the Court of Appeals noted, Paraguay has not ratified Pena's acts, and this alone is sufficient to show that they were not acts of state.

Judgment may be entered for plaintiff Dolly M.E. Filartiga in the amount of $5,175,000 and for plaintiff Joel Filartiga in the amount of $5,210,364, a total judgment of $10,385,364. So ordered.

LIU v. REPUBLIC OF CHINA

United States Court of Appeals, Ninth Circuit, 1989.
892 F.2d 1419.

BOOCHEVER, CIRCUIT JUDGE:

Two gunmen acting on orders of Admiral Wong Hsi-ling (Wong), Director of the Defense Intelligence Bureau (DIB) of the Republic of China (ROC), shot and killed Henry Liu in Daly City, California. Helen Liu (Liu), his widow, appeals the district court's dismissal of her complaint for damages against the ROC. Liu asserted claims against the ROC and various individuals for wrongful death. The district court held that the act of state doctrine precluded Liu from piercing the findings of the ROC tribunals.

We reverse and remand.

The act of state doctrine is not a jurisdictional limit on courts, but rather is "a prudential doctrine designed to avoid judicial action in sensitive areas". The doctrine has "constitutional underpinnings" related to separation of powers concerns and judicial recognition of "the primary role of the President and Congress in [the] resolution of political conflict and the adoption of foreign policy."

The burden of proving acts of state rests on the party asserting the applicability of the doctrine. At a minimum, this burden requires that a party offer some evidence that the government acted in its sovereign capacity and some indication of the depth and nature of the government's interest.

First, we address whether Liu's suit against the ROC for damages for the assassination of her husband is barred by the doctrine. Although the ROC did not raise this argument, we are concerned with the potential for embarrassing the Executive Branch, and raise the issue *sua sponte.*

In *Letelier,* 488 F.Supp. at 673–74, Chile argued that even if its officials ordered the assassination of Letelier, those acts would be immune from review under this doctrine because they occurred within Chile, although the assassination occurred in the United States. The court rejected this argument because:

> To hold otherwise would totally emasculate the purpose and effectiveness of the Foreign Sovereign Immunities Act by permitting a foreign state to reimpose the so recently supplanted framework of sovereign immunity as defined prior to the Act " 'through the back door, under the guise of the act of state doctrine.' "

In *OPEC,* [649 F.2d at 1359–60] this court held that the OPEC nations' price fixing activities, although not entitled to sovereign immunity under the FSIA, were acts of state. We held that the FSIA did not supersede the act of state doctrine because the doctrine addressed different concerns than the doctrine of sovereign immunity. "While the FSIA ignores the underlying purpose of a state's action, the act of state doctrine does not." Consequently, the mere fact that the FSIA confers jurisdiction on this court to hear this type of case does not end our inquiry. We must still determine whether the act of state doctrine mandates abstention in cases alleging that a foreign government ordered the assassination of an American citizen in the United States. We conclude that it does not.

One factor we must consider is whether the foreign state was acting in the public interest. "When the state *qua state* acts in the public interest, its sovereignty is asserted. The courts must proceed cautiously to avoid an affront to that sovereignty." Thus, any injunctive relief "instructing a foreign sovereign to alter its chosen means of allocating and profiting from its own valuable natural resources" would affront the sovereignty of a state. Ordinarily, this type of concern will be generated only when courts are asked to judge the legality or propriety of public acts committed within a foreign state's own borders. In this case, however, we are asked to judge the legality and propriety of an act that occurred within the borders of the United States. Such an inquiry would hardly affront the sovereignty of a foreign nation.

Another factor to be considered is the degree of international consensus regarding an activity. *Filartiga v. Pena–Irala* (E.D.N.Y.1984) (act of state doctrine did not bar court from hearing a wrongful death suit based on a police captain's alleged torture and murder of a person in Paraguay because there was general international consensus condemning the use of torture). There is also international consensus condemning murder. *See* Organization of American States Convention on Terrorism, October 8, 1976 ("The contracting states undertake to ... prevent and punish acts of terrorism, especially kidnapping, murder, and other assaults"); Convention on the Prevention and Punishment of Crimes Against Internationally Protected Persons, Including Diplomatic Agents, Dec. 28, 1973 (article 2 establishes as a crime "[t]he intentional commission of: (a) a murder, kidnapping or other attack upon the person or liberty of an internationally protected person").

Last, this is not the sort of case that is likely to hinder the Executive Branch in its formulation of foreign policy, or result in differing pronouncements on the same subject. Rather, this court would more likely embarrass the Executive Branch if we summarily invoked the act of state doctrine to bar an American citizen from litigating a wrongful death suit for a murder that occurred in the United States. "The decision to deny access to judicial relief is not one we make lightly." *OPEC,* 649 F.2d at 1360. We conclude that none of the factors present in *OPEC* that warranted the invocation of the act of state doctrine is present in this type of case.

The ROC argues, however, that the judicial proceedings in Taiwan are acts of state. Both parties agree that judgments of a court can be acts of state.

A judgment of a court may be an act of state. Usually it is not, because it involves the interests of private litigants or because court adjudication is not the usual way in which the state exercises its jurisdiction to give effect to its public interests.

* * * We need not decide whether the ROC courts' decisions were acts of state because we do not challenge those decisions.

To the credit of the ROC, rather than attempting to hide the sordid circumstances involved in Liu's assassination, it made an investigation and publicly brought to trial individuals involved, even including one in such a high position as Wong. Our decision merely applies California law to the facts as ascertained by the ROC courts. While the result may involve the financial responsibility of the ROC, it does not affront its sovereignty and can cause no more embarrassment than the exposures already made by the ROC courts. Under these circumstances the act of state doctrine is not a bar to Liu's suit.

We hold that the act of state doctrine does not automatically bar a suit against a foreign nation when it is alleged that the nation ordered the assassination of an American citizen within the United States. We reverse the district court's decision dismissing the ROC as a party defendant.

REVERSED and REMANDED.

Questions and Comments

1. Does the act of state doctrine bar the TOCO Plaintiffs' claims against defendants from going forward in this Problem?

2. Would a court find acts of torture to be governmental acts for purposes of the act of state doctrine? What if such acts violated a foreign nation's own internal laws? *See Filartiga v. Pena–Irala* ("we doubt whether action by a state official in violation of the Constitution and laws of the Republic of Paraguay, and wholly unratified by that nation's government, could properly be characterized as an act of state"); *Kadic v. Karadzic*, 70 F.3d 232, 250 (2d Cir.1995) ("[t]he act of state doctrine, under which courts generally refrain from judging the acts of a foreign state within its territory ... might be implicated in some cases arising under [28 U.S.C.A. § 1350 (Alien Tort Statute)]. However, ... we doubt that the acts of even a state official, taken in violation of a nation's fundamental law and wholly unratified by that nation's government, could properly be characterized as an act of state").

3. Because of numerous human rights agreements, might the treaty or controlling principles of law exceptions to the act of state doctrine apply? *See Filartiga v. Pena–Irala*, 577 F.Supp. 860 (E.D.N.Y. 1984) *on remand* (refusing to apply act of state doctrine on basis that "where the principle of international law is as clear and universal as the Court of Appeals has found it to be, there is no reason to suppose that this court's assumption of jurisdiction would give justifiable offense to Paraguay").

4. In *Filartiga*, 630 F.2d at 890, the Second Circuit, stated:

Indeed, for purposes of civil liability, the torturer has become like the pirate and slave trader before him *hostis humani generis*, an enemy of all mankind. Our holding today, giving effect to a jurisdictional provision enacted by our First Congress, is a small but important step in the fulfillment of the ageless dream to free all people from brutal violence.

5.   From the perspective of fostering human rights and the rule of law is it incongruous for a court to decline application of the act of state doctrine for acts of official torture where the foreign nation condemns the act and does not assert sovereign immunity, as in *Filartiga* or *Liu*, but for another court to find the claims barred by foreign state immunity where such defense is asserted, as in *Saudi Arabia v. Nelson*? In *Saudi Arabia v. Nelson*, 507 U.S. 349, 113 S.Ct. 1471, 123 L.Ed.2d 47 (1993), the Supreme Court ruled that the FSIA barred Plaintiff Scott Nelson's claims that he had been tortured and imprisoned by the government of Saudi Arabia for his whistle blowing activities while an employee of a Saudi Arabian hospital. The court found that the employment and treatment by Saudi Arabia of its employee, Nelson, was not commercial in nature, notwithstanding the assertion of amicus Human Rights Watch that the Saudi government "often uses detention and torture to resolve commercial disputes." *Filartiga*, *Marcos* and *Karadzic*, in which plaintiffs' human rights claims were allowed to proceed, each involved defendants who were former government officials or no longer in power of a U.S.-recognized state. These persons, therefore, could not assert foreign state immunity under the FSIA. Would not judicial scrutiny of official acts of torture by CURRENT governments be more likely to deter such conduct? Should *Saudi Arabia v. Nelson* have been decided favorably to Plaintiff Nelson on the basis of a waiver (FSIA § 1605(a)(1)), express or implied in international law or human rights treaties, rather than unfavorably based on the commercial activity exception (§ 1605(a)(2))? Should Congress act in this regard, such as by expanding the torture exception of § 1605(a)(7) to include any nation, not just those classified by the State Department as terrorist-sponsor states?

6.   What if a TOCO employee had been murdered, instead of tortured? Would the act of state doctrine bar suit by the estate/next of kin from going forward? *See Liu*.

7.   The U.S. Federal Arbitration Act makes the act of state doctrine inapplicable to arbitration agreements/awards. Under the Federal Arbitration Act:

> Enforcement of arbitral agreements, confirmation of arbitral awards, and execution upon judgments based on orders confirming such awards shall not be refused on the basis of the act of state doctrine. (9 U.S.C.A. § 15).

*

Part Six

MEDIATION AND
ARBITRATION

Chapter 10

THE NATURE OF MEDIATION AND ARBITRATION

INTRODUCTION 10.0 DEFINITIONS OF MEDIATION AND ARBITRATION, ARBITRATION vs. LITIGATION, AND ARBITRATION RULES

Mediation and arbitration are each forms of alternative dispute resolution "ADR";[1] i.e., alternative to court litigation. ADR has gained widespread use because of the perceived excessive cost, delay and unpredictability of litigation in national courts. ADR is also chosen for numerous other reasons, such as where a party wants to avoid litigation in an alien forum whose laws and procedures are unfamiliar or where arbitration is more culturally acceptable than litigation, such as in Far Eastern nations. ADR is frequently selected in international commerce as it provides parties in separate nations a neutral forum for the resolution of disputes.

Definition of Mediation. Mediation is generally understood as the process of utilizing a neutral third party to help parties to a dispute resolve by agreement their differences. Mediation is usually informal. The mediator generally has no authority, absent agreement by the parties to the contrary, to find facts or enter any binding ruling. Mediators will often act as a facilitator to help each party understand the other's position. Mediators may offer, when requested, a candid evaluation of the relative strengths or weaknesses of a party's position or settlement offer.

The mediation process greatly reflects the temperaments of the mediator and parties. Some mediators tend to push the parties towards agreement and suggest settlement terms. Such a mediator can be most persuasive when discussing the long, difficult and expensive litigation or arbitration process which may await a recalcitrant party! Other media-

---

1. Other common forms of alternative dispute resolution include conciliation, fact-finding, and the so-called "wise person" approach. Under these ADR forms, disputes or certain disputed issues are generally submitted to a neutral party for a non-binding recommendation.

tors see their role as facilitating communication and understanding between the parties. Regardless, the success of mediation hinges on whether the parties have confidence in the integrity and ability of the mediator. The selection of mediator, or method by which he or she is chosen, is therefore crucial. In a complex dispute or one involving many parties it may be helpful to have more than one mediator. The parties customarily share equally the mediator's fees.

Despite its non-binding nature, mediation can be a most effective and efficient means of dispute resolution. Counsel preparing a contract should therefore consider including a well-crafted mediation provision. Many contracts require mediation prior to a party's commencing arbitration or litigation.

Definition of Arbitration. "Arbitration" has been defined as "submission of controversies, by agreement of the parties thereto, to persons chosen by themselves for determination. . . ."[2] The Supreme Court has observed that an "agreement to arbitrate before a specified tribunal is, in effect, a specialized kind of forum selection clause that posits not only the situs of the suit but also the procedure to be used in resolving the dispute."[3]

Arbitration generally occurs pursuant to an agreement of the parties,[4] most commonly in a contract for the purchase or goods and services; or less commonly, at the time a dispute among the parties arises. Arbitration differs radically from litigation, in that the parties have nearly unlimited discretion to structure all aspects of the process. Parties, by agreement, may select the issues to be submitted; the location and arbitrator(s); the substantive law and procedural and evidentiary rules to apply; and the forms and means of enforcing the award. Indeed, the parties can select nearly everything about the dispute to be arbitrated but the result!

Unfortunately, the parties to an arbitration clause often do not take the time to properly consider in advance the full range of issues implicated. In court litigation, the court supplies, among other things, a forum, judge, jury, court reporter, clerks, rules of procedure/timelines, the substantive law, and rules of evidence. In arbitration, all these must be addressed by agreement, as more fully discussed below.

Types of Arbitration. Arbitration may be either binding or non-binding. Arbitration is also often categorized by the nature of the parties to a dispute. Categories of arbitration include: private commercial arbitration, i.e., private parties to a commercial dispute[5]; investor-state

---

2. 6 C.J.S. Arbitration § 1 (1975).

3. Scherk v. Alberto–Culver Co., 417 U.S. 506, 519, 94 S.Ct. 2449, 2457, 41 L.Ed.2d 270 (1974).

4. The clause in a contract by which parties agree to submit to arbitration is known as the "compromis" clause.

5. These arbitrations are generally pursuant to a contract clause between purchasers of goods or services and the provider of same.

disputes[6]; and disputes between governments.[7]

Another significant characteristic of arbitration, which arises primarily in the private commercial dispute context, is whether the arbitration will be "institutional" or "ad hoc."[8] Institutional arbitrations are those conducted by any number of private organizations, known as "tribunals", which exist for such purpose. These organizations generally have their own arbitrators, rules of procedure (which the parties may vary by agreement), fee schedules, etc. Prominent arbitral tribunals include, among many others, the American Arbitration Association, NY, NY ("AAA")[9]; International Chamber of Commerce, Paris ("ICC")[10]; International Centre for the Settlement of Investment Disputes, The Washington Convention ("ICSID"); the London Centre for International Arbitration ("LCIA"); the Stockholm Chamber of Commerce (popular for Russia and former Soviet state matters); the Singapore International Arbitration Center; and the Hong Kong International Arbitration Center.

It is expensive to have one of these organizations administer an arbitration. The AAA Rules set forth the filing and other fees; which fees increase based upon the dollar amount in controversy. Unlike litigation, where the parties are generally not required to pay for the judge, clerks, and courtroom, the parties to institutional arbitration must pay an administration fee and for the arbitrator's time (often at $250 or more per hour per arbitrator). However, the expense is often offset by the administration and rules of the tribunal benefits.

"Ad hoc" arbitrations are those not formally administered by a private organization, such as the AAA and others listed above. The Rules of an established tribunal, such as the AAA, may be selected to guide an ad hoc proceeding. These arbitrations may involve any nature or complexity of subject matter, despite the "ad hoc" title.

Arbitration Versus Litigation. It is said that most golf games are won or lost on the first tee, as players negotiate how many strokes to give to or receive from their opponents. Similarly, disputes are easily won or lost based upon the provisions of the arbitration clause or litigation forum selection clause, often drafted long before the dispute arose. The litiga-

---

6. These arbitrations may arise concerning a private provider of goods or services and a foreign government or by a treaty framework, such as the North American Free Trade Agreement ("NAFTA"). NAFTA, Chapter 11 (providing that any investment dispute between a NAFTA state and a citizen of another NAFTA state may be brought before an International Centre for Settlement of Investment Disputes ("ICSID") tribunal, even absent an arbitration agreement among the parties to such dispute) reprinted in 32 I.L.M. 289, 605 (1993) (signatories: Canada, Mexico, United States).

7. These arbitrations generally occur through international treaty, such as the Treaty establishing the Iran–U.S. Claims Tribunal.

8. Latin, "to this", i.e., for purposes of the dispute at hand.

9. Information on the AAA and its Rules are on the AAA website, www.adr. org. It should be noted that there are different AAA Rules for different types of disputes; e.g., commercial, employment, international, etc.

10. Information on the ICC and its Rules are on the ICC website www.iccwbo. org.

tion forum selection clause requires little verbiage and essentially states the substantive law to apply (U.S., a U.S. state, or other nation's law) and court to hear the dispute (e.g., all disputes to be brought exclusively in U.S. District Court for the Eastern District of North Carolina). Particular risk, however, applies to the arbitration clause. While parties drafting an arbitration clause start with a blank page and are free to include any provisions they wish (i.e., flexibility or tailor-made dispute resolution), often key terms are omitted (choice of law, procedural rules, interim measures, discovery, location, language). Also, concepts which seemed reasonable may prove unworkable in practice. For example, the dispute may involve only $25,000.00 but the arbitration clause provides for each side to pick an arbitrator and the two so chosen to select a neutral third arbitrator, resulting in huge arbitration fees, as each of the three arbitrators charges $300.00 or other substantial hourly rate to attend hearings, read briefs and draft the award.

Once the dispute has arisen, the parties are unlikely to agree on much, including any changes to the arbitration clause. Therefore, it is important that counsel drafting the arbitration clause carefully consider many issues, well in advance of any dispute. Specific drafting issues are discussed below:

ADVANTAGES AND DISADVANTAGES OF ARBITRATION AND LITIGATION

ADVANTAGES TO ARBITRATION

Whatever advantages or disadvantages there may be to arbitration, in international disputes, there are often two overriding considerations which make arbitration preferable:

1. Enforceability. The New York Convention on Recognition and Enforcement of Foreign Arbitral Awards makes arbitration awards enforceable in the approximately 138 nations, parties to the Treaty. Where the opposing party or its assets are located in a foreign country, arbitration is often a must. A U.S. court judgment, particularly a civil jury award in a commercial case, would be enforceable in almost no other country.

2. Neutral Forum. Neither party wants the dispute to be in a foreign court with unfamiliar judges, laws and procedures.

3. Flexibility. Parties may include such procedural rules and timetables as they wish

4. Confidentiality. Arbitration involves no public filings, occurs in a private location and Parties may, by agreement or tribunal rules, make proceedings and the award confidential

5. Finality. The arbitral award, correct or not, will generally be enforced and there is no right to appeal

ADVANTAGES TO U.S. COURT LITIGATION

1. Discovery—The broad scope of discovery under Rule 26, Fed. R. Civ. P. (access to all information reasonably calculated to the lead to the discovery of admissible evidence) and multiple procedures (depositions, interrogatories, requests for production of documents, written interrogatories, requests for admission, inspection of property and things) grant access to the other parties' documents and key facts. In arbitration, the arbitrator may determine the scope of discovery (if any) and there may be no procedure or opportunity to see the other side's documents or question its witnesses or experts prior to hearing. Foreign parties and arbitrators are less likely to engage in discovery than their U.S. counterparts.

2. Jury—There is no jury and the arbitrator(s) decide all matters.

3. Appeal–Court decisions are appealable. There is no right to appeal from an arbitral award and the award will not be set aside, even for most errors of fact or law. In many cases, the arbitrator is not bound by law and may rule in his or her unfettered discretion. Only in very limited circumstances, such as fraud or collusion by the tribunal or violation of fundamental public policy, would an award not be enforced. In many instances, a "reasoned award" stating the rationale of the decision is not required, so the parties may never know the basis of the decision.

4. Cost—In the U.S., taxes pay for the judges, courthouses, clerks, court reporters, translators and other infrastructure and services of the Court System. Despite much recent criticism, the U.S. has excellent, impartial and efficient federal and state court systems. Arbitration is private dispute resolution and all costs are paid by the parties, including the arbitrators, conference rooms or other locations for the hearing, translators, and filing and administrative fees of the tribunal.

Arbitration Rules. The Rules of the established arbitral tribunals cover the arbitration process from start to finish. The rules, however leave much discretion to the arbitrator(s) as to the actual conduct of the proceedings. *See, e.g.*, AAA International Arbitration Rules ("AAA Rules"), Art. 16 ("Subject to these rules, the tribunal may conduct the arbitration in whatever manner it considers appropriate ..."). Counsel should examine the specific rules to be applied before preparing or agreeing to an arbitration clause.

It should be noted that the rules of the major arbitral tribunals may vary in significant respects. *See* AAA Rules, Art. 28(5) ("Unless the parties agree otherwise, the parties expressly waive and forego any right to punitive, exemplary or similar damages...."). *Compare* Rules of Arbitration of the International Chamber of Commerce ("ICC Rules"),

Art. 20(1) (tribunal to establish facts of case); *with* AAA Rules, Art. 19(1) (burden on parties to establish facts relied upon).

What do the AAA Rules, ICC Rules and Arbitration Rules of the United Nations Commission on International Trade Law (UNCITRAL Arbitration Rules) provide with respect to:

Selection and number of arbitrators

Consensus or majority decision-making

Impartiality of arbitrators

Law applicable

Discovery/production of documents and witnesses

Admissibility and weight given to evidence

Interim measures (injunction, seizure or sequestration of property, etc.)

Tribunal administration and arbitrators fees

Form of award (written, reasoned, etc.)

Time limits/length of proceeding (*See* ICC Rules, Art. 24 (six month time limit to final award))?

PROBLEM 10.1   MEDIATION AND ARBITRATION PLANNING: NORTH CAROLINA CEMENT MANUFACTURER ENTERS CONTRACT WITH INDONESIAN CEMENT SUPPLIER

SECTION I.   THE SETTING

Big Block Cement, Inc. (Big Block), headquartered in Dunn, North Carolina, is a regional manufacturer and distributor of cement blocks and other cement products. Big Block, looking to decrease its raw material cost, has entered into negotiations with D.S. Cement, TbK, (DSC) of Jakarta, Indonesia, a large-scale manufacturer of cement in powdered form (i.e., cement mix). The parties desire to enter into a Sales and Purchase Contract for DSC to supply a minimum quantity of Portland type cement of certain specifications to Big Block for a period of years.

The cement would be delivered periodically in 2000 lbs. super-bags by ocean-going vessels to the North Carolina State Ports facility in Wilmington, North Carolina (N.C. Port) under a free out agreement; i.e., cargo delivered and out of the vessel at no cost to buyer. The purchase price would cover the cost of cement and its bagging, loading, stowage, shipment, and unloading/stevedoring at the N.C. Port, and related insurance, fees and expenses. Vessel Charter and these items would, therefore, be the responsibility of DSC.

Payment by Big Block would be by Letter of Credit, contingent upon satisfactory independent test of cement quality and confirmation of quantity by vessel survey at N.C. Port. Ten percent retainage would be withheld by Big Block.

The super-bagged cement would be unloaded from the vessel by crane (ship's gear or Port crane) onto Big Block trucks for delivery into a warehouse leased by Big Block at the N.C. Port. Big Block would extract the cement periodically from the warehouse, as needed by its manufacturing plants.

The parties have had no prior dealings. Associate General Counsel for DSC has proposed the following dispute resolution procedures. Review and comment upon the procedures. You may be counsel for Big Block or General Counsel of DSC:

> **Mediation.** In the event a dispute arises which the parties are unable to settle amicably, the parties agree to submit the dispute, as a precondition to the filing or commencement of any litigation or arbitration proceeding, to mediation as provided in the Commercial Mediation Rules of the American Arbitration Association (AAA) in effect at that time. Request for mediation shall be filed in writing with the other party and the AAA. The parties shall share the mediator's fee and any filing or administrative fees equally. The mediation shall be held in Los Angeles, California. Any agreement reached in mediation shall be enforceable as settlement agreements in any court having jurisdiction thereof.

> **Arbitration.** Any claim arising out of or related to this Contract shall be subject to arbitration. Prior to arbitration, the parties shall endeavor to resolve disputes by mediation as above provided. Claims shall be arbitrated in accordance with the International Arbitration Rules of the AAA, then in effect. Demand for arbitration shall be filed in writing with the other party and the AAA. No person or entity not a party hereto may be joined in any arbitration proceeding. Any award rendered by the arbitrator(s) shall be enforceable as a judgment by any court of competent jurisdiction.

SECTION II. FOCUS OF CONSIDERATION

Prudent counsel should consider, in advance of drafting dispute resolution procedures, the types of disputes which may arise under a given contract. The inquiry then becomes: would the procedures proposed facilitate efficient AND effective (i.e., enforceable) dispute resolution of the problems most likely to arise? The goal is generally cost-effective closure for the parties; NOT to generate complex, involved proceedings for counsel and dispute resolution centers. To this end avoid form language! Always tailor the dispute resolution provisions of any contract. The parties are most likely to pull the contract out and dust it off after a dispute has arisen. Dispute resolution is therefore among the most important contract terms.

SECTION III. READINGS, QUESTIONS AND COMMENTS

Three threshold issues include: (1) cost; (2) timing; and (3) whether the arbitration agreement and any award would be enforceable in a given jurisdiction. Arbitration may be equally or more expensive than litigation since the expenses, including the fees of the arbitrators, are borne by the parties. The parties may also be required to pay fees regarding the arbitral tribunal itself, if a tribunal is selected. Other potential costs of arbitration include travel to and from the selected forum site and room rental.

Moreover, whether an award rendered in a particular forum would be enforceable against the parties must be carefully considered. It would be undesirable for a party to undertake the effort and expense of arbitration and then realize that the award obtained is unenforceable against another party in that party's home jurisdiction.

International conventions exist which generally provide for widespread national enforcement of arbitral awards. These include the United Nations Convention on the Recognition and Enforcement of Foreign Arbitral Awards ("New York Convention") *(Done* June 10, 1958, 7 I.L.M. *1046, implemented at 9* U.S.C. §§ 201–208, *entered into force for the U.S.,* Dec. 29,1970, *21 U.S.T. 2517, T.I.A.S.* No. 6997, 330 U.N.T.S. 3); European Convention on International Commercial Arbitration (Apr. 21, 1961, 484 U.N.T.S. 364); Agreement Relating to the Application of the European Convention on International Commercial Arbitration (Dec. 17, 1962, 523 U.N.T.S. 94); Convention on the Settlement of Investment Disputes Between States and Nationals of Other States Establishing the International Centre for the Settlement of Investment Disputes ("ICSID") (1965,17 U.S.T. 1270, 575 U.N.T.S. 159); Inter–American Convention on International Commercial Arbitration *(Done* Jan. 30, 1975, *104* Stat. 449, 42 O.A.S.T.S. *1, reprinted in 14* I.L.M. 336, *implemented at 9* U.S.C.A. §§ 301–307); and North American Free Trade Agreement ("NAFTA") (Dec. 17, 1992, *entered into force Jan.* 1, 1994, *reprinted in* 32 I.L.M. 289,605 (1993) (signatories: Canada, Mexico, United States)).

However, national requirements for enforcement of awards must be investigated. The United States, for instance, requires that for enforcement of an agreement to arbitrate or of an award under the New York Convention, the corresponding jurisdiction must be a Convention member which enforces U.S. awards reciprocally. Many, but not all, nations are parties to the New York Convention. A list of signatory nations may be found following 9 U.S.C.A. § 201 (West Supp. 2002).

Consent to Arbitration should be carefully considered in advance. Such planning requires a great deal of foresight and implicates a broad range of issues. A partial listing of such issues is:

PARTIES— Know who the parties are, where they and their assets are located, who the principals are of business entity and organization parties, and identify all such parties clearly and by their full and exact names in the applicable contract or arbitration agreement.

Specify whether the arbitration clause shall apply to subsidiaries, parent entities, affiliates or third-parties.

THE DISPUTE—Transaction—What is the nature of the transaction? What issues/disputes may arise? Specify the nature and scope of issues which should be submitted to the arbitration. Will the arbitrator or court determine whether the dispute or a specific claim is within the scope of the arbitration? Consider a provision specifying whether the arbitrator or court is to determine issues of arbitrability, such as "Any issue of arbitrability shall be determined by the arbitrator appointed pursuant hereto."

METHODS OF DISPUTE RESOLUTION—Weigh the options—litigation in a specified forum, arbitration, mediation, fact-finding, etc. If litigation is chosen, a forum selection clause may be inserted in a contract naming the jurisdiction and court to which any dispute shall be submitted; e.g., "any dispute between the parties arising under or concerning the contract shall be submitted exclusively to the U.S. District Court of the Eastern District of North Carolina, Wilmington, NC, and the parties waive any defense or objection to such venue." Counsel should note that selection of federal court may occur only where federal court jurisdiction is proper, as such jurisdiction cannot be created by contract. Common bases of federal jurisdiction include admiralty claims (28 U.S.C.A. § 1333) or diversity of citizenship and amount in controversy exceeds $75,000.00 (28 U.S.C.A. § 1332).

INSTITUTION—Avoid "boilerplate" style and vague clauses; they may create more problems than they solve.

How many arbitrators will be used? One? Three? Are three really necessary (often not)? How will the arbitrator(s) be selected? Specify whether the arbitrators will be neutral or non-neutral. It is permitted practice in arbitration to use non-neutral arbitrators, particularly where each party picks an arbitrator and the arbitrators select a third.

Do not use imprecise names or identify obsolete institutions. Specify the institution, if an institution is desired. Select institutions with established track records, such as the American Arbitration Association, the International Chamber of Commerce, or the London Court of International Arbitration. Avoid selecting organizations located in a parties' home country or whose arbitrators must be chosen from a list of local persons in such country. For instance, the Japan Commercial Arbitration Association is known for strict application of rules and procedures which may appear complex and inefficient to western legal practitioners, for rules resulting in the appointment of Japanese arbitrators, and for lengthy proceedings. See Charles R. Ragan, "Arbitration in Japan: Caveat Drafter and Other Lessons from an American Perspective on Trans–Pacific Dispute Resolution," Private Investments Abroad, at 12–1 (Matthew Bender & Co., Inc. 1996).

Consider not selecting an arbitral institution in order to avoid expensive filing, administrative and arbitrator fees. A sample phrase may read: "While the Rules may generally be applied to the conduct of the proceedings, the arbitral tribunal shall not administer the proceedings, which shall be conducted as a private, ad hoc dispute resolution among the parties."

RULES— What substantive Law will govern the dispute? What procedures will apply? What rules will govern the conduct and timelines of the proceedings?

Discovery—May the parties engage in discovery? Where is the evidence located? Who has it? What means will be necessary to obtain it?

Subpoena—May the tribunal subpoena witnesses or documents from third parties?

Evidence—What if any evidentiary rules will apply?

Address the scope and availability of provisional remedies from the tribunal and national courts, such as injunctions and orders attaching assets to preserve them.

Specify the applicable rules with precision. Established tribunals such as the AAA and ICC have specialized sets of arbitration rules for different disputes: international, maritime, commercial, employment, etc. Simply naming "the AAA (or ICC) Rules" may be insufficient. Go online and compare the Rules; select the Rules best suited to the transaction or dispute at issue. Make an affirmative selection of the rules to be applied to avoid the application of rules by default as provided under certain international agreements and institutional rules *See, e.g.,* Inter–American Convention, Art. 3 (applying rules of procedure of Inter–American Commercial Arbitration Commission in absence of contrary express agreement of parties); Japan–American Trade Arbitration Agreement of Sept. 16,1952 (requiring that rules of Japan Commercial Arbitration Assoc. apply to any arbitration conducted in Japan pursuant to such Agreement); AAA International Rules, Art. 1 (applying AAA rules in absence of express agreement).

Address the issue of confidentiality of the proceedings, of records, of evidence, and other related issues.

LOGISTICS— Where will the arbitration occur? What language will be used? Choice of language may be highly important, not just for the strategic necessity of understanding the proceedings but because translation costs in a complex proceeding may be enormous. See Charles R. Ragan, "Arbitration in Japan: Caveat Drafter and Other Lessons from an American Perspective on Trans–Pacific Dispute Resolution," Private Investments Abroad, at 12–20 (Matthew Bender & Co., Inc. 1996) (revealing translation costs of about $100,000 in single Japanese commercial arbitration).

THE AWARD— Form and Enforcement of Award—Will there be a written award? Will the award contain findings of fact or conclusions of law or just a monetary amount? *How* will it be enforced? In a national court? Do the parties waive any appeal or contest to the award?

Address the issue of costs, interest and attorneys' fees in the award. Can the tribunal award the prevailing party its attorneys' fees and expenses? Does that include arbitrator's fees? How is the prevailing party determined? By the tribunal?

Determine the scope of damages awardable. May the tribunal award special, consequential or punitive damages? May contract performance be specifically enforced or is a party limited to money damages?

Consider including an explicit waiver of immunity from jurisdiction attachment and execution if one party is a sovereign.

Questions and Comments

1. As the mediation contemplated in this Problem would be non-binding, is it necessary that the parties use the American Arbitration Association and pay the related fees and expenses? Use of a tribunal such as the AAA may delay the mediation while the tribunal processes the notice of dispute and appoints a mediator. Consider whether informal, *ad hoc* mediation may be appropriate. Consider imposing a thirty or sixty days deadline to mediate.

2. In this Problem, the parties would likely select a mediator from the AAA list of mediators. Should the parties agree in advance to one or more neutrals to mediate the dispute? Should or must Mediators and Arbitrators be lawyers? In our problem, might a marine surveyor trusted by the parties or another person in the cement business provide valuable experience if selected as a mediator? Provide for alternative mediators to avoid scheduling delays.

3. Why agree to mediate in Los Angeles? Counsel for Big Block would seek mediation and arbitration in Wilmington, N.C., or other convenient location. Why? Often parties to an international contract agree to mediate or arbitrate outside the state at issue in a major city on the seacoast closest to where the work is performed, such as Washington, D.C., New York or San Francisco.

4. Could the provision to make the mediation result binding and court-enforceable chill the parties' dialogue at mediation and ability come up with inventive solutions?

5. What modifications to the mediation provisions in this Problem might you propose?

6. What types of disputes may arise? The commercial disputes will arise from either 1) payment or 2) performance. Here, payment would be automatic under the letter of credit arrangement. However, non-payment of retainage by Big Block may be an issue. More likely the disputes in this Problem would arise from DSC's poor performance. The most likely problems would appear to be poor quality (though the letter of credit arrangement should protect somewhat) or the breakage of superbags from poor quality bags, mishandling or improper type of vessel (i.e., one with sharp protrusions in the hold or which cannot be easily unloaded). The stevedores at N.C. Port may have expensive claims for overtime and extra equipment rental to re-bag the cement and clean the cargo hold. Also delays in loading or discharging the vessel could result in expensive claims for delaying the vessel's departure (demurrage claims) and extra port fees. Is arbitration

desirable to resolve efficiently the disputes which may arise where multiple parties are involved?

7.   Who would be the parties to the dispute? Courts have rules and judicial precedent as to the circumstances in which third-parties to a contract may be joined in the proceedings. Arbitration is a matter of private contract and generally lacks such authority. The arbitration agreement must, therefore, address joinder or non-joinder of third parties. One must also consider the joinder of third parties as an important issue in determining whether arbitration is preferable to court litigation.

8.   As with many maritime or transportation contracts, a number of parties may be involved in a dispute between DSC and Big Block. For instance, if the bags are ruptured or spilled, Big Block may have claims against DSC, the shipping line, the stevedores in Thailand and/or at N.C. Port. The arbitration clause should address the fact that Big Block is only in privity of contract with DSC. As DSC is responsible for contracting and paying for the stevedoring and shipping services under the free out contract, perhaps DSC's contract with Big Block should require all DSC's contracts to contain a compromise clause by all parties that they may be joined in the DSC–Big Block arbitration. Would a vessel owner, shipping line or stevedore be reluctant to sign such a provision? Conversely, would Big Block like to be a named party to arbitrations between DSC and the parties with whom it contracts? What if DSC, as is likely, inadvertently breaches the joinder provision by failing to include the compromise clause in all its third party contracts?

9.   What costs, benefits and disadvantages might arise from the naming of the AAA to administer the proceedings?

10.   Is the arbitration clause clear as to the number of arbitrators? Would one, two or three be preferable in this Problem? How are the arbitrators to be selected? By whom are they to be compensated?

11.   Can the parties seek injunctive or attachment help from a court (provisional remedies) prior to the arbitration panel being appointed? Why might that be important?

12.   Does the proposed arbitration provision in this Problem address the planning issues identified in the above reading? As an example of an arbitration clause contained in an international commercial agreement, consider the following language:

> Any dispute arising between or among the parties concerning the entry, validity, meaning, enforcement, effect or the performance of this Agreement which cannot be resolved by amicable discussion, shall be submitted exclusively to binding arbitration to occur in the city of Raleigh, North Carolina, using the English language. There shall be a single arbitrator agreeable to the parties. Failing agreement, the arbitrator shall be appointed by the arbitral tribunal from its list of arbitrators. The arbitrator shall have the following qualifications: an attorney duly licensed to practice law in North Carolina or the United States and possess at least fifteen (15) years commercial law experience. The arbitration shall be conducted by the American Arbitration Association, applying its rules applicable to

international commercial disputes (AAA International Dispute Resolution Procedures, amended and effective July 1, 2003). The substantive law to be applied shall be that of the State of North
Carolina, excepting conflicts of laws provisions. The arbitrator may
award any relief, including preliminary and injunctive relief ("Interim Measures"), which a Court sitting in the same jurisdiction could
award, and no other relief. The arbitral award and any Interim
Measures may be entered and enforced by any Court of competent
jurisdiction. No party shall contest Court enforcement of an award
on any grounds not expressly recognized under the United Nations
Convention on the Recognition and Enforcement of Foreign Arbitral
Awards done June 10, 1958, commonly known as the New York
Convention. Should a party be unsuccessful in any Court contest to
enforcement of an arbitral award, the unsuccessful party shall pay
interest on the award for the period of delay caused by the Court
proceedings at the rate of ten (10%) percent per month or the
highest rate allowed by law and shall pay the attorneys' fees, costs
and expenses of the prevailing party. Any question of arbitrability
shall be determined by the arbitrator. In the event of a conflict
between the English and foreign language versions of this Agreement, the English version shall govern.

13. Would the proposed arbitration provision facilitate both efficient
and enforceable dispute resolution?

14. What changes might you suggest to the arbitration provision in
this Problem? Would mediation followed by litigation be a preferable alternative to arbitration in this Problem? Would DSC prefer a state or federal
court forum?

PROBLEM 10.2 COMMENCEMENT OF ARBITRATION PURSUANT TO ARBITRATION CLAUSE IN COMMERCIAL AGREEMENT: TAMPA SPANISH LANGUAGE TELEVISION STATION CONTRACTS WITH MEXICO CITY HOSPITAL TO MAKE A PROMOTIONAL TAPE AND DISCOVERS INCOMPETENT PRACTICES IN HOSPITAL; AGREEMENT TO ARBITRATE COVERS CLAIMS OF DEFAMATION

SECTION I. THE SETTING

Television España International, Inc. (TEI) is a Spanish language
television station, headquartered and broadcasting in the Tampa, Florida
metropolitan area. TEI's marketing department has for several years
run a most successful advertising campaign for local hospitals. The ads,
by focusing on the excellent patient care and bi-lingual programs of the
hospitals, including video-taped testimonials of patients and hospital

employees, make the hospitals more appealing to the Spanish-speaking population.

Hospital Central de México, S.A. (HCM), is the owner/operator of five hospitals in Mexico City. Wishing to market itself successfully, HCM entered into a contract with TEI for TEI to prepare five ads for HCM to air on local Mexico City television stations. By the contract, TEI is to be paid a non-refundable, $50,000.00 fee for expenses to visit HCM's facilities in Mexico City, familiarize itself with HCM's programs, and prepare preliminary testimonials and ad concepts for discussion with HCM. The parties are to then discuss the cost and scope of services going forward to finalize the ad campaign.

TEI discovered at each HCM hospital grossly inadequate patient care. There were few physicians, nurses or assistants. Many patients had bed sores, were unattended, and had soiled sheets. Some patients lay on mattresses with no sheets. TEI filmed the wide-spread patient neglect and showed its film to HCM. HCM thereupon terminated TEI, whose employees returned to Tampa. A copy of the film made its way through an unknown source to a Mexico City television station. The station aired the film and its own investigative report supporting the findings of TEI.

HCM thereafter sued TEI in the U.S. District Court for the Middle District of Florida, Tampa Division, for return of the $50,000.00 fee paid to TEI under a breach of contract theory and for the tort of defamation, claiming that HCM's business suffered $10,000,000.00 (U.S.) in damages following the airing of TEI's film.

The TEI–HCM contract contains the following provisions:

Section 8.06. Dispute Resolution. Any dispute arising in connection with this Agreement not resolved through negotiation of the Parties hereto shall be finally resolved in the manner set forth in this Section 8.06 Any Party may notify the other Party of such a dispute by delivery of a written notice (a "Dispute Notice") to the other Party. Upon the giving or receipt of a Dispute Notice, any disagreement regarding the interpretation or the operation of this Agreement shall be determined by final and binding arbitration under the International Arbitration Rules of the American Arbitration Association ("AAA"). This provision shall govern all claims between the Parties, whether sounding in or arising under contract, tort (including but not limited to negligence, fraud, defamation, malicious prosecution or abuse of process), strict liability, statute, code, government order or otherwise. The arbitration shall be conducted in Washington, D.C. in the English language. The arbitration shall be before a single arbitrator agreeable to the Parties and, failing agreement, the arbitrator shall be appointed by the Washington, D.C. courts, upon motion of a party, without the need of showing the refusal of a party to arbitrate. Any issue of arbitrability shall be determined by the arbitrator appointed pursuant hereto. Each Party shall bear its own costs and expenses in preparing for and participating in the arbitration hearing, except that the Parties shall each pay one-half of the compensation payable to the arbitrator and one-half of any other administrative costs related to the hearing proceedings. The arbitration award shall be final and binding on the Parties, and judgment on the award may be entered in any court having jurisdiction. It is explicitly agreed by each of the Parties hereto that no such arbitration shall be commenced except in conformity with this Section 8.06. The arbitration award shall name the prevailing Party and the prevailing Party, as determined by the arbitrator, shall be entitled to recover, in addition to any other relief, an amount equal to all reasonable costs and expenses actually incurred in connection with the dispute, including reasonable attorneys' and experts' fees. This Section 8.06 shall survive any termination of this Agreement. The arbitrator may not grant any relief or award which a court sitting in the same jurisdiction could not grant.

Section 8.07. Interpretation. This Agreement shall be governed by and interpreted according to the Laws of the State of Florida, United States of America, excluding conflict of laws principles.

You are outside counsel for TEI. What do you advise concerning the following issues?

SECTION II.   FOCUS OF CONSIDERATION

Before considering the merits of a dispute, counsel should determine: 1) the forum for the dispute; 2) the law applicable; and 3) the relevant procedures. This is particularly true in international cases. Where there is a contract, the contract may contain dispute resolution provisions addressing these issues. Questions include whether the dispute will be litigated or arbitrated? In what jurisdiction? What law will apply? What procedures will govern?

If the contract provides for arbitration, counsel should examine what international agreements may apply. These provisions may govern the types of claims arbitrable, enforcing an agreement to arbitrate, and enforcing an arbitral award. The United Nations Convention on the Recognition and Enforcement of Foreign Arbitral Awards of June 10, 1958, ("New York Convention"), has been executed by many states. Regional treaties concerning arbitration may also exist, such as the Inter–American Convention on International Commercial Arbitration, to which the U.S., Mexico and other Organization of American States members are Parties. Bi-lateral arbitration agreements also exist between some states. These treaties generally provide for the recognition and enforcement of commercial agreements to arbitrate and arbitral awards by national courts.

Counsel for TEI should first consider the dispute resolution provisions in the contract. Next, counsel should consider the international agreements applicable to arbitration between the parties.

Essential to this Problem are the New York Convention, Arts. I & II, Inter–American Convention on International Commercial Arbitration,

Arts. 1, 2, and 3, and 9 U.S.C.A. §§ 201, 202, 203, 204, 205, 206, and 301–303. These materials are included in the Documents Supplement.

SECTION III. READINGS, QUESTIONS AND COMMENTS

Examine sections 8.06 and 8.07 of the TEI–HCM contract.

What do they provide as to forum, procedure and law for dispute resolution? Does the arbitration clause govern the specific claims of HCM (contract and defamation)? May HCM pursue the defamation/tort claim in U.S. court?

What are the requirements for the New York Convention to apply to an arbitration agreement? Is the New York Convention applicable to the TEI–HCM dispute? Why is the New York Convention applicable only to commercial disputes? *See* Convention, Art. I(3); U.S. Reservations, note 29. What policy underlies this?

MITSUBISHI MOTORS CORP. v. SOLER CHRYSLER–PLYMOUTH, INC.

Supreme Court of the United States, 1985.
473 U.S. 614, 105 S.Ct. 3346, 87 L.Ed.2d 444.

JUSTICE BLACKMUN delivered the opinion of the Court.

The principal question presented by these cases is the arbitrability, pursuant to the Federal Arbitration Act, and the Convention on the Recognition and Enforcement of Foreign Arbitral Awards (Convention), of claims arising under the Sherman Act, 15 U.S.C. § 1 et seq., and encompassed within a valid arbitration clause in an agreement embodying an international commercial transaction.

Petitioner-cross-respondent Mitsubishi Motors Corporation (Mitsubishi) is a Japanese corporation which manufactures automobiles and has its principal place of business in Tokyo, Japan. Respondent-cross-petitioner Soler Chrysler–Plymouth, Inc. (Soler), is a Puerto Rico corporation with its principal place of business in Pueblo Viejo, Guaynabo, Puerto Rico.

On October 31, 1979, Soler entered into a Distributor Agreement which provided for the sale by Soler of Mitsubishi-manufactured vehicles within a designated area, including metropolitan San Juan. On the same date, Soler and Mitsubishi entered into a Sales Procedure Agreement (Sales Agreement) which, referring to the Distributor Agreement, provided for the direct sale of Mitsubishi products to Soler and governed the terms and conditions of such sales. Paragraph VI of the Sales Agreement, labeled "Arbitration of Certain Matters," provides:

> "All disputes, controversies or differences which may arise between [Mitsubishi] and [Soler] out of or in relation to Articles I–B through V of this Agreement or for the breach thereof, shall be finally settled by arbitration in Japan in accordance with the rules and regulations of the Japan Commercial Arbitration Association."

Initially, Soler did a brisk business in Mitsubishi-manufactured vehicles. As a result of its strong performance, its minimum sales volume, specified by Mitsubishi, and agreed to by Soler, for the 1981 model year was substantially increased. In early 1981, however, the new-car market slackened. Soler ran into serious difficulties in meeting the expected sales volume, and by the spring of 1981 it felt itself compelled to request that Mitsubishi delay or cancel shipment of several orders. About the same time, Soler attempted to arrange for the transshipment of a quantity of its vehicles for sale in the continental United States and Latin America. Mitsubishi, however, refused permission for any such diversion, citing a variety of reasons, and no vehicles were transshipped. Attempts to work out these difficulties failed. Mitsubishi eventually withheld shipment of 966 vehicles, apparently representing orders placed for May, June, and July 1981 production, responsibility for which Soler disclaimed in February 1982.

The following month, Mitsubishi brought an action against Soler in the United States District Court for the District of Puerto Rico under the Federal Arbitration Act and the Convention. Mitsubishi sought an order to compel arbitration in accord with the Sales Agreement. Shortly after filing the complaint, Mitsubishi filed a request for arbitration before the Japan Commercial Arbitration Association.

Soler denied the allegations and counterclaimed against Mitsubishi. It alleged numerous breaches by Mitsubishi of the Sales Agreement, raised a pair of defamation claims, and asserted causes of action under the Sherman Act, ... In the counterclaim premised on the Sherman Act, Soler alleged that Mitsubishi and [Chrysler International, S.A.] had conspired to divide markets in restraint of trade.

After a hearing, the District Court ordered Mitsubishi and Soler to arbitrate each of the issues raised in the complaint and in all the counterclaims save two and a portion of a third. With regard to the federal antitrust issues, it recognized that the Courts of Appeals, following *American Safety Equipment Corp. v. J.P. Maguire & Co.,* 391 F.2d 821 (CA2 1968), uniformly had held that the rights conferred by the antitrust laws were " 'of a character inappropriate for enforcement by arbitration.' " The District Court held, however, that the international character of the Mitsubishi–Soler undertaking required enforcement of the agreement to arbitrate even as to the antitrust claims. It relied on *Scherk v. Alberto–Culver Co.,* 417 U.S. 506, 515–520, 94 S.Ct. 2449, 2455–2458, 41 L.Ed.2d 270 (1974), in which this Court ordered arbitration, pursuant to a provision embodied in an international agreement, of a claim arising under the Securities Exchange Act of 1934 notwithstanding its assumption, *arguendo*, that *Wilko [v. Swan,* 346 U.S. 427, 74 S.Ct. 182, 98 L.Ed.2d 168 (1953)], which held nonarbitrable claims arising under the Securities Act of 1933, also would bar arbitration of a 1934 Act claim arising in a domestic context.

The United States Court of Appeals for the First Circuit affirmed in part and reversed in part. It ... rejected Soler's suggestion that it could not have intended to arbitrate statutory claims not mentioned in the arbitration agreement. Assessing arbitrability "on an allegation-by-allegation basis," the court then read the arbitration clause to encompass virtually all the claims arising under the various statutes, including all those arising under the Sherman Act.

Finally, after endorsing the doctrine of *American Safety*, precluding arbitration of antitrust claims, the Court of Appeals concluded that neither this Court's decision in *Scherk* nor the Convention required abandonment of that doctrine in the face of an international transaction. Accordingly, it reversed the judgment of the District Court insofar as it had ordered submission of "Soler's antitrust claims" to arbitration.

* * *

Accordingly, the first task of a court asked to compel arbitration of a dispute is to determine whether the parties agreed to arbitrate that dispute. The court is to make this determination by applying the "federal substantive law of arbitrability, applicable to any arbitration agreement within the coverage of the Act." And that body of law counsels

"that questions of arbitrability must be addressed with a healthy regard for the federal policy favoring arbitration.... The Arbitration Act establishes that, as a matter of federal law, any doubts concerning the scope of arbitrable issues should be resolved in favor of arbitration, whether the problem at hand is the construction of the contract language itself or an allegation of waiver, delay, or a like defense to arbitrability." *Moses H. Cone Memorial Hospital,* 460 U.S., at 24–25, 103 S.Ct., at 941–942.

Thus, as with any other contract, the parties' intentions control, but those intentions are generously construed as to issues of arbitrability.

There is no reason to depart from these guidelines where a party bound by an arbitration agreement raises claims founded on statutory rights. Some time ago this Court expressed "hope for [the Act's] usefulness both in controversies based on statutes or on standards otherwise created," *Wilko v. Swan,* 346 U.S. 427, 432, 74 S.Ct. 182, 185, 98 L.Ed.168 (1953) (footnote omitted); and we are well past the time when judicial suspicion of the desirability of arbitration and of the competence of arbitral tribunals inhibited the development of arbitration as an alternative means of dispute resolution. Of course, courts should remain attuned to well-supported claims that the agreement to arbitrate resulted from the sort of fraud or overwhelming economic power that would provide grounds "for the revocation of any contract." 9 U.S.C. § 2. But, absent such compelling considerations, the Act itself provides no basis for disfavoring agreements to arbitrate statutory claims by skewing the otherwise hospitable inquiry into arbitrability.

That is not to say that all controversies implicating statutory rights are suitable for arbitration. There is no reason to distort the process of contract interpretation, however, in order to ferret out the inappropriate. Just as it is the congressional policy manifested in the Federal Arbitration Act that requires courts liberally to construe the scope of arbitration agreements covered by that Act, it is the congressional intention expressed in some other statute on which the courts must rely to identify any category of claims as to which agreements to arbitrate will be held unenforceable. For that reason, Soler's concern for statutorily protected classes provides no reason to color the lens through which the arbitration clause is read. By agreeing to arbitrate a statutory claim, a party does not forgo the substantive rights afforded by the statute; it only submits to their resolution in an arbitral, rather than a judicial, forum. It trades the procedures and opportunity for review of the courtroom for the simplicity, informality, and expedition of arbitration. We must assume that if Congress intended the substantive protection afforded by a given statute to include protection against waiver of the right to a judicial forum, that intention will be deducible from text or legislative history. Having made the bargain to arbitrate, the party should be held to it unless Congress itself has evinced an intention to preclude a waiver of judicial remedies for the statutory rights at issue. Nothing, in the meantime, prevents a party from excluding statutory claims from the scope of an agreement to arbitrate.

In sum, the Court of Appeals correctly conducted a two-step inquiry, first determining whether the parties' agreement to arbitrate reached the statutory issues, and then, upon finding it did, considering whether legal constraints external to the parties' agreement foreclosed the arbitration of those claims. We endorse its rejection of Soler's proposed rule of arbitration-clause construction.

III

We now turn to consider whether Soler's antitrust claims are nonarbitrable even though it has agreed to arbitrate them. In holding that they are not, the Court of Appeals followed the decision of the Second Circuit in *American Safety Equipment Corp. v. J.P. Maguire & Co.*, 391 F.2d 821 (1968). Notwithstanding the absence of any explicit support for such an exception in either the Sherman Act or the Federal Arbitration Act, the Second Circuit there reasoned that "the pervasive public interest in enforcement of the antitrust laws, and the nature of the claims that arise in such cases, combine to make ... antitrust claims ... inappropriate for arbitration." We find it unnecessary to assess the legitimacy of the American Safety doctrine as applied to agreements to arbitrate arising from domestic transactions. As in *Scherk v. Alberto–Culver Co.*, 417 U.S. 506, 94 S.Ct. 2449, 41 L.Ed.2d 270 (1974), we conclude that concerns of international comity, respect for the capacities of foreign and transnational tribunals, and sensitivity to the need of the international commercial system for predictability in the resolution of disputes require that we enforce the parties' agreement, even assuming that a contrary result would be forthcoming in a domestic context.

Even before *Scherk*, this Court had recognized the utility of forum-selection clauses in international transactions. In *The Bremen, supra,* an

American oil company, seeking to evade a contractual choice of an English forum and, by implication, English law, filed a suit in admiralty in a United States District Court against the German corporation which had contracted to tow its rig to a location in the Adriatic Sea. Notwithstanding the possibility that the English court would enforce provisions in the towage contract exculpating the German party which an American court would refuse to enforce, this Court gave effect to the choice-of-forum clause. It observed:

> "The expansion of American business and industry will hardly be encouraged if, notwithstanding solemn contracts, we insist on a parochial concept that all disputes must be resolved under our laws and in our courts.... We cannot have trade and commerce in world markets and international waters exclusively on our terms, governed by our laws, and resolved in our courts." 407 U.S., at 9, 92 S.Ct., at 1912.

Recognizing that "agreeing in advance on a forum acceptable to both parties is an indispensable element in international trade, commerce, and contracting," *id.*, at 13–14, 92 S.Ct., at 1914–1916 the decision in *The Bremen* clearly eschewed a provincial solicitude for the jurisdiction of domestic forums.

Identical considerations governed the Court's decision in *Scherk*, which categorized "[a]n agreement to arbitrate before a specified tribunal [as], in effect, a specialized kind of forum-selection clause that posits not only the situs of suit but also the procedure to be used in resolving the dispute." 417 U.S., at 519, 94 S.Ct., at 2457. In *Scherk*, ... [a]lthough the contract of sale contained a clause providing for arbitration before the International Chamber of Commerce in Paris of "any controversy or claim [arising] out of this agreement or the breach thereof," Alberto–Culver subsequently brought suit against Scherk in a Federal District Court in Illinois, alleging that Scherk had violated § 10(b) of the Securities Exchange Act of 1934 by fraudulently misrepresenting the status of the trademarks as unencumbered. The District Court denied a motion to stay the proceedings before it and enjoined the parties from going forward before the arbitral tribunal in Paris. The Court of Appeals for the Seventh Circuit affirmed, relying on this Court's holding in *Wilko v. Swan*, 346 U.S. 427, 74 S.Ct. 182, 98 L.Ed. 168 (1953), that agreements to arbitrate disputes arising under the Securities Act of 1933 are nonarbitrable. This Court reversed, enforcing the arbitration agreement even while assuming for purposes of the decision that the controversy would be nonarbitrable under the holding of *Wilko* had it arisen out of a domestic transaction. Again, the Court emphasized:

> "A contractual provision specifying in advance the forum in which disputes shall be litigated and the law to be applied is ... an almost indispensable precondition to achievement of the orderliness and predictability essential to any international business transaction....

"A parochial refusal by the courts of one country to enforce an international arbitration agreement would not only frustrate these purposes, but would invite unseemly and mutually destructive jockeying by the parties to secure tactical litigation advantages.... [It would] damage the fabric of international commerce and trade, and imperil the willingness and ability of businessmen to enter into international commercial agreements." 417 U.S., at 516–517, 94 S.Ct., at 2455–2456.

Accordingly, the Court held Alberto–Culver to its bargain, sending it to the international arbitral tribunal before which it had agreed to seek its remedies.

The Bremen and *Scherk* establish a strong presumption in favor of enforcement of freely negotiated contractual choice-of-forum provisions. Here, as in *Scherk*, that presumption is reinforced by the emphatic federal policy in favor of arbitral dispute resolution. And at least since this Nation's accession in 1970 to the *Convention* and the implementation of the Convention in the same year by amendment of the Federal Arbitration Act, that federal policy applies with special force in the field of international commerce. Thus, we must weigh the concerns of *American Safety* against a strong belief in the efficacy of arbitral procedures for the resolution of international commercial disputes and an equal commitment to the enforcement of freely negotiated choice-of-forum clauses.

At the outset, we confess to some skepticism of certain aspects of the *American Safety* doctrine. As distilled by the First Circuit, the doctrine comprises four ingredients. First, private parties play a pivotal role in aiding governmental enforcement of the antitrust laws by means of the private action for treble damages. Second, "the strong possibility that contracts which generate antitrust disputes may be contracts of adhesion militates against automatic forum determination by contract." Third, antitrust issues, prone to complication, require sophisticated legal and economic analysis, and thus are "ill-adapted to strengths of the arbitral process, i.e., expedition, minimal requirements of written rationale, simplicity, resort to basic concepts of common sense and simple equity." Finally, just as "issues of war and peace are too important to be vested in the generals, ... decisions as to antitrust regulation of business are too important to be lodged in arbitrators chosen from the business community—particularly those from a foreign community that has had no experience with or exposure to our law and values." See *American Safety*, 391 F.2d, at 826–827.

Initially, we find the second concern unjustified. The mere appearance of an antitrust dispute does not alone warrant invalidation of the selected forum on the undemonstrated assumption that the arbitration clause is tainted. A party resisting arbitration of course may attack directly the validity of the agreement to arbitrate. Moreover, the party may attempt to make a showing that would warrant setting aside the forum-selection clause—that the agreement was "[a]ffected by fraud, undue influence, or overweening bargaining power"; that "enforcement would be unreasonable and unjust"; or that proceedings "in the contractual forum will be so gravely difficult and inconvenient that [the resisting party] will for all practical purposes be deprived of his day in court." The *Bremen*, 407 U.S., at 12, 15, 18, 92 S.Ct., at 1914, 1916, 1917. But absent such a showing—and none was attempted here—there is no basis for assuming the forum inadequate or its selection unfair.

Next, potential complexity should not suffice to ward off arbitration. * * * In any event, adaptability and access to expertise are hallmarks of arbitration. The anticipated subject matter of the dispute may be taken into account when the arbitrators are appointed, and arbitral rules typically provide for the participation of experts either employed by the parties or appointed by the tribunal. Moreover, it is often a judgment that streamlined proceedings and expeditious results will best serve their needs that causes parties to agree to arbitrate their disputes; it is typically a desire to keep the effort and expense required to resolve a dispute within manageable bounds that prompts them mutually to forgo access to judicial remedies. In sum, the factor of potential complexity alone does not persuade us that an arbitral tribunal could not properly handle an antitrust matter.

For similar reasons, we also reject the proposition that an arbitration panel will pose too great a danger of innate hostility to the constraints on business conduct that antitrust law imposes. International arbitrators frequently are drawn from the legal as well as the business community; where the dispute has an important legal component, the parties and the arbitral body with whose assistance they have agreed to settle their dispute can be expected to select arbitrators accordingly.[18] We decline to indulge the presumption that the parties and arbitral body conducting a proceeding will be unable or unwilling to retain competent, conscientious, and impartial arbitrators.

The Court of Appeals was concerned that international arbitrators would lack "experience with or exposure to our law and values." The obstacles confronted by the arbitration panel in this case, however, should be no greater than those confronted by any judicial or arbitral tribunal required to determine foreign law. See, e.g., Fed. Rule Civ.Proc. 44.1. Moreover, while our attachment to the antitrust laws may be stronger than most, many other countries, including Japan, have similar bodies of competition law.

We are left, then, with the core of the *American Safety* doctrine—the fundamental importance to American democratic capitalism of the regime of the antitrust laws. Without doubt, the private cause of action plays a central role in enforcing this regime. As the Court of Appeals pointed out:

---

18. We are advised by Mitsubishi and amicus International Chamber of Commerce, without contradiction by Soler, that the arbitration panel selected to hear the parties' claims here is composed of three Japanese lawyers, one a former law school dean, another a former judge, and the third a practicing attorney with American legal training who has written on Japanese antitrust law.

" 'A claim under the antitrust laws is not merely a private matter. The Sherman Act is designed to promote the national interest in a competitive economy; thus, the plaintiff asserting his rights under the Act has been likened to a private attorney-general who protects the public's interest.' " The treble-damages provision wielded by the private litigant is a chief tool in the antitrust enforcement scheme, posing a crucial deterrent to potential violators.

Having permitted the arbitration to go forward, the national courts of the United States will have the opportunity at the award-enforcement stage to ensure that the legitimate interest in the enforcement of the antitrust laws has been addressed. The Convention reserves to each signatory country the right to refuse enforcement of an award where the "recognition or enforcement of the award would be contrary to the public policy of that country." Art. V(2)(b). While the efficacy of the arbitral process requires that substantive review at the award-enforcement stage remain minimal, it would not require intrusive inquiry to ascertain that the tribunal took cognizance of the antitrust claims and actually decided them.[20]

As international trade has expanded in recent decades, so too has the use of international arbitration to resolve disputes arising in the course of that trade. The controversies that international arbitral institutions are called upon to resolve have increased in diversity as well as in complexity. Yet the potential of these tribunals for efficient disposition of legal disagreements arising from commercial relations has not yet been tested. If they are to take a central place in the international legal order, national courts will need to "shake off the old judicial hostility to arbitration," *Kulukundis Shipping Co. v. Amtorg Trading Corp.*, 126 F.2d 978, 985 (CA2 1942), and also their customary and understandable unwillingness to cede jurisdiction of a claim arising under domestic law to a foreign or transnational tribunal. To this extent, at least, it will be necessary for national courts to subordinate domestic notions of arbitrability to the international policy favoring commercial arbitration. *See Scherk*, supra.[21]

---

20. We note, for example, that the rules of the Japan Commercial Arbitration Association provide for the taking of a "summary record" of each hearing, Rule 28.1; for the stenographic recording of the proceedings where the tribunal so orders or a party requests one, Rule 28.2; and for a statement of reasons for the award unless the parties agree otherwise, Rule 36.1(4).

21. We do not quarrel with the Court of Appeals' conclusion that Art. II(1) of the Convention, which requires the recognition of agreements to arbitrate that involve "subject matter capable of settlement by arbitration," contemplates exceptions to arbitrability grounded in domestic law. * * * In *Scherk*, this Court recited Art. II(1), including the language relied upon by the

Court of Appeals, but paid heed to the Convention delegates' "frequent[ly voiced] concern that courts of signatory countries in which an agreement to arbitrate is sought to be enforced should not be permitted to decline enforcement of such agreements on the basis of parochial views of their desirability or in a manner that would diminish the mutually binding nature of the agreements." 417 U.S., at 520, n. 15, 94 S.Ct., at 2457, n. 15. There, moreover, the Court dealt, *arguendo*, with an exception to arbitrability grounded in express congressional language; here, in contrast, we face a judicially implied exception. The utility of the Convention in promoting the process of international commercial arbitration depends upon the willingness of national

Accordingly, we "require this representative of the American business community to honor its bargain," *Alberto–Culver Co. v. Scherk*, 484 F.2d 611, 620 (CA7 1973) (Stevens, J., dissenting), by holding this agreement to arbitrate "enforce[able] . . . in accord with the explicit provisions of the Arbitration Act." *Scherk*, 417 U.S., at 520, 94 S.Ct., at 2457.

The judgment of the Court of Appeals is affirmed in part and reversed in part, and the cases are remanded for further proceedings consistent with this opinion.

PRIMA PAINT CORP. v. FLOOD & CONKLIN MFG. CO.

Supreme Court of the United States, 1967.
388 U.S. 395, 87 S.Ct. 1801, 18 L.Ed.2d 1270.

Mr. Justice Fortas delivered the opinion of the Court.

This case presents the question whether the federal court or an arbitrator is to resolve a claim of "fraud in the inducement," under a contract governed by the United States Arbitration Act, where there is no evidence that the contracting parties intended to withhold that issue from arbitration.

* * *

The key statutory provisions are §§ *2, 3*, and *4* of the United States Arbitration Act of 1925. *Section 2* provides that a written provision for arbitration "in any maritime transaction or a contract evidencing a transaction involving commerce * * * shall be valid, irrevocable, and enforceable, save upon such grounds as exist at law or in equity for the revocation of any contract." *Section 3* requires a federal court in which suit has been brought 'upon any issue referable to arbitration under an agreement in writing for such arbitration' to stay the court action pending arbitration once it is satisfied that the issue is arbitrable under the agreement. *Section 4* provides a federal remedy for a party 'aggrieved by the alleged failure, neglect, or refusal of another to arbitrate under a written agreement for arbitration,' and directs the federal court to order arbitration once it is satisfied that an agreement for arbitration has been made and has not been honored.

* * *

Having determined that the contract in question is within the coverage of the Arbitration Act, we turn to the central issue in this case: whether a claim of fraud in the inducement of the entire contract is to be resolved by the federal court, or whether the matter is to be referred to

courts to let go of matters they normally would think of as their own. Doubtless, Congress may specify categories of claims it wishes to reserve for decision by our own courts without contravening this Nation's obligations under the Convention. But we decline to subvert the spirit of the United States' accession to the Convention by recognizing subject-matter exceptions where Congress has not expressly directed the courts to do so.

the arbitrators. The courts of appeals have differed in their approach to this question. * * *

With respect to cases brought in federal court involving maritime contracts or those evidencing transactions in 'commerce,' we think that Congress has provided an explicit answer. That answer is to be found in § 4 of the Act, which provides a remedy to a party seeking to compel compliance with an arbitration agreement. Under § 4, with respect to a matter within the jurisdiction of the federal courts save for the existence of an arbitration clause, the federal court is instructed to order arbitration to proceed once it is satisfied that "the making of the agreement for arbitration or the failure to comply (with the arbitration agreement) is not in issue." Accordingly, if the claim is fraud in the inducement of the arbitration clause itself—an issue which goes to the "making" of the agreement to arbitrate—the federal court may proceed to adjudicate it.[12] But the statutory language does not permit the federal court to consider claims of fraud in the inducement of the contract generally. *Section 4* does not expressly relate to situations like the present in which a stay is sought of a federal action in order that arbitration may proceed. But it is inconceivable that Congress intended the rule to differ depending upon which party to the arbitration agreement first invokes the assistance of a federal court. We hold, therefore, that in passing upon a § 3 application for a stay while the parties arbitrate, a federal court may consider only issues relating to the making and performance of the agreement to arbitrate. In so concluding, we not only honor the plain meaning of the statute but also the unmistakably clear congressional purpose that the arbitration procedure, when selected by the parties to a contract, be speedy and not subject to delay and obstruction in the courts.

In the present case no claim has been advanced by Prima Paint that F & C fraudulently induced it to enter into the agreement to arbitrate "(a)ny controversy or claim arising out of or relating to this Agreement, or the breach thereof." This contractual language is easily broad enough to encompass Prima Paint's claim that both execution and acceleration of the consulting agreement itself were procured by fraud. Indeed, no claim is made that Prima Paint ever intended that "legal" issues relating to the contract be excluded from arbitration, or that it was not entirely free so to contract. Federal courts are bound to apply rules enacted by Congress with respect to matters—here, a contract involving commerce—over which it has legislative power.

Accordingly, the decision below dismissing Prima Paint's appeal is affirmed.

MR. JUSTICE BLACK, with whom MR. JUSTICE DOUGLAS and MR. JUSTICE STEWART join, dissenting.

12. This position is consistent . . . with the statutory scheme. As the "saving clause" in s 2 indicates, the purpose of Congress in 1925 was to make arbitration agreements as enforceable as other contracts, but not more so. To immunize an arbitration agreement from judicial challenge on the ground of fraud in the inducement would be to elevate it over other forms of contract—a situation inconsistent with the "saving clause".

The Court here holds that the United States Arbitration Act, as a matter of federal substantive law, compels a party to a contract containing a written arbitration provision to carry out his "arbitration agreement" even though a court might, after a fair trial, hold the entire contract—including the arbitration agreement—void because of fraud in the inducement. The Court holds, what is to me fantastic, that the legal issue of a contract's voidness because of fraud is to be decided by persons designated to arbitrate factual controversies arising out of a valid contract between the parties. And the arbitrators who the Court holds are to adjudicate the legal validity of the contract need not even be lawyers, and in all probability will be nonlawyers, wholly unqualified to decide legal issues, and even if qualified to apply the law, not bound to do so. I am by no means sure that thus forcing a person to forgo his opportunity to try his legal issues in the courts where, unlike the situation in arbitration, he may have a jury trial and right to appeal, is not a denial of due process of law. I am satisfied, however, that Congress did not impose any such procedures in the Arbitration Act. And I am fully satisfied that a reasonable and fair reading of that Act's language and history shows that both Congress and the framers of the Act were at great pains to emphasize that nonlawyers designated to adjust and arbitrate factual controversies arising out of valid contracts would not trespass upon the courts' prerogative to decide the legal question of whether any legal contract exists upon which to base an arbitration.

BUCKEYE CHECK CASHING, INC. v. CARDEGNA

Supreme Court of the United States, 2006.
546 U.S. 440, 126 S.Ct. 1204, 163 L.Ed.2d 1038.

Borrowers brought putative class action lawsuit against lender, alleging that lender made illegal usurious loans disguised as check cashing transactions in violation of various Florida state statutes. Lender filed motion to compel arbitration pursuant to provisions for arbitration contained in its contracts with Borrowers.

Justice Scalia delivered the opinion of the Court. We decide whether a court or an arbitrator should consider the claim that a contract containing an arbitration provision is void for illegality.

* * *

Respondents John Cardegna and Donna Reuter entered into various deferred-payment transactions with petitioner Buckeye Check Cashing (Buckeye), in which they received cash in exchange for a personal check in the amount of the cash plus a finance charge. For each separate transaction they signed a "Deferred Deposit and Disclosure Agreement" (Agreement), which included the following arbitration provisions:

> "1. *Arbitration Disclosure*—By signing this Agreement, you agree that i[f] a dispute of any kind arises out of this Agreement or your application therefore or any instrument relating thereto, th[e]n either you or we or third-parties involved can choose to have that

dispute resolved by binding arbitration as set forth in Paragraph 2 below. . . .

2. *Arbitration Provisions*—Any claim, dispute, or controversy . . . arising from or relating to this Agreement . . . or the validity, enforceability, or scope of this Arbitration Provision or the entire Agreement (collectively 'Claim'), shall be resolved, upon the election of you or us or said third-parties, by binding arbitration. . . . This arbitration Agreement is made pursuant to a transaction involving interstate commerce, and shall be governed by the Federal Arbitration Act ('FAA'), 9 U.S.C. Sections 1-16. The arbitrator shall apply applicable substantive law constraint [*sic*] with the FAA and applicable statu[t]es of limitations and shall honor claims of privilege recognized by law. . . ."

To overcome judicial resistance to arbitration, Congress enacted the Federal Arbitration Act (FAA), 9 U.S.C. 1-16. Section 2 embodies the national policy favoring arbitration and places arbitration agreements on equal footing with all other contracts:

"A written provision in . . . a contract . . . to settle by arbitration a controversy thereafter arising out of such contract . . . or an agreement in writing to submit to arbitration an existing controversy arising out of such a contract . . . shall be valid, irrevocable, and enforceable, save upon such grounds as exist at law or in equity for the revocation of any contract."

Challenges to the validity of arbitration agreements "upon such grounds as exist at law or in equity for the revocation of any contract" can be divided into two types. One type challenges specifically the validity of the agreement to arbitrate. See, e.g., *Southland Corp. v. Keating,* (challenging the agreement to arbitrate as void under California law insofar as it purported to cover claims brought under the state Franchise Investment Law). The other challenges the contract as a whole, either on a ground that directly affects the entire agreement (*e.g.,* the agreement was fraudulently induced), or on the ground that the illegality of one of the contract's provisions renders the whole contract invalid. Respondents' claim is of this second type. The crux of the complaint is that the contract as a whole (including its arbitration provision) is rendered invalid by the usurious finance charge.

In *Prima Paint Corp. v. Flood & Conklin Mfg. Co.,*, we addressed the question of who-court or arbitrator-decides these two types of challenges. The issue in the case was "whether a claim of fraud in the inducement of the entire contract is to be resolved by the federal court, or whether the matter is to be referred to the arbitrators." Guided by § 4 of the FAA,[2] we held that "if the claim is fraud in the inducement of

---

2. In pertinent part, § 4 reads:
"A party aggrieved by the alleged failure, neglect, or refusal of another to arbitrate under a written agreement for arbitration may petition any United States district court [with jurisdiction] . . . for an order directing that such arbitration proceed in a manner provided for in such agreement. . . . [U]pon being satisfied that the making of the agreement for arbitration

the arbitration clause itself-an issue which goes to the making of the agreement to arbitrate-the federal court may proceed to adjudicate it. But the statutory language does not permit the federal court to consider claims of fraud in the inducement of the contract generally." We rejected the view that the question of "severability" was one of state law, so that if state law held the arbitration provision not to be severable a challenge to the contract as a whole would be decided by the court.

Subsequently, in *Southland Corp.,* we held that the FAA "create[d] a body of federal substantive law," which was "applicable in state and federal court." 465 U.S., at 12, 104 S.Ct. 852. We rejected the view that state law could bar enforcement of § 2, even in the context of state-law claims brought in state court.

Prima Paint and *Southland* answer the question presented here by establishing three propositions. First, as a matter of substantive federal arbitration law, an arbitration provision is severable from the remainder of the contract. Second, unless the challenge is to the arbitration clause itself, the issue of the contract's validity is considered by the arbitrator in the first instance. Third, this arbitration law applies in state as well as federal courts. The parties have not requested, and we do not undertake, reconsideration of those holdings. Applying them to this case, we conclude that because respondents challenge the Agreement, but not specifically its arbitration provisions, those provisions are enforceable apart from the remainder of the contract. The challenge should therefore be considered by an arbitrator, not a court.

The judgment of the Florida Supreme Court is reversed, and the case is remanded for further proceedings not inconsistent with this opinion.

It is so ordered.

JUSTICE THOMAS, dissenting.

I remain of the view that the Federal Arbitration Act (FAA), 9 U.S.C. 1 *et seq.,* does not apply to proceedings in state courts. See *Allied-Bruce Terminix Cos. v. Dobson,* (THOMAS, J., dissenting). Thus, in state-court proceedings, the FAA cannot be the basis for displacing a state law that prohibits enforcement of an arbitration clause contained in a contract that is unenforceable under state law. Accordingly, I would leave undisturbed the judgment of the Florida Supreme Court.

Questions and Comments

1. The *Mitsubishi* Court found that through the treaty mechanism of the New York Convention and implementing legislation in the U.S. Federal Arbitration Act, the liberal federal policy favoring arbitration in dispute resolution applied with special force in the field of international commerce. "Concerns of international comity, respect for the capacities of foreign and

or the failure to comply therewith is not in issue, the court shall make an order directing the parties to proceed to arbi-   tration in accordance with the terms of the agreement. . . ."

transnational tribunals, and sensitivity to the need of the international commercial system for predictability in the resolution of disputes, all require enforcement of the arbitration clause in question, even assuming that a contrary result would be forthcoming in a domestic context." Is the domestic/international distinction warranted?

2. The *Mitsubishi* Court declared a "presumption" that a dispute is arbitrable and determined there was no reason to depart from this presumption where the party bound by the arbitration agreement raised claims founded on statutory rights; the Sherman Anti-trust act in that case. Would arbitrators, particularly those without U.S. legal training, be apt or qualified to apply uniquely U.S. statutory rights, such as anti-trust, to the proceeding? Would the failure of arbitrators to apply such rights erode the goals of the anti-trust statutes? Would it be fair to foreign parties for U.S. courts to deny arbitration and assert jurisdiction over certain U.S. statutory claims, such as anti-trust or foreign corrupt practices act claims? What factors were advocated by *American Safety* concerning why a court should NOT require the arbitration of certain statutory anti-trust claims? How compelling did you find these factors to be? What difficulties can you envision concerning a foreign tribunal's treatment of U.S. statutory claims?

3. What other significant declarations were made in *Mitsubishi* regarding the role a U.S. court should take with respect to enforcing an agreement to arbitrate? In footnote 20 and accompanying text, the *Mitsubishi* Court suggested that parties might make a stenographic record of the arbitration so that a national court, at the enforcement of award stage, could consider the propriety of the award under U.S. law, such as anti-trust laws. Is not such cost, formality, and attendant delay, arising from an expensive stenographic record and subsequent court involvement and review, the very antithesis of arbitration's advantages touted by the *Mitsubishi* Court of "simplicity, informality, and expedition"? Cf. *Saxis Steamship Co. v. Multifacs Int'l Traders, Inc.*, 375 F.2d 577, 582 (2d Cir.1967) ("Extensive judicial review frustrates the basic purpose of arbitration, which is to dispose of disputes quickly and avoid the expense and delay of extended court proceedings.") What is the time period or procedure for such court review in Japan? Would the Court's logic that court review at the enforcement of award stage may cure misapplication of law by the arbitrators apply equally were the matter to come before a foreign court concerning enforcement of the arbitral award? If the arbitration agreement of the parties failed to specify any national law as applicable, would the arbitrators be required to follow the law of any particular nation, much less U.S. antitrust law? Rather, could they "arbitrate" the dispute and decide it on equitable grounds? On any other grounds, legal, factual or otherwise, which they wished to apply? Could a court properly consider the efficiency or impartiality of the forum or rules under which the arbitration is to proceed? What policy reasons underlie the Court's strong statements favoring arbitration, as opposed to litigation, as a means of resolving disputes among private parties?

4. Close examination should be given the contract provisions and circumstances surrounding execution of the contract. Is there an argument that the contract provisions do not apply? Are they void as against public policy, unsupported by adequate consideration, or otherwise unenforceable? Has the other party waived the provision, either intentionally or uninten-

tionally? For instance, a party who files a court proceeding, or participates in discovery or other aspects of a court proceeding, may be found to have waived its right to compel contractual arbitration. The court in *Hubei Provincial Garments Imp. & Exp. (Group) Corp. v. Rugged Active Wear, Inc.*, 1998 WL 474091 (S.D.N.Y. 1998) observed:

> [A] party does waive its right to compel arbitration when it engages in protracted litigation that prejudices the opposing party. Prejudice, in this context, means "the inherent unfairness–in terms of delay, expense, or damage to a party's legal position–that occurs when the party's opponent forces it to litigate an issue and later seeks to arbitrate that same issue." The expense and delay inherent in litigation does not, without more, constitute sufficient evidence of prejudice to justify a finding of waiver. On the other hand, waiver has been found where a party "engaged in extensive pre-trial discovery and forced its adversary to respond to substantive motions, delayed invoking arbitration rights by filing multiple appeals and substantive motions while an adversary incurred unnecessary delays and expenses, and engaged in discovery procedures not available in arbitration." In determining whether a party has waived its right to arbitration, the following factors should be considered: "(1) the time elapsed from the commencement of litigation to the request for arbitration, (2) the amount of litigation (including any substantive motions and discovery), and (3) proof of prejudice." *Citing PPG Industries, Inc. v. Webster Auto Parts Inc.*, 128 F.3d 103, 107–08 (2d Cir. 1997).

Parties may also choose to expressly waive the provisions and agree at the time of a dispute to a procedure or forum not provided in the contract. Once a dispute has arisen, however, agreement between the Parties may be difficult.

5.   Are either or both of arbitration and litigation an option for TEI in this problem? Could TEI obtain an order from the U.S. District Court, Tampa Division compelling HCM to arbitrate? What U.S. Code provision would permit this?

6.   Is there a more favorable means of dispute resolution or jurisdiction of which TEI may avail itself than that contained in sections 8.06 and 8.07?

7.   In *Prima Paint*, in the domestic U.S. context, the Court, construing the Federal Arbitration Act, ruled that the federal court lacked jurisdiction to adjudicate a claim of fraud in the inducement of a contract where the contract contained an arbitration clause. The Court held that such issue must be submitted to arbitration pursuant to the arbitration clause. However, if a party contended that the arbitration clause itself was procured by fraud (though not the contract as a whole), then the federal court would have jurisdiction to determine such issue. Should the ruling in *Prima Paint* apply with particular force where one of the parties to the contract is foreign? Why or why not? *See* New York Convention, Art. II(1).

8.   Does the Supreme Court's ruling in *Buckeye Check Cashing, Inc. v. Cardegna*, 546 U.S. 440, 126 S.Ct. 1204, 163 L.Ed.2d 1038 (2006) simply apply the holding in *Prima Paint* or make new law? Specifically, does *Buckeye Check Cashing* make it easier or harder for a litigant to challenge in state court the validity of an arbitration clause?

9. Assume that the U.S. District Court for the Middle District of Florida granted a Motion filed by TEI to stay the litigation filed by HCM and directed the parties to arbitrate their dispute pursuant to section 8.06 of the parties' contract. What is the next step the parties must take to commence the arbitration? Must TEI or HCM provide written notice to anyone? Must TEI make a written claim against HCM? Is HCM allowed to respond to a written claim by TEI? Are there any deadlines applicable to the dispute?

In this problem, the parties have agreed that the International Arbitration Rules of the AAA ("International Rules") govern the dispute. Therefore, reference must be had to the International Rules as to matters of procedure and timelines. The International Rules are contained in the Documents Supplement. See International Rules, Articles I, II, III and IV.

PROBLEM 10.3 CONDUCT OF THE ARBITRATION: TAMPA SPANISH TELEVISION STATION PARTICIPATES IN ARBITRATION

SECTION I. THE SETTING

Pursuant to sections 8.06 and 8.07 of the TEI–HCM Contract, set forth in Problem 10.2, TEI and HCM proceed to arbitrate their dispute pursuant to the International Commercial Rules of the AAA (contained in Documents Supplement). The parties selected a single arbitrator from the AAA list of arbitrators. TEI timely submitted its claim within thirty (30) days after commencement of the arbitration to HCM and to the tribunal administrator as provided in Article III of the International Rules. Respondent HCM timely responded within thirty (30) days with its statement of defense, including a counterclaim for its $50,000.00 deposit paid to TEI, with a copy to the tribunal administrator as provided in Article III, Section 2 of the International Rules. Shortly thereafter, the arbitrator, John Smith, sent a letter to the parties, as follows:

March 6, 2008

Television España International, Inc.
1409 North Florida Avenye
Tampa, Florida 33602

Hospital Central de México, S.A.
Blvd. Avila Camacho Manuel 28–7 Piso
Lomas de Chapultepec
1100 Mexico, D.F.

Re: TEI/HCM Arbitration Procedure

Ladies and Gentlemen:

Thank you for selecting me to arbitrate your dispute. I appreciate the confidence you placed in me and my Firm.

By way of full disclosure, I must tell you that I have represented HCM in numerous matters and continue to represent them in various commercial transactions, including purchasing of hospital equipment in the United States. As these matters are unrelated to the instant dispute, however, I am sure they will have no effect on my judgment and I am pleased to proceed as the neutral arbitrator.

I note that the contract provided for arbitration under the International Rules of the AAA, but I had a bad experience once with those rules and will not be using them. Instead, the arbitration will be conducted in fairness and equity in my sole discretion.

I believe that arbitration should be quick and efficient and therefore am not allowing the parties to conduct any discovery. Instead, we will have a one day hearing at a ski resort adjacent my condo in Vail, Colorado on March 15, 2008. I would prefer the parties not be represented by counsel as I find lawyers often confuse the matters and delay the proceeding. I will expect the President of each company to attend the arbitration hearing in person.

I will look at whatever documents the parties wish to present at the hearing. I will not hear testimony from witnesses at the hearing but will let the company Presidents tell me what they think the facts are.

Following the hearing, I will carefully consider the matters presented and provide a reasoned, written award detailing all documents, facts and legal bases upon which the arbitral award is entered. This arbitration sounds interesting and should provide good information for the book I am writing. I reserve the right to follow whatever country's laws or legal precedent I believe applicable to the dispute. Because my calendar is filled through 2008 with trials and business engagements, I expect that the written award, which will be lengthy, will issue sometime in 2009.

The rate for my services will be $1,500.00 per hour.

I will conduct no preliminary conference and will not entertain any pre-hearing motions filed by either party. I look forward to seeing you on March 15.

Sincerely yours,

John Smith

You are outside counsel for TEI. What do you advise concerning the procedural issues raised in the putative arbitrator's letter?

SECTION II.   FOCUS OF CONSIDERATION

The arbitrator's letter, although an extreme example, suggests how procedural issues in arbitration can affect the fairness of the proceeding and determine the outcome of a dispute. The issues raised suggest the need for the parties to select or draft clear procedural rules governing the conduct of the arbitration. As the parties' contract clearly applies the International Rules of the AAA, those procedures govern. The arbitral tribunal may also have standards of conduct for its arbitrators. For example, the AAA/ABA Code of Ethics for Arbitrators in Commercial

Disputes, revised March 2004, sets forth generally accepted standards of ethical conduct for commercial arbitrators, including standards relating to appointment, disclosures, and disqualification. Additional provisions relating to neutrality of the arbitrator, selection of the arbitration, and procedural rules may be set forth in the parties' arbitration clause.

Essential to an understanding of this problem are sections 8.06 and 8.07 of the TEI–HCM Contract (Problem 10.2) and the International Commercial Rules of the American Arbitration Association, found in the Documents Supplement.

SECTION III.   READINGS, QUESTIONS AND COMMENTS

THE COLLEGE OF COMMERCIAL ARBITRATORS, GUIDE TO BEST PRACTICES IN COMMERCIAL ARBITRATION, JurisNet, LLC (2006)

CHAPTER 2

APPOINTMENT, DISCLOSURES AND DISQUALIFICATION OF NEUTRAL ARBITRATORS

In addressing appointment and disclosure issues, the goals of arbitrators are (1) to comply with applicable law, institutional rules, and party agreements, and (2) to ensure that they are, and reasonably appear to be, impartial and independent.

* * *

III. DISCLOSURES

Arbitrators must make appropriate disclosures as required by applicable law, institutional rules, and ethical guidelines.

IV. DISQUALIFICATION

When requested to withdraw by all parties, arbitrators must comply; when requested by only one party, arbitrators should refer to the arbitration agreement, applicable law, or institutional rules for guidance.

V. CONTINUING DISCLOSURES AND LIMITATIONS ON ACTIVITIES DURING THE PENDENCY OF A CASE

Arbitrators should comply with applicable law, institutional rules, and party agreements regarding continuing disclosure obligations and should recognize that the appointment will limit their activities while case continues and for a reasonable time thereafter.

CHAPTER 3

NON–NEUTRAL ARBITRATORS

Since non-neutral arbitrators continue to be used in domestic arbitrations, arbitrators should be familiar with the appointment process and other considerations relating to non-neutral conduct and disclosures.

CHAPTER 4

DETERMINING JURISDICTION AND ARBITRABILITY

Arbitrators should see that challenges to jurisdiction and arbitrability are resolved correctly, promptly, and efficiently by the appropriate decision maker.

CHAPTER 6

PRELIMINARY CONFERENCES AND PRE–HEARING MANAGEMENT IN GENERAL

Arbitrators' goals in managing the pre-hearing process are (1) to work with counsel in devising fair and efficient procedures for the pre-hearing and hearing phases of the arbitration, (2) to monitor the parties' compliance with those procedures, and (3) to resolve promptly any disputes or problems that might delay the arbitration.

I.   THE IMPORTANCE OF PRE–HEARING MANAGEMENT

From the time of appointment to the commencement of the hearing, arbitrators should take an active, hands-on approach to managing the pre-hearing process by working with counsel to establish and implement fair and efficient procedures and schedules that are appropriate to the particular case.

II.   CONVENING THE PRELIMINARY CONFERENCE

A.   Time of the Preliminary Conference

The preliminary conference should be held as soon after the arbitrators' appointment as possible, consistent with affording the parties adequate time to prepare for the conference.

B.   Who Should Attend the Preliminary Conference?

Arbitrators should require that each party be represented at the preliminary conference by the attorney who will serve as lead counsel at the hearing and, in appropriate cases, by senior client representatives as well.

C.   Location of the Preliminary Conference

Arbitrators should determine whether the preliminary conference will be held via conference call or in-person and, if the latter, at what location.

III.   CONDUCTING THE PRELIMINARY CONFERENCE

A.   Arbitrator's Introductory Statement

At the outset of the conference, after all participants have identified themselves, arbitrators should remind those present that arbitration is a private, flexible process that can be tailored to the nature of the particular dispute and needs of the parties involved in order to achieve efficiency, economy, timeliness, and fairness. Arbitrators should make clear that the purpose of the preliminary conference is to enable the arbitrators and counsel to work together in designing such a customized process for the case.

V. MATTERS TO ADDRESS AT THE PRELIMINARY CONFERENCE

Arbitrators should address and resolve at the preliminary conference all matters that may affect the conduct of the arbitration.

VII. SUBSEQUENT PRE–HEARING MANAGEMENT

After the preliminary conference, arbitrators should maintain an active role in managing pre-hearing activities and monitoring the parties' progress to assure compliance with the preliminary conference order and timely completion of the arbitration.

CHAPTER 7

MOTIONS

Arbitrators' goals with respect to motion practice are (1) to encourage motions that are likely to expedite or facilitate the arbitration proceedings, (2) to discourage motions that are not likely to be productive, and (3) to provide a fair, efficient, cost-effective process for party presentations and arbitrator decisions.

II. ARBITRAL AUTHORITY TO HEAR MOTIONS

Consistent with their broad authority to manage the arbitration and to grant relief not available in court, arbitrators have the power to grant any well-taken motion unless there is a specific prohibition in the agreement, rules, statute, or case law.

III. TYPES OF MOTIONS

D. Preliminary Relief

If inclined to grant preliminary relief, arbitrators should ensure that they have authority and, if so, may grant such relief when they determine it is necessary to ensure the efficacy of the ultimate award.

E. Pleadings

Arbitrators must strike a balance between arbitration's informality in pleading requirements and the need of a respondent to obtain enough information about claims to respond effectively.

G. Bifurcation

Arbitrators should bifurcate proceedings in the exercise of sound discretion if it is clear that bifurcation will reduce costs and streamline the arbitration process.

H. Dispositive Motions

To avoid the risk of having an award vacated for refusing to hear evidence, arbitrators should only grant dispositive motions when the party opposing the motion has had a reasonable opportunity to gather and present evidence on the pertinent issues and the arbitrator is confident that, on the undisputed facts, the Movant is clearly entitled to an award in its favor.

I.   Motions in Limine or to Preclude Testimony

Motions in limine or to preclude testimony are within arbitrators' sound discretion; however, granting such motions can imperil an award or subject it to an attack. Such motions should therefore generally be discouraged and the parties reminded that arbitrators will ultimately decide both the credibility and weight of the evidenced offered.

J.   Sanctions

Sanctions may be granted in the arbitrators' sound discretion when and as authorized by the clause, applicable arbitral law, or applicable institutional rules.

K.   Continuances

While motions for continuance are within arbitrators' sound discretion, refusing to grant such a motion can provide potential grounds for vacatur of an award. In addressing such motions, arbitrators should therefore carefully weigh the reasons for the request, the delay in the proceedings, and the risk to the award, and should document the reasons for refusing such a request.

CHAPTER 8

DISCOVERY

Arbitrators' goals in managing discovery are (1) to ensure an efficient and fundamentally fair hearing, and (2) to afford each party a reasonable opportunity to obtain material evidence relating to its claims or defenses.

I.   INTRODUCTION

B.   Absence of a Statutory or Common Law Right to Discovery in Arbitration

When appropriate, arbitrators may remind the parties that most state and federal arbitration statutes, and the common law, do not provide parties with a right to conduct discovery in arbitration.

C.   Relevance of Applicable Arbitration Rules and Parties' Arbitration Agreement

In determining the scope and nature of discovery, arbitrators must comply with applicable arbitration rules and the parties' arbitration agreement.

D.   Soliciting Agreement by Parties Relating to Scope and Nature of Discovery

To the extent the parties wish to conduct discovery beyond that specifically guaranteed by applicable rule or the parties' arbitration agreement, arbitrators should encourage the parties to agree on the scope and nature of discovery and, if the parties are able to do so and there are no compelling countervailing considerations relating to reasonableness and efficiency, should accept and enforce such agreement.

II. DOCUMENT PRODUCTION

A. Applicable Arbitration Rules

As is reflected in virtually all institutional rules, tailored document production is generally allowed in arbitration and is the heart of most arbitration discovery, and arbitrators thus should normally permit at least a limited document exchange.

B. Documents on which Party Intends to Rely

Arbitrators should ensure that all documents on which a party intends to rely during the hearing are exchanged prior to the commencement of the hearing.

D. Computer–Based "Document" Discovery

Arbitrators should recognize that electronically stored information can present unique issues relating to document production and should thus seek creative solutions that best ensure the production of such information.

F. Claims of Privilege

In the absence of an applicable legal exception, arbitrators should not require a party to produce privileged documents.

III. DEPOSITIONS OF PARTY WITNESSES

A. Arbitrators' Authority

In the absence of a contrary rule or contractual provision, arbitrators normally are authorized to permit a discovery deposition of a party witness.

IV. INTERROGATORIES AND REQUESTS FOR ADMISSIONS

A. General Rule

Arbitrators should not normally allow the parties to conduct discovery through the use of interrogatories and requests for admission.

B. Unique Rules

When applicable rules guarantee the right to use interrogatories and requests for admission, arbitrators should limit their number and scope.

V. DISCOVERY OF EXPERT WITNESS

A. Discovery of Experts in General

Due to the complexity of expert testimony, arbitrators often can maximize the efficiency of the hearing on the merits by permitting pre-hearing discovery of expert witnesses.

VI. DISCOVERY FROM THIRD PARTIES

A. Extent of Arbitrators' Authority to Issue Third–Party Discovery Subpoenas

Arbitrators must be aware of constraints on their authority to issue subpoenas to third parties for the purpose of pre-hearing discovery.

VII. SITE INSPECTIONS

Site inspections should be carefully controlled by arbitrators to ensure they are efficient and in compliance with arbitrators' directive.

IX. DISCOVERY DISPUTES

A. Encouraging Parties to Resolve Discovery Disputes

Arbitrators should first approach discovery disputes with the objective of encouraging the parties to resolve their own disputes.

CHAPTER 9

THE HEARING ON THE MERITS

The arbitrators' goals with respect to the hearing on the merits are (1) to provide each party with a fair opportunity to present its evidence and argument, (2) to make the hearing as smooth, efficient, and expeditious as possible, and (3) to provide arbitrators with all the information they need to properly resolve the issues presented.

I. DESIGNING THE APPROPRIATE HEARING PROCESS

Arbitrators should utilize their broad discretion concerning management of the hearing to establish and carry out arrangements and procedures that are fair, appropriate to the particular case, and, to the extent reasonably possible, acceptable to all parties.

III. SETTING THE BASIC CONSTRUCT OF THE HEARING

A. Standards for Admission of Evidence

Arbitrators should advise counsel of what standards will govern the admission of evidence at the hearing and should encourage counsel, in planning their presentations, to focus their attention on evidence that is likely to be accorded greater weight by the arbitrators.

B. Order of Proof

Arbitrators should determine a fair and efficient order of proof for each hearing.

IV. MANAGEMENT OF EXHIBITS

A. Core Exhibits

Arbitrators should require the parties to jointly assemble and submit, as soon after the preliminary conference as is feasible, a tabbed and indexed notebook containing paginated copies of the key documents in the case (sometimes referred to as the "core exhibits" or "the common bundle").

B. Evidentiary Exhibits

Arbitrators should require each party to submit, in advance of the hearing, tabbed, indexed notebooks containing paginated copies of all evidentiary exhibits (beyond the core exhibits) which that party intends to use at the hearing for any purpose other than impeachment of credibility.

VI. MANAGEMENT OF HEARING TIME

A. Introduction

Arbitrators should institute fair, realistic, and reasonable measures to ensure that the hearing is conducted efficiently and that it is likely to be completed in the time allotted.

VII. MANAGEMENT OF LOGISTICS

Arbitrators should ensure that appropriate arrangements have been made for all necessary logistical support for the hearing, including use of technology, appropriate hearing rooms space, transcripts, interpreters and/or signers, access for handicapped participants, and other special needs.

IX. ARBITRATOR CONDUCT DURING HEARINGS

Arbitrators should conduct themselves during the hearing in a manner designed to expedite and facilitate the receipt of the parties' evidence and arguments and to assure the parties of their impartiality and neutrality.

X. DETERMINING REQUESTS FOR FEES, COSTS, AND INTEREST

Arbitrators should determine whether evidence concerning interest, fees, and costs will be received during the main hearing or through supplemental proceedings and should establish the procedures for any such proceedings.

XI. BRIEFING

A. Pre–Hearing Briefs

Arbitrators should determine at the preliminary conference what will be included in the pre-hearing briefs and when they will be exchanged and should include those determinations in their preliminary conference order.

XII. STATEMENTS AND ARGUMENTS OF COUNSEL

A. Opening Statements

Arbitrators should generally allow a reasonable amount of time for counsel to make opening statements at the beginning of the hearing and to respond to any questions the arbitrators might have.

C. Final Arguments

Arbitrators should allow counsel to present their final arguments at a time and in a manner that is helpful to the arbitrators but also affords counsel a reasonable opportunity for advocacy.

CHAPTER 10
AWARDS

In issuing awards, arbitrators' goals are to craft awards that are (1) clear, (2) supported by the evidence and substantive law, (3) appropriate to the circumstances of the particular case, and (4) consistent with applicable law and rules relating to timeliness, finality, and the scope of their authority.

II. FINAL AWARDS

B. Form of Award

Arbitrators should examine the parties' agreement and any applicable rules, and should consult with the parties, regarding whether the award is to contain reasons or findings of fact and conclusions of law.

III. INTERIM AWARDS

In appropriate circumstances, arbitrators may issue "interim awards" that are preliminary and non-final in nature, but which advise the parties of the arbitrators' intended resolution of some, but not all, of the submitted issues.

V. REMEDIES

A. Authority to Craft Remedies

Subject to any limitations imposed by statute, the parties' agreement, or any applicable rules, arbitrators generally have wide latitude in determining the appropriate remedies in an arbitration proceeding.

C. Attorneys' Fees, Arbitrators' and Arbitral Institute Fees, and Costs

In the absence of a specific statute, contractual provision, or rule, arbitrators normally do not have authority to award attorneys' fees, arbitrator or arbitral institution fees, or costs to a prevailing party.

D. Sanctions

When arbitrators formally issue "sanctions" against a party or counsel, such sanctions should be reflected in an award that is final in nature.

CHAPTER 11
POST–AWARD MATTERS

III. POST–AWARD ETHICAL ISSUES

A. Maintaining Confidentiality of the Arbitration Proceeding

Subsequent to the issuance of a final award, arbitrators must ensure the ongoing confidentiality of the arbitration proceeding.

C. Post–Award Relationships with Parties and Counsel

For a reasonable or specific period of time subsequent to the issuance of the award, arbitrators should refrain from entering into relationships with the parties or counsel that could be interpreted as evidencing partiality.

CHAPTER 12

INTERNATIONAL ARBITRATION

Arbitrators who serve in international arbitrations should understand the many characteristics that distinguish such arbitrations from domestic commercial arbitrations as well as the features that they have in common.

II. APPOINTMENT PROCESS

B. Arbitrators' Determination of Willingness, Fitness, and Availability to Serve

In order to determine their fitness and availability to serve in an international arbitration, arbitrators must first gain a meaningful understanding of the nature of the dispute, the underlying arbitration agreement, the applicable procedural rules, the identity of the parties and counsel, and a variety of other potential considerations.

C. Arbitrator Disclosures

Arbitrators must disclose all matters that might give rise to justifiable doubts concerning their impartiality or independence.

III. DETERMINING JURISDICTION AND ARBITRABILITY

A. Challenges to Arbitrators' Jurisdiction

International arbitrators must be prepared to rule on challenges to their jurisdiction to determine the parties' dispute, and should resolve any such challenges in a manner that maximizes the efficiency of the proceeding.

B. Challenges to Arbitrability of a Party's Claims

International arbitrators must also be prepared to rule on challenges to the arbitrability of a party's claim.

IV. PRELIMINARY HEARING

International arbitrators should, to the extent feasible, arrange a preliminary meeting between the arbitrators and counsel for the purpose of organizing and scheduling the arbitration proceeding.

V. TERMS OF REFERENCE

When required or appropriate, arbitrators should actively expedite the finalization of Terms of Reference or other initial framework documents.

VI. MOTIONS AND APPLICATIONS

Arbitrators should require that any motions or applications seeking relief are supported with reasons, and should grant a party opposing such a motion or application an opportunity to respond.

VII. DEPOSITIONS AND DOCUMENT PRODUCTION

A. Depositions

International arbitrators should permit depositions only in rare instances, usually relating to the inability of a witness to appear and testify at the hearing.

B. Document Production

International arbitrators should exercise restraint in authorizing document requests, limiting them to narrow, specific categories of relevant evidence that is in the control of the opposing party and not otherwise available to the requesting party.

VIII. EXPERT WITNESSES

The use of experts differs considerably between different legal systems, and arbitrators thus should consult with the parties to agree on an appropriate procedure.

IX. WRITTEN SUBMISSIONS

Formal written submissions by the parties play a critical role in international arbitration, and arbitrators therefore should establish procedures that will guide the parties on the content and the format of such submissions.

X. THE MERITS HEARING

A. Advance Preparations

Because pre-hearing procedures and preparations play a particularly important role in international arbitrations, arbitrators should ensure in advance of the commencement of the hearing that those procedures have been followed.

B. Structuring the Hearing

Arbitrators should structure the hearing in a manner that fully exploits the nature and extent of the pre-hearing process.

XI. THE AWARD

Arbitrators must ensure that the contents of the award satisfy the requirements of the applicable law and rules and the parties' arbitration agreement, and should only label an award as "final" when all of the issues relating to the award have been finally determined.

Questions and Comments:

1. In this Problem, what substantive law must the tribunal apply? May the arbitrator apply any laws or rules of decision as seem fit? See TEI–HCM arbitration clause, 8.07 and International Rules Article 28(1). What would

happen in the instant case if the parties' contract failed to designate the applicable law? Might that be prejudicial?

2. Where must the arbitration be conducted or may the arbitrator designate any location? See TEI–HCM Contract, section 8.06 and International Rules, Article 13, sections (1) and (2). The Rules also provide that "The parties shall be given sufficient written notice to enable them to be present at any such proceedings."

3. What do the International Rules provide as to whether the arbitrator is to be neutral or non-neutral where the parties' agreement, as here, is silent? See International Rules, Article 7. Does the ongoing representation by Attorney Smith of HCM render him non-neutral? May one or both parties require Attorney Smith to disqualify himself? See International Rules, Article 8. If Attorney Smith refuses, what court remedy, if any, may be had? If a matter has been submitted to arbitration, a court may be reluctant to intervene in the arbitration process and investigate the partiality of an arbitrator. However, some State courts, in domestic arbitration, are willing to undertake such inquiry. See *Arista Marketing Assocs., Inc. v. Peer Group, Inc.*, 316 N.J.Super. 517, 720 A.2d 659 (App.Div. 1998), *cert. den'd*, 158 N.J. 72, 726 A.2d 936 (1999) (ruling that party-selected arbitrator could be disqualified pre-arbitration due to evident partiality shown by legal work done on the case by the arbitrator on behalf of the appointing party prior to selection as arbitrator); *Barcon Assoc. v. Tri–County Asphalt Corp.*, 160 N.J.Super. 559, 390 A.2d 684 (Law Div. 1978), *aff'd*, 172 N.J.Super. 186, 411 A.2d 709 (App. Div. 1980), *aff'd*, 86 N.J. 179, 430 A.2d 214 (1981) ("existence of an undisclosed, substantial business relationship between a party-designated arbitrator in tripartite arbitration and the party designating the arbitrator throughout the arbitration proceeding constitutes 'evident partiality' under N.J.S.A. 2A:24–8(b)."). A non-neutral arbitrator is not excused from his ethical duties and obligation to participate in the arbitration in a fair, honest and good-faith manner. *Metropolitan Property & Cas. Ins. Co. v. J.C. Penney Cas. Ins. Co.*, 780 F.Supp. 885 (D. Conn. 1991) ("Partisan he may be, but not dishonest"). Could assistance from the arbitral tribunal, the AAA in this Problem, be obtained to disqualify a biased arbitrator? See International Rules, Article 16.

4. Do the International Rules permit the arbitrator to vary the procedures and timetables set forth in the Rules? Is there any limit on the arbitrator's discretion in this regard? See International Rules, Article 1(1). May the parties, by written agreement, vary the procedural rules? See id.

5. Under the International Rules, what entitlement do the parties have to:

Participate in discovery? See International Rules, Article 19.

File pre-hearing motions? See Articles 16 and 17.

Present witnesses? See Article 20.

Present evidence? See Articles 16, 19 and 20.

6. Under the International Rules, is there any limit upon the amount of time that an arbitrator may take before issuing an award? See Articles 16(2) and 27(1).

7. If the parties' arbitration clause is silent on the issue, what do the International Rules provide as to the form of the award i.e., whether a detailed "reasoned" award would be issued or whether a simple statement of the relief granted will issue? See Article 27(2).

8. Does this Problem suggest any issues regarding whether one or three arbitrators may be preferable to a given dispute? See International Rules, Article 5. Does Article 5 provide the parties any certainty as to whether one or three arbitrators will be used in the event a dispute arises? What about the additional cost of three arbitrators versus one? Would concerns of cost decrease as the quantum in dispute increases?

9. May the arbitrator require particular individuals, the company Presidents in this problem, to attend a hearing? See 9 U.S.C. § 7. An arbitrator may have difficulty obtaining court assistance to compel attendance of a witness. Absent peculiar circumstances, a U.S. Federal Court or State Court would only have jurisdiction over (1) matters in which personal and subject matter jurisdiction are established; and (2) people and proceedings occurring within their territorial jurisdiction (boundaries of the State for State courts and 100 mile bubble for U.S. Federal courts). A U.S. court, therefore, would not have authority to compel a foreign citizen, the President of HCM in the instant problem, to appear in the United States. Where the arbitrator's subpoena is directed to persons within the court's jurisdiction, however, a court, in certain circumstances, may enforce the subpoena. See *Odfjell, ASA v. Celanese, A.G.*, 328 F.Supp.2d 505 (S.D.N.Y. 2004) (District Court had jurisdiction pursuant to Federal Arbitration Act [9 U.S.C. § 7] to consider motion for an order compelling non-party to comply with two subpoenas issued by chief arbitrator presiding over arbitration, where chief arbitrator was "sitting" in New York); *Stolt–Nielsen, S.A. v. Celanese, A.G.*, 430 F.3d 567 (2nd Cir.2005) (district court had jurisdiction over motion to enforce arbitration panel's subpoena directed to two non-parties' employees, filed by party to arbitration in antitrust dispute arising out of shipment of bulk chemicals via parcel tankers; although provision of Federal Arbitration Act [9 U.S.C. § 7] under which motion was brought did not itself confer jurisdiction, court had admiralty jurisdiction when parties first came before it on motion to stay arbitration, and, after denying motion, court retained jurisdiction over any later petitions arising out of arbitration). Even in circumstances where the arbitrator cannot obtain a court order enforcing a subpoena of the arbitral tribunal, the arbitrator still has strong persuasive powers to compel attendance, such as threatening to construe evidence against a party, exclude evidence a party may wish to present, refuse to consider a claim or defense of a party, or threaten to enter other adverse ruling or penalty. As a practical matter, this leverage possessed by the arbitrator may be more potent than judicial remedies.

10. What actions may an arbitrator take in the event a party engages in misconduct, such as failing to timely respond to a written claim or produce documents or witnesses? What court assistance may be available to the arbitrator? As discussed above in Question 9, in certain circumstances, judicial assistance is available to enforce an arbitral tribunal subpoena to require a witness to appear at the arbitration hearing. This authority exists by virtue of the Federal Arbitration Act, 9 U.S.C. § 7, and analogous provisions of State arbitration acts. The Third Circuit, construing the FAA, 9

U.S.C. § 7, ruled that a court may only compel the attendance of witnesses (including requiring the witnesses to bring documents) at the conduct of the actual arbitration proceeding. *Hay Group, Inc. v. E.B.S. Acquisition Corp.*, 360 F.3d 404 (3rd Cir.2004). The court ruled that a party could not require a witness to appear for a pre-arbitration deposition nor require a party to simply produce documents. Presumably, if the arbitration tribunal were so inclined, it could open an arbitration hearing for the sole purpose of receiving the witness and the witness's documents, then adjourn the hearing, thus creating de facto pre-hearing discovery.

11. Does the problem raise any issues as to whether ad hoc arbitration (without any tribunal involvement) is preferable to involvement of an established arbitral tribunal in a given dispute? What about the cost of the arbitral tribunal filing fees and administrative fees, which can be substantial (thousand of dollars)?

Does this cost concern diminish as the quantum in dispute increases?

12. What do the International Rules provide with respect to hourly rate of arbitrators? See Article 32.

13. What do the International Rules provide as to confidentiality of the proceeding? See Articles 27(4) and (8), 34.

14. If the parties reach a settlement of their disputes, which often happens, may the arbitration be terminated? See International Rules, Article 29.

15. Is a party entitled to have its counsel present at the arbitration? See International Rules, Article 12.

16. The International Rules, like the rules of most tribunals, leave interim measures, such as injunctions or sequestration orders, to the discretion of the arbitrator. See Rules 21 and 27(7). See also, Best Practices, III. TYPES OF MOTIONS, (D) Preliminary Report. In the event a party is not able to timely obtain an injunction or sequestration order, might that effect the outcome of the dispute or effectiveness of the relief ultimately obtained? What if the property in dispute, such as a vessel, leaves the jurisdiction or funds are spent or co-mingled, or confidential or patented technology is pirated? Might these considerations alone counsel against arbitration and in favor of litigation where the nature of the parties' commercial relationship creates a potential for great harm if prompt legal remedies, such as a temporary restraining order or injunction, cannot be obtained?

17. May the tribunal appoint its own experts or seek input from knowledgeable persons? See International Rules, Article 22.

18. Why does the College of Commercial Arbitrator's Best Practices manual contain additional provisions applicable only to international arbitration? What concerns or safeguards do these provisions address?

19. In the final analysis, does there appear to be much difference in procedures or potential time and cost savings between the International Rules and litigation in U.S. court pursuant to the Federal Rules of Civil Procedure? Are not the basic elements present in each instance of Complaint, Answer, preliminary motions and interim measures, discovery, pre-trial conference, trial and award? It may be noted that the International

Rules do not impose any strict timelines and leave such matters to the discretion of the arbitrator. Where then are the often touted time and cost savings of arbitration? Would parties be advised to include strict time limits in their arbitration clause?

PROBLEM 10.4 ENFORCING AN ARBITRAL AWARD: TAMPA SPANISH LANGUAGE TELEVISION STATION RECEIVES MONETARY AWARD IN ARBITRATION

SECTION I. THE SETTING

Pursuant to section 8.06 of the TEI–HCM Contract, set forth in Problem 10.2, and the International Rules of the AAA, a single arbitrator, selected from the AAA list of arbitrators, entered an award in Tampa against HCM and in favor of TEI. The arbitrator found that HCM was entitled to no damages under its defamation claim because the neglect of hospital patients filmed by TEI was not false and because there was no credible evidence that TEI published the information to any third party. The arbitrator further found that HCM was not entitled to the return of any of the $50,000 flat fee paid because TEI performed its contract obligations prior to HCM's termination of the contract. Under section 8.06, the arbitrator awarded to TEI its reasonable attorney's fees, costs and expenses of $100,000.

Counsel for TEI located assets of HCM, specifically several bank and investment accounts in Miami. TEI moved the U.S. District Court for the Middle District of Florida to enforce the award as a judgment of the court pursuant to the New York Convention, as codified in 9 U.S.C.A. §§ 201, 207, and 208 and Inter–American Convention on International Commercial Arbitration, Article IV. HCM objects to enforcement of the arbitral award on the bases of:

a. New York Convention Article V(1)(c) because "The award deals with a difference not contemplated by or not falling within the terms of the submission to arbitration, or it contains decisions on matters beyond the scope of the submission to arbitration" as HCM contends that the tort claim of defamation was not subject of the parties' arbitration agreement. HCM further contends that the decision on defamation is a pre-condition to the decision on breach of contract and therefore, the provision of Article V(1)(c) is inapplicable that "if the decisions on matters submitted to arbitration can be separated from those not so submitted, that part of the award which contains decisions on matters submitted to arbitration may be recognized and enforced";

b. New York Convention Article V(2)(a), "The subject matter of the difference is not capable of settlement by arbitration under the law of that country", for the same reasons as above;

c. New York Convention Article V(2)(b), "The recognition or enforcement of the award would be contrary to the public policy of that country", for the same reasons as above;

d. Inter–American Convention, Article V(1)(c), "That the decision concerns a dispute not envisaged in the agreement between the parties to submit to arbitration;"

e. Inter–American Convention, Article V(2)(a), "That the subject of the dispute cannot be settled by arbitration under the law of that State;" and

f. Inter–American Convention, Article V(2)(b), "That the recognition or execution of the decision would be contrary to the public policy ('Ordre Public') of that State."

SECTION II. FOCUS OF CONSIDERATION

As with recognition of an agreement to arbitrate in Problem 10.2, counsel considering enforcement of an arbitral award should refer first, to the provisions of the applicable contract; and second, to the provisions of any applicable international agreement.

Essential to an understanding of this problem are the New York Convention, Arts. III, IV and V; the Inter–American Convention on International Commercial Arbitration, Arts. 4 and 5; and 9 U.S.C.A. §§ 201, 207–08, 304–07. They are included in the Documents Supplement.

SECTION III. READINGS, QUESTIONS AND COMMENTS

PARSONS & WHITTEMORE OVERSEAS, INC. v. SOCIETE GENERALE DE L'INDUSTRIE DU PAPIER (RAKTA)

United States Court of Appeals, Second Circuit, 1974.
508 F.2d 969.

J. Joseph Smith, Circuit Judge:

In November 1962, [Parsons & Whittemore Overseas Co., Inc., (Overseas)] consented by written agreement with RAKTA [an Egyptian corporation] to construct, start up and, for one year, manage and supervise a paperboard mill in Alexandria, Egypt. The Agency for International Development (AID), a branch of the United States State Department, would finance the project by supplying RAKTA with funds with which to purchase letters of credit in Overseas' favor. Among the contract's terms was an arbitration clause, which provided a means to settle differences arising in the course of performance, and a "force majeure" clause, which excused delay in performance due to causes beyond Overseas' reasonable capacity to control.

Work proceeded as planned until May, 1967. Then, with the Arab–Israeli Six Day War on the horizon, recurrent expressions of Egyptian hostility to Americans—nationals of the principal ally of the Israeli enemy—caused the majority of the Overseas work crew to leave Egypt. On June 6, the Egyptian government broke diplomatic ties with the United States and ordered all Americans expelled from Egypt except those who would apply and qualify for a special visa.

Having abandoned the project for the present with the construction phase near completion, Overseas notified RAKTA that it regarded this postponement as excused by the force majeure clause. RAKTA disagreed and sought damages for breach of contract. Overseas refused to settle and RAKTA, already at work on completing the performance promised by Overseas, invoked the arbitration clause. Overseas responded by calling into play the clause's option to bring a dispute directly to a three-man arbitral board governed by the rules of the International Chamber of Commerce. After several sessions in 1970, the tribunal issued a preliminary award, which recognized Overseas' force majeure defense as good only during the period from May 28 to June 30, 1967. In so limiting Overseas' defense, the arbitration court emphasized that Overseas had made no more than a perfunctory effort to secure special visas and that AID's notification that it was withdrawing financial backing did not justify Overseas' unilateral decision to abandon the project. After further hearings in 1972, the tribunal made its final award in March, 1973: Overseas was held liable to RAKTA for $312,507.45 in damages for breach of contract and $30,000 for RAKTA's costs; additionally, the arbitrators' compensation was set at $49,000, with Overseas responsible for three-fourths of the sum.

Overseas' defenses to this counterclaim, all rejected by the district court, form the principal issues for review on this appeal. Four of these defenses are derived from the express language of the applicable United Nations Convention on the Recognition and Enforcement of Foreign Arbitral Awards (Convention), and a fifth is arguably implicit in the Convention. These include: enforcement of the award would violate the public policy of the United States, the award represents an arbitration of matters not appropriately decided by arbitration; the tribunal denied Overseas an adequate opportunity to present its case; the award is predicated upon a resolution of issues outside the scope of contractual agreement to submit to arbitration; and the award is in manifest disregard of law.

I. OVERSEAS' DEFENSES AGAINST ENFORCEMENT

The 1958 Convention's basic thrust was to liberalize procedures for enforcing foreign arbitral awards: While the Geneva Convention placed the burden of proof on the party seeking enforcement of a foreign arbitral award and did not circumscribe the range of available defenses to those enumerated in the convention, the 1958 Convention clearly shifted the burden of proof to the party defending against enforcement and limited his defenses to seven set forth in Article V. Not a signatory to any prior multilateral agreement on enforcement of arbitral awards, the United States declined to sign the 1958 Convention at the outset.

The United States ultimately acceded to the Convention, however, in 1970, and implemented its accession with 9 U.S.C. 201–208. Under 9 U.S.C. 208, the existing Federal Arbitration Act, 9 U.S.C. 1–14, applies to the enforcement of foreign awards except to the extent to which the latter may conflict with the Convention.

A. *Public Policy*

Article V(2)(b) of the Convention allows the court in which enforcement of a foreign arbitral award is sought to refuse enforcement, on the defendant's motion or sua sponte, if "enforcement of the award would be contrary to the public policy of (the forum) country." The legislative history of the provision offers no certain guidelines to its construction. Its precursors in the Geneva Convention and the 1958 Convention's ad hoc committee draft extended the public policy exception to, respectively, awards contrary to "principles of the law" and awards violative of "fundamental principles of the law." In one commentator's view, the Convention's failure to include similar language signifies a narrowing of the defense. Contini, *supra*, 8 Am.J.Comp.L. 283 at 304. On the other hand, another noted authority in the field has seized upon this omission as indicative of an intention to broaden the defense. Quigley, Accession by the United States to the United Nations Convention on the Recognition and Enforcement of Foreign Arbitral Awards, 70 Yale L.J. 1049, 1070–71 (1961).

Perhaps more probative, however, are the inferences to be drawn from the history of the Convention as a whole. The general pro-enforcement bias informing the Convention and explaining its supersession of the Geneva Convention points toward a narrow reading of the public policy defense. An expansive construction of this defense would vitiate the Convention's basic effort to remove preexisting obstacles to enforcement. Additionally, considerations of reciprocity—considerations given express recognition in the Convention itself—counsel courts to invoke the public policy defense with caution lest foreign courts frequently accept it as a defense to enforcement of arbitral awards rendered in the United States.

We conclude, therefore, that the Convention's public policy defense should be construed narrowly. Enforcement of foreign arbitral awards may be denied on this basis only where enforcement would violate the forum state's most basic notions of morality and justice.

Under this view of the public policy provision in the Convention, Overseas' public policy defense may easily be dismissed. Overseas argues that various actions by United States officials subsequent to the severance of American–Egyptian relations—most particularly, AID's withdrawal of financial support for the Overseas–RAKTA contract—required Overseas, as a loyal American citizen, to abandon the project. Enforcement of an award predicated on the feasibility of Overseas' returning to work in defiance of these expressions of national policy would therefore allegedly contravene United States public policy. In equating "national" policy with United States "public" policy, the appellant quite plainly misses the mark. To read the public policy defense as a parochial device protective of national political interests would seriously undermine the Convention's utility. This provision was not meant to enshrine the vagaries of international politics under the rubric of "public policy." Rather, a circumscribed public policy doctrine was contemplated by the Convention's framers and every indication is that the United States, in acceding to the Convention, meant to subscribe to this supranational emphasis. *Cf. Scherk v. Alberto–Culver Co.*, 417 U.S. 506, 94 S.Ct. 2449, 41 L.Ed.2d 270 (1974).

To deny enforcement of this award largely because of the United States' falling out with Egypt in recent years would mean converting a defense intended to be of narrow scope into a major loophole in the Convention's mechanism for enforcement. We have little hesitation, therefore, in disallowing Overseas' proposed public policy defense.

B. *Non–Arbitrability*

Article V(2)(a) authorizes a court to deny enforcement, on a defendant's or its own motion, of a foreign arbitral award when "the subject matter of the difference is not capable of settlement by arbitration under the law of that (the forum) country."

Resolution of Overseas' non-arbitrability argument, however, does not require us to reach such difficult distinctions between domestic and foreign awards. For Overseas' argument, that "United States foreign policy issues can hardly be placed at the mercy of foreign arbitrators 'who are charged with the execution of no public trust' and whose loyalties are to foreign interests," plainly fails to raise so substantial an issue of arbitrability. The mere fact that an issue of national interest may incidentally figure into the resolution of a breach of contract claim does not make the dispute not arbitrable. Rather, certain categories of claims may be non-arbitrable because of the special national interest vested in their resolution. Furthermore, even were the test for non-arbitrability of an ad hoc nature, Overseas' situation would almost certainly not meet the standard, for Overseas grossly exaggerates the magnitude of the national interest involved in the resolution of its particular claim. Simply because acts of the United States are somehow implicated in a case one cannot conclude that the United States is vitally interested in its outcome. Finally, the Supreme Court's decision in favor of arbitrability in a case far more prominently displaying public features than the instant one, *Scherk v. Alberto–Culver Co.*, *supra*, compels by analogy the conclusion that the foreign award against Overseas dealt with a subject arbitrable under United States law.

The court below was correct in denying relief to Overseas under the Convention's non-arbitrability defense to enforcement of foreign arbitral awards. There is no special national interest in judicial, rather than arbitral, resolution of the breach of contract claim underlying the award in this case.

C. *Inadequate Opportunity to Present Defense*

Under Article V(1)(b) of the Convention, enforcement of a foreign arbitral award may be denied if the defendant can prove that he was "not given proper notice . . . or was otherwise unable to present his case." This provision essentially sanctions the application of the forum state's standards of due process.

Overseas seeks relief under this provision for the arbitration court's refusal to delay proceedings in order to accommodate the speaking schedule of one of Overseas' witnesses, David Nes, the United States Charge d'Affairs in Egypt at the time of the Six Day War. This attempt to state a due process claim fails for several reasons. First, inability to produce one's witnesses before an arbitral tribunal is a risk inherent in an agreement to submit to arbitration. By agreeing to submit disputes to arbitration, a party relinquishes his courtroom rights—including that to subpoena witnesses—in favor of arbitration "with all of its well known advantages and drawbacks." Secondly, the logistical problems of scheduling hearing dates convenient to parties, counsel and arbitrators scattered about the globe argues against deviating from an initially mutually agreeable time plan unless a scheduling change is truly unavoidable.

The arbitration tribunal acted within its discretion in declining to reschedule a hearing for the convenience of an Overseas witness. Overseas' due process rights under American law, rights entitled to full force under the Convention as a defense to enforcement, were in no way infringed by the tribunal's decision.

D. *Arbitration in Excess of Jurisdiction*

Under Article V(1)(c), one defending against enforcement of an arbitral award may prevail by proving that:

> The award deals with a difference not contemplated by or not falling within the terms of the submission to arbitration, or it contains decisions on matters beyond the scope of the submission to arbitration. . . .

This provision tracks in more detailed form 10(d) of the Federal Arbitration Act, 9 U.S.C. 10(d), which authorizes vacating an award "where the arbitrators exceeded their powers." Both provisions basically allow a party to attack an award predicated upon arbitration of a subject matter not within the agreement to submit to arbitration. This defense to enforcement of a foreign award, like the others already discussed, should be construed narrowly. Once again a narrow construction would comport with the enforcement-facilitating thrust of the Convention. In addition, the case law under the similar provision of the Federal Arbitration Act strongly supports a strict reading.

In making this defense as to three components of the award, Overseas must therefore overcome a powerful presumption that the arbitral body acted within its powers. Overseas principally directs its challenge at the $185,000 awarded for loss of production. Its jurisdictional claim focuses on the provision of the contract reciting that "neither party shall have any liability for loss of production." The tribunal cannot properly be charged, however, with simply ignoring this alleged limitation on the subject matter over which its decision-making powers extended. Rather, the arbitration court interpreted the provision not to preclude jurisdiction on this matter. As in *United Steelworkers of America v. Enterprise Wheel & Car Corp., supra*, the court may be satisfied that the arbitrator premised the award on a construction of the contract and that it is 'not apparent,' 363 U.S. 593 at 598, 80 S.Ct. 1358, that the scope of the submission to arbitration has been exceeded.

Although the Convention recognizes that an award may not be enforced where predicated on a subject matter outside the arbitrator's jurisdiction, it does not sanction second-guessing the arbitrator's construction of the parties' agreement. The appellant's attempt to invoke this defense, however, calls upon the court to ignore this limitation on its decision-making powers and usurp the arbitrator's role. The district court took a proper view of its own jurisdiction in refusing to grant relief on this ground.

E. Award in "Manifest Disregard" of Law

Both the legislative history of Article V, *see supra*, and the statute enacted to implement the United States' accession to the Convention are strong authority for treating as exclusive the bases set forth in the Convention for vacating an award. On the other hand, the Federal Arbitration Act, specifically 9 U.S.C. 10, has been read to include an implied defense to enforcement where the award is in "manifest disregard" of the law.

[E]ven assuming that the "manifest disregard" defense applies under the Convention, we would have no difficulty rejecting the appellant's contention that such "manifest disregard" is in evidence here. Overseas in effect asks this court to read this defense as a license to review the record of arbitral proceedings for errors of fact or law—a role which we have emphatically declined to assume in the past and reject once again. "Extensive judicial review frustrates the basic purpose of arbitration, which is to dispose of disputes quickly and avoid the expense and delay of extended court proceedings." *Saxis Steamship Co. [v. Multifacs Int'l Traders, Inc.,]* 375 F.2d 577 at 582 [(2d Cir.1967)].

Insofar as this defense to enforcement of awards in "manifest disregard" of law may be cognizable under the Convention, it, like the other defenses raised by the appellant, fails to provide a sound basis for vacating the foreign arbitral award. We therefore affirm the district court's confirmation of award.

Affirmed.

Comment on Non-domestic Nature of Award

For the New York Convention to apply, the arbitral award must be either (1) made in the territory of another state than the state where enforcement is sought; or (2) not considered as "domestic" in the state where enforcement is sought. New York Convention, Art. I(1). The Convention does not define the term "domestic", and such term is subject to construction by national law and courts. In *Bergesen v. Joseph Muller Corp.*, 710 F.2d 928 (2d Cir.1983), the court ruled that an award made in New York State was non-domestic for Convention purposes where the parties were a Swiss corporation and a Norwegian shipowner. In *Lander Co. v. MMP Investments, Inc.*, 107 F.3d 476 (7th Cir.), *cert. denied*, 522 U.S. 811, 118 S.Ct. 55, 139 L.Ed.2d 19 (1997), the court held that an award was non-domestic where the dispute involved an agreement to distribute shampoo products in Poland, despite the facts that both parties were U.S. parties and the award was entered in the United States.

Recent court decisions may be noted where United States courts refused to enforce an arbitral award under the New York Convention where the arbitral tribunal and parties bore no relation to the United States. This line of decisions creates an entirely new defense to the enforcement of awards under the New York Convention, which was not expressly contemplated by the Convention. Rather, the Convention contemplated enforcement of awards in multiple jurisdictions. See e.g., *In re Arbitration between Monegasque de Reassurances S.A.M. v. Nak Naftogaz of Ukraine*, 311 F.3d 488 (2d Cir.2002) (dismissing action on forum non conveniens grounds where reinsurer based in Monaco, as subrogee of Russian insurer, brought action under New York Convention to confirm Russian arbitration award and to direct entry of judgment against Ukraine and Ukraine company); *Creighton Ltd. v. Government of State of Qatar*, 181 F.3d 118 (D.C.Cir.1999) (dismissing action to enforce foreign arbitral award against sovereign state of Qatar for lack of personal jurisdiction where claim lacked sufficient "minimum contacts" to comport with Constitution's due process clause). Compare *Seetransport Wiking Trader Schiffarhtsgesellschaft MBH & Co. v. Navimpex Centrala Navala*, 989 F.2d 572 (2d Cir.1993) (finding sufficient minimum contacts to assert personal jurisdiction over Romanian sovereign entity in order to enforce French arbitral award pursuant to New York Convention).

SPIER v. CALZATURIFICIO TECNICA, S.p.A.

United States District Court, Southern District of New York, 1999.
71 F.Supp.2d 279.

HAIGHT, SENIOR DISTRICT JUDGE.

Martin I. Spier renews his petition to enforce an arbitration award rendered in Italy by Italian arbitrators against respondent Calzaturificio Tecnica S.p.A ("Tecnica").

In 1969 Spier, an engineer resident in New York and an American citizen, entered into a contract with Tecnica, an Italian corporation, calling for Spier to furnish Tecnica with expertise for the manufacture by Tecnica in Italy of plastic footwear and ski boots, in exchange for the payment of certain fees by Tecnica. * * *

While the intricacies of the Italian courts' reasoning may be partially lost in translation, it seems entirely clear that all three courts nullified the award because they concluded that the arbitrators, casting off all restraints imposed by the contract between Spier and Tecnica, conferred upon Spier a "bonus" or a "pay-off" in a manner and an amount that exceeded the exceeded the arbitrators' powers. In these seemingly inauspicious circumstances, Spier renews his petition to this Court to enforce the Italian arbitration award.

Spier's petition to enforce the Italian arbitrators' award falls under the Convention on the Recognition and Enforcement of Foreign Arbitral Awards. Tecnica defended against Spier's petition in this Court, and cross-petitioned to deny enforcement of the award, by invoking Articles V and VI of the Convention, quoted in pertinent part in *Spier I*, 663 F.Supp. at 873. To summarize, Article V provides that "[r]ecognition and enforcement of the award may be refused, at the request of the party against whom it is invoked, only if that party" proves to the authority where enforcement is sought (here, this Court) that, *inter alia*, the underlying contract was not valid under the law of the country where the award was made (here, Italy), Art. V(1)(a); or the arbitral award contained decisions on matters beyond the scope of the submission to arbitration, Art. V(1)(c); or governing law provides that the award is not binding on the parties, Art. V(1)(e).[1]

Notwithstanding that distinction, [*Yusuf Ahmed Alghanim & Sons, W.L.L. v. Toys "R" Us*, 126 F.3d 15 (2d Cir.1997) ("*Yusuf*")] is instructive in the case at bar because of what the Second Circuit says about the available grounds for resisting enforcement of an award when enforcement is sought in a United States district court.

In *Yusuf,* the arbitration was held and the award issued in the United States, and enforcement was sought in the United States. Those circumstances, the Second Circuit held, were sufficient to entitle Toys "R" Us, the party against whom the award was made, to invoke the FAA's implied grounds for refusing to enforce to the award, in addition to the limited statutory grounds found in the FAA for vacating an award, *see* 9 U.S.C. § 10, or modifying it, *see id.* § 11. The implied grounds for *vacatur* recognized by the FAA are found "where the arbitrator's award is in manifest disregard of the terms of the agreement, or where the award is in manifest disregard of the law." And in those particular circumstances, the principles of domestic American law for *refusing to enforce* an award apply, notwithstanding the fact that a petition to *enforce* the award falls under the Convention.

---

1. As more fully stated *infra,* Article V(1)(e) also provides, as a ground for refusing to enforce an award, proof that the award "has been set aside or suspended by a competent authority of the country in which, or under the law of which, that award was made." In view of the decisions of the Italian courts, all post *Spier I,* that Convention provision now lies at the heart of the case.

However, where (as in the case at bar) an arbitral award is made in one State adhering to the Convention and sought to be enforced in another adhering State, the grounds for resisting the award are limited to those found in Article V of the Convention. In *Yusuf* the Second Circuit explains the difference:

> In sum, we conclude that the Convention mandates very different regimes for the review of arbitral awards (1) in the state in which, or under the law of which, the award was made, and (2) in other states where recognition and enforcement are sought. The Convention specifically contemplates that the state in which, or under the law of which, the award is made, will be free to set aside or modify an award in accordance with its domestic arbitral law and its full panoply of express and implied grounds for relief. *See* Convention art., V(1)(e). However, the Convention is equally clear that when an action for enforcement is brought in a foreign state, the state may refuse to enforce the award only on the grounds explicitly set forth in Article V of the Convention. 126 F.3d at 23.

The Second Circuit's more recent decision in [*Baker Marine (Nigeria) Ltd. v. Chevron (Nigeria) Ltd.*, 1999 WL 781594 (2d.Cir. Oct. 1, 1999) ("*Baker Marine*")] illustrates the "very different regime for the review of arbitral awards" when the award is rendered in one State and sought to be enforced in another. Nigerian and American companies entered into two contracts to provide barges for use in servicing Nigeria's oil industry. The contracts provided for arbitration in Nigeria. Two panels of arbitrators made monetary awards in favor of Baker Marine. Baker Marine sought enforcement of both awards in the Nigerian Federal High Court. The losing parties appealed to the same court to vacate the awards. In that effort they succeeded; the Nigerian court set aside both arbitration awards.

Invoking the Convention, Baker Marine then petitioned the Northern District of New York to enforce the awards. Judge McAvoy denied those petitions, reasoning that "under the Convention and principles of comity, it would not be proper to enforce a foreign arbitral award when such an award has been set aside by the Nigerian courts." The Second Circuit affirmed. It cited *Yusef* for the proposition that where enforcement of an arbitral award is sought in a State other than that where the award was made, "Article V [of the Convention] provides exclusive grounds for setting aside" the award. The Nigerian court having set aside the Nigerian arbitration awards, Article V(1)(e) furnished the ground for a United States district court to refuse to enforce them. The court of appeals said:

> Article V(1)(e) provides that a court may refuse enforcement of an award that "has been set aside or suspended by a competent authority of the country in which, or under the law of which, the award was made." Convention, art. V(1)(e). Baker Marine does not contest that the Nigerian High Court is a competent authority in the country in which, and under the law of which, the award was made.

The district court relied on the decision of the Nigerian court and Article V(1)(e) in declining to enforce the award.

In an effort to preserve the awards, Baker Marine made a number of arguments which the Second Circuit rejected. It is instructive to consider the court of appeals' rejections of those arguments, since Spier also makes them in the case at bar.

First, Baker Marine argued that the Nigerian court set aside the awards for reasons that would not be recognized under domestic United States law as valid grounds for vacating the awards. In aid of that contention, Baker Marine criticized the district court for disregarding Article VII(1) of the Convention, which provides that the Convention shall not "deprive any interested party of any right he may have to avail himself of an arbitral award in the manner and to the extent allowed by the law or the treaties of the country where such award is sought to be relied upon." That language, Baker Marine contended, served to incorporate into the Convention the domestic law of the United States as grounds for resuscitating Nigerian awards nullified by a Nigerian court.

The Second Circuit rejected the argument. It reasoned that "the parties contracted in Nigeria that their disputes would be arbitrated under the laws of Nigeria." Moreover, "[t]he governing agreements make no reference whatever to United States law," and "[n]othing suggests that the parties intended United States domestic arbitral law to govern their disputes." Indeed, the intrusion of United States law on the scene would frustrate that law's public policy, since "[t]he primary purpose of the FAA in ensuring that private agreements to arbitrate are enforced according to their terms." Nor did Baker Marine contend "that the Nigerian courts acted contrary to Nigerian law." The Second Circuit's opinion in *Baker Marine* reminds the reader of its prior holding in *Yusuf* that domestic arbitral law may be applied only by "a court under whose law the arbitration was conducted." Lastly, the *Baker Marine* court cites approvingly a commentator's observation that "mechanical application of domestic arbitral law to foreign awards under the Convention would seriously undermine finality and regularly produce conflicting judgments," the foreseeable consequence of such application being that "a losing party will have every reason to pursue its adversary 'with enforcement actions from country to country until a court is found, if any, which grants the enforcement.'"

Second, Baker Marine argued that because Article V(1) of the Convention begins with the permissive phrase that "[r]ecognition and enforcement of an award *may* be refused" if one of the subsequently enumerated grounds for doing so is proved (emphasis added), rather than a mandatory term, the district court "might have enforced the awards, notwithstanding the Nigerian judgments vacating them." Rejecting that contention, the Second Circuit's pointed response was that "Baker Marine has shown no adequate reason for refusing to recognize the judgments of the Nigerian court."

It is also instructive to note that at that point in the *Baker Marine* text, the Second Circuit dropped footnote 3, which distinguishes a case upon which Spier places primary reliance: *In re Chromalloy Aeroservices*, 939 F.Supp. 907 (D.D.C.1996). In *Chromalloy*, an American company bearing that name entered into a military procurement contract with the Egyptian Air Force (hereinafter "Egypt"). The contract required arbitration of all disputes, recited that "both parties have irrevocably agreed to apply Egypt [sic] Laws and to choose Cairo as seat of the court of arbitration," and further provided that "[t]he decision of the said court shall be final and binding and cannot be made subject to any appeal or other recourse." Disputes having arisen, the arbitrators issued an award which Chromalloy petitioned the District Court for the District of Columbia to enforce. Egypt responded by seeking and obtaining from the Egyptian Court of Appeal a judgment nullifying the award, which Egypt then pleaded in bar to Chromalloy's petition in the district court to enforce the award.

In these particular circumstances, the district court held that Chromalloy could invoke Article VII of the Convention in order to take advantage of the FAA, and enforced the award. The court regarded as central to its decision the fact that Egypt, by appealing the arbitration award to the Egyptian court, "seeks to repudiate its solemn promise to abide by the results of the arbitration," in breach of the contractual agreement that "the arbitration ends with the decision of the arbitral panel." Because the FAA and its amendment to implement the Convention "demonstrate that there is an emphatic federal policy in favor of arbitral dispute resolution, particularly in the field of international commerce, [a] decision by this Court to recognize the decision of the Egyptian court would violate this clear U.S. public policy."

On the facts presented in *Baker Marine,* the Second Circuit distinguished *Chromalloy,* writing in footnote 3:

> The district court [in *Chromalloy*] concluded that Egypt was "seeking to repudiate its solemn promise to abide by the results of the arbitration," and that recognizing the Egyptian judgment would be contrary to the United States policy favoring arbitration. Unlike the petitioner in *Chromalloy*, Baker Marine is not a United States citizen, and it did not initially seek confirmation of the award in the United States. Furthermore, Chevron and Danos did not violate any promise in appealing the arbitration award with Nigeria. Recognition of the Nigerian judgment in this case does not conflict with United States public policy.

In some respects *Chromalloy* bears a superficial resemblance to the case at bar, since Spier is a United States citizen and seeks confirmation of the award in the United States. But I read this footnote in *Baker Marine* to identify as the decisive circumstance Egypt's repudiation of its contractual promise not to appeal an arbitral award. Only that circumstance is singled out as violating American public policy articulated in the FAA, thereby justifying the district court's enforcement of the Egyptian award.

In the light of these recent Second Circuit cases, I consider Spier's several arguments in favor of enforcement by this Court of the award against Tecnica.

First, Spier argues that "[t]he threshold issue . . . is whether or not the award would be set aside under American law," and collects American cases to support the proposition that it should be. But the Second Circuit's holdings in *Yusuf* and *Baker Marine* preclude this Court from reaching that threshold, let alone crossing it. Spier seeks to apply domestic United States arbitral law in order to escape the Italian courts' nullification of an Italian award. That effort cannot survive the court of appeals' observation in *Yusuf* that under the Convention "the state in which, or under the laws of which, the award is made, will be free to set aside or modify an award in accordance with its domestic arbitral law and its full panoply of express and implied grounds for relief." The award at bar was set aside by that state's highest tribunal, the Supreme Court of Cassation of Italy; no American court or statute may be cited to the contrary. In other words, Spier cannot be heard to argue that the Italian courts' decisions should not be recognized on the ground that an American court would reach a different result with respect to the award if it had been rendered in the United States.

Nor may Spier introduce domestic United States law, statutory or decisional, into the case at bar through the vehicle of Article VII of the Convention. *Baker Marine* precludes that effort. There is no basis for applying American law to the rights and obligations of the parties, including dispute resolution by arbitration. Just as did the parties in *Baker Marine,* Spier and Tecnica contracted in a foreign state that their disputes would be arbitrated in that foreign state; the governing agreements make no reference to United States law; and nothing suggests that the parties intended United States domestic arbitral law to govern their disputes.

Spier's reference to the permissive "may" in Article V(1) of the Convention does not assist him since, as in *Baker Marine,* Speir has shown no adequate reason for refusing to recognize the judgments of the Italian courts.

Finally, the *Chromalloy* district court's reliance upon the FAA to disregard an Egyptian court's decision nullifying an Egyptian award was prompted by a particular circumstance not present in the case at bar: Egypt's blatant disregard of its contractual promise not to appeal an award. Spier points to no comparable provision in his contract with Tecnica; and, while Spier deplores the Italian courts' decisions, he does not suggest that Italian domestic law, made applicable to this Italian award by the Convention as construed by the Second Circuit in *Yusuf,* did not entitle Tecnica to challenge the award in the Italian courts.

It remains only to say that even if, contrary to my conclusions previously stated, Spier is entitled to test this award by the measures of domestic United States law, it avails him nothing. That is because all three Italian courts nullified the award on the ground that in making it the arbitrators had exceeded their powers, a ground for vacatur under the FAA. *See* 9 U.S.C. § 10(a)(4).[6]

For the foregoing reasons, Spier's renewed petition to enforce the arbitral award is denied.

Questions and Comments

1. What provisions or limitations are contained in sections 8.06 and 8.07of the TEI–HCM contract, set forth in Problem 10.2, concerning enforcement of an arbitral award?

2. Does the New York Convention or Inter–American Convention apply to enforcement of the arbitral award in the TEI–HCM arbitration? See legislation implementing the Inter–American Convention, 9 U.S.C. § 305. ("When the requirements for application of both the Inter–American Convention and the Convention on the Recognition and Enforcement of Foreign arbitral awards of June 10, 1958, are met, determination as to which Convention applies shall, unless otherwise expressly agreed, be made as follows:

> (1) If a majority of the parties to the arbitration agreement are citizens of a State or States that have ratified or acceded to the Inter–American Convention and are member States of the Organization of American States, the Inter–American Convention shall apply.

> (2) In all other cases the Convention on the Recognition and Enforcement of Foreign Arbitral Awards of June 10, 1958, shall apply."

3. Are the provisions of the Inter–American Convention for refusal of recognition or enforcement of an award similar to those of the New York Convention? *Compare* New York Convention, Art. V *with* Inter–American Convention, Art. 5.

4. In this problem, would the U.S. District Court, Tampa Division, rule in favor of HCM concerning its arguments that the court decline to enforce the arbitral award? See *Parsons & Whittemore Overseas, Inc. v. Societe Generale De L'Industrie Du Papier (RAKTA), supra.*

5. On what grounds does the New York Convention permit a refusal to enforce a commercial arbitral award? What policies are reflected by these exceptions?

6. In his Reply Brief Spier makes the alternative argument that even under the Italian courts' decisions, certain sums awarded by the arbitrators to him survive, and "[i]t would take little effort for this Court to extract from the arbitrators' decision amounts which are clearly due" to Spier. Whether that exercise would be easy or onerous, I decline to undertake it. As a practical matter, the exercise would involve amending or modifying the arbitrators' award or the judgments of three Italian courts or all of the above. Those functions lie well beyond the limited subject matter jurisdiction conferred upon this Court by the Convention and its implementing domestic legislation which, in respect of an arbitral award rendered in a foreign contracting State, empower me to do enter one of only two judgments: enforcing the award, or refusing to do so upon proof of one of the grounds specified in Article V(1) of the Convention.

6. Do the Convention exceptions to enforcement differ from those provided in the Federal Arbitration Act, 9 U.S.C.A. § 10? What policies are reflected in the differences?

7. In note 29 to the Convention, the United States declared, "The United States of America will apply the Convention, on the basis of reciprocity, to the recognition and enforcement of only those awards made in the territory of another Contracting State." U.S. Reservations, 9 U.S.C.A. § 201. To what concerns or policies is the U.S. reservation addressed?

8. May HCM appeal the district court's ruling? See 9 U.S.C.A. § 16.

9. Would the award in favor of TEI against HCM be considered domestic by a U.S. court?

10. On what grounds may a U.S. court modify or correct an arbitral award? See 9 U.S.C.A. § 11.

11. The United States is not a party to any international treaty for the enforcement of court judgments analogous to the New York Convention. Why?

12. May a litigant seek to enforce a foreign arbitral award in a U.S. court where that award has been previously annulled by a court in the country of arbitration? Several courts have considered this issue in light of the interplay between New York Convention Article V(1)(e) (court MAY decline to enforce award where award was annulled by competent authority of country in which or under the law of which award was made) and Article VII (New York Convention SHALL not deprive any party of rights to award to extent allowed under laws of country where enforcement is sought). See e.g., *Baker Marine (Nig.) Ltd. v. Chevron (Nig.) Ltd.*, 191 F.3d 194 (2d Cir.1999) (declining to enforce arbitral award because of previous annulment by Nigerian court); *Chromalloy Aeroservices v. Arab Republic of Egypt*, 939 F.Supp. 907 (D.D.C.1996) (enforcing arbitral award despite its previous annulment by Egyptian court).

13. What if the foreign court annulling the award based its decision on grounds outside the exceptions to enforcement of awards contained in the New York Convention, Article V? See *Spier*:

> In sum, we conclude that the Convention mandates very different regimes for the review of arbitral awards (1) in the state in which, or under the law of which, the award was made, and (2) in other states where recognition and enforcement are sought. The Convention specifically contemplates that the state in which, or under the law of which, the award is made, will be free to set aside or modify an award in accordance with its domestic arbitral law and its full panoply of express and implied grounds for relief. See Convention art. V(1)(e). However, the Convention is equally clear that when an action for enforcement is brought in a foreign state, the state may refuse to enforce the award only on the grounds explicitly set forth in Article V of the Convention.

Would permitting national courts to vacate or modify awards on the "full panoply of express and implied grounds for relief" advance or impede the New York Convention's goals of efficient and binding dispute resolution?

14. Might a court, in deciding whether to enforce an award previously vacated by a foreign court, be influenced by whether the party contesting enforcement violated an arbitration clause that the award or its enforcement would not be contested? See *Spier*, 71 F.Supp.2d at 287 (distinguishing facts from *Chromalloy Aeroservices, supra*, on grounds that Respondent in *Chromalloy* had entered arbitration clause that "[t]he decision of the said [tribunal] shall be final and binding and cannot be made subject to any appeal or other recourse"); *Baker Marine*, 191 F.3d at 197 n. 3 (same). Should a court be influenced by such a clause if there was impartiality, fraud or collusion among the arbitrators?

Index

References are to Problems

†